797,885 Books
are available to read at

www.ForgottenBooks.com

Forgotten Books' App
Available for mobile, tablet & eReader

ISBN 978-0-282-43698-8
PIBN 10851688

This book is a reproduction of an important historical work. Forgotten Books uses state-of-the-art technology to digitally reconstruct the work, preserving the original format whilst repairing imperfections present in the aged copy. In rare cases, an imperfection in the original, such as a blemish or missing page, may be replicated in our edition. We do, however, repair the vast majority of imperfections successfully; any imperfections that remain are intentionally left to preserve the state of such historical works.

Forgotten Books is a registered trademark of FB &c Ltd.
Copyright © 2017 FB &c Ltd.
FB &c Ltd, Dalton House, 60 Windsor Avenue, London, SW19 2RR.
Company number 08720141. Registered in England and Wales.

For support please visit www.forgottenbooks.com

1 MONTH OF FREE READING

at

www.ForgottenBooks.com

By purchasing this book you are eligible for one month membership to ForgottenBooks.com, giving you unlimited access to our entire collection of over 700,000 titles via our web site and mobile apps.

To claim your free month visit:

www.forgottenbooks.com/free851688

* Offer is valid for 45 days from date of purchase. Terms and conditions apply.

English
Français
Deutsche
Italiano
Español
Português

www.forgottenbooks.com

Mythology Photography **Fiction**
Fishing Christianity **Art** Cooking
Essays Buddhism Freemasonry
Medicine **Biology** Music **Ancient Egypt** Evolution Carpentry Physics
Dance Geology **Mathematics** Fitness
Shakespeare **Folklore** Yoga Marketing
Confidence Immortality Biographies
Poetry **Psychology** Witchcraft
Electronics Chemistry History **Law**
Accounting **Philosophy** Anthropology
Alchemy Drama Quantum Mechanics
Atheism Sexual Health **Ancient History**
Entrepreneurship Languages Sport
Paleontology Needlework Islam
Metaphysics Investment Archaeology
Parenting Statistics Criminology
Motivational

EARLY DAYS IN DETROIT

PAPERS WRITTEN BY

GENERAL FRIEND PALMER
OF DETROIT

BEING HIS PERSONAL REMINISCENCES
OF IMPORTANT EVENTS AND DE-
SCRIPTIONS OF THE CITY FOR
OVE

PUBLISHED BY

HUNT & JUNE.

DETROIT, MICH.

PRINT
THE RICHMOND &

EARLY DAYS IN DETROIT

PAPERS WRITTEN BY

GENERAL FRIEND PALMER
OF DETROIT

BEING HIS PERSONAL REMINISCENCES
OF IMPORTANT EVENTS AND DE-
SCRIPTIONS OF THE CITY FOR
OVER EIGHTY YEARS

PUBLISHED BY
HUNT & JUNE
DETROIT, MICH.

PRINTED BY
THE RICHMOND & BACKUS CO.

Copyright, 1906
By Hunt and June

F
574
D4P2

THIS BOOK
IS DEDICATED TO HIM
WHO INSPIRED IT,
MY DEAR LIFE-LONG FRIEND AND COUSIN
THE HON. THOMAS W. PALMER.

৪৭৮

PREFACE.

Several years ago, when I was about to leave for New York, the General, as we always called him, said rather sadly, "It will be very lonesome, when you are away and the hours and sometimes weary."

"Why don't you write your reminiscences? will-keep your heart and mind busy and time will so that I will be back before you have fairly missed me."

"Where will I commence," asked the General.

"Take the river front from the River Rouge to Bloody Run and then zig zag to and fro until you have covered the old city." He did so. He started the papers for the *Detroit Free Press* and they have been published regularly with but few interruptions ever since.

He has woven a story which will interest many in whose veins runs the blood of the pioneers and one which will prove of infinite value to the historian who shall write the story of Detroit and the great Northwest.

General Palmer was my cousin, my friend and my lifelong comrade. For many years he shared my home and at last he closed his eyes forever. In these papers I have all and malice for none.

Yours truly,
J. W. Palmer

PREFACE.

Several years ago, when I was about to leave for New York, the General, as we always called him, said rather sadly, "It will be very lonesome, when you are away and the hours will be long and sometimes weary."

"Why don't you write your reminiscences?" I asked. "That will keep your heart and mind busy and time will pass so swiftly that I will be back before you have fairly missed me."

"Where will I commence," asked the General.

"Take the river front from the River Rouge to Bloody Run and then zig zag to and fro until you have covered the old city." He did so. He started the papers for the *Detroit Free Press* and they have been published regularly with but few intermissions ever since.

He has woven a story which will interest many in whose veins runs the blood of the pioneers and one which will prove of infinite value to the historian who shall write the story of Detroit and the great Northwest.

General Palmer was my cousin, my friend and my lifelong comrade. For many years he shared my home, and in that home he closed his eyes forever. In these papers there is kindness for all and malice for none.

Yours truly

INTRODUCTORY NOTICE.

No work was ever published without omissions or trivial errors, and the publishers claim no better verdict for this volume.

Friend Palmer was stricken with his fatal illness the very day he and the editors were to begin re-editing the manuscript. As these are strictly personal reminiscences, the editors did not feel authorized in making any alterations without the author's co-operation. We therefore present it without rearrangement or amendations.

If the living representatives of the families named herein will notify us of any mistakes or omissions, we will be happy to correct them in future editions.

With a tender appreciation of Friend Palmer's lovable and kindly characteristics, we present his book in its present crude but authentic form.

THE EDITORS,
H. P. HUNT,
C. M. JUNE.

GENERAL FRIEND PALMER.

DIED OCTOBER 9th. 1906

The remains of General Palmer were removed from the residence of former Senator Thomas W. Palmer at 10 o'clock and taken to the Elmwood Cemetery chapel, where the services were held at 2:30 o'clock, Rev. Reed Stuart of the Unitarian Church officiating.

Senator T. W. Palmer, who said, "When I was a boy I read a couplet written, I know not by whom, which impressed me so forcibly that I have remembered it through life. It is as follows:

"'Thou art not a king of terrors, Death,
But a maiden with golden hair.'

MET DEATH QUIETLY.

"This couplet has clung to me through life, and on occasions like this is brought forcibly to my mind. While it does not apply to those who are in the heyday of life, full of health and strength, when life lies all before them, full of achievement and promise of achievement, it is particularly applicable to cases like this.

"The General, as we called him, sank away gradually without preliminary suffering, and went down into the valley so quietly that it seemed to me the maiden with golden hair took him by the hand and led him across the line into the other life.

"He was a member of my father's family when I was born and for seventy-six years we were very near each other. Although we were separated from each other by other family ties, our sympathies were almost always in common. In his youth General Palmer was the friend of all young men in his town, and as they came to manhood their regard for him was not diminished. He was a kind and sympathetic man, and all went to him with their troubles. He met the vicisitudes of life with calm philosophy. He lost his wife and two children, leaving only one behind, and while he grieved for them it never affected his deportment toward others. He was a helpful man and too responsive for his own good in material things.

"Although he may have had resentments he retained no animosities. He was a philosophic man and took the ordinary annoyauces of life with cheerful acceptance. He was a religious man and, although not devout in conversation, believed in the great law of compensation and that time at least would make all things even. His religion was not dogmatic. He was charitable in his judgment of others. He believed in the great hereafter that would bring every wanderer home. He was a man of critical literary tastes, and, although he did not obtrude his conversation on others would astonish his friends when circumstances caused him to expose his knowledge of literature, and particularly of books of travel.

"He will be much missed by me, my family, my household, and all who knew him. I can think of no better way of ending my remarks than by a quotation which a friend repeated to me in the carriage on my way to the cemetery and which I asked him to write out:

> " 'Calmly he looked on either life, and here
> Saw nothing to regret or there to fear,
> From Nature's temperate feast rose satisfied,
> Thanked Heaven that he had lived, and died.'

"Today we place him beside his wife and children in the same ground with his parents and two generations of friends who have preceded him, happy in his life and thrice happy in his death."

The active pallbearers were Charles Miller. Ernest Marson, Henry M. Rice, William Wemp, Henry Grix, Roswell A. Hollister, Clare Bennett and Mr. Marshall.

The honorary pallbearers were Alexander Lewis, Alexander M. Campau, Gen. Henry L. Chipman, Don M. Dickinson, George N. Brady, William Livingstone, William E. Quinby, General L. S. Trowbridge, Colonel S. E. Pittman, Colonel J. D. Lydecker, Richard R. Elliott, William V. Moore, Richard H. Fyfe, C. A. Kent, J. M. Shepard, John M. Wendell, Colonel James M. Shepherd and J. B. Cook.

CONTENTS.

IN DAYS OF DANGER.....................................	17
MY ARRIVAL IN DETROIT, MAY, 1827....................	23
THE EARLY MARINE.....................................	26
EARLIER NAVIGATION ON LAKE AND RIVER..............	30
SLAVERY DAYS IN MICHIGAN...........................	103
THE TOLEDO WAR......................................	108
INCIDENTS OF THE PATRIOT WAR.......................	113
EARLY DAY ARCHITECTURE.............................	120
SURVEYING IN EARLY DAYS............................	123
PERILS OF PIONEER DAYS..............................	124
THE HAPPY FRENCH HABITANT.........................	126
"THE WINNING OF THE WEST".........................	130
THE IRON MEN OF THE BORDER........................	134
IN DAYS OF OLD.......................................	138
EARLY DAYS IN DETROIT..............................	144
OUR CITIZEN SOLDIERS................................	163
OLD EXPRESS DAYS....................................	194
OLD HOTELS OF DETROIT..............................	213
TIPPECANOE AND TYLER TOO...........................	240
REMARKABLE SPECIMEN OF NATIVE COPPER..............	247
WHEN DETROIT HAD A TOWN PUMP.....................	254
ROYALTY SAW DETROIT................................	261
FIRST BAPTIST CHURCH................................	264
DETROIT MERCHANTS OF LONG AGO.....................	269
NO MORE CREDIT AT THE POSTOFFICE...................	275
FIGHTING EPIDEMICS...................................	280
WHEN WOODWARD AVENUE WAS A CORDUROY ROAD......	287
COLONEL MCDOUGALL WAS A RARE OLD SOUL............	294
REV. JOHN N. MAFFITT'S WORK IN DETROIT.............	299
WENT TO PONTIAC BY WAY OF MT. CLEMENS............	304

Tramps Received Ten Stripes	310
When Indians Were Hanged in Michigan	315
Washington Bonnet Inspired a Poet	321
Early History of the Detroit Free Press	325
Fighting Fire in the Old Days	331
Keen Rivalry of Fire Fighters	335
Famous Buildings Destroyed by Fire	341
Darius Clark and M. C. R. R. Fire in 1850	347
Heroic Work of Volunteer Firemen	351
Volunteer Firemen Became Famous	357
Social Functions of Volunteer Firemen	361
Fined $10 if Your Chimney Blazed	366
The Old River Road	370
Early Festivities	374
Down-River Homes	378
The Cass Family	381
Old Mansion House	385
Old River Front	389
Many Old Buildings	393
Tunis S. Wendell	397
Old Jefferson Avenue	401
Dancing Teachers	407
Old Business Men	412, 463
S. L. Rood's Store	418
Mr. John Owen	421
A Son's Tribute	427
Joseph Campau	433
The Campau Family	438
F. & T. Palmer's Stores	443
F. & T. Palmer	449
Old Storekeepers	455
Early Postmasters	459
Makers of Detroit	467
Men of the Forties	473
The Desnoyers Heirs	476
Recollections of Men Prominent in the City's Affairs	481
Colonel Joshua Howard a Man of Note	594
General Isaac DeGraff Toll	601

CONTENTS.

THE NAVARRE FAMILY	606
THE ST. MARTIN FAMILY	614
THE PELTIER FAMILY	619
THE LABADIE FAMILY	623
THE CHAPOTON AND CICOTTE FAMILIES	630
FIVE PROMINENT FAMILIES—RIVARD, LAFFERTY, RIOPELLE, DUBOIS, ST. AUBIN	636
THE CHENE FAMILY	640
THE MERRY FRENCH CARTS	644
HAMTRAMCK	650
THE STREETS IN THE LOWER PART OF THE CITY	665
CHRISTMAS IN DETROIT'S EARLIER DAYS	669
THE OLD BERTHELET MARKET	674
WOODWARD AVENUE IN THE THIRTIES	710
VISITING FIREMEN	802
THE CASS FARM	805
JUDGE SOLOMON SIBLEY	814
A NOTED FIRM	826
CONSPICUOUS MEN IN LIFE OF THE CITY	819, 842
THE LEWIS FAMILY	842
BUSINESS HOUSES IN 1850	852
PERSONS PROMINENT IN THE CITY'S LIFE	856
STATE CAPITOL AND SUPREME COURT	865
DETROIT BOAT CLUB	868
RECOLLECTIONS OF PERSONS AND EVENTS IN YEARS LONG PAST	872
RECOLLECTIONS OF MEXICAN WAR	876
FALL OF FORT DEARBORN (CHICAGO)	880
SOMETHING ABOUT BUSINESS MEN OF THE CITY SEVENTY YEARS OR MORE AGO	886
THE OLD TEN EYCK TAVERN	906
MARRIAGE AND DEATH NOTICES	910
SOME RESIDENTS THAT I HAVE OVERLOOKED	915
THE PLAT OF THE TOWN KNOWN AS WOODWARD'S PLAN	918
BUFFALO TO DETROIT BY STEAMBOAT IN 1821	921
ELKANAH WATSON AND THE ERIE CANAL	925
PRINCE PHILIP AND QUEEN MARY	928

THE FORT STREET GIRLS...............................	934
BELLES AND BEAUX OF BYGONE DAYS...................	944
RANDOLPH STREET....................................	953
FIRST PROTESTANT SOCIETY............................	962
FAREWELL TO JUDGE A. B. WOODWARD..................	965
EARLY SOCIAL CONDITIONS............................	973
RECOLLECTIONS OF THE FIRST THEATRES IN DETROIT......	980
ON THE CANADIAN SIDE...............................	1000

EARLY DAYS IN DETROIT

PALMER

EARLY DAYS IN DETROIT

IN DAYS OF DANGER.

WHEN THE INHABITANTS OF DETROIT AND VICINITY DWELT IN DREAD OF MURDEROUS INDIANS— TALES OF THE BORDER.

"IN 1807 the little town of Detroit was just rising from its ashes. The Indians of the surrounding wilderness were even then seriously threatening the settlements. At that time there was but a small regular force in garrison at the old fort, and, for the purpose of affording additional protection, a body of volunteers was called out and placed under the immediate command of Major John Whipple.

"The main guard was posted at the Indian council house, where the new firemen's hall now stands, and a blockhouse was erected on Jefferson Avenue, on the Brush farm. The town was surrounded by a row of strong pickets fourteen feet high, with loopholes through which to fire. The line of pickets commenced at the river on the line of the Brush farm and followed that line to about Congress Street, and thence westerly along or near Michigan Avenue back to the old fort, to the east line of the Cass farm, and followed that line to the river. At Jefferson Avenue, at the Cass line, and on Atwater Street, on the Brush farm, massive gates were placed, which, daily, at rise and set of sun, grated on their ponderous hinges. Pickets were placed at them and along the line.

"It was rather an exciting time, but many ludicrous scenes occurred. Among others, on a dark, rainy night, a sentinel fired at an imaginary Indian, the drums beat to arms, the troops turned out, and a militia colonel (he was not a native of Michigan), who lived at a distance from the quarters of the troops, hearing the alarm, seized his portmanteau in one hand, and the muzzle of a musket with the other, ran at full speed to the guard house, dragging the but of his gun in the mud. He kept on his headlong way until, encountering a small shade tree, it bent away before him, and he slid up to the limbs, but the recoil of the sapling left the gallant warrior flat on his back in the mud.

"The pickets remained around the town when the war of 1812 began.

"In 1814 General Cass, then a general officer in the army, was in command of the frontier, with a body of troops to protect the country. Our army on the Niagara frontier was hard pressed, and the general, unsolicited, sent to General Brown all his force; only a dozen or so of invalids, unfit for service, remained. General Cass had become acquainted with our people, well knew their courage and patriotism, and determined, with them alone, to defend the country; and they did not disappoint his expectations.

CAPTAIN WESTBROOK AND HIS RANGERS.

"Mr. McMillan, whose widow and children, after the lapse of forty years, are still with us, had joined Captain Andrew Westbrook's company of Rangers. Captain Westbrook was a native of Massachusetts, and had been taken in his childhood by his father to Nova Scotia. He afterwards found his way to Delaware, on the Thames, in Upper Canada, where he was living when the war of 1812 broke out.

"He was too much of a Yankee to be quiet, and they drove him off. He came to Michigan, raised a company of Rangers, and proved to be an exceedingly active partisan soldier, and seriously annoyed the enemy. He made frequent incursions into the province as far up as Delaware.

"He was at that time a man of considerable wealth, had a fine large house, distillery, etc., at Delaware. On his first visit there with the Rangers he called them around him at his own place and, swinging a firebrand around his head, he said:

"'Boys, you have just fifteen minutes to plunder my premises; after that I give them to the flames!' And true to his word he applied the brand and burnt up the whole concern.

"Captain Westbrook afterwards settled on the beautiful banks of the river St. Clair, where we have often experienced the generous hospitality of 'Baronial Hall.' We usually called him Baron Steuben.

INDIAN ATROCITIES.

"McMillan belonged to this corps. He was a gallant soldier and did good service for his country. On the 15th of September, 1814, the morning after his return from the Ronde, in Upper Canada, he, with his young son, Archibald, then 11 years old, went upon the common to find his cow. What follows, I have from an eye-witness, Mr. William McVey, of the Rouge:

"David and William Burbank and myself were sitting down at the Deer park, on the Macomb (now Cass) farm, near where Lafayette Avenue crosses it, watching our cows. Mr. McMillan and Archie passed us. We spoke to them about some apples they were eating. They passed towards some cows that were feeding near some bushes (the bushes then came down to where the capitol stands). We kept our eyes on them, thinking danger might be near. When they approached within gunshot of the bushes, we saw three or four guns fired and saw McMillan fall. The Indians instantly dashed out upon him and took off his scalp. Archie, on seeing that his father was killed, turned and ran towards us with all the speed that his little legs could supply.

"A savage on horseback pursued him. As he rode up and stooped to seize him, the brave little fellow, nothing daunted, turned and struck the horse on the nose with a rod which he happened to have in his hand. The horse turned off at the blow and Archie put forth his best speed again. And this was repeated several times, until the savage, fearing of losing his prize, sprang from the horse, seized the boy and dragged him off to the woods; and thence was taken to Saginaw.

"About the same time a man by the name of Murphy, who lived with the late Abraham Cook, went with a horse and cart into the field on Judge Moran's farm, just back of where the judge now lives. He was shot, scalped and his bowels cut open and left exposed in the field, and the horse was taken off.

BATTLING WITH THE REDMEN.

"The Indians were constantly beleaguering the town, sallying out occasionally, and driving off and killing the cattle, etc., that approached the bushes. Determined to put a stop to this, General Cass called upon the young men to arm and follow him.

"They were ready at the first blast of the bugle, mounted on ponies, such as could be had (for there were but few left), and armed with all varieties of weapons—rifles, shotguns, war clubs and tomahawks, and whatever other instruments of death could be had. As the woods and underbrush were very dense, they expected to have a hand-to-hand fight, and prepared for it accordingly. The company consisted of General Cass, Judge Moran, Judge Conant, Captain Francis Cicott, James Cicott, Edward Cicott, George Cicott, Colonel Henry I. Hunt, General Charles Larned, William Meldrum, James Meldrum, James Riley, Peter Riley, Lambert Beaubien, John B. Beaubien, Joseph Andre, "Ditt" Clark, Louis Moran, Louis Dequinder, Lambert Lafoy, Joseph Riopelle, Joseph Visger, Jack Smith, Ben Lucas and John Ruland. I know nearly every one of them personally, and a better lot of fellows for the business they were on could not be well got together. They were then young and full of spirit.

"After assembling, they rode up along the border of the river, to the Witherell farm, and rode through the lane to the woods. They soon came upon an Indian camp; the Indians having fled, leaving their meat roasting before the fires upon sticks.

"Here they found Archie McMillan's hat, and were in hopes of finding him. The Rileys discovered the tracks of the enemy and a hot pursuit commenced. They were overtaken on the back part of the Cass farm and a hot fire was instantly opened upon them, and was kept up until the word was passed to "Charge!" Then, on the whole body went, pell-mell. It was hot work for the Indians, and after awhile they fled. Peter Riley, who was in advance when the firing commenced, suddenly reigned up his horse across the trail, sprang off, and, firing over the horse's back, brought a warrior to the ground, and in a twinkling took off his scalp and bore it away on a pole in triumph. How many Indians were killed is unknown. A squaw came in with a white flag a few days afterwards and reported that several of their people had been killed. Their chief, Kish-kaw-ko, was carried off in a blanket, but whether wounded or killed could not be ascertained.

"Ben Lucas had a personal encounter with an Indian by the side of General Cass. After the fight the company came out upon the common, except two who were missing. They were the late William Meldrum and Major Louis Moran, now of Grand Rapids. Much anxiety was felt on their account. It was feared that they had been killed. However, after a long while the brave fellows appeared. They had been in hot pursuit of the enemy, and had brought back a scalp, as they said, in token of victory.

"During the whole affair General Cass rode at the head of his men, and when advised by Major Whipple to fall back (for should he be killed it might create confusion), replied, 'Oh, major, I am pretty well off here; let us push on,' and he kept his post."

The venerable Judge Conant, who, as I have before mentioned, was among the volunteers, and to whom, as now, a squirrel's eye at forty yards was a sufficient target, states that General Cass, and in fact every man in the company, behaved with perfect coolness throughout the whole affair. They were nearly all accustomed to the woods and the enemy knew it or they might have been cut off to a man.

"After coming out of the woods the company formed and marched to the River Rouge, drove a band of savages out of the settlement and in the evening returned, having performed a good day's work—one that gave quiet to the settlement until the end of the war.

"Before the return of the company to the town it had been rumored that the whole party had been killed. On their way up from Springwells, the young men of the company raised a shrill war-whoop. This confirmed the rumor and numbers of women and children rushed to the river and put off in canoes, boats and periaguas for safety in Canada.

"I have mentioned the three Rileys, James, Peter and John; they were half-breeds. The latter is yet living on the St. Clair River. They were educated men, and when with white people they were gentlemanly, high-toned, honorable men; when with the Indians in the woods, they could be perfect Indians, in dress, language, hunting, trapping and mode of living. They were the sons of the late Judge Riley, of Schenectady, who was formerly in the Indian trade at Saginaw. The three were thorough-going Americans in every thought and feeling, and were thought to be by the British, after they had gained possession of the territory, too dangerous persons to be allowed at large. They sent an officer and a few soldiers to St. Clair, seized James and sent him to Halifax, where he was kept until the war was over. He was aftedwards killed by the explosion of a keg of gunpowder at Grand Rapids.

"Peter remained about Detroit. He (as well as his brothers) was a great favorite with the Indians, and used occasionally, when a little corned, to annoy the British authorities by putting on the uniform of an American officer, and with twenty or thirty Chippewas at his back, parading up and down Jefferson Avenue, every now and then giving the war-whoop.

"The warriors were, of course, in the British service, but Riley was their favorite, and of their own blood, and they would not suffer him to be injured without a fight. They were proud of his courage and his frolics amused them, so Peter remained unmolested.

"Some months after McMillan was killed, and his son carried off, Colonel Knaggs seized three Indians, the relatives of those who had made the boy a prisoner. They were placed under guard, and John Riley was sent to Saginaw to propose an exchange. The terms were agreed to, and on the 12th day of January, following his capture, Archie was brought in and delivered, as one from the dead, to his excellent mother.

"There were many sufferings endured and danger encountered in those days, which no mortal tongue will ever utter and no pen record."

MY ARRIVAL IN DETROIT, MAY 1827.

THE WINDMILLS—MR. REEDER, NANCY MARTIN AND GENERAL SCHWARZ.

I CAME to Detroit in May, 1827, with my mother and two sisters, on the steamer Henry Clay. We were under the friendly guidance of Mr. Felix Hinchman (father of Mr. Guy F. Hinchman), who took charge of us at Canandaigua, N. Y.

My father, Friend Palmer, had preceded us some two or three months, on account of urgent business matters connected with the firm of F. & T. Palmer, of Detroit, of which he was the senior partner.

Our trip through New York from Canandaigua to Buffalo was by stage and very rough, the roads having been rendered almost impassable by recent rains. It took us, I think, two days and two nights to reach Buffalo. We had to wait at that point two or three days for the steamboat Henry Clay. We did not mind that in the least, for we were quartered at the Old Eagle Hotel, kept by Benjamin Rathbun, a most sumptuous resting place, I thought it, and so it was for those days. Our trip up the lake to Detroit on the Henry Clay was uneventful. We had a pleasant passage that occupied, I think, two or three days. The Henry Clay, Captain Norton, was a floating palace, we thought, and we greatly enjoyed the time spent on it. The Henry Clay had no cabin on the upper deck—they were all below. When you desired to retire for the night or for meals, or get out of the reach of rain and storms, downstairs or between decks you had to go.

MERCHANTS LIVED OVER STORES.

We landed at Jones's dock, between Griswold and Shelby Streets, on a fine day, about 10 o'clock in the morning, and all walked up to the residence of my uncle, Thomas Palmer, corner of Jefferson Avenue and Griswold Street. There were no public conveyances in those days. Thomas Palmer lived over his store, as did many of the merchants doing business here at that time.

Let me refer once more to Captain Norton, one of the most conspicuous and popular captains on the lakes at that early day. The Henry Clay was a crack steamer and, of course, must have a corresponding chief officer. Of commanding presence, Captain Norton, of the "fast steamboat Henry Clay," when he appeared on Jefferson Avenue, clad in his blue swallow-tail coat with brass buttons, nankeen pants and vest, and low shoes with white stockings, not forgetting the ruffle shirt and tall hat, was the observed of all observers. Steamboat captains were kings in those days. All were pleased and anxious to show them every attention.

When the Clay rounded Sandwich point, Detroit lay before us and, though small, the city presented quite an attractive appearance. The most conspicuous object in the distance was the steeple or cupola of the state house or territorial capitol building, that pushed its head up among the surrounding trees, its tin covering glittering in the morning sun.

WINDMILLS ATTRACTED ATTENTION.

The windmills along the river also attracted our wondering attention. Three were located on the Canadian side of the river, one on the point opposite the residence of the late Joseph Taylor, and two just above the present site of Walkerville. The one on the American side was on a small point where Knaggs creek then entered the river and opposite the old Knaggs' homestead (Hubbard's farm), since destroyed. Knaggs creek later on was obliterated by the Ives brothers, who turned the place into a drydock.

The four mills presented to us a wonderful sight on that bright May morning. They were in full operation; their four immense arms, covered with white sail-cloth, were whirled through the air by the force of the wind, and, as said before, filled us with delightful amazement as all New York state could not produce a scene to match it.

Two companies of British regulars in their red coats (they were stationed at Sandwich) were going through their drill on the green in the front of the old Huron Catholic church, its decaying walls propped by poles, and on the open in front was planted a high wooden cross, since destroyed. The parsonage or mission house, however, remained, held up by its two enormous chimneys at either end. The contrast presented by the red of the soldiers' uniforms and the green sward will always remain a vivid picture in my memory, so new and so unique. The Indians in their canoes, to whom a boat propelled without the aid of sails or oars was always an object of wonder, attracted our attention also, as did the horse ferry boat, John Burtis, captain, that plied between Detroit and Windsor, as slow as "molasses in January." The description of the celebrated first steam monitor of the civil war (Ericson's) would aptly apply to this boat of Burtis's, namely, "a cheese box on a raft."

WESTERN HOSPITALITY.

It is needless to say that my father welcomed us gladly at the dock, and my uncle and aunt, Mr. and Mrs. Thomas Palmer, greeted us with a genuine western hospitality that put us directly at our ease. I forgot to mention that the late R. E. Roberts was a fellow passenger on the Clay, it being his first appearance in Detroit, whither he had come to join his brother, John Roberts.

I will try to give my recollections of Detroit and vicinity, and the people at that early day.

The outlook below the present site of Fort Wayne was not quite so inviting as now. The country around the mouth of the River Rouge was low, flat and marshy, covered with a most luxuriant growth of wild grass (marsh hay), that any one could cut if he so desired. What was not cut was usually set fire to in the winter and would burn for days, giving the people of the city quite a scene, at night illuminating the sky above the marsh and showing vividly the flames leaping through the dry grass. The same scene used to be repeated every winter on the Grande Marias, above the city, just beyond the water works.

Where Fort Wayne now is, and extending a little this side, was an immense hill of yellow sand that always looked from the city, like a yellow patch on the landscape. This sandhill, it is presumed, was used in the early days (the memory of man runneth not to the contrary), as a burial ground by the Indians, because in its slow demolition(the sand of which was composed being used for many purposes by anyone who desired to take the trouble to get it), numerous remains of Indians were found who had evidently rested there before and since Cadillac's time.

MR. REEDER.

On the River road (thre was none other at that time), beyond the sand hill, I think, Mr. Reeder lived, on what is now the Crane farm. I will halt a moment to dwell on Reeder. I presume many now living will remember him. He was quite a conspicuous figure in the streets of Detroit—very tall, thin and angular, always dressed in a black swallowtail coat, buttoned to the chin; trousers of the same hue, and a tall hat the worse for wear. He was almost always under the influence of liquor, his frequent potations having lent themselves to painting his face a fiery red. He was known to all at that time and, however intoxicated or in the bonds of the "rosy" he might be, he was always most polite and gentlemanly.

Well, nearly everyone has heard of the passing of Reeder and the Reeder farm, the former to the beyond and the latter to the late Walter Crane and Reeder's heirs.

The next residence, I do not know who occupied it at that time, was an old style French-built house, with huge chimneys at each end. There was an old orchard on the west side. At one time, 1808, I think, it was occupied by Judge James Witherell and family, who, coming here soon after the destruction of the town by fire in 1805, found suitable tenements exceedingly scarce, and had to accommodate themselves to circumstances. It was somewhat perilous at that time for people living so far from the fort, as the Indians were none too friendly. I have often heard Mrs. Thomas Palmer, Senator Palmer's mother and daughter of Judge Witherell, relate how her father used to admonish the family to keep indoors after dark, for fear of being carried off by the redskins.

NANCY MARTIN.

The judge and family did not remain there long. The next tenants I dot remember, but it was occupied by individuals whom many now living will remember,, Walter Harper and Nancy Martin. Of the former little is known, and of what the relations were that existed between the two, just as little. But Nancy Martin's name in connection with Harper Hospital will be remembered long after the present generation are in the beyond. Her property, consisting of eight acres on Woodward avenue, she bestowed as a gift for the purpose of founding a hospital to which she gave the name of Harper, in memory of her old and life-long friend. This hospital is now one of the institutions of the city, an ever present reminder of her generosity. Her name is further perpetuated by a beautiful street leading from Woodward Avenue to the hospital and is named Martin Place in her honor. She died in 1875, February 9, I think.

It may not be out of place to quote here what Chevalier Cadillac, of Detroit's bicennial anniversary celebration, said of her, and it is so true: "In Nancy Martin, contradictory characteristics were mingled. She was sweet, charitable and good; she was coarse, raw and rude; she was gentle, patient and long suffering; she was outspoken, jovial and frank. She had a large store of plain Saxon words more expressive than refined. She was as blunt as a barn hostler, and yet she was loving and forgiving, and as tender-hearted as the noblest of her sex. Her truthfulness, sagacity and integrity were never assailed. Do good, you, too, then you also will be remembered when your bones are dust."

DR. STEWART'S TRIBUTE.

Dr. Morse Stewart, in *The Free Press* a short time ago, had this to say in regard to Nancy Martin:

"When Walter Harper gave nearly 1,000 acres of land situated only a little distance outside of Detroit, also three lots with buildings thereon in Philadelphia, and if my memory serves me rightly some property in the village of Pontiac, to a board of trustees for the purpose of establishing a Protestant charity hospital in Detroit, Mrs. Ann (Nancy) Martin supplemented that munificent gift by conveying to the same board of trustees eight acres of land fronting on Woodward avenue and extending east on the rear part of which Harper hospital now stands; also fifteen acres just outside the city limits. These properties were the accumulations of many years of hard work as huckster in Detroit city markets, the small earnings from which had been wisely invested in real estate of growing value. The hospital very appropriately bears the name of its founder, but to this day there exists no adequate memorial of the large-hearted woman contributor to the enterprise in any part of this rich city so greatly benefited thereby. Tested by the standard which our Lord Jesus Christ set upon money being cast into the treasury, all the charitable contributions of all the rich men of Detroit pale into littleness in comparison with this poor woman's gift, 'for they did give of their abundance, but she of her need did give all her living.'"

In this connection it seems to me that it would not be out of place to perpetuate also in some substantial manner the memory of Walter Harper and that of Rev. George Duffield, he having first suggested the idea to Walter Harper and Nancy Martin. The memory of Harper is sufficiently before the people, perhaps, in having the hospital bear his name, but the memory of the others is not.

I have said this hospital is an ever present reminder of Nancy Martin's generosity, such is the fact, no doubt, to the present generation, very many of whom are familiar with the circumstances attending the birth of Harper hospital, but in the long years to come who will be likely to think of her or tell her story unless something exists in enduring bronze or otherwise to her memory?

My first recollections of her date back to 1839 and 1840, when she and Walter Harper lived in the vicinity of the sand hill, Springwells. She was an almost daily visitor at Sidney Rocd's book store, as a huckster. She paid particular attention to catering to the tastes of the epicures in game, furnishing such choice eatables as woodcock, quail, wild pigeons, ducks, venison, spring chickens, etc. Rood and many that used to congregate at his book store, were generous livers and fond of things good to eat, and Nancy was on the best of terms with them all. Uncle Shubal Conant was an epicure and fond of game. He, too, always patronized her liberally, as did Josh Carew, H. A. Newbould and the gay epicurean bachelors, Randolph Brothers, wholesale dry goods dealers on Jefferson Avenue between Woodward Avenue and Griswold Street, who kept the first strictly wholesale dry goods house in Michigan. Theo. Romeyn, who was the greatest epicure in game of them all, and many others also bought from Nancy.

Mary Jacklin of late years, almost all will remember, was something of the stamp of Nancy Martin, and quite as outspoken.

A GOOD GERMAN.

Gen. J. E. Schwarz also lived down that way about 1830, in a cottage with a veranda in front. The cottage once belonged to Hon. Austin E. Wing, and was occupied as a residence by him. It stood on Bates Street, between Woodbridge and Atwater Streets. The general had a raft constructed and floated the house down the river and anchored it on the bank about where Baugh's iron foundry was built. The general, his wife, who was a highly refined lady, and his daughter Emma, made it an ideal home, many a gay party from the city enjoying their hospitality.

The general was always adjutant-general of the state until his death, it seems to me, and aside from the elite of the city, drew around him all the military officers of the state, as well as the United States army officers stationed here. Aside from Mr. Uhlman, I think Gen. Schwarz was the only German in the city at that time. There were quite a number of English, Scotch and Irish. The French were in the ascendant, of course.

The general was one of the best specimens of a German gentleman I ever came in contact with. I think all those that knew him will sustain my assertion.

His daughter, Miss Emma, long resisted the advances of her numerous American admirers, but was finally captured by "Bob" Woods, a young lawyer from Sandwich, across the river, a gentleman, and well up in his profession. They went to Chatham to reside and I think they are living there yet, and where, I understand, Mr. Woods has gained much distinction in his profession.

The J. P. Clark house next above was built by N. O. Sargent, a boot and shoe merchant of Detroit, but I do not think he lived to occupy it. Mr. Clark bought it and after making some alterations, occupied it with his family and continued to live there until he died. All are familiar with the drydocks he built in front of his house on the river. It is in use and well to the front now. Clark was also owner of the Springwells mineral springs.

EARLIER NAVIGATION ON LAKE AND RIVER.

A VETERAN DETROITER'S INTERESTING RECOLLECTIONS OF PIONEER BOATS AND THEIR COMMANDERS, WITH VALUABLE COINCIDENTAL INFORMATION.

IT is probable that few long-time residents of Detroit retain such an interesting fund of information in regard to lake and river marine matters of early days as did Friend Palmer, some of whose recollections of pioneer boats and their commanders are here set down.

The steamer Henry Clay was one of the fastest boats on the lakes in the early '30s, says Mr. Palmer. Captain Walter Norton, her commander, was a man of fine presence, and he used to cut a swell figure when he appeared on Jefferson Avenue, clad in his blue coat, with its brass buttons; nankeen trousers, white vest, low shoes, white silk stockings, ruffled shirt, high hat, not forgetting the jingling watch chain and seals. Steamboat captains ocenpied a high place in the social ranks in those days and much deference was shown them.

I also call to mind Captain Roger Sherman, who commanded the steamboat Superior, the second steamer on the lakes after the Walk-in-the-Water. The Superior came out on the second Tuesday in May, 1822, and was pronounced a decided success. She was 346 tons burden, 110 feet keel, 29 feet beam, engine 56 horse-power. The accommodations for passengers were excellent, and the ladies' cabin was furnished in a style of great splendor for those days.

Captain William T. Pease was also one of the old school gentlemen of the lakes. He commanded respectively the steamers Niagara first, Pioneer, Superior, Niagara second, and others, including the Boston. He was also at one time master of the schooner Michigan, which afterwards was sent over Niagara Falls.

COMMANDED AN HISTORIC CRAFT.

Captain L. H. Cotton, of Detroit, it is said, commanded the first steamer that ever towed a vessel up the Fort Erie rapids, the steamer being the Monroe and the vessel the Milwaukee. He was also master from time to time of the steamers Ohio first, Pennsylvania, Daniel Webster, Oregon, Baltic, Anthony Wayne, and later on, the then mammoth steamer Western World. At an early period of his life, in 1835, he fitted out the brig Queen Charlotte, which during the war of 1812 was captured from the British by Commodore Perry, and lay sunk for many years at Erie, Pa. Captain David Wilkinson, who died in Perrysburg, O., many years ago, commanded the schooners Eagle and Guirrier, his first steamer being the Commodore Perry, of which he remained master until the close of her career, when he and others caused to be built the Superior second, which he commanded for many years. Captain C. L. Gager was with Captain Levi Allen, James Harrington, Loring Pierce and John Kimberly on the Walk-in-the-Water when she was lost. He was absent from the lakes for several years, and on his return bought the Red Jacket and sailed her, then the General Porter, which he converted into a propeller, and afterwards the steamer Albany, which latter he owned.

RACING WITH A MYTH.

Captain John F. Wight commanded the William Penn, and afterwards the Chicago, a scow craft. It was said of him when master of the latter steamer, that coming out of Cleveland, and passing the then town Ohio City, since absorbed by the former, a heavy fog prevailed. The captain observed, as he supposed, the smokestack of a steamer between his boat and the shore. He at once ordered the engineer to put on all steam, saying he would not allow anything to pass him, if he knew it. The contest kept up, apparently, but when the fog cleared away it was found that the smokestack was nothing but a fire-blackened tree stump on shore. It is also related of him that one time coming from Buffalo the steamer Illinois hove in sight abaft the Chicago and gained rapidly on her, whereupon an anxious passenger said to the captain: "Captain, she is after us, isn't she?" "Never mind," said he, "we will be after her directly." Captain Wight, speaking in praise of the Chicago, said his boat "could run anywhere where the ground was moist."

NAVIGATED LAKE ERIE ALL WINTER.

Captain Harry Whitaker, who died a few years ago at St. Luke's Retreat, Detroit, sailed at one time the schooner Marie Antoinette; then the steamers North America, Monroe, United States and A. D. Patchin. By navigating the United States between Detroit and Buffalo during the entire winter of 1845, Captain Whitaker accomplished something that has never been equaled in the history of lake navigation. I was a passenger with him on one occasion during the fore part of that year. We left Buffalo on the morning of the 10th of March, I think it was. The steamer made its way laboriously through a mass of rotten ice for about five miles, when we encountered a large field that was apparently solid. The captain got all the passengers on the upper deck, and had them run in a body from one side of the steamer to the other, which gave her a rolling motion, as he backed her up, and then let her drive with a full head of steam into the icy barrier. We continued in this way for the greater part of two days in full sight of Buffalo before we got out of the ice into clear, open water.

Captain Augustus Walker was probably one of the best known navigators in aiding and furthering steamboat interests that ever sailed the lakes. He built the Sheldon Thompson, Washington First, Columbus and Great Western. He first commanded the United States and subsequently the others named. In regard to the Sheldon Thompson, I copy an advertisement from a Buffalo paper of July 7, 1830:

"The steamer Sheldon Thompson, A. Walker, master, proposes to leave her dock, August 30th, for Mackinac, Green Bay and intermediate ports. This stanch and elegant steamship is lauded as being a specimen of Ohio architecture. She will remain at Green Bay two or three days and one or two days at Mackinac, to give her passengers a chance to view the delightful scenery of the upper lakes."

On May 30, 1832, the Sheldon Thompson was advertised to leave Buffalo on the 4th of July, and Detroit on the 6th of July, for the same ports. She left her dock (Dorr & Jones', foot of Shelby Street) on the day advertised. I witnessed the leaving of this steamer from her dock as above. She had on board a goodly number of passengers, besides a number of United States troops, with their officers and regimental band, destined for the seat of the Black Hawk war. The band treated the citizens to some fine music.

ASTONISHED THE NATIVES.

The Great Western was the first steamboat on the great lakes provided with upper cabins, and she aroused the curiosity and interest of the entire lake region. I will give a description of her, taken from the *Cleveland Herald and Gazette,* published at the time, 1838 or '9: "Her dimensions are as follows: Length, 186 feet; breadth of beam, 34 feet 4 inches; across the guards, 60 feet; depth of hold, 13 feet; tonnage, custom house measurement, 781; being greater than any craft that ever floated on our fresh seas. She is propelled by a high-pressure engine, made at Pittsburg, said to be the largest, or one of the largest, engines of that description ever made in the United States. The cylinder is 30 inches in diameter; stroke 10 feet; rated at 300 horse-power. Her paddle wheels are 13½ feet radius, and 2 feet in breadth. The Great Western is arranged unlike any other boat. The entire hull is occupied by the boilers and by holds for freight and wood. On the main deck aft is the ladies' cabin and state rooms; above this, on what would be the hurricane deck, the main cabins are placed, running almost the whole length of the boat. The ladies' saloon is aft, the dining cabin next, and the saloon, or bar-room, forward. State rooms are arranged on either side these cabins the whole length. The Great Western has sixty state rooms, with three berths in each, and other berths in cabins, making in all about 300."

I remember well when this steamer first came out. I was residing in St. Clair for a short season at the time, and it was heralded abroad that she was to be fitted with upper cabins, an innovation unheard of on the lakes and hardly believed possible, as it was feared she would prove top-heavy. All the people living along the St. Clair River watched for her passing on her first trip to Chicago. The steamer unfortunately passed up the river in the night. Nevertheless, the people were all out and on the watch. She made a fine sight as she passed up on the Canada side, her cabins all ablaze with light. Captain Walker died at Buffalo many years ago, aged 65 years.

THE FIRST SAILING SHIP.

"Bob" Wagstaff, as he was familiarly called, will not soon be forgotten by many. He commanded the first and finest sailing ship ever on the lakes, the Julia Palmer, in 1836. She was built at Buffalo in that year, and was 300 tons burden. Afterwards she was converted into a steamer. Captain Wagstaff was also a steamboat man for many years. He and Captain "Gus" McKinstry took command of one of Oliver Newberry's steamers in midwinter, and relieved Fort Mackinac, the troops stationed there being short of provisions. He was also in command of Newberry's fine brig Manhattan, when she went ashore on Lake Erie, below Malden. Later on he was appointed collector of customs at Tampico, Florida. He died many years ago in Brooklyn, N. Y.

Captain Chas. C. Stannard commanded the brig Ramsey Crooks, also the steamers Niagara, Bunker Hill and Saratoga, and died on board the Western World as she was leaving the dock at Detroit in 1856. Stannard's rock in Lake Superior took its name from him.

A REMARKABLE OCCURRENCE.

The steamer Chippewa, built at Buffalo, without frames, and with the shape or model of a muskmelon, was sailed by Captain Benjamin Armstrong, who also commanded the schooners Sterling and Brittania, besides other craft. Captain Gil Appleby sailed the schooner New Connecticut, which capsized on Lake Erie; three days afterwards a woman was rescued from the cabin alive, which was conceded to be one of the most remarkable events of the times. Captain Appleby also commanded the steamers North America, Constitution, Ben Franklin and Sultana. He died at Buffalo in 1867.

Captain T. J. Titus commenced his career in sailing vessels, commanding the schooners Aurora, United States and others. He also sailed the steamers Ohio First, Sandusky, Erie, Buffalo, Queen City and Julia Palmer, his first one. His last command was that of the propeller Monticello. While on Lake Michigan he was drowned from the small boat while attempting to land on shore.

THE MAYFLOWER.

The steamer Mayflower, built by the Michigan Central Railroad Co., was by all odds the finest steamer that up to that time had ever appeared on the lakes. As she was of our own production, so to speak, a notice of her first departure from Detroit to Buffalo, taken from a local paper of that day, along in the spring or summer of 1849, will prove of interest. It was as follows:

"This magnificent boat left our city on Monday evening on her first trip to Buffalo this season. She carried many of our worthiest citizens among the crowd of passengers, some of whom have waited for days for her departure. Her kind and gentlemanly commander, Van Allen, appeared as natural as life in his post of 'mine host' on the occasion, and the polite and efficient clerk, Nichols, transacted office business with his usual prompt suavity, while Wormley, the bountiful and accomplished caterer, and Newhall, the experienced engineer, and Farrer, his assistant, were each looking as well as heart could wish at their accustomed vocations."

The Mayflower was wrecked on Point Au Pelee, Lake Erie, in 1854. Before the completion of the Great Western Railway through Canada, passengers journeying east or west would always time themselves so as to catch the Mayflower. I have often waited for her, in company with many others, at Buffalo, twenty-four hours at a time, and when the hour for her departure arrived she would appear to be in an almost sinking condition, loaded as she was with passengers, their baggage and her usual freight. Detroit and the entire lake district bemoaned the fate of the Mayflower. No lives were lost, I think. The steamer Thames was also at one time commanded by Captain G. R. Williams, plying between Buffalo and Port Stanley, Ont. Captain Eberts also at one time was in command of the Thames when she plied between Detroit and Chatham, Ont., and he kept on this route for many years. Captain F. S. Atwood ranks also among the first navigators on the lakes. Besides sail vessels, he commanded at different times the steamers Macomb, Monroe, General Harrison, Troy, Arrow, T. Whitney, Philo Parsons and others. Captain J. L. Edmonds commanded for several years vessels and steamers, such as the North America, Chicago and Southerner. While in command of the latter, and after leaving Buffalo on her second trip of the season, in March, 1850, he was taken suddenly ill, causing the immediate return of the steamer to port, where he died on entering the harbor. Captain Aaron Root sailed the schooner Amaranth, steamers Constellation, in 1836, Bunker Hill, in 1837; and subsequently the propeller Henry Clay. He died at Black River, Ohio. Captain Joel H. McQueen commanded the steamer Constellation in 1837, afterwards the Samuel Ward, and other boats. He also at one time commanded the schooner White Pigeon. Captain John Shook sailed the schooner Cincinnati, besides other vessels at an early period; also the steamers United States and Columbus. He died at Huron, Ohio, some years since. He had the distinguished honor, if it may be called so, while in command of the Columbus, of conveying the Prince de Joinville and suite from Buffalo to Green Bay. They tarried in Detroit two days to see and to be seen. Captain Shook's brother, Captain Jim Shook, sailed the fine clipper brig Illinois, of the Eagle line, in 1836, when it was fashionable to have the peajacket ornamented with a spread eagle. He also at one time commanded the propeller Sciota, besides several small sail craft. He died at Huron, Ohio, many years ago.

MERRY MARINERS OF OLDEN DAYS.

Captain A. H. Squeirs sailed vessels for many years, among others the schooner Leguire, steamers De Witt Clinton and Garden City. He was living in Buffalo in 1883. He had for clerk with him on board the steamer Clinton, Ben Barton, of Buffalo, who, perhaps, some will remember. Ben was a gay and convivial chap, and knew the "boys around town" in every port on the lakes between Buffalo and Chicago. When the Clinton came into port it was the signal for a gathering of the boys, to have a good time, and they always had it. Dan Whipple's place, that was on Bates Street, Detroit, saw many of these gatherings, where fun reigned fast and furious. The captain had a brother, Heber Squeirs, "Hebe," as he was familiarly called. He was a gay young man when I knew him in Buffalo in the early forties. He commanded and owned a tug, the name of which I have forgotten; but "Hebe" I cannot forget. During the winter months he was always the head and front of the gay balls and dances given in the assembly rooms of the old Eagle tavern, on Main Street, Buffalo.

OTHER LAKE PIONEERS.

Captain Amos Pratt, long a prominent lake navigator, will be recollected as the master of the steamer Anthony Wayne, or Mad Anthony, as she was first called. He also commanded one of the first propellers on the lakes, the Sampson (in 1843), afterwards the Princeton and the Globe. He was a popular seaman and a gentleman. His death occurred in 1869 or '70. Captain William Dickinson, who died at Buffalo in 1865, aged 65 years, was reared on the waters and commenced life as a ferryman between Black Rock and Fort Erie. After several years' experience on the lakes, he commanded the schooners Sterling, Merchant, Michigan (second), ship Milwaukee, brig Robert Hunter, propellers Hunter and Illinois.

Captain I. T. Pheatt, who died at Toledo in 1859, came from the lower lakes in command of the schooner Grant. While on the upper lakes he commanded the steamer General Harrison (in 1840), the steamer Indiana (in 1842), the Northern Indiana and Western Metropolis. At the time of his decease he was managing a ferry at Toledo. Captain John Stewart sailed several vessels for the late Oliver Newberry. Among others were the schooners Marengo, La Salle and the brig Manhattan. Previous to his decease, which took place on the River St. Clair, he commanded the steamers Michigan and Northerner. He was a bluff, hearty sailor, and universally liked. I would also like to pay a passing tribute to the memory of other lake pioneers, among whom were Captain Samuel Vary, who died at Sheboygan, many years ago; "Old Ned Burke," as he was familiarly known; Jerry Oliver, who commanded the steamer New England, besides sail vessels at other periods; Captain Paine Mann, Joe Sherwood, John Kline; also Captain John W. Webster, who, with Captain James Hackett, lighthouse keeper at the mouth of Detroit River, were the two oldest vessel masters living in 1833. Webster died at Painesville in 1864, and Hackett died in May, 1901. "Ned" Burke died at Buffalo in 1841. Jerry Oliver died at Buffalo in 1855. Captain Paine Mann died at St. Joseph, Mich., in 1859. Captain Joe Sherwood died at Delafield, Wis., in 1856. Captain John Kline died at St. Joseph, Mich., in 1870. Captain W. P. Stone, once of the steamer Keystone State, and favorably known, died many years ago at a hotel in New York City. Captain Thomas Richards died while in command of the steamer Niagara at Milwaukee in 1849. Captain G. W. Floyd came from the seaboard, and sailed the brig Indiana in 1837, in 1839 the steamer Sandusky, and in 1843 the propeller Hercules, after which he returned to salt water. He died in California.

Captain E. B. Ward was also at an early day a vessel man,

sailing among others the schooner General Harrison. The first steamboat he commanded was the Huron, in 1840. Subsequent events in his career are too familiar to be repeated here. Captain L. B. Goldsmith was navigating the lakes in 1871, and was in command of the steamer Jay Cook in 1883. Captain Fred S. Wheeler, who commanded the propeller Hercules and steamboat St. Louis, was very popular with all classes in every port on the lakes. The Hercules, besides being the largest propeller on the lakes at that time, had another distinguishing peculiarity—her hull was painted checker pattern, red, blue and white. The Hollister Bros., of Buffalo, her owners, had their store on Main Street, in the latter city, painted in the same fashion.

Captain Fred S. Miller was still navigating in 1883. He was tossed about from an early date. There are those, no doubt, who will also remember Captain R. C. Bristol, who sailed vessels, also the steamers James Madison and Niagara, second. He died at Chicago in 1856.

Captain Morris Hazzard came from the east, having had experience on the rivers. He brought out the steamer Milwaukee at Buffalo in 1838, and afterwards commanded the Constellation, Empire State, and also sailed the Monroe. Captain D. H. McBride died in Milwaukee in March, 1871, after a lengthy career on the lakes. He had a long experience on both sail and steam craft. The schooner Havre was the last vessel he commanded (in 1842), and the propeller Ironsides the last steamer. He was second mate of the steamer Erie, which was burned on Lake Erie in 1841, and narrowly escaped being counted among the lost. Captain William Hinton, for several years pilot on the United States steamer Michigan, was first officer of the Erie when she was burned, and he also met with a narrow escape. He served long and faithfully on board of steamers, and commanded the Daniel Webster after her name was changed to the Black Dan. Captain James M. Averill, an old lake man, commanded the steamer Erie (the little one) in 1840, and subsequently sail vessels. Previous to this period the captain was several years at sea. He died at Buffalo in 1875.

In the year 1836, the steamer Little Erie made her first appearance on the St. Clair River. She was the fastest boat of her size on the lakes. She made quite a record during the Patriot war, chasing up the patriots and seeing that they did not violate the neutrality laws existing between the United States and Canada. She was lost in the ice on Lake St. Clair in 1842, and her loss was much deplored.

Captain Jacob Travers, who commanded the steamer Golden Gate, besides several smaller craft, was lost with the steamer Keystone State on Lake Huron in 1861. Captain John Caldwell, who died at Cleveland in 1846, commanded in 1836, '37 and '38, the schooner Hudson, afterwards the Henry Crevolin, and Trenton. Subsequently for several years he commanded steamers to Lake Superior, and in the Northern Transportation Line.

Captain J. C. Benjamin, who died at Prairieville, Mich., in 1864, sailed the steamboat Ben Franklin in 1849. He previously sailed vessels out of Cleveland. With Captain Imson on the steamer Hendrick Hudson as clerk, was Wm. B. Rochester, of Rochester, N. Y. He during the civil war entered the army as paymaster and subsequently became paymaster-general. He is now living in Washington, a retired brigadier-general.

OLD-TIME CLERKS AND STEWARDS.

The steamer Ocean, of the Ward line, Captain C. C. Blodgett, had for clerk Theodore Luce ("Commodore Luce"), and "Bob" Montgomery for steward. The captain and these under officers were immensely popular and made things quite pleasant for their patrons. Captain Whitaker had for his clerk on the steamer United States in the early forties a young man by the name of Bradley, a quiet, sedate, gentlemanly chap, who was very popular. He resigned to become a messenger in Charles H. Miller's Western Express Company, the first enterprise of the kind ever inaugurated between Buffalo and Chicago. Bradley was the first and only messenger of the company except Miller himself. As the venture was not a success, Wells, Fargo and Dunning obtained Miller's interest, and all know the immense success of the present express companies in this direction.

The steamer Great Western, Captain Walker, had at one time a very popular clerk in the person of a Mr. Emerson, who contributed his share in rendering this steamer a great favorite with the traveling public. He, too, after a while (1844) resigned to take a position in Wells, Fargo & Co.'s Western Express as messenger. William A. Bury, now of Grosse Ile, Mich., was a very popular clerk on many steamers and propellers in the early days. He is unfortunately now a hopeless invalid.

"Tom" Gillett, son of the late Shadrick Gillett, was also clerk on various steamboats and propellers in those days, and he, as well as Bury, was a great favorite with all. He died several years since. There were a large number of steamer clerks at that time on the lakes, equally as deserving as those mentioned, but I do not recollect their names.

RIVER BOATS AND CAPTAINS.

Among the river captains that I recall, were Captain Arthur Edwards, master of the steamboat Gratiot, which plied to and from the following ports: St. Clair, Black River and Ft. Gratiot. Monroe, Vistula and Maumee. In noticing the Gratiot a paper of that day (1832) says: "No foolishness about Captain Edwards, for he says his boat will be precise in starting at the hour advertised."

The same paper says (June, 1833): "The River Line is supplemented by the addition of the steamer General Brady, Captain John Burtis, and this year the General Gratiot has changed masters. Captain John Clark succeeds Captain Edwards."

I knew these captains well; have traveled with them often. Captain Clark retired from service and settled on his farm on the banks of the St. Clair, just below St. Clair city. He became a prosperous farmer, wood merchant and general dealer.

All the Chicago steamers of that day (or steamers plying between the latter port and Buffalo) used to wood at his dock. He died many years ago. Captain Edwards passed away since the civil war, in which he served with distinction as quartermaster. Captain John Clark also at one time (1834) commanded the steamboat General Jackson, built at Mt. Clemens, also the Lady of the Lake, built at Mt. Clemens in 1833. Captain Atwood was at one time also on this route. The steamboats General Macomb, built at Mt. Clemens (1837), and Star, built at Belvidere (1837), were also at one time on this route.

Captain E. B. Ward sailed the steamboat Huron in 1840. "She was owned by Captain Samuel Ward, and was a very successful steamer, netting him thousands of dollars, and laying the foundation of his large fortune."

FIRST BOAT THROUGH THE CANAL.

Captain Samuel Ward built and commanded another boat at an earlier day than any of the above. It was a sailing vessel called the St. Clair, and was built in 1820 at Marine City. After the Erie canal was opened, Captain Ward freighted his boat at Detroit for New York city, and took on board two horses to tow her through the canal. On arriving at Buffalo he took down his masts, entered and towed her safely through the canal; arrived at the Hudson River, he shipped his masts, bent the sails and soon came to anchor at the metropolis. Securing a full freight back, he returned, but was somewhat disappointed on being required to pay toll. Captain Ward not only calculated on getting through the canal free of toll, but expected (as should have been the case) to get a premium, as his was the first boat from the lakes to New York.

FIRST DETROIT AND PORT HURON BOAT.

Captain Hanson succeeded Captain E. B. Ward in command of the Huron. These three captains (Ward, Hanson and Clark) sailed the steamers Huron and General Gratiot respectively between Detroit and Port Huron along in the '30s and '40s. Another river steamboat, the first to ply between Detroit and Black River (Port Huron), was the Argo, built at Detroit in 1830 by Captain John Burtis, and commanded by him. I was on hand when she was launched and I made two or three trips on her to St. Clair and return. She was very cranky. On these trips I was in company with Thomas Palmer, father of the senator, who was quite portly, and Captain Burtis was on constant watch to see that "Uncle Tom," as he called him, did not upset his steamboat. She was found too cranky for the business and was put on the ferry route between Detroit and Windsor.

The steamboat General Vance, about 1835, was on the down-river route, Detroit to Truax's (Trenton), and Newport, and was owned and commanded by Captain Samuel Woodworth, son of Uncle Ben Woodworth, of the Steamboat Hotel. She blew up while lying at the dock in Windsor, killing the captain and some of the crew.

GREAT FUR-SHIPPING PORT.

About 1830 Thomas Palmer, father of the senator, owned the schooner Tiger and the scow Independence. The former was not a very large affair, but the latter was of considerable tonnage, and was quite a freighter. Her captain, William Loucks, dubbed her a "square-toed packet."

The Tiger seems to have done considerable business in her time. The *Detroit Gazette,* of July, 1821, says: "The schooner Tiger, Captain Birdsall, sailed from this port for Buffalo with 410 packs of furs, valued at $62,000."

Detroit was the greatest shipping port for furs on the lakes at that time. In addition to the Tiger, the schooner Superior, Captain Keith, sailed for Buffalo with 200 packs, and the account quoted from above says: "There are between 300 to 400 packs remaining at our different wharves, valued at from $300 and $500 to $900 each. The Tiger and Independence both came to grief on Lake St. Clair; no lives lost.

Lewis Godard, of Detroit, about 1830, built a steamboat, called the David Crockett. She was small, and of novel construction in that she was propelled by an immense wheel attached to her stern. She plied between this port and Mt. Clemens.

The steamboat Arrow, built at Trenton in the early forties, by Messrs. Atwood, Davis & Edwards, was a very fast boat, and a great favorite with the traveling public. The *Toledo Blade* said of her when she came out: "It is expected she will take passengers here after breakfast and land them in Detroit immediately after dinner, and be in Toledo before tea time," and she did.

The names and personalities of the early navigators of the lakes and rivers, as well as the various craft they were connected with, all seem to pass before me in a long procession, as in a dream. Many of the captains and all the clerks I knew quite intimately, having traveled on many of the steamers in the early days, when in the employ of the Western and Pomeroy's Express Companies between Buffalo and Detroit.

THE GRIFFIN, THE FIRST VESSEL ON THE LAKES.

It is recorded that the first vessel on the lakes was the Griffin, which was built on the Niagara River at or near Schlosser Landing in 1679. She was schooner rigged with the addition of a topsail, and was sixty tons burden. She took her departure from that place for Mackinac on August 7 of that year, in command of Chevalier De LaSalle, a Catholic missionary, with a crew of six persons. She arrived there in due time, and was laden with furs for a return voyage, but after her departure was never again heard from. Not for many years thereafter do we find any record of craft on the lakes.

From 1771 to 1779 nine vessels were built at Detroit by the English government. They were as follows: Schooner Hope, 81 tons, built in 1771; sloop Angelica, 66 tons, built in 1771; brig Gage, 154 tons, built in 1772; schooner Dumore, 106 tons, built in 1772; sloop Felicity, 55 tons, built in 1774; schooner Faith, 61 tons, built in 1774; sloop Adventure, 54 tons, built in 1776; sloop Wyandotte, 47 tons, built in 1779. During the revolutionary war, the Gage carried fourteen guns, and the Faith, ten guns.

What was the fate of these vessels the record does not disclose.

SOME VERY EARLY BOATS.

It appears from a Buffalo paper, published in 1830, "that the first schooner, fore-and-aft, built on Lake Erie after the Griffin, was in 1797, at Four-Mile Creek, near Erie, Pa. She was called the Washington.

The Union was the name of the first brig. She was built in 1814. She was ninety-six tons burden. She was laid up for a time on account, it was said, of her being too large for the requirements of the period.

The first steamboats ever built on the lakes are said to have been built by the Canadians, one at Brockville in 1816, name not known, and the other the Frontenac. She was built at Kingston in 1817. She was of 700 tons burden, had three masts, no guards, and looked like an ocean steamer. The Frontenac cost £20,000. Captain James McKenzie, a retired officer of the royal navy, was her first commander. It was said at the time that he was not over-confident of his vessel, for advertisements were thus qualified: "The steamer Frontenac will sail from Kingston for Niagara, calling at York (Toronto) on the first and fifteenth days of each month, with as much punctuality as the nature of lake navigation will admit of." She ended her career in 1828.

In 1817 another steamboat, the Ontario, was built, but in American waters, at Sacket's Harbor. She was 110 feet long and 24 feet wide, measuring 246 tons. Captain Francis Mallaby, U. S. N., was her first master.

In 1818 the celebrated Walk-in-the-Water was built at Black Rock.

"In those days a solitary barque now and then sailed lazily along the gentle current of our beautiful river, and the painted savage, in his bark canoe, with his brood of tawny papooses, glided silently along the sea-green waters. The voyageurs and the bois coureurs of the Hudson Bay and Northwest Fur Companies, while their voices kept tune and their paddles kept time, annually departed to the hunting grounds of the red men along the shores of the Slave Lake and the Lake of the Woods, and even to the shores of the far-distant Oregon, where no sound was heard but its own dashing."

The *Detroit Gazette* of May 10, 1822, says: "On Monday last at about 1 o'clock, our noble river presented a very pleasant sight. Nine fine schooners and a variety of small craft, aided by a favorable wind, could be seen bearing into port with all their sails set."

I am led to contrast the foregoing with the account of the number of craft, steam and sailing, that passed up and down the Detroit River, on the 3d of June, 1901. The number on that date was 168.

The *Detroit Gazette* of Friday, July 21, 1820, says: "The arrivals and departures of vessels at this port since the 13th inst. was as follows: Arrivals, 9; departures, 9, including steamboat Walk-in-the-Water, for Black Rock," and the article also states that Captain Rodgers has reduced the rate of passabe (cabin) on his steamboat from Detroit to Black Rock from $18 to $15, and in proportion to intermediate ports.

The *Gazette* of Friday, July 21, 1820, says: "The schooner Tiger, Mr. Birdsell, master, arrived at this port last Sunday from Green Bay, in the remarkably short passage of four days and twelve hours, twenty-four hours of which time she remained at Fort Mackinac. The following gentlemen were passengers on her: Of the Third Regiment, United States Infantry, Colonel Smith, Lieutenant-Colonel Lawrence, Captains Green and Garland, and Lieutenants Dean, Lewis and Curtis. Of the Fifth Infantry, Captain Whiting and Lieutenant Hunt. Of the Corps of Artillery, Major Biddle; also Lieutenants Leib and Harding."

The same paper of Friday, May 18, 1821, says: "Last Saturday morning fourteen schooners, laden with merchandise and produce, sailed from this port for Michilimackinac and the ports on Lake Michigan." It also says: "The steamboat Walk-in-the-

Water arrived here last Tuesday evening. She left Buffalo on the 13th inst. at 11 o'clock A. M., being the first vessel from Buffalo this season. She brought, among other things, several emigrants."

A *Detroit Gazette* of 1827 says: "These boats (referring to the steamboats Henry Clay, Superior and Niagara) will take freight at the usual rates, and every exertion will be made to deliver it to the owners or consignees, but which, as well as baggage of every description and small parcels, will be taken only at the risk of the respective owners or shippers."

There were laid up in port of Detroit in December, 1845, eleven steamboats, one propeller, forty schooners and sixteen wood scows.

STEAMBOAT SUPERIOR.

"The History of the Great Lakes" gives this account of the steamboat Superior, that came out after the wreck of the Walk-in-the-Water: "The hull of the Walk-in-the-Water was damaged beyond repair, and having been a financial success, her owners determined to replace her, and during the following winter the Superior was built on the bank of Buffalo creek by Noah Brown, master carpenter. She was not quite as long nor as wide as her predecessor, but was two feet deeper. She was owned by the Lake Erie Steamboat Co., and was launched April 13, 1822. She was the first vessel of any size built at Buffalo. Some slight work had to be done in the mouth of Buffalo creek in the way of cutting through the sandbars, so as to deepen the waters in order that the Superior might get out into the lake. The shallowness of the water there had caused the owners of this boat to hesitate about building her in Buffalo creek, but as they were assured that the spring freshets would clear the mouth of the creek, and a guarantee of $100 per day was given by responsible citizens for each day that she was delayed in the creek, after she was ready to go out, they decided to build her there.

"When she was nearly ready to go out there was great anxiety lest the guarantee would have to be made good, and the citizens assembled every day in large numbers—merchants, lawyers and laborers alike, with teams, scrapers and shovels and other necessary tools, and labored most assiduously to remove as much of the bar as was necessary to permit the Superior to pass out, and to return to the harbor; and those who could not work sent down provisions of all kinds to those at work, in order to help the good work along. All felt that success in getting this vessel out of the harbor into the lake was vital to the future of that harbor.

"The fatal day arrived, and after some little difficulty in touching the bar, the Superior got out into the lake, being aided by her engine, around the shaft of which a cable was wound and, attached to an anchor, carried ahead. After making a few miles' run on the lake to try her machinery, she returned to the harbor, and everybody concerned breathed more freely, for it then seemed certain that had the Superior failed to get out over the bar at the mouth at Buffalo creek, the harbor for commerce at the lower end of the lake would have been established at Black Rock."

The Superior went into commission in May, 1822, under command of Captain Jeddediah Rogers, and until 1826 was the one steamboat of Lake Erie. This boat also made voyages to Mackinac, which was then the terminus of western navigation.

The Lake Erie Steamboat Line, which was in operation in 1827, was composed of the steamers Superior, Wm. Penn, Henry Clay and Niagara, which plied between Buffalo and Detroit. One of these boats left the above ports every other day, commencing in the early part of May from Buffalo. The Superior left on May 7, the Wm. Penn on May 9, the Henry Clay on May 3, and the Niagara on May 5.

EARLY RECORDS.

The number of arrivals at the port of Detroit, and what they brought from April 8th to 19th, 1830, is as follows: Arrivals—Steamboats and schooners, fourteen. The cargoes consisted of flour, 91 barrels; whisky, 698 barrels; port, 95 barrels; dry fruit, 51 packages; cider, 33 barrels; beef, 16 barrels; salt, 66 barrels; passengers, 72; kegs of lard, 18; bars of iron, 30; packages of furs, 10; skins, 171; hides, 2; bushels of corn, 123; fish, four barrels; butter, 36 kegs; hams, 106; shingles, 11,500; lumber, 990 feet.

It will be seen that whisky had the call.

The Lake Erie Steamboat Line in 1830 was made up of the following boats and captains: Superior, Captain Wm. T. Pease; Wm. Penn, Captain Wright; Niagara, Captain Blake; Wm. Peacock, Captain Fleeharty; Enterprise, Captain Miles; Henry Clay.

Captain Norton. The first boat left Buffalo, April 12. For the season of 1831 there were added to the above the Ohio, Captain Cahoon, and the Sheldon Thompson, Captain Walker, making a daily line.

The steamboat Michigan, Captain W. T. Pease, commenced her regular trips between Detroit and Buffalo and intermediate ports, Wednesday, April 23, and continued through the season, except on July 10, when she started for St. Maries (Soo), Mackinac and Green Bay. On August 10, she started for Mackinac, Green Bay, Chicago, St. Joseph and Grand River—a fine inland voyage.

The following Lake Erie steamboats were in 1834 plying between Buffalo and Detroit:

The Michigan, Captain W. T. Pease; Daniel Webster, Captain Tyler; Governor Marcy, Captain Chase; Ohio, Captain Cotton; Oliver Newberry, Captain Edwards; General Porter, Captain Norton; Henry Clay, Captain Stannard; Uncle Sam, Captain McKinstry; Niagara, Captain Allen; New York, Captain Miles.

There entered the port of Detroit from June 19 to 25, 1832, eight steamers and eight sailing vessels, and cleared during the same time ten steamboats and five sailing vessels.

In October and November of the same year it was some better; from October 29 to November 12, ten steamboats and twenty sailing vessels entered and thirteen steamboats and nineteen sailing vessels cleared.

The *Chicago Democrat* of June, 1834, says: "Arrangements have been made by the proprietors of the steamboats on Lake Erie whereby Chicago is to be visited by a steamboat from Buffalo once a week until the 25th of August. The steamboat Uncle Sam left Buffalo on Monday last, agreeable to the arrangement." It is also stated that "there are four or five schooners which are constantly plying across the lake. The stage has commenced running twice a week to Niles."

A DELIGHTFUL EXCURSION.

On the 12th of August, 1834, the splendid steamboat Michigan left Buffalo for Mackinac, Green Bay, Chicago, Michigan City, St. Joseph and the mouth of the Grand River of Michigan; and the notice of the event goes on to say:

"The trip will embrace a distance of 2,000 miles, and the

passengers will have an opportunity of viewing the splendid scenery of Lakes Erie, St. Clair, Huron and Michigan, and the rivers, straits and bays connected with them. The Michigan is described to be a splendid vessel. We can conceive of no more delightful excursion."

DETROIT IN 1834.

I make a few extracts in regard to Detroit and the lakes, from a letter published in the *Buffalo Daily Advertiser* some time in the year 1834. The letter is from Detroit, without date, and commences: "I have just returned from an excursion among the lakes, having traveled about 1,700 miles and visited some portion of the country bordering the Mediterranean of the west," and among other things goes on to say: "The Detroit River is not surpassed in beauty and grandeur by the majestic Hudson. The city of Detroit has a population of 5,000, and is very rapidly increasing in population and business. I am persuaded that Detroit possesses advantages which have not been fully appreciated. The river at its foot, being very broad and deep, forms a harbor which can hardly be excelled, and which must always form the grand rendezvous for the lake vessels." The letter goes on to say further: "The increase of shipping and the improvement of the vessels within a few years on the lakes are equally astonishing. An excursion of 1,000 miles is a mere matter of relaxation and pleasure. The citizens of Detroit, however, have the honor of bearing off the palm in the construction of steamboats. The Michigan, built wholly at Detroit, challenges the entire American waters to produce her equal."

The first propeller on the lakes was the Vandalia, built at Oswego, in 1841. She was commanded by Captain Rufus Hawkins, and made her first voyage to the upper lakes in 1842. All know how rapidly this class of steamer has accumulated since that time, and how they have increased in size and speed.

The first steamer known to be on Lake Michigan was the Henry Clay. In August, 1827, an excursion of pleasure was made on her to Green Bay, where Governor Cass was holding a treaty with the Winnebago Indians. From that period to 1832, some of the boats went to Green Bay, but no further.

Here are some of the doings of steamboats, vessels, etc., that appeared in the local papers here and at other ports during the season of 1844:

"The steamboat Fairport was got into Buffalo harbor without having suffered any material injury. She was advertised to leave that port to-day, for Detroit, 4th April, 1844."

The *Commercial Advertiser* of Buffalo, March 20, 1844, says: "Travelers from the west say a boat was seen yesterday on the Canada shore near Point Abino. Whether it is the United States (Captain Whitaker) returning, or the St. Clair, is unknown; it is probably the former, as she has had sufficient time to make her trip to Detroit and back."

This no doubt was the return trip of the United States. She left the port of Buffalo, for Detroit, March 10, 1844, and on this trip I was a passenger.

INTERESTING NEWSPAPER REFERENCES.

"Steamer Missouri—This boat arrived here this morning from Buffalo, which place she left on Thursday last. The Missouri is the first steamer from below which has entered our port this season."—*Chicago Express,* April 11, 1844.

The *Buffalo Gazette* of January 17, 1844, says: "The ice is all out of the creek again, and there is but very little prospect that the lake will be frozen over during the winter. There is not much ice yet formed along the shores, and unless we have extraordinary weather during February and March, an earlier navigation than usual may be anticipated. The season thus far resembles that of 1837."

The *Chicago Express* of April 10, 1844, says: "The schooner Oneida arrived this morning from Cleveland, an event quite gratifying to our citizens. Our own port had been opened so long that we had been impatiently awaiting the arrival of vessels from below. The schooners E. C. Merrick and St. Lawrence, also from Cleveland, are in the offing. The Oneida found a great deal of ice in the Straits, and it was generally very thick. She reports, as being this side of the Straits, the brig O. Richmond, and schooners Windham, Baldwin and Havanna."

The schooner Windham got away from Chicago all right, with a fine cargo, but met with disaster, as the *Chicago Express* of the 17th of April, 1844, relates as follows:

"The schooner Windham, which cleared from this port yesterday for Buffalo with 10,000 bushels of wheat, went ashore during the prevailing high wind of last night, north of the north pier, and close to it. She mistook a light on shore for the one on the north pier. There is considerable water in the Windham, but she can be got off without serious injury to the vessel."

The steamer Missouri got away from Chicago all right, as appears by the *Chicago Express* of April 13, 1844, which says:

"The steamer Missouri left this morning for Buffalo with quite a number of passengers. Our present fine weather will hasten the traveling season. A large emigration may be expected.

The *Buffalo Advertiser* of April 17, 1844, thus chronicles the first arrival of the season at that port from Chicago:

"FIRST SAIL FROM CHICAGO.—Captain Gager led in the upper lake fleet, this morning, with the propeller Porter from Chicago, with 8,500 bushels of wheat, and a heavy invoice of flour and other rolling freight from Detroit. The Porter also brought down quite a number of passengers."

LAKE BUSINESS IN 1844.

The picking up of business at the western ports on Lake Michigan, etc., is thus chronicled by the *Buffalo Commercial Advertiser* of April 12, 1844: "Vessels are much wanted for the upper lake lumber trade. Some have been chartered here and others sold for such destination. Chicago, Racine and other leading points on the west shore of Lake Michigan, are improving so fast, and the demand for building materials is so great, that good round prices are now offering for vessels to trade between Green Bay, Kalamazoo, etc., to the places named above."

This appears to be a notice of the first steamboat combination formed on the lakes. It appeared in an evening paper published in Detroit by George L. Whitney, May, 1844, and reads: "The owners of the steamboats on our lakes have completed an association for the ensuing season; the cabin fare from Buffalo to Cleveland is $5; to Detroit, $7; and to Chicago, $14; the steerage to Detroit, $3; to Chicago, $7. We learn that the Julia Palmer and St. Clair do not come into the combination, but run on the "opposition line."

LAKE ERIE FROZEN OVER.

The *Buffalo Gazette* of January 30, 1844, takes back what it said in its issue of the 17th of the same month, in relation to the lakes freezing, and says: "The lake is at last frozen over. A friend who skated out to Point Abino on Saturday informs us that about half way across he made a hole through the ice, and found it to be about five inches thick. The fishermen of course will soon commence bringing in fresh lake trout."

A "FAST" TRIP.

The *Buffalo Advertiser* of April 13, 1844, contained the following: "The *Detroit Free Press* of Wednesday evening acknowledges the receipt by the propeller Hercules, Captain Wheeler, of New York papers of Saturday and of Buffalo papers of Monday evening, in advance of the mail. This trip of the Hercules is an era in the annals of propellers, and fully demonstrates the great value of that class of vessels. The Hercules left this port at 5 o'clock Monday afternoon and was back to her berth again fully loaded at 5 o'clock this morning, thus making her trip in four days and a half, an instance of dispatch rarely, if ever, surpassed by our best steamboats. Her rate of running was about nine miles an hour."

The same paper of April 24, 1844, says in regard to lake freights: "The price of freight is low upon the lakes. From Lake Erie ports to Buffalo, wheat is brought for four to five cents; flour, sixteen to eighteen cents; pork, twenty-five to twenty-eight cents per barrel. For the same to Oswego, wheat is taken through the Welland canal at eight and one-half cents. From the upper lakes to this port, wheat is charged only eleven to twelve cents per bushel, flour thirty-five to thirty-seven one-half cents per barrel, according to circumstances."

CAPTAIN CHELSEA BLAKE.

Captain Chelsea Blake, that veteran sailor, so long and favorably known on these waters as "Commodore of the Lakes," and who for so many years sailed the magnificent steamers Michigan and llinois, built by his earnest and steadfast friend, Oliver Newberry, of this city, also commanded the good schooner General Jackson in 1816, then owned by Messrs. Mack & Conant, of Detroit. At the breaking out of the war of 1812, and while the British fleet was blockading our coasts, Blake was mate of a brig outwardbound, and then lying at Newberryport, Mass., waiting for an opportunity to go to sea. He had been waiting about two months and, seeing no chance of passing the British squadron, determined to remain inactive no longer; and at his solicitation the whole brig's crew joined the American army. Blake, possessing a good business education, was placed in the commissary department, and his regiment belonged to Scott's brigade. He was at the battle of Lundy's Lane, and used to relate an incident thereof. As the two armies were approaching, and a little while before the action, an Indian attempted to pass between the armies, running for dear life. His captain said, "Blake, can't you kill that Indian?" at which Blake leveled his gun and fired, but did not hit the red man. He loaded his gun in an instant and fired again. The Indian gave an upward leap and fell, apparently dead. This Indian proved to be one of a family of five brothers, all warriors, who resided on the Big Bear Creek, on the Canadian side, and were known as the Sha-na-way family. One of them bore the name of Megish, who followed the British army, and was at the battle of Lundy's Lane, where he was killed."

The late R. E. Roberts had this to say of Blake in his work on Detroit:

"For so many years, and so intimately, through ,battles breeze and storm, had our citizens known Blake, from the time he volunteered to sustain his country's flag under General Scott at Lundy's Lane, until through every vicissitude of a sailor's life, he had won for himself the distinguished title which he bore at his death, that his name must be forever associated with the lakes, which became his favorite element. Of almost giant size and commanding presence, no son of Neptune ever united in his composition a rarer combination of the qualities which make a true seaman, a safe commander, a genuine hero. Rough as the billows whose impotent assaults on his vessel he ever laughed to scorn; with voice as hoarse as the tempest which he delighted to rule this gallant son of the sea had withal a woman's tenderness of heart to answer the appeals of distress. Sincere was the grief of many he had relieved, and universal regret among those who had ever sailed with him, when he fell a victim to the cholera at Milwaukee in the year 1849."

Captain Blake was rough, indeed, and rude of speech. Unlike most of the lake captains of those days, who were perfect gentlemen in manners and dress, he affected none of these, no courtly phrases, no ruffled shirt, no blue coat with brass buttons, when in port and off duty, but was ever the hard-headed, rough seaman. Like most men with rough exteriors, he possessed, as Mr. Roberts says, a kindly heart, and rarely ever allowed a cry of distress to pass unheeded. His use or abuse of the king's English was somewhat phenomenal. Indeed, most of the lake captains of those days had the same malady, though to a limited extent, and I presume some of those of to-day have the same characteristics.

A PICTURESQUE PROFANER.

I listened once to Blake's profanity. On this occasion it was directed to no less a person than his employer, Uncle Oliver Newberry himself. The former was in command of a schooner belonging to the latter, and had tied up his vessel at the wharf near the foot of Cass Street. Between this wharf and Mr. Newberry's warehouse was a narrow slip. In this slip another youngster and myself were amusing ourselves in a small canoe. I saw Mr. Newberry come hastily out of his office, bareheaded, and hurry around the rear of the ship, and call to Blake. He began to comb him down for something in grand style. The captain listened to the tirade a brief period; then he let out at Mr. Newberry with such a storm of profanity that the latter was so amazed and nonplussed he turned on his heel, with the remark, "Well, well, have your own way; you are bound to have it, anyway," and went back to his office.

Blake, it was said, stood in mortal fear of death and from the cholera in particular. He went to Milwaukee to escape the latter, but unfortunately did not. A short time before he went to Milwaukee he attended the funeral of a friend as a pallbearer. Bishop McClosky officiated, and as the funeral cortege turned from Jefferson and Elmwood Avenue, the bishop said to Blake, "Well, captain, this is a ride we shall all have to take sooner or later."

"Yes, bishop," Blake said, "I know that, but I shall object just as long as I can, d—d if I don't."

He died in Milwaukee of the cholera in 1849, aged about 65.

Here is a poem from the *Milwaukee Commercial Herald* printed some time in 1843, in regard to Blake:

> Ho, all ye travelers to the west;
> If you are bound across the lake,
> And wish to take the boat that's best,
> Go on the Illinois with Blake.
>
> A veteran, both by land and sea,
> He long has braved the stormy main;
> And amongst the foremost, too, was he,
> In the great fight at Lundy's Lane.
>
> And now the din of battle past,
> And smiling peace returned again,
> See proudly floating from his mast,
> Our nation's banner o'er the main.
>
> Steve Newall, too, is at his post;
> A man of science, as to steam;
> Of engineers he is the boast,
> And none of danger need dream.
>
> The steward, Wyncoop, is on board;
> 'Mongst epicures he has the name
> Of keeping his rich larder stored
> With luxuries of fish, flesh, game.
>
> In short, the boat we recommend
> For safety, comfort and for speed;
> And warmly we advise each friend
> For his own sake this notice heed.
>
> Success attend your bonny boat,
> The pride and glory of the lake;
> And may ye both forever float—
> The Illinois and Veteran Blake.

CAPTAIN H. WHITAKER.

I know I will be pardoned if I have a little more to say about Captain Whitaker and his steamboat, the United States. In a letter from the editor of a Detroit evening paper, dated "Buffalo, May 1, 1844," speaking of the United States and her captain, is this statement: "We arrived here about 8 o'clock last evening, having had the most pleasant trip over the lake that I ever enjoyed. We made the passage from Detroit to Buffalo in less than thirty-four hours, including some five or six hours that we lost in stopping at intermediate ports. The United States surpassed my expectations, in comfort as well as in speed. Her new and spacious upper cabin makes her one of the most comfortable and pleasant boats on the lakes. No boat sets a better table, by which, I mean, a table with a variety of dishes, well selected, well cooked, well arranged, and well attended. The United States has a fine band of music on board, which frequently entertained the company amid the solitude of the lakes. One word of Captain Whitaker, who owns and commands the United States: He has been connected with lake navigation, and most of the time in command of some vessel, for about twenty years. For several seasons, as the public well knows, he has been the first out of and the last into port, and yet he has never had a serious accident befall his boat, nor ever lost a life on board of one, nor ever injured property under his care, so as to incur a dollar's worth of insurance."

The United States was the first steamer to arrive from Buffalo in the spring of 1844, the date being March 18. I was a passenger in charge of the Wells & Co. western express. A Detroit evening paper of the above date thus mentions the event: "As the Buffalo papers announced that the steamboat United States, Captain Whitaker, was advertised to leave Buffalo for this port on the 9th inst., and she not arriving here before the papers of that day came round by land, we had made up our mind that Captain Whitaker had been balked for once; but lo! about breakfast time yesterday, up came the steamboat United States in gallant style to our wharf, being the first vessel out of Buffalo this season. The United States left Buffalo, according to her advertisement, on Saturday afternoon, the 9th. After proceeding some five or six miles, she found herself completely surrounded by the ice, which a strong headwind had blown down the lake; here she was obliged to remain during Saturday night and most of Sunday; towards the close of the day the wind had somewhat moved the ice so as to allow the boat to turn around, and at about 5 o'clock she returned to Buffalo. With characteristic perseverance and energy, Captain Whitaker put out again on Thursday and came through in triumph. We understand that the boat encountered ice 100 miles this side of Buffalo."

At the close of the last century there were on Lakes Huron, Erie and Michigan the following schooners: The Nancy, 94 tons; the Swan and the Neagal; the sloops Sigma, Detroit, Beaver, Industry, Speedwell and Arabaska, and on Lake Superior the sloop Otter.

The steamboat Michigan, "The Pride of the Lakes," the sailing vessels Marengo, Marshall Ney, the steamboat Michigan No. 2 and the brig Manhattan, all of Oliver Newberry's fleet, were built on the river front between Cass and Wayne Streets. The steamboat Michigan No. 1 (before mentioned) was, as many will remember, the "ne plus ultra" of steamboats at that time. She had three masts, two low-pressure engines, and at that date was a wonder and a show, although her cabins, sleeping and eating accommodations were between decks. The splendid brig Manhattan was the pride of Admiral Newberry's heart, and when she was wrecked, after she had been out but a short time, he was, as he said, "badly hurt." Not that he missed the money that she had cost so much, but because she was such a thing of beauty, with her towering masts and fine lines. One of Mr. Newberry's vessels—the Napoleon—was built on the St. Clair River, in front of Captain Westbrook's residence, just above Marine City. I saw this vessel on the stocks myself when it was building.

RELIEF OF FORT MACKINAC.

The Napoleon was the vessel that was afterwards selected to convey supplies to relieve the garrison at Fort Mackinac, in midwinter, and commanded by Captains Bob Wagstaff and Gus McKinstry. December, 1829, news came that by some oversight the garrison and people at Mackinac had failed to receive their winter supplies of provisions. The weather up to this time had been boisterous, and much ice had formed. A favorable change in the weather occurred and it became mild. Mr. Newberry offered one of his vessels in winter quarters here at that time to carry the supplies, if a crew could be got together for that purpose. "Gus" McKinstry (son of Colonel D. C. McKinstry) and Bob Wagstaff, both good, fearless sailors, undertook the job. They succeeded in getting a crew, and about the middle of December they landed the needed supplies on Mackinac Island, much to the delight of the citizens and garrison.

WELL-KNOWN CAPTAINS.

I witnessed the launching of all the craft that I have just mentioned, with the exception of the schooner Napoleon. Captain Van Allen, in command of the steamboat Mayflower when she first came out, was at that time said to be the first favorite of the traveling public on the lakes. Those now living that have sailed with him, either on the Emerald, between Buffalo and Niagara Falls, or on the steamboat Canada, between Detroit and Buffalo, on the same route, I am sure, will testify to his gentlemanly bearing at all times and to his good qualities as a sailor. He retired from the service to take charge of a hotel at Mackinac, which was a success, and died there some years ago. Captain Willoughby succeeded Van Allen on the steamer Canada. He, too, was immensely popular with the traveling public, as many will remember. The Canada, under his command, and the Mayflower, under the command of Captain Van Allen, divided the honors between this port and Buffalo. Captain Willoughby died in Quebec in 1862.

Captain Thomas P. Folger was quite popular on the lakes in the '40s. I knew him quite well, but cannot call to mind the names of any craft that he commanded. He was brother to Judge Folger, of New York, who was secretary of the treasury under President Arthur. He died in California in 1855.

Captain Ira Davis was a very popular captain. I think his entire service was on the route between here and Toledo. He was in command of the steamboat John Owen, when she first came out, I think, and for some years after. He died at his fine home on Woodward Avenue, this city, in 1873, aged 56.

Captain Selah Dustin was on this same route, and also commanded the steamboat John Owen for some time. I presume he was master of other craft, but do not call them to mind. He, too, was very popular and a master of his profession. Many, I am sure, will remember with pleasure the kindly old captain as I do.

CAPTAIN CHARLES L. GAGER.

I have something further to say in regard to Captain Gager. He died in Buffalo, December 2, 1886. The Buffalo paper recording his death goes on to say: "He was well known in marine circles. His career dated back to 1819, when he served on the steamboat Walk-in-the-Water, which was the first steamboat on the lakes above Niagara Falls. She ran from Black Rock to Detroit, and, in addition to her own power, required the assistance of twelve yoke of oxen to get up the current of Niagara River.

Captain Gager about 1848 built the passenger steamer Albany, sailing her himself. He also commanded a number of other steamboats, and later owned and ran the large tug Echo, at this port, which was afterwards converted into a floating elevator. In his early days he sailed on the salt water, and is said to have been engaged in the slave trade. He was bluff and obstinate, but good-hearted, and a decidedly unique benefactor. He leaves considerable property.

Captain Gager, was, indeed, a "rough diamond." He had an interesting family. His wife was a sister of Mrs. George G. Bull, who was the clerk of the United States Court here about 1858 or 1859. He had a beautiful daughter. Mary was her name. Mr. George G. Bull, her uncle, was for many years and until his death (some time about 1870), an attache of the United States Court here, in conjunction with the late Colonel John Winder and Addison Mandel, etc. I record a transaction in which Captain Gager was one of the principal factors:

The steamer Albany was wintering at this port in 1848. Some time in January of that year, the First Regiment, Michigan Volunteer Infantry, destined for service in Mexico, had completed its organization and had reported to the war department for duty in the field. Five companies, under command of Lieutenant-Colonel Alpheus S. Williams, were ordered to march to Cincinnati, to take transportation down the Mississippi, which they did. The other five companies, with Colonel Stockton and staff, managed to secure transportation by water to Cleveland, or thought they had. The river and lake were open and clear of ice, a January thaw being in evidence, and apparently there was no inpediment to navigation in that direction. Captain Sewel L. Fremont, the United States quartermaster at this post at that time, contracted with Captain Gager to take the five companies, with their baggage, etc., to the point above mentioned. Colonel Stockton's command, with their baggage, etc., got on board the steamer Albany, at the foot of Woodward Avenue, and started for their destination. Before leaving the dock it was currently reported that Captain Gager had induced the quartermaster to pay him in advance for transportation of the troops to Cleveland. But on arriving at Malden the steamer was met by a sudden change of temperature and threatening weather. The captain tied his boat up at the dock and informed Captain Fremont that he would not proceed a rod further under the circumstances, as he feared for the safety of his vessel, as well as for the safety of his passengers. He did not budge an inch, notwithstanding the threats of the officers, backed by loaded pistols. They tried the engineer, but he, too, was obdurate. Finally, the colonel and his command were forced to get to Gibraltar, on the American side, as best they could, and that was on foot, across Grosse Ile, and on scows across the river beyond.

How Captain Fremont, if such was the fact (the prepaying of Captain Gager), ever squared himself with the war department at Washington for his blunder, I never knew. As for Captain Gager, he could take care of No. 1, as all who knew him can testify. I was a clerk in the United States quartermasters and commissary offices here at the time, under Captain Whitall, Fifth United States Infantry. Captain Fremont was detailed by the war department on a special duty of equipping and transporting this regiment and Captain Whitall and he had their offices together.

STEAMBOAT ENGINEERS.

The steamboat engineers were not quite so much in the public eye as were the steamboat commanders. Yet here are a few of them that I call to mind, whose names and personalities were almost as much to the front as any of the captains that I have named: Steve Newhall, Ben Briscoe, Joe Cook, Frank Farrer and George Watson. Newhall was one of Oliver Newberry's trusted, reliable subordinates, and was an accomplished engineer wherever placed. I think he was with Blake on the steamboat Michigan when she first came out. Ben Briscoe passed the morning, noon and almost the afternoon of his life in the engine rooms of many of the finest steamers on the lakes, and it is entirely safe to say he was inferior to none. Joe Cook, Frank Farrer and George Watson were also accomplished engineers. I do not call to mind any of the steamboats on which Frank Farrer served, but I know he had the reputation of being A No. 1 in his profession. Joe Cook was for many years engineer on the May Queen, running between here and Cleveland. George Watson was engineer at one time on the steamboat Ocean, one of

Ward's finest steamers. There were hosts of other accomplished engineers on the lakes at that time, as there are now, but I do not call them to mind.

CAPTAIN SAMUEL WARD.

Captain Samuel Ward came to Newport (now Marine City) about 1819 or '20. Shortly afterward he built a little schooner of thirty tons burden called the St. Clair. In this boat Captain Ward got his start, trading in general merchandise. The captain made extensive trips in this little boat, one of which was from Green Bay to New York (of which trip mention has before been made). He built the schooner Marshal Ney about 1830. About 1835 the schooner Harrison (100 tons) came out. E. B. Ward, a nephew of Captain Samuel Ward, afterwards one of the largest vessel and steamboat owners on the lakes, sailed in her as mate. In 1839 he built the hull of the steamboat Huron, but had not the means to complete it. His nephew, Eber B. Ward, took the matter in hand, finished the boat and afterwards developed a rare business sagacity, as all who are familiar with his career can bear witness.

THE STEAMBOAT DETROIT IN 1846.

In 1846 the steamboat Detroit was the only first-class steamer plying regularly between Detroit and the "Soo." In 1855 there were four first-class passenger steamboats, besides several propellers, running regularly between Detroit and ports on Lake Superior, passing through the "Soo" canal. The shipment of the copper output of the fourteen mines in the Ontonagon district in 1855 amounted to nearly 3,000 tons. At the present writing not one of the fourteen companies is in existence. But the mines in the Portage Lake and Keweenaw districts are now (as everyone knows) producing immense amounts of copper, and the stocks of each are held high in the Boston market, particularly the Calumet & Hecla and the Tamarack. It is hard to imagine what the late Mr. Sheldon, at one time one of the heavy owners of the Calumet & Hecla mine, would say in regard to this property now.

In 1866 I was in Houghton, and Mr. Sheldon, whom I knew well, tried to induce me to take some of the stock at $1 per share, but I had been bit in copper to the extent of about $600, and could not be persuaded.

THREE HISTORIC BOATS.

I call to mind three craft that were included in our lake marine, that I have not mentioned before, and that had quite a history attached. They were the brig Queen Charlotte, the barque Detroit and the fore-and-after Lady Provost. They belonged to the British fleet, opposed to Commodore Perry at the battle of Lake Erie, and were captured by him. They were sunk in the harbor of Erie. After remaining under water for a number of years they were raised and put into commission. How long they remained so I do not remember. They all plainly showed in their hulls the marks of the punishment they had received.

The brig Queen Charlotte had to "take crow." I have been told that before the Lake Erie fight she passed up and down the opposite side of the Detroit river under full sail, with the cross of St. George flying at her masthead, and as she passed in front of the city she fired a blank cartridge (cannon), besides lowering and hoisting her topsails. The late Commodore Brevoort related the above circumstance. He knew, if anybody did, as he was here at the time and was an eye-witness of the incident. He afterwards participated in the fight as a volunteer. He used to relate the incident with great glee, and it was memorized in rhyme, as follows:

> The Detroit and Queen Charlotte and Lady Provost,
> Not able to fight or run, gave up the ghost,
> And not one of them all from our grapplings got free
> Though we'd fifty-four guns and they just sixty-three.

Here is a short sketch of what the Queen Charlotte was in her prime:

"On the morning of the 16th of August, 1812, the time of Hull's surrender, the Queen Charlotte, a fine ship of war, 18 guns, ran up the Detroit River, near the sand hill (where the old copper smelting works are now located) and dropped her anchor. Under cover of her broadsides the boats, with General Brock's troops, landed. They instantly formed and marched up to the place where the Michigan Central Railroad crosses the river road, and there defiled into the ravine out of the reach of our cannon."

Referring to the recent move of shipping freight direct by steamers from Chicago to European ports, I would say that it is not the first attempt of our lake shippers to place western products in foreign ports, without breaking cargo at the east. George W. Bissell, of Detroit, freighted a vessel (the Levi Cook), sometime in the early fifties, with an assorted cargo, for Liverpool. What the result of the venture was I never knew.

The St. Helena (sail), among others, chartered by J. and P. Aspinwall, Detroit, to carry staves to Europe in July, 1859. The Sexton, Pierce and Kershaw (sail), were chartered the same season by Captain Pierce, of Cleveland, to carry railroad ties to Russia. Trowbridge and Wilcox, Detroit, in 1859 sent from this port the schooner Grand Trunk, 327 tons burden, Captain Starkweather, to Hamburg, Germany, with a large cargo, consisting of hardwood lumber, and no doubt there were others.

In the fall of 1843, the number of boats remaining in commission on the lakes was sixty, making a tonnage of 17,000 tons; and of these only thirty-five were used when the steamboat combination was in existence.

It was computed in 1845 that the average value of property freighted to and fro on lakes Erie and Ontario exceeded $81,000,000, and the number of vessels exceeded 500, including seventy-eight steamboats and steam propellers, many of which were from 500 to 1,200 tons burden. (This information was obtained from a Detroit Daily of that year.)

SHIPMENTS OF GRAIN, ETC.

The first shipment of grain from Lake Michigan was made in 1836. In that year 3,000 bushels of wheat were shipped from Grand River, Mich., on the brig John Kenzie, owned by Dorr & Jones, Detroit, and commanded by Captain R. C. Bristol. This cargo arrived at Buffalo safely. In 1838 the steamer Great Western carried from Chicago to Buffalo thirty-nine bags of wheat, which were consigned to parties in Otsego County, N. Y. This was the first grain shipped from Chicago. In October, 1839, the brig Osceola carried down from Chicago to Kingman & Durfee, of Black Rock, 1,678 bushels of wheat, this being the first shipment of grain in bulk from that port. In 1840 a small schooner named the General Harrison, of about 100 tons, was loaded at Chicago with 3,000 bushels of wheat for Buffalo. The same years the schooner Gazelle carried from Chicago to Buffalo 3,000 bushels of wheat; the brig Erie 2,000 bushels; and the schooners Major Oliver and Illinois each a small cargo, etc.

WINTER OF 1843.

The *Jackson, Mich., Democrat* said in the winter of 1843: "Just think of it—As soon as the lake is open to Buffalo, travelers can go from Jackson, sixty miles in the interior of Michigan, to Boston or New York by steam. If any man had told us fifteen years ago that such a trip would be performed, or that such a communication would be opened in 1843, we should have called him a Mormon or Millerite."

There was much trouble with the mails in those days (1843), as, for instance, a Detroit paper had this to say: "The steamboats Columbus and Julia Palmer left Buffalo at the same time day before yesterday. The mail was put on board the Julia Palmer; the Columbus arrived here between 8 and 9 o'clock this morning, but the Julia Palmer is not here yet. The result is that we have had no eastern mail since yesterday morning."

BAGGAGE CHECKS.

It appears from the *Buffalo Gazette* of some time in 1843 "that CaptainSquires, of the steamboat DeWitt Clinton, was the first to adopt the plan of metallic checks for baggage, so that when a passenger delivers his baggage to the porter he receives a check, the duplicate number of which is attached to his baggage, which is delivered only on presenting the duplicate—a great and long-felt want."

A WONDERFUL TRANSFORMATION.

A copy of the *Buffalo Commercial Advertiser* of 1843 says: "The present year completes a quarter of a century since the first steamer was launched upon the western lakes. During that period changes of vast magnitude have been effected by the application of the mighty agent—steam. Dense forests which frowned from the margins of great lakes, have been felled to give place to thriving villages, and the moody aboriginal occupant, who gazed with wonderment at the approach of the ponderous vehicle, has become extinct, or is known only as a wanderer beyond the limits of the Mississippi. Changes like those have characterized the introduction of steam upon the lakes and the independent, inquiring spirit which so distinctly marks the habits of the people of this country has kept pace with the progress of steam westwardly, and developed the fertility and abounding resources of the prairies until they have become the granary of the world."

CAPACITY OF SOME EARLY-DAY STEAMERS.

"The largest steamer on the lakes in 1859 was the Western World, 2,002 tons. There were nine others over 1,000 tons each, twenty-one measuring over 400 tons, seventy measuring over 100 tons, sixty-three measuring over 30 tons, and sixty-one measuring under 20 tons.

"In May, 1863, the steamers Western World, Plymouth Rock and Mississippi were taken from Detroit to Buffalo to have their machinery removed, and otherwise to be dismantled. These fine steamers were commissioned in 1855, plied but three seasons, and were among the largest and finest floating palaces ever put upon the lakes; and like everything else earthly they had their time; so had the railroad that scooped them, and there was no further use for them. An extravagant outlay of money to a very small purpose, as they never realized one dollar over expenses."

OVER THE FALLS.

In 1827 the schooner Michigan, having been condemned as unseaworthy, was sent over Niagara Falls. The event was announced in sensational handbills, which proclaimed that "the pirate ship Michigan, with a cargo of furious animals, will pass over the Falls of Niagara on the 8th of September, 1827." Entertainment was promised for all who might visit the Falls on that occasion, which would, "for its novelty and the remarkable spectacle which it will present, be unequaled in the annals of internal navigation." The Michigan was 136 tons burden. The event was witnessed by several thousand people.

This schooner Michigan, that was sent over the Falls, was the same vessel that conveyed Judge Buncer, of St. Clair, and his belongings to Detroit in 1817. He left Albany for Buffalo in April of that year. On his arrival at the latter place, he had to wait some days for the completion of the above vessel, on which he intended to cross, and did cross Lake Erie.

A GALA OCCASION.

In the early days, from 1827 to about 1835, the absorbing event in this community was the arrival of the steamboat from Buffalo. A quaint old custom prevailed on these steamboats, and that was the firing of a cannon on rounding the point at Sandwich, announcing the fact that a boat was coming up the river. The echo of the gun had hardly died away before, down to the wharf would come trooping all the citizens of the town, not otherwise specially engaged, who enjoyed the diversion of seeing the boat come in to her dock. Seeing the boat come in meant a great deal, too, for the boats were few and far between, and those that did arrive over the then uncertain route of inter-communication were indeed welcome, bringing, as they did, friends, news, letters and needed supplies. So the boats let off a gun to announce their arrival and away every one that could hurried to the dock.

I can testify from actual experience, many times repeated, what a welcome sound it was, and how everyone rushed to the dock, as stated. I presume the old steamboat Walk-in-the-Water inaugurated this custom of firing a cannon, which was kept up until steamboats became so numerous that their arrival and departure ceased to be a novelty, and the practice gradually died out. But it was a stirring and exciting experience to all Detroit folks, while the custom lasted, as any one that passed through that time will bear witness. Everything in the way of occupation was dropped when the report of that cannon was heard.

GREAT RIVALRY.

In the early thirties immigration was at fever heat, and every steamboat that came in from Buffalo was loaded to the water's edge. The rivalry was intense, and the boats were, ineed, floating palaces for those days. The agents especially emphasized the assurance that the public might depend on the most exact punctuality in the sailing of the boats throughout the season, from either end of the route, and their absolute safety. One of the most energetic and active of these agents, or runners, at this end, and indeed one of the most lively and truthful, not excepting those at the port of Buffalo, was Billy Burchell. Many, no doubt, will remember him, and what a stirring little chap he was. After hustling around at every hotel and taven in town, and seeing to it that everyone desiring to leave on the daily boat was on hand at the hour of departure, his "passengers all aboard, sir!" to the captain at his post, was the signal for starting, and it was almost invariably waited for.

"FLOATING PALACES" OF THE PAST.

The steamer Michigan, as before mentioned, built by Oliver Newberry, when she first came out was considered a leviathan

(472 tons burden), with her two engines, two walking beams and three masts, and magnificent appointments. Then after a while the steamboat Superior appeared, eclipsing the Michigan; then the Washington (609 tons burden); then the Great Western (780 tons), with the upper cabin, outdoing them both; then came the Empire, Captain Howe, declared by all to be, up to that date, the largest and most magnificent steamboat that had ever appeared on the lakes. She was a fine steamer, and I well remember her first appearance at her dock in this city. She landed at the foot of Woodward Avenue, Grey & Lewis' wharf. The citizens of this goodly town, almost en masse, inspected her admiringly and pronounced her the pride of the lakes, and one not easily duplicated or surpassed. Then came the Western World, 1,000 tons; then the Mayflower, 1,300 tons; then the Plymouth Rock, 1,991 tons; also the Northwest, 1,100 tons; the R. N. Rice, 1,030 tons, etc.

The magnificent examples of naval architecture, taking into account also their size and speed, as are now presented to us, makes all former efforts in that direction dwindle into insignificance; perhaps the efforts of the future may dwarf the present, but it does not seem possible. How significant also is the advance of the steam propeller of the lakes. In the early days sailing vessels or steam propellers capable of taking on a cargo of 15,000 or 20,000 bushels of wheat, were considered large and quite sufficient (copper and iron ore were not factors then in the freighting business only to a very small extent), but now the capacity of the propellers engaged in the grain, ore and lumber trade is enormous. The amount of tons of ore, bushels of grain, and feet of lumber the present lake monsters are able to take all are familiar with.

Comparing the capacity of some of the early freighters with those of the present an illustration is given, taken from a Detroit paper of that time, November 27, 1843.

"The brig Rocky Mountains (which was one of the largest of her class), on her last trip for Buffalo took a full cargo, consisting of 1,042 barrels of flour, 1,776 bushels wheat, 120 barrels fish, 6 casks ashes, 9 barrels cranberries."

Contrasting the time taken by steamers between Buffalo and Chicago from the years 1833-1840, with the present, we find that a steamer left Buffalo June 23 and returned July 18; another left Buffalo July 20 and returned August 11.,

CROSSING LAKE ERIE IN 1815.

The following extract from a letter dated Detroit, September 29, 1815, will give some idea of the tribulations of travelers in those days. It was written by the late Judge James Witherell to a friend in the "states," as they used to say then:

"I arrived in Buffalo on the 19th of August, and was detained until the 31st for want of a vessel. On that day I sailed in a little vessel called the 'Experiment.' The little dirty cabin was crowded with several women, six men and a dog. During the night we ran past Presque Isle (Erie) some twenty miles, and as some of the passengers were to have been landed there, they chose to be put on shore opposite the vessel, and get back as they could. They were landed. Among them was the famous Barnabas Bidwell. On the 20th we ran into the mouth of Grand River in a gale of wind. The mouth of the river was then some three or four rods wide. The wind changed and soon raised a sandbar at its mouth, which prevented the vessel getting out; and in this condition we lay until the 6th of September (sixteen days), when Major Marston and Lieutenant Ballard, of the army; Messrs. Bell and Kane, of Buffalo, and myself (as the prospect of getting out within the next ten or fifteen days was uncertain) concluded to hire a man to take us in a wagon to Cuyahoga (Cleveland). Our baggage was sent on shore to the wagon, but in going myself got jostled out of the boat into deep water, and was compelled to swim some distance. Of course I was thoroughly wet. It was about sunset and we had several miles to go. The teamster said the road was plain and I walked on ahead. When I had gone far enough to feel sure that I was not on the right road, being surrounded by a dense wilderness and no habitation to be seen, I began to retrace my steps. I had walked several miles. The cold night air and my dripping clothes had benumbed my shivering limbs. After awhile I discovered a light and procured a boy for a guide, and after seven or eight miles' walking over a very soft, muddy road, I found the wagon. Arriving at Cleveland, I found that there was but one way to proceed to Detroit, and that was to charter a small schooner, which we did for $40, and sailed the next morning. September 8. We ran to Black River; stopped about an hour and sailed again about 10 o'clock at night some twenty miles towards Sandusky; but the captain, not knowing the coast, was obliged to run back to Black River on account of head wind, where we remained until the 12th of September. On that day we sailed to the mouth of the Vermillion, but could not enter on account of a sandbar. We ran into a small creek and remained until daylight. On the 13th we reached the islands. Here a violent storm of thunder, lightning, wind and rain set in, which placed our little barque in imminent peril. Here we found ourselves out of provisions, and in attempting to leave the islands the wind drove us back. We went on shore to look for food, but the island, being uninhabited, and we having no guns or fishing tackle, we got nothing but a few hard, small peaches, which were divided among us. At night two men were sent on shore to get some sassafras or spice bush to make a drink of, but the men found none. The captain then advised that some buttonwood bark should be procured, which was done, and being boiled an hour or two in an old ash kettle we fell to drinking. To me it was serviceable, as I was suffering from fever occasioned by long fatigue and exposure. In the course of the night the wind became favorable to lay our course to Malden. After being two hours under way a violent storm arose, and our vessel sprung a leak in a place where it could not be stopped; and after our sails had been split to pieces by the wind, we were driven on the Canada shore near the new settlement below Malden. Here we found a house and stayed all night, and in the morning we hired a man to take us to Malden, and there another was employed to take us up the river, and we landed at Captain Knagg's on the 18th of September."

What a difference between then and now!

There have been in the past sailing greyhounds on the lakes, as well as those at present on the ocean; as, for instance, the ships Julia Palmer and Superior, the brigs Manhattan, Ramsey Crooks, Queen Charlotte, the clipper brig Illinois, etc.—all fast sailers, as old lake men can testify.

It was an exhilarating sight and one to stir the blood, to witness one of these vessels fly by the city with a fair wind abaft, carrying a "bone in her mouth" (to use a nautical expression), everything set below and aloft, her colors fluttering in the breeze. Old citizens, and sailors as well, will call to mind with a thrill of delight the stirring spectacle. The picture can be, and is repeated, on the ocean, but it is safe to say never again on the lakes. Gone like a puff of smoke.

CAPTAIN WHITAKER AGAIN.

In the article below, which appeared in one of our local papers, signed by the captain himself, appear the names and descriptions of some of the steamboats and their captains that I have mentioned before, but I do not think that need lessen its interest; besides it presents some new features:

The first steamboat—the Walk-in-the-Water—was built at Black Rock in 1817. John Fish was the master. She was as good a model as those upon which boats of the same dimensions are now built. Her length was 150 feet; breadth of beam, 27 feet; depth of hold, 10 feet, with three feet rise to quarter-deck. Her engine was low pressure and was built in England. It had four feet stroke of piston, cylinder 40-inch bore, diameter of wheels, 16 feet—four times the length of stroke. She always ran from Grand River to Cleveland in three hours and forty minutes in still water, a distance of thirty-one miles by government chart, which gives a speed of eight and a half miles per hour. She was lost at Buffalo on the first day of November, 1821, after running four seasons.

The steamboat Superior, Jedediah Rogers master, was built at Buffalo and came out in May, 1822. She was not as good a model as the Walk-in-the-Water. She was about the same speed, and had the engine and furniture of her predecessor.

A small steamboat called the Chippewa, with a low pressure engine, was built at Buffalo in 1823. She was a failure.

The Enterprise was built at Cleveland in 1825 by L. Johnson. She had a low-pressure engine, which was changed to a high-pressure in 1828-9. She then made money.

The Wm. Penn was built at Erie, Pa., in 1826, with a condensing engine. She was a failure.

The steamboat Pioneer was built at Black Rock (Captain W. T. Pease) in 1825-6. She went ashore at Grand River, Ohio, the same fall; was gotten off and a high-pressure engine put in her. She then performed well. The small boat Niagara, built at Black Rock in 1826-7, received the low-pressure engine of the Pioneer. She was a success.

The steamboat Henry Clay (Captain William Norton) was built at Black Rock in 1826. She was a low-pressure boat, of model and size similar to the Walk-in-the-Water. The Clay was a success.

In the winter of 1827-8 the steamboat Wm. Peacock was built at Barcelona, Chautauqua Co., N. Y. She had the low-pressure engine of the Chippewa and was a failure. She was bought by C. M. Reed, of Erie, who put a high-pressure engine in her. She was then a fair boat of her size.

In 1830 the small steamboat Ohio was built at Lower Sandusky with a high-pressure oscillating engine. She was a failure.

In 1830 the steamboat Sheldon Thompson came out with a low-pressure engine. She was a good model and a fair success.

In June, 1833, the steamboat Uncle Sam (Captain Stiles) came out from Detroit. She had a condensing beam engine, but was not a success.

In the same month, 1833, the steamer New York was built at Black Rock. She had two high-pressure engines and eight boilers, but was a big failure.

The steamboat Pennsylvania, with two high-pressure engines, built by C. M. Reed, at Erie, Pa., was not a success.

From May, 1822, up to July, 1833, the following steamboats were built: Chippewa, Enterprise, Wm. Penn, Pioneer, Niagara, Henry Clay, Wm. Peacock, Ohio, Sheldon Thompson, Uncle Sam, New York and Pennsylvania—twelve steamboats—making fourteen steamboats built during the first fifteen years. The Henry Clay was the only one of the twelve steamboats which came up to the Walk-in-the-Water, or was superior to her in speed or capacity for business. The other eleven were far inferior in speed and capacity.

In the fall of 1833 the steamboat Michigan, with two low-pressure beam engines, built by Oliver Newberry, of Detroit, and commanded by Chelsea Blake, came out. She was then the best rough water boat in this country.

The Daniel Webster came out in December, 1833, and made one trip from Buffalo to Detroit and back. She was built by Pratt & Taylor, of Buffalo, after having false sides. She was a fair boat.

After 1833, with an increase of business, the steamboats built, with the exception of a few failures, were larger and better.

I commanded four of the above-named steamboats during the time stated, and know their speed and capacity.

This account of early steamboating upon our western lakes is drawn from memory and is reliable. I doubt whether records can be found which are reliable. I am pleased to say that during the fifteen years of steamboating, of which I have written, there were but five lives lost, caused by the breaking of a steam pipe on board the Peacock, Captain John Flaherty.

HARRY WHITAKER.

CAPTAIN FRED WHEELER AND THE HERCULES.

Captain Fred Wheeler, of the steamer Hercules, was a gay boy for a steamboat captain, but they were nearly all so when in port and tied up at the dock. Of course, outside, they were sailors all.

The Hercules, on her trips from Buffalo to Chicago, rarely ever stopped at any ports on the way, except Cleveland, Detroit and Milwaukee, and at these three ports Captain Fred had many warm friends. By far the greater number were at this port, Detroit.

The arrival of the boat here was always the signal to the "boys" that a good time with Fred was at hand, and we always had it, in a moderate way. He usually tied up at Alex. Lewis' dock, at the foot of Bates Street, for from twelve to twenty-four hours, leaving in time to get over the St. Clair Flats by daylight, and rarely ever stopping on his downward trips for over an hour or so.

Well, Fred concluded to get married and settle down, which he did, marrying a young lady in Buffalo. Just before the event he left word here with Dan Whipple (of the Bates Street restaurant) to provide a supper and a basket of champagne for the "boys," wherewith to celebrate his nuptials. The supper came off, and they were all on hand and enjoyed it, as much as they did the champagne. There was only one thing that occurred to mar the pleasure of the occasion, and that was the intoxication of the properietor of the house (Whipple), and he was the only one of the crowd to get in that condition.

A MERRY ROW.

After the supper was over and the cigars lighted, it was proposed that a meeting be organized for the purpose of adopting resolutions expressing the friendly sentiments of the crowd toward the bride and groom. Barney Campau was called upon to preside and George Dibble was named as secretary. They were installed in chairs placed on top of the supper table after the cloth was removed. The proceedings had hardly begun when Dan, seeing the boys seated on top of the table, his muddled brain (he having been indulging a little in the "rosy") failed to take in the situation, got furious, grabbed hold of the two chairs and pulled them and their two occupants to the floor. The meeting broke up in a row, of course, and the party left the house highly indignant. Whipple came around to each one the next day and made an humble apology, and the matter was smoothed over and soon forgotten. Dan was always ugly when in that plight, but he was a mighty good fellow withal.

Wheeler concluded to spend his honeymoon on a trip to Chicago and return on the sidewheel steamer St. Louis, instead of his own, the Hercules. The party arrived here in due time, and he received the congratulations of his friends. As the steamer was to remain here for eight or ten hours, one of the boys proposed to take the bride out for a buggy ride, and show her the city. The offer was accepted.

For some reason or other, I imagine designed by the way of a joke on the part of the escort, they did not return until after the steamer St. Louis had left, and with it the groom. Wheeler was in a peck of trouble on account of the non-appearance of his wife, and left word for her to join him at Chicago by rail, which she did. She was awfully indignant, of course. Captain Fred bided his time in which to get in his retaliation work, and he did after a little. About a month had passed after this small episode when one day, along about noon, the Hercules appeared at her dock, on her down trip from Chicago. Fred gave out to the "boys" that it would give him great pleasure to have them dine with him on board the boat at 7 o'clock of that day. Well, we were all on hand at the hour, and had a very enjoyable time. After the cigars were lighted, Captain Fred excused himself for a few moments, and upon his return he resumed his cigar. After a pleasant half hour spent in smoking and relating reminiscences, he said, "Boys, I am afraid I cannot give you an invite to accompany me to Buffalo, but I can do the next best thing, and that is to give you a trip to Malden, and you are taking it right now; no thanks!"

Sure enough, when he excused himself he had given orders to have the cables quietly slipped, and before we knew it we were half way to Malden. On our arrival at the latter place the captain put us ashore, with a "Good bye, boys," and a "safe return home," and sped on his way. We had to hire conveyances at Malden to get us home, which we reached after a tedious, dusty ride of some three or four hours. We failed to see the joke.

MYSTERIOUS LOSS OF THE GOLIAH.

The other propeller, which I have mentioned (the Goliah), was of about the same tonnage as the Hercules, and was owned by Wesley Truesdail, of St. Clair. She was lost on her way to the "Soo" in 1846, I think, on Lake Huron, it was supposed. At any rate she was never heard from after she passed Port Huron. The reason that I mention this boat again is that I knew the captain and have been aboard of her frequently; on her last trip she carried two friends of mine, Edward Cood, a clerk in the employ of Mr. Truesdail, and John Schwarz, son of Gen. John E. Schwarz, adjutant-general of the state. Both were bright young men, the latter particularly so.

Captain T. Langley, when in command of the propeller Mayflower, in August, 1861, received on board his boat at Mackinac Prince Napoleon (Plon-Plon) and his suite, who wished to go to Milwaukee. He gave up his own stateroom to the prince, who testified his appreciation of the pleasures of the trip by presenting the captain at the end of the voyage with his own cane. The cane was a fine one, being surmounted by a massive gold head bearing the prince's own name and crest.

TRIBUTE TO THE STEAMER OCEAN.

The following tribute to the steamer Ocean is from the pen of Ossian E. Dodge, and is an extract from a poem delivered on that boat, on its return to Detroit from the celebration of the forty-fifth anniversary of the battle of Lake Erie at Put-in-Bay Island, September 10, 1858.

> Well, just at half-past seven o'clock,
> The good steamer Ocean pulled out from the dock,
> And while from the river she merrily ran on,
> The ladies all screamed at the sound of the cannon.
>
> There were plenty of soldiers with musket and sword
> And a number of men lost their hats overboard,
> While soon in the cabin we all had a chance
> To each take a lady and all have a dance.

And now I will this opportunity take
To say that steamboats are well manned on the lake;
And you will no doubt all respond to my motion,
That none can be more so than the good steamer Ocean.

To prove that this steamer is rapid and fierce,
She's got an agent, one Gen. Pierce;
And passengers dream of the Cupids and heavens,
While sailing so smoothly with good Captain Evans.

When the steamer is ready and all wish to start her,
The clerk sells the tickets—one good David Carter;
And to be doubly sure that she'll never be late,
One William McKay is the popular mate.

Of danger there never can be any fear
So long as George Watson is chief engineer;
And no one to grumble can ever be able
When the steward, John Greenslade, provides for the table.

Before the advent of Captain John Burtis, with his horse boat, which he brought from Cleveland in 1825 or thereabouts, the traffic between the two points was carried on by small boats and scows, the former for the conveyance of passengers, the latter for teams and passengers as well.

William Baubie, of Windsor, recently deceased, was engaged in this business before Burtis came. He owned a scow and seven row-boats, and has often related to the writer his experience in the ferry marine.

Captain Burtis' boat was called the Olive Branch, a scow-constructed craft propelled by horses. It resembled a "cheese-box on a raft," and Mr. Bolio, one of the old French residents, whose widow is still living in this city, was also engaged in the same business about that time, and with the same appliances. And now comes Captain Ben Woodworth, of Woodworth's hotel, who has this advertisement in the *Detroit Gazette* of April 20, 1820.

OVER! OVER!!

The subscriber has obtained a license to keep a Ferry on the Detroit River, and calls on the public for patronage. He has provided an excellent Flat, and his Boats for passengers are superior to any that can be found on the River. Careful men have been engaged to attend the Ferry, and constant attention will be given, in order that passengers may suffer no delay. Persons wishing to contract for their ferriage by the year, will be accommodated at a low rate, and landed at any point within a reasonable distance of the landing-place on the opposite shore. Freight will be taken over at a low rate.

☞ The Ferry is kept nearly in front of the Steam Boat Hotel. B. WOODWORTH.

N. B.—Persons wishing to cross are desired to give notice at the Steam Boat Hotel.

Detroit, April 20, 1820.

Captain Burtis' horse-boat was a sidewheeler. These wheels were made to revolve by two horses, which trod on a circular table, set flush with the deck in the center, and revolved upon rollers, which, being connected with the shaft, set the wheels in motion. The horses remained stationary on the deck, the table on which they trod revolving under them, and being furnished with ridges of wood, radiating like spokes from the center, and which the horses caught with their feet, thus setting the tables in motion.

The following advertisement in relation to the horse-boat ferry appeared in the *Detroit Gazette* in 1825:

"HORSE-BOAT FERRY."

The subscribers have recently built a large and commodious

HORSE-BOAT,

for the purpose of transporting across the Detroit river passengers, wagons, horses, cattle, etc., etc. The boat is so constructed that wagons and carriages can be driven on it with ease and safety. It will leave McKinstry's wharf (adjoining that of Dow & Jones) for the Canada shore, and will land passengers, etc., at the wharf lately built on that shore by McKinstry & Burtis. The ferry wharves are directly opposite.

Mr. Burtis resides on the Canada shore and will pay every attention to those who may desire to cross the river.

D. C. McKINSTRY—J. BURTIS.

The writer crossed the river on this boat many times in 1827 and afterward.

The "horse-boat" continued on this route until 1833, when Captain Burtis superseded her with the steamer Argo, which Captain Jenkins, of Windsor, built for him in that year. This little steamer I have alluded to slightly in a former article. For the following, in regard to the ferry business, I am indebted to the late Captain J. W. Hall, marine reporter at this port in 1878:

"In 1834 the Argo had a rival on the ferry route called the Lady of the Lakes. The status of the ferry business did not vary materially until 1836, when the United was brought forth. Mr. Jenkins got up this craft for Louis Davenport. The United was 71 tons burden, and continued on the ferry route until 1853. Subsequently she was converted into a lumber barge, and is still (1878) in commission. During her term of service as a ferry she had several masters. Those we at present call to mind were Captains Davenport, W. Clinton and J. B. Baker. In 1842 the Alliance began plying. After a few years her name was changed to the Undine, Captain John Sloss. Tom Chilvers at different times commanded her. The Argo No. 2 came on the route in 1848. Not long afterward an explosion took place on board, killing Captain Foster, her master, and others. After reconstruction she was for several years commanded by Captain W. C. Clinton, father of the present Captain W. R. Clinton, and afterwards by Captain James Forbes until 1872, when she was taken from the route. In 1852 Dr. Russell built and placed on the route the Ottawa, commanded by Captain W. R. Clinton, and subsequently by Captain A. H. Mills. The steamer Gem, built for W. P. Campbell, came out in 1856, and was first in command of Captain J. B. Goodsell, and afterwards by Captain Tom Chilvers, the latter having had for a short time on the route the Mohawk, formerly a British naval steamer. The Windsor was also built in 1856 by Dr. Russell. She was commanded by Captain W. R. Clinton. After a short period of service she was chartered to the Detroit & Milwaukee Railway, and was burned at their dock in March, 1866, with the loss of several lives. Subsequently she was rebuilt, converted into a barge, and is now (1878) in commission on Lake Michigan. The Essex, built by Messrs. Jenkins, came out in 1859, and began ferrying. She was commanded by Captain George Jenkins. After running for some years she was laid up for a time and again took the route, plying more or less of the past (1878) season. The steamer Olive Branch for a time also served as a ferry during the period of 1859. She was owned by W. P. Campbell. The Detroit, built at Algonac for Mr. Campbell by Zadock Pangburn, came on in 1834, and, with others above referred to, continued plying until 1875, when she was retired. The Hope was built in 1870 for George N. Brady and Captain W. R. Clinton, the latter taking charge of her. The present (1878) fleet of ferry steamers consists of the Victoria, built in 1872, Captain W. R. Clinton; the Fortune, built in 1875, Captain Walter E. Campbell, and the Excelsior, built in 1876, Captain W. L. Horn. The last named steamers, in point of superiority, in their get-up and accommodations, are unsurpassed anywhere in the world. And what adds to this is that their officers are obliging and gentlemanly in their deportment, and spare no pains in caring for all who travel over this important thoroughfare."

This statement was made twenty-four years ago, and the great advance the ferry company has made since that time all are quite familiar with.

Another pleasing feature about this ferry business is the liberality of the company in allowing the public to enjoy in season the luxury of riding on their boats from morning until evening for ten cents each person; children in baby carriages and arms free. Just think of it! Nowhere else in the world can this be duplicated, nor the routes either, for that matter. In the early days no such luxury was dreamed of. It was available to a limited extent, but no one ever thought of taking advantage of it.

Although I have copied freely from Mr. Hall's article, I was quite familiar with all the ferry boats, etc., that he mentions. The ferry dock during the time of the Davenports and a little earlier was at the foot of Griswold street. The steamboats Argo, 2d, and United ran every fifteen minutes or so into a slip on which the Davenports, Lewis and his brother, built a commodious structure for a waiting room, saloon and restaurant. The saloon and restaurant were run by John Edwards, whom many, no doubt, will remember as an exceedingly jolly and pleasant Englishman. This waiting room, saloon and restaurant were built over the water on piles.

CAPTAIN BURTIS AND HIS STEAMBOAT ARGO.

I have barely mentioned this mite of a steamboat and her jovial captain in a former article, but think both boat and captain deserve a more extended notice, as it was this city's first attempt in steamboat building.

The Argo was built in this city at the foot of Wayne Street. The captain was a pioneer in the ferry business between Detroit and Windsor, he having, as before mentioned, commanded the horse ferry-boat that plied between the two cities. His ambition in the navigation business was not satisfied, so he essayed the steamer Argo (this was in 1833). She was fashioned out of two immense trees, or logs, hollowed out like canoes, and the two were joined together, fore and aft, but were spread apart and decked over with side wheels. Shadrick Jenkins, father of the Jenkins brothers, Windsor ship builders, was the builder also of several vessels respectively at Detroit, Moy (this side of Walkerville) and Malden. It seems to me that I was on hand almost daily when the building of this boat was in progress, such an interest I took in it.

The boat was finally completed and launched, sideways, into the slip near by. She was a success in a small way, as far as steam propulsion was concerned; but was very "cranky." The *Free Press* published in 1879 (the exact date I do not remember) an article I wrote in relation to Captain Burtis and his steamboat, which I think will bear reproduction here:

INTERESTING RETROSPECT.

"Rambling about the city a few days ago, I found myself in the City cemetery on Russell Street, corner of Gratiot Avenue, and it occurred to me that as the order had gone forth for the removal of the bodies still remaining buried there, I might idle away an hour or so scanning the few remaining tombstones, and that perhaps I might remember something in relation to them that would be of interest to the living.

"Many of our old residents will remember Captain Burtis. His grave is so near Russell Street that the passerby can or could read his name on the tombstone; doubtless many have done so, when it stood erect, and perhaps have wondered who this person was that once owned the high-sounding title of 'Captain.' Quite recently some miserable vandal broke the stone in twain. The

amazon.com   # amazon.com

Amazon Fulfillment Services
172 Trade Street
Lexington, KY 40511

Shipping Address:

susan mazzara
6012 COLONY PARK DR
YPSILANTI, MI
48197-6025
United States of America

YOUR ORDER OF FEBRUARY 11, 2018 (ORDER ID 113-2545738-1613841)

Qty	Item
	IN THIS SHIPMENT:
1	Early Days in Detroit: Papers Written by General Friend Palmer of De Being His Personal Reminiscences of Important Events and Description the City for Over Eighty Years (Classic Reprint) Palmer, Friend Paperback 0282436987 Amazon.com Services, Inc.

This shipment completes your order.

Dr72tpm0k

http://www.amazon.com

Your Account

For detailed information about your orders,
please visit Your Account. You can also print invoices,
change your email address and payment settings,
alter your communication preferences,
and much more - 24 hours a day - at
http://www.amazon.com/your-account.

Returns are easy !

Visit http://www.amazon.com/returns to return any
item - including gifts - in unopened or original condition
within 30 days for a full refund (other restrictions apply).
Please have your order ID ready. Thanks for shopping
at Amazon.com, and please come again !

	Item Price	Total
:oit, of	$27.81	$27.81

amazon.com
and you're done.

WC   813   #7BLMJ   20C4669
02/12/18   Dr72tpm0k

AM04 - 06165V05

captain had the gift of forcible language to a remarkable degree, and I can imagine him standing beside his own grave, in the flesh, giving vent to his feelings against the perpetrators of the useless act, in some of his choicest English. He died in 1836, at the age of 45, so the stone records, and though comparatively young, he had lived long enough to accomplish some few things to help along the growth of this great city and state. He was the first to establish a decent ferry between this city and Windsor. Many will remember his boat that looked something like 'Erickson's cheese box on a raft,' propelled by horsepower. It was a wonder to all the natives as well as a great convenience to the inhabitants on both sides of the river. He continued this for a while until he superseded it by something new and better, viz.: the steamer Argo, the first steamboat built in Michigan. After serving as a ferry boat for a short time, it became the pioneer of steam river navigation between Detroit, Port Huron, Fort Gratiot, St. Clair, etc.

"I well remember the building of this diminutive steamer and the captain's overseeing the same. It was built almost in front of the hardware house of Buhl, Ducharme & Co., on Woodbridge Street. The hull was composed of two immense logs, hollowed out and joined together, making a huge canoe, as it were, and when sufficiently completed to receive her miniature engine, she was helped into the river on rollers. Her trips to Port Huron and other places were trips to be remembered. I ventured on three of them to St. Clair and return, and the incidents connected therewith are as fresh in my memory as though they had happened yesterday. She was awfully 'cranky,' this little Argo, and it required considerable vigilance on the part of her captain to keep his passengers from 'shooting' around and tipping her over. One occasion I remember well. On one of the trips I mention, the late Thomas Palmer was with us, and he, being of goodly proportions, it behooved Burtis, who was at the helm, to keep his eye on him. Every once in a while he would sing out, 'For God's Sake, Uncle Tom, keep in the middle of the boat, or you will have us over,' or 'Trim ship, Uncle Tom,' or 'Look out, Uncle Tom,' until 'Trim ship, Uncle Tom,' came to be a by-word during the excursion. This little Argo soon passed away and was superseded by another and larger steamer of the same name, but not another 'Burtis.' The jovial and genial captain fell a victim to cholera, I think."

RELEASED BY MAN-POWER.

Another funny incident occurred on one of these trips that I have hitherto failed to record. My uncle had imported from the then lumbering state of Maine, an experienced hand, or expert, in the lumber business, for service in his water saw mill, located some miles up Pine River, in St. Clair county. Well, this chap was with us on one of these excursions. Everything went along all right until, steaming quietly and serenely close to the shore, between Algonac and Newport (now Marine City), the Argo sunddenly ran her nose into a dense bunch of alder bushes on the river bank, and stuck there hard aground. The utmost power of the diminutive engine was unable to extricate the boat. My uncle suggested to Captain Burtis that perhaps his man from Maine might do the thing, as he was over six feet tall and quite lanky. Well, the chap was quite willing, and, cautiously letting himself into the water, at the bow of the steamer, where the water was about up to his waist, he, without much effort, released the Argo from her plight. Then the question arose, how was the man from Maine to get aboard again without tipping us over. He was bound to do it, if he tried it where he was, at the bow, so the captain told him he must try getting aboard over the stern. The water there was up to his arm-pits, but he managed to crawl aboard over the stern, with the help of those on board, and we proceeded on our way rejoicing.

UNCLE TOM'S MISHAP.

Here is another incident in connection with the Argo and Uncle Thomas Palmer. On one of these trips the latter found it necessary to go aft. To accomplish this it was necessary to climb over the paddle-box, and as he was executing that feat he broke through and caught his foot in a bucket of the paddle wheel. It was a test of strength between himself and the engine. The engine gave up. Palmer extricated his foot and the Argo proceeded on her way.

It's a long cry from the little Argo to the steamers Promise and Tashmoo, and from these to what——-

Steam tugging was begun in 1844 by the steamer Romeo, a sidewheeler. In 1848 there were also employed at the Flats the steamers Tecumseh, Little Erie, Telegraph No. 2, Chautauqua, propeller Odd Fellow, and others. The number of tugs in commission in 1877, according to Captain J. W. Hall, marine reporter at that time, was forty-two. In his records Captain Hall says: "These tugs, for finish and capacity, are not surpassed in any other part of the world, both as regards towing and wrecking."

The late Governor Jerome and his brother "Tiff" had the charter of the steamer Chautauqua when she was engaged in tugging on Lake and River St. Clair in 1848. Captain David, as we called him then, invited me, in the fall of the above year, to spend a couple of weeks with him "aboard ship," which I did. I had a very enjoyable time, the memory of which will remain with me pleasantly always. Dave did not dream then that some day the governorship of Michigan would be bestowed upon him.

SOME POWERFUL TUGS.

This tugging business was at one time indispensable and assumed immense proportions. Of the forty-two tugs in commission in 1877, I call to mind only four—the Champion, the Sweepstakes, the Crusader and the Gladiator—all powerful tugs. The Champion was without doubt the most powerful tug on the lakes. She was built by the Detroit Dry-Dock Co. and owned by the late John P. Gillett and others. The Sweepstakes was owned by H. Norton Strong. These tugs, with their tows, were a spectacular feature of our river in those days. Strong had his tug, with five or six vessels in tow, perpetuated in a colored lithograph. They made a pleasing picture, taken as they passed the city, bound down, with colors flying. This lithograph was widely distributed, and many no doubt are the fortunate possessors of them.

These tugs filled a long-felt want. I call to mind, along in 1837, 1838, and on to 1840, when our merchants received the bulk of their spring and fall purchases in the east by sailing vessels from Buffalo. These vessels were often detained by adverse winds, sometimes for many days, causing the merchants and their customers considerable anxiety and vexation. I call to mind one such occasion. I was a boy clerk in the general store of C. & J. Wells, Desnoyer Block, Jefferson Avenue, in 1837 or 1838. We had the fall and winter stock of dry goods, groceries, etc., on the way here, by vessel from Buffalo, and the proprietors were looking anxiously for their arrival, as were many other merchants for their goods. Well, one day eight or ten vessels appeared in sight just below Sandwich point. As they were rounding the point a head wind struck them, and there they lay for almost a week, with all those goods in their holds that everybody needed so badly. Finally a fair wind came along and wafted the fleet to the city, and all interested were happy. Now, if the steam tug had been in evidence such a thing could not have happened.

The late Captain E. B. Ward built an iron tug boat about three years before he died. It was the first one built of iron, and the largest on the lakes. She was constructed by the Detroit Dry-Dock Company, but was found to be not adapted for the work and was taken to New Orleans and sold. She was put into the fruit trade in that vicinity.

THE WALK-IN-THE-WATER.

The public has no doubt often heard of the steamer Walk-in-the-Water, her origin and her loss on the beach at Buffalo pier in 1821, but there are some incidents connected with this boat that I don't think have appeared in print before. The "History of the Great Lakes" says of the Walk-in-the-Water:

"The year 1818 is memorable for the construction of the Walk-in-the-Water, the first steamboat on Lake Erie. During the winter of 1817-18 the following named persons associated together to build a steamboat to navigate Lake Erie: Joseph B. Stuart, Nathaniel Davis, Asa H. Curtis, Ralph Pratt, James Durant and John Meads, of Albany, and Robert McQueen, Samuel McCoon, Alexander McMuir and Noah Brown, of the city of New York. Of these Mr. McQueen, a machinist, built the engine, and Mr. Brown, a shipwright, superintended the construction of the hull. Early in 1818 Mr. Brown laid the keel at the mouth of Scajaquada creek. There she was launched on May 18, 1818. On August 25 she departed on her first passage over the waters of Lake Erie.

The scene presented when the boat was ascending the Niagara River was picturesque. The primitive steamboat struggled with the rapid current, aided by several yoke of oxen on the beach, tugging at the end of a long towline. This was the historical "horn breeze" prevalent on Niagara River when the current was stronger than the applied steam power.

According to Captain Barton Atkins, of Buffalo, the origin of the name "Walk-in-the-Water" was as follows: "When Fulton first steamed his boat, the Clermont, up the Hudson in 1807, an Indian standing on the river bank and gazing long and silently at the boat moving up-stream without sails, finally exclaimed: 'Walks in the water.'" The man in the forest saw the boat stemming the current unaided by any power known to him. He observed the paddle wheels slowly revolving, and intuitively comprehended that when a paddle struck the water there was a step forward.

STARTLED THE NATIVES.

It may be here briefly stated that the name, "Walk-in-the-Water," being so long was not generally used, either in conversation or in print. As she was the only one of her class on Lake Erie, she was usually designated as "The Steamboat." Her arrival at Cleveland is thus chronicled by a local historian: "On the first day of September, 1818, an entire novelty, the like of which not one in 500 of the inhabitants had ever before seen, presented itself before the people of Cuyahoga county. On the day named the residents along the lake shore of Euclid saw upon the lake a curious kind of a vessel making what was then considered very rapid progress westward, without the aid of sails, while from a pipe near its middle rolled forth a dark cloud of smoke, which trailed its gloomy length far into the rear of the swift-gliding, mysterious traveler over the deep. They watched its westward course until it turned its bow toward the harbor of Cleveland, and then returned to their labors. Many of them doubtless knew what it was, but some shook their heads in sad surmise as to whether some evil powers were not at work in producing such a strange phenomenon as that on the bosom of their beloved Lake Erie. Meanwhile the citizens of Cleveland perceived the approaching wonder and hastened to the lake shore to examine it. 'What is it?' 'What is it?' 'Where did it come from?' 'What makes it go?' queried one and another of the excited throng.

"'It is the steamboat; that's what it is,' cried others in reply.

"'Yes, yes, it's the steamboat; it's the steamboat; it's the steamboat,' was the general shout, and, with ringing cheers, the people welcomed the first vessel propelled by steam which had ever traversed the waters of Lake Erie.

"The keel had been laid at Black Rock, near Buffalo, in November, 1817, and the vessel had been built during the spring and summer of 1818. It had received the name of Walk-in-the-Water from a Wyandotte chieftain, who was formerly known by that appelation, which was also extremely appropriate as applied to a vessel which did, indeed, walk in the water like a thing of life. The harbinger of the numerous steam leviathans of the upper lakes, and of the immense commerce carried on by them, was of 342 tons burden, and could carry 100 cabin passengers and a still larger number in the steerage. Its best speed was from eight to ten miles an hour, and even this was considered something wonderful. All Cleveland swarmed on board to examine the new craft, and many of the leading citizens took passage in it to Detroit, for which place it soon set forth."

FIRST TRIP TO DETROIT.

The *Detroit Gazette* of that day said of her first trip to this city:

"The Walk-in-the-Water left Buffalo at one and a half P. M. and arrived at Dunkirk at thirty-five minutes past 6 on the same day. On the following morning she arrived at Erie, Captain Fish having reduced her steam in order not to pass that place, where he took in a supply of wood. The boat was visited by all the inhabitants during the day, and had the misfortune to get aground for a short time in the bay, a little west of French Street. At half past 7 P. M. she left Erie and arrived at Cleveland at 11 o'clock. Tuesday at twenty minutes past 6 o'clock P. M. she sailed, and reached Sandusky bay at 1 o'clock on Wednesday; lay at anchor during the night, and then proceeded to Venice for wood; left Venice at 3 P. M. and arrived at the mouth of the Detroit River, where she anchored during the night. The whole time of the first voyage from Buffalo to Detroit occupied forty-four hours and ten minutes—the wind being ahead during the whole passage. Not the slightest accident happened during the voyage, and her machinery worked admirably.

"Nothing could exceed the surprise of the 'sons of the forest' on seeing the Walk-in-the-Water move majestically and rapidly against wind and current, without sails or oars. Above Malden they lined the shores and expressed their astonishment by repeated shouts of 'Taiyoh nichee!' (An exclamation of suprise.)

"A report that had circulated among them that a 'big canoe' would soon come from the 'noisy waters,' which, by order of the 'great father of the "Chemo Komods"' (Long Knives, or Kankees), would be drawn through the lakes and rivers by a sturgeon. Of the truth of this report they were perfectly satisfied.

"Her second arrival at Detroit was on September 7 of the same year, having on board thirty-one passengers, including the Earl of Selkirk and suite, destined for the far northwest.

"The cabins of the Walk-in-the-Water were fitted up in a neat, convenient and elegant style, and a trip to Buffalo was considered not only tolerable, but truly pleasant. She made an excursion from Detroit to Lake St. Clair with a party of ladies and gentlemen, and returned to Buffalo in time to be again at Detroit the following week."

Honorable Henry R. Schoolcraft, Indian agent, gives an account of a trip on the Walk-in-the-Water in 1820, as follows:

"On the 6th of May I embarked on the steamboat, which left Black River at 9 o'clock in the morning and reached Detroit on the 8th at 12 o'clock at night. We were favored with clear weather and part of the time with fair wind. The boat is large, uniting in its construction a great degree of strength, convenience and elegance, and is propelled by a powerful and well-cast engine on the Fultonian plan, and one of the best pieces of the original foundry (McQueen's, N. Y.). The accommodations of the boat are all that could be wished, and nothing occurred to interrupt the delight which a passage at this season affords. The distance is computed at 300 miles; the time we employed in the voyage was sixty-two hours, which gives an average rate of traveling of five miles per hour. The first two miles after leaving Black Rock a very heavy rapid is encountered, in ascending which the assistance of oxen is required. In passing through Lake Erie the boat touches at the town of Erie, in Pennsylvania, at the mouth of Grande River, and at the towns of Cleveland and Portland, in Ohio, the latter situated on Sandusky Bay."

The Walk-in-the-Water had a low pressure engine. Captain Job Fish commanded her when she made her first trip, arriving at Detroit August 22 of the above year. She was afterwards commanded by Jebediah Rogers, and a Buffalo paper of July 9, 1821, says of her:

"The steamboat Walk-in-the-Water will sail on the 27th of July at 4 o'clock in the afternoon for Detroit, Mackinac and Green Bay, and will stop, as usual, at Erie, Grand River, Cleveland and Sandusky."

A "SPLENDID ADVENTURE."

The *New York Mercantile Advertiser* of May 14, 1818, had this to say of her: "The swift steamboat Walk-in-the-Water is intended to make a voyage early in the summer from Buffalo, on Lake Erie, to Michilimackinac, on Lake Huron, for the conveyance of company. The trip has so near a resemblance to the famous Argonautic expedition in the heroic ages of Greece that expectation is quite alive on the subject. Many of our most distinguished citizens are said to have already engaged their passage for the splendid adventure."

To speak of a trip to Mackinac as having a resemblance to the famous Argonautic expedition of the heroic ages of Greece, will provoke a smile in these days, when the same voyage is an every-day occurrence.

The *Detroit Gazette* of August 10, 1821, contained the following:

"The steamboat Walk-in-the-Water left here on the 31st ult. for Michilimackinac and Green Bay, having on board upwards of 200 passengers and a full cargo of merchandise for the ports on the upper lakes. The officers of the army who took passage in her were Colonels Pinckney, McNeil and House; Majors Baker, Larribee and Watson; Captains Garland, Green, Legate and Cass; Lieutenants Tuffts, Baker, Morris, Chambers, Allen and Pomeroy.

WAS UNSEAWORTHY.

General Ellis, at one time surveyor-general of Wisconsin, contributes a paper on the early days in the west, which is printed in the collections of the Historical Society of Wisconsin, in which he gives a description of this steamboat and of his passage on her from Buffalo to Detroit, some time in June, 1821. He goes on to say:

"The new steamboat Walk-in-the-Water, built by capitalists from Albany, and after the North River models, commanded by Captain Rogers, lay at the wharf at Black Rock. We took passage in her for Detroit. She was furnished with what the engineer called 'a powerful low-pressure engine,' but she could not, with all her power, stem the rapids, and go out into the lake, but had to be towed out by nine yoke of oxen going along the beach, at the end of a line of 600 feet, which was cast off as soon as the steamer got out of the rapids into the lake. This boat has great length with but little breadth, was very slender, and proved unseaworthy, having broken in two the next fall in a storm on the lake. She, however, took us safely to Detroit."

A GLORIOUS FOURTH.

The steamboat Walk-in-the-Water assisted in celebrating the Fourth of July in 1821. The *Detroit Gazette* of July 6 says:

"This day, which may be emphatically syled 'The Birthday of our Nation,' was celebrated by our citizens and strangers in this city in a very appropriate and agreeable manner. At 12 o'clock the Declaration of Independence was read to a large concourse at the council house, by Charles Larned, Esq. A procession was then formed, and, preceded by martial music, playing the good old tune, 'Yankee Doodle,' marched to the hotel of Mr. Bronson, where upwards of 150 persons sat down to a bounteous repast, at which Judge James Witherell, as president, and Major T. Maxwell, as vice-president, presided. Both of these gentlemen entered the army at an early period of the revolution, and never laid aside their arms until the liberties of their country were secured. Major J. Kearsley and Captain B. Woodworth assisted as second and third vice-presidents."

The account goes on to say:

"The anniversary of our national independence, in the celebration of which every American heart and hand should join, was also distinguished by a numerous and brilliant assemblage of the ladies of Detroit and its vicinity, accompanied by several of our citizens and the gentlemen of the army at this post, who embarked on board the steamboat Walk-in-the-Water at 11 o'clock. The company were attended by a band of excellent musicians, and their strains of melody,

'Now scarcely heard, now swelling on the gale,
  As down the stream the floating barque is borne.'

conveyed to each listener the truth that the party on the water sympathized amply in the patriotic and joyous feelings of their fellow-citizens on shore.

"The day was extremely fine, and the quarter-deck of the

boat, which, by the politeness of Captain Rogers, had been prepared for the occasion, was occupied by cotillion parties. The Declaration of Independence was read, and, after partaking of an excellent dinner, a set of appropriate toasts were drunk. The boat, after passing Malden, and making a short trip in Lake Erie, returned to her wharf at sunset."

The *Gazette* of the 13th says:

"It ought to be stated that the steamboat Walk-in-the-Water, while passing the British garrison at Fort Malden, was properly noticed by the military authorities at that place."

The Walk-in-the-Water was beached in a storm, a few miles above the Buffalo lighthouse, on the night of the 6th of November, 1821, on her way to Detroit. She left Black Rock at 4 P. M. of that day. She was struck by a severe squall when about four miles out in Lake Erie, which caused her to spring a leak. The boat was at the mercy of the waves until half-past 5 o'clock Thursday morning, when she beached a short distance above the lighthouse. The passengers and crew got ashore without the loss of lives or any material injury. Some idea may be formed of the fury of the storm, when it is known that the boat, heavily laden as she was, was thrown entirely on the beach. Among the passengers were Mr. and Mrs. Thomas Palmer, of Detroit, who were returning home from their wedding trip, accompanied by Miss Catharine Palmer, Mr. Palmer's sister.

WRECK OF THE WALK-IN-THE WATER.

Here follows a more extended account of the disaster, taken from a Buffalo paper of November 6, 1821:

"On Wednesday last the steamboat Walk-in-the-Water left Black Rock at 4 p. m. on her regular trip to Detroit; the weather, though somewhat rainy, did not appear threatening. After she had proceeded about four miles above Bird Island she was struck by a severe squall, which it was immediately perceived had injured her much, and caused her to leak fast. The wind from the southwest continued to blow with extreme severity through the night, which was exceedingly dark and rainy, attended at intervals with the most tremendous squalls. The lake became rough to a terrifying degree and every wave seemed to threaten immediate destruction to the boat and all on board. This was truly to the passengers and crew a night of terror and dismay—to go forward was impossible; to attempt to return to Black Rock in the darkness and tempest would have been certain ruin, on account of the difficulty of the channel; and little less could be hoped, whether the boat were anchored, or permitted to be driven on the beach. She, however, was anchored, and for awhile held fast, but as every one perceived, each wave increased her injury and caused her to leak faster; the casings in her cabin were seen to move at every swell, and the squeaking of her joints and timbers was appalling; her engine was devoted to the pumps, but in spite of them all the water increased to an alarming extent—the storm grew more terrible. The wind blew more violently as the night advanced, and it was presently perceived that she was dragging her anchors and approaching the beach. In such blackness of darkness could her helm have commanded her course, not the most skillful pilot could have chosen with any certainty the part of the shore on which it would be most prudent to land. The passengers on board were numerous and many of them were ladies, whose fears and cries were truly heartrending.

"In this scene of distress and danger, the undersigned passengers in the boat, feel that an expression of the warmest gratitude is due to Captain J. Rogers, for the prudence, coolness and intelligence with which he discharged his duty; his whole conduct evinced that he was capable and worthy his command. He betrayed none but the character of one who at the same time feels his responsibility and has courage to discharge his duty. He was, if we may so speak, almost simultaneously on deck to direct and assist in the management of the boat, and in the cabins to encourage the hopes and soothe the fears of the distressed passengers. The calmness of his countenance and pleasantness of his conversation relieved in a great degree the feelings of those who seemed to despair of seeing the light of another day. No less credit is due to the other officers, Sailing Master Miller, and Engineer Calhoun, and even the whole crew. All were intent on their duty, and manifested that they had intelligence, courage, and a determination to perform it. All were active, and proved that they wanted none of the talents of the most expert sailors, in the most dangerous moments. To them all as well as the captain the undersigned passengers tender their most sincere thanks.

"The boat was at the mercy of the waves until 5:30 o'clock Thursday morning, when she beached a short distance above the light house, when the passengers and crew began to debark, which was effected without the loss of lives, or any material injury. Some idea may be formed of the fury of the storm, when it is known that the boat, heavily laden as she was, was thrown entirely on the beach.

ALANSON W. WELTON,	JEDEDIAH HUNT,
THOMAS PALMER,	ORLANDO CUTTER,
WM. BERCZY,	SILAS MERIAM,
MARY A. W. PALMER,	RHODA LATTIMORE,
CATHERINE PALMER,	MARTHA BEAREY,
CHAUNCEY BARKER,	GEO. WILLIAMS,
THOMAS GAY,	ELISHA N. BERGE,
JOHN S. HUDSON,	EDSON HART,
JAMES CLARK,	GEO. THROOP.

A JOURNEY TO DETROIT IN 1821.

The following is taken from a Detroit paper of March 23, 1874, the particulars of which were given to the writer of them by Mrs. Thomas Palmer, one of the passengers on the steamer. Mrs. Palmer was the mother of Senator Thomas W. Palmer:

"On the evening of October 31st, 1821, the saloons and decks of the Walk-in-the-Water (the first steamboat on the lakes, coming out in 1819) were thronged with intelligence and beauty, all full of animation and joyfulness, in the harbor at Buffalo, destined for Detroit and other western towns—some returning home after the absence of weeks and months, some to seek their fortunes and some on a mission of love and mercy. Among the passengers were to be found Thomas Palmer, merchant of Detroit and his wife; Mrs. C. Hinchman, of Detroit; John Hale, of Detroit; Lieutenant Kenzie, of the United States army for the post at Detroit; Rev. Mr. Welton, Protestant Episcopal minister, and family, destined for Detroit; Mr. Throop, merchant of Pontiac; Rev. Mr. Hart and wife, of the Presbyterian church, for an Indian mission at Fort Gratiot; John S. Hudson and wife and Miss Eunice Osmer, as teachers for the same mission, with some others not important to mention. With this company Captain Jedediah Rogers started from Buffalo at evening for Detroit, all having high hopes of reaching this port in safety. But during the night the storm king walked forth and shook himself fearfully, the wind howled, the storm raged, and everything conspired to make it a fearful night. Every effort to stem the storm was in vain. They were driven back, and at 5 o'clock in the morning of November 1st, 1821, the Walk-in-the-Water was wrecked on the shore in Buffalo bay, at the light-house. Mrs. Palmer was the first one to reach the light-house. Others quickly followed, and all the passengers and crew were saved. This was the first steamboat ever navigated on these inland seas—that ever visited the port of Detroit. She was succeeded the next summer by the Superior, of three hundred tons burden, constructed at Buffalo, 1822, and commanded by Captain Roger Sherman, and not by Captain Rogers, as some have supposed. But what became of the passengers? They were all taken to Buffalo and kindly cared for by the inhabitants for three or four days, when they found other ways of getting to their respective destinations. Thos. Palmer had been away from his business so long that he thought he must secure the most expeditious means of getting to Detroit that he could find. So he engaged a Mr. Williams to bring himself and wife, Mrs. Hinchman, Lieutenant Kenzie, John Hale and a Mr. Throop, of Pontiac, in a large wagon across Canada. The weather was stormy, the roads horrible, and the accommodations terrible. The journey occupied nine days of hard and diligent travel. In the midst of what was then called the long woods the wagon broke down, and, as it was near night, they concluded to walk on to find a house, which they found to be several miles distant. It was wet and the road very muddy, but the ladies courageously walked on. In the meantime they had to cross a river on a bridge composed of a single log. Some of the men having gone before, the man of the house came to meet the ladies with a torch, and so lighted their way and aroused their courage. Weary, wet and covered with mud, they finally reached the house, and were glad to find anything for a shelter, as it was now in November. The house was made of logs and had but one room for all purposes. There were seven in the family—father, mother and five children. Not a very flattering prospect for comfortable accommodations. The family, however, sat up all night and dried and cleaned the garments of the travelers, and left all the lodging room for their guests.

A CANOE FERRY.

"On the ninth day, just at evening, they reached the Detroit River. The only means of ferryage was a canoe. The idea of crossing in such a ferry was perfectly terrifying to Mrs. Palmer, and so affected her that she wept bitterly. There, however, was no other way to cross, and notwithstanding the canoe man was very much intoxicated they passed over safely. It is easier to imagine than to realize the perils and sufferings of such a journey at that season of the year, and through so sparsely settled a country. The trip was so severe on the team that Mr. Williams had to remain a whole week to recruit his horses before he could venture to return with them to Buffalo. Having recruited his team he returned the way he came.

A LONG VOYAGE.

"The other division of the passengers must have had even a worse time than the first division. They embarked on a schooner, or at least Rev. Mr. Hart and his wife, Mr. Hudson and wife, Miss Osmer, Rev. Mr. Welton and family did so, and were four weeks on the way. To have been confined on a small schooner for that length of time must have been even worse than crossing Canada in nine days in an open wagon. As everything must have an end, so had their voyage, and they reached Detroit in safety. Here the missionary family remained a short time to recruit themselves and then went to their mission. They obtained all their supplies through Thomas Palmer. During the time they were here a box of clothing had been left in store in the loft of Mr. Palmer's store for the benefit of the mission. One day one of the men in the store below, hearing a noise in the loft, went up to see what was the matter, and found Mr. Hudson in a sad predicament, for, having put on a coat that was much too small for him, he was not able to get it off, and had to be relieved.

"Of all the passengers on the Walk-in-the-Water at the time of the disaster only one is now residing in Detroit, viz., Mrs. Welton, one of the last survivors, Mrs. Palmer, having died March 23, 1874. Mrs. Palmer to the last retained a lively remembrance of the event, and of the various incidents connected with it. It was a joke for a good while whether she or one of the divines aboard was the most frightened. I am indebted to Mrs.

Palmer for the facts above recited. She was one of the pioneers of Detroit, being a daughter of Judge James Witherell, one of the justices appointed by President Jefferson for the Territory of Michigan when the territorial government was first organized. The judge brought his family to Detroit from Vermont before the war of 1812, but when he saw the clouds of war gathering he sent his family east till the storm had passed over. She, therefore, had seen the city grow up from a very small town. Having seen in the papers a different version of the story above recited, she was very anxious to have the true state of the facts published. 'The truth of history must be vindicated.' I should here also state that Mrs. Palmer went east on the first downward trip of the Walk-in-the-Water. She went east as Miss Witherell and now was returning as Mrs. Palmer. Thomas Palmer having gone east, was married to her and they were now completing their bridal trip.

"We have now, March 23, 1874, to record that since the foregoing was written Mrs. Palmer has deceased, having died quite suddenly on the 18th instant. Her husband had preceded her, having died in 1868. She was 78 years of age, and nearly 79. Thus, one by one, the pioneers of Detroit are dropping away.

"J. H. P."

Come we now to the birch-bark barge and canoe and the French voyageurs—a great come-down, it must be confessed, from the splendid equipment of our present lake and river marine; and it seems as though they ought not to be included in the program; yet they were the beginning, and in Cadillac's time almost the only marine hereabouts. They were quite plentiful in the early days, and with their companions, the wooden dug-outs, were indispensable, and formed quite a feature in the meager panorama of the river. Nearly, if not quite all, were equipped with a mast and sale that could be used at pleasure, the sail consisting usually of a blanket. There were no regular sailboats, as we have them now. The people here and those living on the borders of the river, up and down, on either side, did not seem to appreciate the pleasure and satisfaction that a sail on the surface would afford them. How much it is enjoyed and indulged in now, all know.

It seems a queer thing, too, in the light of the present, that the young men of the city at that time were not fond of sailing or a sailboat, as are the young people, and some of the old, for that matter, now. As far as my experience goes, I can safely say that I never went sailing on the river until after I was 25 years of age, nor did any of the youth of my acquaintance. Such a pastime was never indulged in. A boat club (and the first) was formed in the early forties, composed of the principal young men of the city, such as A. E. Brush, Dr. J. H. Farnsworth, Barney and Alex. Campau and others. (Alex. Campau is the only survivor.) An exhaustive and interesting account of this club was given in the *Detroit Free Press* some two or three years ago.

Henry R. Schoolcraft, in his "Travels," gives a description of the birch-bark barge and canoe. He says: "Those of the largest size, such as are commonly employed in the fur trade of the north, are thirty-five feet in length and six feet in width at the widest part, tapering gradually towards the bow and stern, which are brought to a wedge-like point and turned over from the extremities towards the center, so as to resemble in some degree the head of a violin. They are constructed of the bark of the white birch tree, which is peeled from the tree in large sheets and bent over a slender frame of cedar ribs confined by gunwales, which are kept apart by slender bars of the same wood. Around these the bark is sewed by the slender and flexible roots of the young spruce tree, called "wattap," and also where the pieces of bark join, so that the gunwales resemble the rim of an Indian basket. The joinings are afterwards luted and rendered watertight by a coat of pine pitch, which, after it has been thickened by boiling, is used under the name of "gum." In the third cross-bar from the front, an aperture is cuit for a mast, so that a sail can be employed when the wind proves favorable. Seats for those who paddle are made by suspending a strip of board with cords from the gunwales in such a manner that they do not press against the sides of the canoe. For propelling them the natives use the cedar paddle, with a light and slender blade. They are steered with a large paddle having a long handle and broad blade. A canoe of this size, when employed in the fur trade, is calculated to carry sixty packages of skins weighing ninety pounds each and provisions to the amount of 1,000 pounds. This is exclusive of the weight of eight men, each of whom is allowed to put on board a bag or knapsack of about forty pounds weight. Such a canoe thus loaded is paddled by eight men, at the rate of four miles per hour, in a perfect calm."

THE FRENCH VOYAGEURS.

The French voyageurs were quite numerous here up to about 1837. They manned the "Mackinac barge" and the canoes of the fur traders, and were also ready for service to anyone needing them. They were quite a feature on the river at that time, and, of course, must have been the same from Cadillac's day. I remember them quite well, and have often been one of a party propelled by them in their birch-bark canoes and barges. I copy from the late Bela Hubbard's admirable book, "Memories of a Half Century," a vivid and lifelike description of them, as I saw and knew them: "A wild-looking set were these rangers of the woods and waters. The weirdness was often enhanced by the dash of Indian blood. Picturesque, too, they were, in their red flannel or leather shirts (buckskin), and cloth caps of some gay color finished to a point, which hung over on one side, with a depending tassel.

"They had a genuine love for this occupation, and muscles that seemed never to tire at the paddle and oar. From dawn to sunset, with only a short interval, and sometimes no mid-day rest, they would ply these implements, causing the canoe or barge to fly through the water like a thing of life; but often contending against head winds and gaining but little progress in a day's rowing. Then in came the oars, and down Iopped each mother's son, and in a few minutes was in the enjoyment of a sound snooze. The morning and evening meal consisted almost invariably, and from choice, of bouillon—a soup made from beans, peas or hulled corn, with a piece of pork boiled in it, and hard bread, or seabiscuit. To the northern voyageurs, rations were generally served out of one quart of hulled corn, and a half a pint of bear's grease, or oil, this being the daily and only food.

"The traveler, Henry, says (1776): 'A bushel of hulled corn, with two pounds of fat, is reckoned to be a month's subsistence. No other allowance is made, of any kind, not even salt, and bread is never thought of. The difficulty which would belong to an attempt to reconcile any other men than Canadians to this fare seems to secure to them and their employers the monopoly of the fur trade.'

"As late as the last century, Detroit was one of the principal depots for provisions, and fitting out for the Indian trade; and here, particularly, the corn was prepared, hulled, boiled, and mixed with fat, for the voyageurs.

"After supper, pipes were lighted, and, seated on logs or squatted around the campfire, they chatted until bedtime. This came early and required little preparation. To wrap a blanket around the person, placing coat or shoe-packs beneath the head, and a little greasy pillow—the only bed that was carried—constituted the whole ceremony; and speedy and sound was the sleep beneath the watchful stars.

"The labor of the oar was relieved by songs, to which each stroke kept time, with added vigor. The poet Moore has well caught the spirit of the voyageurs' melodious chant in his 'Boat Song Upon the St. Lawrence.' But to appreciate its wild sweetness one should listen to the melody, as it wings its way over the waters, softened by distance, yet every measured cadence falling distinct upon the ear. These songs are usually half ballad or ditty, and love is of course the main theme. They express the natural feelings of a people little governed by the restraints of civilization."

He gives two specimens of these songs. The words were sung by one of the party and all joined in the chorus. (The songs are too long to copy here; besides they are given in French, and if rendered into English would lose their character.) "These boat songs," he goes on to say, "were often heard upon our river, and were very plaintive. In the calm of the evening, when sounds are heard with greater distinctness, and the harsher notes are toned down and absorbed in the prevailing melody, it was sweet, from my vine-mantled porch, to hear the blended sounds of songs and oar,

'By distance mellowed, o'er the waters sweep.'

"To my half dreaming fancy, at such times, they have assumed a poetic, if not a supernatural, character, wafting me into elfland on wings of linked sweetness.

"Some spirit of the air has waked the string;
'Tis now a seraph bold, with touch of fire,
And now the brush of fancy's frolic wing."

"At other times these sounds harmonize with scenes that are still more inspiring. Seldom have I witnessed a more animated spectacle than that of a large canoe or barge belonging to the Hudson Bay Co., manned by a dozen voyageurs—the company's agent seated in the center—propelled with magic velocity, as if instinct with life, every paddle keeping time to the chorus that rang far and wide over the waters. But times have changed, and with them have passed from our midst the voyageur and his song. French gayety is rapidly ebbing into more sober channels.

"As I call up these memories with the same noble river in my view, I listen in vain for the melodies which were once the prelude to many joyous hours of early manhood. But instead, my ear is larumed by the shriek of the steam whistle, and the laborious snort of the propeller. All announce that on these shores and waters the age of the practical, hard-working, money-getting Yankee is upon us; and that the careless, laughter-loving Frenchman's day is over."

I have myself often listened with delight to these songs as they floated over the water, in the calm, still summer nights, and my emotions in that regard have been so aptly portrayed by Mr. Hubbard that I could not resist the temptation of copying from his book as freely as I have done.

When Governor Cass accompanied Colonel Thomas L. McKinney and party to Lake Superior, he provided, or had constructed, for their use a birch-bark canoe, or state-barge, of unusual dimensions. I forget the size, but it was sufficiently large to accommodate the entire party, with their provisions and other belongings.

The party consisted, I think, of Governor Cass, Colonel McKinney, United States Commissioner Major Robert Forsyth, and C. C. Trowbridge, secretary, besides six French voyageurs. The details of the expedition are related in full by Colonel McKinney, in a book published about that time, a copy of which is in the Detroit public library, and which is very interesting.

The reason why I allude to this event that happened a year before my arrival in Detroit, is that I have often seen this barge, and as often enjoyed a ride in it up and down the river, as the governor retained it until his departure for Washington as secretary of war. What became of it thereafter I do not know.

WAS A RIVER BEAUTY.

There were birch-bark canoes, and birch-bark canoes in plenty, on these waters at that time, but this birch-bark barge eclipsed them all. The stern was amply provided with cushions, and had a canopy, or awning, overhead for protection from the sun. It was usually moored at the foot of the river bank, in front of the governor's residence, in charge of the voyageurs, ever ready for an excursion up or down the river or up into Lake St. Clair. This barge was a feature on the river in those days—more so than it would be now, with all the various attractions that it presents, though no doubt it would cause some stir, even at this day, with its gay flags, colored awnings, and the eight voyageurs, clad in their picturesque costumes, with their crimson-bladed paddles, keeping time to the charming refrain of some French chant, such as "Mal Brooke," etc., which all old residents will remember. These excursions were particularly enjoyable of a moonlight night, as can readily be imagined.

THE GRIFFIN AGAIN.

The hardy friar who accompanied Sieur de la Salle in his expedition, gives this description of the vessel in his published book:

"It was a two-masted schooner, but of a fashion peculiar to that day, having double decks and a high poop projecting over the stern, where the main cabin was located, and over this rose another and smaller cabin, doubtless for the use of the commander. The stern was thus carried up broad and straight. Bulwarks protected the quarterdeck. She bore on her prow a huge figure, skillfully carved, in imitation of an heraldic monster—the arms of Count Frontenac—and above it an eagle."

This in the representation (which appears in the volume) adorns the top of the stern. The ship carried five small cannon, three of which were brass and three harquebusses, and the remainder of the ship had the same ornaments as men-of-war used to have.

"It might have been called," adds Henepin, "a moving fortress." In fine, it "was well equipped with sails, masts, and all other things necessary for navigation."

After describing the natural beauty of the region lying between Lakes Erie and Huron, Fr. La Salle adds: "They who shall have the happiness some day to inhabit this pleasant and fertile country will remember their obligation to those who first showed them the way."

I have received a letter from a lady in St. Clair city (Mrs Anna Brakeman), under date of March 10, in which she says: "I have read with much interest your articles in the *St. Clair Republican,* copied from the *Detroit Free Press,* in relation to the early marine. While reading them I was reminded of a few items my grandfather, the late Captain William Brown, of Cothelville, related to me many years ago. He was born in Detroit in 1784. When 18 years of age (1802) he sailed in the employ of Judge James Abbott, of Detroit. I cannot recall the name of the boat he commanded, but it was a sail vessel, and went down as far as Tonawanda, N. Y. There they loaded with salt for Detroit. I presume it was Syracuse and Onondaga salt. That article was very scarce in this section at that time. After he was 21 years of age he cradled wheat all one day for a farmer in Cothelville for two quarts of salt."

The lady also relates: "My greatgrandfather, the late Captain William Thorn, a native of Providence, R. I., who died in Port Huron in 1842, sailed on the lakes in a very early day; was captain of a sail vessel owned by a Mr. Donsman, and I have been told he took the first boat through the St. Mary's River.

On one occasion his vessel was windbound, near an island at the mouth of that river. He went ashore on the island and found there a frying pan, supposed to have been left by the Indians. He then named it 'Frying Pan Island,' the name it still retains. On another occasion his vessel lay at anchor in a bay in Lake Erie. They were entirely out of provisions, excepting flour, which they stirred in a pot of boiling water, calling it pudding. He then named the bay 'Pudding Bay.' At the present time it is known as 'Put-in-Bay.'

THIS WAS HEROISM INDEED.

He was so well acquainted with the route at the head of Lake Huron and the Straits of Mackinac that he was selected as pilot of the American fleet that went to recapture Mackinac Island from the British after the War of 1812. He was lame at the time from a dislocated hip; could not climb a mast, but sat in a chair securely lashed to the seat, and was hoisted with pulleys to the masthead. As I have been told, it was a very foggy morning, but, understanding the route so well, he took the fleet in unawares to the British.

MORE OF INTEREST FROM THE SAME SOURCE.

She goes on to narrate further in regard to the early lake and river marine, and says:

"By old papers I find that some time prior to the year 1830 there was a sail vessel named the Louisa Jenkins, which brought goods, that came to Buffalo from New York, for the firm of Peter Verhoeff & Co., Detroit. George Jasperson and my father, the late Peter F. Brakeman, were members of the firm. The same year the brig Wellington and the schooner Lady Goderich brought goods from Montreal for the firm. Messrs. Verhoeff and Jasperson had previous to this opened a store at Sandwich, Canada. Mr. Brakeman had charge of the store at Point du Chien. The goods were brought to him from Detroit by small sail vessels, row boats and French batteaux. The names of the sail vessels were the Nation's Guest, Lark, Happy Return, and a sloop called The Forester, commanded by Captain Samuel Hayward. These boats carried grain, furs, lumber and shingles from Point du Chien to Detroit for the firm.

The letter also says: "June 20, 1832, P. F. Brakeman shipped from Point du Chien, on the schooner Pilot, Captain Charles Cauchois (Coshnay), 100 bushels white flint corn to Mackinac for Robert Stuart, agent of the American Fur Co.

"Lewis J. Brakeman, brother of the late Peter F. Brakeman, with four other men—Roswell Newhall, brother of the late Captain Clark Newhall, of Port Huron; Francis Lanzon, uncle of David and Daniel Cottrell, of Cottrellville; a Captain Stevens and a Mr. Roe, on their way from Detroit to Point du Chien, on the schooner Emily, were shipwrecked on Lake St. Clair December 13, 1830. L. J. Brakeman had purchased the boat and was bringing her to lay up for the winter at Point du Chien, now Algonac. Altogether there were seven men on the boat and a boy, Jemmie Burns, whose homes were on the river. They had taken passage on her from Detroit, that being the only way of conveyance for them at the time. Each had some goods and stores with him. It was a very cold and severe time. The boat jumped her mast, but did not sink immediately. The story, as told by the boy, Jemmie Burns, was that as soon as the accident occurred each one put forth his best efforts, which would naturally be the case at such a time, to save lives and goods. The schooner had a yawl boat of sufficient size to carry all the men who were on board, with their goods. One Bela Knapp and brother, with the boy Burns, got themselves in readiness a little sooner than the other five, and were hurrying to the yawl. The men begged them to wait until they could get ready. They paid no attention to their pleadings, but entered the yawl, and Bela Knapp, who had a new broadax with him, cut the rope, which loosened them from the schooner, and they and their goods were all saved. The blame all rested on Bela Knapp, as his brother and the boy pleaded with him to wait until they were all in. We can better imagine than describe the feelings of those who were left behind to perish with the cold. The schooner dashed about for some time. Peter F. Brakeman, then residing at Point du Chien, hearing of the trouble, procured a large yawl and took with him several men, going to the place of the accident, but when they arrived there the sea was rolling so high they could not reach the wreck, but could very distinctly see the men all sitting near each other at the bow—dead, frozen—the stern being under water. Mr. Brakeman recognized his brother sitting, holding his head in his hands, his elbow resting on his knees. They then rowed for shore, built up a fire, spending the night there, thinking perhaps the sea would calm down, and they be able to procure the bodies in the morning. But when day dawned nothing could be seen of the boat. She sank during the night. L. J. Brakeman's body was found the next August by an Indian, having been washed ashore on Squirrel Island. The remains were buried in the old Point du Chien cemetery."

I remember the William Brown the lady mentions. He lived near Cothelville (St. Clair River). I once accompanied my uncle, Thomas Palmer, on a trip to St. Clair, in a sleigh, along shore, in the winter of 1829, and we accepted his hospitality for one night. He was a gentleman of the old school, sported his ruffled shirt, etc., the same as did his neighbors along the river. Colonel Cottrell, grandfather of Hon. E. W. Cottrell, Captain John Clark, Colonel Westbrook and Mr. Smith, the "Father of Algonac." I also remember Captain William Thorn. He was the brother or nephew of Mr. John Thorn, who platted the greater part of the village of Black River, now the city of Port Huron. He was rather a wild boy in the early days—they used to call him "Captain of St. Clair River." I have often heard my uncles, Thomas and George Palmer, relate the mad pranks the lawyers of Detroit, Mr. Thorn, and the members of the Black River bar would indulge in every time the court was in session at St. Clair, (the latter being the county seat then). Conspicuous among the Detroit lawyers, they used to say, were Counselor O'Keefe, Mr. A. D. Frazier, B. F. H. Witherell, etc., though Witherell, not being a drinking man, was rather a "looker-on in Venice" than otherwise.

I also remember quite well the Mr. George Jasperson mentioned. He was a highly educated Swede. When I knew him he was a retired merchant, and lived in quite a pretentious house, surrounded with two or three acres of ground on the corner of Russell and Catherine Streets, nearly opposite the present Arbeiter Hall, which was away out in the country then. He had two promising sons, Henry and Lewis, schoolmates of mine. He also had a beautiful daughter, who became the wife of Alex. Goodell, a partner of Henry M. Campbell, father of Judge Campbell. Campbell and Goodell carried on the grocery business at the northwest corner of Jefferson Avenue and Bates Street. What became of the Jaspersons, I do not know.

SLAVERY DAYS IN MICHIGAN.

NEGROES WERE BOUGHT AND SOLD AND REGARDED AS CHATTELS—WELL TREATED BY THEIR MASTERS.

THE following references to slaves in Michigan have been extracted from an able paper on the subject, prepared and published many years ago by the late James A. Girardin, and also from other sources, and from personal recollections:-

In the olden time the city of Detroit and vicinity had slaves among its inhabitants. The old citizens generally purchased them from marauding bands of Indians, who had captured the negro slaves in their war depredations on plantations. Many were thus brought from Virginia, New York and Indiana, and sold to the inhabitants of Detroit, sometimes for nominal prices. Among our old citizens who were slaveholders in the olden times were the late Major Joseph Campau, George McDougall, James Duperon Baby, Abbott, Finchley and several others. The negro slaves were well treated by their owners. Many of these poor captives when sold and released were at once well taken care of by our ancient inhabitants. Sometimes the price of a slave was regulated according to his intrinsic value, but the price was quite high for those days. For instance, a negro boy named Frank, aged 12 years, the property of the late Philip Jonciere, of Belle Fontaine, now Springwells, was sold on the 22d of October, 1793, by William Roe, acting auctioneer, to the late Hon. James Duperon Baby, for the sum of £213, New York currency, equal to $532.50 of our money. Mr. Baby being the highest bidder, Frank was adjudged to him for the benefit of Mr. Jonciere's estate. In the records of baptism of Ste. Anne's church, we find several persons of color recorded as having received the sacrament of baptism, and, in the absence of family names, we learn that the name of "Margaret," for instance, a negress "unknown," would be entered. Several instances of this kind are entered in the old records.

WERE WELL TREATED.

During the administration of the governor and judges of the territory of Michigan, several negroes received donation lots. Among them was a well known negro named "Pompey," the property of the late James Abbott. As a class the negroes were esteemed by our early time population. Many of them could speak the French language fluently, especially those living with their French masters. But little cruelty was practiced by their owners. There were no Wendell Phillips nor Lloyd Garrisons nor any "higher law doctrine" expounded in those days to disturb the mind of the slave or the slaveholder. Everyone lived in Arcadian simplicity and contentment. The negro was satisfied with his position, and rendered valuable services to his master, and was ever ready to help him against the treacherous Indians. During the war of 1812, several of them accompanied their masters to the battlefield and materially helped them and the troops.

MANY OWNED SLAVES.

By an ordinance enacted by congress, dated July 3, 1787, entitled "an act for the government of the territory of the United States northwest of the Ohio River," there was a clause in Article VI, saying that "there shall be neither slavery nor involuntary servitude in the said territory, otherwise than in the punishment of crimes." This was a safeguard by congress to prevent the extension of slavery northwest of the Ohio River. Notwithstanding this wise provision, our ancestors paid little attention to it, for whenever a spruce young negro was brought by the Indians he was sure to find a purchaser at a reasonable price. Most every prominent man in those days had a slave or two, especially merchants trading with the Indians. Detroit and vicinity was a heaven to the slave compared to the southern states, although slavery was carried on on a moderate scale here, there being no cotton or rice fields to employ them in, their labor being on the plantations near Detroit, or at their master's houses. The master once attached to his "Sambo," a great price would have to be paid to buy him.

The late Judge May had a slave woman, who had come to his hands for a debt owed to him by one Granchin. This faithful slave served the judge some twenty-five years. Mr. Joseph Campau, an extensive trader in those days, had as many as ten slaves at different times. Among them was a young negro named Crow, quite a favorite of Mr. Campau, who had him dressed in scarlet, a decided contrast to his color. This negro, to the amusement of the inhabitants of the old town, used to ascend old Ste. Anne's church steeple and there perform some of his gymnastic tricks. He was supple and elastic as a circus rider. He had been purchased at Montreal by Mr. Campau. He was afterwards drowned from one of Mr. Campau's batteaux.

"Hannah," another intelligent colored woman, was purchased at Montreal by Mr. Campau. This faithful slave, after serving him many years, married "Patterson," also a slave. "Mullett," one of the most honest and faithful of all slaves, also belonged to Mr. Campau, who very often employed him as confidential clerk. This slave died not many years ago, at a very advanced age, respected and esteemed for his great integrity and fidelity. The slave "Tetro" was among the favorites of Major Campau. He, too, was a faithful and as honest as the day was long. The late General John R. Williams also possessed a slave named "Hector." He, too, was faithful and trustworthy.

In the year 1831 Daniel Leroy, Olmstead Chamberlain and Gideon O. Wittemore sold to Colonel Mack, General Williams and Major Campau the newspaper called the *Oakland Chronicle,* the office being transferred here, and the well known slave "Hector" was placed in charge of it. When the late Colonel Sheldon McKnight entered to take possession he was fiercely resisted by "Hector," who showed fight and the colonel (I heard the colonel relate this circumstance) had to retreat. This paper was afterwards merged into the *Detroit Gazette,* and afterwards into the *Detroit Free Press.*

DEATH FOR LARCENY.

Ann Wyley, a former slave, suffered the extreme penalty of the law for having stolen six guineas from the firm of Abbott & Finchley. She was sentenced to death by a justice of the peace, and buried on the spot where Ste. Anne's Church formerly stood on Larned Street, which ground was used as a place of burial in early days. When in 1817 the foundations of the church were being excavated, the body of this unfortunate woman was found face downward. It was supposed that she was in a trance at the time of her burial. This incident Mr. Girardin says was related to him by an old lady some years ago, who knew all about the facts, and who has since died.

The late Joseph Drouillard, of Petite Cote, Canada, had two daughters. Upon the marriage of one of them to the grandfather of Mr. Girardin she received a farm; the other received two slaves as her marriage portion. This goes to show that the negro in those days was considered a chattel. Several of our French farmers on both sides of the river had one or more of them.

Many anecdotes can be related of Africa's sons among our ancestors. They as a class were well cared for and educated by their kind masters.

The question may be asked, "How did slavery die out here?" The owners of slaves, after having received their services for a number of years, would generally liberate them, or sometimes sell them to parties outside of the territory. When the celebrated ordinance of 1787 was extended over the north-west, Michigan assumed for the first time the first grade of government, and the laws were put in force; no more slaves were afterward allowed to be brought into the territory, and slavery was known no more here.

SALE OF THE NEGRO MAN POMPEY.

The following is a copy of a deed furnished by W. W. Backus, of Detroit.

"Know all men by these presents, that I, James May, of Detroit, for and in consideration of the sum of forty-five pounds, New York currency, to me in hand paid by John Askin, Esq., of Detroit, the receipt whereof I do hereby acknowledge, to be fully satisfied and paid, have sold and delivered, and by these presents, in plain and open market, do bargain, sell and deliver unto the hands of said John Askin, Esq., his heirs, executors, administrators and assigns forever; and I, the said James May, for my heirs, executors and assigns, against all manner of person or persons, shall and will warrant and forever defend by these presents.

"In witness whereof, I have hereunto set my hand and seal this 19th day of October, A. D., 1794.

(Signed) "JAMES MAY."

In the presence of

ROBERT STEVENS.

"I do hereby make over my whole right, title and interest in the above mentioned negro man, Pompey, to Mr. James Donaldson, of this place, for the sum of fifty pounds, New York curreney, the receipt of which I do hereby acknowledge, as witness my hand and seal at Detroit this 3d day of January, 1795.
(Signed) "JOHN ASKIN."
Witness:
"WILLIAM MCCLINTOCK."

Through the counties of Wayne, Monroe, Macomb and Oakland, the slave existed. True, he bore the same relation, almost, to his master, as the white laborer of the south did to his master previous to 1861. Yet he was a slave and liable to be bought and sold.

An extensive merchant of Sandwich, Canada, and father of the late Mrs. Judge John McDonell, of this city, owned two or three slaves in the early days. Mrs. McDonell had in her possession her father's account books and papers, and she has often shown the former to me, in which there appear accounts of the expenses of each slave; also an accurate description of them. Their names I have forgotten. She remembered them all, well, and testified to their fidelity quite heartily.

THE TOLEDO WAR.

IT WAS A RATHER FARCICAL AND AN ALMOST BLOODLESS CONTEST—SOME AMUSING INCIDENTS.

THE "Toledo War" has been often ventilated in the public press and through other sources, but there are two or three amusing incidents connected with it that may be news to some people. Although quite young, I was an eye-witness of the feverish excitement that ruled our little community, and of the marshaling of troops in our streets with the beating of drums, flaunting banners and all the "pomp and circumstance of glorious war"—all eager to be led by our plucky governor, Stevens T. Mason, to chastise Ohio. It was related at the time that Major Stickney, of Toledo, and his raft of boys were the only ones they met there that really did any real fighting.

An instance is related concerning Major Stickney's arrest, which caused great amusement at the time. He and his family fought valiantly, but were overpowered by numbers. He was requested to mount a horse, but flatly refused. He was put on by force, but would not sit there. Finally two men were detailed to walk beside him and hold his legs, while a third led the horse. After making half the distance in this way, they tied his legs under the horse, and thus got him to jail in Monroe.

VALIANT MAJOR STICKNEY AND HIS BOYS.

Major Stickney's raft of boys were named One Stickney, Two Stickney, Three Stickney, and so on. In an attempt to arrest one of the boys, "Two Stickney," a scuffle ensued, in which the officer was stabbed with a knife, but the wound did not prove dangerous, and it is believed this was the only blood shed during the war. The officer let go his hold, and Stickney fled into Ohio. On another occasion an officer attempted to arrest a man in the night time. The man had but a moment's warning, and sought safety in flight. He reached the Maumee River, threw himself on a sawlog, and, with hands and feet paddled himself to safety to the other shore.

A very pious man was elected as justice of the peace and fled to the woods, where he lived for many days in a sugar shanty. It was currently reported and generally believed by the Ohio partisans, that a miracle had been wrought in his behalf—that "robin red-breasts" brought him his daily food and drink. The belief in this miracle strengthened the cause of Ohio in many quarters very materially.

BLOOD ON THE MOON.

The Ohio troops, numebring about 600 officers and men, fully armed and equipped, went into camp at old Fort Miami, and there awaited the orders of the governor. Governor Mason, with General Joseph E. Brown, arrived at Toledo with a force, under the immediate command of the latter, variously estimated at from 800 to 1,200 men, fully armed and equipped, and went into camp. Then "blood was on the moon," but the troops did not meet in hostile array, owing to the timely intervention of two commissioners sent by the President of the United States to use their personal influence to stop all warlike demonstrations. The commissioners were men of eminence in the nation—Hon. Richard Rush, of Philadelphia, and Colonel Howard, of Baltimore. Hon. Elisha Whittlesey, of Ohio, accompanied the commissioners as a voluntary peace-maker.

Governor Lucas, of Ohio, believed things were all amicable, and thought he could run and re-mark the line between the two states without serious opposition from the authorities of Michigan, whereupon he disbanded the military he had collected, and directed his commissioners to proceed with the work. S. Dodge, an engineer on the Ohio canal, had been engaged as surveyor to run the line. But Governor Mason was not of the same mind, for it appears from the report of the Ohio commissioners to their governor, that "On Saturday evening, May 25, 1835, after having performed a laborious day's service, your commissioners, together with their party, retired to the distance of about one mile south of the line, in Henry County, within the state of Ohio, where we thought to have rested quietly, and peaceably enjoy the blessings of the Sabbath; and especially, not being engaged on the line, we thought ourselves secure for the day. But contrary to our expectations, at about 12 o'clock in the day an armed force of about fifty or sixty men hove in sight, within musket shot of us, all mounted upon horses, well armed with muskets and under the command of General Brown, of Michigan. Your commissioners, observing the great superiority of force, having but five armed men among us, who had been employed to keep a lookout and as hunters for the party, thought it prudent to retire, and so advised our men. Your commissioners, with several of their party, made good their retreat to this place (Perrysburg, O.). But, sir, we are under the painful necessity of relating that nine of our men, who did not leave the ground in time, after being fired upon by the enemy from thirty to fifty shots, were taken prisoners and carried away into the interior of the country. We are happy to learn that our party did not fire a gun in turn, and that no one was wounded, although a ball from the enemy passed through the clothing of one of our men."

These prisoners were taken to Tecumseh. They were there brought before a magistrate for examination. They denied jurisdiction; six entered bail for their appearance, two were released as not guilty, and one, Mr. Fletcher—refused to give bail and was retained in custody.

Governor Mason was at Tecumseh at the time with General Brown. The former in an interview with Fletcher, advised him to give bail, but he firmly and decidedly declined to do so.

Governor Mason was very anxious that the unpleasantness and difficulties might be settled without any further trouble. General Brown did not have much to say on the subject, but it was believed at the time that he did not desire to have the question amicably settled, but that he secretly wished for a collision between the two states, that he might have the opportunity to distinguish himself, and in a conversation between Fletcher and General Brown, in regard to the arrest of the former and party, the general, in response to the sheriff's regret that the citizens of Ohio were fired upon, replied that "it was the best thing that was done; that he did not hesitate to say he gave the order to fire." He also mentioned giving orders to the sheriff how to proceed; and the latter admitted that he acted under Brown's direction.

"B. F. Stickney, of Toledo, although one of the party engaged in running the line, was confined in the Monroe County jail for, as he says, "the monstrous crime of having acted as the judge of an election within the state of Ohio."

Mr. N. Goodsell, a citizen of Toledo, was also abducted and taken to Monroe. He was obliged to ride on a horse without a bridle; the horse, being urged from the rear, became unmanageable and ran away with him until he freed himself by jumping, and got to Monroe on foot, where he was detained for a day or two, secured bail and returned to Toledo. On the way to Monroe Mr. Goodsell and the party having him in custody were joined by another party having in custody a Mr. McKay, of Toledo. He was mounted with his feet tied under the horse.

THE COMMISSIONERS ESCAPED.

The Ohio commissioners, with their surveyor, again commenced to run the line, previous to which General Brown sent scouts through the woods to watch their movements and to report when they found them running the line. When the surveying party had got within the county of Lenawee, the under sheriff of that county, with a warrant and a posse, made his appearance to arrest them. He arrested a portion of the party; but the commissioners and Surveyor Dodge made their escape, and they ran with all their might until they got off the disputed territory. They reached Pennsylvania next day with clothes badly torn; some of them hatless, with terrible looking heads, and all with stomachs very much collapsed. They reported that they had been attacked by a large force of Michigan militia under General Brown, and had been fired upon and had just escaped with their lives; and that they expected that the remainder of their party were either killed or taken prisoners.

THE ONLY BLOOD SHED.

In regard to the arrest of "Two Stickney" by Joseph Wood, deputy sheriff of Monroe County, Michigan, and of the knifing of this officer, some further particulars are given herewith. Lyman Hurd, constable, of the same county, testifies that he and Wood, the latter having in his hands a warrant against "Two Stickney," went into the tavern of J. B. Davis, in Toledo, where they found Stickney and George McKay, against whom Hurd also had a warrant. Hurd also testified that he informed the latter that he had a warrant against him, and attempted to arrest him. McKay sprang and caught a chair and told him if he attempted that game he would split him down. Hurd also said McKay had a drawn dirk in his hand, and he did not arrest him, presumably on that account. While Hurd was attempting to arrest McKay, Wood attempted to arrest Stickney. They had quite a scuffle and during the melee Stickney drew a dirk out of the left side of Wood and exclaimed, "There, damn you, you have got it now." Wood let go of Stickney and put his hand upon his left side, apparently in distress, and went to the door. Those present asked Wood if he was stabbed. He said, very faintly, that he was. A doctor was called, on Wood's request, who on examination of the wound, thought the latter's recovery very doubtful. But he did recover, and as I before said, this was the only real fight and the only blood shed on this memorable occasion.

For some of the foregoing particulars I am indebted to the History of the Maumee Valley, by H. T. Knapp, Toledo, 1872.

INCIDENTS OF THE PATRIOT WAR.

AN EYE-WITNESS OF SOME OF THE EVENTS OF THE TROUB-
LOUS TIMES OF 1838-9 GIVES INTERESTING DETAILS.

I WILL not say very much in regard to the Patriot war of 1838-39, as it has been dilated upon, so often that the story must be familiar to most people.

I was on Jones' dock, this side of the river, directly in the rear of the old board of trade building on Woodbridge Street, shortly after the Patriots crossed the river on the steamboat Thames. The noise of the exploding musketry, in the short battle between the Canadian militia and the Patriots, in the Baby orchard, woke me early. I surmised what it meant, and, on reaching the dock, I saw the steamer in flames, at the dock in Windsor, a short distance above the present ferry dock, and the barracks, a large yellow building, just this side of the steamer, was also ablaze.

I think the Patriots, who got badly worsted in their short scrimmage with the "Cannucks" in the orchard, set them on fire in their hurry-scurry to get away up the river; part of them took to the Canadian woods. Soon a battery of British artillery, from Malden I think, came tearing up the river road and pushed on in hot pursuit of the fugitives, but they did not succeed in capturing any of the retreating Patriots.

THE PATRIOTS ROUTED.

In the meantime those who had taken the river road reached in safety the two old windmills that stood on the bank of the river, just above the present site of Walkerville. They availed themselves of six or eight canoes, that luckily appeared in sight, drawn up on the river bank, and pushed off for the American shore. Some of them met with disaster before reaching "home." The artillery gained the further mill just about the time the fugitives reached the middle of the river, and from that point they opened upon them with grape and caninster. We could plainly see the

114   EARLY DAYS IN DETROIT.

puffs of smoke at every discharge. They did not do much damage, only wounding three or four slightly. Part got across the river safely, the remainder, including the wounded, were taken prisoners by a detachment of the Brady Guards, Captain Rowland, and under the immediate personal command of General Hugh Brady, who were on the steamer Erie, patroling the river in the interests of the neutrality laws. Those who escaped and remained in Canada got back safely after awhile.

During this time the little steamboat Erie, got away from the dock between Woodward Avenue and Griswold Street, where it was waiting the Brady Guards to get aboard. Atwater Street in that vicinity, and indeed the entire river front, was filled with a howling mob, who deeply sympathized with the Patriots. When the Brady Guards appeared, headed by Captain Rowland and General Brady, a howl of derision went up from the crowd. But General Brady, tall and as straight as a young poplar, Rowland, whose black eyes snapped ominously behind his gold-rimmed glasses, and the boys behind them with their muskets, paid no more attention to the howlers than they would have done to a swarm of buzzing flies, but parted the crowd to the right and left and boarded the steamer without molestation.

SOME PROMINENT PARTICIPANTS.

The reason I surmised that the musket-firing on that December morning meant trouble was that a short time previous to the crossing, I was invited by one of the initiated to an informal meeting of the members of a "Hunter's Lodge," so named by the Patriots. Thes gatherings were held in a building in the Brush garden. The late William Adair ran the garden at that time. While at this meeting, I gleaned from the conversation going on around me, that in the near future, a demonstration would be made against our neighbors on the other side of the river, but the time and place I could not ascertain. It was at this meeting that I first saw and became acquainted with the late John Harmon, who was an ardent Patriot, and the acquaintance ripened into a warm friendship that lasted until his death. At this meeting I also saw Colonel E. J. Roberts, Dr. Theler and others.

I was an eye witness of all the incidents referred to in this connection.

AN IRISHMAN'S ESCAPE.

One of the Patriots that ventured across the river and took an active part in the affair was a clerk in the office of A. E. Hathon, city surveyor, a son of Erin (Hogan I think was his name). He got back to this side safe and without a scratch. He related with much amusement some of the details of the expedition. He said that after they had marched off the steamboat on the Canada side. "Some d—d rascal set it on fire," and there they were, "Sink or Swim." They proceeded down the river road to the barracks, a large frame building occupied by a company or detachment of Canadian soldiers. They fired on the advancing Patriots without damage. The fire was returned with a charge by the Patriots, on the barracks. The enemy left in short order, and retired to the Baby orchard, where the Patriots followed them, and where the latter got worsted and were scattered, some being taken prisoners on the spot, others fleeing for their lives up the river road towards what is now Walkerville, and still others took to the fields and roads leading into the country, all pursued by the victorious Canadians. Our Irish friend said he took to one of the country roads and, being fleet of foot, soon out-distanced his pursuers, though several shots were fired at him, and any quantity of imprecations were hurled after him. He got shelter and concealment in a friendly farmer's barn, whose kindly wife furnished him subsistence. He remained here quiet for a few days, and then ventured into Windsor concealed in a load of hay the farmer was bringing in. He got to the river all right, stole a canoe, and paddled himself across to this side, and out of danger.

Hathon's office was in the Cooper block, and the back windows commanded a clear view of Windsor. I have often seen Hogan go to the windows, and, casting his eyes across the river, syear in an undertone, and then laugh immoderately at the remembrance of some funny incident connected with the affair. He said further, he reckoned the reason the soldiers did not hit him during his hurried flight was because they could not see him for the dust he kicked up.

I have mentioned before in this connection Colonel E. J. Roberts. He was the father of Colonel Horace S. Roberts, of the First Regiment Michigan Volunteers, and was killed at the second battle of Bull Run, while in command of the regiment.

DR. THELER'S EXPEDITION.

Referring again to Dr. Theler. He was an ardent Patriot of the first water, a short, chunky Irishman and full of fight apparently, but the expedition he commanded that set out to capture Malden did not pan out successfully. He got away from here one morning somehow, with I do not remember how many men, and one piece of cannon—I think a brass six-pounder—on the schooner Ann, and sailed away down the river for Malden. Arriving in front of that town, they began blazing away with their gun. The inhabitants, realizing what they were up to, armed themselves and started out in small boats to capture the Patriots, which they did after a short and harmless scrimmage. The doctor and party were sent to Quebec and confined in the citadel and the schooner and equipment were confiscated. The doctor, after a brief confinement in that stronghold, managed to escape, and got safely to this side. He published a book detailing his adventures, escape, etc., which was quite interesting, his escape from the citadel being particularly so.

A NERVY PATRIOT.

One party of Patriots, including Captain James Armstrong, of Port Huron, recrossed the river from Canada, landing on Belle Isle, but before they reached the land a ball from the six-pounder cannon fired from the windmill at Walkerville mangled Armstrong's arm. He was brought to Dr. Hind's office, in this city, where the arm was amputated. Anesthetics were not in use in those days, but Armstrong never uttered a groan during the operation, and when it was finished he picked up the arm, waved it around his head and said: "Hurrah for the Patriots! I'm willing to lose another arm for the cause." Armstrong was afterward sheriff of Sanilac County in 1856 or 1857.

CONVICTS IN VAN DIEMAN'S LAND.

Aaron Dresser and T. T. Wright were engaged with Colonel Von Thoultz, in the affair of the windmill, near Prescott, Canada, November, 1838. They were tried by a militia court-martial at Kingston, and sentenced to death, but were sent to Van Dieman's Land as convicts, where, after residence of nearly four years, they were forgiven and allowed to return to their country by Sir John Franklin, the British governor. In a communication to the *New York Tribune,* February 17, 1844, they appealed to their countrymen to interest themselves in behalf of the fifty-four comrades still in captivity, and to endeavor to procure their release. In addition to the above serving sentence at the same place they said were twenty-two, taken prisoners in the affair at Windsor, opposite Detroit, in the same year. Their names were Chauncey Sheldon, Elijah C. Woodman, Michael Murray, John H. Simmons, Alvin B. Sweet, Simeon B. Goodrich, James A. Achison, Elijah Stevens, John C. Williams, Samuel Snow, Riley M. Stewart, John Sprague, John B. Tyrell, James DeWitt Ferro, Henry V. Barnum, John Varnum, James Waggoner, Norman Mallory, Horace Cooley, John Grant, Lynus W. Miller (student at law) and Joseph Stewart. They said they were five months on the passage from Van Dieman's Land to London, and Mr. Everett, our minister at London, got them a ship to New York. They also said: "We say it with truth and sincerity that we would not of choice pass the rest of our lives in Van Dieman's Land if the whole island were given to us in freehold as a gift. We have not to complain of unusual hardship used to ourselves, and yet both of us have often wished to be relieved by death from the horrid bondage entailed on those who are situated as we were. 'To be obliged to drag out an existence in such a convict colony, and among such a population, is in itself a punishment severe beyond our power to describe."

They also said: "Several parties, in all about 1,500 men, were placed last May, under proper officers of the government, for the purpose of securing four criminals guilty of murder, etc.; we were in one of these parties by whom the criminals were secured; and this and general good conduct procured several persons their liberty, among whom we two were so fortunate as to be included. Morrisset, Murry and Lafore are, we think, from lower Canada. We can speak more decided as to our comrades from Prescott, Windsor, and the Short Hills, above named, because when we got our freedom we visited most of them, though scattered through the interior of the country, following their several trades or occupations. One of us, Aaron Dresser, resides in Alexandria, Jefferson County—the other, Stephen T. Wright, lives in Denmark,

Lewis County, both in New York state. We will be happy to reply to any post-paid letters from the relatives of our comrades. and to give them any further information in our power."

(Signed) AARON DRESSER,
T. T. WRIGHT.

ONE OF THE PARTY CAPTURED AT WINDSOR.

Chauncey Sheldon was from Oakland County, this state, and came into the city with his team and load of produce. He had some friends here that were ardent in the Patriot cause. They persuaded him to visit the Hunters' Lodge in the Brush garden, the night before the crossing, and induced him to join the expedition, telling him it was just a picnic and nothing short of that. Well, he crossed the river with the "gang," leaving his team, etc. He was taken prisoner and sentenced to Van Dieman's Land as above stated.

DR. HUME'S CRUEL MURDER.

The old orchard (Baby's) where the battle came off was nearly opposite the building now occupied by D. M. Ferry & Co.'s seed store, and among other incidents connected with this scrimmage was one of a most melancholy nature, and that was the murder of Doctor Hume, of the British army, who was at Sandwich, and for some reason was detained there, after the militia left, and came up alone on horseback. On the road in front of this orchard was a long, low log house, which was at that time in possession of the Patriots, and from one of the windows or corner of this house he was as far as any one knows, shot without mercy. His body was thrown into a hogpen and partially devoured before his friends had time to rescue it. For this and other atrocities of the Patriots Colonel Prince, of Sandwich, commander of the Canadian militia, retaliated on them with a summary vengeance that has been often detailed.

This taking off of Dr. Hume in such a tragic manner has been often detailed before, and I repeat it now because he was so well known on this side of the river. The distressing occurrence was the talk of the town and was regretted by all. I visited the scene of the battle in the orchard two or three days after it occurred, as also the spot where the doctor fell.

AFTER THE WAR.

The excitement incident to the war was kept up for many months, all along the border, on both sides, after all demonstrations of a hostile nature had ceased. During the summer following the Windsor episode, I spent some months in St. Clair. The village of Moretown, on the opposite side of the river, still contìnned to maintain a company of Canadian militia, who had their quarters over the store and warehouse of a Mr. Sutherland, an extensive English merchant, who was loyalty personified. Many of the present inhabitants of St. Clair and of Moretown will, no doubt, call to mind the personality of the jolly Englishman. Every time the militia company relieved guard, night and morning, the squad that were relieved, would invariably discharge their muskets when they reached the platform at the head of the stairs, on the outside of their quarters. Everyone banged off his piece, singly, before entering the door, waking the sleeping echoes and reminding the peaceful inhabitants on both sides of the river, that, although the "cruel war" was over, still, "eternal vigilance was the price of liberty" and that they were not to be caught napping.

EARLY DAY ARCHITECTURE.

DETROIT'S FIRST BRICK AND STONE STRUCTURES—INTERESTING OLD BUILDINGS.

THE first brick dwelling house in the city, it is believed, was built, or begun, by an Englishman—Mr. Benjamin Stead, who died in 1821. The house was finished soon after his death by other parties. It was a two-story, double brick house, and still stands, nearly opposite the old Michigan Exchange. Part of it was occupied by the late Tunis Wendell, and the other part by the late Col. Whiting, U. S. A. Later portions of it were used by the United States for officers' sleeping rooms. Dr. Farnsworth also had his office in part of it. It is now occupied for various purposes.

The house of David Cooper, that formerly stood on Cadillac Square, was built about 1827. It also was a double brick house and was built by David Cooper and Charles Jackson. Both Mr. Jackson and Mr. Cooper lived there in 1827 and later on. There was also a small brick house on Jefferson Avenue below Wayne Street, occupied for many years by William Berger as a gun-shop, and before him by Hon. John Norvell, with the postoffice. Many old residents will remember this, I think, as well as the old wooden gun Berger had projecting from the roof as a sign. The house on the south side of Fort Street, near Wayne Street, now occupied by Mrs. Whitbeck, was built by Dr. Henry, father of D. Farrand Henry, and was occupied by him for at least five years. It was probably built prior to 1832.

Dr. Hurd built and occupied a two-story brick house on the corner of Woodward Avenue and Congress Street, where is now the Richmond & Backus Co., before 1827. Thomas Palmer, father of the senator, built and occupied as a store and residence a two-story brick house on the south side of Jefferson Avenue, on

EARLY DAY ARCHITECTURE.

the corner of Griswold Street, where the senator first saw the light in 1830.

Levi Brown, the jeweler and inventor of the gold pen, had his brick store and residence on the north side of Jefferson Avenue between Shelby and Griswold Streets, nearly opposite that of Thomas Palmer. There was also a brick dwelling, built by Jonathan Keeney prior to 1830, on Fort Street, north side, between Griswold and Shelby Streets. It is still standing.

Robert Smart built and owned, prior to 1827, a two-story brick store on the corner of Jefferson and Woodward Avenues, the present site of the Merrill Block, which was occupied as a general store in 1827-8-9 and 1830, by Henry V. Disbrow, Esq.

General John R. Williams, prior to 1827, owned and lived in a two-story brick house, on the north side of Woodbridge Street, between Bates and Randolph Streets.

General Hull also built and occupied, prior to 1827, a brick residence of quite a pretentious character, on the corner of Jefferson Avenue and Randolph Street, the present site of the Biddle House. After General Hull vacated it it was occupied for a short time by General Proctor (British), and shortly after by General Brady, until he completed his residence on the corner of Jefferson Avenue and Hastings Street, the present site of the Art Museum.

The Mansion House, that stood on the north side of Jefferson Avenue, near the line of the Cass farm, now Cass Street, was a stone and brick structure, and was built prior to 1827, from the ruins of Fort Shelby. The old Bank of Michigan, or Detroit City Bank, as I think it was called then, built and occupied, prior to 1827, a small brick building on the present site of the Kearsley building, at the southwest corner of Jefferson Avenue and Randolph Street.

Judge Canniff and Jerry Dean, prior to 1827, built and occupied as residences, the two-story, double brick house (still standing), on the south side of Congress Street, a few doors from Shelby Street. Peter Desnoyer also, about the same period, built and occupied as a store, a two-story brick building, on the present site of the Desnoyer Block. The store did not occupy as much ground as does the present block. His dwelling (wooden), built directly after the fire of 1805, stood on the corner of Jefferson Avenue and Bates Street, and the new brick store next to it on the south.

The stone buildings of that time were Ste. Anne's church (Catholic), the old Council House, on the corner of Jefferson Avenue and Randolph Street, on the present site of the water works building, and the old arsenal, on the southwest corner of Jefferson Avenue and Wayne Street.

The state capitol building (brick) was built prior to 1827. There was also a government warehouse, of brick, directly in the rear of Berger's gun shop and fronting on Woodbridge Street.

SURVEYING IN EARLY DAYS.

THE OCCUPATION HAD ITS PERILS IN THIS PART OF THE COUNTRY—EXPERIENCE OF THE JEROME PARTY.

IN October, 1831, Mr. Edwin Jerome left Detroit with a surveying party composed of John Mullet, United States surveyor, and Utter, Brink and Peck, assistants, for that portion of Michigan territory lying west of Lake Michigan, and which is now Wisconsin. Their outfit consisted of a French pony team and a buffalo wagon to carry tent, camp equipage, blankets, etc. Most of the way to the southeast corner of Lake Michigan they followed a wagon track or Indian trail, and had a cabin or an Indian hut to lodge in at night; but west of the point mentioned they found neither road nor inhabitant. They arrived at Chicago in a terrible rainstorm and put up at the fort (Dearborn). This far-famed city at that time had but five or six houses, and they were built of logs. Within a distance of three or four miles of the fort the land was valued by its owners at fifty cents an acre.

After twenty-three days' weary travel through an uninhabited country, fording and swimming streams and exposed to much rainy weather, they arrived at Galena where they commenced their survey, but in two days the ground froze so deep that further work was abondoned until the next spring. The day after the memorable Stillman battle with Black Hawk, while the Mullet party were crossing the Blue Mounds, they met with an Indian half-chief, who had just arrived from the Menominee camps with the details of the battle. He stated the slain to be three Indians and eleven whites. The long shaking of hands and the extreme cordiality of this Indian alarmed Mullet for the safety of his party, but he locked the secret in his own heart until the next day. They had just completed a town corner when Mullet, raising himself to his full height, said: "Boys, I'm going in; I'll not risk my scalp for a few paltry shillings." This laconic speech was an electric shock to the whole company. Mr. Jerome, in describing his own sensations, said "that the hair of his head became then as porcupine quills, raising his hat in the air and himself from the ground, and the top of his head became as sore as a boil."

PERILS OF PIONEER DAYS.

TRAVELERS IN THESE PARTS IN EARLY TIMES HAD TO BEWARE OF WOLVES, INDIANS AND OTHER DANGEROUS PROWLERS.

THE late Judge Z. W. Bunce, of Port Huron, in the spring of 1817 put on board a one-horse wagon $3,000 worth of ready-made clothing and started from Albany, N. Y., for Detroit on the 15th day of April. He passed through Rochester, N. Y., when there were only twenty persons there, and a choice of lots could be had then for $50. In this connection, and referring to the same location record, Judge Jerome, father of all the Jeromes in this state, related once in my presence that he was offered 200 acres, on which was a log house, for 20 cents an acre, but he said his eyes were set for Michigan, and had no use for wild land in New York state.

Our adventurer was detained at Buffalo some days for the completion of the schooner Michigan, on which he intended to cross Lake Erie. The schooner was the one which was subsequently sent over the Niagara Falls with wild animals on board. After three days he arrived in Detroit and stored his goods with James Abbott and engaged board at Colonel Richard Smith's tavern, on the south side of Woodward Avenue, between Jefferson Avenue and Woodbridge Street. He made an effort to see the farming country around Detroit, and for this purpose told Colonel Smith, his landlord, to have a horse saddled for him. He mounted his horse and took his course across what was then called the commons to a French wood road, followed this until he found himself deep in the mud and water. He then tried another and another road, and found all the same. He then returned to the tavern and asked the landlord to put him on to a road that would take him into the country.

"Where do you want to go?" inquired the landlord.

"Out among the farmers, to see what you have got for a back-bone for your city," he replied.

"We have got no such bone. You will find nothing in that direction but swamps, woods, wildcats and Indians. If you want to see our farmers you must go up and down the river."

He took his advice and went as far as Hudson's (now the

Country Club) on Lake St. Clair, by way of the old Stone Wind Mill (once on Wind Mill Point) and was apparently satisfied. He was invited by Colonel Jack Langhan, paymaster in the United States army, to go with him and assist in paying off the troops at the River Raisin, now Monroe. They started at 3 o'clock in the morning, Colonel Langhan and Colonel Dick Smith on horseback, and Chauncy S. Payne and the judge in a one-horse wagon. They crossed the Rouge by swimming the horses and carrying the wagon over in two canoes. In the same way they crossed the Ecorse. The ground over which they passed in the first part of their journey was sandy and they found no great difficulty until they reached Swan Creek. There they mired their horse and wagon, but after one expedient and another they extricated themselves from this quagmire. Here night came on—a dark, dreary night—with nothing to amuse or cheer them but the howl of the wolves, which kept up their serenade until nearly daylight. The last part of their way there was a road made by the United States troops through a dense forest free from stumps, but with no bottom to the spongy soil. They arrived at the Raisin about 9 o'clock in the evening.

After four days at the Raisin they started at 6 o'clock A. M. on their return and, having daylight for the most part of the way, they got along better than when going down, crossing the Ecorse about 9 o'clock in the evening. Half way between that river and the Rouge they found a pack of wolves in the road before them, which opened to the right and left and let the travelers pass, at the same time saluting them with a hideous howl. Payne, badly scared, stuck to the wagon. The judge, having provided himself with a cudgel, posted himself at the hind end of the wagon for defense, but neither of them was injured. The horse suffered most from the effects of Payne's whip. They reached Detroit in the wee hours of the morning.

Mr. Payne was for many years a citizen of Detroit, associated with Levi Brown in the silversmith and jewelry business. Payne married the daughter of Jacob Smith, an Indian trader. Captain Garland, of the army, married another daughter of Smith. These girls inherited from their father an Indian reserve west of this city.

Mr. and Mrs. Payne were both living in 1882. The traffic of this family with the Indians was carried on most through the house of Conrad (Coon) and Jerry Ten Eyck.

THE HAPPY FRENCH HABITANT.

HIS AFFILIATION WITH AND INFLUENCE UPON THE INDIANS HEREABOUTS IN THE EARLY DAYS OF OUR HISTORY.

GEORGE HERIOT, in his "Travels in Canada" (London, 1807), says of the French habitant:
"They were honest, hospitable, religious, inoffensive and uninformed, possessed of simplicity and civility. Without ambition and attached to ancient prejudices they sought no more than the necessaries of life. Many, as a result of happy action, were poor without realizing their poverty; some were well-to-do without boasting of their wealth."

"The stream-haunting habitant has been happily compared to the beaver, or muskrat. At times he seemed to live in waters and marshes around him, building his cabin where it was accessible only to a canoe.

"A century and more after the founding of Detroit, the farms still cling lovingly to the river banks, and a mile back from the stream was still seen the untouched forest. The troops who came from Ohio to Detroit in 1812, found only one muddy road, winding along between stream and wood, a situation which offered the lurking savage every opportunity for ambush and attack. What roads there were, the water-loving habitant despised; but over his rough highways he jogged merrily to market with a two-wheeled Norman cart and rough, dwarfish pony, a curious mongrel animal of unknown pedigree, but with an endurance and possible speed which delighted the simple peasant or his rollicking sons.

AFFILIATED WITH THE SAVAGES.

"It was the hardy, lawless French coureur des bois and bushrangers who hated England cordially, and pushing their way into this coveted country, readily affiliated with the savages and influenced them to hate English, and to look upon the French as their allies. They many times adopted Indian habits, took to wife daughters of their savage friends, and raised a brood of half-breed children.

"When the time came to change French for English control the Indians, it is said, reluctantly consented, and down to the middle of the last century, although the British were generally preferred to the Americans, the French were greatly preferred to either.

"'Whatever may have been the reason,' said Governor Cass, 'the fact is certain that there is in the French character peculiar adaptations to the habits and feelings of the Indians, and to this day the period of French domination is the era of all that is happy in Indian reminiscences.'" (Historical Sketches of Michigan.)

LOVED BY THE INDIANS.

At the Sault de Ste. Marie in 1826 a Chippewa chief, addressing the American agent, thus pathetically referred to the happy days of the French dominion in the west: "When the Frenchmen arrived at these falls they came and kissed us. They called us children, and we found them fathers. We lived like brethren in the same lodge, and we had always the wherewithal to clothe us. They never mocked at our ceremonies, and they never molested the places of our dead. Seven generations of men have passed away, but we have not forgotten it. Just, very just, were they towards us." Mrs. Jameson's "Winter Studies."

DETROIT'S EARLY DAYS.

In his "Life of Cass" Professor Andrew McLaughlin says: "Seventy-five years ago Detroit was still a French settlement. The few Scotch who came in during the later years of the English domination affiliated with the French and appreciated their conservatism. In consequence of this ancestry there has always been a steadiness and sobriety in business and a caution and reserve in society. It has not felt until a comparative recent period the stir of American life, as has Buffalo, or Cleveland, placed in the heart of 'New Connecticut.' It can scarcely be doubted that conservative French Catholicism has had its influence in giving peculiar tone and setting a dignified pace. It is true that after Detroit had been ostensibly an American city for forty years, the introduction of New England life gave the town a look of prosperity and activity which was lacking to the Canadian towns across the river. Not long ago, easily within the memory of men now living in Detroit, the well-to-do French peasant held his acres and refused twice their value or demanded perhaps that the city put a rail fence on each side of the street, which eminent domain had forced through his land. For a long time Detroit was practically Michigan.

"Down to 1763 the city grew slowly. In the time of the English domination there came a few English traders and a few canny Scotch, with their habits of thrift and deftness. But the French habitant does not allow his ease to be interfered with. Everywhere the world presents the same roseate hue to his contented vision. After 1796 some Americans making their way into the territory jostle him about a little, insist on trial by jury, talk to him of popular elections and other incomprehensive problems, suggest the idea that Detroit may become a great commercial center.

"When winter set in, the people gave themselves up to pleasure-seeking. Their shaggy ponies, which had been allowed all summer long to roam the woods or scamper uncontrolled along the river banks, now became their special pride. The swiftest of the herd was dearly cherished; and the highest ambition of the farmer was to drive the fastest horse. The frozen river was the theater of delights, or the 'Grand Marais' a few miles above the city, swollen with autumn rains, offered its icy attractions. Sunday, as in most Catholic countries, was a day for enjoyment as well as solemn worship, and Saturday was generally an occasion of unrestrained merry-making. Sleigh-riding, dancing, feasting and uncontrolled levity filled up the passing winter weeks. A summer's providence was easily lost in a winter's mild dissipation."

In 1817 the *Gazette* thus encouraged the French to effort: "Frenchmen of the territory of Michigan, you ought to begin immediately to give an education to your children. In a little time there will be in this territory as many Yankees as French, and if you do not have your children educated the situations will all be given to the Yankees."

The French were exasperating to the busy Yankee, for they never did today what could be delayed till the morrow.

DIFFERED FROM OTHER SETTLERS.

The late Bela Hubbard, in his "Memorials of a Half a Century," in regard to the French habitant, has this to say: "I have alluded to one trait in which the French emigres differed widely from the English and Spanish settlers in America—their friendliness towards the aboriginal inhabitants. This kindly disposition was appreciated by the Indians; so that the two races, whenever they fairly understood each other, lived in peace together.

"I am not aware that intermarriages were frequent, or that this relationship was often entered into by the peasantry of this part of Canada. It was common enough at the remoter parts, down even to times within my personal knokledge. The Indian trader, whether Frenchman, Scotsman or Yankee, prompted partly by interest, usually took to himself an Indian wife. At such places as Mackinac and Sault Ste. Marie, half-breeds were quite numerous, as they had been at Detroit at an earlier day. The class known as voyageurs—the coureurs de bois of the older times—had become to a very considerable extent of mixed blood. The licentious lawlessness of those wild wood-rangers was not only well known, but was a subject of much complaint at a very early day. Certain it is, that in many points there was greater assimilation between the natives and the people from France than was the case with the emigrants from any other civilized country. In several excursions which I made between 1836 and 1840, in the wilderness portions of Michigan, and along the large streams and channels, it was not uncommon to find the solitary lodge of a Frenchman, with his squaw wife, and sometimes two wives, and a troop of half-breed children. They lived more like Indians than white people, associated chiefly with them, and depended on fishing."

"THE WINNING OF THE WEST."

FRONTIERSMEN IN THESE PARTS LED ADVENTUROUS LIVES IN THE EARLY DAYS.

GEORGE CROGHAN, of Pennsylvania, Sir William Johnson's sub-commissioner, made a visit to the west in 1765, for the purpose of establishing more friendly relations between the English and the more distant western tribes.

He says: "We arrived at Detroit on the 17th of August, in the morning, and went to the fort, which is a large stockade, inclosing about eighty houses. It stands close on the north side of the river, on a high bank, commands a very pleasant prospect for nine miles above and nine miles below the fort. The country is thickly settled with French. Their plantations are generally laid out about three or four acres in breadth on the river and eighty acres in depth. The soil is good, producing plenty of grain. All the people here are generally poor wretches, and consist of three or four hundred French families, a lazy, idle people, depending chiefly on the savages for subsistence. Though the land, with little labor, produces plenty of grain, they scarcely raise as much as will supply their wants, in imitation of the Indians, whose manners and customs they have entirely adopted, and cannot subsist without them. The men, women and children speak the Indian tongue fluently. In the last Indian war, the most part of the French were concerned in it (although the settlement had taken the oath of allegiance to his Britannic majesty). They have, therefore, great reason to be thankful to the English clemency in not bringing them to deserved punishment. Before the last Indian war, there resided three nations of Indians at this place—the Pottawatomies, whose village was on the west side of the river, about one mile below the fort; the Ottawas, on the east side, about three miles above the fort; the Wyandottes, whose village lays on the west side, about two miles below the fort. The former two nations have removed to a considerable distance, and the latter still remain where they were, and are remarkable for their good sense."

BRITISH AND INDIAN ALLIES.

Roosevelt in his "Winning of the West," speaking of the conflict for supremacy between the white element of the infant northwest and the Indian element, says: "They would have found their struggle with the Indians dangerous enough in itself, but there was an added element of menace in the fact that back of the Indians stood the British. It was for this reason that the frontiersmen grew to regard as essential to their well-being the possession of the lake posts; so that it became with them a prime object to wrest from the British, whether by force of arms or by diplomacy, the forts they held at Niagara, Detroit and Machilimackinac. Detroit was the most important, for it served as the headquarters of the western Indians, who formed for the time being the chief bar to American advance. The British held the posts with a strong grip, in the interest of their trades and merchants. To them the land derived its chief importance from the fur trade. This was extremely valuable, and, as it steadily increased in extent and importance, the consequence of Detroit, the fitting-out town for the fur traders, grew in like measure. It was the center of a population of several thousand Canadians, who lived by the chase and by the rude cultivation of their long, narrow farms; and it was held by a garrison of three or four hundred British regulars, with auxiliary bands of American, loyalist and French-Canadian rangers, and above all, with a formidable but fluctuating reserve force of Indian allies.

It was to the interest of the British to keep the American settlers out of the land; and therefore their aims were at one with those of the Indians. All the tribes between the Ohio and the Missouri were subsidized by them, and paid them a precarious allegiance. Fickle, treacherous, and ferocious, the Indians at times committed acts of outrage even on their allies, so that these allies had to be ever on their guard; and the tribes were often at war with one another. War interrupted trade and cut down profits, and the British endeavored to keep the different tribes at peace among themselves, and even with the Americans. Moreover, they always discouraged barbarities, and showed what kindness was in their power to any unfortunate prisoners whom the Indians happened to bring to their posts. But they helped the Indians in all ways save by open military aid to keep back the American settlers. They wished a monopoly of the fur-trade; and they endeavored to prevent the Americans from coming in to their settlements. English officers and agents attended the Indian councils, endeavored to attach the tribes to the British interests, and encouraged them to stand firm against the Americans and to insist upon the Ohio as the boundary between the white man and the red. The Indians received counsel and advice from the British, and drew from them both arms and munitions of war, and while the higher British officers were usually careful to avoid committing any overt breach of neutrality, the reckless partisan leaders sought to inflame the Indians against the Americans and even at times accompanied their war parties.

LIFE AT THE POSTS

"The life led at a frontier post like Detroit was marked by sharp contrasts. The forest roundabout was cleared away, though blackened stumps still dotted the pastures, orchards and tilled fields. The town itself, was composed mainly of the dwellings of the French habitants; some of them were mere hovels, others pretty log cottages, all swarming with black-eyed children; while the stoutly-made, swarthy men, at once lazy and excitable, strolled about the streets in their picturesque and bright-colored blanket suits. There were also a few houses of loyalist refugees, implacable Tories, stalwart men, revengeful and goaded by the memory of many wrongs done and many suffered, who proved the worst enemies of their American kinsfolk. The few big, roomy buildings which served as store houses and residences for the merchants were built not only for the storage of goods and peltries, but also as strongholds in case of attack. The heads of the mercantile houses were generally Englishmen, but the hardy men who traversed the woods for months and for seasons, to procure furs from the Indians, were for the most part French. The sailors, both English and French, who manned the vessels on the lakes, formed another class. The rough earthworks and stockades of the fort were guarded by a few light guns. Within, the red-coated regulars held sway, their bright uniforms, varied here and there by the dingy huting shirt, leggings and fur cap of some Tory ranger or French partisan leader. Indians lounged about the fort, the stores, and the houses, begging or gazing stolidly at the troops as they drilled, at the creaking carts from the outlying farms as they plied through the streets, at the driving to and fro from the pasture of the horses and the milch cows, or at the arrival of a vessel from Niagara or a brigade of fur-laden bateaux from the upper lakes.

DANGEROUS FRIENDS.

"In their paint and cheap, dirty finery these savages did not look very important; yet it was because of them that the British kept up their posts in these far-off forests, beside these great lonely waters; it was for their sakes that they tried to stem the inrush of the settlers of their own blood and tongue, for it was their presence alone which served to keep the wilderness as a game preserve for the fur merchants; it was their prowess in war which prevented French village and British garrison from being lapped up like drops of water before the fiery rush of the American advance. The British themselves, though fighting with and for them, loved them but little; like all frontiermen, they soon grew to look down on their mean, trivial lives—lives which nevertheless strongly attracted white men of evil and shiftless, but adventurous natures, and to which white children, torn from their homes and brought up in the wigwams, became passionately attached. Yet back of the drunken and lazy squalor lay an element of the terrible, all the more terrible because it could not be reckoned with. Dangerous and treacherous allies, upon whom no real dependence could ever be placed, the Indians were nevertheless the most redoubtable of all foes when war was waged in their own gloomy woodlands."

THE IRON MEN OF THE BORDER.

ADVENTURES AND TRIALS OF THE EARLY SETTLERS IN THIS SECTION—INDIAN ATROCITIES.

IN the early conflict for supremacy I do not think it out of place to recount some of the struggles, trials and hardships these men of iron endured in "Winning the West," gathered from various sources, and before which the widely heralded accounts of expeditions to the Klondike in search of gold pale into insignificance.

The times were hard in the early days, and they called for men of flinty fiber. Those of the softer, gentler mood would have failed amidst such surroundings. The iron men of the border had a harsh and terrible task allotted to them, and, though going through dreadful scenes and privations, they never faltered, and wrested this fair land from the dominion of the cruel and remorseless savage, and left it as a heritage to the present owners, who today are scarcely mindful of the splendid gift and the immunity from harm that they enjoy, from within or without, contrasting today with those of the early troublous ones.

The late Judge B. F. H. Witherell, writing of the early days, says:

A DARING FEAT.

"When the United States troops took Malden, during the war of 1812, they found in one of the government buildings, securely packed away, hundreds of human scalps, nicely dressed, and put up in packages of twenty each, and artistically ornamented with various colored ribbons. The scalps were from the soft, silky hair of the infant to the gray and white hair of the aged man and woman.

"A halfbreed Pottawattamie chief, by the name of Robinson, was present at the surrender of the fort at Chicago at the end of the last war with England, and, being somewhat friendly with the American troops, he used his influence to prevent their massacre. He succeeded, however, in saving only Captain Helm, the commandant, and his wife. During the confusion that followed the first volley fired by the Indians, and partly covered by the smoke, he succeeded in placing Captain Helm and his wife in a bark canoe that he had concealed in that vicinity, and carried them to Mackinac, navigating the whole length of Lake Michigan in a bark canoe, and keeping out of sight of land nearly the whole distance for fear of roving bands of Indians."

Probably the whole history of the western country does not furnish a more daring feat than this.

I must confess this is a silver lining to the cloud, for the Indians massacred nearly the entire garrison.

INCIDENTS OF THE WAR OF 1813.

"Immediately after the defeat of General Winchester on the Raisin, which occurred on the 22d of January, A. D. 1813, all the prisoners that were able to travel were taken to Malden; the badly wounded were indiscriminately murdered by the tomahawk, rifle and fire. Our fellow citizen, Oliver Bellair, Esq., at that time a boy, resided with his parents at Malden. He states that when the prisoners, some three or four hundred in number, arrived in Malden, they were pictures of misery. A long, cold march from the states in mid-winter, camping out in the deep snow, the hard-fought battle and subsequent robbery of their effects, left them perfectly destitute of any comforts.

"Many of the prisoners were also slightly wounded; the blood, dust and smoke of battle were yet upon them.

"At Malden they were driven into an open woodyard, and without tents or covering of any kind, thinly clad, they endured the bitter cold of a long January night; but they were soldiers of the republic and suffered without murmuring at their hard lot.

"They were surrounded by a strong chain of sentinels to prevent their escape, and to keep off the savages who pressed hard to enter the inclosures. The inhabitants of the village at night, in large numbers, sympathizingly crowded around and thus favored the escape of a few prisoners.

"Mr. Bellair tells me that at the time these prisoners were brought into Malden, the village presented a horrible spectacle. The Indians had cut off the heads of those that had fallen in battle and massacre, to the number of a hundred or more, had brought them to Malden and had stuck them in rows on the top of a high picket fence; and there they stood, their matted locks deeply stained with their own gore—their eyes wide open, staring out upon the multitude, exhibiting all varieties of features; some with a pleasant smile; others who had probably lingered long in mortal agony, had a scowl of defiance, despair or revenge; and others wore the appearance of deep distress or sorrow—they may have died thinking of their far-off wives and children and friends, and pleasant homes which they would visit no more; the winter's frost had fixed their features as they died, and they changed not.

"The savages had congregated in great numbers and had brought back with them from the bloody banks of the Raisin, and other parts of our frontier, immense numbers of scalps, strung upon poles, among which might be seen the soft, silky locks of young children, the ringlets and tresses of fair maidens, the burnished locks of middle life and the silver gray of old age. The scalps were hung, some twenty together, on a pole; each was extended by a small hoop around the edge and they were all painted red on the flesh side and were carried about the town to the music of the war-whoop and scalp-yell."

"That the British government did not attempt to restrain the savages, is well known; on the contrary they were instigated to these barbarous deeds. Among the papers of General Proctor, captured at the battle of the Thames, was found a letter from General Brock to Proctor, apparently in answer to one asking whether he should restrain the Indians. The reply was, 'The Indians are necessary to his majesty's service and must be indulged.'

"In another communication, the judge says:

"Captain Knaggs, of Monroe, pointed out to me the cellars of buildings in which our wounded soldiers, who were made prisoners at the battle of the Raisin, were burned. They are within a few yards of the brick house on the left, as you approach the north bank of the River Raisin from Detroit. One of them yet remains uncovered.

"Mr. Campau, who, at the time of the battle, lived and yet lives, about a quarter of a mile from the burned buildings, vividly describes the scene—the shrieks of agony, and the howls of despair, that went up to heaven, as the fierce flames rapidly enveloped the burning buildings. Though covered with wounds, many of the prisoners were able to crawl to the doors to avoid the raging fires; but the bullet and the battle-ax met them there and at once ended their miseries. The voices of all were soon stilled in death; and their bones lay bleaching in the sun and storm. The Indians forbade the inhabitants to bury them under pain of death.

"A soldier made prisoner at the battle was taken to Mr. Campau's house by the Indians. Some apples were handed to them. The prisoner happened to receive his first. This was a mortal affront, and the poor fellow was instantly seized, dragged to the door and cut down on the steps.

"Another soldier had hid in a haystack. He was discovered by an Indian boy, who informed the Indians at Campan's house. With a fierce whoop they started for him. Campau called out, 'Chief, give me your word to save that man!'

"'I give it!' said the chief, and this saved the poor fellow from certain death.

"It were endless to relate all the tales of blood that were witnessed on the frontier. The lives of the French inhabitants, in consideration of their former kindnesses to the Indians were generally spared and they exerted themselves to the utmost in behalf of the suffering captives and saved many from untimely graves. Forty years have passed away, and the regent, with all his ministers, who employed the savages, and stimulated them to such atrocious deeds, together with most of the immediate actors in the scenes, have passed to that great tribunal to meet their countless victims, where the crimes of the one and the sufferings of the other have been registered for the final reckoning."

IN DAYS OF OLD.

WHEN INDIANS AND OTHER ENEMIES HARASSED PEACEFUL INHABITANTS HEREABOUTS—INTERESTING TALES.

"IN 1813-14, after the battle of the Thames, and the appointment of General Cass to be governor of the territory, the hostile Indians were everywhere committing depredations on the inhabitants. The lives of the Way-we-te-go-che (French people) were generally spared, because, during peace, they had been universally kind to the Indians; had relieved their distress, fed them when hungry, clothed them when naked, and sheltered them by their firesides from the winter storms—these things they remembered; but though they spared their lives, stern necessity compelled them, as they said, to take all their means of living. All their cattle were killed and their horses taken away; the fences around their land were used for firewood; the fruit from their orchards was carried off, and, in fact, they were left totally destitude.

"Knowing their readiness to take up arms for their country and the patriotic spirit that animated them, the government, at the instance of General Cass, supplied them with the necessaries of life from the public stores until they could raise something from the earth to subsist on.

"This was a slow process for a people without cattle, without teams, without fences. But they murmured not; they looked upon it as the fate of war and cheerfully submitted to it.

"As to the Yankee portion of our population, it was comparatively small and with the Indians it stood on a different footing. All these were either put to death, when in their power, without mercy, or were carried into captivity.

"Mr. McMillan, a respectable citizen, whose widow and children are yet among us, was shot down and scalped, while out on the common after his cow, and one of his children was taken prisoner and carried to Saginaw, as before mentioned. On the same day a chief and his two sons, seeing old Mr. Moran and his son getting rails near the border of the woods, approached with stealthy tread, and when near enough drew their rifles and took deliberate aim. There was but a hair's breadth between the Morans and death. At this critical moment the old gentleman turned the side of his face towards the Indians. The old chief knew him at once, by his crooked nose, to be his former friend. He whistled, the rifles dropped and the Indians went off. After the peace they told Uncle Lewis that his nose had saved his life.

FIGHTING WITH THE INDIANS.

"The forest within sight of the city was filled with these marauding bands and they were daily seen from the city, killing cattle, driving off horses, etc.

"Colonel Croghan built a little fort, which is yet standing, I think, on Judge-Sibley's land, near the Pontiac road, to keep the Indians from the common, and then fired into it from Fort Shelby, to see whether or not he would be able to drive the Indians out if they should take it. There was too small a garrison at Fort Shelby to risk it or any part of it in an Indian fight. Governor Cass called upon the eitzens to come and follow him.

"Detroit then was but a small town and had but few inhabitants, but they were of the right sort. They gathered together at the summons of the general, armed in all manner of ways—muskets, fowling pieces, rifles, sabers, tomahawks, etc., but still armed and willing to use their arms with General Cass at their head, for he always was there.

"They went up the river about a mile, and there took to the woods, intending to gain the rear of the Indian force, but their scouts were on the alert, and when the citizens reached the Indian camp they had just quitted it. A fire was opened upon them, however; one Indian, only, was known to be killed; how many others were killed or wounded was never known. The Indians effected a retreat, followed by the party, for some distance—the dense forest and thick underbrush, however, prevented a rapid pursuit on horseback.

"After returning, the party were informed that the Indians were hanging on the borders of a settlement below, near the River Rouge. General Cass and his party proceeded to that part of the country, and the Indians fled. He afterwards, with the citizens, marched toward the settlements on the Clinton River, which were menaced by the enemy, and the savages again retired and fled to Saginaw.

"His constant, unremitting vigilance and energetic conduct saved our people from many of the horrors of war, and he was well sustained by our habitants. They were brave and fearless to a fault; the Indian yell and the war-whoop had no terrors for them; when they heard 'it in battle they invariably returned it, and rushed upon the enemy, as they did at Monguagon, under the gallant Dequindre. They had great confidence in General Cass, and willingly followed him into any danger.

"Horses were very scarce, and it was with great difficulty that enough were obtained for the expedition. General Cass had several, and his were readily and willingly furnished; one magnificent horse, ridden by one of the bravest fellows in all the west (the late William Meldrum), was accidentally killed during the expedition.

THE INDIAN'S CONSCIENCE.

"Among the unpleasant incidents of the early days of our city were the numerous brawls and quarrels of the Indians.

"Murders, not alone of the whites, but of their own people, also, were frequently committed by the Indians. Being almost at all times drunk, it is not to be wondered at that they so easily and so often immured their hands in human blood.

"In the winter of 1812, on the afternoon of a day in January, a Chippewa was found in the street of Detroit nearly dead from a cut in his head from a tomahawk. Kish-kaw-ko, a notorious war chief, dreaded for his many atrocious murders, was suspected of the crime. He was sought after and found, with his son, Big Beaver; the latter had his father's tomahawk, which was stained with blood. When he was arrested, he said the blood was from some meat he had been cutting. Both went quietly to prison, when told it was the wish of General Cass that they should go there. The governor's jury found a verdict of guilty against Big Beaver, as the principal in the murder, and Kish-kaw-ko as accessory.

"The Indians remained in jail until May, when Kish-kaw-ko was found dead one morning in his cell. A jury of inquest returned a verdict of death from natural causes, but from circumstances afterward ascertained it was rendered probable that he had poisoned himself. The night before, one of his wives brought him a small cup; then went away. Soon after a number of Indians called to see him, and held a long conference, and when they went away he took leave of them with great solemnity and affection. After they left, Kish-kaw-ko asked the jailor to give him some liquor, a request which he had never made before. At an early hour the next morning the people who had visited him the evening previous came again and asked to see him.

"When they found him dead they appeared delighted and as if gratified to find their expectations realized. All but a few of his band started immediately for Saginaw. Those who remained performed the funeral ceremonies. He was buried by moonlight in an orchard on a farm near the city."

HE FOUND THE HATCHET SHARP.

The Moravian missionaries arrived in Detroit in 1781, when the Indians held a war council in the presence of those missionaries and De Peyster, the commandant. The Indian chief, known as Captain Pike, told De Peyster that the English might fight the Americans if they wished; they had raised the quarrel among themselves and it was they who should fight it out. The English had set him on the Americans just as a hunter sets his dog on the game, but the Indians would play the dog's part no longer.

Kish-kaw-ko and another warrior stood by the British commandant. The former carried a hickory cane about four feet long, ornamented—or, rather, strung with scalps of Americans, together with a tomahawk, presented to him by De Peyster, some time previously. He concluded his address to the commandant thus:

"Now, father, here is what has been done with the hatchet you gave me. I have made the use of it you ordered me to do, and have found it sharp."

A few days after this council the Moravians left Detroit for their new homes on the Riviere aux Hurons (Clinton).

The English at Detroit, it appears, suspecting that a certain set of pious Moravians on the Muskingum River were sympathizers with the Americans, called a conference of the tribes at Niagara, and urged the fierce Iroquois to destroy the Moravian Indians. But they failed to see where such a massacre would benefit themselves and would not fall in with the measure. The conference at Detroit, it will be seen, met with like result.

A FEROCIOUS CHIEF.

"He was one of the most ferocious and bloodthirsty chiefs of modern times. His influence with his people was great, although he was unpopular. He was tall and athletic, and of great decision of character. He was always attended by a large retinue when he visited Detroit; was peculiar for carrying his war-ax on his left arm, tightly grasped by his right hand, as if in the expectation of striking. His disposition may be learned from the following:

"One of his band killed another, at Saginaw. The friends of the victim were clamorous for revenge. The murderer's friends were desirous of saving him from their vengeance and negotiated for his life. The conditions were agreed upon and the property offered in fulfillment of the bargain was about to be delivered, when Kish-kaw-ko stepped up and struck the murderer dead with his tomahawk. When asked why he interrupted the proceedings and interfered with their lawful agreements, he merely said: 'The law is altered.'

"Big Beaver, like his father, was a powerful and muscular savage, and one day, when the jailor's son went to see him, he seized him, thrust him to one side, just as he opened the door of his cell, locked the door on him, and escaped to the woods. He was never retaken, but was, not long afterwards, drowned in Saginaw Bay."

HE WAS A BRAVE MAN.

Referring again to General Cass, and the fearlessness and decision displayed in his dealings with the Indians, "Early Western Days" (by Judge B. F. H. Witherell, in the Wisconsin Historical Collections), records:

"In 1820 General Cass was detailed by the war department to make a treaty with the Chippewa Indians, for a tract of land at the outlet of Lake Superior for a military post.

"General Cass took along fifteen or twenty soldiers. Arriving at the straits he sent out runners to inform the Indians of his arrival and business.

"On the day appointed about 600 Indians assembled, a majority of them from the north of the straits. A council was called. General Cass explained at length the object of his visit, which was to obtain, for the Great Father at Washington, a certain district, or county, upon which to build a fort, where the traders could be protected, etc.

"Robinson was uneasy. He noticed that the Indians were mad; they did not look right; and when General Cass had concluded his speech, one of the chiefs rose and, in reply, said he did not like the Americans; he did not like the Great Father at Washington, and that they would not sell him any of their lands, and that if he (General Cass) and his soldiers did not leave they would be killed. The chief then reached back, took a spear with a cloth around it from another Indian, stuck the shaft into the ground and the British flag spread in the breeze to the music of the war-whoop of the entire band.

"General Cass instantly stepped up and took the staff in his hand, jerked it out of the ground, tore off the flag, threw it down and ground it with his heel, fairly hissing out with rage:

"'As long as I live that flag shall not float in my presence on this side of the great lakes!'

"'Then,' said Robinson, 'I was afraid. I expected they would kill us right off.'

"But not another word was spoken for some minutes. General Cass and the chief stood looking at each other. At length the chief advanced towards Cass, took him by the hand, and said:

"'The Great Father at Washington can have the land he wants.'

"The land was selected and a treaty was signed without any further difficulty.

"General Cass," said Robinson, "was the bravest man I ever saw."

EARLY DAYS IN DETROIT.

WALK-IN-THE-WATER, FAMOUS WYANDOTTE CHIEF, AND THE DEATH OF THE GREAT TECUMSEH.

WALK-IN-THE-WATER, the great chief of the Wyandottes, resided at Monguagon (Wyandotte) on the place where the late Major John Biddle built his farm house and resided for several years. Walk-in-the-Water's totem was a turtle (because it walked in the water). He was a famous chief in his day, of fine commanding person, nearly six feet in hight, well proportioned and straight as an arrow. He had none of the ferocious, morose and savage manner that characterized the great chief of the Chippewas, Kish-Kaw-Ko; he was mild in his deportment and appeared pleasant and sociable with those who could converse with him in the Wyandotte language. He could speak only a few words of English. He was highly respected by the whites who knew him and his own people respected him for his wisdom and prudence in council and for his valor in war.

He led his warriors against General Wayne, whom the Indians generally called General Waw-bunk (or General Tomorrow). Nearly all the warriors of his tribe that followed him to that battle, fell in the action, and he barely escaped. After the defeat of Harmer and St. Clair, the old inhabitants used to say, that long poles strung with the scalps of our soldiers were daily paraded through the streets of Detroit, then a British post, accompanied by the demoniac scalp yells of the warriors who had taken them—but after the battle of the Maumee, not a scalp was seen; the bayonets of the Tub-Regions roused them so rapidly from their coverts that they with difficulty brought off their own scalps.

After the commencement of the war of 1812, and after General Hull had arrived at this post, Walk-in-the-Water and his Wyandottes asked to be employed in the service of the United States. General Hull, under orders from the government, declined and advised them to remain in peace at home. They were soon after exposed to the attacks of the British troops and their Indian allies from Malden—these threatened the Wyandottes with extermination unless they would raise the tomahawk for the Saga-nosh (the British). The late Judge James Witherell, who had been an officer of the revolutionary army, at the request of the executive, accepted the command of a battalion of volunteers in the service of the United States. He strongly urged upon General Hull the necessity of establishing a stockade at Monguagon or Brownstown, with a garrison strong enough to resist any sudden attack, for the double purpose of keeping up the communication with Ohio, and to aid the Wyandottes in protecting themselves; the general at last consented and ordered him to take a few companies of troops with entrenching tools and proceed in boats to Monguagon or Brownstown for that purpose. The boats were got ready, the entrenching tools were on board, and the troops embarked, when the vacillating course, which characterized the whole of General Hull's conduct, again showed itself and the following order was received:

MAJOR WITHERELL:

SIR—General Hull has ordered me to call for the entrenching tools you have in your charge or can obtain, including those that were delivered to go to Brownstown; you will be so good as to deliver to the bearer. TAYLOR BERRY, Q. M.
July 27, 1812.

After awhile he again induced the general to make the attempt to establish a post and to open the communication with Ohio. And he was again ordered to proceed with his own command, Dequindre's Rifles, Smith's Dragoons, Forsyth's Artillery, and some companies of the Fourth United States Infantry and a few Ohio Volunteers. They set out for Ohio, expecting to meet the enemy below the Ecorse. On reaching the Rouge General Hull sent an aid with the following order:

SANDWICH, 3d August, 1812.

SIR—I have received your letter of this day. I wish you to cross the River Rouge with your main force, until I send a reinforcement or until you hear from me; take an advantageous position on this side of the River Rouge, and remain until you receive further orders. I am respectfully yours,
WILLIAM HULL,
B. Genl. Commanding.

Walk-in-the-Water and his warriors soon discovered that they were to receive no protection or assistance, and being too few to defend themselves, they joined the enemy, though their hearts were never with the British.

The next year (1813) Tanke, the Crane, one of the great chiefs of the Wyandottes, living with a part of his tribe in Ohio, and who had joined General Harrison, dispatched one of his trusty warriors to the Wyandottes in Malden, requesting them to leave the British service and return home. The delivery of such a message in the camp of the enemy required a high degree of integrity and moral courage, yet the brave fellow "threaded the forest, and swam the rivers" and alone entered the camp of the enemy, and in a bold manner and fearless tone delivered his message. The Wyandottes knew that open compliance would be impossible— instant death would have been their lot—and they returned a negative answer, but sent a band of their bravest warriors to protect the messengers of the Crane, until he reached the Black Swamp, and was in safety. The Wyandottes gradually disappeared from the British service.

Following the treaty of Brownstown Walk-in-the-Water, after some urging, gave to the late Judge Witherell his opinion of the origin and creation of the earth, etc. It shows that he had mingled biblical revelations with his pagan ideas.

Walk-in-the-Water died about the year 1817. He was a man of strong mind and sound common sense, and had he been an educated white man he would have risen to a high position in the nation; yet how dark, bewildered and crude were his ideas of the creation and final destiny of man.

THE GREAT TECUMSEH.

As Tecumseh was somewhat before my time (as also was Kish-Kaw-Ko). I only relate some incidents in regard to him picked up from various sources, that I think will be found to be rather new; also James Knaggs' sworn statement and affidavit, furnished to General Cass, Detroit, September 28, 1853, in regard to the death of Tecumseh, and who killed him, found among the papers of the late Judge B. F. H. Witherell. Mr. Knaggs claimed to be an eye-witness of the affair.

Tecumseh was not only an accomplished military commander, but a natural statesman and diplomat. A strong natural characteristic was exhibited by him at the council, held by General Harrison at Vincennes in 1811. Tecumseh had heard the demands and charges, and in reply made some striking hits at the general. Having finished one of his speeches he looked around, and seeing every one seated, while no seat was prepared for him, a momentary frown passed over his countenance. Instantly General Harrison ordered that a chair be given him. One of the officers presented one, and bowing to him said:

"Warrior, your father, General Harrison, offers you a seat."

Tecumseh's eyes flashed. "My father!" he exclaimed indignantly, extending his arm toward the heavens, "the sun is my father and the earth is my mother; she gives me nourishment and I repose upon her bosom," and then sat down upon the ground.

General Brock at one time took the sash from his own waist, and placed it around the body of Tecumseh, who seemingly appreciated the honor, but the next day he was observed not to be wearing his sash, and General Brock, fearing that something had displeased him, sent his interpreter for an explanation. On reporting, the latter said that Tecumseh did not wish to wear a mark of distinction, while there was an older and better warrior than himself present and hence he had transferred the sash to the Wyandotte chief, Roundhead.

The following was found in the diary of a British officer:

"In the skirmish in which my command and a party of our allies were engaged with the Americans, one of their officers was wounded, when two Indians rushed in to take his scalp. The American officer, bethought himself to give a Masonic signal, when one of the Indians immediately sprang forward and caught him in his arms. The Indian was Tecumseh."

THE DEATH OF TECUMSEH.

Here follows the affidavit in regard to the death of Tecumseh:

DETROIT, September 28, 1853.

GENERAL CASS: DEAR SIR—I read with interest your remarks in the senate of the United States, last winter, relative to the death of Tecumseh, in which you expressed the opinion that he fell by the hand of Colonel Johnson.

Honorably and actively engaged as you were in all the stirring events of the war of 1812, on this frontier, your opinion, made up from circumstances at the time, and being yourself on the field of battle, is entitled to great weight.

The affidavit of Captain James Knaggs, with whom, as with nearly all our old citizens, I believe, you are acquainted, will, I think, set the question at rest.

Being at the River Raisin a few days since, I called on Captain Knaggs, who was a brave and intrepid soldier, in the Ranger service.

He stated to me all the circumstances of the battle on the Thames, as far as they came within his knowledge, and at my request, he made an affidavit (a copy of which I herewith send you), narrating so much of the action as is connected with the death of the great chief.

Colonel Johnson stated at the time, and afterwards often reiterated it, that he killed an Indian with his pistol, who was advancing upon him at the time his horse fell under him. The testimony of Captain Knaggs shows conclusively that it could have been no other than Tecumseh.

Colonel Johnson, when last here, saw and recognized Captain Knaggs and Mr. Labadie as the men who bore him from the field in his blanket.

The transaction is of some little importance in history, as the ball that bore with it the fate of the great warrior dissolved at once the last great Indian confederacy, and gave peace to our frontier.

I am, respectfully yours, etc.,   B. F. H. WITHERELL.

State of Michigan, County of Monroe, ss.

James Knaggs deposeth and saith as follows:

I was attached to a company of mounted men called Rangers, at the battle of the Thames, in Upper Canada, in the year 1813. During the battle, we charged into the swamp, where several of our horses mired down, and an order was given to retire to the hard ground in our rear, which we did. The Indians in front, believing that we were retreating, immediately advanced upon us, with Tecumseh at their head. I distinctly heard his voice, with which I was perfectly familiar. He yelled like a tiger, and urged on his braves to the attack. We were then but a few yards apart. We halted on the hard ground, and continued our fire. After a few minutes of very severe firing, I discovered **Colonel Johnson** lying near, on the ground, with one leg confined by the body of his white mare, which had been killed, and had fallen upon him. My friend, Medard Labadie, was with me. We went up to the colonel, with whom we were previously acquainted, and found him badly wounded, lying on his side, with one of his pistols lying in his hand. I saw Tecumseh at the same time, lying on his face, dead; and about fifteen or twenty feet from the colonel. He was stretched at full length, and was shot through the body, I think, near the heart. The ball went out through his back. He held his tomahawk in his right hand (it had a brass pipe on the head of it) ; his arm was extended as if striking, and the edge of the tomahawk was stuck in the ground. Tecumseh was dressed in red speckled leggings and a fringed hunting shirt; he lay stretched directly towards Colonel Johnson. When we went up to the colonel, we offered to help him. He replied with great animation. "Knaggs, let me lay here, and push on and take Proctor." However, we liberated him from his dead horse, took hs blanket from his saddle, placed him in it, and bore him off the field. I had known Tecumseh from my boyhood; we were boys together. There was no other Indian killed immediately around where Colonel Johnson or Tecumseh lay, though there were many near the small creek a few rods back of the place where Tecumseh fell.

I had no doubt then, and have none now, that Tecumseh fell by the hand of Colonel Johnson. JAMES KNAGGS.

Sworn to before me this 22d day of September, 1853.
B. F. H. WITHERELL,
Notary Public.

Tecumseh left a son about 17 years of age, when he was slain, to whom King George III., in 1814, sent a present of a sword as a mark of respect to the memory of his father.

When Colonel Richard M. Johnson was running for vice-president I heard him deliver a campaign speech here from the balcony of the Russell House, and during the speech some one in the crowd cried out, "Who killed Tecumseh?"

"Well," the colonel said, "while the battle was progressing (referring to the battle of the Thames) "I saw a stalwart Indian warrior approaching me with uplifted tomahawk. I was mounted, and, drawing a pistol from my holsters, shot him dead. On examining the fallen Indian, they all averred that it was Tecumseh, and I have never doubted but that it was."

JOSEPH CAMPAU, THE FRIEND OF THE INDIANS—CHIEF MACAUNSE A BAD INDIAN.

Macaunse was a brave and sometimes sanguinary Chippewa chief and warrior. His home was on the border of Lake St. Clair, L'anse Cruz Bay. I have been to his lodge in company with my uncle, Thomas Palmer (father of the senator), when on winter excursions to his possessions in the village of Palmer (now St. Clair City) in 1830. The chief was well-to-do, and entertained us with genuine hospitality. He often visited the city, where he had many friends among the old French Inhabitants. Joseph Campau, Peter Desnoyers, Major Antoine DeQuindre and others. When I came here in 1827 the half of the first floor of Mr. Joseph Campau's residence on Jefferson Avenue was devoted to a store and office, the store in front and the office in the rear. In this store he had a small stock of Indian goods, to supply, in a measure, the wants of his good friends, the Indians. This he kept up until about 1840, when most of the Indians in Michigan were removed by the government beyond the Mississippi.

Mr. Campau was indeed the friend of the red men of the entire northwest, and they heartily returned the feeling. He could talk their language, and every chief of note knew him intimately, and came to him for counsel and advice. I have seen, often and often, in the summer season, scores of them, bucks, squaws and pappooses, squatted on the pavement in front of his place, invading his front steps and every available space, as on their visits to the city they always made it a point to call on their good friend, the great "Che-mo-Ka-Mun" (white man).

They never failed to give him an ovation every fall when on their way to and from Malden (Canada) to receive their presents from the British government. It was said that he used to make a good thing of it, trading or buying outright the articles the Indians got at Malden that they did not need or want. Perhaps he did. He was not the only one.

The only chief of prominence that I remember visiting Mr. Campau was Macaunse. I think he belonged to the Chippewa tribe of Indians. His lodge and headquarters were on the banks of Lake St. Clair, as before mentioned. I have seen him here very often, and also at the village of Palmer, now St. Clair City. He was a fine specimen of his class, of commanding presence, and spoke English fairly well and on these occasions was costumed as nearly like a white man as it was possible for an Indian to be; black frock coat, confined around the waist with a wampum sash, calico hunting shirt, fringed gaudy vest, broadcloth leggins ornamented with beads and porcupine quills, the outer seams profusely decorated with silver ornaments, that gave out a musical jingle with each step he took, buckskin mocassins hooked with porcupine quills, plug hat ornamented with a broad open worked silver band, five or six silver ear-bobs in each ear, and a silver ring through the cartilage of his nose. All this, added to his fine physique, made him quite the thing.

He was a brave and sometimes sanguinary Indian, quite as bad as the rest of his dusky companions, and any one seeing him in his lodge dispensing his hospitality, or quietly and peacefully mingling with friends in Detroit or in his own village would scarcely believe that he was the murderous savage our friend Gagette Tremble describes him to be, further on.

He was always robed, a state of existence that many of his race could not boast of. Extravagantly fond of whisky were these Indians, squaws as well as bucks. I have often seen the former, when offered a drink of whisky, take a good swig of the article, and then fill their mouths to the utmost limit, and deposit the contents in a little buckskin bag that they carried for the purpose, to enjoy at their leisure.

Among the papers of the late Judge B. F. H. Witherell I find an account of the experience of Gagette Tremble, who lived at Milk River point, fifteen miles above the city, on the borders of Lake St. Clair (now included in Grosse Pointe Village), had with Macaunse, Kish-Kaw-Ko and their bands; also the experience of Richard Connor, Indian trader and interpreter, who lived at Connor's creek, with the same savages. He goes on to say, "His (Tremble's) is a healthy, active, green old age. (He was hale and hearty in 1855 at the age of 78 years, the judge says). I met him a short time since, joyous and merry, driving his pony and charette home from the city, his cheerful countenance beaming with pleasure and delight. Some of the old man's adventures in former years are worthy of notice. The enemy, as is well known, had in 1813 full possession of the whole territory, and all the western tribes of Indians had joined them. After the defeat and slaughter of our troops on the Raisin, Macaunse, one of the chiefs of the Chippewas, came to the house of Tremble, with a bag in his hand, and said: 'My friend, I am hungry, I have brought you some venison. Have some of it cooked for me.' He then emptied the bag on the floor, shaking out the leg of one of our brave but unfortunate soldiers who had been killed a few days before under Winchester at the Raisin.

"Tremble's anger rose, and regardless of danger, and the fact that he was wholly in the power of the chief and his braves, he delivered a volley of the most opprobrious epithets that the Indian language afforded, and with foot and fist, gave the chief a severe pommeling, kicked him into the highway, and told him, at the peril of his life, never to insult a Way-me-ta-goche (white man) in that way again. The old chief threatened to kill him, but Gagette walked fiercely up to him, looked him in the eye, and said: 'If you are a brave man, as you say you are, strike now. You are armed; your young men are all around you; kill me if you dare—strike now; but you are a coward, and no warrior. Puckachee—go, go.' The chief never sought revenge; he felt that Gagette was right in his anger.

"One of Macaunse's band shot one of Tremble's hogs. Gagette discovered it, hauled it to the house, dressed and salted it. The savage begged for a piece—said he was starved, was very hungry, and he would have a piece. 'No,' sternly said Tremble, 'not a morsel. When did a hungry red man ever come to my wigwam and ask for food in vain? Have I not always divided with him when I had little; and when I had much, did I not satisfy his hunger, and feed him and his people? But you come to rob and steal, and maybe to kill me. Not a bite of the cocoche (hog) shall you have.'

"'Well,' said the Indian, 'I'll burn your barn then.' He took a firebrand and ran to the barn. Gagette seized his rifle and ran after him, while the rest of the band looked on to see the result. Arriving at the barn the Indian flourished his brand. Gagette cocked his rifle and leveled it at his head, and cried out: 'Do it, do it, and you are a dead man.'

"'Ty yaw,' said the fellow, and throwing away his fire, he walked sullenly off. After that they never tried by force to get any of Tremble's pigs. His fists and his rifle, and his well known readiness to defend his property, were his protection.

"Whatever could be stolen, however, was considered lawful

prey. One of the most daring feats ever performed by man—one that is not exceeded, if equaled in the history of Indian wars—was performed by Gagette about the same time.

The late Henry Connor, so well and favorably known in the state, was one of the Indian interpreters. The Indians called him Waw-bis-Kin-diss, or white hair. He had once traded at Saginaw, the stronghold of Kish-Kaw-Ko and his band. Connor had in some way incurred the ill-will of the chief, who was impatient for revenge; but he feared Connor, who was a man of dauntless courage and stalwart frame. So the old savage postponed his vengeance until a safe opportunity should occur.

"The war came on and Connor was ordered out of the country by General Proctor. It so happened that his wife and child were at what is now known as Mt. Clemens. It then contained but one dwelling house, that of the late Colonel Clemens.

"Mrs. Connor, who still survives, is the sister of Gagette. Kish-Kaw-Ko, knowing of Connor's absence, thought that the time for revenge had arrived, and started with his guard (he always had some fifteen or twenty armed warriors about him) for Mt. Clemens, with the design of murdering Mrs. Connor and her child. It is an Indian custom to kill the nearest relation of their enemy when he is out of their reach.

"Gagette's younger brother heard of the old chief's designs, and immediately sent word to him of the threatened danger. He was at work in a field, at a distance from his house when the word was brought to him. He was ten miles from Mt. Clemens, and felt that no time was to be lost. His sister might even then have fallen under the war club or battle ax. He was wholly unarmed, had only his shirt and pants, with a blue handkerchief tied around his head. Minutes seemed ages. He instantly leaped upon his faithful Sorrel, as he called his pony, which happened to be feeding near, and, without saddle or bridle, away he flew, cleared the fences at a bound, and through swamp and forest he held his headlong way, lashing his nag to his utmost speed, and in an almost incredibly short space of time, his pony, covered with foam, reached the door of the colonel's house which Kish-Kaw-Ko and his warriors were plundering. He sprang from his horse. His pent-up wrath was burning high as he rushed into the house. Old Kish and his men saw him enter, and knowing his terrible violence when justly aroused and his dauntless courage at all times, and feeling moreover guilty, they instantly sat down and drew their blankets over their heads and were silent.

"Gaggette's wrath exploded with a perfect tornado of Indian billingsgate, he gave full scope to his anger. When his eye caught the giant form of Kish-Kaw-Ko his wrath fairly boiled over, he sprang upon him like a tiger, jerked his blanket from his head and showered his blows like winter rainfall in the old chief's face, till the blood spouted from his nose and mouth; then, rapidly passing to the others, he pulled away their blankets, slapped their faces, and returning to Kish, he gave him another pounding, saying, 'You old murderer, you have come here to kill my sister, have you? You cowardly old villain. You have killed women and children. You are not afraid of squaws and pappooses, but you fear a brave man. If you don't, here is one—try me (striking his fist on his own bosom). Come on, coward—dog, strike. Go home and never show a murderer's face here again. The Green Bird (a brave chief of the Tiger band, and a deadly enemy of Kish), told me that you were a coward and a woman. You are no warrior, no brave.'

"A young brother of Gagette, a mere boy, was present, and says that he fully expected instant death, but Gagette's sudden burst of insane fury seemed to have completely paralyzed the savages. Not one of them stirred; but received his vigorous blows, dealt out, right, left and center, as they were, without a word or motion.

"Having found that Mrs. Connor had been sent in a canoe down the Clinton river (then called the Upper Huron) to a place of safety, before the arrival of the Indians, Gagette gave them a parting blessing in his own peculiar way, and telling them that the next time they went on an expedition to murder women and children, they would find him on hand, he mounted his Sorrel and ambled off at a careless, easy gait, to his home on the point—and though a quiet, peaceable citizen, he is yet ready for another fight, if the like occasion requires it.

"Mount Clemens was then in the Indian country—there was no white man's dwelling between that of Colonel Clemens and the North Pole. The life of the good and brave old colonel was, during the war, often in peril from civilized and savage foes—he was a while in service with the Michigan troops."

RECOLLECTIONS OF THE VISIT OF THE INDIAN CHIEF BLACK HAWK AND HIS STALWART SON.

It was at the Mansion House in Detroit and when Colonel Mack was landlord that I saw the Indian warrior and chief, the celebrated Black Hawk, and party. They were here on July Fourth, 1833, on their way home after their imprisonment in Fortress Monroe. Black Hawk and party put up at the Mansion House, staying there three or four days, and I had the opportunity of seeing them often. I quote from the diary of an English gentleman who was a fellow passenger on the steamer that brought them from Buffalo.

"Black Hawk is a slight-made man, about 50 or 55 years old, and stands five feet five or six inches tall. He is dressed in a short blue frock coat, white hat and leggins tied around below the knee with garters. He carries his blanket folded under his arm. His shirt is not very clean, and his face is of a very dark complexion, much like our gypsies. The cartilages, as well as the lobes of his ears, are loaded with glass bugle ornaments, his nose perforated very wide between the nostrils so as to give the appearance of the upper and lower mandibles of a hawk. He wears light-colored kid gloves and walking stick with a tassel. His son is a fine looking young man, with what might be called an open countenance. He carries his head high and looks about him. He is covered with a scarlet blanket or cloth and wears nothing on his head but a feather or two stuck in his hair, and great bunches of bugles in his ears. His face and bosom are painted red and his forehead either painted or tattooed with a band. His hair is turned up in front and pompatumed. He has many ornaments about him and little bells that jingle as he walks. The prophet is covered with a green blanket or mantle."

As said before, I saw Black Hawk and party many times, and must say that the Englishman has given a good pen-picture of them. The son was, indeed, a fine specimen of the Indian athlete. He looked, as he was, the beau ideal of the Indian warrior, a tall, brawny, muscular fellow, and handsome, too. His scalp-lock was twisted full of gorgeous feathers, silver medals adorned his breast, and silver bracelets clasped his wrists and arms. A scarlet blanket was thrown in the most negligent manner across his shoulders, and his nether garments were plentifully ornamented with porcupine quills and silver bobs. As he stood there on the porch or veranda of the hotel, having taken this pose evidently for effect, he attracted more attention than did all the rest of the party, particularly from the female portion of the community. But he received it all without betraying the slightest interest in what was going on around him, and without a shadow of emotion. Indeed, they all behaved in the same manner; that is where the Indian of it comes in. I have seen many good specimens of the Indian brave, but I think this son of Black Hawk excelled them all, a noble specimen of physical beauty, a model for those who would embody the idea of strength.

Ex-Senator Jones, in a speech made September 29, 1894, said: "When the Black Hawk war came on in 1832, General H. Dodge sent his adjutant and his son, H. L. Dodge, to my home to ask me to serve him as aid-de-camp in the war which seemed inevitable. I readily accepted the invitation, as only a few days before my brother-in-law, who was agent for the Indians who were making the trouble, was killed by the red devils. They cut off his head, his hands and his feet and then cut his heart into chunks, which the young bucks ate, he being judged the bravest who could swallow the largest piece without chewing it."

Mr. J. C. Sabine, who came here in the early days, says that he, too, saw Black Hawk and party, when here. He also says that Senator T. W. Palmer had the proud distinction, when quite an infant, of being held for a few moments in the old chief's arms. His nurse had him out for an airing one morning, and they met Black Hawk and his son, who were out for a stroll. The old chief took notice of the child, and, taking him up in his arms, said, "Fine pappoose, but him too dark for white pappoose," and the senator was dark at that age, two years.

Dr. J. L. Whiting, in his reminiscences published some years ago, says among other things, speaking of Black Hawk and his son: "On their return from Washington they stopped a while in Detroit. I saw them both. Young Black Hawk fell desperately in love with a prominent society belle and wanted to honor her by making her his squaw. She declined the proferred dignity, for reasons best known to herself, but she never married, and is still living in single blessedness at Mackinac."

The lady in question was Miss Sophia Biddle, daughter of Edward Biddle, Esq., of Mackinac.

ADDITIONAL TESTIMONY AS TO THE FINE CHARACTER OF THE FAMOUS INDIAN CHIEF TECUMSEH.

The command of Colonel Dudley, which consisted of 800 Kentucky militia, completely succeeded in driving the British from their batteries on the left bank of the Maumee River and spiking their cannon. Having accomplished this object, his orders were to return at once to his boats and cross to the fort; but the blind confidence which usually attends militia when successful, proved their ruin. Although repeatedly ordered by Colonel Dudley and warned of their danger, and called upon from the fort to leave the ground, and although there was abundant time for that purpose before the British reinforcements arrived, yet they began a pursuit of the Indians and suffered themselves to be drawn into an ambuscade by some feint skirmishing, while the British troops and large bodies of Indians were brought up and intercepted their return to the river. Elated with their first success, they considered their victory as already gained, and pursued the enemy nearly two miles into the woods and swamps, where they were suddenly caught in a defile and surrounded by double their numbers. Finding themselves in this situation, consternation prevailed; their line became broken and disordered and huddled together in unresisting crowds, they were obliged to yield to the fury of the savages.

Fortunately for these unhappy victims of their own rashness, General Tecumseh commanded at this ambuscade, and had imbibed since his appointment more humane feelings than his brother Proctor. After the surrender, and when all resistance had ceased, the Indians finding 500 prisoners at their mercy, began the work of massacre with the most savage delight. Tecumseh sternly forbade it and buried his tomahawk in the head of one of his chiefs who refused obedience. This order, accompanied with his decisive manner of enforcing it, put an end to the massacre. Of 800 men only 150 escaped. The remainder were slain or made prisoners.

TECUMSEH'S IDEAS OF JUSTICE.

Captain Knaggs, who made the affidavit in regard to the killing of Tecumseh, is thus spoken of by the late Judge B. F. H. Witherell:

"Captain Knaggs is a highly respected citizen of Monroe, and was one of the most active and useful partisans during the war of 1812. Almost innumerable and miraculous were his 'hairbreadth 'scapes' from the savages.

"He related to me, when I last saw him, several anecdots of Tecumseh, which will illustrate his character. Amongst others, he states that while the enemy was in full possession of the country, Tecumseh, with a large band of his warriors, visited the Raisin. The inhabitants along that river had been stripped of nearly every means of subsistence. Old Mr. Rivard, who was lame and unable to procure a living for himself and family, had contrived to keep out of sight of the wandering bands of savages a pair of oxen, with which his son was able to procure a scanty support for the family. It so happened that while at labor with the oxen Tecumseh, who had come over from Malden, met him on the road, and, walking up to him, said:

"'My friend, I must have those oxen. My young men are very hungry; they have had nothing to eat. We must have the oxen.'

"Young Rivard remonstrated. He told the chief that if he took the oxen his father would starve to death.

"'Well,' said Tecumseh, 'we are the conquerors, and everything we want is ours. I must have the oxen; my people must not starve; but I will not be so mean as to rob you of them. I will pay you $100 for them, and that is far more than they are worth; but we must have them.'

"Tecumseh got a white man to write an order on the British Indian agent, Colonel Elliot, who was on the river some distance below, for the money. The oxen were killed, large fires built, and the forest warriors were soon feasting on their flesh. Young Rivard took the order to Colonel Elliot, who promptly refused to pay it. 'We are entitled to our support from the country we have conquered; I will not pay it.' The young man, with a sorrowful heart, returned with the answer to Tecumseh, who said: 'He won't pay it, won't he? Stay all night, and tomorrow we will go and see.' On the next morning he took young Rivard and went down to see the colonel. On meeting him he said:

"'Do you refuse to pay for the oxen I bought?'

"'Yes,' said the colonel, and he reiterated the reason for refusal.

"'I bought them,' said the chief, 'for my young men were very hungry. I promised to pay for them, and they shall be paid for. I have always heard that white nations went to war with each other, and not with peaceful individuals; that they did not rob and plunder poor people. I will not.'

"'Well,' said the colonel, 'I will not pay for them.'

"'You can do as you please,' said the chief, 'but before Tecumseh and his warriors came to fight the battles of the great king they had enough to eat, for which they had only to thank the Master of Life and their good rifles. Their hunting grounds supplied them with food enough; to them they can return.'

"The threat produced a change in the colonel's mind. The defection of the great chief, he well knew, would immediately withdraw all the nations of the red men from the British service, and without them they were nearly powerless on the frontier.

"'Well,' said the colonel, 'if I must pay, I will.'

"'Give me hard money,' said Tecumseh, not rag money (army bills).

"The colonel then counted out a hundred dollars in coin, and gave them to him. The chief handed the money to young Rivard, and then said to the colonel:

"'Give me one dollar more.' It was given, and, handing that also to Rivard, he said: "Take that; it will pay for the time you have lost in getting your money.'

"How many white warriors have such notions of justice? Before the commencement of the war, when his hunting parties approached the white settlements, horses and cattle were occasionally stolen, but notice to the chief failed not to produce instant redress.

"The character of Tecumseh was that of a gallant and intrepid warrior, an honest and honorable man; and his memory is respected by all our old citizens who personally knew him."

A DESCRIPTION OF TECUMSEH.

The following letter from the late venerable General Combs, of Kentucky, who bore so gallant a part in the defense of the Ohio and the Maumee valley, in regard to Tecumseh, will, I think, be found interesting. It is copied from "The Records of the Maumee Valley":

Editor Historical Record: You ask for a description of the celebrated Indian warrior, Tecumseh, from my present observation. I answer that I never saw the chief but once, and then under rather exciting circumstances, but I have a vivid recollection of him from his appearance and from intercourse with his personal friends, I am possessed of accurate knowledge of his character.

I was, as you know, one of the prisoners taken at what is known as the Dudley's defeat on the banks of the Maumee River, opposite Fort Meigs, early in May, 1813. Tecumseh had fallen on our rear, and we were compelled to surrender. We were marched down to the old Fort Miami, or Maumee, in squads, where a terrible scene awaited us. The Indians, fully armed with guns, war clubs and tomahawks—to say nothing of scalping knives, had formed themselves into two lines in front of the gateway between which all of us were bound to pass. Many were killed or wounded in running the gauntlet. Shortly after the prisoners had entered, the Indians rushed over the walls and again surrounded us, and raised the war-whoop, at the same time making unmistakable demonstrations of violence. We all expected to be massacred, and the small British guard around us were utterly unable to afford protection. They called loudly for General Proctor and Colonel Elliot to come to our relief. At this critical moment Tecumseh came rushing in, deeply excited and denounced the murderers of prisoners as cowards. Thus our lives were spared and we were sent down to the fleet at the mouth of Swan creek (now Toledo), and from that place across the end of the lake to Huron and paroled.

I shall never forget the noble countenance, gallant bearing and sonorous voice of that remarkable man, while addressing his warriors in our behalf. He was then between forty and forty-five years of age. His frame was vigorous and robust, but he was not fat, weighing about one hundred and seventy pounds. Five feet ten inches was his height. He had a high, projecting forehead, and broad, open countenance; and there was something noble and commanding in all his actions. He was brave, humane and generous, and never allowed a prisoner to be massacred if he could prevent it. At Fort Miami he saved the lives of all of us who had survived running the gauntlet. He afterwards released seven Shawanese belonging to my command, and sent them home on parole. Tecumseh was a Shawanese. His name signified in their language, Shooting Star. At the time when I saw him he held the commission of a brigadier-general in the British army. I am satisfied that he deserved all that was said of him by General Cass and Governor Harrison, previous to his death.

Lexington, Ky., October, 1871. LESLIE COMBS.

A STIRRING INCIDENT.

During the siege of Fort Meigs it narrowly escaped destruction. Many of the enemy's balls were red-hot and were directed to a small blockhouse within the fort where the powder had been removed. Whenever their balls struck they raised a cloud of smoke and made a frightful hissing. An officer seeing the danger cried out, "Boys, who will volunteer to cover this blockhouse?" No second call was needed, and a more than sufficient number sprang to execute the officer's request. As soon as they reached the spot there came a ball and took off a man's head. The spades and dirt flew faster than ever. In the midst of the job, a bombshell fell on the roof, and lodging on one of the braces it spun around for a moment. Every man fell flat on his face, and breathlessly awaited the explosion which they expected would end their days then and there. Only one of the party saw fit to reason on the case. He silently argued that as the shell had not bursted as quickly as it ought, there might be something wrong in its makeup. If it should burst where it was, and the magazine exploded, there could be no escape; it was death anyhow; so he sprang to his feet, seized a boat-hook, and pulling the sputtering missile to the ground, and jerking the smoking match from its socket, discovered that the shell was filled with inflammable matter, which, if once ignited, would have wrapped the whole building in a sheet of flame. This circumstance added wings to their shovels, and the party were right glad when the officer said: "That will do; go to your lines."

MORE PRAISE FOR TECUMSEH.

Mr. Joseph R. Underwood, who was present at the defeat of Colonel Dudley in the capacity of lieutenant in a volunteer company of Kentuckians, commanded by Captain John C. Morrison, has this to say:

"Colonel Elliot and Tecumseh, the celebrated Indian chief, rode into the garrison. When Elliot came to where Thos. Moore, of Clark County, stood, the latter addressd him, and inquired 'if it was compatible with the honor of a civilized nation, such as the British claim to be, to suffer defenseless prisoners to be murdered by savages.' Elliot desired to know who he was. Moore replied that he was nothing but a private in Captain Morrison's company and here the conversation ended.

"Elliot was an old man. His hair might have been termed, with more propriety, white than gray, and to my view he had more of the savage in his countenance than Tecumseh. This celebrated chief was a noble, dignified personage. His face was finely proportioned, his nose inclined to the aquiline, and his eye displayed none of the savage and ferocious triumph common to the other Indians on that occasion. He seemed to regard us with unmoved composure, and I thought a beam of mercy shone in his countenance, tempering the spirit of vengeance inherent in his race against the American people. I saw him only on horseback."

A PARTING WORD.

For the Indian, cruel and revengeful as he was, there is some apology, and time has in a measure conceded it. Since the landing of our forefathers on Plymouth Rock until the present day the crusade has been ever against the Indian. He resisted the invasion of the whites on his domain, with all the means in his power, throughout all the wide empire we claim to own, which once called him master. They have fought the relentless crusade step by step (as we white people would have done), until the last remnants of that once numerous and powerful race are few in number and scattered to the winds, as it were; soon they will be nothing but a memory—a tradition.

"Ye say they all have passed away,
  That noble race and brave—
That their light canoes have vanished
  From off the crested wave;
That 'mid the forest where they roamed
  There rings no hunter's shout;
But their name is on your waters,
  Ye may not wash it out.

"Ye say their cone-like cabins
  That clustered o'er the vale
Have fled like withered leaves
  Before the autumn gale;
But their memory liveth on your hills,
  Their baptism on your shore;
Your everlasting rivers speak
  Their dialect of yore.

"Ye call these red-browed brethren
  The insects of the hour,
Crushed like the noteless worm amid
  The regions of their power;
Ye drive them from their father's lands
  Ye break the faith, the seal,
But can ye from the Court of Heaven
  Exclude their last appeal!"

OUR CITIZEN SOLDIERS.

DETROIT MILITARY COMPANIES IN THE EARLY DAYS AND AT THE PRESENT TIME.

THE City Guards were the first uniformed infantry company. The present Light Guards are the lineal descendants of the Brady Guards, and the Brady Guards of the City Guards. The City Guards were organized at a meeting held in the parlor of the old Steamboat Hotel in the winter of 1830-1. Among those present were General John E. Schwarz, Colonel Edward Brooks, R. E. Roberts, Chas. R. Desnoyers, Joseph Alexander, Jas. W. Sutton, Geo. Moran, B. B. Moore and Virgil McGraw. Colonel Brooks, who was an officer under General Harrison at the battle of the River Thames, was chosen captain, and Isaac T. Rowland, a graduate of West Point, was first lieutenant, and R. E. Roberts was orderly sergeant.

In 1831 there was one other military company in the city, but it was one of cavalry, commanded by Chas. Jackson, an artillery company, raised previously by Captain Ben Woodworth, having been broken up.

CITY GUARDS SWORN INTO SERVICE.

The Black Hawk war broke out in Illinois in 1832, and Michigan troops were called upon to aid the United States forces. Accordingly the militia, under the command of Major-General John R. Williams, were ordered to appear for muster at Ten Eyck's, near Dearborn, on the 24th of May, the only uniformed companies in the command being the City Guard and the Light Dragoons, of which Chas. Jackson was captain, Garry Spencer first lieutenant, John Farrar second lieutenant, and James Hanmer third lieutenant. At the muster of the First Regiment, Michigan militia, it was ordered to furnish a detachment of 250 men to be under the command of Col. Edward Brooks, who was promoted from the captaincy of the guard to the colonency of the regiment, Lieutenant Rowland being promoted to the captaincy. Volunteers were called for, and not a member of the company except the commissioned officers stepped forward. General Williams, who had been told that all would volunteer, asked what the apparent mutiny meant, whereupon First Sergeant R. E. Roberts advanced and said that "the City Guard is an organized military company and ready to obey orders." The order was then given, "City Guards, five paces to the front, march!" The command was obeyed, and the men sworn into the service. The detachment, with the cavalry, went as far as Saline, and was then ordered to return to Detroit. This order was countermanded, and while the troops were at Ann Arbor, they were ordered to join General Brown's command at Dexter, and, there being no camp equipage provided, the men contributed their money, watches and other valuables to raise a fund for its purchase, but before another twenty-four hours had elapsed the company was again ordered back to Detroit, and this time there was no revocation. General Williams with the dragoons went on to Chicago and thence to the Naper settlement in Illinois, remaining there until the termination of the war.

On the return of the detachment it encamped on the commons, near the old capitol, where a bountiful mess was prepared and the men had the first square meal since leaving home. Hard bread and raw salt pork was all that was supplied them on the march. Some managed to cook the pork on sticks stuck into the ground before the camp fires. The young men of the guard were unused to such fare and several died shortly after, and others were so broken down in health that they never mustered with the company again. Many of the guard in the absence of blankets, had green Scotch plaid cloaks, then the prevailing fashion, which, when strapped on their knapsacks, gave them the appearance of highlanders.

The field officers connected with the Detroit command, aside from General Williams, were Colonel Edward Brooks, Lieutenant-Colonel Jonathan D. Davis, Major Benj. Holbrook and Dr. John L. Whiting, surgeon; Captain Louis Davenport having charge of the baggage train.

THE CAREER OF TOM WILLIAMS.

Tom Williams, son of General John R. Williams, was fourth corporal in the City Guards. When the Guards were ordered back Thomas joined the Dragoons under Captain Jackson, and went to Chicago, and on arriving there news had just been received that the Indians were massacreing settlers at Napier settlement, some miles beyond. Thomas joined a party of volunteers, under Colonel Brooks, and went to their rescue that night, arriving at daybreak next morning. This Tom Williams afterwards entered West Point Military Academy, graduated after the usual course, entered an infantry regiment as second lieutenant and during the civil war was killed a brigadier general at Baton Rouge on the Union side. In this engagement he received his death wound while leading his command with a ringing cheer, mounted, saying to the Twenty-first Indiana Volunteers: "Boys, your field officers are all gone. I will lead you."

Tom Williams also served through the Mexican and Florida wars, with distinction.

General Williams was also accompanied to Chicago by Major Chas. W. Whipple and Major M. Wilson, escorted by Captain Jackson's dragoons. Jackson returning to Detroit, the company was in command of First Lieutenant Garry Spencer, Second Lieutenant John Farrar and Third Lieutenant James H. Hanmer.

While the command was in Chicago the people of the city, on the 18th of June, at a public meeting, adopted and published an address to General Williams and the officers and soldiers of his command, warmly thanking them "for the prompt and efficient aid rendered them when the citizens of Chicago were without protection and had not means of defending themselves."

THE CITY GUARDS GO TO TOLEDO.

The City Guards were again called upon, and this time a proclamation of Governor Mason to go to Toledo armed and equipped to defend the soil and sovereignty of Michigan against the invasion and attempt of Ohio "to steal their neighbors' landmarks," and to capture certain judicial officers, "who were attempting to hold a session of an Ohio court at that place in defiance of the statutes of Michigan and the peace and dignity of the people thereof." And they went. Under command of General Joe Brown and the immediate orders of Colonel Warner S. Wing, they entered Toledo at 1 o'clock in the morning, and saw the coattails streaming in the air of the Ohio judges and troops as they flew from their secret court room. The City Guards, after having at the city of Monroe, in a hollow square, with about 2,500 more Michigan volunteers, sworn "eternal hostility to Andrew

Jackson, Ohio and all their legions, and eternal fidelity to Stevens Thompson Mason as governor of Michigan," returned to Detroit amid the beating of drums and flaunting banners, and were welcomed by the people, as were the Roman legions of old on their return from a foreign conquest. Among the names of those who composed or went forth on this expedition were such men as Jacob M. Howard, Franklin Sawyer, Conrad Ten Eyck, Daniel Goodwin, Peter Desnoyers, Marshall J. Bacon, Charles M. Bull, George D. Bull, George C. Bates and others.

THE CITY GUARDS ESCORT GOVERNOR CASS.

In 1831 the City Guards escorted Governor Cass from his residence to the boat on his departure for Washington to enter the cabinet of President Jackson as secretary of war. A carriage had been provided for the governor, but he declined it and took his position with Captain Brooks at the head of the company, and walked bareheaded from his residence on the river bank at the west line of the city to the foot of Woodward Avenue, where he took the steamer Henry Clay.

The exact date at which the City Guard ceased to exist is not known, but it was previous to the organization of the Brady Guard, many of its members being among the original members of the latter company.

THE ARTILLERY COMPANY.

The artillery company mentioned as having been organized by Uncle Ben Woodworth, and that had such a brief and uneventful life, was made up of the young element, many of whom, after it ceased to exist, entered the ranks of the City Guard, notably Anson Burlingame, B. B. Moore, R. E. Roberts, James Sutton, and, I think, Geo. Doty. They were not uniformed, but had one gun, an iron six-pounder, attached to the gun carriage; no horses. Thy hauled their piece around with drag ropes, as the "fireladdies" used to haul their machines in the old days. They seemed to have a considerable amount of fun, getting the gun out, hauling it around the streets and banging it off on slight provocation. But they got it off once too often, and with disastrous results. The occasion was on a Fourth of July. They were engaged in firing a national salute on the Campus Martius, where the Bagley bust now is. I do not know who had charge of the breech of the gun, but I do know that the late Levi Bishop, who was one of the members of the company, was at the muzzle ramming home the cartridge. A premature discharge sent a large portion of the ramrod into one of his arms, the right one, injuring and lacerating it to such an extent that it had to be amputated. I was an eye-witness of the accident and the amputation of the arm as well. The latter operation was performed by Dr. Hurd in his office, corner Woodward Avenue and Congress Street. Mr. Bishop was at that time a journeyman shoemaker, working at his trade. On his recovery he concluded to abandon shoemaking and enter the law, and all know his subsequent career in that profession. In after years it used to be said of him, "That Fourth of July accident was the means of spoiling a poor shoemaker and making a good lawyer."

OUT OF COMMISSION.

The artillery company was dead after this. Their gun came to grief also. It was said the cause of the accident lay in the gun itself, being, as artillerymen term it, "honey-combed at the breech." "Tom" Peck, a jolly, genial chap, and a member of the company, too, procured a sledge-hammer and knocked the gun off its carriage, injuring it in such a way that it was fit only for old iron, saying, as he did so, "he'd be d—d if that gun would ever have a chance to injure another man." No one appeared to object. "Tom" Peck—perhaps some may call him to mind—kept a large shoe store in what was called the "Rpublican Block," corner Jefferson Avenue and Bates Street. I think Bishop was in his employ at the time of the accident.

THE MICHIGAN LEGION.

Before going further I call to mind that there is an account somewhere that during the war of 1812 four independent, ununiformed companies called the "Michigan Legion," commanded by Major James Witherell, then one of the territorial judges, who had been an officer in the American revolution, and was grandfather of Senator Thomas W. Palmer. They and their leader saw hazardous and arduous service on this frontier during the entire war. They were included in Hull's surrender, and Major Witherell was taken down the lake as prisoner of war, and only submitted to parole at Kingston.

THE BRADY GUARDS.

In 1835 a force of 100 men or more was employed in grading down the high river bank in front of the Cass farm. One day, having been given an unlimited supply of whisky, they got into a fight. They were too drunk to do much injury to each other, but blood flowed freely. The sheriff's posse was powerless to stop the fight or make arrests, and as there was no military organization to call upon, there was nothing to do but let them fight it out, until night put an end to the battle. This disgraceful scene showed the importance of having a military company to call upon in such cases.

Accordingly, in February or March, 1836, John Chester, Isaac S. Rowland, Andrew T. McReynolds and Marshal J. Bacon met in a room in the old "Smart Block," where the Merrill block now is, discussed the question of raising a military company, and resolved that they would use their utmost efforts to interest other young men in the project, and with such success that on the 2nd of April a formal meeting of those favorably disposed, was held, with an attendance of thirty-three young men. Colonel John Winder was chosen chairman and Geo. C. Bates and John Y. Pretty, secretaries. The unanimous conclusion was soon reached that a company should at once be formed, and that a number of committees were appointed for that purpose. The committee on names were discussing earnestly, when Peter E. De Mill suggested the name of General Hugh Brady as one which it would be a pleasure to honor, and the suggestion was so appropriate that it was unanimously accepted by the committee, who reported it to the company, when it was adopted by acclamation and a committee appointed to ask the general's consent to the use of his name, which consent was accorded with thanks for the compliment.

General Hugh Brady was an officer in the war of 1812. He was especially distinguished in the battles of Chippewa and Niagara Falls (Lundy's Lane), and was commander of the department of the lakes, with headquarters at Detroit, from 1825 to the time of his death, April 15, 1851, aged 83 years. He had been for fifty-nine years continuously an officer in the United States army.

The committees on membership, at a subsequent meeting, reported the results of their endeavors in that direction. The committee also presented a "Pledge of Membership," drawn up by

Andrew T. McReynolds, and engrossed on parchment by John Chester, which had received fifty-seven signatures, which, with those added subsequently, swelled the entire membership to ninety-seven names, which constitutes the celebrated.

ROLL OF 1836.

The following is a list of officers elected at this meeting:

Captain—Isaac S. Rowland.

Lieutenants—First, Marshal J. Bacon; second, James H. Mullett; third, George B. Martin.

Surgeon—Abram E. Sager, M. D.

Quartermaster—Henry G. Hubbard.

Sergeants—Orderly, George C. Bates; second, George C. Leib; third, John Chester; fourth, Peter E. DeMill.

Corporals—First, Jacob M. Howard; second, John J. Ashley; third, Caleb F. Davis; fourth, John McReynolds.

I am under the impression that the first appearance of the Guard, fully armed and equipped, was on the 22d of February, 1837, on which occasion the first standard was presented to them at the American hotel (now the Biddle house) in the presence of Governor Stevens T. Mason and a large concourse of citizens, who had watched with eager interest the development of this organization embracing as it did the elite of the male portion of Detroit, in every walk of life. At this their first turnout they numbered nearly 100 muskets. The flag, presented to the Guard, I think, is now in the possession of the state quartermaster general at Lansing.

General Brady subsequently presented the company with a handsome flag from the steps of the American hotel (Biddle House). One side of the flag bore the arms of the city of Detroit, and on the reverse was a portrait of one of the Guards, Charles W. Penny, and said at that time to be the handsomest man in the company.

The flag was painted by Tom Burnham or Caleb F. Davis, I forget which. Both were artists well up in their profession.

FIRST PARADE OF THE BRADY GUARDS.

The Brady Guards, on their first parade, mustered nearly 100 (as before mentioned) muskets, and made a fine appearance. Their captain, Isaac Rowland, was every inch a soldier, and the

Guards, on this, their first appearance, plainly showed by their superb drill and soldiery bearing, that they had been under the keen supervision of a West Point graduate. They were given a splendid ovation by the citizens, who had watched with eager interest the formation and the nightly drilling of the company in the streets.

Soon after the "Bradys" had completed their organization and perfected their uniforms, equipments, etc., the patriot war suddenly loomed up on the horizon. Their services were soon required to aid the United States in the enforcemnet of our neutrality laws, and which became an imperative necessity. So General Scott made his requisition for an armed military force from Michigan and the "Young Bradys," like the Coldstream guards, rushed to the front and during the winters of 1837 and 1838, for three months of each year, were mustered into the service of the United States as common soldiers, subject to the rules and articles of war. And, as George C. Bates said, "We faithfully performed all the duties as such and won the special commendation and praise of Generals Scott, Worth and Brady, and the secretary of war, as the records will prove.

AT THE FRONT.

"During all this time we pooled our pay, secured a very large sum of money, with which we burnished our muskets, mounted them with mahogany stocks instead of the old black walnut, purchased a magnificent camp equippage, and so, at Goat Island, at the Falls of Niagara, on July 4, 1838, we took the highest prize as the best drilled, most thoroughly uniformed and equipped troop on the frontier. We numbered about 100 muskets and our officers were Captain L. S. Rowland, Lieutenants A. S. Williams, Edmund Kearsley and James A. Armstrong. Our sergeants were George C. Bates, John Chester, George Doty and one other, whose name escapes me. Our men, every one of them, were the elite of Detroit, who voted always as they shot, and who would gladly have shot any and all men who violated the laws or defiled the flag of the nation."

The front, to which the guards were ordered, was at Fighting Island, near Ecorse and within the boundaries of Canada. General Brady had his headquarters directly opposite the island, on the American shore.

A DEFIANT BRITISH OFFICER.

By Lieutenant Ed. Kearsley and one other officer, General Brady sent a message to Colonel Basden, of the Twenty-first British foot, in command at Malden, the purpose of which was that he (Brady) and his command would see to it that the Patriots on Fighting Island would be prevented from crossing the river as they had threatened. Lieutenant Kearsley returned from his interview with the British commander, and proceeded to General Brady's headquarters, where he reported to him that on reaching Malden they found Colonel Basden and all his officers at the mess table, where they were dining and wining deeply; that on being introduced by the orderly to Colonel Basden and delivering their message from General Brady, they were not even asked to be seated, but were answered by Colonel Basden "that while he had the highest possible respect for General Brady, whom he had not met since the battle of Lundy's Lane in 1814, where the two regiments repeatedly crossed bayonets, yet he had none for the United States civil service officers or their disposition to enforce their neutrality laws; that he should, regardless of General Brady or his command, attack the d—d vagabonds on Fighting Island before daylight the next morning; that he would clean them out with grape and canister from his batteries and if they retreated to the United States he would follow them there and destroy and kill them wherever he could overtake them."

IN LINE OF BATTLE.

The moment this message was delivered the bugle call sounded, the drum beat the alarm, and the entire command fell in, formed into a hollow square with General Brady in the center, who, in a firm, clear voice repeated most distinctly his message to Colonel Basden and Basden's unsoldierlike and insulting reply, and calling upon Captain Rowland for a half-dozen Brady Guards with guide flags he ordered them to pace off the distance on the ice from the American shore to mid-channel, which was the boundary line between the United States and Canada, and to place those flags about 100 rods apart up and down, so as to mark clearly and distinctly that portion of the ice which covered American soil and that which covered the British boundary. When this was done Brady moved the command back into line of battle, up and down the river, and, taking his place about five paces in front of the line, pointed to those guide flags and straightening himself up like the old hero that he was, said:

BRADY'S ORDERS TO HIS TROOPS.

"Soldiers, you see before you clearly marked out by yonder guides the boundary line between the United States and Canada. We are here to enforce our laws and to arrest and punish all offenses and offenders against the United States on this side of that line, and to see to it that no foreign power shall intermeddle with our rights and duties. My orders to you are as heretofore, to arrest and prevent all armed men from proceeding over to Fighting Island, to capture and to turn over to the United States marshal as prisoners all men who shall retreat from Fighting Island to our shore; but if a British officer or soldier in arms crosses inside of our lines I charge you all to beat them back, to capture and to kill them, if it be necessary to protect our sovereignty, and to guard our soil against the impress of a British soldier's foot. I have confidence that we can and will successfully defend our soil against the intrusion or insolence of a British foe."

"These orders," Geo. C. Bates, orderly sergeant of the Brady Guards, says, "were received by the troops with the wildest huzzahs, and then our sentinels resumed their cheerless and chilly round. The camp fires were piled high with hickory, beech and maple and ash, and the suppers were cooked and the coffee boiled. We all waited and watched for what was next to come. That fearfully cold night wore on. The officer of the night made his grand rounds repeatedly and reported all was well on the Detroit. The old general, enveloped in buffalo robes and blankets, knee deep, was sleeping in his headquarters. But every man slept with his piece loaded, and his right ear listening sharp and keen for the call to arms. About an hour before day an attempt was made by the Patriots to run a gun carriage over on the ice in order to mount their sole piece of artillery, but this was prevented, and the men in charge of it arrested. Almost simultaneously therewith the rumbling of heavy artillery was heard on the Canadian shore, and very shortly thereafter the whole British Twenty-first regiment moved directly up, opposite Fighting Island, took up their position on the ice and commenced a heavy cannonade upon the Patriot camp. With the first gun fired, the whole of our command turned out under arms, and as the shot from the British batteries, struck through the branches of the trees on Fighting Island, and knocked off the snow and ice, in one instance carrying away a Patriot's arm, their track could be followed as distinctly as that of the locomotive of a railway train. No sooner had Basden's battery fairly opened, than the poor devils on the island began to retreat by tens and twenties, and soon the Detroit River was dotted all over with the fragments of this grand army, and just so fast as they came inside our lines, we picked them up, arrested them and turned them over to the United States marshal, who sent them up by sleigh loads to Detroit, where they were confined in jail.

"About 10 o'clock, with drums beating and flags flying, Colonel Basden's entire regiment, in two divisions, one above and one below the island, marched around in line of battle to cut off the retreat and capture these retreating ones. No sooner had they uncovered themselves from behind the island than our entire command was formed in line of battle, and thus awaited the movements on the other side, and of course with a strong hope that no collision should come. The two British detachments marched close down to our flags on the boundary, saluted each other, and marched back whence they came, but not a British soldier stepped inside the American line. The pluck and coolness and prudence of General Hugh Brady, aided by the Brady Guards and their comrades, vindicated the rights and maintained the peace and dignity of the United States and the people thereof."

Dr. Theller (Hero of the Schooner Ann) has something to say about the Brady Guards on this occasion in his book, "Canada in 1837-8." It appears there was a party of Patriots congregated in this city, who conceived the idea of seizing the little steamer Erie, lying at her dock in winter quarters, and joining the forces at Fighting Island. "Hearing the cannonade they hurried their movements, and took possession of the steamer and got their arms, etc., on board. At this juncture fresh troops (Patriots) came in from St. Clair, Macomb and Oakland Counties, all choice riflemen, and joined their comrades on the Erie. They accomplished all this before any alarm was sounded, an excitement was created at once by the ringing of bells, and a general feint simultaneous from all directions. However, before they could raise steam on board the Erie, the Brady Guards were turned out with the United States marshal at their head, and an attempt made to seize the boat. Finding all entreaties, commands or threats unavailing, the marshal ordered them to be fired upon. The Bradys of course obeyed the order, but being most of them good fellows, took good care to fire over their heads, with the exception of one who let his bullet strike a barrel of provisions a hardy old Patriot was handling, who coolly, and as if a little offended, cried out, "Take care there; d—n it, you had a ball in your gun."

FIRST BALL OF THE GUARDS.

February 22, 1839, the first ball of the company was given at the National Hotel (Russell House). The élite of the city were present, as were the officers of the United States army stationed here and those of the British army stationed at Sandwich and Malden, in full uniform. There being quite a large number of United States officers stationed here at that time, they, the British officers and the officers, non-commissioned officers and privates of the Guards, all in full uniform, aided by the gay toilettes of the ladies present, made a most brilliant spectacle.

The day before the ball the following resolution, offered by Private Geo. G. Bull, was adopted:

"Resolved, That all who go to the ball ought to keep sober."

EXCURSION TO BUFFALO.

July 2, 1838, the company, on the invitation of the Buffalo City Guard, left on the steamer Michigan to spend the Fourth at Buffalo and Niagara Falls. The Burgess Corps of Albany, the Williams Light Infantry of Rochester and the Buffalo Light Guard of Buffalo were at that period considered to be the crack volunteer military companies of the union.

Writing of the Buffalo excursion of the Brady Guards, the late Geo. C. Bates says: "During our active service upon the frontier and under the special teachings and thorough drillings given in person by Gen. Worth, Scott's aid, and by Maj. Payne, U. S. A., the latter one of the most perfect drill sergeants that ever shouldered a musket, we had acquired a reputation that not only extended through the state of Michigan, but all along the frontier, and so on the 4th of July, 1838, we were invited by the mayor and common council of Buffalo to visit that city and spend the day with the Buffalo Light Guard and the Williams Light Infantry from Rochester, on Goat Island at Niagara Falls. The invitation was joyously accepted and the whole command, numbering 119 muskets, some nineteen or twenty of whom were distinguished young lawyers, among whom I remember especially the Rev. Jack Atterbury, then a mad wag, a fellow of infinite jest, were carried down on the old steamer Illinois or Michigan, and were received at the docks in Buffalo by a grand military escort and two-thirds of the population of that busy city. They were marched to the park in front of the old court house, and in the square above the splendid hotel—such an one as Buffalo has never since had—where we spent the 3d, and were feasted and feted and wined and juleped and punched and addressed by Mayor Taylor and the various members of the common council as if we had been revolutionary soldiers. Finally at early dawn on the 4th we went to Goat Island, where we pitched our tents, set our marquee, planted our batteries and there contested with Williams Light Infantry from Rochester for the palm of victory. We justly won the premium, then and there awarded to us, as the best citizen soldiers along the national frontier, who had no superiors in promptness, efficiency and perfect knowledge of the school of a soldier, the company and the battalion."

On this trip to Buffalo, on the invitation of the Buffalo City Guards, the Bradys must have had a "high old time," judging by the steamer's bill for refreshments, which amounted to $480, of which $268 was for champagne at $2 a bottle, and $212 for meals at thirty-seven and a half cents a meal. The question seems to present itself, why they spent so much money on their eating."

VISIT OF BUFFALO CITY GUARD.

The Buffalo City Guard having accepted an invitation to pass the Fourth of July, 1839, in Detroit, elaborate preparations were made to entertain them handsomely, and on the evening of the first (Saturday) the Bradys went into camp, with the Washington Lancers, the camp being named in honor of Maj. Payne, under whom the Guard had served during their enlistment in the patriot war, and was located on the Cass farm, where the residence built by the late Gov. Baldwin now is. Monday, July 3, the battalion from Buffalo arrived, the whole being under the command of Col. McKay, and went into camp with the Brady Guards and Lancers. July 4 at 10 a. m. all were under arms, and Captain Rowland, on behalf of the Brady Guards, presented a stand of colors to the battalion of the Buffalo City Guard. Private Norman Rawson, secretary of the Bradys, then presented a pair of pistols to Captain Allen and silver cups to Messrs. Barton and Mosier, all of the steamer Michigan, as tokens of appreciation of their attentions on the occasion of the visit of the company to Buffalo in 1838.

The Bradys also gave a ball in honor of their guests at the National hotel that was graced by the beauty and fashion of the city, as well as by the presence of the United States officers stationed here, and the British officers stationed at Sandwich and Malden, all in full uniform. Notably among the latter were Colonel England and Captain Eyrie, both of whom later on won distinction in the Crimean war, the former attaining high command in the line and the latter on the staff, rising to the position of quartermaster-general of the English forces. The affair was a brilliant success, eclipsing the one given February 22.

The music at this ball was furnished by a colored band, which came with the Buffalo Light Guard, and it was particularly fine, as well it might be, when it is understood that the band and its leader (whose name it bore, which I have unfortunately forgotten) had a national reputation at that time. It had its headquarters at Philadelphia, I think.

THE WASHINGTON LANCERS.

The Washington Lancers was a juvenile company, composed of youths, all about 16 years of age, commanded by Captain William P. Doty; Albion Turner, first lieutenant; Edward M. Pitcher, second lieutenant. This latter company usually did guard duty while their older soldier brothers were away on social and pleasanter duties. Their uniform was white pants, blue jacket, blue cloth cap and they were armed with a lance instead of musket. This lancer company was exceedingly short lived.

The military, at 11 a. m. on the 4th, united with the civil authorities and attended the Presbyterian church, corner of Woodward Avenue and Larned Street, and listened to the oration in honor of the day, by George C. Bates in his civil capacity as member of the Detroit Young Men's society, after which there was a grand dinner at the National hotel. At half-past 6 o'clock p. m., the guard, accompanied by the common council, escorted their guests to the steamer Buffalo and gave them a salute by way of a parting compliment.

VISIT OF THE WILLIAMS LIGHT INFANTRY.

The above company, from Rochester, N. Y., having accepted an invitation to visit the Bradys, arrived here on the Steamer Lexington, Wednesday morning, July 16, 1846, and having been received by the Guards, was escorted to the corner of Jefferson Avenue and Rivard Street, and went into camp on the spot where the Jefferson Avenue Presbyterian church now stands.

After morning parade the two companies and a large number of invited guests participated in a cold collation, which was given on the camp ground by the Bradys, in a large marquee tent. On this occasion the late Hon. John Patton, then a somewhat obscure wagonmaker, read an address suitable to the occasion, and he delivered it in such a masterly manner as to challenge the admiration of all his listeners. This, and his prominence in the volunteer fire department, were great factors, no doubt, in elevating him to the position of Mayor of the city, which office he filled acceptably for two terms.

In the evening the visiting company was complimented with a ball at the National Hotel (now Russell House), which was graced, as all the former balls were, by the fashion of the city, as well as by the officers of the United States Army stationed here, and the British officers stationed at Malden. The next day they were invited to a dinner at the Michigan Exchange, and in the evening started on their homeward trip, evidently highly pleased with their visit.

General Brady and Colonel Basden first met at the battle of Lundy's Lane (as before intimated) June, 1814. General Winfield Scott, as all know, was in command of the American forces, and, as most people know, was a giant in stature, being six feet four inches high. On this occasion, it is said, he wore in his hat a white plume nearly two feet long. With his aids, Worth and Wool, he stormed the British battery, but was repulsed by the Twenty-first British Infantry, commanded by Colonel Basden, until finally about 8 o'clock in the evening, just as the moon rose over the carnage that raged there. Scott organized a division, consisting of Hugh Brady's Twenty-first Pennsylvania Infantry and the bloody Ninth recruited in Maine, and forming them into column of four deep and placing himself on his white horse in front, he said:

"Boys, I am satisfied that you can carry that infernal British battery. Now, I want you to follow me, and wherever you see this white plume you will know that Winfield Scott is under it, in advance. Charge!"

Shortly the white horse and the white plume were seen rolling over and over in the dust, but on rushed Hugh Brady and on clashed the arms of that gallant battalion until shortly Worth and Wool, Scott's aids, were both knocked over, and Colonel Brady wounded by a ball striking his sword and driving it into his groin, was picked up and cared for. Basden and the British troops encamped upon the field and slept upon and under their guns, while Scott and Worth and Wool and Brady, and many others were carried off the field and transported in batteaux to Buffalo, where they all recovered.

THEY MET AGAIN.

Strange to say, twenty-four years thereafter these old warriors met again on the frontier at Malden and Detroit, and by their arms and true patriotism prevented another war between Great Britain and the United States.

They, Brady and Basden, met again (and the last time) at the Michigan Exchange in 1847, where they and their fellow soldiers, English and French, as the guests of the Brady Guards, rushed into each other's arms and embraced like boys from school, until the dining-hall of that glorious old-time hostelry echoed and rang with joyous cry, "God Bless Brady and Basden: God bless the queen and the president of the United States; God grant that henceforth in sunshine and in storm, in times of plenty and of poverty, on the land and on the sea, everywhere the sun shall shine, that Great Britain and the United States shall be firmer friends, and that their only contests and controversies hereafter shall be which can most and best promote the blessings of commerce, education, religion and liberty. Let all the people of both nations forever shout Amen." And thus the feast ended.

THE WHTE PLUME.

A further account of this dinner, from the pen of Geo. C. Bates, orderly sergeant of the Bradys, is given below. He is also responsible for the story that General Scott, at Lundy's Lane, sported a white plume, in imitation of Henry IV. of France at the battle of Ivry:

"The king has come to marshal us
  In all his armor dressed,
And he has bound a snow-white plume
  Upon his gallant crest.

"And if my standardbearer fall,
  As fall full well he may
(For never saw I promise yet
  Of such a bloody fray),
Press where ye see my white plume
  Shine amidst the ranks of War
And be your oriflamme today
  The helmet of Navarre."

A FAMOUS DINNER.

"The troubles along the border had substantially ceased and were finally ended by the treaty made by Lord Ashburnton with Daniel Webster, our secretary of state, in 1847. The federal government had placed in its fortifications at Buffalo, Cleveland, Detroit, Fort Gratiot and Fort Brady, and the Sault Ste. Marie detachments of regular troops, between whom and the British troops on the Canadian side a warm friendship soon sprang up and invitations to lunch and to dine from one side to the other, were constantly given and accepted. This finally led to an invitation from the Brady Guards to the officers of the British and federal armies to a dinner to be given at the Michigan Exchange, including, of course, Colonel Basden at Malden, and General Brady at Detroit, where for the first time after a quarter of a century, they should meet face to face, not with bayonets and sabers and guns, and drums and wounds, but with knives and forks and wines and wassail, and where once more they could embrace each other, not in the arms of death, but in those of friendship, love and truth. "The invitations to the dinner were cordially accepted by all parties—the day fixed and the old dining room of the Michigan Exchange on the corner of Jefferson Avenue and Shelby Street was decorated, not with flowers as of modern dates, but draped upon one side with the battered banners of Basden's regiment, prizes captured in the peninsula campaigns at Badajos, Salamanca, Corunna and other victories in Spain, and on the other side the walls were hung with the banners captured in the war ued, the organic law of the Brady Guard that in the event of the sounding of the tocsin of war, the Guard should instantly disband. But he had sat down for hours and listened to the warlike reminiscences of the veterans of the Guard, who at the conclusion of their bloody recitals always drew forth their land warrants to prove the terrible statements."

DINNER IN HONOR OF COLONEL GRAYSON.

Mr. Geo. N. Brady has kindly furnished me a copy of the *Free Press* of March 10, 1901, in which is copied an account of the dinner of the Grayson Light Guards in honor of their commander, Colonel J. B. Grayson, which account appeared in the *Detroit Evening Tribune* of Saturday, Deecember 21, 1850. Among the distinguished guests present were Lieutenant (afterward general) Grant and other distinguished men of affairs, both in military and civil life.

"At the head of the table," reads the article, "was seated the commanding officer of the guards, Lieutenant E. R. Kearsley; seated at his right were Colonel Grayson, Colonel Whistler, of the Fourth United States Infantry, and Major Daniel H. Rucker; on his left were General Hugh Brady, U. S. A., and General Schwarz and aid. At the tables on the right and left were Lieutenants James E. Pittman and Wm. D. Wilkins, of the Grayson Light Guards; Lieutenants Henry and Grant, of the Fourth United States Infantry; Lieutenant Freeman Norveil, of the marines; Hon. John Ladue, mayor; Judge Whipple and Messrs. Rufus Hosmer and Henry Barnes, of the press. Lucker's Sax Horn band discoursed sweet music during the evening, adding much to the pleasure of the occasion. After the removal of the cloth, and ample justice had been done to the rations furnished for the occasion, the president announced that they would charge for a toast, which introduced the guest of the evening, Colonel John B. Grayson. Colonel Grayson's toast was followed by others, responded to by the following prominent men: Adjutant and Quartermaster-General Schwarz, Governor John S. Barry, Mayor Ladue, Chas. E. Whilden, Lieutenant Wm. D. Wilkins, Lieutenant Kearsley, Captain Phin Homan, aid-de-camp to the adjutant-general; Rufus Hosmer, of the *Advertiser;* Lieutenant James E. Pittman, Lieutenant Henry, of the Fourth United States Infantry; Major Rucker, Sergeant Jas. B. Witherell, Joe L. Langley,

Charles Dibble, Henry Barnes, of the *Tribune;* Lieutenant Freeman Norveil, Corporal John B. Palmer, Alex. K. Howard, Sergeant John Robertson, Lieutenant Grant, Fourth United States Infantry; Judge Chas. Whipple, S. J. Mather, Charles S. Adams, Charles Brewster, J. E. Martin, Calvin C. Jackson, J. Cook, Chas. Berkey, Sergeant Geo. Davie, James W. Sutton, Corporal V. W. Bullock and Thos. S. Gillett.

"A letter of regret was read from Surgeon Chas. S. Tripler, U. S. A. Among the toasts proposed was one to the press of the city by Colonel Wm. D. Wilkins, wishing the pencil-pushers long life and prosperity, to which was added, in brackets, by the printer that set up that part of the article ('Sensible to the last—Compositor.')

"When the name of the immortal Grant was announced he arose and in his characteristically modest style said he 'could face the music, but not make a speech.' He proposed the toast, 'The Grayson Guards—should their services be required, may they be rendered in proportion to the confidence placed in them and their worthy commander.'"

Of the above named men Colonel W. D. Wilkins will be remembered by *Free Press* readers as the writer of the best series of foreign letters ever penned; Lieutenant, afterwards Colonel Freeman Norveil, was one of the early proprietors of the *Free Press;* Sergeant Robertson was adjudant-general of Michigan during the civil war; Calvin C. Jackson, at one time private secretary to Governor Stevens T. Mason, was afterwards purser in the navy during the civil war; Colonel, now General Jas. E. Pittman, is still alive (1901) and one of the most respected veteran residents of Detroit. Sergeant James B. Witherell entered the United States service as first lieutenant Third Dragoons, and was accidentally drowned at Point Isabel, Texas, just as his regiment was on the point of embarking for the north at the outbreak of the civil war."

Of the above named persons the only ones now alive (1902) are General D. H. Rucker, U. S. A, retired), Washington, D. C., and Joe L. Langley, Chicago, Ill.

When the Brady Guards disbanded the arms and accoutrements that the state had furnished them with reverted to the Grayson Guards and from them to the Light Guard. While in use by the Bradys the possessor of each musket became attached to it to that degree that, as Geo. C. Bates said, he replaced the ordinary wood of the stock with the mahogany or cherry, and otherwise embellished it with silver mountings. When the civil war broke out these muskets were taken possession of by the state quartermaster-general (being flintlock), and percussion lock arms substituted in their stead, and the Light Guard took these latter with them out of the state. These same flintlock muskets were changed into percussion lock, as indeed all flintlock muskets in possession of the state were, the demand for arms being so urgent, and issued to troops in the service of the United States. After the war closed the state claimed pay for all ordnance stores, in its possession, that were issued to troops in the service of the United States and taken by them out of the state and not returned. (Included in these stores were the Brady Guard muskets, 79 in number.) The state demanded the cash for them, or the return of the stores. After some years the general government concluded to allow the claim in cash, and the state, in due course, got the money.

The present Light Guard, learning of the payment of the claim by the United States, petitioned the state military board for pay for the 79 Brady Guard muskets. What the nature of their demand was, or what it was based on, I do not know. The board allowed the claim, the state paying the same amount to the company for the muskets that it received for them from the general government. So the Light Guard, luckily, were ahead so much.

The Detroit Light Guard, the successors of the Bradys and Graysons supplied over thirty officers, for various Michigan regiments in the civil war, and I presume the Scott and Montgomery Guards did their share. Greusel, one time captain of the Scott Guard, became colonel of an Illinois regiment in the war.

WHEN THE BRADYS WERE ORGANIZING.

Referring again to the Brady Guards: When they were organizing I was a boy clerk in C. & J. Wells' grocery store, Desnoyer Block, corner of Jefferson Avenue and Bates Street. Mr. John Wells, one of the firm, was a Brady, and, being quite popular, our store seemed to be headquarters of the company as it were, where the members used to meet daily and "talk shop." The drill rooms of the company were in the Williams building, where Edson, Moore & Co. now are, in the fourth story. So I became deeply interested in the company, its formation, etc., and when it turned out on its first public parade, nearly 100 rank and file (with its brass band), completely armed and equipped, it seemed to me the climax was reached. Of all that number I think but one survivor remains, and that one is George Doty. In an article on this company contributed to one of the daily papers some months ago by Mr. Richard R. Elliott, is given the first roster of the company, and if this meets the eye of any fortunate owner of it, by referring to it, will readily see, if he is an old timer, that it contains the names of nearly all the bright, promising young men of that day. Men in every walk of life, that have contributed their shares to make Detroit what it this day is.

THE GRAYSON GUARDS.

The Grayson Guards that followed the Bradys was composed of about the same material as its predecessor, and flourished like a "green bay tree" during the sojourn of its founder (Colonel J. B. Grayson, U. S. A.,) among us. When he was ordered away it languished, and died a natural death. There are many living who were members of this company who will remember more about it than I. Suffice it to say, I knew most of the members of the company intimately, Colonel Grayson and his assistant, Major Whilden, as well, and I am sure scores and scores of our people will call to mind the personalities of the two latter gentlemen with the same emotions of pleasure and regard that I do.

Most of all those that composed the foregoing military companies have passed to the beyond and many of them on the field of battle in the service of their country.

"On Fame's eternal camping ground
Their silent tents are spread,
And glory guards with solemn round
The bivouac of the dead."

TARGET SHOOT AT BLOODY RUN.

The Grayson Guards had an amusing target shoot (their first, I think) up at Bloody Run. The firing was from this side of the Run, where the stove works are now; the target was planted on the opposite bank of the stream. The day was all that could be desired, the commissary had everything provided in the way of eatables and drinkables that could be required. I was not present, but full details of the affair were not wanting, given by participants, the next day. Joe Law, a member of the company, had the first crack at the target. His bullet bored a hole clean through the center of the bull's-eye, much to his surprise. The rest followed in quick succession, their bullets apparently taking the same course that Law's did, through the bull's-eye, as there were no other marks on the target. On examination it was found that the bank of the run on each side of the target was heavily charged with lead, so they were compelled to award the prize, whatever it was, to Private Law. Whereupon they had the greatest kind of a jollification then and there. Their march back to their armory was said to be a laughable affair by those who witnessed it. Geo. Conkling, a member of the company, and an engraver in Geo. Doty's employ, got up a cartoon of the return march, which was most graphic and amusing, as all will testify who saw it, and their number must be many. The memory of this target shoot in its entirety must also be fresh in their remembrance. It was quite fortunate that there were no dwellers at that time on that side of Jefferson Avenue in the rear of the target. If there had been their lives might have been in dangr.

SCOTTS AND MONTGOMERYS.

I never was very familiar with the Scott or Montgomery Guard, except that they were old organizations, well drilled and efficient. The former furnished some capable officers of the First Michigan Volunteer Infantry in the Mexican war—notably Major Reuhle and Captain Nick Greusel. One conspicuous feature in the Scott Guard parades, that many no doubt will remember, was the "pioneer" (Mr. Crongeyer), who marched at the head of the company, clad in a uniform copied, I think, from that of Napoleon's pioneers of the Imperial Guard—blue with buff facings, bearskin shako, white leather apron coming down below the knees, buff gaiters and carrying over his shoulder a broad or battle ax. It is presumed the great captain got up this kind of a soldier to clear away the underbrush, as it were, from the path of his guarl, that they might have a fair show. Our friend, Crongeyer, was mindful of the position he held in the company and bore the honor with becoming dignity, as all who ever saw him in that capacity will recall to mind.

The Scott Guard also furnished a company for the Second Michigan Volunteer Infantry, in the civil war (Company A):

Captain, Louis Dillman; first lieutenant, John V. Reuhle; second lieutenant, Gustavus Kast. At Fair Oaks Major Dillman was in command of the regiment; he was also in command at Centreville, August 28, 1862, but this time as lieutenant-colonel (Poe being in command of a brigade).

Referring again to the Detroit Light Guard, which today is so well to the fore, and to which I once had the honor to belong, when it was first organized, I think it quite appropriate to include in this article, an extract from one in relation to it that appeared in the *Detroit Journal* some time in the fore part of 1898:

"This grand old company was an outgrowth of the Brady Guards, which was organized by the young men of the city as an independent and volunteer military company April 2, 1836. The name was derived from that famous hero, General Hugh Brady. To this organization belonged the best class of young men in the city. Matters of social as well as military interest were taken up, and the company made many trips up to various parts of the state and country, reflecting great credit upon Detroit.

"When the Mexican war broke out, the Brady Guards responded to the call for men at once. They served with distinction and gave three men to the cause whose names are well known. These were General Alpheus S. Williams, General James E. Pittsman and Colonel Wm. D. Wilkins.

"Shortly after the close of the Mexican war, and on the death of General Brady, the Brady Guards were disbanded and merged into the Grayson Light Guard, which was organized in 1851. This latter company was named after and commanded by Colonel John B. Grayson, U. S. A., who was at that time stationed in Detroit. But it was destined to a short life, and on November 16, 1855, it became the Detroit Light Guard.

"The original roll of the new organization was signed by 100. Many of them went to the front in '61 and earned honor for themselves and their state. One of the most prominent of these was General A. S. Williams. Among the original first signers of the roll who are still living in Detroit are General James E. Pittman, Colonel Jerome Croul, General Friend Palmer, Hon. Thomas W. Palmer, William A. Moore, George Doty, John Patton, Alfred Russell, Thomas P. Sheldon, Henry R. Mizner, Edward J. Smith, R. R. Howard, David R. Pierce and Henry C. Penny.

"The record of the Light Guard in the war is magnificent. It was the first company in the state to volunteer its services to President Lincoln. The call was made April 16, 1861, and the Light Guard volunteered on the next day. Nearly the whole company of 79 men who were enrolled in the organization at that time were mustered into the army. Many were anxious to go with the boys and in several instances the members were offered large sums of money for their places.

"The company was in command of Colonel Charles M. Lum as captain, John D. Fairbanks, after whom Fairbanks post is named, was the first lieutenant and Wm. A. Throop second lieutenant. General Eugene Robinson was at that time second sergeant of the company. It will be remembered that it was General Robinson who drilled the Detroit Commandery, Knights Templar, and made it what it is.

"The Light Guard became company A of that famous regiment the First Michigan. It was the first company west of the Alleghanies to report for duty at Washington. To it, also, belongs the distinction of being the first company of the entire north to cross the Long Bridge into Virginia, and so enter hostile territory. The First Michigan led the army, and as company A, the Light Guard was at the head of it. The company sacrificed two men to the government in the battle of Bull Run. They were William A. Cunningham and David A. Jones.

"At the end of three months, the Light Guards' term of service closed. The members returned to Detroit and were given a most enthusiastic greeting. But they were not grand stand players. Their country still needed them and nearly every man went back to reenlist for three years, and the Light Guard furnished the government with eighty-three commissioned officers.

"Prominent among these were Major-General A. S. Williams, Brigadier-Generals Henry M. Whittelsey, Henry M. Mizner, William A. Throop, F. W. Swift, Jas. E. Pittman and John Robertson; Colonels Henry L. Chipman, Horace S. Roberts, W. W. Duffield, William D. Wilkins, Huber Le Favour, Edward Hill, William S. Whipple and Charles M. Lum; Majors John D. Fairbanks and Robert T. Elliott, and Captains Charles E. Wendell and William J. Speed.

"While the company was fighting bravely at the front, the Detroit Light Guard reserve corps did good service at home.

There were at times stirring scenes even in Detroit. Many rebels lived in Windsor and attacks were expected at almost any moment. In 1863 the negro riots had to be put down, and there were raids of various kinds. During all these troublesome times, the reserve corps did good service in patrolling the streets, guarding the jails, and protecting the city generally.

"They did good work at the time of the negro riots," said Colonel Fred E. Farnsworth, speaking of the matter. "The city was aroused one night by the ringing of all the bells, which was the signal agreed upon for calling the troops to arms in case of danger. The reserve corps came to the rescue at once, and had it not been for their aid, bloody scenes might have been the result.

"And since the war the Light Guard has showed the kind of men that composed it. In 1874, it was ordered to Ishpeming to quell the riots among the iron workers in that locality. Its services were so well appreciated that one of the iron companies sent it a check for $500. In 1877, with other military organizations, it helped suppress the railroad strikes. Again, in 1885, they were called to Bay City during the lumber workers' strike.

"The Light Guard has always been a great advertisement for the city. The boys took part in the parades connected with the Centennial in Philadelphia in 1876, and won compliments galore by their fine appearance, splendid marching, and superb drilling. It was the same way in New York, where the company stopped on its return home. The organization has taken its due share of first prizes in drills held in Toledo, Cleveland, Grand Rapids and other cities.

"It has always made a fine showing at all state encampments. It inaugurated the governor's levees, which have been among the prominent social functions of the city.

DETROIT LIGHT INFANTRY.

This company is an offshoot from the Detroit Light Guard, which occurred some time in 1877. I am not at all well informed on this military company, except that it is composed of the same element as is the Light Guard, and not behind it in any way in the manual of-arms or proficiency in drill. I saw them once on parade when the audience was the nation, as it were. The place was Washington, and the occasion the dedication of the Washington monument, February 22, 1884. It was a stinging cold day, as many members of the company must remember. They formed in the procession part of its military display, which latter was composed of crack independent military companies from all parts of the union.

I witnessed the passing of the procession from the office of the depot quartermaster, U. S. A., corner of Fifteenth Street and Pennsylvania Avenue, and when the Light Infantry came marching down Fifteenth Street in open order and wheeled into Pennsylvania Avenue, they came around, or wheeled, with admirable precision, as one man, eliciting the applause of the vast crowd that were gathered at that point, an ovation of the like no other military company in the procession called forth.

AGAIN THE BRADY GUARDS.

During the month of June, 1847, the company known as the Brady Guards of Detroit was enlisted and mustered into the service of the United States on the 18th of the above month, with Morgan L. Gage, Detroit, as captain; Alex. K. Howard, Detroit, first lieutenant; Wm. F. Chittenden, Detroit, second lieutenant, and Asa W. Sprague, Detroit, third lieutenant. This company garrisoned Fort Mackinac and Fort Brady at the Soo, taking the place of United States regulars sent to the front (Mexican war). These forts were commanded respectively by Captain Gage and Lieutenant Howard. The company was mustered out of service at the close of the war. Though assuming the name of "Brady Guards" there were none of the old members of the guard in the ranks, but made up of new men recruited for the emergency.

The commissioned officers, however, were, or had been members of the old guard. They were mustered into service by Captain J. A. Whitall, Fifth United States Infantry, who was stationed here at that time.

THE CITY GUARD.

Referring again to the City Guard, that they had an arduous time during their Black Hawk campaign may well be believed, when I state, that I was an eye-witness of their return, somewhere about the latter part of July. They came into the city, mounted, via Chicago turnpike (Michigan Avenue) to Woodward Avenue, then down that avenue to their armory somewhere in the vicinity of Woodworth's Hotel on Woodbridge Street east. Horse and man were a sorry sight, particularly the former. Their reception by the citizens was most cordial, every one was out, apparently, and the guard was delighted with the generous welcome accorded them.

Later on the Cavalry horses belonging to the general government, came into the city, by same route, tied together in fours, then came cannon, caissons, traveling forges, etc., four horses to each, the latter were skeletons, bedraggled with mud, indeed the whole business was, as it had rained quite hard the two days previous. Well, it was a wretched sight; but Black Hawk and his savage followers had been snuffed out like the flame of a candle.

DEAR MR. EDITOR:

An old and esteemed friend, as he says, who has perused my articles published in your paper on the military companies of Detroit, writes me in relation to the Brady Guards, and clears my memory in regard to that company in two or three particulars, as for instance:

The music that the Buffalo City Guards brought to Detroit at the time the Bradys entertained them on the Cass farm, was the band of the Philadelphia Firemen, led by the celebrated bugle player, Frank Johnson (colored). The band gave a concert at the old city hall while in Detroit, which was then the only hall in the city. It was crowded with the elite of Detroit. (I now call to mind the incident, as I was present). He further says that John A. Rucker, of Grosse Ile; George Doty and Stanley G. Wright of this city, are the sole survivors of the Brady Guards.

Another point: I stated in one of the articles that the portrait painted on the flag presented to the Bradys by General Brady represented the handsomest man in the company, "Charles W. Penny." It was my impression that it was so understood at the time, but it appears there was another claimant in the field, George G. Bull, clerk United States Court. George was, indeed, a handsome man, a fine soldier, as many will remember, and might easily have been selected to represent the company as its handsomest member, but which of the two it really was I do not know. I presume John Rucker, Stanley G. Wight or George Doty, can say.

I understand there is in existence in this city, a full-length portrait of Mr. George G. Bull, taken at the time he was a member of the Bradys, and in the full uniform of the company. A most interesting relic, it seems to me.

RETREAT OF THE BRADY GUARDS.

In this connection, I repeat what is related in regard to the Guards, in my article, "Incidents of the Patriot War," that appeared in your journal some time during the early summer. It was with the Patriots who invaded the soil of Canada on that December morning of 1838 that the Guards had to do. After their defeat in the Baubie orchard, Windsor, the Patriots dispersed at once; some of them took to the Canadian woods, but most of them took the river road towards the Windmills (now Walkerville) that stood on the bank of the river. They availed themselves of six or eight canoes that luckily appeared in sight, drawn up on the river bank, and pushed off for the American shore. Some of them met with disaster before reaching home. The British atillery, in pursuit, gained the further windmill, just about the time the fugitives reached the middle of the river, and from that point they opened upon them with grape and cannister. They did not do much damage, only wounding three or four slightly. Part got across the river safely, the remainder, including the wounded, were taken prisoners by the Brady Guards, Captain Rowland, and under the immediate personal command of General Hugh Brady, who were on the steamer Erie, patrolling the river in the interest of the neutrality laws.

The march of the Guards from their armory to the steamer Erie, which was at her dock between Woodward Avenue and Griswold Street, waiting for their arrival, appeared to be somewhat perilous. Atwater Street in that vicinity, and indeed the entire river front, was filled with a howling mob who deeply sympathized with the Patriots. When the Brady Guards appeared, headed by Captain Rowland and General Brady, a howl of derision went up from the crowd; but General Brady, tall and as straight as a young poplar; Rowland, whose black eyes snapped ominously behind his gold-rimmed glasses, and the boys behind them, with their muskets, paid no more attention to the howlers than they would have done to a swarm of buzzing flies, but parted the crowd to the right and left, and boarded the steamer without molestation.

FAILINGS OF GENERAL SCHWARZ.

Another incident in regard to the Bradys that, until now, had lapsed from my memory, and of which I was an eye-witness. It has also to do with the late General T. E. Schwarz, quartermaster-general of the state. The general was intensely military, and donned his uniform on the slightest occasion. Although a fine, scholarly gentleman, and one of the old school, he was not much up in military matters, particularly parade duty and manual of arms. He did very well caring for the military property of the state, but when it came to other duties—the "shoulder arms" part —he was minus, although I do not think he was conscious of it. The instance I allude to in which he betrayed his lack of knowledge in this regard was a public inspection of the guard. When the Bradys were in their prime the general was requested by Captain Rowland to inspect the company in his official capacity. He signified his willingness to do so, and the Guards were occordingly drawn up in open order for inspection on the designated day on the east side of Woodward Avenue between Jefferson Avenue and Woodbridge Street. The general, in full uniform, passed up and down the ranks, minutely examining the men, accoutrements and muskets. I think there is a regulation way of handing a musket, by a private, to the inspecting officer and also a regulation way of returning it. Without heeding the rule, whatever it is, the general had nearly concluded his job without a miss, apparently, when he came to Sergeant George Doty, who was away up in the manual of arms. The latter handed him his musket for inspection. The general looked it over critically, proceeded to return it to George, but not "according to Gunter." The latter did not see it, so to speak, and the musket fell to the ground with a clang, causing much surprise. and suppressed merriment by the members of the company and the bystanders gathered to witness the parade. The general did not appear to notice the incident in the least and concluded his inspection and expressed himself as being highly pleased with the superb condition of the company. Doty used to enjoy relating this affair. FRIEND PALMER.

OLD EXPRESS DAYS.

REMINISCENCES OF THE TIME WHEN THE BUSINESS WAS IN ITS INFANCY.

NOTING by the papers, some months ago, that the American Express, the United States Express, and the Wells-Fargo Express Companies contemplate consolidating under one head with capital of $30,000,000, brings to my mind the early days of the express business, when its was in its swaddling clothes, and giving then but little evidence of growing to the giant it has now become. Perhaps my memories of those days may be of interest to some, and therefore they are here presented:

All know what a mighty business this express venture has grown to, and probably do not realize what a small and insignificant beginning it had. How much the people of this great country, and, indeed, the world, owe to its progenitors, they, perhaps, will never stop to consider. From its very start and inception the enterprise was a success, in a small way, and proceeded to fill a great and long felt want was, instantly, as it were, appreciated by all classes of the community. It fast became an absolute necessity, and it is now impossible for the business portion, at least, to get along without it.

Well, I was connected with this express business, in a moderate way, when it was first started in Buffalo, and was with the company for a few years afterwards. Early in January, 1842, I left Detroit for Buffalo, to fill, or try to fill a position in the book and stationery store of Wm. B. and C. E. Peck, on Main Street in that city. The Pecks were also agents for Pomeroy & Co.'s Express.

FROM CANADA TO BUFFALO.

The journey through Canada to Queenstown, was uneventful, except that it took six days to get through to that point, traveling by day and putting up nights at the comfortable taverns on the route, where wines and liquors were free, and the juicy round of beef was always in evidence. The only thing the stage passengers "kicked" at was the price of cigars, and that was four cents for the best Havanas, the price never having been but three cents on the American side for the best Principe Havana could produce. We could not see why they did it; they did not offer any explanation and we stood it.

From Lewiston, opposite Queenstown, a horse railroad took us to Niagara Falls, thence by steam railroads to Buffalo. Buffalo was quite bewildering to me, being so much larger than Detroit, 25,000 inhabitants. Detroit at that time had only ten or twelve thousand, I think. I was soon installed in my new position and, among the rest of my duties was the care and charge of this express business. Its small limit can be imagined, when I relate that I was easily able to take care of my part in running the book store and attending to the business of the express as well, no porter, no delivery wagon, etc.

The parties comprising the firm of Pomeroy & Co. were Geo. E. Pomeroy, Henry Wells, Crawford Livingston and Wm. A. Livingston. Mr. Pomeroy and W. A. Livingston had their headquarters in Albany, and Crawford Livingston in New York. The chief office was in Albany. Mr. Wells had his headquarters in Buffalo, and was almost always traveling on the railroad, between the former city and Albany, soliciting business and making the new enterprise known. He was a great factor in founding the express business and placing it on the firm and stable basis it now enjoys.

Of commanding presence, possessed of a most kind and genial manner, Mr. Wells was a most companionable man, full of joke and fun. He had a pronounced impediment in his speech, a stammer and a stutter combined, which in some might be considered a great affliction, but in him it seemed to lend piquancy to his jokes, stories and remarks of men and things. He had, as said before, a fine presence, and in addition, affected a peculiarity in dress. Ruffle shirt, always a blue broad cloth cloak in winter, with ample, flowing sleeves, and always a peculiar black silk velvet cap that fell over the left side of the head and ended with a gold tassel. He was sure of being the conspicuous, central figure wherever he happened to be, and if any one on the route wished to know anything in relation to the express business, if Mr. Wells was on the railroad train, most every one knew it, and could readily point him out. His personality was his greatest card, and did more to fasten his ideas of the express business, its benefits, etc., on the minds of the public than any other factor did, or could. He won and always had hosts and hosts of warm-hearted friends, and they, as a natural consequence, became the friends and patrons of his express company, an enterprise so novel and so new.

Mr. Crawford Livingston was the resident New York partner at, then, No. 2 Wall Street. I never came in contact with him except through correspondence. He was a fine business man and did much to promote the express business in New York, now the head center. He died early, but lived long enough to realize what his exertions in that direction would blossom into.

Mr. Wells performed twice the feat of bringing the president's message from Albany to Buffalo in advance of the mails, riding on the locomotive, the train composed of the latter and its tender only. He used to say in his inimitable way "the engineer just pulled the plug and let her rip."

TRIBUTE TO EXPRESS MESSENGERS.

Mr. Pomeroy was considered the "Great Mogul," or assumed to be, but in my opinion Henry Wells and Crawford Livingston were the two men who gave to the weak child a healthy, sturdy growth, which kept on increasing, and which it has today in a most marked manner.

To the express messengers is also due a large share of the success that came to the enterprise. They were hustlers, all of them, and untiring in the interest of the company. I call to mind the names and personalities of some of them who were considered the best, viz., Sam Lee, who always had what was termed the "Bank Run." To explain, most of the country banks and bankers kept their accounts with the Albany City Bank, and made their remittances weekly by this "Bank Run" and this Messenger Lee. Then there was Daniel Dunning, a pink of suavity and politeness, as also Schyler, Thad Pomeroy, Powell Hurd, Wheeler, and last and not by any means least, Wm. G. Fargo. The assumed duties of these messengers were something that the messengers of the present day do not feel called upon to perform, or are not, I presume, only in some isolated cases. These were executing messages, errands of all sorts, taking charge of ladies traveling from one point to another on the railroad without escort, seeing to their baggage, etc., taking charge of young children without their parents, and doing many other things for the public that they had long desired some one to step in and do. Thus they made themselves exceedingly popular, as well as the express company they so well and ably represented.

Messenger Dunning (before mentioned) was most polite and winning in manner, particularly to the fairer portion of creation; he gained their good-will, and I might say, admiration, both old and young, if they were journeying unattended between Albany and Buffalo, by his assiduous attentions to their wants.

NO PICNIC IN WINTER.

The journeys between the above points were something different from what they are now. Instead of four continuous tracks, there was only one (strap rail), and that was not continuous. Four or five different companies, I do not remember their names, operated their several roads and had their depots at the various termini. So it can be readily imagined that a woman, unattended and with or without baggage, would not have much of a picnic traveling in those days, particularly in winter. It was on such occasions that our friend Dunning 'got in his work," so to speak, and, as said before, gained their admiration, also their appreciative regard, besides advertising the merits of the express company, which then was in need of all the favorable publicity it could get.

I do not know, with but one exception, what ever became of these messengers that I have mentioned, but presume they continued with the company, and retired with honor. They seemed to drop out of the business in the ordinary course and never heard of afterwards, but with Wm. G. Fargo it was quite different. He entered the service of the company as messenger the fore part of the winter of 1842, at a salary of fifty dollars per month. He came originally from Pompey, Onondago County, New York, where he was born and to the employ of the express company, from the position of freight agent on the Auburn & Syracuse Railroad. "This employment" his biographer, Francis F. Fargo, truthfully says, "gave him the employment of his life," and he readily proceeded to take advantage of it. "It awakened conceptions of the possibilities in transportation facilities which he so grandly wrought out and carried to such completeness in later years.". Mr. Fargo says he was one of the original projectors of the express business of the Pomeroy and American Express. He was not, but he was of the Western Express, and says also "at the time William G. came on the road the rails were only laid to the east from Batavia, and packages were carried between the latter place and Buffalo by stage coach." Not so. The rails were there, all right, from Buffalo to Batavia and Rochester, January, 1842. He also says "W. G. was appointed agent for Pomeroy & Co. at Buffalo." Not so, he was never agent for that company at Buffalo. Not but that he would have been competent enough to fill the bill, but he had other "fish to fry," and little did he or anyone connected with the express business at that time, dream that he would die as early as he did, a broken down old man at 63, but worth, it was said, $20,000,000. In addition to this he had been mayor of Buffalo twice, during the civil war. He was a war Democrat, and in 1868, was candidate for governor of New York, but failed to get the nomination. Don't think he cared much for it.

PECK'S BOOKSTORE.

Peck's bookstore was located on Main Street, Buffalo, north side, in the block between Swan and Seneca Streets, and was, as all bookstores were in those days, headquarters for book lovers, literary and business men, those scientifically inclined—a place where the society gossip and the affairs of the day of every phase were discussed and commented upon. The express venture, so new an innovation and a novel but much needed enterprise, claimed and had its full share of commendation and ardent wishes for its success. The winter of 1842 will be remembered by old railroad and express men as one of unusual rigor. The railroad between Buffalo and Albany was ironed with the strap rail, and where any deep cuts occurred, or any cuts at all, the flurry of snow would put a quietus on railroad travel until the cause could be got rid of by gangs of men armed with shovels. Snow plows were not in evidence in those days.

ALWAYS ON DUTY.

The express company was put to its trumps to maintain a daily express between New York and Buffalo during that winter, but did it in spite of cold and snow. When the railroad was tied up or snowed under the company had to resort to the stage coaches, and thus it was through snow, or rain or shine, the express messenger was on hand daily to meet the wants of the community, and the people soon learned to appreciate its benefits and rely on its service, more especially banks and bankers. It soon came to be a necessity, same as the daily mail, the daily paper, etc. I have seen the snow on a level with the tops of the fences, yet there was the express messenger.

The expense and difficulties attending the enterprise at this early day seemed to be insurmountable, but the American pluck and energy of the people composing the company pushed aside all obstacles, and their hold on the country at large was assured.

The express people realized they were building for a far future, and at the present time, though they of that day have gone to the other shore, the small structure they then erected, and the enterprise they inaugurated, has grown, as all know, to gigantic proportions and has "girdled the globe." The express company had the confidence of the people from the very beginning, so much so that banks and bankers, in fact all, intrusted their business to them, giving into their care vast sums and packages of valuables for transmission, without even the formality of a receipt for the same, and neither the company nor the public at that time demanded or required a receipt for money or valuables.

To illustrate some of the difficulties encountered during that winter of 1842. Three or four times I was called upon to make a messenger's run to Rochester, as from that point east the railroads managed to make reasonable time, but between Buffalo and Rochester the snow kept up an almost continuous blockade, necessitating the services of additional messengers between these points. Communication was kept up by the stage company by means of coaches on runners. During these trips it was a common occurrence to experience two or three tip-ups in the snow going, and about the same number returning. On one of my trips to Rochester, the stage was crowded with passengers. I had in my custody a valise containing money packages, value not known, besides six boxes of silver coin, the latter stowed away in the bottom of the stage. While we were, or the horses were, floundering through the snow, which filled the air and everything with a blinding blizzard, the team came up against a huge snow bank, and in trying to wallaw through it, over we went completely. The sudden shock

threw us all in a heap, and the six boxes of coin, weighing about seventy pounds each, went bang through the stage window, and into three or four feet of snow. We managed after a little delay and much trouble to right the coach and rescue the six boxes of specie from the snow, and went on our way rejoicing, none the worse for our rough experience in the snow, and arrived at the end of our journey in time for an enjoyable dinner, which was made the most of.

Rochester at that date called itself quite a city, crediting itself with 25,000 inhabitants, 5,000 more than Buffalo, I think. My impression of Rochester, that wild, first stormy night, will ever remain with me. One peculiar feature was this: I noticed that Buffalo did not have, though she needed them badly, night watchmen, who, clad in their long cloaks and leather headgear, with lantern and club, guarded the streets and slumbers of the people and cried the hours, "Two o'clock, and all's well."

My return trip with the express was quite as stormy. The snow was on a level with the tops of the fences, and the stage tipped over several times between Rochester and Buffalo, as I said before. The railroad did not resume operations for many days. The messengers had a hard, weary time that winter. They never came into Buffalo without long accounts of their hardships, and angry complaints against the various railroad superintendents between Albany and Buffalo, and more particularly against Mr. J. W. Brooks, late superintendent of the Michigan Central railroad, and Mr. Higham. They alleged that Brooks and Higham arbitrarily restricted them to much less than their quota of freight and extra baggage, when all the cities between Albany and Buffalo were clamoring for the extras that the express had afforded them, the which they had never had before so promptly; they kicked because they were now and then deprived of them. They were beginning to realize what a wonderful benefit the advent of the express company was to the country and community.

FIRST WESTERN EXPRESS.

Early in the spring of 1842 Mr. Charles Miller, a German, and a retired oil merchant of Buffalo, started the first western express. He had his headquarters with the Pecks, and designed running the business in connection with Pomeroy & Co. He made two or three preliminary trips to Chicago, as did his one messenger (Bradley). After looking the ground over pretty thoroughly, as he thought, he concluded the task was too heavy and gave up the venture. There were at that time no railroads between the west and Buffalo. Communication was had in summer by water and in winter by stage.

Some time during the summer of 1842 the Pecks changed their location for a more central one further down Main Street, on the same side, to Brown's building, midway between Seneca and Exchange Streets, and with them went the express company. By this time the business of the company had increased to that extent that it became necessary to hire a porter and equip him with a horse and wagon. The clerical force was not increased, Mr. Henry Wells giving his almost undivided attention to the business when in the city, and it also necessitated my sleeping at the store, which I had not done before, as the express messenger came in at midnight and I had to be on hand to receive him and take charge of the money packages, etc. For fear something might happen when the messenger and porter routed me out, the company provided me with a revolver, a six-shooter, the same as the messengers carried, a clumsy affair, though I never had occasion to use it.

The railroad depot at that time was located on the outskirts of the city, away out on Exchange street, and the messenger and porter had a trying time in bad weather getting their express matter into the city and to the office.

LUXURIES EASILY OBTAINED.

Shortly after removing to the new location the company entered into an arrangement with Hagerman & Cowell, fruit and sea food dealers, of Albany, to supply them daily with oranges, lemons, pineapples, etc., when in season; also fresh oysters, lobsters, hard and soft shell crabs. This was a great and unheard-of accommodation to good livers, all along the line from Albany to Buffalo, and, indeed, to all who could afford to indulge in such luxuries. The people used to say, "Just think of it, oranges and lemons in midwinter, and fresh oysters and sea food, and all you want if you pay the price," and the latter was not heavy. It became possible for the wealthy citizen to have all these hitherto unobtainable luxuries at his winter entertainments. I am reminded of a retired Buffalo capitalist, a Mr. Coe, living on Niagara Street, who gave three entertainments at that time, one week apart, on the nights of Thursday. He ordered 1,500 fresh oysters in kegs for each function. It was the talk of the town for quite a while.

Occasionally during the season of 1843 a messenger was sent west in charge of packages, etc., that had accumulated from time to time, for points beyond Buffalo. A young man by the name of B. B. Cornwell was employed in that capacity, the first express messenger, except Mr. Bradley, of Miller & Co., that was ever sent west. The principal agents west were Mr. C. Younglove, bookseller, Cleveland; B. L. Webb, forwarding merchant, Detroit, and S. F. Gale & Co., booksellers, Chicago.

The business kept on increasing to that extent that the company were forced to abandon their agency with the Pecks, and seek quarters for themselves alone. They selected offices in the Mansion house, then kept by Philip Dorsheimer, on the Exchange Street side, and moved in early in the fall of 1843.

SUCCESSFUL FROM THE START.

As said before, about this time was organized the Western Express, under the name of Wells & Co., and it was a success from the start. The company had but one regular messenger, Mr. Nichols (Cornwell having resigned.) They selected a number of steamboat clerks, who acted in that capacity in addition to their other duties, so they managed to fill the bill quite well. Some time during the winter of 1844, Mr. Dunning came to Detroit, as resident partner, and established his office with C. Morse & Son, booksellers. In 1845 Mr. Dunning withdrew from the partnership, and a year later Mr. Wells sold his interest fo William A. Livingston, of Albany, and the firm name was changed to Livingston & Fargo. "Mr. Livingston took charge of the Buffalo business and Mr. Fargo removed to Detroit, where he remained a year and returned to Buffalo."

No messengers went west of Detroit, either by boat or rail, until after 1845. Business did not warrant it. The Michigan Central railroad was finished to Marshall only at that time, at which point the express company established an agency, with Mr. Kimball as agent. Communication between the latter point and Chicago was by stage. Money packages destined for the east from Milwaukee, Racine, Kenosha and so on found their way by private hands to the Chicago agency.

MADE RAPID STRIDES.

In October, 1894, I had a communication from Mr. Charles Fargo, second vice-president of the American Express Company, Chicago, which I copy, and which will show what giant strides the express business made west of Buffalo, from 1844 up to the above date. He said: "We have in the western department (which means all the lines of the American Express Company west of Buffalo) 6,136 men employed in the forwarding, receiving and delivery of express packages at offices. In addition we have 807 men employed as messengers on trains, steamboats and stage lines. We use in handling our business in this department 1,223 horses. We have, arriving and leaving Chicago every day, from all points, seventy-four messengers bringing in from one package each up to seven or eight carloads of express matter. In addition to this we have established at convenient locations in all cities in the west agents for the sale and payment of our money orders. They do not handle express packages of any kind, simply being what we call branch money order agents, where patrons can at all times and conveniently purchase money orders. In many large cities a large portion of the gas bills each month are paid by means of these orders. In the city of Chicago alone we have 250 of such branch agencies, and in the west nearly 1,500."

At that time (1845), as before mentioned, the Buffalo agency could boast of but two clerks, one porter and one delivery wagon, while at Cleveland, Detroit and Chicago there were none at all. Verily, the projectors of this express business "built better than they knew."

When the company had got well into their new quarters on Exhange Street, Buffalo, their legitimate business had increased to the extent that they abandoned the oyster and fruit business.

Mr. Dunning, when he came west, was the first regular messenger of Wells & Co. He left Buffalo for Detroit in January, 1844, with quite a large consignment of goods, money, etc., and a few valuable packages for Chicago. He had a large Pennsylvania wagon that looked like a schooner on wheels, with a driver and four horses. Thus equipped, he made the journey in about seven days, I think. He said he had a prety rough time. After that the express left Buffalo weekly. The messengers were Parks, Emerson and Geer (Kye Geer.) When navigation opened these same messengers continued, but to Detroit only, I do not know when messenger service was established between Detroit and points west, as I left the service in the fall of 1845.

I had a little fun with this Western Express messenger business myself three or four times. The first trip was March 10, 1845, out of Buffalo on the steamboat United States, Captain Whitaker. We were two days and two nights in the ice in sight of Buffalo light before we got into clear water.

The Hemingways, of Buffalo, owned and operated the line of stages between the latter point and Detroit, through Canada, and they had their stage office with the express company on Exchange Street. The stages arrived and departed from this point, so it was quite the thing to get newspapers and small packages to the Detroit office ahead of the mails through the courtesy and kindness of the stage drivers.

Pomeroy & Co. had some little opposition after they got fairly on their feet. A firm by the name of Pullen & Copp, seeing what a good thing it promised to be, thought they would join in. They did start in, but they soon found that the "longest pole was bound to knock the persimmons." Pomeroy & Co. appearing to have it, they soon backed out. Adams, of Adams & Co.'s Boston and New York Express, occasionally came to Buffalo, with a lonesome carpet bag in his hand, presumably to look the land over. He soon quit, however.

The excessive postage on letters charged by the United States had been for many years a matter of complaint among all classes. The express companies determined to "beard the lion in his den," and advertised to carry single letters to and from all points where they had their offices established, for ten cents each, which included delivery. They had stamps printed and gummed. The stamps were from a wood-cut and oval in form. The design on them I forget. Anyway, the innovation took with the public, and the company was rushed with business. But it did not continue long. Uncle Sam got his "dander up," pitched into the company, served an injunction and got a decision from the United States Supreme Court that knocked the express company out of the letter-carrying business. In the meantime about two bushels of letters had accumulated in the Buffalo office. These the company turned over to the postmaster at Buffalo to forward to their destination. Those to them they were directed had to fork over the amount of Uncle Sam's charge for postage. What the outcome of the matter was I never knew. It, however, paved the way to the adoption of cheap postage.

STIMULATED BUSINESS.

The express company was the means of stimulating the newspaper and periodical business, and to it, in a large measure, is due the credit of affording them facilities that have enabled them to achieve the enormous business and circulation they now enjoy. The same can be said of the book trade. I well remember what an experience it was in Buffalo to get the New York dailies the next day after publication. Two rival newsdealers, Hawks at the postoffice, and Burke in the Mansion house in that city, received all the New. York and Albany papers and all the magazines then published, which were only two or three, if my memory serves me. How rapidly they have grown since, under the distributing facilities afforded them, all know.

The express company was also a great factor in the fish, oyster and fruit trade, placing the great public out of New York almost on an equal footing. It was also a great factor in the millinery, jewelry and fancy goods trade at that time. The small and pressing wants of dealers in these lines could be readily supplied. I call to mind, aside from quite a number in Buffalo, a firm in Detroit, Freedman & Goodkind, in the millinery and fancy goods trade. The first express that went west from Buffalo in the winter of 1844, and every one thereafter, carried for that firm a large bale of millinery goods, dress trimmings, etc. The express charges were excessive, necessarily, but the house glady paid them in view of the increased custom the early receipt of the goods gave them —an innovation Detroit people had not been used to. Freedman, one of the firm, from the small store on Jefferson Avenue, branched out into one of larger dimensions on Woodward Avenue, and was for quite a period the proprietor of the largest dry goods house in Detroit, or in Michigan—Freedman Brothers.

The express company also at that time did a large business buying foreign silver coin, German thalers, Spanish milled dollars, etc.

TRANSPORTATION VIA THE CANAL.

The company (Pomeroy & Co.) sent a messenger weekly by canal packet boat during the season of navigation to Buffalo to Lockport and Rochester and return. Lockport at that time had no communication by rail with the outside world. This was a very enjoyable trip, though a little slow, but it gave one ample time to enjoy the beauties of the country through which the canal passed, and also ample time and opportunity to study that odd specimen of humanity, the "canal driver," and also to experience the pleasurable sensation of passing through the canal locks at Lockport.

The packet boats (the "Old Red Bird Line") on the canal between Buffalo, Lockport and Rochester at that time (1843) were new and acknowledged to be the finest and fastest packets that ever floated on the canal. Their names were the Empire and Rochester. They were 110 feet long by 12 feet wide, and elegantly fitted up with saloons, wash rooms, etc. The Empire was commanded by Captain D. H. Bromley ("Dan Bromley") and the Rochester by Captain J. H. Holmes, both princes of Captains, as many old Buffalonians and others, perhaps, will remember. The fare was $2, meals extra, and they were fine. The boats left from the Commercial Street bridge daily, and their departure was almost as much an event as that of an upper lake steamer; indeed, quite so.

There are so many more people in the world now and so many travel for pleasure only, and to while away the time, perhaps travel by canal may be revived, as pleasure travel is now revived between Detroit and Buffalo by two magnificent steamers, forming a daily line. What a contrast between them and those of the early days!

As said before, the company had not been in the habit of giving or taking receipts for packages; their customers did not demand it, neither did they. This custom of mutual confidence continued for two or three years, until the company got a rude awakening. In the early spring of 1844 Richard Mott, of Toledo, delivered to the express messenger, as he supposed, a package of money, said to contain $3,000. The package never reached its destination. A fuss was made about it, of course. I was sent to Toledo to see about it. I saw Mr. Mott, and he said he had occasion to make a remittance to Buffalo of the amount stated, and arriving at the Indiana House, in that city, just as the stage was leaving, he inquired at the stage window if the express messenger was inside. Some one answered, "Yes." He handed the package over, and that was the last of it. I made inquiries in regard to Mr. Mott's standing and veracity, and satisfied myself that he was all right, and so reported to the company, and they paid the $3,000 without any further talk. A few months after this Pomeroy & Co.'s express messenger, Powell, was robbed of his money trunk at the Syracuse House in that city, kept by Phile Rust. The trunk was said to contain $7,000. I don't think the money was ever recovered, or the thief found; anyway, the company paid the loss, and ever after the receipt business, to and from, was in vogue and rigidly adhered to, as all know. These two happenings served to strengthen still more the confidence of the public in the company.

A TRIP ALONG SHORE AS EXPRESS MESSENGER.

It is amusing, in the ligt of the present, to call to mind a trip (one of many) along shore from Buffalo to Detroit in charge of the express, say on the steamboat New England, for instance, in 1844. She was very slow, light of draft, and her captain boasted that she could run anywhere. She used to touch at Dunkirk, Erie, Ashtabula, Conneaut, Painesville, Milan, Vermillion, Cleveland, Toledo, Monroe, and so on. These were all small places at that time, and the only towns that made anything of a show were Cleveland and Toledo. The former boasted of two lighthouses, as it does now, one at the mouth of the river, the other on the high bluff overlooking the lake. There were three or four warehouses near the lighthouse at the mouth of the river, but not another structure of any description on what was then called the "Flats." There were quite a number of good business houses, besides a fine hotel, the Weddell House. There was a town across the river, Ohio City, I think it was, connected with Cleveland by a bridge. Toledo at that time was the most forlorn, uninviting looking place that it is possible to imagine. The authorities had been cutting down the bank of the river Maumee, where is now Summit Street, and filling in along its front for dock purposes.

There was not a structure of any kind on Summit Street until you got down the street some distance, and that, I think, was the residence of Richard Mott. There were warehouses on this front (two only, I think), newly erected, not very pretentious, and occupied, one by Alonzo Goddard, the other by King Bros. But the Toledo people said, notwithstanding the apparently gloomy outlook, there was a "silver lining to the cloud," and that was the Wabash canal, which had just then been completed to their city. All know what that canal has done for Toledo, and what its citizens have done for themselves. There was only one hotel at Toledo at that time of any pretensions, and that one was the Toledo House, a two-story brick building, on the corner of Perry and Summit Streets. It was afterwards added to and renamed the Indiana House.

Monroe was more of a shipping point then than now. The steamboat ran up the short canal from the lake to the dock (which I think was about two miles from the city), where were several quite pretentious warehouses. Considerable shipping was done at this point, and for many years after, but I think now it has almost entirely ceased.

There were no other points between Monroe and Detroit, except, perhaps, Brest and Gibraltar, but they were of no account. The trip was rather enjoyable than otherwise, when the weather was fair, and it took some three or four days to accomplish it.

Of the large number of people, except in a clerical way, connected with the express companies (Pomeroy and American) at the times I mention, only one, I think, is alive and still remains "in harness," and he is the present efficient president of the American Express Co., James C. Fargo. His brother, W. G. Fargo, secured him a place in the Buffalo office on Exchange Street, in 1843 or 1844, a country lad fresh from the farm. He has passed along up from office boy, through a period of over 50 years, to the head of the largest business of the kind in the world. His brother Charles came into the business later, and was a good second. He died in Chicago a short time ago, vice-president, I think, of the same company. Nothing further need be said, I think, in regard to the Fargos that I have mentioned, and their connection with the express business, except this, their record speaks for itself now and always. In this connection Fra Elbertus, the "high daddy" of the Roycrofters, East Aurora, N. Y., says in the *Philistine:*

"There is no such thing as a science of education, any more than there is a science of medicine. Both are systems of experiment and guesswork. Some of the very strongest and most influential men who have ever lived were men who had no "advantages." Almost without exception, the men who have built up and who managed our great railroad were untaught country boys. Many of the strong men in all our great cities—the men at the heads of the factories, great enterprises and banks—were boys who never had college advantages."

HENRY WELLS.

I do not call to mind the date of the death of Henry Wells. He, too, departed this life a millionaire, I think. At any rate, he established a young ladies' seminary at Aurora, in New York state, or some point near Buffalo, and endowed it liberally. He, too, was on "his uppers" when he took hold of the express business. He was at one time, I was told, captain of a canal packet or passenger boat. He was also at one time employed as a runner for steamboats plying between New York and Albany on the Hudson River.

An article that appeared in the *New York Sunday Sun*, of recent date, in relation to pioneer steamboat days, on the Hudson, has this to say of him in that regard:

"The rivalry between the steamboats brought into existence an army of persistent and strenuous runners. Not a few of them rose in after years to distinction and wealth as railroad men and in other lines of transportation, as well as in politics. I remember one who operated on the New York docks. We used to call him stuttering Wells, on account of an impediment in his speech. Wells was a hustler in his line, but not much of a fighter. One day in a hand-to-hand contest over a passenger, a runner for an opposition boat knocked him down. Wells got up, pondered a moment as he saw his opponent bearing the passenger away in triumph, shook his head and walked away. He did not come back to steamboat running any more, but took to carrying parcels, packages, letters and the like to their destinations. He built up such a business in that line that he founded an express company. That company made him a millionaire and bears his name today as the "Wells-Fargo Express Company." So that knock-down argument of an opposition runner on the steamboat dock that day was rather a good thing for Stuttering Wells."

He often used to tell of his selling tickets on the curb in front of the Park Theatre in New York, and also of opening a school to cure stammering, although a confirmed stammerer himself. He said he was quite successful in the latter vocation. But how he effected a cure on his patrons he did not divulge.

ORIGINATED THE C. O. D.

Although my services with the express company lasted only for a brief period, about three years, yet I was in almost at its beginning, and claim to have "billed" the first goods that ever went west by express from Buffalo. Not much of a job, to be sure, and one that some one else would and could have performed, if I had not. Yet it is something to tell, seeing that after all these years, I am alive to tell it. I also claim to have originated the initials "C. O. D." that are often seen on express packages in place of "Collect on Delivery." If any one living is disposed to dispute these two propositions, let him "rise up and speak."

The principal points between Buffalo and Albany were Rochester, Canandaigua, Syracuse, Auburn, Geneva and Utica. Canandaigua was at one time head center of the stage lines in the state of New York, the home of some of the most prominent and wealthiest men in the state. Also the head and front of the Masonic Fraternity, where it was said the taking of Morgan was concocted. Anyway, in regard to this latter, two of its prominent citizens and Masons were imprisoned in the county jail at Canandaigua, on suspicion of being engaged in the affair. Their names were Cheesebro and Sawyer.

I may be pardoned for getting off of the express track, as it were, and dwelling over much on Canandaigua, but the fact is, it was my birthplace, and also the home of the first clerk the Pomeroy & Co. express employed after their move into their new quarters on Exchange Street. And all old expressmen will remember "Bill" Blossom, I am sure. He was a nephew of that prince of landlords, Col. Blossom, the proprietor of "Blossom's Hotel," known so well the country through.

Geo. Bemis, son of Mr. J. D. Bemis, bookseller, was the efficient agent at this point, assisted by a young man by the name of Shepard. All these were factors in favor of the express company. (except Morgan, perhaps). Canandaigua also, was one of the places Lafayette deigned to honor with his presence, when he visited this country in 1824. He was dined and wined by the citizens at Blossom's Hotel.

Rochester was another prominent and important point, more so, I think than any other between Albany and Buffalo, (more so than the latter.) D. Hoyt, the principal bookseller in the place, was the agent and had two efficient assistants, Starr Hoyt, his nephew, and Henry Hastings, two popular young men in Rochester, as many will remember. These young men were untiring in their efforts to serve the interests of the express company in season and out of season. The other points on the route were of importance, of course, but these I have mentioned, with the exception, perhaps, of Syracuse, were the most talked of and most heard from.

Erastus Corning, head of the Albany City Bank, also chief of the great hardware house of Erastus Corning & Co., was a great friend and patron of the company, as also was Dean Richmond. In fact all men of prominence along the line from Albany to Buffalo lent their aid and gave their good words for the success of this new venture.

When the ice went out of Buffalo Creek, in the spring, it was a sure sign, and noted as such, then that the Hudson River was open, from Albany to New York; a gratifying event to the express company, as during the closing of the Hudson, the only communication between Albany and New York was by the Housatonic Railroad, and that was very unsatisfactory and uncertain. They used to call it "The Ram's Horn."

The founder of the express business in the Unied States was William F. Harnden, who commenced the transportation of bundles and parcels between Boston and New York March 4, 1839. A year later (1840) a competing express was started by P. B. Burke and Alvin Adams, the sole ownership and management of which soon passed into the hands of the latter. In 1841 Mr. Adams associated with himself as partner William B. Dinsmore, of New York, and placed him in charge of the New York office. Following this enterprise were the companies started by Gay & Kinsley and Pomeroy & Co., and the Wells & Fargo. Mr. Harnden died in 1848.

Contrasting the business of the express companies the present, in Michigan only, with that of 1842, 1843 and 1844, I copy an article that appeared in one of the daily papers in Detroit.

"The American Express Company paid its annual taxes in March, 1902, and in its report to the auditor-general stated that it had 555 agencies, and the National Express, which is under its control, in Michigan, 88. The number of miles under which the former does business in the state is 4,191, and the latter 780.

Receipts for 1901:

American in Michigan were.................... $370,825 81
National in Michigan were..................... 76,672 63

Total $447,498 44

In closing this article all I have to say is: All the express people had to do in the early days, and since, was to get in ahead on every new route that was opened and to take care of the business that came to them. Once firmly seated in the saddle they could not be easily unhorsed, nor were they.

OLD HOTELS OF DETROIT.

REMINISCENCES OF THE HOSTELRIES OF EARLY DAYS, THEIR PROPRIETORS AND THEIR GUESTS.

WOODWORTH'S STEAMBOAT HOUSE.

WOODWORTH'S HOTEL was in the early days the center of almost everything, all the stage lines started from there and nearly everyone of any note put up at this hostelry. "Uncle Ben's" was as well known as any house of its kind in all the northwest. Here were held many of the festivities and functions of importance, military or otherwise.

I remember one occasion, a ball held directly after the conclusion of the Patriot War and Washington's birthday. It was a brilliant affair. All the British officers stationed at Malden and Sandwich were invited and attended in full uniform, which was quite elaborate with hussar jacket, dependent from one shoulder, with side arms, saberstache, aigulettes, scarlet bobtailed coats, knee breeches, silk stockings, etc. This was the same kind of uniform it was said, that the British officers wore at Waterloo, minus the silk stockings and knee breeches. The originators of the ball anticipated a rumpus at the ferry dock, foot of Woodward Avenue, on the arrival of the guests, on account of the ill-feeling entertained by our people on the border, engendered in consequence of the then recent patriot disturbance. A large crowd did gather at the ferry landing, but happily nothing unpleasant occurred. Another rather interesting event happened there, an auction for the benefit of the Free School Society which was running a free infant school, in a building which had been part of old Fort Shelby, which building stood on the line of Cass farm. The auction was held in the dining room of the hotel and the articles to be disposed of were, fancy goods, needle work, etc. Colonel Edward Brooks, a humorous and witty man, was the auctioneer. One of the articles put up was a roasted turkey, donated by Oliver Newberry, for which Landlord John R. Kellogg, of the National

Hotel (now the Russell House), and Landlord Wales, of the Michigan Exchange, bid against each other until it was finally knocked down to Kellogg for $200. My eye came across another version of this auction sale and I give it below:

"After the sale, Mr. Lillibridge, of the Tontine restaurant, in the old council house, nearby, had a turkey waiting for a purchaser. It was proposed that this turkey be obtained and sold for the benefit of the society. Mr. Kellogg and Mr. Wales went for the turkey, and it was proposed that the two draw lots for it and give it to the ladies. Thereupon Lillibridge declined to sell, but shouldered the turkey, brought it to the sale and donated it to the ladies, and it was sold over and over again and finally knocked off for $200."

I was present at this auction and I think the first version is the correct one. I know Mr. Newberry presented a turkey. Various articles brought large prices. For instance, a doll made of raisins excited such competition that it was finally knocked down at seventy-five or a hundred dollars. The successful bidder, I think, was Oliver Newberry. People had some money to burn, even in those early days of Detroit. The fair netted $1,656.

"Uncle Ben" retired from the hotel business after awhile, and settled on his farm, near St. Clair City. Milton Barney succeeded him in the keeping of this house. But its glory had departed. Barney continued it for a while, until the fire of 1848 swept it away.

IN THE FLOWER OF HER YOUTH.

Mr. Barney had a beautiful daughter, Caroline. She was highly accomplished and all that, and the father set great store by her. She did not happen at that time to be in the social swim, but soon attracting the attention of some of the young men of Detroit's society, they chose to introduce her into their set if she so desired. She was not adverse to the idea and the opportunity soon came. The "boys," as they termed themselves, had formed a dancing club (this in the winter), and met once in every two weeks at their homes, each gentleman inviting his own lady. Miss Barney was invited and was escorted, in the first instance, by the gentleman giving the party. She was well received, and ever afterwards did not lack for "invites" and a welcome from all. But during the early summer following death came to her in the shape of malignant erysipelas. She was widely mourned, and her funeral was largely attended.

THE WOODWORTH FAMILY.

Uncle Ben Woodworth had two sons and two daughters. One was drowned at the foot of Randolph Street in 1829. One of the daughters was married about 1830, to whom I have forgotten; the other daughter, Ann, was married to Mr. Simon Brown, who afterwards became colonel of a Michigan cavalry regiment in the civil war, and attained the rank of brevet brigadier-general. The other son, Samuel, must be remembered by many. He was his father's right-hand man. Prompt and energetic, he was always "on deck." After quitting the hotel business he purchased and became captain of the steamer Vance and was blown up on her shortly afterward while the steamer was lying at her dock in Windsor.

Ann Woodworth was a sprightly, quick-witted, black-eyed lady and was the boss in the kitchen and upstairs as well.

Following were the lines of stages running from Woodworth's Steamboat hotel in 1832, daily:

Sandusky line, passing through Monroe and Maumee; St. Joseph line, passing through Ypsilanti, Saline, Clinton, Tecumseh, Jonesville, Mottville, White Pigeon and Niles; Ann Arbor line, passing through Pekin, Plymouth and Panama; Pontiac line, passing through Rochester, Stony Creek and Romeo; also a line to Mt. Clemens, three times a week, Ypsilanti daily, in the morning and sometimes an extra at 12 o'clock, noon.

AN INTERESTING PICTURE.

I copy an article written in 1877, in regard to Sam Woodworth, and the hotel, by the late Geo. C. Bates. The latter was a citizen of Detroit in 1835 and later.

"Come a little closer to the front (Steamboat hotel) and there you see that same old omnibus having on its white panels over the door in great gilt letters, "Woodworth's Steamboat Hotel," and standing, aiding passengers to alight, is a stout red-haired, blue-eyed, very polite young man, about 28 years of age, whose green frock-coat is buttoned very tightly about his person, his dazzling-striped pantaloons fitting very closely, while a black string and broad rolling shirt collar gave the Byronic appearance to Sam Woodworth, the son of its proprietor—the major domo, the man-of-all-work, who accompanied the omnibus to all steamers, whose politeness, affability and knowledge of all men and things, made him a very different hotel clerk from the diamond-studded clerk of modern days. Everyone, man or woman, who ever entered 'Uncle Bens,' as the Woodworth's hotel was called for short, will remember Sam's suavity of manner, his graceful, smiling politeness, smacking a little of Sam Weller's, but still, a kind-hearted, truly polite, and quite well-educated son of a brave old father, who, after serving in the capacity of general manager of Woodworth's hotel, for years, became possessed of the vaulting ambition to step up the ladder, and become the master of a steamboat, to stand, like old Commodore Blake, on the pilothouse, pull this bell, that, and shout in loud tones, 'Avast, there!' 'Port, sir!' 'Port sir!' and, who having purchased a very small steamer called the General Vance, commenced his regular trips to Truax's (Trenton) and Newport, down the river and back, all in a single day, touching at Windsor, Sandwich, Springwells, Ecorse and all the intermediate points, 'wind and weather permitting,' until one day, when lying at the Windsor dock, the teakettle engine of poor Sam exploded, and the last ever seen of him was when he was observed with outstretched arms and widespread limbs going up higher than a kite, where many of the old sailors on the steamers of those days followed him.

"The steamer was split up into matches, and what was left of poor Sam was followed to the old cemetery—Sexton Noble and his pipe managing the hearse—by all the old habitues of that inn, and no man ever deserved more justly the tears that were shed over his remains than he did."

RARE CHARACTERS.

Mr. Bates also speaks about Uncle Ben Woodworth in this wise: "But come, let us enter this hospitable old home and first pay our respects to Uncle Ben, a broad-shouldered, gray-eyed man, then nearly 60 years of age, with very firm lips, mild in his outward seemings, but when enraged a perfect old volcano, whose increasing pallor, and deepening of the wrinkles on his face, told of the higher barometer of passion within; a great-handed, strong, old-fashioned Yankee, whose heart was as open as the day, and whose industry and cordiality made his home the headquarters of all the steamboat men, and pioneers of the Straits."

Mr. Bates also mentions a noted character of those days, William Clay, and says this of him: "Having shaken hands with 'Uncle Ben,' we pass into the barber shop, and, behold, here is William Clay, the learned tonsorial artist, the cultivated, educated barber from England, a man sui generis, who could cut your hair in the very latest fashion, and chop logic with you ad interim; who would give you a superb shave and simultaneously discourse on the Greek roots; who would furnish an elegant shampoo and all the while interesting you by quotations from Socrates, Longinus, Thomas Aquinas; who would give you the catalogue of his private library—where the very finest editions of the Greek, Latin and English classics could be found; a man who would make you a wig and at the same time weave you a web of philosophy, of metaphysics and religion that would carry you to your grave; a learned, scholarly, thoroughly educated barber, who only went to rest these last few months (about 1875) and who was indeed a marvel of the bygones of Detroit. 'When shall we look upon his like again?'—a scholarly barber; a logical wigmaker; a classical hairdresser; a most learned shampooer; a tonsorial artist, and expounder of Greek philisophy, all combined; a marvelous conjunction of the vulgar art of living, with the aesthetics of the academy, the homely drudgery of everyday life, united with the beautiful teachings of Plato, Socrates and Cicero on the banks of the Ilyssus."

Mr. Bates goes on to say further of the Steamboat Hotel:

A QUAINT HOTEL.

"But let us look the Woodworth Hotel over—it will take but a moment. Observe it is only two stories over the basement; it is plain in construction and model. On entering from the street you find the stage office, the bar, wherein those days one could get a glass of pure Monongahela whisky, old Jamaica rum, brandy imported from Quebec, that had no adulterant in it—bygones now giving place only to liquid hell fire, composed of all sorts of ingredients. Then came a large sitting room; then a large dining room, all neatly and simply furnished, but all most comfortable. In the next flight of stairs was the ladies' parlor, a very large room, which we used to occupy for Whig meetings; several large double rooms, where you would find not infrequently at least eight members of the legislative council, all living and sleeping there. The carpets were not velvet nor Royal Wilton, but three-ply, softened by heavy linings of hay, which gave rather frowzy odor to the room., The furniture was very substantial, not wahogany; the forks were steel, not silver, and the knives had bone instead of ivory handles; but every room and bed in that hotel was full, year in and year out.

"In February of each year, after the session of the Supreme Court of the territory, around that table were wont to congregate the members of the bar; and the annual bar dinner was given when Judge Woodbridge, that witty old gentleman at the head of the table, was flanked by Chief Justice Sibley and Justice Morrell. At the foot sat Harry Cole, with Ross Wilkins on his right, and midway between the two was General Charles Larned, one of the most elegant, dashing and princely of all that bar, having on either hand George McDougall, the father of the bar, and Charles Cleland, his poet, editor, toastmaster; while on the other side sat Augustus S. Porter pulling his nose in nervous enjoyment of the wine and wit, when every member was condemned to give a toast, tell a story, make a speech, sing a song or drink a glass of salt and water, and when Cleland's last toast was always to old McDougall, a legal Falstaff, redivius, the quondam father of the bar, then lighthousekeeper at Fort Gratiot, and which was drunk standing, somewhat in these words:

"'Brethren of the Bar: We drink now to the Nestor of our bar, George McDougall, who, in early life, shed the light and brilliancy of his genius over our profession in beautiful Michigan, but who now, in his old age, illuminates the dark waters of Lake Huron with his magic lantern, and so guides the tempest-tossed mariner safely through storms and dangers of the lake down to the silvery streams of St. Clair.'

"At which three cheers were given, heel taps all around, and then, after a valedictory from Judge Hand, the bar went back into chancery."

THE MANSION HOUSE.

Melvin Dorr, city auctioneer, occupied the first house this side of the Cass residence, and on the line of the farm. The next was the Mansion House, about where Cass Avenue crosses Jefferson now. This and Uncle Ben Woodworth's Steamboat Hotel were the only hotels of any consequence in the city then. This Mansion House was built and owned by Judge Woodward and was built in 1824 of the brick and stone taken from the ruins of old Fort Shelby when it was demolished. It was not very large (three or four stories, I think), and, with the out-building, extended back to what is now Larned Street. It had a high, open porch that occupied its entire front, supported by large wooden pillars. Across the street from it was a large summer house, built apparently for the pleasure of the guests of the house, and where a band, when they had one, discoursed music, such as it was. The high bank in front of the Cass farm extended to and a little beyond the Mansion House. This summer house was on this bank and had a long flight of steps leading from it down to Jefferson Avenue, where the latter deflected from its course, about where Cass Avenue crosses, and ended in the river. It was a pleasant experience to spend a summer evening on the hotel porch or in the summer house. Perhaps there are some living who can remember the pleasure, and with myself regret that the needs of business and commerce necessitated the destruction and obliteration of this, the fairest part of the city. It is hard to realize the change it has undergone.

ENTERTAINED MANY NOTABLES.

Here at this Mansion House and at Uncle Ben Woodworth's Steamboat Hotel all the notables of the country visiting the city were entertained. General Scott and suite made the former their headquarters in 1832, as also did Black Hawk and his suite, on their way from Washington to their homes, after receiving a wholesome chastisement from Uncle Sam. Here also the citizens of Detroit banqueted General Cass on the eve of his departure for Washington to accept the portfolio of the secretary of war. I got into this banquet for a short time through the good offices of Charles Mack, who was a chum of mine, and son of the proprietor, Andrew Mack. I remember quite well the appearance of the whole affair, the company present, etc. I also remember Major Henry Whiting's recitation of his poem, "Michigania."

Mr. Alvah Bronson was the first proprietor, General J. E. Schwarz the next and Andrew Mack next, Mr. Uhlman next, and then Mr. Boyer.

The hotel was demolished in 1834, when the Cass farm front was graded down and dumped into the river, making some dozen or more acres of available river front. A singular fact in regard to General Schwarz and Mr. Uhlman was that they were the only two native-born Germans in the city at that time.

THE FIRST PROPRIETOR.

Colonel Andrew Mack was the first landlord after I came, or shortly after. He was also United States custom house officer, and the office was in a small building adjoining or near the hotel. I think he afterwards kept the American Hotel (where the Biddle House now is) for a short time when it was first opened. A fine man was the colonel. Of commanding presence and a "Chesterfield" in manners, he easily won the esteem of all. He was ably seconded by his amiable wife. He subsequently moved or retired to a farm on the St. Clair River, between Port Huron and St. Clair City, where he died many years ago.

Charles Mack, son of Colonel Andrew Mack, proprietor of the old Mansion House, was a handsome boy, and grew to a fine manhood, but had no adaptation for business. He tried to be an artist; had a studio here, worried a while at portrait painting, but soon gave it up, not meeting with success. He entered the United States revenue service, and continued in it until he had to be retired on account of rheumatism, which finally caused his death, I think. He married one of the Clark sisters, who at one time (1838 or 9) was playing at the old brick theatre near the public library building, with their brother-in-law, William Sherwood. They were very pretty, bright and attractive, and were great favorites. They made a great impression on the "boys," and I did not wonder at Charley Mack's falling in love with the prettiest one. Among other gifts the sisters were fine singers, and, accompanied by Sherwood, who was himself a fine singer, they rendered such songs as "Hail Columbia," "Star Spangled Banner" and others of the patriotic order, that set the house wild with enthusiasm.

Mrs. Mack is living yet, and is, with her daughter, Mrs. Fitz Talman, somewhere in North Carolina.

THE OLD MICHIGAN EXCHANGE.

The late George C. Bates, in some of his reminiscences (1877) has this to say in regard to the old Mansion House and of its closing days, in 1834, when it was demolished, and the glory of the old house was transferred to the new Michigan Exchange:

"In those 'by-gones' the Detroit River in turning around so as to swing Sandwich Point, made a huge detour just at the foot of Cass Street, and, sweeping away inland, made a second Tappan Zee. Its banks at that curve were the Cass farm, the Jones, Woodbridge, Baker and Thompson farms, very high and bold, and General Cass' orchard came almost to the edge of the bluff. High up on the bank just below Cass Street stood this dashing old home, the Mansion House, built many years before our visit of today (July, 1835). It was made of stone, some three stories high, with a veranda along its entire front and huge pillars reaching clear away to the roof, and then extending back some 200 feet deep. From that veranda you could look right down over old Uncle Oliver Newberry's warehouse, across the Detroit Iron Works, and have an exquisite view of the river, the dwellings and gardens at Windsor and Sandwich down around the Point, Springwells, and the smoke of the upcoming steamer could always be seen far away around Sandwich Point. The old porch was very cool and delightful, and there today you see grouped on the veranda young Governor Tom Mason, so handsome and genial; prim John Norvell, Lieutenants Alex. Center, John M. Berrien, Heintzelman, the latter all drawn up with rheumatism; Lieutenant Poole, Captain Russell, Major Forsyth, of the army; Judge Wilkins, Judge Morrill, Thomas Sheldon, Justin Burdick and numerous other long-time habitues of this old inn—for today was a gala day in Detroit.

"The records of that old Mansion House, if they could be exhumed and read now, would furnish a sketch of Detroit, its old citizens and guests that would astonish, interest and amuse.

"On that veranda in 1837 Daniel Webster was welcomed to Detroit and in General Cass' orchard—afterwards graded down by Abraham Smolk, and dumped into the river, making some 17 acres of new river front—made one of those God-like speeches, which no other man ever had, ever can or ever will make. At that dining table during a whole season was Silas Wright, New York's greatest senator, with Judge Morrell, wife and daughter, Captain J. B. F. Russell, of the United States artillery, and his gorgeous wife, a splendid beauty. At the same table Stephen A. Douglass was not an infrequent guest, and there I have seen in brilliant army costume side by side Generals Scott, Worth, Wool, McComb, Whiting, Larned and an army of subalterns. But now here today (1834) the glory of dear old Mansion House departeth."

WAS A BRILLIANT AFFAIR.

Mr. Bates also discourses quite at length in regard to the opening of the Michigan Exchange. I have already given above quite a space to this hostelry, yet I did not refer to its opening, as I was a young schoolboy in those days and do not remember much about it, although I knew of it, as Edwin A. Wales, son of Austin Wales, was a schoolmate of mine at the time. I will let George C. Bates tell the story.

"Now the Michigan Exchange is opened and all the crowd are about to go there and aid in its christening. So in fall all the gentry, and in double files, led by Governor Stevens T. Mason and John Norvell, we march to Shelby Street, corner of Jefferson Avenue, where at the door the entire party are welcomed by Shubal Conant, the owner and builder of that then magnificent palace, and by Austin Wales and his brother, E. B. Wales, then its proud and youthful landlord. Prodigious, indeed, is this grand new hotel, one hundred feet front on the avenue, the same in depth on Shelby Street, four stories high, of pressed brick, with stone trimmings. It begins a new era in Detroit. Old times are passing away and commerce and fashion are westward bound today. Of the building itself I need not speak. Like the monument of Bunker Hill, 'there it stands, and the first rays of the morning sun greet it, and the last hours of expiring day linger and play around its base.' "

"The dining room in that day was upstairs over the corner store, at the conjunction of Jefferson avenue and Shelby street, where Webb, Douglass & Co., of Albany, the junior partner of whom was John Chester, who for many a long year had the first wholesale and retail crockery establishment. Directly from the street you entered the office, and on the right was a large well-lighted, airy, elegant bar, with a mahogany rail, rested on plated silver arms or braces in front, and where, on this opening day, everybody, young and old, grand and humble, drank pure liquors to their hearts' content, for then we had no red ribbons; '"tis true, 'tis pity, and pity 'tis, 'tis true.' Everybody shakes hands with Shubal Conant, then a teetotaler of the strictest kind, like old Solomon, who had found 'wine and strong drink to be a mocker.' Everybody congratulated Wales & Co. and everybody drank with everybody and all 'went merry as a marriage bell.' Late dinner was served, and around that first table were gathered John A. Welles, George B. Martin, Walter Newberry, Rufus Brown, John Chester, Judge Hand, Colonel Daniel Goodwin, Ambrose Townsend, John L. Talbot, Bill Alvord, Morgan L. Martin, while at its head sat Judge Conant, a Vermont giant—who occupied that same seat until he was upwards of 80 years of age—and a great number of invited guests, including all who came over from the Mansion House.

"The register of that first day of the Michigan Exchange, Irish John used to shriek it out, 'Passengers for the Michigan Exchange, omnibus going up now,' will furnish over 150 names of the Detroit guests, and out of that number not a dozen remain to this day (1877) to read these 'Bygones,' or to recall the pleasures of youth and hope there gathered around the first table ever spread in that now universally known hostelry. Underneath that old roof lived Fletcher Webster, the favorite son of Daniel Webster, and wife; Anthony Ten Eyck and lady; Marshal F. Bacon and wife; John A. Welles and wife; Robert McClellan and wife, and nearly all the quondam guests of the Mansion House, while Judge Conant, Uncle Gurdon Williams, Salt Williams ('Stammering Alph'), Young Gurdon, poor Bill Alvord, John L. Talbot, and multitudes of others either actually lived in the house or left it to die somewhere else.

"Forty-two years have come and gone since that opening day of the Michigan Exchange—an epoch in Detroit (July, 1885), and of the multitudes then in our streets only here and there can you see a gray-haired man plodding wearily on, waiting for the carriage that will be his escort to Elmwood—but even to this day, with its old-fashioned front, its simplicity and plainness of outward seeming, whosoever shall enter there will find every comfort and care that heart can desire or money command. Like the old homes of Detroit, its latchstring is always on the outside, and the weary and dust-stained traveler will ever find a cordial and hearty welcome."

THE MICHIGAN EXCHANGE.

The Michigan Exchange was built by Shubal Conant about 1837 and opened by Austin A. Wales, who was succeeded by Orville B. Dibble, and the latter by Daniel Goodnow, formerly of the Macomb Street House, Monroe. Mr. Goodnow had associated with him his son, William. They were succeeded by Fellers & Benjamin, the latter having been keeping the old National Hotel, the present Russell House; they were followed by Edward Lyon. I don't remember who had it after that. During Mr. Lyon's reign Homer Barstow, George W. Thayer, now of Grand Rapids, and Farnham Lyon, now of the Bancroft House, Saginaw, were associated with him from time to time in running the house. The hotel was a success from the start, and to accommodate the constantly increasing business, Mr. Conant was obliged to enlarge the building on towards Wayne Street, and towards the river on Shelby Street to Woodbridge Street. The original building occupied but one-half of the lot on the corner of Jefferson Avenue and Shelby Street; that is, it extended back from the avenue about 100 feet. In the rear ran an iron balcony the width of the hotel, the reading and dining rooms opening out on to it.

On one occasion under Mr. Goodnow's supervision, a public dinner of some sort was given, and among the guests was Curtis (Curt) Emerson. Many people will remember him. After the wine had circulated pretty freely, he became quite jolly and uproarous. Mounting the table, he proceeded to promenade up and down, kicking the dishes right and left. His father, Thomas Emerson, was sitting in the reading room quietly reading during all this. Mr. Goodnow informed him of what was going on in the dining room and entreated him to go in and see if his son "Curt" could not be induced to simmer down. The old gentleman readily assented and, going out on to the balcony, through the open windows (it being summer), he saw his son "Curt" dancing up and down the table and raising the old "Harry" with the crockery. He looked on for a minute, chuckling, and this is what he said, "Yes, that is my son Curt, sure enough. I used to do the same thing myself when I was his age. Go it, Curt." He returned to the reading room and resumed his paper as though nothing unusual had happened.

THE GOOD OLD DAYS.

The Michigan Exchange, in the "forties," was also a famous place for the gay and dancing portion of Detroit's society, young and old, to assemble during the long winter months and "chase the hours with flying feet;" Detroit was always gay in those days, more particularly in the winter season. When the "frost king" locked the lake and river in his icy embrace, cutting off all communication from the eastern world, fun and frolic had full sway. It was here in the ball room of this hotel, during the time the Fourth United States Infantry (Grant's regiment) was stationed here, that all Detroit's gay "400" or less, whatever there was, the creme de la creme, met in weekly cotillion parties, gotten up by subscription. That they were exclusive goes without saying. You could not get within the charmed circle, had you ever so much money, unless you were in the swim; would not even be asked to subscribe; no, sir! The officers of the army stationed at this post, on detached duty (and it being the headquarters of the "Michigan department of the lakes"), there was always quite a number of them who contributed to their success. General Grant, then a brevet-captain in the Fourth United States Infantry, was a subscriber also, and with his bride, formerly Miss Dent, was in attendance at all these parties, as well as the other officers of the regiment and their ladies during its stay here. Grant himself did not dance, but his wife did. He used to stand around or hold down a seat all the evening. One thing I noticed in him. He was always ready to join the boys when they went out to "see a man." This they did pretty often, as boys and men will, but I never saw him under the influence of liquor, and I saw him as often as anyone here, anyone, I mean, outside of the members of his regiment and family; and why I came to know so much in regard to him arose from the fact that I was at that time in the employ of Major E. S. Sibley, U. S. A., quartermaster for the military department of the lakes, with headquarters in this city, as quartermaster's clerk. Captain Grant was acting assistant quartermaster and commissary of that portion of his regiment stationed at Detroit barracks. He drew all his funds and orders for supplies for his command from our office; consequently I was in frequent communication with him. He was always very taciturn, talking no more than the business would allow, making his wants known in the fewest possible words, and that was about all. I attributed it to his youth and diffidence, for he certainly was very "backward about coming forward." This latter trait in him led me to ask his quartermaster-sargeant why the colonel of the regiment appointed him acting quartermaster. He said he really did not know why; just happened to do so, he guessed, "but," he said, "the captain, I will own is not much good when you come to papers, accounts, returns and all that sort of thing, but when you get to the soldier part of it, drill, manual of arms, etc., (shoulder arms business we used to call it) he could handle the regiment as well, if not better, than any other fellow in it." This sergeant's name was Smith. I once repeated the above, in relation to Grant, to Mr. H. Garland and think he published it among other things about the general in a magazine a few years ago.

TORE THINGS LOOSE.

These gatherings were always delightful and a source of much pleasure to those who had the entre. Mr. Lyon was the most even-tempered landlord, except Mr. Goodnow and his son, William, that ever held sway over the fortunes of this hotel. No matter how gay or wild the "boys" would get, nor how "Curt" Emerson and Josh Carew and that set would rush things, he never got off his balance. If things did get smashed, he always knew well that there was always someone to foot the bill, and no talk back. I call to mind one occasion. (It was New Year's eve, 1845 or 6; I forget which year.) There had been a New Year's ball in the hotel that night, and on its conclusion (and it was an unusually brilliant and gay affair), some eight or ten gentlemen of the younger set hied themselves to the dining room on the ground floor to pass the remainder of the evening. Champagne was freely indulged in, and to the extent that it made the boys quite jolly. They occupied the table next to the street, on which were many remains of the ball supper, such as crockery, glassware, etc. Soon the fun began, fast and furious, and in a very short time there was not a thing left on that table. During the performance Mr. Lyon would look in now and then to see how they got along, but never an angry word nor remonstrance on his part, as to the noise they were making or the havoc they had caused in the crockery and glassware line. He knew the party well, and that they were amply able to pay for what they called for or for any damage his property might sustain at their hands. They did pay the next day or two, and no mistake, and all parties were satisfied.

HAWLEY'S BEER ROOM.

Under the corner of the Michigan Exchange on Shelby Street, and directly after its completion, a Mr. Hawley, from Cleveland, opened a place for the sale of "Cleveland Beer" and a sandwich; nothing else. It was called "Hawley's Cleveland

Beer Room." The beer was fine; much better than Thomas Owen's brewery had supplied to the people of Detroit. He directly had a large run of custom and continued there for quite a while, making money. There in that little downstairs room he laid the foundation for a fortune. Afterwards he established a brewery of his own. Many will remember "Hawley's Brewery and Malt House" on Bates Street, between Woodbridge and Atwater Streets.

THE MICHIGAN EXCHANGE.

Here is a list of people of note who have lived at the Michigan Exchange, from time to time. Tubal Conant, General Brooke, U. S. A.; Colonel J. B. Grayson, U. S. A.; Colonel Jas. R. Smith, U. S. A.; Colonel J. B. Kingsbury, U. S. A.; Colonel Electus Backus, U. S. A.; Major Hunter, paymaster, U. S. A. (afterwards brigadier-general in the civil war); Captain Irwin McDowell, U. S. A. (later on commander of the Army of the Potomac); Lieutenant De Lancey Floyd Jones, U. S. A. (afterwards colonel Third United States Infantry); Lieutenant J. M. Berrien, U. S. A.; Lieutenant Center, U. S. A.; Captain J. A. Whitale, U. S. A.; Captain Robinson, U. S. A. (afterwards brigadier-general in the civil war); Josh Carew, Mr. Carnes, Curtis Emerson, Thomas Emerson (father of "Curt"); Governor Austin Blair, George C. Bates, Mr. Van Husen and family, Judge Warner Wing, Doctor T. B. Scovell, Colonel Rucker, of Grosse Ile; Lieutenant Holabird, U. S. A. (afterwards quartermaster-general United States Army); Lieutenant Hawkins, U. S. A. (afterwards commissary-general United States Army); Colonel John W. Alley, U. S. A.; Colonel J. P. Taylor, U. S. A. (brother of President Taylor); Colonel Chilton, U. S. A. (afterwards on General Lee's staff, United States Army).

SOME NOTED GUESTS.

Alex H. Newbould made his home at the Exchange most of the time, as also did Henry J. Buckley, Colonel E. H. Thompson Flint, Colonel Grosvenor, Colonel Hammond, General Fountain and General Giddings of the state military department, during the first two or three years of the civil war. Whenever Gil Davidson, of the wholesale hardware house of Erastus Corning & Co., Albany, came to visit Alex Newbould and the "boys," the Exchange prepared itself for feasting, wine and wassail. In the private dining room would gather Alex Newbould, Josh Carew, Joe Clark, Curt Emerson, Colonel Grayson, Sam Suydam, Alph Hunter (Ypsilanti), Charles Ducharme, Fred W. Backus, etc., when fun, fast and furious, ruled the hour.

Captain Meade, United States Army (afterwards in command of the Potomac); Lieutenant M. C. Meigs, United States Army (afterwards quartermaster-general, United States Army, during the civil war), were also guests of the house most of the time they were stationed here. Among those who lived at the Michigan Exchange in the early 40s was Joseph Clark ("Joe," as he was familiarly termed), and his wife. Clark was a popular and genial man. He trained in the crowd composed of Josh Carew, Colonel Grayson, Curtis Emerson, John T. Hunt, Samuel Suydam, etc. His wife belonged to the fashionable set, and was a very bright, pleasant lady. She was the daughter of Colonel Fenton, of Flint. Her sister, Miss Jennie Fenton, lived with them at the Exchange. They were there continuously through two winters, and added much to the gayeties of that hostelry. General Brooke was a soldierly-looking man, as all who ever saw him will call to mind. He served with great distinction in the Mexican war, and came here with his regiment, the Fourth United States Infantry (Grant's regiment).

Lake Superior magnates, the copper kings of the early days, usd to make this their headquarters also, when in the city. Among them were Simon Mandelbaum, that genial, nervous, energetic German, close friend of the Sibleys and the Bradys, as also of all the Lake Superior people. Among the latter were James Carson, John Senter, Ransom Sheldon (the father of the Calumet & Hecla mine); C. C. Douglass; Hon. Peter White (the delegate from Carp River, Marquette), Holland, etc.

General Custer, in 1861, then a fresh graduate from West Point and second lieutenant in a cavalry regiment, danced attendance on Governor Blair, waiting his pleasure, for an advancement to the colonelcy of a Michigan cavalry regiment. The latter hesitated, being distrustful of his flowing, yellow locks, and his otherwise effeminate appearance. He succeeded in gaining his opportunity after a brief period, and all are familiar with the brilliant use he made of it. Chief Justice Charles W. Whipple made this house his home after the death of his wife. Chamberlain, the Democratic sage from Three Oaks, also had his headquarters here, when in the city.

The members of the legislature, before the capital was removed to Lansing, bestowed their patronage about equally between the Exchange, American, National and Woodworth's, though I am inclined to think that Uncle Ben Woodworth got the lion's share, on account of old associations, etc.

A MELANCHOLY REMINDER.

Well, the glory of the old hotel has departed, I fear never to return. What was almost the center of the city, around which, and in the immediate vicinity, ebbed and flowed nearly all the life there was here then, and I might say of the whole state, in either the social, political or business world, is now almost deserted, and the old hostelry has been given up to the rats. What a change it presents, seeing it then, as I did, and seeing it now, as I do.

It seems to me the present site of the old Exchange would be an ideal one for the contemplated new hotel. Take the entire block, if it can be acquired, and have the house eight or ten stories high, with a summer garden on top, balconies to all rooms fronting on the river, above the third story. What a magnificent outlook all this would have. Not another city in the Union could match it.

THE DIBBLE FAMILY.

After Mr. Dibble left the Exchange he retired to private life, from which he emerged in company with his son Charles to take charge of the Biddle House, of which they were the first proprietors.

Dibble had a very interesting family. They were all together when he kept that hostelry—two boys, Charles and George, and three girls. Sue was the eldest; the other two were quite young then. I have forgotten their names. George entered the navy as midshipman. His father was very proud of him—he was truly the "apple of his eye." When he was home on leave for the first time, and sported his midshipman's uniform, the "admired of all admirers," it did seem as though the father could not make enough of him. Indeed, he was a handsome, bright and genial youth of great promise, and a great favorite in the gay circles of Detroit's young society and with all guests of the house. But, sad to say, he met a violent death, just before passing to a lieutenantcy, in California, at the hands of a desperado. The latter, for some cause, was never brought to justice. It was a terrible shock to the family, and I do not think the father or mother ever recovered from it entirely.

Charles was associated with his father in the management of the Exchange, as also in that of the Biddle (as mentioned). Many will remember Charles L. Dibble, who was an ideal hotel Clerk, and all-around landlord as well. He was a favorite in society and with the public also. Strange to say, he, too, met a violent death, as did his brother George. It happened in an oil mill, near the foot of Dequindre Street, that himself and Mr. Higham (a civil engineer and formerly superintendent of one of the separate railroads between Albany and Buffalo in 1842-3), were operating. It suddenly blew up one morning, killing both men instantly.

Sue Dibble was a bright, charming society bud, the gayest of the gay. She had many admirers, but death came to her early, before she was out of her teens, and shortly after the death of her brother George, which seemed to add still greater weight to the burden of affliction already borne by the parents. The other two daughters married, and are living in Syracuse, N. Y., or near there. One of them married a Mr. Stanton, who was at one time conductor on the Detroit & Milwaukee Railway; the name of the other gentleman I have forgotten. I may be pardoned for dwelling so long on the Dibble family. I was on almost as intimate terms with them as I was with my own before they took charge of the Biddle House.

THE AMERICAN HOTEL.

The American Hotel was built somewhere about 1830, the Governor Hull residence being utilized in its construction; and it was extended to Randolph Street, the first story of the extention being used for stores. Its first proprietors were Austin Wales & Bro., or John Griswold, I forget which. Many others succeeded these in its management, until the great fire of 1848 wiped it out. It was always a first-class hotel, fully on a par in every way with the Mansion House, Woodworth's National or the Exchange. During Mr. Griswold's occupancy it was the headquarters of the officers of the Fifth United States Infantry, five of which companies were at that time stationed at the Detroit barracks, out on Russell Street. Nearly all of the officers of these companies boarded at the American. Many of them had families.

All these, in conjunction with the other United States officers on staff duty stationed in the city, added much to the social swim, and there was a constant whirl of gayety at this hostelry, until the Mexican war rudely broke it up, but not before Griswold's pretty daughters, Martha and Clara, had been captured and made soldiers' brides by two officers of the Fifth, Captain Carter L. Stevenson taking the former, and Lieutenant Paul Guise (brother of our old and lamented friend, A. H. Guise) taking the latter. After this, it always was more or less a military hotel. Mr. Griswold was the father of Attorney George R. Griswold, for many years county clerk; Charles, deputy county register, and Dr. John Alexander. Many must remember these gentlemen. After thinking the matter over I am satisfied that John Griswold was the first proprietor of this house, and that Austin Wales & Bro. succeeded him. It was not quite so gay as it was under Griswold's rule, though reasonably so.

The first bachelors' ball that was ever given in Detroit came off at this house, directly after Wales took it. It was a brilliant affair, graced by the elite of the city, men and women. One peculiar feature about it was, there was a committee appointed to see that the ladies invited had an escort to and from the ball. The invitations stated that the recipient would be called for about a certain hour and also that it would be seen to that she had an escort to her home. So all anxiety on that score was done away with, and those that didn't have a beau got there and back to their residence all right. Rather unique, don't you think?

Wales, after quitting this house, retired to his farm at Erin, a short distance out on the Gratiot Road, where he died many years ago. A large number of our people must remember him, as well as his brother, and his son, Edwin A. Wales. Mr. Wales had two charming daughters. One died in the early 40s; the other, Cornelia, married La Fayette Knapp, son of Sheriff Knapp, who declined or shrunk from the task of hanging Simmons, the wife murderer, in the early 30s. He died after a brief married life, and she afterward married Alex. H. Newbould.

FIRST MESMERIST IN DETROIT.

I think Petty & Hawley succeeded Austin Wales in the management of this house, and after them J. W. VanAnden. It was at this hotel, during the proprietorship of Austin Wales, that Professor DeBonnville, a disciple of Mesmer, gave exhibitions of his wonderful powers, and performed his wonderful cures, particularly of rheumatism.

I have seen lots of people go to his rooms on crutches and come away without them, their aches and pains entirely dispelled. But I do not think the cures were lasting. The professor had two attendants, who seemed to be entirely under his influence. They were young men by the name of Williams and the other E. N. Lacroix. The latter most all old residents will remember. Whenever DeBonnville gave a lecture on mesmerism, these two were always in evidence. The professor was the first exponent of this wonderful science that Detroit had ever seen, and of course he drew crowds, and he no doubt made much money.

Before leaving the American Hotel I will relate an incident with it, or, more properly, with the General Hull residence, which it afterwards absorbed. Mrs Nancy Hubbard, in a paper read at a meeting of old settlers at Port Huron, Mich., on July 3, 1886, in which reference was made to the early days in Detroit, says: "My father left Painsville, Ohio, in 1811, in an open boat, for the territory of Michigan, taking his family with him. We came around the shores of Lake Erie and were two weeks in making the trip to Detroit, stopping wherever night overtook us. When we reached Detroit, we landed where is now Randolph Street, but there was no street there then, and where Atwater Street now is was covered over entirely with water. There was but one dock, and it belonged to the United States government. The only church in Detroit was Ste. Anne's Catholic church. Father Richard was the pastor. There were no settlements back from the river, the Indians being the only inhabitants of the forests, and a dense wilderness covered the state. Most of the inhabitants of Detroit at that time were French."

Speaking about Hull's surrender, Mrs. Hubbard relates that, "A guard was placed around Hull's house, which stood where the Biddle House now stands, and the public buildings were all burned. After Hull was taken to Canada, General Proctor occupied his house and he offered $5 for every American scalp the Indians brought to him. I have seen twelve Indians go in at one time with scalps. At such a time the Indians would form a circle in Proctor's yard, with the scalps hung on a pole in the center, and would whoop and dance to the music of a small drum beaten by one of their members."

NATIONAL HOTEL AND RUSSELL HOUSE.

The corner where the Russell House now is in the early days was inclosed by a cedar picket fence. In the inclosure was a small yellow house occupied by Dr. William Brown before he changed his residence to Jefferson Avenue, north side, just above Bates Street. Adjoining was a log house used as a schoolhouse. It had for a teacher a Mr. Healy (an Irishman), who was clerk of the steamer Henry Clay when I was a passenger on her to this city. After some years the National Hotel succeeded this log house and Dr. Brown's corner. It was built (if I don't mistake) by Mr. Chase, of the hardware firm of Chase & Ballard. Mr. Chase was a retired British army officer, and a grandfather of the Casgrains. Mr. Chase and family made their home at this house until his death. The National was a fine structure in its day, first-class in every respect and on an equal footing with the Mansion, Woodworth's, Exchange and the American. Its first proprietor, I think, was Mr. S. K. Haning. He was succeeded by John R. Kellogg, H. D. Garrison, Edward Lyon, Fellers and Benjamin and, I think, the last proprietor was Mr. Russell, after whom the present house gets its name. It is my impression that it has always, up to the present time, been successful. The spacious dining and dancing hall of this hostelry was a favorite place for concerts, balls, etc., in the 40s and early 50s—much more so than any of the others, with the exception of the weekly cotillion parties at the Michigan Exchange in the winters of 1845-6. The dances of the Brady Guards were always given at the National, as also were the annual balls of the fire department, which were all brilliant affairs. The firemen's balls were a feature of the year, looked forward to with eager anticipation by every member of the department, and the fairer portion of the city as well. They came off about midwinter usually, and for months before the function the office of the secretary of the department in the hall, corner of Larned and Bates Street, was besieged by anxious inquirers to ascertain for a certainty that their names and those of their fair friends were on the list of the secretary.

When the night came it seemed all too short to suffice for the eager longing, and the fuss and worry of preparation. Every phase of society attended these department balls. From the highest to the lowest all met on a common footing, and everything went as "merry as a marriage bell." Many, I presume, will remember them. Perhaps there are some that can call to mind the gay society that in the latter 30s, through the 40s and early 50s used to congregate in assembly rooms of the Michigan Exchange, American and National (Russell) Hotels during the winter months. I have given something of a description of the balls given by the Brady Guards at the National Hotel in a former article on our "Independent Military Companies."

FAMOUS PEOPLE PERFORMED THERE.

Every concert of any note was given at this house (the National). The great English singers, the Brahams, sang here, as did Henry Russell, the greatest of them all. Who that ever heard him render "The Brave Old Oak," "The Ivy Green," etc., will ever forget them or the singer? Others of reputation sang here, but their names have passed from my memory. Signor Martinez always gave his inimitable guitar concerts here. On this instrument he had no equal, as those that ever heard him will remember. Mr. Siddons and his niece at different times gave readings here. They were lineal descendants of the immortal Sarah.

Looking through a package of old letters, etc., I came across an invitation to attend a ball to be given the evening of February 15, 1844, at this hotel, for the benefit of Mr. Noverre, an Italian music teacher here at that time, by the following gentlemen: Thomas C. Sheldon, Douglass Houghton, Orville B. Dibble, A. L. Williams, Edmund A. Brush, Lewis Cass, Jr., Alex H. Sibley, Samuel Lewis, John Bradford, John T. Hunt, John Watson, E. P. Seymour, Lieutenants George Deas, J. L. Folsom, J. L. Jones, of the Fifth United States Infantry, stationed here, Walter Ingersoll, William N. Carpenter, T. W. Lockwood, James M. Welch, E. S. Truesdail, Charles S. Adams, J. B. Campau and Henry M. Roby. It was a gay affair, all the beauty and fashion of the city, as well as from the opposite side of the river, were present. The owners of the names appended to the invitation have all passed away, without an exception. Not more than five or six persons, myself among the number, are now living who attended the brilliant, crowded ball room of the National Hotel that night.

COSTUME PARTIES.

In the early 50s, costume parties were quite in vogue among Detroit's 400. Two, particularly, I call to mind, at both of which I was present.

The first one was given by Mr. Thomas C. Miller at his residence on Jefferson Avenue, corner of Hastings Street, where is now Dr. Jennings's office. It was a notable affair, attended as it was by the youth and beauty of the city, all in costume. The other was given at the National Hotel, now the Russell House, February 19, 1857, by a committee of gentlemen. The chronicler of the event at the time says:

"The costume party at the National Hotel on Thursday evening, February 19, notwithstanding the embarrassment under which the committee suffered, was entirely successful. So brilliant an assemblage was never before witnessed in the 'City of the Straits,' and all who participated in the delineations of that evening will long remember the enchanting scene and recur to it with emotions of pleasure and satisfaction.

"Messrs. Fellers and Benjamin contributed much to the enjoyment and comfort of their guests, by their preparation and attentions."

Here follows a list of some of those present and the characters they represented:

Mr. John C. Bonnell, as Lord Shaftesbury, in a rich court dress of blue and gold. He escorted Miss E. C. Green, who was prettily dressed as a Swiss peasant in a blue skirt and cherry waist. Mr. L. E. Higby, as the great financier, Sir Giles Overreach, escorting Mrs. L. E. Higby, as the beautiful Catherine Parr, first wife of Henry VIII. The costume of Mr. Higby was a court dress of crimson and gold. Dr. Gunn represented a Highlander and dressed in the tartan of his clan. Mrs. Gunn was the Goddess Flora, with her hair pleated in the form of a basket and filled with flowers. Mr. Wareham S. Brown wore a remarkably rich costume of crimson velvet and gold, of the court of St. James, made expressly for the occasion. Mr. Nat Pitcher wore the dress of a German courtier. One of the most perfect disguises of the evening was worn by Mr. John W. Strong, as a zouave. His dress consisted of scarlet pants, tied at the knee and falling to the ankle, blue jacket and scarlet cap. Mr. H. T. Stringham, as a Turk, was also completely disguised. He wore a very long beard, large turban of blue and white silk, with silver crescent; jacket and wide flowing pantaloons of silk, red sash and sword. Mrs. H. T. Stringham, in her dress, represented most charmingly an Italian peasant girl, in her gala dress—a very beautiful costume. The impersonation of Night by Mrs. J. Talman Whiting was admirable.

Mrs. Horace S. Roberts was prettily dressed as "Snow;" Mr. Charles P. Crosby as a courtier of St. Petersburg; Captain A. D. Dickinson as Paudeen O'Rafferty. His correct representation of the character contributed much to the amusement of the evening. Mr. M. Howard Webster wore a remarkably rich dress of the court of Louis XV. Mrs. Henry H. Welles appeared as Lady Rowena. Miss Higby personated Sir Walter Scott's charming character of "Die Vernon." Mr. Henry H. Welles was King Charles II., in a maroon velvet trunk and jacket trimmed with gold lace, black velvet mantle with a wide border of ermine and cavalier hat and plumes. Mr. Moses W. Field was an Italian peasant. Mr. G. W. Hunt was "Alonzo," in a rich dress. Messrs. George W. Jarvis and E. M. Biddle were appropriately costumed as Athos and Porthos, and made excellent guardsmen. Messrs. A. J. Fraser, Thomas W. Mizner and T. D. Wilkins were Italian brigands, in rich, fierce-looking costumes. Mr. Walter Ingersoll was very becomingly costumed as a Spanish courtier. Mr. H. Norton Strong was a Calabrian brigand. Dr. Louis Davenport appeared as Don Juan, and Captain Alpheus S. Williams the postillion de Longumeau, with his pretty little daughter as La Fille du Regiment. Mr. James F. Bradford was Master Modus.

Among the Shakespearean characters came Mr. Thomas H. Hartwell as the Duke of Buckingham; Mr. Julius E. Eldred, as Romeo; Mr. Theodore H. Hinchman looked Hamlet well; Mr. Henry P. Sanger was richly dressed in ermine as Richmond.

Mr. George W. Bissell appeared in perfect continental dress; Mrs. George W. Bissell in her mother's wedding suit; Miss Bissell as a country school marm of 1800; Miss Sarah Palmer was Young America in short dress skirts of red satin, striped with white; blue waist spangled with silver stars and red velvet cap with red and white plumes. Mr. G. B. Stimson as Don Juan, in a purple velvet Spanish jacket, doublet and trunks slashed with white satin and silver lace, buff boots and Spanish hat with plumes, look the part. Lieutenants C. N. Turnbull and C. M. Poe, United States Army, wore the becoming full dress uniforms of the United States engineers. Mr. William Biddle was very handsomely costumed as Mercutio. His dress consisted of a delicate pink silk trimmed with white satin and cap of same material, with elegant drooping plumes. Mr. Horace S. Roberts was Don Caesar. King Charles II. was represented by Messrs. A. N. Rood, Henry R. Mizner and Allyn Weston. Mr. Samuel Lewis as Chinese Koryan, looked very odd. Mr. Julius Movius was King Charles I. Mr. Tom P. Shelden appeared as the brave Count Rudolph. Miss Sallie Webster was beautifully dressed as the Maid of the Mist;

> "And gracefully, to the music's sound,
> The sweet, bright nymph went gliding round."

Mr. Thomas C. Miller was richly costumed as Cassio; Mr. Jesse Ingersoll danced in Highland costume, and Mr. Nath G. Williams in the rich green silk costume of Vicentio. Mr. J. C. Van Anden was the Count of Monte Cristo. Mrs. W. Y. Rumney was appropriately costumed as "Night." Mr. L. L. Knight was a page of the court of Louis XIV. Mr. C. H. Wetmore was in a field marshal's uniform.

Two of the most elegant dresses of the evening were those worn by Mrs. Alex J. Fraser and her sister, Miss M. Miles, as Grecian sisters. The skirts were short, of white silk, striped with silver, over which was a blue silk tunic covered with spangles; a beautiful white plume encircled the head, securing a rich veil of white lace trimmed with spangles, which hung gracefully over all. The effect was beautiful, and the costumes, in exquisite taste, elicited much admiration.

Mr. John Rumney was a Spanish courtier. Mr. Sears Stevens was a gentleman of the old school. The queenly Miss Louisa Whistler wore a blue dress, straw hat, and skirt looped up with a choice collection of flowers, and carried a bouquet on her arm. Mrs. DeGarmo J. Whiting as a tambourine girl wore a rich scarlet skirt, white bodice, short outer jacket of scarlet, trimmed with gold lace and richly spangled, and carried an ornamented tambourine. Mr. Preston Brady as a cowled monk, escorted Mr. Fred W. Backus as Mephistopheles. Major Charles E. Whilden was an Italian brigand. Mr. Joe L. Langley was an excellent Scotchman in the Fraser tartan. Mr. John B. Palmer was costumed as a gentleman of colonial days. He was dressed in black slik, velvet, knee breeches, silk stockings, low shoes and diamond buckles, powdered hair, etc. Mrs. E. F. Alery was a Spanish peasant, and was dressed in a crimson merino skirt, trimmed with deep black plush, green silk velvet waist, laced in front, and trimmed with crimson ribbon; corn-colored silk apron. Mr. E. F. Alery was a Spanish muleteer, in black velvet, knee breeches, Spanish sandals, crimson velvet jacket trimmed with corn-color, crimson sash and long cap of red falling on the shoulder. Mr. C. C. Cadman appeared in the style of a citizen of the French republic. Joseph Law, F. Palmer and E. A. Lansing wore rich court dresses. Mr. T. V. Reeve was Ruy Gomez, in a full suit of blue, with blue and white plumes, curls and mustache. Mr. Nathan Reeve was a Tyrolean peasant. Messrs. C. K. Gunn and Benjamin Vernor were Knights Templar. Mr. George A. Baker was in Mexican costume. The court of Louis XIV was represented by several characters, all of which were beautiful—Mrs. John Rumney and Mrs. R. T. Elliott, Mr. W. J. Chittenden in scarlet and gold, and Mr. F. G. Goodwin in black and purple. Mr. W. J. Rumney, dressed as a clown, had the most comical dress of the evening.

The author of the foregoing description of this party, etc., was Mr. Henry R. Mizner, then a law student, but now a retired brigadier-general, U. S. A.—a title won by distinguished service during the civil war as colonel of the Fourteenth Michigan Infantry, and subsequent service as colonel of a regular regiment on the Indian frontier.

As stated before, the first proprietor of this house was Mr. S. K. Harring, who was followed by Hon. John R. Kellogg and others. Kellogg had a very beautiful daughter (Amanda), and while he was the landlord she died in the house of malignant smallpox. Strange to relate, her death with that dread disease caused scarcely any flutter among the guests.

A SUCCESSFUL HISTORY.

This house has had various fortunes under various proprietors, successful and otherwise, and thus, all down through the years, it has continued to be one of the centers of the social and dinner-giving world of Detroit. When merged into the Russell House many years ago, it continued on the same plane, and has kept up the reputation of the locality in a marked degree. Its career under the admirable management of Chittenden & Whitbeck, and, after Mr. Whitbeck's unfortunate demise, by the present proprietor, Mr. W. J. Chittenden, I am told, has been marked with deserved success. The present house has been in the public eye for the past thirty or forty years, and should be familiar to all.

TIPPECANOE AND TYLER TOO.

RECOLLECTIONS OF HARRISON CAMPAIGN OF 1840—DETROITERS WHO PARTICIPATED.

THE Whigs of Detroit participated quite heartily in the Harrison campaign of 1840, and were almost wild in their espousal of the cause of the "Log Cabin," "Hard Cider" and "Coon Skin" candidate for the presidency.

A large vacant lot opposite the American Hotel (now the Biddle House) on Jefferson Avenue was selected on which to build a log cabin, in which the faithful could meet. The logs for the structure were cut by the Harrison and Tyler Club on the Jones farm out on Grand River Road, and hauled into the city. Alex H. Sibley and Henry M. Roby drove a four ox team for about two days. It was no boys' play either, as the Grand River Road then was turnpiked quite high, and muddy at that, and it was difficult to keep from getting into the ditch. There were others engaged in the same pastime, but these are the only ones I remember particularly.

I was one of the party cutting the logs and building the cabin, though not quite old enough to vote. The log cabin was of ample dimensions and of the most primitive kind. The front was decorated with dried coonskins, with the hair on. The interior was garnished with festoons of dried apples, dried pumpkins, and corn ears, while a barrel of hard cider, on tap, occupied a prominent position, and over the speaker's primitive seat was placed a stuffed raccoon.

The ladies were requested to send in contributions of coarse eatables for the dedication feast, and they responded liberally. The tables groaned under a generous supply of pork and beans, cold boiled ham, rye and Indian bread, corn dodgers, etc.

On the occasion of the dedication of the Log Cabin, a procession was formed, in which were included the orator of the day, Colonel Edward Brooks, distinguished visitors from abroad, various Harrison and Tyler Clubs, as also the Glee Club, composed of Chas. T. Adams, Henry M. Roby, Dr. Terry, Morris M. Williams, James Sutton, Chas. A. Trowbridge and two or three others whose names have passed from my memory. Two or three log cabins on wheels, drawn by yokes of oxen, were also in the procession. One of quite large dimensions, large enough to accommodate four or five persons, who dispensed hard cider to the thirsty crowd. Perched on the ridge pole was a live raccoon, to which it was attached by a chain. It took four or five yokes of oxen to haul this cumbersome affair. Another feature of the procession was our stalwart Whig friend, fireman and ship carpenter, Matthew Gooding (Zip-Coon) in his picturesque backwoodsman's costume, bearing on his shoulder a tame live raccoon. Gooding followed directly after the large log cabin, and attracted universal attention.

The dedication was a very hilarious affair. Colonel Edward Brooks, president of the club, presided, and, after a characteristic speech from him and a song by the Glee Club of "Tippecanoe and Tyler, Too," he gave the signal to pitch into the eatables. There was a wild scramble, and soon the tables looked as though a cyclone had struck them.

Well, the Whigs had many a good enthusiastic meeting in that log cabin that were remembered by the participants for many long years.

After the nomination of Harrison, a Washington correspondent of a Baltimore paper, who subsequently became a Harrison man, referred to the candidate of the Whig party as one whose habits and attainments would secure him the highest measure of happiness in a log cabin with an abundant supply of hard cider. This ill-chosen and hapless phrase, coming from a Democrat, was seized upon by the crafty Whig politicians, and made to form the keynote of the campaign. Log cabins constructed after the frontier style of rude architecture, their walls ornamented with coon-skins and their interior abundantly supplied with hard cider, which was generally drank from gourds, or in tin cups, constituted the "wigwams" where all indoor gatherings of the Whigs were held.

A GREAT GATHERING.

The Whig celebration of Fort Meigs, Ohio, was held in June, 1840, on the anniversary of the raising of the siege of that fort, and on the ground it had occupied. A chronicler of that time says of it:

"There assembled at the appointed time and place, a concourse of people variously estimated at from thirty-five to forty thousand and embracing representatives from every state and territory in the Union. Probably never before or since in the annals of the country has there occurred a more enthusiastic or impressive pageant. All classes and conditions, rich and poor, aged and young, 'fair women and brave men,' lent their presence and ardor. General Harrison's veterans and many of the country's rare statesmen, orators and humorists were there to honor, each in his own attractive way, the hero of the siege. The merchant left his counter, the farmer his fields, the mechanic his bench, to join in the shouts of applause and exultation, while cannon, musketry, church bells and martial music rent the air again and again. Nature, too, smiled from her brightest sky upon the green banks, the glancing waters, the beautiful towns of Perrysburg and Maumee, the gleaming banners waving over the victory—honored fort and British batteries—all combining to give the celebration the pride and glory, if not magnificence, of a Roman triumph."

MICHIGAN WELL REPRESENTED.

A large number of distiguished speakers were present, among them General Harrison himself, who, it was said, delivered an eloquent and scholarly address. Governor Woodbridge, of Michigan, was also among the speakers, as was Geo. C. Bates, Geo. Dawson, Colonel Edward Brooks and Jas. A. Van Dyke, of Detroit. A large number of our citizens attended, among whom were nearly all the young Whigs of the city, voters and non-voters. They provided themselves with tents and subsistence for the occasion. That they had a good campaign and enjoyable time was evidenced by the rubicund nose each one had on him when he returned. Most of them laid it to the sun and some to the hard cider, and things they had to encounter. Of all the number that went from here on that occasion, Stanley G. Wight is the only one living, I think. He can remember, no doubt, the festive time the boys had at the function, and going and returning on the steamer. I was prevented from being one of the crowd, much to my disgust. My employer, "Sid" Rood, his brother, "Gil" Rood, and the foreman of the bindery going, kept me at home.

SOME DETROIT WHIGS.

Geo. Dawson and Morgan L. Bates ran the *Detroit Daily Advertiser* (Whig) at that time.

Geo. Dawson wàs, as the late Eben N. Wilcox happily said, the very impersonation of muscular politics and was also endowed with great power to enforce the pleasure of his will against all questions. His phrenological and physiognomical features adorning such a figure impressed one instantly with the idea of the man's intellectual superiority. You saw at once a man of force, a born leader, and as such he was accepted by the Whigs of Michigan, whom he was largely instrumental in leading to the grand victory won in that fall of 1840. He had a most able helper in the person of Morgan L. Bates ("Morgan the Rattler"). Many must remember his energetic personality and his green spectacles.

Among other political writers and speakers of the Whig persuasion of that day were Franklin Sawyer, John L. Talbot, Henry Chipman (father of the late Hon. J. Logan Chipman), William Woodbridge, Jacob M. Howard, Geo. C. Bates, Jas. A. Van Dyke, Asher B. Bates, Colonel Edward Brooks. The Democrats had among their foremost rank of writers and speakers such men as Henry N. Walker, John S. Bagg, John Norvell, Daniel Goodwin, Anthony Ten Eyck, Wm. Hale, Randolph Manning, Dan Munger, Geo. R. Griswold, Colonel E. J. Roberts (father of the lamented Colonel Horace S. Roberts, who fell at the Second Bull's Run), Theo. Romeyn, Marshal J. Bacon, Chancellor Farnsworth.

We will recall the names of some of the most prominent co-workers (Whigs) in this memorable campaign: Abram C. Canniff, A. C. and Virgil McGraw, Ed. King, Dave Smart, that gushing Scotchman, Henry Roby, one of the celebrated minstrel quartet who enlivened the rafters and sawdust of the Log Cabin nightly, Alanson Sheley, Judge Canniff, Zach Chandler, Francis Raymond, Franklin Moore, Wm. N. Carpenter, Wm. Harsha, N. Prouty, Oliver Newberry, with his brigade of noted lake captains, headed by Captain Bob Wagstaff, Wm. Cole, sailmaker, the Desnoyers, P. J. and son, DeGarmo Jones, J. R. Dorr, N. T. Ludden, Phin Davis, Theo. Williams, the Abbotts, James and sons, Morris Williams, Sid. and Gil. Rood, Wm. Gooding, James Sutton, Stetson, the giant vulcan, Cullen Brown, John, Ellis and

R. E. Roberts, Doctors Pitcher, Rice and Whiting, Chas. Jackson, John Farrar, Jerry Moors, John Mullett, John Farmer, Thomas Mason and John Palmer, Frank Hall, Charley Adams, C. C. Trowbridge, John and Howard Webster, Alex. H. Sibley, the most youthful voter of all but a most strenuous worker, and a young man that "feared no noise." Eb. Wilcox, myself and a large, number of young Whigs were under age at that time, but that did not deter us from "working in the vineyard," and we did the best we knew how. Wilcox was an exceedingly bright youth, and could more than hold his own in our lyceum debates, pitted against such rising lights as Anson Burlingame, Wm. B. Wesson, J. Hyatt Smith, Jed P. C. Emmons, and others. He was quite a poet, besides, but I think he never essayed anything loftier than carriers' addresses or something of that sort. He might have done better, perhaps, if he had only let his muse have full swing. I give a verse from his first carriers' address, composed for Geo. Dawson's paper, January 1, 1840:

> "Time, inexorable tyrant; ever on,
> Remorselessly thou hold'st thy rapid flight;
> Thous't traveled ages; still thou art not wan
> But hale, as when God said, Let there be light."

Dawson, he said, praised him very much for the effusion, and he said further, what surprised him more than anything else was that the former should have pitched on him to write the address, when there were so many others more capable, but he had a copy of the address written the year before for the same paper by E. M. McGraw (brother of A. C. McGraw), a superb production, he said, and worthy of Byron, and what better could he do than follow in his footsteps. Here is the opening stanza of E. M. McGraw's production, or part of it:

> "Hist! 'tis the tread of ever fleeting Time;
> Another year is buried in the tomb of years,
> With all its scenes of virtue, vice and crime,
> Its buoyant hopes, and bitter, burning tears."

Wilcox also pays a glowing tribute to G. W. Dawson, that I am sure, all who knew the man, will concur in:

"Peace to thee, dear Dawson; if we pictured thee too brusquely in the opening lines of this diffusive tribute to thy memory, it was with no unkind thought. The whirligig of time has let us come to know thee in thy gentler moods, as a lover of nature and thy fellowman, an enthusiastic disciple of beloved Isaak Walton. May your lines be as pleasant as his, now that they are cast in the ocean of eternity."

I think it proper in passing to mention some of the young boy Whigs who, with Eben Wilcox and myself were active in this campaign, many of them in after life gaining distinction, viz: Anson Burlingame, Wm. B. Wesson, J. Hyatt Smith, O. B. Wilcox, Ed. M. Pitcher, Joseph Cook, Henry R. Mizner, Frank Farrar, La Fayette Knapp, E. A. Wales, David Lum, Stewart Lum, Abijah Joy, Stanley G. Wight, Henry A. Wight, Sylvester Larned, Albion Turner, L. H. Cobb, Geo. Jerome, Wm. Duncan, Kin S. Dygert, Jed Emmons, L. W. Tinker, Ed. King, Henry P. Dequindre, John T. Walker, W. L. Woodbridge, Anson Eldred, Ed. Kearsley, Harrison and Tyler boys, all, and as enthusiastic in the cause as they could be, and whose efforts no doubt contributed much to the success of the Whigs, particularly in Detroit. Senator Palmer, though a lad of only ten years, was always around, and quite lively, too.

I may be pardoned for referring again to Eben N. Wilcox, the friend of my boyhood, and of my maturer years whose premature taking off was the cause of so much regret. He will be remembered for his promising opening youth, his brilliant career at the bar, and his stirring speeches in the cause of the Union at the outbreak of the civil war. His effort before the crowd convened at the old firemen's hall on the fate of Fort Sumpter, was like a bugle blast. Peace to his ashes.

> "The moving finger writes; and, having writ,
> Moves on; nor all thy piety nor wit
> Shall lure it back to cancel half a line,
> Nor all thy tears wash out a word of it."

Colonel Richard M. Johnson, of Kentucky, the candidate for vice-president on the Democratic ticket, came up this way during the campaign on an electioneering tour and put up at the old National Hotel (Russell House). From the balcony of this hotel he made a stirring speech to a large and enthusiastic crowd of his admirers and others. I was among the latter. During the harrangue, some previous cuss in the audience interrupted the orator with, "Who Killed Tecumseh."

"Well," said the colonel in answer, "in the thickest of the

fight, at the battle of the Thames, I saw a stalwart and fierce-looking Indian, with his war paint on, coming at me with uplifted tomahawk. I was mounted at the time and drawing one of my pistols from its holster, shot him dead. Some one coming up at the time said that it was the noted chief (Tecumseh) ; he was also recognized by many others. I believe now, as I believed then, that the individual who is now addressing you, did kill Tecumseh."

I guess there is no doubt about it. I think I have alluded to this incident slightly, in a former article.

During the campaign, the Whigs had an immense mass and barbecue meeting on Fort Street where the Governor Baldwin house now stands. They had a rough building improvised for the purpose, with dining hall, speakers' stand, etc. Representatives from adjoining states were present, also distinguished Whig orators from outside the state, including Wm. M. Evarts, at that time a rising young lawyer, and a fine orator even then. The gathering was a great success, particularly the barbecue part of it.

REMARKABLE SPECIMEN OF NATIVE COPPER.

ITS TRANSFER FROM THE BED OF THE ONTONAGON RIVER TO THE SMITHSONIAN INSTITUTION.

AS AN indication of the mineral wealth of Michigan that was so soon to make many men millionaires, the recovery of an immense mass of copper in the bed of the Ontonagon river in 1843, and its transfer to Detroit and to Buffalo, and finally to the Smithsonian Institution, Washington, are facts of considerable interest. The valuable find was discovered by Gov. Cass, H. R. Schoolcraft and others, and the huge mass was brought down by Julius Eldred, of Detroit, in 1843.

The *Buffalo Gazette* of that year says of it:

This celebrated rock of pure copper, which has caused so much speculation among the scientific and others, arrived in this city on board the revenue cutter Erie, Capt. Knapp. This rock has attracted much attention since its discovery, about one hundred years since.

"This rock has been brought from the shores of Lake Superior through the enterprise of Mr. Julius Eldred, of Detroit, and is to be placed in the national institution at Washington. After several visits and two or three unsuccessful attempts to remove it, Mr. Eldred left Detroit on the 11th of June last, with apparatus and machinery, fully determined to fetch away this great mineral curiosity. After almost incredible efforts—being compelled to overcome a hill fifty or sixty feet in hight, the party at length reached the lake, having an affective force of twenty-one men to assist in the removal.

The copper was shipped on board the schooner Algonquin and transported over 300 miles to the head of the Falls of St. Mary. It was then transferred to a Mackinac boat, and after passing through the canal and around the rapids, it was shipped on board the schooner Brewster for Detroit, where it arrived on the 11th of October last.

"At Detroit, it was taken on board the revenue cutter, and arrived here, as stated, in charge of Mr. Eldred. Mr. Eldred has presented to us a piece of the rock, which was flaked off in moving. It is pure native copper, and such is its malleability that it may easily be hammered into any shape or form without heating.

"The weight of the rock has never been definitely ascertained. It has been differently estimated—by Schoolcraft at 2,200 pounds, and he gives its dimensions at 3 feet 3 inches long, by 3 feet 4 inches broad. Dr. Houghton, the state geologist for Michigan, who has good opportunities for forming a correct estimate, thinks it will weigh not far from 4 tons. It is the largest specimen of native copper in the world, and Mr. Eldred assuredly deserves the thanks of the country for his indefatigable and successful efforts to bring it forth into the civilized world."

The canal around the St. Mary's Falls was not in existence at that time. The rock was transported across the portage on the horse tramway.

WAS INSPECTED IN 1840.

Mr. Hubbard with Dr. Houghton visited this copper rock in 1840, in the bed of the Ontonagon River. At that time nothing was known of all this mineral wealth locked in the rugged hills of Lake Superior, except now and then traces of copper were seen at a few places along the shore, and this large mass of native metal in the bed of the Ontonagon River was known. It was long revered by the Indians as a Manitou, and was mentioned in the relations of the early French historians. Large masses (larger even than this celebrated mass) have since been mined in the Lake Superior district, and smelted at the old copper smelting works at Springwells. They came from the Minnesota, Isle Royal and Cliff mines.

This Ontonagon river copper rock arrived in Buffalo when I was residing there. I think it came in the fall of 1843. While in transit from the revenue cutter Erie to the railroad depot on Exchange Street, it was under the immediate charge of Capt. S. P. Heintzelman, United States quartermaster (since major-general, U. S. A., in the civil war), who was stationed at Buffalo at that time.

The captain, to gratify the curiosity of the citizens, had it paraded up and down the principal part of Main Street and down

Exchange Street on a four wheeled truck, behind two spans of horses and a driver. The horses were gayly decorated.

Many of the citizens, eager to possess a clipping from the rock, as a souvenir, provided themselves with hammers and chisels for that purpose, hoping to get a clip at it as it passed through the streets, but they were foiled in this, as Captain Heintselman was close to the rock on foot and it kept him busy keeping the people back.

The history of this copper mass is familiar to many, and more particularly to Lake Superior people, and I mention it more from the fact that in the winter of 1845 or 6 I kept Julius Eldred & Co.'s tannery books in this city during my unoccupied evenings, and at that time Mr. Eldred was trying to collect from the government money to repay him for the expense he had sustained in getting the rock to Detroit, and of course, heard from the old genteleman more or less about it. He recovered something I think from the United States, but how much I do not know.

GOVERNOR CASS'S VIVID DESCRIPTION.

H. R. Schoolcraft, in company with Governor Cass and party, visited this copper rock June 28, 1820. His description of it is much like the rest. I quote a few remarks of his in regard to it and its surroundings. He says: "I do not think the weight of metallic copper in the rock exceeds 2,200 pounds. The quantity may, however, have been much diminished since its first discovery, and marks of chisels and axes upon it, with the broken tools lying around, prove that portions have been cut off and carried away.. Notwithstanding this reduction it may still be considered one of the largest and most remarkable bodies of native copper on the globe, and is, so far as my reading extends, only exceeded by a specimen found in a valley in Brazil weighing 2,666 Portuguese pounds."

In regard to its surroundings, he says: "Mostly immersed in water reposes the copper rock; on the left the little island of cedars divides the river into two channels, and the small depth and rapidity of the water is shown by the innumerable rocks which project above its surface from bank to bank. The masses of fallen earth—the blasted trees, which either lie prostrate at the foot of the bluffs or hang in a threatening posture above—the elevation of the banks—the rapidity and noise of the stream, present such a mixed character of wildness, ruin and sterility, as to render it one of the most rugged views in nature. One cannot help fancying that he has gone to the ends of the earth, and beyond the boundaries appointed for the residence of man. Every object tells us that it is a region alike unfavorable to the productions of the animal and vegetable kingdom; and we shudder in casting our eyes over the frightful wreck of trees, and the confused groups of falling-in banks and shattered stones. Yet we have only to ascend these bluffs to behold hills more rugged and elevated; and dark hemlock forests, and yawning gulfs more dreary, and more forbidding to the eye. Such is the frightful region through which, for a distance of twenty miles, we follow our Indian guides to reach this unfrequented spot, in which there is nothing to compensate the toil of the journey but its geological character and mineral productions."

After Governor Cass and Thos. L. McKenney as joint commissioners on the part of the United States to negotiate a treaty with Chippewa Indians at Fond du Lac in 1826, had concluded the same, they ordered Geo. F. Porter to accompany the detachment sent to the Ontonagon River for the purpose of procuring this mass of native copper.

The result is given in his report, part of which follows:

REPORT OF THE COPPER ROCK.

"We left Fond du Lac on the first day of August, 1826, with two boats, containing 20 men, including our French and Indian guides; and after a short passage of something less than four days, arrived in the mouth of the river. We immediately proceeded up the river. About 28 miles from its mouth the river is divided into two branches of equal magnitude. We continued up the right branch for about two miles further, where we found it necessary to leave our boat and proceed by land.

"After walking about five miles further over points of the mountains from 100 to 300 feet high, separated every few rods by deep ravines, the bottom of which were bogs. We at length, with some difficulty, discovered the object of our search, long known by the name of Copper Rock of Lake Superior.

"This remarkable specimen of virgin copper lies a little above low water mark on the west bank of the river, and about 35 miles from its mouth. Its appearance is brilliant wherever the metal is visible. It consists of pure copper, ramified in every direction through a map of stone (mostly serpentine, intermixed with calcareous spar) in veins of from one to three inches in diameter, and in some parts exhibiting maps of pure metal of 100 pounds weight, but so intimately connected with the surrounding body that it was found impossible to detach them with any instruments we had provided.

"Having ascertained that, with our means and time, it was impossible to remove by land a body weighing more than a ton (two-thirds of which I should have observed is pure metal) we proceeded to examine the channel of the river, which we found intercepted by ridges of sandstone, forming three cataracts, with a descent in all of about 70 feet, over which it was impossible to pass; and the high and perpendicular banks of sandstone rendered a passage around them impracticable. Finding our plans frustrated by unforeseen difficulties, we were obliged to abandon our attempt, and proceeded to the Sault Ste. Marie."

This mass of native copper appears to have been known to the Indians for a very long period. Pierre Boucher, in his Historie Veritable et Naturelle, Paris, 1664, says "that the Frenchmen who went with Father Menard told me that they had seen a nugget of copper at the end of a hill which they estimated to weigh more than 800 pounds."

INDIANS' BELIEF.

At the conference in 1826 with the Ojibwa at Fond du Lac, for the purchase of these lands, one of the chiefs said in reference to this nugget of copper:

"This, fathers, is the property of no one man. It belongs alike to us. It was put there by the Great Spirit, and it is ours. In the life of my father the British were busy working it. It was then big like that table. They tried to raise it to the top of the hill, but failed. They then said the copper was not in the rock, but in the banks of the river. They dug for it by a light, working under ground. The earth fell in, killing three men. It was then left until now."

In 1843 the weight of this rock was estimated between 6,000 to 7,000 pounds, and its purity at 95 per cent, it was removed to the Smithonian Institution at Washington as before stated, and at a cost of about $3,500.

ITS HISTORY SHOULD NOT BE FORGOTTEN.

I have seen this rock many times at the Smithsonian Institution, Washington, as I presume many thousands have done, but I do not remember if it bore on its surface anything to indicate its strange history, and the various vicissitudes it had passed through before reaching this, its final resting place. If it does not, it seems to me it should, considering the vast wealth it has already heralded, and the prospect of millions yet to come, the contemplation of which almost makes the senses reel.

This silent rock, in its bed on the rugged shore of the Ontonagon, bore on its metallic face its story and its significance. The untutored savage read it partly, but it was left for Fur Trader Henry and Cass, McKenney, Schoolcraft, Houghton, Hubbard and others before them who visited it from time to time, to read aright the tale it had to tell and its great import.

It seems to me no mineral specimen in the world at this day possesses the interest and significance that this rock of copper does now, reposing so quietly in the halls of the Smithsonian Institution in Washington, and there should be some fitting recognition of the great part it played in making known to the nation the vast wealth that lay hidden in the copper region of Lake Superior, only waiting to be sought after.

The Calumet and Hecla people could afford alone to furnish a golden pedestal for it, let alone a marble one, surmounted by a golden scroll, with its history blazoned upon it.

Aside from seeing this copper rock in Buffalo, when it was on its way to Washington, and listening to Mr. Julius Eldred's account of his experience with it, I some years before this (1830), heard of Mr. J. O. Lewis, who was with Governor Cass and Colonel McKenney as sketch artist on their trip in 1826, relate his account of it to my uncle, Thos. Palmer.

After my uncle was burned out, on the corner of Jefferson Avenue and Griswold Street, in 1830, he moved his books and papers to the first floor of a frame building in the rear, on the corner of the alley and Griswold Street (where the Michigan Mutual Life is now), belonging to Shubal Conant. This Mr. Lewis, who was by trade a steel and copper plate engraver and printer, occupied the rooms in the rear of my uncle's.

Lewis often talked of this trip and this rock with my uncle and others. I was most of the time in evidence, and an eager listener. Early impressions, it is said, are always lasting, so the story of hunting up this copper rock, told by J. O. Lewis, I never forgot.

It has been told that the one hundred pounds of copper that the fur trader, Alexander Henry, cut from this rock in 1766 is now in the British Museum and is held to be one of its rarest mineral specimens.

Schoolcraft, as a further evidence of what a terrrible spot this rock had for an abiding place, quotes a passage from Walter Scott, which I give:

> "It seemed the mountain, rent and riven,
> A channel for the stream had given;
> So high the cliff of sandstone gray,
> Hung beetling o'er the torrent's way.
> Where he who winds 'twixt rock and wave,
> May hear the headlong torrent rave;
> May-view her chafe her waves to spray,
> O'er every rock that bars her way.
> The foam globes o'er her eddies glide,
> Thick as the scheme of human pride
> That down life drive amain,
> As frail, as frothy, and as vain."

It is fair to presume that the vicinity of Ontonagon, to which this refers, wears something of a different aspect from what it did when this was quoted.

Mr. J. O. Lewis above referred to made a sketch of the copper rock as it appeared lying in its bed on the margin of the Ontonagon River, and I presume the engraving of it that appears in Schoolcraft's narrative, is taken from it."

FRIEND PALMER.

WHEN DETROIT HAD A TOWN PUMP.

HOW THE CITY GOT ITS WATER SUPPLY BEFORE THE PRESENT FINE SYSTEM WAS ESTABLISHED.

MANY people now living in Detroit can remember when all the people were supplied with water through tamarack logs, bored out to make pipes. It was not long before that when there was a town pump at the foot of Randolph Street, free for the use of all citizens.

The development of the water system included the discarding of plants that in their day were supposed to be large enough to take care of Detroit for years to come. At times people in some sections of the city found that they could get no water during the day, and some member of the family had to get busy at midnight, when the demand fell off in other sections of the city, in order to draw water to supply his family through the next day.

The issue of the *Detroit Gazette* July 20, 1820, contains this notice:

"Resolved, That the board of trustees of the city of Detroit will meet on Thursday, the 10th of August next, for the purpose of receiving proposals to furnish the city with water for a certain number of years. "GEO. McDOUGALL,
Attest. "Sec'y pro tem."

But it does not appear that any further action was taken until the 4th of June, 1822, at a meeting of the citizens convened at Bronson's Hotel, situated on the south side of Woodward Avenue, midway between Jefferson Avenue and Woodbridge Street. The *Detroit Gazette,* in 1822, had this item:

STEAM COMPANY.

"At a meeting of a number of the citizens of Detroit, convened at Bronson's Hotel on the evening of the 4th of June, 1822, A. B. Woodward was elected chairman and Geo. A. O'Keefe, secretary.

"Certain proposals for supplying the city with water were exhibited to the meeting by George Deming and his associates, and were read and considered by the meeting, whereupon,

"Resolved, Unanimously, as the opinion of the meeting, that it is expedient to promote the enterprise of George Deming and his associates to supply the city of Detroit with water, and it will be agreeable to us that the legislative authority should give him an exclusive privilege for·a certain number of years, under equitable conditions.

"Ordered, that the secretary transmit a copy of these proceedings to the *Detroit Gazette* for publication."

And then the meeting adjourned. But it does not appear that any further progress was made until the legislature, August 5, 1824, passed the act in relation thereto, mentioned in the "History of the Detroit Water Works," by Jacob Houghton, superintendent, in his report December 31, 1853. But this was only an act empowering Mr. Peter Berthelet to construct a wharf at the foot of Randolph Street and on it erect a pump, for the purpose of pumping water from the river, to which all citizens should have free access.

Previous to this meeting, however, the *Gazette* of April 12, 1822, in an editorial, had this to say: "A respectable fellow-citizen has received a letter from a gentleman in Ohio, in which inquiries are made as to the encouragement which a person would receive from the citizens of Detroit in undertaking to supply them with water from the river by means of hydraulic machinery. That water can be carried from the river to the door of every inhabitant by means of hydraulics is evident to every person least acquainted with the subject—and it is equally certain that were it once effected, a vast number of our citizens would be saved an expense of from $15 to $25 per year. It is perhaps out of the power of our corporation to erect the necessary works, but it is not out of the power of the citizens of Detroit to grant certain privileges to individuals who would undertake and properly accomplish the business. It is·to be hoped that the trustees of the city of Detroit generally will turn their attention to this important object; and as its great utility cannot for a moment be questioned, let foreign enterprise derive a portion of the benefit of its accomplishment, if a company of our own citizens cannot be formed to secure the whole to ourselves."

THE FIRST STEP.

The efforts of the citizens of Detroit to devise some plan or means through which they could be supplied with water became —as Jacob Houghton says in his report—noised abroad, until it reached the ears of Bethuel Farrand and Rufus Wells, residents of Aurelius, Cayuga County, New York, who came on and submitted to the common council, February 17, 1825, their proposition for supplying the city with water, a full detail of which is given in Mr. Houghton's report.

I witnessed the erection of the pump house on the Berthelet wharf, foot of Randolph Street, and saw it in operation, in free use by the citizens. I also saw it pumping water into the reservoir erected on the rear of the lot now occupied by the water board (formerly Firemen's Hall), and witnessed the boring for water on the site designated for that purpose by Mayor Jonathan Kearsley and Alderman Thomas Palmer, on the south side of Fort, between Shelby and Wayne streets, and the building of the reservoir at that point. I also gathered at the boring works quite a quantity of water-worn pebbles that the borer brought to the surface from a depth of between two and three hundred feet.

I was also quite familiar with the pumping works erected by the Detroit Hydraulic Co. on the north side of Woodbridge Street, between Cass and Wayne. I was well acquainted with Uncle Chas. Howard, who ran the engine, and was around there often when Captain John Burtis was building his steamboat Argo, close by. I think it will be interesting to many of the old settlers, as well as to many of the new, of our goodly Detroit. To the latter it will, no doubt, be fresh news

I give herewith facts from the History of the Detroit Water Works, up to the time (February 14, 1853,) the state legislature passed the act creating the board of water commissioners and for which history I am under obligations to my good friend of these many, many years' standing, Jacob Houghton, Esq., superintendent, who, I am happy to say, is with us yet.

The history is quite lengthy, I know, but I give from it facts as they appear in his report of the condition of the department under his charge for the year 1853. The report was presented to the common council.

THE TOWN PUMP.

On account of the stiff and impermiable clay upon which the city was located the old residents did not find wells satisfactory, for the water in them drained into them only from the surface. As a result the river was the unfailing source of supply.

The water was at first furnished to the people by men who hauled in carts, casks and barrels of it. Buckets were suspended at the ends of wooden yokes, borne on the shoulders of worthy pioneers. The ordinance of the trustees compelled each citizen to keep on his premises a cask containing a certain amount of water, for use in case of fire.

A free pump was arranged for at the foot of Randolph Street in 1824, and it was erected by Peter Berthelet, by permission of the governor and legislative council. All citizens had free access to the wharf on which the pump was located. It continued in use until 1835, when it was taken down, by order of the common council.

Bethuel Farrand, father of the late Jacob S. Farrand, and a pump maker, Rufus Wells, both of Aurelius, Cayuga County, New York, learned that Detroit wished an up-to-date water system and came to this city on foot in 1825 and submitted a proposition to the council which was accepted, and Mr. Farrand was given the "sole and exclusive right of watering the city of Detroit." Mr. Farrand later withdrew from the enterprise and the plant was established by Mr. Wells.

The pump house was located on Berthelet's wharf at the foot of Randolph Street. This was in 1827. The house was a frame building 20 feet square, with a cupola 40 feet high. The pumps were driven by horse power, and the water was pumped into a 40-gallon cask at the top of the cupola.

The water passed through tamarack logs from this cask to the reservoir which was located on the rear of the lot later occupied by the Firemen's Hall at the corner of Randolph Street and Jefferson Avenue. This reservoir was 16 feet square and 6 feet deep, and held 9,580 imperial gallons.

From the reservoir a line of logs was laid down Jefferson Avenue as far as Schwartz's Tavern, between Cass and First Streets, through parts of Larned and Congress Streets and east on Jefferson as far as Brush Street.

FIRST WATER FAMINE.

The city had a water famine one day, because a man in a residence on Larned Street left a plug open, and the water ran until it filled his cellar. At this time the city had about 1,500 inhabitants. Families were uniformly charged $10 per annum, quarterly in advance. Mr. Wells remained sole proprietor until 1829.

In that year the right to supply the city until 1850 was given Mr. Wells, Phineas Davis, Jr., Lucius Lyon and A. E. Hathon. They formed the Detroit Hydraulic Company and bored on the south side of Fort Street, between Shelby and Wayne, going down 260 feet, getting no water, but running into a bed of salt that gave an indication of the future wealth to be obtained in this state from this source.

The company secured an extension of the life of its charter in 1865, and prepared to build a pumping station and reservoir. They were placed on the same lot where the boring took place. The power was furnished by the second stationary engine brought into this state, and water was supplied in the fall of 1830. The reservoir was constructed of brick, was 18 feet square and 9 feet deep, housed in a wooden building. The engine also furnished power for the Detroit Iron Works, at the corner of Jefferson and Cass.

The city was supplied through two lines of wooden logs, of three-inch bore. During the winter of 1830-'31 all but four of the hydrants were rendered useless by freezing and remained in that condition until spring. Many of the logs, which had not been laid at sufficient depth, also were frozen. The reservoir was extremely defective and in 1831 the company constructed another, 40 feet square and 10 feet deep, made of oak planks.

THERE WERE KICKERS THEN.

The Detroit Hydraulic Company soon after erected an engine house on the north side of Woodbridge Street, between Cass and Wayne streets. Instead of a rotary pump a double action force pump was used. The water was declared not to be clear, pure and wholesome, and not furnished continuously, and the company was losing money, but it continued to extend its system.

Frequently the common council discussed the proposition to buy the works, and a committee reported to that body that the company had forfeited its charter by the character of service rendered. It was recommended that the works be located on land up-river from the city.

A committee conferred with the company to learn on what terms it would give up its interest, the committee consisting of Aldermen Julius Eldred and Thomas Palmer. The price fixed was $20,500. This report was accepted and the plant was purchased in 1836. Noah Sutton, as agent for the city, visited eastern water works and soon a site was purchased at the foot of Orleans Street.

The plan of piping water from springs near Farmington was considered and forgotten. During 1837 the foundation of a new reservoir was laid, nearly a duplicate of the old Manhattan works in New York. The next year the reservoir was completed.

The construction of the new plant included the laying of nine miles of hollow tamarack logs and four and a half miles of iron pipe. Water was pumped into an iron reservoir at the foot of Orleans Street and from there it ran by gravitation to the old reservoir on Fort Street, and from this point it was distributed through the old system of logs.

BIG LEAKS.

A report made to the council in 1841 said that there was leakage through the old logs at the rate of 116,000 gallons in twenty-four hours. It was recommended that the new system be used entirely, and provision was made for keeping a map of all connections. Digging at random was found expensive, even in those days. In 1838 six hundred and thirteen persons were assessed for water, and in 1841 only 335. The deficiency was probably occasioned more by the defects in the old works than the absence of persons wishing a supply of water.

Soon after this report was made the engine and pump on Woodbridge Street were abandoned and the new Orleans Street pump was brought into use to supply water to the Fort Street reservoir for distribution. December 14, 1841, the works was accepted by the council. Early in 1842 the Fort Street reservoir was abandoned.

When the plans for the new system were decided upon in 1836 the city contained 8,000 inhabitants. In 1849 the number was more than 20,000, and nearly twice the contents of the reservoir was required each twenty-four hours. It was difficult to find time to make the necessary repairs. Contracts were made for a larger engine and new engine house. The new engine was put in use in November, 1850.

Early in 1851 four acres of land on the Mullet farm, between Russell and Prospect Streets, opposite the city cemetery, were purchased by the council as a site for a new reservoir.

GOT WATER ONLY AT NIGHT.

For several years there had been many complaints of insufficient supply, as the population increased. People had to draw water at night for use the following day, and there were large districts in which a supply could not be secured before midnight. There was plenty of power to raise water to the reservoir, but inadequate means for distributing it. Joined to the four and a half miles of iron pipes, the largest having an interior diameter of ten inches, were about thirty-five miles of logs, principally of two-inch bore, and those were in many cases connected with a five-eighths inch lead pipe. These were laid regardless of any system. and the common council was besieged by complainants. More than $181,000 had been spent on construction, and there had been a deficit in fifteen years of more than $85,000.

In 1852 the control of the water works was placed in the hands of five trustees, Shubael Conant, Henry Ledyard, Edmund A. Brush, James A. Van Dyke and William R. Noyes. Jacob Houghton was appointed commissioner. Iron pipes were laid to those sections of the city from which the most complaints had come.

The trustees were made a board of water commissioners February 14, 1853, by an amendment of the city charter, on application by the common council, and special powers and authority were given to them. Shubael Conant was the first president of the board. He later resigned and E. A. Brush was appointed.

The city had grown from 1,500 to 35,000 people. Water-works constructions, supposed to be large enough to care for increased population, were repeatedly found inadequate after a few years. This lesson was learned.

Be sure to build large enough; you will find it difficult to overestimate.

ROYALTY SAW DETROIT.

PRINCE DE JOINVILLE AND SUITE SPENT A DAY HERE, WHILE DAUPHIN-HUNTING.

ALONG in the latter thirties and early forties, I was clerk in the book store of Sidney L. Rood in the Cooper Block on Jefferson Avenue, this city. I recall an incident that happened, in which the Prince de Joinville and his suite figured.

They visited this city while en route to Green Bay, Wis., on the steamer Columbus, in charge of Captain Shook. The steamer lay at her dock one entire day, giving the distinguished party ample time to see Detroit. They visited our store and remained quite a time looking over the French books in stock that I submitted for their inspection, and they purchased quite liberally.

Many of our people were curious to know why the prince and his party should be bound for Green Bay. The question appeared to be answered when it was remembered that the Reverend Eleazer Williams, the alleged Dauphin of France, son of Louis XVI. and Marie Antoinette, lived there, and it was known afterwards that the prince called on the Reverend Eleazer Williams, on the steamer's arrival at Green Bay, and had a prolonged interview with him. I think the prince did call and see Williams, but he disclaimed afterwards that there was any significance attached to it. Yet the people continued to wonder.

KNAGGS WAS INTRODUCED TO THE PRINCE.

In this connection, George Knaggs, in Robert B. Roy's history of the Knaggs family, says:

"While on a visit to my relatives in Detroit, I met General Lewis Cass, who said: 'You are the very man I wanted to see.'"

He went to the Cass residence, where he was introduced to the Prince de Joinville and the Duke d'Aumale, sons of King Louise Phillippe, of France. who with their suite had just returned from Green Bay, Wis. Their suite consisted of Marshal Bertrand, Count Montholon, Viscount Montesquieu and several servants.

It appears that Louis Phillipe had heard that a man named Rev. Eleazer Williams, an Indian missionary in the Episcopal church of the United States, claimed that he was the son of Louis XVI. and Queen Marie Antoinette, who had been beheaded, was consequently the dauphin end entitled to the throne of France. To ascertain whether the story was true, the young princes came to the United States, chartered the steamer Columbus at Buffalo, and proceeded to Green Bay, where Williams was preaching to a tribe of Indians.

DID NOT BELIEVE HIM.

When they saw and spoke to him, however, they became convinced he was either a wilful imposter, or a person deceived by foolish stories. Williams was well-known in Detroit. When the first St. Paul's church on the east side of Woodward Avenue, between Larned and Congress Streets, was consecrated, on August 24, 1837, he read the consecration service and he was frequently in this city afterwards. He died at Hogansburg, N. Y., in 1858.

When the two princes were on their way back they stopped at Detroit and were entertained by General Cass. They had great curiosity to know the situation in the surrounding country, which was once under French rule. Cass was much gratified on being able to furnish a historian on those subjects like George Knaggs, who was gentlemanly, finely educated and spoke French like a native. George accompanied the princes on their steamboat trip to Buffalo, where he bade them farewell, and went to New York, via Lake Champlain.

The Prince de Joinville and the Duke D'Aumale were accompanied by Marshal Bertrand, Count Montholon and the Viscount Montesquieu. Something in regard to their attire may be interesting. I copy a description of the same from an article that appeared in one of our daily journals, of date, November 27, 1892, and written by Richard R. Elliott, Esq.

"The princes, who were tall and sallow, but well shaped, wore dark cloth frocks, buttoned; light cassimere trousers, made rather collant, patent leather boots and blue traveling caps. De Joinville wore a Byron collar and black silk cravat once around with sailor fashioned knot; D'Aumale a straight collar, black lace scarf run through a gold filagree ring; Montesquieu was dressed somewhat like D'Aumale, neither wore mustache nor beard, nor was there any sign of jewelry visible.

"There was, however, a small oval ring badge on the cap of De Joinville, on which was displayed an anchor, and the letters L. B. P., La Belle Poule, the name of his man-of-war frigate.

"The marshal presented the type of the retired generals of the army. His bronzed face, short white mustache, long blue frock, buttoned to the chin, loose blue trousers which partially concealed his legs, which had become bowed from the constant use of the saddle, his black cravat without collar, his erect and commanding appearance, all indicated the hero to whom bistorians had already assigned a distinguished place in European history.

"Montholon, confidential companion of his exiled master to the last, wore a bourgeois claret frock, buttoned, gray trousers, straight collar, black scarf and horseshoe coil scarf pin. He had in the upper button-hole of his frock the small ribbon of the Legion of Honor. His face was cleanly shaved, and both he and the marshal wore 'compromise' silk hats, i. e., neither bell-shaped, which was royalist, nor cone-shaped, which was republican."

Mr. Elliott says, further, the dress of the princes and suite was described to him at the time by the junior of the firm of A. and J. McFarlane, merchant tailors here.

FIRST BAPTIST CHURCH.

REMINISCENCES CONCERNING MEMBERS OF THE EARLIEST CONGREGATION IN DETROIT.

A COPY from the Michigan Christian Herald, of October 16, 1902, a portion of an article on this society, in 1827-8. As I was closely intimate with some of the persons mentioned in it, I give it herewith, and follow it with some personal remembrances.

The growth of modern Detroit dates in almost every particular from the period from 1820 to 1830. It was in this period that the anomalous rule of the governor and judges, who combined in one body executive, legislative and judicial functions, gave way first to an appointive council to act with the governor in administrative measures, and afterwards to an elective council. It was about this time also that the first steps were taken toward the establishment of the University of Michigan; that the first State Medical Society was organized; that the first territorial roads were laid out; that emigration to the territory commenced on a large scale.

"In this transition period from the lethargy of the old French settlement to the modern American city, the religious life of the place received a new impetus. It was along in this period that the first Episcopal, Methodist and Presbyterian churches were organized, and at this time, also, that a few Baptist brethren began to move for the establishment of religious services according to their own faith.

FIRST IMMERSION.

"It was providential that Brother Henry Davis, who was just completing his studies for the ministry, had his attention turned in this direction, and in the August of 1826 he paid the brethren here a visit. In the course of the following winter a 100m was fitted up in the old Academy, a historic building, which long stood at what is now the west entrance of the city hall. Two brethren and three sisters constituted his first congregation. At the first meeting all related their Christian experience, and covenanted together to strive for the establishment of their faith in the city. Stated meetings were thereafter kept up in the Academy for preaching, prayer and business. On the 19th of August Mrs. Nancy Cabell was added to their number by baptism, the first baptism by immersion that ever took place in the Detroit River. Later in the same month two others were also baptised.

"October 20th, 1827, at the call of these brethren, a council convened, and, after examination of their letters, declaration of faith and covenant, gave them recognition as an organized body of believers, under the name of the First Baptist church at Detroit. The council consisted of lay delegates from the churches in Pontiac, Troy and Farmington. No minister of the denomination is known to have been then settled in the state except Rev. Elkanah Comstock, of Pontiac, who, from some providential cause, was not present. The fact is historically suggestive that the nearest ministers whose presence could be secured for the occasion were Rev. Elisha Tucker, of Fredonia, Rev. Jairus Handy, of Buffalo, N. Y., and Rev. Asahel Morse, of Ohio. The sermon on the occasion was from the text, 'Walk About Zion,' etc., by Brother Tucker, the moderator of the council, and the charge and hand of fellowship by Brethren Morse and Handy. The constituent members of the church were, Henry Davis, pastor; Leonard Loomis, Reuben Starr, and Sisters Eliza H. Davis, Mary Loomis, Martha Rhodes, Hannah W. Gordon, Sally Moon, and Thankful Newberry. Brother Francis P. Browning was considered a member, though his letter from Pontiac was not received at that time. To these four brethren and six sisters was thus given a banner to be diisplayed because of the truth, and in the name of their God, they set it up.

REV. HENRY DAVIS' GOOD WORK.

"Of the further labors of Brother Henry Davis, Rev. Samuel Haskell said in his Half Century Memorial of the Church: 'The records of the church during the first year are incomplete. They mention, however, the painful exclusion of one who was among the first baptized into their number, the dismissal of several others, and the disablement of the pastor by sickness, which compelled him to leave the field at the opening of navigation, before he had finished a year's labor on it. He left in April, much debilitated, intending, however, by appointment of the church, to serve it for a few months in collecting funds to build a house of worship, and then return. But these expectations were disappointed. His work here was finished. He had accomplished good under great hindrances, and deserves our grateful remembrance, especially for the leading part he acted in procuring from the city the grant of these most eligible and beautiful lots on which our house of worship stands. This grant was secured only by coping with great opposition, and owed its passage very much to the friendly advice and active co-operation of Governor Cass, whose sympathy with the young interest and its young pastor is still spoken of by the latter with affectionate gratitude.'

"For more than three weeks after Brother Davis' departure the church was without a pastor and was refused admission to the Michigan Baptist Association. The reason given for this refusal was that the body was too small to be considered a church, and that it chose to receive as members persons who had been baptized by pedobaptist ministers. Through this period the church membership varied from eight to twelve. But the little band with a noble zeal and firm purpose, continued to hold meetings regularly from house to house. Brother Browning was an acknowledged leader among them, and he was accustomed to expound the Scriptures, read a published sermon, conduct a Sunday School, and exercise a general presidency over the church. Though unsolicited by agents this little body of faithful workers made regular contributions to foreign missions and tract and Bible organizations, and erected a small building for the uses of the church.

"The history of the denomination in the state contains few records of more devoted service and deeper Christian love than were shown by this little body during its day of small things."

FRIEND PALMER'S ERCOLLECTIONS.

Of those first members that met on the 20th of October, 1827, the following, as a boy I knew well: Rev. Henry Davis and his wife, Sally Moon, Thankful Newberry and Francis P. Browning. I have always been told that my father, Friend Palmer, who was a devout Baptist, was mainly instrumental in inducing Brother Davis to turn his eyes in this direction. He came in 1826, as the *Herald* says, and one year before the advent of my mother and two sisters and myself.

In July, 1827, the trustees of the city gave Rev. Mr. Davis permission to use the lower room of the academy as a place of public worship. This academy was a historic building, as the *Herald* has it, but it was located on the corner of Bates and Congress Streets, instead of where the west entrance of the city hall is. He held forth there accordingly every Sunday morning and at 2 o'clock in the afternoon. During his pastorate here he baptized my mother, Thankful Palmer, and at my father's death in May, 1827, officiated at the funeral. Shortly after this my mother and myself became inmates in his family, for how long I do not remember, but it appears to me for nearly a year. He lived then on the Corner of Hastings and Woodbridge Streets in the rear of the present Blodgett Terrace. He was a charming man and a most devout Christian. His wife was a most estimable woman, and so neat and trim. They were a very devoted couple, and during all the years that have intervened, their memory dwells with me fresh and fragrant, "like the vase in which roses have once been distilled."

Mrs. Thankful Newberry was the wife of Uncle Henry Newberry, and a most intimate and dear friend of my mother. Miss Sally Moon was quite prominent here in those days. She was associated with her brother, Geo. C. Moon, in the millinery and fancy goods business, and what Miss Moon said in regard to the prevailing style in female attire "went," as the saying is.

MR. FRANCIS P. BROWNING.

Mr. Francis P. Browning was a most estimable man, and extensive operator in lumber, real estate, etc., a true, unselfish Christian gentleman, if there ever was one. The firm of F. & T. Palmer was intimately connected with him in many business ventures, all of which were mutually beneficial. He was a sure Baptist from the crown of his head to the sole of his foot. He died, much lamented, of the cholera, in 1834. He left a son, Samuel Browning, who is at present in the hardware business in this city.

Francis P. Browning was the father of the Baptist Sunday School in this city, as were John J. Deming and Horace Hallock of that of the Presbyterians.

My uncle, Thos. Palmer, was intimately connected with the building of the first Baptist church on the corner of Fort and Griswold Streets. Though not a member of that persuasion, he assisted in the erection of the building in many ways, principally in money and lumber, the latter from his sawmill at St. Clair. So much was he identified with it that he was considered one of the "pillars of the church," and Rev. Mr. Turnbull, its first pastor, was always an honored and welcome guest at his house, corner Fort and Shelby Streets. Senator Palmer when a boy was a regular attendant at the Baptist Sunday School, as I was myself.

After Rev. Mr. Davis left the society erected a small wooden building for church and Sunday School purposes on the corner of Fort and Griswold Streets, and it continued there until it made way for the fine new brick structure that took its place. In addition to those I have mentioned as being at that time members or regular attendants, I recall the names and personalities of the following: Lewis Goddard and wife, Mr. Crocker and wife, Mr. Ambrose and wife, Henry Glover, James Burns, Solomon Davis and wife, John Bloom and wife, the three Dwight families, Samuel Goodell and wife, Miss Urilla Bacon. The last named was a niece of Lewis Goddard, an inmate in his family. In her James Burns met his fate, then and there. After marriage, I think, they joined the Methodist Church. Anyway, they were mighty good people, good enough for any church. Henry Glover also met his fate here, in the person of Miss Laura Dwight, a daughter of Mr. Amassa Dwight. She was his first wife, and a charming woman she was.

HIS MOTHER'S BAPTISM.

Referring again to Rev. Henry Davis, and my mother's baptism, it was by immersion and it occurred on the river front, between Hastings Street and Bolivar Alley. The latter alley is now obliterated, but it ran between the residences of Theo H. Eaton and Wm. G. Thompson, from Jefferson Avenue to the river.

Most of the river front along here was composed of a sandy beach, shallow water out for quite a distance, with hard, sandy bottom. It was an ideal place for the purpose, much better I used to think, than the one in front of the Cass Farm. When the new church was erected on the Corner of Fort and Griswold Streets a large tank, for use in immersions, was put in the basement. I think after this no more baptisms happened on the river front, except those that got into the water by accident, or mistake, without the aid of a minister.

DETROIT MERCHANTS OF THE LONG AGO.

INTERESTING FACTS GLEANED FROM THE COLUMNS OF THE DETROIT GAZETTE OF 1820-1822.

THE old *Detroit Gazette* was an insignificant sheet both in size and appearance. The *Democratic Free Press* that followed it was a trifle larger, and a decided improvement, as regards typography, paper and contents. The first page of the *Gazette* was almost entirely taken up with the laws of the United States and the territory of Michigan. It was fairly patronized by the merchants and others with advertisements.

I have a file of the paper from July 21, 1820, to June 28, 1822, from which I make some extracts, coupled with some personal remembrances of parties, and incidents mentioned in its pages, that may be of interest to many and of no moment perhaps to others. Anyway they will serve to show the difference in many things between then and now. "Joining in Contrast Lieth Love's Delight." In the issue of July 21, 1820, I find:

George McDougall, Sec'y pro tem of Board of Trustees, orders that the assize of bread be 4lbs. 4oz. for 12 1-2 cents; and 2lbs. 2oz. for 6 1-4 cents.

It also has an article taken from the *New York Columbian,* viz:

"Shameful procedure—Some persons at York (now Toronto) in Upper Canada recently thought proper to show their loyalty to the British and hatred to the American cause, by seizing on a wax figure of General Jackson, which had been exhibited in that place, and after a mock trial, hanging it and destroying it. This pitiful evidence of malice appeared to give great satisfaction, and even a newspaper expresses much approbation at the triumph. We have, however, been gratified in seeing, in another part of the province, sentiments of a very proper disapprobation of this procedure."

From July 13th to the 21st the *Gazette* chronicles nine arrivals at this port and nine departures. Among them were the steamboat Walk-in-the-Water, Rogers, master; and the schooner General Jackson, Chelsea Blake, master.

SOME OF THE ADVERTISEMENTS.

Tunis S. Wendell & Co. advertise in the same space a general assortment of goods, just received from the east (at the new store in Mrs. Dodemead's house).

This Dodemead house was on the northeast corner of Jefferson Avenue and Shelby Street.

John S. Roby advertises for sale at his auction and commission store, on the wharf, between Shelby and Wayne Streets, quite an assortment of merchandise, consisting of whiskey, beer, flour, pork, tobacco, furniture, boots and shoes, etc.

June 26th, 1821, the steamboat Walk-in-the-Water, Jebediah Rogers, master, advertises to sail from Black Rock on the 9th of July next, at 4 o'clock in the afternoon, for Detroit, Michilimackinac and Green Bay. She will sail from Detroit on her return trip on the 23d of July.

FOUNDING OF A GREAT BUSINESS.

M. Chapin & Co. say that they have received from New York a very extensive assortment of drugs, medicines, groceries, paints, oils, dye-woods, dye stuffs, etc., and offer the same low for cash, at the store adjoining the house of Mr. Roby.

Mr. Roby's house was just below the Michigan Exchange. The "Co." was John Owen, and after this the firm was John Owen & Co., Dr. Chapin retiring, and Theo. H. Hinchman taking his place. Mr. Owen, after some years, retired and Mr. James A. Hinchman took his place.

The firm then became T. & J. Hinchman. Mr. J. A. Hinchman, after a brief session, retired, and T. H. Hinchman's three sons took his place, under the firm name of T. H. Hinchman & Sons. After the death of T. H. Hinchman the concern was merged into the present extensive one of Williams, Davis, Brooks & Hinchman Sons.

I imagine it is the only firm in the entire west that has maintained a continuous organization (so to speak) for nearly ninety years, and with unimpaired credit.

It appears the paper, itself, was in trade. Their issue July 21, 1820, has this notice:

Quills, etc.—Just received at this office. Also Flutes, Fifes, Flute Preceptors, Fife do, Blank Music Books, Record Books, etc.

James Abbott, postmaster, has quite a List of Letters in his office uncalled for.

Another advertisement reads:

Paul Clapp.

Has on hand, and will constantly keep for sale, at wholesale and retail, a large assortment of Hats, Beaver, Castor, Roram, Napt and Felt.

Also—Ladies elegant Beaver Hats, with trimmings complete. The whole will be sold very cheaf for CASH or PELTRY.

Clapp's place of business was between Bates and Randolph Streets, on west side of Jefferson Avenue.

BIG FOURTH OF JULY CELEBRATION.

July 6th, 1821, the paper records a 4th of July celebration, by the citizens and strangers in the city. At twelve o'clock, the Declaration of Independence was read to a large concourse, at the Council House by Chas. Larned, Esqr. A procession was then formed, and preceded by martial music playing the good old tune of "Yankee Doodle," marched to the hotel of Mr. Bronson, where upwards of one hundred and fifty persons sat down to a bounteous repast; at which Judge James Witherell, as president, and Major T. Maxwell, as vice-president, presided. Both of these gentlemen entered the army at an early period of the revolution, and never laid aside their arms until the liberties of their country were secured. Major T. Kearsley and Captain Ben Woodworth assisisted as second and third vice-presidents. A set of appropriate toasts were drunk.

Aside from the foregoing a number of ladies and gentlemen of this city and vicinity, also officers of the army at this post, embarked on the steamboat Walk-in-the-Water at 11 a. m. The company was also attended by a fine band. The day was extremely fine, and the quarter deck of the boat, which by the politeness of Captain Rogers had been prepared for the purpose, was occupied by cotillion parties.

The boat, after passing Malden and making a short trip into

Lake Erie, returned to her wharf at sunset. The British troops at Malden saluted the steamer on passing.

In the issue of August 10, 1821, A. C. Canniff (Judge Canniff) says he has opened a boot and shoe shop in the small building two doors east of Colonel Henry J. Hunt's store, where he intends to carry on the business in all its branches.

Colonel Hunt's store was a few doors east of Shelby Street on the south side of Jefferson Avenue.

A VALUABLE CARGO.

In the issue of August 17 is a notice of the arrival of the schooner Decatur from Chicago and Mackinac, having on board 500 packs of furs, valued at $100,000. The schooner Red Jacket sailed from this port with 200 packs of furs.

James Abbott, auctioneer, says he will sell (same date) a large quantity of maple sugar in barrels, kegs and mocoocks, and take his pay in fine flour at the, then, cash price.

December 1, 1820, the proprietors of the *Gazette* offer for sale a large and fine assortment of miscellaneous books, much the finest that has ever been brought to the territory.

In this same issue F. T. & J. Palmer have nearly a column ad. but dated November 15, setting forth that they have received and are opening their fall stock of goods, comprising almost everything in the line of dry goods, groceries, liquors, hardware, crockery and glass ware, which can be had low, for cash.

December 29, 1820, records the marriage of Mr. David Cooper to Miss Lovicy Mack, also that of Captain Henry Whiting, of the Fifth Regiment, to Miss Eliza Macomb. Both couples were joined by Rev. Mr. Monteith.

David Cooper was father of Rev. David M. Cooper, of this city. Captain Whiting was afterward Major Whiting, and stationed here for many years as quartermaster.

In the issue of February 16, is a notice of the marriage of Doctor J. L. Whiting, at Hudson, N. Y., on the 18th of January to Miss Harriet C. Talman, daughter of Doctor John Talman, mayor of that city.

Scores of our citizens will remember Dr. Whiting with pleasurable emotions, I am sure.

Chauncey S. Payne, says, he has, for sale, Cheap for Cash, at his shop on Jefferson Avenue, south side (between Shelby and Griswold Streets) a large assortment of jewelry, clocks, watches, military goods, pocket knives, Indian jewelry, etc.

The *Gazetter* Office offers school books of all kinds, wrapping paper and law blanks. John P. Sheldon, of the same office, has a few axes for sale of excellent quality.

PRAISE FOR OAKLAND COUNTY.

A stranger contributing a long article to the *Gazette,* on the country around and adjacent to Detroit, among other things has this to say about the country around Pontiac.

"The little lakes I have mentioned (twenty-one of which I visited and from the best information I could obtain there are upwards of sixty of them in all) abound with fish of various kinds, many of which I saw would weigh twelve pounds each; they are also in great abundance. The grey and black duck was frequently seen in large flocks on these unfrequented waters. These lakes are of various dimensions, from one to four miles in circumference. Here may be found some of the most delightful retreats for gentlemen of taste and fortune, and only a week's journey from the city of New York. When the great Erie canal to Lake Erie is completed, you need not be surprised at seeing gentlemen with their families coming to spend the summer months on their country seats near Pontiac."

THE OLD-TIME FERRY.

In the issue of July 21, 1820, and continued through the files of the *Gazette* that I have, is the notice that B. Woodworth has obtained a license to keep a ferry on Detroit River, and calls on the public for patronage. He has, he says, provided an excellent flat, and his boat for passengers is superior to any that can be found on the river. Careful men have been engaged to attend the ferry, and constant attention will be given, in order that paasengers shall suffer no delay. The ferry is kept nearly in front of the Steamboat Hotel.

Ben Woodworth's Steamboat Hotel was on the southwest corner of Randolph and Woodbridge Streets, and the ferry landing was at the foot of Randolph Street.

In the same issue and continued through subsequent issues for quite a period, is a notice of the forming of a land agency, by Ball & Petit, and that an office has been opened at the office of the surveyor of the Michigan territory in the city of Detroit, for the purchase, sale or exchange of lands, public and private, lying within this territory, the western district of New York and Upper Canada, or the adjacent parts of the state of Ohio, etc.

This firm of Ball and Petit was dissolved before my advent here, by the death of Mr. Petit. Mr. Ball, the survivor, when I knew him, was in the employ of Sheldon & Reed as assistant editor or business manager of the *Gazetter,* I think in latter capacity. He was quite competent, however, to fill both positions. He at the time boarded in my uncle's family, adjoining the *Gazette* office, and with him was his sister, a charming girl in her teens, Sophia Ball. The latter was here temporarily. What became of Ball I do not remember, but his sister returned to her home somewhere in the south and married Mr. Hancock, a southern planter who owned many slaves.

SLAVE GIRL WAS ABDUCTED.

Miss Ball, her father, and Miss Elizabeth Clemens, of Mt. Clemens, the latter a daughter of Judge Clemens, were inmates of my uncle's homestead for a year or more, the young ladies attending school here. Two or three years after Miss Ball's marriage, she visited her former brief home here, with her two children and they were guests in my uncle's family. She had with her a young colored girl, one of her husband's slaves, as a nurse.

The fact became known to Doctor E. W. Cowles, a partner of Doctor E. Hurd, through a colored barber on the steamer that brought them here. The doctor, a pronounced abolitionist, interested himself in the affair and the girl was abducted; her mistress never saw her again, and, I remember so well, much to her disgust.

I don't think Doctor Hurd had any knoweldge of the affair, though I know his sympathies were all with the colored people.

Mr. R. B. Ross, in his sketches of Detroit in 1837, has already dilated on this incident, and the reason I repeat it is that I know the lady well who is mentioned and the circumstances connected therewith, also think I furnished Mr. Ross with some of the facts.

Mr. Petit, who, as I have said, died before my arrival here, left a widow and one child, a boy. The Petits lived on the southeast corner of **Woodward** Avenue and Congress Street, and owned through to Griswold Street. The son, Dudley Petit, a bright youth, a schoolmate of mine, died in the early thirties. The widow married Mr. Eurotas P. Hastings, president of the Old Bank of Michigan.

NO MORE CREDIT AT THE POSTOFFICE.

WHY IT WAS ABOLISHED IN 1821 BY POSTMASTER JAMES ABBOTT.

THERE are many interesting articles in the old *Detroit Gazette,* from which I quoted last week. They throw a great deal of light on life in Detroit in the early twenties.

For example, in the issue of July 21, 1821, I found that W. Leonard & Co. inform their friends and the public, that they have commenced the Saddling and Harness business at Spencer's Tannery a few rods above the city, and ask for a share of their patronage.

This Spencer's tannery was situated on the river front, just west of Hastings Street. Spencer, whoever he was, had docked out into the river quite a space and filled it in with earth. It was said that an Indian chief with uplifted tomahawk chased a man by the name of Scott into this tanyard with murderous intent but Scott hid in one of the tanning vats and thus got rid of his pursuer.

It was quite a busy locality in the early thirties. Mr. Dequindre, a brother of Major Antoine Dequindre, had an extensive store close by. The Detroit & Black River Steam Mill Co. had their saw mill and lumber yard just west; and opposite the tannery yards were quite a number of saloons, a French dancing house and billiard room; also located in the vicinity were two or three other dance houses, and it was said a seeker after a chance and place to "trip the light fantastic toe" had only to get on top of any of the lumber piles nearby to determine where it was located by the sound of the fiddle. Those dances were always "on tap."

Harvey Williams had his extensive blacksmith shop near here, and Alanson Sheeley had an extensive lumber yard near, when he was agent for some Black River (Port Huron) steam saw mill company. On this tannery dock was built the steamboat Argo, No. 2.

ADVERTISEMENTS.

Storage and Commission Business.

(At the Steamboat Wharf),

D. C. McKinstry informs the public that he has taken the commodious store house, wharf and yard of Austin Ewing (foot of Bates Street) and will transact the above business on accommodating terms.

Auction and Commission Store.

James Abbott has just received N. Y., Penn., and Ohio Whisky, Smoked Hams, Bacon, Lard, Butter and Genesee Cheese, Flour, Garden Seeds, Pecan and Hickory Nuts, Domestic Goods by Box or Piece, Buffalo Robes, Playing Cards, Soap, Tar, Linseed Oil, Grind Stones, Stoves, Boards & Scantling, etc.

Also—a few barrels of Whisky, four years old, and best Jamaica Spirits.

Jerry Dean has

Saddles, Bridles, Harness, Portmanteaus, Valises, etc., Jefferson Avenue, west side, between Griswold and Shelby Sts.

The proprietors of the steamboat Walk-in-the-Water have come down in their price for cabin passage from Detroit to Black Rock, from 18 to 15 dollars. J. ROGERS, Master.

Henry I. Hunt says in addition to his usual assortment of Dry Goods, Groceries, Hardware, Crockery and Shoes, he has just received 100 barrels of Flour, 3 do of Maple Sugar, 50 do of Pork, 100 do of Whisky, 200 do of Salt, 14 kegs of Butter and 7 crates of Bottles and 3 boxes Domestic Factory Cottons. All of which he will sell low for cash. He says further, Bills on the Bank of Muskingum, Ohio, will be received in payment for the sugar and for part of the flour, butter and pork. Also, he again solicits those who owe him to make payment without delay; by so doing they will avert the mortification of being sued, and relieve him from that painful duty.

JOHNSY MCCARTHY says he has established a bakery at the southeast corner of Griswold and Woodbridge Streets, where may be found at all times loaf bread, sea biscuits, rusks, hot rolls, etc.

McCarthy was in the same business, and at the same location, when I came here and after.

WILCOX & BEACH inform their friends and the public, that they have commenced the Hatting business in this city, and will manufacture and keep on hand a good assortment of well finished Hats, warranted equal in style and quality to any manufactured in this country.

Wilcox was the father of Eben N. and General O. B. Wilcox.

NO MORE CREDIT AT POSTOFFICE.

Detroit in the early twenties was governed by a board of trustees, of which James Abbott was the chairman and Jas. D. Doty secretary.

In the issue of January 12, 1821, James Abbott, postmaster, says:

"The trouble, exclusive of the loss, I have lately experienced in crediting postage, renders it necessary for me to discontinue it. Notice is therefore give that from and after the first day of February next no letter will be delivered out of the office unless the postage is paid, except to persons who receive letters on public business. Postage on newspapers is required by the seventeenth article of instructions from the general postoffice, to be paid in advance, without which they will not be delivered, even should the money be tendered for them singly. N. B.—Persons who are dissatisfied with the above arrangement, and others who do not like to carry change in their pockets, may be accommodated by depositing the probable amount of one quarter's postage in advance."

PONTIAC IN 1821.

In the issue, Friday, February 2, 1821, the editor has this to say in regard to Pontiac village:

A gentleman recently from Pontiac gives us the following information in regard to the progress and improvement in that new settlement:

"In December, 1818, the first house was erected, and in July, 1820, the first County Court was held.

"There is now within the limits of the spot laid out for the shire town of Pontiac one large grist mill, one saw mill, one tanner and currier, one shoemaker, one blacksmith, one cabinetmaker, one wheelwright, three carpenters and one brickmaker.

"From the 21st to the 28th ult. sixty-three sleighs, each loaded from thirty to forty-eight bushels of grain, arrived at the grist mill, and all from a distance of more than twenty-five miles.

"In March, 1819, there were but four families in the County of Oakland—there are now about 200—all of the best class of emigrants."

In a communication to the *Gazette* from a correspondent, February 2, 1821, he has this to say in regard to Sault Ste. Marie, the expedition of Governor Cass and party the year previous and the Indians:

"It (the Soo) is the key to the country around and north of Lake Superior, and equally important to the savages and the English. Accordingly the English government has established a post on Drummond's Island, at the mouth of this (Soo) river, and made that a deposit of presents for the Indians. When the exploring party last season landed at Sandy Lake, many of the head men of the bands were receiving cordial greetings at this island; and to reach this happy spot, where fortune always smiles, it is absolutely necessary they should pass the Soo. Here is an extent of country of 500 miles, in which British flags and British medals are not unfrequent sights. It is by this same route, likewise, the North-West Company make their largest and most valuable returns. At this time an easy, free and avowed communication is had annually with these Indians by this place. It is with regret and displeasure that both sides (British and Indians) try to intercept this wide-trod path.

"This dislike was strongly evinced last season when a treaty was held by Governor Cass at the Sault for a cession of a certain tract situated there, claimed by our government under Wayne's treaty. It was with the greatest difficulty that cession was obtained. One of the chiefs who was called the 'count' appeared in the council in the full dress of a British officer, and during the conference showed the greatest aversion for the Americans. When the chiefs were about to retire, this fellow standing by the presents, which lay in the center of the marquee where the council was held, with great contempt, kicked them aside and rushed out of the marquee.

GOVERNOR CASS'S BRAVERY.

"In a few moments a British flag, and not a North-West flag, was seen flying within thirty rods, and in front of the governor's camp, and in the midst of the Indian lodges. Immediately the governor, unattended by any of the party, walked to the lodge where the flag was raised, and by which the chiefs who had been in the council were standing, and seizing the flag, he flung it upon the ground and trampled it under his feet.

"The Indians appeared panic-struck by this daring act. The governor called to the interpreter and remonstrated with them upon the impropriety of their conduct, and upon the hostile feelings they displayed towards the United States. He also stated the inevitable result to which such conduct must lead, and that a repetition of it while we were there, would not pass unpunished. In less than fifteen minutes, the squaws belonging to the lodges, with all their children, had abandoned their camp and were safely landed on the British shore, and appearances indicated an immediate attack. On the part of the exploring party preparations were instantly made for defense against any attack which might be made by the Indians. But the firmness of the party effected what had already been despaired of. In a short time the older chiefs sent for the governor and disavowed the rash act which had been committed. They attributed it to the young men, and expressed their sincere regret at its occurrence. They also requested a renewal of the council, and proposed their readiness to make the small concession, being only sixteen sections which was asked. The council was accordingly renewed and in a short time the treaty was signed. These same Indians had before insulted American officers who had visited the Sault, and their object was undoubtedly to ascertain how far their insolence might be carried with impunity. During the whole of this transaction, in their conduct and in their language, a positive attachment to the English was very evident."

(An allusion has been made to this incident previously, but differing from it in many respects.)

FIGHTING EPIDEMICS.

HOW DETROITERS DEFENDED THEMSELVES FROM CHOLERA IN 1832 AND 1834.

DETROIT had memorable epidemics of cholera in 1832 and 1834. I was but a strip of a lad then and do not remember much about it, only in a general way. I was too young to realize the grave import of the calamity.

The bonfires of tar and rosin that the common council ordered lighted at the corners of the principal streets throughout the city, as a sanitary precaution, made the whole affair look to me like a continuous Fourth of July celebration, so I rather enjoyed it than otherwise and gave no thought to the cholera.

An immense iron potash kettle was located in the center of the square at the intersection of Jefferson Avenue and Woodward, and was kept constantly full, night and day, with burning tar and rosin.

A portion of the troops under General Scott were quartered here for a short time, while on their way to Green Bay, Wis., to attend to Black Hawk. They occupied the government warehouse on Woodbridge Street, near the corner of Cass. The cholera broke out among them, as it did, indeed, among his whole command. Many of them died here, I think. I know many of them did die of the dread disease after they embarked on the steamer Henry Clay and were buried along the shore of the St. Clair River. All old settlers on the St. Clair will confirm this statement.

CHOLERA IN 1832.

Four steamers, the Henry Clay, Superior, Sheldon Thompson and William Penn, were chartered by the United States government for the purpose of transporting troops, provisions, etc., to Chicago during the Black Hawk war; but owing to the fearful ravages made by the breaking out of the Asiatic cholera among the troops, the crews on board two of these boats, the Henry Clay and Superior, were compelled to abandon their voyage, proceeding no further than Fort Gratiot.

On the Henry Clay nothing like discipline could be maintained. As soon as the steamer came to the dock each man sprang on shore, hoping to escape from a scene so terrifying and appalling. Some fled to the woods, some to the fields, while others lay down in the streets or under the cover of the river bank, where most of them died, unwept and alone.

Their remains were subsequently gathered up and buried at Fort Gratiot. Among the dead was a son of Henry Clay, to whom a monument was erected in the cemetery at that post.

The Sheldon Thompson arrived in Chicago about the first of July with her complement of troops and munitions of war, and supplies for Fort Dearborn. Out of the number of soldiers aboard of her twelve had died of the disease after she left Detroit, and their bodies were cast into Lake Michigan at the mouth of the Chicago River.

DEATH OF FATHER RICHARD.

Father Richard, the venerated and well-beloved Catholic priest, also fell a victim to the disease, contracted in his tireless devotion to the stricken, a martyr to the cause of humanity. I was at his funeral, as indeed the whole community were, far and near. His remains were deposited temporarily in the grounds adjoining St. Mary's Hospital and shortly after found, as was then supposed, a permanent resting place in the vaults under old St. Anne's church, corner Larned and Bates Streets. When the latter was destroyed, I think they were removed to the new St. Anne's.

His body lay in state for two or three days in front of the high altar in the church that he built almost entirely through his own exertions. It was his pride and he loved it well. His body was so arranged that it reposed clad in its priestly robes, half reclining in his coffin, so that the features could be distinctly seen the moment one entered the church.

A sorrowing crowd filled the church almost constantly, during the time his body lay in state, and on the occasion of the funeral the obsequies were most solemn and impressive.

CHOLERA IN 1834.

From about the middle of July, 1834, to a date about 40 or 60 days thereafter, this dreadful disease visited all ages, sexes, conditions and colors in Detroit, and out of a population not exceeding 3,500, more than 10 per cent were cut down amidst a panic of dread and misery, such as had rarely visited any of our cities before.

Among the earliest victims was Governor Geo. B. Porter, who died very suddenly in the very meridian of his life. He passed away down at the brick house then in Springwells, which he was erecting and furnishing for his own habitation. It was afterwards occupied by the late Sylvester Larned. The death of Governor Porter left Stevens T. Mason, then but 20 years old, the secretary and acting governor of Michigan, which place, notwithstanding his youth, he filled with dignity and honor until in 1836 he was elected by the people of Michigan to that same office and held it until 1839.

EFFORTS OF MAYOR TROWBRIDGE.

At this time, 1834, Charles C. Trowbridge was the mayor of Detroit. No better man or braver officer for such an emergency ever held an office of so much importance to the safety and welfare and the protection of a terrified and terror-stricken people. The alarm that spread all over Detroit was created and extended not merely by the sudden and awful deaths which occurred on the steamers, on the docks, among the woodpiles and merchandise strewed along the river, not merely among the laboring, the dissipated, the filthy and reckless portion of the community, but by the deaths among the most temperate, the most cleanly and apparently among the most calm and courageous. Those who have read Eugene Sue will not forget that when Father Rhodan met the cholera as he came out of the gates of Paris and demanded of him "for what purpose he had been mowing down that population like blades of grass before the scythe," the cholera responded to the reproach that he "had carried off only one-third, while fear alone had destroyed the remaining two-thirds." As it was true in Paris, so it was in Detroit.

GEO. C. BATES'S REFERENCE.

The late Geo. C. Bates, writing about it in 1885, says: "It is impossible now after fifty years have rolled away, to describe the terror, alarm and panic that prevailed, to depict or portray with the pen the blanched cheeks and the husky voices of brave men who met at the corners of the streets or in the reception room and drinking room of the old Mansion House (for brandy was prescribed by Drs. Rice and Whiting and other leading physicians). Standing upon its gallery, they could look up and down the avenue and see carts, drays and all kinds of vehicles on their way to the cemetery, filled with corpses, many of whom but a few hours before were in full health and strength. Neither can I portray the absolute alarm and panic which emptied that old Mansion House of nearly all its inmates on the death of its matron, Mrs. Boyer—a woman huge in size, with a heart in full proportion to her body, and courage that seemed to bid defiance to death itself. About the 25th of August the bulletins reported the death of thirty-six on that one day, among whom were General Chas. Larned, F. P. Browning, Tom Knapp, the sheriff, E. B. Canning, Mrs. B. F. H. Witherell, and others like them.

"Dr. Randall Rice declared, with an oath, that in 1832 he had saved nearly all his patients by bleeding and calomel, yet at this season every single patient whom he had thus far treated had died upon his hands.

"To obtain nurses at night and aids and assistants to remove and bury the dead became almost impossible. Despair was fast settling upon all who remained. The stages were loaded down each succeeding morning with load after load of frightened people, who fled in terror to Pontiac, to Ann Arbor, to Jackson or Monroe, and who not unfrequently died on their way, or immediately after reaching their destination of supposed safety."

WORK OF FATHER KUNDIG.

In the midst of all this desolation there appeared, to aid Mayor Trowbridge in his efforts to arrest the progress of the disease, to roll back by force of will and courage the tide of anxiety and fear that existed, one who was then and long afterwards regarded almost a savior of Detroit, whose heroism and Christian pluck and power did more than all other things to rescue his people from the grave. He won from them a record and testimonial never to be effaced. His benevolence, humanity and devotion to duty equaled any upon the field of battle, or exhibited in the wildest and most fearful storms at sea. I mean Father Kundig, a Catholic priest, who many a long year afterwards was an honored bishop in Milwaukee of Holy Mother church, and who carried with him to his grave the affections of all who ever knew him.

The good father on his own responsibility went to work as utterly regardless and fearess of death as if God had vouchsafed to him the power to crush it in the hollow of his hand or stamp it out as he would the burning brand planted by an incendiary. He organized and improvised a hospital just behind where the Russell House now stands. Calling to his aid some twenty-five or more of the daughters of his church, young, bright and beautiful girls, like Josephine Desnoyer, Anne Dequindre, the Knaggs and Campau girls, he infused into them at once by his teachings and by his holy example an absolute conviction that it was their duty to visit the sick, to perform the most irksome and sickening duties for the poor, filthy and drunken wretches that were gathered up each morning from the docks, steamers, lanes and highways of Detroit, and to nurse them and to save them if possible from death, and after death to prepare them decently and carefully for the grave.

So thoroughly did he arm them with his own courage and religious zeal and pluck that almost at once the minds of all the people began to realize that indeed cholera cut down only about one-third, while panic and fear finished the work by laying low the remaining two-thirds. Let it be borne in mind and never be forgotten that of that noble old Catholic priest, and all those bright, beaming, beautiful and blessed Catholic girls, not one of them, although exposed day by day and night by night for weeks together during the existence of that dreadful epidemic, ever were even attacked by that hideous monster, the cholera.

MUTUAL INSURANCE COMPANY.

Let it not be forgotten that immediately after the death of Mrs. Boyer at the Mansion House, when the house was deserted by everybody who could leave it and the city, fifteen young men, of whom the writer was one, organized themselves into a mutual insurance company and agreed that they would not leave their home, but would occupy the old ball-room in the third story of that old hotel and would watch over, aid and assist one another to guard against disease, and if necessary, would faithfully watch over and nurse and protect one another. Of all that number one only was ever taken ill or died, and it was the victim of his own folly—in drinking mint juleps and eating green cucumbers, as if determined to invite an attack from the disease.

That Mutual Insurance organization, like the work of Father Kundig and his lady aids and assistants, soon banished all fear, panic and mental anxiety for ourselves, and demonstrates in the clearest and most absolute manner that whosoever cooly and courageously pursues the ordinary habits of his life and his daily business may bid defiance to cholera or yellow fever or any other epidemic, and outlive its dangers and its destruction.

From about August 3, of that year, down to September 15, the cholera continued its ravages, and furnished a death list from day to day that was appalling, until at the final summing up of the figures the balance-sheet showed that about one-eighth of all our population had been carried off to the cemetery.

About the middle of September, 1834, it was announced that the cholera had abated entirely and that the theatre under Dean & McKinney in old Colonel McKinstry's building, would open. Our club went enmasse to listen to Dan Marble's humorous performance of "Black-eyed Susan." That was a happy crowd, you may be sure, until on returning late at night the old sexton, Israel Noble, mounted on his horse and followed by half a dozen drays and carts, each one laden with dead bodies, warned us all to shut up the theatre and wait until a later day, when finally the cholera disappeared as suddenly and as strangely as it came.

OLD CHURCH USED AS HOSPITAL.

The Presbyterin church that stood on the corner of Woodward Avenue and Larned Street was sold to the Catholics and moved to the corner of Cadillac Square and Bates Street, where, in the cholera time it was occupied as a hospital under the charge of Father Kundig, as he says, John Canann, an Irish ditch digger, was employed to bring the sick to the hospital and to take away the dead for burial. He used a horse and cart for the purpose.

On one occasion as he was taking bodies away in his cart for burial, he seized and undertook to carry out a man by the name of Rider, who was noticed to be alive. On being remonstrated with, John said that it made no difference, as he would be dead anyway before he got him to the cemetery. Rider was still living near St. Louis in 1860.

The hospital that Bates mentions as being improvised by Father Kundig, just behind the Russell House, was the place, as Mr. Bates says, where thirty-five died in one day.

Such was the panic of the public that at one time there were supposed to be not over 1,500 people left in the city, those who were well not being sufficient to take care of the sick.

During the epidemic of 1832, J. M. Howard, Lawyer Harding, Thomas Palmer, A. P. Mormon, A. H. Stowell, Sidney L. Rood and Levi Cook advertised that they would at all times be ready to take care of those who had cholera, and they at once had all they could do. The senate chamber in the old state capital was also utilized and filled with the sick.

Uncle Thomas Palmer lived at that time on Woodward Avenue at the corner of Jorn R. Street, where is now Schwankovsky's music store, and made it a point to visit the capitol building twice a day at least, going and returning from his place of business down town. I was there myself, often more out of curiosity than anything else, being too young to realize the gravity of the situation.

My uncle's great remedy was brandy and, indeed, stimulants of all kinds, and he was quite successful, as I have heard him say, in saving the lives of many who came under his care. As said before, Drs. Rice and Whiting and other leading physicians prescribed the same, with the addition of calomel. Dr. Hurd was also quite successful in his treatment of the dread disease, though he failed to save the life of a favorite servant of his, a young girl from the River Rouge. She was about 20 years old and was stricken with cholera. She was a great favorite in the family, as she was of myself. The doctor and his good wife used every effort to save her, but, as I said, in vain. I happened to be present when she passed away, and, boy that I was, I shall never forget that death-bed scene. I may say, in passing, that Dr. Hurd and Uncle Thomas Palmer worked in unison in treating the disease. The cholera visited this city twice after this, but I was not here either time.

WHEN WOODWARD AVENUE WAS A CORDUROY ROAD.

TRIP TO OAKLAND COUNTY, 28 MILES, REQUIRED TWO DAYS—EXTRACTS FROM THE OLD DETROIT GAZETTE.

FRIDAY, November 10, 1820, the editor of the *Detroit Gazette* says:

"We delayed the publication of our paper until this evening, in the expectation that the steamboat would arrive with some late and important news, but we are disappointed. The mail arrived in due season last Wednesday, but brought nothing of interest."

EARLY ROAD MAKING.

The paper of the same date has this to say of the Pontiac Road, Saginaw Turnpike:

"The six miles of this important road which Major S. Mack contracted to complete, and the progress of which our citizens have watched with so much interest, are now finished, and we are happy to say, in a manner highly to the reputation of the contractor and the satisfaction of the public. Considerable more than one-half of the road made by Mr. Mack is formed of very large logs laid closely together, across the road, on which are piled small timber, brush, clay and sand, making a dry, and at the same time a durable highway.

"The principal objects encountered in making the road were the immense number of large and small trees with which the country immediately in the rear of this place abounds.

"It is, we believe, admitted on all hands, that Major Mack has completed the most **difficult** part of the road between this place and Pontiac. Still considerable labor remains to be done, for the track beyond the Six Miles does not deserve the name of Road—we refer more particularly to the portion lying this side of the cranberry marsh and that near Mr. Woodford's and beyond Mr. Thirber's.

"We will not insult the good sense of the inhabitants of this city and of Oakland County by saying that they do not seem, from the little that has been done on those parts of the road alluded to, to understand how much of their true interest is involved in its speedy completion, but it will not be improper to say that the exertion already made to accomplish the object has not been proportioned to its palpable importance."

WOODWARD AVENUE AS A CORDUROY ROAD.

Those that witnessed the large quantity of heavy logs unearthed by the contractors when preparing the bed for the asphalt pavement recently laid on Woodward Avenue (Pontiac Road) to the Six Mile Crossing and wondered how and why they were there, can now account for them, if they did not before. And in the above connection I give the late Mrs. John Palmer's experience over this turnpike a short time after its completion. She said:

"We had Mack and Conant's turnpike on the north (Woodward Avenue), then it was a new corduroy road extending from the Grand Circus north six miles. Mack and Conant built it for the general government, receiving $6,000 for it."

Mrs. Palmer said further: "You can get an idea of what its condition was then, when I tell you that Mrs. John P. Sheldon and myself, each with an infant in our arms, started to visit Mrs. Sheldon's father, who lived in Oakland County, 28 miles from Detroit. We made the six miles over Mack & Conant's turnpike and 22 miles along an Indian trail in just two days. Rather slow, wasn't it?"

A. Edwards advertises a large stock of merchandise among which is 200 barrels of whiskey and only 50 barrels of pork, also boots and shoes of his own manufacture.

HE WANTED MUSKRAT SKINS.

De Garmo Jones wants a few thousand prime muskrat skins, for which he will pay the CASH, at his warehouse foot of Shelby Street.

F. T. & J. Palmer, say "they have recently received a fresh

supply of merchandise, and they are daily expecting to receive an extensive assortment, which together with what they now have on hand, will make their assortment as complete as can be found in the territory. Their former practice of not being undersold by their neighbors is rigidly adhered to."

TO PURCHASE FIRST FIRE ENGINE.

The board of trustees of the City of Detroit, through their secretary, Geo. McDougall, called a meeting of the citizens at the Council House on Monday, the eleventh of September, at 4 o'clock P. M. to determine on the propriety of voting on a tax to be applied in the purchase of a fire engine for the use of the city. This was for the purchase of the first fire engine.

The Postmaster-General advertises August 31, 1820, for proposals for carrying the mails from Detroit by Pontiac to Mt. Clemens once a week, 53 miles.

October 27, 1820. John P. Sheldon of the *Gazette,* has a few barrels of good old Ontario Whisky for sale, also a few barrels of flour.

GOVERNOR CASS'S EXPEDITION.

Governor Cass, it appears, in 1819 was impressed with the importance of an expedition for exploring the extreme northwestern regions of the Union—the great chain of lakes, and the sources of the Mississippi River, which were the continued subject of dispute between geographical writers. He presented a memorial to the Secretary of War upon the subject in which he proposed leaving Detroit in the ensuing spring, in two or three Indian canoes, as being best adapted to the navigation of the shallow waters of the upper country, and to the numerous portages which it would be necessary to make from stream to stream.

The specific objects of this journey, as presented in the memorial of Governor Cass, were to obtain a more correct knowledge of the names, numbers, customs, history, condition, mode of subsistence and disposition of the Indian tribes—to survey the topography of the country, and collect the materials for an accurate map, to locate the site of a garrison at the foot of Lake Superior, and to purchase the ground, to investigate the subject of the northwestern copper mines, lead mines and gypsum quarries, and to purchase from the Indian tribes such tracts as might be necessary to secure to the United States the ultimate advantages to be derived from them. To accomplish these objects it was proposed to attach to the expedition a topographical engineer, a physician and a person familiar with mineralogy.

The Secretary of War, Mr. Calhoun, not only approved of the proposed plan, but determined to enable the Governor to carry it into complete effect, by ordering an escort of soldiers and enjoining it upon the commandants of the frontier garrison, to furnish every aid that the exigencies of the party might require, either in men, boats or supplies.

The expedition left Grosse Pointe (Lake St. Clair) in three canoes May 26, 1820, and consisted of the following persons:

His excellency, Lewis Cass, Governor of the Michigan Territory.

Alexander Wolcott, M. D., Indian agent at Chicago, physician to the expedition.

Captain David B. Douglass, civil and military engineer.

Lieutenant Aeneas McKay, Third United States Artillery, commanding the soldiers.

James D. Doty, Esq., secretary to the expedition.

Major Robert A. Forsyth, private secretary to the governor.

Mr. Charles T. Trowbridge, assistant topographer.

Mr. Alexander R. Chase.

Also ten Canadian voyageurs, seven United States soldiers, ten Indians of the Ottawa and Shawnee tribes, an interpreter and a guide, making thirty-eight persons all told.

TREATY OF 1820.

The treay at the Soo was signed by Governor Cass on part of the United States and by sixteen chiefs on the part of the Indians (Chippewa) on the 16th of June, 1820, and witnessed by Robert A. Forsyth, secretary; Alex Wolcott, Jr., Indian agent, Chicago; Captain D. B. Douglass, United States Engineer; Aeneas McKay, lieutenant corps artillery; John J. Pierce, lieutenant artillery; Henry R. Schoolcraft, mineralogist to the expedition; James Duane Doty, Charles C. Trowbridge, Alex R. Chase, James Ryley, sworn interpreter.

This is the treaty referred to by "a correspondent" in the issue of February 2, 1821.

From May 2d to 11th, 1821, there were thirteen arrivals of schooners from lower lake ports, with emigrants and merchandise.

ORGANIZING ST. CLAIR COUNTY.

Governor Cass in his proclamation May 8, 1821, says:

"And I do further declare that the seat of justice to be temporarily located at the town of St. Clair, and as soon as the building, contracted to be built by the proprietor of said town, for court house and jail is completed, then the county seat, shall be permanently located in St. Clair.

This proclamation did not "hold water," or did not stick. The building for county purposes mentioned, was completed in due time at a cost of over $6,000, by the proprietor of said town, Thomas Palmer, and the county seat located at St. Clair, permanently (as was supposed). It continued there peaceably and quietly until the death of Mr. Palmer, when it was removed to Port Huron.

The subject of its removal was slightly agitated before Mr. Palmer's decease, but I have heard him say the people of the county dare not remove the county seat while he was on earth. Why he said so, I don't know, but any way the thing was not consumated until after his death.

DETROIT ELECTION.

At an election on the 7th of May, 1821, for trustees and officers of the city corporation, the following gentlemen were chosen trustees: Joseph Campau, A. G. Whitney, Shubael Conant, Levi Cook, Jacob Ellert; secretary, Jeremiah V. R. Ten Eyck; assessor and supervisor, D. C. McKinstry; marshal and collector, Robert Garratt.

The issue of the *Gazette,* Friday, May 18, 1821, contains a notice of a meeting of the citizens of Detroit, to meet at the council house on the coming Monday (21st), at 4 o'clock in the afternoon, to take into consideration the propriety of exhibiting a mark of public attention to Major-General Macomb, on the occasion of his expected departure from this territory.

A subsequent issue has this to say in regard to Major-General Macomb:

"The citizens of Detroit and its vicinity have at a public meeting resolved to present to General Macomb a silver tankard, with appropriate engravings; the tankard will be made in this place by Mr. Rouquet. It was also resolved to present the general an address, expressive of the high respect and sincere friendship which his fellow citizens entertain for him. The address and tankard will be presented on Monday next (the 21st). The proceedings of the meeting above alluded to, and the address will appear in subsequent issue.

"It is expected that the general and his family will depart for Washington on Wednesday or Thursday next."

FOR GENERAL MACOMB.

At the meeting of the citizens of Detroit convened at the council house on Monday, May 21, 1821, in pursuance of the notice published in the *Detroit Gazette,* Governor Cass was called to the chair and Geo. McDougall was elected secretary. At this meeting it was resolved to appoint a committee of five persons to prepare an address to the general, and it was also resolved that a piece of plate be procured and presented to the same, by the citizens of Detroit, with an appropriate inscription thereon. The committees were to report their proceedings to this meeting on Saturday next (the 26th). The committee on address consisted of A. B. Woodward, William Woodbridge, Solomon Sibley, Henry I. Hunt, and Austin E. Wing.

The committee on procuring the piece of plate consisted of James McCloskey, A. G. Whitney and Thomas Rowland.

The citizens again met on May 26, pursuant to adjournment, Governor Cass in the chair and Geo. McDougall secretary.

Judge Woodward, on behalf of the committee, reported the address, which was adopted and a committee was appointed to present the same to Major-General Macomb on the coming Monday. The above committee consisted of A. B. Woodward, William Woodbridge, Solomon Sibley, Henry I. Hunt, Austin E. Wing, James McCloskey, Andrew G. Whitney and Thomas Rowland, with the chairman and secretary.

Monday, the 4th day of June, the citizens of Detroit met agreeably to adjournment.

Colonel McCloskey, from the committee appointed for the purpose, reported the following inscription for the piece of plate to be presented to the general:

(Arms of the Territory.)

PRESENTED

to

MAJOR-GENERAL ALEXANDER MACOMB

by

THE CITIZENS OF HIS NATIVE PLACE, DETROIT,

AS A TESTIMONIAL

OF ATTACHMENT AND RESPECT

FOR HIS

PERSON AND CHARACTER.

June 4, A. D., 1821.

The inscription was unanimously adopted, whereupon the citizens proceeded to the house of Gen. Macomb, presented to him the piece of plate and delivered the address.

The general responded to the address in feeling terms, and accepted the plate which the citizens were pleased to offer, with (he said) the utmost pleasure.

COLONEL McDOUGALL WAS A RARE OLD SOUL.

AMUSING RECOLLECTIONS OF THE EARLY TWENTIES AND EXTRACTS FROM THE *DETROIT GAZETTE*.

GEORGE McDOUGALL, who acted as secretary at the General Macomb demonstration, referred to last week, was a lawyer of great ability and distinction in Detroit in the early days. The late Geo. C. Bates, in an article written in 1877 in relation to Ben. Woodworth's Steamboat Hotel and to a dinner to the bar given there, refers to Mr. Geo. McDougall, one of its members present, and says: "When Lawyer Cleland, who was toastmaster, gave his last toast, it was always to old Geo. McDougall, a legal Falstaff, redivivus, the quandom father of the bar, then lighthouse keeper at Fort Gratiot, and which was drunk standing, somewhat in these words: 'Brethren of the bar, we drink now to the Nestor of our bar, George McDougall, who in early life shed the light and brilliancy of his genius over our profession in beautiful Michigan, but who now, in his old age, illuminates the dark waters of Lake Huron with his lantern, and so guides the tempest-tossed mariner safely through storms and dangers of the lake down to the silvery stream of St. Clair.'"

I was living at Palmer (now St. Clair) when Lawyer McDougall was keeping the Fort Gratiot light. He used often to visit Palmer and always put up at Tomlinson's St. Clair Exchange Hotel. Landlord Tomlinson kept a model hotel, much better indeed than Black River (Port Huron) could boast of. The civil engineer and the army of others connected with the St. Clair & Romeo Railroad, then under construction, as also the judges and lawyers having business at the county seat, called for most everything desirable in the way of eatables and drinkables, particularly the latter. Now McDougall used to enjoy his "otium cum dig" at this hostelry, things were so different from his cooped up lighthouse quarters and indifferent fare. He was always accompanied by a colored youth, who was his valet, and seated comfortably in the bar-room of the hotel, his gouty foot resting easily on a cushioned chair, with his brandy toddy at his elbow, and his valet combing, oiling and brushing out his voluminous wig (for he was as bald as a billiard ball), and cracking his jokes and making witty comments on the passing show, he was a pleasure to behold.

In after years, when I had become familiar with Dickens, and with the transactions of the Pickwick 'Club, the picture of the baldhead and rotund body of Mr. Pickwick always put me in mind of Mr. McDougall.

Another character always suggested the colonel, and that was Shakespeare's Falstaff as Hackett was wont to render it.

McDougall Avenue is named after his brother, whose daughter married Barnabas (Labie) Campau, the father of Alex M. Campau, who is with us still, enjoying a hale, hearty old age, and far beyond the reach of want.

HIS SERVICE WAS DECLINED.

Further about the colonel, it is said, that during the war of 1812 he marched with twelve mounted volunteers to join General McArthur, who was then in Canada, but the general sent him back, as it took too many men to help him on and off his horse. He was very patriotic, but fat and gouty. The old colonel, it was said, was a bundle of eccentricities. His habit of ridiculous exaggeration, his pounds of flesh, and his fondness for "sack" reminded one of Shakespeare's fat knight.

The colonel died at his post, his lantern of life flickering out, many, many years ago.

It was also said he made many laughable attempts at suicide, and for what reason no one seemed to know.

In the *Detroit Gazette* of June 8, 1821, Mr. T. Young says he has opened an English school on Woodbridge Street, and will teach the English language, penmanship, arithmetic, geography, etc., at the moderate price (just think of it!) of $2.50 per quarter.

In the same issue J. E. and J. G. Schwarz make their first bow to the public, and inform them that they will pay the highest market price for furs and peltries, and that they have likewise at their store and for sale domestic cotton goods, cloths, blankets, calicos, etc.

John E. Schwarz (Gen. Schwarz) was in after years and until his death, adjutant and quartermaster-general of the state.

He was also at one time landlord of the old Mansion House, a most estimable gentleman and good citizen.

In the issue of Friday, June 18, 1821, the editor says in regard to gas lights:

"By the Louisville (Ky.) *Public Advertiser,* we perceive that some of the inhabitants of that place have begun to use gas lights."

On the score of expense the editor says: "We are convinced that the expense of lighting up a room in which twelve or twenty lights would be requisite, is not one-fourth the amount that would be required by the use of tallow candles."

In the issue of June 22, 1821, is a notice that I consider quite interesting and therefore copy it.

"PROCESSION."

"According to ancient custom, the solemn procession in commemoration of the institution of the blessed sacrament, commonly called the Lord's Supper, will take place on Sunday next, at 5 o'clock P. M., within the enclosure of the Church of St. Anne. A short address, explanatory of the ceremony, will be delivered at half past 4. Christians of all denominations disposed to witness the procession are welcome. It is expected, however, that they will conform to all the rules observed by the Catholics—by standing, walking and kneeling. The military on duty, only, may remain covered. It is enjoined on all persons to preserve profound silence during the whole time of the cermony. N. B.—A collection will be made, the proceeds of which will be employed in completing the steeples of Church of St. Anne, and covering them with tin."

In later years I myself have witnessed these same processions within the enclosure of the Church of St. Anne on Larned Street, and the same were conducted by Father Richard. They were to me, always, most impressive.

In the issue of July 6, 1821, the editor says that "Major A. Edwards, of this city, has completed an excellent team grist mill with two run of stones. It will, we learn, require four oxen to work it, yet it is believed, notwithstanding the expense attending a mill of this kind, that sufficient business will be done by it to award the enterprising proprietor; for there is not a grist mill in any direction nearer to this place than Pontiac, which is worthy of notice; and our windmills, of which there are a considerable number, never produce good flour. From the inconvenience which the inhabitants of Detroit and the adjacent country have suffered for the want of good grist mills, which will now in a great measure be removed, we must place that of Major Edwards's among the most useful establishments in the territory."

I have often been in this mill and witnessed its operations and the ceaseless tread of the oxen propelling it always interested me. When I saw it, it was run by Julius Eldred (French & Eldred) as a woolen mill. It was situated near the foot of Randolph Street, between it and the railroad depot. I saw it burn one night in 1835.

The editor says, in the issue of Friday, June 22, 1821, in regard to drains, etc.:

"For several days past we have heard frequent complaints of the intolerable stench arising from gutters or drains of cellars, etc., which are suffered to run into the streets, and form in many places such masses of putridity as cannot fail, in this warm weather, of producing disease. Every one who frequents Woodbridge Street and some others near the river is annoyed by the execrable odors arising from these gutters, few or none of which are carried further than that street, where they form green, stagnant pools, equally offensive to the sight and the smell. Is it not necessary, in order to preserve the health of the town, that a main gutter should be made through Woodbridge Street, say from Woodworth's to the public wharf? Two or three channels from this main one would carry the offensive matter into the river, and render the air in that part of the town pure and wholesome."

This public wharf was at the foot of Woodward Avenue.

FARMERS LAMBASTED.

In the *Gazette* May 11, 1821, see how the editor lambasts the farmers of the territory:

"There are not three families that manufacture their wearing apparel—and it is believed there are not five looms in the territory. There is not a carding machine or fulling mill within, perhaps, a 100 miles of Detroit. There is not a farmer in the territory that ever had sufficient enterprise to cultivate any article for exportation, although we have thousands of acres of the best hemp land in the world. On Tuesday last a small vessel from Ohio was lying at Roby's wharf, laden with potatoes, for which five shillings a bushel was received for several hundred bushels. This can justly be attributed to the indolence and improvidence of our farmers. Since navigation opened this spring there have been upwards of fifteen arrivals of vessels in the port of Detroit, laden with produce to feed the farmers and other inhabitants of this territory."

TO BUY FIRE ENGINE.

In the issue of April 6, 1821, is a notice of a public meeting of the citizens of Detroit at the council house on the 9th inst. at 3 o'clock P. M. to determine on the propriety of voting a tax to be applied to the purchase of a fire engine for the use of said city.

It is presumed the meeting was held accordingly and the tax voted, though I do not discover any notice of it, as when I came here the city owned a fine new fire engine, Protection No. 1.

The tax was voted, it appears, and paid and the engine ordered. It arrived here on the 26th of December, 1825, on the schooner Superior. It was made by Jacob Smith, Jr., of New York. Another fire engine was also in commission when I came (No. 2). I think the city acquired it some time in April, 1827.

REV. JOHN N. MAFFIT'S WORK IN DETROIT.

PERSONAL REMINISCENCES OF THE EVANGELIST'S LABORS HERE IN THE LATE '40s.

IN the issue of the old *Detroit Gazette* of December 7, 1821, the editor has this to say in regard to a book, then recently published, entitled, "The Life of John N. Maffit:"

"A book has been recently published in some of the states of the Union, entitled 'Tears of Contrition, or Sketches of the Life of John M. Maffit,' (by some editors called the 'Second Whitefield') in which the author gives incidents of his life in a very peculiar style. Mr. Maffit, who has been often mentioned in newspapers as a very eloquent and powerful preacher, was from Ireland, and landed with his brother in New York in April, 1819, where he experienced many difficulties, which led him to indulge in gloomy reflections, etc. While in the city, his brother visited a camp meeting in Hebron (Conn.) and on his return told him to be of good courage—that there was an opportunity of his doing well as a preacher in Connecticut, to which state he advised him to go. Instead of adopting the ordinary phraseology which one brother would use in giving advice to another, Mr. Maffit says he was addressed by his brother, on his return from Hebron, in the following strains:

"'Up go and possess thy Eden. Thou hast crossed the Red sea and traversed the desert, behold the little stream of Jordan rolls between. Fear not to launch away—pluck up fresh courage—gird up thy loins—address thyself to Satan's Conqueror—view your eastern shores—go proclaim a Saviour's name and let the starry pennant of the Manger's God wave through Connecticut's farthest bounds.'

"We cannot resist the wish to give a farther specimen of this celebrated preacher's style of writing; and therefore extract the paragraph immediately subsequent to the one above, in which, we think, he would be understood as having considered his brother's advice feasible, and that he adopted it as soon as possible.

"'Quick as the rapid stream which rushes o'er some deep mouthed, rocky bed, I started from my couch, and drawing the glittering falchion from my bosom, that had slept ingloriously at ease, and flying to the arms of hope, she clasped me to her peaceful bosom, and spreading forth her broad and downy pinions, cut the air till within the peaceful woods of Thompson, I beheld the crowded tents of Israel's camp, and mingling with the happy throng, from the bending willows snatched my lone and silent harp, and touched the first strains which burst from a grateful heart.'"

The editor goes on to say: "A little indulgence in style like Mr. Maffit's may be allowed when writing about 'Tears of Contrition,' but in giving 'Sketches of Life,' it is presumed that most readers of judgment would prefer a mode of telling a story, in which plain matter of fact were not so liable to distortion and misrepresentation, as they certainly are by the figurative and flowing manners of Mr. Maffit."

HE WAS POPULAR.

Many of the present day will no doubt remember well the above mentioned Methodist, distinguished in his day as a revivalist preached. He held forth here during the summer of 1848 or '49, for about six weeks, in the Methodist church that stood where the new county building now is. He created quite an excitement, crowds flocked to hear him, and a large number were plucked "like brands from the burning" through his ministrations. He was a natty, neat little gentleman, always faultlessly dressed, and apparently on intimate terms with the fairer portion of his congregation. He had quite a number of young society buds, of that day, "on a string," so to speak, and they ignored in many instances the escort of the worldly boys of their set from these meetings to their homes.

I remember particularly there were three or four upper Jefferson Avenue young girls that gave their boy friends and admirers the cold shoulder, preferring instead the escort of Judge Ross Wilkins. The judge, a devout Methodist, was a close attendant of these meetings, and always occupied the "amen corner," and therefore the proper thing.

I attended these meetings very often, was much taken with Maffit's style of oratory, as also the way he worked his congregation. During prayer time, which took up most of the evening, when nearly all heads were bowed, he would walk up and down the aisles, and if his eye lit on a comely fair one, occupying the first seat in a pew, he would kneel down in the aisle close by, and earnestly plead with her to go forward to the anxious seat. I have seen him do it often. One instance in particular: There was Mrs. Perry, a very pretty woman, the wife of a boss carpenter here, who had attended these meetings regularly, but had not been induced to go forward to be prayed for. I was there one evening and so was Mrs. Perry. I had a seat in the gallery where I could see things, Mrs. Perry had one in the body of the church close to the aisle. It was during prayer, the reverend gentleman was walking up and down the aisle as usual, when he spied Mrs. Perry whose head was down, and whose fair plump hand, ungloved, was resting invitingly on the top of the pew.

What did he do but kneel down in the aisle at that pew door and quietly lay his hand over that of Mrs. Perry. She looked up, of course, and after a few, it is presumed, persuasive words, he brought her up "into camp," so to speak.

DID MUCH GOOD.

Myself and the Rev. Mr. Maffit were quite friendly, and it arose from the fact that he had a son, then a midshipman in the navy, of whom he was quite proud. On leave here at that time was Midshipman George King, a brother of the late J. L. and J. E. King, a very promising young officer. King and I used to now and then attend these meetings. The first evening that King accompanied me, when we got to the church, the congregation were engaged in prayer. We halted in the vestibule and saw Brother Maffit pacing up and down the aisle as usual. King being in uniform instantly attracted his attention. He threw whatever he had on his mind to the winds, apparently. Rushing down the aisle he grasped King by both hands, apologizing for the sudden action by saying: "My dear boy, you must excuse me for this demonstrative greeting, but I have a son in the navy, a midshipman, and the sight of the uniform is always a forcible reminder of my dear boy, perhaps you know him, sir?" King said he knew him well. I think they had served on the same ship together, whereupon Mr. M. invited us to take seats in the gallery, which we did. On all our subsequent visits he was equally cordial.

Much to our surprise he did not once broach the subject of religion, the one thing that was apparently nearest his heart. He thought we were good enough already, and no room for improvement, I presume. It was said he did a great amount of good here.

AN APPEAL.

Like the country papers of the present day, the patrons of which are proverbially tardy in paying up, was the *Detroit Gazette* in 1822. The *Detroit Gazete*, like many of the country journals of the present day, had hard sledding to get along and keep its head above water. In its issue of June 13, 1821, it makes an appeal to its patrons. As it is quite lengthy, I quote only a portion of it:

"*To Our Patrons:*

"In this number of our paper, which closes the fourth year of our labors as printers and editors in the territory, we are induced from the appositeness of the time, and, more particularly, from urgent necessity, to call upon all our patrons, real and nominal, to discharge the demands we may have against them."

After a long detail of its situation financially, and an urgent appeal to the citizens to aid and foster emigration to the territory, he goes on to say:

"We beg leave before concluding this article, to revert once more to our own concerns. Our neighbors have frequently said to us, when presented with a bill, 'You must be making money—you have a terrible price for your paper and a good many advertisements, and you must be getting rich. Now, in relation to the value of our little *Gazette* to us, we will only repeat what we did some time ago, when under the necessity of dunning: If we calculate the annual value of the labor, the materials consumed and other necessary expenses in printing our *Gazette,* and deduct from the amount our annual receipts, both on account of subscriptions and advertisements, our loss will be found to amount to more than $500. This can be easily accounted for. The French population have very little inclination to know the contents of newspapers, because they have never been taught their value, and only eight or ten of the most intelligent are subscribers for our paper, and so far from receiving from our subscription enough to pay for the value of the labor alone required to print the *Gazette,* we do not hesitate to say that were our subscribers increased fourfold, we should not receive more than enough to pay the necessary expenses of the establishment. We have but two subscribers in the county of St. Clair, four in Macomb, one in Oakland, two at Mackinac, fourteen in Monroe, and about one hundred in Wayne, and many of them, perhaps, are unable to pay their subscription.

As to subscribers who receive our papers by mail, they may be considered as a loss, for from a few to whom we send them we have never received enough to pay for the labor and expense of enclosing them. In fine, we have been enabled to keep up our establishment from our receipts on account of contingent support, and as we have before said, from the generous forbearance of a great portion of our creditors. We assure our patrons, however, that such are our expectations of future support from a continued increase of enlightened population, that we shall, with God's blessing, still continue our exertions and do all we can in our vocations, to benefit the country.

"Farmers who wish to become subscribers and who are prevented on account of the scarcity of money, are again informed that all kinds of grain, butter and cheese will be received in payment for them."

The editor's remarks in regard to the lack of interest, taken in his paper on the part of some of the French residents here, at that time, is too true, sorry to say. I was well acquainted with one of our French residents, rich and quite intelligent, who down to about 1850, at least, did not take a newspaper, but would, every morning, send over to a Yankee neighbor of his to borrow his *Free Press.* I have been in the latter's residence often when the request for the paper came. Nor did he take water from the city, but for a long time had it hauled in barrels from the river, in the old way. Nor did he take gas from the gas company for quite a while after they had it introduced. Now this French gentleman, though many, many times richer than his neighbor, was not penurious in hardly any sense, his purse was always open to calls of charity, and a free giver to many laudable enterprises. Why this backwardness on his part in coming forward to the support of the press, gas and water I never could fathom.

WENT TO PONTIAC BY WAY OF MT. CLEMENS.

REMINISCENCES OF SOUTHEASTERN MICHIGAN IN THE DAYS OF THE STAGE COACH.

IN the old *Detroit Gazette* of Friday, May 31, 1822, is this notice:

"Judge Clemens, one of the proprietors of Mt. Clemens, has recently established a Stage, to leave this City Weekly, after the arrival of the Steam Boat, and arrive at the Seat of Justice of Macomb Co. on the same day. Seats may be taken at the very low price of One Dollar, by Applying to Colonel Richard Smyth, the Agent at Detroit. Extra accommodations will be furnished to strangers who may wish to visit Pontiac, St. Clair or the other new villages in the country. This is the first public Stage ever established in Michigan."

The late Judge B. F. H. Witherell, in 1855, writing about Colonel Christian Clemens and Mt. Clemens, has this to say:

"Emigrants to the territory (Michigan) after the war of 1812 had passed by, will remember the colonel's generous, boundless hospitality to those seeking a new home in the wilderness. The only passable road for carriages for years to the country about Piety Hill, Pontiac and north of them, was by the shore of Lake St. Clair to Mt. Clemens, and thence up the Clinton, making a journey of some sixty or seventy miles to get eighteen or twenty; it then occupied from four to six days, and is now performed in one hour by railroad.

The allusion to Mt. Clemens in the *Gazette* suggests the following extracts from some articles I wrote last summer for the *Mt. Clemens Monitor,* in regard to the early days of the "Bath City," and to the country between here and there and through which the rapid transit electric runs. Note the difference between then and now. It is almost a part of Detroit.

EARLY MT. CLEMENS.

My stepfather, George Kellogg, settled in Mt. Clemens, on a farm that he purchased on the Clinton River, a short distance below the village, and opposite the Connor farm. This was about 1835. He built an ideal log house, i. e., the logs were square, and the chinking filled in with plaster instead of mud, and nicely furnished inside. The chimney and fireplace were built of brick; the latter was of ample size, sufficient to take in nearly one-half a cord of wood; an immense crane swung in it from which depended the pots and kettles needed in the culinary department.

Cooking stoves were a great rarity in those days. The nearest approach to one was the tin open oven that was placed on the hearth before the glowing fire, containing fish, flesh or fowl, as the case might be, fitting it for the family consumption, and splendidly it did its duty, I can testify. And often turkeys and geese, in cooking were suspended by a cord from the ceiling, and slowly turned by a willing hand, the drippings from the bird being caught in a tin dish, directly under it, and returned back over it by the attendant with a pewter or wooden spoon, they used to call it "basting." Cannot some of you remember with delight this process of cooking or roasting a turkey, and how appetizing the bird was? And the short cake and biscuit of those early pioneer days baked in the iron spider, the latter containing the white dough turned up to the glowing fire. I say "white dough" because it was not always in evidence in the settlers' houses of those days. Wheat flour was considered almost a luxury, rye and Indian corn predominated all through that section and St. Clair County as well, and mighty good bread rye and Indian meal, mixed, made, as I can testify. I include St. Clair County because I had personal experience in that locality.

When a lad on my uncle's (George Palmer) farm on the St. Clair River, where the Oakland Hotel now is, I spent quite a portion of my early days on this farm, and must say that the surroundings on this farm were not near as pleasant as those on my stepfather's farm on the Clinton River. The log house was much more primitive, logs not square, the chinking done with mud, no such ample fireplace, and my quarters under the roof were reached by a ladder instead of stairs.

Referring to the trip to Mt. Clemens on my mother's wedding day; it was a beautiful day in June. I remember that much, and some little more in regard to the event and the trip. Mr. Kellogg during the time he was courting my mother was a guest of Uncle Ben Woodworth (Woodworth's Hotel), and when the interesting event occurred he had no difficulty in persuading his host to place at his disposal his private carriage, with "Jabe," his coachman, as Jehu. This carriage was quite a pretentious affair, and about the only covered one in the territory at that time. We journeyed to Mt. Clemens in fine style via the Gratiot turnpike and arrived at Mr. Connor's residence along late in the afternoon. "Jabe" and the coach returned the next day.

There was very little settlement along the turnpike between here and Mt. Clemens, after you left the confines of the city. There was a tavern at Connor's Creek, five miles out, and another ten miles out, called the Half Way House. Aside from these two houses I think there were but five or six others the entire distance. I know there was but one between the Half Way House and Mt. Clemens, and that was five miles this side of the latter town.

To this house from the Half Way tavern the pike ran through an unbroken forest. On this piece of road the people had allowed the brush to encroach to the extent that there was insufficient space left for the passage of vehicles, and when it came to turn-out, as did happen now and then, it was a rather difficult matter.

I am reminded of another trip through these same woods nearly ten years later on and they had changed but very little in that time. A young lady relative of mine desired to attend the funeral of a mutual friend in Mt. Clemens, a daughter of Colonel Stockton, and requested me to drive her up there in a buggy. I undertook the business, and we started about nine o'clock. Fine day and all that, road in good condition, but the horse was poor, not much of a goer, and we did not reach the Half Way House until long in the afternoon. We tarried long enough to refresh the horse and ourselves, and started on our journey. We had not gone far before the shades of evening began to fall and soon it got as dark as a "stack of black cats;" could not see your hand before you; had to let the horse take his own course, which he did.

Reader, were you ever out in the woods on a dark night, and the custodian of a young lady and a horse and buggy? If you ever have been you will know just about how I felt. I did think at one time that I was just a little bit scared and asked my lady cousin what she thought of the situation. She was plucky and said she did not care if I didn't, and to let the horse take his own sweet will as he was doing. So I did not worry.

A BAD SCARE.

The silence was most profound, broken only by the rattle of the buggy and harness, as the horse felt his way. We had proceeded a mile or so thusly, when all at once from the side of the road, apparently in the dense forest and from out the inky darkness, came the sounding rattle of a snare drum. Goodness, gracious! how it startled us, the horse swerved into the bushes on the side of the track, but thanks to his docility he stopped there.

After getting the horse on the right track again and finding my cousin was all right, I sung out to some one to find what all this disturbance was, and the cause. A voice in German-English said that the owner of it and the drum had been a short distance up and off the road to a friend's house where a rehearsal of a brass band they were forming had been going on, and hoped his sudden serenade had not rattled us and the horse. I told him I thought it a queer time and place to raise such an alarm without notice. Well, we reached Mt. Clemens in due course without further mishap. I have often been to Mt. Clemens before and since by this route, but never encountered a like experience or had such a scare.

A WEDDING.

My first visit to this interesting village was in 1834, on the occasion of the marriage of one of the daughters of Judge Clemens to Sidney D. Hawkins, of Detroit, who was a prominent merchant and auctioneer. Mr. Hawkins was a relative of Mrs. Thomas Palmer, and as the latter's family and that of the judge were closely allied, socially, it became a sort of family affair and all our house attended and were the guests of the judge over night, getting home next day. The senator, (T. W. P.) was on hand with the rest, then a chubby four-year old. We had also on this occasion for our conveyance Uncle Ben Woodworth's coach and coachman "Jabe." The wedding was a fine affair and participated in by the then elite of Macomb County. The knot was tied by Elder Colclazer, the handsome presiding elder of the Methodist church, who it was thought was at one time a suitor for the fair bride's hand. Miss Caroline Whistler, a niece of Mrs.

Judge James Abbott, was the bridesmaid and Mr. John V. R. Scott, a young society man of Detroit, and partner of Mr. Hawkins, was the best man. I may be pardoned for dwelling a little on this happy event, as all the participants were of the first prominence, socially and otherwise. After a brief and happy married life passed in Detroit, Mr. Hawkins died, and his widow returned to Mt. Clemens, to live with the judge, her father. After a fitting season had elapsed she married Mr. E. C. Gallup, of Mt. Clemens. Both passed the rest of their days there, and all old settlers will remember them both with pleasurable emotions, I am sure.

Mt. Clemens wears a different aspect now from what it did then. It was at best only a straggling village, with the business, etc., centering around the square in which was the old wooden court house, jail, and meeting house as well, patterned after the St. Clair county court house, or the latter was patterned after the former, I don't know which. They were identical in structure, as I can testify, having been in both of them many times, and quite a different affair from the present fine brick building.

THEN AND NOW.

The passenger to and from Mt. Clemens at the present day, comfortably seated in the luxurious electric cars, can hardly realize, in passing over the road, the different aspect the same route presented in the '30's and '40's Then it was almost a dense wilderness, relieved now and then by a settler's log dwelling; now it is a continuous settlement the entire route of prosperous farmers, with their commodious dwellings, in lieu of the rude log cabin. I have had it forcibly brought to mind when passing over this electric road what a wonderful change has taken place on this route from that period to this.

I have tried often to locate the site of the old Half Way House, that was in the early days such a desirable point to reach, a haven of rest, as it were, particularly if one was journeying from Mt. Clemens to Detroit. The woods were so dense, the settlers so far between, and the way seemed so long to the tavern, it used to seem as though it never could be reached.

The sign, a large swinging one, painted white, hung away out over the road, a prominent reminder that when you reached it you would be ten miles nearer your destination, one-half way home, and sure of ample refreshment for yourself and horse, if you were not on foot. That delusive white sign, how often have I when journeying from Mt. Clemens to Detroit eagerly watched for the first sight of it, and when it did loom into view white over the road, five or six miles in the distance, it seemed, as said before, as though it never could be reached, like the mirage on the plains, "so near and yet so far." It was awfully tantalizing. There are very few living I imagine that have had the same experience on this route, and to those the incidents I relate I am sure they will readily testify to.

In the *Gazette* of July is a notice of the arrival, in the steamboat Walk-in-the-Water, of Rev. Eleazer Williams, missionary to the Oneida Indians, with a deputation from the Six Nations, who were on their way to visit their brethren in the vicinity of Green Bay. The object of those who composed the mission (under the auspices of the general government), was not only to endeavor to plant the gospel among the western Indians, but treat with them for a tract of their territory, with a view to locate themselves and such of their brethren as might be disposed to remove to that region.

This Rev. Eleazer Williams, many will remember, became quite conspicuous at one time, later on, as an aspirant to the throne of France. He claimed that he was the son of Louis XVI. and Marie Antoinette. The Prince de Joinville, about 1838 or '39, visited Green Bay for the express purpose of seeing this Williams, to ascertain for himself what grounds there were for this assumption. On an interview with him the prince was convinced that his claims were groundless.

The *Gazette* says Austin E. Wing was sheriff of Wayne County in 1821, J. V. R. Ten Eyck was secretary of the board of trustees of the city, and Thomas Rowland was clerk of the Wayne County Court.

There were seventeen arrivals (schooners) at the port of Detroit from 1st to the 10th of May, 1822.

TRAMPS RECEIVED TEN STRIPES.

WHEN WHIPPING POST WAS LOCATED ON WOODWARD AVENUE—SERVICES OF VAGABONDS WERE SOLD.

THE old *Detroit Gazette* of November 23, 1821, says:

"By the act of this territory for the punishment of idle and disorderly persons, it is provided that any justice of the peace, on conviction may sentence any idle vagrant, lewd, drunken or disorderly persons to be whipped not exceeding ten stripes, or to be delivered over to any constable to be employed in labor not exceeding three months, by such constable to be hired out for the best wages that can be procured, the proceeds of which to be applied to the use of poor of the county.

"Under this act sometime last summer the services of a drunken vagabond were offered for sale in the market house, and some wags on board the steamboat Walk-in-the-Water, then in this port, persuaded one of the hands, a black, to attend the sale and buy the man. The black actually purchased the vagrant's services for ten days, for which, we think, he paid $1.

"From this circumstance, a writer in the Ontario (N. Y.) *Respository* has made up a pretty good story, which, however, would have passed without observation from us had not the story been in a measure calculated to mislead those unacquainted with the provisions of the law alluded to. By the story one would think that the vagrant or drunkard, when sold, becomes the slave for life, but the law provides that his services cannot be disposed of to exceed three months. It remains to state, that the citizens of Detroit and the adjoining counties have derived many benefits from the operation of the law, and feel no desire to part with it. It has had the effect of sending from the territory very many drunkards and vagabonds that thronged into it from Canada, Ohio and the state of New York."

This practice of selling or disposing of a vagrant's time was continued until way along into 1830. I have witnessed a number of instances where the like occurred in front of the old market on Woodward Avenue, and on King's Court. I remember seeing the whipping post, that was close by the market, but I never saw anyone whipped there, nor do I think any unfortunate underwent that ordeal after 1826.

Imagine it must have been tough from the fact that the sheriff at that period, whose duty it was to administer this punishment, was a tall and powerful man, who no doubt got in his work to his own satisfaction, if not to that of the culprit. Some, no doubt, will call to mind this officer of the law. His name was "Swan," and he was brother-in-law of Thos. C. Sheldon.

SOME ADVERTISEMENTS.

In the year of November 30, 1821, F. T. & J. Palmer say: "They have just received a new stock of goods, which they are opening, at their new brick store, on the corner of Jefferson Avenue and Griswold Street, and a short distance from their old stand." They fill nearly a column in the paper enumerating the various kinds of goods they have for sale.

John Hale, in the same issue, makes his first bow to the public, and says he is receiving and has for sale at the store formerly occupied by F. T. & J. Palmer, a general assortment of goods, such as dry goods, crockery, groceries, hardware, etc.

A notice of the death of Benjamin Stead, a native of England, and for many years a respectable and public-spirited inhabitant of the town, appeared in the old *Detroit Gazette,* September 28, 1821.

This Mr. Stead was the father of all the Steads, well-known residents here thereafter. Mr. Stead built the first brick dwelling that was ever erected in this city, except the one built by Governor Hull, where the Biddle House now is.

This residence of Mr. Stead is still standing and nearly opposite the Michigan Exchange. It is occupied at present, I think, by commercial agents who sell goods by sample.

The issue of Friday, September 7, 1821, says in regard to the treaty of Chicago:

"On Tuesday last Governor Cass and Mr. Sibley, the commissioners appointed to treat with the Indians, returned from Chicago, together with the gentlemen who attended at the treaty," and says further: "Governor Cass, on his route to Chicago, ascended the Miami to Fort Wayne. From thence his canoe was transported over a portage of about nine miles to the head of the Wabash. This river he descended to the Mississippi. The latter river he ascended to the mouth of the Illinois, one of whose tributary streams approaches within ten miles of Chicago.

EARLY ERIE CANAL BUSINESS.

September 7, 1821, the editor says, in regard to the Erie canal:

"A friend who has lately traveled in the interior of New York, has brought with him on his return, the subjoined exhibit of the business done on the canal in that state, between Utica and Cayuga, from the first day in May up to the 22d of July, in the present year. This canal is complete, and extends eight miles below Utica, and will in about twelve months be finished to the Cohoes, within a mile and a half of Troy, and as far west as the Genessee River by the same period. Elegant boats for the accommodation of passengers ply daily between Utica and Montezuma, near Cayuga lower bridge. So much adds our informant, and we respond, for the spirit and well directed resources of this great state.

"Account of property transported on the middle section of the Erie canal at Utica from May 1 to July 22, 1821: Barrels of flour, 18,993; do of salt, 7,007; do of provisions, 4,200; do of ashes, 2,243; bushels of wheat, 12,529; feet of boards, 44,065; bushels of water lime, 34,583; galons of whisky, 38,827; tons of gypsum, 212; tons of merchandise, 989; feet of timber, 14,269." It will be seen that whisky held its own.

POSTOFFICE ON WOODWARD AVENUE.

James Abbott, postmaster, in the issue, October 12, 1821, advertises 120 letters uncalled for.

The postoffice was then located on the west side of Woodward Avenue, midway between Woodbridge and Atwater Streets. Judge Abbott lived in a cottage with a fine garden in the rear on the corner of Woodbridge Street; next was the postoffice, next was his store and warehouse.

This issue, and many thereafter, informs the public that the proprietors have received and have for sale "Schoolcraft's Travels," through the northwest regions of the United States, performed as a member of the expedition under Governor Cass in the year 1820.

The book is now out of print, and a very scarce volume; if you doubt it, try to get hold of one by purchase and see what a time you will have.

The *Gazette* says, October 19, 1821:

"Governor Cass, when in the City of New York, presented Dr. Mitchell with a piece of the petrified tree alluded to in our article respecting the treaty of Chicago. The fragment was, with divers other things, on the 29th ult., deposited in one of the columns which adorn the grand avenue (now erecting) of the park."

I wonder what park?

The same issue has an extract from the *Pittsfield Sun,* which says, in regard to the New York city hall:

"The iron railing, now enclosing the grand public square and city hall, has been imported into New York from Liverpool, though it might have been had cheaper in this country. This want of patriotism as well as economy has called forth not a little raillery and irony from the friends of the city and the country."

THE SCIAWASSA COMPANY.

The issue of the 8th of October, 1821, contains a notice of a meeting of the Sciawassa Company, at the council house (corner of Jefferson Avenue and Randolph Street), Thursday, the 25th inst., for the transaction of important business. It was signed by Obed Wait, secretary.

This Obed Wait was the architect of and superintended the erection of the capitol building.

October 12, the *Gazette,* in an editorial, calls attention to the Sciawassa Company, whose avowed mission was to encourage immigration to the territory, and to disseminate full information in regard thereto, and says in part:

"It is peculiarly favorable to the interests of the territory that a measure like that entered upon by the Sciawassa Company should be taken at this time—for, so far from our citizens having hitherto been able to spread a knowledge of the advantages of this territory to any considerable extent among the people of the eastern and northern states, it may be said with truth, that a general ignorance prevails relative to them. Indeed, the traveler **from Michigan** is frequently asked (by persons whose standing **in society** would seem to imply at least a knowledge of the geography of their native country), 'if Detroit belongs to the British or the United States.'"

SCARCITY OF BRICKMAKERS.

In this same issue of October 12, 1821, complaint is made in regard to the scarcity of brickmakers.

"Much inconvenience has been sustained by the citizens of Detroit for the want of a few good and industrious brickmakers. But two brick buildings have been commenced during the past summer—a store of the Messrs. Palmer, 40 feet square, and one of Mr. Peter J. Desnoyers, 44 x 36. The former, after several delays, is completed; the latter is nearly so, but the masons discontinued work two weeks ago for want of brick. Three other buildings would have been erected if brick could have been obtained."

The Palmers, before their new store was erected on the northeast corner of Jefferson Avenue and Griswold Street, occupied with their stock of goods a wooden building on the corner of Larned and Griswold Streets, where is now the Campau building.

Peter Desnoyer's new brick building stood on Jefferson Avenue, where the store recently vacated by the Richmond & Backus Co. now is.

November 23, 1821, the editor says in regard to the progress made in building the Erie canal:

"On Thursday, the 1st inst., the water was let in from the termination of the Utica level to the Little Falls, which is 22 miles below Utica. This event was celebrated by a party of gentlemen from Utica and many others who joined them on the passage down. Their arrival at the Little Falls was announced by a national salute, and the cheers of a great number of people who had assembled to witness the scene. On landing a procession was formed, which marched to the house of Colonel Myers and partook of a dinner prepared for the occasion."

December 14, 1821, Melvin Dorr makes his first bow to the citizens of Detroit, and says he has just received a fresh supply of dry goods and groceries, which he desires them to inspect, and which he will be glad to exchange for cash, furs, produce, dried ginsang, clean linen and cotton rags.

Melvin Dorr was brother to J. K. Dorr, and when I knew him he was city auctioneer.

WHEN INDIANS WERE HANGED IN MICHIGAN.

EXTRACTS FROM THE FILES OF THE OLD DETROIT GAZETTE OF 1821-1822.

THERE is in the old *Detroit Gazette* of December 28, 1821, an interesting account of the hanging of two Indians for murder. It reads as follows:

"Execution—Yesterday, Ke-tan-Kah and Ke-wa-bis-Kim, the Indians who were sentenced to death, at the last September session of our Supreme Court, the former for the murder of Dr. W. F. Madison, and the latter for the murder of Charles Ulrick, were, agreeably to their sentence, hanged by their necks until they were dead.

"The First Regiment Territorial Militia, under arms, and a guard of United States troops attended the execution. The spectators were very numerous—not many of whom had ever witnessed a similar scene.

"They appeared throughout the whole solemn preparatory steps to be perfectly collected—they walked firmly to the gallows, and previously to ascending to the drop, shook hands with Rev. Mr. Janvier, Mr. Hudson (one of the gentlemen belonging to the Mission family), the sheriff and marshal, and several other gentlemen who stood near them. They ascended the steps of the drop in a manner peculiarly firm, after which they asked through the interpreter the pardon of the surrounding spectators for the crime they had committed. They then shook hands and gazed for a few minutes on the assemblage and on the heavens, when their caps were drawn over their faces and they launched into eternity."

January 4, 1822, Henry Sanderson says he has for sale twenty-five barrels of the best kind of Michigan apples, and twelve barrels of good cider, also an elegant one-horse sleigh, two chaises and two sets of harness complete; also continues the harnessmaking business at his old stand, and will attend to all orders for painting or glazing, also for fire buckets (leather).

Mr. Sanderson's place of business and dwelling was on Woodbridge Street, between Bates and Randolph Streets. He was the father of Mrs. Bissell, wife of the late Geo. W. Bissell.

BUCKET SHOPS.

The business of making fire buckets in those days was quite an industry, as every citizen was compelled by law to provide himself with two, to be kept in a conspicuous place in his dwelling, those in business of any kind to keep two additional wherever such business was carried on. These to be used in case of fire.

It was quite interesting on the occasion of an alarm of fire to see the citizens, each with their two leather buckets, rushing in hot haste to the blaze, wherever it might be located. Some of these fire buckets are preserved. Three or four are in possession of the present fire department, and two, that were once the property of Judge James Witherell, grandfather of Senator Palmer, are in the log cabin at Palmer Park.

In same issue, J. L. & H. S. Cole, attorneys and counsellors-at-law, say they have opened an office in the north apartment of the Steam Boat Hotel.

Harry S. Cole, of the firm, married the daughter of Peter J. Desnoyers, and was the father of the late Mrs. Eben N. Wilcox and Charles S. Cole. He was a very popular lawyer and elegant gentleman.

In the issue of November 2, 1821, O. & L. Cook announce that they have just received from New York and offer for sale a fine assortment of dry goods.

This firm was composed of Levi and Orville Cook (brothers) and they occupied a part of the brick store of Levi Brown. It stood on the west side of Jefferson Avenue, midway between Griswold and Shelby Streets. At the time of my advent here this firm had dissolved, Orville giving place to his brother Olney. The latter firm continued for a while and were succeeded by Cook & Burns, Levi retiring. This latter firm continued for some years at the old stand, when Olney Cook retired, and was succeeded by Timothy L. Partridge, a young man from St. Clair, who had been in their employ for a long period. The firm then became James Burns & Co., whom scores of the present day will remember.

In the issue of November 9, 1821, is a notice of the marriage (on the 5th) by Rev. Mr. Janvier of Mr. Peter Desnoyers to Miss Caroline Leib.

Miss Leib was the daughter of Judge Leib (Leib farm, Hamtramack) and aunt to Clevil and W. Q. Hunt, of this city.

November 16, 1821, the paper contained this announcement:
"Good news! The following is taken from the Albany *Gazette* of October 29:

"'Wheat sold in this market on Saturday at 16s 1d sterling per bushel.'"

The newspaper carrier had his troubles in those days as well as in these. Sheldon & Reed say, January 11, 1822:

"GIVE THE DEVIL HIS DUES."

"Our carrier informs us that several persons to whom he presented his New Year's address requested him to tell Messrs. Sheldon & Reed to charge the address to their account. To those we have to say that the moneys raised by the carrier from the address belong entirely to himself; and that, on that score, he is at full liberty to open an account with whom he pleases."

February 8, 1822, James McCloskey, cashier of the Bank of Michigan, gives notice to the stockholders that an election will be held at the bank on Monday, the 11th day of March next, at 12 o'clock M., for choosing directors for the ensuing year.

The bank building was a small brick one, of one story, and stood where is now the Kearsley building, corner of Jefferson Avenue and Randolph Street.

In the paper of Friday, March 29, 1822, is the notice of marriage (on Wednesday evening last) by Rev. A. W. Welton, Mr. John Farrer to Mrs. Hannah Mack, all of this city.

Mr. Farrer was the grandfather of Ford Starring, of this city.

THE STRONGEST BOAT.

The *Gazette* in its issue of Friday, May 31, 1822, announces the arrival of the elegant new steam boat Superior, Captain J. Rodgers, with a full freight of merchandise and ninety-four passengers, sixty-eight of whom were citizens of or immigrants to Michigan, and goes to say:

"This excellent vessel was built at Buffalo during the past winter, under the immediate superintendence of Captain R— and is owned by the proprietors of the old steam boat Walk-in-the-Water, which was wrecked in the fall of last year. She is

346 tons burthen, 110 feet keel, 29 feet beam, and has an engine of 59 horse-power. In her construction great exertions have been made to render her secure in the most tempestuous weather, and it is the opinion of many that she is the strongest boat on the continent. Her accommodation for passengers are excellent, and the ladies' cabin, particularly, is furnished in a style of splendor, highly creditable to the liberality and taste of her owners and commander."

In the issue of June 7, the editor has this to say in regard to United States troops being stationed at Sagana Bay:

"We learn with much pleasure that a post is to be established at Sagana Bay, and that Captain Perkins, military storekeeper at this post, has received orders to procure implements for erecting barracks, etc., as early as practicable. This post is to be formed by a detachment of the Third United States Infantry, and will be under the command of Major Baker, now at Green Bay."

THE OLD ARSENAL.

This Captain Perkins was in charge of the government arsenal here until it was transferred to Dearborn. This arsenal occupied the square, bounded by Jefferson Avenue, Wayne, Larned and Cass Streets. The arsenal building was of stone and was on the corner of Jefferson Avenue and Wayne Street. The captain's quarters were on the corner of Jefferson Avenue and Cass Street.

Major Baker was the last commandant (then Colonel Baker), of Fort Shelby. He died here in the early thirties, much regretted. He was indeed a most estimable man, and gallant soldier. He owned what is called the "Baker Farm," at the time of his death.

The editor also has this to say, in regard to British troops on this frontier:

"On Saturday last (June 1) about 150 British troops passed this place in the American schooner Michigan. They are to be stationed at Drummond's Island. It is obviously the intention of the British government to maintain, if possible, its influence over the Indian tribes to the northwest, and to do this, the maintaining of a force as large as any which our government may send to that quarter is necessary. This reinforcement for Drummond's Island is probably intended to counterbalance the effect which our new post at Sault Ste. Marie would produce upon the Indians."

MANY IMMIGRANTS.

In same issue (June 1), the editor has this to say in regard to emigration to this territory of Michigan:

"So numerous have been the arrivals of immigrants to this territory, since the opening of navigation, that it is difficult, at this time, to ascertain with any degree of certainty, their actual numbers—and by making inquiries among those of our citizens who would be most competent to form a correct opinion on the subject, we have found a material difference in calculations. Almost every vessel which has touched at this port has brought immigrants, and last week a schooner (the Erie from Buffalo) landed forty-five. They were mostly from the counties of Monroe (formerly Genesee) and Ontario, N. Y., and came well prepared to take immediate advantage of every facility which our delightful country extends to the enterprising immigrant. It is worthy of notice, also, in relation to this body of immigrants, that they were not induced to leave their homes, in the most fertile portion of the state of New York, and remove to this territory by any high wrought and vivid descriptions of its excellence, by interested speculators. On the contrary, they had the consoling certainty that they should not regret their removal, because their providence had sent those on whose judgment they could depend, to 'spy out the land' and from whom they had obtained a good report.

"The interest which is awakened in many parts of the Union, in relation to this territory, and, above all, the arrival of numerous intelligent immigrants and gentlemen who come to see the country, induce a conviction that the barriers to emigration are giving way, and that a tide has begun to blow which nothing will retard. It is also a pleasing reflection that those who have arrived in our territory were not from any particular part of the Union, Vermont, Massachusetts and Pennsylvania having furnished a portion of our population, and Ohio is also giving us a liberal share. Last week the schooner Sylph landed ten farmers from that state, and we are informed that many more are preparing to follow them. But from New York we have received and, perhaps, shall continue to receive, the greatest number of immigrants. In that great state this territory begins to be known, and it is with much pleasure that we observe, in some of the newspapers of the western district of the state, publications relating to the advantages of certain portions of this territory, which seem to have been written by those who have carefully examined them."

NAMING THE CLINTON RIVER.

He also has this to say in regard to the Tetibawassa River:

"This river, the largest which empties into the Sagana, has recently received the name of Clinton. The reasons for a change of this kind must be obvious to all. Tetibawassa is at best an uncouth, ill-sounding term, and if by varying it a better can be substituted, the measure must meet with general approbation. To DeWitt Clinton, the principal and most active projector of the New York canal, this country has been and will be infinitely indebted. Hence the propriety of sending him every suitable demonstration of gratitude and respect."

In the issue of Friday, June 21, 1822, the editor has this to say in regard to the steamboat Superior:

"The steamboat Superior, Captain Rodgers, arrived here from Buffalo on Friday last and sailed for Michilimackinac on Saturday, having on board a considerable number of passengers and a full cargo of merchandise destined for the Indian trade.

"The trip-sheet of the Superior contained the names of ninety-nine passengers, more than half of whom were for this territory, and have since left this place to examine the United States lands in the interior.

"The trip to Sault Ste. Marie will be made as soon as the Superior returns from her next trip to Buffalo."

He also says in regard to whitefish:

"Last fall a gentleman in this city sent a barrel of whitefish to a friend in New York, from whom he has recently received a letter, in which the highest commendation is given to the fish. Those who had the opportunity of tasting them were of the opinion that in flavor they far exceeded shad. We have not the least doubt but this opinion of our whitefish will become more general as the exportation of them increases."

How truthfully this prediction of the editor has been verified. I can testify of their present scarcity, scarce in comparison to what they were in the early thirties. You could then buy, any morning in the season, at any of the markets and from the canoes of the French habitants at the foot of Woodward Avenue fine fresh fish, as many as you desired, for five cents each, and at any of the fishing grounds along the river you could have as many as you could carry away conveniently, for nothing.

WASHINGTON BONNET INSPIRED A POET.

I HAVE never seen this parody by Woodworth before, and doubt if many have.

The *Detroit Gazette* of November 30, 1821, contained a song by Samuel Woodworth, author of the "Old Oaken Bucket," and is a parody on the latter, delivered at the cattle show and exhibition by domestic manufacturers of the New York Agricultural Society.

At the exhibition, it appears, there were presented five bonnets manufactured from spear grass by American ladies. They were pronounced superior to the best Leghorn. The finest of the number received the name of the Washington bonnet and subsequent to the fair was sold at auction for more than $100. The following excellent partriotic song, from the pen of the American Poet Woodworth, was in circulation at the fair:

THE WASHINGTON BONNET.

AIR—"The Old Oaken Bucket."

"The Bard who has so often sung Independence
    And wakened his lyre to the praise of the brave,
Now hails a new spirit among their descendants,
    Imparted from heaven that blessing to save.
The delicate white-fingered hands of the lasses
    Have opened the era their virtues adorn,
By making alone from American grasses
    A delicate bonnet that rivals Leghorn.

Chorus—
    A pretty grass bonnet—a dear native bonnet,
    The Washington bonnet that rivals Leghorn.

No foreign intrigues can now disaffect us,
    Since we can oppose them with courage and wit;
Our masculine valor has made them respect us,
    Our feminine genius will make them submit;
No more shall we send them our eagles and dollars,
    Our fair from our soil can their persons adorn
With necklaces, bracelets and corsets and collars,
    And delicate bonnets that rival Leghorn.

Then hail to the arts that secure independence,
    And draw our resources from liberty's soil.
Our national banner derives new resplendence
    From feminine genius and masculine toil.
Our valor shall teach all the world to respect it,
    Tho' some have affected that valor to scorn;
And Amazon damsels have armed to protect it
    With helmets or bonnets that rival Leghorn."

Some of the readers of the *Gazette* now and then dropped into poetry. Listen to this one in its issue of December 7, 1821:

THE RULE REVERSED.

The devil once, to execute his plan,
Tempted woman, and she tempted man,
    Whence rose, we read, the origin of evil;
But wiser grown and better skilled to stray
Through every devious maze of folly's way,
Man now tempts woman—woman tempts the devil.

                      QUIZ.

Friday, June 7, 1822, the paper gives notice of the sailing of the steamboat Superior, from Buffalo to Michilimackinac on June 11 next at 9 o'clock A. M., and will touch at all intermediate ports up and back.

ASA PARTRIDGE.

The name of Asa Partridge appears in the *Gazette* now and then in 1820 as drawing sheriff's fees, charges for the care of paupers, etc., from the county treasury. This Asa Partridge was sheriff of Wayne County before Austin E. Wing. He came here as captain and commissary in the army during the war of 1812.

He moved to Palmer (St. Clair) in 1826, and shortly after died there. His widow married Doctor Harmon Chamberlain, of that city. Partridge left four children, three boys and one girl. One of the boys, Benjamin, was colonel of the Fourteenth Michigan Infantry during the civil war, and rose to the rank of brigadier-general. He was afterwards state land commissioner for four years. Another of the boys, Timothy, entered the service of Cook & Burns, this city, about 1840, and on the retirement of Mr. Cook he succeeded to his place, as before stated, and the firm name became James Burns & Co.

The daughter married Marcus H. Miles, of St. Clair, who became register of deeds of that county, and afterwards a captain and quartermaster in the civil war.

September 26, 1827, James Abbott says he has 240 acres of land on Pontiac road, five miles from Detroit, that he would like to dispose of on the most reasonable terms.

If his heirs only had it now in 1903.

October 2, 1827, Alexander Campbell, a baker at the corner of Griswold and Woodbridge Streets, advertises a runaway apprentice to the baking business. All persons are forbidden harboring or trusting him on his (Campbell's) account, as he won't pay a cent.

Campbell was father of the late John Campbell, bookkeeper for the board of public works.

In March, 1828, James Abbott says he continues to pay cash for deer skins in any quantity. He also has a few barrels of fine old whisky (now hear him) which he will sell cheap to the thirsty.

In October, 1829, Emmor Hawley advertises saddles, harnesses, trunks, valises, etc., at the red building, north side of Jefferson Avenue.

This red building was midway between Woodward Avenue and Griswold Street. Mr. Hawley married the sister of Shubal Conant.

Thomas Palmer advertises December 29, 1829, about 1,000 acres of land, where St. Clair City is now, for sale at auction on the first Monday of June, 1830, at the county court house in the village of Palmer. The climate is mild and healthy, and the situation is decidedly the most pleasant and beautiful in Michigan. Terms made known at time of sale.

LIBERAL WITH UNCLE SAM'S LAND.

Aaron Greeley was the land surveyor in those days. He surveyed the 10,000 acre tract, and in doing so was rather liberal with Uncle Sam's land. When Thomas Palmer came to dispose of the portion he received from the general government for building the capitol building, some 7,000 or 8,000 acres, it was found in re-surveying it into parcels (metes and bounds) as purchasers desired them, many of the quarter sections over-ran. In some instances there would be quite a strip of land running clear across a quarter section (after the purchasers had got all the land their deeds called for), that no one appeared to own, so they divided it up among themselves. For instance, two parties purchasing a quarter section would have the surveyor divide it equally, eighty acres to each. When the survey was completed it appeared that there was a strip of land from sixteen to twenty feet wide between the two eighties that there was, apparently, no owner or claimant for, so the parties gobbled the sixteen or twenty feet and set their fences accordingly. I don't know whether Thomas Palmer ever detected the error or not, don't think he did. Perhaps, if he had, he would have been very apt to have made a fuss about it. I think some of the quarter sections through which Woodward Avenue is laid out, that were reserved by the governor and judges, are in the same predicament.

EARLY HISTORY OF THE DETROIT FREE PRESS.

ACCOUNT OF EARLY NEWSPAPER WORK IN DETROIT, WITH SOME PLAINLY-WORDED AND INTERESTING POLITICAL LETTERS.

IN the year 1829 Daniel Leroy, Olmstead Chamberlain and Gideon O. Whittemore sold to Colonel Andrew Mack, General John R. Williams and Major Joseph Campau the newspaper called the *Oakland Chronicle,* the office being transferred here, and Hector (colored), the well-known slave of General Williams, was placed in charge of it. When the late Colonel Sheldon McKnight, who in the meantime had made arrangements to take charge of and run the concern, entered to take possession, he was fiercely resisted by Hector, who showed fight, and the colonel had to retreat. I presume the former had not been advised. I heard the colonel relate this incident. This paper was afterwards merged into the *Detroit Gazette* and after into *The Free Press.*

Shortly before the destruction of the office of the *Gazette* by fire in 1830, Mr. E. Reed, one of the proprietors of the paper, seeing, no doubt, that the concern was traveling on the "ragged edge of the whirlwind," hied himself to Washington in search of office under President Andrew Jackson, and while there wrote a number of letters to a well-known Democratic political leader and influential citizen here on his prospects there, and about things political in Detroit. Letters were all franked by Hon. John Biddle, M. C.

Copies of them are given here; they will explain themselves, and no doubt will be found interesting, particularly to old settlers.

The following is an extract from a letter of E. Reed, one of the firm of Sheldon & Reed, publishers of the *Detroit Gazette,* dated Washington 27th, December, 1829:

POLITICAL LETTERS.

"Coon Ten Eyck's backsliding does not surprise me. A man so utterly selfish cannot be expected to hold on to anything without being paid for it. He would sell his Saviour for a halfworn Indian blanket. His big talk about his influence (Good Lord!) was always a good joke. I don't believe he ever controlled a vote except those of the ragged thieves that he has about him, and that he pays with whisky for their work. Doctor Sloss, of Dearborn, also, I am told, has sworn vengeance because Judge Witherell was removed. If you had a real newspaper, the influence of such apologies for men might be set right. Catch them telling some damned lies, and then prove it on them in the paper.

"In relation to the next election, who will oppose Biddle? How will the Masons go? The anti-Masons? The French? The mining country? You ought to be damned if you are beaten this time—but, so help me God, I believe you will be. The battle once on, our good-natured easy Democrats fall to billing and cooing and frolicking with the aristocrats and sharpers, and they take advantage of them. The price of liberty is eternal vigilance, so somebody has said. It is equally true, that the Republican party, which must exist in all places in the country, can only triumph by being true to itself, and wide awake all the time. The war should never cease, nor should any compromise be made. That business of compromise is always one of the acts of the devil, which he puts in the heads of the aristocrats in order to defeat the people. Our party in Michigan is cursed with false friends.

DEPEND ON THE COUNTRY.

"You will have to depend on the country, and let the town people, the aristocracy of tape-cutters, pill-peddlers, bankmen and pettifoggers go their own way. It is not necessary to waste a word upon them. Show them that they cannot kick out of the traces without getting hurt. All the little appointments in the country should be looked to. Not a constable should be appointed or elected, unless he be a good man and true, if possible to prevent it.

"But the worst feature of Michigan politics is the practice of electing nincompoops to the legislature, merely because they can be elected. The lines of party should be drawn taut, and no man put in nomination who is not a thorough whole-hog party man. It is never too late to begin to do good, and you may as well begin now as later. You can never have a legislature fit to depend on until this practice is introduced.

"Why the devil don't you get that paper started? Never mind an editor—better have none at all than a half-way man. Tell Wells if he will start it I will give him two columns weekly from here, until he can get someone who will go the whole hog. For God's sake keep it out of the hands of any milk-sop politician, and tell Wells not to place too much reliance on Parson Hasting's advice, or that of any sectarian who catechises babies on Sunday mornings at the academy. The paper ought to have a man, and not an old woman in pantaloons at the head of it. It cannot be made profitable in any other way. Tell him to avoid the 'no party' man as he would a pestilence. They are always a set of crafty, speculating wretches, who have their own ends to gain. I believe there are more of this species of knaves in Detroit than any other place, and now is the time to set them before the public in their true colors, before they contaminate the state government, and make it offensive to the eyes of the others, as they have succeeded in regard to the territorial government. Michigan can never have any influence here until she possesses a strong party character, and he who succeeds in giving her that desirable character will deserve most at the hands of her people.

"Yours truly,
(Signed) "E. REED."

SECRETARY WITHERELL IN DANGER.

The following is a copy of a letter from E. Reed, dated Washington, January 24, 1830, and marked private and confidential:

"DEAR TOM—I saw Eaton, secretary of war, last night—he is a fine fellow. I mentioned your case, and stated that when the news arrived at Detroit of the vote of Ohio and Jackson's election was rendered certain, our Secretary Witherell raised up his hands and said he 'hoped God would interpose and take Jackson to Himself and prevent the nation from being disgraced by his taking the presidential seat.' Eaton's reply was exactly in these words: 'Make out and substantiate that fact, and by God, sir, I pledge, my life he will be removed. Your statement is sufficient for me, but get all the affidavits you can."

"And now, for God's sake, get affidavits of that fact, and keep dark. Don't show this to any one—for if we fail, the least said the soonest mended. Write often.

"Dear T——, I find myself a strong man here—a much bigger fellow than at home. If I told you all, you would think I was a vain, bragging man.

"I don't leave until I get an appointment.

(Signed.) Yours truly, "E. REED."

OPPOSED TO WING.

The following is a copy of a letter from E. Reed dated Washington, January 26, 1830, and marked "private:"

"DEAR TOM:

"I have tried to keep Biddle on the turf, but he won't and told me today that he would not be a candidate again. What will you do? Will you turn in and support Wing? If you do, you ought to be damned, and will be. Do you think I say this without reason? No, I do not, and I will tell you why you ought to be damned, in the event of that contingency.

"In the first place, if you go for Wing, you acknowledge that there was no principle in your support of Biddle. Think of that! In the next place, by electing him, you give the aristocracy of Michigan a lift which it will take a good Democratic editor five years to pull down again. Think of that again! And, thirdly (which is the best reason I shall give you just now, for I am in a hurry), by sending Wing here, you cut your own noses off. He is well known here as the devoted friend of Clay, and a bitter anti-Jackson man. He could do the territory no good.

(Signed.) "E. REED."

On the back of the last letter, or one dated January 24, someone has written or made the following "Mem:"

"The statement about the secretary is a lie from beginning to end."

The "Wells" mentioned was Stephen Wells, bookseller, and "Parson Hastings" was Eurotas P. Hastings, president of the Bank of Michigan. "Coon Ten Eyck" was Conrad Ten Eyck, of Dearborn, United States marshal at that time.

OLD STYLE OF INKING.

The office of the *Gazette* was located on Griswold Street directly in the rear of F. T. & J. Palmer's store. There was quite a space between the store and the *Gazette* office, that was used as a woodyard, etc., by Mr. Thomas Palmer. On the rear of this yard was a two-story wooden kitchen, carriage house, etc., that joined onto the printing office.

As I was located so near the *Gazette* office, and the typesetting and printing process so new to me, and so interesting, it became a habit for me to visit it, particularly when they were working off the paper. The way of inking the types was quite amusing. The ink was spread out over the surface of a table near by the printing press and pressman. Two great round leather cushions, stuffed with sheep's wool, and in each of which was a wooden handle, were used in the process. The operating "printer's devil," taking a cushion in each hand, by the handle, dabbed them in the ink on the table and then briskly jabbed them together many mines, thus distributing the ink equally over their surfaces. Then he dabbed them on the types—quite different from the present way.

THE DEMOCRATIC FREE PRESS.

The fire that destroyed the *Detroit Gazette* and much adjoining property happened on the evening of April 26, 1830.

The late Judge B. F. H. Witherell, writing to a friend in Washington the next day, says of it, in part: "Judge McDonnell, who was one of the losers, said, while his house was in full blaze, 'There is no evil without a corresponding good; there will be no more dispute about public printing.' The *Gazette* people saved their type, I think, for which I am not glad nor anyone else. A sword in the hands of a mad man is a dangerous weapon, and no matter how he uses it. A fellow set the office on fire to avenge himself on McKnight; he is now in jail."

McKnight was a nephew of Mr. Sheldon, one of the proprietors of the *Gazette*. The judge does not say who this mad man was.

Sheldon McKnight busied himself directly in getting out a new paper, and succeeded in establishing The Democratic *Free Press*, the first number of which was issued May 5, 1831. It was published every Thursday morning from the office, corner of Bates and Woodbridge Streets.

The first number was very little larger than the *Detroit Gazette*, being 19½x14 inches. It is better printed than the latter and on much better paper. The dimensions of the *Gazette* were 15½x10½. The issue was almost entirely taken up with the proceedings of a public meeting of the Democratic Republicans of the County of Wayne, who were opposed to the election of Austin E. Wing for delegate to congress. The meeting was held in the session room March 14, 1831. John R. Williams was chairman and Chas. W. Whipple and John P. Sheldon were secretaries.

At this meeting a committee of five was appointed to draft an address to the citizens of the territory. John R. Williams, John P. Sheldon, Oliver Newberry, David C. McKinstry, and Colonel Andrew Mack were appointed the said committee.

They met and drafted an address to the citizens of the territory, setting forth the views of those present, and on the evening of the 24th of March met and adopted the address.

Later on John R. Williams was nominated for delegate against Austin E. Wing. The former was defeated.

The career of The Detroit *Free Press* since then is familiar to all.

FIGHTING FIRE IN THE OLD DAYS.

THE BEST LADIES OF THE CITY ON ONE OCCASION ASSISTED THE VOLUNTEER DEPARTMENT.

I DO not undertake to give a full and complete history of the old volunteer fire department, as that has already been done in an admirable "History of Our Firemen," compiled and edited by Mr. Charles S. Hathaway, and issued in 1894, but merely give some incidents connected therewith that came under my personal observation while I was a member of the department and "ran wid de machine," and some from competent history and hearsay.

I joined the department in 1838, and became a member of No. 4. I ran with the machine for many years, until four or five before the paid fire department with its steam fire engine took the place of the hand engines and the volunteer companies.

A MAN OF NERVE.

William Green was foreman of No. 4 when I joined. He was a man of nerve, exceedingly prompt and dignified when on duty. He commanded to a very great degree the respect of the members of his company. He was at that time foreman for Sidney L. Rood in his book bindery. He was succeeded as foreman of No. 4 by William B. Wesson, who was also a prompt and energetic fireman.

The rivalry among the various companies was great indeed. The excitement in striving to be first at a fire was blood tingling, as all who have experienced it will remember, and when one company washed another, as it was termed, it was glory enough. I do not know how it was among the members of the other fire companies, but among the members of No. 4 it was all engine; they talked engine, thought of hardly anything else but engine, and dreamed engine.

I will endeavor to give an account of the fires and other incidents, of which I was an eye-witness and participator, that were connected with the volunteer fire department.

A fire broke out in the *Detroit Gazette* office, on Griswold Street, about 8 o'clock of an April day in the year 1830. The building was destroyed. F. & T. Palmer's brick store was damaged and the wooden kitchen and carriage house adjoining, on the corner of Jefferson Avenue and Griswold Street, were destroyed, as well as the wooden dwelling of Judge John McDonnell, adjoining Palmer's, on Jefferson Avenue. Dr. Thos. B. Clark had his office and a small stock of drugs and medicines in a small building next to McDonnell's, which was pulled into the street by the citizens to prevent the fire from extending to Major Dequindre's wooden store and dwelling adjoining it.

This was about the first fire of any consequence that had visited Detroit for some years. Happening, as it did, in the office of the only paper published in Michigan at that time, and threatening the destruction of one of the few brick buildings in the town occupied as a store and residence by a prominent citizen, it brought to the scene nearly the entire community. All joined in, men, women and children, to assist the firemen; also to assist in saving property, furniture, etc.

Many of the first ladies of the city worked like heroines, passing buckets to the fire brigade, and aiding the Palmers and McDonnells in saving as many of their effects as possible. People became almost beside themselves, and there was wild excitement for a time. I remember quite well seeing men throwing looking glasses and frail furniture out of the windows, and carrying feather beds down stairs, and depositing them out of reach of all possible harm.

Thomas Palmer had disposed of the remaining stock of the old firm to Phineas Davis, so was not much of a loser. What losses the other sufferers sustained I do not know.

BEER RAN IN THE DITCH.

Jack Smith's dwelling, on the corner of Griswold and Woodbridge Streets, was also destroyed, with the stable in the rear. In the lower part of the McDonnell house was the hat store of H. Griswold and auction house of Colonel Edward Brooks. Thos. Owen, the brewer, had about 300 barrels of beer in McDonnell's cellar which, I think, was a total loss. Beer ran down Griswold

Street gutter nearly all the next day—a great chance for free lager. The fire was the work of a drunken or crazy printer (Ulysses J. Smith), who pretended to have some grievance against Sheldon & Reed, the proprietors of the *Gazette*.

I have said the Palmer's brick store was damaged. Only the doors, window casings and eave troughs on the side towards the fire suffered. The wooden kitchen and carriage house that joined on to the *Gazette* office were the only buildings of the Palmers that were totally destroyed.

The city owned at that time but three engines. There was the new "Protection No. 1" and the "Old Engine," said to have been taken from Fort Shelby when it was demolished. Any way, it was in commission that night and manned by the "boys" did good service. There was also the new one belonging to No. 2 Company.

The *Gazette* building was an unpretentious one, a small wooden two-story affair with a small cupola, and in it hung a bell. Office and editorial rooms were on the first floor. The upper one was devoted to printing and composition. This fire knocked the *Gazette* out. It never appeared again. It was merged somehow into The Detroit *Free Press*, under the management of Sheldon McKnight.

A rather humorous account of the fire is contained in a letter written the day after it happened, by the late Judge B. F. H. Witherell to a friend in Washington, a copy of which appeared in The Sunday *Free Press* recently.

"FRENCHMAN TOOK DE BUCKET."

The next fire that occurred, of any note, happened during the winter 1832-33. As I was an eye-witness of the affair, I will endeavor to detail it, as memory serves me. It broke out early one intensely cold Sunday morning in Jerry Dean's saddlery and harness shop, that was situated about midway between Griswold and Shelby Streets, on the north side of Jefferson Avenue, and before it was mastered, consumed the building in which it started, also the book store of Stephen Welles, adjoining on the west, and the general store of Oliver & Walter Newberry, that stood on the now so-called Ives' corner, Griswold Street. The buildings, being of wood, burned like tinder.

It was at this fire that Mr. Joseph Campau (he lived almost opposite the fire, as did my uncle and family) in his excitement, rushed in among the crowd summoned there by the clanging bell in the church steeple, corner of Woodward Avenue and Larned Street—some to render assistance and others to look on, as usual—and exclaimed:

"Frenchman took de bucket, white man took de engine."

Engines No. 1, 2 and 3 were stationed as near the burning buildings as prudence would permit, and two lines, composed of the citizens, were formed and extended from them to the river at the foot of Griswold Street. There was not any dock or wharf there at that date. A hole was cut in the ice and some citizen volunteered to station himself at it and pay particular attention to filling the fire buckets as fast as they came to him, which was pretty fast, and handing them to his nearest neighbor, who in turn passed them to the next, and so along the line to the fire engine. The empty buckets came back along the other line in due course, and so on.

It was a bitter cold job, and before the affair was over nearly all those who participated in keeping up the lines, as well as the men at the brakes, were covered with icicles. There were no convenient hydrants, reservoirs or hose in those days, and the engines had to depend on the "bucket brigade" to keep them supplied with water.

This "bucket brigade" was a most necessary institution. Each householder was obliged to provide himself with two leather buckets for use in case of fire. When an alarm was sounded he would grab his buckets and rush to the scene of danger. They would form lines, as said before, and hurry up the water. After the fire was over the buckets were thrown into a heap and then each owner claimed his buckets, names being conspicuously painted on them. I think the present fire department owns three or four of these self-same leather fire buckets. Senator Thomas W. Palmer has two of them, in the "Log Cabin" at Palmer Park. They used to belong to his grandfather, Judge James Witherell.

KEEN RIVALRY OF FIRE FIGHTERS.

STORIES OF THE OLD VOLUNTEER DEPARTMENT AND THEIR AMUSING DEEDS SEVENTY YEARS AGO.

AT the time of the burning of the old *Detroit Gazette* newspaper office, in 1830, the members of No. 1 Protection Fire Engine Co. that I knew personally in after life were: David C. McKinstry, chief engineer; Obed Waite, engineer; Asa Madison, Shadrach Gillett, John Farrar, Timothy Fales, Dexter Merrill, Jeremiah Moors, Francis Leterneau, Perez Merritt, Thomas C. Sheldon, John Wright and Harvey Williams; and of Engine Company No. 2 were: Robert A. Forsyth, Edmund A. Brush, Ralph Wadams, Darius Lamson, Felix Hinchman, Charles C. Trowbridge, Henry S. Cole, Walter L. Newberry, John L. Whiting, David Cooper, Joseph W. Torrey, Marshal Chapin, Wm. G. Abbott, Simon Poupard, Curotas P. Hastings, Theodore Williams, James W. Hinchman, Josiah R. Dorr, Melvin Dorr, John J. Denning, Shubal Conant, Alanson M. Hurd, George F. Porter and Thomas Rowland.

THE RELIC.

There was one other fire engine besides Protection No. 1 when I came here, and that was a very crude and cumbrous affair. It was said to have belonged to Fort Shelby and a relic of Perry's fleet. It had solid wooden or iron wheels. A faithful representation of it is to be found on page 26 of the book entitled "Our Firemen."

In March, 1827, the common council appropriated $127 to put this "old engine" in repair and to keep the same in good condition for one year.

Robert Hopkin, the well known and venerable artist, in "Our Firemen," page 118, has described the first fire engine (Boys' Company) and to which I have alluded. He said:

"I not only remember the first fire engine in Detroit, but

when I was a lad I painted and decorated the machine, which was to be a feature in some public parade. At that time—it was along about 1852, I think—I know it was said that the little apparatus was about forty years old, and it looked it. The thing consisted of an iron-bound oblong box or reservoir, about 6 feet long by 2½ feet wide, and 18 or 20 inches deep. It was mounted on four small iron wheels, just such as you now see on hand trucks used in wholesale houses. In the center of the box was a copper dome or air chamber some 15 or 18 inches high, and in front of and behind this dome were two small pumps set on an angle and operated by long brakes extending to the front and rear of the reservoir. There was a suction opening—and only one—on one side of the reservoir, and a long curved handle or tongue by which the vehicle was hauled. When the suction failed to provide a sufficient quantity of water—which was almost invariably the case, it was said—the deficiency was overcome by lines of bucketmen passing water and emptying it at either one of the open ends of the little reservoir.

PUMPS FROM PERRY'S FLAGSHIP.

"Of course, I know nothing first-hand as to the pumps, but I recollect that when I was decorating the engine many persons called to look at it, and I heard it said repeatedly that the pumps were from the flagship of Commodore Perry's fleet, and that the engine had been devised and built by the soldiers garrisoned at Detroit. I do not think it weighed as much as an ordinary lumber wagon, and, as I remember it, the suction opening was not much over an inch and a half in diameter."

Mr. Hopkin made a sketch of this engine from memory, and it is quite a faithful reproduction of the "Old Machine," as I remember it.

The boys of No. 3 supplied themselves with fire hats from the stock of privates' uniform hats in the United States storehouse. They had seen service in the war of 1812, and were condemned. Seymour Rossiter, son of Old Rossiter, the dyer, one of the members of the company, and quite an artist, painted something on the fronts of these hats that represented a building in full blaze, and the letters "F. E. Co. No. 3" above it. These hats were of glazed leather.

GOT THERE FIRST.

On one occasion a member of the company, who was employed in some occupation near the foot of Cass Street, discovered a fire in a building adjacent to the place where he was at work. He directly, without giving a general alarm, quietly posted five or six of his fellow members, who were in hailing distance, of the fact; they repaired at once to the engine house, and when the general alarm was sounded their engine was out in no time, and the first at the fire, of course. This member of the company who first discovered the fire was Henry (Hank) Mullett. I have often heard him in after years relate the circumstance and with much amusement. I have also heard Henry M. Roby, a member of same company, tell the same story. The incident is alluded to in "Our Firemen."

This younger element of the city that had before 1830 organized this sort of fire company (they were present at the *Gazette* office fire), gathered around the "old machine" mentioned, and had it housed in a small wooden building, on the northeast corner of the alley that crosses Wayne Street, between Larned and Congress Streets. Fire Engine Company No. 4 occupied this building afterwards, and for many years.

PETITION FOR NEW COMPANY.

Well, the boys after a while came to see that they were not having a proper show in the fire department and, accordingly, in the early part of 1830, they petitioned the common council for the organization of a new fire engine company. The petition was granted and the members (named in the grant) that I knew personally at that time and for long years after, were: Henry J. Canniff, Benjamin F. Stead, John McCarty, William W. Miller, William H. Wells, William N. Carpenter, Lewis C. Rowland, Seymour Rossiter, George Doty, Henry M. Roby, Francis Eldred, Rufus W. Griswold, James H. Mullett, Henry H. Snelling, Henry L. Chipman, Benjamin R. Keeney, Willis Garrison, Charles Mack, George W. Keeney, Henry C. Wagstaff, John Dackett and John Watson.

Their engine was named officially No. 3, and to stimulate the members it was said that the common council agreed by a resolution to pay a premium of $5 to said company if their engine was the first to operate on any fire.

And it was further said that in April, 1830, when the *Gazette* office fire happened, the members of the company claimed they were the first to get a stream of water on the fire and put in their bill for the $5. But from some unexplained cause the claim was rejected. It is my opinion that the claim of the boys' company was valid, as they were all quite young. None of them could have been over 18 years old, handy and full of snap and boyish enthusiasm.

EXCITING SPECTACLE.

A short time after that fire, the common council requested the three companies to appear at the public wharf on a stated day at 4 o'clock in the afternoon, for the purpose of making certain experiments in the operation of said engines in concert, and to ascertain more fully the expediency of procuring hose for Engines Nos. 1, 2 and 3.

The three engine companies with their engines appeared at the "Public Wharf," foot of Woodward Avenue, according to request, and gave the common council and citizens of Detroit (the latter gathering in large numbers) a full taste of their quality, and so convincing was it that the hose was ordered a few days later. I witnessed this parade and display of the prowess of that fire department, in its infancy, and must say it was to me, though quite a small lad, a most exciting spectacle.

The companies all took suction from the river, and as they had no hose the foreman of each company, standing on the top of his "machine," held the pipe that was screwed tightly on to the "goose neck," and with his thumb pressed tight over the mouth of the nozzle, held the stream of water back as long as he could, while the boys at the brakes were putting in their best licks, with "down with her" and "now she feels it" constantly repeated.

SOAKED EVERYONE.

When the water was releasel, then the excitement culminated, and each company did its best endeavor to outdo the other in the distance thrown, as well as in the time the stream of water was maintained. When they did get started, the foreman directed the water to the tops of the adjacent buildings (they were not very high then), on to the sidewalks, in at any open door or window, onto any careless pedestrian that happened to be in reach, and onto members of rival companies, until they were as wet as a lot of drowned rats. I believe he would have squirted on Governor Cass if he had been handy. Such fun!

I have seen almost the same scene enacted many, many, times in after years. I call one or two to mind. One was at an annual parade of the department (I have forgotten the date). It was announced at this parade that the top of J. L. King's store (King's corner) was to be the objective point, the goal, as it were, and the first company to attain it with a line of hose and a stream of water was to have the "broom" and carry it until it was wrested from them by some similar achievement by a rival company.

Well, the day came, and the department was on hand, all eager for the fray. The engines were posted at the reservoirs near by, one on the corner where the Merrill Block is, and one a little farther up Jefferson Avenue. I do not remember what engines were at each reservoir, except No. 4, and that was at the reservoir on the Merrill Block corner. Well, the foreman of each company with their assistants were at the foot of the ladders, with lines of hose, the brakes manned and all eagerly awaiting the signal from the chief engineer to pitch in. When the signal did come, the mad and perilous rush to get to the top of the building was a thrilling experience to those engaged in it, as well as a thrilling sight to the spectators. No. 4 it was, I think, that got the broom that time.

LEE'S BRASS TRUMPET.

The other occasion was a parade of the department held on the vacant space in front of the Russell House, where is now the Bagley fountain. I do not call to mind much in relation to this parade or what the various companies set out to do, except it was to see which engine could throw a stream of water the farthest. Well, they got to work and soon the usual wild excitement possessed each company, and the cries of "Down with her, now she feels it," etc., were universal. I do not remember which company bore the palm, but what I do remember—and it is principally for the following incident, in connection with it—was that William Lee (Bill Lee) was the foreman of No. 3. The company just before this had purchased a fine large brass trumpet, and "Bill" had it on this occasion, of course. His position, or the one he took, was on the body of the "machine," between the brakes.

After the signal from the chief engineer to commence playing was given, the excitement was as usual on such occasions, until after a few moments it seemed to increase, and "Bill" in his eagerness, every time he shouted "Down with her" to the boys, he banged this brass trumpet against the "goose neck" until it lost all semblance of what it had been, and was but an unshapen piece of brass. I have a cut of this affair among my effects somewhere, clipped from a paper of that date.

FAMOUS BUILDINGS DESTROYED BY FIRE.

FURTHER REMINISCENCES OF CONFLAGRATIONS THAT RUINED POPULAR LANDMARKS IN THE 30'S AND 40'S.

SOME time during the summer of 1832, French & Eldred's woolen mill, a short distance to the east of the foot of Randolph Street, was destroyed by fire. The same blaze ruined the pumping apparatus of Farrand & Wells, and Mr. Eldred's store and dwelling near by. It happened on a moonless night, about 2 A. M. The buildings were dry and burned like tinder. The flames lit up the whole county of Wayne and part of Canada, apparently. Out where we lived on Woodward Avenue, corner of John R. Street, the illumination was so great one could see to read by it.

One early summer morning in 1837, a fire broke out in the row of wooden buildings adjoining Dr. J. L. Whiting's warehouse on Woodward Avenue. It was thought to have commenced in a bakery adjoining McKenzie & Greaves's store, which was nearly enveloped in flames before the alarm was sounded. From there it extended with ungovernable fury in all directions east of Woodward Avenue, crossed Atwater Street, and swept over the buildings between Atwater and Woodbridge Streets. The buildings between Woodbridge Street and the river, from Woodward as far as the low block (Berthelet row) in front of Woodworth's Hotel, on Woodbridge, with two or three exceptions, were a mass of ruins.

On Atwater Street the fire was arrested at a small building below and next to the tavern called the Market Hotel, in the rear of the Berthelet market. Included in the loss, besides the warehouse of Dr. Whiting and McKenzie & Greaves's grocery store, were the extensive grocery house of Franklin Moore, on the corner of Woodward Avenue and Atwater Street; the grocery store of Garrison & Holmes on the opposite corner of Woodward Avenue (where Eaton's now is); the Arthur Bronson tavern, northeast corner of Woodward Avenue and Woodbridge Street; John

Farrer's store, on the southeast corner of Bates and Atwater; the Detroit Public Garden, with buildings, etc., on the northwest corner of Bates and Atwater Streets; the entire plant of John Roberts, on Atwater Street, between Bates and Randolph, fronting on the river, consisting of a general store, soap and candle factory, etc.; Charles L. Bristol's wooden stores, on the south side of Atwater, between Woodward Avenue and Bates Street; Knowles Hall's carriage factory and Mr. Sanderson's carriage and saddlery shop; the dwelling of H. H. Leroy & Co.

The late George W. Foote was at that time bookkeeper for Franklin Moore, and during the fire he brought the books and papers of the concern over to the store of Loomis & Jaquith, opposite (in which store I was a clerk at the time), and established a temporary office there until things could be straightened out.

The Detroit Garden was the only place of the kind in the city at that time, and its loss was deeply deplored. Dr. Marshal Chapin's residence, midway between Bates and Randolph Streets, on Woodbridge Street, was also destroyed.

BURNING OF STEAMER GREAT WESTERN.

One important fire, and so considered at the time, the book entitled "Our Firemen" does not make mention of at all, and that was the partial burning of the then finest and most magnificent steamer on the lakes, the Great Western, while lying at her dock (Gillett & Desnoyer's), near foot of Shelby Street. It happened about 1838, on a summer Sunday afternoon about 5 o'clock. I have forgotten the exact date. She had arrived that forenoon on her down trip from Chicago to Buffalo. I was present at the fire with engine company No. 4 (that far-off time, it seems but yesterday). She was the pride of the lakes, and of her owner and commander, Captain Augustus Walker. She was the first steamer to have her cabins on the upper deck, passengers heretofore having had to dive down between decks if they had any idea of sleeping or eating, and most of them had. The news that this steamer was ablaze spread like wildfire and hurried everyone to the scene; indeed, all Detroit was on hand. The engines hustling down Wayne and Shelby Streets came near running over the men and boys who had hold of the drag ropes, so wild was the excitement. No. 4 engine company came first in this encounter. It had its station on the dock, between the warehouse and the burning steamer, and three of its members had the post of honor during the fire. William Green, the foreman, who had the pipe, was assisted by Barney Campau and Kin Dygert. They held the fort, so to speak.

They were stationed on the upper deck of the steamer, abaft the wheelhouse. The scene lives in an oil painting by Thomas Burnham, a well known local artist of that day. This painting is now the property of some citizen of this city, who should, it seems to me, donate it to the Art Museum, or to the present fire department. The upper cabins of the Great Western, abaft the wheelhouses, and the ladies' cabin below, were badly wrecked, otherwise the steamer did not sustain much damage. But it was a most exciting fire while it lasted, as any one now living who was present at the time will, I am sure, bear witness.

FIRE OF JANUARY 1, 1842.

Early on the night of January 1, 1842, a fire broke out in the New York & Ohio House, situated on Woodward Avenue, midway between Jefferson Avenue and Woodbridge Street, and swept away the entire block bounded by Woodward and Jefferson Avenues, Griswold and Woodbridge Streets.

"It was a fire, as was a fire," and tried the mettle of our volunteer firemen to the utmost, as no fire that ever preceded it had done. The night was mild but windy, with the wind from the south; no snow or rain had fallen for quite a while. We were in the midst of a January thaw. All things conspired to give the flames a good time and they had it. Aided by the high wind, they came near crossing Woodward Avenue and would have done so, perhaps, had it not been for the gallant efforts of our brave firemen. The foremen of No. 2 and No. 4 engine companies, aided by their assistants, ran lines of hose to the top of of J. L. King's store, on the corner of Woodward and Jefferson Avenues, and there, protected by a high wooden balustrade, were enabled to keep the fire brands and sparks from getting a foothold on the roof of King's store, as well as on the brick building adjoining, occupied by McArthur & Hulbert.

The Bank of Michigan building on Griswold Street had all the plate glass in its windows so badly cracked that they had to be replaced by ordinary glass. The plate glass had been imported from France and was the first of its kind to appear in the state.

The panes were not very large, to be sure, only eight by ten, but then they were plate glass, nevertheless. The destroyed buildings along Jefferson Avenue were speedily replaced by others of brick.

In addition to Hallock & Raymond's clothing store, Warren's candy and confectionery place, the Howard restaurant, and Geo. Dawson's, the *Detroit Advertiser,* the following firms and concerns were wiped out: A. C. McGraw, boots and shoes; G. & J. G. Hill, drugs; Nelson, groceries; Gardner & Mather, crockery; Edward Bingham, drugs; Salisbury, grocer, and the United States customs offices. Our engine, No. 4, was stationed that night at the reservoir, corner of Jefferson and Woodward Avenues (the Merrill Block corner).

FIRE OF 1848.

Early in the forenoon of a June day in 1848 a fire broke out in a large yellow warehouse on the river front, between Bates and Randolph Streets, occupied by John Chester & Co., and J. Nicholson Elbert. A portion of the upper stories was used by a fur dealing firm, the name I have forgotten, for the storage, repacking and cleaning of furs, ridding them of the fatty portion adhering to them. Captain J. A. Whitall, United States quartermaster, one other person and myself were at the time looking out of the back windows of the captain's office that was over the Peninsular Bank building on Jefferson Avenue, noticing two or three propellers that were passing up and down the river. One of these propellers was just steaming away from the dock of the yellow warehouse, when suddenly an immense billowy cloud of inky smoke streaked with jets of flame burst from the rear of the building, and in less than a minute the whole structure was a roaring mass of fire. Sparks from the propeller had a fine chance to get in their work through the open windows of the portion used by the fur dealers, and they did it. The cleaning benches and floors were so saturated with the grease and oil from the furs that they were as tinder. The flames, fanned by a fierce east wind, raged despite the efforts of almost the entire population of the city until quite along in the afternoon, by which time nearly every building in the following described areas was destroyed:

The entire square now occupied by the Biddle House property, including the residence of E. A. Brush on the corner of Brush Street, and the residence of Major John Biddle adjoining;

the entire square bounded by Woodbridge Street, Atwater, Brush and Randolph; the east half of each square fronting on the west side of Randolph Street, between Jefferson Avenue and the river. The principal buildings destroyed were the Old Council house, in which Sandford Britton had a stock of furniture; the Berthelet market, the Berthelet row, Woodworth's Steam Boat Hotel, American Hotel (the old Governor Hull mansion), the Indiana Hotel in the rear of the Berthelet market, on Atwater Street; the house of engine company No. 3, the *Daily Advertiser* office, the large warehouse belonging to Alex. M. Campau next adjoining the yellow warehouse on the east; also the boat house and all the fine boats of the Detroit Boat Club.

300 FAMILIES HOMELESS.

About 300 families were rendered homeless by this disaster.

In the first story of Alex. Campau's brick building adjoining the council house on the west, Bill Clare kept a billiard room, and when the fire broke out the two tables were in full blast, but, notwithstanding, the game progressed until the iron shutters in the rear became so heated that the party thought it prudent to quit. This building, however, did not sustain much damage on account of its heavy walls, only a small portion of the roof being destroyed. This disastrous fire dealt this portion of the city a blow from which it has never recovered.

The American Hotel, formerly the old Governor Hull mansion, was a historic building, and its loss was much regretted on that account. Hull built the house for his own use on taking command of this post in 1812. It was a substantial brick building, and the first brick structure of any pretentions erected in Michigan. After his unfortunate surrender of this post he was succeeded in the occupancy of it by the British General Proctor, who made it his headquarters during his brief stay. General Hugh Brady, on being assigned to the command of this department, made it his headquarters until his own residence was completed, where the Art Museum now is.

The destruction of Ben Woodworth's old Steam Boat Hotel was also keenly felt by all, and deeply deplored by the old settlers particularly. It had been for years the principal hostelry in all the northwest, the headquarters, so to speak, of all the social and political life of Detroit and the state. All grand entertainments, military balls, social parties, bar dinners, etc., were given there after the war of 1812, until the completion of the National Hotel (Russell House), which latter then shared the honors.

I was an eye witness (though quite a lad) of a brilliant ball given at Woodworth's Hotel on Washington's birthday, shortly after the termination of the Patriot war. All the officers of our army on duty here were present, as also were the officers and members of the Brady Guard and General John R. Williams and staff, all in full uniform. The British officers then stationed at Sandwich and Malden, were also present, in full uniform. Quite an unusual significance was attached to the presence of the latter at this ball. The battle of Waterloo had been fought but a little over twenty years at that date, and nearly every British officer present had participated in that battle. Some bore scars of the conflict, and all who were entitled to do so displayed conspicuously on their breasts medals struck in commemoration of that event. The fame and genius of that great captain, Napoleon Bonaparte, had so filled the world, while he compelled its attention, that a little more than twenty years after his death had passed, way out here on the confines of civilization his name and his exploits were as fresh as though they had happened the day before, and therefore these men that had been pitted against him on that memorable day were objects of peculiar interest. The side arms worn by some of them that night were the same that they wore on the day of the battle.

DARIUS CLARK AND M. C. R. R. FIRE IN 1850.

THIRD PAPER OF REMINISCENCES REGARDING THE OLD VOLUNTEER DEPARTMENT AND ITS WORK.

NOVEMBER 20, 1850, in the early morning, fire broke out in the large cupola of the Michigan Central freight building, an immense structure for those days, and quite as extensive, it seems to me, as the present one. The building and all its contents were lost, including 10 freight cars, 15,000 barrels of flour, 25,000 bushels of wheat, 2,000 bushels of corn and a quantity of miscellaneous freight.

Of the flour, some 1,000 or 1,500 barrels happened to be piled on the dock, on the river front. Most of this was rolled into the river to save it from the flames, and settlers all along both sides of the river to its mouth got the benefit.

The fire was supposed to be the work of an incendiary, through the agency of some kind of an apparatus confined in a small box filled with combustibles. It was set to explode at a certain hour. As free access was had to the cupola during the day by persons desiring to get a fine view of the river and opposite shore, it was an easy job for a visitor to deposit such an article in that locality if so disposed, and quietly and safely wait the result.

I think the fact of the burning of the depot by one of the railroad conspirators was established at their trial for lawless acts on their part perpetrated against the Michigan Central Railroad Company. I presume many will remember this trial. It came off at the Firemen's Hall, this city (I do not remember the date), and attracted wide attention. Eminent counsel were engaged on both sides, prominent among whom were Colonel John Van Armen, of Michigan; Hon. W. H. Seward, of Auburn, N. Y., and Hon. Eli Cook, of Buffalo, N. Y. I was in the court room many times during the trial.

THE SECRET AGENT.

Mr. Darius Clark, formerly of Marshall, Mich., was quite a factor in unearthing this conspiracy. He was a secret agent of the railroad company, employed for the very purpose of ferreting out the "gang." The fact of his appointment was kept a profound secret. It was so well guarded that Clark was enabled to join this secret conclave of railroad wreckers, and did join, taking all the prescribed oaths, and, of course, became one of the "gang," attended all the meetings of the "lodge," etc. It is needless to say the information he gained was divulged to the railroad people. Hence the trial and break up.

Clark received for his reward from the railroad company, among other things, the appointment as its agent in New York City, which important position he held for many years to the entire satisfaction of the company and the community in general. Scores and scores of people, citizens of Michigan particularly, will, I am sure, remember Darius Clark, with pleasurable emotions—a gentleman of elegant manners and most engaging address.

The conspirators, for the part he took in their undoing, swore vengeance against him, and in consequence Clark steered clear of Michigan, and I don't believe he ever visited this or any other locality in the state until some time in 1865 or '66.

DARIUS CLARK'S GUESTS.

During the civil war, in the fore part of 1863, Governor Blair and party, consisting of Mrs. Blair, Mrs. Gorham, of Jackson; Dr. Tunnicliffe, also of Jackson; John J. Bagley, Colonel Fred K. Morley, assistant adjutant-general of the state, and the writer visited the army of the Potomac. On the way, we tarried some days in New York City, the guests in a great part of Darius Clark, who rendered us every attention in his power. The chief of police of that city, through Clark's request, put one of the small harbor steamers belonging to that department at the disposal exclusively of Governor Blair and his party during their stay in the city.

Clark had some months previous to this solicited of Governor Blair the appointment of state sanitary agent at New York City, without pay, asking only that he be commissioned colonel with the rank of colonel in the state volunteer service, which Governor Blair did. There were at that time large numbers of invalid officers and soldiers of Michigan regiments on leave going to and from the army of the Potomac and southern battlefields. They necessarily drifted through New York City and there were large numbers of sick and wounded soldiers of Michigan regiments who had been sent to the various hospitals in and around New York, particularly the extensive hospital at David's Island.

To all these Colonel Clark gave a large share of his time and attention, visiting them almost daily. He, however, was reimbursed by the governor's order for money expended on account of the soldiers, their small expenses, such as tobacco, stationery, periodicals, newspapers, etc. These accounts were paid regularly by the quartermaster-general of the state.

ASKED FOR RELIEF.

After the war closed, Colonel Clark resigned his agency of the Michigan Central in New York City and engaged in the wholesale drug business with his brother, Emmons Clark, colonel of the celebrated Seventh New York regiment, and another gentleman. He also engaged in other ventures. Time passed and sorry to say, all of thm came to naught and left him almost penniless. In his dilemma he sought relief from the state of Michigan, which he claimed to have benefited by his aid and assistance rendered to the wounded and invalid soldiers. He at the same time acknowledged that in his hour of plenty and supposed remoteness from want, he had solicited and taken this state agency without the expectation of pay, still he concluded, under the circumstances to make an appeal to the legislature of the great State of Michigan for relief in this his hour of need.

He did not in his petition state any sum for services, but merely cited the amounts paid to the other sanitary agents of the state, Messrs. Benjamin Vernor, Dr. Tunnicliffe and Luther B. Willard, i.e., $200 per month and office expenses, and left it to the discretion of the state officials to pay whatever amount they saw fit. Well, a joint resolution looking to Clark's relief was introduced in the legislature, second term of Governor Bagley's administration, instructing the board of state auditors to examine and adjust his claim and make him whatever allowance was found to be his due.

THE OUTCOME.

The resolution was passed along towards the latter part of the session. Clark himself and his friends thought, then, he would have some show for obtaining relief, not giving themselves the least apprehension in regard to the fate of the resolution at the hands of the governor, as the latter had not, as far as was known, signified the least hostility to the measure.

Well, Mr. Bagley put the joint resolution in his pocket and it never made its appearance from that receptacle. What his reasons, good or bad, were, for so doing, I never heard.

Clark was much cast down on account of the result, and finally accepted a subordinate position on the then New York & Harlem Railroad, and died in harness, not many years ago, and was buried through the kindness of friends (I have understood), beside the remains of his wife in the cemetery at Marshall, Mich. Peace to his ashes.

Referring again to the trial of the railroad conspirators, it was said at the time that Colonel Van Armen also ingratified himself into the good graces of the conspirators, and became, with Clark, one of the "gang." How true this is I do not know.

Along in 1870 Clark visit Detroit and, during his stay here, he made a trip on the Michigan Central Railroad to Jackson, Marshall, etc. On the way, when passing the village of Leoni, he pointed out to me from the car windows the very house in which the secret conclaves of the conspirators were held, when he joined them. He was always quite reticent in regard to the part he took in the affair, scarcely ever alluding to it. Why he was so shy, I never inquired.

HEROIC WORK OF VOLUNTEER FIREMEN.

SEEN DURING THE BIG BLAZE OF 1837—WINDSOR GAVE DETROIT DEPARTMENT A SILVER TRUMPET.

EARLY on the morning of January 10, 1854, a fire broke out in the shoe store of Smith & Tyler, at the northeast corner of Woodward Avenue and Larned Street, and before it could be gotten under control—the structures being of wood and a high wind prevailing—the entire north half of that square was destroyed, including the grocery store and sample room of George Davie and John Fay, also Bates's merchant tailoring establishment.

Shortly after this fire had been mastered by the firemen, a small jet of flame was noticed by a few lookerson (myself among the number) issuing from a point high up on one of the wooden pillars of the Presbyterian Church on the northwest corner of Woodward Avenue and Larned Street. No one appeared to pay much attention to this, when all of a sudden, like a flash of lightning, a volume of flame was seen to shoot up in the interior of the steeple in which was the belfry and almost in a twinkle it was an immense torch of fire. This steeple being of goodly dimensions and quite tall, made a most magnificent spectacle, lighting up as it did the city and adjoining country. I heard afterwards, many citizens of Windsor, Sandwich, Canada, declare that the illumination furnished on that occasion was most grand. It appears that the fire or flame that was discovered burning on one of the pillars in front of the church, proceeded from a pine knot, fat with rosin, located in the outer casing of the pillar, it being hollow. It soon worked its way through, and then asserted itself, to its heart's content.

It was beyond all reach and just rioted. The church was completely destroyed, nothing but the walls being left standing. It was feared for a while that the burning steeple would fall, either into Woodward Avenue, or on the stores of Holmes & Co., adjoining on Woodward Avenue, and it was watched with intense interest by the spectators. Considerable anxiety was also felt, from the fact that the establishment of Holmes & Co. was crowded with citizens assisting that firm in removing their stock of goods to a place of safety, as they had come to the conclusion that their premises must go.

THE STEEPLE FELL.

Well, soon the steeple was seen to waver, and finally, and fortunately fell, with a loud crash into the body of the church, Holmes & Co. did not sustain much damage, fortunately.

The bell of the church was melted by the fierce heat, and the metal was cast into a large number of tea bells, and distributed among the church members as souvenirs. Dear reader, perhaps you are the fortunate possessor of one.

WILLIAM DUNCAN.

The compiler of "Our Firemen" aptly says: "No man living put in more years of active service or took a greater or more practical interest in the affairs of the old volunteer fire department than did Wm. Duncan. He has been assistant foreman, foreman, assistant chief and chief engineer; he was a member of the original fire commission, and as a member of the common council did a great deal of work as a member of the committee on fire department. On the Fourth of July, 1875, he entertained the entire fire department of the city at his home on Miami Avenue, the members of which, together with other invited guests, constituted a company of considerably over one thousand persons who partook of his hospitality on that occasion. I was present, and it was a lavish and most enjoyable entertainment and the host was at his best.

It is sad to relate, that his last days were chilled by the presence of want, and of the very many that he had assisted when in affluent circumstances, very few came to his rescue in his hour of need.

I first knew him when he was an apprentice to Cullen Brown, in the saddlery and harness business. He was at the same time a member of Engine Company No 4, of which company I was also a member. We used often in after years, even until a short period before his death, to talk over, with a wonderful amount of pleasure, the stirring times that we had experienced, "running with the machine." A thorough fireman was "Bill Duncan," and an all-around good fellow withal.

THE FREE PRESS FIRE.

I also copy from "Our Firemen" Mr. Duncan's account of a fire that partially destroyed the Sheldon Block, now the Willis Block, on Jefferson Avenue. I copy it because I was present at the fire and can verify the truth of his statement. Mr. Duncan said:

"Just after 3 o'clock on the morning of January 4, 1837, fire was discovered in what was then called the Sheldon Block, now known as the Willis Block, on the north side of Jefferson Avenue, between Griswold and Shelby Streets. The weather was intensely cold, so that the fire department, in addition to working with inadequate apparatus, met with many annoyances and much delay in handling the hose. The fire, while it was at last brought under control, succeeded in destroying *The Free Press* office, Henry A. Naglee's confectionery store and bakery, Amos Chaffee's blacksmith shop and Dr. Rufus Brown's general store, groceries, wines and liquors, the total loss amounting to about $23,000—a very considerable blow in those days of wild-cat panic.

"Near the close of the fire two of the younger members of the fire department passed through a scene of danger that was considered most thrilling and gave a display of cool-headed determination which was the talk of the town for the rest of the winter. The store occupied by Doctor Brown was largely filled with drugs, oils, turpentine and liquors. It was two stories high, built of brick and having a steep pitched roof, so high that the roof-tree and gable peaks were ten or fifteen feet higher than the adjoining buildings. Owing to the character of its contents Doctor Brown's store burned rapidly, untily only the bare brick walls remained. Meanwhile the late Mr. John Owen had a position astride the ridge of the roof of the adjoining building—a frame structure occupied by Cook & Burns as a dry goods store—and only about ten feet from the burning building, where he sat holding the hose nozzle, and directing a stream on the flames. At the top of a ladder, which rested against the eaves of the dry goods store, stood the late James Sutton, holding the hose which led up to Mr. Owen.

BRAVE WORK.

"Suddenly a cry arose from the several hundred people who, standing in the street below, were watching the picture that the walls of the Brown building were weaving to and fro.

" 'The wall is falling!' shouted a fire warden. 'Get away from there!' Still Messrs. Owen and Sutton held their position. 'Get back further,' 'look out, John!' 'Slide down the ladder, Jim!' and other warnings sounded, but to no avail.

"Evidently the young firemen did not hear the cries, for presently a large section of the wall came down with a crash, forcing its way through the roof of the dry goods store, and sending up a great cloud of smoke, cinders and fire, completely hiding Messrs. Owen and Sutton from view, and so far as the crowd could guess, carrying the entire roof and the two men down among the ruins. In a few minutes, however, when the smoke had cleared away, this anxiety was relieved by the sight of Mr. Owen still astride the ridgepole and sending water down into the flames, while Mr. Sutton, fairly covered with ashes, dust and smoke, was clinging to the hose in his old position. They had not been hurt, although the wreck made by the falling wall was within six feet of them; so close, indeed, that when the falling brick had ignited the crushed-in roof, Mr. Owen found it advisable to retreat about ten feet. There he remained, however, with Mr. Sutton, a loyal companion, until the fire was stopped. By this act the entire eastern one-third of the block in question was saved from destruction."

BIG FIRE IN WINDSOR.

In 1849, while Mr. Duncan was chief engineer of the Volunteer Fire Department, a fire broke out in Windsor on the night of April 6, and as far as appearances from this side indicated, the City of Windsor was in danger of being wiped out by fire. Dougall's large brick store on the west side of Ferry Street and abutting on the river, was a mass of flames and a high wind was prevailing. After a delay of an hour and a half, owing to the absence of the ferry boat, Duncan was enabled to send only one engine (No. 5) across, and that was by a small steam boat called the Hastings, that he happened to see make a landing at the foot of Shelby Street. The reason why only one engine was sent across the river was owing to the smallness of the Hastings. Duncan, however, at the timely suggestion of Mr. John Owen, took over at the same time 250 feet additional of hose, which addition saved the City of Windsor many, many thousands of dollars.

When Chief Duncan and his men reached the scene nearly an acre of territory had been burned, and the northwest wind was sending a mass of cinders and flame directly towards the large frame hotel known as the Windsor Castle, which stood directly opposite the site of the present Crawford House.

About two hours and a half after the landing of the boat, the Detroit firemen being augmented in the meantime, by the arrival of Engine Company No. 2, on board the steamer Ariel, the flames were subdued, the fire completely checked. It was a fierce, stubborn fight, and the firemen that particularly distinguished themselves in connection with Chief Duncan, as hoseman and pipeman were: Andrew Young, A. P. Copeland, Joseph P. Rhodes, William Hopkins and J. P. Rosenburg. For reasons unexplained the ferry boats did not visit Detroit that night.

LOSS WAS $30,000.

Following is a list of the buildings that were destroyed: Dougall's dry goods store, two warehouses, Hunt's hardware store, and packing house, customs office, a restaurant, the Queen's Hotel, brick school house and dwelling, Mr. Richard's bakery and dwelling, four large frame barns (and four horses) besides several small outbuildings. The total loss was $30,000. Had it not been for the Detroit firemen the loss would, at least, have been double the amount.

The Windsor people entertained the Detroit firemen right royally, "gave them the best they had in the shop," of course, and the day following called a public meeting of citizens which was held at the Windsor Castle Hotel, at which meeting an address of thanks was unanimously adopted to Wm. Duncan, chief engineer of the fire department of the city of Detroit, and the two fire companies under his command on the occasion. They also voted a silver trumpet to the volunteer firemen of Detroit. The trumpet was procured, properly inscribed and on July 2, 1849, the same was presented to Mr. Duncan, as chief engineer of the volunteer fire department of the City of Detroit.

The firemen were drawn up in a hollow square at the foot of Woodward Avenue, and received the committee on presentation, consisting of Colonel Arthur Rankin, chairman; John McEwan. Esq., sheriff; P. E. Verhoeff, merchant; H. Kennedy and J. McCrae, also merchants, preceded by the German band, playing "God Save the Queen," and escorted by the mayor, chief engineer and officers and member of the fire department.

THE CEREMONY.

The presentation speech was made by Colonel Rankin and the same was responded to by Chief Duncan, who received the gift in behalf of the department. Hon. Jas. A. Van Dyke then made a brief but interesting and eloquent address, after which the committee on presentation, accompanied by President James A. Van Dyke, of the fire department; Vice President Georg Foote, Chief Engineer Duncan, and the assistant engineers, honorary members, General Cass, Doctor Pilcher, Wm. Barclay and others, with invited guests, partook of a dinner at the National Hotel, given by the fire department committee, consisting of James A. Van Dyke, David Smart and Stanley G. Wight.

The trumpet in question is at present among the most valued mementoes of the Detroit Fire Department and is in the keeping of its chief.

I mention these incidents in regard to Chief Duncan almost at length, as I was an eye witness to all.

The pages of "Our Firemen," where a complete account of the Windsor fire is given, served to refresh my memory in some particulars.

VOLUNTEER FIREMEN BECAME FAMOUS.

MANY OF THE OLD DETROIT DEPARTMENT GAINED DISTINCTION AS SOLDIERS, STATESMEN, DIPLOMATS, SCIENTISTS, POLITICIANS OR ARTISTS.

AMONG the good firemen of the old Detroit volunteer department were many men whose names became famous in the history of this city and are familiar to the old residents. Among the capable fire fighters were:
Wm. Duncan, Wm. H. Lum, Wm. Moors, Peter McGinnis, Wm. R. Noyes, Jr., Wm. C. Ryan, Benj. Sparling, Wm. B. Wesson, Morgan L. Gage, John J. Garrison, Henry H. Leroy, Hugh Moffat, John D. Fairbanks, John Pulford, Alpheus S. Williams, Henry R. Mizner, Mark Flannigan, Wm. D. Wilkins, Chas. M. Lum, Jacob Houghton, Chris. Baby, Ananias McMillan, Cornelius Ockford, Geo. W. Patterson, Wm. Lee, Ben Clark, Jas. W. Gilbert, Abijah Joy, Kin Dygert, Oliver Bourke, Frank Eldred, Henry J. Canniff, Ed. Kearsley, Wm. Barclay, Alvah Ewers, Wm. P. Doty, Dave Esdell, D. J. L. Whiting, Jerome Croul, Robert W. King, John Kendall, Wm. Adair, Sam Clements, Ben Keeney, Charles A. Trowbridge, Henry M. Roby, John Y. Petty, Chas. S. Adams, Jacob S. Farrand, Chas. R. Desnoyers, Geo. Foote, Nick Greusel, Chauncy Hurlbut, Theo. H. Hinchman, John Owen, Robt. E. Roberts, James W. Sutton, Christian Buhl, Jas. A. Van Dyke, Chas. Vail, Henry T. Buckley, Barney Campau, Lucretius H. Cobb, Harman DeGraff, Lafayette Knapp, David O. Lum, Sam Lewis, Henry L. Newberry, Geo. Doty, Francis Raymond, Eben N. Wilcox, O. B. Wilcox, Stanley G. Wight, Wm. N. Carpenter, P. E. Demill, Anson Eldred, Elisha Eldred, Matthew Gooding, Jeremiah Godfroy, J. S. Jenness, Ben G. Stimson, David Smart, Pierre Teller, Anson Burlingame, John Campbell, Henry P. Dequinder, Theo. Williams, Robert McMillan, James R. Elliott, Robert T. Elliott, Andrew J. Brow, W. S. Penfield, Tom Gillett, John Patton, Ben Vernor, A. A. Rice,

Edward Shepard, Noah Sutton, Asa P. Morman, Joseph Leroy, William Green, first fireman No. 4, David R. Pence, George Osborne, Tom Hurst, Samuel G. Caskey.

MANY GAINED DISTINCTION.

A large number of the members of the old organization gained distinction in after life on the battlefield, as statesmen, diplomats, scientists and otherwise. The late Zachariah Chandler and the late H. P. Baldwin head the list as United States senators; Anson Burlingame, as minister of the United States to China; J. Logan Chipman, as a congressman, and the following as distinguished soldiers: General O. B. Wilcox, Colonel Marshall Chapin, Colonel John D. Fairbanks, Colonel Whittlesey, General John Pulford, General A. S. Williams, General Henry R. Mizner, Colonel Mark Flannigan, Colonel Wm. D. Wilkins, Colonel Chas. M. Lum, Colonel Nick Greusel and Colonel Robt. T. Elliott; Robert Hopkin in art; and in science Jacob Houghton; in diplomacy, Anson Burlingame. Many filled the office of mayor of the city, as, for instance, Zach. Chandler, John Patton, O. M. Hyde, Wm. C. Duncan, Hugh Moffat, Alex. Lewis and some others. Henry L. Chipman, brother of Hon. J. Logan Chipman, died a lieutenant in the United States navy. Colonel J. B. Grayson, United States commissary, at one time stationed here, was foreman of No. 3.

RUNNING ON THE SIDEWALKS.

I copy from "Our Firemen" what it says in regard to the opposition the firemen met with from the citizens in regard to the former using the sidewalks in running to fires:

"One of the chief obstacles met by the hand engine men was the continuous effort to prevent their use of the sidewalks in running to fires. The most persistent objector in this respect was Major Kearsley, who, whenever a fire alarm was sounded, at once took a position in front of his property, at the corner of Jefferson Avenue and Randolph Street. Being somewhat crippled he carried a crutch, which he would shake at the racing men as they would refuse to get out of the way, and so cause the firemen to turn into the street. At last this obstacle was overcome by detailing two men to run ahead, whenever there was a run in front of Major Kearsley's place.

"These men would very carefully and good-naturedly pick up the irascible old gentleman and carry him out of the way, hold him there until the machine had passed. An opposite to the major was the late General John R. Williams, who lived at the corner of Woodward and Grand River Avenues. On one occasion, in making a run over the sidewalk in front of the general's house, the wheels of No. 5 ripped off thirty or forty pickets from the fence, besides taking off the gate hinges. The general appeared at his front door en deshabile to wave his hand deprecatingly at Foreman George C. Codd, but when the boys returned from the fire they repaired, by special invitation, to General Williams' residence, where they were most hospitably supplied with an abundanc of hot coffee and lunch."

FUN ENROUTE.

I can testify to the truth of the foregoing as far as regards the annoyance the citizens sustained, as also the damage done to the sidewalks. I myself used, sometimes, to wonder why the citizens took it as patiently as they did. It did not make any difference what the condition of the street was—good, bad or indifferent—on an alarm being sounded, out would rush the engines and up or down the sidewalks they would go, regardless. The foreman hallooed himself hoarse through his trumpet, the two stalwart men hold of the tongue guiding the machine into every box, barrel, or wood pile in its way or out of it, and knocking it into "kingdom come." It was just glorious, the boys a-hold of the drag ropes almost wild with excitement—what could the average citizen do under the circumstances, except protest as Major Kearsley used to do? But I am satisfied, it is quite safe to say, that no detail of men was ever made to run ahead, whenever there was a run in front of the major's premises, and carefully and good-naturedly pick up the irascible old gentleman and carry him out of the way, holding him there until the machine had passed. It would not have been a healthful proceeding at all, as all who knew him will bear witness.

HOT COFFEE.

I also copy from the same source (because it is so true) what is said in regard to the gratuitous furnishing of hot coffee by the ladies of the neighborhood in which the fire happened to be located.

"Speaking of hot coffee. It was an invariable and necessary feature of the life of a fireman in those days. No matter as to the locality of the fire, it was a certainty, if the fire amounted to anything worth mention, that the ladies in that neighborhood would appear with their big pitchers of hot coffee, royally brewed and delightfully served. Then, too, if the fire was a mere trifle, or if the alarm had been a false one they were certain of finding a good, stiff pot of hot coffee awaiting them on their return to the engine houses."

SOCIAL FUNCTIONS OF VOLUNTEER FIREMEN.

ANNUAL BALLS WERE GREAT EVENTS—THE VISIT OF THE SYRACUSE, N. Y., COMPANY WAS MEMORABLE.

A GREAT feature of the Volunteer fire department in the early days was its social side, i. e., the annual firemen's ball, a function that was kept up for years. These balls always took place in midwinter and were looked forward to as the event of the year. Every woman of a dancing age, high and low, was invited, and months before the happy event came the office of the secretary of the fire department was besieged by anxious male visitors to ascertain if the names of their female friends were on the indexed invitation book of the secretary.

The latter's position was no sinecure at that time and he had to call in outside help to pull him through. I myself with many other members of the department, used to spend hours and hours correcting the lists and names, adding new ones, etc., also assisting in filling in names in the blank spaces on the printed invitations and directing them. Each invitation to give it greater significance had to bear on its face the broad seal of the department. This was plainly impressed on a large disc of gold surfaced paper, and then pasted on to the face of the invitation—quite an elaborate affair, that consumed some time and called for considerable care in getting them just right.

WHAT A FLUTTER.

These balls were always given at the National Hotel (Russell House), and for weeks almost before the long-looked-for night came decorators were busy making ready for the event the large dining hall of the hotel.

And when the night did come, ah, me! what a flutter the fair portion of the town was in, to be sure. Their particular flutter consisted in, wondering if they would be called for by some one of the committee designated for that purpose and mentioned in the invitation ("All ladies will be called for, and after the ball escorted to their homes"). Well, I never knew of any mishap on account of facilities in getting the fair portion of the town to and from these balls.

Here once a year all the city, high and low, met on the same level. The first society was always largely represented, particularly the younger, dancing, portion, the boys of their set nearly all being active members of the department. Any way, they were very democratic affairs, all around, enjoyed by all who participated in them, I am sure. I neglected to say that the invitations desired all ladies who required an escort to the ball to so inform the secretary, and some one of the committee would call for them.

THE FIRE WARDENS.

The fire wardens, "Leather Heads," as the boys used to call them, were quite a feature in the Volunteer fire department. It was their business to provide recruits from the idle and curious spectators present at a fire, to man the brakes when the firemen became exhausted, which was often the case, particularly at a protracted, stubborn fire.

They wore the usual fireman's uniform and leather hat and carried as a badge of office and authority a staff about six feet long, painted white and tipped with gold leaf. They were clothed with sufficient authority to arrest anyone who refused to work on the brakes.

I recall these names of some of our citizens who at various times served as fire wardens, men most of whom had served as active firemen, but who were incapacitated through various causes from serving as such any longer: Levi Cook, Mason Palmer, John Palmer, James Williams, Alex. H. Adams, Alvah Ewers, Jonas Titus, John Farrer, John Farmer, Darius Lamson, M. F. Dickinson. They rendered most efficient service, and often without their aid the boys at the brakes would have had a weary time, and the devouring element a better show.

VISIT OF SYRACUSE FIREMEN.

The *Free Press* in its issue April 9, 1899, has a very faithful reproduction of the old Fort Wayne engine that was manned by No. 3 boys, also of a hand pump engine built in 1830, presumably the new No. 3 that usurped the place of the old one. The hand pumping engines that followed Protection No. 1 and 2 were about all alike.

Our volunteer fire department came to be so efficient that its name and fame were heralded abroad, as was the name and fame of our Brady Guards and many invitations from eastern fire companies to tournaments were received and accepted, leaving the city to the care of their brother firemen of other companies. The tournaments consisted of quick runs, laying lines of hose, pumping streams to a great distance and other contests which put into requisition all their speed and strength and skill. Eastern fire companies used, of course, to return these visits, which were considered field days by the members of our department.

One visit of this kind I call to mind, and that was by a company from Syracuse, N. Y. They came without an invitation and unheralded. The first intimation our department had of their arrival was a notice from Uncle Oliver Newberry that a fire engine company from Syracuse, N. Y., with their apparatus had landed at his dock and wanted to know what he should do with them, and at the same time suggested that the department officials look after them. The fire alarms were sounded at once and out came the whole fire department. In cases where the location of a fire was not known the practice was to assemble at the corner of Woodward and Jefferson Avenues, and ascertain its whereabouts, then pitching for all they were worth. On coming together at the point I have named, the chief engineer gave the information that an eastern fire company was at our gates, knocking for admission. The entire department with its apparatus headed by the chief engineer and James A. Van Dyke, its president, at once repaired to Newberry's dock at the foot of Second Street, where they found the Syracuse Company modestly waiting, as their foreman said, to see what their welcome would be, coming as they did, uninvited and unannounced, though down in their hearts they were sure it would be cordial, as indeed it was.

A HEARTY WELCOME.

President Van Dyke, in his usual happy manner, welcomed them to the city and to its hospitalities, assuring them that they could have the best there was "in the shop." Then all hands repaired to the Firemen's Hall, corner of Larned and Bates Streets, where more speech-making was had, a brief welcome by the mayor, etc. The foreman of the Syracuse company was elevated to the top of a convenient barrel in No. One's house, and told his story amid much laughter and applause—that his company had determined to visit the Detroit fire department, willy nilly, whose reputation was being continually buzzed in their ears, and see for themselves. He at the same time alluded to General Lewis Cass in happy terms, intimating that the citizens of Detroit ought to be proud to count among them as one of the citizens such an eminent statesman, and intimated that it would give himself and his brother firemen from the salt district great pleasure to pay their respects in person to the general, if the opportunity was afforded them. Word to that effect was gotten to the general directly, who responded, saying he would be much pleased to welcome the Syracuse firemen, as well as the Detroit fire department, at his residence on West Fort Street that afternoon at 3 o'clock.

ENTERTAINED BY GENERAL CASS.

At the appointed hour the fire laddies were on hand. The general and family welcomed them very cordially; the house, crowded with rare paintings, statuary and bric-a-brac, gathered during their residence in Paris, was thrown open for their inspection. Refreshments were served in the large dining room, and after the boys had made a terrible slaughter of the sparkling champagne and rare wines that the general had brought from France, the foreman of the visiting company, 'a nervous little chap, made an eulogistic speech to the host that fairly staggered him.

The general, perhaps, had no idea, until he was informed of it on that occasion, that he was so distinguished a personage. He, however, replied quite briefly, and in chosen words expressed the pleasure and gratification it afforded him to welcome at his home the Detroit firemen and their guests.

INTERESTING PORTRAIT.

An interesting incident occurred on this occasion that has always remained fresh in my memory, so much so that I will relate it. In the generals' dining-room a full length portrait of Marshal Soult, in full uniform, occupied a conspicuous position at its head. It attracted the attention of all, of course, and par-.

ticularly that of the visiting firemen, who expressed much curiosity in regard to its history. The general said, that during his mission at the Court of St. Cloud, as the representative of this government, the marshal and himself (the former being minister of war) were on the most intimate terms, diplomatically as well as socially (a mutual admiration society, as it were) and that on the eve of his departure from France the marshal had this portrait of himself painted, and presented to him, as a memento, and as a mark of his regard. The general said, further, that it was a fine likeness of Napoleon's celebrated marshal, as he then was, and that he set great store by it. I presume the painting is in existence somewhere yet.

The general did not say that he gave his picture in return, but it is fair to presume that he did. After a characteristic speech from President James A. Van Dyke, the firemen took leave of their host and his family, with warm expressions of pleasure the visit had afforded.

VISITORS WERE DELIGHTED.

The Syracuse firemen left for their homes the following day, highly delighted with their visit, and, as they put it, "overwhelmed with hospitality." I do not remember whether any of our Detroit fire companies returned the visit or not, but presume they did. There are no doubt some members of the old fire department living that will call to mind this visit of the Syracuse fire company.

There were many other fires that occurred during my membership in the Volunteer fire department, that I have not mentioned in this connection, as I did not happen to be present at them. Those that I do mention, I was an eye-witness of. The burning of the Detroit *Gazette,* the burning of the French & Eldred's woolen mill, also the fire of 1832, corner of Jefferson Avenue and Griswold (Ives' corner), happened before I became a fireman, but I saw them all the same. It is needless to say I did not witness the fire of 1805.

FINED TEN DOLLARS IF YOUR CHIMNEY BLAZED.

EARLY FIRE REGULATIONS IN DETROIT NOW READ LIKE AMUSING JESTS—ADDITIONAL REMINISCENCES.

THE action of our early town fathers upon the subject of fires forms a curious chapter in our municipal history, especially when taken in connection with the fact of the entire destruction of the town by fire soon after. But it is easily accounted for by the fact that the town within the pickets were mainly composed of old dry wooden buildings, standing close together upon very narrow streets—mere lanes—and crowded into a space between where Griswold Street now is on one side and Wayne on the other, and extending from the river, which then came up near to Woodbridge Street to a lane a little north of Larned Street, covering but little more than two acres of ground.

The trustees of the town first met February 9, 1802. There being no printing press here to give the inhabitants notice of the act of incorporation, a meeting was called by the trustees for February 15 to have the act read to them, of which meeting written notice in both French and English was served upon each householder. This meeting held, the first official act of the trustees was to pass an ordinance of seventeen sections, "for the better securing of the said town against injuries by fire." Some of its provisions are worthy of attention.

EARLY REGULATIONS.

Chimneys were to be swept once in two weeks in winter and once in four weeks in summer, before 9 o'clock Saturday evening. If a chimney took fire there was a fine of $10. Every householder was to be provided with a tight barrel, to have ears of ropes on each side with lever to pass through, so as to enable two men to move it when full, to where it was wanted. The barrel was always to be kept full of water, where it could not freeze. They were also to be provided with two buckets of three gallons each, and a ladder on the roof to each chimney, and one from the ground to the roof. In addition each shopkeeper was to provide one bag, afterwards two, to hold three bushels, which, on the first alarm, he was to take with his buckets of water, to the fire. On the first cry of fire, the housekeepers were to turn out every male capable of assisting, and the men thus turned out were to form in a line to carry water from the river. These and various other regulations were enforced by penalties varying from $5 to $25.

MANY FINES.

Committees were appointed to visit every house, and report to the board violations of the ordinance. A large portion of the town records for three years is taken up with these reports, and with the fines inflicted for the breaches of the ordinance. The ordinance was adopted on March 10, and by the 29th, less than twenty days, fifty-one fines had been imposed. These fines seem to have been distributed with remarkable impartiality. Many of the first citizens were among the victims, including four of the five trustees, John Asher, John Dodema, James Henry, and Joseph Campau, and the well known secretary, Peter Andrain. Among the others fined were Robert Abbott, Peter Desnoyers, George Meldrum, Dr. Scott, Dr. Eberts, Judge McNiff, and Rev. Mr. Bacon (father of the late Rev. Dr. Bacon, of New Haven, Conn., who was a native of this city).

The reports of these committees of examination were sometimes very curious. Some families had frozen barrels, others empty ones; others barrels with one ear, others with no ears, and some had no barrels at all; some no buckets, some but one; others had no levers, others had two short ones; some shopkeepers had no fire bags—some had them filled with flour, others with goods, and Mr. Ten Eyck is reported as having his filled with muskrats.

John R. Williams was fined 75 cents because the water in his bucket was frozen. Elijah Brush (father of the late Edmund A. Brush) was complained of for having ladders that were too short in front and at the rear of his house. Mr. Woolsey was fined because he had neither poles, buckets nor barrels about his premises, and Robert Abbott was fined $3 for failing to have his chimney cleaned.

FOOLED THE EXAMINERS.

Authentic tradition informs us that one of our most respectable matrons on seeing the examiners coming, and finding her barrels without water, as they approached crept into the barrel, exclaiming, "Gentlemen, you can't say that my barrel is empty." That woman was not fined. The very last recorded act of the trustees before the great fire of 1805 was to provide that these examiners should go over the whole town once a week. This was on the 11th of May, 1805, just one month before the destruction of the city.

THE DISASTROUS FIRE OF 1805.

The fire of 1805, which destroyed "Old Detroit," has often been described by eye-witnesses. Some of the descriptions have already been published, but I think this clipping from one of our morning papers in 1855, in relation to it, may not be out of place:

The boundaries of the town at the period of the fire were as follows: the western extremity was on a line with Wayne Street, the northern Larned Street, the eastern Griswold Street and the southern the river. The houses were usually composed of logs, clapboarded, and one story in height. The number of inhabitants may closely be estimated by the list of losses published below multiplied by four. The fire broke out about 9 o'clock in the morning of June 11, 1805, in the stable of a baker named John Harvey. The stable stood between Wayne and Shelby Streets, on the north side of Jefferson Avenue. The wind was south by southeast, and was so violent as to carry cinders as far as Grosse Pointe. The flames spread so rapidly that in spite of the exertions of the citizens nothing remained but an old warehouse located on Wayne Street, subsequently occupied by Henry J. Hunt. Few of the inhabitants saved any of their personal property except those who were wise enough to cart their effects to the commons. An old fire engine formerly owned by the British was brought into requisition, but to little purpose. The only recourse for the afflicted families was to find shelter in residences along the river. These were too few to accommodate all the sufferers, and common board shanties were erected on what was then called the commons, which at that time extended from Griswold to Randolph Streets. Fortunately the weather was mild. When a violent storm arose the inhabitants would rush out of doors for fear that their frail shelters would tumble down. One evening a blind horse owned by Henry Berthelet walked into one of the board shanties occupied by Conrad Seek and family, and full possession was given before the brute would be expelled.

The following is nearly a complete statement of the losses, as presented by heads of families to the committee authorized to receive their clams. The original inventory was in the possession of the late Peter Desnoyers:

James May, £1,000.
— Mackintosh, £1,000.
John Watson, £550.
Dr. Brown, £550.
James Dodemead, £4,060.
G. Meldrum, £3,000.
R. J. Abbott and Mary Abbott, £2,000.
James Henry, £2,300.
Church and Presbytery, £6,000.
Conrad Seek, £260.
Robinson & Martin, £2,500.
James Fraser, £500.
Peter J. Desnoyers, £392.
John B. Piquet, £320.
G. Godfroy, Jr., £850.
John Connor, £420.
Rev. G. Richard, £250.
Augustin Lafoy, £800.
A. Horne, £256.
William Allen, £120.

Joseph Voyez, £800.
John Gentle, £500.
Mrs. Cote, £400.
— Lafleuer, £400.
Mrs. Provencal, £400.
Mrs. Coates, £450.
Mer Gobiel, £450.
Daniel McNeal, £480.
D. McClain, £240.
Peter Audrain, £650.
John Harvey, £400.
John Williams, £150.
Mr. Frere, £240.
George Smart, £372 5s.
Daniel Lazelete, £701 3s. 4d.
Joseph Thiebault, £7,711 7s.
Abraham Cook, £955.
Jacques Girardin, £400.
Thomas Welch, £215.
Peter Chartron, £31.
Archibald Horner, £637 5s.

The statement of losses suffered by Joseph Campau, Forsyth & Smith, Messrs. Saunders & Donovan, William Robertson and Dr. Wilkinson are not to be found.

THE OLD RIVER ROAD.

REMINISCENCES OF PEOPLE AND RESIDENCES ON THAT HISTORIC THOROUGHFARE.

THE Knaggs house (Hubbard farm), built about 1790, long since destroyed, stood on the, west side of Knaggs Creek, twenty feet back from the road, on what is now the corner of River Street and Swain Avenue. As I have already mentioned, Knaggs Creek was obliterated by the Ives Brothers when they built their dry dock there. The latter was taken down in 1845. A windmill stood on the river bank in front of the Knaggs house.

The mouth of Knaggs Creek was said to be in 1812 about 300 feet wide, and came up to within a few yards of the Knaggs house. At the mouth there were growing in 1827 about three acres of wild rice that attracted vast multitudes of wild duck and large numbers of blackbirds.

In connection with this old house I quote from remembrance of the late Colonel James Knaggs, son of Whitmore Knaggs, who was born in the house. It may be of interest to some to repeat it here:

"Whitmore Knaggs, my father, was born in Detroit in 1763, the same year Pontiac tried to carry out his famous plan of driving the English out of Detroit and the other forts on the western frontier. On July 31, 1763, a party of the Detroit garrison under Captain Dalzell made a sortie, and at Bloody Run were defeated by Pontiac with great loss.

"After his triumph Pontiac invited the leading French residents, including Peter Descompts Labadie, who afterwards became the father of my mother, to a grand feast in honor of the victory. There was plenty of fish and fowl but no liquors. After the feast was over Pontiac said to Labadie: 'How did you like the meat? It was very good young beef, was it not? Come here, I will show you what you have eaten,' and Pontiac then opened a sack that was lying on the ground behind him, and took out the bloody head of an English soldier. Holding it up by the hair, he said with a grin, 'There's the young beef.' Labadie took one look, his stomach turned and he ejected all he had eaten. The dusky warrior jeered at him and said he was nothing but an old squaw. He described the young beef as very tender and quite appetizing until Pontiac's revelation. He also says that General Hull was also a frequent visitor at the old house. Governor Cass and Governor Woodbridge called frequently. Tecumseh, the celebrated Indian chief, and his brother called several times to see my father."

James A. Armstrong lived down that way on the River Road, but considerably later than 1827. He lived near the "Labadie house," still standing, just below the Governor Porter house, since owned and occupied by Colonel Sylvester Larned.

After Mr. Armstrong vacated the house Judge Bacon, of Lake Superior fame, was its tenant. He was a jovial man and all-around free liver. Many of the present day will no doubt recall him. The house owned and occupied by Colonel Larned near the gas works, mentioned above, was commenced by Territorial Governor George H. Porter, but never finished by him. He was carried off by the cholera in 1834. The house was of brick and designed to be the finest in Michigan. It had reached only one story and a half at the governor's death and then stopped. It was roofed over in a sort of way to protect it from the weather and remained in that condition for many years, when it was taken by Colonel Larned, who put on a substantial roof without increasing the height of walls and it so remains to this day.

GOVERNOR PORTER.

I remember Governor Porter very well. He was a Pennsylvanian, a fine-looking gentleman and well liked here. He was exceedingly horsey and brought with him a fine stud of thoroughbreds. Mrs. Porter was a fine-looking woman but rather stout, whereas the governor was of slight build. He had two sons, Hume and Andrew, who remained here with Mrs. Porter for quite a while after the governor's death. Hume was a lawyer and moved to Washington to practice his profession. He was at one time Assistant Secretary of War under Polk. Andrew got an appointment in the army and became colonel or brigadier general. He was provost marshal general at Washington and

Alexandria, Va., at outbreak of the civil war and had for his aid Captain Trowbridge, U. S. A., son of C. C. Trowbridge. He married Maggie Biddle, daughter of Colonel John Biddle, after whom the Biddle House was named. Hume and Andrew are both dead.

The Brevoort house, occupied by Commodore Brevoort, was built by Robert Navarre about the year 1740, that and the Labadie house, built the same year, were standing in 1885, just above 24th Street, on what was commonly known as River Road, but now River Street. The Lafferty house, which was demolished some years ago, was built about 1750.

THE LAFFERTY ELM.

On the River Road, in Springwells, in front of the old Lafferty homestead, was a conspicuous mark in the landscape. It is known to have been planted a few years before the close of 1750 and was a striking example of the period required for the elm to produce a respectable shade. In 1862 the trunk measured four feet from the ground, was ten feet in circumference, which dimensions it held to the limbs. At ten feet the trunk parted into seven branches, each of which was in size a considerable tree. It stood within the fence and its limbs extended over 100 feet. One by one its seven limbs were ruthlessly cut away by the axe and finally the main trunk succumbed to the iron march of improvement; otherwise it might have stood for centuries the glory of the neighborhood. I myself have often rested under its shade while a boy in the early thirties and forties and wondered at its vigorous aspect. The Loranger house, part of which was standing in 1885, was built about 1730. The Lafontaine house was standing just below the Loranger farm, between the river and the road. It was occupied as a school house about 1835, the Lafontaines having moved to Monroe, Mich. I attended a spelling bee or spelling school there one night sometime along in 1835. The late Edward Jerome was the pedagogue par excellence of that time. He accepted a challenge from the Springwells school teacher to see which school could spell the other down. Well, it was a pretty tough job, but we came off victorious. During all the long years after between that time and Mr. Jerome's death, whenever I met him, he would always allude to that time and with the greatest glee. He was a model teacher, as many now living can testify. He understood his business in all the minor branches, but did not go into Latin, Greek and that sort of thing. He was most kind and considerate to those scholars that got their lessons and behaved themselves, but a terror to those who did otherwise. Some of the most unruly boys that ever existed lived in Detroit at that time and our friend Jerome had his hands full teaching the young "idea how to shoot." Aside from the city boys he had some pretty rough specimens during the winter months, boys who drifted into the city from the lakes after navigation closed. But he was equal to the occasion and always came off best.

The Lafontaine house, though seemingly strongly built, tumbled down of itself soon after this, leaving only its stone chimneys standing, bare and naked for some years after.

Peter Godfroy lived on the Godfroy farm, fronting on River Road. The house was of recent construction compared with the others I have mentioned. I think Mr. Godfroy once lived at corner of Woodward Avenue and Woodbridge Street, about 1827, and while living there he built the house I mentioned on this farm and occupied it about that time. The corner I mention belongs yet to the Godfroy estate.

This side of Godfroys lived later on Mr. Charles Bissell, dry goods merchant, and later on in the forwarding and commission business, in which he was engaged at time of his death. Charley Bissell was a handsome man but exceedingly brusque and sometimes overbearing, a terror to his clerks. One of the clerks in his dry goods store on corner of Jefferson Avenue and Griswold Street (site of the old store of Thomas Palmer), J. Hyatt Smith, afterwards a distinguished Baptist divine, and a member of Congress, and one of my particular chums used to repeat to me some of his grievances in that direction. But in his home and private life it was said Mr. Bissell was all he should have been.

Later on Ladue & Eldred had a large tannery opposite the old Lafferty house, and just below them Brooks & Adams had a lumber yard, and this side of them Hubbard & King had a saw mill and lumber yard. The Bissell residence, Ladue & Eldred, Hubbard & King's lumber yard are all within the memory of the present generation, and I think all have given place to other uses.

EARLY FESTIVITIES.

REMINISCENCES OF DETROIT'S FAMILIES AND THEIR GAY DOINGS MANY YEARS AGO—FAMILIAR NAMES IN THE NARRATIVE.

BEFORE leaving the old French residences down the river, let me try to picture the gay scenes enacted in them in the early days, particularly during the long winter months. From the sand hill in Springwells to Grosse Pointe, on the river front, and from the latter point to Milk River Point on Lake St. Clair they formed an almost continuous settlement. All the dwellers in them considered themselves near neighbors and almost one family.

The French residents were proverbial for the love they bore their horses; and the traditional French pony, wiry, strong and fleet of foot, gave them all they desired in that direction. Every French family owned two or three ponies, at least, some of them more, particularly the Cicottes, Laffertys and the Campaus. Joseph Campau owned a vast number. Go where you would through the woods adjacent to Detroit, nearly all of every drove of horses you came across had the letters "J. C." branded on the flank. So numerous were these ponies that they would venture into the city in droves during the warm summer nights, attracted by the salt that the merchants had stored in barrels in front of their places of business. Convenient "saltlicks," as one might say, and they were.

When winter shut down and Jack Frost locked the river and lake in his icy embrace, cutting off all communication with the outside world, then the fun commenced. Young men and maidens were in abundance and sleighing, dancing and other festivities ruled the hour. I have attended many of these dances, and have often made one in a sleighing party and can testify to the fun that ruled.

SUBSTANTIAL REFRESHMENTS.

The music, furnished by one or two violins—fiddles, they then called them—was quite all that was needed. French four and reels comprised about all the dances, no cotillion or round dances.

EARLY FESTIVITIES.

Refreshments were not elaborate, but were quite ample, consisting in nearly every case of cider, apples, doughnuts, venison dried and roasted, hickory nuts, black walnuts, etc., and sometimes a little whisky.

I do not think the early pioneers of this section were much addicted to whisky, though the late George Moran, who kept a roadhouse in Grosse Pointe and whom many will remember quite well, once told me that his father made his own whisky and drank it fresh from the still. The old gentleman passed away at the age of 80 years. I asked George once how much whisky he thought his father had gotten away with during his lifetime, and he said about eighty barrels. The old gentleman drank it all himself. Just ponder on it! But he was an exception.

These gatherings were usually kept up to the early hours of the morning. The ride home in the carry-all, behind the fleet pony, and your best girl, for the nonce, by your side, will long be remembered.

THE WIDOW WEAVER.

But to return. The Widow Weaver used to keep a hotel about where Twelfth Street comes down to the river. Mrs. Weaver owned the so-called Thompson Farm. She was assisted by her daughter Polly, who was quite pretty, charming and all that sort of thing. She had many suitors, many admirers, among those who were wont to patronize the hostelry, but none seemed to gain favor in her sight until Mr. David Thompson, who was at that time sheriff of Wayne County, laid his heart at her feet.

She accepted the sheriff's offer and became Mrs. Thompson. Mr. Thompson brought his bride to the city and lived in a house that I well remember. It was a white frame house and on the present site of the Hotel Normandie on East Congress Street. While living there Mrs. Weaver, the mother, died and Mrs. Thompson became heir to the Thompson Farm, an ample fortune in itself. She at once proceeded to build a handsome residence on the corner of Fort and Shelby Streets, the present site of the State Savings bank. All will readily remember it. It was a palatial dwelling in its day. Mrs. Thompson developed quite a taste for the arts, the walls of her house were decorated with some fine paintings by celebrated artists, and in the yard adjoining the house on the Shelby Street side was an artistic bronze fountain, as well as a fine copy in bronze of Kiss's Amazon.

THE THOMPSONS.

On its completion Mr. and Mrs. Thompson occupied the house and she continued to do so until her death. Mr. Thompson passed away years before her.

Mrs. Thompson's life was full of charitable, kindly acts. Her ears and purse was always open to the cry of the needy. The crowning act of her life was the establishment of the Old Ladies' Home in this city, which will be a pleasant reminder of her memory when those of the present are dust. I think she endowed this home in her will. She lived to a good old age and died without a "blot on her escutcheon."

May's Creek, named after Judge May, who once lived just below and adjoining it, was once quite a stream, boasting at one time of a large grist mill, about where Fort Street crossed it, but has been entirely obliterated by the tracks of the Michigan Central Railroad. It was a splendid place to skate in the early days, being quite wide at the mouth. It was always frozen earlier than the river, and, besides, not so dangerous. All the boys in the early days used to skate there.

ROBERT ABBOTT.

On the north side of May's Creek was the home of Robert Abbott, brother of James Abbott, then postmaster of Detroit. Unlike his brother James, he was tall, spare and stoop-shouldered. He had the appearance of being quite feeble, but he was not. He and his wife were devout Methodists and scarcely ever were they absent from church service, walking all the way from their home to the house of worship in the city. He was auditor-general of the state in 1838-9 and had his office in the same room with A. E. Hathon, city surveyor, and Thomas Palmer, in the Cooper Block, on the present site of Rev. D. M. Cooper's white store on the south side of Jefferson Avenue, between Griswold and Shelby Streets.

Contrasting the duties and scope of his office with those of the present auditor-general at Lansing, with his spacious quarters and army of clerks, the comparison seems wonderful. Mr. Abbott had but one clerk, Mr. Church, but it was ample force for the business then. It would look as though these four gentlemen had crowded quarters, but I don't think any of them suffered on that account.

Mr. Abbott, at times, was inclined to be quite peppery with

some who came in contact with him in his official capacity. I call to mind one instance in particular of which I was an eye witness. Hon. Lansing B. Mizner (father of General Henry R. Mizner), at that time was one of the commissioners appointed by Governor Mason, to disburse the five million dollars the state borrowed for public improvement purposes from the Morris Canal & Banking Co., of New Jersey. One morning Mr. Mizner called on the auditor-general officially, and in the course of their conversation the latter made some disparaging remarks in regard to a written report of expenditures, etc., that the former had submitted for auditing some days previous. Mr. Mizner, as many who knew him will remember, was the pepperiest of the peppery, when rubbed the wrong way. Well, our friend Abbott got it back hot, so hot that Mizner came off first best. However, Mr. Abbott was, notwithstanding, a fine, genial gentleman of the old school.

Mr. and Mrs. Abbott died many years ago, and what disposition they made of their property I never knew. They had several children, one a daughter, married the late E. V. Cicotte, sheriff of Wayne County.

DOWN-RIVER HOMES.

REMINISCENCES OF DAYS WHEN PROMINENT FAMILIES LIVED ON THE RIVER FRONT NEAR THE PRESENT SEVENTH STREET.

GOVERNOR WILLIAM WOODBRIDGE was a neighbor of the Abbotts on the north side of the old May's Creek. The family residence was a quaint cottage of the villa style, with dormer windows, and veranda in front. It was set back quite a distance from the River road, nearly as far back as the present Fort Street. A fine farm the governor had. Its front extended two French farms in width on the river to the line of the Baker farm, and ran back two miles into the woods. Beyond and in the rear of the house was a fine orchard, full of apple, pear, peach and plum trees that, it seemed to me, were always in a full bearing mood during the season. I have been in it often, though it had in the front and the rear a high board fence to keep out intruders. I got in in the regular way.

The governor was a conspicuous figure in the early days of Detroit and many no doubt will remember him well. His career, personality, etc., have been publicly recounted often by others, so won't bear repeating here. His oldest son, William, and myself were schoolmates. Mrs. Woodbridge was the daughter of Hon. Jonathan Trumbull, the author of "McFingal," a poem that many are familiar with (it is in most libraries and is not yet out of print). Trumbull died in the Woodbridge homestead and was buried in the family lot in Elmwood.

COLONEL BAKER.

Lawyer John S. Abbott married a daughter of the governor. His residence was on the line of the Baker farm, River road. Colonel Baker, U. S. army, lived in an unpretentious house a short distance back from the River road (Baker farm). It had three or four of the fine old French pear trees in front. Colonel Baker was the last commandant of Fort Shelby in 1823. It is said he was engaged to be married to the widow of Henry I. Hunt, who died mayor of Detroit, in 1826. The colonel became ill and unfortunately died October 12, 1838, but in compensation for his taking off he left the widow, in his will, the front of the Baker farm, extending back from the river to Fort Street.

Mrs. Hunt was the daughter of Angus McIntosh, a Scotchman of good family who had been a merchant in Detroit both under British and American rule.

After four years of American rule, McIntosh moved across the river into Canada, above Windsor, and afterwards built a large residence, still standing (this side of Walkerville), which he named Moy Hall, after the home of the family in Scotland. I have been to the Moy house often when it was in its prime. He also built a warehouse and dock in front of his residence or a little this side. A fine place to fish was this dock, and many an afternoon I played truant to fish on the McIntosh dock. Both dock and warehouse disappeared a few years ago. I remember Colonel Baker well and also Mrs. Hunt. The colonel was a fine-looking man, a gentleman and a soldier. As for Mrs. Hunt, it goes without saying, she was a fine, beautiful woman and highly accomplished.

THE MULLETT HOUSE.

The Mullett house (John Mullett), next above Colonel Baker's, was an unpretentious residence and had some fine old pear trees in front of it. Mr. Mullett was a surveyor, civil engineer, etc. He surveyed most of the land in Michigan and the northwest. He was at one time surveyor-general of the northwest, being at the head and front in his calling. He died many years ago. One of his daughters married Frank Hall, a banker of Aurora, Ill. He was lost on the steamer Lady Elgin, Lake Michigan. Another daughter married Mr. Forster, a mining engineer. One of the boys, Henry, came near being a graduate of West Point. He was there about two and one-half years, but, as he said, he could not bear confinement any more than a "liberty pole," and the strict rules were irksome to him, so he quit and came home. He had ability enough and all that sort of thing, but, as he himself said, he could not and would not think of the rules in time. The rest of the family went into the interior of the state to live, on a farm near Lansing.

Between the Mullett house and the next one (Kercheval's) was a street, now Seventh Street, the first one that was opened down to the water's edge at that time in that section. The Kercheval residence was an unpretentious one, but quite as good as its neighbors, built in 1825 or 6, I think (it was there at any rate in 1827). The Kerchevals have occupied a place with the first in Detroit society ever since I knew them or of them. Mr. B. B. Kercheval was an ideal host, as was also his wife, and, aided by their four charming and attractive daughters, made their home a center for all the society people of the forties and early fifties. Many a dancing party I have attended there, and can speak "by the card." Strange it may seem, but it is a fact, the Kerchevals were the only down-the-river family that entertained to any extent, and drew around them the younger society of Detroit.

HON. AUGUSTUS S. PORTER..

The residence of Hon. Augustus S. Porter was the next above the Kerchevals of any prominence. It was an old-fashioned house with pillared veranda in front, and stood somewhat back from the river road. Mr. Porter was a prominent lawyer and was a partner in the law business with the late Henry S. Cole, and was at one time United States senator from Michigan. He was a genial, pleasant gentleman, and his change of residence (he moved to Niagara Falls) was much regretted by his Detroit friends.

The next residence above the Porters was that of DeGarmo Jones. The house was a story and a half cottage, had two wings with bay windows, after the villa style, and with its front garden ornamented with a profusion of flowers and two fine pieces of statutary, "Spring" and "Autumn," was the prettiest of all the down-the-river residences, surpassing those up-the-river or in the city, for that matter. It was situated on the line of the Cass farm, and what became of it after the Jones family abandoned it I do not know.

The Savoyard River, or more properly Creek, came down through the Cass farm, passing under a stone culvert on the Jones farm line to the river. The advent of the Michigan Central Railroad, with its numerous tracks swept away all the dwellers on the river front to May's Creek, and forced them to seek other and more desirable abiding places. How changed is that locality at the present from what it was when I first saw it, can scarcely be imagined. Fancy DeGarmo Jones coming back to earth and starting out to look for the charming home he occupied when here! He would get lost sure.

THE CASS FAMILY.

INTERESTING REMINISCENCES OF GOVERNOR CASS AND A DESCRIPTION OF HIS RESIDENCE, BUILT ABOUT 1743.

THE Cass orchard extended to the line of the Jones farm, and occupied the space between what is now Congress and Fort Streets. Between the orchard and the River road and fronting on the road, was a large warehouse, called the Indian council house; it stood about where the locomotive works and Buhl iron works were.

Between the Indian house and the lane that led to the barns and outhouses of the general were two or three houses (two and a half stories) belonging to him. Mrs. Hinchman, mother of Guy F. Hinchman, occupied one of them for a while. I do not know who tenanted the other two. In front of these houses, and on the river, was Thomas Owen's large brick brewery and dock. I presume he leased the ground from the general, being on the Cass farm. This brewery of Owen's was a fine one and so was the dock. The latter, it seems to me now, had about one hundred feet front, but it might not have been so great, as things look larger to young eyes than they do to the eyes way long in the seventies. I remember Thomas Owen well; he was a bluff, hearty Englishman, of goodly proportions, and, I have been told, he knew how to brew beer. He died many, many years ago.

Just east of this brewery the high bank in front of the farm began to assert itself and continued to a little beyond the further line on the river. This bank was very high. Look across the river, below Windsor, and you will see a repetition of this bank with this exception, the bank on this side had considerable slope to it and was covered with a growth of fine large trees that afforded a delicious shade in the hot summer months. It was, indeed, the only public park we had. A high and close board fence, from the tenement houses to the ornamental picket fence in front of the general's house, kept out intruders. One could not look over it.

GENERAL CASS'S HABITS.

The Cass residence itself has been so often described that I will not repeat it here. I have frequently seen Governor Cass sitting on his front porch on warm afternoons, in straw hat and dressing gown in addition to his other light clothing, or taking his constitutional up and down the broad plank walk in front, that went from the Mansion house down to opposite the Owen brewery site. He rarely visited other parts of the city on foot, at least I never saw him do so. He seemed to me to keep himself within himself. He was quite stout; perhaps that was the reason.

This plank walk that skirted the farm front between it and the River road, afforded a fine promenade for the city people; a delightful place it was for a stroll on a summer's day or a moonlight night. Indeed, it was the only place in the city where its citizens could get a small taste of a park and, save for the trees that intervened, an uninterrupted view of the broad and beautiful Detroit River that got out of sight at Sandwich Point. If we had this site for a park now, what sum of money would buy it!

The Savoyard ran in the rear of the Cass residence, through the orchard, sometimes quite a stream. Its outlet I have already mentioned. This orchard was a fine one. I often visited it with the rest of the boys and not by invitation, either, and can testify to the excellence of its fruit. It was in this orchard that Daniel Webster once addressed a meeting of the citizens who had assembled to do him honor. No public hall was large enough to accommodate the crowd. I saw him on that occasion. This was sometime after General Cass and family had left for Washington.

When the front of the farm was tumbled into the river in 1835 or 1836, to prepare for wharfs and for business purposes, the house was moved back to Larned Street, where it remained until some years ago, when it was torn down to make room for a more pretentious building for business purposes.

QUAINT PORCH.

The quaint porch at the old house looked like a Chinese pagoda and the governor used to say that it was a puzzle to decide which was built first, the porch or the house. As to the builder, some authorities say Cadillac, others "Mons. Taberneir dit St. Martin." The latter once owned the Cass farm and sold it to the Macombs in 1787 for $1,060, and they sold to Cass. The house was supposed to have been built about 1743. The governor said he was satisfied that the house was built anterior to or about Pontiac's time, there being on it numerous marks of bullets shot into it.

One thing about the house that I remember in particular was the large knocker on the front door. It was a lion's head in bronze, had a large ring through its nose for a clapper. It was there when the governor took the house. There was a deep mark across the lion's face, as if made by some sharp instrument wielded by a powerful hand. The general used to say, he was told that it was made by Chief Pontiac, who, after a stormy interview with the then occupant of the house, who was commandant at that time in Detroit, left in high dudgeon and when the door had closed upon him, he drew his tomahawk from his wampum belt and dealt the lion's head a fierce back-hand blow with it that left a mark. I have seen this lion head often and knowing the story, always looked at it (the mark being plainly visible), with a great deal of interest. When the general vacated the house he took the knocker, and it afterwards adorned for some years the front door of his own house at the corner of Cass and Fort, and after he retired from Mr. Buchanan's cabinet in 1861 the front door of his private apartments and office which he had added to the residence of his daughter Mrs. Canfield, corner First and Fort, and which he occupied until he died. I don't know where it is now, I presume some of the family have it, and no doubt set as much store by it as did the general.

CHARMING FAMILY.

The general had a charming family, though the son, Lewis, was inclined to be odd.

Lewis went with his father to Washington and accompanied him to France when he was appointed minister to the Court of St. Cloud. He was appointed a major of cavalry in a regular regiment raised for the Mexican war but too late for service in that war. About 1852 he was appointed minister to Rome. He returned to Detroit about the commencement of the Civil War, and in 1866 returned to Paris where he died about 1879. His most intimate friends were the late E. A. and Alfred Brush, also the late Doctor Rufus Brown. Doctor Brown, in particular, was the most intimate friend of all, after he returned and made Detroit his home and after his mission to Rome was ended.

Mrs. Cass, it goes without saying, was an estimable lady, beloved by all. The four daughters were fine looking girls, slight, with features of the madonna type, except Elizabeth, the eldest, I think, who was a brunette. She did not have the "Cass look" (as they used to call it), out of the eyes which all the rest had. She unfortunately died early, before the general and family went to Washington. It was said at the time that she was engaged to the late Edmund A. Brush, and it was also said the engagement was "in his mind," only. Whether it was so or not, who knows? That he was not, was the common opinion then. He put on mourning for her, however. He at that time used to wear a tall white hat and the crape on it in her memory was quite conspicuous. Her remains are in Elmwood Cemetery.

FAMILIES WERE INTIMATE.

As for the other daughters, most people are familiar with their after life and knew them as Mrs. Canfield, Mrs. Ledyard and Mrs. Von Limburg. They are all dead now, Mrs. Ledyard quite recently. I had opportunities of knowing the Cass family pretty well, by sight at least, as I was a lad in my teens. Our people, my uncle's family and the Cass's were on quite intimate terms, also attended the same church, the old Presbyterian, that stood on the corner of Woodward Avenue and Larned Street, where the Waldorf now is. The governor's pew was in the same aisle as ours and directly across. They were pretty regular in their attendance at morning and evening service, and my aunt, Mrs. Thomas Palmer, made me go to church, it seemed to me, all the time. So with seeing them so often in church and elsewhere I knew them and of them quite well.

I may be pardoned for giving so much space to the Cass family when it is remembered that Detroit was then virtually the capital of the great northwest, and everything centered here. It was also headquarters of the military department of the lakes. This family, of course, held the first position socially, for was not its head the governor of this wide domain, and what transpired in his family and in connection with it was, of course, interesting to all in this then small community, and besides, was not my aunt's father, Judge James Witherell, his secretary of state?

THE OLD MANSION HOUSE.

RECOLLECTIONS OF THAT WELL-KNOWN DETROIT HOTEL AND ARSENAL, WITH THEIR INTERESTING SURROUNDINGS.

JEFFERSON AVENUE ended on the eastern line of the Cass farm. At that point the River Road (which would have been Jefferson Avenue if continued) took a sharp turn, skirting a bay that put in from the river, between the Mansion House and Owen's brewery. This bay was in the shape of a crescent and on the farm front, affording a fine place to skate in the winter; it was also used by the Baptists, both white and colored, to immerse their converts in, summer and winter (how different from the practice of today). I have witnessed many baptisms in this bay; the ceremony was interesting at all times, but particularly so in the winter, when a large space had to be cleared in the ice for this purpose on the edge of the bay. Sometimes the cold was so severe that the constantly forming ice had to be removed with rakes. Yet, for all that, the minister and those to be immersed walked into the freezing water calmly and seemingly without fear or dread. It is said that no one ever suffered from after effects. It always seemed to me to be the height of heroism to do those things under those conditions. An abiding faith seemed to sustain them which was reflected in their faces, as they entered and emerged, singing, from the freezing water, clad in their baptismal robes. Was it not heroic?

This bay was obliterated when the excavation of the farm front was accomplished, as was also Owen's brewery. "Sic transit."

THE MANSION HOUSE.

Mr. Melvin Dorr, city auctioneer, lived in the first house on Jefferson Avenue, on the Cass farm line, and next was the Mansion House, about where Cass Avenue crosses Jefferson now. This and Uncle Ben Woodworth's were the only hotels of any consequence in the city then. This Mansion House was built by

Judge Woodward and of brick and stone taken from the ruins of old Fort Shelby when the latter was torn down. It was not very large, two or three stories, I think, and, with out-buildings, extended back to what is now Larned Street. It had a high open porch that occupied its entire front, supported by large wooden pillars. Across the street was a large summer house, built apparently for the pleasure of the guests of the hotel, and where a band, when they had one, discoursed music, such as it was. The high bank in front of the Cass farm extended to and a little beyond the Mansion House. This summer house was on this bank and had a long flight of steps leading from it down to Jefferson Avenue, where Jefferson Avenue deflected from its course (about where Cass Avenue crossed) and ended at the river. It was a pleasant experience to spend a summer evening on the porch of the hotel or in the summer house. Perhaps there are many living who can remember the pleasure and, with myself, regret that the needs of business and commerce necessitated the destruction and obliteration of this, the fairest part of the city. It is hard to realize the change that this locality has undergone.

Between Jefferson Avenue, at the foot of the summer house steps, and the river, Mr. Scanlon lived, as did also John Cannan; the latter was an "Irishman of the Irish." He was the boss ditch digger and turnpike builder, also house mover and sometimes undertaker. My uncle, Thomas Palmer, had him constantly in his employ, it seemed to me, for aside from his store business he was always having a ditch dug, a road built or a house moved, and John was always the man to boss the job. There was also at the water's edge a large yellow brewery; I do not remember whom it belonged to, but I think to Mr. Hoadley. From it a long wharf extended into the river, at which wharf the steamer Niagara of those days used to tie up when she reached here. I think Cass Street was open to the river at that time, at least there was a street open to the river from Jefferson Avenue, and it seems to me it was about where Cass Street is now. Well, be that as it may.

POWERFUL TURNER STETSON.

The Detroit City Engine & Foundry Co. occupied the southeast corner of this short street. Their works were quite extensive, extending to and on Woodbridge Street. J. R. Dorr was the president and W. B. Alvord was the secretary and treasurer of the company. DeGarmo Jones and Harvey Williams were also of the company. Turner Stetson, many will remember him, I presume, was the chief man in the engine and foundry departments. He was tall and gaunt, but had a frame of iron and was gifted with the strength of a giant. The works boasted a trip hammer, located in a large shop on Woodbridge Street, and it used to be a picnic for us boys to see how and with what ease this stalwart Stetson could handle the immense masses of red hot and yielding iron, and to see the sparks fly from under the blows of the ponderous hammer. Of course, he had hold of the comparatively cool end of the iron, but he handled it like a toy. With all his powerful strength, he was kind, genial and gentle as a child. A little later on (1844), Armstrong, Sibley & Co. had a large warehouse opposite this foundry, fronting on the river.

I think Alvah Bronson was the first landlord of the Mansion House, 1824 to 1827. General Schwarz succeeded him for a short time. Colonel Andrew Mack was the landlord when I came, or shortly after, at least he was the first one to occupy it that I remember. He was also United States customs house officer and the office was in a small building adjoining the Mansion House, or near it. He afterwards kept the American, where the Biddle House now is. A fine man was the colonel, of commanding presence, and a Chesterfield in manners, he easily won the esteem of all. He was ably seconded by his amiable wife. He moved or retired to a farm he had purchased on the St. Clair River, between Port Huron and St. Clair City, where he died many years ago. Mr. Uhlman, a German, succeeded him in the Mansion House and was the last landlord, I think.

THE ARSENAL.

The government arsenal grounds covered the entire space from the custom house to Wayne Street, running back to Larned (Cass Street was not open then through these premises). Captain Perkins, U. S. A., was the officer in charge. His residence was about where is what is now the center of Cass Street. A high white fence inclosed the square, the stone arsenal building being on the corner of Wayne Street, where was the wholesale store of Phelps, Brace & Co. The arsenal grounds, except the space given to the captain's house and garden, were filled with unmounted cannon, cannon balls and empty bombshells, piled in pyramids. The arsenal was filled with muskets and infantry and cavalry accoutrements. These were afterwards removed to the Dearborn arsenal upon its completion.

The arsenal property was sold by the government, I think to Oliver Newberry. At any rate, he erected a brick building, about on the site of Captain Perkin's house, which afterwards became the Garrison house. The Wayne County register of deeds occupied the ground floor in the rear, on Cass Street, as an office, for two or three years. Josiah Snow was register, W. T. Young was deputy. I was also a clerk in the office at that time. Snow did not give the office much attention and Young and myself ran the whole business and had a good easy time, too. Compare the two offices of register of deeds then and now. Often when searching the records in the office of the register of deeds in the city hall of late years and coming across specimens of my penmanship, memory used to leap back to the office on Cass Street, with its small force of two; and comparing with the present ample quarters and the army of clerks required to get away with the increased business of today, made me "tired." The stone arsenal building was afterwards turned into a hotel, and continued so for many years. Mr. Uhl, a German, was the first landlord. I am told he was the father or grandfather of the late United States minister to Germany, how true it is I don't know. The bar was in the basement, corner of Cass Street, and it was open nearly all night, summer and winter. The proprietor used to hang out, at night, a green light. We boys, when all the other places were shut up, would look for the green light, and if it was going we were sure of a place to spend the balance of the evening and regale ourselves with the savory pork and beans, and the beer (not lager) that the house afforded, and the latter was always on tap, as was the pork and beans.

THE OLD RIVER FRONT.

REMINISCENCES OF BUSY DAYS IN THE WAREHOUSE DISTRICT FROM WOODWARD AVENUE TO THIRD STREET.

ACROSS Jefferson Avenue from the arsenal was the residence of our postmaster, Hon. John Norvell; he was appointed to succeed James Abbott, I think. The house, one and a half stories, with dormer windows, was on the corner of Wayne Street, set a little distance back from the avenue, with peach trees in front, and had been the residence of the late Hon. Henry I. Hunt, mayor of Detroit in 1826, who died there in that year. The postoffice was in a little brick building of one story, and it had a hip roof. This building was just below the residence of the postmaster. The office had been maintained there only a short time when Mr. Norvell fitted up a room in his dwelling and moved the office and its belongings into it. It was quite a different affair from the old postoffice on Woodward Avenue when James Abbott was postmaster, although the office was up-to-date at that time. Mrs. Norvell and their son Joseph ran the office almost entirely and gave universal satisfaction; indeed, it could hardly have been otherwise. Mrs. Norvell was a beautiful woman, highly cultured, and Joe was a bright, active, sturdy youth. "Jimmy" Norvell, broker, of the present day, is a living image of him.

In the rear of the postoffice was a large brick building, belonging to the government and used as a warehouse for government purposes. General Scott quartered his troops there for a short time while on his way to Green Bay, Wis., to attend to Black Hawk.

FINEST WAREHOUSE ON THE LAKES.

At the foot of Wayne Street was a slip and on the opposite side from the Oliver Newberry warehouse was another warehouse, but I do not know who occupied it, although I presume the dock was owned by Mr. Newberry, as he subsequently built a fine, substantial brick warehouse there, the finest on the lakes, and now used by the Detroit & Cleveland Steam Navigation Co. The first warehouse I mentioned was sold by Mr. Newberry to the United States government and was used by the quartermaster's and commissary departments of the United States army during the Mexican war.

It was on the border of this slip, foot of Wayne Street, that Captain John Burtiss built his steamer Argo.

This warehouse was afterwards torn down and its place occupied by a brick building put up to accommodate the pumping engine of the Detroit Hydraulic Works. "Uncle Charles Howard," as he was familiarly called, was the engineer. The reservoir was located on the corner of Fort and Wayne Streets, south side of Fort, opposite the present site of the *Journal* office. It was not a very extensive affair, but sufficient for the time, I presume; I do not know how long it lasted, but the city records will tell anyone who has the curiosity to inquire.

B. L. Webb (the late Duncan Stewart at that time was warehouseman for Webb) occupied a warehouse next to Armstrong, Sibley & Co. Between the two warehouses there was a slip. The warehouse adjoining was Oliver Newberry's. Here were built the steamer Michigan, "the pride of the lakes," the sailing vessels Marengo and Marshall Ney, another Michigan, and the brig Manhattan. The steamer Michigan No. 1 (commanded by Captain Blake) was, as many will remember, the "ne plus ultra" of steamboats of that day. She had three masts, two low pressure engines, and at that time was a wonder and a show, although her cabins were between decks. No upper cabins were built at that time.

WAS A SMALL BUILDING.

The next warehouse on the river, I think, was Shadrack Gillett's, and is yet standing. As can be seen it is a small affair compared to its neighbor, the Cleveland line warehouse, yet it was considered a large worehouse in 1827, '29 and '30. It was in front of this warehouse that the steamer Great Western was burned while laying at the dock.

The next warehouse, it seems to me—although I think there was another warehouse between, but I do not remember positively—was the De Garmo Jones. Nearly all the steamers and boats at that early time used to tie up at Jones's dock. He had an enormous stock of steamboat wood on hand at all times; that was one inducement; another was that it was the river center of the city. Lawson F. Howard and General James E. Pittman subsequently occupied it, as did the Cleveland line of steamers. The next warehouse was used by Captain E. B. Ward and John Hutchins.

J. W. Strong, Charles Bissell, Gurdon Williams & Co., F. W. Backus, George W. Bissell, John Hurlbert and O. Newberry & Co., were in the forwarding and commission business on the dock between the foot of Cass Street and the Michigan Central depot. E. W. Bissell, successor to his father, A. E. Bissell, is on deck yet at th same old stand, at the foot of First Street.

In later years and before the Great Western Railway was opened through Canada to Buffalo, in 1855, the following (in addition to those mentioned) were in the forwarding and commission business on the dock in the same and other localities: John Chester, Door, Webb & Co., Brewster & Smart, Littlejohn & Crarey, Hicks & Palmer, B. L. Webb, Poupard & Petty, Hunt & Roby, L. W. Tinker, J. P. Mansfield, J. & P. Aspinwall, C. D. Farlin & Co., Brewster & Dudgeon, Graves & Wickware, Backus & Bissell, L. P. Brady, H. H. Brown & Strong, Bridge & Lewis, A. E. Bissell, Chas. Howard & Co., Howard, Stewart & Co., Kercheval & Collins, Armstrong, Sibley & Co., Armstrong & Guise, Ives & Black, Gillet & Desnoyers, E. W. Hudson, Lewis & Graves, Backus & Armstrong, W. M. Whitcomb & Co., Bissell & Farlin, J. Nicholson Elbert, E. P. Hastings & Co., J. A. Armstrong, W. T. Pease, Nichols, Whitcomb & Armstrong, Alex. Lewis & Co., Grey & Lewis, N. Norton Strong, J. L. Hurd & Co., Duncan Stewart and John W. Strong, Sr.

A NOTE FROM MR. C. M. BURTON.

To the Editor of The Free Press:

In last Sunday's *Free Press* there was an article on the Mansion House by Friend Palmer. Mr. Palmer stated that the building was of stone, was put up by Judge Woodward, and that the stones were taken from Fort Shelby. I think Mr. Palmer is at least partly in error: The lots on which the Mansion House was erected were purchased by Judge Woodward of James May, March 21, 1811, for the consideration of $8,000. I judge from the value of the property, that the building must have been erected before that date.

Judge Woodward remained in Detroit as judge until he was rotated out of office in 1824. Just before he left Detroit, in that year, he advertised his property for sale, and gave quite a description of it. The judge went south as far as Washington at this time, but returned the following year and sold this property to General John E. Schwartz for $7,500. He then returned to Washington, and from that place went to Florida, where he had received an appointment as territorial judge, and died in Florida in 1827.

Fort Shelby was not abandoned by the United States until 1826. I do not know but that some portions of it had been torn away before that date. Mr. Palmer will probably know whether the fort buildings remained intact or whether they were demolished. It seems to me quite improbable that the Mansion House buildings were erected out of the old fort.

I have heard that after the fire of 1805 the old stone chimneys and whatever other stone there was in the old village were collected and used for this hotel. There was no stone in the neighborhood of Detroit that could be readily obtained sufficient for a building of this size. Perhaps some old resident of Detroit may be able to give us some information on this point.

Respectfully yours,

C. M. BURTON.

Dated November 26, 1903.

MANY OLD BUILDINGS.

INTERESTING RECOLLECTIONS CONCERNING THEIR TENANTS AND HISTORY IN THE '20's—THE BIG STEELYARDS.

ON the corner of Jefferson Avenue and Wayne Street, opposite the arsenal, was a small frame building used as a tailor shop by Ezra Rood. Adjoining was a large brick building of three stories erected by Henry S. Cole. The first floor was used for stores, the upper floors for offices and sleeping rooms. The frame building and the brick one made way for the present fine wholesale stores, erected by the late Henry Glover. Adjoining the Glover Block and still standing, is, it is believed, the first brick residence built in Detroit. It is said it was erected or at least begun by an Englishman, Mr. Benjamin Stead, who died in 1821. The house was finished soon after his death by other parties. It is a two-story, double brick house and is nearly opposite the old Michigan Exchange Hotel.

In 1827 and later, part of it was occupied by the late Tunis Wendall (I think he died there in 1851 or '52), and the other part by Colonel Henry Whiting, assistant quartermaster, U. S. A. Tunis Wendell's eldest son and Colonel Whiting's two sons, Henry and William, were playmates and schoolmates of mine and we had many good times together, of course. Henry Wendell went off to sea and never returned. A younger son, Charles E., was killed in the civil war. Henry Whiting entered West Point, graduated into the infantry and served with his regiment in the Mexican war. He died in this city and is buried in Elmwood. William Whiting entered the navy and died a short time ago, an admiral, having served with distinction during the civil war. A few years before his death he was afflicted with total blindness.

OTHER TENANTS.

Colonel Whiting occupied his part of the building until about 1837 or '38, when he moved to his new brick residence on Fort Street, at present owned by the Lothrop estate. The colonel was ordered to another station just before the war with Mexico and I don't think he ever returned to this city. He was succeeded by Captain S. P. Heintzelmann, U. S. A., since major-general, in the late rebellion. During the Mexican war the premises were used by the United States for quartermaster's, commissary and recruiting offices. Later Doctor Farnsworth had his office there until he died. It is now occupied for many purposes in a mercantile way. Some of the upper rooms were occupied from time to time as sleeping apartments, by Axel. H. Newbold, Josh Carew, Seelah Reeves and others.

Adjoining was an old wooden building, with dormer windows, set some distance back from the street, and occupied by the Thiebault sisters, two old maids, relics of a pioneer French family. Some people averred that one of them was a witch, for, it was said, on one occasion, when their chimney was discovered to be on fire, she flew out of the house on a broom-stick, with a water bucket in her hands, down to the river and back again to the chimney top, with the bucket filled with water, which she emptied into the chimney and directly the fire was out. But I never believed the yarn and don't imagine any one else did, either.

SLOSS'S STORE.

Adjoining and on the corner of Shelby Street, Mr. Sloss had a small store, dry goods, notions, etc.; the family lived upstairs over the back part. He continued there a few years, then moved to Dearborn with his stock of goods. His son, William, succeeded to the business there, and, I believe, is in it yet, or was up to a few years ago. Opposite the Cole building on the corner of Wayne Street was a large wooden tenement building, set some distance back from the street and occupied by several families. I don't know who owned it.

RUGER, THE HAY SCALE MAN.

Adjoining was the house of Mr. Ruger, the hay scale man, where he lived with his two daughters. Ruger was a scrubby looking little man, hair and whiskers frosted by sixty or more winters. Always attired in a suit of rusty black, a low-crowned, borad-brimmed black beaver hat, from which the fur had been worn by constantly chalking on it the weight of loads of hay, etc., that had gone under the scales.

Ruger had two daughters who kept his house, the mother

being dead. They were of an uncertain age, and not very attractive. Still, damaging stories were circulated around about them, to the extent that some of the unruly boys around town used to gather on the opposite side of the street and stone the house. Ruger stood but two repetitions of this sort of fun, when he retaliated by firing into the crowd. The gun fortunately did not contain any lead or things, so no harm was done. But the stoning experiment was not repeated. I never heard that the stories about the daughters were ever substantiated. I am satisfied they were not.

The city hay scales were located on the corner of Larned and Wayne Streets, where are now the fire department headquarters.

THE OLD WAY.

These hay scales were somewhat curious in construction and quite primitive, but not any more so, I imagine, than any other city or town in the country possessed at that time. A pair of immense steelyards were suspended from strong oaken beams, protected by an overhanging shingled roof, that sheltered the whole business. Under these steelyards the load of hay or other property was driven, and by some process—I think it was done by the aid of a windlass—it was swung clear of the ground, vehicle and all, and then the weight taken and chalked on old Ruger's hat. The steelyards were plentifully supplied, of course, with iron 56's and other heavy weights, that have in a great measure gone out of date; indeed, I think quite so, and are scarcely ever seen nowadays, except in the circus ring, when the "strong man" tosses them around, swings them over his head, etc. The advent of the platform scale relegated all this mode of heavy weighing into the corner. I have often witnessed old Ruger and his assistant go through the process of weighing a load of hay and other things.

Adjoining this building was the two-story office and residence of Doctor Hendry. It was quite pretentious, had dormer windows and a square roof. The doctor was a Virginian and quite up in his profession, I have heard said. His family occupied a high social position. The doctor died there about 1835 or '36, and his widow married Lawyer Charles Cleland, whom many will remember, I presume. Adjoining the Hendry house lived the widow Roby. Her husband died before 1827. He had a warehouse and wharf on the river front (Roby's wharf), where he did quite an extensive business in the forwarding and commission way. Adjoining Mrs. Roby's was an old unoccupied building that was soon torn down to make way for the Michigan Exchange Building, which all know about, as it is still standing, though almost tenantless and in a forlorn condition.

MR. BURTON IS RIGHT.

DETROIT, MICH., December 2, 1903.

To the Editor of The Free Press:

In reply to Mr. C. M. Burton in your edition of last Sunday, I desire to say that, on second thought, I think he is right in regard to the stone used in the building of the Mansion House, and that it did not come from Fort Shelby. I was here before the fort was completely demolished and do not remember having seen any stone that had been used in its construction. The magazine, a bomb-proof structure of stone, was situated outside the embankments of the fort, and in the center of Congress Street, midway between Shelby and Wayne Streets. This magazine was in the process of demolition when I came, and what I learned about the Mansion House having been built out of the stone taken from Fort Shelby was from hearsay only.

Most of the buildings of the fort called the "cantonment" were standing on my arrival here. They were shortly after disposed of by auction, except the row on the west side that extended from the present east line of Fort Street, out towards Michigan Avenue.

My uncle, Thomas Palmer, purchased quite a number of the buildings at the sale, as did many other citizens, and moved them to different localities about the city. The Presbyterian congregation bought the assembly building that had been used for dances, court-martial, lectures, etc., and moved it to the rear of their church, then in process of erection, at the corner of Woodward Avenue and Larned Street, and used it for a session and Sunday school room for many years. After that, it did duty as a place of worship for the colored Methodist Episcopal congregation, near the corner of Brush and Champlain Streets, and I think it did so for many years. Yours truly,

FRIEND PALMER.

TUNIS S. WENDELL.

SEDATE, EXEMPLARY MAN COULDN'T REALIZE THE FACT THAT THE OLD BANK OF MICHIGAN HAD GONE TO THE WALL.

OPPOSITE the Michigan Exchange Hotel on Jefferson Avenue Tunis S. Wendell had a general store on the northeast corner of Shelby Street.

Tunis S. Wendell was a sedate, wholly religious and most exemplary man. In business his integrity was unquestioned and his faith in his neighbors and others with whom he came in contact was unbounded. When the Old Bank of Michigan was tottering to its fall, he had such confidence in the officers of that institution that he turned a deaf ear to the rumors that were afloat affecting the solvency, and continued to take the notes of the bank a long time after it had suspended specie payments. He said that the bank managers had assured him of its solvency, and that its assets were ample to secure all bill holders and not to worry. He did not worry, but continued to take the notes in exchange for goods until he was forced to the conclusion that the concern was dead, completely so. There is no question that the bank officers did assure our friend Wendell that it was sound; and to my personal knowledge they did so to many others—Sidney L. Root (with whom I was clerking at the time) among the number; he sustaining a serious loss. I never heard Mr. Wendell say how much he was out, but the amount must have been large, as he showed me once a drawer in his desk that looked to be nearly full of Bank of Michigan bills.

THEY WERE HONEST.

There is no doubt that the bank officers were perfectly honest in their assertions to their customers and to the bill holders that things would come out all right, but they themselves were badly deceived by the Dwights, bankers of Geneva, N. Y., who owned the controlling interest in the bank, and had promised to stand by, but did not do so when the time came, so the institution had to go under. Many creditors took real estate for their holdings. Among them was Judge Canniff and he took the farm ("Canniff farm"), out Woodward Avenue. Why Wendell and Rood did not take real estate for what amounts they held, I do not know. Real estate being a poor asset at that date, was the reason, perhaps.

I think this loss made Mr. Wendell more sedate than ever, and evidently preyed upon his health. When I bought out the concern of G. F. Rood & Co., in 1857, Mr. Wendell had been their bookkeeper for some little time and on taking possession he continued with me for six months or so, at my request. He could have kept on longer if he had so desired, but as he sought employment more for recreation than otherwise, he elected to quit. He did not live long after that.

MRS. WENDELL.

Mrs. Wendell was a Hunt, sister of Henry J. and Wm. B. Hunt. She was a widow at the time of her marriage to Mr. Wendell. Her first husband was Captain Gleason, U. S. A.

The Wendells had two sons and two daughters. Henry, the eldest son, was a schoolmate of mine. He went off to sea, made a voyage to China, returned home, after a brief stay started off again, and never was heard from. Charles, a most promising young man, was quite an efficient telegraph operator and when the civil war came on he raised a company and went to the front and was killed.

I have mentioned elsewhere about the Wendells living at one time in the brick dwelling opposite the Michigan Exchange. Well, while this is on my mind, there comes to me the vision of the old colored "mamma," who was a domestic in the family when I came here, and so continued many years until her death. There was an entryway on Jefferson Avenue to the cellar kitchen of the house, and on every fine afternoon in the summer this "mamma" would plant herself in this entryway arrayed in her best "bib and tucker," a bright-hued handkerchief bound around her head, her face wreathed in smiles. She knew nearly every passer by, and they her, and kindly greetings were always in order. She was especially motherly to us boys, as she had a son of her own, "Dick," who was a playmate of ours, and one of us on most all occasions then. Perhaps some living may remember her.

PETER E. DEMILL.

After Mr. Wendell in that store came Peter E. Demill. Mr. Demill came here along in the thirties, and seemed to me to have been always in the mercantile business, until he associated himself with the Detroit Gas Light Co. He was an ardent church man and an Episcopalian of the Episcopalians, a good citizen, a kind neighbor and a most exemplary Christian gentleman. He was a bachelor when he came here, and so remained for years. So long was it before Cupid snared him that his friends thought him incorrigible, but at last along came Miss Henrietta Westbrook, daughter of Colonel Westbrook, of St. Clair (a soldier of 1812) he met his fate and they were married. They had two children, a son and a daughter, the former a most promising young man (Peter E. Demill, Jr.) Unfortunately he was accidentally drowned at Chicago during the World's Fair. The daughter, possessed of a most charming and attractive personality, as nearly all know, and married Mr. George W. Moore, a prominent member of the Detroit bar.

Both Mr. Demill and wife passed away but a few years ago, widely regretted.

MRS. CHARLES JACKSON.

Mrs. Charles Jackson owned the ground and building. She acquired the property from her husband, Mr. Dodemead, who erected the building. After his decease she married Mr. Dyson (who had been a captain in the war of 1812) and after his decease she became Mrs. Charles Jackson. Mr. Jackson was a stone and brick mason, also a master builder, and a prominent citizen. He did his share in the building line, and had the contract for the stone and mason work on the territorial capitol. He built many other buildings in the city, among them a double brick house on Cadillac Square where the central market is, as residences for himself and David Cooper.

Mrs. Dyson had two children by Mr. Dyson, Sam and Jane; many will remember "Aunt Jane" as she was familiarly called. "Sam" most always held some city office.

About the date the Exchange was completed, the Thiebault residence and the Sloss store, opposite, were swept away and gave place to a brick building of four stories called the Waverly Block, built by C. C. Trowbridge, Elon Farnsworth and Colonel Henry Whitney. Avery & Eldredge had a dry goods and grocery store in this block on the corner of Shelby Street.

MR. LILLABRIDGE.

Before going any further I will mention that Mr. Lillabridge occupied the building below the Wendell house, on the corner of Wayne Street, instead of Mr. Rood. It was the next building that Ezra Rood occupied as a tailor shop. Lillabridge claimed to be most intimate withe Edwin Forrest, whether this was so I do not know, but this I do know: When the Detroit Juvenile Library and Debating Society circulated a subscription papers for the purpose of raising funds with which to purchase books for a library, he put himself down for ten dollars and Edwin Forrest for a like sum and the money was paid. He was a house decorator in a small way and had a small stock of fancy wall papers, etc. He made a specialty of cutting tissue paper into fanciful shapes and decorating the ceilings of stores, the hanging lamps, etc., with them to accommodate the flies. They were quite pretty and attractive. He also had a very pretty wife, and people used to say that he was inclined to be jealous. There might have been some foundation for it and perhaps was. There was Captain Walsh, an Englishman (Mike Walsh), who kept the "Shades" under the Republican Hall on Jefferson Avenue, who was and had been quite attentive to Mrs. L——, so much so that it raised Mr. L.'s "Ebeneezer." He determined to have satisfaction the next time he met this disturber. They met—and the alleged "wrecker" got his eyes full of snuff and his head punched through the injured husband's efforts. I saw Walsh directly after the affair in Mr. Scoville's office, upstairs in the Republican Hall Block, where the doctor was busy getting the snuff out of Walsh's eyes and patching up his face. He presented a pitiable appearance, with his blood-shot eyes and disfigured countenance. I don't think anything ever came of it, a least I never heard of anything. I think this Walsh was afterwards prominent in New York politics.

OLD JEFFERSON AVENUE.

REMINISCENCES OF MANY OLD STOREKEEPERS, WITH THE STORY OF A PROPOSED EAST-SIDE PARK.

C. H. JAQUITH & CO. occupied a store (boots and shoes) on Jefferson Avenue, below the Michigan Exchange. It was a branch of an eastern house. (Captain Arthur Edwards married a sister of Jacquith's). His right-hand man was Smith, who for many years kept a shoe store on Woodward Avenue, at the corner of Larned Street, where Swan now is. J. W. Tillman had a furniture store in the Waverly Block. Morse & Bro. had a book store in the same building. C. C. Trowbridge and Chancellor Farnsworth also had their offices in this building, up stairs in the second floor. W. B. Alvord had bachelor quarters there also. The entrance was by a flight of iron steps on the Shelby Street side. R. E. Roberts also had at one time a dry goods store in this block.

The widow Coates owned the ground and building, and occupied it until her death. After her Z. Vollum occupied the store as a book bindery. I do not remember who came after. On the northwest corner of Shelby Street, and opposite the Waverly Block, H. H. Brown occupied a small wooden building adjoining, as an insurance and exchange office, with Walter Ingersoll as his assistant. The Shelden Block, of brick, adjoining, was occupied by Almar & Shaw, books and stationery. C. W. Barnum had a hat store in the same block. The postoffice at one time was located in this building. Shelden McKnight was postmaster and he had Mr. Adams, his brother-in-law, for an assistant. Geo. M. Rich, Eugene Laible and D. C. Holbrook were clerks. George M. Rich was first with Postmaster John Norvell. The *Detroit Free Press* and Harsha & Wilcox had their quarters in this building, up stairs, and occupied most of the upper part, I think. The widow of Orville Cook lived in a wooden dwelling in this locality in 1827 or 1828. Mr. Cook had been a dry goods merchant and I think was in partnership with Levi Cook (O. & L. Cook), at the time he died. Mrs. Cook was a sister of John Hale (Hale & Bristol).

FIRST SODA WATER SALOON.

Afterwards this building was occupied by Henry A. Nagle, who sold ice cream, candy, soda water, etc., the first saloon of the kind established in this city. In relation to Mrs. Cook, the former occupant of this building, and John Hale, perhaps it may not be out of place to say that Mrs. Cook, as said before, was the sister of John Hale, and John Hale married the sister of Mrs. Thomas Sheldon. The latter was the wife of Mr. Piquette (Mrs. Sheldon was a Labadie, a daughter of one of the old French families and a most estimable woman). Mr. Piquette died, leaving two children, John B. and Charles. Mrs. Piquette married Mr. Reed, who died shortly after, leaving no issue. Mrs. Reed then opened a boarding house, not for the income it promised, but more for the sociability attached to it. She soon had all the boarders she needed, it being so home-like. My uncle, Thomas Palmer, boarded there before his marriage, as did my father, when here from the east, and many others.

Among them was Thomas Sheldon. He at that time was a gay young bachelor, and at once laid siege to the widow's heart —and won. The fruit of the union was two daughters and a son. This was after the removal of the family to the corner of Fort and Wayne Streets, now the *Journal* office site, where Mr. Sheldon owned a lot and built a residence. They retired into the country, as it were, and as they fondly hoped.

George Tucker, a cultured colored barber and hairdresser, was opposite the F. & M. Bank and kept a fine stock of perfumery, hair goods, and toilet articles. William Bond had a looking glass and picture frame factory in this locality. In the Levi Brown brick block, Olney and Levi Cook, brothers, had a general store, the firm name being O. & L. Cook, afterwards Cook & Burns. The latter continued in business some years. Mr. Cook then retired from the concern and Mr. Burns removed to Woodward Avenue, between Jefferson Avenue and Larned Street, opposite the Merrill Block. Mr. Cook retired to his farm on the Grand River Road, near the railroad crossing, where he died. Mr. Burns took into partnership Tim W. Partridge and Hamilton Miller, clerks in the former firm. They continued in the business until the death of Mr. Burns.

FINE MEN.

The Cooks and Mr. Burns were men of the highest integrity and of the first standing in the community. In their store one could find almost everything adapted to the wants of man at that time. They all spoke French fluently, as did their clerks. They catered to the French trade, which was a great factor in the business of the city in the early days, and they enjoyed the largest share of it.

Later in life Mr. Burns had the misfortune to be elected to the legislature. While a member of that body a bill was introduced authorizing the City of Detroit to issue bonds for the purpose of raising money to buy a park. The ground to be purchased (its locality was named in the bill) was the fine piece of woods on the Cook farm, opposite Belle Isle, in Hamtramck. Mr. Burns and John Owen owned this land. The price per acre to be paid was incorporated in the bill, and was $450.

Great opposition to the bill at once sprang up. It was contended, aside from the personal interest Mr. Burns had in the matter, that it was giving too much to the eastern part of the city, while the southern and western part had nothing in the way of a park except the Grand Circus. Mr. Burns and the advocates of the bill contended, if it passed, it would give the city a beautiful piece of woods and grounds ample for park purposes, and at the same time the city would acquire title to the property that in the near future would more than double in value.

A STRONG REASON.

It happened to be the desire of Mr. Burns and Mr. Owen, and the former in a feeling speech before the house expressed it, that aside from the bargain the city was getting, it would, of course, give a needed resort to all classes, more particularly to young men, clerks, etc., who, on Sundays and other days of recreation, hied themselves to all sorts of vicious resorts on this side and the other side of the river. Canada was a great mecca for the youth in the early days. I used to go there on a pilgrimage myself, now and then. Well, Mr. Burns and the other advocates of the bill got "busted." The opposition were too strong for them, carried too many guns. Mr. Burns may have been a bit selfish in his efforts, as it would undoubtedly have enhanced the value of the adjoining property, which was owned by Mr. Owen and himself. Let me recall—the bill did pass, but it was left to the citizens of Detroit to decide whether they desired a park or no, at a mass meeting to be called by the mayor. Well, Mr. W. W. Wheaton, mayor at 'that time, did call a mass meeting of citizens to assemble in front of the rear entrance to the city hall, on Griswold Street, to determine the question. Those who were in favor of the park were to bunch themselves together on one side of the entrance, and those opposed on the other. The mayor, stationed at an upper window, was to decide. After all had taken their places he took a long and critical look at the assembly beneath him, and decided no park. I was there, and it seemed a mighty close squeak. The people had another try at it while Mr. Henry Moffat was mayor. They were called together in the same place on the same business. They did get together and bunched themselves as did the citizens at the former meeting, and with the same result. Mayor Moffat could not see it. This time, too, it seemed to be a mighty close squeak. After this the matter was dropped. Referring to the prophecy of Mr. Burns that the property would greatly increase in value in the near future, it is verified, for today the property is valued at $2,500 or more per acre.

And I am strongly of the opinion that the heirs interested at present in this property are mighty glad that the park question went as it did.

A GOOD RESULT.

Well, after all, the opposers of the park builded better than they knew. If the tide had turned the other way we would not now, perhaps, be the owners of the finest park in the world, Belle Isle. "All's well that end's well." In the light of the present, what a queer proceeding the foregoing was, to determine a question. I don't imagine that such a thing could happen now.

At one time later on a German by the name of Hahn kept a fur store, dyeing and repairing furs, etc., nearly opposite the old Joseph Campau residence and next to Cook & Burns, Jefferson Avenue. He was successful in business, I think. He had two fine daughters. One of them married Charles H. Duncks, who was at that time with Charles Piquette, jewelry, gold pens, etc. He afterwards removed to Flint, and engaged in the manufacture of spring beds. The other daughter married Robert T. Elliott, who was major of the Sixteenth Michigan Volunteer Infantry, who was killed in action in Virginia in 1864. He was a fine officer and soldier.

To the Editor of the Free Press:

I have read, with a great deal of interest, the articles of Mr. Friend Palmer, and I believe, with many others of our city, that we can give him hearty thanks for the work he is doing, and also thank *The Free Press* for the space it gives in publishing them.

I do not believe that Mr. Palmer will think me captious or critical if I suggest a few corrections and additions to his last week's paper. He has twice referred to our second mayor as Henry I. Hunt. Mr. Hunt's full name was Henry Jackson Hunt, and the "I" has crept into some records, because of the peculiar manner in which Mr. Hunt wrote his middle initial.

I am personally acquainted with several members of the Dodemead family, and therefore am able to correct one statement regarding them that Mr. Palmer made. John Dodemead, the Detroit ancestor, left ten children. Robert M. died in 1828 without issue, David died in 1836 without issue, Isaac died in 1818 without issue, John died in 1813 without issue, James died in 1818 without issue. Alice married Joseph Wilkinson and died in 1850; Betsey married Charles Jouet, at that time Indian factor at Chicago, where she died shortly after her marriage, in 1809. She left one daughter, Jane, who married Samuel Northington. Ann married Captain Dyson, and after his death she married Charles Jackson; she died in 1850, leaving Samuel T. Dyson, who was known as a good fellow and a politician in Detroit; Jane M. Dyson, familiarly and lovingly known as Aunt Jane. Nearly everyone in Detroit knew her and loved her. The third child of Ann Dodemead was Anna Jackson, who married a Mr. Watkins, and afterwards married Jonathan Thompson; she left three children, Mrs. Overton, Mrs. Smith, and Miss Kittie Watkins. One of Mrs. Overton's daughters has recently become well known as a novel writer. The ninth child of John Dodemean was Maria, who died in 1821, and the youngest child was Catherine, who married Jacob B. Varnum. At the time of her marriage, Mr. Varnum was Indian factor in Chicago. His brother was acting vice-president of the United States during the war of 1812. One of Mr. Varnum's sons, Dr. Varnum, now lives in Los Angeles.

The property at the southeast corner of Jefferson Avenue and Shelby Street was the homestead of John Dodemead during his life, and there his wife, Jane, and his family lived after his death. The wife, Jane, was a very energetic woman, and carried on a boarding house or hotel on this corner, which was a famous resort in its time. The Supreme Court of the territory held its sessions part of the time in the building on this lot. This property afterwards came to be owned by Aunt Jane Dyson and her stepfather, Charles Jackson, by purchase from the other heirs of the Dodemead family, and by partition proceedings. It was never owned by Mr. Dodemead. The ancestor of John Dodemead acquired this lot by purchase from John Askin, January 22, 1799, and the title for the property remained in the family nearly one hundred years, until it was sold to Mr. Frederick E. Driggs, November 1, 1897.   C. M. BURTON.

DANCING TEACHER.

MISS BARKER HUMMED MUSIC AT HER SCHOOL, AND ADAM COUSE ALMOST DANCED HIMSELF TO DEATH.

OVER the store of Cook & Burns, on Jefferson Avenue, Miss Barker had a dancing school, the only one in the city then (1840). She lived there with her brother and family. The dancing was done in the parlor. Barker was a musician and played on a number of instruments, the violin being the chief. He furnished the music when sober, but was so rarely in that condition that Miss Barker had to sing or hum dancing tunes, and we would do fairly well, considering the orchestra. She had quite a class of boys and girls from the first families and, although her methods were crude, she succeeded in making her pupils pretty fair dancers. Many that I know and remember received their first and only lessons from Miss Barker—some of them pretty good dancers, too. Fancy a dancing school waltzing to the tune of the song, "Dark-eyed one, dark-eyed one, come hither to me," hummed by the teacher.

Levi Brown occupied the other part of this brick store (his family lived upstairs) for many years, until into the forties, and then moved to New York. He dealth in jewelry, clocks and watches. Chauncey S. Payne was his partner and succeeded him in the business for awhile, then moving to Flint. Levi Brown was the inventor of and the first to manufacture the gold pen in the United States or elsewhere. He used to charge five dollars for the nibs alone and people thought them cheap at that. A nice man was Levi Brown and a Christian gentleman. After Mr. Payne, Mr. Sibley, from Canandaigua, N. Y., occupied the premises and dealt in the same kind of goods as Messrs. Brown and Payne.

ADAM COUSE.

Speaking about dancing schools, somewhere in the forties these buildings were swept away to make room for the Masonic Hall, with stores underneath, and in one of these stores Mr. Adam

Couse, assisted by C. F. Amsden, opened a music and piano store, and had a dancing school in one of the rooms attached to the hall. Mr. Couse was a finished dancing master and introduced here all the new dances as fast as they appeared on the carpet east. He had a large class at once and gave universal satisfaction. He almost danced himself to death and had to give it up.

While in this locality I will take the occasion to mention Chauncey S. Payne again. He was the brother of Mrs. Levi Brown. He married Miss Smith, a daughter of Jacob Smith, who was here before 1805 as a merchant or Indian trader. Captain Stockton, of the United States engineers, married another daughter of Jacob Smith. He was appointed colonel of the First Regiment, Michigan Volunteers, at the outbreak of the Mexican war, and went to Mexico and returned with them. After that he resigned from the army and went to Flint to live and died there some time after the civil war. He also was appointed to a Michigan regiment as colonel during that unpleasantness, the Sixteenth Infantry. Jacob Smith had still another daughter whom Colonel Garland, United States army, married. The colonel built and occupied a residence on the site of the former residence of the late Mr. Beattie on Jefferson Avenue. Colonel and Mrs. Garland had four children, two girls and two boys. The two boys, I think, went into the army. Of the two girls, Bessie and Louise, the former married Lieutenant Deas, adjutant of the Fifth United States Infantry, and Louise, I think, married Lieuteant Longstreet, U. S. A., afterwards lieutenant-general of the confederate army

LIEUTENANT GEORGE DEAS.

I presume there are but a few living who remember Lieutenant George Deas, adjutant of the Fifth United States Infantry. He was a soldier from the crown of his head to the sole of his foot; the finest looking man in the regiment. He made an excursion into Canada, visiting the officers of the British regiments stationed at Malden, Toronto, Montreal and Quebec, and was by them pronounced without peer in any service.

Deas was in the confederate army also and was killed during the war. Many paid court to Bessie, but Deas held the winning cards. She was a beautiful and attractive girl, Louise not so much so, yet enough to capture Longstreet. The latter had quite a rival in the person of Lieutenant Gordon Granger, U. S. A., who was then stationed here in Detroit, but it was of no use; Gordon Granger, as we all know, got to be brigadier-general during the civil war. He was a fighter from "way back" and indeed a "rough diamond."

He was the roughest specimen of a West Point graduate I, or any one else, ever saw, I think; as for myself, I know he was so, I had ample opportunity to know him well when he was stationed here in Detroit. In the absence of any other officer of the United States army who were stationed here and who had been ordered to Mexico, he was detailed to assume command of the quartermaster's and commissary departments. I was quartermaster and commissary clerk at the time and, of course, was in daily communication with Granger and we came to know each other well. He was all right, except that he was rough and uncouth, and got along well enough with the boys, but with the girls he was a back number. Henry Mullett, of this city (son of John Mullett), who had been to West Point, said to me one night at Whipple's, on Bates Street, when Granger was present, after looking him over for awhile: "He is the roughest specimen of a West Point graduate I ever saw, but," he said, "if he passed the West Point ordeal he is all right and no mistake. There is something in him, sure."

During the civil war it came out as it did in General Grant's case.

The country is still indebted, and so was Phil Sheridan, to Gordon Granger, for unearthing and bringing the former into prominence. Sheridan at the time was a captain of cavalry, U. S. A., and on staff duty at General Halleck's headquarters near Farmington, Miss., never expecting, as he himself said, to get higher in rank than major. Granger had been colonel of the Second Michigan cavalry, but was promoted to brigadier-general, leaving the position of colonel of the regiment vacant. He recommended Sheridan for the place, to Governor Blair, who had been looking around for a suitable person to succeed Granger. The governor caused the commission of colonel to be issued to him, May 25, 1862, and the country is quite familiar with his subsequent career. I think General Alger was the officer that conveyed the commission of colonel to Sheridan.

Well, to resume. The space between Levi Brown's and the corner of Griswold Street, about 1830, was occupied by a law firm, Cole & Porter; Jerry Dean's saddlery and harness shop, Stephen

Wells's book and stationery store ond O. & L. Newberry's general store. The law firm's office was a small one story building, pillars in front; the late Senator Jacob M. Howard was a law student with this firm, as I had occasion to know, because at that time he was my Sunday school teacher in the Baptist Sunday school. He was an ideal teacher, to my mind. His clear and interesting expounding of the meanings of the various passages of Scripture included in our lessons made it quite easy for our young minds to grasp them. In all his after life, until death took him so suddenly, he was, in my mind, always my Sunday school teacher.

A NOTE FROM MR. PALMER.

To the Editor of the Free Press:

In reply to Mr. C. M. Burton in yours of Sunday last, say: Instead of thinking him captious or critical in suggesting a few corrections and additions to my articles that appeared the 13th, I thank him very much. In calling to mind the personalities, etc., of various old residents of Detroit who have passed away, I did not, and do not intend to give, only in a partial way, their antecedents, nor the after career of their descendants, as in some instances it would be impossible. All those old residents that I have mentioned, and those that I may hereafter mention, I knew personally, and those of that time that I did not know, I do not write about.

In regard to Mr. Hunt. I never heard him called by any other name than Henry I. Hunt. He being such a prominent man in this community, and having died such a brief period before I came, his name was, so to speak, in everyone's mouth. Have no doubt his name was as Mr. Burton puts it.

As regards the Dodemeads, Dysons and Jacksons, I only know about the first named that Mrs. Dyson was a Dodemead, and that the property referred to, corner Jefferson Avenue and Shelby Street, was always called the Dodemead corner. I knew Sam Dyson and Aunt Jane intimately (think I have mentioned them before). I also knew Anna Jackson well. Was an admirer of hers myself, and when she married Mr. Leonard Watkins ("Len" Watkins) I was his best man. In a future article I shall have something to say in regard to Anna Watkins's three daughters, as also her second husband, Jonathan Thompson.

Referring to Mr. Tunis S. Wendell, whose name was mentioned in a former article, I omitted to say that two of his daughters are still living; one, the widow of Mr. Geo. E. Curtiss (formerly leather dealer here) at 374 Cass Avenue; and the other, widow of Mr. Reuben Doolittle, who was an extensive paper dealer in Chicago, lives in the latter city, at 174 Oakwood Boulevard. I also mentioned a son of Mr. Wendell, Captain Chas. E. Wendell, as having been killed in the civil war. I desire to add that he fell while leading the First Michigan Volunteer Regiment at "double quick" immediately after the fall of Colonel Horace S. Roberts, his most intimate comrade in arms. This at the second battle of Bull Run. FRIEND PALMER.

DETROIT, December 22, 1903.

OLD BUSINESS MEN.

ON Jefferson Avenue, adjoining the Dodmead house (T. B. Wendell's store), Judge Abraham Canniff had a boot and shoe store, he being a shoemaker by trade. Charles M. Bull, next to him, kept a general grocery store. Along here a woman had a millinery shop, she afterwards became Mrs. Chauncey Hulbert.

David Cooper had a general store, and Conrad Seek had a tailor shop about 1830. Afterwards on part of this property was built the Granite Block, so-called. It was not granite, however, but an imitation, being brick covered with stucco. Later on, 1845, G. F. Rood & Co. occupied a story and a half building as a stationery store and book bindery adjoining..

Dr. Hoyt built and occupied a four-story brick building that adjoined the F. & M. Bank. This was afterwards occupied as a billiard saloon and dwelling by Tobias Love. The billiard saloon was the first floor. It was afterwards occupied by the Peninsula Bank on the first floor, and the upstairs as offices by William Hale, lawyer.

CASS PARK.

Lawyer Hale, as he was more familiarly termed, was at one time a member of the Common Council, and when General Cass proposed to donate to the city the present Cass Park. The subject came up before the council May 8, 1860 (it had been up before, it appears), through the following resolution, offered by Mr. Hale:

"*Resolved*, that the resolution and proceedings of the Common Council in relation to the acceptance of a parcel of ground to be conveyed to the city for a public park by Lewis Cass, be, and the same are hereby rescinded."

Mr. Hale was much opposed to the acceptance by the city of the land proposed to be donated under the terms attached to the gift by Mr. Henry Ledyard, the agent of General Cass. It appeared that Mr. Hale had formed the idea, and so stated in his remarks on the resolution, that Mr. Ledyard desired the city to spend much more money in beautifying the ground to be donated, laying out walks, fencing, setting out trees, planting flowers, building a fountain and doing other things tending to make the grounds attractive, for the sole purpose of enhancing the value of the lots surrounding and adjacent the property of the general. He also stated that in case the council did not accept the terms, the proffer of the land would be withdrawn for an indefinite period. He made quite a lengthy and spicy argument against it, in which he handled the general and Mr. Ledyard without gloves. What decision the council came to then I do not know. Perhaps Mr. Ledyard modified his demands, or the council swallowed them whole. Anyway, the city now has the park, and a lovely piece of ground it is, with its abundance of fine trees, its flower-bordered walks, and its fine fountain, the finest for the amount of water thrown of any in the city, with the exception perhaps of the fountain on Washington Avenue, near the Hotel Cadillac, and that only within the last year or so. I imagine the people of Detroit would not hold Mr. Hale in grateful remembrance had he succeeded in inducing the Common Council to reject the gift of General Cass.

Mr. Hale at one time kept the National Hotel (Russell House). He went to California and died there. Something of a coincidence, his brother-in-law, Wm. J. Chittenden, is the present proprietor of that hostelry.

A bright young man, Frank Pixley (I think he was a relative), was a student in Mr. Hale's office about 1849. I do not know whether he was admitted to the bar here or not. Anyway, he went to San Francisco and became editor and proprietor of *The Argonaut,* published in that city, a journal widely and favorably known. He died in San Francisco a few years ago. I presume many here and elsewhere will call him to mind.

Colonel Grayson, commissary; Major Sibley, quartermaster, and Major Hunter, paymaster, all of the United States Army, also had offices in the building. Later on G. F. Rood & Co., in place of their wooden building, erected a four-story brick building which they occupied until Mr. Rood's death. John Owen & Co. occupied a store in the Granite Block, before mentioned, as did Jacobs & Garrison. The F. & M. Bank, next to "Tob" Love's, was erected sometime in the thirties. It was a fine building, of cut stone, four stories high with basement. Joy & Porter and George C. Bates at one time had their offices here, as also did the American Express Co. when Wm. G. Fargo was agent. The David Cooper block covered the site of his old store as well as that of Conrad Seek's tailor shop, and the millinery shop or store.

The Cooper Block was of brick, three stories high, and a capacious unfinished attic, and was built along in the thirties. Mr. Cooper occupied the first store as a general store for some years, until he retired. Mr. David Cooper was a most methodical man in all he said or did. A conscientious Christian gentleman, he was quite thrifty and most modest in all his desires, owing no doubt to his early training with the firm of Mack & Conant. From a humble beginning he acquired position and a large fortune. In trade he was exactness itself. He was his own bookkeeper always, and when you received an invoice or statement of account from him, where fractions occurred in either, it was always 6¼, 12½, 18¾, 37½, 62½, 87½, pro or con, as the case might be, in every instance. I have seen his day book often, and it did look too odd. He used to say he only wanted what was his own, and desired to accord to others their own. I do not think he ever sued a debtor, or foreclosed a mortgage. I never heard that he did the latter, though he must have had from time to time large amounts out on that class of security. In addition to his Jefferson Avenue store, he had a lime house situated on the slip at the foot of Wayne Street. It was a small brick structure and contained the lime burned at Sibley & Cooper's stone quarries down the river, just this side of Wyandotte or Trenton. I think he was the only one in the city at that time who had lime for sale. He also kept building stone for sale from the same locality. This double duty, store, lime house and building stone kept the old gentleman, his clerk, George Woods, and his son, George A. Cooper, quite as busy as they desired to be. I always wondered why Mr. Cooper got rid of his interest in the stone quarry so easily and cheaply as he did. He had the entire management of the business and occasional differences would arise between the Sibley's and himself in regard to his methods in carrying on the business. On one occasion, and I was present—in fact the only one present but the two parties concerned,—the meeting occurred in May, E. S. Sibley's office. In discussing the affairs of the company a little heated talk occurred, whereupon Mr. Cooper said: "Major, I'll tell you what I'll do. I will give you $10,000 for your interest in the business or take $10,000 for mine." The major said on the instant. "Mr. Cooper, it is a bargain." The affair was closed then and there. I was Major Sibley's clerk at the time. I say the affair was closed at the time and at the figure I have named, as I never heard anything to the contrary. I thought then and have always thought since that Mr. Cooper did not expect that the major would take him up so promptly. Mr. Cooper had two sons and one daughter. The daughter, Adeline, married Dr. Sprague, of Rochester, Mich. The eldest son, George A., died many years ago. He was a schoolmate of mine and always an intimate friend. He was a young man of much promise and his early taking off was much felt by his family, as well as by the gay young society in which he moved. The next son, Rev. David M. Cooper, is with us yet, and all know him so favorably that it would be useless for me to say anything further in his direction, only to join with all who know him in expressions of esteem and regard.

T. H. EATON.

Then T. H. Eaton had it for a drug store, groceries and dye stuffs. A spruce individual was T. H. Eaton and well up in the drugs, dye woods and grocery business. He came here from Buffalo about 1841, and had there been a member of the firm of Wm. Williams & Co., druggists and grocers, I do not suppose there was ever before his advent here or since, a more suave bidder for trade and position than he. He was connected by marriage with Bishop McCoskrey, and John A. Welles, the banker. He soon acquired both position and comparative wealth; wealth that as the years went on continued to increase until at his death it must have been a most comfortable fortune. He first established himself in the American Hotel Block, corner Jefferson Avenue and Randolph Street, succeeding David A. McNair, the latter having succeeded Riley & Ackerly, both concerns in the drug and grocery business. After the fire of 1848 he moved to the Cooper Block, further down Jefferson Avenue, and from there to the fine new store corner Woodward Avenue and Atwater Street, where his son, who succeeded him, is now located. He was the first to introduce here a machine to grind the brown Muscovado sugar. As many will remember, it was about the only quality of sugar in general use here at that day, white and loaf being considered luxuries. The sugar came in large hogsheads, and on opening the contents would be mostly in large hard lumps that took much time and hard work with axes and hammers to bring them to a granulated state. The machine obviated the difficulty and was a great boon to the trade. He was a neat penman and kept his own books at that date. He was particularly proud of his work in that direction. He used to show with a great deal of satisfaction a copy of an inventory taken of the stock of Wm. Williams & Co., of Buffalo, just before he left that concern, and it certainly was a model. He was always a neat dresser and a most precise, methodical man. He certainly was fond of acquiring money, and it is my impression his charities were large and mostly in the direction of the Episcopal Church, of which he was a member. I came to know him fairly well because a chum of mine, Chas. T. Paddock, nephew of Mr. Chas. Jackson, was his confidential as well as his prescription clerk. I also heard much of him in Buffalo after I went there, as the drug house of Wm. Williams & Co. was on the same block on Main Street, as was the bookstore of Messrs. Peck, in which house I was a clerk. They all spoke of him as a very bright young man. He built himself a palatial residence (now occupied by his son) on Jefferson Avenue. He was a familiar figure on the avenue in those days, riding home from his Woodward Avenue store on that white horse of his that the coachman brought down regularly every afternoon for his use. Many will call this to mind no doubt. Mr. Eaton was politeness and consideration itself to his clerks and employees during the early part of his career here, and I presume he kept it up until his life's end.

Mr. Thomas Cranage, now of the extensive lumbering firm of Pitts & Cranage, Bay City, was at one time, and for quite a period, clerk for Mr. Eaton. The business habits he acquired in Eaton's house have no doubt stood him in good stead through all his life.

COLONEL BERRIEN.

A frequent visitor to the Eaton mansion was Col. John M. Berrien, engineer of the Michigan Central Railroad, when it was the property of the state. The colonel was a West Pointer, and graduated into the engineers, resigning to enter the employ of the state in laying out the road. He had for an assistant Lieutenant Center, who had also been a West Pointer.

The mother of Theo. H. Eaton, Maria Montgomery, was the granddaughter of Judge John Berrien, lineal ancestor of Colonel Berrien, engineer of the Michigan Central Railroad. It is said General Washington wrote his farewell address to the army while a guest of, and in the house of Judge Berrien's widow at Rocky Hill, near Princeton, New Jersey, December 1st, 1783.

Many of the present day will remember Colonel Berrien, whose commanding and soldierly figure was often seen on the streets. He died many years ago. In this connection it may not be out of place to mention John A. Welles, the banker, who married a sister of Mr. Eaton.

S. L. ROOD'S STORE.

IT WAS THE HEADQUARTERS FOR THE JOLLY SET OF DETROIT'S BUSINESS MEN MANY YEARS AGO.

CHAPIN & OWEN had the next store with the same class of goods, and Snow & Fisk with books and stationery had the next. Josiah Snow, of Snow & Fisk, I presume many will call to mind—a fussy, plump, nervous little man, always on the go, always a cigar in his mouth and scarcely ever was lighted. He was engaged in all sorts of enterprises after he left the book business. The last I heard of him was directly after the war. He was then engaged in building telegraph lines. His right-hand man here was Scott W. Updike, who some will, perhaps, remember, for everyone knew him at the time. He was an enthusiastic fireman, as well as one of the trimmest members of the Brady Guards. He was a master in the art of dancing, and no firemen's or Brady Guards' ball was complete unless Scott Updike was on hand to call the sets. Standing on the lower step of the platform on which the music was stationed, his trim figure on these occasions always arrayed in the uniform of the Brady Guard, his loud and commanding voice would sway and direct the gay crowd before him through all the mazes of the giddy dance, as none other in all my experience has ever done. The last I ever saw of him was at a military encampment in Cleveland many years ago. He was then captain of a military company from Rochester, and myself and the late Dr. Lucretius Cobb were his guests for two or three days. He gave us a good time.

OTHER CONCERNS.

The upstairs portion was used for offices and sleeping rooms. William Patterson (late of the old book store on Michigan Avenue) had a job printing office here. Robert Abbott, auditor-general of the State of Michigan, had his office here, as did Thomas Palmer and A. E. Hathon, H. R. Schoolcraft, Indian agent, and Dr. Marshall Chapin, Mr. Owen's partner.

The firm of Chapin & Owen was dissolved through the death

of Dr. Chapin, and Theodore H. Hinchman, head clerk in the late concern, took his place, and the firm name changed to John Owen & Co. After a few years here they moved a few doors down into the Granite Block. John W. Strong occupied this John Owen store along about 1848, '49 and '50' with a stock of groceries, wines and liquors. John Owen & Co.'s neighbors in the same block were Jacobs & Garrison, corner of Jefferson Avenue and Shelby Street, as mentioned before, and they were in the same line of business. Snow & Fisk were succeeded by Sidney L. Rood & Co., in the same line, Sidney L. Rood and Morris F. Williams purchasing the stock of Snow & Fisk. After a brief period M. M. Williams retired and took a position in the post-office, which he retained through all administrations until his death. I might say in passing that I succeeded to the business of G. L. Rood & Co. after Mr. Gilbert Rood's death, which occurred in 1851.

"GIL ROOD."

This G. F. Rood ("Gil" Rood) was a queer combination. He was rough, though kind and genial, and fond of a joke. Honest to a fault, his word was as good as his bond. He always expressed himself as a follower of Tom Paine, as did his brother Sidney, although whether they really believed in his teachings or not, I do not know. At the time of his death "Gil" expressed a wish that a band of music should play "Yankee Doodle" on the way to the cemetery, and "Hail Columbia" on the way back, which was done.

I was clerk and bookkeeper for S. L. Rood after Mr. Williams left, for nearly three years, until he quit business and removed to Fredonia, Chautaqua Co., N. Y. From the latter place he removed to Milwaukee, got rich and died there about 1873. Sidney L. Rood was an out-and-out Whig in politics, an all-around good fellow, genial and most charitable, his purse ever ready to respond to the cry of want. His store was the headquarters of the jolly set of Detroit's contingent (the old heads), Whig or Democrat. In those days it was customary for loiterers and customers of the proprietors to occupy chairs in front of the premises on the pavement under the awning in the summer time. Here, in front of Rood's, of a hot summer's afternoon would gather such genial spirits as Judge Canniff, Levi Cook, David Thompson, Charles Jackson, Jerry Moores, Virgil McGraw, Frank Hall, Mr. Meredith, Judge Backus, John Farmer, Thomas

Palmer, A. E. Hathon, Uncle Henry Newberry, John Mullett, Oliver Newberry, Ezra Rood, John Scott (father of "Jim" Scott), Joseph Campau, who was always an amused spectator), and many others. The topics of the day would then and there be discussed and whatever fun there was in the crowd was sure to come out. The same parties did not get together every day, of course, but they did not skip very often. Oliver Newberry would never tarry long, but would linger a few moments on his way to the Bank of Michigan, quiet and taciturn, listen to a joke or two from Canniff and others, and pass on with a grim smile.

UNCLE HENRY NEWBERRY.

Uncle Henry Newberry was almost a daily attendant. He was crusty and taciturn, but kind-hearted, loved a joke but rarely indulged in perpetrating one. He always persisted in being on the wrong side of nearly all questions discussed there or elsewhere. To illustrate: One day he made his appearance, looking rather the worse for wear and exceedingly crusty. He was questioned by Judge Canniff and said "he had passed through an experience that would make any man crusty, ill and sour-tempered, and that was he had been summoned on a jury and had passed the entire night sitting up with eleven of the contrariest men he ever met." I think John Farmer was the most argumentative and persistent talker of the lot. Rood was the publisher, so to speak, of Farmer's maps of Michigan, consequently he was a frequent visitor.

Mr. Rood, in addition to his book and stationery business, carried on quite an extensive book bindery and blank book factory in a small wooden building in the rear of the store. Rood, with all his good points, was apt sometimes to be a little rough. He said to me, directly after entering his employ:

"Palmer, have you ever kept a set of books?" I said "No, sir." Then he said: "Williams has left and, damn you, if you want to stay with me you have got to keep those books." It is needless to say I kept the books.

SUPPLIES FOR THE LEGISLATURE.

Rood used to furnish the legislature, until the capital moved to Lansing, with paper and stationery—quite a good thing those days, no contract and no grumbling at price. On the start, at the opening of the session, the order always was: Sixty bunches quills, sixty Roger's penknives, sixty sand boxes, sixty wafer cups, sixty rulers, sixty papers of black ink powder, sixty wafer stamps, sixty pieces of red tape, sixty dozen of lead pencils, sixty small bottles of pounce, sixty erasers, sixty inkstands, sixty papers of black sand, and, besides all these articles, quite a quantity of letter and fool's-cap paper, envelopes or wrapping paper, red ink, wafers, sealing wax, etc. "Something of a starter."

I slept in the store, on a bed made up on the counter, and boarded in Mr. Rood's family. They did not give much salary then. My princely compensation was $50 the first year and board, $100 the second, and $150 the third, and so on. I thus worried through three years rather happily.

One of Mr. Owen's clerks, Reuel Roby, and myself were great chums. After closing at night, at 9 o'clock, we would spend the evening together, either at his place or mine. While clerking next to John Owen's, I never lacked, in a small way, for candy, nuts, oranges and cigars. Wines of the finest brands and other strong liquors were always on tap, but neither Reuel nor myself partook of the latter. For some cause or other we had no desire to do so.

REUEL ROBY.

Reuel Roby was the son of Mr. John Roby, who did an extensive forwarding and commission business at the foot of Shelby Street (Roby's dock and warehouse), until the time of his death about 1825 or 1826. A widow, three sons and one daughter survived him. The widow and daughter passed away soon after, and of the three boys, Henry, the eldest, went into the employ—I think—of Wm. Brewster, forwarding and commission merchant, as bookkeeper. He continued in the same capacity, with various firms, until he went into business on his own account, associating himself with John T. Hunt (Hunt & Roby).

Reuel, the next, entered the employ of Chapin & Owen and remained with them, as principal prescription clerk, for many years. John, the next, entered the service of a forwarding and commission house on the dock, who had a business connection with the firm of Hollister Bros., Buffalo. This latter firm had a branch of their concern located at Monroeville, Ohio, then a great railroad transfer center. John, being an exceedingly bright young man, soon attracted the attention of the Hollisters, and they made him a flattering offer to take charge of their branch at Monroeville, which he accepted, and ever after made that town his home.

A change in the railroad system of Ohio served to divert much of the business from Monroeville, so John Roby went into the malting business quite extensively on his own account, the Hollisters in the meantime having withdrawn their interest. The malting business, which had assumed large proportions, and what little remained of the railroad freight business, taxed John's capacity to the utmost, so he summoned Henry and Reuel to his aid, Henry having severed his connection with Hunt. They responded, and the three brothers undertook the business together. Shortly after Henry's advent in Monroeville he married a sister of Hon. Thomas W. Palmer, of this city, and took up his permanent residence there. After a married life of a few years' duration, the wife died, leaving a daughter, who subsequently married Major Frank Hamilton, Fourth United States Artillery, a native of Monroeville. The latter was military attache to the United States legation at the court of Madrid, Spain, during Senator T. W. Palmer's mission there. Mrs. Hamilton accompanied him.

The Robys acquired a comfortable fortune in Monroeville, but they are all dead, as are Captain Hamilton and wife.

The major was a graduate of West Point. His wife was a most estimable woman. There are but very few of the present residents of Monroeville that do not hold in loving memory the Robys and Major Hamilton and his wife.

MR. JOHN OWEN.

STORY OF THE GREAT AID HE GAVE TO THE STATE OF MICHIGAN, AT THE OPENING OF THE CIVIL WAR.

RIGHT here, let me dwell for a few moments on Mr. John Owen. A wonderful business man he was then and continued so for many years, almost to the time of his death.

He was apt to be at times somewhat harsh with the clerks in the store and sometimes with his sons. He was very pleasant in his family always. He was the same among his fellow Methodists, in the church and in the Sabbath and singing school. He was an ardent Methodist and was a familiar figure in the choir of the old wooden church on the corner of Woodward Avenue and Congress Street, of which he was the leader. He was the mainstay of the Methodists for years in this city and state.

I think it was his nature to be prompt and exacting in business matters, hence his success. When he came to the store in the morning or at any time, it would always be with a rapid, hurried walk. He would march with the same step directly to the bookkeeper's desk, at the rear of the store. On reaching his destination off would go his plug hat and in his quick and decisive way would summon either Theo. Hinchman or Roby, the confidential clerk, to his presence and then would begin the business of the day. Senator Palmer, when a boy, roughed it in Mr. Owen's store for about a year, as a coarse hand clerk.

I, myself, stood in wholesome awe of Mr. Owen and, indeed, it never entirely wore off, though we were always on friendly terms. I think he believed in me somehow (though it took me a long time to find it out), as, for instance, during the civil war, he was state treasurer, and part of that time I was assistant quartermaster-general of the state.

TWO HUNDRED THOUSAND DOLLARS WORTH OF BONDS.

While I was acting in that capacity Mr. Owen had succeeded in placing $200,000 worth of the bonds of the state, authorized to be issued by the legislature for the purpose of raising money to pay state bounties. The cash was in the bank to the credit of the state, and the quartermaster-general was out of the city, in Washington. On this money the bank was paying interest to the state. Mr. Owen, the president of the bank, did not like the situation. He came to the office one morning and said he desired to turn this money over to our department and so stop the interest. I said to him:

"The quartermaster-general is in Washington and I am not properly in condition to receive it, as I am not under bonds to the state."

"I know it," said he, "but it will be all right, and if you will take the money and receipt for it it will be passed to your credit at the bank."

I assented, gave a receipt, and the $200,000 was passed to my credit. To say that I was surprised would not express it. You might have knocked me down with a feather. Ever after I looked upon Mr. Owen in a far different light.

At the outbreak of the civil war, as said, Mr. Owen was state treasurer. The treasury was almost empty. In this emergency the governor (Blair) convened the legislature at once, to devise ways and means for the purpose of equipping the troops of the state destined for the service of the United States (President Lincoln having called for 75,000 men to aid in putting down the rebellion). In the meantime, in response to the appeal of the president through our governor, the First and Second regiments of infantry were rapidly recruited and came in to camp the first at Fort Wayne and the second at Camp Blair, out Woodward Avenue.

MR. OWEN'S GREAT SERVICE.

Clothing, tents, equipments, ammunition, etc., were needed at once; the necessity was imperative. In this dilemma Mr. Owen came to the front, and on his own individual responsibility guaranteed to A. T. Stewart & Co., New York, the payment of an invoice of army cloth sufficient to clothe the First and Second regiments. Colonel Henry M. Whittlesey, acting for the state, was dispatched at once by the governor to New York to negotiate its purchase. It is needless to say the goods came on with quickest dispatch. A little later on Colonel E. O. Grosvenor was dispatched on a like errand and under the same auspices to the New England factories for the purchase of underclothing, socks, etc.

Most all citizens of Michigan at the present day know with what promptness the first two regiments of Michigan troops were put into the field, armed and equipped for immediat service. When recounting the deeds of Michigan's citizens in the civil war, to uphold the union, the name of John Owen, it seems to me, should stand pre-eminent. War without its principal sinew (cash) would be but a rush in the dark.

I think it may be pertinent to say in this connection that the purchase from A. T. Stewart & Co. could not have beeen duplicated in any northern city one week later, as the demand for army cloth was so urgent.

JUDGE CANNIFF.

In passing I will halt for a brief space to say a few words about Judge Canniff. Where or how he acquired the title of "judge" was not apparent, but he was always addressed as such. He was an inveterate joker and gave as good as he got. He was for many years the agent for Suydam, Sage & Co., wholesale grocers, of New York, before their failure and after. They had large interests here and throughout the state, all of which the judge settled up to the satisfaction of the firm. I was in a good position to know, as I made up his final statement to the firm and closed the account.

The judge was mighty fond of money and strictly honest. When I had closed the account I speak of, he handed me a two dollar bill, saying at the time:

"Don't let Jim or Ann (his son and daughter) know anything about this, as they might make a fuss."

I presume he feared they might think he was throwing his money away. He left quite a large estate to his children, but mostly to his son James, who was his idol. I rather think James must have played it on the old man, as during the last sickness of the latter James would allow scarcely anyone but the doctor to see his father, not even his adopted son, Henry Canniff. James did not live long to enjoy what he got, a few years only. He divorced his wife, married his ward, and built himself a fine residence on the Canada side, opposite Belle Isle. He had a stroke of paralysis, lingered along two or three years almost helpless, and then passed to the "beyond." And thus it is.

DANIEL J. CAMPAU.

Daniel J. Campau, father of the present Daniel J., built himself a wooden building, two stories high, on his father's lot, next to Rood's, in which he carried on the dry goods business in all its branches, kept a fine line of goods and did a fine business. A good business man was Dan, the most capable of any of his father's sons, except Joe, who was the old gentleman's favorite and man of affairs. The latter died many years ago, in 1838 or '39, I forget which. Dan was considered quite a high roller, loved fast horses and all things else in their train. Nevertheless, he made money and retired from business with a competency, which, added to that his father left him, made him a rich man. His success in the dry goods business, I think, was partly due to his able assistants, the late Charles Vail and a nephew, the late Henry Campau, the latter for so many years in the county register's office.

When Theo. Hinchman first came to Detroit, himself and Charles Vail were great chums and were "boys about town," into most everything that was going of a lively nature. They used to relate to Reuel Roby and myself, when they came into Mr. Owen's store late at night, an account of their adventures around the city. They were always in high glee, not from intoxicants, but from the fun they had had attending French dances, etc. But a stop came to all this. Mr. Theo. Parker, a Presbyterian revivalist, came along and preached his stirring sermons, morning, noon and night. He created quite a furor. Hundreds were drawn into the fold, among them Hinchman and Vail. They became devout Christians, as much down on their former follies as they had been eager in their pursuit, and so each continued to his life's end.

A SON'S TRIBUTE

REV. D. M. COOPER CONTRIBUTES SOME INTERESTING FACTS CONCERNING HIS REVERED FATHER.

To the Editor of The Free Press:

I appreciate very highly the kindly reference made to my revered father by my old friend, Mr. Friend Palmer, in the Sunday *Free Press* of January 3. One or two qualifications of statements are nevertheless necessary. He said:

"In trade he was exactness itself. He was his own bookkeeper, always, and when you received an invoice or statement of account from him, where fractions occurred in either, it was always 6¼, 12½, 18¾, 37½, 62½, and 87½, pro or con as the case might be in every instance. I have seen his day book often, and it did look too odd."

But really I cannot see anything "odd" in his style of bookkeeping. It was the one in vogue in his time, before the introduction of the decimal system and was the outcrop of the pounds, shillings and pence period. It was the mode in which I was instructed in my youth, and it always was pleasing to me by its exactness.

It would interest Mr. "Friend" to see an account now before me, when my father was clerk to one Richard Pattison, in Sandwich—probably his first clerkship before he fixed himself in Detroit.

· I recollect my father point out to me the old Sandwich store shortly before it was burned. The credit side of the account reads:

Cr.

By year's wages from 14 June, 1811, to 2 January, 1812, 6 mos. 19 Ds. at £80 per annum £44 3s 4d. Due Mr. Cooper £28, 16s 8d. Sandwich, 16 March, 1812.

E. E.

A LEGACY.

His old account books I have stored away, as a legacy for my children. If I supposed it would interest your readers I could give some choice tracts from these old-time accounts. I never saw more beautiful penmanship, and that done with the old quill pen. Steel pens, of course, were unknown. And I remember, as if it were yesterday, the glee with which coming home from the store one day he exhibited his first gold pen purchased from Mr. Levi Brown, a watchmaker, and deacon in St. Paul's church, for which he paid $5 and whose shop stood on the site of the present Willis Block. I supposed then, and have never seen it contradicted, that Mr. Brown was the inventor of the gold pen. Mr. Brown subequently sold out to Mr. Payne and removed to New York City. His chief workman, Mr. Griesbach, continued until quite recently the business of repairing gold pens. Since his death, at an advanced age, his son carries on like work at his residence on Orleans Street.

TRANSFER OF THE LIME QUARRY.

The transfer of the lime quarry to Judge Sibley was on the basis of $12,000 instead of $10,000, as Mr. Palmer states. At least so I have always understood.

Solomon Sibley, one of the most noted of the early residents and judge of Michigan territory, came here in 1797, and some years after that acquired title from the government to a valuable tract of land in what is now the Township of Monguagon, while Colonel Mack, also one of the earliest American residents, obtained possession of the adjoining tract. The Sibley property went by descent to Frederick B. Sibley, while Colonel Mack's parcel came into possession of his son-in-law, David Cooper. There were outcroppings of an excellent quality of limestone on both tracts, and Mr. Cooper opened a quarry about the year 1840. Three or four years later the general government commenced the construction of Fort Wayne, and in order to obtain the material leased a portion of Mr. Cooper's quarry. From the stone there obtained all the concrete used in the first fortification at the fort was obtained, as well as the stone, in blocks, out of which the officers' quarters and barracks were built. One of these structures burned down during the period that the fort was unoccupied after the war. The other, the large stone structure inside the fortifications, has been used as barracks down to the present time. This work of construction was carried on by General Meigs, afterwards quartermaster-general of the army.

HIS FAITHFULNESS.

As an example of the faithfulness of Mr. Cooper as a clerk for Mack & Conant this anecdote has often been told of him:

One of the habitues of the store was the eccentric Judge Woodward, who was in the habit of calling every evening and helping himself to a glass of whisky. This he would place before him and while discoursing pedantically on history, politics, metaphysics and every other conceivable subject, would sip the liquor until the tumbler was empty. As he never offered to pay, the bookkeeper felt it his duty to make an entry of each glass on the back page of the daybook.

One day the judge was presented with a paper which, on unfolding, he found to be a bill of some seventy-five half pints of whisky at five cents each.

"What?" he cried, "do you charge for such a thing as a little whisky?"

"Not for a little," was the answer. "This amount shows that you have had four gallons and a half."

The judge came off his high horse and paid the bill but unwillingly and with a very bad grace.

A FILIAL DUTY.

And now, as my "Friend" has opened this topic, allow me before I conclude to occupy a little more of your space to discharge a filial duty to one to whom I owe so much. Possibly so suitable an opportunity may not occur again.

Many years ago I accompanied my father on his first visit to Montreal since his birth, in search of some reminders of his childhood. The old streets were there in the French quarter where he acquired a knowledge of the French language which served him so well when in subsequent years, as a merchant in a city where the use of that tongue predominated, he did business. But nothing seemed familiar to him except the old Bonsecour Catholic church.

Strange that we should have then missed St. Gabriel's, in which he received the rite of baptism shortly after its erection in 1786—the oldest Protestant church in Montreal, whose centennial celebration occurred March 12, 1886.

THE MARBLE TABLET.

The building is now occupied as an annex to some municipal structure. While examining it I noticed that the marble tablet on the outside, announcing the fact of its antiquity, attracted to it a constant file of visitors. Standing, it preserves the memory of Christian courtesies in early days between the three leading Christian communions.

While the church was being built the good old Recollect fathers offered the congregation the use of their chapel to worship in. The sturdy Scotchmen accepted the offer, and when they moved into their own kirk they presented the fathers with a hogshead of canary wine and two boxes of candles.

Subsequently, when the Anglican church was burned, the Presbyterians, doubtless remembering how they had been indebted to others, came forward promptly and put St. Gabriel's at the entire disposal of the Anglicans for the half of every Sunday until their church could be rebuilt.

The knowledge of its continued existence came to me in a curious way. One of those "New Year's Greetings" which I was accustomed to present annually to my congregation, and in which allusion was made to the fact that I built the Memorial church in memory of my father, by some chance came into the hands of Rev. Robert Campbell, pastor of St. Gabriel's. It led him to address me the following note:

"68 Jainville St.,
"Montreal, Nov. 5, 1886.

"Dear Brother—My friend and co-presbyter, Mr. Jordan, mentioned the circumstance of your father's birth in Montreal in 1789 to me the other day, and being curious in the matter I turned to the old church register used in common by the Protestants of the city in those days, and I found the following entry: 'David, son of Mr. Alexander and Elizabeth Cooper, born the 24th day of November. Baptized the 19th day of December, 1789.'"

MR. COOPER IN DETROIT.

In 1799, three years after the first flag that ever floated in Michigan bearing the Stars and Stripes was given to the breeze, we find Mr. Cooper in the City of Detroit—then only a military post—a lad 10 years of age, without influential friends and no relative excepting a widowed mother of slender means, whose residence, a little one-story wood colored house, was on the site of the present Union Trust building.

The necessity of earning his own livelihood led to his apprenticeship to Mr. James Henry, a merchant then doing business in a store on St. Anne Street (now Jefferson Avenue), just west of the present site of the old Michigan Exchange.

To Mr. Henry he was largely indebted for those business habits which formed the basis of his after success in life. He ever entertained an affectionate remembrance of his old employer, and after him named one of his children. At the close of his apprenticeship he became chief clerk in the mercantile establishment of Thomas Emerson & Co., afterwards known as the firm of Mack & Conant, where his integrity secured him general confidence.

UNIVERSALLY ESTEEMED.

Perhaps no resident trader was more universally esteemed by the old French inhabitants and the Indians, over whom he always had great influence. At the age of 35, in the full vigor of manhood, with a valuable mercantile experience and an unsullied character he carried into execution his long-cherished projects of establishing business for himself. In 1820 he was married by Rev. John Monteith to the daughter of Colonel Stephen Mack, a pioneer from the State of Vermont—the first Yankee merchant in the City of Detroit—a man of remarkable energy and public spirit, as the schemes he set on foot for the development of the resources of the territory will abundantly testify. But these schemes were frustrated by an untimely death. He lies buried in the cemetery at Pontiac, a city which he was mainly instrumental in founding.

Thence onward to the date of his death, July 27, 1876, at the advanced age of 86, Mr. Cooper pursued the even tenor of his way, honored as a citizen, beloved as a husband, revered as a father.

His first place of business was in a story-and-a-half frame building standing immediately in the rear of the site of Macauley's millinery store, corner of Jefferson and Woodward Avenues. The space in front on Woodward Avenue was occupied by the town market and surrounded by a wooden paling.

A GRAND LIFE.

The only official positions he ever filled were those of alderman, trustee of Harper Hospital, and elder in the First Presbyterian church of Detroit. All I claim for him whom I revere as earthly father is a life like that of David Elginbrood, "intelligently met and honestly passed," which, McDonald truly says, "is the best education of all"—except it be that higher one to which it is intended to lead and to which it did lead.

What wealth he acquired was the result of slow accumulation in legitimate trade, rigid economy, incessant toil and patient waiting, and not a "dirty shilling" in it. He avoided debt as he avoided sin and would have no more thought of defrauding a man of a farthing than of taking his life.

Hence his life was not one of feverish anxiety but one of quiet. His sleep was sweet and refreshing—the sleep of a man whose conscience was void of offense toward God and man, as it was his daily prayer it should be.

His remains repose peacefully in Elmwood, in this city, where he passed seventy-six years of his active life, and which he saw grow to its present size and beauty, and in close proximity to the noble river upon which he gazed in boyhood—a locality and a stream as familiar to his eyes a hundred years ago as it is to ours today.

> His youth was innocent; his riper age
>   Marked with some act of goodness every day;
> And watched by eyes that loved him, calm and sage
>   Faded his late declining years away.
> Meekly he gave his being up and went
>   To share the holy rest that waits a life well spent.
>
> That life was happy; every day he gave
>   Thanks for the fair existence that was his;
> For a sick fancy made him not her slave,
>   To mock him with her phantom miseries:
> No chronic tortures racked his aged limb,
>   For luxury and sloth had nourished none for him.
>
> And I am glad that he did live thus long,
>   And I am glad that he has gone to his reward:
> Nor can I deem that Nature did him wrong
>   Softly to disengage the vital chord;
> For when his hand grew palsied and his eye
>   Dark with the mists of age—it was his time to die."

D. M. COOPER.

JOSEPH CAMPAU.

INTERESTING RECOLLECTIONS OF THIS SUBSTANTIAL OLD CITIZEN, AND OF CHIEF MACOONCE.

THE JOSEPH CAMPAU residence (most all will remember it) was built, it is said, on the foundations of the former residence of Mr. Campau, erected before the fire of 1805. One curious feature about the house was that not a nail was used in its construction, hickory pegs being substituted instead, at least so all the Campau boys asserted. It was a one-story house with high finished attic, dormer windows, etc., and was always painted yellow with white trimmings. It has been so recently removed that I will not attempt to describe it further, as all will probably remember it.

From Dan's store to his father's residence was a line of red cedar pickets set closely together, about six feet high with a double entrance gate in the center. Half of the first floor of the house was devoted to a store and office, the store in front and the office in the rear. In this store, when I first came here, Mr. Campau had a small stock of Indian goods, to supply, in a measure, the wants of his good friends, the Indians. This he kept up until about 1840, when most of the Indians in Michigan were removed beyond the Mississippi by the government.

Mr. Campau was indeed the friend of the redmen of the entire northwest, and they returned the feeling. He could talk their language, knew their peculiarities, and every chief of note knew him intimately and came to him for counsel and advice. He always met them with a smile of welcome. I have seen often and often, in the summer season, scores of them—bucks, squaws and papooses—squatted on the pavement in front of his place, as on their visits to the city they always made it a point to call on their friend, the great "Che-mo-ka-mun (i. e., Whiteman). They never failed to give him an ovation every fall when on their way to and from Malden, Canada, to receive their presents from the British government.

SUCCESSFUL TRADER.

It is said he used to make a good thing of it, trading for or buying outright the articles the Indians got at Malden that they did not need or want. If he did do so, it was what all the other merchants did. I have seen a list of the presents they received, some of them I have forgotten. Those that are now in my mind were shot-guns, rifles, lead, powder, shot, bullet molds, gun flints, hunting knives, axes, tomahawks, vermillion, blankets, broadcloth, calico, brass kettles, seine twine, fish-hooks, fish-lines, glass beads, thread, needles, silver ear-bobs and other silver ornaments. The glass beads were always very much in evidence, as were also the silver ear-bobs and other silver ornaments.

An eye-witness has described the distribution of these presents:

"I noticed the effect each gift had on this expecting multitude, as it was brought out from the store house. New joy would sparkle in every eye. The little naked children would run about almost frantic; the squaws would utter the exclamation 'neau,' which is peculiar to the women; the boys and girls clap their hands and toss themselves about, whilst the old men smoked away like steam engines. And as the dispensers of these gifts would go round every eye would follow them, and with an imploring look, when every now and then a fear would manifest itself lest they who indulged it might be passed."

CHIEF MACOONCE.

The only chief of prominence that I remember visiting Mr. Campau was Macoonce. His lodge and headquarters were on the banks of Lake St. Clair. I have seen him here very often. He was a fine specimen of his class, always sober, a state that many, many of his race could not boast of. Awfully fond of whisky, were these Indians, squaws as well as bucks. I have often seen the former, when offered a drink of whisky take a good long swig and then fill their mouths to the utmost limit and deposit the contents in a little buckskin bag that they carried for the purpose, to enjoy at their leisure.

This Macoonce spoke English fairly well and was costumed nearly like a white man—black frock coat, tied around the waist with wampum, fringed calico hunting shirt, vest, broadcloth leggins, ornamented with porcupine quills, the outer seams profusely decorated with silver ornaments that jingled with each step he took; buckskin moccasins worked with porcupine quills, plug hat ornamented with a broad silver band, five or six silver ear-bobs in each ear, and a silver ring through his nose. All this, added to his fine physique, made him quite conspicuous.

My uncle used to visit St. Clair once every winter at that time and generally took me along with him. We always used to stop at this chief's lodge, on L'Anse Cruche Bay, Lake St. Clair, and enjoyed his hospitality.

Macoonce was one of those chiefs of the Chippewa tribe that were compelled to join the enemy during the war of 1812, but, like Walk-in-the-Water, the Wyandotte chieftain, his heart was never with them.

A BRAVE BUCK.

Among the savages the chief was not only the judge who pronounced sentence on the culprit, but was frequently executioner of his sentence. The late Thomas Coquillard related to Judge Witherell this circumstance in connection with the above:

"In 1813 he saw many Indians one day gathered about what is now the foot of St. Antoine Street. He went up to them and found that the death penalty was about to be inflicted on a young savage for killing a young squaw of Macoonce's band.

"The chief sent word to the culprit to come at the appointed time and place and be killed; the young Indian came alone; no fetters, no guard, no sheriff or constable to prevent the escape of the murderer. Alone he came to meet his fate. He cast one long, lingering look upon his people, put a handful of salt in his mouth, fell on his hands and knees, drew his blanket over his head, and submitted to his fate. The chief, with a single blow of his tomahawk, dismissed his spirit to the red man's heaven—the happy hunting grounds, in the islands of the blest."

Macoonce, when visiting the city, always stopped at a tavern on Woodbridge Street that stood in the rear of the present Cooper building. He also used to put up, when visiting the college of Palmer (St. Clair), at Cross's tavern in that town, where I have seen him often.

My uncle Thomas lived, at the time I write of (after being burned out), in a house next to Mr. Campau's, so we were pretty near neighbors. I have given an account of this fire in a former article on "Our Old Volunteer Fire Department."

This dwelling of ours belonged to Uncle Shubal Conant and was set back from the street line twenty-five or thirty feet. It was afterwards moved and its place taken by a brick building three stories high, occupied as a dry goods store by Mr. C. M. D. Bull and as a boot and shoe store by Mr. N. O. Sargent for quite awhile, until their death. John Palmer afterward had a dry goods store in the same building.

As said before, we were near neighbors of the Campaus, and of course quite intimate. Two of his boys, Dennis and James, about my age, and myself were great chums. We used to have great times playing, in the winter evenings, in the cellar kitchen, which was quite large and boasted of an immense fireplace. We had some help, of course. Mr. Campau had a very pretty daughter, Adelaide, who was the apple of his eye. He set great store by her, and she was, indeed, a dainty piece of humanity. A Scotch gentleman of fine presence by the name of Johnson came along who quite captured her. He was a widower, represented himeslf as a scion of the Scotch nobility and exhibited much family silverware, linen, etc.

Mr. Campau would have none of him and threatened his daughter with excommunication from his heart and wealth if she persisted in marrying him, which she did without anybody's consent but her own, and the old man did as he said he would— divorced her from his heart and wealth and never had say with her thereafter. I never knew what became of them. Her brother, Daniel J., however, treasured his sister's memory, for he named his daughter, now Mrs. Campau Thompson, after her.

The old merchant was always kind, affable and neatness itself. He was always arrayed in black broadcloth, coat, vest and pants, coat cut swallow-tail, with plug hat and white cravat. He was for some reason or other a foe to the Catholic priesthood, so much so that he let no occasion pass to express his hostility, and for this reason, I suppose, he was denied burial in the consecrated ground of Mt. Elliott Cemetery. But perhaps he will get there quite as soon as some of the rest of us. Notwithstanding his trouble with the priesthood, he was a Christian and, I think, a good Catholic at heart, as were all the family. Mrs. Campau particularly. But it appeared to be the priests he was after and not the faith.

Joseph Campau was buried in Elmwood Cemetery, the moss-covered foundations of a monument are over his remains, but no-monument was ever erected upon them. Upon a massive marble slab near by is the record of the man who was to be honored. It reads:

"In memory of Joseph Campau, born in Detroit, February 20th, 1769; died July 22d, 1863, in the ninety-fifth year of his age. American by birth, French by descent and education, he was a merchant for over sixty years and distinguished as the wealthiest man in the State of Michigan."

His grandfather was a French officer under M. de La Mothe Cadillac, the founder of Detroit in 1701. Theo. J., his son, aged 50, is buried near him.

THE CAMPAU FAMILY.

ADDITIONAL INTERESTING FACTS ABOUT MR. JOSEPH CAMPAU, HIS DECENDANTS AND HIS WEALTH.

MR. JOS. CAMPAU had something to do with slaves, as it appears from an old document, a bill of sale in the possession of his heirs, that on one occasion Mr. Campau bought of Margueritte de Boucherville, in Montreal, a negro boy named Thomas, aged 9 years. The price paid for him was £25 sterling, and it was one of the conditions of the sale that the boy should be brought up in the Catholic faith and manumitted at the age of twenty-one years. Another bill of sale dated November 25, 1791, shows that a negro named Pompey was sold by George Lyons to George Leath & Co. for the sum of £40 sterling. In June, 1792, the same chattel was sold to James May for £38 sterling. He had one or two other slaves besides this one.

Still another document of interest, especially in these days of thoughtless hurried and unceremonious marriages, is a contract drawn up with imposing formula, the principals in which were Sieur P. J. Desnoyers and Demoiselle M. Louis Goberille. The date of this interesting relic of an obsolete custom is July 30, 1798. All old settlers remember Peter J. Desnoyers.

The pioneers of Detroit were, it seems, not adverse to social pleasures, which fact more definitely appears from the following:

"January 17, 1807.

"Mr. Campau will please furnish for the Grand Marais party on Saturday next, provided there is good carioling, a qr. of roast beef and a pair of fowls ready for the spit.

"MAJOR ERNEST,
JAMES ABBOTT."

Of all the wealth that Mr. Campau did leave, and it was very large, none remains in the heirs except that possessed by Daniel J. Campau and his sister, Mrs. Thompson, though I think the widow of James, "Jock Campau," the late Mrs. James Scott. owned some of the property left by her first husband, at the time of her death.

MR. CAMPAU'S CHILDREN.

The eldest son, Joseph, who was his father's right-hand man, died along in the early forties. He was a very quiet, level-headed young man, and the old gentleman felt his loss keenly.

Daniel J., as before mentioned, was a successful merchant on his own account and did not pay much attention to his father's affairs. He married Miss Palms, the sister of Francis Palms, and they had three children, two boys (Daniel J. and Lewis P.) and one girl. This girl, as said before, he named after his discarded sister, Adelaide, showing that her memory was ever fresh in his mind.

Lewis, one of the sons, died only a few years ago, a bright, promising young man; the other, Daniel J., is still alive and with us. All know what an influential Democratic politician he is, and all-around turf man as well. I do not profess to know a thing about horses, races or race tracks—on those matters I am all at sea. But I am told, and judge by observation, that the Grosse Pointe race track, with all its appliances, is the finest in the country, and all owing mainly to our fellow citizen, Daniel J. Campau.

Adelaide, the daughter, became the wife of a former mayor of this city, Wm. G. Thompson, as all know.

RICHEST MAN IN MICHIGAN.

Theodore and Dennis attended more or less to their father's business, and managed with his aid and that of a French bookkeeper (as his books were kept in that language) to keep things in order, until the old gentleman died in 1863. Then Theodore and Dennis took almost the entire charge of the estate, which was considered large, as it was said at the time of Mr. Campau's death that he was the richest man in Michigan. Daniel was incapacitated from attending much to business, on account of a paralytic stroke that deprived him of the use of his lower limbs. Theodore married Miss Mesels and built himself a palatial residence next above that of C. C. Trowbridge, and died there. Jerome Croul bought it after the death of Theodore, tore it down and replaced it with a residence more pretentious than its predecessor.

Dennis continued in the old homestead on Jefferson Avenue until his death. Most all at the present time will remember the old Campau homestead that was torn down only a few years ago, and also Dennis on his white horse, taking his usual outing of a fine afternoon. James, "Jock," as he was familiarly called, married a daughter of Colonel Abram Edwards, of Kalamazoo, and busied himself in attending to what property his father left him. I think quite a bit of it came into the hands of his widow, who subsequently became the wife of our good and genial friend, "Jim" Scott. She died a short time since. I think one son, by Campau, survives her.

THE YOUNGEST SON.

Timothy, the youngest son, and the pride of his mother's heart, married the sister of Mr. J. B. Howarth, of this city. He died some years ago, leaving a widow and one daughter. The former survived him but a short time; the latter is married and is living now with her husband in Grand Rapids. Whether Timothy left any property or not, I do not know.

Joseph Campau had four daughters. One, Adelaide, married in the early thirties, Mr. Johnston, a Scotch gentleman of winning address, a widower.

"TASH" CHAPOTON.

Another daughter, Matilda, married "Tash" Chapoton, son of Eustache Chapoton, of this city. Tash used to clerk for Mr. Brown, who kept an extensive clothing store in the Smart building, which is now the Merrill Block, in the early thirties. He continued with him some years, went to Chicago, and engaged in the same business on his own account, was quite prosperous, and during the civil war did an enormous business in his line. But the acquisition of more wealth through his wife, one of the heirs of the Joseph Campau estate, made him reckless in regard to money, and he, a genial, whole-souled chap and inclined to be a little horsey withal, soon came to grief. Himself and wife are both dead and I do not think they left any estate. I met "Tash" Chapoton often in Chicago during the civil war and he was always anxious to give one a good time while there, and did do so.

Another daughter, Emily, married a man by the name of Lewis; they both died many years ago. Whether they left any children or property I do not know.

Another daughter, Catharine, married Mr. Francis Palms. She died many years ago, leaving a daughter, who became the wife of Dr. Book, of this city. I imagine Mrs. Book must be quite wealthy.

MR. BRIGHAM'S EXPLOSION.

Next beyond us was a two-story and a half frame building, half of it occupied by Mason Palmer as a general store, and the other half of it as a hardware store by William Wells. (Wells was an enthusiastic fireman as well as Brady Guard.) He also dealt in a particular kind of lamp, in which burning fluid was used instead of oil, and he dealt in this fluid as well. The fluid was, by some process, distilled from spirits of turpentine. The process of distillation was a secret at that time and known only to Mr. Brigham. The manufacture of this fluid was carried on directly in the rear of John Palmer's dry goods store in the cellar of an unoccupied dwelling on the alley that runs from Griswold Street to the line of the then Campau lot. The approach to the cellar was by a flight of hewn log steps on the outside, laid in the earth down the incline, the house being built on the side hill towards the river.

The business was prosperous and continued for some time and quite a demand was created for the fluid, when all of a sudden something terrible happened. One morning the whole thing blew up, with Brigham in the cellar or laboratory, busy with his still, his furnace, his fluid and his turpentine. I happened to be in the Palmer store at the time and was sitting at the back window looking into the alley, when, Bang! came the noise of the explosion, a great puff of black smoke shot out of the chimney and then all was silence for a moment or so. I ran out into the alley and just as I reached the house Brigham was being led up the steps outside, his clothes nearly all burned off of him, groaning piteously. He was taken to a house occupied by a widow in the same alley, where his burns were attended to.

The doctor, after examining his injuries, found that he had inhaled some of the burning gas and pronounced his case serious. Brigham lived but a short time afterwards and with him vanished his illuminating fluid business till a later time when its manufacture was surrounded with more proper and better safeguards.

Brigham was a very handsome man, a neat dresser and all that sort of thing, a favorite in society. He had a profusion of curly hair and luxuriant whiskers, all of which vanished when the explosion took place. On looking at himself in the glass in the parlor of the house to which he had been taken, he saw what had come to him—hair, whiskers, eyebrows and eyelashes all gone, lips drawn and blistered by the heat. He looked once and exclaimed, with hands raised, "My God! My God!" and no more. It is needless to say that the affair gave the whole city quite a shock.

HERRICK'S CIRCULATING LIBRARY.

Mr. Palmer retired from business after awhile; so did Mr. Wells, the latter moving to Monroe. Their places were filled by Mr. J. A. Herrick, who used the entire building as a book and stationery store. He had also a circulating library—something new then. Next to him Lewis Hall had a watch, clock and jewelry store. After awhile all the buildings were swept away, including the Bull store, and their places supplied by the present Conant Block.

Before going any further I will go back again to 1827 to say that Dr. Marshall Chapin in that year occupied the store where Mr. Herrick held out in 1842 or '43, as a drug and grocery store. John Owen was his clerk. (I think he was his partner.) Mr. Owen was a little inclined to be wild at that time, and with his chum, the late Captain Arthur Edwards, used to have a heap of fun bothering the then city marshal, Adna Merritt, a nervous, excitable little body, who used to get himself all tangled up trying to stop these two from starting and throwing fire balls, balls of cotton wicking soaked in turpentine and reenforced with twine. It was quite common then on Fourth of July nights, and on other nights as well, during the summer season, for the boys to ignite and throw these balls up and down Jefferson Avenue. Merritt tried to put a stop to it, but Owen and Captain Edwards were dead against his doing so and supplied all the fire balls necessary from Dr. Chapin's store. Did you ever see fire balls thrown, or did you ever throw them yourself? 'Tis great fun and attended with some danger to the hands and some to property, although I never knew of any harm to come from them. After a short season both Owen and Edwards joined the Methodist church, having gotten religion. No more fire balls from that quarter after that.

F. & T. PALMER'S STORES.

REMINISCENCES OF SENATOR PALMER'S FATHER'S LIBERALITY IN THE PRESENT TOWN OF ST. CLAIR.

THE lot on which the old Bank of Michigan building stands (now occupied by the Michigan Mutual Insurance Co.) was nearly vacant in 1827. In 1828 Thomas Palmer erected a double brick building on the lot for a New York concern. A part of it was occupied by B. B. Kercheval as a general store for awhile; I don't remember who occupied the other part of it. This building was afterwards torn down and the Bank of Michigan building took its place.

On the opposite corner, same side, was the brick store of F. & T. Palmer. The upper part was used as a dwelling by Thomas Palmer. They kept a general stock of goods. a much larger assortment than any house west of Buffalo. They dealt largely in furs and Indian goods and did not scorn to undertake almost any other venture on the side, as, for instance, the contract for building the territorial capitol, portions of the Saginaw (Pontiac) turnpike and the Gratiot, Grand River and Michigan Avenue (Chicago) turnpikes. Besides, they ran an ashery and pottery where West Park now is, on the line of the Cass farm. The ware turned out at the pottery was called "Jackson ware" and was used extensively in those days. This latter business was carried on for some time after my father's death in 1827.

My uncle, in the fall of every year, used to fill a wagon body with this ware weekly, and in charge of a trusty man it was peddled out to the farmers between the city and Milk River point on Lake St. Clair, taking in exchange apples, cider, vegetables, etc. I used often to accompany the man on these trips and enjoyed them ever so much, as well as the hospitalities of the French farmers. It took sometimes three or four days to get around and back again, but it was a heap of fun, and I look back upon these trips as among the most pleasant episodes in my life. Every farm had its cider mill.

MR. CONANT'S BUILDING.

The lot on which the Bank of Michigan erected its building was not entirely vacant in 1827, as Mr. Conant some time before that year put up a wooden building, two stories with basement, in the rear of this lot on Griswold Street, on the corner of the alley.

On this alley, which is still open, and in the rear of the Michigan Mutual Insurance building, lived some of the first families in the city at that time, among them Mr. Hawley, a merchant doing business on Jefferson Avenue, near Griswold Street. He married a sister of Shubal Conant. They had three children, two sons and one daughter. What became of the sons I do not know. The family moved to Kalamazoo, and the daughter, Jane, married a man by the name of Marsh, and their daughter married William Stephens, a son of John Stephens, grocery merchant, of this city.

The wooden building remained there for many years. The basement was occupied by Thomas Palmer as an office after the fire which wrecked the F. & T. Palmer store on the corner of Jefferson Avenue and Griswold Street. J. O. Lewis also occupied a room in the rear of this basement. He was an engraver and was at work particularly at that time, engraving on steel the likeness of General Cass and Father Richard, from which to take impressions. Some of the impressions are still extant and are wonderful likenesses of the originals. I used to be very much interested in his work while the two engravings were under way. The rest of the building up stairs was used by Mr. Conant for offices and sleeping apartments for bachelor tenants.

INVESTMENTS AND LIBERALITY.

In addition to their business here, F. & T. Palmer carried on a store in Canandaigua, N. Y., another at Ashtabula, Ohio, and another on the St. Clair River, now St. Clair City. Besides this they owned the two sections of land upon which the City of St. Clair is platted and had a water sawmill some miles up the Pine River, where the pine timber was then abundant and of the choicest quality. Later on, after my father's death, Thomas Palmer built an extensive steam saw and lath mill on the St. Clair River, at Palmer, now St. Clair, and abandoned the water mill up the Pine River.

The mill he ran for many years, until the supply of pine in St. Clair County gave out; then he gave up the mill. Before my father died in 1826 the firm found that they had so many irons in the fire that they had to suspend payment. Things were in a state of chaos for awhile, but the surviving partner, Thomas, cleaned everything up and paid the debts of the concern out of its assets, one hundred cents on the dollar. Thomas Palmer was a father, so to speak, to nearly all of St. Clair County at that time, and particularly of the village of Palmer. I passed two or three years of my boyhood there, off and on, and have often heard them say to him:

"Uncle Tom, when you go back to Detroit, I wish you would send me a barrel of flour or a barrel of pork or a bushel of beans" or something. These things were always sent. I don't know that he ever got his pay for them, but I don't think he did in many instances.

He tried yet further to help the village by organizing a company to build a railroad from there to Romeo. A great deal of money was expended in clearing the way and on the superstructure, but after getting that far the money gave out and, no one coming to the rescue, the project had to be abandoned, Mr. Palmer being out about $20,000. The superstructure can yet be traced along the Grand Trunk Railway that runs into St. Clair.

In payment of all the money spent in the locality and the worry and fuss endured, the villages of Palmer, or St. Clair, when they found out "Uncle Tom" could not and would not do any more for them, changed the name of the village "Palmer" to that of St. Clair, through petty spite or something. He had donated the public square and had built a court house and jail, while it was the county seat, that cost over $6,000. The question of moving the county seat to Port Huron was mooted during his lifetime, but he told them he would go for the public square and for the lot on which the court house was built if such a thing happened while he was on earth. The matter rested until after his death and then the transfer was made directly.

My uncle Thomas Palmer's varied interests in St. Clair County, and particularly in his village of Palmer, took him often to that locality. On one of these excursions I accompanied him. I was but a lad and delighted with the prospect of a long sleighride. We had it. The sleighing was fine, the ice in the Detroit River,

Lake St. Clair and River St. Clair was good. We started out in our one-horse French carriage, and took the river road to Grosse Pointe and Lake St. Clair. On reaching "Milk River" point on Lake St. Clair, which river empties into L'Anse Cruz Bay, Lake St. Clair, we struck right across the bay to about where New Baltimore now is. The bay puts miles into the land, as all know, and it was quite a venture to take the course we did, besides there was a slight flurry of snow, but not sufficient to blot out the shore of the bay.

WAS A LITTLE IN DOUBT.

My uncle was a little apprehensive, as he, in company with Mr. Jerome (Geo. Jerome's father), the winter before, had a rough time crossing this same bay. They were caught in a snowstorm and came near perishing, but General Brady with double sleigh and span of horses had preceded us about an hour before, on his way to Fort Gratiot. The tracks of his team and sleigh were plainly visible and we followed them closely and reached the opposite shore all right. We put up for the night at what is now New Baltimore, with a Frenchman by the name of "Yax," who kept a tavern there in a long, low log house. It was very comfortable, this log tavern, with its only one room divided off into sleeping rooms by curtain calico strung on wires, and a general room at the end of which was an immense fireplace, and a bar, where was dispensed the prevailing beverage, whisky. Yax and his companions played cards and caroused all night. They woke us up occasionally with their wrangling merriment.

We left in the morning bright and early for the village of Palmer. We halted a short time at Algonac, which was scarcely any town at all, to see Mr. Smith, a pioneer of that village. He almost overwhelmed us with his hospitality. I saw him often in after years. He was a nice gentleman, one of the old school, sported a ruffled shirt and all that. I think some of his descendants are prominent in Algonac yet. We also met on the way (after Algonac) and made a brief stop with each, Captain Sam Ward, Colonel Cottrell, Colonel Westbrook and Captain Wm. Brown. In front of Westbrook's residence the schooner Napoleon was on the stocks, nearly completed. Colonel Westbrook was building her for Oliver Newberry.

Westbrook was a noted character on the river in those days. It was said he had served under General Scott in the war of 1812, and that he had been captain of a privateer in the early part of that war. He was rugged appearing and of giant stature, reminding one of Captain Blake. I saw him often in after years and every time I saw him the conviction grew on me that he really might have been what they said, though it was no disgrace. We reached my Uncle George Palmer's log residence, one mile from Palmer, about dusk the second day out of Detroit.

This log house of my uncle's was situated on the bank of the river, just below where the Oakland now is, and was as primitive as it well could be. The logs were not hewn or squared, but in their native state; wooden latch to the door, with the "latch-string" always out. It boasted one luxury not found in all the log cabins of those days, and that was a brick chimney. It had an ample fireplace, of course, that would hold all the wood that could be piled on. Down stairs the "cabin" had three rooms, one general room and two sleeping rooms. Upstairs could boast only of one room and that directly under the rafters. This room was reached by a short ladder.

I became well acquainted with this room and the rest of the log cabin in after years. When about 12 years old my Uncle Thomas thought it would be a good thing for my general health to rough it on a farm. So I was sent to live for a short season with my uncle on the banks of the St. Clair. I did not make much of a fist at farming, but did the best I could and liked it fairly. My aunt, a New England girl, was kindness itself, and treated me in a most motherly fashion. My uncle was all right, too. After five or six months I contracted the fever and ague. This disease shook me up so, and hung on so persistently, that I was obliged to come home. I did not get rid of the pest for nearly a year. But I think my experience at farming in St. Clair and my tussle with the fever and ague were a lasting benefit, as I have never been sick over a day or two since.

ON THE WAY HOME.

We remained in Palmer (St. Clair) three or four days and then started for home. After reaching Yax's tavern, where we put up for the night, we skirted L'Anse Cruche Bay on the ice, instead of crossing it. On the shore of the bay, a short distance above the mouth of the Clinton River, which empties into it, the Indian chief, Macoonce, had his lodge. My uncle, who knew him quite well, called on him. He welcomed us cordially and seemed much pleased with the visit we made him. We also stopped for a warming on our way down at the tavern of Mr. Moross at the mouth of the Clinton River. The tavern was a large two-story frame building, with dormer windows and painted yellow, with white trimmings. It stood on the site of the once thriving village of Belvidere, and became a part of it. The tavern and Belvidere have both passed away, and I think scarcely a vestige remains. Belvidere was quite a village at one time, evolved through the brain and energy of Colonel James L. Conger, of Mt. Clemens. I visited there once for three or four days when it was in its prime. It boasted of quite a large warehouse and dock, a few stores and a number of substantial dwellings. My visit was to a friend who kept the lighthouse at the mouth of the Clinton at that time. He and his family lived in the village in a pretentious two-story house, and the surroundings seemed to bid fair for a healthy growth to the town, but something struck it, don't know what, and, as said before, it has vanished. Well, we reached Detroit all right, much pleased with the trip.

F. & P. PALMER.

STORY OF THEIR LARGE DEALINGS—COLONEL McKINSTRY, A. C. McGRAW, SAMUEL G. CASKEY AND OTHERS.

MY uncle, Mr. Palmer, also built for the Detroit & St. Joe Railroad, now the Michigan Central Railroad, a car track from the depot, where the city hall now is, down Woodward Avenue to Atwater Street, and along the latter street to the DeGarmo Jones warehouse. I don't just remember the year this was built, but it was before the Patriot war. This track, laid above the level of the street, made Woodward Avenue from the city hall to Jefferson Avenue awful in muddy weather. I have often seen loads of wood, etc., completely stalled in front of what is now the Merrill Block. Why the track was abandoned I do not know, but I always supposed it was because of this muddy business and the difficulty the locomotive had in getting up Woodward Avenue to Jefferson Avenue. I have seen the engine puff and snort, some time for half a day, before it could get up to the level of the latter street.

The firm got from the United States, in payment for building the court house, about eight thousand acres of land in the ten thousand acre tract, so-called, and three hundred city lots. The government reserved all the quarter sections on each side of Woodward Avenue and called them Park lots. F. & T. Palmer got the remainder. The ten thousand acre tract came down to the railroad crossing on Woodward Avenue, so it would seem; if they could have held the land until the present day what a good thing it would have been for their heirs.

LAND WAS SOLD CHEAP.

Most of the quarter sections near the city were cut up into five-acre lots and sold for from $7 to $8 per acre. The land in the back part of the tract, then almost a howling wilderness, they were glad to sell for from $3 to $4 per acre. The city lots, many on Woodward Avenue, sold for $300 and $400 each, being sixty feet front. The one that Metcalf brothers used to occupy was sold for $300. Many lots on Miami Avenue, near Grand Circus, sold for $75 each, also those adjoining West Park and so on. I merely mention this to show the difference in the prices asked for real estate then and now.

Next to the Palmer's store on Jefferson Avenue, was the residence of Judge John McDonnell, who occupied the upper part, and the lower was used by Mr. H. Griswold as a hat, cap and fur store, and by Brooks & Hartshorn, auctioneers; the cellar, by Thomas Owen, the brewer, for the storage of beer. Dr. Thos. B. Clark occupied the next building as an office; he also had a small stock of drugs and medicines. Next, Major Dequindre had his store and residence. He dealt largely in Indian goods and furs, and owned the Dequindre farm. Mr. Dequindre was a fine French gentleman, one of the old school.

Next to Mayor Dequindre's was the store of Gray & Noble. They kept a general stock of goods. Mr. Noble was quite a small man, while Mr. Elliott Gray, his partner, was of commanding presence, about six feet two inches tall, but slender. He always wore the conventional outer garments of black, a ruffled shirt, tall hat, etc. I think he always carried a cane. I remember these gentlemen well. The firm finally dissolved and Mr. Gray went into partnership with Mr. Gallagher in the forwarding business at the foot of Bates Street. I think the late Samuel Lewis and his brother Alex clerked for them at that time. Afterwards the firm was Gray & Lewis, and after that it was Lewis & Graves.

A POLITICAL MEETING.

The Palmer building on the corner of Jefferson Avenue and Griswold Street, after the fire that swept it away, gave place to a fine large four-story brick building erected by Lewis Goddard, that extended from Jefferson Avenue to the alley in its rear. In this building were located, on the corner of Jefferson Avenue, Charles Bissell, dry goods merchant; next to him, on the same street, were Enoch & Grif. H. Jones, also in dry goods. On the Griswold Street side, Colonel Edward Brooks had his office, as collector of the port, Jacob Farrand was his deputy. The second story was occupied as lawyers' offices, etc., the third and fourth stories were occupied by Colonel D. C. McKinstry for a museum and for theatrical purposes, lectures, political meetings, etc.

One political meeting there is in my mind quite vividly. The young men of the city had organized a party, irrespective of politics and had up a ticket for the city offices that they had pledged themselves to support. At the head of the ticket was the name of Curtis ("Curt") Emerson for mayor. At this meeting "Curt" was in the chair and when called upon for a speech, he gave one in his characteristic manner, ending up with: "Gentlemen, although the consumption is preying on my vitals, yet will I go with you to the brink of the grave, g—d d—n you."

Their ticket did not carry.

THE MUSEUM.

The museum, under the charge of the late William Adair, contained many rare and curious objects, among which were three Egyptian mummies, a fine collection of wax figures, also a variety of beautiful and rare specimens of birds, beasts, minerals, shells, etc.; with many interesting curiosities in nature and art. There were many splendid cosmoramic views, and in the evening phantasmagora and phantascopal illusions were exhibited. The museum was quite popular and a source of considerable revenue to the colonel.

Dramatic exhibitions of a light vaudeville character were given in the fourth story, and laughing gas was also administered to those who desired it. This giving of laughing gas was somewhat dangerous to the operator and to spectators as well. A partition extending from the floor to ceiling hemmed in the partaker of the gas from outsiders. Many funny incidents occurred connected with this pastime. While under its influence the partaker usually acted out his peculiarities or proclivities, laughing boisterously, dancing, boxing with an imaginary foe, declaiming, etc. It was quite a feature and always attracted a large crowd.

MAN OF MANY PARTS.

Colonel D. C. McKinstry, owner of the museum, was indeed a man of many parts, enterprising, public spirited and somewhat of a Bohemian. He was tall and heavily built, rather abrupt in manner and speech, yet of a warm, genial disposition which made him quite popular. He was fond of parade and show, was either a major or colonel in the militia—anyway, everyone used to call him colonel. He was engaged in many ventures, besides the theaters, and the Michigan Garden and Museum. Notably, he was associated with F. & T. Palmer in the contract with the general government for building the state capitol. After the work had made fair progress the other contractors bought him out and went on and finished the structure. Through them all he acquired considerable means. His success in most every venture led someone to call him "Silver Heels," a name that stuck to him through life. A fair representation of the colonel is given in the picture painted by Thomas Burnham entitled "Election Day at the Old City Hall," when Stevens T. Mason ran for governor against C. C. Trowbridge. This painting is, I think, in the possession of Mrs. General A. T. Williams, this city. Colonel McKinstry died in Ypsilanti in 1856, aged 78 years.

MC KINSTRY'S SONS.

Of the sons of Colonel D. C. McKinstry, Charles was a lawyer in New York City, and died there many years ago, of consumption. Augustus (Gus) sailed the lakes. I have mentioned him before in an article on the "Lake and River Marine," that appeared in the Sunday *Free Press* quite a while ago In it allusion was made to himself and Captain Robert (Bob) Wagstaff volunteering to take charge of Oliver Newberry's schooner Napoleon, loaded with provisions for the troops at Fort Mackinac, and the inhabitants of the island as well. Although in midwinter, their heoric and dangerous mission was successfully accomplished. James P. entered the navy, served through the Mexican war, as also the civil war, with distinction, rising to the rank of commodore. He at the outbreak of the rebellion brought the United States squadron stationed in the China Seas safely to this country. He at one time during the civil war had command of a gunboat on the Mississippi River, and, I think, was severely wounded in an encounter with the rebel batteries on shore. He was the second in command on the U. S. steamer Michigan when she first came out.

Elisha, after passing sufficient time at the law school in New York City, hied himself to California some time in the early '50s, became a judge, and is still alive and fairly active.

Another son, Justus, entered West Point and graduated, but into what branch of the service I do not know. After a while he entered the quartermaster's department, U. S. A., as captain and departmental quartermaster. I think he was in the Mexican war. Anyway, he served in the civil war, was Fremont's chief quartermaster at St. Louis, when organizing his army to invade the south. The transactions of his department were on a gigantic scale.

The McDonnell building that had been destroyed by fire was replaced by a wooden one and was used by Edward Bingham as a drug store (Jacob S. Farrand was at one time his clerk). He furnished Bingham's "Red Cordial" for summer complaints, and it is yet on sale at the various drug stores in the city. It was a great remedy then, and I think it is now.

A. H. Newbold and John W. Strong put up a three-story brick building on the site of Dr. Clark's former hardware store, Webb, Chester & Co., dealers in crockery and glassware, occupied a store somewhere along here before they moved to the Michigan Exchange building. It was the first of its kind in Detroit, crockery and glassware exclusively. John Chester some time afterwards went into the forwarding business on the dock. Major Dequindre retired from business and A. C. McGraw occupied part of the major's former premises with a boot, shoe and leather store, as did G. & J. G. Hill with drugs and groceries the other part.

MR. A. C. MC GRAW.

Mr. McGraw came here, I do not exactly know when, but he had been here two or three years or more when the fire of 1842 wiped out the his boot and shoe store. I remember his store quite well, from one circumstance, if from no other; and that was on the night of the fire mentioned, I was a member of fire engine company No. 4. Our machine was stationed at the reservoir, corner of Jefferson Avenue and Woodward Avenue (Merrill Block) and we had a line of hose run through McGraw's store to the alley in the rear. The fire progressed so rapidly that everything was in flames before the danger to the hose was fairly realized. Then the foreman sent four members of the company (of which I was one) to help the pipe man and his two assistants to drag the hose out of danger, which we did, and a warm and perilous job it was.

Samuel G. Caskey, late of the firm of A. C. McGraw & Co., was then a sturdy youth, just off the farm from somewhere down east, and serving his apprenticeship at the boot and shoe business.

He slept in the store on the counter, as all boys did in stores then, and on this occasion was suddenly awakened by the uproar, and rushed half dressed as he was, and barefoot at that, to Mr. McGraw's house on Congress Street and gave the alarm.

MEN WHO HAVE RISEN.

Caskey was a sturdy, awkward youth, not unlike some others that have commenced way down at the foot of the ladder and slowly and patiently won their way to the topmost round—as for instance John J. Bagley, Dexter M. Ferry, Philo Parsons, Moses W. Field, William N. Carpenter, Alex Lewis and many others that could be named.

I, myself, commenced way down the ladder, slept on the counter, swept out the store, took care of the horse, sawed and brought in the wood and all that, but somehow did not reach the top financially. The trouble was, I suspect, I was not saving; they were. Well, it's all right, anyway, and I have managed to get a heap of fun out of life.

I never knew Mr. McGraw personally very well, but knew of him and about him in the early days, through the late Edward C. Walker, who was a brother-in-law of his, he having married Walker's sister. "Ed" Walker, as we boys always used to call him, on his advent here entered the school of D. B. Crane, and in the higher and advanced classes; he was also a member of our young debating society, that wrestled weekly in the upper rooms of the school building with the stirring questions of the day. As Walker was so much further advanced than the rest of us, and apt to worst anyone pitted against him in debate, we concluded to hold him in reserve for lectures before the society, on subjects of interest to all. These lectures were very interesting and instructive, and were open and free to all. They were remarkably well attended and highly appreciated.

Another thing that somewhat interested me in Mr. McGraw, he married for his third wife a Miss Metcalf, who was a great friend of Sidney L. Rood and family, and they of her's. I being clerk in Rood's establishment at the time, my thought and attention were called more or less to the subject of this brief sketch. Something rather remarkable in Mr. McGraw's life was that he lived to celebrate the fiftieth anniversary of his wedding with his third wife.

OLD STOREKEEPERS

STORIES ABOUT INTERESTING CHARACTERS IN BUSINESS IN DETROIT FIFTY YEARS AGO.

THE Gray & Noble building, they having retired from the business, gave way to a fine large four-story brick building, with an attic. The store stood on a corner of Jefferson Avenue, and was occupied by Horace, Hallock & Raymond, as a clothing store, the next one by Mr. Warren as a candy and confectionery store. The entrance to the upper floors was on Jefferson Avenue, between these two stores. What use these upper floors were put to I do not remember, but I think that the top story and attic were used by the *Detroit Daily Advertiser* as a publication and printing office.

In the basement Mr. Howard kept a first-class saloon and restaurant. Previous to Mr. Howard, a jolly, rotund Parisian Frenchman, kept this restaurant. It was much frequented nights by the youth of the city to a large degree, and particularly the boys of No. 4 engine company. When the time between ordering refreshments, liquid or solid, seemed longer than usual and things got dull, he would say:

"Come boys, why for you no do som tings for make ze pot boil; you be one lot good for nottings."

I never knew what became of him. Howard was there in the same location when the fire of 1842 wiped the premises out.

Next to this building on Woodward Avenue was N. B. Carpenter's meat shop (Sheriff Thompson was interested with him for a while); the New York and Ohio House, formerly Arthur Bronson's Tavern, and the dwelling of Mrs. Colonel Anderson and Miss Taylor, her sister, on the corner of Woodbridge Street.

A HORRIBLE DEED.

An incident in relation to the atrocities committed by the Indians at an early day and with which this locality is in a measure associated, may not be out of place, and is from the pen of the late Judge B. F. H. Witherell.

"Among the many instances of the atrocities and horrid cruelty of the savages on our frontier was the murder of Mrs. Snow and child. Doctor Coleman, of Ashtabula, Ohio, saved her daughter. (Coleman was surgeon in the army under General Harrison). After the mother was killed Snow, at the commencement of the war, was living with his family at Pipe Creek, near Sandusky. He made maple sugar in that neighborhood, and to prevent his sap from being stolen, he had set some pitfalls, in which a few squaws had accidentally been caught. The savages, on the breaking out of the war, determined to kill him (Snow), and went to his shanty for the purpose, but he was absent; so they took all his family, with some neighboring women and children, prisoners, and started for the great scalp depots, Detroit and Malden.

"Mrs. Snow was enciente, and in feeble health. After proceeding a short distance they found that they could not well carry Mrs. Snow's youngest child, which was some two or three years old. A blow of the hatchet saved them any further trouble. The death (and such a bloody death) of her lovely child before her eyes, filled the mother's heart with unutterable agony. She struggled on with her demon captors a few yards, her strength gave way, and she fell to rise no more. The devils incarnate tomahawked and scalped her, and stripped her naked, jumped with their feet upon her naked body, jammed it in the mud, and left her.

BROUGHT TO DETROIT.

The children and other prisoners were brought to Detroit. One of Mrs. Snow's daughters, Electa, a girl of seventeen years, shortly afterwards (not knowing of the death of her mother, as they were separated at the time she was murdered) was standing at a window in Doctor Scott's house (afterwards Colonel Anderson's) on Woodward Avenue—where the Mariner's church now stands—and saw a party of Indians passing with her mother's scalp on a pole. She knew it by the long beautiful auburn locks, and cried out:

"Oh, my mother is killed, there is her scalp and there is her shawl on an Indian."

It was so.

This transaction was so horrible, that General Harrison not only reported it to the government, but issued a proclamation calling the attention of the world to the manner in which the war was carried on by the enemy.

In the rear of Mrs. Anderson's house was a barber shop, kept by an antiquated Frenchman, whom the boys had nick-named "Dusty." They used to steal his barber pole every chance they got and he got his name, I presume, from the manner in which he used to "dust" after them when he knew of the affair.

The museum corner, after the fire of 1842, was occupied by the Michigan Insurance Bank, H. H. Brown, cashier. This bank was the depository of the Michigan Central Railroad Company during the railroad conspiracy troubles. Having been warned that their funds might be in danger (as one of the gang had reported that, at one of their secret meetings, it was resolved that the bank should be raided in the near future) the bank provided a night watch consisting of Walter Ingersoll, assistant cashier; William L. Whippe, teller, and myself, an outsider, to fight off the robbers if they should make themselves manifest. We were provided with shotguns and revolvers as well as with dark lanterns. We had a cot bed made up against the vault door upon which we took turns napping it. This fun continued for two or three weeks, but no robbers put in an appearance, so we were mustered out. I really do not know what we would have done if they had made an attempt. There was no organized police force on duty night and day then.

O. M. Hyde occupied the rear of this building then as collector of customs, William Goodnow being his deputy. The stores along Jefferson Avenue erected after the fire of 1842 were occupied from time to time by John Palmer, dry goods; Henry Glover, merchant tailor; Graham & Lacey, dry goods; G. & J. G. Hill, drugs and groceries; H. P. Baldwin, boots and shoes; Moore & Bradford, dry goods; Hallock & Raymond, clothing, and the Farmers & Merchants Bank, on the corner of Woodward and Jefferson Avenues.

THE MARINER'S CHURCH.

Down Woodward Avenue, after the 1842 fire were Hiram Walker, groceries and liquors; Kirby, leather; Gleason F. Lewis, and David Preston, brokers and dealers in land warrants, etc., and the Mariner's or Bethel church, on the corner of Woodward Avenue and Woodbridge Street, which still holds its place there. This church was given the lot on which it was built, extending through to Griswold Street, and the money with which to build it, by Miss Taylor, the survivor of Mrs. Colonel Anderson. By the terms of the will, as I always understood it, the church was to be called the "Bethel," the seating was to be entirely free and devoted particularly to the use of the mariners and sailors on the lakes. I do not know that she endowed it, but the rents received from the stores underneath have always been sufficient, I imagine, to maintain a minister and a sexton. The Episcopalian church has always had this church under its special charge and control. The question of proprietorship, as to the rights of the Episcopalians in the premises, has sometimes, in the past, been mooted. I am not sure that the question has ever been fairly settled, but think it has been. I have always understood that there was no provision in the will of the testator that gave to any one denomination the exclusive right to run this church, but that the pulpit and seating were free to Protestant and Catholic alike.

Mr. Mason Palmer, who was one of the executors of Miss Taylor's will, was an "Episcopalian, of the Episcopalians," and, good man that he was, considered it a desecration of the pulpit of the Episcopalian churches to have any but the regularly ordained ministers of that denomination occupy them, and thus it was, I have always understood, that Mr. Palmer handed the control over to the Episcopalians, and as no one has taken the trouble to make a fuss about it this control still continues. In my mind it makes but little difference anyway what denomination controls the church, be it Protestant or Catholic, as long as the gospel is preached from its pulpit and the seats are free to all. Mr. Richard R. Elliott gives an exhaustive account of this business in one of the daily papers.

EARLY POSTMASTERS.

REMINISCENCES OF THE FIRST POSTOFFICE, JUDGE ABBOTT, JOHN NORVELL, SHELDON McKNIGHT AND OTHERS.

THE postoffice first occupied the store under the church on the corner of Woodward Avenue and Woodbridge Street, moving from its quarters in the basement of the Bank of Michigan building, that it had occupied for many years after leaving its quarters in the Sheldon Block. The postoffice continned there until Uncle Sam provided for it a home of its own, in conjunction with the United States custom office and the United States courts, on the corner of Griswold and Larned Streets, a home that was then considered ample for its uses for a score or more of years to come. But meantime the city had grown beyond, far beyond, its swaddling clothes and these then ample quarters were found too small to meet the demands of the public, so Uncle Sam, after five or six years of weary waiting, on the part of the city, provided another, a much larger and more magnificent home, into which the postoffice, the customs, judges and jury have lately moved.

The business of the courts and of the postoffice and customs has increased so within the five or six years that it took the government to build the new home, that the present quarters are now found to be too small to meet the wants of the public. There is ample room, however, for expansion on the square it occupies on the corner of Fort and Shelby Streets.

The first postoffice in Detroit under the federal government was establishment in the year 1796, with the late Judge James Abbott as postmaster. During his administration the office was kept in the river end of his residence on the southeast corner of Woodward Avenue and Woodbridge Street. Adjoining was a small red warehouse containing his stock of merchandise in bulk, and furs.

In the latter he was the largest dealer in the northwest, being agent of the Astors and the Northwest Fur Company. Mr. Abbott retained his position until 1830, when he was superseded by Mr. John Norvell, who retained the position till 1836, when he was elected United State senator. During Mr. Norvell's administration, the office occupied a small brick building then standing on Jefferson Avenue, midway between Wayne and Cass Streets, and adjoining his dwelling, on the southeast corner of Wayne Street, that had formerly been the residence of Henry I. Hunt, mayor of Detroit, in 1826. The little brick building used for the postoffice had been Mr. Hunt's private office. The latter was found to be too small to accommodate the increased business of the postoffice, so Mr. Norvell had the south end of his dwelling fitted up and converted into an office sufficient for his needs. The little brick building stood for many years, after the postoffice left it, and, as many will remember, was occupied by Mr. Berger as a gun shop until it was torn down to make way for the present brick block.

MR. SHELDON MCKNIGHT.

Mr. Sheldon McKnight succeeded Mr. Norvell in the office and moved its location in 1837 to the corner of Griswold Street, where C. & A. Ives formerly had their banking house for so many years. In 1839, under same postmaster, the office was removed to the Sheldon Block, fourth down Jefferson Avenue, same side. In 1841 Major Thos. Rowland, securing the appointment of postmaster, the office was again removed to the corner of Griswold Street in the basement of the then new stone structure erected by the Bank of Michigan for its own use. The building is now owned and occupied by the Michigan Life Insurance Company. During the administration of John G. Bagg, who succeeded Major Rowland, the office remained in the same location.

In 1850, under the administration of Colonel Alpheus T. Williams, the office was removed to the basement of the Mariner's church, then just erected on lower Woodward Avenue. It remained in this locality until the completion of the then new building at the corner of Larned and Griswold Streets. In the Mariner's church building, after Colonel Williams, came Thornton F. Broadhead, who succeeded him in 1853, and retained the office until July 1, 1857, when Cornelius O'Flynn was appointed. Mr. O'Flynn was superseded on the 10th of May, 1859, by Henry N. Walker, Esq., and it was under the latter's administration that the new building was finished, and he removed into it in January, 1860, and at noon on the 30th of that month it was thrown open to the public.

OPENING OF NEW POSTOFFICE.

I copy from *The Free Press* of January 31, 1860, a short account of the opening:

"At noon yesterday the spacious new building erected for the accommodation of the postoffice and other federal offices in this city, situated on Griswold Street, between Congress and Larned, was thrown open to the public. The portion intended to be ocenpied by the postoffice is so far completed as to permit of its immediate occupancy, and the business of that office will hereafter be conducted there. The occasion of the opening attracted a large concourse of people, hundreds of whom rushed into the corridor as soon as the doors were thrown open, each anxiously striving to be the first to get a letter from the new office. "The location of the boxes being somewhat different from those of the old office, of course, much confusion ensued, the pushing and rushing and hurrying and crowding reminding one of the scenes in California in olden times on the arrival of a mail from the Atlantic states. Everybody went to the office, whether they expected any mail or not, and made as much fuss in finding their boxes as though their dispatches were of the utmost importance. Throughout the day the excitement and curiosity were kept up to a considerable extent, the office being filled with persons desiring to secure eligible boxes or curiously inspecting the place."

The amount of labor performed in the Detroit postoffice at that date, the same paper says, can be estimated from a few general figures. There are fifteen mails received and the same numher sent away daily. These mails convey an average of over 15,000 letters, exclusive of the large amount of newspapers, books, packages of valuables and other articles transmitted through this channel. This amount of mail matter requires the use of from sixty to seventy-five large mail bags, which are received and sent away daily. The sale of postage stamps averages $100 per day. The department of registered letters, which is a comparatively new branch of the service, now occupies the entire time of one clerk, and having increased 125 per cent within the past year, promises soon to require additional force.

FOSSILS IN THE STONE.

Referring again to the Bank of Michigan building, attention is called to the quality or rather make-up or formation of the stone used in its construction. It seems to be a hard sandstone, capable of sustaining a high finish, but it is to the countless number of fossils it contains that particular attention is called. They have always been an interesting study to the curious and to the geologist as well, these specimens of extinct life that moved and had their being thousands and thousands of years ago and are imprisoned in this stone. The high finish given to the surface of the stone has brought out the presence of the fossils so as to be easily seen, particularly at the Jefferson Avenue entrance and in the pillars adorning it. Go and look at them, it will richly repay you.

The first animals that ever walked on the earth lived about twenty million years ago. Scientists call them "trilobites" and declare that they were undoubtedly the first animals that had legs. They were the ancestors of modern lobsters and crabs and great numbers of them have been preserved in the rocks in some parts of this country.

Quantities of them are found in the neighborhood of Cincinnati. Being clad in armor made of an imperishable substance known as "chitine," their forms have been preserved in a wonderful way, and, the mud in which they became buried having hardened into stone, they are dug out today by curiosity hunters, who call them "petrified butterflies" or else "fossil locusts."

OLD BUSINESS MEN

REMINISCENCES OF MANY MEN WHO SOLD GOODS IN DE-
TROIT LONG AGO—THE CAPTURE OF ANDRE.

IN 1827 and early thirties, directly opposite the Palmer building, on the corner of Jefferson Avenue and Griswold Street, was a two-story wooden building. I don't remember who occupied it at that time, but later on it was occupied by Mr. Dwight, the father of the late A. A. Dwight. He kept a miscellaneous stock of goods and lived on the corner of Woodward Avenue and State Street, where Rolshoven's jewelry store now is. Afterwards Stowell and Rood kept a bookstore there, having a book bindery upstairs. Stowell and Rood dissolved partnership and Rood remained there until he bought out Snow & Fisk. I don't remember who followed, but I think it was Banks, a colored man, with clothing. Spencer & Calhoun kept a fancy grocery store next door; they had on sale the first pineapples that I ever saw.

Next came Mrs. Calhoun, who kept a millinery shop; J. Hawley, harness and saddlery; Charles Piquette, jewelry and gold pens; Chase & Ballard, hardware, and C. Wickware & Co., drugs, liquors and groceries. Their store afterwards was occupied by Knight & Pitcher, with boots and shoes. Dr. Thomas B. Clark, with a drug store, occupied the corner of Woodward and Jefferson Avenues, after his forced removal by fire from across the street. Mr. M. Paulding had at one time a hardware store in this block and John B. Piquette had a jewelry store in the same building, as did also George Doty.

WERE TAILORS BY TRADE.

Garry Spencer and Mr. Calhoun were both tailors by trade and it seemed out of place for them to be in the grocery business. They dissolved partnership soon after and each went his way in the pursuit of his old calling. Mr. Chase, of Chase & Ballard, was a retired British officer, from Quebec. How he came to get into the hardware business with Mr. Ballard is not known, but they kept a large stock, did a large business and were quite successful. Mrs. Chase, a French lady, a native of Quebec, was a very charming and attractive woman and her daughter, Charlotte, was her counterpart. The latter married Dr. Casgrain, of Windsor, who since has been elected a member of the Dominion parliament; and their son is now quite a prominent attorney of Detroit. Mr. Chase was a quiet, dignified gentleman of small stature. Chase & Ballard were succeeded by F. A. Hickox. Mr. Chase built and owned the National Hotel (Russell House).

The two Piquettes were the sons of Mrs. Thomas Shelden, by her former husband and half brothers of Mrs. Storrs Willis and the late Mrs. Harry Guise.

Mr. Paulding's father was one of the three men who captured Major Andre during the revolution.

HOW THEY CAUGHT ANDRE.

Paulding used often to refer to the part his father played in the capture of Major Andre, not by any means in a self-asserting way, as much as did his friends. He being of a jovial, genial nature, was possessed of many friends. Indeed, nearly all the then small community knew him well.

Paulding's ancestor, it appears was the master spirit of the party that captured Andre (namely John Paulding, Isaac Van Wart and David Williams), and the only one that could read and write, and when they hailed Andre he (Paulding) advanced with present musket and bade him stand and announce his destination.

"My lads," he replied, "I hope you belong to our party."

They asked which party he meant.

"The lower party," he answered, and on their saying that they did, he betrayed an exultation that was unmistakeable.

"Thank God, I am once more among friends," he cried.

Paulding happened to have on a royal uniform at the time, which further mystified Andre. None but Paulding (as before mentioned), was able to read Arnold's pass which he produced, and he treated it with little respect after the previous avowal. Paulding said after, if he had pulled out General Arnold's pass first, he should have let him go.

SEARCHED HIM.

They at once proceeded to examine his person. He warned them of Arnold's displeasure, but they vowed they did not fear it, and while by their compulsion he threw off his clothing, piece by piece, Williams was deputed to the examination. Nothing appeared, however, till one boot was removed; then it was evident that something was concealed in the stocking.

"By——," cried Paulding, "here it is," and seizing the foot while Williams withdrew the stocking, three folded half-sheets of paper inclosed in a fourth indorsed "West Point" were revealed. The other foot was found similarly furnished.

"By ——," repeated Paulding, "he is a spy!"

They questioned him as to where he obtained these papers; but, of course, his replies were evasive. They asked him whether he would engage to pay them handsomely if they would release him and he eagerly assented. He would surrender all he had with him, and would engage to pay a hundred guineas or more, and any quantity of dry goods, if he were permitted to communicate with New York. Dry goods, it will be remembered, was the general term for articles peculiarly precious to our people. Paulding peremptorily stopped the conversation, swearing, determinedly, that not ten thousand guineas should release him. In answer to further questions Andre prayed them to lead him to an American post, and interrogate him no more.

It is also asserted that, but for the strong, energetic spirit of Paulding, there is a probability that Andre would have gotten off, and that his resolutions and sagacity are shown by the course pursued on this discovery. I will not go further into a detail of this disastrous affair, disastrous as far as Andre and the British cause were concerned, as all school boys and girls throughout the land, as well as the average citizen, are familiar with the story. But I presume it is with them, as it is with me, the account of Andre's capture and unfortunate fate is ever new.

JULIUS ELDRED.

Julius Eldred, in the latter thirties, erected a block of three brick stores on the north side of Jefferson Avenue, between Woodward Avenue and Griswold Street, and removed his hardware store to one of them, his son Elisha and Mr. Marvin joining him. Another son, Anson, with Mr. David French, continued the ground plaster, French burr millstone, lumber and wood business at 84 Atwater Street, in the "blue building."

Randolph Brothers occupied one of the stores with wholesale dry goods, the first of its kind in Michigan. There were four brothers, bachelors to their life's end. They were a gay, genial, hospitable quartet, bon vivants if you will, and for whom Nancy Martin saved her choicest tid-bits. Whether they made much money, or what became of them, I never knew, but from about 1835 to 1845 or '6, they were quite in the public eye.

After occupying the corner of Jefferson and Woodward Avenues for awhile, Dr. Clark was burned out and a four-story brick building was erected on the place by the owner of the lot, Barnabus Campau or "Labie" Campau, as he was sometimes called. This building was occupied by A. C. McGraw & Co., boots and shoes, for many years; afterwards by M. S. Smith & Co., with a jewelry store. They also remained there for many years.

On the Merrill block site, in the early '30's, was a brick building owned by Robert Smart and occupied by the dry goods merchant, Henry Disbrow, afterwards by a Scotch gentleman with the same line of goods (I have forgotten his name); then by M. M. Brown as a clothing store, and finally by Campbell & Jack and Campbell & Linn, dry goods merchants. All will remember Colin Campbell and James Jack and Mr. Linn. The last named is with us yet, a fine, courteous gentleman, who has quite recently retired from the employ of Newcomb, Endicott & Co., after many years of service with them. Aug. L. Wells was on this corner in 1847. He sold dry goods.

MAKERS OF DETROIT.

ALEX. McFARREN, PETER J. DESNOYERS AND HENRY S. ROBY, EARLY BUSINESS MEN OF THE CITY.

AROUND these four corners—Jefferson and Woodward—and in the immediate vicinity for many years ebbed and flowed the life of the city. It was its business center, and to be located far from it, even in a small way, meant disaster. Adjoining Campbell & Linn, Alex McFarren kept a book and stationery store. Mr. McFarren had been a boss carpenter, but went into the book and stationery business. He secured the agency of the American Bible and Tract Society publications, and being a Presbyterian, easily obtained nearly all the patronage of that denomination. He was a fine, genial man and enjoyed a large trade from the general public as well. After some years in the business, having secured a competency, he retired to his comfortable home out Woodward Avenue, and passed the remainder of his days in quiet. He had for principal clerk a very popular young man, Frank Brainard, who drew a large amount of custom, particularly from the younger portion of the community, in want of school books, etc. He was a brother of Mrs. McFarren, as also of Mrs. A. E. Hathon. There are many, no doubt, who will call to mind the persons I have mentioned. The late Don C. Henderson, editor of the Allegan *Journal,* was a clerk in McFarren's book store for quite a while, before he joined the editorial staff of the New York *Tribune,* under the tutelage of Horace Greeley.

Next to McFarren Pierre, Teller kept a store, having for sale drugs, wines and liquors, and next to him George Wales had a wholesale liquor store. Some now living may perhaps call to mind George Wales. He was a short, chunky, genial chap, not unlike the late William P. Moore, whom many will remember, I know. Wales kept an extensive stock of liquors and sold cheaply. I recall that he had a particular make of brandy that he sold by the barrel for 75 cents per gallon to the trade and to the tavernkeepers in the interior of the state. If any of the latter's guests desired to "wet their whistles" (and most all of them did) and made any objection to the "goods" handed out, the proprietor would say, "Why, that is George Wales's best, and cost me 75 cents a gallon." What more could be said?

On the site of Mr. Desnoyers's residence William and J. E. King had a clothing store, and next was the Desnoyers Block.

Peter J. Desnoyers was born in Paris, France, on the first of August, 1772. He received an excellent education and served with his father as a silversmith until he was 18 years of age. Just previous to the French Revolution a company had been formed in America known as the Sciota Land Co., which opened an agency at Paris, and offered large inducements to mechanics and artisans of moderate means to invest in its lands. It was represented that they were eligibly located on a large stream called "La Belle River," abounding with fish of an enormous size, embracing magnificent forests, filled with wild game; that there were no military enrollments and no quarters to find for soldiers. A large number of mechanics and artisans were allured by such represensations to invest in these lands, and many of them came over and took up their abode here.

Mr. Desnoyers made some purchases for his son, Peter J., who, with many others, stimulated by a spirit of adventure, and influenced by the political disturbances at home, embarked in an emigrant vessel, and after a voyage of 60 days reached Havre de Grace, Md., and thence proceeded to Gallipolis, Ohio, which was said to be within the company's domains. They arrived there in 1790. Upon reaching this spot they found that the title deeds which they held were worthless, the company of whom they purchased not owning a foot of the land they had sold. They had parted with all their worldly goods, merely to reach a wilderness, in the midst of a people of whose language, manners and customs they were ignorant and at a period when the Indians were carrying death and destruction to most every white man's home. They endured many hardships and privations, and had frequent struggles with the hostile savages, which resulted in the death or capture of many of their number. One of the emigrants, a Mr. Melcher, of the same profession as Desnoyers, was missing for a long time, and it was thought he had been killed by the Indians. A few years afterwards Mr. Desnoyers met his old friend at a French farm house in Springwells. Melcher had been purchased from the Indians by some of the Canadian French on the Detroit frontier, and thus his life had been saved. The meeting between the two friends was of the most cordial character.

The French settlement at Gallipolis did not flourish. A few of the emigrants remained there and cultivated the ground according to the limited knowledge and skill which they possessed. But the Sciota Land Company failed entirely, and the settlement was ultimately broken up. Mr. Desnoyers went to Pittsburg, whence, in company with Michael Dousman, a well-known merchant of Mackinac, he accompanied Wayne's army, it then being on its way to the northwestern territory. He arrived in Detroit in June, 1796, being then 24 years of age. In July of the same year his services were called into requisition by the government as an armorer, his commission being signed by Colonel Hamtramck. He continued in the service as an armorer until November, 1803, when he resumed the business of silversmith, manufacturing chiefly Indian silverware, and trinkets, so highly valued by the savages. He formed a copartnership with John B. Piquette, the father of the late John and Charles Piquette, and first husband of the late Mrs. John P. Sheldon.

The firm carried on a successful business as jewelers and silversmiths until the great fire of 1805, when they dissolved. Mr. Desnoyers lost nearly all his earnings, the result of his industry and prudence for nine years.

WHEN LOTS WERE CHEAP.

After the fire, Jefferson and Woodward Avenues and that portion of the city from Griswold Street to Randolph and north to Adams Avenue, was surveyed and regularly laid out into lots. These lots were the property of the United States, and were sold at auction. The highest price of the most eligible lots in the city was seven cents per square foot, and the whole average, not more than four cents. Mr. Desnoyers purchased the lot or lots on the corner of Jefferson avenue and Bates Street, now occupied by the buildings known as the Desnoyers Block, where he erected a small building, one story high, and an attic with dormer windows. It had two wings, in one of which, for some years, he kept a general store, and in the other carried on his business as silversmith.

The Desnoyers Block also occupied the site of another building of brick, built a few years after the wooden one. This latter was designed for a dwelling and for store purposes as well, and was occupied some time after 1825 or 1826. Anyway, the two structures were standing there in the early thirties. The old wooden homestead was trundled off to Beaubien Street, beyond Congress, where it "held the fort" for many years. The brick one was torn down when the present block was built.

Mr. Desnoyers was about the first merchant here (that I remember), to keep marbles, the delight of the average boy's heart in the early days, and I presume they possess the same charm for those of the present day. All the boys attending the old University School on the corner of Bates and Congress Streets, nearly, used to patronize him extensively. I myself squandered many a penny for marbles at the old gentleman's store.

Aside from marbles, Mr. Desnoyers kept in his store as great a variety of articles as possible. It was a common remark, when a citizen was in quest of an article that was difficult to be obtained elsewhere, that it could be found at Desnoyers's, which generally turned out to be true. This became so proverbial that on one occasion a gentleman made a wager with another that he could name an article that Desnoyers could not furnish. It was agreed. They entered the store, and one of them very seriously inquired of the salesman of versatile resources if he had any goose-yokes. "Oui, monsieur," was the prompt reply, and he proceeded to a drawer and produced the article asked for. The merriment of the party was beyond reasonable bounds, Mr. Desnoyers entering as heartily into it as his customers.

FINE CHARACTERISTICS.

Mr. Desnoyers's personal habits were plain. He was a man of great perseverance and industry, of strict integrity, and was a devoted Catholic. He was quite facetious and jovial, and never failed to perpetrate a good jest when occasion called for it, and no man perceived more readily the point of his own jokes and laughed more heartily at them when uttered. For many years previous to his death he lived in affluence and ease in the fine brick house which he, on retiring from business in 1835, purchased from the Frances P. Browning estate, situated on the corner of Larned and Griswold Streets, where is now the old postoffice building. This fine mansion was built by Mr. Browning for his own use. He was a merchant well known here many years, for the philanthropy and the zeal with which he supported his political opinions. He was also the head and front of the Baptist church here, and he was, besides, an Abolitionist of the most radical stamp. He died in 1834, of the cholera.

Mr. Desnoyer's house was the center of attraction for many of our most refined citizens. The elegant, old-fashioned furniture and plate, costly wines and luxurious tables were suggestive of wealth, good taste and pleasant associations.

Mr. Desnoyers died suddenly at his residence on Griswold Street on the 3d of June, 1846, aged 74 years. He left a handsome estate which was divided among his heirs. Some of them or their survivors are with us yet.

HENRY S. ROBY.

Perhaps none of the present day will remember Henry S. Roby, a contemporary of Shubal Conant, Peter T. Desnoyers, Thomas Palmer, Oliver Newberry and other merchants who flourished here in 1810-11-12. He was an enterprising citizen (the father of Henry M., John S. and Reuel Roby), and I think built the first private wharf in Detroit. At one time during his business career, there was a scarcity of small change, and Mr. Roby initiated a system of shinplasters, which became quite current. Mr. Roby had occasion to visit Monroe, and the landlord at whose hotel he stopped, not knowing him, in the course of conversation, inquired somewhat anxiously about the Detroit shinplaster system and Roby's responsibility. Roby's reply was brief and rather equivocal; in fact, he expressed strong doubts whether "this man Roby was worth a damn cent."

"I have in my pocket," said he, "a considerable amount of his shinplasters, and though they seem to pass current in the community, I doubt whether they will ever be redeemed. I have often been tempted to burn the damn things, and I'll tell you what I will do. I have more of them than you have; yet, if you will burn yours, I'll do the same thing, and then we will get rid of the trash." He had no idea that the landlord would asquiesce, but he did. "Done!" said he. Roby deposited his in the stove; the landlord did the same. Roby enjoyed the joke quietly, but said nothing. A few days afterwards Mr. Desnoyers, General Cass and other distinguished citizens of Detroit, visited Monroe, and Roby's shinplasters again became the subject of discussion—the landlord,

I believe, refusing to receive them. Mr. Desnoyers assured him that they were current and that Roby was sound. Said mine host, in reply: "I am informed by a gentleman from Detroit that they are worthless, and he and I burned up several dollars' worth the other day." A description of the gentleman from Detroit was demanded and Mr. Roby's unmistakable physiognomy and dress were described. The company were convulsed with laughter.

Upon their return to Detroit Desnoyers had his fun. Said he to the shinplaster banker: "Vy you burn up your bills, eh? You tink 'em no good, I suppose. I give you Michigan bank bills for all of dem, if you burn de Michigan bank bills, too." Roby declined the proposition and his shinplaster exploit was a standing joke for a long time.

MEN OF THE FORTIES.

ANOTHER CHAPTER OF INTERESTING REMINISCENCES OF DETROIT IN EARLIER DAYS.

PIERRE TELLER had a store in the Desnoyers Block at the corner of Jefferson and Woodward Avenues when he first came to Detroit, and afterwards he located further down the street. His new location used to be headquarters for many notables of that day (the late '40s) and among them were David Smart, James A. Van Dyke, Doctor J. H. Farnsworth, Doctor Rufus Brown, Doctor J. B. Scovill, Tom Edmonds, John McReynolds, Doctor W. Egge, Walter Ingersoll, Theo. Williams, and Edgar Randolph. He had for clerks at that time Henry N. Munson and Robert Dermont. The former, after leaving Teller, went into the insurance business and continued in it until his death. Dermont went into the drug and liquor business on the northwest corner of Woodward Avenue and Congress Street and continued there until he died.

Doctor Ware had his office over Teller's store, as did Doctor J. H. Farnsworth. Doctor Ware was a dentist of great skill. The late Doctor J. H. Farnsworth learned the profession of dentist from him, and all know what a skillful practitioner he was, and how he would joke and jolly a fellow when it hurt. He had me in chancery occasionally, and I can speak by the card. Aside from his social and genial qualities, the doctor's loss was keenly felt by the large number of our citizens who had for years and years looked upon him as the only dentist and would have none other. But I presume they have become reconciled ere this.

Doctor M. Ware went to New York City many years ago, became quite wealthy and had houses and lands. Along in the early fifties I visited New York quite often and used to see and hear of the doctor through Geo. F. Macey (once of the firm of Macey & Driggs), who was located in New York and carried on a general agency there—insurance, collecting, rents, etc. He had quite a number of houses under his charge in different parts of the city belonging to the doctor, and he busied himself chasing up the tenants.

C. & J. Wells occupied the next store with groceries and liquors. My first experience in clerking was with this firm in 1837-8. I slept on the counter, took care of the horse, sawed and brought in all the wod, swept out the store and was a general all-around coarse hand clerk. I enjoyed it very much, though; having worked on a farm two or three years I was used to roughing it and did not mind it a bit. Besides I was my own master after the store closed and could go to the theater, of which I was passionately fond, as often as I liked.

It was an interesting situation in one respect; the store was the headquarters, so to speak, of the Brady Guards, then just forming, and I seemed to live in an air of excitement constantly.

Doctor Edwin Desnoyers later on occupied the store on the corner of Bates Street and Jefferson Avenue with a stock of drugs, etc. The C. & J. Wells store was, in 1844, occupied as a book and stationery store by C. Morse & Son. C. Morse & Son came from Canandaigua, N. Y. The father had been for years in the same line of business with his brother-in-law, Jas. D. Bemis, in the above place. The firm of Bemis & Morse was well and familiarly known throughout the state of New York and all along the lakes. They were extensive manufacturers of blank books, and during the early days—say from 1818 to 1830—furnished nearly all the blank books and office stationery needed by the merchants here and Mackinac. The firm of F. & T. Palmer alone seemed to me to have a cart load of ledgers, journals and day books made by this firm.

C. Morse & Son did an extensive business in their line. Wells & Co.'s Western Express had their office with this firm—the first regular express office established in this city. Daniel Dunning was the agent and resident partner. This express company was afterwards merged into the American Express Co.

Morse & Son after many years retired from business; the father to his quiet home on Selden Avenue, this city, where he died not many years ago. Charles entered the service of the Michigan Central Railroad Co., in whose service he died four or five years ago. Charles was musically inclined; indeed, very much so. I used to tell him he was always at it. He was a modest, quiet, retiring, genial gentleman, as all who knew him will bear witness. There were two daughters that Mr. Chauncey Morse brought here with him from Canandaigua. Jane, the eldest, married Geo. G. Bull, a member of the Detroit bar and clerk of the United States court. George was also an enthusiastic Brady Guard and divided the honors of being the handsomest man in the corps with Chas. C. Penny. Mr. Bull died many years ago, as did his wife, leaving a daughter, who, I think, is at present employed in the Detroit postoffice. The other daughter of Mr. C. Morse (Sarah) married Lawyer Van Rensaeler, of the Detroit bar. The latter died many years ago. Mrs. Van R. is still living.

I understand that Geo. G. Bull's portrait, painted full length in the unifrom of the Brady Guard, is in the possession of his daughter.

THE DESNOYERS HEIRS.

INTERESTING HISTORY OF THE DESCENDANTS OF ONE OF DETROIT'S PROMINENT EARLY SETTLERS.

THE upper part of the Desnoyers Block was used for offices as well as for bachelors' sleeping rooms. John Webster, hardware merchant, had a suite of rooms here, called "Crimson Hall," from the color of the paper used in decorating the walls. Zeke Truesdail (brother of Wesley), L. W. Tinker, Mr. Abbott, Thomas Edmunds and others also had rooms in the same block. Sometimes they and their friends used to make things quite lively in the old building.

THE DESNOYERS HEIRS.

Peter Desnoyers was the eldest son, the next was Charles and the next was Frank. They assisted the father in the store until he went out of business. Peter went into business on his own account, and at the same time looked after his father's affairs. In 1821 he married a daughter of Judge Leib, a sparkling, brilliant brunette. They had two children, Edmund and Emelie (Totts). Peter's second wife was Annie Hunt Whipple, daughter of Captain John Whipple, U. S. A., and sister of Chief Justice Charles Whipple, Kate, a daughter of this second marriage, became the wife of J. Newton Powers, Fanny, another daughter, married William B. Moran, son of Judge Charles Moran.

Peter Desnoyers held many offices of public trust, particularly that of state treasurer for two terms. He died in 1880, widely known and widely lamented for his sterling qualities of head and heart. A truly good man.

Marie Rose, a daughter of Peter J., who I never saw, married in 1817, Louis Dequindre, brother of Major Antoine Dequindre.

Emilie, another daughter, married Louis Leib. She died young and left no heirs. Victoire married in 1825 Henry S. Cole, a most able lawyer, from Canandaigua, N. Y., who had settled here. They had three sons and four daughters. Marie Louise married Eben N. Wilcox; Isabelle died a nun of the Sacret Heart; Marie Antoinette and Harriett S. never married, but their beautiful and pious lives were a repetition of that of the mother and grandmother.

Elizabeth Desnoyers married, in 1835, James A. Van Dyke, one of the most brilliant lawyers of his time, who died before he had fulfilled the bright expectations his talents promised, and who left a large family, as follows: George W., married Fanny Perley, widow of Charles Piquette; Marie D., married Wm. Casgrain, a member of that distinguished family of Canada. They did reside at Milwaukee, Wis.

Philip James Desnoyers married, first, Marion King, a daughter of Daniel King, of Green Bay, and niece of Mrs. Geo. Doty, of Detroit, and second, Sarah Beeson, daughter of Jacob Beeson, produce dealer of this city. He was one of the most known lawyers Detroit has ever produced, inheriting in an eminent degree the brilliant talents of his father. When he came to be prosecuting attorney of Wayne County he was a terror to evil doers, and they stood in awe of him. He had the misfortune to become quite bald in early life, and adopted no means or device to conceal the defect; and it is reported of him that on one occasion a number of criminals were lined up at the county jail, to be escorted to the court room, in order to learn their fate, when a chap standing by whose time had not come, but had evidently been in limbo before, said: "Now, boys, mind your eye, if that bald-headed cuss down at the court room gets after any of you, you are gone, sure;" and it was pretty often the case. He died in the flower of his age.

Rev. Ernest D. Van Dyke is the very worthy and respected pastor of the Pro-Cathedral (St. Aloysius), Detroit. Josephine D. Van Dyke married Henry F. Brownson, an officer in the United States army. He resigned in 1871, became a lawyer and partner of Philip Van Dyke. He is a son of the celebrated writer, D. Orestes Brownson. Victoria Van Dyke is a nun of the Sacred Heart order. Elsie Van Dyke married Wm. B. Moran, son of Judge Moran, as before mentioned. She died in 1874, leaving one child, Catherine, who married Strathearn Hendrie.

Charles Desnoyers, son of Peter J., went into the forwarding and commission business on the dock with Shadrich Gillett (Gillett & Desnoyers). Many will remember the old firm. They remained together many years. He married Elizabeth Knaggs, of the well known Knaggs family that lived down the river. A beautiful girl she was, with such a wealth of golden hair. The wedding was a brilliant affair. The knot was tied in St. Anne's Church, on Larned Street. I was present at the ceremony and remember it well. It seems to me that Father Richard officiated on the occasion. Charles was a tall, handsome man; and together they made a very fine looking couple, indeed.

Francis Desnoyers married Louise Baird, of Erie, Pa., and settled at Green Bay, Wis. His children still reside there. I knew Frank better than any of the other Desnoyers boys. He was of a jovial, kindly disposition, much like his father. He invariably came to see me when he visited Detroit, which he often did.

Josephine Desnoyers married Professor Henry Barnard, of Hartford, Ct. Mr. Barnard was at one time president of St. John's College, Md., chancellor of the University of Wisconsin, and United States commissioner of education. One son and two daughters are the children of this marriage. The son, Henry, an accomplished, studious gentleman, took up his residence in Detroit, and entered the law. I understand he was quite successful and gained distinction. He married, in 1878, Kitty, daughter of Judge Chas. Moran and Justine McCormack. He died some years ago. His widow survives him.

The two children of Marie Rose Desnoyers, who married Louis Dequindre in 1817, were Annie and Henry P. The former married Edward A. Lansing, who for many years was in the insurance business here, at one time a partner of Ben Vernor's, and later a partner of Anderson, under the firm name of Lansing & Anderson. The latter firm dissolved and Lansing continued the business until he died. Four or five children were the fruit of this union—three boys and two girls, I think. One of the daughters married Judge Riley, some years ago. I do not now know what became of the others. We all know the happy, contented life the judge and his wife lead.

There are very many of the present day, who I am sure, will call to mind "Ed" Lansing and his agreeable and gentlemanly personality, as I do; as also his brother, "Gat" Lansing, who was one of the same stripe. The latter was engaged in business here, the nature of which I do not just now remember, but he was somewhat conspicuous from the fact that he was the "Grand High Priest" of that mystic order, the Druids—which afterwards merged into the Sons of Malta, another mystic order.

Henry Dequindre and his sister, Annie, lived with their grandfather after the death of their father and mother. Henry was a schoolmate of mine, a handsome, bright, intelligent boy. After leaving school he was for many years clerk for Mason Palmer, and then for Palmer & Holmes, with whom he continued until they retired from business. What business he followed after that I do not call to mind. He married and, after a brief married life, he died in this city. His widow secured a clerkship in some department in Washington, where she was only a few years ago.

Emelie (Totts) Desnoyers, daughter of Peter, married, as I said before, Professor F. Allerie. At this wedding Senator Palmer was the professor's best man. Edmund, the brother of Mrs. F. Allerie, after passing the usual time here at school, was ambitious to be a doctor of medicine, so his father sent him to the Philadelphia Medical College, where, after the stated period, he capturd his "sheepskin." On his return here he practiced his profession only to a very limited extent. He at once opened a drug and prescription store on the corner of Bates Street and Jefferson Avenue (Desnoyers Block), where he continued until he died, many years ago. The doctor was a very companionable, genial man, and a favorite with all. He was also an accomplished druggist and chemist. Many will, no doubt, call him to mind, and remember what a neat dresser he was, after he returned from Philadelphia. His attire was stunning, particularly in waistcoats, scarfs and cravats. But for all that he was a fine, all around good fellow.

Of the sons of Henry S. Cole and Victorie Desnoyers, Augustus Porter went with the First Regiment, Michigan Volunteers, to Mexico in the sutler's department. While there he contracted typhoid fever, which hung on to him until after his return and which after a time caused his death. Chas. S. studied law with his uncle, James A. Van Dyke. I cannot say that he was admitted to the bar. He, however, never practiced the profession. Many will remember him and his companionable, genial ways. He died many years ago, unmarried, and much lamented, at his sister's (Mrs. E. N. Wilcox) house, out Woodward Avenue (Wilcox farm). Henry S. died when quite a youth, of consumption.

Referring again to Josephine Desnoyers and Annie Dequindre, I am reminded of the last rites of the church on the occasion of the funeral and burial of Father Richard. I was present at Ste.

Anne's during the ceremony, and also at the burial of that saintly priest, as was almost the entire community, without regard to creed. But out of all that great concourse of mourners, I fail to call to mind but two, and they were these young maidens I mention. After all these years, I seem to see them as I saw them then, both at the church and at the grave, overwhelmed with grief. At the grave they lingered long, as did many others, after the body had been deposited in its temporary resting place. I lingered with the rest and could not help but remark, boy that I was, the deep and almost uncontrollable sorrow shown by these two young girls at the loss of their spiritual father, who had always been near and dear to them from their earliest youth until his death.

I am indebted for a large number of incidents in the life of Mr. Peter J. Desnoyers to an article published in a Detroit paper in 1863, from the pen of Mr. Geo. L. Whitney, who many years before was the editor of a daily paper here (the name of which has escaped my memory). The article in question was kindly loaned to me by Rev. D. M. Cooper.

I am also indebted for many facts in regard to the descendants of Peter Desnoyers to that charming and interesting volume, "Legends of Detroit," the author of which was that bright and accomplished daughter of the late Mrs. Eliza Watson (nee Godfroy), Mrs. Caroline Watson Hamlin, whose early death was so widely and so deeply regretted.

RECOLLECTIONS OF MEN PROMINENT IN THE CITY'S AFFAIRS.

THE store on the corner of Bates Street and Jefferson Avenue, opposite the Desnoyers Block, was occupied by Campbell & Goodell (H. M. Campbell, father of the late Judge Campbell). William Brown occupied the dwelling adjoining. It boasted of a very pretty front yard, filled with roses, etc.; also had fine shade trees in front. Mr. Howard Webster occupied it as a residence some time after. Mr. Webster, as many will call to mind, was quite a florist, and was given to raising rare plants and flowers; among the latter was the night blooming cereus. The specimen he had was a fine one, and when the time for its flowering approached, he gave notice that on the nights, naming them, when the plant would be in full bloom it would be on free exhibition in his parlors. The plant did show itself in all its fragrance and glory, as all will remember who saw it. I never saw one before nor since, and all had to thank the gentleman for the rare treat he so generously gave.

Further along, Wilcox & Beach, at an earlier day, had a hat store, and next to them a Mr. Swan kept a tavern. Counsellor O'Keefe resided along here next to the present Kearsley residence (the latter still standing). Freedman & Goodkind were doing business along here later. Major Kearsley had his residence next, beyond Doctor Brown's, before he built on the corner of Randolph Street. Freedman & Goodkind were the first merchants in Detroit to order goods from New York by express in the winter. They dealt largely in ladies' trimmings, embroideries, jet goods, laces and fine fancy goods. Every trip the express messenger made to this city during the winter he carried one or more bales for this firm. This was an innovation in the dry goods business here and it established their reputation to such an extent that the firm sought larger quarters on Woodward Avenue and afterwards became the extensive dry goods house of Freedman Brothers that many will remember. Along here some years later Doctors Bissell and Lauderdale had a drug store. They also practiced their profession, and enjoyed a large share of patronage. They were very genial, companionable young men. Doctor Bissell married the sister of Mrs. Theo. A. Eaton, and what became of them I have forgotten. Doctor Lauderdale, on the breaking out of the civil war, entered the service as assistant surgeon Twenty-fourth Michigan Infantry, and served to the end of the rebellion.

The present Kearsley house occupied the old Bank of Michigan site (standing in 1827).

COUNSELLOR O'KEEFE.

Counsellor O'Keefe was an eminent Irish barrister, brim full of wit and repartee. He kept bachelor's hall and continued to until after the arrival of his maiden sister from Ireland, who, after the counsellor's death, married Judge Strong. I used to see much of the counsellor in the early thirties, as he frequently visited the office of my uncle in the Cooper Block that I have mentioned before. Robert Abbott, auditor-general, and A. E. Hathorn had their offices in the same room. He was always interesting and at that time was just past his prime. It appeared that previous to his departure from Ireland he had a misunderstanding with some of his fellow students and had it out with them on the college green in Dublin, and, as he said, he quit the latter place in disgust but not in disgrace. In relating the circumstance and also the tame reception the bar of Detroit gave him when he came to this city, he would warm up with the subject, and with passionate eloquence he would give them all particular fits. He was of commanding presence, over six feet tall and straight as a poplar, and with his ample cloak thrown across one shoulder, his right arm free, he would stride up and down, gesticulating and rolling out his adjectives, to the intense wonder and amusement of his audience, myself included. He died poor, I think, but left a memory that is cherished by relatives now here. He was a member of the legislature before the removal of the state capitol to Lansing, and always when he had occasion to address the house he kept them in a roar of laughter. He was quite as witty as "Willie" Gray (whose relative he was), which is saying a great deal.

O'Keefe was at one time in the early days prosecuting attorney of St. Clair County, and this is how it came about. The story is taken from the "History of St. Clair County," published in Chicago in 1883, and is as follows:

"At a very early date, about 1820, O'Keefe came to Detroit. He was a liberally educated and thoroughbred lawyer, but was extremely intemperate in his habits. His drinking sprees were frequent, sometimes lasting for weeks. He became acquainted with Judge Bunce, of St. Clair County, visiting him often, sometimes prolonging his visits for weeks, and through the judge's influence became prosecuting attorney for the County of St. Clair. O'Keefe on one of his visits to Judge Bunce, expressed a wish to represent St. Clair in our legislative council at the next sitting, and he stated that the judge favored his election, which was doubted by the leading men of the county. In the following year O'Keefe came up from Detroit to canvass the county, and made his first call on the father of Anna P. Stewart. He introduced his subject by stating that he had quit the use of intoxicating liquors, that he had decided on thorough reformation, and was about to take up his abode permanently in St. Clair County. Relying on his reformation and ability, he had come to offer himself as a candidate to represent our county in the legislature. In reply Mr. Stewart said: 'Counsellor, I am glad to hear of your proposed reformation, and as to your abilities, no one can doubt them. Come and make your home among us for one year, and give us proof of your reformation, and there is not the least doubt that you will become a favorite among the people, who will certainly give you their hearty support; but to be candid, counsellor, I must insist upon one year's reformation before I can give you my support.'

At this O'Keefe became angry and said: "Sir, I wish you to know I was educated at two of the best seminaries in England, and I was bred at the Irish bar; and, sir, .I can write your governor down."

After this outburst of passion there was a pause. Mr. Wolverton who was present remarked:

"Counsellor, you remind me of the story of the calf who sucked two cows."

"Indeed," said O'Keefe, "and what of that, sir?"

"Nothing in particular," said Wolverton, "only it is said the more he sucked the larger he grew."

At this remark O'Keefe smiled and became apparently good natured, when the three went into a calm discussion of the matter. Mr. Stewart and Wolverton tried to convince him that Bunce did not intend to support him, but on the other hand was seeking his own election. O'Keefe said: "It may be so, but if I thought there was such deception in professed friends, I would throw myself on the mercy of the Lord."

From the first organization of St. Clair County up to 1830, O'Keefe practiced in the county court, most of the time as prosecuting attorney. A soldier at Fort Gratiot had murdered a comrade, and was delivered over to the authorities for trial; at the time Judge Sibley, of Detroit, was the circuit judge, and O'Keefe prosecuting attorney. This was the first time that Mr. Stewart ever sat on a jury. The jury in this case found a true bill of indictment. The bill was drawn up by O'Keefe while visiting Judge Bunce. In order to dress in the backwoods style of that day, O'Keefe procured a pair of buckskin pants, which he wore on visiting Mr. Stewart.

MR. WILLCOX, OF WILLCOX & BEACH.

Mr. Willcox, of Willcox & Beach, was the father of the late E. N. Willcox and General O. B. Willcox, U. S. A. Mr. Beach was the father of the late Eben Beach, who built a fine residence on Lafayette Avenue. The latter at an early day, became a member of the firm of Rathbone & Co., stove manufacturers, of Albany, New York, acquired a fortune and came back here to pass his days in affluence and quiet, loaned his money to the Michigan farmers, at a good rate of interest, and proceeded to enjoy himself and his money, until the grim destroyer death stepped in and stopped it all. Eben's daughter married a son of the late L. M. Mason. Doctors Allen and Stewart, botanical doctors, had at one time an office in this locality.

Major Kearsley, who lived in the house he built on the corner of Randolph Street, is, of course, remembered by many old residents. His whole bearing and appearance gave one the idea that he was a very stern man, but he was not. He was prompt and decisive and not much given to levity, but he was full of the "milk of human kindness." He was a fine Greek and Latin scholar and a terror to the classes in those languages in D. B. Crane's and Professor Fitch's school, in the university building that was on Bates Street. He was always invited, on examination days, to hear the classes recite and was sure to be present. I seem to hear him now, stumping up the stairs leading to the recitation room, and the cold chills are chasing down my back, as I write. Woe betide the scholar who made a slip, for the major was sure to haul him up with a round turn. J. Howard Webster married a daughter of his, and Edmund Kearsley, his son, was a schoolmate of mine at Crane's school. He (Edmund) was a good scholar and was an assistant to old "D. B." (as we used to call him), in the chemical laboratory. The major was engaged in the battles of Niagara (or Lundy's Lane), Stony Creek, and Chrysler's Field, and the sortie from Fort Erie, September 17, 1814. In the latter engagement he received a wound which resulted in the loss of a leg. This was a source of life long pain to him. The amputation was delayed in the hope of saving the leg, and then was improperly done.

The major was held in high esteem in the army for his attainments and his bravery, and it was much regretted when his wounds compelled him to retire to private life. He was appointed receiver of public money for the district of Michigan in 1820, and made Detroit his home until his death, August 31, 1859. I think he retained the office of receiver of public money until his decease. He was at one time mayor of this city, and on account of his ability as a linguist was for many years a regent of the University of Michigan. He was held in highest respect for his upright and honorable character, and for his fidelity in the administration of public trusts. A sword presented by General Washington to his father, Captain Samuel Kearsley, was given to Major Kearsley by him in 1819. This sword, I understand, descended to his son, Captain Edmund R. Kearsley, of Bucyrus, Ohio—lately deceased. I presume it is in the possession of the latter's heirs.

The sword above referred to was presented to its recipient in recognition of the valuable and timely aid rendered by the captain and his amiable wife, providing the soldiers with flour and meat, to the extent of their means, in the dark days at Valley Forge. This charitable act, coming to the ears of Washington, touched his **great** heart. The commander-in-chief ordered the troops paraded **at headquarters**, and calling Captain Kearsley to the front, commended him for his meritorious services as an officer and his philanthropic efforts for the relief of the soldiers, and presented him with his (Washington's) own sword. It is a sharp three-edged **French rapier**, which Washington wore at Braddock's defeat in 1755, and upon which is engraved:

"**Draw** me not without reason; sheath me not without honor."

It is related of the major that towards the end of his life he frequently visited his farm at Grosse Pointe, to and from which he drove in a two-wheeled gig. The road ran close to the river, and in some places there was no room for two vehicles to pass. One day, while on a return trip, he found an ox lying in the middle of the road at the narrowest place, so that he could not pass. He called to it in an endeavor to drive it out of the road, but the ox paid no attention. Finally, losing patience at the inactivity of the animal, the major drove his horse upon it, when it quickly rose and overturned him into the river. Having but one leg he found some difficulty in righting his gig and getting into it.

Upon telling of the occurrence (with much amusement), and being asked why he drove onto the ox, the major replied that he had told the ox if it did not get out of the way he would drive over it, and as the animal paid no attention there was nothing else for him to do, for there was not room to go around.

An extensive hardware merchant of Detroit, Mr. Howard Webster, married a daughter of Major Kearsley (Martha). The latter and Eliza Chipman, daughter of Judge John Chipman, who was a near neighbor, were almost inseparable in their girlhood days. Miss Chipman married William Baubie, of Canada, a writer of prominence, afterwards in the government service in the Dominion. A son survives him, William E. Baubie, a prominent attorney of Detroit, who is also a writer and compiler of merit. The latter married Julia P., daughter of James Beatty, of Detroit, their children being Marie Logan and Raymond Perrier Baubie. A daughter of Webster (Sarah) married Colonel J. T. Sterling, who commanded an Ohio regiment during the civil war. Another daughter, Rebekah, married a son of Lawyer Oscar Heyerman. The latter was at one time law partner of the late James B. Witherell. Young Heyerman entered the United States navy as a cadet, and during the civil war rose to the rank of commodore.

He died at sea on his way to visit his mother in Germany. Commodore Heyerman had the reputation among his fellow-officers of being one of the bravest men that ever trod the deck of a ship. I think his wife is dead also. "Major," a son of J. K. Webster, married a daughter of Thornton F. Brodhead, who was colonel of the First Michigan cavalry in the civil war.

A son of Colonel Sterling, following in the foosteps of his grandfather and those of his father, gained a cadetship at West Point, passed with honor through that strict ordeal, and is now a full-fledged officer in the regular army.

Colonel Sterling's wife is still living and resides on Grosse Ile.

Edmund Kearsley, son of the major, whom I have mentioned as attending D. B. Crane's school, and as one of his assistants in the chemical department, after completing a college education at Kenyon College, Ohio, in 1832, returned to Detroit, and became asistant receiver in the United States land office under his father. He proved so efficient in this position that Major John Biddle, registrar of the land office, requested his transfer to his department, and made him chief clerk of that important office, which position he filled until 1840, when his health failing from too close application to business, he retired to a farm belonging to his father in Oakland County, remaining there until he returned to Detroit and resumed active business, his health having been restored. Among other things he superintended the erection of the Biddle House, one of the largest hotels in the state of Michigan at the time, built by a company of which his father and Major Biddle were the principal stockholders. Inheriting the military spirit of his ancestors, he took an active interest in organizing the Brady Guards, and was at one time captain of the company. This organization was pronounced by General Scott the best drilled company that came under his inspection, and equal to any troops in the regular service.

During the "Patriot" disturbance of 1837-8 the Brady Guards were called out and mustered into the United States service, where they remained for nearly a year and a half, quelling disturbances and protecting the border. During this time Kearsley was captain of the company.

The subsequent history of some of these young men (members of this company) it would be interesting to trace. Several of them occupied prominent places in the councils of the nation, in both houses of congress, upon the bench, at the bar and in pulpits. Some of them served their country in the Blackhawk and Mexican wars; and not a few fell at Gettysburg fighting under command of their former comrade, Lieutenant Williams, of the Brady Guards, then a brigadier-general.

Years after the guard had been disbanded General Brady was thrown from a carriage, receiving injuries which proved fatal. Captain Ed Kearsley, upon learning of the death of their old commander and patron, returned to Detroit, from which he had removed, and the old company, many of whose former members were now solid business men and men of note of Detroit and different parts of the country, turned out as the Brady Guard—for the last time—to escort the remains of the general to their last resting place in Elmwood cemetery.

During his life in Detroit Captain Kearsley was for a number of years secretary of the fire department and assistant chief engineer. He was also for a time assistant quartermaster-general of the state, and while in that position served with Captain U. S. Grant while located at Detroit.

In 1851 Captain Kearsley removed from Detroit to Bucyrus, Ohio, where he remained until his death.

ANSON BURLINGAME AND OTHER MEN.

King's corner, opposite the Merrill Block, before King put up his building, was occupied by a Mr. Phelps as a saloon and eating house, and was called "Phelp's Corner." The building was one story high, with porch and pillars in front. The whipping post was located near it, on the Woodward Avenue side, close to the curb. I saw the post often, but never saw any one whipped there. There are people, however, who came here after I did, who say that they have seen culprits being punished there, but I doubt it. I don't believe it was used for that purpose after 1826. If it had been I should certainly have been an eyewitness, or should have heard of it, as I lived only a block from it, down Jefferson Avenue, and was always on the "qui vive" for anything of that kind. This was a great corner for auctions, anything and everything. I have seen the sheriff sell a man's time here, having been sentenced by the court for some petty offense, or for vagrancy. If he could not pay the fine imposed by the judge his time was sold to any one who would pay for it and board him while he worked it out, as was the custom in those days. The sheriff, of course, had to put the culprit on the "limits," and to see to it that he did not skip the town.

*THE OLD MARKET.

The old city market (it has often been described), was in the center of Woodward Avenue, about fifty feet from Jefferson Avenue. This market, as I recollect it, was a pretty good one, and was well supplied. The French housewives from the other side of the river furnished most of the eggs, poultry and vegetables needed. They usually occupied the space between the market and Jefferson Avenue, and I do not know what the people would have done without their assistance. Delicious whitefish, in season, were here abundant and cheap. J. L. King became the owner of this corner and replaced the old wooden building with a new brick one, four stories high, the highest one in the city at that time (about 1829). It was the custom of the old fire department, at its annual parade and on other occasions, to assemble all the engines on this corner or in the immediate vicinity, and then at a given signal to see which company could first reach the top of King's building with a line of hose, taking water from the reservoir on the Merrill Block corner. It was an eager, hustling rush, and no mistake, for a few minutes after the signal was given to plant the ladders and gain the top. The feat was also attended with considerable danger. The winning company always got a wild ovation, and were entitled to display a broom fastened at the "goose neck" of their engine, which they carried until some other company knocked them out.

BULL & BEARD.

The basement of the King building was occupied by Charles M. Bull and George Beard (Bull & Beard), as a saloon and restaurant. Here at last was a place where almost everything in season could be had, and it became quite a resort, continuing so for many years. Here is was that Mr. Avery, a bookkeeper in one of the banks (Michigan, I think) met his death at the hands of Sheldon McKnight. Mr. Avery was a quiet, reserved gentleman, not given to intoxicants, but genial withal, whereas McKnight was of a rather fiery and peppery disposition, and on the evening of the tragedy was somewhat under the influence of liquor, though this was not his habitual condition. Some words of a trivial nature, buf heated, passed with them. McKnight gave Avery an openhanded blow, not intended to be a crusher, but it was sufficient to cause Avery to stumble over something on the floor. He fell heavily, striking his head, and expired almost immediately. The event made quite a stir, of course; McKnight was arrested and tried. He plainly showed that he had no intention of injuring Avery and that he had always been on the most friendly terms with the deceased, whereupon he was acquitted. McKnight ever afterwards felt the sting of remorse for this act and in many ways assisted the widow of Avery and her children, particularly Charles H. Avery, a son, who became a protege of C. C. Trowbridge and by him was given a position in one of the banks—the Bank of Michigan. I myself have many times heard McKnight regret bitterly that the sad accident happened.

LAWYER HANSCOM'S JOKE.

There was another famous restaurant started by a man by the name of Carson, but at a somewhat later date than Bull & Beard's. It was on Griswold Street, somewhere between Jefferson Avenue and Larned Street. When the legislature held out in Detroit the members used to go down there for lunch. Carson had a huge cast-iron image of a man, life size, on top of his large stove. It was said that Hanscom, a waggish member of "the house," drew up a resolution, authorizing the clerk of the house to purchase this image for Representative Hall, and succeeded in prevailing upon Charles O'Malley (the Irish member from Mackinac County) to introduce it, in perfect innocence of its being a huge joke. It is unnecessary to say that the resolution was laid on the table.

Many no doubt will remember Hanscom. He was a lawyer of good repute, was also captain in the First Regiment, Michigan Volunteers, that went to Mexico. He was member of the legislature from Oakland County, and a "high roller."

The first and second stories of King's building were occupied as offices and I think the fourth floor was occupied by either *The Free Press* or *Advertiser,* I do not remember which. At any rate there was a printing office there. Counsellor Charles Tryon had his office on the first floor front, above the clothing store. He was a confirmed bachelor, quite eccentric in many ways. He was a fine penman and did a large business drawing up deeds, mortgages and conveyances of all sorts. They did not have the neat and convenient law-blanks and the typewriters of the present day, so most law-papers had to be written out.

ANSON BURLINGAME.

Anson Burlingame was a protege of Tryon's and a student in his office. It has been said that Burlingame was not so especially indebted to Tryon as has been the popular belief. Now I know that he was deeply indebted to him in many ways. The latter was the first one to take hold of him, pull him up out of obscurity, and give him a show. I would like to know what he would have been if Tryon had not lent a helping hand when he did. Burlingame and myself were schoolmates, sitting side by side at the same desk. The school was in an alley in the rear of the *Evening News* office and a Mr. Clark was the schoolmaster. Burlingame was bright, studious and ambitious, which I was not, I am sorry to say. His father had been a butcher and drover, as well as a local Methodist preacher in Ohio, but at that time he kept a tavern in some part of the city—just where I am not certain, but I think it was in the vicinity of the Berthelet market. Anson went from this school into Tryon's office, then into the law office of Zepheniah Platt, attorney-general, and then into the office of Atterbury & Williams. General A. S. Williams, L. B. Mizner and others helped him through Cambridge. He made speeches before the Whig Club of Boston, attracted the attention of the Whig Central Committee and was employed by that body to stump the state of Massachusetts. His western style of eloquence was new in that section and he at once became popular. Briggs, then governor of Massachusetts, took a great interest in him, and paved the way for him to a seat in the legislature of that state in 1846 and afterwards to a seat in the thirty-fourth, thirty-fifth and thirty-sixth congresses of the United States.

Senator Hoar in his autobiography, recently published, says of Burlingame, in connection with the presidential election of 1848: "Anson Burlingame, afterwards minister to China, captivated large crowds with his inspiring eloquence." In a footnote, he relates the following: "Shortly after Burlingame came into active life, he made a journey to Europe. The American minister obtained for him a ticket of admission to the house of commons. He was shown into a very comfortable seat in the gallery. In a few minutes an official came and told him he must leave that seat; that the gallery where he was was reserved for peers. They are very particular about such things there. Burlingame got up to go out, when an old peer who happened to be sitting by and had heard what was said, interposed. 'Let him stay, let him stay. He is a peer in his own country.' 'I am a sovereign in my own country, sir,' replied Burlingame, 'and shall lose caste if I associate with peers.' And he went out."

DUEL THAT DIDN'T COME OFF.

While in congress, Burlingame denounced in no measured terms the cowardly and brutal attack made by Preston S. Brooks upon Senator Sumner. Brooks sent him a challenge and it was accepted, the meeting to be held at Niagara Falls, with rifles as weapons. Brooks, for reasons best known to himself, did not put in an appearance, but Burlingame did. This exhibition of pluck on the part of the latter gained for him a wide reputation. President Lincoln appointed him minister to Austria in 1861, and soon afterwards to the China mission. This mission he held for a few years, resigned and took a position at the head of the Chinese embassy commission, appointed by the Chinese emperor to negotiate treaties with the United States and the European powers. He was stricken down with congestion of the lungs, with this great work unfinished, February 22, 1870.

Burlingame visited Detroit directly after the Brooks affair and Eben Wilcox gave him a reception at his home on Jefferson Avenue, next to Doctor Cobb's residence. All his old friends were invited to meet him, myself among the number. At the reception the subject of the duel that did not come off was freely discussed, and the guest of the evening got a good deal of chaffing. It seemed to me that he was quite satisfied that the affair took the turn it did. I know I should have been.

THE KING BROTHERS.

A few words, in passing, in regard to J. L. King ("J. L.," as he was familiarly called). He was a fine, genial man and always had a strict eye to business. Nothing pleased him better than to get hold of a customer and make him believe that the particular coat or garment he was inspecting was just the thing he wanted. He would grab it in the back and say, "My friend, it fits you like a glove," and it almost always did. Any of the "boys" could get almost unlimited credit of "J. L." if he knew them well or knew of them. He was first located at the corner of Atwater and Randolph Streets, in company with a Mr. Trowbridge, and there he accumulated enough capital to purchase the site on the corner of Woodward and Jefferson Avenue and erect his store. His brothers, William and John E., were associated with him in the business as clerks, and were of the same type of manhood—all very fine.

AT THE OUTBREAK OF THE MEXICAN WAR.

At the outbreak of the Mexican war, the state raised and equipped a regiment of volunteer infantry with T. B. Stockton for colonel, A. S. Williams for lieutenant-colonel, and James E. Pittman for adjutant. John E. King was commissioned lieutenant in this regiment, helped raise a company and went with it to the war. At the close of the war the regiment returned to this city—with King as captain of his company—and was mustered out of the service. William and John E. then went into the clothing business in the block opposite J. L.'s store, on Jefferson Avenue, and continued there for awhile, until John E. married Miss May Baughman. The firm then dissolved partnership and John E. went into the lumber business with Bela Hubbard and Collins Baughman. The firm name was Baughman, Hubbard & King.

On the same floor with Tryon, in the King building, Ezra Williams, lawyer and justice of the peace, had an office. He was commonly known as "Pope Williams." McArthur & Hulbert, grocers, occupied the store next to King's on Woodward Avenue. Between this and Woodbridge Street, were located, from time to time, A. S. Bagg's book store, the law office of Judge B. F. H. Witherell, M. F. Dickinson, stoves and hardware, John Thompson, liquors, and Jonas H. Titus and Silas Titus, auctioneers. In 1830 the law office of Judge Witherell was in a small wooden building; he afterwards put up a brick one in its-stead. The corner of Woodward Avenue and Woodbridge Street was then occupied by the Godfroy House, built just after 1805 by Peter Godfroy, owner of the Godfroy farm, down the river. The lot also included the present site of the police station. The corner is now occupied by a brick building and the property is still in the hands of the Godfroy family. It is said that Tecumseh and his brother, the Prophet, and "Walk-in-the-Water" often visited there, when the family occupied the corner. Peter Godfroy was at one time extensively engaged in the fur business in company with his brother, in Monroe. It is said that John Jacob Astor was their principal customer.

In the block from King's store to Bates Street, on Jefferson Avenue, about this time (1837), George C. Moon and his maiden sister had a millinery store, Zach Chandler and after him, Chandler & Bradford, had a dry goods store, Hicks & Palmer also had a dry goods store, and Darius Lamson (afterwards Lamson &

Butler), had a dry goods store. Lamson was a quiet, unobtrusive man, of undoubted integrity and in whom it seemed there could be no guile. His partner, later on, Wm. A. Butler, most of the present generation are familiar with, as he died but a few years ago, a banker on Griswold Street.

In this block also John Hale kept a general store. Associated with him was Charles L. Bristol. John Hale had the reputation of being a sharp trader and always looked out for "John," hit or miss. He also carried on an extensive ashery and soap factory and had a number of teamsters collecting ashes throughout the city. There were no hard or soft coal ashes at that time. In return for these ashes the people were given printed orders on the store, payable in goods. The orders bore the legend, "Honesty is the best policy," which created considerable amusement in the then small community.

THE BUHL BROTHERS.

F. and C. H. Buhl, on their arrival here, occupied a store in this same block, with hats, caps and men's furnishings, also manufacturing hats and caps. The factory was in the rear of the store and separated from it by a wooden and glass partition. The stock of furnishings was fine, though limited. All the gentlemen of that day attending the swell parties, balls and dances used to go to Buhl's for their white kid gloves, etc. With George Winter to assist in attending to the wants of their customers, they had a large and profitable trade. Right here no doubt they laid the foundation for the large fortunes they both acquired later on. I have often seen, through the glass partition, both of the brothers, coats off, working hard at their trade and they continued to do so until the necessity for it vanished. They were in this location nearly twenty years.

George Winter succeeded the Buhls, and carried on the business in the same locality for many years. George was a familiar figure on the avenue for two decades at least. He was the first to introduce the "Conformateur," a Paris invention to take the measure of the head, a contrivance that all are now familiar with, but which was then quite a novelty. He was also the first to introduce illuminating gas jets over his store, spelling his name, "Winter's."

It may not be out of place to note somewhat briefly the after-business career of the Buhl brothers, though I presume it is known to scores of people.

After dissolving partnership, F. H. continued in the business, later—in 1852—moving down the avenue to 146-148, Shubael Conant's (then) new brick block, adjoining the Bank of Michigan—now the Michigan Mutual Life Insurance Co. building—where he carried on a successful trade, also going into furs extensively.

HENRY A. NEWLAND.

When the civil war broke out Mr. Buhl had in his employ a young man by the name of Newland, who appeared to be his head or confidential clerk. Anyway, he was bright, energetic, always present, and most strenuous in his endeavors to secure trade for his principal. I speak of all this in regard to Newland, from the fact that I was a personal observer of his early career with Mr. Buhl. At the breaking out of the civil war I was at once installed into the office of assistant quartermaster-general of the state. I had seen some service in the United States quartermaster's department during the Mexican war. Our department had the furnishing and equipping of the first eleven regiments of infantry of the state, as well as the Coldwater battery.

Right here was where our young friend Newland "got in his work." He early made friends with all the attaches of the office, was on hand almost daily, and if anything in his line in the way of forage caps or military equipments in general was wanted, he always found it out. The establishment he was connected with being the largest in the city or state, and fully competent to execute all orders of the military nature I mention, almost on the "drop of the hat," so to speak, and as time was the essence of all contracts then, he most always got the "job." So, if 500, 1,000 or 5,000 infantry caps were wanted, and wanted quick, the department knew who to depend upon. Through our office he also secured the patronage of nearly every officer in the military department, as well as that of almost every officer belonging to the Michigan regiments. Their wants in the military line were many, consisting in part of forage caps, swords, silk sashes, sword belts, shoulder straps, epaulettes, chevrons, spurs, gauntlets, etc. So it can readily be seen what a splendid trade this young man picked up for his principal, and when Mr. Buhl took him in as a partner, no one wondered. They continued together some years successfully, when Mr. Newland finally branched out for himself in the same line. All will remember the tragic instantaneous death of Mr. Newland and wife, which occurred in a collision on the Grand Trunk railroad at Battle Creek in 1893. They were on their way to the World's Fair in Chicago.

Mr. Buhl kept on in business until 1877, accumulated a large fortune, and passed away a few years ago (1890) honored and respected by all. Full of years and good works he was gathered, as was the Patriarch Abraham of old, to his people.

The firm name after Mr. Newland became the partner of F. Buhl, was Buhl, Newland & Co., the "Co." being Walter Buhl, son of F. After Mr. Newland left the concern, and Mr. Buhl had passed to his fathers, the son of the latter carried on the business for some time, then disposed of it and the stock to Edwin S. George.

C. H. Buhl, after the separation, got hold of the Detroit Locomotive Works. It was merged into the Buhl Iron Works, which concern made much money and continued nearly forty years. C. H. Buhl was also head of the wholesale hardware house of Buhl & Ducharme, which concern is still in business under the name of Buhl Sons & Co.

He also, in company with Albert S. and Henry Stevens—and, I think, the late Wm. H. Stevens—was interested in 1871 in the building of a railroad thirty-five miles long from Champion, Marquette County, to Huron Bay on Lake Superior, projected for the purpose of transporting ore, timber, etc., to the lake. But from some unexplained reason it was not a success, though completed and equipped with locomotives and cars. It turned out an utter failure, the Stevens brothers losing more than $250,000, Wm. H. Stevens all he put in, if any, and Mr. Buhl more than $600,000. But, notwithstanding all this and other losses, the latter was able at the time of his death to leave to his heirs the snug sum of nearly $6,000,000, it is said.

Reflecting on the successful career of these two Buhl brothers, I seem to see them now as I saw them then—coats off, sleeves rolled up, and hard at work in that little room in the rear of their store on Jefferson avenue—amid the steam arising from the vast open copper boiler in which the hat bodies were stewing. And it would have been hard to realize then that in after life both would attain large wealth, and one, C. H., would become so rich that he could afford to lose $600,000 almost at a blow, without a ripple; and, when called away from earth, could leave his heirs nearly $6,000,000. They were both fine, splendid men, of the most rigid integrity and very successful, but for all I don't think that either of them got much fun out of life.

THE BANK OF MICHIGAN.

The Bank of Michigan built its first banking house in this block—from King's store to Bates Street on Jefferson Avenue—and it was a fine structure, with a cut stone front. When the bank vacated for its new quarters on the corner of Griswold Street, the Michigan State Bank, John Norton, cashier, took the building and after they quit business the Bank of St. Clair, with W. Truesdail for cashier, occupied it. W. N. Carpenter had a dry goods store in this block, also. W. N. Carpenter I seem to have known always. We were schoolmates, and the friendship contracted then continued through life. He sprung from an eminently respectable family. His father, N. B. Carpenter, was one of the magnates of the town, and was almost as much of a character as Judge Canniff or John Farmer. He and David Thompson were in the provision business on the south side of Woodward Avenue, between Jefferson Avenue and Woodbridge Street. I think their establishment was wiped out in the fire of 1842. N. B. was short of stature, rotund and one of the jolliest of men.

William N. entered into the employ of Franklin Moore's dry goods store on Jefferson Avenue, between Woodward Avenue and Bates Street. After awhile the firm name was Moore & Carpenter, later it was William N. Carpenter alone, and finally it became Carpenter & Rice (A. A. Rice, who was afterward with Beecher, Rice & Ketchum). I think that after the separation between himself and Rice, Carpenter retired partially from active business, having acquired a competency—and that through his own exertions entirely, as he inherited scarcely anything from his father's estate. He early entered the fold of the Episcopal church, and was ever prominent in it. Of pleasing address, he soon won the affections of Miss Gibbs, the sister of Mrs. Theodore Eaton, and they in due time married.

Carpenter erected a fine house—fine for those days—next to that of Doctor Morse Stewart on Jefferson Avenue, and lived there until his untimely death. While his house was in the builder's hands he used to take me into it often, for my inspection and admiration. It was certainly fine (particularly the interior decorations), though small. He himself was quite in love with it and often pronounced it a "perfect gem."

It is a pity he could not have lived the fullness of years, to have enjoyed it, and the fortune he had acquired as well.

He was, as many people know, thrown from his buggy and instantly killed while on the way from his coal yard and dock, in the lower part of the city, to his home. He used to visit the above place of business almost daily. I was with him on two or three occasions, and took him to task for driving around the streets unattended. But he reminded me that he had always been used to a horse and did not fear. "Watch out, for ye know not."

In 1827 Felix Hinchman, father of Guy F. Hinchman, had a store on the corner of Bates Street in the same block, and A. S. Bagg also had a book store here in the early forties, after leaving his former store on Woodward Avenue to the use of Mr. Miller, father of Thomas C. Miller, who carried on the tobacco business for awhile. He was succeeded by his son, Thomas C., who continued the business until his death. John J. Bagley got his knowledge of the tobacco business in this store, as did also Daniel Scotten. Bagley succeeded to the business and Scotten went with Granger and Lovett into the same business. How they all prospered everybody knows.

With A. S. Bagley was a young man, Peter R. L. Pierce, who was his right hand man while in the book business; a bright, curly-headed, handsome chap. He went to Grand Rapids and engaged in business, the nature of which I do not know. He was county clerk of Kenty County during the civil war, and after that a member of the legislature. He died some years ago.

Mr. Felix Hinchman lived at that time on the opposite corner from his store (the northeast corner of Bates Street), in the John R. Williams homestead, a yellow cottage with a large willow tree in the front yard. The Williams family had vacated it for their new brick dwelling on Woodbridge Street between Bates and Randolph Streets.

The Hinchmans, after leaving the Williams homestead to make way for the Republican block, moved directly in the rear on Bates and opposite Durell's cabinet shop. The house was a unique affair, and was perched on top of a high bank. Its approach was made by a flight of hewn log steps let into the bank.

Mr. C. C. Trowbridge, who came to Detroit with Felix Hinchman, was an inmate of his household, after the latter's marriage with Mr. Thomas Palmer's sister, Catherine. He seemed and, indeed, was almost like one of the family, the bonds of friendship between the two young men being so close. Mr. Trowbridge continued an inmate of the Hinchman family until his marriage with Miss Sibley, daughter of Judge Solomon Sibley.

Hinchman and Trowbridge remained firm, fast friends during the life of the former, and for years and years after his death Mr. Trowbridge and family remembered the wife and children of his deceased friend most liberally at Christmas time and also on other occasions.

It is not necessary for me, here, to speak of the career of Mr. Trowbridge. It is known to nearly all our citizens of the present day, as he passed away so recently. His kind, fatherly ways, genial and gentlemanly bearing, which he retained through life, will also be remembered.

The splendid banquet given in his honor by his admiring fellow citizens at the Russell House not long before his decease attested the regard they held him in and will long be remembered, by those who were present, with pleasing emotions, and he himself, it will be impossible for us to forget.

It has been said of Mr. Trowbridge that the most earnest applications for loans coming from his personal friends would be declined by him when it was not safe or convenient for the bank to discount, with an air and politeness that really did the applicant almost as much good as the loan itself could have done, if it had been obtained.

Inexorable, and yet courteous, he never gave offense. With these traits, it may be supposed that he was an invaluable bank officer, and that the administration of his department gave high satisfaction to the friends of the institution. He resigned in 1836 and was succeeded by H. K. Sanger.

Mr. Trowbridge, speaking of Judge Sibley, his father-in-law, said: "I am reminded of a remark made to me not long since by the venerable General Cass. The general said, that, while a stout boy, he was one morning occupied at a hollow stump standing before his father's on the Muskingum River, pounding Indian corn for the family breakfast. He looked down the road and espied two persons approaching on horseback. They proved to be Mr. Sibley and his young wife, the daughter of Colonel Sproat, of Marietta, Ohio, on their way to Detroit, where Mr. Sibley had decided to practice law. According to the custom of the country, they alighted without ceremony, partook of a welcome breakfast, and resumed their long journey."

In the rear of the Hinchman store, on Bates Street, was the furniture and cabinet shop of William Durell. The next on the corner of Woodbridge Street was the old store of John R. Williams, occupied by his son, Theodore (of blessed memory), as a grocery store. Opposite Durell's lived David Isdell, whom some may remember. He and his son Dave were quite well known her at the time. Dave was an enthusiastic fireman.

Continuning on up Jefferson Avenue, there were located, as near as I can remember, between Bates and Randolph Streets, Ellis Doty's residence, Pat Palmer's tavern, with a large elm tree in front of it. Pat Palmer was the father of Perry Palmer. The latter was captain of the propeller Goliah, which was lost on Lake Superior, and nothing heard of vessel, passengers, cargo or crew. Captain Palmer fortunately for him, did not happen to be on the vessel at the time, having got a friend to take his place temporarily. The propeller was owned by Wesley Truesdail.

BARNABAS CAMPAU.

Barnabas (Labbie) Campau was a fine specimen of the French gentleman, of commanding presence, quite unlike the two brothers Joseph and James, who were thin and small of stature, comparatively. Mr. Campau had two sons and two daughters. One of the daughters married John B. Piquette; the other never married. The two boys, Barney and Alex. M. upon the death of the father, came into their inheritance, which was large, and proceeded to enjoy it judiciously. After a while Barney married Miss Alexandrine Sheldon, daughter of John P. Sheldon. After many years of an apparently happy married life, Barney was accidentally drowned at the foot of Bates Street. He left two sons, fine, promising boys, who might have made their mark in life, but they died early, just after they had reached their majority. Barney Campau was a fine, manly, generous and all around good fellow, as all will say who knew him and there are scores and scores of people here and elsewhere, who did, and his early taking off was deeply deplored. His widow married R. Storrs Willis, a brother of the poet, N. P. Willis, and himself no mean composer of verses. He was also a close student of literature and the arts, music being one of his principal accomplishments. He died not long since. He was for many years connected with the Detroit public library.

The children of John B. Piquette I am unable to follow intelligently.

Alex M. Campau is with us yet, and in the full enjoyment of all his faculties, and one to look at him and mark his erect figure and elastic step would think he could never grow old.

GEORGE DOTY.

A little later on, where Doty and Palmer had been, Robert Rumney had a dry goods store, as also did Saunders and Kittredge. Where Oliver Miller had been, George Doty, jewelry, put up a four-story brick building, the first and second floors of which he occupied for his own use with a stock of jewelry, clocks, watches and sporting goods. The remainder of the building was used for offices, etc. In his store front Doty introduced the first plate glass windows of any dimensions (and they were large) that had ever been seen in Michigan. They attracted wide attention and at that time were a wonder and a show.

Doty at that time was the jeweler of Detroit, and also kept the finest stock of sporting goods in the state. Old Mr. Lebot, Berger, William Wingert and Dygert (father of Kin Dygert) had previously attempted to do a little in the latter line, but Doty beat them all "out of sight." Any one having arrived at the point where he thought he could afford a fine gold watch, always went to George Doty, or if a diamond ring, Doty's was the place to procure it. I bought one there once, myself, and Hon. Peter White, of Marquette, speaking in praise of Doty and his jewelry establishment, not long ago, said he procured from George his engagement ring. It was a stunner, of course, though the Hon. Peter did not say so. Morrison J. S. Conklin, Ed. J. Smith, of Chicago, and many other young men acquired their knowledge of the watch and jewelry business under the tuition of George Doty. The latter also made the first Detroit city clock.

George married a sister of J. L. King (Rachel King). How

. The subsequent careers of these two (Elwood and Howe) are known to most people of the present day. I am under the impression that it was with Dow Elwood that Dexter M. Ferry first took service in this city, as all around clerk and bookkeeper. Dexter was a stalwart youth at that date, faithful and prudent, and he feared no noise. I, being in the same business as Elwood & Howe, further down the avenue, had frequent transactions with him and came to know Dexter well (Elwood I had known previously in Rochester.)

BEGINNING OF A GREAT BUSINESS.

When Howe succeeded Elwood, Dexter Ferry staid on, until he went into the seed business. It is not necessary, except briefly, to follow his successful career further, as all are familiar with it. I little thought, at the time I speak of, that he would attain the wealth he possesses, nor the prominence in the community which he now enjoys. Our relations during all these years have been most friendly, and I am right glad that he is as he is. His seed venture was with M. T. Gardner, the firm name being M. T. Gardner & Co. I had at the time a steam job printing office, and did a large amount of printing for the new concern, and having in my book bindery the only paper cutting machine in the city, cut all the paper used in making their seed bags, etc., thus being a factor in a small way in helping to the front this early bird that now overshadows the country with its wings. They were in a measure something like the express business—they filled a long-desired want. A seed company in Rochester, and Frisbee & Co., of Fredonia, N. Y., and the Shakers had for years flooded this state and the west with garden seeds and it was time for some one to call a halt, some one nearer home that could fill the bill equally as well, if not better, than a foreign concern. M. T. Gardner & Co., tried to experiment, and time, care and attention, developed the infant it was into the giant it has now become.

Shortly after the advent of the Markhams here they were joined by James C. Parsons and Jerome Croul from Rochester, N. Y. I say joined—they did not do so in the book business but did in the family circle, making their home with the Markhams. They entered at once into the tanning business—leather, hides, wool, sheep pelts, etc., and later on leather belting. The firm continued some time. I do not know how long, and was very successful. Mr. Parsons retired from the firm, moved to Chicago, where I think he engaged in the same business. He passed through the great fire there losing heavily, went to New York and engaged in the stock brokerage business with Frank C. Markham. I do not think they were very successful. The former is living at present in Whitestown, Long Island. He married while here a daughter of the late Doctor Thos. B. Clark of this city; she is also living. Many will remember "Jim" Parsons and his estimable wife with kindly, pleasurable emotions, as I do. Jerome Croul was at the time he left Rochester a most active member of its volunteer fire department, and on his arrival here, as a matter of course, identified himself directly with the like organization in this city. He continued an active fireman until the volunteer department went out of business. He served one or two terms with marked ability, as all know, as fire commissioner in the paid department. At the outbreak of the civil war he was appointed on the governor's staff as colonel, and a member of the state military contract board. In relation to this board Adjutant-General Robertson had this to say at that time: "Individual ability and great energy, coupled with exemplary economy, characterized this board, relieving the quartermaster-general of much labor and responsibility." I was in a position to know very much of the workings of the board, and in my opinion Colonel Croul was by far the most efficient member of it. His subsequent career in business all are familiar with, as he died so recently. I presume it is almost needless to mention, as a matter of news, that he married a sister of his partner (Parsons), who survives him, a most estimable woman.

The Markhams resided in the Elisha Taylor house (still standing) on Jefferson Avenue, south side, between Brush and Beaubien Streets. Their home was made most attractive by the presence of its presiding genius, the charming wife of Fred P., a Rochester lady. Croul and Parsons, as before mentioned, made it their home with this family, and in addition the presence of a few outside congenial friends, almost always of a Sunday, met them around their hospitable board, to discuss the bountiful spread, made these occasions most enjoyable for all the participants. There were usually present besides the family above mentioned, Geo. Sam Rice, freight agent of the Michigan Central railroad; J. Hargrave Smith, pay department, United States army; Major Whilden, George Jerome, the writer, and occasionally W. Van Miller, of Monroe. Time has dispersed all that crowd, and but three are now living, viz.: Frank C. Markham, James C. Parsons and myself.

The firm that succeeded Parsons & Croul was Croul Bros., of which our jolly and genial friends "Joe" Croul was a most efficient member, and contributed much to its success.

Fred P. Markham, after leaving Detroit, was at one time United States consul at Samoa. He died many years ago, as did his charming wife.

> "Make merry with the world as best you may,
> Ere you, like them, are called to pass away.
> All pleasure ceases with our loss of breath,
> And all is ended with the one word death."

The other occupants of the old council house were the *Advertiser* Printing office, Patrick Tregent's billiard saloon and M. Martz, bootmaker.

THE VINGT CLUB, AN ORGANIZATION THAT FLOURISHED BEFORE THE WAR—ITS MEMBERSHIP.

Referring again to the Doty building, I desire to say that Mr. Doty used the second and third floors for his business and the entire fourth floor was occupied by the "Vingt (20) club," an organization similar to the present Audubon club. It was founded in 1848, by Mr. Charles E. Whilden (Major Whilden), a clerk in the office of Colonel J. B. Grayson, United States commissary of subsistence stationed here at that time, and some others. It differed in one respect from the present Audubon club inasmuch as liquors, eatables and cigars, were furnished to the members and a monthly assessment of $2 each was found to be sufficient to cover all expenses, except on some extraordinary occasion when a special call would be made. It was intended at first to limit the number of members to twenty, but the club soon gained great popularity and the membership limit was done away with, though the club still retained the name of "Vingt."

This was the first club of the kind ever organized in this city, and, as said before, it rapidly grew into favor and carried on its list of members such names as Charles E. Whilden, Benjamin Vernor, J. C. Parsons, Jerome Croul, James E. Pittman, S. Dow Elwood, William Gray, W. D. Wilkins, Theodore Luce,

Horace S. Roberts, Alexander Lewis, T. W. Palmer, John B. Frink, George Doty, Mr. Duff, Dr. L. H. Cobb, George A. Cooper, V. W. Bullock, Colonel John Winder, City Treasurer Bushnell, Henry A. Wight, James W. Sutton, H. J. Buckley, David R. Peirce, John B. Palmer, J. B. Witherell, Robert H. Brown, Friend Palmer, and many others whose names I fail to recall. It continued to flourish until some time before the Civil War and then fell to pieces on account of the repeated indulgence in gambling of some of the members, which the by-laws strictly forbade. The good members simply would not stand it.

The first meetings of this club were held in a small room over Peter Babillion's saloon on Griswold Street, and later in two rooms in the fourth story of the Williams block (Republican hall), corner of Bates Street (where Edson, Moore & Co. now are). One of the two rooms was devoted exclusively to whist, the other to noise, and plenty of it. I was caterer, as well as secretary and treasurer at that time, but on account of the smallness of the income was able to furnish only bread and butter, crackers and cheese, herring (smoked), brandy, whisky, lemons, sugar and cigars. The refreshments were all displayed on a sideboard in the noisy room, and every one helped himself. The club began to grow and becoming too large for its quarters in the Williams block, it secured larger and more commodious ones in the George Doty building.

It was the custom in the early days of the club, when one of the bachelor members married, for him to give a dinner to the members, in the club rooms, the spread being provided from outside by a nearby restauranteur. This pleasant custom was discontinued after the club took up its quarters over Doty's store. The list of members had increased to such an extent that it was found to be impracticable.

Here in their new quarters, as in the old, one room was devoted exclusively to whist and silence, which room fronted on Jefferson Avenue. The next room, in the rear, was given up to euchre, checkers, dominoes and noise; the next, in the rear of this, and fronting on the river, was used (as the members termed it) as "Feasting Room." Here in a moderate and primitive way were the appliances for preparing eatables and drinkables— chafing dishes, ordinary table furniture, etc. "Jim" Sutton was here the caterer par excellence. The two dollar assessment against each member would not admit of a much more elaborate larder than in its early days, and "Jim" did the best he could on the limited income. In addition to the bill of fare in the Williams block, we had oysters, and fresh eggs, in season, pigs feet, pickled, ready to serve, canned lobster, now and then a cold boiled ham and pickles always. No waiters, no cooks, it was every one for himself as formerly, and deliciously free and easy. As remarked, the liquids furnished were confined to brandy and whisky. Lager beer was not in it those days. It was before the Civil War, and liquors of all kinds were remarkably cheap, as many will remember. The finest, the purest brandy, imported, was only from three to four dollars per gallon, and whisky of the first quality and age (Luke Whitcomb's best) was way down, down. Cigars, the finest Havana, were only from three to four and a half dollars per hundred. So you see, a lot of "fellers"' could have, and did have, a pretty good time on a small amount of money.

The club met on Saturday nights, and on no other, except special occasions. This was in conformity with the by-laws, and was for a long time, three or four years, rigidly adhered to, but after a while some of the pokerishly inclined members (gambling being strictly prohibited) procured keys of their own to the rooms and met there when they pleased, on other nights besides Saturday, thus violating the rules of the club and consuming its provender. They were remonstrated with, but to no purpose, the consequence being that the club disbanded.

I know that some of the members of this club are still alive, and I am sure if this article meets their eye their thoughts will travel back to those good old days, those happy days, or those nights, of mild revel and keen enjoyment, when William Gray, Wm. D. Wilkins, John B. Palmer, Major Whilden, Dr. L. H. Cobb, Horace S. Roberts, Jerome Croul, V. W. Bullock, Henry Buckley, J. B. Witherell, "Jim" Sutton and others were at their best; when

"All hearts with pleasure bounded,
The laugh was laughed,
The song was sung,
And loud the revel sounded."

Visitors out of town used often to enliven the club with their presence. I particularly call to mind "Charley" Little, from Saginaw. Charley was musically inclined; could sing a good song, tell a good story, and being an all around good fellow, his company was always welcomed. He used to sing one song that always brought down the house. The name of it I have forgotten, unfortunately, but it always used to tickle Bullock (that sweet singer) so immensely that he almost tired poor Little out getting him to repeat it. I visited Saginaw two or three years ago, and made quite a protracted stay there, with some friends. It was in the summer time, and Saginaw looked its best. While there the gentleman I was visiting drove me over to see Little (I think he lived on the east side). We found him at home, in his fine residence embowered in splendid trees. He was pleased to see us, of course. We (he and I) had much to talk over, discussing the early days, and I am satisfied that he enjoyed it quite as well as I did. I think he is living yet, indeed I hope so.

The following effusion (mentioned an a former article) in regard to our friend Willie Gray, a distinguished member of the "Vingt club," occurs in a "Post Prandial Rhyme" recited at a bar supper in Detroit on the evening of January 28, 1857, by D. Bethune Duffield:

> Next to Levi (Bishop) sits his favored friend,
> Whom much he loves, nor ever would offend;
> A ruddy youth, adorned with smiles and curls,
> And once, and still, the fav'rite of the girls;
> His graces those of Ganymede excel,
> And Ganymede's vocation loves he well;
> Give him a cask of old Falernian wine;
> 'Round his fair brow let boys the roses twine;
> Close to his side, and ere the wine has run,
> Plants generous Toms, all dripping with his fun,
> Let goblets pass as often as they are drained,
> And wit flow free, unpruned and unrestrained.
> And ere the midnight hour has come and gone,
> You've seen young Bacchus and Anacreon.
> But he of whom we sing, the rosy boy,
> Is still a man, and knows each manly joy;
> Effeminacy soft, he never knew,
> Save when he knocked a dandy all askew,
> His thirst for wine has never been paralleled.
> Nor powers of suction ever been excelled.
> No matter how or where the night was spent,
> Next morning finds him o'er his table bent;

No sluggish blood within his veins e'er lay;
He works at heavy tasks with each new day.
With him Fraser alone an oracle can shine,
And 'Old Lemaiee' is Bible-truth on wine—
For all his brands read 'Henkle on the Rhine.'
A mean or sordid breath he never drew;
For all his friends he ever has a chew;
The juices of his heart are ripe and rare,
For Mumm's best vintage ever bubbles there;
Indeed his body might be called a vine,
Since all his blood is ripe and rare old wine!
In him no error lies except in name,
For this father is alone to blame,
And had he known him as some others do,
Instead of Gray, he'd named him William Blue.

The records of this club, which were faithfully kept during his life, would now afford most interesting reading to any of the surviving members, but unfortunately they are lost. Robt. H. Brown was the last secretary, and on his departure from the city he left them in charge of the late Tim Campau, who was never a member of the club. On the latter's demise an effort was made to discover them among his effects, but the search was fruitless.

THE REPUBLICAN HALL AND OTHER BUILDINGS AND THEIR OCCUPANTS.

The Rumney and Kittridge stores and the General Williams homestead were after awhile swept away and were replaced by the Republican hall, Brick Block. In this block were located from time to time, T. & J. Beaubien, Charles Moran, T. & J. Watson, Benjamin Vernor (with Jed P. C. Emmons for clerk), and Horace Hill, dry goods dealers; Truax & Booth, wholesale grocers; James Nall & Co., dry goods, and C. D. Crossman, dry goods. Walsh, whom I have mentioned before, in connection with Lillibridge, occupied a large portion of the basement as the Tontine Coffee house. A large hall occupied the fourth story, about the center of the block, and was used as occasion offered, for political meetings, lectures, balls and dances, the latter patronized exclusively by the second four hundred of Detroit. The remainder of the upper floors was occupied as doctors' and lawyers' offices, sleeping rooms, etc. Devereaux Williams had rooms in the third story of this building, on the Bates Street corner, and at one time had for a roommate Charles Barstow, a gifted, courteous gentleman from Boston—a Yale graduate—who was here in the interests of some eastern firm. He had an unfortunate appetite for intoxicants, and during a fit of delirium he threw himself from the corner window of the room to the pavement below and was instantly killed.

The Grosvernor residence was enlarged and extended to the corner of Randolph Street. The corner was occupied for a time by Riley & Ackerly with drugs and groceries—until 1838, when they became embarrassed. Theo. H. Eaton, then of the firm of Wm. Williams & Co., Buffalo, bought their stock, through his agent, David A. McNair, and the latter carried on the business until the dissolution of the co-partnership of Wm. Williams & Co. in 1842, when Mr. Eaton came on and took control of the business in person.

This is slightly different from the account given of this corner in my article of January 3, and D. A. McNair's, Riley & Ackerley's and the late Theo. H. Eaton's connection with it. For this revision I am indebted to his son and successor, Theo. H. Eaton.

Cicott Brothers had a dry goods store next beyond Eaton. The upper part, in connection with the old Hull residence, was occupied by Austin Wales as the American hotel. He kept it for some time and then retired to his farm at Erin, in Macomb County. He was the father of Edwin A. Wales and Mrs. Alex H. Newbould. Later, John Griswold kept this house until his death. He was the father of George R. Griswold, John and Doctor Alexander Griswold, also Mrs. Captain Stevenson and Mrs. Captain Guise, of the United States army. Petty & Hawley also kept this house, as did J. W. Van Anden.

The opposite corner of Jefferson Avenue and Randolph Street, which was occupied, in 1827, as a residence by Judge Solomon Sibley, was well surrounded by shade trees, flowering shrubs, and extensive gardens. The rest of the block was vacant, except a house on the corner of Brush Street, although Caleb F. Davis had a paint shop here later. This vacant space was used for a long time as occasion required by circus people, menageries, etc.

Here, in the campaign of 1840, "Tippecanoe and Tyler, too," was located the Log Cabin, in which the stirring meetings of that memorable time were held.

"Cale Davis," as he was familiarly called, was a noted citizen in the early times. Beside being an expert at his trade, he was an energetic fireman, a trained body guard, and at one time was city clerk or city treasurer. I forget which. Anyway his signature at that time became a familiar one, as it was attached to the first "shinplasters" the city ever issued. They were of various denominations of the fractions of a dollar, and I presume some of them are still extant, pasted in the scrap books of collectors. Davis, I think, saw service in the Civil War, but in what capacity I do not know. Anyway he was employed for some years in the war department, Washington, as clerk or head of the bureau having charge of the rebel archives captured at Richmond, Va. Whether alive at present I do not know. He was the artist of one of the banners presented to the Brady Guards, the one that General Hugh Brady presented from the steps of the American hotel (Biddle house).

Adjoining the American hotel on Jefferson Avenue was the residence of Major John Biddle and next was that of Edmund A. Brush, neither dwelling being very pretentious. The Brush house was on the corner of Brush Street, a two-story wooden structure. The Brush estate was not at that time quite as valuable as it is at the present day, but nevertheless it yielded a very comfortable income and revenue. After the death of Colonel Elijah Brush, the family were quite as poor as some of their neighbors. The late C. C. Trowbridge once said, "Colonel Elijah Brush died in 1813. (Edmund A. Brush was at college), widow and children very poor, living in Canada, in Sandwich, farm not very valuable, not worth much and producing nothing," this in 1819. But under the fostering care of Edmund A., the Brush farm became very valuable and what is left of it now in the hands of the heirs is worth much money. Colonel Brush left four heirs, Charles R., Edmund A., Alfred and Sumantha. Charles R. was a jolly, easy going man, unlike the rest; Alfred was a West Point cadet and graduated into the infantry but soon after resigned and, returning to Detroit, remained ever after under the wing of E. A., until he died. His chief occupation was horticulture, which he pursued for amusement. In his office in the Michigan or Brush garden that occupied the square where now the Lyceum theater stands, and also the D. M. Ferry seed store, etc., he kept a history of the various trees, shrubs and flowers growing there and entered in a small blank-book their daily progress, fruition, etc. He was also a great pedestrian, and, in company with Doctor Farnsworth and Doctor Rufus Brown, took daily outings, rain or shine. They would "pedest," these three, as though the "old Harry" were after them. Charles R. died leaving a daughter to the care of his brother, E. A.; Sumantha married George R. Meredith, a lawyer living in Detroit. The union was not a happy one. Meredith was a thoroughly good, happy-go-lucky fellow, came of a fine Baltimore family, was a good lawyer and a gentleman in every way, but dissipated, I am sorry to say. After living together for a time they were divorced. The fruit of the union was a daughter. Mother and daughter died soon after the separation, as did also Meredith. Much to the latter's credit he reformed some time before his death and gave temperance lectures here and elsewhere. The daughter of Chas. R., who became the ward of Edmund A., married a gentleman by the name of Boggs. They went to Chicago, where they still reside. Edmund A. Brush after awhile absorbed the whole of the estate and made it the study and aim of his after life to keep the Brush farm as much as possible off the tax rolls, as other than farm property, and fighting assessments of various kinds. He rarely sold any property, preferring to give what was called a "Brush" lease, the party of the second part paying a cheap rent therefor and also the assessments on the property, ordinary and extraordinary. He died quite suddenly, some years ago at his Grosse Pointe residence. He left to his widow and two other heirs all of his vast estate.

MAJOR BIDDLE.

Major Biddle was a fine gentleman of commanding presence, courteous and polished, one of the old school. He was the brother of Nicholas Biddle, president of the old United States Bank. The Biddle house was named after him. He died in Paris, France, I think.

From 1837 to 1850 there were located from time to time, between Randolph and Griswold Streets, on Jefferson Avenue, firms that I knew, such as Jas. G. Crane & Co., hats and caps; Watkins & Shaw, harness; Farnsworth, Mather & Hall, general store; Benjamin LeBritton, drugs; Charles W. Penny, clothing; Eldred & Son, and Eldred & Marvin, hardware; J. Sabine, harness; John McReynolds (after Doctor Clark), drugs, on the corner of Jefferson Avenue and Woodward Avenue; McCormick & Moon, hats, caps and millinery; Doctor Rufus Brown, liquors (opposite S. L. Rood); J. M. Berger, books; E. & H. Doty, dry goods; Hutchinson & Titus, dry goods; Ingersol & Kirby, leather; Martin & Townsend, hardware; F. H. Stevens, president of the Michigan State Bank, hardware; Stevens & Zug, furniture, below the Michigan Exchange; R. W. King & Company, crockery, and F. Wetmore, in the same line.

McCormick, of the firm of McCormick & Moon, was the brother of the late Mrs Judge Moran, as also the late Mrs. J. B. Vallee. Mons. Vallee was deputy collector of customs under Colonel Andrew Mack. The customs office was located just one side of the Mansion House hotel on Jefferson Avenue, when the colonel was its proprietor. When I think of that customs office I seem to see it as it was then, with its large sign over the door, on which was painted an eagle with outspread wings holding in its beak a scroll, on which was inscribed "U. S. Customs," and a representation of the stars and stripes as well.

THE WILLCOX FAMILY.

Mr. Watkins, furniture dealer, occupied the house on the opposite corner of Brush Street (where Haight's drug store now is), which was wiped out by the fire of 1843. Next to Haight's store, Jonathan• Thompson after awhile built the brick row of tenement houses still standing there. Elisha Taylor built and resided in the house next adjoining for many years; after him, for awhile, Mr. Fred P. Markham occupied it. The house is still standing. Adjoining this house lived the widow Willcox, the mother of Eben N. and General O. B. Willcox. Mrs. Willcox lived there until Eben N. purchased the farm at Highland Park and went there to live. His mother joined him and spent her last days there. A motherly, kind, benevolent and Christian lady was Mrs Willcox and it is owing to her exertions alone that the people of Greenfield (Highland Park) are enabled to enjoy the little brick church on Woodward Avenue, just this side of the six mile road crossing.

Besides Eben and Orlando (the latter's second name was Bolivar, and he went by the name of Bolivar among the boys, much more than by the name of Orlando), Mrs. Willcox had three daughters. One married David A. McNair, druggist, another Mr. George Davis and the other Chas. A. Taylor. Eben did and Orlando does owe much to this good mother of theirs, for any success or prominence that they attained in after life. Eben was as fine a stump and after dinner speaker as I ever knew. Orlando's career in the Civil War all are familiar with.

Another son of Mrs. Wilcox (Charles), was a printer by trade, and for some years carrier on a job printing office in company with Wm. Harsha, under the firm name of Harsha & Willcox. He died many years ago.

Mrs. Chas. A. Taylor, it appears, is alive, and, in the *Chicago Tribune* of September 20, 1903, she states that she started for that city in May, 1832, her sister, Julia, going with her in a prairie schooner. After the fifth or sixth day they came to Calumet, and put up at a two-room tavern kept by a French Canadian. One room was used for sleeping, divided off by blankets. The half breed wife of the Frenchman, with her infant, shared the bed, but in spite of the discomforts they slept well. The next morning they resumed their journey, though in fear and trembling as they had received the disquieting news that Black Hawk was on the warpath and headed for Chicago. They arrived safely at their destination, however, and went at once to one of the two taverns kept at the post and that by J. B. Beaubien—but they were scarcely asleep before being aroused by an alarm, and told that the Indians were really coming. They took the children from their beds, dressed in a hurry and rushed to Fort Dearborn. Colonel J. V. D. Owen, U. S. A., met them en route, and gave them a warm welcome to his own quarters. They afterwards opened a boarding house, and felt rewarded when two or three young men applied for board. One of them was a young Englishman, Geo. Davis, who later on became a brother, he marrying the sister Myra.

Mrs. Taylor says further: "In the winter of 1834-35 a piano which had been brought from London, England, by a Mr. Brooks, then the only one in the place, or in the state—was taken from the store, and Mrs. Brooks, assisted by Geo. Davis and others, gave several concerts to the great delight and amusement of the citizens. Davis was the life and soul of any company he might be in. There are many old citizens yet in Chicago who will remember the comical songs, 'The Great Mogul' and 'The Blue Bottle Fly,' for instance, that always brought forth rounds of applause."

I, as well as many of the citizens of Detroit, have often heard Mr. Davis get off the above songs. He rendered them finely, and they were most amusing. Mr. Taylor, I did not have the pleasure of knowing.

George Davis was in the employ of the Michigan Central railroad in this city as cashier in 1852-3.

Eben N. Willcox was the father of our street railway system, securing from the common council the original franchise in 1862, and organizing the company which built the earliest lines. Frank B. Phelps was associated with him.

On the occasion (July 4, 1866) of the delivery of the battle flags of the various Michigan regiments and batteries to the state by the general government, Bishop McCroskrey made the opening prayer, and Mayor M. I. Mills, the welcome speech to the 123 bearers of the flags, and to about 125 other veterans, who accompanied them. General O. B. Willcox followed him with a presentation of the colors to the state, and Governor Crapo followed in an address of acceptance. The day before, the latter submitted his manuscript to Colonel Fred Morley, assistant adjutant-general, for his opinion. The document being quite lengthy and verbose, the colonel, after its perusal, advised the governor to cut it nearly one-half, giving as a reason that he thought the veterans would become uneasy before its conclusion. The governor did cut it, but when about half through his manuscript, a squad of artillery men, who had charge of a Parrott gun stationed on the Campus Martius, about where the Bagley bust now is, getting impatient on account of the lengthy address, let the gun off prematurely. At the sound of the discharge every bearer dropped his flag and, with the other veterans, with a yell, rushed over to the cannon, leaving the governor with a very meager audience. The address was hastily concluded as the standard-bearers and veterans did not return, of course. According to program the squad in charge of the piece were to fire a salute on the conclusion of the governor's address, but they could not bear the strain, and started in on their part of the celebration without notice, much to the delight of the standard bearers and the rest of the veterans.

In July, 1863, General Willcox had command of the department of the Ohio, headquarters at Indianapolis, and at the time of the Morgan raid. I think Morgan made his escape, although a large number of his force were captured, and confined in the prison at Indianapolis. One of the Michigan batteries, M, Captain Hilliar commanding, and of which the late George A. Sheeley was second lieutenant, was on duty there at the time, having been ordered out during the raid above mentioned, but fortunately their services were not required. General Willcox generously and humanely made an offer to the captured Morgan men—that they would be set free if they would enlist in this battery and as an extra inducement each would receive the bounty of $50 the state of Michigan was at that time paying for recruits. Somewhere between fifty and eighty of these rebels accepted the offer and I was sent by the quartermaster-general of the state (Hammond) to pay this bounty. Well, I did pay it, and to the scaliest lot of chaps I think I ever set eyes on. But the funny part of it was after they had got washed up and shaved and had donned Uncle Sam's uniform every mother's son-of them deserted with uniform, overcoat and blanket, not one of them stuck. On my return to Detroit the general and one of his staff (Lieutenant Howard, Son of Senator Howard, I think it was) came on also. On the same train as ours to Cleveland were General Morgan's wife, her sister and Morgan's brother (the latter a non-combatant). The brother was genial and affable, but the ladies were as bitter and discourteous as they could well have been, except to General Willcox and his aide. When any of the other union officers or soldiers on the train passed their seats they would draw the skirts of their dresses to one side so as to avoid contamination, and turn their faces away with the most pronounced looks of disdain in their eyes. It was very amusing.

Eben Willcox was something of a poet, as well as a lawyer, ready debater and an all around good fellow. At the conclusion of a post-prandial rhyme recited by the late D. Bethune Duffield at a bar supper on the evening of January 28, 1857 (which I have mentioned before), he contributed the following appendix:

To these smooth rhymes of our beloved Bethune,
Pray let me add a short impromptu tune.
Too faithful limner, he portrays us all,
From ermined judge to pettifogger small;
Hits off a foible, here—there, praise bestows.
To satirize, too kind; in verse or prose,
His humor, like an Irving's, genial flows.
Welcome, dear Duffield, with your funny pen,
Welcome your shafts, tho' wounding now and then.
You love the Muse—you love your dog as well;
Write well in prose—disdain not doggerel.
To "Babes in Heaven" sometimes address a verse,
And win cheap fame with many a pretty nurse;
While weeping mothers hug you in their arms,
In Grief-Eyed Fancy yielding all their charms.
Classic in costume, see his flowing hair
Adorn the Forum and the Banker's chair;
Beset for discounts, turning from his brief
To give a briefless brother kind relief;
At Education's call devotes a willing life,
And urges unwashed urchins to its strife.
Zealous in party, his "resolves" are classed
The best in all conventions, and are—passed.
Whilom an Honest Whig penned many a line,
And knelt devoutly at the Union shrine;
But now, alas! in want of strength of nerve
(Naught else), behold him, tim'rous; shake and swerve,
Join the mad factions, yelping "bleeding" crew
Forget his friends, and swallow "Kansas," too.
Oh! how much brighter would thy laurels shine
Had'st thou proved steadfast like the "Sixty-Nine!"
In deeds benevolent, he foremost ranks,
Active in good, nor stays to gather thanks;
With mind well filled from Learning's ample stores.
Enriched by travel to her classic shores;
With all the virtues beaming from his eye,
So deep, so dark, so full of poesy,
To him may turn, in honest pride, our bar,
And in his genius hail a risen star.

And at this same bar supper Bethune Duffield had this to say to our friend, Eben N. Willcox:

>Wilcox (who once had bent a hopeful eye
>Toward chancery honors and sweet poesy,
>And who, if his ambition had held out,
>Would long ere this have brought his schemes about.)
>Inclines to raising pigs and pony mares,
>Working off mining stocks by thousand shares;
>And lately, when the nation heard and hoped,
>And strong men trembled as tho' all was lost,
>Lest the great Union should begin to slide,
>Bearing off pigs and ponies on its tide,
>He boldly raised the Fillmore banner high,
>Shouting "The Union" as his battle cry,
>And with an army numbering "sixty-nine"
>He saved the Union with its sacred shrine,
>Then marched his army home with him to dine,
>While Gray stepped in to quaff the flowing wine.

General O. B. Willcox is also something of a poet, as is evinced by the following, which emanated from his pen, and was sung at the New England dinner given here in 1854:

VIVE LES VOYAGEURS—

>Huzzah for the mighty men of old!
>   Vive les voyageurs!
>Men of the ancient lordly mould,
>   Brave, chivalrous, though poor,
>See o'er the mountain waves they plow
>   Look through the forest dim
>Lit with the western sun their brow,
>   Sing them a choral hymn.
>Huzza for the lily girls of France!
>   Vive les bons garcons!
>Sing to the glittering sword and lance—
>   Frenchmen for honor draw.
>Sing to the courier—his bark
>   Floats o'er the silvery lakes!
>Chant with the fur-trader! and hark
>   How the forest shakes!

> Huzzah for the fathers old!
> Honor the cross they bore—
> Not by the path to fame and gold,
> But persecutions sore;
> Sing to the soldiers of the cross,
> Fighting the way they trod!
> Chant! for the gain is ours—the loss
> Fell on those men of God.

Our friend Orlando was a creator of fiction also. He wrote quite an interesting book of the early days in Detroit entitled "Shoepac Recollections." It was very entertaining and had a wide sale at the time. I think it is out of print.

In the early days, a solitary barque now and then sailed lazily along the gentle current of our beautiful river, and the painted savage, in his bark canoe, with his brood of tawny papooses glided silently along the sea-green waters. The voyageurs and the couriers du bois of the Hudson Bay and North West Fur companies, while their voices kept tune and their paddles kept time, annually departed to the hunting grounds of the red men, along the shores of Slave Lake, the Lake of the Woods, and even to the far distant shores of the Oregon "where no sound was heard save its own dashing."

There are some now living, and who are to the manor born, amid whose earliest recollections linger and float the musical strains of the old canoe songs, and to those who have (as I have) personally shared the wild pleasures of the voyageur's life, the memory lingers with us like a pleasant dream, or like a charming story that has been told to us.

The word voyageur throngs the mind of the habitan, whether of French or American descent, with a thouasnd pleasant associations. Visions of sport, of mad-cap rollickings, of jigs and feasts—of dangers, braved with bold hearts —or hardships endured with patient heroism arise to cause him to gaze regretfully on the olden time, and wish that in the present we had more of the light-heartedness, the easily won content of the "vieux habitans" of the northwest. Who is there born here to the soil, or who was here in the twenties and thirties, who does not remember the simple and innocent pleasures of these men? Who, whose memory does not turn to the sturdy French pony, flying with the carriole over the ice; to the snowshoe and canoe race, or the dashing winter ride in the traineau? Who is there whose mind is not stored with the wild tales of the strife of the northwest fur trade, or the weird legends of the camp-fire? Of all these—of the feast and the superstition, the wassail and the ghost tale—the voyageur, the gay, reckless, brave, honorable courier of the wood and the lake, was the exponent, ever ready to engage in the one, and relate wild mystical tales of the other. They were a singular race, these old voyageurs. With the Indian and Buffalo they may now be found retreating before the tide of civilization, unchanged, the same that their fathers were one hundred and fifty years ago. They have played an important part in the history of this continent. Where they made their camp-fire, or erected their trading post, the towns and the great cities of the northwest have sprung up. Their trail through the wilderness has grown to the pathway of a nation's progress. We who today have found prosperity and happiness in the country they opened to the world, owe them a debt of everlasting gratitude.

It was in Mrs. Willcox's barn in the rear of the Jefferson Avenue house that the youth of that day got together at the instance of Eben N. Willcox to form a library and debating society. After repeated meetings, a society was formed and a constitution and by-laws were adopted. The society, now full-fledged, secured rooms in the upper part of the old University building on the corner of Bates and Congress Streets and proceeded to business. More in regard to this society anon.

This corner (the southeast of Jefferson Avenue and Beaubien Street) was, during the Henry Clay presidential campaign, occupied by the Whigs as a meeting place. A rough board structure of ample dimensions, they built for their use. Many, no doubt, will call it to mind, and the stirring speeches delivered there, as also the campaign songs, given by that admirable glee club, composed of such (then) well known members as Chas. S. Adams, Henry M. Roby, Morris M. Williams, James M. Sutton, Chas. R. Morse, A. H. Sibley, Chas A. Trowbridge.

After this building had served its purpose it was torn down, and a Mr. Bouchard kept an extensive blacksmith shop there, but for a short time only. This was succeeded by the Congregational church, a brick structure, which is there yet, though turned into a livery stable—or was once.

The Mr. Bouchard mentioned above was a lieutenant in the First Regiment, Michigan Volunteers, that saw service in the Mexican War. During the progress of the 1848 fire that destroyed the American Hotel (Biddle House) the steeple of this church was accidentally set on fire by the flying sparks, and completely wrecked.

* * *

In this connection, and before it slips my mind, I do not think it out of place to tell the story of the fate that befell the Log Cabin, opposite the American (Biddle House), the headquarters of the agitators in the celebrated campaign of 1840, "Tippecanoe and Tyler, too." The story is given to me by Mr. Richard R. Elliott, who says:

"The destruction of the Log Cabin was quite dramatic. On the morning of the festival of SS. Peter and Paul, June 29, 1848, was to occur the dedication of the new cathedral. On such occasions generally the relics of some saint are deposited under the altar stone of the main altar of the church to be dedicated. The Episcopal residence at the time was on the west side of Randolph Street, between Larned and Congress Streets. At 8 A. M. the procession started, a band of music leading, followed by acolytes and priests, then the relics on a white silk-covered table, covered by a canopy, held by four priests, with four acolytes swinging incense censors, following were the bishops, and last of all the Archbishop of Baltimore, Eccleston, all in rich vestments. The crowds of people were unusually large; Randolph Street was a compact mass of men, women and children. Major Kearsley's house, windows and roof, were occupied, but the greater crowd was on the large roof of the Log Cabin. As the procession was passing a rush was made on the roof to get to the front, and during this rush the upper structure collapsed and the crowd were precipitated below; what the casualties were I do not remember. The debris was cleared away, but that was the end of the Log Cabin.

* * *

On the northwest corner of Brush Street Mr. J. Bour built for himself a wooden residence, not very pretentious, that was possessed of one peculiarity in its construction, the absence of nails, wooden pegs being used instead, as in the Joseph Campau residence. Mr. Bour used to say that he got the idea from his ancestral home in Germany. Mr. Bour was the pioneer fine bootmaker of this city. Gentlemen's and ladies' boots were his specialty. He was quite successful, and after his demise his son, Joseph Bour, succeeded to the business. After the fire of 1848 their shop and store were in the Biddle House Block. Many will remember Mr. Bour and his son Joe. The latter was quite lame.

Dr. R. S. Rice lived in the house adjoining. The doctor for years was one of the most noted physicians here, and his house, presided over by Mrs. Rice and their daughter, Adelaide, was one of the centers of the gay young society of that day. Simon Poupard, of Poupard & Petty, built for himself a brick residence adjoining, which was afterwards occupied by Mr. William Brewster for some years. It is still standing.

Simon Poupard was a polished French gentleman, an accomplished bookkeeper and an expert accountant. He was acting in that capacity when I came to Detroit, for the firm of F. & T. Palmer, with whom he had been for many years, and was almost like one of the family. Besides, being a master of the French language, he was equally at home in the Indian dialect. He continued with the above firm until they went out of business, and then entered the service of Phineas Davis, who succeeded the Palmers. He afterwards went into the forwarding and commission business with Mr. John Y. Petty under the name of Poupard & Petty. The warehouse was at the foot of Bates Street. This was about 1838. They continued there for some time and then disolved the partnership, Petty going with B. L. Webb in the same business. Poupard retired to Hamtramck and built himself a brick residence on Jefferson Avenue, north side, that is still standing, just this side of Belle Isle bridge. He married a daughter of old Lambert Beaubien. He died in Grosse Pointe many years ago. Many of my earliest memories cluster around genial Simon Poupard.

Mr. Justus Ingersol lived on the southwest corner of Jefferson Avenue and Beaubien Street for a while. He was the father of Mrs. Frank Phelps, the late Mrs. Anthony Dudgeon and the late Mrs. Alexander Lewis. Mr. Ingersol was a very estimable gentleman. He was connected with the firm of Ingersol & Kirby in the leather business.

The opposite corner on the same side of the street was vacant at that time but was occupied soon after by the present building. Next was the brick residence of Eustache Chapoton (father of the present Chapotons), a most reliable brick mason and builder. It was enough to say to a would-be purchaser that the house had been built by old Mr. Chapoton; no further talk seemed necessary.. It is fitting here to record that his descendants in the same business fully sustain the old gentleman's reputation.

Mr. John Traux built and lived in the next residence, a most pretentious house at that day; it is still standing. Traux, a widower, took for his second wife the beautiful daughter of Robert Rumney. Mrs. Traux's daughter, Fanny, married John A. Rucker, of Grosse Ile, and is still living.

One of the firm of P. & J. George, furriers, lived in the double house adjoining, Barney Campau, at one time occupying the other half. Mr. E. V. Cicott lived along here and next to him were two small two-story houses, the first occupied by a Doctor Smith, the other by Washington A. Bacon ("Old Bacon"), in the rear of which was his first school for boys. Many a boy, now grown to manhood and still with us, can testify to his efficiency as a teacher and to his skill in handling the birch as well.

Some years after Doctor Smith and W. A. Bacon vacated these two houses; they were occupied, one by Thomas W. Blackmar, and the other by the writer. The latter, which was where Mr. Bacon had his school, is still standing. His old pupils ought to club together and purchase it.

Doctor Egge lived in this Bacon house at one time, but only for a brief period—after his marriage with Miss Matilda Connor, sister of Mrs. Darius Lamson, and Mrs. J. H. Farnsworth, and daughter of the Connor, of Connor's Creek. All Detroiters of David Smart's, Pierre Teller's and Doctor Farnsworth's time will call to mind the genial, skillful doctor and gentleman, as also his amiable wife. They are both dead. Mrs. Egge passed away in this house a short time after her marriage, and the doctor died a few years later, I think, in this city.

A Mr. Trowbridge, who was the partner of J. L. King in the clothing business, on the southeast corner of Randolph and Atwater Streets (opposite the Berthlet market), also married a sister of Mrs. Lamson. He died before I came to Detroit, as did his wife. Their daughter, Miss Emily Trowbridge, was brought up in Mrs. Lamson's family, as was Miss Matilda Connor. Miss Trowbridge married a gentleman from Rochester many years ago. I think they are both dead. The head of the Connor family, Richard Connor, of Connor's Creek, the intrepid Indian fighter, Indian trader and interpreter, I knew well by sight. He was quite a familiar figure on the streets here in the thirties.

Andrew J. (Jack) Connor I knew better than any of the rest of the boys. He was for many years connected with the United States lake survey, and on the breaking out of the Civil War entered the service as sergeant of Company A, Fifth Michigan Infantry. He resigned as captain October, 1864, on account of disability contracted in the service. He died not long ago at the Soldiers' Home, Dayton, O. Next, and almost adjoining this Bacon (school) building, and my dwelling, as well, was a small wooden building, with but one room, erected by some one for school purposes, lectures, ward and other public meetings. One of the Scott sisters used to keep a Children's school in this building. It was here that the first services of the Jefferson Avenue Presbyterian Church were held. It caught fire one night and was so badly wrecked it had to be carted off.

The corner of St. Antoine Street was built upon by James Sherlock, and although the houses are there yet, they are not very sightly. The corner of Beaubien Street, opposite Boucherd's shop, where now is Sievers & Erdman's, was ocenpied by Professor C. M. Fitch (with a girls' boarding and day school, which was well patronized by the best families in Detroit as well as those outside of the city), and afterwards by Lawyer Geo. B. Porter. The next residence was that of Theodore Williams, who lived there until his death. The brick building lately adjoining was erected by F. H. Stevens, the hardware merchant and president of the State Bank of Michigan. Mr. Stevens's brother was his partner in the hardware business. I think his name was George B. He had two fine daughters, the elder, a dashing brunette, was quite a belle, the second not quite so much so. I do not know what became of the elder; the younger married in Detroit and I think her daughter is the wife of ex-Mayor Pridgeon. The two families entertained handsomely, particularly that of F. H. Stevens. Mrs. Stevens was quite a society woman and gathered around her all the gay people of that day. I think a daughter (Elizabeth) survives, unmarried. Both brothers were fine gentlemen and first class business men. F. H. was the father of our late tax title friend, Sears Stevens. Mr. E. A. Brush once told me that he feared him more than anyone else in the business and that he was always getting hold of one or more of his lots that the tenants had failed to pay the taxes on and giving him no end of trouble. And Sears did enjoy so much getting Brush in a tight corner. He was a tax title expert, and often acted as agent for many owners of real estate who had property scattered around the city, looking after their taxes and watching the tax sales, which he did with lynx-eyed vigilance, seeing to it that no other tax title shark got hold of any of it, as he himself used to express it. And there were some of them always camping on his trail, particularly Land Agent Johnson and Lawyer Ebenezer Rogers. In addition to his tax title business, he was for some years librarian of the Detroit Bar library.

Sears married a niece of Christian H. Buhl, and spent the latter years of his life in Utica, Macomb County, though transacting business in this city. He died there in 1888, leaving a widow and six children.

The Sisters of the Sacred Heart occupy the adjoining lot with a fine building, a convent and young ladies' seminary that all are familiar with. Antoine Beaubien gave them this property, to the corner of St. Antoine Street, and sufficient cash with which to put up the building, at least I have always understood that he did so. This fine building, erected by the Sisters of the Sacred Heart, replaced the homestead of Mr. Beaubien (where he died). Mr. B. was an exceedingly kind and polished French gentleman. Perhaps there are some who will call him to mind. He used to be quite a familiar figure on Jefferson Avenue in the early days, driving behind his span of little black French ponies.

Judge James May's widow occupied a small wooden house on this lot from 1827 to 1829. Judge May was a native of Birmingham, England, and came over to Montreal in early life; was there at the capture of Ethan Allen; came to Detroit during the American Revolution, and often saw the savages parading the streets of ancient Detroit with strings of scalps. Judge May was the type of a fine old English gentleman; gave splendid dinners and kept the richest "Valerian." He held many offices in the territory, among them chief justice of the common pleas, and in 1810 he was made adjutant-general of the Michigan militia. He died on the 19th of January, 1829, and his grandchildren and great-grandchildren are still living. Mr. Alex. D. Frazier married a daughter of Judge May, so did Colonel Edward Brooks. I have often seen the judge, a plump, rosyfaced little man. His son, Ben May, was a schoolmate of mine, as also was Andrew Porter, son of Governor Porter. The latter, being the son of the governor, was inclined to put on airs and bully the younger boys. He tried it on Ben, but the latter wouldn't stand it, pitched into him and combed him down nicely. We did not hear any more from Porter after that.

Judge May at one time—in 1805—occupied the old Cass House, and in September of that year the Michigan territorial court, consisting of Judges A. B. Woodward, Frederick Bates and John Griffin, got May's consent to meet there (this was directly after the fire). Indeed, there was no other place. In May, 1806, they met at the Dodemead house, erected directly after the fire, and on the south side of Jefferson Avenue, corner of Shelby Street. Later the court was held at so many places that its course cannot be followed. It has been said that some over-critical person even complained at the time that it had been known to meet on a woodpile. Certain it is that one or two judges have been known to convene the court in a tavern or private room without notice to colleagues, sheriff, clerk, crier, counsel, witnesses or litigants, and, to adjourn without even a pen or paper having made record thereof.

Judge A. B. Woodward, for eighteen years on this bench, it is said, was the source of nearly, if not quite all, the grotesque rulings and erratic acts which mark the court as the most peculiar that ever administered justice in Michigan, and yet he was very far (it is said) from being an ignoramus, and was a gentleman by birth and education.

The commandant of Fort Shelby, vexed that his soldiers resorted to Mr. Dodemead's hotel to slake their thirst, placed a sentinel at the door to prevent their ingress. It so happened that one of the courts occupied an apartment in this hotel for its sittings, and the records of the day show the discussion and reference to the district attorney of the grave question whether the court was not in duress by reason of this military order. The learned counsel, who loved a joke, returned a long report, full of legal phrases and hypothetical cases, but ingeniously avoided the question at issue. The court ordered its approval of the report to be entered of record as quite clear and satisfactory, and there it stands to this day for the inspection of any antiquarian who may have the curiosity to look for it.

The present building on the corner of St. Antoine Street, and belonging to the Sisters, was erected by Mr. Beaubien and leased to the late Hon. Zach Chandler, who occupied it directly after his marriage to the lady who died his widow so recently. Chandler, while living in this house, got into a little trouble with the late General (then lieutenant) U. S. Grant. The latter, with a half dozen officers of his regiment stationed at the Detroit barracks, then located on the corner of Gratiot Avenue and Russell Street, in their daily walks to and from their barracks and the American hotel, had to, or did, pass this residence of Chandler's. The latter was quite remiss in cleaning the snow from his sidewalks. Grant made a complaint and after a lively time on both sides, the affair was amicably adjusted, but Mr. Chandler was highly incensed at the time. When Chandler came to be a power in running the business of the United States, during the civil war, it was feared by the friends of Grant that this early trouble might have some influence on his advancement, but on the contrary, Chandler gave him all the support in his power, which was much.

When I came here this block, bounded by Jefferson Avenue, Beaubien and Woodbridge streets, contained the Beaubien homestead dwelling and the orchard on Woodbridge Street. The orchard was in the rear of the dwelling and took up nearly one-third of the block on Jefferson Avenue from Beaubien to St. Antoine Streets. I have been in the orchard many times and knew it so well.

The homestead on Woodbridge Street was a long, low structure, in the French style, with a row of fine pear trees in front. There were no houses at all between it and the river, only a beautiful green pasture or lawn. In the orchard and where Theodore Williams built his residence, the old Indian chief Kish-kan-Ko, was buried. I have often seen his grave, in a small inclosure and covered with bark. What disposition was made of the old chief's remains when Williams invaded the premises I never knew, but presume they are there yet. I have often seen old Lambert Beaubien, brother of Antoine, during the summer days wandering around wearing a blue and white cotton handkerchief tied around his head instead of a hat, as was his custom.

The lot on which the cathedral of SS. Peter and Paul and the priests' residence are situated, was vacant until Antoine Beaubien donated it to the Catholics for church purposes. The late Charles Moran erected on adjoining lots, three two and a half story brick dwellings, that were occupied respectively by Andrew Ladue, O. B. Dibble and Judge Ross Wilkins. These were afterwards replaced by the present Jesuit college. Adjoining these three dwellings was the residence of the Hon. Zephaniah Platt, a handsome cottage with a pillared verandah in front. Judge Charles Moran built and resided in the old-fashioned brick building adjoining, recently torn down. Here he died, leaving to his heirs the extensive Moran farm, almost intact, that he had nursed during his long life, and as to leasing and keeping down the taxes, did as Edmund A. Brush did with the Brush farm. I once leased a lot from him on Larned street, on the Brush plan, rental sixteen dollars per year and taxes, and presume that I could have retained it at the same rental until the Judge died if I had desired to do so.

A large number of our people will remember the judge and most of his characteristics. He was genial, charitable and honesty itself, but he had a keen eye to his estate and the geeting in of dues from his tenants, and there is no doubt that he loved to accumulate money. He had many peculiarities in that direction. He was neither mean nor stingy, and always listened to the appeals of the needy and responded liberally.

The late Judge Charles Moran was the only son of Charles Moran and Catherine Vessier, dit Laferte, and born in 1794. The founder of the family came to Quebec from France, somewhere about 1678. His descendants came to Detroit before the English conquest in 1760. Charles (Judge) Moran married for his first wife, in 1822, Julie Dequindre, daughter of Antoine Dequindre. The children were Matilda, Charles, Julie, Virginie, Mary and Josephine. Matilda married James B. Watson, grandson of Judge James Witherell, and also of Hon. Elkanah Watson, of New York and Washington. The wedding was a brilliant one and occurred in the old brick Moran mansion on Jefferson Avenue, lately demolished. At it were gathered all the elite of Detroit. The young couple went to housekeeping directly, in the little wooden cottage (still standing) corner of Jefferson Avenue and Riopelle Street. After a brief married life of a little more than a year the wife passed away. Charles, after a career in the dry goods business in the Republican block (where Edson, Moore & Co. are now), went to Cleveland and was there for some years engaged in the same business. Before his departure from this city he married a young miss by the name of Pryer, a very pretty girl, indeed. I met the couple two or three times in Cleveland. Whether they had any children or not I do not know. The wife died in Cleveland, I think. Charles was of a frail constitution. He contracted consumption, returned home, and here, after a short period, died. He was like the scions of all the old French families, possessed of elegant manners and a kindly and generous disposition. Julia married Captain Isaac D. Toll.

Toll saw service in the Mexican war. He was captain of Company E, Fifteenth United States Infantry. In May, 1847, three companies were recruited in this state and mustered into the above regiment, of which Company E was one. The field officers of the regiment were Geo. W. Morgan, of Ohio, colonel; Joshua Howard, of Detroti, lieutenant-colonel; Frederick D. Miles, of Iowa, and Samuel Wood, of Indiana, majors. Thornton S. Brodhead, of Detroit, was adjutant. The regiment entered early on the Scott campaign, and was engaged in the battle occurring on that line of operations, sustaining a most creditable record for energetic, galant and effective service, ending with the surrender of the city of Mexico. The regiment was mustered out of service August 21, 1848. Wm. D. Wilkins, of Detroit, was also an officer in this regiment, being second lieutenant of Company G.

Mary Josephine Moran married Robert Mix, of Cleveland, O. Virginia married Francis St. Aubin, of Detroit.

Mrs. Captain Toll died many years ago. The captain resided at Fawn River, this state. One of his daughters married Colonel Frank Croul, a son of Colonel Jerome Croul.

August 3, 1836, Judge Moran married for his second wife Justine McCormick, of New York, sister of Mrs. J. B. Vallee, of Detroit, by whom he had the following children: James, Wm. B., John Vallee, Alfred and Catherine. James, the oldest, was accidentally shot by a companion. The two were out duck hunting, in a canoe, in the Grand Marais, above the water works. James was in the forward part of the boat, and as they were going cautiously along, a flock of wild ducks arose suddenly just in front of them, when his companion, who was in the stern, raised his gun on the instant and fired. Strange to say the whole charge of shot entered the head of young Moran. Death was instantaneous. It was a grievous shock to the judge and his wife, as may be supposed. James was his father's right hand man, attended to his office business, collecting rents, etc. The judge had quite a large number of lots on the Moran farm, let out to tenants on long leases, Brush leases, and the special business of the son was to look after these.

Wm. B. married, in 1872, Elsie, daughter of James A. Van Dyke, and for his second wife, in 1875, Frances, the daughter of Peter Desnoyers. John Vallee married, in 1880, Emma Etheridge, daughter of the distinguished orator and statesman, Hon. Emerson Etheridge, of Tennessee, Catherine married, in 1877, Henry D. Barnard, of Hartford, Conn. Alfred married, in 1878, Miss Latilda Butterfield.

Judge Moran died in 1876, leaving the most valuable estate, with the exception of the Brush and Campau estates, in Detroit.

With the members of the second family of Judge Moran I was not so familiar, though I had always known the judge well, and I knew Miss McCormick, who became his second wife, as also her brother, who was a partner in the hat and cap business here with Geo. C. Moon. I also knew her sister, Mrs. J. B. Vallee. Judge Moran's first family and the family of Judge B. F. H. Witherell were very near neighbors for years, and were on the most intimate and cordial terms, almost like one family, as it were. The charming personalities of the judge's four daughters and their winning ways made of their house a Mecca, so to speak, and what wonder is it that they were captured soon.

Lawyer Alexander D. Fraser owned the house and lot on the southeast corner of Beaubien Street, opposite the cathedral, and lived there until his death. He was eminent in his profession, as many will remember. David Smart occupied the adjoining house. All will recall David, that bluff, hearty Scotchman, a prince of good fellows, whose heart and hand were as open as the day. David Smart had always made his home with his uncle (Robert Smart) in the little two-story wooden house on Woodward Avenue, previously mentioned. What his occupation was before his uncle's death, I do not know, but directly after he was a partner of Wm. Brewster's, in the forwarding and commission business (Brewster & Smart). They did not remain long together, the latter turning his attention to improving the property left him by his uncle (he being his sole heir). The result was the the various business structures that appeared adjacent to what was then called "Smart's Corner." After a while the late Mr. Charles Merrill leased the Smart property for a long term of years, swept away the old buildings and new, and erected in their places the present "Merrill Block," which has been a familiar landmark for more than fifty years. Before this, however, he and Henry M. Roby, who had been bookkeeper for Brewster & Smart, made a pleasure trip to Europe, visiting his old home in Scotland, and the various points of interest in England, Ireland, and Wales, and also on the continent.

Many will remember David's brusque, hearty, genial manner, his wide charity, that was dispensed to every needy and worthy object with an open hand. He was a king, so to speak, among the Odd Fellows, which order was a popular institution, at that time, and embraced within its folds the cream of the young men of this city. They could boast of such names as Colonel John Winder, Chas. S. Adams, Morris M. Williams, Henry M. Roby, James E. Pittman, Sax Kellogg, Doctor Edward Desnoyers, Chas. Richmond, Henry R. Mizner, Geo. S. Rice, and many others in the foremost walks of life. Many no doubt will remember the dedication of the Odd Fellows hall—in this building of which Smart was a moving spirit—somewhere about the year 1845 that occupied the site of the present establishments of L. B. King & Co. and Wallace Sons. It was an imposing affair; nothing approaching it had ever before been witnessed in this city. David was also an active and enthusiastic member of the old fire department. He was always made a welcome guest by the social element that ruled here, and it was a matter of wonderment why he did not forsake bachelordom, and take to himself a life partner. After a while the wonder ceased. He succeeded in capturing the affections of Miss Mary Williams, only surviving daughter of General John R. Williams, and she became Mrs. Smart. She was a beautiful girl with the rosiest of lips, and the blackest of eyes, that sparkled behind her gold-rimmed eyeglasses. After some years of happy married life, David died, leaving to his wife all his possessions, which, coupled with the property she inherited from her father, made her a wealthy widow. She did not remain in the latter state long, however. Commodore Jas. McKinstry, of the United States navy, and son of Colonel D. C. McKinstry, wooed and won her. After a brief married life he too passed away, leaving her again a widow. She died a few years later in Egypt, while on a foreign tour. Her property, all or nearly all, went to the children of her brother, General Thos. Williams, U. S. A., and included the present Merrill Block.

Judge Solomon Sibley abandoned his residence opposite the American Hotel and built and ocuupied the house adjoining Fraser's. It was a large, plain, square brick house, and here the Sibley family lived until the judge died. William Brewster afterwards purchased and occupied it for some years.

William Brewster was a queer specimen of humanity, but not by any means a bad man. He was much opposed, though, to his family having any fun or enjoying themselves. He never had any fun himself he said, and did not see why they should. I note one occasion. Mrs. Brewster and daughters, being in the social swim, decided to give a dancing party. Mr. Brewster objected and said the affair should not come off, but come off it did. The invitations were issued and, on the eve of the party, before the guests had assembled, Mrs. Brewster managed to lock her spouse in his room up stairs. During the evening when the music and the dance were fast and furious, the company was startled by a pounding on the floor overhead. The cause was explained by the mother and daughters, much to the amusement of the guests, and no one paid any further attention to the rappings but let him rap. Yet Brewster was a first-class business man, and of the strictest integrity.

Darius Lamson occupied the adjoining house, which is still standing, though modernized. Mrs. Lamson was a leader in society and, with her sisters, the late Mrs. Doctor Farnsworth and Miss Matilda Connor, and her niece, Miss Emily Trowbridge, made a very attractive household, that drew within its circle the elite of Detroit.

Mrs. Lamson was the daughter of Henry or Richard Connor, of Connor's Creek, the Indian trader, scout and interpreter. In the latter capacity he accompanied Governor Cass and Colonel Thomas L. McKenney, commissioners, to Fond Du Lac in 1826, whither they went to conclude a treaty with the Chippewa Indians. The remainder of the party was composed of Colonel Abram Edwards, secretary; Geo. F. Porter, assistant to Colonel Croghan, U. S. A.; Major Whipple, comissary; T. O. Lewis, sketch artist; Jas. W. Abbott, son of Judge Jas. Abbott, and E. A. Brush, assistants in delivering provisions to the Indians.

Mr. Connor owned the ground on the southwest corner of Jefferson Avenue and Bates Street, in the early days, and about 1825 or 6, built on it a substantial brick building that was occupied from time to time by Franklin Moore, Moore & Carpenter, Wm. N. Carpenter, and Carpenter & Rice. Doctor Morse Stewart had an office in this building, as also did Doctor H. P. Cobb. This building gave way to a more pretentious one, erected by Doctor Jas. H. Farnsworth, which is still standing.

Colonel Garland, United States Army, occupied the adjoining house, which was a plain brick structure and was built by him. Mr. Harrington, a lawyer from Port Huron, built and occupied for a time, a house adjoining Colonel Garland's. It was of brick and of the villa style. Edward Lyon and family afterwards occupied it, about 1849, while he was keeping the Exchange Hotel. During the occupancy of this house by Mr. Lyon, in the fall of 1850, he and his wife gave a dancing party. It was a brilliant affair and was attended by the élite of the city, military and all, the latter in full uniform. A short time before issuing the invitations he told the "boys" he intended giving a dancing party, and charged them all to be on hand as it was going to be a stunner. Well, it came off in good time and it was a sure enough stunner. I have attended many functions of this kind in my time, and think this affair "took the cake." The supper room, located in the upper part of the house, was open from the beginning of the party until its close. Whisky in the gentlemen's dressing room, and champagne in the supper room; the latter flowed like water. It is a wonder the whole male portion did not get tipsy; but they did not, except two or three. Most of the rest, though, it must be confessed, became quite hilarious. Dancing to the music of Gilliam's String Band, was kept up until a late hour. Lyon said on the start that he was going to give the boys all the wine they could get away with, and a general good time. He did it. This "blow out" of his was the talk of the town for quite a while after it occurred. General Garland and his staff, on their way through the city, were present.

General Hugh Brady, United States Army, and commanding this department, accupied the house adjoining, which was a plain brick one. It was replaced by the present Museum of Art. The General was a splendid entertainer, and this city at that time was eminently a military one. There was always quite a number of troops stationed at the Detroit Barracks, the officers of which augmented by the various staff officers on duty at headquarters, made of the General's house a mecca, as it were. From time to time, when their husbands were on duty here, Mrs. Colonel Backus and Mrs. Captain Thompson, U. S. A., made it their home with him. He also had with him, until her marriage with Judge B. F. H. Witherell, his daughter, Cassandra, who managed his household. That she was an adept in the culinary art, it is needless for me to say, in view of the many living witnesses who can testify to her gifts in that direction. I, for one, can give appreciation of her skill. A fine officer and gentleman was Colonel Backus, and an admirable lady was his wife. They had a charming daughter, Mary, who married Captain Ward, U. S. A.

At the time of the marriage of Colonel Backus with Miss Brady, the General was living in the General Hull Mansion, where is now the Biddle House. I remember the occasion well, as I was present, though quite a lad. The affair was a festive one and drew together in the General's parlors, the elite of the city, including all the military stationed here, as also the British officers stationed at Sandwich and Malden, all in full uniform. The officers wore their side arms and spurs, as was the custom at the time. I seem now to hear, as I heard him then, the rattling of their accoutrements and the jingling of their spurs, as they whirled through the mazes of the giddy dance. The custom of wearing the spurs on festive occasions was annoying to the ladies as they made sad havoc with their dresses. The practice soon died out, however, as did the wearing of side arms, except when on duty.

Colonel Backus, at the outbreak of the Civil War, was stationed here as mustering officer, and was assisted in performing those duties by Lieutenant (now General) Henry R. Mizner, U. S. A.

On the corner of Hastings Street and Jefferson Avenue, where now stands the Blodgett Block, Major B. F. Larned, paymaster United States Army, built and occupied a brick residence, and lived there for many years until ordered off for duty in the Mexican War. Colonel Whistler, United States Army, lived there afterwards, until he was ordered elsewhere. He was colonel of the Fourth United States Infantry. The colonel had a beautiful, attractive daughter, Louise Whistler. I presume many will remember her. When once seen, it was not easy to forget her. She was bright, sparkling and vivacious, and when she appeared on Jefferson Avenue, as she often did, she drew the attention of all passers. She was spirited and pugnacious withal, i. e., would not allow any nonsense from the "boys" or young men of her acquaintance. On one occasion I remember, at a party given by a prominent family, she was present, and among the young gentlemen also present, was Mr. Charles S. Adams, one of the society leaders and a good fellow. Now Charles had always been in the habit of being quite free and easy, in a jovial and harmless sort of way, with the young ladies of his acquaintance. He tried some of his pleasantries on Miss Louise, that evening, but she would not have it, and drew a dagger on him, which she always carried, and made him apologize, which he did gracefully and with a good deal of amusement. I was not at the party but I heard the young woman herself give an account of the affair the next day at the house of another young lady, a mutual friend. She married a young gentleman from Louisville, Kentucky, a Mr. Helm, who went into the Confederate service and was killed during the Civil War. I saw her here in company with her mother, some time after the war, but she was very much changed and looked quite unlike the brilliant girl I had known in former years. They came on a visit to Mrs. Whistler's sister, Mrs. Judge James Abbott. Colonel Whistler and Mrs. Abbott were members of that distinguished family which in addition to a colonel in the United States Army, who rendered marked service to his country, furnished a trained and most accomplished engineer to the Russian government, building its first railroad, and continuing in its employ for many years. There was born to the latter, in Lowell, Mass., in 1834, James A. McNeill Whistler, who in later years became a distinguished artist, his death occurring but recently. It was said at his demise "We had not another painter, the announcement of whose death would have attracted such widespread attention." He was also an etcher and executed some fine examples, as the "Pool on the Thames," "German Rag Picker," "The Lime Burners." Among his paintings was a fine portrait of his mother, made when the family were in St. Petersburg. It is said, that the world has known only two etchers as great as Whistler, Rembrandt and Hayden, president of the Royal Society, London. He was educated at West Point, but why he did not enter the army was not known. A number of pictures from this artist's brush are owned in this city, also several etchings.

Eurotas P. Hastings, president of the Bank of Michigan,

owned the next dwelling; it was in cottage style, with pillared front, and I always thought the house and grounds were most attractive, more so than any other place on the avenue. The front yard was quite ample, and Mr. Hastings always showed fine taste in adorning it with flowers and flowering shrubs. The spring display of fine tulips was always a most attractive feature, and drew exclamations of delight from passers-by. It was afterwards owned and occupied by Hon. Robert McClellan.

The Christ Church congregation for some years occupied the next lot with a barn-like structure, until it was replaced by the present fine edifice. The Sibley family built and occupied the adjoining house, which is still standing and used by members of the same family. Robert Stewart built and occupied the adjoinng brick house, now the residence of Doctor Morse Stewart. Robert Stewart came from Mackinac, where he had been in the employ of the American Fur Co., as also was his uncle, David Stewart, who came with him. They both went to Astoria, Oregon, overland, in 1812, in the employ of John Jacob Astor. They are often mentioned in Washington Irving's "Astoria." David, a sturdy Scot, resided with his nephew, Robert, until his death.

It is said of Robert Stewart that he was a severe man in all things, and he looked it. He was severe in his family, and when he experienced religion, he was severely religious. At one time, which I well remember, he attended a party at Woodworth's Hotel, and when the waiters brought in the refreshments on trays, they were halted by Mr. Stewart, who quickly gained the attention of all present, and then and there, in a ballroom, in a most reverential manner, he asked the divine blessing on the good things about to be served, all present bowing their heads devoutly and all accepting the interruption as an entirely desirable feature of the occasion. I know I always thought him severe, and no doubt he was. Two of his boys, John and Robert, with whom I was very intimate, did not hesitate to say so. Mr. Stewart used the remaining space between his house and Hastings Street as a garden.

The two boys I mentioned both entered the navy. They died early, after attaining the positions of first lieutenants. John, the elder, married a Miss Field, of New York, and Robert married a sister of the first wife of the late R. Storrs Willis. She married again, and I think she is still living. They were two fine, promising young men. David Stewart, the eldest son, I was not very intimate with. He was a brilliant lawyer and became a member of congress. He was a very handsome man, as many will remember. He removed to Chicago, where, through causes entirely of his own creating, he was not successful. He entered the service on the outbreak of the Civil War, as lieutenant-colonel in an Illinois regiment and served with distinction. He died many years ago.

Robert Stewart had two daughters. Kate, a brilliant, fascinating brunette, married a gentleman by the name of Baker, from somewhere in the south. She died some years ago. I understand that Mr. Baker is alive and is a resident of this state. The other sister—I have forgotten her first name and personality—married a gentleman by the name of Turner. Wm. N. Ladue married a daughter of theirs. He is a banker somewhere out west.

Mr. Ladue was at one time deputy city controller under Mr. Redfield. On the breaking out of the Civil War he entered the service and was first lieutenant and adjutant of the Fifth Michigan Volunteer Infantry, June 19, 1861, to September 15, 1862.

My goodness! how those straight-laced old fellows of the Robert Stewart type used to freeze the hearts of their children. I presume, though, they did not mean to be harsh, for Stewart, during that young adventurous life of his must have been "one of the boys" himself.

Opposite Major Larned's and across the street from Judge Moran, resided Colonel A. T. McReynolds (lately deceased). He lived there before the Mexican War, for which he raised a company of dragoons. The colonel and his command participated in the war, he being severely wounded at the capture of the City of Mexico. He continued to live there after his return until his removal to Grand Rapids.

Andrew Ladue, of Ladue & Eldred, lived in the adjoining house. Andrew Ladue came here somewhere along about 1848 or '49, and at once entered into copartnership with the Eldreds in the tanning business. They established an extensive tannery on the river front directly in the rear of the present Jefferson Avenue residence of Hon. Wm. G. Thompson. They did a large and successful business there for some years, when they removed their establishment down the river to the Lafferty farm front.

Mr. Ladue brought his family with him, consisting of his wife, two sons (I think) and three daughters. With them came a brother's widow, her two sons and one daughter. What became of these two sons I fail to recall. Suffice it to say they were bright, temperate young men, and I presume they turned out all right. The daughter, an interesting and quite attractive young lady, after a while married Anson Eldred, son of Julius Eldred, who took her and her mother to his home, somewhere in Wisconsin. With the careers of the sons of Andrew Ladue, James and William N., most of the present generation are familiar. Of Andrew's three daughters, two are alive. One married (now) General Wm. P. Duffield, who served with distinction in the Civil War, and who is (I think) engaged in some civil capacity under the general government. He resides with his family in Washington. The other daughter (I think) has a responsible position in the Detroit public library. I beg pardon for taking up so much space with the Andrew Ladue family, but the fact is, James Ladue and myself were, from the start, warm personal friends, and so continued to his life's end. And so for the young ladies, the one that Anson Eldred carried off, and the one that General Duffield captured, had in me one of their most ardent admirers. Had I been at that time in a different financial condition, don't know what I might have said or done.

Shortly after the advent of Andrew Ladue here his brother John and family also took up their residence in the city. John was in the same business as Andrew, but confined his attention (I think) almost exclusively to the tanning of sheep pelts and dealing in wool as well. He was quite democratic and was often seen passing through the streets driving his own wagon, piled full of sheep pelts, and he seated on the top. He became quite popular and was elected mayor of the city once, or twice. Thousands, no doubt, will remember Mayor Ladue, his son, Tom Ladue, and all about them. He had daughters and other sons, but I fail to recall what became of them. They or some of their representatives are living here yet, I understand. Tom Ladue was a bright young man and full of business.

James F. Joy lived next to Mayor Ladue. Mr. Joy lived in this locality at an earlier date than did the Ladues (Lawyer Clelland living here before him), but at the same period as did Judge Witherell. It was, I think, his first attempt at housekeeping in this city. I was quite intimate with the Witherells, my uncle Thomas having married a sister of the judge (and I way long in after years married a daughter of his). I therefore saw much of the Joys.

James F. Joy, when he first came to this city, had a class of boys in the Presbyterian Sunday School, that met in the little brick session room on Woodward Avenue, between the two churches (First Presbyterian and St. Paul's). I had the pleasure of being one of the members of his class. I say pleasure, because it was eminently so, besides being most instructive. His clear exposition of the Scriptures, was a complete revelation to me, as well as to the rest of the class. I had, a few years before this, been one of a class of boys under the tutelage of Mr. Jacob M. Howard, at the Baptist Sunday School, and gained much instruction from the clear way he put things, but being some futher advanced in years when a member of Mr. Joy's class my mind was better prepared to "catch on," so to speak, to his plain and terse elucidation of the various scriptural passages that appeared in our Sunday lessons. I met Mr. Joy in after life only a few times, and then in a business way when he was connected with the Michigan Central Railroad, but I have never forgotten my experience with him as a Sunday School scholar and he my teacher.

* * *

Next to Mr. Joy lived Judge B. F. H. Witherell. Judge Witherell built his residence about 1830, while occuping a small yellow cottage that stood where is now the Detroit Opera House. On its completion he changed his location. He was chosen judge of Wayne County in 1855, and continued in that capacity until his death.

On the occasion of the dedication of the new Wayne County court house building, October 11, 1902, in an address delivered on "The Early Bench and Bar of Detroit," a distinguished member of the profession had this to say of Judge Witherell:

"Who among the older members of the Detroit bar can ever forget his dignified bearing, benignant smile and friendly address? He came of an old Detroit family, his father having been secretary of the territory, had lived here since the early years of the century, and was never known to have done a dishonorable act. He was perfectly honest, and his perceptions of justice were rarely at fault. His memory was replete with anecdotes of the early settlers, and he was never so happy as when recounting stories of the old territorial life. He knew and was known by everybody, and no one who ever passed him on Jefferson Avenue, where he lived for many years, failed of a winning smile or a cordial greeting. It was one of his pleasantries, and one which lent itself to his natural bent, to catch the bar napping, and if another case were not ready when the jury went out, he would call the entire docket and continue the cases over the term, though a dozen might have been ready upon a day's notice. But it was impossible to be angry with the dear old man. He died in 1867, respected and beloved by all and mourned by every one with whom he had been brought into social contact."

Judge Witherell, for some years and until his death in June, 1876, was the only civil court judge of Wayne County. He performed the duties unaided, for the small consideration of fifteen hundred dollars per year, and when the Civil War was on Henry A. Morrow, then city recorder, raised the Twenty-seventh Michigan Infantry, and went with it to the front. Judge Withell took charge of the recorder's court in addition to his other duties, and continued to do so until Colonel Morrow resigned, or his term expired. The judge drew the salary for recorder's unexpired term and handed the same over to Mrs. Morrow.

* * *

Judge Witherell contributed a large number of interesting articles to *The Detroit Free Press,* on "Early Detroit," over the signature of "Hamtramck." Nearly all of these articles were reproduced and published in the transactions of the Historical Society of Wisconsin, an evidence of their appreciation. He it was who first proposed the idea of erecting a monument to the brave soldiers and sailors of the state who fell while fighting the battles of the country during the Civil War, and he lived to see the idea carried to the certainty of a successful termination. On the organization of the Monument Association he was chosen president, an office he filled till the day of his death. In fact, nearly his last moments were spent in presiding over the deliberation of the board of directors of that association. He was also president of the Historical Society of Michigan during its existence.

I am fully alive to the fact that the amount of court business has increased in a most remarkable degree, and shows as much as any other factor can the great growth of the city and county. In Judge Witherell's time, as said, the one judge and the one city recorder were considered sufficient to handle all the business in that line in the city and county, except what came before the United States judge, whereas now it takes six judges to run the business.

R. B. Ross, in his admirable sketches entitled "Winder's Memories," published some seven or eight years ago in the *Evening News,* had an article entitled "Judge Witherell Going Through the Docket," and a cut heading it showing just how the judge did it.

Judge Witherell was married three times, and survived each of his partners. He was first married to Miss Mary A. Sprague, of Poultney, Vermont, in 1824, by whom he had four children, Martha E., James B., Harriett C. M. and Julia A. His first wife died in 1832, being the first victim to the cholera which prevailed to such an alarming extent in that year. In 1837, he married for his second wife Miss Delia A. Ingersoll, by whom he had one child, Charles I. She died in 1847, and in 1849 he was married to Miss Cassandra S. Brady, daughter of General Hugh Brady, and who died in 1864, from the effects of a lamp explosion. Martha, the eldest daughter, a saint if there ever was one, died just on the verge of womanhood. Harriett, the next daughter, married the writer and after thirty years of a happy married life she too passed away to a glorious immortality. The next, Julia, married Herman A. Lacey. The latter was at one time a partner in the dry goods house of Graham & Lacey on Jefferson Avenue, east side, between Woodward Avenue and Griswold Street, and after in the real estate business. He served with distinction through the Civil War as captain and assistant quartermaster from its commencement until its close. He was with the army of the Potomac at the battles of Fredericksburg, Chancellorsville and Gettysburg, as on Sherman's line from Louisville to Atlanta, and from Atlanta to the sea, quitting the service in Texas, March 13, 1866. He afterwards engaged in the street paving business with Mr. Walton, under the firm name of Walton & Lacey. This firm paved a large number of streets in this city, notably Jefferson Avenue. They also had the contract for paving the principal streets in Little Rock, Arkansas, which they completed to the entire satisfaction of the citizens of that city. Captain Lacey, later in partnership with Mr. Walton and Mr. Walker, had the contract to put in the receiving basin, build the docks and perform other work at the new water works, up Jefferson Avenue, involving large expense and much executive ability. Captain Lacey's health became so much impaired through the various strenuous pursuits in which he had been engaged, that he passed away July 4th, 1881, leaving behind an unblemished name. Captain Lacey served as city clerk for two terms, and was also deputy city controller under B. G. Stimson. His widow and a daughter are still living.

One of the sons of Judge Witherell, James, was a graduate of the University of Michigan. After graduation he joined a party of fellow graduates, five in number, Senator Palmer among them, and made the tour of Southern Spain, including Gibraltar and Tangier, Morocco. They sailed from New York in a vessel loaded with lumber, and after a rather hazardous voyage entered the harbor of Cadiz one Christmas morn. Now just see how eloquently Senator Palmer puts the incident in his Decoration Day address, delivered in this city May 30, 1879:

"On a Christmas morning, many years ago, I stood upon the deck of a merchantman, in the harbor of Cadiz, in Spain. The cathedral and convent bells were ringing out their carols in commemoration of that event which, two thousand years ago, brought tidings of peace on earth and good will to men, and, as I leaned on the taffrail infused with the glamor of youth, enveloped in the Indian summer haze of that delicious atmosphere which predisposes the most stolid to reverie, I gazed on the beautiful town, that rose like a city of pearl from the sea, and mused. I could hardly realize my own identity; that I, a boy born and reared on the margin of the great lakes, was floating on the same waters that had borne the Phoenician fleets three thousand years ago; that I was looking on a city contemporary with Carthage, and which was old before Rome was born; on the distant mountain side I could see the towers of Ronda, where Julius Ceasar had fought a pitched battle of which he said, that 'although he had fought many times for victory, he had fought but once for his life.' And here was the spot; and Hannibal had here probably stopped when starting on that march which was to end only in Rome's abasement or her triumph. I thought of the advent of Christianity, and the dethronement of the idols of Baal; of Roderick, the last of the Goths, and his fateful love; of the coming of the Moors, and of the empire they reared; of the sorrows of Boabdil, 'the man without a country, the king without a throne;' and as these imaginings floated across my brain as pinnaces before a soft south wind, a strain of music struck upon my ear. As its cadences floated across the tremulous floor of the sea, it sounded wonderously familiar. It was our national hymn. I turned and there, thank God, our flag was flying at the peak of a man-of-war. A great lump arose in my throat, great drops rolled down my cheeks. I reached out my arms as if to enfold it. What to me were the historic scenes of Spain and its fables; what its olive groves and acacias, what Xeres, Saguntum, the Alhambra or the Guadalquiver?

"Yet, to those who knew not its significance, it was a piece of bunting, with hues harmoniously blended, not half so attractive as a painting or a landscape; but no Murillo, nor the gardens of Atlantis, could have awakened any such emotions in my breast.

"What was it that endowed it with power? It was the emblem of all I held dear on earth. It was home, country, power, protection, inspiration, restraint, society in solitude, wealth in poverty. From it as from a camera were thrown upon my heart visions of those I loved, of the beautiful city where I was born, of my companions in its streets, of the primeval forests of my state, of its environing lakes, of my country and its happy homes. It was not because it floated above the deck once trod by Decatur that it had character to me. It was not that it represented half a continent. It was not because it had been triumphant on land and sea, but because from its rustling folds, as from the unpent lips of a phonograph, came to me words of cheer, expressions of affection, voices of friends in the old town, the speakers on the campus, the shouts of the hearers in response or applause, the traditions of our history and the assurance that 25,000,000 of people looked up to it only to bless it. I was no longer away from my native land. The shadow of the Flag annihilated space."

* * *

The senator's fine allusion to "Old Glory" no doubt met a thrilling response in the breast of everyone who had the pleasure of hearing the address, and, I presume, its reproduction or a portion of it at this time will cause like emotions in the breasts of those under whose eyes this article may pass. Americans at least, and particularly those that have been abroad. Twice from our shores have I wended my way across the Atlantic, and neither time did I cast my eyes upon the Stars and Stripes, with exception of seeing it displayed at two or three consulates after I left New York until I saw it flying at the mast-head of one of our men-of-war, in the harbor of Villefranche, on the Mediterranean; nor did I see it again that trip. The second trip I do not think I saw it at all, unless it was, as before, at two or three consulates, and, in addition, at the United States legation at Madrid, Spain, until I saw it flying from the mast-head of a small brig in the harbor of Cadiz. Among the vast number of ships that crowded that harbor, flying the flags of every nation, sometimes two or three times repeated, this diminutive brig was the only one that had "Old Glory" at its mast-head. It was as big as a large tablecloth, seemingly, and the strong breeze did shake it out good, saucy and defiant. I just wanted to get up and yell. I think every American has felt like doing the same under similar circumstances. The senator and wnole party besides myself felt the inspiration the incident caused.

* * *

After the party of graduates had concluded their tour, they separated at Cadiz. Young Witherell and one of the party, Dave James, going to Granada, and the rest sailing for Rio Janeiro. Witherell and James took up their quarters in the old Moorish Alhambra and there they remained for several months. Dave James and young Witherell, before leaving New York, took a course of lessons in the Daguerrean art, and became familiar with it, so much so that they themselves were competent to give instructions to others. They also provided themselves with the necessary apparatus for taking the pictures, etc. On their reaching Granada they directly set up shop in the Alhambra, and with giving instructions in the art and taking pictures they had all they could do. They were the first to introduce this art into Spain, and it created no little curiosity and interest among the natives. I have before me now one of the old plates that they took of the "Court of the Lions" in the Alhambra with themselves shown among the marble lions. It is almost as distinct now as it was on the day it was taken. On their return to this country James went to Kansas City, and Witherell went into the law and real estate business with J. Logan Chipman. He served as city attorney for two terms. After a time, tiring of the law, he turned his eye on the army, and in 1855 procured a lieutenancy in a new cavalry regiment then forming, the Second, of which regiment Albert Sidney Johnson was colonel, Robert E. Lee lieutenant-colonel, W. J. Hardee brevet lieutenant-colonel and George H. Thomas major. The regiment completed its organization the summer of the above year at Jefferson Barracks, Missouri, and was ordered to Texas. In December, 1856, Lieutenants Witherell and Owens, with a detachment of men of this regiment, defeated a party of Indians near the Rio Grande and drove them across into Mexico.

* * *

Lieutenant Witherell, in November, 1858, with a small detachment from that regiment, came up with a party of Indians who had robbed the mail party of a number of mules, near the head waters of the Nueces, Texas. A short and severe contest took place, the Indians being routed and defeated. Lieutenant Witherell and three of the soldiers were wounded. The most desperate and the main fight of the year was fought by Captain Earl Van Dorn with a detachment of the Second Cavalry, against the Comanches in Texas, who were, it was said, the best riders in the world. Their horsemanship was truly remarkable. Writing about this battle in 1865, Colonel Albert G. Brackett, chief of cavalry of the department of the Missouri during the latter year of the Civil War, and who was present, says of it, in part:

"It was soon over. The Comanches fought without giving or asking quarter until there was not one left to bend a bow, and would have won the admiration of every brave soldier of the command but for the intrusive reflection that they were the murderers of the wives and children of our frontiersmen, and the most wretched of thieves. A too high meed of praise for gallantry and unflinching courage cannot be awarded to the officers and men who achieved this success over so desperate and skillful a foe. Although superior in number to the Indians, it nevertheless required the coolest and most undaunted individual bravery to advance upon the danger that presented itself in this fearful ravine—a danger as imminent as it was unseen—without a single one of those immediate incentives to chivalric deeds—the open field, the charge, the shout of defiance, the gallant overthrow of an enemy by a comrade, the clank, clank and glitter of steel—without one of these, the troops of this command moved, as it were, into darkness, and with a courage that challenged admiration, felt for the danger they were called upon to encounter."

Among the officers he mentions as having participated in this battle occurs the name of Lieutenant James B. Witherell.

* * *

The act of secession was passed by the convention of Texas after that of South Carolina, and in March, 1861, those of the Second Regiment who had not joined the Confederacy, including Lieutenant Witherell, had to get out of Texas in short order. They proceeded to Point Isabel at the mouth of the Rio Grande, for the purpose of embarking for the north on a steamer that lay at anchor a short distance out in the Gulf of Mexico. The night before the regiment left the officers occupied quarters on the small steamboat lying at the dock that was to convey the regiment to the large steamer in the offing. During the night, by some unaccountable mishap, Lieutenant Witherell was drowned from off this boat. How it happened has always remained a mystery. It is supposed that he left his stateroom during the night for some purpose or other, and being quite near-sighted, stumbled over the low railing on the upper deck, and thence to his death. His body was recovered the following morning. It had a severe bruise on the forehead, showing that in his fall he must have come in contact with the dock or something and been rendered at once unconscious. Sad to say, that was the end of what no doubt would have been a brilliant career in the conflict that came a little later on, and in which so many of the officers of his regiment gained distinction, for or against the union. Those that were against the union, we sorrow for their sin, though they did achieve renown for their bravery.

The surviving son, Charles, younger than James B., and also a graduate of the Michigan University, a young man of much promise and scholarly attainments, died just on the verge of manhood. He was an intimate and bosom friend of Hon. Don M. Dickinson and a classmate. .Had he lived he might perhaps have attained as deserved honor and renown as has the distinguished gentleman I have named. He passed away highly esteemed and regretted by his associates, and also by all those with whom he had come in contact.

In connection with the foregoing it may be of interest to say that after fort-one years had passed Senator Palmer returned to Spain, to Cadiz. Not as a college graduate, just released from his Alma Mater and on a voyage of pleasure or adventure, but as the accredited minister of this great republic to the court of Spain. It was also Christmas time at Cadiz. The same bells from the towers of the cathedral across the square from the hotel and from various other towers in the city were ringing out their joyous notes as they did when the senator and his fellow graduates sailed into its harbor on that Christmas morn forty-one years before. With him were Mrs. Palmer, Captain Hamilton, U. S. A. military attache, and Mrs. Hamilton, Mr. Wm. Livingstone and myself. We celebrated the day at our hotel by an old-fashioned New England Christmas dinner. The conventional turkey, as well as the plum pudding, were in evidence, as also the "cup that cheers," but the pumpkin pie was missing. While here the party visited many points of interest, and one afternoon in walking around the ramparts we came across a somewhat dilapidated Spaniard who was seated on the outer wall, fishing in the bay, the water at that point being quite deep. Senator Palmer accosted him in Spanish and said:

"Well, my friend, I see you are fishing here yet, after all these years."

"Yes, Senor, but how many years?"

"Forty years," responded the senator.

"Oh," said the chap with the rod, "that was my father," and they two had by constant use all the years at that point worn quite an indenture in the stone coping of the wall.

A CORRECTION.

EDITOR DETROIT FREE PRESS: In the interest of historical accuracy, permit me to correct an error by Friend Palmer in his article in today's Sunday *Free Press*, "Detroit in Earlier Days." He says: "And when the Civil War was on, Henry A. Morrow, then city recorder, raised the Twenty-seventh Michigan Infantry and went with it to the front. Henry A. Morrow raised and was colonel of the Twenty-fourth Michigan Infantry, and joined us at Washington, D. C., 1862, after the Pope campaign, and shortly before the battles of South Mountain and Antietam, in Maryland.

I know this to be correct for our lieutenant-colonel, Frank Graves, of the Eighth Michigan Infantry, was a brother-in-law of Colonel Morrow, and he and I called on the colonel at his tent shortly after his arrival. JAMES C. WILLSON, M. D.,
Major and Surgeon, Eighth Michigan Infantry.
FLINT, July 10.

Next to Judge Witherell lived Buckminster Wight, whose house is still standing. Buckminster Wight built his fine residence somewhere in the early forties, I think. His son, Henry A. Wight, had preceded him to this city quite a while, how long I do not call to mind. Anyway we were schoolmates as well as most intimate friends and both attended D. B. Crane's school. At that time Wight made his home with his uncle (Rice) on the Cass farm, on Fort Street, where the dwelling of Allan Shelden now is. After his term of schooling with Mr. Crane had expired, he went to Boston and entered the wholesale dry goods house of another uncle, named Rice. After some years he returned to this city, and went into the lumber firm of Wight & Coffin (The Wight being his father). This firm succeeded the Detroit & Port Huron Steam Mill Lumber Co. (Rice, Coffin & Co.), who had their sawmill near the foot of Beaubien Street. They carried on business here for many years and quite successfully. Nick Greusel (captain of the Scott Guards and later a colonel of an Illinois regiment in the Civil War) was in their employ for many years, and I think was their foreman for quite a while. I do not know when Mr. Coffin quit the concern, but quit he did, and Henry, the father, and Stanley G., a younger brother, continued the business there until the father passed away. Henry and Stanley, finding their quarters too limited, went further up the river to the foot of Wight Street, and erected for themselves a model steam sawmill, unquestionably, at that date, the finest in Michigan.

The firm was H. A. & L. G. Wight. They did a successful business in their new location, for quite a while, until fire wiped out the fine plant completely. They never rebuilt. After this the firm met with varied fortunes. Henry died, leaving a widow, two sons and one daughter. The widow died a short time ago. The two sons and daughter survive. Stanley G. Wight is still with us, and is, I am pleased to know, in fairly good health, and in comfortable circumstances. The Wights built the block of residences between the corner of Hastings Street and their homestead, all of which are still standing. They also built the block of brick residences on Jefferson Avenue, between the late Senator McMillan's home and that of Mrs. Chas. Wetmore. Edwin B. Wight, younger brother of Henry and Stanley—I do not know whether he was in the firm or not—went into the Civil War, served with distinction and was in the fight at Gettysburg, where he lost an eye. * * *

Henry married Miss Sara Davenport, scion of one of the first and oldest families here. She was the daughter of Louis Davenport, the first proprietor of the Detroit and Windsor Ferry, and one of the jolliest and pleasantest of men. Another daughter of Davenport's (Ann) married our lately departed friend, Doctor Geo. B. Russel, and another (Matilda), married General John King, U. S. A. Mrs. Davenport's maiden name was Walker, and she was the sister of Lieutenant John T. Walker, U. S. Navy. The Davenports, when I came here, had a charming cottage residence on Woodward Avenue, west side, nearly half way between Larned and Congress Streets. The house was set back quite a way from the street, the intervening space being made attractive with trees, flowering shrubs and flowers. This locality presents quite a different aspect now from what it did then. I think it is the property of the Davenport heirs yet.

Doctor Louis Davenport, a most skillful surgeon, was a son. He did not see service in the regular army, during the Civil War, but often went to the front as volunteer surgeon, and rendered most efficient and timely aid, particularly after the second battle of Bull Run. It was said of him that he had the steadiest hand and the coolest head of any man on the job. The doctor was quite clever as a caricaturist, and would have made his mark in that direction had he so desired. Some of his sketches, particularly imitations of "Holbein's Dance of Death," were startling. He died not many years ago, widely lamented.

Captain Bob Wagstaff married for his first wife a sister of Mrs. Louis Davenport. Wagstaff was honored by Oliver Newberry, who gave him command of his fine brig, "Manhattan," then the pride of the lakes, and also of Uncle Oliver's heart. Wagstaff had the misfortune to lose her. She went ashore in a heavy gale on Lake Erie, just below Malden, and was almost a total loss.

Wagstaff also had the proud distinction, in connection with Captain "Gus" McKinstry, of taking the schooner Napoleon (one of Newberry's fleet) in the depth of winter, loaded with provisions to Mackinac to relieve the dwellers on the island as well as the United States troops stationed at the fort, who by some unexplained reason happened to be short and almost on the verge of starvation. (This incident as well as the loss of the Manhattan has appeared in print before, but it may not be out of place now, in this connection).

* * *

General John King was a protege of General Hugh Brady. The latter procured for him, when a lad, the appointment of cadet at West Point. After the usual four years' ordeal, he graduated into the infantry, serving with distinction in the Mexican and Civil Wars. He died not many years ago, a retired brigadier general, U. S. A. He was severely wounded in the hand, at the battle of Shiloh. All who knew John King (and they were a host) knew him only to love and admire him. He died just as he had commenced to enjoy life and his well won honors. His widow and (I think) two daughters survive him.

* * *

Oliver Bellair and Richard Hopson lived in this block also. Bellair was one of the old French residents, and quite prominent. He was in the war of 1812, and held some important position on the American side. He was present at Hull's surrender. I have seen the old gentleman often, and knew him quite well.

Hopson kept a grocery store in an addition to his dwelling. The lot on this upper corner of Hastings Street was vacant. James Nall, later on, built a fine residence in this block and resided in it for quite a period.

* * *

Thomas C. Miller, a tobacconist, lived on the opposite corner of Hastings Street, where are now a drug store and Doctor Jennings' office. Miller lived here until he erected a house of his own a little further up the street and moved into it. It was just beyond or adjoining the Congregational church. I think he lived their until he died.

Thomas C. Miller, an agreeable gentleman, succeeded his father, who was the pioneer in the tobacco business here. Miller's store and factory was on Woodward Avenue, between Jefferson Avenue and Woodbridge Street. It was quite extensive for those days, and in fact the only one in Michigan. Dealers of every sort kept tobacco in stock, but Miller's was the first establishment that dealt in that most desirable commodity exclusively, and their wooden Indian was the first to appear on any street in Detroit. John J. Bagley served his apprenticeship at the business with Miller and his father, as did Daniel Scotten.

While occupying this house, Miller gave a fancy dress party, that was attended by all the elite of the city, in costume, none being admitted that were not so dressed. It was a brilliant affair, and the first of the kind ever held here, with the exception of one given three or four years before by Captains Grant and Gore, which (in my opinion), the one at Miller's eclipsed. The latter at that time kept bachelor's hall, and it was hinted, that he was on the lookout for a fair partner, and had adopted this means of paving the way into society, for that purpose. Be that as it may, he, after a while, married, not to any fair one that was present at his house that night, but to a charming young lady, highly accomplished, the daughter of a fine French family (Quelos), not long here from their native country. After a brief but happy married life, of a little more than a year's duration, the wife died leaving an infant daughter. Miller himself followed, not many years after, the daughter surviving him.

* * *

A young sister of Mrs. Miller, a bright, vivacious young lady, and also highly accomplished, had many admirers, and among them was, Wellington (Duke) Hunt, a scion of one of the old Hunt families, who succeeded in capturing her. After many years of happy married life Hunt passed away, leaving her a widow with three boys. The eldest (Wellington) is married, and he with his wife and his mother at present occupy the family homestead on upper Jefferson Avenue. The other two boys are also alive, and are all well and favorably known to the present generation. Many will call to mind the father, "Duke" Hunt. A most strenuous, vigorous hustler after this world's possessions. He managed, through much up-hill work, to secure a competency, which his widow is now enjoying. I think the present "Duke" Hunt is successful in the real estate business. I hope so, at least.

Hunt served in the Civil War as captain in a Michigan cavalry regiment. There were other Hunts in this war, cousins of his, notably Lewis C. Hunt, a West Pointer, who rose to the rank of brigadier-general; another cousin, Henry I. Hunt, also a West Pointer and later a brigadier-general, and chief of artillery of the Army of the Potomac, and rendered most distinguished service as such at the battle of Gettyburg.

* * *

After Thomas C. Miller, there lived along here from time to time Zebulon Kirby, Samuel G. Watson and others whose names have escaped my memory. Zebulon Kirby was of the firm of Ingersoll & Kirby, leather dealers. Captain John Pridgeon most all of the present day will remember. Anthony Dudgeon scores of our citizens will recall with pleasure and regret that he parted from our midst so early in life. He married a daughter of Mr. Justus Ingersoll, sister to Mrs. Alex Lewis, Mrs. Frank Phelps and Mrs. Carman, and sister also to Jessie and Jerome Ingersoll. Two children were born to the Dudgeons, a son and a daughter. The son, a promising boy, just verging into manhood, was acidentally drowned, as was ex-Mayor Barker, from the latter's yacht, between the city and Grosse Ile. The daughter, as fair and comely as her mother and aunts ever were, which is admitting much, married Mr. Harry Newberry, son of Mr. John G. Newberry. Mr. and Mrs. Newberry have resided abroad during most of their married life, in Paris and Madrid, Spain. Mr. Newberry was appointed secretary of the United States legation at the latter capital a short time before Minister Palmer resigned the post. After the latter retired Mr. Newberry became virtually minister, until the appointment of Mr. Palmer's successor. It is, perhaps, needless to say, that Mr. Newberry and his gifted wife fully sustain the reputation of Minister Palmer and his estimable consort in upholding the dignity of this nation, both politically and socially, at the Spanish court. They remained there until Mr. Newberry was transferred to Constantinople. How long he remained at the latter post I do not know.

* * *

Lawyer Samuel G. Watson was an eminent member of the Detroit bar and one time was a partner of Judge B. F. H. Witherell. He was a genial, companionable gentleman. He died many years ago, leaving a widow and three attractive daughters. One of the latter married a Captain Hart, U. S. A. Another married Mr. Lovett, of Scotten & Lovett. The other married the youngest son of John Stephens, of the firm of Stephesn & Field, wholesale grocers, Woodward Avenue. Mr. Lovett died a few years ago. Mrs. Lovett survives him. I do not know whether Mrs. Hart and Mrs. Stephens are alive or not.

Colonel J. B. Grayson, United States Army, followed Mr. Miller in the occupancy of the house on the corner and lived there for a time, while his family were here with him. They returned to New Orleans, from whence they came, and the colonel took up quarters at the Michigan Exchange, until ordered to New Mexico, just before the Civil War. Between Mr. Miller's house and Russell Street, "Ferd" Parker, grocer (brother of the late T. A. Parker), built a fine brick residence which is still standing, though completely modernized. Mr. Townsend, of Martin & Townsend, afterwards of DeGraff & Townsend, built and occupied a comfortable wooden dwelling adjoining the residence of Mr. Parker, and lived there until his death, which occurred many years ago.

A portion of Russell Street, adjoining, was in dispute, as regards dedication to the city or something of that nature. Anyway, Patrick Tregent concluded he would take the bull by the horns, and squatted on it and put up a four-story brick residence which nearly blocked the street. The authorities pitched into him and after a long fight Tregent removed it. I don't know whether he reaped anything from his venture or not, but think he did. He was not apt to go short on anything of that sort. Beyond Robert Stewart, on the opposite corner of Hastings Street, where Alex. Lewis is now, Cullen Brown lived in a modest wooden dwelling until he moved into a brick house on the present site of the Mandell residence near the corner of St. Aubin Avenue. The Brown corner was afterwards occupied by Mr. Lewis, with the present fine brick residence.

Mr. A. C. McGraw built a fine brick residence adjoining the house of Mr. Lewis, and it still belongs to the McGraw estate. Chancellor Farnsworth owned and occupied a large wooden residence adjoining and lived there many years, until his death, which occurred in the same house. The chancellor's holdings continued to Boliver alley, now obliterated.

The chancellor built this residence while living on Fort Street, and occupied it somewhere about 1835. Many, very many of our old citizens will remember Chancellor Farnsworth, the amiable, kind-hearted, Christian gentleman, who, I used to think, was absolutely without guile. His accomplished wife was one of the principal leaders in society, a society that was as brilliant as any in all the northwest. They had two daughters. General O. B. Willcox won the eldest for his first wife, when he was second lieutenant, U. S. A., and shortly after he graduated from West Point. She died many years ago. The second married a young lawyer from New York, whose name has escaped my memory. And here the chancellor and his gifted wife passed the remainder of their days, honored by all, and, when they passed from earth, regretted by all.

Ellis Doty, father of George and Henry Doty, built and occupied, before 1830, a fine residence at the foot of this alley on the River Road. On the corner of this alley, next beyond Chancellor Farnsworth's, was a yellow cottage, occupied by Mrs. Hinchman, mother of Guy F. Hinchman, who lived there a short time only. Its place was taken by the present Eaton residence, which was built by Theodore H. Eaton.

Mr. C. C. Trowbridge built and occupied the adjoining residence which is still standing. It was where Jefferson Avenue then came to a stop. This avenue was not opened beyond the Trowbridge line or the line of the so-called Mullett farm for two or three years after 1827, a rail fence crossing the avenue at that point. People had to use the River Road if they desired to proceed further. When the avenue was opened up to Mt. Elliott Avenue it was done with a great deal of difficulty and met with much opposition from the old French settlers, who regarded the innovation as downright robbery. Some years later Ezra Rood built two houses where the late Senator McMillan's residence now stands.

Mr. Rood had been for about four years the receiver of public moneys here, and at the end of his term of office, found $6,000 in his hands, surplus, that he could not account for, and reported the fact to the treasury. They said his accounts were O. K. and closed, so he took the $6,000, built these two houses, and he and his wife took a trip to Europe. Upon his return the United States treasury officials informed him that on a re-examination of his accounts, through an oversight in the settlement when he closed his official relations with the United States government, it was found that he was in debt in the sum of $6,000. On a showing of the facts, Rood at once paid up the amount, but he had the two houses and a trip to Europe to show for it. Not so bad after all.

Captain Gore, Fourth United States Infantry, occupied the first one of these two houses for a while, and after him, Lieutenant U. S. Grant, of the same regiment, lived there. Washington A. Bacon, a well remembered school teacher, took possession after Grant vacated the premises. He had his school in the rear in a building on the corner of Larned and Russell Streets. The next house was occupied by Captain S. P. Heintzleman, United States quartermaster at this post, during his station here. Afterward, in the Civil War, he became general. The row of brick houses that extended to the residence of Mrs. Charles Wetmore, were erected by Mr. Buckminster Wight and are still standing.

The brick dwelling now occupied by Mrs. Wetmore was built by her father, Alex. H. Buel, a distinguished lawyer, member of congress, etc. There were no buildings of any note between this and Jefferson Avenue bridge, except the Benson house, on the corner of Jefferson Avenue and Orleans Street, two brick dwellings erected by P. & W. Fisher, jewelers, and a wooden dwelling occupied by the late Colonel W. D. Wilkins. All of these above mentioned are still standing.

The next dwelling beyond Mr. Trowbridge's, same side, was that of D. J. Campau. The next was that of Horace Hallock. The stone residence of the late Sidney D. Miller is on the site of a wooden dwelling erected by Mr. C. Morass and occupied along about 1848 by Dr. Ebenezer Hurde. Mr. Morass also built the brick residence, still standing, next beyond that of the late R. P. Toms, and now owned by Mrs. Chas. Lathrop. The house adjoining was built by the late Dr. H. P. Cobb and occupied by him until his death. His widow and his son, Dr. L. H. Cobb, lived there until the son's death, the widow dying soon after. There were no residences of any consequence between the house of Dr. Cobb and the railroad bridge except the brick dwelling right at the bridge, built by the late Dr. Desnoyers, now owned by the William Gray estate, and occupied by the latter's widow.

The depot of the Detroit and Pontiac Railroad was, at an early date, on the southwest corner of Jefferson Avenue and

Dequindre Street. It was a temporary wooden affair and the road was equipped with very ordinary cars, in the light of the present, and the track was laid with strap rails that curled up on the least provocation, the end coming up through the floors of the cars and endangering life and limb. I have been to Pontiac often on this road and have been a scared witness on two or three occasions, when the "snake heads," as they were termed, made their sudden appearance, but am happy to say that no very serious accident ever occurred on their account.

After using this terminus for a while the company, instead of building a depot and shops at the foot of Dequindre Street, as it was supposed they would do, concluded that they would rather get into the heart of the city than on to the river front, so they tore up and abandoned their track through Dequindre Street to Gratiot Avenue, and came in on the latter thoroughfare, establishing their depot in the rear of Andrew's Hotel (where the Detroit Opera House now stands).

After the company had thus used or occupied Gratiot Avenue for some years, the citizens doing business on the street began to make a fuss, and continued it, threatened to tear up the track, etc., until finally the company was compelled to vacate the avenue and return to their old occupancy of Dequindre Street.

When the Detroit & Pontiac Railroad was first contemplated, Major Dequindre, Judge James Witherell and other property owners interested, and the projectors of the road, entered into a written agreement whereby the latter bound themselves, if the former would permit them to run their tracks into the city over their land, and to the river front, to establish their depot and other buildings there, making it the permanent terminus of the road; and further, in consideration of the expected benefits to adjoining property to be derived, through the location of the depot, etc., on the river front, the property owners agreed to grant the railroad people a right of way 100 feet wide over any of their land. The route selected was between the Dequindre and Witherell farms, down what is now called Dequindre Street, to the river.

Well, the road did come in but only to this depot on Larned Street, and the company never established a depot nor buildings of any sort at the foot of the so-called Dequindre Street. During the time they abandoned the above location and came in on Gratiot Avenue down to the Campus. They quietly acquired the title from the Dequindre heirs to forty feet of the so-called Dequindre Street, and, in connection with the Witherell heirs, for and in consideration of the purchase from them of thirty-five feet on Jefferson Avenue and running along their track to Woodbridge Street, for street purposes, and also some other minor considerations, they relinquished to them their interest in all but sixty feet of the 100 feet right of way mentioned in the original grant in the early thirties. They also at the same time acquired right of way from Woodbridge Street at its intersection with Dequindre to their present location. Having accomplished this clever move, they abandoned Gratiot Avenue, as said before, but instead of laying their tracks on Dequindre Street down to Atwater, they switched off at Woodbridge Street and came in on the river front where they now hold out. A most desirable change for the railroad company, but not quite so much so for the holders of property at the foot of Dequindre Street, the Witherell and Dequindre farms.

In the early days when the railroad was projected, there was scarcely anyone living along its line, or in the vicinity. There were not at that time 500 inhabitants scattered over the then Seventh Ward and on the Witherell and St. Aubin farms adjoining (the latter then in Hamtramck). It was all farming land beyond Gratiot Avenue, and the danger to life and limb was scarcely thought of, nor were the benefits of a thoroughfare to the river taken into account. Who was there to use it? But now what a difference and what a benefit it would be to the thousands living in the immediate vicinity of the railroad to have it abandon its present tracks and come into the city, if it could, on the Michigan Central loop line, Beaufait Avenue, or some other street beyond it, and give the city a chance to open Dequindre Street to the river. "A consummation devoutly to be wished" and one that would greatly enhance the value of real estate in that section of the city.

The railroad company has had its innings for the last sixty years. The benefits the kind-hearted and credulous people expected to derive from the grant of 100 feet right-of-way were never realized. The railroad went its way, regardless and rejoicing, and now they ought not to howl if they are compelled to do what they most certainly should do, in the interests of the public, and what they must do in time.

The title to the twenty feet of the Witherell farm, the railroad company has not acquired, so far.

Repeated attempts have been made by citizens of the old Seventh Ward along the line of this road, through the common council, to make the road remove its tracks, or do something, but without success.

The heirs of the Witherell farm, after it was divided, occupied most of the space on each side of Jefferson Avenue to the line of the St. Aubin farm, with their residences, as, for instance, Dr. and Mrs. Hurd, Judge B. F. H. Witherell, Mr. and Mrs. Thomas Palmer and James B .Watson. On the line of the St. Aubin farm, Cullen Brown lived in a two-story brick residence, where is now the Mandell house, as before stated, and after him Mr. Carne, the brewer, occupied it.

Beyond this there were no residences of any note, except that of the Hon. John Norvell, which is still standing this side of the Ducharme place. On the bank of Bloody Run one of the Hunt brothers lived in a small, attractive cottage. He married, as before stated, a daughter of Jonathan Keeney, who lived on Fort Street. His memory has been perpetuated by our friend, J. B. Ross, in his admirable articles in the *Evening News*, entitled, "Detroit in 1837."

Where Jefferson Avenue crossed Bloody Run, near the Pontiac tree (now gone), were the remains of a grist mill, the foundations, some of the timbers and the mill stones half buried in the soil. The mouth of Bloody Run, was, when I came here, crossed by the same log bridge or a large portion of it, that spanned it that July day in 1763, when Captain Dalzell and his command met disaster at the hands of Pontiac and his warriors. This bridge had been repaired from time to time of course, but it was practically the same bridge. The old Parent residence at the mouth of the "Run" was then standing where many of the defeated troops sought shelter after their repulse on the bridge. This house bore many bullet marks fired into it during the melee. The battle of Bloody Run has been so often described that I will dwell on it here, only briefly.

In regard to the battle, Mr. Trowbridge said, in an address before the "Historical Society of Michigan," of which Judge B. F. H. Witherell was president: (There is no date to the newspaper clipping giving an account of it, kindly loaned me by the

Rev. David M. Cooper, of this city, but it must have been delivered many years before Mr. Trowbridge's death).

"We of this generation, although the silver cord is appointed to be broken at three score years and ten, have shaken hands, as it were, with Cartier and La Salle and Marquette, to whom Charlevoix assigns the discovery of the Mississippi, with Hennepin and Charlevoix and La Hontan and Carver and Henry and Pike. Nay, we have actually talked with the friends of Pontiac, and listened with breathless interest to their simple and truthful narratives of his daring conspiracy with the western tribes for the extermination of the British power from the country claimed by the conspirators as the special gift of the Great Spirit, to his red children, and especially of that dreadful massacre of British troops on the 31st of July, 1763, at Parent's Creek, now and ever since the event called Bloody Run, and at this time within the boundaries of our city. You and I, Mr. President, were well acquainted with Mr. Peltier, the grandfather of the late Chief Justice Whipple; with Mr. Charles Gouin, our near neighbor; with Madame Meloche, a resident at Parent's Creek; with Jacques Parent, of Connor's Creek; and Gabriel St. Aubin, of Sandwich. These were all eye-witnesses of the massacre. Mr. Peltier was lying upon the roof of his father's cottage, near the creek, looking over its ridge upon the horrid spectacle, and Mrs. Meloche was a young bride, living with her father-in-law upon the bank of the creek, and but a few hundred yards from the bridge upon which so many brave men met an inglorious death. It was my privilege, just forty years ago, to take from the lips of each of these venerable persons, while yet in the full possession of their memories, such of the principal incidents of the siege of the fort at Detroit as were most vividly recollected by them. Their relations, just as they were then taken, with a lead pencil, have, as you are aware, been presented to your society, together with a literal copy in ink, covering about fifty pages of foolscap, in order to insure their better preservation."

Parkman says, as most all have read, that the designs of Pontiac were told to Major Gladwin, the commander of the fort, by a beautiful dark-eyed daughter of the forest, named Catherine, who had won the major's affections. Parent says that Pontiac told him this was done by "an old squaw" of that name, who communicated not with Gladwin, but with some Pawnee servant woman in the fort; and that he sent two young men to bring her to his tent, where he gave her a severe beating with a crosse, a stick used by the Indians in playing ball.

Colonel McKenney in his "Tour of the Lakes," in 1826, says he visited the battleground, "Bloody Run," and that the remains of the old bridge were there then, "The Bloody Run Bridge," and its remains.

> "Tell ye where the dead
> Made the earth wet, and turned th' unwilling waters red."

And also that Mr. St. Aubin, who with Mr. Chapoton, were Captain Dalzell's two guides, on that fatal July morning, told him that on visiting the battleground on the morning after the battle he saw upon the bridge alone from eighty to 100 dead bodies. The passage over it was stopped by them. Pontiac, on the day after the battle, sent for some Canadians who lived near, and pointing to the dead bodies on the bridge, and to the batteaux in the creek, said:

"Take these dead dogs—put them in those boats of mine and take them to the fort."

The order was obeyed, so far as the removal of the bodies were embraced in it, but they were buried in the cellar of a Mr. Sterling's house. It is also said Captain Dalzell's head was chopped off and stuck on one of the pickets of the fence in front of Parent's house.

I think this Mr. Sterling's house must have been inside the palisades, and situated between what is now Jefferson Avenue and Woodbridge Street, in the rear of the Mutual Insurance Company building, as the late Judge B. F. H. Witherell said he had often, when a boy, seen the inclosure containing the remains. Presume they are now reposing quietly in the alley in the rear of the Michigan Mutual Insurance Company building.

Bloody Run was called Parent Creek before this Pontiac affair. Its name being changed afterwards to the one it now bears or rather to the one it did bear before it was obliterated.

The hearth and chimney stones of this old Parent residence were lying around on the ground a few years ago, and I presume some of them are around there yet.

As said before, Jefferson Avenue was not, in 1827, opened up further than to the residence of C. C. Trowbridge. The travel for quite awhile was by the river road. On this river road was located the residence of Ellis Doty at the foot of Boliver Alley. Adjoining was a tavern kept by Pascal Potvin (the old Frenchman also drove a cart in the city, hauling water, etc.). Mr. Abraham Cook, father of Mrs. Thomas Knapp and Mrs. John Owen, occupied the next residence, then came Colonel Marsaac's residence, then the Riopelle and Dequindre homesteads. Judge Witherell occupied the next residence. The latter was not of the old French style. It had a fine orchard and quite a number of fine old French pear trees attached to it as did the Marsaac, Riopelle and Dequindre homes. The pear trees around the Witherell home were particularly fine. Three large ones at the entrance gate, on the river front, three on the line of the apple orchard in the rear of the house and five or six on the line of the Dequindre farm. They bore delicious fruit, as did also the apple orchard.

The judge was a man of commanding presence, more than six feet tall, quite different from his immediate neighbors who were small in stature, but at this time he had begun to feel quite a little the weight of the years that were upon him. He, however, proved to me one day that he was not as far gone as he appeared. We were on his back porch and I called his attention to a black squirrel that was disporting itself in the top of one of the tallest pear trees. Said he, "You just wait, keep your eye on the squirrel, I will get my shot gun and see what I can do with him, think I can fetch him." He got his gun, raised it to his shoulder and fired, bringing down the squirrel. Then he turned to me and said, "you didn't think I could do it, now did you?" I said, "no, sir, I did not think you could." Then he chuckled.

The St. Aubin farm and homestead were adjoining, then followed the Chene, Campau and McDougall farms. The St. Aubin, Chene and Campau homesteads I remember quite well. They were of the conventional French type. All these residences had fine pear trees in the front and fine apple orchards in the rear.

Mr. Wm. H. Coyle, who was a resident of Detroit, in the latter thirties, wrote a poem about the pear trees, which shows how they were loved and almost made sacred by the French pioneers. The few verses which follow give the tone of the poem:

"An hundred years and more ye have stood,
    Through sunshine and through storms,
And still like warriors clad in mail,
    Ye lift your stalwart forms.

When the ancient city fell by the flames,
    Ye saw it in ashes expire,
But like true sentinels kept your posts,
    In the blazing whirl of fire.

The lingering few "vieux habitans"
    Look at ye with a sigh,
And memory's teardrop dims their gaze,
    While they think of the times gone by.

Live on, old trees, in your hale green age,
    Long, long may your shadows last,
With your blossomed boughs and golden fruit,
    Loved emblems of the past."

Many of the present residents of Detroit must remember that eccentric genius, W. H. Coyle.

There were, along here, fine fishing grounds, where in the season innumerable whitefish were caught with the seine. The best ground was on the Chene farm, where the plant of Parke, Davis & Co. now is. There was a sort of a middle ground about twenty or thirty feet from the shore, and on it were located the reels for the nets, two log shanties for the fishermen, and a large inclosure for the catch. I have often spent the night there, witnessing the operation of seining. I quote from some one, I do not know who, in regard to the catching of whitefish. It expresses my sentiments:

"And truly it was an interesting spectacle to see boats leaving the shore with nets coiled on the stern shelf as the men pulled up the stream, until reaching the channel bank the net was quickly paid out and the boat pulled rapidly back to land, the floats following in a graceful curved line, while often a song kept time with the oars; then as both ends were drawn briskly in, to see the beautiful white silvery bodies glancing through the water and finally tossed, all glowing and active, on the beach."

The Campans (Labie), the father and his two sons, Barney and Aleck, carried on the catching of whitefish at the upper end of Belle Isle for many years, and after the death of their father, the sons continued for some time, until, I think, the death of Barney. The grounds were considered the finest on the river, and yielded every season great quantities of fish. I have often been there during the fall and saw their expert French boatman haul in the seines almost bursting with their finny prey. To my mind it was an exceedingly interesting experience, and one I imagine that but few of the present day can recall.

> "Come hither from Parnassus' hill,
> Of melting whitefish eat your fill,
> And from your lubricated throats
> Will glide such smooth and pleasing notes
> As never yet the pipes did follow
> Of your precentor—bright Apollo.
> In the fall weather, cool and hazy,
> When the slow sun is getting lazy,
> And from his cold bath in the river
> Comes out all red with many a shiver,
> With feet too chilly as they pass
> To melt the hoar frost on the grass.
> Northward his yearly journey takes
> The shining 'white deer of the lakes.'
> Swift through the lymph, in countless herds,
> Thicker than the thickest flight of birds.
> The living shapes of silver dash,
> Till all the rustling waters flash,
> As when beneath the breeze of June
> Their myriad waves reflect the moon.
> Then all the dwellers in the land
> Come trooping gaily to the sand;
> Through day and night the populous shore
> Echoes the clanking of the oar.
> The meshes of the spreading seine
> Are tried with many a grievous strain,
> And the gay crowd with jovial din,
> Hail the rich harvest gathered in."

And then to eat a whitefish, cooked by one of the natives, man or woman, was a delicious morsel to be long remembered.

so unlike the present methods. You that have tasted a whitefish cooked on the fishing grounds by a French fisherman know what I mean.

> "This fish is a subject so dainty and white
> To show in a lecture, to eat or to write,
> That equals my joy; I declare on my life,
> To raise up my voice or to raise up my knife,
> 'Tis a morsel alike for the gourmand or faster;
> White, white as a tablet of pure alabaster,
> Its beauty and flavor no person can doubt
> When seen in the water or tasted without;
> And all the dispute that opinions ere makes
> Of this king of lake fishes, this deer of the lakes,
> Regards not its choiceness, to ponder or sup,
> But the best mode of dressing or serving it up."

This fish in its season was the mainstay of the community, rich and poor alike. Just think of it, you could go to market any morning in the season and get as many whitefish as you wanted for five cents apiece. On the fishing grounds you could have for the asking as many as you yourself could well carry away.

The salting and packing of the surplus stock of whitefish was a great industry, giving employment to a large number of persons up and down the river. These salted fish were considered a great delicacy here and elsewhere, during the summer months. No household was regarded as fixed for the summer season unless it had one or two half barrels of salted whitefish in the cellar. Tom Lewis, the "Governor of Grosse Ile," had an extensive whitefish fishery on his farm on that island. He had a peculiar way of curing his fish that kept them always in great demand and only a favored few could get them.

All the whitefish that were salted down by the proprietors of the various fisheries in this vicinity, and up the lakes, before they could obtain a market for them in the east and elsewhere, had to undergo the examination of a state inspector here. This inspector was a man by the name of Clark, quite a conspicuous figure in those days. The inspection of the fish was conducted in a long open shed that occupied the space on the dock between the warehouse of Shadrach Gillett and DeGarmo Jones. It was rather an interesting process to me, and I used often to witness it. The fish had to be re-packed, and gone over one by one, re-salted and otherwise put in a marketable condition. Clark's son, Ben, who was his father's deputy, was a schoolmate of mine, and another attraction that drew my attention to this business. The decline in the catch, owing to the absence of whitefish, made the services of an inspector useless, and the office was therefore abolished, I think.

The James Campau (brother of Joseph) homestead was a large log structure, a story and a half with dormer windows, huge chimneys, etc. It was situated about opposite where Pitt's saw mill used to stand. In this house, a large number of British soldiers, on their retreat from Bloody Run, took refuge. Campau hustled them into the upper part of the house, the entrance to which was reached by a ladder and closed by a trapdoor. Before they all got out of harm's way the Indians swarmed into the house and fired on the last few who were on the ladder, but did not do much damage. I have often seen the bullet marks on the wooden beams of the ceiling. Judge Witherell had at one time a barbed arrow that came from an Indian bow on this occasion. It did not harm anyone, but lodged in the front door frame of the Campau house. One of the latter's descendants presented it to the judge and he gave it to the State Historical Society. Campau claimed to have sustained a serious loss in this affair and in 1772 sent a petition "to the king's most excellent majesty," stating that he had sheltered two hundred and fifty of Captain Dalzell's troops on their retreat, had suffered much damage on that account and asked for three hundred dollars in payment of same. It is not known whether he ever got it or not.

The diminutive old French church or chapel that stood next below the James Campau house and partly in the orchard, on the river road, is probably well remembered by many old settlers. No service was ever held in it in my day; it always remained tightly closed. It used to be a curious relic of the olden time to me, and I have often rested on its front steps, in my boyhood days, and pondered over its origin and the many scenes enacted in and around it. The late Colonel W. D. Wilkins wrote an interesting description of this little church, for the Detroit *Free Press*, in 1878, and it is such a faithful one that I reproduce it here:

"It seems a pity that we have not a little of this reverence for the olden time in Detroit, or rather that we did not have it before, for except the old Joseph Campau house on Jefferson Avenue, all the buildings that might have recalled the joyous, adventurous and romantic age of the French habitant and the British garrison and trader, are gone. I remember a dear little wooden chapel that once stood close by the river side, in what is now the western part of the Tenth Ward. It was built by one of the earliest French settlers, I believe by an ancestor of the late Joseph Campau and Barnabas Campau, in fulfillment of a vow made to the Blessed Virgin during a great storm on his voyage from Normandy to Canada. It stood on solid oaken foundations and frame, though with crumbled weather-beaten sides, with moss covered belfrey, with the tiny but musical bell that came from "La Belle France," and with massive iron handles to the double leaves of the door, each bearing the fleur de lis, proud badge of the Bourbons. It was here that the adventurous voyageurs and coureurs des bois heard their last mass and took farewells of friends and relatives and gave the parting kiss to one who was dearer than either, before departing on their long and perilous canoe voyages over stormy lakes, through unknown streams, amidst dense forests, through savage bands, more inhospitable than wood, lake or storm, to the far, far distant La Pointe or Lake of the Woods or Mississippi's sources, or wherever the quest of commerce led their dauntless, patient, merry hearts. Here the gay voyageuer, returning with haloo and song and gun fire from his long and perilous voyage, decked with red sash and bead work, and passing rich from the perils and profits of journey and chase, was wedded to the bright-eyed demoiselle who had been patiently waiting for him in the high-roofed, one-story farm house by the bank of the stream; and here they drove in gay procession through the narrow streets of 'La Fort' to display the gallantry of the groom and the beauty and the fine attire of the bride.

"It was a most interesting little building, almost the only one left in historic old Detroit City of three dominions and five wars, hallowed with the most romantic and sentimental associations; but it stood in the way of a projected sawmill, the few feet of space occupied by its venerable and sacred walls were needed for lumber piles, and in 1848 the little church disappeared, and I presume its very existence has been forgotten except by the older inhabitants, among whom I am beginning to class myself. It would have cost but a trifle to preserve the time honored chapel, and think what a precious relic it would be now."

In "Shoepac's Recollections," a story of the early days in

Detroit, by General O. B. Willcox, U. S. A., the writer says of the River Road (already mentioned) :

"In front of the houses on the river bank are the cherry trees and in the rear the apple and pear orchards—fruits brought from sunny France and planted by the skillful Jesuits; apples red to the core, large and luscious; cherries that rival nectarines, and pears of every variety, and of every season from July to November.

"'Bright gleam the apples, pears and cherries.'

"Nor will the patch of onions escape his notice; it is the Frenchman's flower-garden—the invariable concomitant of every family who may claim a foot square of mother earth. The fish net or seine is stretched on the fence." I can bear most willing testimony to Shoepac's statement in regard to the cherry, apple and pear trees, as I have spent many an hour in my boyhood in their branches and beneath their shades; also enjoyed the luscious fruit; and then the sweet cider and perry (the latter the juice of the pear). Every farmer on the river owned a cider mill, and on Judge James Witherell's farm was a fine one. Reader, did you ever, when a boy, suck cider through a straw? If you have, then you know what a delicious pastime it is, and what a delightful memory of your boyhood's days.

"The fish nets. Have you ever been on the fishing grounds and witnessed the paying out and the hauling in of the net or seine, and joined in the excitement, as I have done many times, and after, of melting whitefish eat your fill?

"'The shining "White deer of the lakes"
Swift through the lymph in countless herds,
Thicker than the thickest flight of birds,
The living shapes of silver dash,
Till all the rustling waters flash
As when beneath the breeze of June
Their myriad waves reflect the moon,
Then all the dwellers in the land
Come trooping gaily to the sand;
Through day and night the populous shore
Echoes the clanking oar.
The meshes of the spreading seine
Are tried by many a grievous strain,
And the gay crowd with joyous din,
Hail the rich harvest gathered in.'"

Shoepac goes on to say:

"The long flint-lock gun, with leather pouch and powder-horn is hung on wooden hooks in the hall. The canoe is drawn up on the beach. But hark! You hear the sound of distant voices come stealing over the water. Turn towards the river. See a long pirouge (birch bark canoe) or more ample Mackinaw boat, perhaps a little fleet of them in a single line manned by voyageurs or coureurs de bois, and loaded with packs of furs. The oarsmen have fitted out at Mackinaw, to appear in style at Detroit—the greater station and nearer civilization. Each garcon has a red sash around his waist and pulls a red oar, or short-handled paddle, the blade of which is a bright crimson. They keep perfect time and it is a joyous, quick time—with the notes of a French song which was chanted in France a century or more ago.

" 'Malbrooks s'en vat a guerrah!'

"Or, perchance the air is one you may not recognize—

" 'A Lon-don day
S'en va coucher!'

"And this, one verse of which is given—

" 'La Jeune Sophie
Chantait l'autre jour,
Son echo repete,
Que non pas d' amour
N'est pas de bon jour.'

"The words were sung by one of the party of boatmen and all joined in the chorus. No music could be more lively and inspiring. It comes over the water—is accompanied by the splash of oars. It is roared out with the utmost spirit, too, by that most glorious of all instruments, the human voice. It has pealed through the woods, and over the rivers and lakes for thousands of miles. It has animated those brave adventurers in camp, at portage through summer and winter, rain and snow, sickness, peril and death; and now joy! joy! it greets the steeples of St. Anne! The children run out of the houses, down to the river shore to hear it; the maiden turns pale, and blushes, and hurries to the door; the old man hobbles out and waves his hat. Troops of people rush down to the wharves to see them land; and such shouts of welcome and rejoicing never were known before. Witness the fiddling and dancing on Sunday evenings whenever there was any little neighborhood of French people on the great wide porch, or beneath trees on the grass; or, if in the house with the doors and windows thrown wide open. And there were the prettiest and most mischievous-eyed French girls dancing away for dear life with the good-looking, frank-mannered voyageurs or coureurs de bois, in their red, yellow or green sashes, long black hair, and blue calico shirts.

"Then was there not the racing to church the year round and racing home again? And were there not regular trotting matches on the afternoons of the great days of the church, which brought the people in from the country up and down the river? Especially, was there anything like it in the winter season, when the wicked river would even wink at these atrocities by freezing over, so that nothing was seen on Sunday afternoons but carioles, turned up in front, in a curl like a skate, gliding or rather flying over the ice, two and two? The little Canadian ponies held their tails up in the air like banners and their noses protruding into the clouds, or snorting between their legs—they trotting like mad, while the garcons whooped like Indians.

"Then on Easter morning, was not the churchyard of St. Anne fairly riotous with boys cracking painted or dyed eggs?"

General Wilcox speaks also of the "Shoepac," the name he gives his book. The Shoepac, as all old timers know, was an article of foot wear used almost exclusively by the French habitant. It was an article of general merchandise, the merchants of those days keeping it always in stock. The Palmers kept a large quantity on hand, as did Joseph Campau, Peter Desnoyers, and others. A few of the French residents of the city used to wear shoepacs habitually, summer and winter, as, for instance, Lambert Beaubien, Mons Cote (the latter lived on Woodward Avenue, where is now the store of Marvin Preston), and others.

How Judge James Witherell used to treasure his flint-lock gun, with its leather pouch and carved powder horn, relics of his Revolutionary days. He, too, had it hung on wooden hooks in his hall, and it was from these hooks he took it, at the time he shot the squirrel that was disporting itself in the top of one of his loftiest pear trees, and to which I have alluded at length in a former article. And those birch bark canoes, and Mackinaw boats manned by those gay, sturdy voyageurs! The store of F. & T. Palmer used to swarm with these coureurs de bois, when navigation was open, and I became as familiar with them as with other frequenters of the establishment. Governor Cass had a fine barge, the best of its class, made of birch bark, and manned by nine of these voyageurs, four on a side, and a steersman. Had a cushioned stern, and an awning over it. It was truly a swell affair. It was in this barge that he, with Colonel McKinney and party, journey to Fond du Lac and return in 1826. I have alluded to this barge somewhat at length in a former article, and only refer to the refrains "Shoepac" mentions. I was so familiar with them I seem to hear them now, as I heard them in that far off time, the music of their voices floating over the water of a calm, still summer night, when hardly another sound interfered. I call to mind one evening in particular. It was a moonless summer night, calm and still. A party of us young folks were gathered in the summer house of the "Mansion House Hotel," the latter directly in front of the hotel and across Jefferson Avenue, when all at once the refrain started from Hog Island (Belle Isle) apparently, anyway in that vicinity, and it was kept up by the voyageurs without let or hindrance until they passed the city on the Canada side of the river. There was more to the songs than is here given, but the lines quoted are the ones that always remain fresh in my memory. It proved to be the governor's barge with a small party on board. The same thing was ofttimes repeated, and so weird and entrancing was the music that the memory of it will remain with me always. As the late Bela Hubbard says in his "Memorials of half a century," published in 1888:

"The boat-songs were often heard upon our river, and were very plaintive. In the calm of evening when sounds are heard with greater distinctiveness and the harsher notes are toned down and absorbed in the prevailing melody, it was sweet, from my vine-mantled porch, to hear the blended sounds of song and oar—

"'By distance mellowed, o'er waters sweep.'

"To my half-dreaming fancy, at times, they have assumed a poetic if not a supernatural character, wafting me into elf-land, on wings of linked sweetness.

> "'Some spirit of the air has waked the string,
> 'Tis now a seraph bold, with touch of fire,
> And, now the brush of fancy's frolic wing.'"

I think I have quoted this passage or a portion of it from Bela Hubbard's book, in an article some time ago, but perhaps a repetition of it here may not be out of place.

There are but few living, I imagine, who have heard these Canadian boat songs, and if there are any I am sure they will join me in praising them as I do, a charming episode of the long ago that will never be repeated. Yes, times have changed, and with them have passed from our midst the voyageur and his song. French gayety is rapidly ebbing into more sober channels. Even the church has set its face, in a great measure, against balls and merry-makings.

This barge of the governor's (as I think I mentioned in a former article) he kept for use of his family and friends until he went to Washington as secretary of war. I, myself, enjoyed a ride on it several times, evenings, up and down the river, but there was no such charm in the music heard on board the barge as there was listening from the shore, in the stillness of the night. What became of it I never knew. It ought to have been preserved, as it was unique in its way. These voyageurs brought from the upper country from time to time, large quantities of Indian maple sugar, in a granulated state, packed in birch bark mococks. A mocock is a receptacle of a basket form, and oval, though without a handle, made of birch bark, with top sewed on with wattap (the fine roots of the red cedar, split). The smaller ones were ornamented with porcupine quills, dyed red, yellow and green. These ornamented mococks held from two to a dozen tablespoonfuls of sugar, and were made for presents, or for sale to the curious. The larger ones were not ornamented, and contained from 10 to 30 pounds of sugar. This was an article of exchange with those who made it. They bartered it for labor, for goods, etc., generally at ten cents per pound. The Indians often lived wholly upon it, and the explorer Henry says he has known them to grow fat upon this sugar alone. Fish bones and the bones of dogs and deer were often found in the large mococks, mixed with the sugar, showing of course that while the sap was boiling they used it for cooking purposes, instead of water.

In conjunction with these birch bark canoes, and the voyageurs who manned them, was the "Dog Train," a most important feature. The dog train was made of a light frame of wood, and covered round with a dressed deer skin. The part in which the feet went was lined with furs, and was covered in like the fore part of a shoe. The bottom was a plank, about half an inch thick, some six inches longer than the train, and an inch or two wider. In this train a lady was very comfortable and could take a child in her arms while her husband or friend, standing on the part of the bottom that projected behind, gave the word to the well-trained dogs, who, it was said, were capable of trotting with such a load forty miles in a day.

What Shoepac says in regard to the fiddling and dancing among the French habitants is true to life, as I can testify, having seen so much of it and participated in so much of it. I think I have mentioned elsewhere how the young fellows in the early thirties used to get on the top of the lumber piles of the Detroit and Black River Steam Mill Lumber Co., near the foot of Beaubien Street, to locate the dance by the sound of the fiddle. That part of the town then was decidedly French and scarcely a night passed without one or two dancing parties. They were orderly, too; no nonsense permitted. I have seen, as Shoepac has, the racing to church on Sunday and other festive days, and racing home again, and the trotting matches on the ice, up and down the river on the Rouge; have seen,

> "The rapid pacers come and go
> Like phantoms o'er the beaten snow!
> And jumper, cutter, train and pung,
> Behind the nimble ponies swung.
> The swan neck carioles make the scene
> Lively with scarlet gold and green,
> The brightest pacers, roan and bay,
> Caper like little boys at play,
> And toss their heads as if they knew
> As much as human horses do."

Then he mentions Easter morning. How often have I of an Easter morning been with the boys in Ste. Anne's Church yard cracking eggs. Weeks before I would prepare my colored eggs for the occasion and when the day came I was always on hand. There was scarcely an Easter Sunday went by I did not capture four or five dozen eggs, and that was considered pretty good luck where the whole crowd were sharp.

ON THE RIVER BANK IN EARLY DAYS.

"The cottage homes so closely stand,
Their numbers stretching up and down
In front of each continuous town,
In front of each upon the bank,
A narrow wharf of single plank
Stretched out to where a single hand
Might fill a bucket to the brim,
Sinking it down below the brim,
Yet never touching the bottom sand;
While to this simple jetty tied,
Canoes float safely by its side."

"Whenever Monday's morning ray
Brings to the world its washing day,
The busy housewifes and their daughters,
There with their labors vex the waters.
The garments in their fingers gathered,
With vigorous rubbing drenched and lathered,
And paddled with cunning knack,
Resound with many a rousing whack,
While the fair laundresses at work
In no Carthusian silence lurk,
But skilled enough to wash and speak,
Gossip enough for all the week."

Even as their ancestors did in old France.

Any one who has traveled in the south of France—and there must be many such—cannot have failed to notice the peasant girls and women, clad in their bright and gay attire, washing clothes on the banks of the streams adjacent to their homes, and partienlarly can this be witnessed at Nice, where any morning the visitor may see on both banks of the shallow little river (Paillon) that runs through the city, scores of French women residents of the "Old Town," busy washing and paddling the garments with their short wooden paddles and skilled alike to wash and speak gossip enough for all the week. The services of these French women are in almost constant demand taking care of the laundry of the various hotels with which Nice is crowded. During the season from November to April, it is a luxurious city with the attractions and resources of the great northern capitals.

TRAFFIC IN DETROIT AT AN EARLY DAY.

In the old *Detroit Gazette* of January 29, 1819, may be found a report made to the Lyceum, of the business of the town for the year 1818. The shipping then belonging to Detroit was 849 tons. The whole shipping on Lake Erie was 2,384 tons. The value of exports was $69,630, most of which went to other trading ports on the waters above. The value of imports was $15,619.

The United States commissary brought here from time to time from Ohio for the use of the troops, 1,042 beef cattle, and 1,439 hogs. So situated were our domestic resources. The wheat and flour seems also at that time to have been brought from Ohio. These two articles of food (staff of life) were almost exclusively brought from the latter state as late as 1837-38, to which I can testify. In an address delivered some years ago the late G. V. N. Lothrop said:

"This is the oldest town in the whole northwest except Kaskaskia, and far the most important. Its central position in the lake basin and its inviting site early arrested the ambitious sagacity of the French. It soon became the key to their empire on the Mississippi. If one would bid the past again return and walk reanimated before him, this is the very spot for the invocation.

"The clear, sparkling waters of the Detroit River played and wore away its natural shore.

"The canoe of the savage with its freight of squaw and papoose, or peltries, often rested on the sands of the beach, and here the oars of the voyageur returning after long absence, has kept time to the music of his boat songs. And here, happy in the joys of home and welcome the sweet summer evenings have sped swiftly by in merry dance on the green carpet of the river banks, reflecting here in the new world the manners of the parent land —gay sparkling land of mirth and social ease."

DETROIT IN 1787.

Roosevelt in his "Winning of the West" (Volume III, page 31), writing about the post of Detroit in 1787, has this to say:

"At such a post those standing high in authority were partly civil officers, partly army officers. Of the former, some represented the provincial government and others acted for the fur companies. They had much to do, both in governing the French townsfolk and countryfolk, in keeping the Indians friendly and in furthering the peculiar commerce on which the settlements subsisted. But the important people were the army officers. These were imperious, able, resolute men, well drilled and with a high military standard of honor. They upheld with jealous pride the reputation of an army which in that century proved again and again on stricken fields no soldiery of continental Europe could stand against it. They wore a uniform that for three hundred years has been better known than any other wherever the pioneers of civilization tread the world's waste spaces, or fight their way in the overlordship of barbarous empires. A uniform known to the southern and northern hemispheres, the Eastern and Western Continent and all the islands of the sea. Subalterns wearing this uniform have fronted dangers and responsibilities, such as in most other services only gray-haired generals are called upon to face; and at the head of handfuls of troops have won for the British crown realms as large and often as populous as European kingdoms.

The scarlet-clad officers who serve the monarchy of Great Britain have conquered many a barbarous people in all the ends of the earth, and hold for their sovereigns the lands of Moslem and Hindoo, of Tartar and Arab and Pathan, of Malay, Negro and Polynesian.

"In many a war they have overcome every European rival against whom they have been pitted. Again and again have they marched to victory against Frenchman and Spaniard, through the sweltering heat of the tropics; and now, from the stupendous mountain passes of mid-Asia, they look northward through the wintery air, ready to bar the advances of the legious of the Czar.

"Hitherto they have never gone back, save once; they have failed when they sought to stop the westward march of a mighty nation, a nation kin to theirs, a nation of their own tongue and law, and mainly of their own blood."

THE MACOMB FAMILY AND ITS BRANCHES—WELL KNOWN AND DISTINGUISHED NAMES.

John Macomb came to America from the north of Ireland about 1784. He settled in New York and made his famous purchase from the United States of 38,000 acres of land situated in New York and Vermont. He had three sons, David,

William and John, who together owned all the American islands in the Detroit River, having made the purchase of the Pottawatomie Indians, and also owned all the islands in the River St. Lawrence on the American side, with the exception of Carlton Island, on which was Fort Haldiman. They also owned what are the Cass and Stanton farms. They were merchants in Detroit during the Revolution and furnished the English army with their supplies, and also largely the American army.

Another account says that William Macomb was an English officer, of Scottish extraction, and came to Detroit with the English troops in 1760. Macomb obtained an Indian grant for Grosse Ile, as well as all the islands in the Detroit river. Hog Island (Belle Isle), John and David joined him in claiming. This island contained 704 acres, was surveyed by Mr. Boyd in 1771, and purchased from the Indians of the Ottawa and Chippewa nations in council under direction of his majesty's commander-in-chief, and conveyed to Lieutenant Geo. McDougall, whose heirs sold it to Wm. Macomb in 1793. Hog Island (Belle Isle) after this somehow came into the possession of David Macomb, and he sold it to L'Abie (Barnabas) Campau for $5,000, and the heirs of the former assert that the amount paid was in "wild cat money," and that he never realized one dollar from it. It is presumed, however, that he took this money with his eyes open. At all events it is pretty certain that the Macombs one time owned all the American islands in the Detroit river. William, the younger, died on Grosse Ile in 1827, leaving three daughters and one son; the son went to California in 1849 and never returned. One daughter married for her first husband William Abbott, son of Judge James Abbott, of this city, and for her second husband, Colonel Brodhead; the second daughter married Henry Brevoort; the third daughter married John Wendell, of Albany, N. Y. This John Wendell was a nephew of Tunis S. Wendell, one of our old time merchants. His widow survives him and is living at Grosse Ile. A daughter (Kittie) married a gentleman by the name of McLaughlin. She has lately become a resident of this city.

Four chilren of Colonel Brodhead are living. Lieutenant John Brodhead, a son, late of the U. S. marine service, died in Detroit, March, 1904. Thornton F. Brodhead had quite a military career. He was first lieutenant and adjutant, Fifteenth United States infantry, April 9, 1847; brevetted captain August 20, 1847, "for gallant and meritorious conduct at Contreras and Churuboso, Mexico;" full captain, December 2, 1847; disbanded July 31, 1848; colonel First Michigan Cavalry August 22, 1861; died September 2, 1862, on the battlefield of wounds received in action at the second Bull Run, Virginia, August 30, 1862. Brevet brigadier-general of volunteers from latter date. Colonel Brodhead was mortally wounded while gallantly leading his men to the charge. On his death bed on the field, almost the last words to his attending surgeon were, "The flag will triumph yet." In his last to his wife he writes: "I fought manfully, and now die fearlessly." A heroic ending of what gave good promise of being a brilliant career.

The Brodheads, Wendells and Brevoorts are descendants of William Macomb. Mrs. John Anthony Rucker, a sister of William Macomb, left numerous descendants on the island. Her husband had obtained a large quantity of land there and their children still own several large tracts. Long ago, when William Macomb's daughters were little girls, it is related that the Indians would come across the river in canoes from Canada with mococks of sugar (described in a recent paper) for sale.

In the war of 1812 William Macomb was captured by the British and taken prisoner to Montreal, together with Judge James Abbott, of Detroit. During his absence the Indians attacked "The Mansion House," which stood on the Wendell place, and burned it. William Macomb's wife, Monique Navarre, with her baby of only three weeks old, fled to the woods to escape the savages, and shortly afterward died in consequence of the exposure.

A. and W. Macomb were extensive merchants here as far back as 1777, as evinced by the fact that they were in the practice of drawing upon their correspondents in Montreal and elsewhere bills ranging from £30 to £40,000 and upwards; one bill as high as £53,740 18s 8d. The fur trade at that time was very heavy. The Macombs appeared to be engaged as agents of the British government as well as extensively employed in the fur trade. They were intelligent merchants and must have carried on a very large business in the way of exchange.

Mrs. Col. Rucker, of Grosse Ile, was a Macomb. The colonel died in the 30's, I think. He was a familiar figure on the streets of Detroit in the early days—of commanding presence and gentlemanly, courtly address, and always faultlessly attired in the conventional swallow-tail, ruffle shirt, etc. The Ruckers were quite intimate with the Whitings, Mrs. Whiting being a Macomb. The Whitings were Colonel and Mrs. Whiting. The colonel was United States quartermaster of this post and had been for many years; he conitnued to hold the same position until the breaking out of the Mexican war, when he was ordered to the front. Of the children of the Ruckers, Daniel H. was at one time clerk for Oliver Newberry. He afterward entered the United States service as second lieutenant of a dragoon regiment, October 13, 1843, and saw adventurous and hazardous service against the Indians on the plains and around Santa Fe, New Mexico, when it was scarcely known and could be reached from the states only by a primitive wagon road of 800 miles through a hostile country. He served through the Mexican war, was promoted to major February 23, 1847, for gallant and meritorious conduct in the battle of Buena Vista. He was transferred to the quartermaster's department August 23, 1849, and rose in that difficult and responsible branch of the service to the position of colonel and assistant quartermaster-general, U. S. A., and brevet major-general of volunteers.

After the breaking out of the civil war, and during its continuance, the services he rendered at Washington, D. C., as depot-quartermaster and as assistant quartermaster-general, was most efficient. I have no doubt but that many a Michigan officer will call to mind General Rucker's impressive manner and vigorous expression when called upon to furnish transportation and supplies that he did not think according to regulations. He married Miss Irene Curtiss, niece of Colonel William Whistler, U. S. A., and daughter of Captain Curtiss, U. S. A.

The general has been retired from service for many years and with his estimable wife is passing the remainder of his days in Washington, D. C., that Mecca of the retired army officer. He has the proud distinction of being the father-in-law of the late Lieut.-Gen. Phil H. Sheridan, who, when the civil war broke out, declared he would remain with the north, and if in the then coming conflict he should be lucky enough to attain the rank of a major of cavalry the measure of his ambition would be full to overflowing. How his wish was gratified the entire nation knows. From an obscure lieutenant of cavalry, he rose to be lieutenant-general of the army, and one of that immortal quartet of America's greatest captains—Washington, Grant, Sherman and Sheridan.

Another son was, and I think is now, a major and paymaster in the United States army. John A. Rucker, another son, was, in his youth, or when a young man, clerk in the United States quartermaster's department in Detroit under Colonel Henry Whiting, and continued in his employ until the colonel was relieved by Captain S. P. Heintzleman, assistant quartermaster United States army. He then took up his permanent residence on Grosse Ile and on the old homestead farm where he has lived ever since the quiet and retired life of a farmer and country gentleman, happy in his family and in his competency. He married some years ago Miss Fannie Truax, daughter of John Truax, of Detroit. Mr. Truax was the first merchant in Detroit or the northwest to break away from the retail system of selling goods and of selling by the package only.

There were but two daughters. I think one of them married Captain J. A. Whitall, Fifth United States infantry. The captain was stationed at this post during the latter part of the Mexican war. He was aid to General Hugh Brady, as well as in charge of the quartermaster and commissary departments for the space of two years and over. He mustered into the United States service the First regiment of Michigan volunteer infantry and then went to Mexico. He also subsisted them at the Detroit barracks while they remained there and while en route to Cincinnati. He also furnished quarters at the barracks, fuel, straw and subsistence to that portion of the Fifteenth United States infantry that rendezvoused there. It was my good fortune to serve under him in the capacity of quartermaster and commissary clerk. He was always the kind, considerate officer and courteous gentleman. While on duty here he was an applicant for the position of major and paymaster, United States army. After a while he obtained the promotion and was stationed at Santa Fe, N. M., where he died some years ago, leaving a widow and daughter. The former has since died, I think; the latter still survives and is living at Grosse Ile.

The captain also furnished the First Michigan volunteers on their return from Mexico, quarters, fuel, straw and subsistence until they were mustered out of service.

The other daughter married Rev. Mr. Fox, who was for so

many years the able assistant to Bishop McCoskrey. He died some years ago, leaving a widow and three sons. The widow, I think, is dead, and one of the sons (Colonel E. Crofton Fox) died quite recently at Grand Rapids. The career of the two other sons I am not familiar with.

General Alexander Macomb, who died commander-in-chief of the armies of the United States, married his first cousin, Catharine Navarre, Wm. Macomb's daughter. Gen. Macomb was the son of Alex. Macomb (called the great land speculator). General Macomb was in command here about 1821 and on being ordered away was presented by the citizens of Detroit with a service of plate.

A descendant of the Macombs—a charming lady—has charge of St. Luke's Retreat, that delightful, soothing, quiet haven of rest where weary souls "lapped in quiet bide their time." I have had occasion to visit friends there in former years; as, for instance, Captain Whitaker and his wife (the former of the early lake marine); August Palm, that quiet, unassuming gentleman, for so many years connected with the Detroit & Milwaukee railway. My own sister spent some time there; Mrs. Williams, widow of Morris W. Williams, formerly of the Detroit postoffice for so many years; the late Alvah Bradish, the well-known artist, who passed almost his whole life in our midst; Amoray A. Rice (of Beecher, Rice & Ketchum), and others.

I have been told recently by an inmate, who is an old-time friend of mine, that under its present management the retreat is indeed a haven of rest—"Rest'for the Weary."

Abraham Cook was born at Trenton, N. J., in 1762, his father being a farmer. It is said that he served as a drummer boy during the revolutionary war, and in after years when he now and then came across a drum he would take it up eagerly and beat the charge in handsome style.

He joined the militia here in the war of 1812 and was wounnded in one of his hands, in a brush with the enemy, losing a finger. In Detroit he engaged in the lumber business and general trading, and was quite successful. His name appears on the election roll of 1799 as a voter on December 15 of that year, when three representatives to the general assembly of the northwest territory at Cincinnati, O., were voted for.

He came here an orphan and had no relatives except one

sister, Mrs. Dickson, who in after years lived at Ypsilanti. It is thought he came with Col. Hamtramck's army in 1796, at which time he was 22 years of age. Of course his army experience as a drummer boy preceded that date. He was also here in the fire of 1805, but suffered a small loss only.

He was present at Hull's surrender, and when General Proctor ordered many citizens to leave the town in 1812, he was passed over and remained at home. One day several English officers who were boarding at his house indulged in some slighting remarks about the American army in his hearing. He resented their language in a spirited way, but was not called to account for it.

Mr. Cook vigorously advocated the extension of Jefferson Avenue about the years 1828-29, through the town of Hamtramck, from C. C. Trowbridge's line in Detroit to Grosse Pointe, and of course passing through his (Cook's) farm. The French settlers, through whose land the avenue was to go, were bitterly opposed to it, particularly Antoine Dequindre. Antoine Rivard, one of the Campau's (James, I think) and others. They threatened all sorts of things. I well remember the controversy. They (the opposers) petitioned the legislative council, asserting that the opening of the avenue through their farms would be an illegal proceeding, and also alleging that Cook favored it "because he has a legal title to a large estate which will greatly enhance in value by the opening of the road." The avenue was finally opened without serious trouble, as is well known.

Both of Mr. Cook's wives were of the name of Thorn. The name of the first was Jane, and she was the daughter of John Thorn, of Black River (now Port Huron). About 1826 she died and he removed with his remaining family nearer the city on to the river front adjoining the Marsack residence and in the rear of C. C. Trowbridge's Jefferson Avenue house. For several years after he married Jane Thorn he kept boarding house in this city, which was patronized mostly by army officers and the best citizens and which, by his wife's careful and energetic management, became a profitable business. He purchased 240 acres in Hamtramck in 1811 of Gabriel St. Aubin for $650. In 1816 he purchased from Francois Rivard 167 acres for $1,000 and in 1818 purchased from Robert J. McDougall 160 acres. He afterwards married Mrs. William Thorn, whose maiden name was Elizabeth Cottrell, and who was a daughter of Colonel Cottrell (St. Clair river), and the widow of Cook's deceased wife's brother. She was also aunt to our esteemed fellow citizen, Hon. Eber W. Cottrell. There was no issue by the second marriage.

John Thorn, of Black river, was a gay man in his day. I do not remember to have seen him, but I have seen his brother, of the same locality, who was a fine looking man, and of the most genial nature. During my repeated sojourn in St. Clair, on my uncle's farm, I often listened to the tales the dwellers along the borders of the St. Clair river had to tell of the gay times the lawyers of Detroit and others had with John Thorn, the hospitable entertainer of Black river, when court business led them to the county seat of St. Clair county (Palmer). Thorn was almost always assisted in making it lively for the foreign element by some of the dwellers along the St. Clair river, as, for instance, the Fultons, Cottrells, St. Bernards (Sambineaus), Wards, Westbrooks, Wm. Brown and others. Those from Detroit, usually, were Lawyers Frazer, O'Keefe, Fletcher, Witherell, McDougall, Backus and others. What wild tales they told of unrestrained harmless fun and frolic. John Thorn was a gay character in the early days, and well known all up and down the St. Clair river.

As before said, the Cook residence was in the rear of the Trowbridge house and on the river front. I have often seen the old couple sitting on the front porch of an evening, when I was going to and fro in charge of "our cow" that was pastured on the Witherell farm—and this cow, I want to record right here, gave me a world of trouble. They (the Cooks) were great friends of the Indians, who often in the summer time used to pitch their tents in front of their house, as also in front of the Marsack's, the Riopelle's and the Dequindre's, and up to the Witherell residence. The narrow road in front of the last named would not accommodate them, otherwise they were quite welcome. Often have I seen them and often have I lingered in their tents unawed by the fearful tales told by the old residents, of the cruelties practiced by them in Pontiac's time and later.

Mr. and Mrs. Cook were often seen in the city, visiting the Knapps who, at that time, lived on the north side of Griswold street, between Larned and Congress streets. They always came either in their French cart or their one horse sulky.

The Cook house in Hamtramck was an old-fashioned brick dwelling, large and roomy, and the only brick house above Detroit and the north pole except that of Captain Samuel Ward at Newport, now Marine City; hence, quite peculiar and interesting on that account. It occupied, with its immediate grounds, the present site of Owen park.

Mr. Cook had sons and daughters. The eldest daughter, Eliza, married Thomas Knapp, who was sheriff of Wayne county at the time Simmons was hanged—and fine man he was. After the death of Mr. Knapp, which occurred about 1830, she married Mr. John Owen. After some ten or twelve years of happily wedded life passed together, she died. Miss Jane Cook, who had for many years made it her home with her sister, Mrs. Owen, married Mr. Owen.

James H. Cook, the eldest son, married Miss Drew, daughter of Hon. John Drew, of Mackinac, and of the firm of Biddle & Drew. James H. was an extensive Indian trader. He had sons and daughters and in 1837 was a ship chandler in this city and resided at 30 Griswold street. He died in Canada while lumbering for his brother-in-law, John Owen. Otis Cook, an intimate friend of mine, a remarkably handsome and promising young man, died early in life of consumption. Joseph Cook was also an intimate friend as well as schoolmate. He graduated into a marine engineer. "Joe" was first-class in his profession. He was engineer of the steamboat May Queen, that plied between here and Cleveland for many years, and was also on other steamers. He was an all-around good fellow, as all who knew him will bear witness. A man every inch of him. He was alderman of the seventh ward in 1887-88, United States inspector of hulls from 1868 to 1878, United States supervising inspector of steamboats from 1878 to 1885, and from 1890 to the time of his death, on May 29, 1891.

John Cook, a fine, stalwart youth, went to California in 1849 and died there.

As said, Miss Jane made it her home with her sister, Mrs. Owen. She was possessed of a most charming personality, bright and gentle, but, when occasion required, aggressive. She was a great favorite in society and was conspicuous in that bright galaxy of "Fort street girls" of whom she formed a part. She had many admirers, of course, myself among the number; and two or three of them that I could name were most persistent, but all of us failed to capture her. An unsuspected suitor appeared on the scene in the person of Mr. John Owen, the husband of **her** late sister. Well, after a sufficient season had elapsed for Mr. Owen to bury his grief (as before remarked), the two were married. I was one of the regretful witnesses of the marriage ceremony. I have the satisfaction of knowing, however, that through all the years that intervened between that time and the death of Mr. Owen, the relations existing betwen the two were of the most happy character. Mrs. Owen is still with us, enjoying the society of her children and the competency left her by Mr. Owen and her inheritance in the Cook farm.

Mr. Abraham Cook was a very quiet, steady, retiring, gentlemanly man, and he looked it. He always, when I knew him, sported a black broadcloth swallow-tail coat, white cravat, and low crowned, broad-brimmed black beaver. But for all the good things the neighbors and friends of Mr. Cook said about him, it was intimated that he had his streaks, as most of us have, and when the situation required it, he was as strenuous as any. When I was about 15 years old I received an invitation from a schoolmate to spend a short season with him on this "Cook Farm." His father, Judge Jeddiah Hunt, had leased it for a term of years from Mr. Cook. I had a most enjoyable time, and always remembered it with great pleasure. The judge realized the most profit from the farm by raising produce for the Detroit city market, also poultry, turkeys, geese, eggs, etc. The daily morning trip down to the city with the load of "garden stuff" will long be remembered. Jefferson Avenue, as before stated, extended only to the upper line of C. C. Trowbridge's residence lot. Access was had to the city along what was called the "River road," that skirted the French farms. Judge Hunt, I think, was about the only farmer around Detroit, except, perhaps, Mr. Peter Van Every, who paid any attention to supplying the Detroit market with farm produce. The city market in the center of Woodward avenue, and a little below Jefferson, and the Berthlet, corner of Randolph and Atwater, were supplied with farm produce, etc., mainly by the wives of the French farmers, residents of the Canada side of the river. There was a hard-surfaced space, kept scrupulously clean, between the market front and Jefferson Avenue, on which these French wives used to "squat," surrounded by their "garden truck," etc. I used to be in that locality so constantly that the faces of these French housewives were almost as well known to me as my own people. Their names I never knew, but it is fair to presume that some of their fair descendants have chosen for their lords residents of this side of the river, sons of the New Yorker and of the New Englander, so intimate were the relations existing between the residents of the Canada side of the river and this.

What became of Judge Hunt and his family I never knew, nor do I know why he was called judge. He was a fine man, and really looked the judge. He had a very fine family, and to account for the intimacy that existed between our people and theirs, state that the judge and his family were passengers on the steamboat Walk-in-the-Water when she was wrecked off Buffalo harbor in 1821, and on which also were Mr. and Mrs. Thos. Palmer, my uncle and aunt, also Mr. Palmer's sister, who afterward married Felix Hinchman.

This Judge Hunt and Geo. Jerome's father resembled each other in appearance very much. When you saw one it was hard to believe you did not see the other.

I do not remember who the tenants of the farm were after Judg Hunt left, except Monsieur Woolaire, a French gentleman, and one of Napoleon's Imperial Guard, who at the time had a wine and liquor store on Woodward Avenue, below Jefferson. He occupied it as a residence and not as a road house. The premises always remained in the ownership of the Cook family.

Some time after the death of Mr. Cook, which occurred at his residence on Atwater street, December 28, 1874, aged 73 years, the property was leased to (I think) the Hamtramck Driving Park Association, and the Cook homestead was turned into a public road house. The state fair was held there one year, and the First Michigan Cavalry, Colonel Brodhead, rendezvoused there. Headquarters in the public house and the regiment quartered on the race grounds. A Mr. Pond was at one time the proprietor of this road house. He had a son, Charles Pond, who was a talented portrait painter. He transferred to canvass the likenesses of many of our citizens, among them Mrs. Palmer, the wife of Senator Palmer, and presume he is well and pleasantly remembered. This road house had numerous proprietors and varied fortunes until the race track was removed farther up the river to its present location, when it was abandoned, and its site donated to the city as Owen park—a much more savory and pleasing institution. The present condition of that locality all are familiar with. The property is still in the hands of the Cook and Owen heirs, that portion remains unsold. A charming locality for a residence, situated as it is in the immediate vicinity of the Detroit river with Lake St. Clair in full view.

Eliza Cook, by her first husband, Dr. Thos. Knapp, had three children: Thomas, who when quite young was accidentally shot while hunting in the Cass orchard, and died from the effects. Lafayette, a very bright, promising and agreeable young man, attained his majority and was with Mr. John Owen for some years as clerk in the drug store, and finally branched out for himself in the same business on Woodward Avenue (east side), between Fort and Congress Streets; he married Miss Cornelia Wales, daughter of Austin Wales. After a brief married life, he died at Erin, on the Gratiot road, between this city and Mt. Clemens, the country seat of Mr. Wales, Eliza (Puss) Knapp, who was one of the brightest and one of the most vivacious of that charming group of Fort Street girls who held all of us young men and boys in bondage. She had hosts of admirers, of course, and was finally captured by Mr. Frank Hunt, a son of Judge Hunt, of Washington, D. C., and brother of Mrs. Wesley Trusdell and John T. Hunt. There were born to them three children: Tom Hunt, whom many will remember as being quite prominent in the newspaper business and in amateur theatricals in this city. He died here a few years ago of Bright's disease. A daughter married a gentleman in Sault Ste. Marie (Canada) by name of Hughes, and died there some years ago. A son, Harry Hunt, is a resident of this city, and is now publisher of this book. After some years of married life, the Hunts separated. Frank Hunt emigrated to Manitoba, and remained there until his death, a few months ago. Mrs. Eliza Hunt after a while married Honorable Albert Prince, son of Colonel John Prince, of the Park farm, Sandwich, Ont. • Mr. Prince was a distinguished Canadian barrister, and member of parliament from Essex. They had their home down the river on the Canadian side at Petite Cote (The Firs), where they entertained lavishly. They had five children. Albertina, who arrived at womanhood, was possessed of a charming personality, bright, intelligent and skillful on the harp and piano. She died in this city in 1898 quite suddenly. Albert, a son, is at present in the employ of the Canada Southern railroad and holds quite a responsible position. John, another son, arrived at maturity and married, and was identified in some way with the newspaper business. He died some seven or eight years ago. Constance, a daughter, who is richly endowed with all the charming attributes of her sex, resides at the Park farm, Sandwich, in the Prince homestead, with her aunt, Miss Belle Prince, and her brother, Albert Prince, and his wife.

Mrs. Eliza (Cook) Knapp had by Mr. Owen two sons and one daughter, Griffith, who attained majority, and was a captain and assistant quartermster, U. S. A., during the civil war, died of consumption some years ago. Edward T. also attained majority and was in service during part of the civil war as first lieutenant, Fourth Michigan Cavalry. He died many years ago. The daughter, Catharine, married Mr. Horace Turner, at one time auditor of the Michigan Central Railroad. He is alive, is in business in this city and is well and favorably known. Mrs. Turner, a lovely character, died some years ago, leaving two daughters.

The fruit of the marriage of Mr. John Owen and Miss Jane Cook was three sons, Edward, Lafayette and John, and one daugter, Fannie. Edward died not many years ago. Lafayette and John have charge of the large Cook and Owen estates. Fannie married Mr. Chas. Lothrop, a distinguished member of the Detroit bar and son of the late Hon. Geo. V. N. Lothrop. He died a few years ago.

THE GODFROY FAMILY AND ITS BRANCHES—THE FIRST COMERS WERE PIONEERS.

The name of Godfroy is among the oldest in Normandy, and some claim that it is a descent from Godefroi de Bouillon, the Crusader.

Several of the family were eminent as priests and historians. Denis (Dinie), councillor in the parliament of Paris, 1580, was the author of several valuable legal works. His son Jacques was secretary of state. His grandson was made historiographer of France in 1640 and wrote the history of the Constables and Chancellors of France. A branch of this family resided in Normandy in 1580, whose head was Pierre. His son, Jean Babte, came to Canada about 1635.

In 1715 Pierre Godfroy, grandson of Jean Babte, came to Detroit. He married, 1724, Catherine Sanduge. He was followed shortly afterwards by Jacques Godfroy. In 1750, Jean Babte Godfroy, called the chevalier, came to Detroit with his wife, and died here in 1756. Pierre and Jacques both married into the same family. Like others of the name, they were interested in the fur trade, which was originally a monopoly carried on by a company called the Hundred Associates, and later by the "Companies des Indies." As early as 1680 it was said that 25,000 beaver skins alone were exported from Quebec in a single ship.

Pierre's line died out, but the children of Jacques were Catherine, who married November 21, 1733, the Chevalier Alex. Trotier des Duisseaux, of an illustrious family. He was the first trustee of St. Ann's, and the first captain of militia. Jacques, born in 1722, was very young at the time of his parents' death, and was brought up by his eldest sister, Catherine des Ruisseaux. Like his father, he was interested in the fur trade. He was thorough with the Indian tongues, and exerting great influence with the chiefs by reason of his bravery and family connections, he soon became widely known as interpreter and negotiator between the savages and whites. When Pontiac, in 1763, attacked the fort at Detroit and other English posts, Jacques Godfroy and Dr. Chapoton were sent by the English commander to parley with him and endeavor to persuade him from his purpose, but the savage chieftain could not be influenced.

Jacques married Louise Clotilde Chapoton, daughter of Dr. Chapoton, surgeon in the army. She died in 1764, leaving one son, Jacques Gabriel. Jacques devoted the remainder of his life to the care of his son, and the rebuilding of his fortune, which had suffered since the English conquest. He figures prominently in many of the Indian transfers of land. In the American state papers is a curious deed in French from Jacques Godfroy to his son, conveying to him farming lands, implements, cattle, silver and slaves. The land conveyed comprised the tract between Twentieth and Twenty-second streets, this city, from the river to some three miles back, some of which is still owned by his descendants (Godfroy farm). He died in 1795. He evidently was very popular and generous, for he seems to have been for several years godfather to almost every child that was born, for pages of baptisms on the records have his name affixed, in his strong, bold handwriting. This Jacques Gabriel was born in 1758, within Fort Ponchartrain. He was named Gabriel from his godfather and uncle, Gabriel Le Grand Chevalier de Sintre. About the year he became of age the American revolution was in progress. Though the colony was far removed from the scene of war, Gabriel's sympathies were with the colonists. His early years were spent in extending the fur trade and establishing trading posts on a large scale, from Monroe to Fort Vincennes; the firm of Godfroy & Beaugrand was one of the largest in the west, as well as the firm of Godfroy & Le Shambre. The latter firm established a warehouse about 1809 at Ann Arbor on the west bank of the Huron river, back of the Occidental hotel. It was called "Godfroy's on the Pottawattomie trail." This trail crossed the river where the Congress street bridge (Ann Arbor) is now. In 1811 this firm received a patent for 2,500 acres of land, signed by President Monroe. It is said that, what is believed to be the key of this old warehouse was found a short time ago on its site, and at present hangs on the wall of Archie McNicol's shop in the Hewitt block, and the account of the find indulges in the following remarks in regard to it: "If that key could talk what a tale it might tell of Indians and bales of deer and beaver skins that were brought into the building and exchanged for guns, powder and shot and knives. Imagine the canoes and flat-bottomed boats coming up the Huron river (as they must have done) with supplies. All that is perhaps now left of this warehouse is the big rusty key."

After the American possession Gabriel received the appointment as sub-agent and deputy-superintendent of Indian affairs from General Harrison (aftedwards president of the United States). The records which have been preserved of his success in negotiating with the Indians are abundant, and he retained the position until his death in 1832. Gabriel was major of the first regiment of the territory, and on the resignation of Augustus B. Woodward, was made colonel. He married Angelique de Conture, by whom he had five children. Gabriel, Jr., married Elizabeth, daughter of Judge James May; his descendants reside at Grand Rapids. Jean Baptiste settled at Fort Wayne, Ind. In 1796 Gabriel married for his socond wife, Therese Douaine de Bondy, by whom he had several children. He died in 1831. He was one of the few who lived under French, English and American rule in the same place and saw a change of flags five times. He married a third time, Monique Campau, by whom he had no issue. The only child by his second wife, Susanne, married James McCloskey. Her children were: Henry, married Therese Souland, of St. Louis; Elizabeth, married Hon. Isaac P. Christiancy, of Monroe. Hon. Isaac P. Christiancy was at one time justice of the supreme court of Michigan, later United States senator from this state, and still later United States minister to Peru. Caroline married Mr. Calwell. Susanne married Mr. Morton, of Monroe, brother of the late Julius Morton, of Detroit (father of Hon. J. Sterling Morton). Melinda married John Askin, of Sandwich. I think both of the latter are living. Pierre (Peter), "La Prince," as he was generally called, was born 1796. He, in company with Colonel Marsaack, Captain Wm. P. Patrick, Dr. and J. H. Bagg and Robt. J. Graveraet (the latter an Indian interpreter, removed the last remnant of Indians in Michigan, and particularly about Detroit, to their reservation beyond the Mississippi. He was active and enterprising, and the firm of P. and J. Godfroy was well known throughout the northwest. He married Marianne Navarre Marantette, daughter of Dominique Gode de Marantette and Archange Louise Navarre; she and her sister, Mrs. Dequindre (afterwards Mrs. Wm. B. Hunt), were considered the most beautiful women of their time in the territory of Michigan. It is a family tradition that Prince Godfroy once won a wager by paddling himself in a wheelbarrow across the Detroit River to visit his fiancee, who lived on the Canada shore, a feat quite as difficult as Leander swimming the Hellespont and no less romantic. The children of this union that I well remember were William, Elizabeth, Caroline Anne. Alexandrine Louise, Nancy and Jaques B. William, who was a schoolmate of mine, went early to Pueblo, New Mexico, and engaged in the land agency and mining business, and where I think he is yet. I used to hear from him occasionally some years ago. Caroline Anne (Carrie Godfroy) is with us yet, and unmarried. Alexandrine Louise married Mr. Theodore P. Hall. They are now living in quiet, refined retirement at Grosse Pointe. Mr. Hall was for many years a successful member of the Board of Trade. He is a book lover of the most pronounced kind. Nancy married Mr. Joseph Visger, a name well and favorably known here in the early days. Jacques B. was educated at Bardstown, Kentucky; he studied law, but abandoned the profession of it on account of ill health. He was a partner for many years with his father in the fur business, under the firm name of P. & J. Godfroy. He married in 1820 Victorie, daughter of Colonel Francis Navarre, of Monroe. He died in 1847, leaving many children. The only ones I knew anything of were Zoe, who married Benjamin Abbott, son of Robert Abbott, auditor-general of the territory of Michigan; Sophie, who married James Whipple, of Monroe (his first wife), son of Major John Whipple, U. S. A., of Detroit.

I can well believe the assertion that Mrs. Peter Godfroy and Mrs. Dequindre were two of the most beautiful women in the territory at the time of their marriage and for some years after. The first that I remember of Mrs. Dequindre was when she was living with her first husband, Dequindre, in their little dwelling adjoining the latter's store, that was on Atwater Street and on the upper line of the Beaubien farm. I used to pass there morning and night for two or three years in charge of the family cow that was pastured on the farm of Judge James Witherell (I think I have mentioned this briefly in a former article). Mrs. Dequindre, being quite intimate with all our people, knew me well, and always noticed me in a most kind and pleasant way that I never can forget. The bakers of those days used to have for sale molasses ginger cakes, cut rudely into the shape of horses, dogs or cats, that were the delight of the youngsters, of which class I was one. Mrs. Dequindre most always had one in readiness for me when I passed. After all these years I can taste them yet. Well, boy that I was, her striking beauty impressed me strongly, and I seem to see her now, with her sparkling black eyes, dazzling white teeth and bright, winning smile. No wonder that after a brief widowhood she captured the widower, William B. Hunt, one of the handsomest men of that day, and father of Wellington and Cleveland Hunt. The other sister, Mrs. Godfroy, I do not remember but a little about until later on in the early forties. When they lived down the river I used to visit them there occasionally. I remember one visit particularly, and that was a New Year's call in 1842, the day before the big fire. All the female portion of the family were present, this being before Miss Elizabeth was married to John Watson. I, at that time, remarked Mrs. Godfroy and her striking resemblance to her sister, Mrs. Dequindre. I never until then had had a real good look at her. She, in her conversation, confined herself to French, and I was told that she could speak English only quite indifferently. Peter, the father of Mrs. T. P. Hall and Miss Carrie Godfroy, died, I think, in 1831 or 1832. I knew him quite well by sight, as the Palmers (F. and T.) had quite extensive dealings with the Godfroys in furs and Indian goods from the time of the advent of the former in the territory until they quit business. The family at one time, in the early days and before my advent here, occupied quite a pretentious residence (high stoop with pillars, etc.), on the corner of Woodward Avenue and Woodbridge Street, adjoining what is now the police station. It was standing in 1830. This corner is in the possession of the Godfroy heirs at the present day.

CORRECTION.—In Mr. Palmers's article on the Cook family, the birth of Abraham Cook was said to have been in 1774. It should have been about the year 1762.

COLONEL JOSHUA HOWARD A MAN OF NOTE.

COL. JOSHUA HOWARD, A MAN OF NOTE—HIS MILITARY SERVICE AND HIS FAMILY.

COL. JOSHUA HOWARD entered the Army in 1813, and served first in the infantry, afterwards in the ordnance department, the artillery, and as commissary of subsistance.

At the outbreak of the Mexican War, he accepted the lieutenant colonelcy of the Fifteenth U. S. Infantry, and led his regiment gallantly over the walls of Chapultepec, for which he was breveted colonel. The gallant and lamented Broadhead was his adjudant and received the sword of the commander of the fortress. Colonel Howard prevented the notorious General Pillow from carrying off and appropriating to his own use several brass cannon captured from the enemy.

The field officers of the Fifteenth U. S. Infantry were Geo. W. Morgan, of Ohio, colonel; Joshua Howard, of Detroit, lieutenant-colonel; Fredrick Mills and Samuel Wood, of Iowa, majors. Three companies of the Fifteenth Infantry were recruited from this state under the supervision of Colonel Howard. The officers of the Michigan companies were: Company A—Captain, Eugene Vandeventer, Flint; first lieutenant and adjutant, Thornton F. Broadhead, Detroit; second lieutenant, Samuel Beach, Pontiac; second lieutenant, Edwin R. Merrifield, Lansing. Company E—Captain, Isaac D. Toll, Fawn River; first lieutenant, Thomas H. Freelen, Kalamazoo; second lieutenant, John B. Goodman, Niles; second lieutenant, Platt Titus, Jackson. Company G—Captain, Frazer M. Winans, Monroe; first lieutenant, Ahira G. Eastman, Adrian; second lieutenant, Wm. D. Wilkins, Detroit; second lieutenant, Michael Doyle, Detroit. They rendezvoused at the Detroit barracks, were mustered into service by Lieutenant Frank Woodbridge, U. S. A., aide to General Brady; clothed and equipped by Major Henry Smith, quartermaster, U. S. A., who accompanied them to Vera Cruz, Mexico. I was in the U. S.

quartermaster and commissary department here at that time and assisted in equipping this portion of the Fifteenth Infantry.

It is said that Colonel Howard came to Detroit first in 1815 and held a position in the revenue department under Austin E. Wing, deputy collector, and later he secured an appropriation to build an arsenal in Detroit, which was located on Jefferson Avenue and the southwest corner of Wayne Street. He built the arsenal at Dearborn, the corner stone of which was laid with appropriate ceremonies July 30, 1833, Major Henry Whiting, U. S. A., making the address, which was pronounced fine and scholarly. Colonel Howard was at one time a member of the Michigan legislature, was also appointed United States Marshal of the district of Michigan. He was also elected sheriff of Wayne County over E. V. Cicotte in 1854: the latter was a prominent French citizen and Democrat. On the outbreak of the Civil War Colonel Howard was appointed an additional paymaster, U. S. A., and served as such until its end. I accompanied him once, on an exceedingly cold day, to Flint, to pay the Tenth Michigan Iufantry. A frigid ride we had from Holly to Flint in the stage. No railroad then between the two points. Colonel Howard with his estimable wife and sons and daughters, occupied for some years in the late thirties and early forties the dwelling used by General Cass after his return from France. Its site is at present taken up by the late Governor Baldwin's house. I think they came into Fort Street to reside after the colonel had completed the arsenal at Dearborn. At any rate they were there when I fi:st knew them. Of the sons, Alexander K., Henry Dearborn (Duff), and Daniel were the only ones anywhere near my age. Alexander K. was always an assistant to his father. He was an enthusiastic Brady Guard. During the month of June, 1847, the company known as the "Brady Guard" was enlisted and mustered into the service of the United States, for the purpose of garrisoning Fort Mackinac, Fort Brady, Sault Ste. Marie, taking the place of regulars sent to the front during the Mexican War. Morgan L. Gage was captain, Alex K. Howard first lieutenant, Wm. F. Chittended second lieutenant, Ara W. Sprague second lieutenant. The above forts were garrisoned respectively by Captain Gage and Lieutenant Howard.

Scores of people will no doubt call to mind "Marg" Gage, "Alec," Howard and "Bill" Chittenden and the genial, witty city constable, Ara Sprague, "Duff" Howard, who was an accomplished machinist. He was at one time foreman of the extensive engine works of Jackson & Wiley of this city. The last I knew of him he held a responsible position in the Alger Iron Works, Boston. Daniel was, during the Civil War and for a time after, of the firm of Howard & Welch, claim agents, this city. Alexander K. Howard married for his first wife, Mary, daughter of Charles Larned, and for his second wife, Lizzie, daughter of Dr. J. L. Whiting. One of the daughters, the eldest, was at that time or shortly after, married to a lawyer, Mr. C. K. Green. The other two (with whom I was on friendly terms), were Cornelia and Julia. They were prominent in that bright galaxy of femininity that dominated Fort Street and Jefferson Avenue which was composed of (besides themselves) Eliza and Mary Inman, Frances Gillett, Marion Forsythe, Eliza (Puss) Knapp, Mary and Julia Palmer, Harriet, Eliza and Mary Williams, Rose and Alexandrine Sheldon, Louisa Heath, Jane Cook, Martha Palmer, Mary (John) Palmer, Sarah Gilman, Mary Larned, Lizzie Whiting, Mary Brooks and others. Three or four of the young ladies named did not live on Fort Street but in the immediate vicinity, but for all that they were noted to be of the Fort Street crowd. Cornelia Howard married John W. Strong and Julia Howard married Walter Ingersoll.

Brig.-Gen. Henry R. Mizner, U. S. A., married one of the daughters (Lizzie) of Colonel Howard. She was not of my time, but later, though I knew her and of her and was at the general's wedding.

Listen to the following poetic effusion from the pen of our gifted friend, the late Colonel William D. Wilkins, addressed to Miss Lizzie Howard. Colonel Wilkins prefaces his verses thus:

"Miss Lizzie—I promised you when we were dancing last night some lines, if you would not album—ize them. La Voila Howard is such a pretty name to rhyme to, that it is a pity you should ever change it.

"I'll try some lines to improvise
  With most exceeding pleasure,
For, when I think of your bright eyes
  My thoughts all flow to measure,
And should the Muses silent stand
  They'd be the worst of cowards,
For now I write at your command,
  The lovliest of the Howards.

A single glance from those soft eyes,
    Bewitching and entrancing,
Makes my heart a certaint prize
    And sets my spirits dancing.
I pray for some low rustic cot,
    In woodbine all embowered,
And that it there might be my lot
    To dwell with Lizzie Howard.

You'd make a paradise on earth
    Wherever you resided,
And comfort, happiness and mirth
    Should dwell where you and I did.
We'd laugh at sorrow's chilling tide,
    And when misfortune lowered,
You'd be my angel and my guide;
    Wouldn't you—Lizzie Howard?

Alas! These visions never can
    Meet with realization:
I'm the most melancholy man
    In all this mighty nation,
I see—with a prophetic eye—
    My cup of bliss all soured,
And all that's left me is to die
    For love of Lizzie Howard."
Friday morning, July 9, '52.

The Brady Guards above referred to of which Alexander Howard was first lieutenant, did not include among its numbers any members of the old original Brady Guards, except Captain Gage and Lieutenant Howard, but was recruited from the general public, the same as Uncle Sam gets all his soldiers. Lieutenant Hiram Dryer, of the regular service, was, after a little, assigned to this company of Brady Guards as second lieutenant. Dryer had been a soldier in the ranks in Mexico, where he especially distinguished himself. It is reported of him that in the course of a siege of some fortification by General Taylor a volunteer was called for to plant "Old Glory" on the wall or embankment of the fort. Hiram Dryer volunteered and did it, in the face of the enemy's fire. He was made second lieutenant in the regular service on the spot. He came north and was detailed to join the Brady Guards at Fort Mackinac. He afterward served in the

Civil War as a captain in some regular regiment (I forget now which).

When Governor Blair and party (of which I was one) visited the Army of the Potomac just after the battle of Chancellorsville, Captain Dryer entertained us hospitably in his tent. He was a thorough soldier. Perhaps some may remember him. He married a daughter of the late John J. Garrison of this city. I think they are both dead.

I am indebted to Hon. Peter White, of Marquette, for the incident in regard to Captain Dryer's experience in Mexico.

* * *

Colonel Howard was the chief marshal on the occasion of the celebration of Cadillac's day, July 24, 1858, aided by Colonel Cyrus W. Jackson and Signor Angelo Paldi. John Patterson was mayor at the time. They had an immense procession, which was participated in by the mayor, common council and officers, Detroit Light Guard, Scott Guard and Shield's Guards, the volunteer fire department with twelve hand engines and one hook and ladder company, all the organized labor societies, and thousands of other citizens.

The exercises came off in Firemen's Hall. Hon. C. L. Walker was the orator of the day. E. N. Lacroix delivered an address in French. A grand banquet was given in the evening at the Russell House, at which Judge B. F. H. Witherell presided, assisted by Joseph Campau, Maurice Moran, Pierre Desnoyers, Charles Beaubien, Richard Godfroy, William Woodbridge, Shubael Conant, Henry Chipman, David Cooper, Levi Cook, Ross Wilkins, S. V. R. Trowbridge, and others. Rev. F. A. Blades pronounced the benediction.

D. Bethune Duffield composed a poem for the occasion, which he read.

A record of the toasts given and speeches delivered on that occasion is not preserved, but it is safe to say a good time was had.

Cyrus W. Jackson was of the firm of Jackson & Wiley, the iron founders and steam engine builders, and Signor Paldi was an esteemed Italian citizen, who had been bandmaster of the Fifth United States Infantry, coming here with that regiment before the Mexican War. He served with his regiment through that war, and when it closed, his term of service having expired, he made this city his home. He built and resided in the first house erected in the vicinity of the Detroit Barracks, with the exception of the Jasperson residence. The Signor's house was of the Italian villa order, and stood on Catherine Street, opposite the barracks. The Jasperson dwelling was on the northwest corner of Russell and Catherine Streets, and quite unpretentious.

* * *

In this connection it may not be out of place to give the following from the Grand Rapids Sunday *Herald* of June 5, 1904, over the signature of General Isaac D. Toll, of Petoskey, president Michigan Association of Veterans of Mexico. It relates some of the operations of the Fifteenth United States in Mexico:

EDITOR GRAND RAPIDS HERALD—The *Herald* of May 15, under caption, "Horse in the World's History," you give General Scott's horse "Rolla" the distinction of being a "beautiful bay." Now the horse he rode at Contreras and Churubusco was a very large horse, quite eighteen hands high, but roughly coated, very dark brown, anything but handsome, angular in shape. Captain R. E. Lee, who rode a magnificent bay, pointed out to us of the Fifteenth U. S. Infantry, and led the way to the Mexican rear, commanded in person by Santa Anna, then rejoined General Scott at Nativitar.

Major Mills of ours rode a hard-mouthed mare to his death (he was unable to control her) at the city gate (San Antonio). I knowing her, warned him against his joining the dragoons, and had before done so. Redpath in his school history, page 287, writes of the "heights of Churubusco carried by Generals Twiggs and Pillow."

Now the battlefield was mostly as level and flat as land could be. There were heights at Contreras on August 19th and 20th, 1847, we had to cross the rock pedregal and storm the entrenched works on the morning of the 20th.

Colonel Riley in the van, your then captain, afterwards Colonel McReynolds, had command of Company K, Third Dragoons, could, if still with us, corroborate the above. I had command of Company E, Fifteenth U. S., and the colors in these affairs, and lost severely at Churubusco. Yours truly,

ISAAC D. TOLL,

President Michigan Association of Veterans of Mexico.
PETOSKEY, Mich.

This pedregal was a great obstacle in an advance on the Acapulco Road through San Antonio directly to the southern gate of Mexico City. It was an immense field of broken lava lying in front of the Mexican General Valencia's camp, battle of Contreras, August 20th, 1847. It was in this battle that Captain F. D. Callender's battery did such good service. Captain Callender, before the Mexican war, had command of the Dearborn Arsenal.

Isaac D. G. Toll

GENERAL ISAAC DE GRAFF TOLL

GENERAL ISAAC DE GRAFF TOLL was born December 1, 1818, on Toll farm, near Schenectady, N. Y. Is a resident of Petoskey, Mich., since 1880, of which city he was President in 1881-1882, and to which he presented the site for the Lockwood Hospital. He was also chiefly instrumental in having built the breakwater that has so vastly improved the harbor.

The account given before does not fully cover his actions in the Mexican war, for at the battles of Contretras, 19th and 20th of August, 1847, and Churubusco, 20th of August, 1847, he was in the thick of the fray, and his charge with the bayonet at the latter battle, against orders, after having gone three times through a fierce fire to ask permission to charge, which was refused, was the cause of the American troops winning the day in that part of the field, with the assistance of the New York Volunteers and the Palmetto Regiment of South Carolina and others.

On this occasion Captain Toll was in command of Company E, the 15th U. S. Infantry, recruited in Michigan, his being the color company. He was also engaged at El Molino del Rey, September 8, 1847. The subjoined letters from his companion-in-arms Samuel E. Beach, first lieutenant Company A, 15th U. S. Infantry in Mexican war, and colonel of the 5th Michigan in the War of 1861, and from Governor Ransom, of Michigan, will show the estimation in which he is held by th Ransom, on the 23rd of December, 1847, wrote in part as follows:

"Allow me to congratulate you on account of the high character you have won for yourself by your gallant conduct and bravery during the period, and amid scenes and events of the most brilliant military campaign ever witnessed. I pray God that the laurels you have gained may garland your brow in unfading freshness through a long and happy life, and I most cordially welcome back to Michigan.

Most sincerely and truly,

E. P. RANSOM."

Isaac G. Toll

GENERAL ISAAC De GRAFF TOLL.

GENERAL ISAAC DE GRAFF TOLL was born December 1, 1818, on Toll farm, near Schenectady, N. Y. Is a resident of Petoskey, Mich., since 1880, of which city he was President in 1881-1882, and to which he presented the site for the Lockwood Hospital. He was also chiefly instrumental in having built the breakwater that has so vastly improved the harbor.

The account given before does not fully cover his actions in the Mexican war, for at the battles of Contretras, 19th and 20th of August, 1847, and Churubusco, 20th of August, 1847, he was in the thick of the fray, and his charge with the bayonet at the latter battle, against orders, after having gone three times through a fierce fire to ask permission to charge, which was refused, was the cause of the American troops winning the day in that part of the field, with the assistance of the New York Volunteers and the Palmetto Regiment of South Carolina and others.

On this occasion Captain Toll was in command of Company E, the 15th U. S. Infantry, recruited in Michigan, his being the color company. He was also engaged at El Molino del Rey, September 8, 1847. The subjoined letters from his companion-in-arms, Samuel E. Beach, first lieutenant Company A, 15th U. S. Infantry, in Mexican war, and colonel of the 5th Michigan in the War of 1861, and from Governor Ransom, of Michigan, will show the estimation in which he is held by those who know him. Governor Ransom, on the 23rd of December, 1847, wrote in part as follows:

"Allow me to congratulate you on account of the high character you have won for yourself by your gallant conduct and bravery during the period, and amid scenes and events, of the most brilliant military campaign ever witnessed. I pray God that the laurels you have gained may garland your brow in unfading freshness through a long and happy life, and I most cordially welcome you back to Michigan.

Most sincerely and truly,

E. P. RANSOM."

Letter from Colonel Samuel E. Beach, first lieutenant of Company A, 15th U. S. Infantry, to Lieutenant Merrifield, also of the same company, who was left in hospital at Pueblo, Mexico, when the 15th advanced to the City of Mexico, August 10th, 1847. Colonel Beach also served as Colonel of the 5th Michigan, war of 1861:

"PONTIAC, July 10, 1886.

My Dear Mr. Merrifield, Lansing, Mich.

In progress of time you and I naturally recall the more prominent events of our youth, you of the assault at Pueblo, Mexico, where you led the Forlorn Hope, I of the terrible fire and overwhelming odds at Churubusco, where the Michigan companies, the right, Company A, commanded by me, and the center, with the colors, E, commanded by Captain Toll, gloriously sustained the honor of our state.

I must state to you, my old comrade, that Captain Toll, after he had thrice gone back amid the fire, to get permission to charge, was refused, himself ordered it, and reformed the regiment, which then, at the critical time, charged the masses of the enemy successfully, and none too soon, for the New York and South Carolina Volunteers, on our left, had just 'gone in,' in their part of the field. I hope justice will be done this opportune and gallant act, and the men of the companies A and E of the 15th regiment of U. S. Infantry from our state have that justice accorded them which has been delayed.

The battle of Churubusco was the deciding battle of the war with Mexico, the infantry did the work there, while all had their share, but on this arm all relied. Of the nearly two hundred men of those companies which we helped to form, my dear friend and comrade, how many will answer roll-call? Perhaps twenty. Eight dollars a month and found for all this empire of the Pacific, and yet how these twenty survivors are remembered.

Ever sincerely your comrade,

S. E. BEACH."

Also in Burton & Cutcheon's History, 3rd Vol., p. 203:

"In the battle (Churubusco) Company E carried the colors of the regiment and especially distinguished itself, Captain Toll leading the charge, the 15th covering itself with glory, suffering heavy loss."

Captain Toll's company was in the front in this charge, and the heaviest loss was sustained by it.

General Toll comes naturally by his military spirit, for in his veins runs the blood of the Vikings, his paternal ancestor coming from Norway to the then Province of New York, where he took up a large tract of land in the Mohawk Valley, near Schenectady. He was for many years a member of the Provincial Assembly that sat at Albany, N. Y.

Captain Philip R. Toll (father of the subject of this sketch) served in the War of 1812 in Canada, as captain of Schenectady Mounted Artillery; removed to Ovid, N. Y.; and in 1834 to Centerville, Mich., where he conducted a large department store; and on the soldiers' monument lately erected there his name is engraved; later he erected flouring and saw mills at Fawn River, St. Joseph, Co.; then removed to Monroe, Mich., where he died August 17, 1862, survived by his widow, Nancy De Graff Toll, daughter of Major Isaac De Graff, who served through the entire period of the War for Independence. She was the mother of General Isaac De Graff Toll. She was born September 18, 1797, and died at Monroe, Mich., March 27, 1898, having lived over a century.

The De Graffs were equally warlike as the Toll side of the family. It is recorded that at the battle fought near Schenectady, July 18, 1748, on the Toll farm, Captain Daniel Toll, the great-great grandfather of General Toll, and three of his great-great uncles were killed. John I. De Graff (uncle of General Toll) was a member of the U. S. Congress twice, and it was he who furnished the means to equip the fleet of Commodore MacDonough with which he won the battle of Lake Champlain.

The cause of this was that Washington, having been captured and burned by the British in the raid General Ross made upon it, the departments of the government fled the city, and Commodore MacDonough could get no reply from the Navy Department to his requisitions for money and supplies for his fleet then fitting out to repel the British attack, which was known to be preparing rapidly near the foot of Lake Champlain. In this crisis, as every moment's delay might mean the loss of all Northern New York and Vermont to the Union, John I. De Graff pledged his private means and credit to the amount of $100,000 for the necessary equipment, and with this aid Commodore MacDonough was enabled to meet and destroy the enemy's fleet at Plattsburg Bay, this being the final victory that proved that the lion of England, invincible on the waters to all the world, was, on more than equal terms, unable to withstand the valor of Uncle Sam's blue jackets.

Perry's victory on Lake Erie had only partially destroyed the English naval force on the Great Lakes, but MacDonough's utterly destroyed the last vestige of it, and at greater odds against him than Perry had.

The "ingratitude of Republic" is amply shown in the attached letter from Commodore MacDonough and the remarks attached thereto:

"U. S. SHIP SARATOGA, 15th Sept., 1814.

My Dear Sir—You will oblige me by giving any attention to Lieutenant Criswick that may be of service to him while with you in Albany or in your vicinity. He, by the fortune of war, is with us. For him I feel interested, and I know you will attend to him. I am again short of funds and cannot supply him. I have not yet received the draft which was promised me (as you saw when I was with you) by the Secretary's letter. The delay must be attributed to the derangement produced by the capture of Washington. The aid I obtained through your influence and responsibility enabled me to get the fleet ready. When I go to Washington, which will be I hope very soon, I shall not fail to represent to the Secretary your kindness. Be pleased to present to Mr. Walton and Messrs. Bleekers my best regards, and believe me to be, dear sir,.

Your obedient humble servant,
T. MACDONOUGH.

While John I. De Graff was widely known as a public benefactor, the first president and one of the main projectors of the Mohawk and Hudson Railroad, one of the first, if not the first (as has been claimed) for passenger travel in the United States, thrice mayor of his native city, Schenectady, N. Y., and twice in Congress, in justice to his memory and the truth of history, I give above copy of a letter written to him by Commodore MacDonough, showing that by the aid rendered by Mr. De Graff to that gallant officer, he was enabled to get the fleet ready to meet the enemy on Lake Champlain, Sept. 14, 1814, the victorious result of which we know; and will add that Mr. De Graff in his advances to the government lost, by depreciation of treasury notes, thirty thousand dollars, eight thousand of which only was paid to his executor, Judge Jesse D. De Graff, in 1856, the death of Mr. B. Bleeker, of Albany, his most important witness during the prosecution of the claim, cutting off the remainder. The capture of Washington by the British rendered the government powerless to aid the gallant Commodore, so he appealed successfully to Mr. De Gräff. The "responsibility" (see letter) involved a loss as stated.

General Toll is the only living officer of the U. S. Army that served in the Mexican war now residing in Michigan. He served the state as member of the house of representatives and as state senator, 1847; while in the house he prevented the Lake Shore railroad from going south from Coldwater, although one hundred thousand dollars were offered for the route; was chief of division of U. S. Pension, 1853-4; examiner of patents seven years, and holds commissions that show he passed through every grade from lieutenant-colonel to major-general in the service of the State of Michigan.

Among the various public addresses he has made since a resident of Petoskey are those made at the obsequies of Presidents Garfield and McKinley in that city, at both of which he presided.

General Toll is a member of G. A. R. Post 170 from his service in April, 1861, as commandant of the guards at Washington, D. C. Later he received a commission as recruiting officer from Governor Blair, October, 1863.

General Toll was married January 9, 1849, to Julia Victoria Moran, daughter of Judge Charles Moran. She died in 1865. The General is now a resident of Petoskey, where he has lived since 1880, and is as much alive to all that is transpiring, and with as youthful a heart and soul, as though since his birth the steam railroad and telegraph had not been invented in his youth, nor the telephone, phonograph and automobile since he was old enough to be a grandfather.

Let one of us now living be placed in the social and economic conditions that prevailed in 1818, and he would be as helpless as though he were transported to the Middle Ages.

THE NAVARRE FAMILY.

HENRY OF NAVARRE AT THE BATTLE OF IVRY.

Now by the lips of those ye love, fair gentlemen of France,
Charge for the golden lilies, upon them with the lance.
A thousand spurs are sinking deep, a thousand spears in rest,
A thousand knights are pressing close behind the snow-white crest;
And in they burst and on they rushed, while like a guiding star,
Amidst the thickest carnage blazed the helmet of Navarre."

* * *

The Navarres trace back their ancestry in an unbroken line to Antoine de Bourbon, duke de Vendome, father of Henry IV. of France. (The latter the Plumed Knight).

Robert de Navarre came to America and landed at Quebec. He was appointed under the French government subdeleque and royal notary at Detroit. He married here in 1743 Marie Lothmand deBarrois.

Robert Navarre's children were Marie Francoise, born 1735; married Geo. McDougall, lieutenant in the British Army, by whom she had two sons, Jean Robert and George. In 1774 she married Jacques (Jock) Campau, father of Joseph and Barnabe, by whom she had no heirs, but Barnabe, in 1820, married her granddaughter, Archange McDougall, whose sons were Alexander and the late Barnabe (Barney) Campau.

Marianne, born 1737, married, in 1760, Jacques A. St. Martin, frequently called La Butte, a celebrated interpreter. They lived in the old Cass house, which was the St. Martin homestead, the ground being deeded to him in 1750. St. Martin died in 1766, leaving a young widow with three children. His executors conveyed the property in 1787 to the well known Scotch merchant, Alexander Macomb, for $1,000, and in this house was born his grandson, who became famous as Major-General Macomb and died the commander-in-chief of the Federal Army. Previous to this sale it was occupied by George C. Anthon, father of several sons, who distinguished themselves as classical scholars and otherwise.

Of the St. Martin children, one died unmarried; Finon married Philip Fry, Archange married Angus McIntosh, who later on inherited the estates which belonged to the earldom of Moy in Scotland, the earldom itself having been forfeited in the rebellion against the House of Hanover. The McIntosh homestead was on the Canadian shore a little this side of Walkerville, and was celebrated along the Detroit River for the princely and lavish hospitality of its genial owner. The house is still standing, though somewhat modernized.

Ten children were born to Angus McIntosh. The boys went to Scotland to take possession of their estates. Two of the daughters were much loved and esteemed in Detroit—Mrs. Henry I. Hunt and Miss Catherine McIntosh.

In 1770 Marianne Nevarre, widow of St. Martin, bestowed her hand upon Dr. George C. Anthon, who had come to Detroit in 1760 with Major Rogers. She died in October, 1776, leaving no heirs by Anthon.

Robert Navarre, eldest son of Robert, Sr., surnamed Robishe the Speaker, was born in 1739. He married in 1762, Louis Archange de Mersac, daughter of Francois and Charlotte Bourassa. Another Charlotte Bourassa, a cousin, married in 1760, Charles de Langlade, the pioneer settler of Wisconsin, whose family belonged to that of the count of Paris. To Robert (Robishe) was deeded by the Pottawatomies their village, which was on a beautiful eminence, commanding a fine view, which even then was pronounced by them "Ancient Village." "We, the chiefs of the tribe of the Pottawatomies nation at Detroit, have deliberated and given of our own free will a piece of land of four arpents in width, by the whole depth, situated at our Ancient Village, to Robishe, son of the scrivener. We give him this land forever, that he might cultivate the same, light a fire thereon, and take care of our dead, and for surety of our words we have made our marks." This grant was ratified by Henry Bassett, commanding at Detroit, July 15, 1772, in presence of George McDougall. On one of Navarre's quit rent receipts it is stated that this tract was confirmed by General Gage. Robishe resided on his land and in the house known later on as the Brevoort homestead, which stood on the River Road, just about where Twenty-fourth Street crosses it. (It was torn down after the commodore's death, which occurred about 1855 or 1856). It was enlarged by the commodore (Robishe's son-in-law). Robische was the great-great grandfather of Mrs. W. Y. Hamlin, author of the "Legends of Detroit."

This Robische was blessed, like all French of that period, with an exceptionally large family. Jacques, born 1766, settled on the River Raisin. Francois, born 1767, early removed with his brother and Jean Marie to Monroe where twenty-six arpents of land had been deeded to the Navarres by the Ottawas. Francois was colonel during the war of 1812-1813, and figured most conspicuously. His house was the headquarters of Generals Wayne, Winchester, St. Clair and others. Thirty-six Navarres, it was said, served in his (Francois's) regiment. He was thoroughly conversant with the peculiar habits and warfare of the savages, and spoke with facility several other languages. He was captured at Brownstown, whither he went ahead of Colonel Johnson to negotiate with the Indians. He was taken prisoner to Sandwich, but escaped. His son served under Captain Richard (Dick) Smythe. The only French pear trees along the Raisin are those that were taken there by Colonel Navarre from his father's place in Detroit. Francois was the personal friend of Wayne, Winchester, St. Clair, Cass, Macomb and Woodward, and his correspondence with several of them has been preserved by the heirs, it is said. Isadore, born 1768, married (1795) Francoise Descomptes Labadie, daughter of Alexis and Francoise Robert. Their eldest son, Isadore, born 1790, though a mere strippling, served in the war of 1812. He married, 1790, Marie Suzord, daughter of Louis and Maria Dosette Lebeau. The children were, Robert, born 1792; Francois, born 1793; Victoire (married, 1822, Jacques Godfroy, son of Colonel Gabriel and Therese Couaire de Bondy); Agathe, who was exquisitely beautiful, according to all accounts; Monique (married John Askin, eldest son of Colonel Jas. Askin, of Sandwich). Archange Louis, born 1770, married, 1796, Dominique Godie de Marentette, whose daughter Jeanne married, first, Timothey Dequindre; second, William B. Hunt. Charlotte, another daughter of Archange Louis, born 1774, married Cajetan Tremblay. Antoine Freshet, born 1772, married, 1806, Madeline Cavallier. He served with distinction during the war of 1812. Marianne, born 1780, was a great belle. She was very gifted, possessing fine musical ability and decided talent for painting. Colonels Hamtramck and Gratiot were rival suitors for her favor. Both pleaded in vain. She was faithful to the memory of a former lover who had died suddenly. Several of her letters have been preserved, it is said. The style is admirable, the handwriting characteristic and beautiful. Catherine, another daughter (named after her aunt, Catherine Macomb), born 1782, married Commodore Henry Brevoort, of Lake Erie fame, and a member of the Brevoort family of New York. The children of this marriage were: John, married Marie Navarre; Robert, died young; Anne, who was a celebrated beauty, married Charles L. Bristol, who was the partner of John Hale; Elias, settled in Santa Fe, New Mexico; Henry, married Jane, daughter of Wm. Macomb, and Jeannette Francheville de Marentette, who left three sons—William Macomb, who fought bravely and fell in battle during the Civil War; Henry Navarre, who was at one time the popular prosecuting attorney of Wayne County, later on judge of Wayne County court, and at present practicing his profession; Elias Thornton, connected with the Canada Railroad.

Henry Brevoort, son of the commodore mentioned, was for a long time clerk for Hale & Bristol, and after entered the employ of John Mullett, surveyor-general of Michigan, and spent the remainder of his years surveying in Northern Michigan and the Upper Peninsula. He was a fine, manly, handsome fellow, and died too early. Elias, another and a younger son of the commodore, cast his lot in New Mexico (as before said), in the early forties, and I don't think that he ever returned here, but once, and that was at the time of the death of his father, the commodore. He passed a stirring, adventurous life in that once far-off, wild region of the country. He was an intimate friend and associate of General Fremont's famous guide and scout, Kit Carson. Both Henry and Elias were schoolmates of mine. Elias died March 12, 1904, at Sialo, Mexico, whither he had gone for the benefit of his health. He was unmarried.

He passed through many exciting scenes and had many perilous adventures in that "Wild and woolly" country. He was on intimate relations with nearly all the old army officers in the early days. The late General Sturgis was then lieutenant of dragoons and Brevoort led him as guide and trailer, into his first Indian fight. Brevoort said that he (Sturgis) behaved himself with great credit, but forgot all he had told him he was to do or how to do, in case the "Reds" were overtaken, which they were, and

120 head of mules recovered, and they killed nine out of ten of the band. He told Sturgis he never was guilty of killing Indians on paper, but always took a voucher from the dead Red. Sturgis asked him what he meant by voucher. He said, "A scalp, of course." Which he said he did in this case, and fastened them to his belt. He said the Red was bound to get his scalp if he could, and he thought the Indian's scalp was far better in his belt, than his in that of the hostile. That was in the winter of 1854-55. He said it was a hard trip to Sturgis, but a very valuable lesson to him. His gallantry won him promotion to a captaincy. He also said in relation to events in and around Santa Fe at that time. "If I could be with you for six months, I could give you some very interesting data that would fill a good sized volume, which would be brim full of exciting, thrilling events in which I participated. I always had a fine mount in those days, accompanied by the best rifle made, including a pair of Colt's ivory-handled six-shooters and a keen knife. Could sleep mounted as well as upon a mattress, and ride further in twenty-four hours than any two men could with a change of mounts." He also knew and was quite intimate with Major J. A. Whitall, paymaster, U. S. A.; Major E. S. Sibley, quartermaster, U. S. A.; Major Dan H. Rucker, quartermaster, U. S. A.; and others.

Brevoort was quite a voluminous writer, and it is to be hoped that he left some account of the exciting life he led in New Mexico. In a letter to me last December, from Sante Fe, he said in relation to Carson: "Yes, Kit was a personal friend who saved my life and that of my companion, in the fall of '50, when crossing the plains, by riding 150 miles with a troop of dragoons in less than twenty-four hours, arriving the night before myself and party were to be massacred by a band of bandits and robbers of the worst kind. I had in connection with my companions (a party of gentlemen) and under my protection a large amount of specie (gold and silver). It was a gay night when Kit crawled into camp the night before, and informed me of the contemplated attack of the robbers. They somehow got wind of the aid that had come to us, consequently the affair did not come off."

He also sent me copy of communication that he had addressed to the commissioner of Indian affairs in relation to the servant girl problem, but no notice had been taken of it by that official. Brevoort's assumption was that the article had been pigeon-holed, because (as he wrote) the commissioner of Indian affairs and all of his employes, numbering hundreds, would be against any such move as he recommended, simply because they would eventually have to look for some other occupation. The Indian girls were said to be well trained in all home and domestic work, and to speak English. I sent the article to *The Free Press,* and requested its publication. It appeared in the columns of that paper November 15, 1903. Brevoort said he thought if President Roosevelt's attention could be brought to the subject some good might result from it, and this servant girl question arrive at a solution.

Monique, another daughter of Robishe, born in 1789, was the first wife of William Macomb. She inherited the traditional loveliness of her race and added, among other accomplishments, that of a daring and superb equestrienne. She died young, leaving one son, Navarre Macomb.

Pierre (Peter), another son of Robishe, born in 1786, settled at the mouth of the Maumee about 1807. He was a trusty scout to General Harrison during the war of 1812. His thorough knowledge of the Indians and of the country enabled him to render many important services.

It appeared from "Knapp's History of the Maumee Valley" that near the mouth of the Maumee River, opposite Manhattan, about 1806 or 1808, a French settlement, near the Ottawa (Indian) Village was established. Conspicuously among those French adventurers was Peter Navarre, a grandson of Robert de Navarre, an officer in the military service of France, who came to this country in 1745. The Ottawa village, Navarre asserted, had been in existence since the days of the Pontiac conspiracy, and the head chief of the nation was a descendant of Pontiac.

This Peter Navarre joined Hull's Army on the Maumee, went to Detroit, and then returned to the Raisin, where he enlisted in Colonel Anderson's regiment. He was at Raisin when the British Captain Elliott, accompanied by a Frenchman, and a Wyandot Indian, came with a flag to inform Colonel Brush and the troops at Raisin that they were included in the terms of surrender of Hull. Navarre and his four brothers acknowledged themselves as prisoners, and were permitted to depart on parole.

Peter Navarre and his four brothers, rendered valuable aid to the United States as scouts during the war of 1812, and it was said, had General Winchester listened to their sagacious and timely suggestion, the disaster at the Raisin would not, probably, have occurred.

"Navarre and his brothers were employed as scouts by General Harrison as soon as Fort Meigs was completed. When the Indians first made their appearance, Navarre discovered them crossing the river at the foot of the island. On reporting this to Harrison, he gave him three letters—one to Lower Sandusky, one to Upper Sandusky, and a third to Governor Meigs, at Urbana. Navarre departed, and at the end of the fifth day handed the message to Governor Meigs."

Peter Navarre, who was living in 1872, near Maumee Bay, was born in Detroit in 1786 (as said) and was then (1872) 87 years of age. An editorial in the Toledo *Blade* of May, 1872, gives the following in addition to what has been hitherto sketched, upon the authority of this venerable patriot:

"At the battle of the Thames on the 1st of October, Navarre was under Johnson, in the immediate vicinity of Tecumseh, of whose death he speaks as follows: 'He was standing behind a large tree that had blown down, encouraging his warriors, and was killed by a ball that passed diagonally through his chest. After death he was shot several times, but otherwise his body was not mutilated in the least, being buried in his regimentals, as the old chief desired, by myself and a companion, at the command of General Harrison. All statements that he was scalped or skinned are absolutely false.'"

While at Malden General Proctor, of the British Army, offered the Indians $1,000 for the scalp of Navarre, and was informed that if he wanted it he must secure it himself, as in times of peace they had taught him all their knowledge of woodcraft, and now it was almost impossible to capture him."

It is said that his portrait, taken at the age of 70, is still possessed by his descendants. This portrait, with a short history of Peter Navarre, was given in the *Evening News* of August 27 last. In relation to the advice given to General Winchester, by Peter and his three brothers, Robert, Alexis and James, before the battle of the Raisin (and to which allusion has already been made), the article goes on to say: "It was these four brothers who discovered Proctor's proposed attack on the settlement at Frenchtown, but whose warning was set at naught by the conflicting and false report of Jacob La Salle, an unsuspected spy in the service of the British."

For the early history of the Navarre family, before about 1830, I am greatly indebted to the late Mrs. Caroline Watson Hamlin, who, in her admirable book, "Legens of Detroit" (compiled mostly from the records of St. Anne's Catholic church), has given an account of the advent of the first pioneer of this family as well as of most, if not all, of the old French families, who came here after or about Cadillac's time. After I came to Detroit, about 1830, I became personally acquainted with most, if not all, of the surviving members of these old French families, whose forebears were the pioneers of this section, and what I may relate in their connection, after the latter date, is from personal observation and recollection.

In the article printed Sunday, September 4, I said that General Alex. Macomb died commander-in-chief of the Army of the United States. I should have said, "in immediate command." All know that the president is the commander-in-chief of the Army. Also, the compositor made me say, "General Macomb was in command here about 1812." It should have been "about 1821."

THE ST. MARTIN FAMILY.

THE ST. MARTIN FAMILY, A BRANCH OF THE NAVARRES—
DR. ANTHON AND HIS DISTINGUISHED SONS—
THE OLD CASS HOUSE.

TO the St. Martin family belongs a branch of the Navarre family (the Anthons of New York, the Scotch branch of McIntosh). Antoine St. Martin was appointed a royal notary at Quebec as early as 1660. He came from Haut Languedoc, France. He married twice. His descendants by his first wife are still in Canada. By his second wife, Michelle Cusson, whom he married in 1687, he had one son, Jean Baptiste, born in 1689, who, in 1709, came to Detroit and married Marie Louise Dogon, by whom he had five children, one of whom, Jacques, surnamed La Butte, married in 1760, Marianne Navarre, daughter of Robert, the sub-intendant. A daughter, Margaret, married in 1758, Colonel Louis Jadot. She is the ancestress of the Anthons, of New York. Another daughter married in 1760, Jacques Code de Marentette.

Jacques St. Martin (La Butte) was a noted interpreter. He was brother-in-law of Lieutenant Geo. McDougall, whom he accompanied with Major Campbell to Pontiac's camp at that chief's suggestion that he wished to treat with them. The office of interpreter was a very important one, and the English suffered much owing to the rescality of some of these men. The French missionaries and French officers were mostly familiar with the Indian languages and were seldom imposed upon. Bradstreet and Sir William Johnson complained of their interpreters, but always made honorable exceptions of Chabeat de Joncare Chene, Jacques St. Martin, and later of Henry Connor and Whittemore Knaggs—Jacques St. Martin married Marianne Navarre, who, after his death, in 1768, married Dr. George Christian Anthon. She died at the age of 36, leaving no heirs by Anthon, but three by St. Martin. They resided in the Old Cass house, which then belonged to St. Martin. One of these children, Archange, born in 1766, married Angus McIntosh, who inherited the estates which belonged to the earldom of Moy, the earldom itself having been forfeited in the rebellion against the house of Hanover. He was noted for his lavish hospitality. The sons of this marriage returned to Scotland. Two of the daughters were well known in Detroit, Mrs. Henry I. Hunt and Miss Kitty McIntosh, who died some years ago. Mrs. Hunt died many years before the latter (as has been mentioned before).

THE ANTHON BRANCH.

Marguerite de St. Martin married, in 1758, Colonel Louis Jadot, an officer in De My's regiment. He was the eldest son of Jacques Jadot, former alderman and mayor of Recrois (France), and Marie Boland. Colonel Jadot was killed in 1765 by the Indians. His wife had died in 1764, leaving an infant daughter, Genevieve, to the care of her brother Jacques and his wife, Marianne Navarre. Litttle Genevieve was kindly taken care of by her aunt, Marianne Navarre who, becoming a widow, married Dr. Anthon. In 1773 Mrs. Anthon died, and Genevieve was left with her cousins, the St. Martin children, as the wards of Dr. Anthon and their uncle, Alexander Macomb. When Genevieve reached her fifteenth year Dr. Anthon married her; he was at the time forty-five.

A brief sketch of the doctor, whose life was an adventurous one, and who gave to America its most celebrated classical scholar, Charles Anthon, may be interesting to many.

Dr. George Christian Anthon, born at Salzugen, Germany, in 1734, died in New York City in 1815. He studied medicine in his native place, afterwards at Gerstungen. In 1750 he passed his examination before the medical authorities of Eisenbach. From thence, in 1754, he went to Amsterdam, passed two examinations before the College of Surgeons, and was appointed surgeon in the Dutch West India trade. He made several voyages, but the vessel he was on was captured in 1757 by a British privateer from New York, and was carried into that port. At the age of 23 he found himself in a new and strange country without friends, and with no other resources than his profession. Confident of his ability he applied for a situation in the military hospital at Albany. His talents were recognized, and he was appointed assistant surgeon in the First Battalion, Sixtieth Regiment, Royal Americans. In 1760 he was detached with a party which, under Major Rogers took possession of Detroit. He married twice—first Marianne Navarre, the widow of Jacques de St. Martin, by whom he had no heirs; in 1778 he married Genevieve Jadot, her orphan niece, on the St. Martin side. In 1786 Dr. Anthon removed with his family to New Montreal. Three of the doctor's children were born in Detroit. It appears the doctor had eleven children in all. Henry, born in 1795, died in 1861, became the Rev. Henry Antion of St. Mark's Church, New York City. Charles, born in 1797, died in 1867, the most accomplished Greek and Latin scholar in America. The remainder of his children died in New York without attaining special prominence. "Anthon's Classics" were at one time in use in all the colleges and high grade schools in the United States. During my experience in the bookselling business I sold thousands of copies of "Anthon's Classics." Harper & Brothers were his publishers. Do not think they are in use now, but will be remembered quite vividly, no doubt, by many of the present day who in their college days sweat over these productions of Dr. Anthon and damned him up and down.

CASS HOUSE.

At the time of the demolition of the Cass or St. Martin House it was suggested by some one that the City of Detroit buy it and remove it to East Grand Circus Park, but no one in authority took any interest in the matter, the idea died out and the old historic relic went to the rag bag, so to speak. What an attraction it would be at the present day, not only to our own citizens, but to the citizens of the entire country as well. Just witness in the season how the crowds of visitors from abroad press and crowd through the halls of the rustic log cabin at Palmer Park, a structure so suggestive, in a way, of the early days, and besides it is situated quite near (little over a stone's throw) Mad Anthony Wayne's road through the woods to Pontiac, over which his army marched with its artillery and wagon train so long ago.

This Cass (St. Martin) house has been described many times. Notwithstanding, I think an account of it in this connection will not be out of place. It is taken from Colonel McKinney's "Tour of the Lakes," published in 1827. I was quite familiar with it, indoors and out, and can testify to the truthfulness of the colonel's description.

In a letter to his wife, he says: "At 2 o'clock (June 17, 1826), I dined with the governor (Cass), and as you may be curious to know what kind of a mansion he occupies, I will give you a sketch of it. It is not exactly in, nor entirely out of the city —I mean its settled parts; but stands by itself on the bank of the river, with the roadway from the city to Springswells, between it and the precipice, or edge of the bank, down which a diagonal and rough way has been cut to the river. The house is of cedar logs, and weather-boarded, one story, with a high sharp roof, out of which, and near the center, comes a short stone chimney of enormous thickness, and on which the roof leans, being a little sunk round about it. Before the front door, which is nearly in the center of the building, the building itself being some fifty feet front, is a porch that being a little out its perpendicular position inclines north. Its figure is nearly that of a square as of any other figure, with a sharp Chinese-looking top that shoots up some three feet above the eaves of the house and seems to have in no one place the least connection with the building. I told the governor that my puzzle was to decide which was built first, the porch or the house. He acknowledged his inability to decide the question, but added, 'the house itself is anterior to the time of Pontiac's war, there being on it now the marks of bullets which were shot into it then.' I learned afterwards that the porch had once ornamented the garden as a summer house, but had been advanced from its retirement to grace the front of the residence of the executive of the Michigan Territory. A post and board fence runs between the house and the road, the house standing back from the line of it some ten or twelve feet. Two gateways open into the inclosure, one having been intended to admit, and the other to let you out, over a circular gravel walk that gives figure to a green plat in front of the door, and between it and the fence. One of these has been shut up, but how long I don't know— so we go in and come out at the same gate. The position occupied by this relic of antiquity is very beautiful, not on account of the views to it, and from it, only, although these are both fine, but it is sustained on either side and in the background, by fertile upland meadows, and flourishing orchards and gardens which give it a most inviting appearance, and serve to impress one with the idea of old age surrounded by health and cheerfulness. In front are the shores of Canada, with the beautiful river between, and to the right the Huron Church, etc., the sound of the bell from which strikes gratefully upon the ear.

"Now for the inside of the building. You enter first into a room, or saloon, of some ten feet square in which the governor receives his business visitors, and where lie scattered about in some tolerable confusion, newspapers and the remains of pamphlets of all sorts, whilst its sides are ornamented with Indian likenesses, and pipes, and snow shoes, and medals, and bows and arrows, etc. On your left is the door which leads into the dining apartment, back of which is another room (in which is a fireplace) of about the same size, divided from it by folding doors. This dining room is warmed in winter by one half a stove, whilst the other half, passing through the partition into the saloon, keeps that comfortable. From the right of the audience room or saloon, you enter the drawing room, and in place of the back room, in the left division, two rooms are arranged, one which serves for the library, and the other for a lodging room. These rooms being all well carpeted and curtained, and furnished in excellent, but plain style, present a view of comfort which forms a striking contrast to the exterior; and you are made to forget, in the midst of these interior accommodations, the odd-shapen and ancient appearance from without. There is much of the simplicity of republicanism in all this. Extrinsic appearances are to a reasonable extent disregarded, and the higher value is attached to the interior, and this is not an unfit emblem of the governor himself. You are not to imagine, however, that this applies to his person, which is portly, and altogether governorlike, and in regard to which he is neat in his dress, and though plain, polished in his manners."

THE PELLETIER FAMILY.

THE PELLETIER FAMILY AND ITS BRANCHES, IN WHICH ARE FOUND MANY WELL-KNOWN NAMES.

HISTORY states that when La Mothe Cadillac landed at Detroit he was greeted by two couriers des bois, Pierre Roy and Francois Pelletier (pronounced in my time Peltier, also Pelk). This latter name stands very high in Canada and is found in every department of science and politics. Nicholas, the first of the name, came from Beance, France, and married, in 1675, Jeanne Roussy, and settled in Canada. A grandson married at Detroit, 1718, Marie Louise Robert, whose son, Jean Bapte, married Marie Cornet. The children were: J. Bapte, married, 1769, Catherine Valle dit Versailles; Therese, married, 1780, Jean Bapte Chapoton; Andre, married, 1763, Catherine Meloche; his son, J. Bapte, married, 1809, Catherine Williams, daughter of Thomas Williams and Cecile Campau, she was a sister of General John R. Williams; Jacques, married, 1778, Madeline LeVanneur at Quebec. Their children were: Archange, born 1782, named after her godmother, Archange Barthe, wife of John Askin, governor of Mackinac. She married in 1800 Maj. John Whipple of Manchester, Mass. "The children of this union blended the happier traits of the Puritan with graceful charms of the dark-eyed Norman race." James Burbick Whipple married, 1812, for his first wife, Sophie Godfroy, daughter of Colonel Gabriel Godfroy, and for his second wife a daughter of Judge Jas. May. Charles Wiley Whipple, the well known lawyer and chief justice of the Supreme Court of Michigan, which office he held at the time of his death, married Marguerite Anne Brooks, daughter of Colonel Edward Brooks, and Marguerite Anne May, daughter of Judge May. Anne Hunt Whipple married Peter Desnoyers (his second wife). Henry L. Whipple married Caroline Buckley, of Monroe, a most interesting young lady of great beauty, who after Whipple's death, married Mr. Harvey Mixer, of Buffalo, and then of Monroe, and then of Detroit. A fine gentleman and a business man of the strictest integrity. His wife died not many years ago. I knew Mr. Mixer well in Buffalo in 1842-3-4-5, and our acquaintance has continued pleasantly all down these years. Henry L. Whipple when he died was deputy auditor-general of the state. William L. Whipple married Louise Fairchild, sister of Mrs. Benjamin Vernor, of Detroit, and like her sister (Mrs. Vernor) was a very attractive and beautiful woman. His only child, Marie Louise, married Edgar, son of Alexander Lewis. She died on the very threshold of life, as beautiful and as charming as was her mother. William L. Whipple was a schoolmate of mine, and we were always close friends until he died. We were at school together, clerked it together here and in Monroe, and when the Mexican War came on he joined the First Regiment, Michigan Volunteers, Thos. B. W. Stockton, colonel; A. S. Williams, lieutenant-colonel, and James E. Pittman, adjutant, and proceeded with the regiment to Mexico. When peace was declared the regiment returned to Detroit and was mustered out of service. He obtained a situation as teller in the Michigan Insurance Bank, which he retained until he associated himself with the writer in the paper and stationery business under the firm name of Palmer & Whipple. On the death of his wife he parted with his interest in above concern and after a while accepted a situation in the Detroit postoffice. This he retained until the breaking out of the Civil War, when his military ardor and valuable experience gained in the Mexican War impelled him to raise a company for the Second Michigan Volunteer Infantry, J. B. Richardson, colonel, and went with it to the front. He was captain, April 25, 1861. The Second Michigan, with the Third, although they did not participate in the first battle of Bull Run, covered the disastrous retreat. The regiment was with McClellan's army during the Richmond campaign, and with it on its retreat to Harrison's Landing, where it remained until April 15, 1862. Whipple in the meantime was promoted to the lieutenant-colonelcy of the Twenty-first Michigan Infantry, for gallant and meritorious services, August 13, 1862. A rapid rise from a captaincy to lieutenant-colonel in little over a year. The Twenty-first bore an important part in the battle of Perrysville, Tenn., October 8, 1862. In Colonel A. A. Stevens's report of the battle he says among other things: "Lieutenant-Colonel Whipple,

Major Hunting and Adjutant Wells each filled their respective positions nobly, and rendered very efficient service upon the occasion."

Something significant in the fact that Colonel Stevens made his report to Colonel Nicholas Greusel, for many years prior to the war a citizen of Detroit, and uncle to Hon. Joseph Greusel, also a warm friend of Whipple's. At the time of making the report referred to Greusel was colonel of the Thirty-sixth Illinois Infantry and commanded the Thirty-seventh Brigade, Eleventh Division, Army of the Ohio. Whipple died at Nashville, Tenn., November 16, 1862, of typhoid fever, just on the threshold of a brilliant career. He was exceedingly fond of a soldier's life, and during his brief career in that direction, saw more service fighting the battles of his country than did any of his ancestors, except, perhaps, Admiral Whipple, the brave and distinguished head of the family. It is a matter of record that Commodore Abraham Whipple struck the first blow on the water for the cause of independence. When the French and Indian war broke out, he took command of the English privateer Gamecock and captured twenty-three prizes in one cruise. In 1772 he led the secret expedition that burned his majesty's armed schooner Gaspe in Narragansett Bay.

Eliza Susan Whipple married Chas. Conagham, of Cincinnati, O.; Margaretta Torry Whipple married Charles Hyde, also of Cincinnati; Catherine Sophia married Edwin Skinner. Skinner was at the time in the employ of the Michigan Central Railroad. Later, on the breaking out of the Civil War he joined the Tenth Michigan Volunteer Infantry as first lieutenant and quartermaster, and served in that capacity with distinction and marked ability, during the entire war. Their children, who are alive, reside in this city, except Dr. Strong and wife; Henry W., who married in 1877, Nannie Avery, of Detroit, for his first wife. and for his second Miss Dana, daughter of R. H. Dana, author of that exceedingly entertaining book, "Two Years Before the Mast." Archibald married, 1887, Norton Strong, surgeon United States Army, son of H. Norton Strong and Helen Chapin, of Detroit. Bernard Skinner is unmarried. Mary Walcott Whipple, who inherited all the fine characteristics of her race, died unmarried, and quite recently, at an advanced age, preserving to the last her fine conversational powers and all her faculties almost unimpaired.

. The Whipple family in the early forties and fifties drew around them in their modest but comfortable home on Congress Street, between St. Antoine and Beaubien, all the gay young society of the city. Charles Peltier, who held many important offices in the city and county, and who was also prominent in insurance circles, was the son of Charles Peltier and Cecil Marthe Chapoton, whose sister married Major Antoine Dequindre, of Dequindre farm. He married Eliza Vameter Cicotte (his cousin, I think). Charles, a son of his, succeeded his father in the insurance business. A daughter of his, Madeline, married Joseph Belanger, a branch of whose family came to Detroit in 1715 from Canada. These two young men (Peltier and Belanger) joined forces in the insurance business under the firm name of Peltier & Belanger. They were deservedly popular and successful. They finally concluded to dissolve partnership. They are now pursuing the same business, each on his own account.

Lucy Peltier—the daughter of which Peltier she was I do not know—was a charming girl, very beautiful, and a great favorite in the family of Mr. Felix Hinchman, as also in that of ours. She married a gentleman by the name of Lacey, a banker in Niles, Mich., in 1838. "Lucy Lacey" were household words in the Hinchman family for years. What became of her and hers during all the past time I do not know. I presume some of her descendants are living in Niles now.

THE LABADIE FAMILY.

THE LABADIE FAMILY AND ITS CONNECTIONS BY MARRIAGE INCLUDES MANY WELL-KNOWN NAMES.

THE name of Labadie was borne in France, 1732, by Alexander Etyenne Ravielt Claude Labadie, colonel of an infantry regiment. A descendant of his came to Detroit about 1747 and immediately took a foremost rank in the affairs of the colony. His son was Louis (Badichon) Labadie, married, 26 February, 1759, Angelique Campeau, who died in the parish of l'Assumption (Sandwich, Ont.), 11 December, 1767. She left six young children. Louis (Badichon) Labadie then fell in love with the daughter of an Indian chief. Though no record can be found of his marriage to this Indian woman, yet it is known that he lived with her seventeen years, and when she died she left seventeen children. He was then married, in St. Anne's Church, Detroit, October 18, 1784, to Charlotte Barthe, widow of Lieutenant Louis Reaume, of the British army. By this marriage he had ten children, so as he had thirty-three children by his three wives, he may claim to have aided materially in populating Detroit and its vicinity. One of the children of Louis Labadie married John Hale, an extensive merchant here until into the forties (Hale & Bristol). One of his daughters (Antoinette) married Joseph Langley, then of New York, but now of Chicago; the other (Lizzie) married William S. Driggs of Macey & Driggs, real estate, etc. Her son is an officer in the United States navy (he invented a gun). Another daughter of Louis (Badichon) Labadie, Eleonore, married first, Mr. J. Reid, who was one of the editors and proprietors of the old *Detroit Gazette* (Sheldon & Reid); second, in 1806, Jean Baptiste Piquette, son of John Baptiste Piquette and Francoise Archeveque de Rouen, by whom she had two sons, John Baptiste and Charles; third, in 1825, Thomas C. Sheldon, by which marriage she had three children. Thomas P. married Winnie Clark, niece of Governor Fenton of

Michigan; Rose married A. Henry Guise, of a distinguished Philadelphia family, an estimable man and courteous gentleman. Her daughter Nellie married Mr. Orville Allen, of Grosse Ile. She died some years ago. One of the sons (Thomas Guise) possessed a fine voice and is now on the operatic stage; another son (Richard) is also upon the operatic stage; another son (Philip) was a bright young man of scholarly attainments, he was at one time engaged in newspaper work and was on the *Evening News,* and bid fair to become a success in that line, but unfortunately he has been the victim of rheumatism for years to such an extent that it has almost totally incapacitated him from attending to any business that requires much out-door work. Alexandrine Macomb, another daughter of Thos. C. Sheldon, married first, Barnabas Campau, son of Barnabas (L'Abbie) and Archange McDougal, by whom she had three children; Charlotte died in infancy; Thomas S., and Albert, two bright, promising young men who attained majority. Thomas died after a brief illness in Yokohama, Japan, where he had gone for his health. Albert studied medicine under Dr. E. L. Shurly, of Detroit, was admitted to practice, with the prospect of a brilliant career before him, but from some cause became a hopeless invalid and died at the Catholic Retreat, Dearborn. These two young men were quite celebrated for their courteous and elegant manners. Alexandrine M. Campau married a second time to Mr. R. Storrs Willis, brother of the poet, N. P. Willis.

Mrs. Alexandrine Burt, who recently died in Paris, and who was well known in Detroit, was quite a celebrated opera singer. Years ago Mrs. Burt sang at several sacred concerts given for charity in Detroit, and it was said her voice compared favorably with that of her personal friend, the renowned Adelina Patti. Oliver P. Burt, her husband, was at the time of his death a prominent Michigan lumberman of Saginaw. Mrs. Burt was a descendant of the Labadies (L. Descomtes, called by the Indians, Badachon) and was a sister of Mrs. L. J. Archambeault, now living at 31 Elizabeth Street, West, with her daughters, Mrs. Chas. M. June and Mrs. Josephine Kelly. She is a cousin of Mrs. R. Storrs Willis, and also connected with the Campaus, Marentettes, Montreuil and other French families of Detroit and vicinity. She was born in Canada, at the Labadie farm, at what is now known as Walkerville. Mrs. Burt's daughter (Nina), a sweet singer and ing young woman, has been on the operatic stage in Europe, singing in Paris, Naples, London and other continental capitals for several years, and now resides at Milan, Italy. She also sang in concert in Detroit about eight or nine years ago. Judge James May married for his second wife Marguerite (a Labadie), and daughter of a third branch of this family, and by her had many children. Marguerite, Anne married Colonel Edward Brooks. Her children were mostly girls (had two boys). The girls were celebrated for their beauty and charming personality, and they were also quite musical. Emma, Octavia and Mary were almost the mainstay of the Presbyterian Church choir. Marguerite Anne married Charles W. Whipple, son of Captain Whipple, U. S. A., and brother of Lieut.-Col. W. L. Whipple, Michigan Volunteers in the Civil War. Charles was a distinguished member of the Detroit bar, and held the office of chief justice of Michigan. She died at the early age of 30 years, leaving two daughters—Eunice, who married Judge William Jennison, of Detroit, and Adeline, widow of Josiah Johnson, a wholesale dry goods merchant of Detroit, west side of Woodward Avenue, just above Michigan Avenue. Adeline Brooks died unmarried, as did Emma. Rebecca married Dr. J. B. Scovell, a most skillful physician of Detroit, and a genial gentleman. Two children were the fruit of this union—Edward Brooks, whose wonderful voice has won him an enviable reputation (Chevalier Scovelli), married Marcia Roosevelt, a daughter of Judge Roosevelt, of New York City, and a cousin to President Roosevelt. Mary (May) married Mr. Richard Cornell, of Buffalo, N. Y. After separating from her husband she went on the stage and was known to the theatrical world as May Fielding. After quite a successful career she again married, and at present she and her husband live at Cobourg, Canada, that pleasant retreat, the summer home of many society people from this side. Octavia married Mr. J. C. W. Seymour, for many years connected with the old Farmers & Mechanics, and also other banks in operation here at that time. Two children of this marriage, I think, are still living—Elizabeth, wife of Captain Waterbury, U. S. A.; Marguerite, wife of Mr. Rush Drake, formerly of Detroit, but now of Denver, Col. Mary Brooks (Mollie) married Mr. Whitney, of Philadelphia. Mr. Whitney was a capitalist, and at an early day invested largely in Texas bonds at a low figure (Lone Star State). When the state was admitted into the Union the general government assumed the payment of these bonds, and so Mr. Whitney came into much money. Mrs. Whitney was at one time noted in New York society as one of its most brilliant and accomplished women. She is, I think, yet alive and in New York. Emily Brooks married Mr. Francis Markham, of the Woodward Avenue dry goods house, of Markham & Thompson. They afterwards resided in New York. Elizabeth married Harry Scoville, son of Dr. J. B. Scoville, who was connected with the Detroit *Free Press* when it was under the management of Wilbur F. Storey, and afterwards with the same gentleman on the *Chicago Times*. Carrie married Mr. Philip Gulliger, and resided in New York. She possessed musical talents of a high order, both vocal and instrumental. It is said she gained a great reputation in the former. William died young. Edward went to Colorado, and at one time was chief of police of Denver. I met him in Washington, D. C., in 1884 or 1885.

Colonel Brook's house on Woodward Avenue, west side, about midway between Congress and Larned Streets, was the center of the gay life of Detroit of that day. None other possessed so much the potent charm to draw within its magic circle all that went to make up the social swim. Adeline, as said, died unmarried and, I think, of consumption, but she was in her prime one of the most queenly looking women that ever trod the streets of Detroit. I saw her one evening, in the Brooks' parlor, standing beneath and in the full light of the chandelier engaged in animated conversation with John W. Strong, Jr., who was then in his very prime (both in the pride of youth and beauty) and I thought then, as I think now, that I never saw a handsomer couple. John had just returned from New York, where he had spent two or three years in mercantile pursuits, was fresh from the east, so to speak, and had all the glamor of the big city about him. Sad to think she had to die so young. Emma (as said) also died unmarried. She was strikingly beautiful, differing somewhat from the others in this particular: she was a brunette, the others were not. She showed Labadie blood. There were a half dozen of us boys who used to attend Rev. Mr. Cleveland's (Presbyterian) Church in the gallery, and for no other reason than to see Emma, Octavia and Mary Brooks. Ah, me, poor boys, they are all dead and gone but myself, but I am sure if any of them were alive they would make the same confession. Emily,

Elizabeth and Carrie were a little after my time and I know of them only. I know there are some two or three now living who will call to mind Colonel Edw. Brooks. He took some part in the Black Hawk War and was always identified with what little military we had here at an early day. He was also the most prominent and efficient auctioneer that the city could boast of. He could never get through a sale without repeating some funny story or getting off some witty anecdote or saying which always made those occasions quite interesting, besides putting his audience in good humor with themselves, and stimulating the bidding. He was also the most prominent figure here, and in the state for that matter, during the campaign of 1840 ("Tippecanoe and Tyler, too"). His witty speeches at the "Log Cabin," that was opposite the American Hotel (Biddle House), and elsewhere will long be remembered. He was appointed by President Harrison collector of this port. How long he served in that capacity I do not know, nor do I know when and where he died. Another daughter of Judge May, Nancy, married James Whipple, of Monroe, another son of Major John Whipple, U. S. A. James Whipple was at one time register of deeds of Monroe County. Another daughter of Judge May, Caroline, married Alex. D. Frazer, a highly distinguished member of the Detroit bar for many years. The only fruit of this union was Alexander, whom many will call to mind, a very pleasant and agreeable young gentleman. The latter married Miss Milly Miles, of New York, daughter of Dr. Miles. The latter, in company with Dr. Bannerman (Bannerman & Miles), were in this city temporarily, exploiting some medical specialty, the nature of which I forget. Dr. Miles had with him here Mrs. Miles and three beautiful daughters. One of them (Milly) captured Alexander, Jr. (as said). The husband died, leaving one daughter (Carrie), who died in her teens, unmarried, a bright, charming girl. Another daughter, Mary Miles, married Mr. Herter, of New York, a dealer in antique furniture and an artistic house decorator as well. The remaining daughter is married, I think, and is living in Paris, or was the last I heard of her. Mrs. Frazer and her sister attended the costume party at the National Hotel (Russell House) on the evening of February 19, 1857, and the chronicler of the affair (General Henry E. Mizner, U. S. A.) has this to say of the costumes worn on that occasion by the two ladies I have mentioned:

"Two of the most elegant dresses of the evening were those of Mrs. Alex. J. Frazer and her sister, Miss Mary Miles, as the 'Grecian sisters.' The skirts were short, of white silk, striped with silver, over which was a blue silk tunic, covered with spangles. A beautiful white plume encircled the head, securing a rich veil of white lace trimmed with spangles, which hung gracefully over all. The effect was beautiful, the costumes in exquisite taste, elicited much admiration."

That it was a function of the swellest kind may be gathered from the same account of it, which goes on to say: "So brilliant an assemblage was never before witnessed in the 'City of the Straits,' and all who participated in the delineations of that evening will long remember the enchanting scene, and recur to it with emotion of pleasure and satisfaction." I was present on this occasion, and do not suppose there are but four or five besides myself who were of that notable gathering now living. Lawyer Frazer, his wife, their son Alex, and his wife and their daughter Carrie, were all of them on the most cordial terms imaginable, and when together seemed like a party of children. All even before Alex was married, father, mother and son, were as chummy as a trio of boys and girls. Many of the present day will call these characteristics of the Frazer family to mind, I am sure.

One of the Marentettes (Canada) married a Labadie. James Godedet Marentette to Elizabeth Labadie in 1821. This Marantette was born at Assumption, Sandwich (Ontario), in July, 1798. This Elizabeth Labadie was born at Assumption, Sandwich, in September, 1801, and was daughter of John B. Labadie.

The Marentettes were widely celebrated for their musical talents. One of the descendants of the above-mentioned Marentette is Mr. Victor E. Marentette, who now conducts a wholesale and retail book and stationery business at Windsor, Ontario; he is married to Delphine, youngest daughter of Captain Chas. F. Labadie, of Windsor, a direct descendant of Louis (Badachon) Labadie, thus combining in this union two branches of the Labadie family. Members of the Godfroy and Dequindre families married into the Marentette, Navarre, Labadie family, of Sandwich, as will be seen by reference to my article on the Godfroy family.

JOHN B. AND CHARLES PIQUETTE.

John B. was for many years, indeed from their first advent here until they quit business, one of the most trusted clerks of F. & T. Palmer. He was well posted in French and Indian dialect, almost the main requisites in business here at that time. Charles was in the employ of Levi Brown, jeweler and gold pen maker, and when he quit he branched out for himself, also continuing the manufacture of gold pens. John married, 1836, Angelique Campau, daughter of Barney (l'Abbie). Their children were: John, died unmarried; Elsie, married first in 1870, to Lieut. Armsby Mitchell, U. S. A., son of the distinguished astronomer and soldier, General Mitchell, U. S. A.; second (1880), James Hoban, Washington, D. C.; Charles married, 1876, Fanny Elston Perley. He died in Paris, France, the same year. Emilie married, 1876, Francis P. B. Sands, a prominent lawyer of Washington, D. C., son of Rear Admiral Sands, U. S. N.

John B. Piquette was a happy-go-lucky genial soul. What business he followed after his marriage I do not call to mind: attending to the large estate belonging to his wife, I think, was sufficient to keep his time employed. The Piquette family was originally from Picardie, and the name is frequently seen in the *Armorial General* of France.

The first in this country was Eustache, 1680. He settled in Canada and married, his descendants drifted to Detroit, and John Baptiste Piquette married in 1808, Eleonore Descompts Labadie, as mentioned. To this family belongs the celebrated Sulpician, Francois Piquet, who in order to attack the Iroquois confederacy to the French, founded a mission at the mouth of the Oswegatchie River in 1748. He erected a substantial stone building and placed this inscription on the corner stone:

"Francois Piquet laid the foundation of this building in the name of the Almighty God in 1749." This inscribed corner stone occupies a conspicuous place in the New York State Armory, erected in Ogdensburg in 1858.

THE CHAPOTON AND CICOTTE FAMILIES.

THE CHAPOTON AND THE CICOTTE FAMILIES, WITH THEIR NUMEROUS BRANCHES.

THE first of the Chapoton family and name in Detroit was Jean, son of Tendrez Deame Cassaigne. Cazolle, diocese of Duges, Languedoc, France. He was a surgeon in the French army, with the rank of major, and was ordered to Fort Ponchartrain (what a tedious journey it must have been!) to relieve Doctor Forestier, the first physician who came to the post. For forty years Doctor Chapoton's elegant and stereotype-like signature is affixed to every death notice in the colony. He retired from the army several years previous to the English conquest, and settled on the land which he had received as a grant. He died in 1762, one year before the battle of Bloody Run. He married in 1721 and had twenty children. A son of Doctor Chapoton was Jean Baptiste, born in 1721. He also was a doctor, and was the one who held an unsuccessful parley with Chief Pontiac in 1763, just before the battle of Bloody Run. Eustache Chapoton was born here in 1792, and was son of Jean Baptiste Chapoton and Theresa Peltier (Pelky). He was married in 1819 by Bishop Flaget, of Bardstown, Kentucky, to Adelaide Julia Coquillard (Curkeaw). He died in 1872 at his residence on Jefferson Avenue, just above Beaubien Street. Many will remember him. He was a fine looking, sturdy man, and was a Frenchman in manners as well as in ancestry. It was said that through some unfortunate accident his father lost the large property which had been granted to Doctor Chapoton No. 1.

Eustache was a builder, a stone and brick mason all the years that I knew him. His name alone was a sufficient guarantee of good, relible work. By energy, industry, and untiring perseverance he acquired considerable wealth, which he left to his children. He was honesty and integrity itself, which qualities have also descended to his children in a marked degree. His wife, as before said, was a Coquillard; a brother of hers lived where J. L. Hudson's store now is. He also was a most reliable stone and brick mason. A brother of Eustache Chapoton located in Mt. Clemens about the time Judge Clemens died. I think he followed the same trade as did his brother. I used to see him there in 1835 and later. He had a son who was a playmate of mine, when as a boy I sojourned there on visits to my mother. This son is alive yet. Josephine, daughter of Alexander, married Raymond Baby, of that well known Canadian family, and resides at Sarnia, Canada, or did some years ago.

A daughter of Doctor Jean (Charlotte) married in 1760 Pierre Barthe, a brother of Charles, the ancestor of the families of Askins and Brush. Her daughter Charlotte, born in 1763, married twice; first, an English officer, stationed here, and who participated in the battle of Bloody Run, July, 1763; second, in 1784, Antoine Labadie (Badachon), whose descendants are Mrs. R. Storrs Willis and the late Mrs. Henry Guise. Another daughter, Catherine, married in 1808 Major Antoine Dequindre.

Alexander, a son of Eustache, married a daughter of St. Luc Labadie. Several children blessed this union; first, Alexander, Jr., married Marianne Peltier, daughter of Charles Peltier and Eliza Cicotte; second, Elizabeth, married Alex Viger, at the time an extensive coal merchant, and brother of Captain Viger, of the steamboat May Queen, Detroit & Cleveland line; Emilie, married Edward Bush. A fine fellow was Ed. Bush, and when he married Miss Chapoton his prospects were brilliant, none more so. He was a nephew of Mrs. Chas. Ducharme, and at the time of his marriage he was in the grocery business on the corner of Jefferson Avenue and Brush Street, and was conducting it quite successfully, and so continued. He subsequently removed to the corner of Congress Street and Cadillac Square, where is now the new county building, and continued there for a while until disaster overtook him, and he vanished to I do not know where. His widow survives him.

Edmund Chapoton, one of the rising doctors of Detroit, married in 1883 Martha Sherland, of South Bend, Indiana. Eustache, son of Eustache and Miss Coquillard (Tash) married Matilda Campau, daughter of Joseph Campau. Therese, his sister, married Louis St. Aubin (St. Aubin farm); William (his brother) married Sarah Connor, of Connor's Creek. Felice (his sister) married Captain Paxton (whom I knew well); he was of the river and lake marine. It will be seen that there have been, thus far, three doctors in the family, besides one of the daughters marrying a doctor (Cicotte), Dr. John R., and brother of Sheriff Cicotte.

Dr. Jean Baptiste Chapoton and St. Martin were Captain Dalzell's guides on that disastrous march to Bloody Run, July, 1763.

* * *

The founder of the Cicotte family in America was Jean, born in 1666 in the diocese of Rochelle, France, and said to have descended from the same family as the celebrated de la Rochejacquelien, the Vendean chief. Jean came to Detroit in 1730 as a merchant. The quantity of handsome plate possessed by this family has frequently been mentioned. With the exception of that of Miss St. Martin, afterwards the wife of Angus McIntosh, there was no such collection of silver in the colony. The fate of war, pillage by the Indians, extravagant living and reckless trust in the honor of others soon scattered this superb property. A few remnants, it is said, are still in the possession of the descendants.

The present Godfroy farm was at one time owned by the Cicottes.

Catherine Cicotte married about 1855 Doctor Allen, of the Botanic drug store of Stewart & Allen, that was on Jefferson Avenue, north side, between Randolph and Bates. Doctor John Cicotte, a bright, handsome young chap and a good dentist, married a daughter of Eustache Chapoton (Julie); Madeline Cicotte married F. W. Lawson, of the firm of Lawson & Howard, forwarding and commission merchants, DeGarmo Jones warehouse, foot of Shelby Street. Francis X., son of Jean Bapte Cicotte, born 1787, married Felice Peltier, the widow of Capt. Peter Tallman, an artillery officer in the United States army. Francois was commissioned as captain by General Hull in 1812. His small company, composed mostly of men inured to the toils, dangers and privations of frontier life, were noted for their discipline and undaunted bravery. After the defeat of Winchester at Monroe an Indian chief brought Doctor Brown, a Kentuckian, to Francois X. Cicotte to sell as his prize. The Indian wanted $100 for the ransom of his captive, which was paid by him. Doctor Brown afterwards visited his deliverer when he came again to Detroit with General Harrison's army. Francois died in 1860. He was a fine specimen of the early Frenchman, possessing that rare charm of manner which seemed a peculiar legacy to these descendants of the first pioneers.

His son Edward V., married, first, Miss Bell, of New York, by whom he had one son (George). He married a second time, Lucretia Abbott, daughter of Robert Abbott, auditor-general of Michigan. Edward V. held many positions of trust, and was for two or three terms, sheriff of Wayne County. He was a remarkably fine gentleman, polished and of the most agreeable manners. He died not many years ago, and hosts of our people will remember him pleasantly. Francois X. married, first, Victoire Beaubien, daughter of Lambert Campau, by whom he had two daughters. Victoire married Charles R. Bagg, son of Asahel S. Bagg, and for many years clerk of the recorder's court; Phillis married a Mr. Rankin. Francois X. married a second time Elizabeth, daughter of Dr. E. A. Theller, of patriot war fame or notoriety, by whom he had three girls and a son. The son resides in California (San Francisco) with one of his sisters, who married a son of William B. Hunt, of this city. Emma and Anne married two brothers and, I think, reside in Detroit. F. X. Cicotte held many offices of public trust. He was at one time city clerk or city treasurer, as his name appears on the Detroit city "shin plasters" as clerk or treasurer. He was an affable gentleman. There is extant a curious and interesting marriage contract between J. B. Cicotte and Angelique Poupard, executed July 27, 1770, before Philip De Jean, royal notary, by act of law residing in Detroit, at the signing of which twenty-five or thirty prominent people (friends and relatives) of Detroit were present and signed the document with the principals. Mrs. Hamlin in her book, "Legends of Detroit," gives the document in full, with the names of the signers, etc. An uncle of Sheriff Cicotte, father of Jim Cicotte (the latter a noted character and Democratic politician, was a great lover of fast horses, and had quite a local celebrity in that line. He and Lieutenant U. S. Grant, Barney Campau, Major Bob Forsyth and many others used to make it lively in the winter racing down Jefferson Avenue from the bridge, and also on the River Rouge when the ice was in condition. He went by the name of Captain Cicotte, and in 1835 built and occupied the second frame house that was erected in the third ward on Congress

Street east. It was occupied after by Israel J. Beniteau, father of Captain Beniteau, of the Detroit Light Guard. I think the house is still standing. Captain Cicotte's father was the second white male child born in Wayne County.

* * *

In relation to the sad condition of the people of Monroe after the battle of the Raisin, Judge B. F. H. Witherell says:

"It was reported at the time, that on learning a few teams were mustered here and sent down, among the rest Captain Francois Cicotte and his brother, Jean B., went down, with each a pony and traineau. A traineau is a peculiar kind of sledge, useful for traveling in deep snow. Arriving at the Raisin, they beheld the unburied bodies of the fallen braves. Cutting large quantities of thorn brush, they covered them up, and with the inhabitants, started on their return—Captain Cicotte happened to drive the foremost team, and said that as he approached the place of Blue Jacket's, a noted Indian chief, a little below Trenton, he noticed a robust, hardy looking young white man standing by a tree. While wondering how and why he should be there alone he heard the sharp crack of two rifles. The poor fellow sank down to earth, the balls from the Indian rifles had passed through his heart, the crimson life current spouted from the wounds, and he gasped and died. The savages cut off his feet and carried them away in triumph. The white man had been made a prisoner—had escaped —got bewildered in the deep forest—was overtaken and shot. He had doubtless marched to our frontier among the gallant men of Kentucky and Ohio, thousands of whom perished and their heart's blood saturated our soil, their bodies became a prey to the famished wolves and their bones for many long years lay bleaching in the summer suns and winter storms.

"General Cass gave Captain Cicotte and his men great credit for the skill and bravery with which they met, fought, and beat the enemy, with such disparity of numbers.

"Afterward Captain Cicotte and his company were ordered to scour the banks of the River Rouge, several miles up, to drive off the Indians and protect the inhabitants; arriving at old Francis Chavan's farm, he divided his company. With some of the men he crossed the river on a raft made of fence rails, and marched to the Hicks's farm. Old Jesse Hicks, the owner, a brave old scout, was along in the ranks, and as they approached his house they discovered several Indians at a distance on the run. One of them, the hindmost, had a large roll of blankets, which he had plundered, on his back. On the outside of the blankets hung a large pewter basin, such as our fore-mothers were wont to keep brightly burnished on "the dresser." The Indian was at a great distance when Cicotte turned to old Jacox, a gallant Scotchman from Grosse Ile, and said, "Jacox, give that fellow a pill." He instantly leveled his rifle and fired. The Indian tumbled head over heels, then sprang to his feet and ran off. When the scouts came up they found that the ball had entered the center of the basin, but the blankets had stopped it, and the red warrior escaped."

FIVE PROMINENT FAMILIES.

THE RIVARD, LAFFERTY, RIOPELLE, DUBOIS AND ST. AUBIN FAMILIES AND THEIR BRANCHES.

IT is said the founder of the Rivard family in this country was Nicholas Rivard, born in 1624, but it does not appear that they came to Detroit until about 1713, as among the earliest marriages celebrated at Fort Ponchartrain.(Detroit) is that of Francois Rivard (the interpreter) and the widow of a distinguished officer, which occurred October 13, 1713, the witnesses being the commandant and seven or eight prominent citizens. Francois Rivard was an ensign in the First Regiment of militia organized in the territory. His daughter Archange, born, 1774, married, 1795, Paul Plessis Bellair. A son, Oliver Bellair, married his cousin, Rose Rivard.

Oliver Bellair lived for many years on Jefferson Avenue in the same block as did Judge B. F. H. Witherell, Mr. McKibbon and others, as I have mentioned in a former article. He gained much distinction in the war of 1812, and was present at Hull's surrender. Rivard Street gets its name from this family. Mr. Weiss, a former well-known music dealer of this city, married a daughter of Oliver Bellair, as did Fred Watson, son of Eugene W. Watson. A daughter of Mr. Weiss is now Mrs. Fred C. Whitney, wife of the well-known theatrical manager. Both daughters of Mr. Bellair were faithful repetitions of their mother, who was a very beautiful woman.

LAFFERTY OR LES FERTÉ.

The Lafferty farm takes its name from Joseph Lafferty, a descendant of Antoine Ferrault dit Lafferty, who served in the regiment of M. de Tubercasse and was stationed at Fort Ponchartrain as early as 1710. He married, at Montreal, Michelle Fortin, whose mother, Louise Sommilliard, was the daughter of the sergeant-at-arms and sister of Soeur Bourgois, founder of the Order of Notre Dame, Montreal.

I knew only one of Joseph Lafferty's descendants, Clemence, though was often in the old homestead down the river on the Lafferty farm, and often on a summer day sheltered myself under the spreading branches of the elm that stood in front of it, the branches of which spread nearly across the River road. Clemence died not long ago.

It appears that a branch of the Riopelle family moved to Detroit shortly after the English conquest in 1760. Dominique, born 1787, married, in 1818, Clotilde Gouin. She was the widow of Antoine St. Bernard. The latter was of the St. Bernards of St. Clair River, one of whom at one time was a famous pilot of the United States steamer Michigan, one of the steamers that carried a portion of General Scott's cholera stricken army to Chicago during the Black Hawk war. Domonique, a son, also married a Gouin (presumably a cousin). One of their children, a son, is a member of the Detroit bar. A daughter married Michael G. Payment, who was so many years with Chauncey Hulbert in the grocery business on Woodward Avenue, and who, notwithstanding his constant intercourse all his life with English-speaking people, could not very fluently speak the language. I used often to worry him about it.

Dominique and myself used to be schoolmates at "Old Crane's" in the University building on Bates Street.

Riopelle Street is named after this family.

DUBOIS.

It appears that the one who left his name to the present Dubois farm, came from Montreal to Detroit several years previous to the American possession. In 1792 he married Marguerite, daughter of Alexis Descomptes Labadie. James, a son of this union, married in 1829 Sophie Campau, a daughter of Jacques and Josette Chene. He died some years ago, leaving to his children his large estate, and the reputation of an honest man and upright citizen. One of his daughters, a remarkably beautiful girl, married Julian Williams, grandson of General John R. Williams. Louis Charles (a son) married Julia St. Aubin, daughter of Louis St. Aubin, and Therese Chapoton. Louis was a fine, sturdy fellow. He was many years in the employ of Grey & Lewis, Lewis & Graves, and other firms. James Dubois lived for many years on the east side of Jefferson Avenue, corner of Dubois

Street. I knew him well. How surprised he would be if he could see the stupendous and splendid apartment house (the Pasadena) that now occupies the site of his late homestead. The homestead of the pioneer of the family was on the river front of the Dubois farm.

Dubois Street gets its name from this family.

ST. AUBIN.

Mrs. Hamlin says: "This family was formerly called Casse and is one of the very oldest in Detroit. Jean Casse dit St. Aubin came to Fort Ponchartrain as early as 1710. Francois, a descendant of his, born here in 1775, was intimately identified with the history of this city. He was the owner of the St. Aubin farm, and resided on it, in the old homestead on the river front house next above that of Judge James Witherell. The late Judge B. F. H. Witherell gathered from him many detailed accounts of incidents that occurred in the early days of the English conquest, information he had received from his father, Louis St. Aubin, which he (the judge) gave us through the columns of the *Free Press* some years ago (1855-6) over the signature of Hamtramck.

Francois St. Aubin married Basaline Campau. She survived her husband forty years, and died in the old homestead, aged 84 years. They had nine children. Louis St. Aubin married, first, Therese Chapoton; second, Madeline Cottrell, of St. Clair. Francois married Virginie Moran, daughter of Judge Chas. Moran. Another daughter married Mr. Louis Groesbeck. Another daughter married Pierre Provencal, of Grosse Pointe. Another daughter, Matilda, married Eugene W. Watson, U. S. N., and grandson of Judge James Witherell. Another daughter married Richard Connor, of Connor's Creek. Another daughter married Mr. John F. Godfroy, of Grand Rapids. Another daughter married Mr. Henry Beaubien. Another daughter married Antoine Moross.

I saw Mrs. St. Aubin often when I was a boy, in the old log homestead on the river front of the St. Aubin farm, when nearly all, if not all, the above nine children were unmarried and living at home.

I never knew much about the after life of the St. Aubin boys and girls and those that they married, except Pierre Provencal;

Francois, who married Virginie Moran, and Matilda, who married Eugene W. Watson.

Pierre Provencal, of Grosse Pointe, was a fine gentleman of commanding presence and possessing all the courteous manners of the old French resident in a marked degree. There are many, I know, who will call him to mind.

Mrs. Judge James Weir, of this city, is a daughter of his. Judge Weir's daughter impersonated Madame Cadillac on the occasion of the Bicentennial celebration of the founding of this city, July 25, 1901. Her untimely death, a little later on, was deeply and widely deplored.

St. Aubin Avenue takes its name from the St. Aubin family.

THE CHENE FAMILY.

(Sometimes Called Chesne in the Early Days.)

THE Chenes are a (French) Hamtramck family, and the earliest to invade this section of the country. Mrs. Hamlin says in her book, "Legends of Detroit":

"As early as 1717 the name of Chene appears on the records of St. Anne's, and one is attracted by the beautiful and picturesque signature, so clear, precise, full of character and individuality."

It appears that Pierre Chene, the founder of the race on the soil of the new world, married in 1676 at Montreal, Jeanne Bailly, of a family of considerable importance. Two of his sons, Charles and Pierre, came to Detroit as early as 1717 (as said), and are the ancestors of that name in Michigan. They were active and enterprising, and at once took leading positions in the colony.

One of the Chenes (Pierre) married, in 1747, Clemence Chapoton, daughter of the surgeon. Charles, another son, was a noted interpreter; he married a Labadie. Isadore, another son, married, in 1758, Therese Bequet. Isadore was noted for his great bravery and figures conspicuously in the military annals. To him was deeded a tract of land by the Pottawatomies at the same time as the one to Robishe Navarre. This grant to Isadore was confirmed by Lieutenant-Governor Hamilton in 1777.

The descendants of Isadore married into the Joncaire, Labadie, Campau, Chapoton, Dequindre and Baby families.

In 1753 a large body of French from Canada moved to the southeast and erected forts—Presque Isle, on the site of Erie, Pa.; La Boeuf, on French Creek, and Venango on the Allegheny river. In April of that year Mr. Joncaire was sent with a small detachment of regulars and a number of friendly Seneca Indians, to visit the Indians on the Ohio and its branches. When Joncaire reached the Miami, he marched into their towns with great ceremony. The Indians were frightened and promised again to become the children of the French. Joncaire assured them of protection and succeeded in inducing a large number to accompany him to the fort on Maumee.

Rev. Rufus W. Clark, in his address, or sermon, delivered before the Sons of the American Revolution in the First Congregational Church, this city, April 30, 1899, has this to say in regard to the Chenes:

"During the revolution and long after peace was declared Detroit was the center of the military operations of the British in the northwest, and furnished the base of supplies for their incursions. The first expeditions fitted out here were those which appeared before Harodsburg and other points in Kentucky in the spring of 1777. The attack on Fort Henry at Wheeling was in the fall of the same year. The expedition of 1778, consisting of a force of four hundred Indians and eleven Canadians, led by Captain Chene, of Detroit, against Boonesborough, Ky."

It was reported and generally believed that Isadore Chene parted with the entire island of Grosse Ile for two satin dresses, desirous that his wife and daughter should be the two best dressed women in the community. The grant of land mentioned as going to Chene from the Pottawatomies and confirmed by Governor Hamilton in 1777 may have been this same island of Grosse Ile. He might have thought he was well paid in what he got for the island, as land was worth scarcely anything in those days.

The Joncaires, one of whom married into the Chene family, were highly educated and cultured gentlemen. It is no wonder that they were such an acquisition in their new home. Francois Chabert de Joncaire was a son of Gabriel, captain of infantry, and Marguerite Fleury de la Gorgendiere, one of the most aristocratic and powerful families of Canada. The chevalier was a man of great ability and took an active interest in promoting the growth of the city of Detroit. He married Josette Chene, by whom he had ten children, sons and daughters. They are represented today by the families of the La Fontaines, Lorangers, McBride, F. Van Miller, Kellogg, of Monroe, and Mrs. Fitzsimmons, of Albany, N. Y. The grandmother of the foregoing, Catherine Chabert de Joncaire, born 1784, married, 1808, Francois La Fontaine. He was a merchant and considered a man of wealth. He also had a large property in Canada. To him belonged the "La Fontaine Farm." He was a man of much ability, energetic and persevering. Five children were born to them, Julia, Charles, Margaret, Louis and Lucy. Louis was a banker in Monroe; he died some years since. Lucy La Fontaine married James McBride, a prosperous merchant of Monroe. A daughter of theirs (Josette) married a Mr. Clark, of Monroe. He passed away and the widow married W. Van Miller, of Monroe, son of the late Hon. Dan B. Miller, of that city, cashier of the Wyandotte Savings bank, and brother of the late Sidney D. Miller, president of the Detroit Savings Bank, and Mrs. Alex H. Sibley, of this city. Another daughter married Mr. Fitzsimmons, of Albany, N. Y., at one time a partner in the extensive firm of Erastus Corning & Co., hardware and railroad supplies. Another daughter (Nellie) is single and resides in Monroe. Another daughter married Mr. James Kellogg, of Detroit, for many years connected with the late wholesale hardware house of J. James & Son, and after with the United States customs in this city until his death. He was the half brother of Mr. Friend Palmer, of this city. A son of Mr. McBride (James) is a prosperous furniture manufacturer in Grand Rapids.

Captain Chene, mentioned in Mr. Clark's address, was the great great grandfather of Mrs. Serena Kellogg and the rest of the Monroe descendants. The Joncaire mentioned was their great grandfather (Chabert de Joncaire). Joncaire was, as before said, at one time in command of a detachment of Indians and coureurs des bois that marched to the Ohio.

The Chene homestead was standing when I came here, and occupied a portion of the present site of Parke, Davis & Co. It was a hewn log structure covered with clapboards. One of the Chenes (they used to call him "Old Man Chene") occupied it at that time, and he died there. I remember the funeral quite well. He was buried from St. Anne's church with most imposing ceremonies, and his body deposited in the vault beneath the high altar, where reposed the remains of Father Richard; for which privilege his estate paid $500, a most munificent sum in those days.

The Chene heirs claimed, through Gabriel Chene, who in 1827 paid $50 (it is said) for it, a large tract of land skirted by the river front and extending from the Boulevard to Baldwin Avenue, which takes in Beller's establishment, Kling's brewery and a large number of handsome dwellings. When the land was originally purchased a stipulation in the contract called for a reservation for a burial ground by the Catholic diocese. Bishop Riese was then officiating. A chapel was built (St. Phillips'). The property was never used for the dead, as far as I know.

Mrs. Catherine Baby Chene, the wife of Mr. Charles Chene. who died at the family home on Jefferson avenue, May, 1904, was a Baby, scion of the distinguished Canadian family of that name. In her obituary notice it was stated that her grandfather, Colonel Baby, was in command of the Second Regiment of Essex Militia in the War of 1812. It was also said, in the obituary notice, that the first deed of land in Detroit was held by the ancestors of Gabriel Chene. The deed was given by Cadillac.

Chene street takes its name from this family.

THE MERRY FRENCH CARTS.

THAT WERE USEFUL IN ALL SORTS OF WEATHER AND FOR MANY PURPOSES.

IN the earlier days the streets of Detroit, in the absence of pavements, were very bad in the fall and spring; mud seemed to predominate. Cabs and public hacks were in a very limited number. Peter Cooper, colored; Jackson, a colored barber, and George Herron, an English barber, were about the only persons owning and operating public conveyances, and their services, as may be supposed, were taxed to the limit. Men wore their heavy boots, pants tucked inside, and in the outskirts of the city a few boards and planks were laid down lengthwise, so that people could manage, with difficulty, to get along.

In such a state of things the single two-wheeled horsecart was very much in evidence and was a most important institution. It was an invention of the old French habitants of the country. They were used by all classes and were convenience itself. A buffalo robe or blanket was spread on the bottom of the cart, two or three ottomans or stools were put in (in the absence of other covering for the bottom or floor of the cart, hay or straw was used), and the horse, understanding his business as well as his master, off he plodded, ofttimes half leg deep in mud, to church, shopping or to make fashionable calls. The carts were mighty enjoyable, as I can testify, having time and again been the driver on many, many occasions, sitting perched up in front, and the ladies enjoying the bottom of the vehicle, protected from the rough boards by soft buffalo robes or other means; occasionally the lynch pin that apparently held the cart together would get out of place, and the occupants be dumped in the mud. It was quite a sight, when the streets were in bad condition of a Sunday, to see the long line of carts backed up against the curb in front of the two churches (Presbyterian and Episcopal) on Woodward avenue, between Larned and Congress streets, waiting the pleasure of their owners.

Indeed no other conveyance would have been practicable, when mud prevailed, which was always the case, and to the fullest extent when wet weather set in. I have often seen in those days the feminine portion of the families of General Cass, Commodore Brevoort, John Millett, Governor George B. Porter, Thos. Palmer, B. B. Kercheval, Governor Woodbridge, Honorable Augustus Porter, DeGarmo Jones, Colonel Baker, U. S. A., Judge Jas. Witherell, Judge Sibley, Judge Leib, Judge Moran, C. C. Trowbridge, and others enjoying a ride to church or on a shopping tour, or paying a social call. They could be backed up anywhere, and get into all sorts of places, and to get in and out of them was just too easy. Governor Porter maintained a stud of fine horses, but as far as memory serves me, he did not sport a four-wheeled carriage. I do not think there were four-wheeled carriages in the city at that time. Judge B. F. H. Witherell was the first to start one, that I remember, and the Kerchevals followed.

The carts were great factors in removing the earth composing the Fort Shelby embankments, as also the quite prominent knoll that was where the city hall now is. Thos. Palmer, the senator's father, had the contract for removing the earth from the latter place, and I used often to wonder where all the French carts came from. The feminine portion of the community attending the singing school under the leadership of Eurotas P. Hastings and his brother, in the Presbyterian session room, adjoining the church, as also the school in the basement of the Methodist church, on the corner of Congress Street, in bad weather, always came in these carts, but—

> "They contained a deal of fun
> Like mourning coaches
> When the funeral's done."

Mrs. John H. Kenzie, of Chicago, in her interesting book, "Wau Bun," writing of the early days in the northwest, says:

"We took passage at Detroit on the steamer Henry Clay in September, 1830, for Green Bay. Our ride to the dock, through the dark by-ways in a French cart, the only vehicle which at that day could navigate the muddy, unpaved streets of Detroit, was a theme for much merriment, and not less so, our descent of the narrow perpendicular stairway by which we reached the little apartment on the Clay called the ladies' cabin."

When General Macomb visited Detroit Mrs. Hester Scott took him around the city in one of these French horse carts, borrowed for the purpose from Mr. H. D. Harrison, the Jefferson Avenue dry goods merchant, and it was said that the general enjoyed it hugely. Mrs. Scott and her three daughters are no doubt well remembered by many residents of this city and elsewhere. They taught a select school for young ladies, and that it was select, may be gathered from the appended list of pupils, daughters, of Detroit, that graduated from or at one time attended this school. Mrs. Scott came of a distinguished family. Her father, Hon. Luther Martin, was an eminent Baltimore lawyer. He defended Aaron Burr and Blenerhassett when they were tried for conspiracy against the United States.

PUPILS AND PARENTS.

NAMES OF PUPILS.	PARENTS OR GUARDIANS.
Andrews, Miss C.	H. R. Andrews
Brady, Sarah	S. P. Brady
Brewster, Martha	Wm. Brewster
Brewster, Harriet	Wm. Brewster
Barney, Mary	Milton Barney
Barton, Harriet	S. Barton
Briscoe, Frances	B. Briscoe
Bell, Sarah	Mr. Bell
Bingham, Sarah	E. Bingham
Bullock, Mary	H. Bullock
Brooks, Elizabeth	Col. Edw. Brooks
Brooks, Emily	Col. Edw. Brooks
Boggs, Elizabeth	D. E. Harbaugh
Chapoton, Julia	E. Chapoton
Chittenden, Miss	Wm. F. Chittenden
Campau, Caroline	Mrs. A. Beaubien
Coe, Adelaide	Israel Coe
Drew, Elizabeth	John Drew
Drew, Ellen	John Drew
Desnoyers, Ellen	P. Desnoyers
Davenport, Matilda	Lewis Davenport
Davenport, Sarah	Lewis Davenport
Dixon, Florence	Mrs. Green
Dibble, Helen	Col. O. B. Dibble
Dibble, Mary	Col. O. B. Dibble
Dibble, Susan	Col. O. B. Dibble
Elliott, Elizabeth	Mrs. R. T. Elliott
Fairbain, Margaret	T. Fairbain
Forsyth, Marion	Col. R. A. Forsyth
Flood, Julia	Mrs. Flood
Gallagher, Mary	Thos. Gallagher
Garrison, Margaret	H. Garrison
Godfroy, Caroline	Peter Godfroy

Green, Emily	Mr. Green
Gooding, Caroline	Matthew Gooding
Hallock, Mary	Horace Hallock
Hamilton, Sophia	Mrs. S. Clement
Harvie, Mary	Andrew Harvie
Hammond, Isabella	Chas. G. Hammond
Howard, Eliza	Chas. Howard
Hurd, Henrietta	Dr. E. Hurd
Johnson, Isabella	Mr. Johnson
Jack, Mary	I. R. Jack
Kercheval, Mary	B. B. Kercheval
Larned, Harriet	Mrs. Sylvia Larned
Lamson, Cornelia	Darius Lamson
Le Roy, Ann	H. H. LeRoy
Low, Lucy	Mrs. Bushnell
Lee, Fanny	Mrs. E. O'Keefe
Lyon, Cornelia	Edward Lyon
Manning, Camilla	Randolph Manning
Merrill, Julia	Samuel Pitts
Mizner, Eliza	L. B. Mizner
Mizner, Mary	L. B. Mizner
McReynolds, Julia	Col. A. T. McReynolds
Moon, Harriet	Miss M. Moon
Moran, Mary	Chas. Moran
Moran, Julia	Chas. Moran
Moran, Virginia	Chas. Moran
Norvell, Emily	Hon. John Norvell
Platt, Mary	Z. Platt
Pitts, Julia	Samuel Pitts
Poupard, Elise	Simon Poupard
Raymond, Mary	Frances Raymond
Sheldon, Alexandrine	Thomas C. Sheldon
Swan, Margaret	Thomas C. Sheldon
Sheldon, Rose	Thomas C. Sheldon
Strong, Eliza	John W. Strong
Town, Elizabeth	Reuben Town
Tomlinson, Isabella	N. Tomlinson
Wagstaff, Miss	Lewis Davenport
Whipple, Margaret	Chas. W. Whipple
Williams, Mary	Ezra Williams
Watson, Margaret	W. Richardson
Witherell, Julia A.	B. F. H. Witherell

The school house, I think, was situated on Larned Street, below St. Antoine, and along about 1854 they lived opposite me on Larned Street, between St. Antoine and Hastings. Next to them lived Morris M. Williams and next Alex. H. Adams. One night during the summer months these three unprotected females were assailed by burglars. They gained access by means of a ladder raised to one of the upper windows of their sleeping apartments. The whole neighborhood was alarmed by their cries of alarm. I hastened across the street and found that the uproar they raised had scared the burglars off, and the ladder that they had used, in the possession of Max Allor, now the well-known detective, who, though a mere lad, had partially succeeded in quieting their fears. They were all right in a little while, when they found that they had not been carried off bodily, nor robbed of any of their earthly possessions.

* * *

These French carts were very enjoyable also in fine weather on short excursions with the girls into the surrounding woods, particularly in October, when they had put on their gay autumn attire and the hickory nuts and hazel nuts were plentiful. How full of pleasure those trips were! The distance to the woods was not great; they came down to Elizabeth Street on the west side of Woodward Avenue and down to about Hancock Avenue on the east side, and out on Grand River Avenue on the Jones farm, not far from Perkins's tavern, and out on Michigan Avenue they came down to where is the hay market (once Woodbridge grove), and just in the rear of this grove was an immense field of hazelnut bushes which in the season were loaded down with nuts. Out Woodward Avenue, about where is Farnsworth Street, were many acres of blackberry bushes, loaded with their delicious fruit in the season. And then the excursions in these carts down to that lovely driveway, "Lovers' Lane," in the vicinity of what is now Fort Wayne. The lane came into the River road about where Winterhalter's beer garden was, and extended out quite a distance toward the Dix settlement. My friend, Ross, in one of his articles in relation to early Detroit, says of this lane, and as the incident he relates to it is true, I copy it:

"Mrs. Tunis S. Wendell, the daughter of Colonel Thomas Hunt, and widow of Captain Gleason, U. S. A., and Miss Isabell Cass, daughter of General Cass, at one time were riding on horseback with a party of officers, when they came to a narrow country road which was on the present line of Junction Avenue. It was a beautiful pathway, and overshadowed with stately trees, many of them covered with clinging vines, and Belle Cass said: "We ought to name this lovely spot." "Why not call it 'Lover's Lane?'" said Mrs. Gleason. So said, so done. This pathway was for many years a favorite trysting place for enamored young people, and was generally known by that name, 'Lovers' Lane.'"

Afterwards, in 1857, the common council confirmed the name officially. I have often been through this lane on foot and on horseback, sometimes alone, and sometimes in the company of a fair friend, when the scent of summer was strong and luscious, and "where wild honeysuckles scented the air," and can testify to its attractive and sylvan beauty, that appealed to every sense. My cousins, the senator's (Palmer) sisters, used to say: "Come, harness the horse to the cart; we will get one or two other girl friends, and off we will go to 'Lovers' Lane' on a picnic." So said, so done. The same thing happened often for some years. I think these outings were more enjoyable during the fall months, say October and the early part of November, than in the summer. The soft, hazy, dreamy Indian summer, that always prevailed here in the fall of the year, threw its glamour over everything animate and inanimate, which, coupled with the gorgeous attire of the trees and shrubbery, made it an ideal spot for a picnic, and an ideal place for lovers. The memory of those delicious days can never be forgotten. It seems strange that the Indian summers that were always with us during a great part of the autmun months, in the early days, should have ceased to put in an appearance, as a rule, only coming now and then, and when we are favored, tarrying with us only for a brief period. In the old days, it seems to me, Indian summer never missed us, and when the warm, dreamy, hazy season did come, it tarried with us for two or three weeks and sometimes longer. Presume clearing off the forests has caused it. The late Judge Campbell says in his poem, "A Legend of L'Anse, Creuse," a few words in reference to Lovers' Lane:

> "And the cool shades of Lover's Lane
> Heard a low murmur as of bees
> Humming among the linden trees ,
> As up the Rouge the pony sped."

HAMTRAMCK.

THE township with this unpronounceable name is the oldest in the state—the mother of all the others. It takes its name from Colonel John Hamtramck, of the United States army, who was left in command of this post by "Mad Anthony" Wayne. The army under General Hull crossed to Canada from this town. Colonel Joseph Watson, the son-in-law of Judge Jas. Witherell, it is said, was the first man, and Major John Whipple the second, that landed in Canada at the commencement of hostilities. Colonel Hamtramck purchased the farm, afterwards owned by the late Hon. James A. Van Dyke, some two miles above the city, and from this circumstance the town received its name.

Colonel Hamtramck was a native of Canada. He joined the American army in 1775 and continued in that service nearly twenty-seven years. As a disciplinarian he was exemplary, as an officer highly respected. Having received the approbation of Washington, he received from him the most honorable testimonials. He was colonel of the First Regiment, United States Infantry. He died at Detroit April 11, 1803.

Colonel Joseph Watson was the father of the late Eugene Watson and grandfather of the late Lewis Watson.

The old residents above Bloody Run that I recall are Judge Leib and William B. Hunt.

William B. Hunt was the son of Thomas Hunt, heretofore mentioned, who volunteered at the battle of Lexington, and was subsequently a colonel in the First Regiment of United States Infantry, stationed at Fort Wayne, Ind. He removed from Watertown, Mass., to Fort Wayne in 1798, and shortly after came to Detroit. Thomas Hunt's wife was Eugenie Wellington, whence the late George Wellington (Duke) Hunt, son of William B. Hunt, gets his name. William B. was the brother of Henry I., and all the rest of the family of Hunts here and in Maumee, as also the brother of Mrs. Captain Josiah Snelling, U. S. A., Mrs.

Tunis S. Wendell and Mrs. Major Abraham Edwards, of Kalamazoo, and mother of late Mrs. James Scott, of this city. Major Edwards was deputy quartermaster-general at Fayette, Pa., until the close of the war of 1812, when he moved to Detroit and entered into business with Henry I. Hunt, his brother-in-law, keeping a general store.

* * *

Wm. B. married a daughter of Judge Leib, by whom he had George Wellington and Cleveland Hunt. The former died in 1881; Cleveland is with us yet, a prominent member of the Detroit bar. The first Mrs. Hunt died many years ago, and Wm. B. married the beautiful widow of Timothy Dequindre, brother of Major Antoine Dequindre. Mrs. Dequindre was the daughter of Louis and Archange Navarre, and was the sister of Mrs. Colonel Jas. Askin and of Mrs. Peter Godfroy. Mrs. Dequindre and Mrs. Godfroy had the reputation of being the most beautiful women on the frontier. To this latter assertion I can bear willing testimony, as I have seen both of the ladies often, when almost in the pride of their youth and beauty. The former I knew intimately. Four children were born to Mr. and Mrs. Hunt, two daughters and two sons. One daughter is a nun of the Providence Hospital at Washington, D. C.; the other daughter was the late Mrs. Thos. Paxton of Detroit. A son (Wm. B. H.) married Miss Cicotte, a daughter of Francois Z. Cicotte and Elizabeth Theller. They reside in California. Roland Hunt, the brother, passed away at Los Angeles in April last. He was quite a musical genius, and a very lively boy. I also knew Wm. B. Hunt; knew him when he was state librarian, during the time that I had much business at the state capitol on Griswold Street, in the latter thirties, when Sidney L. Rood, my employer, had the contract for furnishing the state with paper and stationery. He (Hunt) was a remarkably nice man and gentleman. R. B. Ross, writing in the *Evening News* some years ago, on Detroit in 1837, gave quite an exhaustive history of the Hunt family.

This Hunt family descends from William Hunt, born in 1611, in England. He was promoted to colonel in the British army during the parliamentary wars. For his successful defense of York against Cromwell he was knighted in 1644 by Prince Rupert. Defeated in the battle of Marston Moor, July 2, 1644, he took refuge in America, under the name of a deceased cousin, Ephraim

Hunt. He settled at Weymouth, Mass., where he married Ann Richards, daughter of Thomas and Weltheau Richards. His great-great-grandson, Thomas Hunt, born at Watertown, Mass., in 1754, enlisted in the American army during the war of independence, and was at the battle of Lexington. He was an officer under Anthony Wayne in August, 1796, and became commandant of Detroit in 1800, where his family followed him.

* * *

Payee, who lived on the bank of the river, just above Judge Leib, was a jolly, rollicking Frenchman, and it was at his house more than any other up the river that the French dances came off, almost weekly, during the winter. They were liberally patronized by the young bloods from the city, who were always eager to bask in the smiles of the pretty French girls, whom they knew, and whom they were sure to meet. Have any of you that read these lines ever been to a French dance given in a French farm house, not in a tavern? If you have, then you know all about it. The large kitchen and living room, with its polished floor, quaint old-fashioned furniture, the tall clock in the corner, the huge cast-iron plate stove of two stories, brought from Montreal in the early days, in which a scorching heat could be engendered in short order. "Music in the corner posted," which consisted of two violins. And then the gathered company, eager to begin, which they did always early in the afternoon, and kept it up until the small hours in the morning. No round dances, only Money-musk, Virginia reel, Hunt-the-grey-fox, French four, the pillow dance and occasionally a cotillion. It did not seem to me as though the feet of the dancers would ever grow weary moving to the inspiring music of "French four," given on a violin, and as a Frenchman alone could give it. Refreshments were also ample, served in primitive style, of course, and of good quality.

Then the going home with your best girl, if you had one, or the going home with any of the girls, was a pure delight. "In the lingering by the wayside and the tarrying on the door-step, in the light of the winter moon, there were many tender words spoken and solemn vows exchanged, and many a good-night kiss stolen before the pretty girl, her cheeks painted by the frost and rosy with the touch of her rustic lover's lips, went blushing into the kitchen to say 'good-night' to the wife of the house and to dream of her joy in her little low chamber, where the same moon stole in that had witnessed their plighted vows on the doorstep.

"I can't remember what they said,
  'Twas nothing worth a song or story;
Yet that rude path by which they sped
  Seemed all transformed and in a glory

The snow was crisp beneath their feet,
  The moon was full, the fields were gleaming;
By hood and tippet sheltered sweet,
  Her face with youth and health was beaming

Perhaps 'twas boyish love, yet still,
  O listless woman, weary lover;
To feel once more that fresh, wild thrill
  I'd give—but who can live youth over?"

But there were other houses besides Payee's where the inmates were quite as jolly. Abraham Cook owned the farm a short distance above Payee. All these had to be reached by the River road. Jefferson Avenue was then opened up only as far as the residence of the late C. C. Trowbridge. I do not call to mind the names of the owners of the farms between the Cook farm and the water works, but think they were all of them of French descent. One of them must have been, as is evidenced by the small apple orchard, and the group of sturdy French pear trees yet remaining. The apple and pear trees are entirely unprotected, and it seems to me the owner, whoever he is, ought to look to it that they are not destroyed. They have survived the wear and tear of all these years, and deserve to live as long as possible.

* * *

The water works occupy the site of the Peter Van Avery homestead. The homestead was a long, low frame structure, painted yellow with white trimmings. It had a fine apple orchard in the rear river front, and a row of fine French pear trees on the Jefferson Avenue side. I knew Mr. Van Avery and his family well, and visited there often. In addition to carrying on and attending to his large farm, Mr. Van Avery owned and operated a grist mill, which I think was located on Connor's creek. When a mere boy, Colonel Peter Van Avery shouldered his musket and volununteered to defend the territory, and with the army of General Hull was surrendered to the enemy, and carried a prisoner of war to Montreal, where he was paroled. He shouldered his knapsack and started off alone and on foot, with but twelve shillings in his pocket, a journey of some two hundred miles to Albany. On his solitary journey, at Poultney, in Vermont, he heard some one call out, "Holloa, Peter, where are you found?" and, to his great surprise, found another prisoner of the same army, also on parole. He turned in, rested himself awhile, and then resumed his weary journey, and finally reached Albany, with his pocket replenished to twenty-four dollars, the donations of the Vermonters, who kindly added to the little store of the soldier-boy. During the long march, he found but one man who would take pay for his entertainment.

* * *

The Connor family, from whom the creek derived its name, lived a short distance up the stream on the Connor farm. The Connors of this and Macomb Counties came to the state with the Moravians, and were always well-to-do people in both counties. The Connors of Connor's Creek identified themselves more with Detroit society and people than did any other family outside of its limits. Richard, the head of the family in this county, improved the southeast corner of Jefferson Avenue and Bates Street with brick stores, in the latter thirties. Darius Lamson, a prominent merchant, married a daughter, as did Dr. J. H. Farnsworth and Dr. Egge. Another daughter married a Mr. Trowbridge, clothing merchant here in the early days, and one time partner of J. L. King. Richard, a son, a merchant here, married a daughter of Mrs. Ellis Doty. He died in California. James, another son, was a prominent young man, as was also "Jack" Connor, another son. The latter was in the Civil War, and died at the Soldiers' Home, Dayton, Ohio. William, another son, died recently in this city.

* * *

I have omitted thus far the "Church farm," so-called, this side of the Cook farm. I think Beller's garden is a portion of it. I do not call to mind the name of the original owner (I think the Chenes claimed some ownership), but I well remember the small Catholic church that stood on the bank of the river above Beller's and just this side of the late Levi

Dolson's tannery. It was called St. Phillippe's. "When the rays of morning creep down the gray spire of St. Phillippe's and cast its shadow o'er the way, just at the foot of Grand Marias, the wooden cock that at its peak stood opening wide his gilded beak." Also the St. Phillippe's college for boys, adjoining the church. This school was quite celebrated in its day, and many scions of our first families used to attend it. There were some fine French pear trees on this farm, and they were included in the Beller property. They remained of vigorous, sturdy growth until quite recently, but their constant use as hitching posts gradually killed them and they went the way nearly all their kind have gone in the past few years.

Next this side of the residence of Abraham Cook (Cook farm), between it and St. Phillippe's, lived one of the Chapoton families. There were sons and daughters, but their personalities have faded from my memory. The only thing in relation to them that I remember is that they kept tavern, as did Peter Van Avery.

Somewhere between Connor's Creek and Hudson's (Fisher's) lived the McQueens. Along in the early thirties, our hired man and myself used every fall to make excursions in a two-horse wagon to Grosse Pointe, and Milk River points, exchanging Jackson ware, that my uncle turned out at his pottery, where is now West park, for apples, cider, potatoes, and other farm products. These trips usually occupied two or three days' time. We were welcome guests, wherever night overtook us. One night, I remember, caught us at McQueen's. It is the only all night stopping place that I do recall, and the reason that it remains in memory, arises, I presume, from the fact that during the night there was quite a fall of snow, the first of the season, and in the morning the ground was covered to the depth of nearly two inches. That night we had bargained for a quantity of apples, which we were to gather ourselves. The orchard was located in front of the house, between it, the road, and the river, and it is the gathering of those apples I never can forget, nor the McQueen's. My companion was some inclined to use cuss words, and on this occasion he outdid himself. This family had sons and daughters. One comely daughter, the late Captain E. B. Ward captured for his first wife.

The Van Dyke Farm, so-called, next above the residence of the late Wm. B. Wesson, I have failed to mention also. The original owner was Stephen Mack of the old firm of Mack & Conant, but it was on this farm, river front, that Colonel Hamtramck built his residence in the early days, when he was in command here. It has been recently destroyed. It has been often described and written about and sketched, and its history, etc., is quite familiar to all of the present day. Judge James Witherell occupied it for a while after Hamtramck's demise. It was hoped that the associations connected with the old house might enlist sufficient interest in our community in the historical structure to warrant and ensure its preservation, but while all were waiting for some one else to do something, the old house tumbled to the ground of itself.—"Vale."

Victor Morris was the original owner of the tract now known as the Wm. B. Wesson plat, and from whom the latter purchased it. It extends from the channel bank of the Detroit River, north above Gratiot Avenue. One of the grandsons, Cleophus, lives in Chatanooga, Tennessee, or did in 1902. A granddaughter, Mrs. Chas. Burnett, lives on the old farm on Gratiot Avenue, or did two or three years ago. Another granddaughter married Mr. C. Frazer, of this city, and I think they are both living.

The "Grand Marais," what a garden it has become! A few years yet, and it will be hard to realize (and even now it is), that the present broad fields of corn and waving grain, and the splendid grounds and buildings of the Blue Ribbon race track were in the early days, and not so very remote either, one vast swamp or quagmire, covered with a most luxuriant growth of marsh grass and bull-rushes, the home of the muskrat and all kinds of horrid snakes.

> "The bullfrog with his croaking harsh,
> And the fat muskrat, haunt the marsh;
> The wild duck floats among the reeds."

I have often been through it in its wildest state, have many times skirted its borders on the river to Windmill Point, and when a little more than a year ago, I gazed over the same country from my seat in the electric car, it was hard to believe the evidence of my senses. I have been up along the Grosse Pointe road often while this change has been going on, but it never struck me so forcibly as it did the time of which I speak.

In those days Windmill Point, with its roofless stone tower slowly falling to decay, was always an object of great interest to me. The Point, as now, was quite a high piece of ground, and had the same stunted apple orchard. Why the mill was abandoned I never knew, nor who was the builder of it. I think it has now entirely disappeared.

Just this side of the Century Club, on the river bank, lived Henry Hudson—"Old Hudson" everyone called him. He and his family were considered for some reason an unsavory lot, and were known far and wide through this section of the country. Besides Hudson and wife there were three or four boys. They were stalwarts all, parents and the boys, and when the sheriff or any of his deputies had occasion to visit their premises in their line of duty, they went prepared, for they were fully aware that they might meet with trouble. On one occasion Sheriff Wilson had a warrant for Hudson for some alleged misdeed. He went up to the house to serve it. Mrs. Hudson saw him coming, and divining his mission, she at once provided herself with a large basin of scalding water and stationed herself behind the open front door, so she could give it to him good and plenty. The sheriff fortunately discovered the enemy and her means of defense through the crack of the door, and struck the basin from her hands with the heavy but of his riding whip, spilling its scalding contents over her bare feet. The outcome tickled the officer immensely. Mrs. Hudson was a masculine looking woman, marked with smallpox. She wore a broad-brimmed straw hat, winter and summer, and out of doors when the weather demanded it, a sailor's heavy sea jacket.

At the French dances the boys were most always on hand, and almost sure to get into a muss of some kind before the party was over. One occasion I call to mind. The dance was given at a house on Jefferson Avenue, just above the present water works. About the usual number and quality of people were on hand, as were two of the Hudson boys, also some five or six youngsters from the city, myself among the number. The dance proceeded merrily for quite a while, and everything bid fair for an enjoyable, peaceable party. But along in the small hours it became apparent that some of the party had partaken quite liberally of liquid refreshments, so much so that it made them inclined to be ugly, particularly the two Hudson boys, and they appeared to be spoiling for a muss of some kind. The opportunity soon came. John Demas, whom very many will remember, was present on this occasion, and as usual was very busy enjoying himself. He was quite a favorite among the French girls, and his attentions were eagerly sought. It seems that John had been during the evening more than polite to the elder Hudson's "fancies," a young Grosse Pointe beauty. This angered Hudson to that degree that he determined to put a stop to it, and he did. A dance was called, the couples including Demas and his partner, (Hudson's girl), and were in their places on the floor; the music and everything was ready and waiting for the "caller," when in rushed Hudson, nothing on but pants and shirt (it was in summer), a short iron bar in his hand and crazed with drink. He at once proceeded to stampede the party; pell mell, dancers, music and spectators hustled for the doors and windows, any way to get out. Hudson, after they were all out, proceeded with his bar of iron to smash the furniture in the room, knock all the plastering off the walls and put out the lights, and broke up the party completely. I never learned the outcome of the matter. I presume, though, that John Demas, being the better man, came out first best.

What finally became of the Hudson family I never knew. I have, however, one pleasant remembrance of them. Adjoining their homestead was a fine cherry orchard, and I have often visited it during the season. Visitors for cherries were always welcome, whether they brought the price or not, showing that they were not so bad as they were painted. A Mr. Fisher succeeded them. I think he bought the Hudson property. He opened a roadhouse there, and "Fisher's" was known as a house of entertainment for years and years. Who have not danced at "Fisher's," dined and otherwise enjoyed themselves under the hospitable roof?

Fisher in the early thirties was a grocery merchant on lower Woodward Avenue. He married a daughter of Coon Ten Eyck, of Dearborn, then sheriff of Wayne County. Directly after his marriage he disposed of his grocery business in the city and moved to Grosse Pointe. Mrs. Fisher carried on the business quite successfully at the Pointe for many years after her husband's death.

I never at any time was very familiar with Grosse Pointe, or the residents there. I knew George Moran very well and who did not know George Moran? His place on the bank of Lake St.

Clair, a mile or so above Fisher's, was a welcome spot to all journeying in that direction, besides those that made it their special business to call on George. He was full of reminiscences of the early days, and took special delight in relating them. He married a daughter of the adopted son of Commodore Grant, who commanded the British government vessels on the lakes before the surrender of the country to the United States in 1796 under the Jay treaty, and he once owned the farm where George lived. The commodore died there about 1813. The homestead is there yet, or was a few years ago. It stood directly opposite Moran's place, a short distance back from the road and had a large pine or evergreen tree in front of it. The late Judge Witherell (Hamtramck) has this to say of the adopted son: "The first distinct recollection that he (Grant) has of his childhood is that he was a captive boy about three years old among a wandering band of Chippewa warriors. Whence he came, his name or lineage he never knew. The Indians had brought him to Detroit and while roaming about the street, the little captive attracted the attention of the lady of the late Commodore Grant. He was a kind-hearted old sailor, and his wife was one of the excellent of the earth. As they were riding out one day, she discovered the little blue-eyed prisoner among the savages, and his condition aroused all the sympathies of a mother's heart. She pointed him out to her husband, and asked him to buy the boy. The old tar was ever ready when a good deed was to be done. So, dismounting from his carriage, he went among the Indians, and finding the owner, he gave him $100 for the little Che-mo-ka-mun, and carried him home, giving him his own name, John Grant. The little captive was a great favorite of the commodore, who raised him to manhood, and he well repaid the kindness shown him by his unremitting care and attention to the interests of his benefactor. Captain Grant, as he grew up to manhood, understood that he was a native of the United-States, and never for a moment wavered in his allegiance, though as the adopted son of a British officer, it might have been supposed that he would have acted differently." The captain was alive in 1854.

* * *

Reynard Creek (Fox Run, a short distance above Connor's Creek, and where the Grosse Pointe Road crosses), about five miles from the city, was the turning point in the supremacy of some of the Indian tribes. Great numbers were slain in the battle, and it is believed the vast number of human bones found in the fields of George Moran, of Grosse Pointe, are the remains of some who fell in the fight. They are evidently of great age and some have the mark of the spike of the war club in their skulls. Mr. Moran had quite a collection of these relics, also rusty knives and tomahawks, as well as quite a number of small tomahawks measuring about four inches, wrought out of native copper. They give quite conclusive evidence that the Aborigines had a knowledge of the copper deposits in the Lake Superior regions, and the skill to mine the mineral and to fashion it into various articles of use.

* * *

Commander Alexander Grant married, in 1774, Therese, daughter of Chas. Barthe and Marie Therese Campau. He was of the clan of Grants, of Glenmoriston, Scotland. He entered the navy at an early age, but resigned in 1757 to join a Highland regiment raised for the army of General Amherst in America. In 1759 he reached Lake Champlain. General Amherst, desiring able officers for his fleet on the lake, commissioned Lieutenant Grant to the command of a sloop of sixteen guns. After the conquest of Canada, Grant was ordered to Lakes Erie and Ontario. Detroit was then an English garrison, and it was here that he met his fate in Therese Barthe. He built his castle, as it was called, at Grosse Pointe (its site is at present occupied by T. P. Hall's summer residence, "Tonnancour.") It was a place noted for the courtesy of its host, and his open, generous hospitality. Tecumseh and his warriors were frequent guests at the Grant castle. In 1805 the commodore belonged to the executive council of Upper Canada. In a letter to his brother "Alpine," dated from York (Toronto), July 5, 1811, he says:

"My duty where my naval command requires me is such a distance from here that I cannot travel in the winter when the legislature meets, but I come down at my ease in the summer and take some sittings in the council. A gentleman who has served his country upwards of fifty-five years requires some indulgence and my superiors allow it to me."

He was a man of commanding presence, a great favorite and a good officer. He had ten daughters who are represented by the English-Canadian families of Wrights, Robinsons, Dickinsons,

Woods, Duffs, Gilkersons, Millers, Jacobs and Richardsons. Mr. Jasper Gilkerson, of Brantford, has been in charge of the Indians in Canada for many years. So faithful has he been to his charge that any promise made to the Indians by him has always been kept by the government. A worthy representative of his grandfather, Commodore Grant, who, when administrator, with the power of giving free grants of land, never granted any to his family or their connections.—(Mrs. Hamlin in "Legends of Detroit."

* * *

Commodore Grant was connected by marriage with the Labadies. An uncle of the commodore's wife (Pierre Barthe Labadie), in 1760, married Charlotte Chapoton, daughter of Dr. Jean Chapoton, surgeon in the French army. Their daughter Charlotte, born in 1763, married in 1780 Lieutenant Louis Reaume of the British army, who left her a widow within the year. In 1784 she became the second wife of Antoine Louis Descomptes Labadie, surnamed "Badichon," and was the mother of Mrs. Thomas C. Sheldon. She is buried in the same lot in Mount Elliott cemetery, Detroit, as is Mrs. Thomas C. Sheldon, her daughter, and her grand-daughter, Mrs. Laura J. Archambault, mother of Mrs. Chas. M. June and Josephine Kelly, both of Detroit. The commodore was also related by marriage to the Askins and McKees, of Sandwich, and the Brushes, of Detroit. Grant was also concerned by marriage with the family of Colonel Edward Brooks and that of Lawyer Fraser. The two latter persons married daughters of Judge James May, by his second wife, who was a Labadie. The Labadie homestead is still standing, and is on the river road or River Street, just below the residence of the late Colonel Sylvester Larned (the Governor Porter house).

* * *

Mr. Provencal, a French gentleman, owned a farm a short distance above George Moran's. He was one of the old school, and of commanding presence. Presume many will remember him.

* * *

Judge Leib owned and lived on the farm adjoining the Hunts, across Bloody Run. The judge and his wife came from Philadelphia, when, I do not know. They were living on the Leib farm, at any rate, when I came to Detroit.

The judge was from a distinguished family in that city. His brother, Dr. Michael Leib, also of Philadelphia, died at the age of 63, January 28, 1823, and his obituary notice said of him: "He was a man of considerable talent and great energy of character, qualities which qualified him to be a conspicuous politician during the arduous conflicts of party. He was a member of the legislature of the state of Pennsylvania, a representative of the state in congress, a senator of the state in congress and again a member of the legislature of his own state."

Their residence was situated where Berry Bros.' varnish factory is now. Their dwelling was floated down from Grosse Pointe on a raft and was, with much difficulty placed on its foundations. After the judge and his wife had passed away it was moved back to the corner of Jefferson and Mt. Elliott Avenues, where it did duty for many years as a road house. I think it was then the property of Flattery brothers. Many of the present day will remember this house.

I call to mind the judge and his good lady quite well. He was a rosy-faced, jolly, rotund man, short of stature, and of the old school in every way. I used often to meet them coming into the city, on the river road. They knew me and always passed a pleasant word with me. They always came in their one-horse calache or shay, such as Judge James Witherell, Judge Sibley and Joseph Campau used. Very few of the residents here at that time sported this kind of a conveyance (the one-horse French cart being most in use), hence they were more noticeable.

The Leibs were fine people. They had one son, I think. He was a fine, handsome young fellow and highly gifted. I saw him directly after his return from Tangier, Morocco, where he had been serving the United States as consul, and think I never saw a finer looking man. He died soon after his return.

Mrs. Leib was a Quakeress, and always attracted my attention in her dove colored satin Quaker bonnet, and her plain but rich dress.

It was said that Colonel Hamtramck was in love with the beautiful daughter of Robert Navarre, Marianne. He first saw her with her father when they visited Philadelphia in 1786, on the organization of a government for the North West Territory, which comprised all the American possessions west of the Alleghanies. General St. Clair was appointed governor, and a number of the most popular officers of the revolution were given important positions. A court was established and the judges were authorized to prepare a code of laws. Major-General Samuel Holden Parsons, the rival of St. Clair for the appointment of governor, was appointed chief justice with Judge Cleves Symmes and General Joseph M. Varnum as associate judges. The former was a great-grandfather of Theodore P. Hall, of Detroit and Grosse Pointe, and the descendants of Judge Symmes reside in Louisville, Ky. In this first court of the northwest Judge Solomon Sibley, General Lewis Cass, Colonel Ebenezer Sproat and others well known in Detroit took their first lessons in law.

These pioneers, who had crossed the mountains of Pennsylvania on horseback, settled on one of the picturesque bends of the Ohio. Here they founded Marietta, so called after the lovely and ill-fated Marie Antoinette of France. Louise St. Clair, who had not forgotten the little Norman friend whom she had met in Philadelphia, wrote to her as soon as she was settled at Marietta; challenging her to cross the intervening "Black Swamp" and visit her in her new home. Marianne came from too good a pioneer stock to shrink from any hardship, especially where it promised an adventure. So, accompanied by her relative, Antoine Garelin, a guard of friendly Indians, and her faithful serving woman, she performed the perilous journey in safety. On her arrival she found Marietta a scene of life and excitement. The newly organized first regiment of United States Infantry was then on its way to garrison Vincennes. Its corps of gay officers, among whom was Major John Francis Hamtramck, made the days speed merrily and happily for the young maidens. Major Hamtramck made desperate love to the Navarre beauty, and was almost constantly by her side. For some reason she doubted the young officer's fidelity to her, and finding a convenient pretext, returned to Detroit whilst Hamtramck was away upon temporary official business. Shortly afterwards St. Clair was attcked by the combined savage tribes of the west, and sustained a disastrous defeat. It is said Washington, on hearing of it, for once in his life, swore such a volley of oaths as to make his secretary's hair stand on end. After the battle of the Maumee Colonol Hamtramck was ordered to Detroit, and here he again met his former sweetheart, and pressed his suit a second time. Marianne again refused him. "Well," said he, "since we cannot be uited in life, in death I shall be near you. I shall give orders to be buried by your side."

"Oh, that is romantic, colonel, but you are a soldier and cannot say where your last sleep shall overtake you," she replied.

"No matter, mark me, I shall slumber within the shadow of your tomb."

In 1803 Hamtramck died, and was buried near the Navarre lot in the old St. Anne's Churchyard. On the abandonment of the old St. Anne's cemetery the remains were placed in Mt. Elliott, as well as the tombstone, over them, with its voluminously worded inscription.

Fifty years later Marianne died, and her body was removed some years ago from the Navarre to the Godfroy lot in Mt. Elliott, which is opposite the spot where Hamtramck is buried, and he slumbers within the shadow of her tomb, as he said he would.

* * *

One of the Trombleys (Gazette) lived at Milk River Point during the Indian Chief Tecumseh's time, as also that of Macoonse and Kish-Kan-Ko. Himself and Richard Connor, of Connor's Creek, had many thrilling experiences with the three noted Indian Chiefs. Mrs. Connor was the sister of Gazette Trombley. Both were living as late as 1856.

THE STREETS IN THE LOWER PART OF THE CITY.

BEYOND Jefferson Avenue, out Gratiot Avenue way, from Hastings Street up, was sparsely settled and continued to be so until about 1850. Away out Russell Street were situated the Detroit barracks, erected just previous to the Mexican war. Before these barracks were built here, the troops stationed at this post were quartered in the old Government warehouse at the foot of Wayne Street, which was ill adapted for such a purpose. But here the quarters for the troops, the officers' quarters and the public offices, etc., were quite commodious. The barrack enclosure took in three or four acres on the corner of Gratiot Avenue, Russell and Catherine Streets, and including in it the old brick powder magazine that many will perhaps remember. It stood a short distance back from Catherine Street, and, before the barracks invaded that part of the city, was way out in the country, as it were, and considered beyond any possibilities of danger to the citizens in case its contents should by any accident blow up. At that time there was a wide open common around this locality. The only house I remember near there was that of Mr. Jasperson, a merchant in the city, and that was in a two-acre lot on the northwest corner of Russell and Catherine Streets, and house of the bandmaster of the Fifth United States Infantry. There were no houses out Gratiot Avenue beyond Russell Street until the Bloody Run was reached. The rifle range for target practice was set about where St. Joseph's Catholic Cathedral now is and there was no possibility of any one getting hit by a stray bullet unless one wanted to bad.

One great benefit to that part of the city at that date was in the building of a plank walk by the government, from Jefferson Avenue out Russell Street to the barracks, and on to Gratiot Avenue, and one from Russell Street along Catherine Street, down to Gratiot Avenue, where it joined the latter street. But for this walk, the barracks and that part of the city would have been almost isolated in bad weather. The location of the barracks out that way was a great factor in settling that part of the city. The officers' quarters were on the southwest corner of Russell and Catherine Streets, and were occupied at various times by many officers afterwards distinguished in the Civil War, notably Lieutenants Grant, Gordon Granger, Longstreet, Canby, afterwards General Canby, of Modoc Lava Beds fame, and many others. This building is still standing and adjoining Arbeiter Hall on Russell Street. The barracks served a good purpose before and during the Mexican War, also during the Civil War. The necessity for their continuance ceased after the latter war ended, and they passed away. The land on which they were built was owned by General Cass, of Detroit, and James Schoolcraft, of the Soo.

Woodbridge Street was not opened for some years, only as far as Chancellor Farnsworth's line. Between it and the river there was not much to note for many years. Between Bolivar Alley and Hastings Street, on the river front, the ground was low and marshy and continued so until it was filled in and reclaimed.

When the river was high, the water always washed over the road, along its border, between Hastings Street and Bolivar Alley (that was). Consequently most of the portion of that section between the above two points and Woodbridge Street was a swamp, of no use whatever, and never had been, so far as known. This was a capital bathing spot, and freely patronized by the small boy and his elders. The water was shallow for quite a distance out, and the bed of the river hard and sandy. It was often used by the Baptist persuasion for baptising.

Eldred & Ladue built their tannery here along in the forties, which they carried on for many years. Alanson Sheley had a small dock, office and lumber yard at the foot of Hastings Street. He was agent for the Black River (Port Huron) Lumber Co. Louis Moran, brother of Charles Moran, lived at the foot of this street, on the River Road. There was a row of low buildings between Moran's house and the line of the Beaubien farm, occupied principally as drinking saloons, billiards, etc.

Mr. Timothy Dequindre had a general store on the line of the Beaubien farm. He was a brother of Major Dequindre and an exceedingly nice gentleman, one of the old school. He passed away, leaving a beautiful widow and two young and handsome daughters. The widow afterwards married Mr. W. B. Hunt, a widower and the father of Cleveland and G. W. Hunt. One of the daughters married Lawyer W. H. Wells, afterwards lieutenant-colonel of a Michigan regiment in the Civil War and provost marshal-general of Alexandria, Va. The other daughter married Rev. Rufus Nutting, of Ohio.

In front of the row of buildings I mention was a filled-in dock of considerable size, and on this dock was built the steam ferryboat Argo No. 2; there was also a small tannery on this dock, carried on in the early days by Joe Spencer.

Mr. Gilbert Dolson, brother of Levi Dolson, who for so many years operated a tannery just above Beller's garden, on Jefferson Avenue, related an incident in connection with this tannery. He said:

"At the time of Hull's surrender, the Indian allies of the British were very jubilant and insolent, and a terror to the inhabitants. The brutal Indian chief Kish-Kan-Ko chased Doctor Scott into Joe Spencer's tannery, and, as he entered, threw his tomahawk at him, which stuck in the door casing."

In the rear of Chancellor Farnsworth's residence was a fine orchard of French pear trees, consisting of at least a dozen trees, all in a bunch (called the twelve apostles). Who planted them or when they were planted is not known, but they were the finest and largest specimens of their kind anywhere along the river or on the shore of Lake St. Clair. The last owner of them caused them to be destroyed to make room for a lumber yard. It was a great pity that they were not preserved.

The old Moran homestead was on Woodbridge Street, between Hastings and St. Antoine Streets. It was so recently demolished that most all will remember it. J. L. King built and occupied a fine brick residence with ample grounds on this street, living there until his demise a few years ago. He also had some fine peach trees. Think the house is there still. The old Beaubien homestead was, in build and character, like the Moran house, only the former was of a natural wood color, never having been painted, while the latter always boasted of a coat of yellow paint with white trimmings. It stood on Woodbridge Street, between St. Antoine and Beaubien Streets. It had a row of pear trees in its front yard and an apple orchard in its rear towards Jefferson Avenue.

The officers and soldiers stationed at Fort Gratiot used always when visiting the city to camp at the foot of Beaubien, and they came quite often during the summer months. They always came in their large green barge; this before the advent of river steamers—before Captain John Burtis had started his little steamer, Argo, on the route between here and Black River (Port Huron), Fort Gratiot, Village of Palmer (St. Clair), etc. The soldiers were always in charge of two or more officers, and the latter, on these occasions, had pressed upon them the hospitalities of our citizens.

I think I have already mentioned that the Indians often times selected this locality for their camping grounds, and it was thought that they did so from the fact that one of their most noted chiefs, Kish-Kan-Ko, was buried near by in the Beaubien apple orchard. I have already mentioned this chief, and his place of burial in a former article.

On the corner of Woodbridge and St. Antoine Streets lived Mons. J. B. Vallee, a French gentleman of the old school; he was deputy United States custom officer under Colonel Andrew Mack.

Mons T. R. Vallee, married Miss McCormick, sister of Mrs. Judge Moran. There were two daughters and, I think, one son. What became of the latter I do not know. One of the daughters married ex-Mayor Langdon, and the other Mr. Wheeler, an accomplished druggist, for some years (about 1879 and '80) in business on Griswold Street near the Moffat block. What a pleasant family, and what a pleasant polite suave gentleman was Monsieur Valee. Many no doubt will call him to mind, and the family as well.

There were no houses on the Beaubien farm front, from St. Antoine Street down, for some years, until 1837, when the first steam saw mill was started. It was located at the foot of St. Antoine Street and was called, if I do not mistake, the "Detroit & Black River Steam Saw-mill Co." Mr. E. A. Brush and Dr. Justin Rice were, I think, the principal stockholders. It was in operation quite a while, until the increase of business necessitated a larger mill. Then the old mill gave place to a new one, thirty-four by eighty feet in size, which was owned by Rice, Coffin & Co., afterwards by Wight & Coffin. This mill was followed shortly afterwards by another one built by Mr. Samuel Pitts, further up the river, and, in three or four years, four more mills were built to keep pace with the demand for lumber. But now nearly all have disappeared.

CHRISTMAS IN DETROIT'S EARLIER DAYS.

HOW THE RESIDENTS OF THE CITY CELEBRATED THE HAPPY OCCASION IN THE EARLY THIRTIES AND FORTIES.

CHRISTMAS was generally observed in the early days, but nowhere near to the extent that it is now. It was not then as at present a church or religious festival, but more of a social one. None of the religious denominations participated in it as such or paid any attention to it; had no services in their houses of worship, except the Roman Catholic. The last named paid marked attention to the day. The ceremonies at St. Anne's were elaborate and imposing. Christmas after Christmas have I witnessed them. Those under Father Richard, I think, impressed me more than any that followed. I also attended a Christmas festival at St. Phillip's in Hamtramck, which was most impressive, and which remains in my memory vividly. The ceremonies were conducted by Father Vanderpool (I think his name was). He died shortly after this and his remains were deposited in the vault under St. Anne's Church. I witnessed his elaborate obsequies.

RACED THE PONIES.

Stores and places of business, as a general thing, closed at noon. If the snow was in good condition on Jefferson Avenue, the horsey portion of the male community were all out with their fast French ponies and an animated scene presented itself, from the Dequindre Street bridge to the Michigan Exchange. In the absence of snow on the avenue, this scene was transferred to the river, if the ice permitted.

The starting point was from in front of the residence of DeGarmo Jones (about where Third Street now is.) The objective points were usually Mother Weaver's, near the foot of Twelfth Street, and "Coon" Ten Eyck's, on the Rouge, this side of Dearborn. Major "Bob" Forsythe with his fast pony "Spider," and Lieutenants Grant and Henry, U. S. A., Cicotte, Daniel J. Campau, the Beaubiens, etc., all with the most spirited French nags, made things hum. There are some, perhaps, that can call to mind the races on the avenue and on the river in that far off time, when all hearts with youth and pleasure bounded.

IN THE HOMES.

Then as now there was the usual hanging up of the stocking, and the interchange of presents, but not quite to the extent it has attained at the present. The usual Christmas dinner, something more elaborate, than on ordinary days, as now, with the conventional turkey, with the pumpkin and mince pies; white fish and always the new cider, that had just commenced to sparkle. In some farm houses in the country the Yule log was hauled in and put into the huge fireplace, that would take in almost a half cord of wood, and soon before it would appear the turkey suspended by a stout cord, and then and there put through the process of fitting it for the table. I have witnessed two or three times the above hauling in of the Yule log, roasting the turkey, etc., in the "Log Farm House" of my stepfather, Mr. George Kellogg, on the Clinton River, just below Mt. Clemens, in the thirties. Have myself watched, turned and basted the bird that Doctor Russel used to say "was too much for one, and not enough for two."

CHRISTMAS VISITS.

The gay portion of the community used now and then of a Christmas to visit Lieutenant F. D. Callender, U. S. A., at the Dearborn Arsenal, also Royal Oak, Mt. Clemens, Fisher's and Payee's up at Grosse Pointe. On all these occasions Brad Thompson with his four-horse turnout was the "Jehu," and held the reins. It is almost needless to remind the reader, that much fun and pleasure was had at these festivities, "where youth and pleasure met to chase the hours with flying feet." It also goes without saying, that an elaborate dinner was always served on this day at Dan Whipple's and continued to be until into the late forties.

The Protestant denominations, as said before, did not appear to take much notice of the day. I do not call to mind a solitary service, in its commemoration, held in either the Presbyterian, Episcopal or Methodist Churches, until after the dedication of St. Paul's Church by Bishop McCoskrey. Then service was had there every Christmas morn and the church inside elaborately trimmed with evergreens, holly, etc. The splendid choir, composed of Mrs. Dr. A. R. Terry and a lady assistant, whose name has escaped me, Chas. S. Adams, Chas. A. Trowbridge and Dr. A. R. Terry accompanied by the pealing organ—rendered the Christmas anthems to the entire satisfaction of the delighted audience. Did any one, living, ever hear Mrs. Terry sing "I know that My Redeemer Liveth?" If so, then that person will know.

MIDNIGHT MASS.

The midnight mass at St. Anne's, was most imposing, with the so-called "Crib of Bethlehem" erected at the end of one of the side aisles—a most elaborate affair, resplendent with lights profusely decorated with evergreens and flowers. This "Crib of Bethlehem" was made to represent the manger in which our Lord was born, with representations in miniature size of the animals said to be present on that occasion, of the Blessed Virgin and St. Joseph, and the shepherds coming to adore their Lord, as also the "Three Wise Men of the East" bearing their presents to lay at his feet.

This impressive and striking adjunct to the other ceremonies was inaugurated to appeal more particularly to the senses of the juvenile portion of the congregation, and it was instilled into them then and there that their "Divine Lord and Master" was once a little, helpless babe, as they had been, and it was a pleasing incident they ever remembered.

It must not be inferred from the seeming apathy of the Protestant portion of the community to notice this day with any appropriate church ceremonies, that they did not in the fullest sense acknowledge the sovereignty of their Divine Master and hold themselves second to none in their fealty to Him. On the contrary the devotion of the early pioneer dispensers of the holy truth and their devotion to the cause of Christ, as evinced in the Methodist circuit rider and the Moravian missionary, will fully attest their faith in Him who was crucified at Golgotha and before whom all knees shall bend.

WELCOMED WITH NOISE.—

It was quite the custom the night before Christmas to usher in the day with the blowing of horns and firing of guns, commencing at 12 o'clock and keeping it up until daylight. This custom was most prevalent among the German portion of the community. Woe betide the English speaking or Protestant family who had a German girl for a domestic. Her admirers would commence at the appointed hour and keep it up till morn. The German maid would be in eager anticipation of the opening of the fusilade and grievously disappointed if it did not occur according to program.

Thanksgiving was more of a holiday than was Christmas among the English-speaking people because they were mainly from New England where the former custom prevailed. They inaugurated also the New England practice of hanging up the stocking and the pleasant custom of interchange of presents. They also introduced here the Christmas tree, the mistletoe bough, the holly branch, English ivy, etc., which customs they had derived from their English ancestors, where

> "The mistletoe hung in the castle hall
> The Holly branch shone on the old oak wall
> And the Baron's retainers were blythe and gay
> Keeping their Christmas holiday."

Perhaps if it had not been for the New Englanders, the early French settler and his descendants would not have heard of Santa Claus, the patron saint of childhood dear to the heart of every child in the land—nor of the poem that will live always and that all are familiar with:

> " 'Twas the night before Christmas
> When all through the house," etc.

THE INDIANS CELEBRATED.

The Indians were also quite a feature here at Christmas time, before they were removed beyond the Mississippi by the general government. They had early learned of the present-giving custom, that the eastern element had brought with them and inaugurated here. So on Christmas and New Year's, those that had their abiding places or lodges anywhere near the city, were sure to be on hand bright and early to secure their share of the good things that were going. They were always more than eager for whisky, but the prevailing sentiment was against furnishing them the article at all freely. Still, in spite of all the precaution exercised, some of them would manage to get as boozy as they make them. But under any circumstances they were always peaceable. On these occasions they used to levy generous contributions on Joseph Campau, Peter Desnoyers, Antone Dequindre and other early French settlers they knew and whom their fathers had known. They also always gave Governor Cass an ovation before they got out of town. I call to mind one occasion when the clothier, J. L. King, decorated a number of them with headgear. He had in stock quite a lot of tall white hats that were many years out of date and unsaleable, so he concluded to pass them to the Indians, as far as they went. They cut quite a ludicrous figure, as may be supposed. Yet, Mr. "Injun," every one of him, that got a hat was as proud as Lucifer. "Everything was grist that came to the Indian's mill."

Contrasting the present elaborate ceremonies in all the churches on Christmas day, with those at an early day, Elder Blades knows what good old Elder Gildruth would say, if he was permitted to attend Divine service at the Central Methodist Church this Christmas morning.

THE OLD BERTHELET MARKET.

PROMINENT CITIZENS WHO LIVED ON THE STREETS IN ITS VICINITY.

THE Berthelet market, on the corner of Randolph and Atwater Streets, was named after Mr. Peter Berthelet. It is said that the Savoyard River, or creek, also obtained its name from this same man, as he bore the nick-name of "Savoyard."

Henry Berthelet, a son of the proprietor of the Berthelet market, was at one time in the dry goods business here, went to Wisconsin and engaged in the lime business, and became rich. He married a Knaggs. It is said he is still living.

Near the market, on this street, were located, Matthew Moon, grocer, and S. B. Morse had a stall in the market. Howard & Wadhams occupied a warehouse at the foot of this street. Henry Howard, of Howard & Wadhams, was at one time mayor of the city. I think he removed to Port Huron. After them came Hartshorn & Howard, and then Morse & Co., then J. N. Elbert. The Market Hotel was in the rear of the market on Atwater Street. Mr. Norton, father of Mrs. Jas. A. Hinchman, had a grocery store opposite this market. Nearby on Atwater Street, Eldred & Co. had a grocery store, called the "Blue Store," a lumber and wood yard and a lime and stone yard. The Eldreds also owned a woolen mill, near the foot of this street, a tread mill operated by oxen. It was from this mill that Farrand & Davis got the power to run their water pumping apparatus, which was located at the foot of the street. Mr. Julius Eldred and family lived over the store. Opposite Mr. Eldred's was the gunsmith shop of Mr. Lebot, (father of ex-Alderman Lebot). Lebot had been a member of Napoleon's Imperial Guard, was at Waterloo and was immensely proud of it. He was a worshipper of his emperor, as he termed him. He was indeed a grizzled veteran in appearance, tall, thin and as straight as an arrow. He was wounded during his service and often used to allude to it. The "boys" used to chaff him once in awhile and say, "Mr. Lebot, how did you get your wound?" his reply always was, (straightening himself), "Joost as I shall say, Vive L'Empereur, I receive a ball."

"And what did you say then, Mr. Lebot?" "I shall say joost de same, all de time, wot I been say before, 'Vive L'Empereur,'" he would always respond, with the greatest enthusiasm.

Among the prominent citizens who resided (from about 1830 to 1848) in the near vicinity of the American Hotel (Governor Hull House), Woodworth's Hotel, Berthelet market, Jefferson Avenue and Randolph Street (the latter from Congress Street to the river) were:

Judge Sibley, Major Kearsley, Edmond A. Brush, Colonel John Biddle, Barnabus Campau, Judge Henry Chipman, Ellis Doty, General John R. Williams, Peter J. Desnoyers, Eustache Chapoton, Counselor O'Keefe, John Truax, Wm. Brewster, Dr. R. S. Rice, Simon Poupard, John Y. Petty, Felix Hinchman, Henry M. Campbell, Dr. Wm. Brown, Widow Wilcox, Father Richard, the Watsons, Johnstons, Fearsons, Clarks, Ords, Andres, Whipples, Dr. McCloskey, Sheriff Wilson, Dr. Marshall Chapin, Thomas Rowland, Oliver Miller, Henry Berthelet, Julius Eldred, Henry Sanderson, Austin E. Wing, Knowles Hall, John and R. E. Roberts.

On Jefferson Avenue, where is now the water office, was the old council house, and on Bates Street, northeast corner of Atwater, was the Detroit Garden. Mr. Kunze, a prominent German citizen, also lived on Randolph Street, southeast corner of Woodbridge Street.

Noyes's extensive livery stable was located near by on Randolph Street, as were the vacant grounds always selected at that time by the circus people for giving their performances.

So it will be seen that Randolph street from Larned Street to the river, and the four corners on Jefferson Avenue were quite the business and social center of the city, where throbbed its life and its activity. Some of the above have been before mentioned in connection with this locality.

The residences of Generals John R. Williams, Dr. Marshal Chapin, Thomas Rowland, Oliver Miller, Henry Berthelet, Henry

Sanderson and Knowles Hall were on Woodbridge Street between Randolph and Bates Streets.

Colonel Garry Spencer, justice of the peace, had his office at one time opposite the American Hotel. The colonel at that time usually wore ruffled shirt, gold rimmed spectacles, and broadcloth cloak with ample velvet collar (the latter in the winter)—a most polite, suave gentleman. The public hay scales were located in front of his office.

A Mr. Freeman had a grocery store on southwest corner of Jefferson Avenue and Brush Street. He lived over the store. He had for a clerk our good friend (who lived with him), now Hon. Peter Wh.te, of Marquette; this in the early forties. Peter, while filling this situation, aspired to be a soldier and to serve his country in that capacity. Colonel A. T. McReynolds was at that time raising a company of dragoons for service in the Mexican War. Peter offered himself to the colonel for enlistment as a private, but much to his disgust he was rejected on account of age —too young.

In 1808 Oliver Williams, brother of Uncle Harvey Williams, and father of O. B. Williams, of Owosso, was a merchant in Detroit and became one of the largest dealers in the peninsula. He bought his goods in Boston, bringing at one time a stock amounting to $64,000, and conveying them overland in covered wagons to Buffalo, thence to Detroit by sail vessels. In 1811 the sloop "Friend's Good Will" was built for him. It was captured by the British and called afterwards the "Little Belt." Williams was in business in Detroit when F. and T. Palmer started their store here. He afterwards moved to Owosso. At a meeting of the State Pioneer Society, held in Lansing, June, 1882, B. O. Williams, of Owosso, son of Oliver, was requested to prepare a biography of his father, and also to contribute further important facts for the sketch of his uncle, Harvey Williams. Whether he did so or not, I do not know.

Beyond Eldred's, Harvey Williams carried on a large blacksmith shop. Mr. Williams was a soldier in the war of 1812 and came to Detroit in 1815. In 1828 he purchased an engine in Buffalo and set it up in his shop in Detroit, which was the first engine ever set up on land in the territory of Michigan. In 1826 he made all the mill irons used by Thomas Palmer and Horace Jerome in the erection of two water sawmills on Pine River, four miles from St. Clair. In 1829 he constructed and used the first engine ever built in Michigan. The cylinder was six inches in diameter and three feet stroke. He removed to Saginaw City in 1834, and was living there in 1882. He made a journey to Saginaw in 1822 with supplies for the troops stationed there, had to ford the Clinton River at five different points. The Indians and first American settlers at St. Clair knew Uncle Harvey well. Though not a trader in the full sense of the term, his dealings with the savages, as well as with the civilized inhabitants, were extensive and honorable.

Opposite Harvey Williams's was the old Brush homestead. This was an unpretentious old-fashioned wooden structure, two stories with an attic, with dormer windows, devoid of paint. It was situated in the center of a spacious lot that took in the entire width of the Brush farm. The dwelling was surrounded with trees, currant bushes, roses, and other flowering shrubs. It was an attractive place, and must have witnessed many stirring scenes in the early days, and no doubt, many times,

> "Every rafter
> Has rung with shouts of laughter."

I passed it often when a mere lad, and have often tasted of the currants from its garden. David French had a lime and stone yard in this locality. Eugene St. Armour had a wagon shop near, on Atwater Street. A. Leadbeater had a tavern on the corner of Brush and Atwater Streets.

* *

WOODBRIDGE, RANDOLPH AND BATES STREETS AND OF PERSONS WHO RESIDED THERE.

On Woodbridge Street, between Randolph and Bates Streets, were the residences of Oliver Miller; also Geo. Doty and Edmund Kearsley, who were great friends of his; John R. Williams, Dr. Marshall Chapin, Knowles Hall, carriage maker, and Mr. Sanderson, cabinet maker. The latter had a daughter who was adopted by Mr. Levi Cook and became the wife of the late Mr. George W. Bissell. Thos. Rowland at one time lived on this street.

I do not call to mind any business houses or residences of any note on Woodbridge Street, between Bates Street and Woodward Avenue, except the residence of Hon. Austin E. Wing, on the corner of Bates Street, nearly opposite the present police station, and the store of John R. Williams, afterwards Theodore Williams, on the corner of Bates Street, where is now (or was) Mr. Parker's wholesale grocery. Down Bates Street from Woodbridge Street, Orson Eddy had a tin and copper shop (his widow married Hiram R. Andrews), there were also the New York and City Hotel (about No. 34), and Gray & Gallagher. had a warehouse at the foot of this street, as did Poupard & Petty. Alexander Lewis afterwards occupied one of these warehouses, as did Hunt & Roby, and after them, L. W. Tinker, agent of the Mt. Clemens glass works, and also engaged in the Lake Superior trade. He was at that time the largest shipper of copper here, except the Minnesota Mining Company. My uncle, Thomas Palmer, had at one time in the thirties an extensive lumber yard, at the foot of this street. The lumber was the product of his St. Clair saw mills.

The Wing residence on the corner of Woodbridge Street was a cottage with a pillared veranda in front. When the judge vacated it and went to Monroe to live, General J. E. Schwartz bought it and floated it down the river on a raft to the locality that I have mentioned in the fore part of these recollections.

* * *

It was said that Austin E. Wing, as much as to any one, the city owes its obligation for the magnificent grant of the Military Reserve, including all the land north of Larned Street, west of Griswold Street and extending to Michigan Avenue on the north, and to the Cass farm land on the west. This splendid work he accomplished while delegate to congress from Michigan. A fine man was Austin E. Wing, possessing talent of the highest order. He was very handsome and always faultlessly dressed, almost the counterpart of General Chas. Larned, and those who ever saw the two men, will I am sure agree with me. I was quite intimate in the family, as Wing's son Talcott and myself were boys together, schoolmates under the various pedagogues that from time to time held sway at the old University school building on Bates Street. Ever after until the day of his untimely death we were close friends, although his lot was cast in another place (Monroe).

When D. B. Crane was on deck at the old University building on Bates Street, Talcott was his chief assistant in the chemical department, which was quite complete in the various chemicals and chemical apparatus, and he was just the funniest boy in the whole school. The cabinet containing the bottles of the various chemicals used was located at the end of the school room on the Woodward Avenue side and just over the boys' desks, within easy reach. When Talcott required any of the chemicals in his experiments, he had to mount the desk to get them. During this he would cast his eye towards "Old D. B.," as the boys used to call him, and if he was not looking, Talcott would get off all sorts of antics and gymnastics for the benefit of the rest of the boys, and directly the school was in an uproar of hilarity, to the astonishment of the "Old Man." No one seemed to know from whence the disturbance had proceeded, and Talcott was always as demure as a lamb. He used often to refer to this pleasant boyish incident in after days with much merriment. Edmond Kearsley had charge of the chemical laboratory in the basement of the building, evolving gas from the black oxide of manganese and other experiments of like character. Edmond was also full of circus. During recess he was constantly walking on his hands, turning cart wheels, hand springs, etc. He had some of the other boys enlisted and they partitioned off a portion of the basement, with Mr. Crane's permission, and gave a sort of acrobatic exhibition, admission two cents, which was patronized to the limit. A son of Talcott Wing is in business here at the foot of Woodward Avenue.

* * *

The "Detroit Garden" was on the northeast corner of Bates and Atwater Streets. It occupied about 150 feet of space along the former street, and about 50 feet along the latter and was kept by Dean & Campbell. It was quite a resort, being the first thing of its kind ever started here. It was here that, for the first time, I ever saw or tasted ice cream; it was served in small wine glasses, ten cents a glass. On the corner of Atwater Street was a small theater belonging to the garden, the auditorium being out of doors under the shade trees. The show was always on when the weather would permit, and the acting, to my mind, was always very fine.

The house was a long, low cottage structure—with dormer windows—set back from the street about 50 feet, the intervening space being filled with trees, roses and other flowering shrubs. Two or three vine-covered arbors found place there, which did duty as all other structures of like character do. It was really quite an ideal retreat. It was said that the Hudson family, who were mentioned in my article on Hamtramck in *The Free Press,* December 5, owned this corner and lived in it before they took up their residence in Grosse Pointe. Anyway, they lived on this (Bates) street, between Woodbridge and Atwater before I came here, as I have been reliably informed, and on this corner. Bates Street from Jefferson Avenue to the river, was quite an important locality in the twenties and thirties. On it, in addition to those I have mentioned, lived others whom I rememebr quite well: Mrs. Hancks, whose husband, Lieutenant Hancks, was killed inside of Fort Shelby, by a cannon shot fired from a British gun on the other side of the river two or three days before Hull's surrender. The Durrells, the Isdells, the Hinchmans on the southeast corner of Jefferson Avenue, and Henry H. Le Roy.

While the American army, under General Hull, was stationary at Sandwich, a British force was despatched from the Canada side to take possession of the Island of Mackinac. The whole garrison of this post was only fifty-seven men, under command of Lieutenant Hancks, and the first intimation which this officer had of the declaration of war was the arrival of a body of British troops, supported by more than a thousand Indian warriors, consisting of Sioux, Winnebagos, Ottawas and Chippewas. The savages, it appears, had been directed, in case of resistance, to show no quarter, and the odds being so fearfully against him, the American officer immediately surrendered.

On Atwater Street, between Randolph Street and Woodward Avenue, were located the stores of Charles S. Bristol, Mr. Bain, tailor; Peter Beaubien, grocer; Gilbert Dolson, dry goods; John Farrer, dry goods; John N. Gott, grocer; Arthur and Jesse McMillan, grocers; Eleazor Ray, grocer; Van-Antwerp, blacksmith; Peleg O. Whitman, carpenter; John Robert's brick store, ashery and soap factory (the latter's holdings extended to the river, and were midway between Randolph and Bates Streets), as also the carriage factory of Knowles Hall.

THE OLD BERTHELET MARKET.

Knowles Hall was quite prominent in those days. He was an extensive carriage builder for the times. When he died he was buried in the cemetery out on Beaubien Street where is now Clinton Park. In the process of time this cemetery became quite neglectd (Elmwood having superseded it), and the headstone that markd Hall's grave had been broken in two by some vandal and lay on the ground. His widow, who directly after his death had, with her two daughters, removed to Buffalo, was informed of this circumstance. She came on here with one of her daughters. They, in company with Mr. David, procured a new stone, had the body removed to Elmwood cemetery, and the stone placed at its head. One of Hall's daughters married Mr. Bronson Rumsey, of Buffalo, an extensive shoe dealer.

* * *

HORSE FERRY BOAT.

The horse boat ferry used to leave from the foot of Bates Street in the early thirties. To verify this statement I give copy of the notice to the public below:

"The public are informed that the horse boat has been thoroughly repaired, and will ply regularly between Detroit and the opposite shore. The decided advantages of this conveyance over the sail ferry boats will readily occur to all, and it is hoped that the liberal patronage which it has hertofore received will not only be renewed, but increased. The boat will leave the foot of Bates Street every half hour during the day and every exertion will be used to accommodate and please. Those persons who may wish to subscribe for ferriage by the year will leave their names at the store of John R. Williams, corner of Bates and Woodbridge.

"May 4, 1831."

On the southeast corner of Woodward Avenue and Woodbridge Street was at one time Bronson's tavern, where is now what used to be called the Wardell Block.

Arthur Bronson, who kept this tavern, was in some way related to the family of De Garmo Jones. There were two daughters, Sarah and Mary. The Bronsons were interested in the French Spoliation claims. Sarah was quite busy only a few years ago trying to get something from the general government on that account; whether she succeeded or not, I never knew. Mary, the other sister, died many years ago. Mr. Bronson was much esteemed and widely known here in the early days.

R. H. Hall built this block for the Wardell's, a wholesale grocery firm in New York. M. S. Bishop had a grocery store in this block, as also did John Rumney and Hutchins & Jenness; also G. & J. G. Hill, after the fire of 1842. On the opposite side of Woodward Avenue John Bull, brother of Charles M. Bull, had a variety store, R. & W. Stead at one time had a grocery store, and also William Phelps, O. M. Hyde and Morgan L. Gage had a hardware store. Ingersoll & Kirby dealt in leather and hides. Dennis Mullane had a clothing store on the corner of Woodbridge Street, H. D. Waller & Co. had a grocery store. Monsieur Woollaire, a Frenchman, kept a wine, liquor and cigar store, his liquid goods being imported from France direct. M. Woollaire was a giant in stature, and had been a member of Napoleon's imperial guard. He had for an assistant a Frenchman, Monsieur Vickar, who was as nervous, talkative and erratic as his principal was staid and dignified. I presume many will call them to mind.

Charles G. Hammond, late of the Illinois Central railroad, located at Chicago, at one time had a dry goods store on the west side of Woodward Avenue, between Jefferson Avenue and Woodbridge Street. He was also at one time collector of customs at this port. Nathan Goodell, brother of Lemuel Goodell, at one time sheriff of Wayne county, had a restaurant on the east side of Woodward Avenue, between the same two streets. Afterwards he was with Oliver Newberry as manager of his vessel and steamboat interests.

Mr. Goodell was the steward of the steamer Henry Clay when I was a passenger on her in 1827.

Colonel Anderson, of the United States army (as said before), occppied the residence where is now the Bethel or Mariners' church. In this connection:

Colonel Anderson was on duty at Fort Shelby at the time of General Hull's surrender, in command of a twenty-four pounder cannon, and when General Brock marched up from Springwells to the fort on August 16, 1812, Colonel Anderson was not allowed to fire, by General Hull's orders. As the British troops advanced on the fort the American troops eagerly awaited the orders to fire. Cannon loaded with grape stood on the commanding eminence of the fort, ready to sweep away the advancing columns. The troops then heard the order, "Retire within the fort," with shame and mortification it is said, but obeyed it. It is further related that Lieutenant Hull, a brother of the general's, while trying to raise the white flag, said to Captain Snelling, who was near by, "Snelling, come and help me raise this flag." "No, sir," was the indignant response, "I will not soil my hands with that kind of flag."

My uncle, Senator Palmer's father, who was one of the surrendered, told me that the artillerymen in charge of the cannon could have swept into "Kingdom Come" the advancing force, if they had been permitted to fire, but he said the British troops came up the narrow causeway leading to the fort as if on dress parade, and evidently knew the surrender had been cooked and dried beforehand.

It is related however brave Hull may have been personally, he was, as a commander, a coward, and, moreover, he was influenced, confessedly, by his fears as a father, lest his daughter and her children should fall into the hands of the Indians. His faculties had become paralyzed by the intemperate use of alcoholic stimulants, which produced a cowardly fear—fear that he should fail—fear that his troops, whose confidence and respect he could not but discover he had lost, would prove untrue to him—fear that the savages would spare no one if opposed with vigor—fear of some undefined and horrible evil impending. His conduct throughout was such as might be expected from a man who had reached premature dotage and of physical decay.

B. B. Kercheval & Co. were adjoining the store of Loomis & Jaquith, in the forwarding and commission business. Their warehouse extended to the river. In this connection I would like to say that at that time I was a clerk in the store of Loomis & Jaquith, and Detroit depended on Ohio for its supply of flour. All of our flour came to this dock from Cleveland, and it used to be my fun to roll the barrels from the vessel to the store.

Dr. J. L. Whiting had the warehouse opposite, once the ferry dock, and did a large business in the commission and freighting line. One early summer morning in 1837 a fire broke out in a row of buildings adjoining Whiting's warehouse and swept it and them away; also Franklin Moore's store, Garrison & Holmes, on the corner, where Eaton's now is; John Farrer's store, on the corner of Bates Street; the "Detroit Garden" and buildings, the entire plant of John Roberts and all the concerns and dwellings located on Atwater and part of Bates Streets. The late George W. Foote was at that time bookkeeper for Franklin Moore, and he brought the books of the concern over to our store (Loomis & Jaquith's) and established a temporary office there until things could be straightened out. I was present at this fire, an account of which I have given in a former article. Directly after this fire I do not remember who occupied the two stores on the corner of Atwater Street, but think that John T. Garrison did the corner one for a while. Benjamin G. Stimson carried on the grocery and ship chandlery business where the Eaton store now is, in 1845 and after. I think he continued there until Eaton succeeded him. Chauncey Hulbert erected and occupied the adjoining building for many years as a grocery store and residence.

J. and P. Aspinwall were grocers on the corner of Woodward Avenue and Larned Street in 1845, and Atkinson & Godfrey, painters and paper hangers, were on Woodward Avenue, near Atwater Street.

Between Hulbert's and Woodbridge Street was a dive called the "Loafers' Paradise," where the lowest element of the city congregated. Judge James A. Slaymaker, as he was familiarly called, was a candidate for the office of alderman of the ward and he was elected. His supporters and admirers desired to present him with a hat in token of their esteem and it was at the "Paradise" where the thing came off.

The judge was present, of course, as well as Colonel J. B. Grayson, J. Nicholson Elbert, Major Whilden, J. B. Witherell, Robert Bullock, Major W. D. Wilkins, Willie Gray, myself and many others whose names I do not now recall. The presentation speech was made by a club-footed hatter in the employ of F. & C. H. Buhl, by the name of "Bob Hittel." He was an "out-and-outer" sure enough.

Just before the speech was made the hat had been passed around among the crowd to give them an opportunity to admire it, and when Hittel came to the part of the speech, "Allow me, judge, to present you with this hat," he was minus the hat and halted for a second, and then, continuing, said: "Where in h— is that hat?" The article was speedily forthcoming and the festivities went on.

Colonel Grayson was a most conservative and democratic individual, for he had this whole crowd at his house a few nights afterward and entertained them right royally. I was there, and the behavior of the crowd was ludicrous; they were orderly enough, to be sure, but quite out of place. On the refreshment table, among other things, was a large dish of macaroni and cheese. Upon perceiving it, Hittel said: "Now, boys, mind your eye, this is macaroni." I presume that neither he nor his pals had ever seen or heard of the dish before.

Judge Slaymaker was a fine, scholarly man, originally from Philadelphia, and in his younger days was a partner in an extensive iron manufacturing concern, a "high roller," and was a chum of Chevalier Wyckoff and his set. He was for some years clerk in the dry goods house of Holmes & Co.

William Cole carried on the manufacture of sails, awnings, flags, etc., on Atwater Street, between Woodward Avenue and Griswold Street. John Ask had a tailor shop on the corner of Griswold and Atwater Streets. John was a big, bluff, Yorkshire Englishman and a great pugilist. Nelson Tomlinson kept the Mansion House, formerly John Hanmer's tavern, at the foot of Griswold Street, where is now the Seaman's home, in the same old building. Mr. Hanmer owned and kept this house in 1827. The ferry dock later on was also at the foot of Griswold Street. The boats, Argo and United, made the trip every fifteen minutes, and ran into a slip on which the Davenports, Lewis and his brother, built a commodious structure for a waiting room, saloon and restaurant. The saloon and restaurant were run by John Edwards, whom many will remember as an exceedingly jolly and pleasant Englishman. This waiting room, saloon and restaurant was built over the water on piles, and it is said that John made a pretty penny smuggling stuff over from Canada, even as people do nowadays. He had a trap door in the floor, inside his bar-counter, and it was said that row boats, in the dead of night, with contraband goods aboard, would somehow get under this trap door and be quickly delivered of their contents.

Edwards was also (1845) agent for the line of stages between Detroit and Buffalo, through Canada. He advertised that "Stages will leave Windsor every morning, during the close of navigation, at 9 o'clock, for Buffalo and intermediate points. Fare to Buffalo $14.00, including ferriage. Through in three days."

It took me longer to make this same trip in the winter of 1842. Then it consumed seven days. Such a sea of mud, most of the way, and the fare I paid was $18 to Niagara Falls.

Dr. E. A. Theller of patriot war fame had a grocery and drug store near the Mansion House on Griswold Street. On Woodbridge Street, in 1837, D. B. Cole had a grocery store as also did James Crabb, whom I presume many will remember. Crabb was a very pleasant fellow, an Englishman, always neatly dressed, invariably wearing a white cravat.

George Miller, afterwards county treasurer, had a grocery store along here also, Gideon Paul had a variety store and Nathan Prouty groceries, and William Shaw had a harness and saddlery shop, and William Winget a gun store, all on this street.

BRUSH STREET.

At the foot of Brush Street, where is now the Detroit, Grand Haven & Milwakee railroad depot, Mr. Charles Howard built two large warehouses (immense for those days). One of them was occupied by himself and the other by Brewer & Dudgeon. They gave place afterwards to the Detroit, Grand Haven & Milwaukee Railway Co., which established the present depot there.

Randolph Street, from Jefferson Avenue to the river, was quite a business center in the early days. Woodworth's hotel was on this street, on the corner of Woodbridge Street (as before mentioned). George Heron, barber and ladies' hairdresser, was also on this street. William Clay, the intellectual perfumer and wigmaker, was in the Woodworth hotel block. Opposite the hotel on Woodbridge Street was the Berthelet row, and on the Randolph Street corner of the same was a large grocery kept by Stead Bros. Dr. McCoskrey (the doctor was an uncle of Bishop McCoskrey) lived on the opposite corner (east), and with him Sheriff John Wilson, his son-in-law. Mr. Kunze, a German and a fine gentleman, had his store and soap factory adjoining.

The northwest corner of Woodbridge and Griswold Streets was vacant for many years after the 1805 fire until Thomas Gallagher erected a wooden building on the site, which he occupied for quite a while as a grocery store, with a sample room attached. He did a prosperous business for the many years that he remained in this location. He afterwards removed to Fireman's hall and still later to a store on Cadillac square.

A splendid, whole-souled, genial, Irish gentleman was Tom —generous to a fault. He died quite poor, I think, at the early age of 53 years. He had two boys, fine, bright, handsome fellows they were. They both got into the regular army as commissioned officers. One in the Sixteenth United States Infantry and the other in the First United States Artillery. What their career was in the army I do not know. I think they are both dead now.

This corner above mentioned was afterwards occupied by the *Detroit Free Press,* and Bagg, Barns & Co., with a fine brick building. In 1827 and later the corner opposite, towards the river, was occupied by a small bakeshop run by a Mr. McLaren. The Eagle tavern adjoining was put up shortly afterwards by B. F. Farnsworth, I think; John Campbell, father of the late John Campbell (at one time bookkeeper for the board of public works), I remember, was instantly killed when this building was in process of erection by falling from one of the upper stories.

This tavern was well patronized and was kept at various times by Mr. Davis, Tomlinson & Graves, Horace Heath, lately deceased; by the father of Mrs. John Drew (whose name I do not remember. Mrs. Drew owns or did own the old Board of Trade building on the corner of Jefferson Avenue and Griswold Street.) Other parties continued there in the tavern whose names I have forgotten.

The father of Mrs. Drew came very near losing his life here in this house. In the office sitting-room he noticed a small box standing on the floor, and, presuming that it belonged to some guest in the house, he picked it up and tossed it into the baggage room adjoining. No sooner had it touched the floor, when, bang! it went off like a cannon, knocking the old man down and making a total wreck of the baggage room. The box contained an infernal machine and was waiting for something of the kind to happen to it. For what particular person it was intended to surprise, was never known or found out.

In 1827, Asa Madison occupied a large building just below the Eagle, as a blacksmith and repair shop. Some years after it was turned into the Buena Vista hotel.

Opposite the Eagle tavern was the dyeing establishment of Rossiter, the only one in the city, and his dwelling as well; adjoining was Joseph Campau's barn (the Campau lot extended through to Woodbridge Street.) A short distance from this barn was a double frame dwelling, one story and attic, with dormer windows. Adjoining was the Meldrum house, a large wooden building, brown and unpainted, and, when I first knew it, it was used as a tenement house. It was said that Sheldon & Reed, in 1817, before removing to Griswold Street, printed the *Detroit Gazette* in this building. The building was destroyed by fire about 1848.

Opposite this Meldrum house was the United States hotel, kept by a Mr. Crawford, on the corner of a narrow street that led from Wodbridge Street down to DeGarmo Jones's dock, where the steamer Henry Clay used to land, also the steamers Peacock and William Penn. When we landed from the Henry Clay in 1827 we all came up this street afoot, across Woodbridge Street, and on up through a narrow alley, between the Campau lot, the Meldrum house and Cooper building to Jefferson Avenue.

Just below the United States hotel was the small storehouse of Henry I. Hunt, the only house saved from the fire of 1805. It was taken down in 1830.

Mr. James Williams carried on for many years, until he died, a flour, feed and produce business between this United States hotel locality and Wayne Street. Mr. Williams built and ocenpied the brick dwelling that stood on the corner of the alley and Griswold Street, where is now the Moffat block.

Adjoining the Jones warehouse was that of Shadrach Gillett, afterwards Gillett & Desnoyer (Charles R.) It is still standing, I think, and has been mentioned before. And how diminutive it looks, alongside of its neighbor, the Detroit & Cleveland line brick warehouse. Yet in its day it was considered quite the thing and was sufficiently large for all purposes.

Canniff & Scott in 1837 had a general grocery store on the northwest corner of Shelby and Woodbridge Streets, and carried on the business there until the death of Mr. Scott. It was quite a lounging place for the old heads of Detroit. Mr. Scott was the father of our well-known genial and witty friend, Jim Scott.

Diagonally across from Canniff & Scott's, a Mr. Clark had a bakery. It had a square corner with a wide double door, which, when Shelby Street was in good condition in the winter, the boys took for use in sliding down hill. The street where it crossed Woodbridge Street diverged a little to the left, and the cousequence was that, sometimes losing control of their sleds, by design or otherwise, the boys would run bang! through these corner doors into the shop, creating no end of a row with the old man Clark. But boys will be boys. Besides Clark had two boys himself.

What a glorious pastime this sliding down hill was. In those early days Woodward Avenue from the market to the river, as well as Griswold, Shelby and Wayne Streets, were in use night and day, in the winter time, when in condition by the boys with their sleds at the peril to themselves of life and limb and to pedestrians as well.

Larned Street was opened up to the Dequindre farm in 1827 but Congress street was not opened up any farther than St. Anne's church until a short time after. When it was opened up through the church property, it left a triangular lot, fronting on Congress Street and Cadillac Square, which the church, or Bishop Foley, still holds, I think.

I do not call to mind any residents of upper Larned Street in the early times, except "Chris" Babe. Chris was C. C. Trowbridge's hired man for years and years, and always drove the cart when the family took an outing. He was an all around good fellow and faithful man. He was an especial favorite of the boys. His house was on the west side of Larned Street, just above Russell. His wife, a slight built German woman, was a merchant in a small way. She kept in the front part of the house a small stock of worsteds, patterns, needlework and all sorts of small articles dear to the woman's heart. Mr. Bacon, a little later on, had his school on the southeast corner of Larned and Russell Streets.

There were no buildings or residences beyond Brush Street, of any note, except, later on, the United States Barracks, which have been mentioned before. The rest of the land here was a wide common, relieved occasionally by some market gardener who had an acre or two under cultivation. It remained so for many years, but of course now it presents a widely different aspect, with its compactly built streets, stretching far beyond the old barracks site, teeming with a busy population. That it was a wide common, may be inferred from the fact, that, in 1826 or 1827, the city bought some few acres here, on the Beaubien farm, for a cemetery, Protestant and Catholic. My father was the first person to be buried out there in May, 1827, and I remember, the bars of the lane, skirting the line of the Beaubien farm, where now Beaubien Street crosses Jefferson Avenue, had to be taken down to let the funeral cortege through. Not a house in all that wide expanse. And now how changed!

Major Whipple lived on the corner of Larned and Randolph Streets in a large, commodious house built of hewn logs that were always whitewashed. He was the father of Judge Whipple, Lieutenant-Colonel Whipple, Michigan Volunteer Infantry, and Miss Mary Whipple. The major had been an officer in the United States army and had served with distinction in the war of 1812.

The southeast corner opposite was occupied by the Clark and Andre families and Captain Phearson, old French residents. Jim Clark was quite a noted individual; perhaps some will remember him. He was a fighter from "way back" and always prominent on election days. I think General Ord, United States army, was a relative of the Andre family. Adjoining the seminary towards Jefferson Avenue, was the Watson residence, parents of John and James Watson, the dry goods merchants, also of Mrs. Judge O'Flynn.

On the opposite corner was the St. Clair Catholic seminary, where many of the daughters of prominent citizens, both Catholic and Protestant alike, were educated. The building is still standing. Before this, about 1832 or 1833, Mr. Edwin Jerome had rooms in the upper part of this building where he taught day and night school, his first attempt at school teaching here. I was one of his pupils. The Jerome family occupied the rest of the building.

Adjoining Major Whipple's was Noyes' livery stable, but some little distance back from the street. Partly in front of the livery stable and the lot adjoining was where the circus companies of those days used to pitch their tents—Blanchard, Dan Rice and many others that I fail to recall. They were all single ring circuses, too, where one could see, hear and enjoy the whole business to his heart's content, and not lose one jot of those side-splitting jokes that came from that wonderful individual, the clown, in his motley garb. His "here we are again" rings in my ears now.

Adjoining this space was the school of the Lyon sisters, for young ladies, in an old-fashioned, typical, French house. Opposite was the residence of Father Richard, which he occupied until his death. The house was a large, unpretentious wooden building, with a large double door in the center, but significant in this, it was said (and at the time it was the common belief), that in donating the square of land on which this house and St. Anne's church were located by the governor and judges, it was stipulated that the gift would hold good only so long as the building stood. Whether this was so or not I do not know, but I do know that Father Richard's successor had the building entirely encased in brick and it was said that it was done for the purpose of holding the property agreeably to the requirements of the grant made by the governor and judges.

It was said that Father Richard was so studious and patient in his search after knowledge that he actually counted the eggs in a whitefish. How many millions, history fails to tell. Here, too, in this priest's house, ate, slept and told their beads, Jos. Mettez, sexton of St. Anne's (who tolled the bells), the philanthropist, Father Kundia; Father Shaw, who in his youth was an officer in a British cavalry regiment, and was at the battle of Waterloo; Pere Badin, Bishop Rese and, last of all, the good, genial, laughing Bishop Lefevre.

Across Cadillac Square, where now the county buildings are, was an old French built house, belonging to the Brush estate, presumably a farm house, and in the rear was quite an orchard.

Mr. Horace Jerome, father of the late George and Governor Jerome, occupied this house, among others, for a while, when the family first came to this city. Alpheus White, livery stable keeper, afterwards occupied it for many years, until it was torn down and the old orchard passed away.

Colonel Garry Spencer lived on the corner of Randolph Street, adjoining, and did for some years. Peggy Welch, a notorious character, owned a house on the opposite corner to Colonel Spencer's, much to the disgrace of the good name of the neighborhood. She had received repeated requests from her neighbors to vacate the premises and had been threatened that if she did not comply she would be forced to do so, to all of which she turned a deaf ear.

Dr. J. H. Bagg was a member of the common council at the time this occurred and he originated and carried through that body the resolution or order to tear down this house of "Peggy's" as a public nuisance. She, learning of the proceedings of the council, said she would not go, hit or miss. The house (after seeing that all the inmates were safely out and the goods and chattels set out in the street) was torn down and destroyed, in pursuance of the order of the council, in the face of day, by the late Alexander H. Stowell, then marshal of Detroit. Of this affair, Mr. Stowell, in his biography read before the Detroit Pioneer Society, says: "It was rather a high-handed measure thus to invade and destroy private property, but being directed to do so, Alexander did it." If there are any living who knew Stowell they may well believe him. I was an eye-witness of the destruction of this house.

There were two or three houses besides those I have mentioned on Cadillac Square, then Michigan Avenue. One of these was the double brick occupied by David Cooper and Charles Jackson. It stood about where the central market now is. There were only two or three buildings on Larned Street between Randolph and Bates Streets, one of these being St. Anne's stone church, built by Father Richard and his congregation, directly after the fire of 1805. It was demolished so recently that it is not necessary to go into a description of it here. But I may be pardoned if I dwell on a few incidents in its connection.

Father Richard I remember quite well. I often heard him preach and witnessed him officiate at high mass frequently. He was a familiar figure in the streets of Detroit in the early days, particularly at the time he was running for Congress. All respected, esteemed and loved him, and at his death, by cholera, brought on by his personal devotion and attention to those affected by that dread disease, the entire community went into mourning. For nearly three days his body lay in state, propped up in his coffin, in front of the high altar in St. Anne's, and I am sure nearly every one in the city and county round about considered it his loving duty and privilege to take a last look at the face of the spiritual father, the friend of all, the loved and honored citizen.

My earliest recollections center around this St. Anne's Church. I attended the Branch University School, directly opposite on Bates Street, for many years, and all the boys were more or less in evidence on the festal days of the church, and sometimes at high mass. I seem to hear now, as I did in reality hear then, on week days, the pealing of the organ of St. Anne's and the chanting of the choir as the music swelled out into the summer air and was wafted over the street, filling our school room with melody and hushing its hum.

Another feature of St. Anne's, and indeed of all Catholic churches of that day, was the presence at church of the young men of the parish, who invariably came, on their little French ponies, from up and down the river, fastening their animals during service to the fence palings that surrounded the edifice. The fairer portion of the worshippers, elderly persons and children, came in their French carts, the younger riding standing up. I presume the girls feared to muss their dresses. The carts differed from the one-horse carts used in the city in this respect: the body was composed of slats and was high enough to enable the occupants to ride in an erect position, and in this way the cart would hold more passengers. I presume many will bring this to mind, as I do. These carts used to be quite a feature on the Canadian side of the river, as well as here, on a summer Sunday, the objective points being the Catholic church at Sandwich and St. Anne's here, the two churches drawing all good Catholics to their folds from up and down the river. After church, to see the long procession of carts filled with gaily dressed French girls, wending their way homewards along the road that skirted both sides of the river, was a sight to be long remembered. Those who came on ponies, after church let loose, used to scurry home at a breakneck pace, running their ponies as though they had been sent for the doctor. I used to think that they just came to church to have a good race home.

On the east side of Bates Street, between Larned Street and Jefferson Avenue, where is now the Franklin House, John Garrison built and occupied what was called the "Yankee Boarding House." He was the father of the late John J. Garrison. He also had a son, Willis, younger than John J., who was a great chum of mine, and with whom I used to spend much of my time, at the Yankee boarding house, when not in school. Willis was quite a genius, one of his acquirements being the painting of interiors with patterns, called theorems, I think, cut from paper by himself, and designed by himself. Wall paper at that time was quite expensive; indeed, I do not think it was in use here at all at that date. He decorated the walls of the rooms of the boarding house in this manner, and I was much interested in the proceeding. This Yankee Boarding House enjoyed a large country patronage. On the corner opposite, the widow McMillan lived in a commodious house (log), and she, too, kept boarders. Mrs. McMillan was a quaint, Quakerish, motherly old lady, with bright red hair, the champion and good friend of all the boys who attended the nearby school, for one reason among others because she had boys herself, who attended this school. I remember one in particular. Ananias was his name; he was a refractory youth, and she seemed to be always wanting him, and he never seemed to be on hand. She used to stand at her door (I seem to see her now) and sing out at the top of her shrill voice, "AN-A-NI-AS." It was repeated so often that it became very familiar; so much so that one of the boys of the school, the late Henry M. Roby, while on a trip to Lake Superior, many years after the good old lady had gone to her reward, remembered it to good advantage. The steamer on which he was making the trip called at Silver Islet, at which point Alex H. Sibley (a former schoolmate who also knew Mrs. McMillan) was located. After stepping on the dock Roby sang out, "AN-A-NI-AS" at the top of his voice, which soon brought Sibley to his side. Mrs. McMillan's husband was shot by the Indians, a short distance from their home, on the outskirts of the city, near the Campus Martius, in 1812.

In after years Dan Whipple occupied the premises opposite the present Franklin House, with a bowling alley, saloon and restaurant. It was for many years the chief place of its class in the city, and held precedence above all others.

For at least fifteen years Dan held sway there, keeping up always the first-class reputation of his establishment, and acquiring a comfortable fortune. He abandoned it only to go into a less trying business, the keeping of a billiard saloon, and the second one of any note in the city. All will remember it, and also the name of his marker and assistant, John Seereiter, the almost champion billiard player of the United States. I say "almost," because at that date his friends and admirers claimed for him the title of champion and maintained it until Mike Phelan, of New York, defeated him in an arranged game, of which I was an eye-witness, that came off at the Fireman's Hall, lasting from early gaslight until broad daylight. Thousands of dollars changed hands on the result, as it attracted crowds of interested people from all over the United States. All will remember that match, of course, as the details have been many times repeated in the newspapers of that day and since.

It was at Whipple's that the "boys" of that day gave all their "Petite Soupire," the premises not being large enough for an extensive banquet. Barney Campau gave us a Fourth of July spread on his coming into his inheritance, which was a swell affair for those days; Wm. G. Lee, of the Bank of St. Clair, on his birthday, and Captain Fred Wheeler, of the propeller Hercules, on the occasion of his marriage. The boys entertained the Detroit officers of the First Michigan Volunteers that went to Mexico, the night before they left. Their guests were Lieutenant-Colonel A. S. Williams, Adjutant Jas. E. Pittman, Captains Jas. M. Williams, Walter Deane, and Lieutenants Pitcher, King, Whipple, Schwartz and McNair. On every Fourth of July for years the gay boys of Detroit made of this locality their headquarters, and it is safe to say that not before or since, with the exception, perhaps (and that in a limited way), of Bull & Beard's restaurant under King's corner, and Wm. Carson's further down Jefferson Avenue, has there been in this city an establishment just like Dan Whipple's. The premises were far from being pretentious, inside or out, but the larder was beyond criticism, and another attraction was the absolute freedom Dan accorded his guests—for you see, he was a *bon vivant* himself.

Well, I quit all this after I married, and Dan, too, quit this particular line, as before mentioned. Before leaving the subject, however, I call to mind some of the older heads of that day, who were well up in this community, who used to frequent "Whipple's Coffee House," such as David Smart, Alex Newbould, the brothers Randolph, Charles Ducharme, Walter Ingersoll, Jed Emmons, Willie Gray, Wm. Lyster, Dr. Eggie, Dr. Scovell, Colonel Grayson, Josh. Carew, Curt Emmerson, Marsh Mead, Theo. Williams, Tom Edmonds, General A. S. Williams, Geo. C. Bates, and many others whose names I do not now recall, but the place was the Mecca of that day towards which all masculine faces, on pleasure bent, were turned.

Some of those who were to be found at the Bates Street coffee house any evening in the week have distinguished themselves in politics, law or arms; some today are found among the solid and substantial business men in the city. When the place was in the full tide of its popularity the Brady Guards—Detroit's pioneer military organization—was in its glory. Distinguished visitors were always entertained with a bird supper at the coffee house, and after drill was over the gallant guardsmen were in the habit of repairing to Whipple's.

Strellinger, the brewer, kept this place along in the early sixties, his family occupying a portion of it. A sort of a literary club used to meet there evenings. Among its members were Colonel Fred Morley, Wm. Gray, Dr. J. B. Scovell, Lyman Cochrane, Thos. Shields, John Hosmer, Frank Baker, myself and others whose names have escaped me. No cards were ever played; it was "a feast of reason and a flow of soul" truly. It would be interesting reading at this date if a record had been kept of the good things said and discussed at those gatherings. One of Strellinger's sons, the one that went upon the stage, begged the privilege from his father to wait on this crowd, and was allowed to do so. He assigned as his reason for the request that it gave him opportunities to enjoy the literary treat that was nightly presented there. This early experience of his led him to adopt the stage as a profession.

I used to meet him often in after years, and he always assured me, as well as others, of the fact that his early contact with the members of that club convinced him that he was fitted for better things than running a lager beer saloon. All know of the phenomenal success that he attained in his profession. It is safe to say, I think, that the elder Strellinger did not lose money in this venture.

"Buck" Birmingham and then Chas. Richter succeeded Dan Whipple and Strellinger. They kept up quite well the reputation the place had acquired under its former proprietors. Charles Richter was and is one of our most reliable German citizens, and knows how to keep tavern, as I can testify, having boarded with him at one time for about five years.

On the University lot, where is now Farrand, Williams & Clark's drug house, "Protection Engine Company No. 1" had its engine house, a small wooden structure, just large enough to accommodate the "machine." Hose carts were not known then, the hose being realed on the engine.

In the rear of the engine house, on the corner of Congress Street, was the brick schoolhouse (branch of the University) where the youth of that day and for many years afterwards wrestled with the various pedagogues, and the worrying lessons and tasks given them.

The first teacher in this school house that I remember was Juba Barrows. He was competent enough but was irritable and passionate to almost the last degree; he had no patience with the boys and they, on their part became so unruly, that he was forced to quit. The next one was Edwin Jerome, who was a success. He ruled with kindness and discretion but was exceedingly firm with the bad boys, and there were many such. He used to join the boys in their sports after school-hours, particularly in the ball games. He was always either pitcher or catcher, when the "ins" were out, and woe be to the boy making bases, when he was on deck, as his aim was unerring. He was followed by Charles Wells, who made a very good teacher, but he had a bad lot to govern. He was assisted by his brother, John Wells. The latter had charge of the younger and quieter pupils down stairs, and the former, those older, and inclined to be fractious, upstairs. It was during the fall, winter and spring season, only, that the reign of the older boys lasted.

When the boats laid up in the fall, many of the younger hands employed on them took advantage of the time until navigation again opened up, to acquire as much book-knowledge as was possible. This element was inclined to be rough and unruly. Charles Wells had many a tussle with some of them, but being a large, athletic man, always came out ahead.

A climax came, along in the early spring, about ball playing time. All of the boys were the owners of one or more balls, and were continually dropping them on the floor in the schoolroom, which was strictly against orders, and Mr. Wells was sure to chuck any into the fire that he got hold of. One forenoon a ball rolled directly in front of his desk. He grabbed it at once and into the stove it went. In a brief space of time there was a deafening report, the stove was wrecked and the ashes were scattered all over the room. The ball had been filled with powder to catch the old man. Well, we had a vacation that day and next. Mr. Wells tried the best he could to find the culprit, but failed.

The next teacher was D. B. Crane. He was well up in Latin and Greek, and taught those languages successfully. Taking him all in all, he was the best all around teacher that had appeared in Detroit up to that time. He was also a student in chemistry, had an extensive laboratory in the building, and gave weekly lectures to us boys, illustrated with interesting and brilliant experiments, that were a marvel to us. His chief assistants in the chemical departments were the late Edmund R. Kearsley, of Berea, Ohio, and the late Talcott E. Wing, of Monroe.

Mr. Crane's younger brother, Ambrose, had charge of the younger boys in the minor branches. Old "D. B.," (as the boys used to call him), ruled more through kindness than the rod, though he did not spare the latter when occasion demanded it. He used quantities of snuff, almost constantly flecking it from off his ruffle shirt bosom.

When Mr. Crane quit the school, I quit my school days also, having got as much learning, I thought, as I could stagger under. Prof. Andrew Fitch succeeded to the school, I think, with Andrew Harvey as assistant. The old school building and extensive grounds passed away years ago to make way for the buildings and improvements that at present occupy the site. Before leaving this locality I may be pardoned for referring to two societies that dominated things in the old building outside of school hours, during Mr. Crane's and Professor Fitch's administration—the "Detroit Juvenile Library and Debating Society" and the "Detroit Thespian Society." The former had its birth in Mrs. Wilcox's barn. At first the membership of these two societies was confined to the pupils attending the "University branch," but after a while their scope was enlarged and many outsiders were admitted. Among the members of these two societies, I now recall the names of many a member who afterwards became well known in the many walks of life: Anson Burlinghame, J. Hyatt Smith, Orlando B. Willcox, Eben N. Willcox, E. C. Walker, William B. Wesson, Henry and William D. Whiting, John Biddle, Charles and Elisha McKinstry, Richard R. Elliott, L. H. Cobb, William Woodbridge, Edward M. Pitcher, Edwin A. Wales, J. Tallman Whiting, John A. Tucker, John and Robert Stuart, Seth P. Ranger, W. L. Whipple, Revel Roby, Levi B. Taft, and others. Burlingame, Smith and O. B. Willcox acquired a national reputation, Henry Whiting entered the army, became captain, was in the Mexican war and died in this city soon after; his brother died a few years ago, a commodore in the United States Navy. Charles McKinstry became a prominent lawyer in New York; his brother Elisha got to be a judge in San Francisco. John and Robert Stuart both served with distinction in the United States Navy, and W. L. Whipple died lieutenant colonel of a Michigan volunteer regiment of infantry, during the Civil War, at Nashville, Tenn. Levi B. Taft entered the law and became a judge. The others I have mentioned stayed in Detroit and were well and favorably known.

The society debates were often quite animated, and the interest taken in the organization by its members was marvelous, particularly when the election of officers was on. The excitement ran high and centered on the office of president especially. W. B. Wesson was the first to hold that office and he bent all his energies to hold on to it and he did. The opposition resorted to all methods of electioneering, buying votes, etc., to down him, but they never did so.

Wesson displayed the same spirit, or characteristic, as a member of "Engine Company No. 4." He was always after the office of foreman of the company, and he had it as long as he wanted it. I know something about his ambition in regard to the debating society and the engine company, as I was secretary of both.

The Thespian Society, during its life, put two or three plays on the boards, that were quite successful and proved that there was considerable talent among its members in that direction. Two plays that I remember particularly were the tragedy of "Douglass" and the farce of "Jeremy Diddler." In the former, J. Hyatt Smith took the part of Norval, a Mr. St. Clair, that of Lord Douglass and Edwin A. Wales, that of Lady Douglass. Smith was very effective as Norval and in the death scene his "Mother, oh, my mother," brought down the house. His rendering of "My Name is Norval," etc., was considered fine. Edwin A. Wales was a handsome boy and made a charming Lady Douglass, so much so that Eben N. Willcox, who played Sam in "Jeremy Diddler," could not keep from throwing his arms around him when the curtain was down.

To procure the necessary costumes challenged the ingenuity of the society. McKinstry's father, the colonel, owned the Detroit Museum, and the wax figures in it had to be denuded now and then to help out the Thespians. Mrs. M. M. Fisher, wife of a Woodward Avenue grocer, and daughter of Conrad (Coon). Ten Eyck, sheriff of Wayne County, who were boarding with the widow Willcox (mother of Eben N. and O. B.), and she a bride of a month, kindly loaned her wedding dress to Wales, and George Tucker, the hair-dresser on Jefferson Avenue, furnished the black ringleted wig, turning the young, smooth-faced boy into a most charming Lady Douglass. Smith and St. Clair were helped out by the museum wax figures. Charles McKinstry and E. N. Willcox in "Jeremy Diddler" were most effective, the former as Jeremy and the latter as Sam, his servant. J. Hyatt Smith, also, did some very good work, it was said, in female characters, as did Elisha McKinstry and the writer.

The Fireman's Hall, a two-story brick structure, with cupola and bell, took the place of the old wooden house on Engine Company No. 1. The upper part was devoted to the uses of the common council, the fire department and of R. E. Roberts, the then city clerk and secretary of the fire department, while the lower floor gave larger and more commodious quarters to the engine company and hose cart, which was duly appreciated.

In January, 1831, the city council house was the old hall, used for balls and other purposes in the Cantonment (Fort Shelby), which was removed when the fort was destroyed, to near the corner of Bates and Larned Streets in the rear of the Presbyterian Church. Before this the city fathers had used the first floor of the council house, corner of Jefferson Avenue and Randolph Street (where the water offices now are), but having leased that part to George R. Lillibridge for a coffee house (The Tontine), and a portion of the upper part to a Mr. Sears for a boys' school, they used this building, or hall, in conjunction with the church, the latter using it as session and Sunday school room.

The city and church continued to occupy this building until it was removed to make way for a new brick structure, in which were located the city offices in the upper part, and Fire Engine Co. No. 1 and Hose Co. No. 1, lower part, the church moving the Sunday school into their new brick session room on Woodward Avenue, adjoining it.

Opposite the University building on Congress Street, about the middle of the block, was a court or "cul-de-sac" that grew rushes and fleur-de-lis, survivors, it is presumed, of the Savoyard. In this court in an old-fashioned French house lived the widow Savenack. She was the mother of Charles Savenack, whom many must remember as the proprietor of the railroad eating house, located in the F. W. Backus warehouse, at the foot of Third Street, along in the early fifties. He did a large business and his place was quite popular.

I mention this Charles Savenack to show what pluck and perseverance will do. When a mere lad he used to peddle molasses candy to the schoolboys at one cent a stick. The sticks of candy were of goodly size and were stuck on a shingle that the vendor always had in evidence. Everybody patronized him, he was in with all the boys, and his business flourished to such an extent that he called in an assistant. He saved his money and one thing led to another until he blossomed out into the proprietor of the business I have mentioned. He died many years ago, comfortably well off. Many of the present day will call him to mind, I presume.

A very few traders were located on Michigan Avenue, now Cadillac Square, at that date, and they were not much in evidence until the vegetable market was built and occupied, and then they flocked to the place in great numbers.

Solomon Davis, with his brass, bell and key foundry, lived and flourished on the corner of Bates Street and the little park that once graced that locality, the latter having since been wiped out by the present police headquarters. This park was of small dimensions, it is true, but it was a charming little breathing place, wits its dense growth of trees, "an oasis in the desert," as it were. Robert P. Toms lived there for many years.

Uncle "Sol" Davis was a familiar figure to us boys and he always had a kind word for us and indeed for all others. He passed away a few years ago at a ripe old age, respected and honored by all.

During all the years "Uncle Sol" lived adjoining the little park he was captain of the "Big Fiddle" in the Baptist Church Choir.

Opposite Sol Davis's was the home of John Farrar, an early pioneer, who was the contemporary of his neighbor, Davis, and of the late Judge Caniff, also of Shubael Conant, Charles Jackson, Levi Cook, John Farmer, the Palmers, John Mullett and many others as well, and enjoyed the full confidence of all the community. He was the grandfather of Ford Starring, the present efficient cashier of the custom house. Farrar Street was named after him. He had a son, Frank, who was a schoolmate of mine, a sturdy, fearless boy. After leaving school he blossomed out into a marine engineer and carried his fearless spirit with him.

Another schoolmate, Joe Cook, brother-in-law of the late

John Owen, was of the same ilk. He, too, became a marine engineer.

Well, boys will be boys, and will get into queer places sometimes, and we were no exceptions to the rule. Whenever we did blunder into anything, if we had Joe Cook or Frank Farrar along with us, or both of them, we did not fear the consequences, as they were just "fighters" and athletes for a fact. Good, true men, they have both passed to the beyond.

The Brush garden was in this immediate locality. All the present generation will remember it as the residence of E. A. Brush and it is now supplanted by the Lyceum Theater, Ferry's seed house, etc. The fire of 1848 wiped out the Jefferson Avenue dwelling of Mr. Brush, and he then occupied the garden as his future home. Previous to this it was a free garden for the public. Most of the time it was run by D. C. McKinstry, who in addition to this was the proprietor of the two theaters near the present public library, as also of the museum that was on the corner of Jefferson Avenue and Griswold Street. Most of the actors performing at the theaters boarded at the garden, which lent an additional attraction to it. The garden boasted fine fruit and shade trees, shrubs, flowers and other attractions. Vine covered arbors were plentiful, in which patrons could have served to them almost anything in the way of refreshments, ices and soft drinks in the season, they might desire.

When the museum was destroyed by fire, the wax figures and curios that were saved were transferred, under the care of William Adair, to this garden, where they furnished another attraction. It was the only place of the kind in the city and was well patronized.

The following in relation to the "Michigan Garden" is taken from McCabe's Detroit City Directory of 1837, and is quite correct:

"Among the many improvements in the city, one of the most prominent is the Michigan Garden—laid out with much skill and taste by our enterprising citizen, Colonel D. C. McKinstry, and opened during the summer of 1835. It is situated in the northern extremity of the town, the entrance from Randolph Street, and occupying about four acres. The walks are admirably arranged, and fruit trees of every description, besides a choice selection of foreign and domestic plants, are distributed in graceful elegance throughout the numerous beds. It is decidedly a summer retreat from the bustle and cares of business, of no ordinary character, combining utility and gratification with pleasure, there being a commodious bath and splendid recess attached to the concern—also tasty summer houses in every part of the garden. The major with his usual 'go ahead' disposition has attached a choice menagerie to the establishment, and in short, spared neither pains nor expense to render it worthy the patronage and support of a liberal and discerning public."

Colonel Elijah Brush, father of E. A. Brush, was buried in the northeast corner of this garden. The grave and quite a plot of ground were enclosed by a high picket fence and the enclosure was filled with a dense growth of alder bushes, through which the headstone could be plainly seen. When Elmwood was opened the remains were removed to that place, as well as this headstone.

Had I been older I might have had unpleasant memories of this garden. My father, anticipating the arrival of his family here, had leased this ground and residence for a term of years. While making some needed repairs on the house, and ridding the cellar of one or two feet of water, he contracted a cold, which rapidly developed into inflammation of the lungs and resulted in his death. I was too young to realize our loss. I confess, though, to harboring a slight grudge against this locality, for if it had not been for my father's unfortunate connection with it he might have lived out his three score and ten years, whereas he died at the early age of 40, just on the threshold of life.

Beyond this Michigan Garden, on the north, all was farming land, except here and there a log cabin. The garden was also the headquarters of the patriots before and after the border war of that name (Hunter's Lodge No. 1).

On the triangular block, now the Hilsendegen block, were the German Lutheran Church and parsonage. Fire, I think, swept them away.

Colonel John Winder built and occupied a cottage where is now the St. Clair Hotel. He continued there for a number of years until he made the then considered mad purchase of ten acres of land out ·Woodward Avenue, paying, I think, $50 an acre for the same. There were only one or two buildings beyond the colonel's and they were private residences. I lived in this Winder cottage myself for five years after I married, succeeding S. Dow Elwood.

Croghan Street, that was, was open only across the Brush farm. One of our common councils recently had the name of this street changed to the one it now bears, ignoring the memory of the gallant soldier, Colonel Croghan, U. S. A., whose name it bore for so many years. "How soon we are forgotten."

Gratiot road, as it was then called, could boast of only a few scattered dwellings and now and then a business place. Breitmeyer's corner was a cow pasture of one or two acres and was owned by Sidney L. Rood, bookseller and stationer, who considered it of sufficient value to off-set a claim of $800 some eastern papermaking concern had against him. They accepted it reluctantly, but I imagine they got their money out of it, if they held it long enough. The transaction tickled Rood, much.

Monroe Avenue was occupied by private residences exclusively, on the east side from Farrar Street to near the corner of Woodward Avenue. Elisha Eldred's is the only one that I remember.

The widow Doty, mother of Henry, George and W. P., lived on the northeast corner of Monroe Avenue and Farrar Street and continued to until her death. Quite a number of the bachelor gentlemen in the thirties, forties and early fifties, made their homes with Mrs. Doty, from time to time, among them, David Smart, Charles Ducharme, Wm. Lyster, Addison Mandell, Thos. J. Cummings, Henry M. Roby, Alex. H. Newbould, James S. Conklin, David R. Pierce, Tom Edmonds and Dr. Egge. The Davenports lived adjoining Mrs. Doty for quite a while. I think John Farmer lived on the opposite corner of the same streets, in a frame dwelling on the rear of his lot and I also think he carried on his map-engraving and printing in the same house. This building was once a part of the old wooden building that stood on the corner of Griswold and Larned Streets, where is now the Campau Block. When Griswold Street was widened it was found that this building was in the way, so Joseph Campau, the owner, was notified to accept the award of the street opening jury or remove it, and he refused to do either. The common council ordered it sawed in two and John Farmer bought the part that was in the street and moved it to his lot on Monroe Avenue.

Farmer was a wonderful man in his way, a most competent surveyor and a finished engraver, as the work on his maps will show. Endowed with surprising energy, it always seemed to me that the steam engine within him, so to speak, must sooner or later wear him out, and it did. I do not think I ever met his counterpart. I knew him intimately and when I was in business sold thousands of dollars' worth of his maps.

The late Judge B. F. H. Witherell lived in a two-story dwelling where is now the Detroit Opera House. The judge lived here until later on in the early thirties, when he built and moved into his new residence on Jefferson Avenue, nearly opposite Christ Church. It was from the roof of the judge's woodshed on the Campus Martius that the late R. E. Roberts and myself saw Simmons hanged.

The hanging of this man Simmons and the details have been so often dwelt upon that I will not go into a lengthy description of the affair, but the scene of the hanging is, after all these years, vividly impressed upon my memory. I seem to see him now, marching at the head of the county and jail officials, preceded by a band of music consisting of drums and fife. His bearing was erect and defiant and he kept time to the music. After gaining the platform on the scaffold, which he mounted with a firm step, he came to the front, examined the crowd critically, glanced up at the noose dangling over his head and listened quietly to the prayer of the officiating minister; then the noose was adjusted around his neck, the white cap drawn down over his face, and he was swung into eternity. Thomas Knapp was the sheriff at the time, but his heart was too tender to permit him to do a job of that sort, so his friend, Uncle Ben Woodworth, kindly volunteered to do it for him. Ben was made of sterner stuff. There were no buildings to obstruct the view of the jail and the scaffold, and not a very large audience to witness his taking off, except the company of riflemen from Oakland County in their fringed hunting shirts, plug hats, etc., who acted as a body guard and formed in a hollow square around it.

Simmons was a large man, full habit, florid face, and when the drop fell it seemed as if his heavy weight must break the rope, the strain was so great. The great body swayed to and fro for a minute or so, the legs contracted two or three times convulsively and then all was still. I have witnessed since then, three executions by hanging at Sandwich, and this taking off of Simmons impressed me more than all the rest on account of the nerve he exhibited on the occasion, and his apparent disregard of death. Besides it was more spectacular.

The only buildings in the vicinity at that time were the jail, John Farmer's, Israel Noble's, the Methodist Church, and a few tenements occupied by colored people on the northeast corner of what is now Gratiot Avenue and Farrar Street. This church, of brick, built for the society by Charles Jackson, is still standing. It has experienced various fortunes, first a church, then a theater, then a private residence and now a restaurant. The Methodists had quite a struggle to build this church, and, after it was built, to maintain it. For a considerable time its only seats were boards placed on blocks, and the pulpit and its immediate surroundings were of planed pine boards, devoid of paint. After a time these things were remedied and the church flourished. I have heard all the noted Methodist divines of that day, in this section, hold forth in this church: Elder Gilruth, Elder Frazee, Elder Colclazer, Elder Baughman, Elder Blades and my esteemed friend, Elder Hickey; also many circuit preachers who now and then filled the pulpit.

Elder Gilruth was, I think, the most athletic and vigorous preacher of them all. He was a man of large frame and impulsive temperament, and, when he got warmed up in his work of warning his hearers to flee from the wrath to come, off would come his coat, vest and neckwear, he would pound on the pulpit with his fists and also with the Bible, and arouse the congregation to the utmost, some, in their fervor being hardly able to restrain themselves. One old colored woman, I remember in particular. She would always get the "power," but more so under Elder Gilruth's preaching than that of any of the others. On these occasions she used to jump from her seat near the pulpit (the "Amen" corner,) and continue to jump and shout "amen," "glory," etc., until she reached the church door when she would quiet down and return to her place.

Colonel Dorus M. Fox, in an article written some time ago, tells of being present on one occasion at this church and witnessing the scene I relate. I think he must have been there at the same time I was.

An itinerant Methodist preacher by the name of Mitchell while delivering a sermon in this church, said to Generals Cass and Macomb, who happened to be present: "You, General Cass, and you, General Macomb, will burn in hell fire if you do not repent." What effect this fierce warning had upon the distinguished gentlemen is not recorded.. And on another occasion, said, when the choir began to sing the hymn given out, he said: "Stop that ungodly big fiddle till we get done worship."

Elder Baughman had the most stentorian voice of any Methodist preacher I ever heard. There were but half a dozen houses around the church, and in the summer time with the windows open his voice could be heard all over the neighborhood. We used to live, then, on the corner of Woodward Avenue and John R. Street and I have often heard his voice at that distance.

The late Elder Hickey, like Elder Baughman, was once noted for his powerful voice. The Indians gave him the name which in their tongue meant "thundering man." It was reported that his voice, while preaching, could be heard one mile away in the quiet of an evening hour. An aged lady said to him once: "I used to hear you preach over fifty years ago." He replied: "And you didn't have any trouble to hear me, did you?" She answered "no."

Elder Colclazer was a handsome man and an effective preacher. He was a bachelor and the idol of the feminine portion of his congregation, could boast of any number of pairs of slippers and had dressing gowns galore, the gifts of his admirers.

The church continued here until it was sold to Colonel D. C. McKinstry, who turned it into a theater. With the proceeds of the sale the society purchased a lot on the corner of Woodward Avenue and Congress Street, where now is Rayl's hardware store, and erected a small wooden building for their own use.

Israel Noble, sexton and caretaker of the church, lived on the southeast corner of Farrar Street, opposite, in a small two-story house. His wife and the wife of Charles Howard, engineer of the city water works on Woodbridge Street, (Sisters Noble and Howard), were the mainstays of the church choir at that date.

The jail, in front of which Simmons was hanged, was an imposing stone structure, with a cupola containing a bell. This jail has often been described; it occupied the present site of the public library. I was inside of this jail quite often, visiting my chum and schoolmate, Brad Thompson, son of Sheriff Thompson, the then keeper, who, with his family, used the living rooms. Over these were two rooms used to confine delinquent debtors. I used to be quite interested in these two rooms. In one of them an inmate had cut his throat, the blood from the wound bespattering the walls and leaving a stain which, it seems, was never gotten rid of. In this room was a large coffee mill, fastened securely to a wooden bench so that it would not wobble. Brad Thompson used to say that the mill went like fun every night, operated presumably by the spirit of the suicide I have mentioned. The other room had been used by an insane person who had covered the walls with the most comical charcoal sketches imaginable. Why they were allowed to remain there I cannot imagine.

Sheriff John M. Wilson succeeded Sheriff Thompson and it was during his administration that the negro riot occurred. It was about the middle of June, 1833, occasioned by the arrest of Thomas Blackman and wife, fugitive slaves from Kentucky. The woman escaped from jail and the man was rescued from the sheriff by a crowd of colored people as he was escorting him from the jail to a carriage to convey him to the dock en route for Kentucky. His rescuers hustled him across into Canada. Sheriff Wilson was borne down by the crowd and beaten with a club, having endeavored to defend himself by discharging his pistol. His injuries, it was feared for a time, would prove fatal. Great excitement ensued, the Presbyterian Church bell rang an alarm, the cry "To Arms" was shouted through the streets and men with guns, pistols and swords were seen coming from all directions. The city council was convened by the mayor and a stringent ordinance passed which prohibited all colored people from being on the streets after nightfall without a lantern and a lighted candle in it. A curious ordinance, in the light of the present. It was many days before the excitement died entirely out. I was a distant witness to the whole affair, from my window in the University school building; from it I had an unobstructed view of the jail, I saw the crowd gather, saw Sheriff Wilson come out with his prisoner, the rush of the crowd, the flash of a pistol and heard the report. Then all was confusion in the school, all the scholars, ignoring Mr. Crane, broke for the outside and for the jail, where we spent the remainder of the day watching them bring in the scared colored people who were considered in any way connected with the uprising.

At that time and long after, the name "Kentuckian" inspired the greatest dread in the hearts of the colored people of this locality, and, indeed, among us boys he was looked upon as an ogre and a walking arsenal, and as if anything and everything horrible might be expected from him.

Grand Circus Park was then an unoccupied piece of ground, a common. Beyond, all was farming land, along the Pontiac turnpike, now Woodward Avenue. On the west side the dense woods came down to Elizabeth Street. On the east side of Woodward Avenue, out to about Warren Avenue, the woods were pretty well cleared off and the land was most of it under cultivation.

Major Kearsley owned a large farm out this way, beyond and adjoining the residence of the late H. C. Parke. Out on this road, near Royal Oak, lived quite a noted character, known to all the country round about, "Mother Handsome" she was called, and she kept a roadhouse. I often saw her and I think she was the homeliest woman I ever looked upon. She was of slight build and stature, with a face much disfigured with smallpox. The late A. C. McGraw relates of her the following. Himself and his father, with two or three others, started on a trip of discovery out on the Pontiac road, in the early part of 1830. He says:

"The day was warm and some of the party becoming thirsty, they inquired of two or three persons they met if they would soon come to water, but were told that 'Old Mother Handsome's' near Royal Oak, would be the first place. Mother Handsome was so homely she was called handsome. She had been through the war of 1812 as a camp woman, (laundress). When they arrived at the cabin, she stood in the door with a broom in her hand. My father was naturally polite and, hurrying up to her, said: 'Mrs. Handsome, you don't know how glad we are to see you.' 'Damn you,' she said, 'if you call me Mrs. Handsome again, I will break the broomstick over your head.' My father's surprise can be imagined. Her other name was 'Chapel.'"

She, however, was a kind, motherly, old lady and gave good entertainment to man and beast.

WOODWARD AVENUE IN THE THIRTIES.

TRIALS OF THE PIONEER RESIDENTS

I CALL to mind but a very few dwellings on Woodward Avenue in 1830, or for some years after. Where the Holden Road (now Palmer Avenue) came into Woodward was a dense forest; it seemed when you entered it as though you were about to explore the unknown. There is a small house now standing on the corner of Woodward and Warren Avenues that was there in 1830 and before. The Brush estate had a farm house at about Eliot Street, fronting on Woodward Avenue.

Considerably later on, B. G. Stimson purchased quite a plot of ground on the corner of what is now Stimson Place, and on it erected the dwelling that is there still. Many wondered why he went so far out when so many more eligible sites were available much nearer the city. Mr. Stimson and his wife were both young, genial and, being quite socially inclined, attracted the young, the gay and the dancing element to their hospitable residence. The only seeming drawback was the trouble getting there during the winter and spring, and sometimes it was more than seeming, as occasionally the snow or mud so blocked the avenue that it was quite an undertaking to do so, and taxed the capacity of the limited number of hacks and cabs to take care of the crowd. On these occasions the French cart was much in evidence.

B. G. Stimson learned the ship chandlery business, or what the needs of a sailing craft were in that line, on a voyage around the Horn before the mast, and up along the South American coast, on a sailing vessel, collecting hides, etc. He was a fellow sailor with R. H. Dana, Jr., who wrote that highly entertaining book, "Two Years Before the Mast." Our esteemed townsman, Harry W. Skinner, married a daughter of his.

Referring again to attending parties at the Stimson's: The pleasure derived more than paid for the discomforts.

Woodward Avenue (Saginaw turnpike), clear to Pontiac, during the rainy season, and particularly in the spring, was dreadful on account of the mud, and sometimes it took the stage coach the best part of two days to make the journey, and then the passengers had, at times, to get out and help pry the coach out of a mud hole with fence rails, and so on. I have witnessed the operation and thought at the time what dreary fun it must have been for a stage load of passengers to go bumping over a corduroy road for a long distance and then get suddenly landed in a quagmire and be forced to help the coach out of its plight.

Referring to the hardships of the early settlers in getting into the interior of Michigan from Detroit, I quote from the late Mr. S. V. R. Trowbridge's (father of General Chas. A. and Edward Trowbridge and brother of C. C. Trowbridge) account of his experience in that direction, published in the Pontiac *Gazette* some time in 1858:

"When I arrived in Detroit with my family some time about the first of May, 1821, I was obliged to hire a wild pair of French steers; no teams in the country.

"I loaded and started for the new home; quite late in the day arrived at Mrs. Chappel's, or "Mother Handsome," as she was commonly called. A turnpike had been made for five miles, and then a horrible road through swamps and marshes. After passing some distance it became dark, road terrible; wife walking, leading one, and carrying a great boy of thirty pounds. Oxen wild and ungovernable; spirits sunk; almost sorry that I ever undertook to bring my family to suffer and die in those wild woods. Presently two men came up who cheered us on, and agreed to stick by, if all night, to help with the team and children.

"Noble fellows! and long to be remembered; one was Mr. Miller, father of Mr. Miller, merchant of Rochester, Mich. Those men were indispensable at that time. I have often wished since then that I could do something for some of their children, as token of thanks to them. About 10 o'clock he saw a light from a window and finally got to White's tavern, and camped on the barroom floor; house filled with lodgers. Next day started in good spirits on a firm road for a few miles, and came to the Royal Oak tree—a tree named by John J. Hunt, Azra Baldwin and David C. McKinstry, commissioners to run a road to Pontiac. The other gentlemen had stuck the stake near this tree, and Judge

Hunt said, 'We will call this the Royal Oak.' I said to Mrs. Trowbridge, 'Perhaps you had better walk around this mud-hole; I am afraid you may be thrown from the wagon.' Mrs. Trowbridge got down with the children, and then commenced a continuous mud-hole that ran for six miles. That was a hard day's travel, through a heavily wooded country, mud to the wagon bed, children constantly becoming fast in the mud, my wife unacquainted with such a life—obliged to carry a heavy child. At one time I saw her sitting on a log crying, children fast in the mud. I then said, 'Cheer up, we are near the promised land. See that light ahead, that is the land of promise.' I called at Dr. Swan's and then came up to our new place, where we have lived ever since, the recipients of manifold blessings, temporal and spiritual.

"The only settlements in this peninsula then were a few in Oakland County. Oliver Williams, father of Gardner, Ephraim, Benjamin, Alpheus, Alfred and James, rolled the first wagon ever started from Detroit for the interior.

"I arrived on my land the 22d of October, 1821."

Rev. O. C. Thompson said that when he came to Michigan in 1831 the hospitality and good cheer of the pioneer families would never be forgotten by him, and he mentions particularly that of S. V. R. Trowbridge. From Detroit he went out in every direction, visiting all parts of the territory in search of a location, and finally settled on St. Clair.

* * *

The late Colonel John Winder built his residence (still standing) on his ten-acre lot about the same time that B. G. Stimson built his, and it was wondered why he, too, went so far out. Some years after, Rev. Dr. Duffield built and occupied a fine brick residence opposite Colonel Winder's. Both himself and Mrs. Duffield died there. After awhile the residence gave place to the present block of stores. At about the same time General John Robertson owned and occupied the lot on which is now Blessed's grocery store, his dwelling being on the rear of the lot.

In the rear of the Duffield residence, near the corner of High and Park Streets, was the fortification or earthwork erected by Colonel Croghan, protecting the outskirts of the city. It was called "Fort Nonsense," and was for the protection of the farmers against the Indians, a place where the former could rally in case of an emergency. It was surrounded by a moat which was crossed by means of a draw-bridge. The guns of the fort commanded it. In after years it was a great resort for picnics and pleasure outings. Why it was called "Fort Nonsense" I never knew. It was leveled many years ago.

Where the Methodist Church now is, John R. Williams had a large barn, and some distance back from it was a large two-story and a half brick house, also belonging to him. And that is all there was in that vicinity for many years.

As said before, Grand Circus Park was nothing but a common. The west side was an extensive pond of water, that furnished good skating during the winter and good shooting of ducks, plover, snipe and tip-ups during the season.

Just south of this pond, on a slight rise of ground, was Cliff's tavern, now the Whitney Block. When I first knew this tavern it was kept by an Englishman by the name of Busby, who came direct from London, England, with his family. He also brought with him three or four farmers from that vicinity with their families, who located in this county. They, the men portion, were typical English farmers, with their smock frocks, gaiters and hob-nailed shoes.

Mr. Busby always put me in mind of Mr. Pickwick, ever since I knew of the latter through our lamented friend, Charles Dickens, and whenever I see a picture of Mr. Pickwick I seem to see Busby. He had a beautiful daughter, a typical English girl; her name was Grace, I think. She married James Frazer, of Bay City.

This tavern used to be well patronized by the farmers living near the city, and by the general public. It was a grand place for shooting turkeys, geese and chickens Thanksgiving and Christmas. The fowls were securely fastened to a box or something some distance in the rear of the tavern, about where the Bagley residence now is, I should think. The crowd would load and fire from the back shed of the tavern, and when the day's fun was over they would spend the night in the bar-room, raffling off the victims of the day. There were no houses beyond the tavern in the direction of the firing, so there was not much danger from a stray bullet.

H. H. LeRoy afterwards occupied this tavern site and grounds with his dwelling and garden, he having been burned out on Bates Street in the fire of 1838.

Nearly opposite Cliff's tavern, where John R. Street comes into Woodward, lived Thomas Palmer, my uncle, in what was called a "rought cast house," two and a half stories high. It was quite a commodious dwelling and was occupied by him during the building of his new residence on the corner of Fort and Shelby Streets. Adjoining and including the ground on which stood the house, he owned one or two acres, which were enclosed at the rear and on the Woodward Avenue and Grand Circus Park sides by a rail fence, and were devoted to garden purposes. There were no business houses of any kind, from this point, on either side of Woodward Avenue, down to Jefferson Avenue, it being given up entirely to private residences and continuing so for some years.

Those that I can call to mind as residing on this avenue the time we lived there and up to 1850 were, next to Mr. LeRoy, Mr. Petty, he being in the employ of the American Express Co.; Mr. Manchester, clothing merchant; William King, clothing merchant; Benjamin Vernor, Dr. Brodie, David R. Pierce, George McMillan and William Stead. The last-named lived on the northwest corner of Clifford Street. On the opposite side of Woodward Avenue, to John R. Street, were Dr. Stone's sanitarium, a double dwelling owned by Dr. Scovell, and the residences of James Abbott, Dr. Kane and Dr. J. A. Brown. Samuel Bates owned and lived on the corner of Clifford Street, where is now the "Sugar Bowl" candy store; he also owned the house and lot adjoining. I think the property is in his heirs to this day. I think M. F. Dickinson owned the two adjoining houses. General John R. Williams owned and lived in a small cottage on the corner of Grand River Avenue, where is now William H. Elliott's dry goods store. The general died in this house, and this property is now in the McKinstry heirs.

* * *

Those who lived on the opposite side of the avenue, between John R. and State Streets, I am unable to recall, except N. T. Ludden, Alanson Sheely, John Atkinson, Lemuel Goddell, and David Dwight, father of the late David Dwight, the lumberman. Mr. Dwight lived in a small cottage where Rolshoven's store now is.

On the same side of the avenue with Elliott's dry goods house, and on the opposite corner of Grand River Avenue, lived, previous to 1849 and after, Edward Shepard, the hardware merchant, in quite an attractive residence, surrounded by fine trees and shrubbery. Mr. Godfrey owned some lots adjoining, and, I think, lived there; at all events, later on he improved the property by building the substantial Godfrey Block thereon.

Dr. Joseph H. Bagg also lived, in 1839, where is now the Godfrey Block, and next to them lived Lawyer Ezra C. Seaman. Frank E. Eldred lived directly opposite.

Where Hunter & Hunter's dry goods house now is Labie (Barnabas) Campau built for himself a brick residence, and lived there until he died. His son, Barney Campau, occupied it afterwards for some time. The space between this and the corner of State Street was vacant for many years, until Mr. Wesson erected the present building. Continuing on the west side of the street, on the corner of State Street was the Methodist Church, afterwards St. Andrew's Hall. Perhaps some of our Methodist friends will recall Rev. Mr. Thompson, who presided so long and so ably over this church. Perhaps they will remember, too, what an ardent, earnest preacher he was. He was always carried away with his subject, and at the conclusion, he would almost invariably drop back into his seat in the pulpit, seemingly in a trance, eyes closed, with a happy smile lighting up his face. Thus he would remain for a brief moment, entirely oblivious to all surroundings.

I do not recall what was on the remainder of this block except what was called the "Checkered Store" and Farnsworth's shoe store, the latter on the corner of Michigan Avenue and demolished only a few years since. I think Martin Story lived along here about where Heyn's Bazaar now is. Story was quite a prominent citizen in his day. He held many offices of trust in city affairs. I knew him quite well when he was city marshal. He seemed always to hold the latter office. Mrs. Story was a daughter of Conrad Seek, who divided the honors with Colonel Garry Spencer of being the first merchant tailors in Detroit, about 1830. I recollect Conrad Seek well. He lived and had his shop on Jefferson Avenue, where the D. M. Cooper White building now is. He had a son (Bill Seek) who was a chum of mine. It is my impression that Alex. H. Stowell married a sister of Martin Story.

Alfred M. Story, a son of Martin, is still a resident of this city. He is quite well known, particularly among the theatrical fraternity.

On the corner of State Street and the avenue, where now is Kern's dry goods house, was Finney's Hotel. Daniel Goodnow, after retiring from the Michigan Exchange Hotel, resided in this block for some time. W. K. Coyl had a dwelling and grocery store on the corner where are now, Wright, Kay & Co.

The present city hall site (Campus Martius) was occupied mostly by the Michigan Central Railroad depot and by a female seminary. The depot buildings, or sheds, were on the corner of Michigan Avenue and Griswold Street; the seminary was on the latter street, and engine company No. 2 had its house on the northeast corner of Griswold and Fort Streets. The remainder of the campus was devoted to circuses and outdoor public meetings. R. N. Rice, superintendent of the Michigan Central Railroad, kindly donated a pagoda here for the use of speakers, bands of music, etc. "The Yellow Seminary," as it was called, from the fact that it was built of yellow Milwaukee brick, three stories high, occupied a portion of the site of the city hall. It was erected prior to 1835 by a corporation organized for the purpose of establishing a female seminary. The site for the school building was contributed by the governor and judges, with the understanding that when it ceased to be used for educational purposes the ownership should revert to the state. Mr. Kirkland was the first principal and was assisted in his work by his talented wife. Mrs. Kirkland was in fact the principal, and the school soon became known as "Mrs. Kirkland's school." The Kirklands remained for a few years and then other teachers followed. The association finally gave it up as a bad job financially and passed the property back to the state. The building was afterwards used by state officials and as a state armory, the latter under Adjutant-General Schwartz. When the city acquired possession of the building it was used for the offices of the mayor and other public officials, until torn down to make room for the present city hall.

Professor Kirkland, though learned, was a small, undersized man, meek and retiring, while Mrs. Kirkland was a woman of commanding presence, quite determined and somewhat aggressive. She was fully competent as a teacher and filled her part to the satisfaction of the seminary organization. She was an author, also; but I do not recall anything that she wrote before she came to Detroit. After leaving here and going west, she wrote "A New

Home in the West—Who Will Follow?" a very entertaining book which, I presume, many have read.

My uncle, Thomas Palmer, was one of the incorporators of this seminary, as I had sufficient reason to know. During the first winter of the Kirkland rule I was a member of my uncle's household, on the corner of Fort and Shelby Streets, and it came about somehow that I had to act as a sort of janitor of the building, sweeping out the school rooms and building the fires in the mornings. I do not remember that I brought in the wood, but don't think I did. But it was not much of a task anyway, only some mornings it was stinging cold, and besides the early rising did not quite suit me. But then I used to see the girls—some consolation.

The corner where the Russell House now is, in the early days, was enclosed by a cedar picket fence. In the enclosure was a small yellow house occupied by Dr. William Brown before he changed to Jefferson Avenue. Adjoining was a log building used as a school house. It had for a teacher Mr. Healey, who was clerk of the steamer Henry Clay when I was a passenger on her in 1827. It is said Eben N. Willcox was born in this yellow house.

After some years, the National Hotel succeeded this log house and Dr. Brown's corner. About the same time, the then new city hall occupied the center of Cadillac Square. It was considered a fine structure at the time, as was the National Hotel, S. K. Harring was the first proprietor of this hotel, I think. It had varied fortunes under proprietors, successful and otherwise, until, as the Russell House, under its present management, it has achieved permanent and deserved success.

This point was then as now one of the municipal centers of the city, full of life and business, notwithstanding the mud and ill condition of the streets at times. It was also the only polling place in the city. Sixty years ago there was not a stone pavement in Detroit and wood sidewalks were not too plenty.

Previous to 1835 not a single street in Detroit was paved. In this year Atwater Street, between Woodward Avenue and Randolph Street, was paved with cobble stones, through the efforts and influence of the late R. E. Roberts. In an article written by Colonel Nick Greusel on Old Times in Detroit, and published in *The Detroit Free Press,* September, 1866, he says: "Speaking of unpaved streets and mud. if Mrs. H. H. Brown is still alive may be she will remember when I carried her across Jefferson Avenue through mud two feet deep with her arms around my neck. I carried her from the Tontine Coffee house (old Council house) across to Major Kearsley's house on Jefferson Avenue, corner of Randolph Street. How many ladies would venture on such a journey these days, and yet it was a common practice for gentlemen to stoop down and carry ladies on their back across the muddy streets along in the thirties and early forties."

The first attempt at wood pavement was made by Julius Eldred, in front of his hardware store on Jefferson Avenue. It was composed of octagon shaped blocks of pine wood, a foot and a half each way, I would think. They remained down some years and wore well, and I don't know why the experiment was not repeated at the time. The city again tried its hand at paving, with stone after awhile, and paved with cobble-stones the square at the intersection of Woodward and Jefferson Avenues, and about twenty feet (in width) in to center of the latter avenue, down as far as some point just below the old Michigan Exchang, to First Street, I think. This pavement remained down for some time, two or three years, or until Jefferson Avenue was paved with the same kind of stone from curb to curb, its entire length, as far up as Dequindre Street.

It was an amusing sight, in the fall and winter, to see the horses hitched to the various conveyances, after ambling serenly along over this twenty feet of pavement, look around in wonder and surprise, when the wheels struck with heavy jolt the sea of mud, at the upper line of Woodward Avenue where it crossed Jefferson. I presume they thought it a "put up job." Woodward Avenue in the early forties was planked with two-inch pine, from Jefferson Avenue to the river, but it did not remain down for long.

Jackson, the colored barber, was the first in the city to start the running of one-horse cabs. He had two or three, and they were a great convenience. His headquarters for them were at his shop, one or two doors below the Ives Bank, on Jefferson Avenue.

There was one other public conveyance, which was always kept quite busy in the season, and that was a covered sleigh omnibus, the first and last one I ever saw with a stove in it. Mighty fine of a cold, frosty night, particularly when going to or returning from a party, with your best girl and the thermometer at zero or thereabouts. The remembrance of the enjoyment of the occasions in this sleigh omnibus is, at the present time, like the memories of a pleasant dream.

Land speculation ran high at that time, and almost every man that came here had his pocket full of money, expecting to invest it so as to make his pile before breakfast, as it were. Cities and villages were springing up in every direction, and city lots were being sold at auction and at privete sales at prices that doubled and trebled very quickly.

James Stilson, a name and personality well remembered by old settlers, was a prominent auctioneer in the earlier days. He had his rooms on Woodward Avenue, near Jefferson, and auctioned off lots upon lots in paper towns, at about $10 each. It was a glorious time for Stilson and bad for the other fellow.

Stilson was no less prominent in politics; he was an enthusiastic Democrat and an ardent supporter of the young and brilliant Stevens T. Mason, when he ran for governor on the Democratic ticket in opposition to C. C. Trowbridge.

Stilson was also a leader, and to quote a writer of that time, alluding to him:

"And here, too, he was again in his glory. No ordinary campaign would answer his purpose. The season had been wet and Woodward and Jefferson Avenues were about half a leg deep in mud porridge. Yet a grand Democratic procession was organized to pass through it. Mr. Stilson was the grand marshal. He rode a horse which was completely covered with a cloth of gold, and he himself was decorated with all the glories of a Grand Legion of Honor. And the way he rode at the head of the column was like Mars on the Captoline Jupiter. A small schooner, fully rigged and manned, and mounted on wheels, and drawn by six or eight horses, was an important feature in the line. And there the Democracy marched to the music of the Union."

Unfortunately for the narrative this schooner-rigged craft did not figure in this or any other Democratic procession, but it did occupy a prominent position in a Whig procession the day of the election for governor. The only polling place in the city was at the old city hall, now Cadillac Square, and, as may be imagined, things were quite lively in and around that locality on that day. The schooner was manned by a crew of Whig shipcarpenters from Oliver Newberry's shipyard, all stalwart, fearless men, prominent among them being George Irving, lately deceased, a host within himself. Irving was their leader. He was foreman at the shipyard as well, and not anticipating that trouble would happen to either schooner or crew, was tardy in joining his fellows. He got a tip from Uncle Oliver, who had just returned from the polls. While there he had detected signs in the air that there would be a scrimmage. On his way to the office, through the shipyard, he called Irving to him and said: "George, I have just been up to the polls, and it seems to me that our boys in charge of that schooner on wheels are going to have trouble. I think you had better take some more of the yard men up there and see about it."

And he did. Shortly after Irving had reached the scene the Democratic procession, headed by Stilson on his panoplied charger and himself in martial array, met the Whig procession, headed by the schooner, opposite where is the present city hall. The meeting was a clash, and a rush was made by the Democrats to capture the schooner. Then the fun began. It was a wild, fierce fight for a time, but the brawny ship carpenters came off victorious and were allowed to go on their way yelling. George told me this himself, and he related the circumstances with great glee.

The scene I have attempted to portray is vividly pictured in a painting by Thomas Burnham, a local artist of that time, and which is now the property of Mrs. Samuel Carson, of Detroit, mother of the late Mrs. A. S. Williams. Mrs. Carson recently loaned the picture to the Detroit Museum of Art. It is a true representation of the event. I was an eye-witness of the whole business.

The late Eben N. Willcox described the painting thus:

"At the right rises in magnitudinous proportions, with all the self-assertion of the reddest brick, with stone capped lintel and window and its little belfry, what was then known and accepted as a great architectural triumph, the city hall of Detroit, our Hotel de Ville. Scarcely less imposing, on the immediate right, with his banners flaunting in the third-story windows, proclaiming 'No Monopoly' and 'Stevens T. Mason for Governor,' sits Stilson, the Magnificent, under his cocked hat and on his grand war horse, marshaling the Democratic hosts to votes and victory—'Bumble the Beadle' not more important. Immediately under him an excited group, consisting of your whilom delightful 'By-Gones' correspondent, George C. Bates, Franklin Sawyer, editor of the

Whig paper, and Kingsbury of the Democratic sheet, with N. T. Ludden and Alanson Sheley—interested spectators, are hotly discussing the all-absorbing questions of the day. Apart in the right foreground stands a conspicuous figure, recognizable at once as that of the most noted Democratic politician of his day, the most public-spirited citizen, the most open-hearted friend of the poor—a peer of the realm—David C. McKinstry."

* * *

Stilson was a tall man of blonde complexion, notwithstanding which he entertained the idea, somewhat, that he resembled Napoleon, in person and mind. Like most auctioneers, he was impatient when the bidding was inadequate to the value of the goods he was selling. "I am a mean man, as mean as dirt," he would say, "but I feel quite at home in this company." On one occasion he was selling some furniture in a private house and put up a pier glass mirror worth about $50.

"How much am I offered for this fine French mirror," he asked repeatedly; but no one seemed inclined to bid. Finally some one bid a dollar. He was nettled but continued to sell until the bid went up to $4.

"All done," he said, holding up his hammer, and lingering, "all done? Well, gone."

As he said the last word, he struck the glass with his hammer, smashing it into a hundred pieces. I have mentioned before his extensive sales of lots in Michigan paper cities hundreds of miles from civilization. One in particular was White Rock City on the shore of Lake Huron, about ten miles north of Port Huron. It looked fine on the draughtsman's plans, but it is still innocent of human habitation.

Years after I saw this same Stilson, at the first state fair ever held in Michigan. It was located out Woodward Avenue, west side, about where Alexandrine Avenue is now. He had on exhibition in a tent four or five trained dogs of peculiar breed. They were certainly very cute and remarkably intelligent animals. The major in his old time style and manner expatiated on the wonderful things his dogs could do, and they bore out what he said of them. It was said that he died somewhere in Virginia.

General John R. Williams owned the corner where is now Kanter's Bank, and about 1835 built on it and the lots adjoining, a brick block extending to what was then the residence of Mr. David Cooper. The Wright Brothers occupied this corner for a long time with a general grocery store, and quite extensive, too. They had been stewards on Mr. Newberry's steamboats.

Adjoining the log school house on Woodward Avenue that I have mentioned, was the residence of a Mr. Gagnier, an old-time Frenchman, who was a woodturner and from whom all the boys bought their tops.

The Methodist Church stood on the corner of Congress Street. This church was dedicated July 20, 1834, and was a small wooden building with a basement, the latter being used for a Sunday school. In the rear of the church, on Congress Street, was the court martial and dancing hall of the Old Cantonment of Fort Shelby. It was formerly in the rear of the Presbyterian Church, corner of Woodward Avenue and Larned Street, where it did duty as Sunday school and session room and city court room.

The opposite corner, where is now Brown's drug store, was vacant up to the Presbyterian session room.

I imagine that the entire front of the block on Woodward Avenue, east side, between Congress and Larned Streets, must at one time have been used for cemetery purposes, for, in digging to place the foundations for St. Paul's Church and the new brick Presbyterian Church, the latter to replace the old wooden one, on the corner of Larned Street, the workmen disturbed a large number who were in the last sleep. I witnessed the laying of the corner-stone of St. Paul's Church, as also that of the Presbyterian, and the installation of Bishop McCoskrey, after the completion of the former. I think the bishop's sermons, his genial personality and his commanding presence can never be forgotten by anyone who was ever brought in contact with him.

I presume that many will call to mind Rev. Mr. Fox, his able assistant, who for so many years, with the bishop, "held the fort" in old St. Paul's Church. He lived at Grosse Ile, where he married a daughter of Colonel Rucker. Mr. Fox and his wife are dead. They left three sons. One of them, C. Crofton Fox, died at Grand Rapids not long ago. He was at one time, under Governor Luce, a member of the state military board, with the rank of colonel. What befell the other two boys I do not know.

For ten years, at least, during the ministration of Bishop McCoskrey, I scarcely ever missed a Sunday morning service, if in the city. A number of young clerks, with myself, owned a pew in the gallery of the church, and the bishop used to say, if he did not see us in our accustomed places of a Sunday morning, he knew that something must be up.

A charming man was the bishop. St. Paul's Church had the only organ in the city, except the one in St. Anne's Church. The leaders of the choir were Dr. and Mrs. Terry, Mr. Charles S. Adams and Charles Trowbridge.

The Presbyterian session room was a small brick building used by the society for Sunday and singing school purposes, also meetings and debates of the Young Men's Society, lectures, etc.

The Young Men's Society drew within its folds all the talented young men of the city, and their debates were always largely attended and eagerly listened to. They were intensely interesting and highly instructive; could hardly have been otherwise when the contestants were such men as Jacob M. Howard, James F. Joy, M. J. Bacon, G. V. N. Lothrop, Samuel Barstow, Jas. A. VanDyke, Jed P. C. Emmons, Geo. C. Bates, D. Bethune Duffield, William Gray, Levi Bishop, Franklin Sawyer and others of equal note.

The lectures that I recall particularly were those on chemistry by Dr. A. R. Terry, also his lectures on Morse's telegraph system. At that time the telegraph wires were nowhere beyond Buffalo, and nearly all were ignorant of its workings. The doctor had the wires stretched along on the walls, inside, with the operating instrument on the president's desk, and gave a satisfactory and enlightening description of transmitting messages by telegraph.

Dr. Douglas Houghton and Franklin Sawyer were the founders of the Detroit Young Men's Society. "Its object was the general diffusion of knowledge and a condensation of the talents and acquirements of the young men of Detroit, for intellectual and moral improvement. Lectures were delivered befort it, and debates conducted, which for the most part were characterized by a deep thought, acquirement and research." In 1837 it had 300 members, professional, mercantile and mechanical.

Here is a list of presidents of the society: Douglas Houghton, Jacob M. Howard, George E. Hand, George C. Bates, James A. Van Dyke, Samuel T. Douglass, James V. Campbell, E. C. Walker, D. Bethune Duffield, H. H. Emmons, G. V. N. Lothrop, C. I. Walker, Levi Bishop, H. P. Baldwin, Luther S. Trowbridge, S. Dow Elwood and Richard R. Elliott.

The society was organized in 1833 and ceased its existence in 1882.

Richard R. Elliott was, I think, the last secretary of the society, and I understand he is engaged in writing its history in full, from its beginning to its close, for publication in the near future. It cannot fail to be of the highest interest.

* * *

The singing school was quite an institution at that time and was conducted by E. P. Hastings, and his brother, David French, ran the "Big Fiddle." The young people of all denominations attended, but I record with sorrow and regret that many of the boys (myself among the number) did not do so for any good it might bring, but for the mischief there was in it. They had formed an aggressive society called the "Rowdy Club No. 1," the captain of which became a distinguished northern officer during the Civil War and is now a retired brigadier-general. The other members in after life filled various responsible positions. "Boys will be boys."

One of the objective aims of the club was the disturbance of the Presbyterian and Methodist singing schools, and they did it most effectually, by running in and out and slamming the entrance door, loud whispering, putting red pepper on the stove, greasing the big fiddle bow, and many other annoying things, until finally Alexander McFarren, the bookseller, volunteered to stand guard in front of the Presbyterian session room on singing school nights and keep the boys out. He knew them all, and managed to curb them somewhat.

The club finally met its Waterloo at the Methodist singing school. Two of its members went one evening arrayed in female attire, under the protection of one of its most stalwart and fearless members (since an officer in the Unites States Navy). A large delegation of the club was on hand, of course, distributed around in various parts of the room, away from the "wolves in sheep's clothing" and their champion.

The strange actions of these three soon attracted the attention of the singing master, Mr. Philbrick, and some of the girls in the class. One of the latter, more venturesome and plucky than the rest, proceeded to investigate them and found to her amusement that the two supposed females were among her most intimate boy admirers. The latter, with their escort, fearing exposure, broke for the door, but before they could reach it, it was shut and securely guarded, catching them in a trap. An officer was sent for, and they were bound over to appear at the recorder's court in the city hall. Well, they appeared before his honor at the stated time. They pleaded guilty, and the recorder, in view of their youth, let them off with a scathing lecture, that, I will venture to say, no member of the club present, and indeed no one of the large audience in attendance, ever forgot. I know myself and the three culprits never did. One of them, the captain of the club, was moved to tears when the recorder alluded to his widowed mother, the other two received the lecture with apparently stolid indifference. The recorder was Asher B. Bates, and when the three got clear of the court room, they vowed vengeance then and there, and if a fitting opportunity ever presented itself, they would take it out of his hide. But as time went on and the sober second thought asserted itself, they came to see that he was right and their animosity gradually died out.

As before said, one of these three, the captain, is now a retired brigadier-general, one died an officer in the United States Navy, and the other became an officer in the Mexican War, a merchant on Jefferson Avenue and a California Forty-niner, and died there. I record with sorrow, and also some little gratitude, that the sympathies of the girls attending these two singing schools were always, from some cause or other, on our side. This affair broke up the club, and the singing schools went on in peace.

The vacant lot on the corner of Woodward Avenue and Congress Street, adjoining St. Paul's Church, was afterward occupied by a two-story wooden building, in which L. Y. B. Burchard had a stock of general merchandise. Dr. John Ellis, almost the first homeopathic physician in Michigan, had his office in the second story. He died some years ago in New York City. Mr. Burchard was about the first one to venture into business on Woodward Avenue beyond Larned Street.

The Presbyterian Church on the corner of Larned Street, when I first knew it, was a small wooden building with an unpretentious steeple. The steeple boasted of a good, fair-sized bell, which was used for all church and city purposes. It was rung at 7 o'clock in the morning, at noon, at 6 o'clock in the evening, and at 9 o'clock at night by a city official. The bell rope came down into the pillared entrance of the church, so that anyone, in case of a fire, could give the alarm. "Hank" Wagstaff, brother of Captain "Bob" Wagstaff, was the bell ringer.

The Reverend Noah M. Wells was the pastor and continued in charge until the church building was sold to the St. Peter's Catholic Society and was removed to the corner of Bates Street and, what is now, Cadillac Square, the present site of McSweeney's billard room. It remained there for some years, until its removal into the Eighth Ward.

Colonel McKinney in his "Tour of the Lakes," in 1826, has this to say of Mr. Wells: "On seeing this minister, the Rev. Noah M. Wells, I was forcibly impressed with his fitness for the sacred calling. His countenance not only wears the expression of benignity but his entire appearance is that of a man of feeble health, which alone was calculated to interest me. The thin partition that seemed to be between him and the eternal world, made his exercises the more appropriate, and gave to his discourse a deeper interest."

I often heard Mr. Wells preach, and can bear witness to the impression the colonel got of his feeble and frail appearance in the pulpit; but outside, and in the daily walks of life he was most energetic. It is my impression that he outlived the colonel. He was a very loveable man. His son, William Wells, was a prominent hardware merchant here for years, an enthusiastic fireman and Brady Guard. This son died a retired farmer at Vienna, near Monroe, a few years ago.

The fine brick edifice that succeeded the wooden one was an ornament to the city, and all were justly proud of it. The Rev. J. P. Cleveland was, I think, the first pastor of the new church, and will be remembered by many as a most eloquent divine. He died quite recently, I think. This church was destroyed by fire in 1854, and the society built a new one where Hudson's store now is.

The choir of the Presbyterian Church was one of its greatest attractions, and quite equal to that of its neighbor, St. Paul's (though unassisted by an organ), which at the time would have been considered sufficient praise. The ladies composing the choir were Mrs. Henry H. Brown, Misses Emma, Octavia, Rebecca and Mary Brooks, Kate Hinchman, Harriet, Eliza and Mary Williams, Sophia Griswold, Miss Wendell, Miss Hastings and one or two others whose names I do not now recall. The gentlemen were—the leader, Eurotas P. Hastings, Mr. Henry H. Brown, Wm. B. Alvord, James M. Bradford, George Watson and others, and sometimes the brother of Mr. Hastings. David French presided at the bass viol, accompanied by Henry T. Cole on the flute. Mr. E. P. Hastings and his brother were born musicians, the latter being a teacher of music and followed the calling for a living.

The present site of the Merrill Block was owned by Robert Smart ("Bob" Smart, as he was familiarly called), who built the brick store on the corner of Woodward and Jefferson Avenues that I have before alluded to. He also had his residence in a two and a half story wooden building about midway between Larned Street and Jefferson Avenue, unpretentious and devoid of paint. It was set back from the sidewalk about twenty feet, with a row of trees in front.

Mr. Smart was a genial, jolly, Scotch bachelor and drew around himself all the "old boys" of that day. I have often seen sitting with him under the trees in front of his house of a summer's day, many of his old cronies, among whom I recall Commodore Brevoort, Austin E. Wing, Dr. Wm. Brown, General Charles Larned, Judge Caniff, Ben Woodworth, Peter Desnoyers, Joseph Campau, and many others. Mr. Smart passed to his fathers and soon after his homestead was swept away, and his heir and nephew, David Smart, replaced it with wooden and brick buildings for business purposes.

Mr. Amberg occupied the brick store adjoining the corner one on Jefferson Avenue, with a stock of clothing. Adjoining Amberg were Doty & McReynolds, auctioneers, and next was L. L. Farnsworth (Gothic store) with boots and shoes. The wooden stores were occupied by various tenants, the names of whom I fail to recall except George Davie and John Fay, who had a grocery and liquor store on the corner of Larned Street. The fire of 1852 swept away all these wooden buildings, and in due course of time (1854 or 1861) the entire Woodward Avenue front, from Larned Street to Jefferson Avenue, was replaced by the present Merrill block.

Later on Wm. S. Penfield was in the hardware business, with seeds and agricultural implements, about where O'Brien's grocery store now is. When the building was demolished, he removed to 210 Woodward. Penfield was an enthusiastic fireman. Mr. C. H. Buhl married a sister of his. Samuel Browning, son of F. P. Browning, who in the forties was clerk for the Noyes Bros. (hardware), later on started in the same business for himself at 117 Woodward Avenue. Thos. Berry, of the Berry Bros., glue manufacturers, had Browning for one of his first customers. Sam Browning said the glue was of such superior quality that it soon asserted itself and practically drove the foreign or eastern article out of the market. The public is quite familiar with it now.

John Owen, about 1830, occupied a house on the corner of Woodward Avenue and Fort Street, where is now McMillan's grocery store. He vacated it after the death of his first wife and Judge Horace Jerome, father of the late Governor Jerome and George Jerome, occupied it until his death, which occurred a short time after he moved into it. I attended his funeral.

I do not recall who succeeded the Jeromes; the next tenants I remember were John and Howard Webster, with stoves and hardware. I think the McMillans occupied this corner shortly after the Websters vacated it and they are still there. The McMillans, before this occupied the premises where is now the Metropole.

Adjoining the John Owen residence on Woodward Avenue was the residence of John Scott, father of our Jim Scott, and adjoining was the log cottage of a Widow Jones; she had a son Ansel, who was a schoolmate of mine. Next to Mrs. Jones was a blind alley fifteen or twenty feet wide, in which lived two or three French families. Mr. Eutache Chapoton, father of the late Alex. Chapoton, lived adjoining this alley in a two-story frame dwelling. Sometime after this he moved to then upper Jefferson Avenue and replaced the wooden tenement with a substantial brick block, still standing. Dr. Ebenezer Hurd owned and lived in an old-fashioned brick dwelling adjoining, on the corner of Congress Street, where is now the Richmond & Backus Company store. The doctor was an eminent physician and surgeon, particularly the latter. It was said that he was the most skillful surgeon in all the northwest, when he was in his prime. His practice extended all up and down the river, on the borders of Lake St. Clair, and up the Rivers Rouge and Ecorse. He always went when he was called, regardless.

As evidence of the doctor's surgical skill I relate a little anecdote, though I think it has been mentioned before. I repeat it here because I knew of it personally at the time it occurred.

"One party of patriots, including Captain James Armstrong, of Port Huron, recrossed the river from Canada, landing on Belle Isle, but before they reached the land a ball from a six-pounder cannon mangled Armstrong's arm. He was brought to Doctor Hurd's office where the arm was amputated. Anesthetics were not used in those days but Armstrong never uttered a groan during the operation, and when it was finished, he picked up the arm, waved it around his head, and said:

"Hurrah for the patriots, I'm willing to lose another arm for the cause."

Armstrong was afterwards sheriff of Sanilac County in 1856-7.

Dr. Hurd also amputated the arm of the late Levi Bishop, that was shattered by the premature discharge of a cannon, while he was assisting in firing a Fourth of July salute on the Campus Martius.

The doctor had a brother who was quite an artist (Gildersleve Hurd), a designer and portrait painter of much skill. He had his studio on Jefferson Avenue one door north of F. P. Browning's store. He painted the portraits of some of the notables here, in 1826-7 and later, among them Judge James Witherell and wife (now in possession of Mrs. Julia A. Lacey, Jefferson Avenue), Judge B. F. H. Witherell and wife. He also painted the portrait of Chemick, the son of the noted Indian chief, Kish-Kan-Ko, which I think is now in possession of the Yondotega Club.

Mrs. Pettie lived on the corner opposite Dr. Hurd (southeast corner of Congress Street), and I think she owned the property through to Griswold Street. Mrs. Pettie, in the course of events, became Mrs. E. P. Hastings.

This corner was afterward occupied by a brick building, and I think it was first used by the Baggs as a bookstore and a home for *The Free Press*. Adjoining was the residence of Colonel

Edward Brooks, city auctioneer, etc., where Fenwick's restaurant is now. A portion of the lower part of his residence, toward the river, was, at an early date (1837, and for some years after), occupied by William R. Noyes with a hardware store, about the first store on the avenue. Adjoining was a small wooden building that was used for a children's school. This children's school was taught respectively by Miss Crawford and Miss Campbell. Senator Palmer, when quite a lad, was a pupil here. Uncle Solomon Davis took Miss Campbell for his second wife.

Afterwards a Mr. Goodrich, sexton of the Presbyterian Church, opened up there with a small stock of confectionery, notions, etc., which appealed to the pockets of the youth attending the school nearby. He drove a brisk trade, particularly on the Fourth of July.

Adjoining, Louis Davenport, proprietor of the Detroit & Windsor ferry, lived in a neat cottage, set back from the street some distance, the front yard being liberally supplied with trees and flowers. The property is in the hands of his heirs yet. One of his children, Lewis, became a skillful surgeon and a good physician.

Adjoining the last named house was the residence of a typical French gentleman, Presque Cote; it was a typical French house of an early period. There were only himself and wife and I used often to see them sitting on their front porch, of a summer's afternoon. Mr. Cote was the only resident that I remember at that time who toted water that the household needed for drinking purposes, from the river; he used two wooden buckets, dependent from a yoke across his shoulders. There were hosts of others, of course, that did the same thing, but he is the only one that I can recall in particular. Rain water supplied their other wants.

The lot adjoining Mr. Cote's was vacant for some years until some one erected a wooden building there, in which Stephen Smith kept a shoe store for a long time, until his death, I think.

On the opposite corner of Larned Street (southwest), was the cottage residence of General Charles Larned, father of the late Sylvester Larned. His law office adjoined his house. The general was an exceedingly handsome man, of commanding presence, with dark curly hair and ruddy complexion. He usually wore in summer a dark blue coat with brass buttons, nankin vest and pants, black silk or satin stock, ruffled shirt and silk hat, a watch fob from which depended a large bunch of seals that jingled as he walked along the streets. The jingling of the seals heralded his approach. One could always hear him before one saw him, from this circumstance. He was unselfish and generous and a friend to the poor; also a good friend to the entire French contingent. The Honorable J. M. Howard, Franklin Sawyer and Samuel Pitts, all studied law in his office. He died of cholera in 1834.

The late Daniel Goodwin, Jr., of Chicago, said in regard to General Larned:

"After Samuel Pitts had graduated at Harvard and studied law with Judge Story, he went to Detroit about 1833, with a letter of introduction from General H. A. S. Dearborn to General Chas. Larned, who had served under the elder Dearborn in the war of 1812. Larned was major of a Kentucky regiment under General Harrison which was incorporated into the regular army and stationed at Detroit. He was mustered out in 1816, and remained in Detroit the remainder of his life and reared a large and influential family there. One of his sons-in-law was General Alpheus S. Williams, who distinguished himself in the Mexican war and in the war of the rebellion. He (the latter) was father-in-law of the late lamented and talented Colonel Francis U. Farquhar of the regular army. Mr. Pitts succeeded to General Larned's practice. A partner for some time of Mr. Pitts was Senator Jacob M. Howand a lawyer of most eminent ability, whose eloquence was admired by almost every citizen of Michigan."

A widow and interesting family survived General Larned, one son and five daughters. The son, Colonel Sylvester, took to the law and became an eloquent member of the Detroit bar. During the Civil War he served as lieutenant-colonel of the Second Michigan Infantry, from July 16, 1861, to March 6, 1862. He married first a daughter of Colonel Lansing and sister of Edward A. Lansing; second a. daughter of C. Edwards Lester, who was the author of that widely read book "The Glory and Shame of England," and at one time United States consul to Liverpool. Colonel Larned died not many years ago in London, England, whither he had gone to visit a married daughter residing there. A large number of our citizens are quite familiar with the colonel's career. He was intensely persuasive before a jury and was fitly termed the "Silver-tongued Larned."

732   EARLY DAYS IN DETROIT.

General Larned's daughters were married as follows: Catherine to Lawyer Samuel G. Atterbury (who afterwards entered the ministry); Julia to Lewis D. Allen, lawyer; Jane to General Alpheus S. Williams; Mary to Alex. K. Howard, son of Colonel Joshua Howard, U. S. A.; Harriet to William Rumney, son of Robert Rumney, of this city.

After General Larned's death the family vacated the cottage for their new residence on the corner of Congress and Shelby Streets, where was St. Paul's Church. Afterwards the cottage passed into the hands of Orris Field, who opened a public house there, calling it the "Detroit Cottage." He continued there for quite a while when he made way for the brick building that now occupies its site.

The cottage, during the general's life, was the scene of many charming entertainments and social functions. I call to mind one in particular, a gay gathering, to witness the marriage of Lieutenant Sproat Sibley, U. S. A., and Miss Hunt, the daughter of Judge Hunt, the father of John and Frank Hunt. The beautiful bride was a niece of Mrs. Larned. It was a military wedding, the groom was in full uniform as well as the many officers stationed here, who were present, making a brilliant spectacle. I, luckily, happened to be an eye-witness. Sylvester Larned and myself were playmates and close friends at the time and through him I rceived an invitation.

The Larned heirs and the Barnabas Campau heirs owned the entire front of this block to Jefferson Avenue, and most of it is in their possession yet.

* * *

The other firms engaged in business on Woodward Avenue between Jefferson Avenue and the Russell House, up to 1850, were Lyon & Co., dry goods; Holmes & Babcock, dry goods; Albert Ives, grocer; Reuben Town, dry goods; D. W. Fiske, hardware; P. & J. George, furs; John Brown, dry goods; Chase & Cargill, auctioneers; Cogshall Hardware Co.; Coe & Coit, bankers; J. & P. Aspinall; R. H. Hall, grocer; Hayden & Baldwin, harness and saddlery; Robert Dermont, drugs and liquors; Freedman Brothers, dry goods; Holmes & Co. (Silas M. and Jabez), dry goods; S. Reeves, dry goods; James Burns & Co., dry goods; Van Husan & Haynes, dry goods; Markham & Thompson, dry goods; Eagle & Elliott, clothing; N. P. Jacobs, drugs; L. W.

Tinker, grocer; Tinker & Webb, grocers; Ephraim Brown, dry goods; P. T. Lowe, hardware; T. K. Adams, boots and shoes; LaFayette Knapp, drugs; Wilder & Hunt, hardware; Noyes Bros., hardware.

Griswold Street, from Jefferson Avenue out, had but a very few buildings on it and none at all beyond the State house, in 1830. The dry bed of the Savoyard with its well defined banks crossed the street diagonally, from Congress Street to the alley by the old postoffice building; across it on that side, was a small wooden bridge with a hand rail on either side of it. This same bridge was in evidence when the Savoyard was a live thing, so I have been told.

Thomas Knapp, the sheriff, lived about the center of the east side block, in a cottage surrounded by fruit trees and flowering shrubs. On the corner of the alley in the rear of the Ives Bank, Edwin Jerome, our one time schoolmaster, had a grocery store, assisted by his brother, "Tiff" Jerome. The latter died a few years ago in Saginaw, almost if not quite a millionaire.

* * *

On the corner of Larned Street, where is now the Campau Block, was an old wooden building with a cupola on top, in which there was a bell. The bell was used to call together the children who attended the school kept there by Mr. McKinney and his wife. They kept school there until the building was sawed in half, and one half with the bell was sold to John Farmer and moved away, as before mentioned. F. & T. Palmer once occupied this building with their stocks of goods, before the completion of their brick store on the corner of Jefferson Avenue and Griswold Street. In 1827 there was a short section of cedar pickets standing in Larned Street, midway between it and Shelby Street, the sole remains of old Fort Ponchetrain.

Later on, Peter Desnoyers occupied until his death the fine brick building (where is now the old postoffice building), which was built by Francis P. Browning. His office was in a small wooden building adjoining on Larned Street. Here he also had the remnants of his old stock of goods from his Jefferson Avenue store. Uncle Peter was a genial gentleman, fond of a joke and a good anecdote.

As the city increased in size, the one polling place, at the city hall, was found to be inadequate to accommodate the increased number of voters, so the city fathers divided the business and had extra polling places, at Woodworth's Hotel, on Randolph Street, and at Uhl's tavern, in the old arsenal building, on the corner of Jefferson Avenue and Wayne Street. On three occasions I was one of the election clerks, once at the city hall and twice at the latter place. Each time Uncle Peter was one of the election inspectors, another was Levi Cook, the other one I do not now remember. Cook was an inveterate joker and between the two they had a heap of fun among themselves and the voters as well. Uncle Peter's quizzical questions to the voters, in his broken English, with a merry twinkle in his eye, always excited the risibilities of those present. The questions sometimes were entirely foreign to the business on hand. If they were puzzlers, Uncle Peter would let it go at that, receive the ballot and drop it into the box with an amused and enjoyable chuckle.

* * *

Mr. Desnoyers, just after he purchased this residence on the corner of Larned Street, built two other houses on Griswold Street, between his own and the alley. One of them was occupied by Dr. Terry and the other by Dr. Farnsworth. Henry V. Disbrow, in 1827, occupied a house further along, on the corner of Congress Street. A little later on Lewis Goddard built a small brick residence on the southwest corner of Congress Street, and I think he lived in it until his death. Barnabas (Labie) Campau afterward occupied it until the completion of his new residence on Woodward Avenue. James Williams built a fine brick residence on the corner of the alley, where is now the Moffat Block, and lived there until his death. John Palmer, in 1829, also built a fine brick residence adjoining, on the corner of Fort Street. He resided there until 1870 or thereabouts, and removed to make room for the Moffat Block. These two houses were the first really good brick dwellings in the city, except the Hull house. A little later Judge James Abbott built opposite John Palmer's, where is now the Hammond building, a fine brick residence, vacating the premises on the corner of Woodward Avenue and Woodbridge Street. The judge lived there until his death, the family afterward removing to Woodward Avenue, between John

R. and Grand Circus. I think the Abbott heirs sold the property and it was devoted to various uses until the Hammond building went up.

Judge Abbott was very fond of bees and had some forty or fifty hives in the rear of his house, on the Fort Street side, and the boys used to fight shy of that locality for fear of being stung.

* * *

There was a house warming in 1833 at the old Abbott house, George C. Bates, who was at the function, on a visit to the city after an absence of nearly forty years, writes about it. The house had been transformed into a restaurant, kept by Mike Bowen, and he looking for a light lunch, as he says, stepped into this restanrant, ordered a cup of *cafe au lait* and a sandwich. As he sat there his eye wandered out to the city hall, the soldiers' monument and the Russell House, the street cars with their tinkling bells, memory carried him back to the by-gone days of forty years before. He says:

"Sipping my coffee, the scene changed, and I saw in my mind's eye on this identical location—including that occupied by the city hall, the old Baptist Church and all this high ground or knoll—a herd of cows, wearied cows, muddy and worn out by long travel, stretched here and there, just brought from Ohio by Mr. Wight for his milk ranch below town on the Cass farm, he then being a hale, hearty, middle-aged man, engaged in the milk business. Between that herd of cattle and the old capitol, now that beautiful Union school house (High School), not one single building was erected either on Griswold Street or Michigan Avenue, but a long narrow plank walk over the green sward (for it was May, 1833) to the capitol where the Supreme Court of the Territory of Michigan was then in session, was the sole isthmus that connected Detroit with that beautiful suburb.

"At the same time on the west side of Woodward Avenue, corner of Woodbridge Street, stood a low two-story old-fashioned wooden building, probably over fifty years old—standing perhaps ten feet back from the avenue, with a steep roof, dormer windows and a high brass knocker on the door on which was cut in deep letters 'James Abbott.' The latch-string of that old door was always on the outside, for there lived for many a long year one of Detroit's most active and successful old-fashioned merchants— a man of figures and of wealth, a sturdy descendant of an English family, born in Montreal about the year 1791, who in the fur trade, in commission business and supplying the military posts of Michigan and the northwest, had accumulated a very large estate, for he owned nearly half of that whole block, and who maintained to his death the character of the fine old English gentleman, 'all of ye olden time,' and who, amidst a long business life, entertained with true hospitality all who made his acquaintance, and sought society under his roof."

In those days the merchant princes of Detroit, and Mr. Abbott especially, lived in small, snug, cosy houses, richly furnished with real mahogany—table spread with solid silver—the finest linen; cellars full of pure old brandy, Jamaica rum, London port, luscious Maderia and sherries that would make the blood dance in one's veins; and the richer they grew the more hospitable they became, the more they entertained with elegant dinners. After business was over splendid supper and dancing parties were the order almost every evening after navigation was closed until the next summer came.

No better representative home of Detroit fifty years ago could be found that of James Abbott on Woodward Avenue; and he himself, his genial, jolly wife, his beautiful daughter Sarah, too soon to die; Aunt Cad Whistler, Miss Caroline Whistler, an antique sister of Mr. A., the most graceful dancer and waltzer then in Detroit; his then two roystering wild sons, Madison and Bill Abbott, who sometimes in grand frolic rode their horses up into the old Mansion House and drank julep and toddy with Jack Smith from the counter there. All these grouped in a photographic gallery would tell the story of bygones of Detroit.

"But commerce had increased. The old steamers Niagara, Clay, Sheldon Thompson, had given way to the New York, the Michigan and such floating palaces. The docks were crowded in summer with vessels, and Judge Abbott found he must move away from the busy, crowded port of Detroit to a quiet retreat in the country—remote from all business—and so he built the then elegant home in which I was now sitting taking my lunch. At that time, except the homes of John Palmer and James Williams directly opposite and where the Moffat block now stands, and a small wooden building at the rear of what was the Baptist Church, then occupied by Mason Palmer, and Mechanic's Hall, then a small, rickety old shanty, there were no buildings in the neighborhood, and when his new home was completed Judge Abbott flattered himself that he was forever outside of and beyond the reach of business wants, or business property; that in future years there he and his children and his children's children could have a quiet country home, where in peace and quiet they could live and die. Of the house itself, it may be said, that, when finished, it was one of the most substantial, costly and elegant buildings in Detroit. "Now stands it there; none so poor, so low as to do it reverence." But the house was finished—the grass plot prepared, and the rose bushes were transplanted from the old home, and with true old-fashioned hospitality there must be a "House Warming," and so invitations, written in Mr. Abbott's round English hand—bespeaking order, firmness, health and true nobility—were sent to all the elite of Detroit to come and help dedicate that home to comfort, enjoyment, pleasure and hospitality, and they came. As I looked into my coffee cup, nearly drained, and closed my eyes to the present, memory and fancy—blessed gifts to man—gave me back that brilliant scene, and replaced it in those, then large parlors, dining rooms, chambers and anti-rooms, long since gone, never, never to return. There stood Mr. and Mrs. Abbott, two sturdy specimens of the old English and French Canadian stock, most richly and elegantly dressed—not in the Parisian styles, but the true English mode. Miss Whistler, as aide-de-camp, waiting to receive their guests, who came to exclaim from their very heart of hearts, "Peace be upon this house and all beneath it," and who were welcomed without ostentation or ceremony, but with true old-fashioned western hospitality. There was General Hugh Brady, one of the noblest, bravest, truest soldiers that ever trod with undaunted step the field of battle, in full uniform, with his staff; General Frank Larned, with his suave and elegant address; Captain Backus, the son-in-law of General Brady; ex-Governor Tom Mason, Governor Woodbridge, Judge B. F. H. Witherell, Augustus L. Porter, Judge Goodwin and a large number of the old lawyers of Detroit, always ready for a big fee, a frolic, or a flirtation. Major Bob Forsyth, a superb, elegant paymaster, U. S. A.; Pierre Desnoyers, Chas. Moran, Chancellor Farnsworth, Edmund Brush, Alex. Centre, Lieutenant J. M. Berrien, Alfred Brush, General J. E. Schwartz, all in complete uniform, Chas. C. Trowbridge, John A. Welles, aye, all the men and women of that day full of life, hope —joyous, generous, fraternal, hospitable—were gathered there and then; and the feast of viands, of music, and of joy, and of wine went merrily on. Such a supper of elk steaks, roast venison, prairie chicken, buffalo tongues and beaver's tails was never excelled in Detroit; and the claret and sherry and Maderia flowed like water, while Jamaica toddies, apple toddies, egg-nog, Canadian shrub and hot Scotch and Monongahela whisky punches came and went, until the long and joyous feast was over, and even now here, as memory brings back the aroma of that old Jamaica toddy and Monongahela whisky, my red ribbon trembles with the pleasant memory of long ago."

The Baptist Church was on the opposite corner from John Palmer's, where the Walker building now is. It was of brick, with quite a commanding steeple. Its first pastor, I think, was Reverend Robert Turnbull. Adjoining was the Mechanics' hall, a two-story wooden building. This hall was used from time to time by various school teachers. As it was after my school days, I call to mind only four or five who taught school there. One was an old-time pedagogue, George B. Eastman (the boys used to call him "Old Eastman"). He taught along in the early thirties, and a good school he kept, too, his scholars and their parents used to say. Another old-timer kept school here in 1838. His name was Marsh. I never came under his tuition, but I did come under his instructions in military discipline, as he was captain of Company A, First regiment, Michigan Militia, and when I was first warned to train, having arrived at the age of 18, I found that it was to be in his company. Well, we did have a time of it, and Captain Marsh put us through our paces good. He was a scholarly man, and gave good satisfaction as a teacher. The others I call to mind were Patrick Higgins, afterwards police justice. The latter and myself boarded together with my aunt, Mrs. Hinchman, on Larned Street, while he had charge of this school. A pleasant and agreeable gentleman. He was rather slight in stature, but always quiet, determined and dignified.

Other teachers were Mr. Bissell (later on Bishop Bissell), assisted by his son, Lawyer Bissell, of this city, and Philo M. Parsons. The latter I knew intimately and admired him greatly. No one deplored his early death more than I.

Mr. W. W. Wilcox was president of the Mechanics' society, 1856-7-8. He was also a member of board of estimators in 1860; grade commissioner, 1855-1861; drain commissioner, 1860-1862; alderman, 1854; city assessor, 1857-1863. During the time he held the last named office he had for employes, Henry M. Whittlesey, J. L. Langley, George W. Osborn, James C. Latham, Eugene Robinson and John I. Teller. Wilcox Street was named after him. This street was formerly Grand River east. Silas Farmer was one of the committee to rename the street, and it was so named from the fact that the Wilcox homestead was on the corner of John R. Street and Miami Avenue, built over sixty years ago. The main part is now doing service as a store.

Mr. Wilcox was a heavy contractor, carrying on a very extensive establishment; many of the most prominent buildings in Detroit were erected by him. In 1865, at the earnest solicitation of his old friend, James F. Joy, then a C., B. & Q. director, Mr. Wilcox was induced to abandon his large interests in Detroit and remove to Aurora, Ill., to assume the responsible position of superintendent of the entire car and wood work department of the C., B. & Q. road, a position which he held for many years. He died in Aurora, May, 1880. A son of his, George G. Wilcox, was clerk in the state adjutant-general's office in this city during the civil war and after, and later a clerk in the United States customs for many years.

* * *

General John R. Williams, at one time had his residence opposite the capitol, on the corner of State Street. Timothy Fales lived in the rear of the capitol, on the corner of Grand River Avenue, where is now the Bennett block. Later on Lawyer Lewis Allen lived opposite the capitol, where later stood the Capitol Square theater, as did also Eralsey Ferguson.

The Capitol building, many will remember, and it has so often been described, I will not repeat an account of it here, except to relate one or two incidents connected with it. The members of the legislature, convening here, used occasionally to have a high old time, particularly at night sessions and on days of final adjournment. Some among the members of the lower house had a trick of smuggling liquor within the walls and having it charged as stationery. At the night sessions when it got along into the small hours, the fun, aided by the "stationery," got fast and furious, and it was kept up until the speaker's gavel rapped adjournment. The brilliant and eloquent member of the lower house from Mackinac, McLeod, was particularly conspicuous on these occasions. He was almost the counterpart of the late "Curt" Emerson and, like him, possessed unusual gifts. They used also to have mock sessions of the house, at night, and at these McLeod was always elected speaker. It can readily be imagined what a wild time they had.

Of all the speakers of the house, the only ones that I remember and, who, at that time, impressed me so much, were Judge Henry T. Backus and Robert McClellan.

The Territorial library was in the Capitol building, and was established by act of legislative council, June 16, 1828. William B. Hunt was appointed the librarian by Governor Lewis Cass, for a term of two years. Mr. Hunt continued to act as librarian until March 7, 1834, when Gershom Mott Williams was appointed by Governor Geo. B. Porter. Wm. B. Hunt was the father of the late Geo. Wellington Hunt, also of our present fellow citizen, Cleveland Hunt. Mr. Williams seems to have acted as librarian until the organization of the institution as a state library.

The honored names of Henry R. Schoolcraft, Charles Moran, Daniel S. Bacon, Calvin Britton, Elon Farnsworth, Chas. C. Haskell and others are found in the list of members of the library committee.

Gershom Mott Williams was the son of General John R. Williams.

The location of the state capitol was away out in the country, as it were, surrounded by a wide common, that for some years could not boast of a single dwelling. The only resident in the immediate vicinity in 1827 that I call to mind was Thomas Rowland, at one time postmaster, and he lived where St. Aloysius Church is now, on Washington Avenue.

Captain John Burtis, of the steamer Argo, lived in a small cottage (Locust cottage), that had a row of locust trees in its front. It was located about 100 feet from Grand River Avenue, on the north side of what is now Bagley Avenue. The captain was asked why he went out so far to "pitch his tent," and he replied, "I want and must have sea room."

The wide commons in the rear of the capitol were, during the summer months, covered in many places with a dense growth of weeds that grew almost as high as one's head. On this common and through these weeds the horses and cattle roamed at will, and among them was a stubborn donkey, the property of Colonel D. C. McKinstry. This donkey was an especial pet of boys, and many tried to ride him. He would allow them to get on his back and get comfortably seated; then he would start off at a canter, with a loud bray, up would go his heels and over his head would go the boy. After a time he met his master, though, in a boy by the name of Nige Pickett, a harum-scarum youth who was utterly fearless. He tried Mr. Donkey several times without success. There came a time, however, when he stuck on despite the efforts of the animal to throw him. Ever after that the donkey would allow Pickett to ride him whenever he pleased. George Jerome, when a boy, often tried to ride this donkey, but failed.

My uncle, Thomas Palmer, owned quite a number of lots between the line of the West park and the line of the Cass farm, and on them had located quite a number of houses bought at the government sale of the cantonment buildings of Fort Shelby, and established quite a colony there. He also had in operation there an ashery and a pottery. The latter turned out what was called "Jackson ware," a very coarse pottery, but just suited to the needs of those who did not care for a better article.

On the line of the Cass farm and on the west side of Michigan Avenue was the cottage residence of Charles M. Bull, the only dwelling that I remember on that avenue or in the immediate vicinity at that time. Mr. Bull lived there for many years and died there. His house, as I have said, was the only one on Michigan Avenue that I recall, and Michigan Avenue continued on its way houseless until one reached a log farm house on the Woodbridge farm, where now is the wood and hay market. This house of Mr. Bull's was turned into a "Cheap John" furniture store, and many will remember the great display of odds and ends the proprietor used to make in front of his store.

General Fairchild, of Wisconsin, married a daughter of Charles M. Bull. Fairchild was afterward governor of Wisconsin. Charles M. and the late George G. Bull, clerk of the United States court, were brothers. Mrs. Captain Gager, whose husband commanded the steamboat Albany, was a sister.

Fort Shelby, when I came here, was in the first stages of demolition. The earthworks had been leveled and but two or three rows of the cantonment buildings remained intact. They were speedily disposed of at public sale, except a portion of the western row, the council hall going to the Presbyterian society, which moved it to the rear of its new brick church on the corner of Woodward Avenue and Larned Street, where it did duty as a Sunday school room, lecture room, etc. I attended Sunday school there and remember with pleasure the names and personalities of two of the Superintendents, John J. Deming and Horace Hallock. Two good pious men, and, if there is a bright hereafter, they, no doubt, are in its very midst.

John J. Deming's daughter Mary married Mr. Chas. Crocker. The latter in after years was one of the Pacific railroad crowd of millionaires, another of whom was Mark Hopkins, formerly of St. Clair. They both erected fine houses on Nobb's Hill, San Francisco, the aristocratic quarter. The mansions, though now vacated by their former owners, are with all their contents kept as show places.

Mr. Crocker was a poor, struggling youth in this city, in the early thirties. Mark Hopkins was at the same period a young boy (perhaps 16 years) dependent on and living with his brother, Samuel Hopkins, in the village of Palmer (now St. Clair). I lived there at the same time; we were boys together. He passed out of my life, and the first I heard of him after that was his wonderful career in California, where he rolled up wealth, " n measures that Alladin never knew." Samuel Hopkins was in the early days the principal cabinet maker and boss carpenter of the village. He was a fine, square man, member of the church, leader of the choir and all that sort of thing. He was the mainstay of the congregation that used to meet in the court room of the old county seat building, before the dwellers there had any stated preacher. Samuel Hopkins was always on hand. When Reverend O. C. Thompson was assigned to St. Clair as the resident preacher, Hopkins continued, a mainstay. Along in the after years, I used to meet him, now and then, and the early times were gone over, you may be sure.

The last time I saw my friend Hopkins he was sitting in the office of the Oakland hotel, St. Clair. He had just completed it, and he looked with great satisfaction on what he had aecomplished, a feat that did not enter his wildest dream in the early days. He said further that after he had gotten hold of the generous "lump" that Mark had left to him it was a new and queer experience for him to have if not an unlimited bank account, a very generous one, and a still further pleasurable experience was to draw a check on a bank.

I saw lately in the papers that Charles Crocker, son of the deceased millionaire, paid a fee of $20,000 to Dr. Doyen, of Berlin. The doctor treated his wife and asserted that she had a cancer. She died under his hands. After her death it was ascertained that she did not have a cancer at all and died from other causes. Mr. Crocker has instituted suit against the doctor for malpractice.

John J. Deming, as stated in a former article, was superintendent of the First Sunday school (Presbyterian) I ever attended in this city; he was a brother of Mrs. John Palmer. He held many offices of trust and his beautiful, clear-cut handwriting appears on many of the city records. A beautifully written card from his pen is before me now, and bears the legend,

JANE M. PALMER, DETROIT.
1835.
"Awake, my soul, to sound His praise.
Awake, my harp, to sing."
—BARLOW.

He died many years ago in California.

* * *

Larned, Congress and Fort Streets all ended on the line of the Cass farm, and beyond there were very few dwellings, except on the river front. The large log farm-house belonging to Governor Cass stood where is now the residence of Allan Shelden. This log house was for the use of the person having immediate charge of the farm and was of ample dimensions.

A line or row of fine locust trees ran across the Cass farm, on the present line of Fort Street. The stone bomb-proof powder magazine, belonging to Fort Shelby, was situated in the center of Congress Street in front of the Caniff & Dean house and midway between Shelby and Wayne Streets. It was torn down shortly after I came here. The quarters for the officers stationed at Fort Shelby (not the commanding officer), were situated on part of the property now the site of the present postoffice. Judge John McDonnell occupied them after the burning of his dwelling in the fire of 1829 or 30, until his death.

* * *

Judge McDonnell and his family were so intimately connected with our family that I must give them some little consideration here. The judge was a most kind-hearted, genial, and intelligent Scotch gentleman, and, although a young lad myself, he challenged my admiration. Mrs. McDonnell was a most estimable lady, a daughter of a Mr. Smith, a Scotchman, who was an extensive merchant in Sandwich in 1812 and previous. Aside from his other possessions, the judge owned two or three slaves, as did other families here and on the border in Canada. He also cared for three old men, pensioners on his bounty, in his home on Fort Street. I have often seen them sunning themselves in the summer, on the front porch, and, in the winter, enjoying the huge kitchen fire.

On the corner of the alley, in the rear of the Widow Coate's house on the corner of Jefferson Avenue and Shelby Street, Amos Chaffee carried on a horseshoeing and blacksmth shop and continud there for some years.

Along in after years, a small, cosy brick dwelling occupied the site of this blacksmith shop. It was the residence—and at the same time—the gambling rooms of "Ike" Flowers, whose personality so many must call to mind. Flowers had the reputation of being among the best principled of that fraternity; he was never known to take advantage of a novice. This assertion I have often heard vouched for by frequenters of his establishment. He always appeared on the streets faultlessly dressed, and invariably alone when on foot, although the owner of a very pretty woman for a wife. He and Mrs. Flowers used often, on fine afternoons, to enjoy an outing behind a spirited nag. The family lived over the gaming rooms, and consisted of Flowers, his wife, and a sister of the latter, a very pretty unasumming damsel. They all lived there until down to about 1853-4, when they vanished. I never knew what became of them, except "Ike" and his pretty sister-in-law. The latter I heard of some years after, as being married to the son of a well-known wealthy manufacturer in Springfield, Mass. Flowers turned up in this city many years after, as keeper of a restaurant, first on Griswold Street, next nearly opposite the Michigan Exchange, the last, in the Desnoyer block on Jefferson Avenue. He had another woman for a wife, the widow of a scion of one of the old French residents. The appetizing "petite soupire" that "Ike" used to provide for the frequenters of his rooms on Shelby Street, were remembered, and drew many who had partaken of them, to patronize him in his new venture. Mr. Harry Guise and myself were guests of his from start to finish, although neither one of us ever visited his place on Shelby Street. He was singularly reticent in regard to his former life, his wife, etc. It was presumed his former wife was divorced from him, although Guise and myself never made the slightest allusion to his past. He died while keeping the restaurant in the Desnoyer block, April 6, 1887.

Flowers began life as a hand on board a Wabash canal boat. He was no sooner able to earn $5 or $6 a month than he learned to gamble. One day when 15 years old he won the piles of the entire boat's crew with whom he worked. Immediately afterwards he quit work and thenceforth became a professional gambler. In 1845 or 1846 he opened his first gambling house in Columbus, O., in company with Sprad Betts and John Brown. His house prospered greatly, and as his wealth increased so did his ambition. He broke from his partners, came to Detroit and opened a gambling saloon on Shelby Street.

During the thirty-eight years which Flowers spent on and off in Detroit he was the proprietor of numerous "high-toned" gambling houses.

It was said that Flowers was one of the most audacious gamblers in the entire west. His losses one night, it was said, exceeded $12,000, and his friends aver that during his career he won and lost over $1,000,000.

* * *

A row of Lombard poplars stood in front of the McDonald house on the corner of Fort and Shelby Streets. I remember them as prominent landmarks on approaching the city from below. It was said that the seed from which they were reared came from France.

In the rear of the McDonnell residence was the wagon and blacksmith shop of Marsh and Chittenden. They occupied the entire lot from the alley to Lafayette Street. The latter street, from Shelby to Griswold Streets, had but two or three dwellings on it. On the northeast corner was a saloon; about the middle of the block on the north side was the residence of Mr. Heath, a produce dealer; opposite were the cottage residences of Gilbert F. Rood and William P. Patrick. Adjoining the residence of Mr. Heath were the freight buildings of the Michigan Central railroad, which extended through to Michigan Avenue. The buildings were in charge of William F. Chittenden, of Marsh & Chittenden, who was freight agent and master of transportation of the railroad at that time. Mr. Chittenden was an amiable man in many ways, possessed more than ordinary culture, had the gift of expressing himself admirably, and managed to acquire quite a competency for those days; altogether a remarkable man.

Opposite the shop of Mr. Chaffee was the two and a half story dwelling of Alvah Ewers, the cooper, and one of the city magnates. He had his shop on the corner of Larned and Cass Streets where is now the wholesale grocery house of Messrs. Lee & Cady. Dr. Ewers, his son (deceased), was at one time the United States consul at Windsor.

Adjoining Mr. Ewer's place, across the alley, was a large double, wooden tement house, belonging, I think, to Levi Cook. It occupied the site of the building formerly occupied by the Calvert Lithographing Company. On the corner where is now the Tribune building was the saloon and residence of John Horn. He made a specialty of brown stout and English ale, keeping both on tap. The excellence of his goods attracted a large custom. He prospered in his business, so much so that he moved to more extensive quarters near the foot of Woodward Avenue. Later he and his boys and a Cincinnati capitalist, who had married Horn's daughter, went into the ferry business between this city and Windsor. Their career in this line is familiar to almost everyone. On the opposite corner, where stands the building formerly occupied by *The Free Press,* were located the stables and headquarters of the various stage lines in which DeGarmo Jones was interested. They occupied quite a large space, extending to the alley crossing Shelby Street and about 100 feet on Larned Street.

Adjoining on Larned Street was the residence of the widow Roby, and opposite, Joseph Campau had a row of five or six tenement houses. Later on, after Mrs. Roby's death, the house she had occupied was replaced by Geo. W. Howe's brick livery stable, the first good livery established here with the exception of John Long's in the rear of the National hotel, now the Russell house.

Referring once more to Horn's corner: It was the property of the late Dr. Rufus Brown, he having purchased it in 1836, paying for the lot $300, and he hung on to it with the greatest tenacity to the day of his death, when the representatives of his estate consented to part with it for the sum of $15,000.

Adjoining Horn's, on the corner of the alley, lived John Y. Petty, of the firm of Poupard & Petty, forwarding and commission merchants.

Larned, Congress, Fort nor Lafayette Streets were not opened up any farther than to the line of the Cass farm in 1827, as before said. The first houses and business places that I recall on Larned Street, between Shelby and Wayne Streets, were, on the south side, the residences of Henry S. Cole and the widow Hinchman (mother of Guy F. and the late Joseph B. Hinchman). Adjoining Mrs. Hinchman's, on the corner of Wayne Street, after some years, was the brick grocery store and residence of E. W. Jones. Adjoining the Horn corner, also, lived Charles Howard, the engineer of the Detroit Hydraulic Works, and next to him was the residence of William Duncan Brewer and Ezra Rood. Later on Duncan became mayor of Detroit. He married for his first wife the daughter of John Hanmer, an esteemed citizen.

My earliest recollections center about Jas. Hanmer's tavern, foot of Griswold Street. When I came here there was no dock at the foot of Griswold Street. The water of the Detroit River washed up here on a pebbly beach, the Indian, the French voyageur and the habitant pulled his canoe up on the shore unobstructed. Here in the season they brought great loads of whitefish from the various fisheries up and down the river. How often when a slip of a boy, have I trudged of a morning down to the foot of Griswold Street, from my uncle's house, corner of Jefferson Avenue, to procure the daily supply of whitefish. The catch was often so large that aside from their excellence as an article of food, their cheapness recommended them, and you could buy from five to ten, nice hard, plump fellows for 25 cents. So plentiful were they that scarcely a household in the city but what had them on their tables if they so desired. They were almost the mainstay of our people in the early days, and when cooked by any of the French housewives of that time, what a delicious morsel they were. I have dwelt somewhat on the white fish in former articles.

Hanmer's was well patronized, mostly by lake and river-going men. It was headquarters for them during the winter months, a "haven of rest," as it were. When the fire (spring of 1830) visited and wrecked the Detroit *Gazette* office on Griswold Street, and the brick store of F. and T. Palmer, adjoining on the corner of Jefferson Avenue, the weary citizens composing the bucket lines formed from the engines stationed on Jefferson Avenue to the foot of this street for the purpose of supplying them with water. Hanmer was on hand with a bountiful supply of hot coffee, etc., that was most gratifying to the inner man. He repeated the same thing the winter following when the fire occurred on the corner of Jefferson Avenue and Griswold Street (Ives old corner), sweeping away a number of wooden buildings. It was an intensely cold Sunday morning and the water froze wherever it touched. It may well be supposed that the firemen and the "leather bucket brigade" had a hard time of it. A person could not stand in the line long without being covered with icicles, and the boys manning the brakes were in about as bad a condition, so it may be imagined our Friend Hanmer's donation on this particular occasion was most welcome. Though quite a lad, I was at both these fires, and helped pass the empty buckets, too small to handle the full ones. This tavern, after Hanmer left it, was occupied by Nelson Tomlinson, who, while the Patriot disturbance was on, had been keeping tavern in Palmer (St. Clair). He changed the name to "The Mansion House," and that name it bore until it was changed to "Seaman's Home." It is still standing, and I think it bears the same name. The Detroit and Windsor ferry boats (Davenport's) landed at the foot of this street, and near by at the docks of DeGarmo Jones and Shadrack Gillett landed most of the large steamboats from Buffalo. Ward's line of steamers landed near by at John Hutching's dock.

Many will call to mind Jas. Hanmer and his personality, as he passed away not so many years ago. He was an ideal landlord, and one of the quietest and most genial of men. After gaining a competency he quit the tavern business, and retired, in a measure. He owned at one time the southwest corner of Woodbridge and Bates Streets, where had stood the home of Hon. Austin E. Wing, and operated there a wood yard, somewhat extensively. He left three daughters and two sons. The name of the oldest was Charles. He died in his teens. What became of the other I do not know. Wm. Duncan, the brewer, married a daughter of Hanmer's, the eldest. An individual by the name of Ryckman (who I think was in the employ of Josh Carew) married another daughter. They did not remain long together and separated for good. The fault could not be hers, as she was one of the most gentle and amiable of mortals. She shortly after married Mr. James Carson, of Lake Superior, and it is presumed lived happily, at least I never heard anything to the contrary. The other daughter married Wm. Ashley, a bright young man connected with William Duncan in the brewery business. Duncan's early married life was passed in a small two-story dwelling on Larned Street between Shelby and Wayne, and nearly opposite my boarding house (Mrs. Hinchman's) so that I became quite familiar with them and their surroundings. After a time I went to Buffalo for three or fours years, and in the meantime Duncan had improved his fortunes, and had gotten into more pretentious quarters and pleasanter surroundings. I do not remember at what time his wife died, leaving a boy and a girl. After some years the widower married a young woman of this city by the name of Heath, pretty and attractive as most people of the present day know.

Duncan was quite successful in the brewery business and as a maltster, and I think associated with him from time to time were Curt Emerson, Josh Carew, Nate Williams, ex-Mayor Langdon and others. His brewery was at 186 Woodbridge Street west, and his malt house, 29 Bates Street. The Collins brothers were in his employ, it seems to me always, particularly John Collins, lately deceased, who was for so many years connected with the Wayne County Savings Bank, and in charge of the safety deposit vaults. A man whose sterling integrity, all who knew him were delighted to acknowledge.

John, while in Duncan's employ was his special delivery and collecting agent, and was a conspicuous figure on the streets at that time driving his delivery wagon himself. He was good nature itself, and always had a place on the seat beside him for the many youngsters of his acquaintance, who swore by him, particularly Thomas W. Palmer, Warner Newberry, Billy Ewers, Guy and Joseph B. Hinchman and many others. Then they were a bit useful to him, too, holding the horse in case of need, etc. When he went a good man passed to his reward.

Duncan after a while essayed politics, though he had been before this alderman of his ward (first) 1854-5-6, and ran for mayor on the Democratic ticket in opposition to H. P. Baldwin. The contest was quite spirited on both sides. The staid Mr. Baldwin had quite a new and to him novel experience visiting the saloons and slums soliciting votes and acquainting himself with the rough element. It was different with Duncan from the nature of his business, which brought him in contact and made him familiar with the saloonkeepers and those that frequented their places. Besides all this he was more a man of the people than was Baldwin, an easy going, generous, genial individual. Mr. Baldwin had all the elements of respectability to a marked degree, but they were not sufficient to win, and his Democratic opponent was elected by a large majority. I heard Duncan in one of his speeches say in regard to his adversary: "Mr. Baldwin, who is opposing me, is a very nice, good man and all that and I have not a word to say against him, except that he is not a Democrat, and besides he wears a No. 6 hat." That was all he said for or against him, no more.

Duncan served the city as mayor for two terms, quite successfully. Some time either during his term of service as mayor, or before or after, there occurred here an alarming scarcity of small change, to relieve which Duncan came to the rescue through the issue of $15,000 worth of fractional currency, on his own individual responsibility. They were welcomed by all classes of the community, and taken without question, or hesitation.

Duncan built for himself a fine residence on Lafayette Avenue, where he hoped to pass the declining years of a busy life in peace and contentment, but he was doomed to disappointment, for death came to him only a few years after he had ceased the worry and hustle of business, and not much past the prime of life, widely regretted, leaving a widow, a son, and daughter by his first wife, and a very comfortable fortune. The widow, after some years married Dr. Donald McLean, who died not long ago. His widow survives him and resides in this city. The son died here only a year or so ago. The daughter married Lieutenant (now Captain) Cecil, U. S. A. He is at present stationed at Fort Cook, Omaha.

On the corner where is now the fire department headquarters stood the old city hay scales, the Washington market afterwards taking its place, and then the present fire department. The arsenal grounds took up the entire square bounded by Wayne and Larned Streets, Jefferson Avenue and Cass Street, except the arsenal building itself on the corner of Wayne Street and Jefferson Avenue, the dwelling of Doctor Houghton in its rear on Wayne Street and the residence of the keeper, Captain Perkins, on the corner of Jefferson Avenue and Cass Street. William Nesbitt had a grocery store and dwelling where is now the Detroit News Co. Between Cass and First Streets after Larned Street was opened up, lived William Harsha, Duncan Stewart, William Warner, stage agent; George W. Howe, William Stewart and others whose names I do not now recall. I lived there myself the second year after I was married (1853).

In the rear of the Washington market, on the corner of the alley, was the house of fire engine Company No. 4, of which I was a member, having joined the company about 1838. This was what was then called the young men's and boys' company, scarcely any of the members being more than 21 years of age, and it is needless to say that the fire engine business eclipsed all else in the minds of the boys. They thought engine, they talked engine and they even dreamt engine. If they succeeded in getting to a fire before any of the older companies, or if they succeeded in washing any of them, it was a victory indeed, and was hailed with yells of delight. The term "washing" used to mean that when any of the companies were taking water or suction from another company and were furnished more water than they could get away with, then they were "washed."

There were some three or four dwellings in the alley corner of the *Evening News* building; and in one of them, as I have before mentioned, Anson Burlingame and I attended school. Across the alley, in the rear of the *Free Press* job office on Shelby Street, was the residence of Colonel Levi Cook; the first story is yet standing and is used as a carpenter shop. The Savoyard used to run down through this alley, and right here was a large elm tree (on its border). Colonel Cook lived here many years. In this house the late George W. Bissell was married to Miss Eliza Sanderson, an adopted daughter of Colonel Cook. He and John Hale owned nearly all the land in this block, bounded by the alley,

Shelby, Congress and Griswold Streets. John Hale built for himself, on Congress Street, a fine large frame dwelling, immense for those days. It stood where is now a part of the Buhl block and opposite the present site of the Wayne County Savings Bank. From the Hale residence to the corner of Congress and Shelby Streets were Colonel Cook's garden and plum and peach orchard. The plum and peach trees yielded delicious fruit, as I can testify.

On the west side of Shelby Street, from the *Evening News* building, there were no dwellings until one reached the residence of Henry Newberry, on the corner of the alley in the rear of the present Tecumseh Block. Oliver Newberry lived with his brother, Henry, and his nephew, Henry L. On the present site of the Tecumseh Block Thomas Palmer, father of Senator Palmer, built for himself a frame residence that, at that time, was the peer of any of a like character on Fort Street. He occupied it until his removal to the Witherell farm on Jefferson Avenue. As an evidence of the rise in value of property in that immediate vicinity, my uncle sold this property for $7,000, and his son, the senator, subsequently bought it for $45,000. I imagine there was some little sentiment on the senator's part connected with this purchase.

There were very few houses on Congress Street from Shelby Street down, before its extension through the Cass farm. Judge Caniff and Jerry Dean built and occupied the brick residence that is still standing nearly opposite the present Shelby Block. The judge continued to occupy his portion of it until his death, nearly thirty years ago. He was an eccentric character, and where he got his title of "judge" no one seemed to know, but nevertheless he was a "Sir Oracle" in many respects in this community at an early date. His decisions on mooted questions that used to be discussed by the city solons in front of "Sid" Rood's book store were nearly always taken as final. The judge was withal the most genial of men and an inveterate joker. He addressed every one, high or low, by his given name. He commenced his career here as a shoemaker in a little shop on the south side of Jefferson Avenue, a short distance this side of Shelby Street. Later on he entered into partnership in the grocery business with John Scott, father of our present fellow townsman and capitalist, "Jim" Scott, on the corner of Woodbridge Street near the foot of

Shelby Street. The business continued until the death of Mr. Scott, when the surviving partner closed it out. The judge, though strictly honest, was very close in money matters and would not spend a cent in any way if he could avoid it except for his just debts. While I was clerk in the quartermaster's office here I used to run across him quite often and his usual salutation was, "Come, Friend, haven't you got ten cents about you? I am awful thirsty," and later on, when I was in the paper and stationery business, he used to have a desk in my store where he kept his books and papers. I used to assist him in taking care of his accounts, etc. In closing his accounts in relation to the Scott estate, of which he was administrator, I made out the final settlement for him. But now and then he used to indorse my paper for four or five hundred dollars, and I was satisfied that he would not do the same for anyone else, so I was content. Take him all in all and he was a good man and an upright citizen.

Jerry Dean, saddler, died in the thirties. His daughter married a Mr. Armstrong, who was with Edgar & Co., sugar dealers, for many years. Mrs. Snelling, widow of Captain Snelling, U. S. A., kept a boarding house opposite the Caniff and Dean house and also at one time kept a boarding house in the Hull residence on Jefferson Avenue, directly after General Hull left there. Among those who boarded with her on Congress Street was the Rev. J. E. Chaplin, a most eloquent and gifted Methodist divine. He laid siege to the widow's heart, and succeeded in capturing it. I think he was the most earnest and persuasive preacher that I ever listened to. He did not have the lungs and voice of Elder Baughman, but in the directions I have named he could not be surpassed. He had a son, an exceedingly bright, clever youth, with whom I was intimate. He was a prominent member of our debating society and a first class debator for a boy. Mrs. Snelling had a son, James, who was a lieutenant in the United States army and was killed in the Mexican war. He also was a schoolmate of mine. Another son, Henry H., was in the seed and horticultural business here for some years and then went into the same business with Grant Thorburn in New York.

The story of General Pickett, of the confederate army, and his men—by his wife, La Salle Corbell Pickett—has this to say in regard to Lieutenant Snelling: "In the Mexican war, among others, Brevet-Major George Wright, Captains Rumford and

Larkin Smith, First Lieutenant and Adjutant James Longstreet, Second Lieutenant James G. T. Snelling and George Pickett, of Eighth Infantry, were all distinguished at the battle of Churubusco. The eighth being one of the two regiments which crossed the Rio Churubusco and held the causeway which led to the City of Mexico," and again; "of the storming party that General Worth sent against the 'Mill,' in the battle of El Molino del Rey (this most bloody of the battles of the Mexican war), he (Pickett) emerged without a scratch. His brother lieutenant (Jas. G. T. Snelling) was less happy, being severely wounded during the charge."

Adjoining Mrs. Snelling's was a large lot that occupied the rest of that side of Congress Street to Wayne Street. In the center of it, and about one hundred feet from the line of the former street, was situated the quarters for the officer in command at Fort Shelby. He was housed in a wooden mansion of considerable pretensions, that stood with its porch and gable end somewhat toward Shelby Street; beautiful and attractive in summer, surrounded as it was by trees of a fine growth, and eglantine and morning glories creeping around the pillars of the porch and climbing up over the gable. Its rear abutted on Wayne Street and the alley. Inside the house along the entire front towards Congress Street was a large banqueting room, with a pillared alcove with raised platform for the musicians. It is needless to say that in this room from time to time gathered, either at feast or dance, all that composed the gay Detroit society of that day, both civil, and military. I have heard one citizen—prominent at that time, but no longer with us—say that he attended a ball here once, given by the officers stationed at the fort. General Hull and staff and other officers of the army stationed here and on duty outside of the fort were present, as well as all the elite of the city. This citizen said further that it was the most brilliant gathering he had ever witnessed. The officers were in full uniform and the ladies were in the gayest attire.

This building stood for some years after the fort was demolished, until Oliver Newberry, who owned the property, carted it off somewhere. I have been in the old house often.

In the winter season at the time Fort Shelby was garrisoned by troops, the younger people always early made arrangements for a series of weekly assemblies for dancing. The *Detroit*

Gazette summoned the gentlemen to the preliminary meeting. Committees were appointed—on wine, music, suppers, invitations, and there was a general committee of reference. The officers of the army stationed at the post always participated in these arrangements and in the general management. The British officers at Fort Malden and Sandwich and the principal citizens of Malden, Sandwich and Petite Cote were invited. In return they generally gave a dinner and ball to our citizens. Among other regulations, no gentleman was allowed to appear in the ball-room except in full dress, officers in uniform. Boots were not permitted, and knee-breeches were the rule.

General Macomb commanded the post of Detroit for several years, and some of the most accomplished men in the army were on his staff or under his command. These officers improvised a theater in the upper story of a large brick storehouse—belonging to the government—that stood at the corner of Cass and Woodbridge Streets. It is said that they made the scenery—painted in a style exceedingly creditable to their taste—and that their plays were all well chosen. Tickets for the winter were issued to the families invited, and at the close of the season a ball in return was given by the latter to the military. As the ladies did not perform, the gentlemen were compelled to assume their dress and parts. It was said the late James Watson Webb, when stationed here as second lieutenant in the army, figured as one of the prettiest brunettes ever seen inside of that playhouse. James Watson Webb was later editor or proprietor of the New York *Courier and Enquirer,* and was also at one time our minister to Brazil.

My aunt, Mrs. Hinchman, occupied the place for two or three years, and during that time I was a very frequent visitor there, and have often, when in its banqueting room, pondered on the gay and distinguished company that had in the past from time to time gathered there.

> "When their hearts beat high and warm,
> With music, song and dance and wine."

The ample kitchen that abutted on Wayne Street and the alley leading to it, with its immense fireplace, would, it seemed to me, take in a quarter-cord of four-foot wood at once. Its immense swinging crane with the great array of pots, kettles and tin baking ovens needed to prepare the viands—all must have been a sight to see. The kitchen, the fireplace and the swinging crane were there when I was, but my aunt did not have use for as many appliances as did the former occupant.

* * *

The Mason family occupied a house on the south side of Congress Street, midway between Shelby and Wayne Streets. Hon. John T. Mason was appointed governor to succeed Governor Cass, and his son, Stevens T. Mason, was secretary of the territory. Governor Mason died in office and his son succeeded him as governor, with Kintzing Pritchette as secretary of the territory. The deceased governor's family continued to live in the old house, and to it Stevens T. brought his new wife, a young lady from New York.

The young governor's inauguration of the Toledo war, his being succeeded by Hon. John Horner (from the east somewhere, September 5, 1835), and his nomination and election as governor of the state after its admission to the union, in opposition to Hon. C. C. Trowbridge, are matters of history.

The notice of the appointment of his successor to the territorial governorship came to Governor Mason while he was addressing his troops, in Toledo, his first intimation. It made the soldier boys, his friends and adherents, fighting mad. Horner was not regarded with much favor, and after a brief reign he quit in disgust. I remember him quite well; he was a tall, slim, dyspeptic looking individual, and what made him most talked about was that when the weather was cool he always sported a fur muff and tippet when out of doors. Horner was succeeded, I think, by Governor Porter.

In the interim, between his being ousted by Horner and his election as governor of the new state, Mason and his adherents had a lively time. Among the latter were Kintzing Pritchette, Isaac Rowland, Franklin Sawyer, Dr. Farnsworth, George C. Bates, Dr. Rufus Brown, Dr. Scovel, Humes and Andrew Porter, Alfred Coxe and many others whose names I do not recall. All the young element were with him, "tooth and nail." The older element opposed him, principally on account of his extreme youth, he being but a little over 21 years of age. Excitement ran high and led to occasional encounters on the streets between the different parties. I call to mind one of which I was an eye-witness that happened on what is now Ives corner. It was quite a lively tussle for a time, Mason's party coming out ahead, but with some little damage to their attire.

Stevens T. Mason was a very handsome man, as his portrait in the state capitol at Lansing will testify. Genial, generous, gifted, fearless and strenuous withal what wonder is it that he enlisted the admiration and devotion of his adherents? After serving his term as governor of the new state he removed with the entire family to New York, I think, except one, a sister (Kate), who was captured by Isaac Rowland and induced to make this city her future home, as Mrs. Rowland.

* * *

Stevens T. Mason's father, John T. Mason, served as secretary of the territory of Michigan until 1831. In that year Governor Cass went into President Jackson's cabinet as secretary of war. The elder Mason saw that here was a chance for the elevation of his son. He also resigned and put forth a request for the appointment of his son as his successor. Jackson appointed Geo. B. Porter as governor and Stevens T. Mason as secretary. The latter appointment created great indignation all over the state, many protests being made against it. The appointee was only 19 years of age and in his position would be acting governor during the absence, illness, death or resignation of Porter. Meetings were held all over the territory and delegates appointed to a central body, with the intention of demanding the resignation or removal of young Mason. In Detroit an indignation meeting appointed Oliver Newberry, Andrew Mack and John E. Schwartz as a committee to report whether Stevens Thompson Mason was 21 years of age. They reported July 25th, 1831, that he was not of age, and that President Jackson knew it. A few days after, Mason responded in a conciliatory manner.

A banquet was given by Governor Cass at his residence, just before leaving for Washington, at which all the notables and officials of the city and territory were present. After appropriate addresses by Cass and Major John Biddle, toasts became the order of the evening.

Austin E. Wing arose and said, "Gentlemen, fill your glasses." After the glasses were charged, he held up his own and said: "The health of the ex-secretary of state." It was a ticklish toast, as both John T. Mason and his son were being fulminated against by everybody. But the elder Mason saw a chance of recovering lost ground, and he promptly took it. He thanked the assemblage for the compliment, and said he had always tried to do his duty. Then he talked about his son and successor. "My boy is smart, gentlemen," he said. "He understands the duties of the office. I hope you will not condemn him unheard." He then placed his right hand upon his heart, and continued in broken tones. "Try the boy, gentlemen, try the boy. President Jackson is not to blame. If any blame can be attached, it is in the affection of the father for the son." It was an effective plea. Tears sprang to the eyes of nearly all his auditors, and the indignation at the appointment of a lad who had not attained legal manhood, passed away like a summer cloud. Mason's subsequent career as acting governor and the real thing are a matter of history.

Colonel Winder said of Miss Emily Mason, a sister of the governor: "She was the most beautiful and accomplished woman of her time, and I can give you no idea of the beauty and elegance of her appearance when she was bridesmaid at my wedding."

Governor Stevens T. Mason died in New York, and his remains repose in a vault in that city. It was proposed at one time to ask the legislature for an appropriation for the purpose of returning the body to Michigan, probably Lansing, for sepulchre. Thus far nothing has been done in that direction.

* * *

Prominent residents on Congress Street, between Woodward Avenue and First Street in the early days, were Doctor Hurd, corner Woodward Avenue and Congress (west); Mrs. Pettie, afterwards Mrs. Eurotas P. Hastings, (east); Henry V. Disbrow, southwest corner of Congress and Griswold; Lewis Goddard, northwest corner of Griswold; John Hale, east side, between Griswold and Shelby; Dr. John R. Ellis, in the double brick house near Shelby; S. P. Brady, H. K. Sanger, at one time cashier of the Old Bank of Michigan, along about 1835 or '36, lived at No. 40 Congress Street (west). The house is still standing. Mr. Sanger came here from Canandaigua, N. Y., and remained with the above bank until it went out of business in 1841, when he returned to Canandaigua for quite a time. He returned to Detroit however, and entered the Michigan Insurance Co.'s bank as its cashier, where he remained until his death. I think he was also at one time internal revenue collector. Henry P. Sanger, one of his sons, is now or was—secretary of the Wholesale Grocers' Association of Michigan. General Joseph P. Sanger, U. S. A., was born in the house No. 40 Congress Street. He has been in the United States military service since the outbreak of the Civil War, and gained so much distinction in that war the Cuban War, and in the Philippines, that from the rank of lieutenant in the First Regiment Michigan Volunteer Infantry, he has risen grade by grade, until quite recently President Roosevelt retired him as a major general of the United States army. There were three daughters, one married Bishop Paddock, another Colonel DeGarmo Jones, who was at the outbreak of the Civil War assistant adjutant general of Michigan. The third married Charles Grimscoe. Phineas Davis lived along here on Congress Street, as did John J. Garrison, and A. C. McGraw. Dr. Stebbins, Peter E. Demill, between Griswold and Shelby; the widow of General Chas. Larned and family, corner of Shelby. Where is now the Shelby block was a brick dwelling occupied by Captain Whipple, U. S. Topographical Engineers; also a wooden building occupied at one time by Mrs. Snelling, widow of Captain Snelling, U. S. A., as a boarding house, and after by John W. Strong and Sheriff A. S. Johnson.

Mr. Johnson had three daughters—interesting, bright, vivacious girls. Annie, the second daughter, was particularly charming. They all belonged to the dancing element, and Annie, at one of the Firemen's balls, given at the National Hotel (Russell House) was the belle of the evening. She married Ephriam Brown, a prominent dry goods merchant here in the forties. His store was on the southeast corner of Woodward Avenue and Congress Street. Another daughter married Lewis F. Tiffany, of the boot and shoe firm of Tiffany & Cushing, and for many years manager of the boot and shoe firm of H. P. Baldwin & Co. To him the latter firm was indebted for the large city trade that it enjoyed, as he was very popular among all classes, particularly the younger. He was also a Brady Guard. Another daughter mrried Mr. Cushing, of the firm above mentioned. Annie married for her second husband Mr. Higgs, and she is now living with her married daughter at Glendower, Va. The others are all dead, I believe.

On the opposite corner lived Dr. Geo. B. Russell. Adjoining lived Judge Abraham C. Canniff, and Jerry Dean in a double brick house which is still standing. After they vacated it Dr. A. R. Terry resided there for a while, as did Lawyer David E. Harbaugh. Along here, between Shelby and Wayne Streets, lived from time to time Governor Stevens T. Mason, Lawyer Wm. Hale, Cleaveland Hunt, Fred Buhl, Captain J. N. Macomb, U. S. topographical engineer; Will H. Biddle, Major Macklin, paymaster U. S. A.; Jonathan Thompson, M. S. Smith, Lieutenant Rose, U. S. A., (son-in-law of Governor Baldwin), and Allan Sheldon.

The Mason residence, after they vacated it, had various tenants. The last before it was replaced by the "Austin House," was, I think, Lawyer Hale. Adjoining, on the corner of Wayne Street, was the residence of G. Mott Williams, son of General John R. Williams. It is still standing.

* * *

On the southeast corner of Congress and Wayne Streets lived Dr. J. L. Whiting. The house was built for him and he lived there for many years. All will remember the genial doctor, as also his son, J. Talman Whiting, the latter a pioneer in Lake Superior navigation, associated with Sheldon McKnight.

Dr. J. L. Whiting, from the time of his advent here until the day of his death, was one of Detroit's most esteemed and influential citizens. He came here in 1817 from Auburn, N. Y., where he had been practicing medicine. He married, at Hudson, N. Y., on the 16th of February, 1821, Miss Harriet Talman, daughter of Dr. John Talman, mayor of that city. Mr. A. G. Whitney, who was a prominent citizen here in the twenties and early thirties, married a sister of Mrs. Talman at Hudson, N. Y., April 3, 1820. Mr. Whitney's name appears often in the early records of Detroit and Wayne County.

Doctor Whiting quit the general practice of his profession about 1836, and ventured in the forwarding and commission business at the foot of Woodward Avenue, east side. He worked up a fine business and was prospering successfully until the disastrous fire of 1837 wiped him out completely. What his next business ventures for some years were I do not know. He afterward formed a co-partnership in the land and insurance agency business with Charles G. Adams. The firm was successful for many years. The untimely death of Mr. Adams was a grievons blow to the doctor, but the latter continued the business until his death. Doctor Whiting, during the cholera seasons of 1832-4 and later, rendered most efficient service, particularly during the first scourge, when the citizens of Detroit and vicinity were almost paralyzed with terror.

The doctor's first trip to Detroit was most eventful. His account of it that appeared in one of the city's papers some twenty-five years ago is quite interesting and amusing, besides showing the hard times the early settlers of this city had to submit to. He relates his experience thus:

"I had been practicing in Auburn, N. Y., for about two months, when a couple of acquaintances came along, each with a sleigh load of dry goods stock which had been unsalable and with which they proposed to start business in Detroit. They revived my original intention and we made up a party for the long journey. I bought a tandem harness, and hitching up my horse before one of their train, I made a definitive start westward.

"Four days of brisk travel over crisp snow brought us to Buffalo, then a small village which was trying to do some 'Phoenix' business by rising from the ashes in which the British had left it during the war. It was in a pitiful plight from the scourge of fire to which it had been subjected, but its people were hopeful and brought brave hearts to their work of rebuilding the fortunes of the place.

"A few miles east of Buffalo we were overtaken by a young man who had already been to Detroit, and who was returning thither in a cutter drawn by one horse, while another was led behind. He proposed that I should join him and go by way of Canada, thus saving two hundred miles in distance and four days' time. Assenting, I placed my horse ahead of his and on Tuesday, February 15th, 1817, we started for Black Rock, where we intended crossing the Niagara River. This, however, we found to be impracticable as the river was full of floating ice, and the winds were blowing great guns from Lake Erie. We had to wait until the following Friday for a change of wind, when we embarked with our horses and possessions on the solitary scow or flat-boat of the place.

"This movement nearly deprived me of the pleasure of telling you the story. We were slowly floating in the eddy, up-stream, when the ferry-man raised a sail, a movement which so frightened the horses of my friend Knapp, that they immediately jumped overboard. The day was one of the coldest I ever experienced, before or since, and the work of fishing the poor animals out was desperately chilling. I was left in the scow with my horse Charley, to contemplate the pleasing prospect of being crushed by a floating cake of ice, or driven over the ledge of rocks, which, I had learned from the venerable Jedediah Morse in early life, existed some twenty miles down the river.

"However, I was rescued at length, and while we were laboring to restore life to our frozen horses, a small boat came across from Fort Erie with a party, among whom were Colonel DeGarmo Jones and Shubael Conant, both of whom advised us to abandon our contemplated journey through Canada, and travel by the south shore of Lake Erie.

"This course we followed, retracing our steps through Buffalo and passing the first night at Hamburg, eight miles west. We headed next day for Cleveland, passing through Dunkirk, Cross Roads, Conneaut and Painesville, then all mere clusters of from six to a dozen log cabins, surrounded by a dense primeval forest.

"The roads, to give them their title of courtesy, had been merely cut out of the woods and were full of stumps.

"At Conneaut we quartered ourselves in the only tavern in the place. I was wofully alarmed at the prospect of being taken ill in such a place, far from home and friends, and among a lot of Irish emigrants, who were busily engaged in disposing of villainous whisky. But the doctor of the place gave me a mixture of boiling water, vile sugar and whisky, yet warm from the still, and I was placed in bed and covered with blankets, coats, etc., to give the whisky and the covering a chance to knock out the chill, which they did, and in the morning I was as well as ever.

"When we reached Cleveland, a village of some fifteen or twenty houses, we found the ground bare. The snow was all gone and with it the road. The country was a wilderness and there was no guide. Progress seemed impossible, unless we chose to go by the ice on the lake, and that did not appear either safe or practicable. We took the advice of the oldest inhabitant, Doctor Long, who said that as the winter had been very cold, the ice was probably pretty firm to Huron, forty-five miles distant.

"So we bought a jumper of 'pung' and got to Rocky River, some seven or eight miles distant, the same evening. Next morning the ice on the lake was covered with from eight to ten inches of snow, the day grew bright and warm, with a strong wind from the south, the snow thawed and we plodded on through heavy slush. Cracks appeared in the ice, at first but a few inches wide, but toward evening, as the wind became stronger, increasing to a yard or more, ugly looking crevasses, below which we knew there were seventy-five feet of lake water.

"As evening approached we came to one frightful chasm in the ice. We had jumped a good many during the afternoon, but none so formidable as this gap. My friend Knapp was for going back, but this I opposed, insisting that as we had made forty miles of our journey, we should not back down before the other five. Besides we were on a rock-bound coast, there were no landings, and there was nothing for us to do but to push ahead or lose ourselves in the yawning holes which we had already passed.

"So giving the horses a cut each, I made them jump the crevasse, which they did very neatly, indeed. We reached Huron before nightfall, and after a hearty supper, slept the sleep of the weary.

"At sunrise I went down to the shore to examine the condition of the ice. There was none to examine. Every particle had floated off during the night to the Canadian shore.

"Here was another stoppage—our ice gone. There was nothing for it but to leave the 'jumper' we had bought, at Cleveland, and take to our saddles.

"We waited four or five days for the mail-carrier, Barron, then young to the service, to act as our guide through the Black Swamp of Ohio, for, with the disappearance of the snow, the overland route had completely disappeared also. When Barron arrived we started on horseback on the dreariest portion of our way, reaching lower Sandusky late in the afternoon.

"The river was greatly swollen by a freshet, but it had to be crossed if we did not want to stay out in the cold at night, for there was no shelter on the east bank. Lusty shouting brought out an Indian who paddled over in his canoe and ferried us across for a small fee. We led our horses as they swam behind us.

"The next day, Monday, February 24, we plunged into the Black Swamp, a terrible, dismal, bottomless, almost impassable stretch of nearly thirty miles of black ash. We forded the Carrying River in its very midst and reached Maumee about 4 P. M.

The swamp was trodden about with hoof and footprints, the only indications of a trail, save the blazed trees. So long as the frost lasted these indications of the trail lasted, but when the thaw came, it disappeared and the blazed trail alone remained.

"When we were about three parts through the swamp, Barron lost the trail of blazed trees and placed us in a new and most painful dilemma. He insisted that the trail lay to the left, while I was equally positive that it lay to the right. So to settle the matter we placed Knapp in the center to act as a rallying point and started out in opposite directions. I recovered the trail after tramping about one-third of a mile, summoned my companions by shouting like a trooper, and well contented with our luck, we pushed along afresh, completing our passage of the Black Swamp in a single day, a very astonishing feat in those primitive times.

"On Tuesday we reached the River Raisin, whose east side, then as now, was known as Frenchtown, and spent the night with Gabriel Godfroy. We successively crossed the Rivers Raisin, Swan Creek, Huron, Ecorse and Rouge, and reached Detroit February 26, 1817, at 4 P. M.

"Detroit was then the extreme western point of white civilization, and considerably mixed with white and red at that. I made my first home with the late Major David C. McKinstry, on Jefferson Avenue, between Shelby and Griswold Streets, and nearly opposite the old Campau homestead. I rented a room in a store kept by Thomas Palmer, father of Senator Palmer, in a house belonging to the late Joseph Campau, and in it I conducted my practice as a physician for three years.

"My practice increased to such an extent that I was obliged, in 1820-1, to move over to the corner of Jefferson Avenue and Griswold Street, where stood a two-story wooden building, in which I had half of the first floor.

"This was then the center of the city, which was bounded on the south by the river, on the east by Brush Street, on the north by Larned Street and on the west by Cass Street.

"The people were suffering bitterly from the effects of the war with the British. They were only a handful in number, some 900 souls in all, white or native born, English-speaking Americans; outside of the garrison there were only about fifty. They had lost pretty much everything during the war and were suffering from the want of the very necessaries of life. All their provisions, their oxen, hogs and sheep, came from Ohio, through the Black Swamp and were very dear.

"There was a full regiment of infantry at the fort, with two companies of artillery and a few engineers. General McComb was in command, and had a staff of officers who made a very pleasant society for a number of years. You could scare up a dance almost any evening by merely snapping your fingers, as I might say, and you were not expected to half ruin yourself by laying in vast stores of expensive refreshments. The society of the day, if restricted as to numbers, was cultivated and refined, and life was very pleasant."

Dr. Zina Pitcher built on the northwest corner of Congress and Wayne Streets a residence and office which he occupied for many years, until his death. Nearly all the old settlers will remember Doctor Pitcher. The house is still standing.

Edward Kanter at one time lived along here between Wayne and Cass Streets, as did Allen A. Rabineau and James Hanmer, John Stephens (of Stephens & Field) lived in a fine brick residence on the northeast corner of Cass Street (afterwards Gray & Baffy furniture factory).

* * *

John Stephens was of the firm of Stephens & Field, wholesale grocers, Woodward Avenue. The first acquaintance I had with Mr. Stephens was in Mt. Clemens along in the forties. He and his brother carried on an extensive grocery business in that town, made much money there, and after a while drifted to this city, going into the same business, but not together. John went with Moses W. Field, corner of Woodward Avenue and Woodbridge Street (Mariners' Church). The brother opened up in the checkered store that stood where the present Majestic building looms up, its top almost out of sight. Mrs. Stephens and her attractive daughters drew around them in Mt. Clemens all that went to make up the social life of the place, and almost of Macomb County as well. It is quite safe to say that upon the advent of the above family to this city, they at once took here the same position socially that they had occupied in Mt. Clemens. Any one of the present day who had the pleasure of enjoying their splendid hospitality, in their fine residence, corner of Congress and Cass Streets, will, I am sure, bear witness to my statement that their family circle was a most charming one to be drawn into. Mr. and Mrs. Stephens passed away many years ago.

One of the daughters married George Lamson, son of Darius Lamson; another married Lieutenant J. Kemp Mizner, U. S. A., who served with distinction through the Civil War as colonel of a Michigan cavalry regiment, and died a few years ago a retired brigadier-general, U. S. A. Another married Captain Van Vliet, U. S. A., and another Mr. Little. One of the boys, William, enlisted as quartermaster-sergeant in the First Michigan Volunteer Infantry (three months), went to the front and was in the first Bull Run battle. At the expiration of his term of service he was mustered out in this city. Afterward he married Miss Marsh, a society belle of Kalamazoo, a grandniece of Uncle Shubael Conant. The wedding at Kalamazoo and the reception given here were quite brilliant affairs, and a nine days' wonder. The other son married a daughter of Lawyer Samuel G. Watson.

I know that some of the members of the Stephens family are dead, but think Mrs. George Lamson is alive and residing in Santa Barbara, Cal., and Mrs. Captain Van Vliet, living at Fort Slocum, New York harbor. I think the son that married Miss Watson is alive, as also the daughter that married Mr. Little.

* * * *

Reynolds Gillett, father of the late John R. Gillett, occupied the southwest corner of Congress and Wayne Streets, and lived there for many years. The old house is replaced by the fine building erected by Mr. Croul for storage purposes. Charles Lum lived adjoining. He was the father of the late Charles M. Lum, and a master builder of wide reputation. The "Old Brick Brewery," whose ample dimensions loomed up so conspicuously for so many years on the corner of Congress and First Streets, has disappeared and its site is now occupied by the William Dwight Lumber Co., a much more sightly point than it was a few years ago. It was a famous brewery in its day, when Thomas Owen, Curt Emerson, Josh Carew, Carne, Carew & Co., Davis & Moore, William Duncan and others operated it. The ale product turned out was of the finest quality and much money was made there. But lager beer came and knocked the heavy beers and ales out of the market and killed the old brewery.

John Bloom, the sailmaker, lived opposite this brewery, on First Street, in a plain brick dwelling. He died there. The house is still standing. Old John Bloom was of foreign birth, came to America about 1830, from Boomusaund, Sweden, and to Detroit in 1834. He started business as a ship chandler and sailmaker, near the foot of Wayne Street, thence to the foot of Cass Street, thence to the foot of the De Garmo Jones warehouse, foot of Shelby Street, thence to the Abbott block, foot of Griswold Street, and finally to the foot of Woodward Avenue, where he was in business when he died. The business was carried on by his son, Nelson, who died a few years ago.

After awhile the lower part of Congress Street, between First and Third Streets, became quite aristocratic. D. Bethune Duffield, Eben N. Willcox, R. N. Rice, George Jerome, Charles Howard, Samuel F. Barstow, U. Tracy Howe, Captain Gager (of steamer Albany), Judge Longyear, Mr. Emmons, father of Judge and Jed P. C. Emmons, and a number of others, living there. The brick mansion (still standing), on the northwest corner of Second Street, was built and first occupied by Charles Howard (at one time mayor), afterwards by Gurdon Williams. It was a palatial residence in its day and witnessed many a festive scene, but now dilapidated. Its glory has departed, as has the glory of the rest of that section, so far as sites for private residence are concerned.

The house on the southwest corner of Cass Street and Lafayette Avenue was occupied by Lawyer Charles H. Stewart, father of Mrs. William Gray, and afterward by Mr. John Drew. Mr. Stewart was an exceedingly sharp lawyer and practitioner. He, Theodore Romeyn and John A. Welles (the latter not a lawyer, however, but an exceedingly clever banker) were almost always concerned in some enterprise where money-getting was the final issue. Kinsing Pritchette and Governor Stevens T. Mason were sometimes mixed up with the rest in some way. This was about the time the state got the $5,000,000 loan from the "Morris Canal & Banking Association" of New Jersey. Mrs. Stewart was an intellectual lady and a fine musician, whom he married in Ireland.

While occupying the premises on the southwest corner of Lafayette Avenue and Cass Street, vacated by Drew, Mr. Stewart built for himself the fine wooden residence (still standing) on the southwest corner of Fort and Second Streets, in which he lived quite a while. Afterwards the residence of Henry K. Sanger and after him Henry A. Newland; it is held by the heirs of the latter yet. After Mr. Stewart left this city he lived in Washington, New York and St. Louis, spending the summers on Staten Island during the following twenty years. He then removed to San Francisco, where he died, January 20, 1871.

The mother and daughters were familiar figures on Fort Street and vicinity, and always drew marked attention to themselves when taking an outing on account of the rapid pace with which they proceeded; the three always arm in arm, Mrs. Stewart in the middle. There were other rapid walkers living in the immediate neighborhood of the Stewarts, and I presume it was from the former they caught the infection. They were John Owen, Theo. H. Hinchman, the Hall brothers (Lewis and William), and most citizens of the present day know what rapid pedestrians they were.

My recollections of the Stewarts are very pleasant, particularly from the following incident. One afternoon, passing up Shelby Street, where the alley crosses the street in the rear of the present *News* building, I found a lady's gold watch lying on the sidewalk, evidently dropped by some passerby. Shortly hand bills appeared telling of the loss, and also that $30 reward would be paid to the finder if delivered at the Stewart residence, corner Cass and Lafayette. I hastened to get the watch into the hands of the owner, but declined the promised reward, which was pressed upon me, though I hated to, I must own. Thirty dollars was such a fortune to a small boy. But Mrs. Stewart did not forget me. Two or three days afterward she and her daughters called at our house, corner Fort and Shelby Streets, and presented me with an elegant bound book, one of those handsome and interesting keepsakes that were annually issued from the press in those days. I treasured it for years and years until some one stole it. One of the daughters married Lawyer William Gray, and the other Lieutenant W. D. Whiting, afterwards a commodore of the United States navy.

* * *

Mrs. John Drew at that day was a handsome, attractive woman, and drew around her quite a sprinkling of the Fort

Street feminine society, as well as many of the gay bachelors of that period, among whom were David Smart, H. M. Roby, John and Frank Hunt, Josh Carew, Walter Ingersoll, the Randolphs, Alexander H. Newhould, Sam Suydam, Ed M. Pitcher, Dr. L. Cobb, Barney Campau and others. Many a pleasant gathering was had in her parlors, some of which I participated in. After vacating these premises the Drews removed down the river, in the vicinity of the Governor Porter house (Sylvester Larned). Mr. Drew died here. Mrs. Drew married Mr. "Sol" White, M. P. P., of Windsor.

Mr. Drew was of English birth—a quiet, easy-going gentleman, well liked as far as I knew. He erected and owned the brick building on the southeast corner of Jefferson Avenue and Griswold Street, at one time occupied by the board of trade after it vacated its old quarters corner of Woodbridge and Shelby streets. At his death his widow inherited the property. It passed through various hands, until quite recently it reached those of Senator T. W. Palmer, who has, after all these years, the satisfaction of becoming the owner of the property where was located the dwelling of his father (Thomas Palmer) and the mercantile establishment of Friend & Thos. Palmer as well. The brick store, with dwelling overhead, was erected by the two brothers somewhere about 1823 and 4. The upper part, in which Senator Palmer was born, was used as a dwelling by Thomas Palmer (as was the custom then) until the fire of 1830, which so damaged the building that he was forced to vacate it, and he allowed it to pass from his hands. Aside from being at one time the location of the Palmer store and homestead, and the place of his birth, Senator Palmer values the spot as being historic ground, for it is but a few feet outside of where at one time (before 1805) was located the only block house and entrance gate on the eastern side of Fort Pontchartrain, the gate through which Pontiac and his dusky warriors were admitted on that memorable morning on an alleged mission of peace. How his murderous designs were frustrated by Gladwin and the Indian maiden or some other redskin, most all are familiar with, but I prefer to put faith in the pleasing story of the Indian maiden warning Major Gladwin of Pontiac's bloody intent. Major Richardson, in his romance of Wacousta published many years ago, intended, no doubt, to depict this Indian maiden in the character of "Oucanasta;" Major Gladwin in that of "Major DeHaldimer," and Pontiac in that of "Wacousta." The story of Wacousta was dramatized, and Dean & McKinney, theatrical managers from Buffalo, about 1837, gave a representation of it, at the old brick theater near where is now the public library. The play was very fine, and the characters were well rendered. Mr. McKinney took the part of "Wacousta," and Mrs. McClure that of "Oucanasta." I do not call to mind who acted "Major DeHaldimer." Mr. McKinney made as bad an Injun as can well be imagined, and Mrs. McClure personated the devoted, confiding Indian maiden to perfection. Major Richardson, the author, was in the city at the time, a guest of Governor Stevens T. Mason.

It was through this gate also that Captain Dalzell and his brave followers passed to their disaster at the mouth of Bloody Run, and through it the shattered and bleeding remnants of his command returned. If the spirits of Pontiac and his warriors and those of Dalzell and his men ever haunt this earth they must, one would think, be much in evidence on this very spot. Through this same gate trooped in and out, for more than a hundred years, the dwellers sheltered behind the pickets of Fort Ponchartrain, who sought an eastern egress. At the foot of Griswold Street and only two blocks or so distant from this corner, is the very spot upon which Cadillac landed when he founded Detroit more than 200 years ago.

The location of the office of the *Detroit Gazette*, the only journal in the northwest for many years, adjoined the Palmer premises, and also gave much prominence to this locality. In and around the editorial rooms of this paper gathered from time to time all the politicians and the influential men of that day. Austin E. Wing, Sheldon McKnight, Colonel John Biddle, Judge McDonnell, Solomon Sibley, Judge Jas. Witherell, Judges Griffin and Woodward, Colonel McDougall, Governor Cass, General Charles Larned, Judge Conant, Father Richard, Judge May, Judge Abbott, Commodore Breevort and many others. To my mind no other locality in Detroit possesses so much interest as does this.

After the English came, the large number of officers of the garrison, coupled with Scotch and English merchants who soon followed, contributed to form a society that could hardly have been more attractive.

It is said the English and Scotch merchants kept within the confines of this little stockade immense stocks of goods for the purpose of trading with the Indians. Their accumulations at one time amounted, it is said, to the large sum of $5,000,000. This was the most important trading post, and indeed almost the only one in all the northwest, and to which, as to a Mecca, all the Indian tribes and noted Indian chiefs bent their steps. Pontiac, Tecumseh and his brother, the Prophet, were here or in close vicinity constantly. Pontiac's dream of capturing this and other posts from the British kept him ever vigilant, and when his scheme in regard to Detroit failed ignominiously he was filled with rage and chagrin and later at Bloody Run poured the vials of his wrath on the ill-fated Captain Dalzell and his followers.

John Logan, the Cayuga chief, whose speech to Lord Dunmore, Governor of Virginia, is familiar to every school boy, was here in 1774, and after the treaty of Chillicothe, O., he resided for many years in this vicinity.

Alexander and Wm. Macomb were extensive merchants here in 1777. They drew at one time on their correspondents in Montreal for over $250,000, and frequently for as high as $150,000 and $200,000 against furs they had shipped.

* * *

In these sketches of the old settlers I have seldom mentioned any except those that I knew well, or their descendants—some of the latter are with us yet. To the later resident of Detroit or the newcomer, these recollections may not be of much interest, but to the descendants of those hardy pioneers—whose early career here of industry and frugality, and whose wise forecast not only laid the foundations of their own private fortunes, but whose enlightened enterprise and liberality contributed so much to render Detroit what she now is, a wealthy, prosperous city, with an honorable record in the archives of commercial enterprise—they ought to possess interest of the most absorbing character.

In this connection the newcomer in our midst may, if he stops to consider and dwell upon the fact, be reminded that the pioneers from Cadillac's time down (with their descendants) have lived, moved and had their being right here where is our goodly city; walked the streets in old Fort Ponchartrain, and later, after the fire of 1805, trod the streets of New Detroit, and busied themselves in all the walks of life as we do now here today, but with this difference—they carried their lives in their hands, ever in dread of the hostile savage. Pontiac, Tecumseh, Kish-Kon-Ko, Walk-in-the-Water and their savage followers from time to time were held by the dwellers of the town in the direst dread, and were familiar figures on the streets of both the old and the new town and the country round about in time of peace. There were plenty of Indians here after my advent, streets thronged with them during spring, summer and autumn, but they were always most peaceable and friendly.

I presume there is hardly a rod square of ground underlying the city from Beaubien Street to First, and from the river back to Fort Street and in the immediate vicinity of the latter, that does not contain the remains of a human being. When the Cass farm front was excavated into the river over a hundred dead bodies of Indan warriors were exhumed. Their bones went into the dirt carts, the implements of war and the chase, as also the various ornaments buried with them becoming the spoil of the lucky finder.

Jefferson Avenue in the immediate vicinity of where was old St. Anne's Church before the fire of 1805, must now contain the remains of many who were in the old church cemetery. Years ago, when ditches were being dug in that locality, I repeatedly saw workmen uncover coffins of those that had been buried there (for 105 years it was a burying ground).

Detroit, I think, may be called one vast cemetery. When excavating for the foundations of buildings now occupying the old St. Anne's Church square on Larned Street, many, many dead bodies were disturbed and scattered. Even Colonel Hamtramck's remains might have met the fate of the rest if some kindly hand had not seen to it that they got safe sepulchre in Mt. Elliott cemetery.

Those that fell at the battle of Bloody Run, tradition says, were buried between Jefferson Avenue and Woodbridge Street, below Griswold. The ground we tread on is sacred because of the martyrs in the cause of civilization and religion who have suffered and perished here. It is said that Pope Pius V., while crossing the piazza of St. Peter's in Rome, with the Polish ambassador, suddenly stooped down and gathered a handful of dust, saying, "Take this (as a relic) for it has been reddened with the blood of martyrs." The same might with equal propriety apply to the soil in and around the location of Fort Ponchartrain and Old Detroit.

> If you but stop a moment on the way,
> When passing o'er the road from day to day,
> Perhaps a voice long silent with the dead
> Will you admonish for your careless tread.

For more than 100 years the small community within the stockade of Fort Ponchartrain (Old Detroit), and on Griswold street and vicinity were most of the time at outs with the Indians, who swarmed around the little picketed enclosure, eager to put a bullet into the first white man who gave them the least show. And it is quite safe to say that those inside the fort were equally as alert and eager to return the compliment. One can readily imagine what a dusty, perilous time the inhabitants of our old town must have had, particularly during Pontiac's siege. In this connection I think it would be appropriate to give a description of the old town of Detroit before the fire of 1805—its streets, names of some of its residents, etc., which I found among the papers of the late Judge B. F. H. Witherell.

DETROIT IN 1805, BEFORE THE FIRE.

The old town, previous to the fire, occupied a site embraced within the following limits: Griswold Street on the east and Cass Street on the west, and extended from the river to Larned Street, secured by a stockade on the east and west, running from the river to Fort Shelby (present north line of Congress Street). In the rear of the fort were the royal military gardens, on the east the commanding officers field, and east of the stockade, on the bank of the river, was the navy garden. Where Woodward Avenue now is and between Woodbridge and Atwater Streets was the navy yard. The names of the streets in the old town were St. Louis, St. Anne, St. Joseph, St. James, St. Honore and L'Erneau. The width of the widest street, St. Anne, was but twenty feet, at either end of which were gates, forming the only entrances into the city. A carriage-way, called the Chemin du Ronde, encircled the town just inside the pallisades. A large creek called the "River Savoyard," bordered by low marshy ground, separated the high ridge upon which the old town was built, from the high grounds along the summit of which runs at present Fort Street. That part of town not required for public use was subdivided into fifty-nine lots.

The names of the freeholders of the old town were Askin, Abbott, McDougall, Meldrum, Parke, Grant, Chagrin, McGregor, Campau, McKea, Oadney, Macomb, Roe, Howard, Tremble, Sparkin, Leith, Williams, Ridley, Frazer, Haines, Dolson, Jayer, Lefoy, Thebauld, Duhamel, St. Cosmo, Belanger, LaFleur, Cote, Scott, Bird, La Fontaine, Starling, Andrews, Hardy and Ford.

* * *

Lewis Hall, the jeweler, built and occupied the house where Dr. Brodie now lives on Lafayette Avenue. Hall was succeeded by Judge Jennison, I think. Henry Doty built on and occupied the southeast corner of Lafayette and Cass Avenues, and I think he also built an adjoining building on Lafayette Avenue.

Below this there were a number of residents between Lafayette and Michigan Avenues on Cass and these were Jerry Moore, Mr. Greenwood, Mr. Lothrop, builder, and G. and J. Gibson, carriagemakers. The last named left a comfortable fortune, if we might judge from the fine marble tomb with its tall obelisk that covers the remains of one of the brothers—John, I think—in Elmwood cemetery, near the E. B. Ward monument. They were the sons of old man Gibson, the court crier, who succeeded Day. Jerry Moore, stone mason, and one of the solons of the town, and the widow Stevens, mother of Sears Stevens, lived on Wayne Street, between Fort and Lafayette; Jonathan Keeney and his son Ben operated an extensive foundry here (extensive for those days) on the corner of Shelby and Lafayette Streets, where is now the Philharmonic building. After his father's death the son associated with him William Barclay, and the firm became Barclay & Keeney. The firm did a successful business for several years and then dissolved partnership. Keeney wandered to Panama and took service with the company then building the railroad across the Isthmus, as a civil engineer. Barclay branched off in a foundry of his own, near the foot of Hastings and Atwater Streets. The foundry of Barclay & Keeney had no steam power to furnish wind for the big bellows that kept the blast furnace going, so had to depend on horsepower for that purpose. They had in their employ a comical French boy, who had charge of the horse and the "merry-go-round." The boys used to call him "Drive" in lieu of a better name. You could hear the wheeze of the big bellows for a half mile or more across the commons. Ben Keeney married "Drive's" sister, a pretty French girl. She died shortly after and he married for his second wife a daughter of Mr. John Drew. The family name of the boy "Drive" was "Janeau." He in time blossomed out as one of the most skillful locomotive engineers on the Michigan Central, as did his brother, Noveau.

Fort Street in the early days was an aristocratic street, indeed; it has always been so until within the last eight or ten years. It was more so then than was Jefferson Avenue. Its dominion was contracted, to be sure, extending only from about Griswold Street to Second and Third Streets, but it had plenty of blood. Mrs. Clitz, widow of Captain Clitz, U. S. A., occupied the house on the corner of Fort and Cass Streets, where the Governor Baldwin residence now is. She later on occupied the Norton Strong house, on the southeast corner of Fort and Cass.

John Clitz was a lieutenant in the Second U. S. infantry in 1819, and stationed at Plattsburg, N. Y., when he married Mary Gale Mellen, of Walpole, Mass., and daughter of Gilbert Mellen. They were married at Sackett's Harbor.

Lieutenant Clitz had been a soldier in the war of 1812, being wounded at the battle of Plattsburg. He was for many years aide to the late General Hugh Brady. Mrs. Clitz followed her husband to the various frontier posts, at which he was stationed, enduring the many privations which the families of United States soldiers at remote points were called upon to encounter in those days. When the command was sent to found Fort Brady at the Soo, early in the twenties, she had to live for six months in a tent during severe weather. The lieutenant had attained the rank of captain, and was in command at Fort Mackinac, where he died in 1836, leaving his widow with eight children.

The four sons were John, Henry, William and Edward M. John entered the U. S. navy, and died a rear admiral. Henry entered West Point, and graduated into the infantry. He died a brigadier general. John Clitz and Henry Clitz saw distinguished service in the Mexican as also in the Civil War. The former was with Commodore Perry on his mission to Japan many years ago.

William was for fourteen years in the employ of the late John Owen, in the drug and grocery business, and later went to South America to buy rubber for the Goodyear company. He afterward entered the government service as paymaster's clerk to his brother-in-law, Colonel Pratt, and in 1883 embarked in gold and silver mining in Montana. He was obliged, on account of ill-health, to abandon the latter business, and on the advice of his physician in Montana returned to Detroit. He entered Grace Hospital for treatment for Bright's disease. But from the beginning there was no hope for him, and he died there some time in July, 1893, being cared for by loving and devoted friends. "Billy" Clitz will be remembered by many of the present day as a faithful friend, a man of gallant parts and of sterling character. Edward M. is living, a resident of New York city. He saw service in the Mexican war, and was for some years with A. T. Stewart, the New York dry goods king, in the fifties and sixties. The daughters were all beautiful and highly accomplished. Mary, after rejecting many suitors, at length married Major Pratt, paymaster, U. S. A. Frances married Lieutenant DeRussey, U. S. A., who saw service in the Mexican war, as also in the Civil war. He was retired as a brigadier general, U. S. A., in November, 1882. He died in this city, May 29, 1891. Harriet L. married Lieutenant Sears, U. S. A. Sara married Lieuetnant Anderson, U. S. A., who during the Civil war entered the Confederate service, and became a brigadier general. Afterwards he was chief of police at Savannah, Ga., for many years. They were all fine, lovable people, worthy descendants of a worthy sire and gallant soldier. John and Henry Clitz were boys here, and schoolmates of mine and James Snelling, Henry and William Whiting, John King, Anson Burlingame, the Willcox boys (Eben N. and Orlando B), Tom and Devereaux Williams, Wm. B. Wesson, J. Hyatt Smith, and others. All of the above, with one or two exceptions, attained distinction in the army, in the navy, in diplomacy, etc. Mrs. Clitz died at an advanced age, in 1890, at the residence of her son, General H. B. Clitz, 664 Woodward Avenue.

After Henry Clitz left this city for West Point I did not set eyes upon him again until I met him in New York in the spring of 1852, at the Irving House, corner Broadway and Chambers street. I was east for the purchasing of goods and had under my charge (who were on a visit to the metropolis) Mrs. Judge B. F. H. Witherell, Mrs. B. B. Kercheval, and Mrs. Chas. Bissell, all of this city. Clitz was then a lieutenant and assistant professor at West Point (having graduated into the infantry some years before). He had been informed of the arrival of our party at the Irving House, and came down from the Point "post haste" to meet us. The meeting on his part was quite boisterous. He kissed the ladies, of course, and he threw his arms around me, giving me a regular bear's hug and rubbing his bearded cheek against mine.

I call to mind this latter incident particularly, as when he first left for West Point, or when I last saw him, he was a slight-built youth, with cheeks and chin as fair as a maiden's—while mine when we met were almost beardless—and from a slight figure he had increased much in size. Mr. Zach Chandler was in the city at the time, though not stopping at the same hotel. He called on the ladies, and he requested permission to dine with us, which was readily granted, of course. Clitz was of the party. We had a private dining room, and it goes without saying that we had an enjoyable time. Mrs. Chas. Bissell (nee Ellen Hunt) was then in her prime. I do not remember whether Mr. Chandler was married then or not, but, anyway, he paid particular court to the fair lady. Who could help it? He was quite attentive to our party—took us to Burton's theater on Chambers Street, also escorted the ladies through Stewart's dry goods store, whose white marble palace was directly opposite the Irving House. To make a tour of Stewart's New York dry goods house was something to talk about long after. I did not see John Clitz after he left Detroit to enter the navy as midshipman, until I met him at Asbury Park in the summer of 1889. Then he was a rear admiral of the United States navy, retired. How on the wings of the wind time does travel!

> "Quick! We have but a second,
> Fill round the cup while you may;
> For time, the churl, hath beckoned,
> And we must away, away!"

Kossuth, the Hungarian patriot, was at the Irving House at the same time we were.

Colonel Joshua Howard, U. S. A., on the completion of the arsenal at Dearborn occupied this (Baldwin) house after Mrs. Clitz. The next occupant was, I think, Governor Cass, who purchased the property after his return from France. When Mrs. Canfield, his daughter, completed her residence on the southeast corner of First Street, the governor took up his abode with her, occupying a portion of the Fort Street front as his office. He died there in 1866, aged 83 years.

Governor Cass was not present at Hull's surrender, as all readers of history know, but was very indignant in consequence. Senator Palmer's father was present, as was his grandfather, Colonel James Witherell (alluded to in a former article) with his command; also his uncle, James Cullen Witherell. All were included in the "give-up" and put upon their parole. I think, however, that Witherell, his son and Palmer were taken to Malden as prisoners of war for a short time.

Governor Cass, when he vacated his home for that of his daughter, Mrs. Canfield, left nearly all his pictures, statuary, art-treasures and bric-a-brac, that he had collected during his sojourn in Europe and the far east, in charge of his son, Major Lewis Cass. In the meantime, the governor's daughter, Isabella (Belle Cass) married Baron Von Limbourg, minister to the United States from the Netherlands. She died in Florence, Italy, and left all her property to the gouty old baron. Mr. Halstead, in the New York *Times,* sometime during 1885, relates among other things in regard to the late Major Cass, that "he was in love with and proposed to Miss Emily Mason, sister of Governor Mason, and also was at one time a cadet at West Point." Well, he no doubt might have admired the young lady, as all the young and old bachelors of that day did.

Our people, at that time, lived on the corner of Fort and Shelby Streets, opposite the present postoffice, and the Masons lived in the house that formerly stood where the Austin house on Congress Street now is. My uncle, Thomas Palmer's family, and the Mason and Cass families were quite intimate, and, although a lad of 15 or 16 at the time, I can remember quite vividly the happenings in those days; I was quite old enough to see and remember.

In regard to the intimacy existing at that time, I recall one instance of it. One summer the entire Mason family went east on a pleasure trip for a short season and left the governor's grandmother, Mrs. Moore, aged about 90, in charge of the servants. During the time they were away my aunt, Mrs. Palmer (who was a warm friend and admirer of the old lady), made me sleep there every night they were away, as a sort of a protection to "grandma." But I do not think, nor did I think then, that I would have been of much use in case trouble had appeared. I was a great admirer of the young governor as were all of the young boy element. His dashing manner, military bearing, as well as the sort of heroic glamor thrown around him through his attitude in connection with the so-called Toledo war, just caught the sympathy and admiration of us· youngsters. His gorgeously attired color-bearer on all political occasions (Stillson), on his panoplied charger more than attracted our attention, and when Mr. C. C. Trowbridge (good man that he was and a Whig) was defeated, the young element of the city were tickled.

Thomas H. Hartwell, former president of the board of education, in his recollections of Detroit, published some years ago, has this to say of Governor Stevens T. Mason:

"Mason was a bachelor, and made his home with his mother and sisters. The eldest of the latter, and the reigning belle of Detroit, was Miss Emily Mason. Their residence was on Congress Street between Shelby and Wayne. Great entertainments were given at their house, and all of the bon-ton of the city were invited, and Emily Mason did the honors of the gubernatorial mansion with that elegance of manner, stateliness and grace characteristic of one well versed in all the courtesies and amenities of high social life."

In the early part of 1847 a company (K) was recruited in this city, for the Third United States dragoons, in which regiment, Lewis Cass, Jr., of Detroit, served as mayor. The company was officered by Andrew T. McReynolds, Detroit, as captain; John T. Brown, Tecumseh, as first lieutenant; J. C. D. Williams, Detroit, and Frank Henry, of Wisconsin, as second lieutenants. This company and regiment served in the Mexican War with much distinction, in the army of General Scott, on his advance from Vera Cruz, and participated in the several engagements on his line of operations and especially in the celebrated and successful charge of Captain Phil Kearney on the Gareta San Antonio, in the capture of the City of Mexico. Captain McReynolds received a wound while leading his company, disabling for ever after one of his arms. Lieutenant Williams also was wounded quite severely in one of his arms. The company was mustered out of service July 20, 1848.

While minister to Rome Major Cass fell in love with Miss Ludlow, daughter of an eminent banker of New York, and married her. After a brief married life in Rome she died.

On his return from his mission to Rome cupid again got hold of him and the object of his quest this time was Miss Cornelia Platt, daughter of the Hon. Zephenia Platt, attorney-general of the State of Michigan. Engaging in every particular, slender and graceful, with clear cut features, large, mournful gray eyes that looked as if they could flash stormily at times, a colorless skin and a glory of golden hair, what wonder that she enthralled the major! I think there are but two or three living that remember her as I do. As charming a creature as that sun which brings to early maturity flowers and women alike, ever shone upon. The intimacy on both sides continued for a year or so, and became, from the position the two occupied in society, most marked and commented upon. It was said at the time that the admiration was more upon the major's side than upon that of Miss Cornelia. Be that as it may the intimacy got a sudden chill, and for some unexplained cause Miss Platt packed her trunks and started for a visit to friends in New York, under the charge of Jas. A. Hicks, a prominent merchant here at that time. Before reaching New York they met with disaster. They were passengers on that unfortunate steamer, the Swallow, which was wrecked on the Hudson a short distance below Albany. Many passengers were lost, among them being the mother and father of the late Hon. W. G. Thompson, of this city. Mr. Hicks had the good fortune to save his own life as well as that of his charge, Miss Platt. They managed to get hold of a settee and were held up by it until rescued.

There were about 300 passengers on board, and an article in an Albany paper at the time, giving the particulars, says among other things in regard to it: "Miss Cornelia Platt, a young lady of Detroit, who was on her way to New York, under the charge of Mr. Hicks, of that city, left the boat on a settee, and were taken up a short distance below nearly exhausted. Mr. Hicks, when he went over, had his overcoat on, but finding that he could not do anything with it on, and it requiring great exertion to keep the settee up straight, he succeeded in getting it off. The coat was found this morning nearly five miles below—in one of the pockets was a draft for a considerable amount. Wm. N. Carpenter, of Detroit, was also on board the Swallow at the time of the disaster."

I do not think Miss Platt ever returned to this city. She married, three or four years later, a gentleman engaged in business in New York City, and they lived in Brooklyn.

Mr. Hicks returned to Detroit and of course was made quite a lion of on account of his gallant rescue of the young lady.

A younger sister of Miss Cornelia Platt married Sam Agnew, a son of Professor Agnew, of the University of Michigan. They were living in New York in 1868. I saw them there. Old graduates of the university will remember Professor Agnew and his son, "Sam."

Major Cass, on his return from France, continued to occupy the Cass house, as it was called, until it and its contents were finally sold to Governor Baldwin. During his occupancy he performed a graceful act by permitting the public to see and inspect the art treasures and bric-a-brac it contained. Every Wednesday of the week, the lower part of the house, consisting of the drawing rooms, library, padded sleeping room, etc., were thrown open to the free inspection of the public. What seemed odd was that no one was present to look after things, the sight-seers came and went as they listed. The Major, in addition to his collection of curios lying about loose, would, as if to tempt the cupidity of his visitors, leave around small amounts of gold coin and greenbacks that any one could appropriate if he so desired. But I used to note that this money was always displayed on a small table placed near the closed door of apparently, a bed room. I have been told that this door had a number of small gimlet holes bored in it and by this means the Major could see what was going on. He was, if behind the door, now and then enlightened in regard to his carelessness. Be that as it may, no theft was ever reported nor small articles purloined.

The major went to Paris to spend his last days in retirement and there passed to the beyond. Dr. Rufus Brown, who knew him as intimately as any one in the city, used to say that the major was misunderstood by the community in general;

that he was full of all kindly and generous impulses, ever ready to assist the unfortunate when their cases were brought to his notice.

On the corner of Washington and Michigan Avenues, where is now the Cadillac, William Champ kept the Railroad Temperance House. Champ's father, Nathaniel, occupied the jail after Sheriff Wilson, as sheriff. The father of Nathaniel Champ was sergeant-major of cavalry during the revolution and served under Major Henry Lee. His exploit in attempting to abduct Major-General Arnold, and bring him into the American lines, I presume, is well known by all readers of American history.

Washington conceived a plan for abducting Arnold and bringing him into the American camp. The plan was: Champ was to desert from the American Army and enlist in the British service, for that purpose. He did so and directly formed his plans to capture Arnold. But on the very day when Champ was to execute his plan, Arnold changed his quarters to superintend the embarkation of troops for an expedition southward, to be commanded by himself, and of which expedition Champ was to be a member. By this unexpected movement the latter's plans were entirely frustrated, and he took the first opportunity to desert from his majesty's service and rejoin his command in the American army.

Sheriff Champ was a fine looking man, spare, tall and straight as a young poplar. He had the manner's of the "Old School." Some of his descendants are living in this city yet. I am told that Rob Roberts, son of the late R. E. Roberts, married a granddaughter of his.

F. M. Latourneau, builder, lived on Washington Avenue. Hugh Moffatt, builder, lived on Lafayette Avenue. Latourneau and Moffatt were the boss builders of that day. The latter's skill in that line is shown in the Moffatt block of the present day. The former built the wooden dwelling of Thomas Palmer, corner of Fort and Shelby Streets, conceded to be at that time the finest and best constructed wooden residence in the city. The carved mantels, the carved fan light over the front entrance on Fort Street, as well as the covering for the attic window in the gable on the same street, were wonders in their way. He also built the family residence on Jefferson Avenue, Witherell farm, after Mr. Palmer had disposed of the Fort Street house.

Dexter Merrill, city marshal, lived on Lafayette Avenue, near Griswold Street. A. H. Stowell lived on Griswold Street, near Grand River Avenue. James M. Sutton had his pail and tub factory on the corner of Griswold and State Streets, and later moved to May's Creek. Mr. Sanderson had his stone yard on Lafayette Avenue, adjoining Keeney's foundry. W. F. Chittenden lived on the corner of Michigan Avenue and Rowland Street. Later on Jas. Burns lived here, as also did Rowe, the oyster dealer. The latter died here, and I think he was the last tenant.

Later on, on the south side of Lafayette Avenue, between Shelby and Wayne Streets, lived John Owen, Sidney L. Rood and M. F. Dickinson.

Edward McGraw, brother of A. C. McGraw, lived on Lafayette Avenue near Cass. He was quite a poet and was called the poet McGraw. A specimen of his poetry is extant, I think. It is a New Year's address written for Geo. W. Dawson's paper, *"The Detroit Daily Advertiser,"* and commences thus:

> "Hist, 'tis the ever fleeting tread of Time,
> Another year is in the tomb of years,"

and pronounced by Eben N. Willcox and others at the time as equal to anything Byron wrote.

Bishop McCoskrey lived in a house owned by John Owen on the northeast corner of Lafayette Avenue and Wayne Street, still standing.

Dr. Abbott, brother of Lawyer John T. Abbott, built a fine brick residence on the southeast corner of Fort and Cass Streets. Mrs. Clitz occupied it after Dr. Abbott, and after her Mr. Daniel Dunning, of Wells & Co.'s Western Express, as a first-class boarding house. There had been boarding houses and boarding houses in Detroit before this, and first-class ones, too, but this house of Dunning's exceeded all of its predecessors in the appointments of its table, service, etc. Mr. Dunning and his wife had been in the hotel business in Albany, Syracuse, etc., and were fully up to the requirements of that day. They were ideal hosts. Among their patrons were Captain Inman, of the U. S. steamer Michigan, and his family, consisting of his wife, two daughters and a son; John A. Welles, the banker, and his wife; Colonel Berrien, chief engineer of the Michigan Central Railroad, and his associate, Mr. Center; Colonel McIntosh, U. S. A.; Albert Crane; William Welles, brother of the banker, John W. Strong, and many other people of note whose names have escaped me. I boarded with the Dunnings for over a year. Mrs. Captain Inman was a sister of Theo. H. Eaton, as was also Mrs. John A. Welles. The daughters of Captain Inman, Eliza and Mary, were both young and attractive and were a great addition to the society of Fort Street, which at that period was at its zenith. Eliza married a son of Bishop Odenheimer. The other daughter, Mary, died unmarried, I think. The son was for some years clerk with T. H. Eaton in the drug and grocery business. Captain Inman was a fine officer and gentleman. He was the first commander of the steamer Michigan. Mr. John A. Welles was a banker, pure and simple, and managed the affairs of the old Farmers' & Mechanics' Bank with singular ability. His ideas of monetary affairs, economics, etc., were of the highest order, and under his immediate eye was reared the present Mr. T. H. Eaton, and to Mr. Welles, no doubt, he owes, through the latter's teachings and advice, much of the business ability he now possesses, although one would think the mantle of his father falling on him would give him all the aid he needed in that direction. Be that as it may, I think he himself will concede that John A. Welles was a great factor in shaping him for the care of the mercantile knowledge he acquired through his father. I am told, though his givings are large, he has added much to his bank account since his father's death. John A. Welles was a tall, fine looking man, of polished manners, always faultlessly dressed. Mrs. Welles was a fine, attractive looking woman, and one to see them together on the street, which was no uncommon occurrence, would think they were lovers on the eve of marriage.

* * *

Colonel John M. Berrien was a West Pointer, and graduated into the Engineers. He resigned to take charge of the engineering department of the Michigan Central Railroad, after its purchase by the state. He was a relative of Mrs. Inman, Mrs. John A. Welles and Theo. H. Eaton. In a former article referring to the father of Theo. H. Eaton, I alluded to the farewell address of General Washington as having been written at the home (Rocky Hill, New Jersey) of the great-greatgrandmother of the present Mr. Eaton, Mrs. Judge Berrien, who was born Margaret Eaton. It is a matter of history (see Lossing's Year Book of the American Revolution). Colonel Berrien's fine, soldierly figure was familiar to all Detroiters for years; he was a fine gentleman and a most accomplished engineer.

To the last day of his life, he supported his old negro nurse, who fostered him in infancy. He boarded at the Michigan Exchange the latter years of his life and died there. Aside from his qualities as a civil engineer and soldier, he was an artistic flute player, and an ardent lover of music.

Colonel McIntosh resembled in physique General Wheeler, U. S. A. (formerly of the Confederate Army). McIntosh was a fiery, irascible man, but a soldier every inch of him. He was killed in the Mexican War, on General Taylor's line.

Albert Crane is of course well remembered by many of the present day, his career as member of the extensive real estate firm of Crane & Wesson is also familiar. Their sub-divisions in various parts of the city at that early day have led to some confusion in straightening out streets, etc. Mr. Crane removed to Chicago years ago, embarked in the same business. Walter Crane, a brother, lately deceased, who was part owner of the Reeder farm, Springwells, it is said, remembered him quite generously in his will.

John W. Strong, Jr., many will remember, as he passed away not so many years ago. He was well and favorably known.

* * *

U. S. STEAMER MICHIGAN.

The U. S. steamer Michigan was launched at Erie, December 5, 1843. She was built at Pittsburg, Pa., and transported in sections by canal and wagon. The launching drew thousands to witness it, owing to the fact that she was the first craft on the lakes of iron construction. Her first commander, Wm. Inman, saw service on Lake Ontario in the war of 1812, under Commodore Chauncey, and after under Commodore Perry in the West Indies. Lieutenant James P. McKinstry, second officer, saw service on the ocean and the lakes. Sailing Master Stevens was a son of Captain Thos. Holdup Stevens, who commanded one of the gunboats under Perry at the engagement on Lake Erie, September 10, 1815.

In a series of articles on "Old Express Days," which appeared in the Sunday *Free Press* in the winter of 1902-3, I had this to say of our friend Dunning, and think it will bear repeating in this connection:

"Then there was Daniel Dunning, a paragon of suavity and politeness, as also Schuyler, Thad Pomeroy, Powell, Hurd, Wheeler and others. The assumed duties of these messengers were something that those of the present day do not feel themselves called upon to perform, I presume, except in isolated cases. These were executing messages, errands of all sorts, taking charge of ladies traveling from one point to another on the railroad without escort, seeing to their baggage, etc., taking charge of young children without their parents, and doing many other things for the public. Thus they made themselves exceedingly popular, as well as the express company they so well and so ably represented."

Messenger Dunning was most winning in manner, particularly to the fairer portion of creation; he gained their good will, and I might say, admiration, both old and young, if they were journeying unattended between Albany and Buffalo, by his assiduous attentions to their wants. No picnic in winter, these self-imposed duties.

The journeys between the above points were quite different from what they are now. Instead of four tracks, there was only one (strap rail), and that was not continuous. Four or five different companies (I do not remember their names) operated the several roads, and had their depots at the various termini. So it can be readily imagined that a woman, with or without baggage, would not have much of a picnic traveling in those days, particularly in winter. It was on such occasions that our friend Dunning "got in his work," so to speak, and gained their appreciative regard, besides advertising the merits of the express company, which then was in need of all the favorable publicity it could get.

ON THE ERIE CANAL.

Travel by rail through New York was far more expeditious than by canal, of course, but by the latter route during the season of navigation, particularly the summer months, was delightfully comfortable. Take it in the month of June, for instance, on one of the splendid packet boats of that day, which plied between Albany and Buffalo. They were 110 feet long by 12 feet wide, and elegantly fitted up, with saloons, wash rooms, etc. The charming rural portion of New York state through which they slowly passed, presented a delightful panorama to gratify the eyes of the passengers. It was somewhat monotonous at times, of course, but what a change from the crowded, lumbering stage coach, with all its discomforts, no one who has not experienced both can realize. And what kings the packet boat captains were. Their personalities were familiar to almost every man, woman and child all along the route. The bright dark sides of the "Raging Canawl" were depicted in song and story on the boards of every theater in the state. I witnessed some amusing scenes sometimes, particularly when a packet boat crowded with passengers, and they nearly all on deck enjoying the air and scenery, there suddenly came the cry from the pilot or captain of "low bridge," then such a scattering of the lazy ones who had been lost in day dreams to get clear of being knocked into the canal. It was a heap of fun. What a bright, knowing, independent chap was the "canal driver." No one could teach him a thing. The cowboy of the plains puts me in mind of him; like him resourceful and ever ready for a muss or a heroic action.

I have lugged in one or two allusions to the Erie Canal in these remarks, and do not think it out of place, now that we are at it, being also a matter of record, to say that the canal was not opened through its entire length, until in 1825 or 1826. Before this goods had to be teamed from Albany to Buffalo, and it took about three months to get goods up from New York. Stages were two days to Sandusky in 1837. Mails were brought on horseback until 1827 through the Ohio Black Swamp. Stages to Chicago in 1837 were four and five days reaching there.

The dwellers on Fort Street west in the thirties and early forties were opposite the city hall, Chas. R. Desnoyers, whose residence was adjoining what is now McMillan's grocery store. Desnoyers was the son of Peter J. Desnoyers and of the firm of Gillett & Desnoyers. The James Abbott brick residence was on the corner where is now the Hammond building. On the corner where is now the Moffatt Block, was the house and ornamental grounds of John Palmer. Adjoining the latter on Griswold Street, was the house and ornamental grounds of James Williams. Elon (Chancellor) Farnsworth lived in the house on Fort Street, adjoining that of John Palmer. He soon vacated it, however, for his new residence up Jefferson Avenue.

Judge C. I. Walker succeeded him. James Penny, boot and shoe merchant, owned and occupied the house adjoining Farnsworth's. He was the father of Mr. Henry Penny, who is at present a resident of Detroit. This property was purchased by Mr. Simon J. Murphy, on which he erected his fine office building "The Penobscot."

The Pennys were related to Chauncey Hulburt, late president Detroit water works board. The fine brick residence of Mr. and Mrs. David Thompson adjoined the Pennys, and was where is now the State Savings Bank. It is safe to say, however, that aside from the house erected by John A. Welles, the Thompson mansion and the grounds were the pride of the street. Thomas Palmer, the father of Senator Palmer, erected his residence on the southwest corner of Fort and Shelby, about 1834. It was built by Mr. Latourneau, the builder "par excellence" of those days, and was a most substantial structure, as those employed to tear it down found out. It was ornamental as well. It remained there, although altered a little, until it was replaced not long ago by Senator Palmer's present fine brick building called the "Tecumseh Block" and devoted to business purposes. The noted Indian chief Tecumseh, it is said, was often in evidence around this corner during the 1812 trouble, as the officers' quarters of Fort Shelby were on the opposite corner, and his spirit haunts this locality, accordingly.

* * *

The next house was that of John H. Kinzie. Mrs. John H. Kinzie in her entertaining book "Wau-Bun, The Early Days in the North West," telling of their first leave taking of it, says:

"It was on a dark rainy evening in the month of September, 1830, that we went on board the steamer Henry Clay to take passage for Green Bay. All our friends in Detroit had congratulated us upon our good fortune in being spared the voyage in one of the little schooners which at this time afforded the ordinary means of communication with the few and distant settlements on Lakes Huron and Michigan. They arrived at the bay (Fort Howard) in due course, and it appears Mr. Kinzie remained there in his official capacity, disbursing agent of the Winnebago Indians, until July, 1833, when they returned to Detroit under escort of Governor Geo. B. Porter and E. A. Brush, Esq."

It is presumed the present building was erected by Mr. Kinzie a short time before the above year (1830). This Mr. Kinzie was the son of the John Kinzie who was present at the Chicago massacre, April, 1812. John H. Kinzie removed permanently to Chicago about 1835 or 1836. This house is still standing.

The late George C. Bates's first wife was of this family of Kinzies. She was, I think, the widow of a son of John H. Kinzie. The latter at one time owned some 140 acres of land near the mouth of the Chicago River (north side). Mrs. Kinzie was reputed to be a wealthy widow when Bates married her. They had one child, he a son, who became an officer in the U. S. Army, Captain Kinzie Bates. He was stationed at Fort Wayne at the time of the negro riots, October, 1862, which occurred in the vicinity of the Brush Garden, on Brush, Lafayette and Congress Streets. The affair had got beyond the control of the city authorities, whereupon the mayor called upon the commandant at Fort Wayne for assistance. Captain Bates and a squad of men were ordered to the scene of trouble.

I was standing on the corner of Fort and Brush Streets, a block or so from the burning tenements, when Bates and his little command came marching up Brush Street from Jefferson Avenue, he and a sergeant side by side at their head, the former with drawn sword, the latter and the rest of the men with muskets at a ready. Near by me stood the then notorious Arthur Gore. Just as the soldiers were passing us he sung out in a tone of derision, loud enough for Bates to hear distinctly: "See, boys, I am damned if Uncle Sam isn't sending our soldiers to protect the damned niggers." Bates did hear it, his face grew more scarlet than ever. He did not take the slightest notice of Gore, but marched steadily on at the head of his men, looking neither to the right nor the left, straight for the dense crowd of rioters who were surrounding the burning buildings. They scattered like chaff before the wind. Bates and his squad of soldiers were masters of that situation. At which there was not quite as much laughing on the back seats.

If I recollect right the disturbance had assumed such a magnitude that the aid of a regiment of troops, partially organized for the Civil War, and rendezvousing at Dearborn, had to be called on before it was put to a final stop.

Bates was a private in the First Michigan Infantry (three months), and after November, 1861, first lieutenant in First United States Infantry. He was promoted to brevet captain in October, 1862, for gallant and meritorious service in the battle of Corinth, Mississippi, was breveted major July, 1863, for gallant and meritorious service during the siege of Vicksburg, Mississippi, and made full captain in March, 1866.

* * *

Dr. Zina Pitcher lived in this house for a short period after Kinzie; after him Dr. A. R. Terry, and after Terry Mr. Byram, furniture manufacturer (Byram & Philbrick), and then came Thomas W. Lockwood, a partner in the law firm of Barstow & Lockwood. The latter did the office work of the firm, being well equipped for this department of the profession. An impediment in speech deprived him of the opportunity of oratorical display either in court or as a political speaker. He was of a quiet, retiring nature, and devoted to home pleasures and the duties of religion. He was active in literary and intellectual pursuits, and was a leading member of the Detroit Young Men's Society, being chosen president of that body in 1847. He was one of the incorporators of the old Board of Trade in 1848. He died here April 18, 1866.

Samuel Barstow, his partner, died in Buffalo of cholera in 1856. He was an excellent lawyer, a man of good sense, strict integrity and universally respected. He was very prominent in educational affairs. He was one of the school inspectors in 1840, and so continued until his death. The Barstow school was named after him. The late Rev. J. Hyatt Smith, who knew him intimately, used to say of him that, when he was speaking and got thoroughly warmed up with his subject, he always put him in mind of a bunch of wormwood. Intimately associated with Barstow & Lockwood (though not in partnership) was Lawyer Anthony Ten Eyck, who was quite prominent here in the latter forties and fifties. He served during part of the Civil War as paymaster in the army. Mrs. Thomas W. Lockwood was a sister of his. He was a fine, quiet gentleman and much esteemed.

Mr. John Owen owned the two vacant lots (100 feet) between Thomas Palmer and John H. Kinzie, but did not build upon them until about 1846.

After the death of my father, my mother was paid $600 by Lewis Goddard for her dower interest in the lot, southeast corner Jefferson Avenue and Griswold Street. This sum her friends urgently advised her to invest in the purchase of these two lots (100 feet), but she declined, and they subsequently became the property of Mr. Owen.

John Scott, after he left Woodward Avenue, lived adjoining and beyond the Kinzie-Lockwood house. He died here in 1846, aged 49 years. Jim Scott, after the death of his father, sold the property to ex-Mayor Wm. C. Duncan, for, I think, $14,000, cash, western currency. I remember the transaction quite distinctly, as Jim showed me the money done up in several packages. He went west or south somewhere, and returned only at long intervals, for quite a period, then he came to stay, and is here yet. Duncan, I think, rebuilt the Scott house or replaced it with brick, and then sold it to N. G. Williams. H. H. Brown built a fine brick residence where the old reservoir had been.

Simon Mandelbaum, one of the copper kings of Lake Superior, became the owner of the house built by H. H. Brown on Fort Street west, after the death of the latter, and I think his widow owns it yet.

Many will remember Mr. Mandelbaum, a genial gentleman. All Lake Superior people in the early days in that region I am sure will. He and Alexander Sibley were close friends, and interested together in many Lake Superior ventures, as also were Holland, Sheldon M. Knight, Carson, Close, Ransom, Sheldon, S. B. Brady, Breitung, Peter White, C. C. Douglass, Charles A. Trowbridge, Slawson, Senter and others.

I mention Alexander Sibley particularly because it was in his company I first saw Mandelbaum. It was in Major Sproat Sibley's office (he was a brother of Alexander and United States quartermaster here). They had just returned from a business and pleasure trip to New York and Boston and were in high glee relating the various happenings they had experienced on their journey. It was quite the custom then for the porters and baggagemen employed on the railroads, steamboats and in hotels throughout the country to wrestle with a passenger's baggage in the wildest manner; it seemed as if they did not care how they handled it. Protests from the owner did not appear to count. "Baggage smashers," they were aptly termed. Sibley and Mandelbaum constituted themselves a committee of two to put a stop to the abuse, as far as they were concerned. On this trip each of them had a considerable amount of baggage, and they made it their business to keep close tab on their belongings. At every railroad station, on every steamboat, they personally saw that their "traps" were handled with care, and woe betide any luckless "baggage smasher" if he did otherwise. They did have many encounters with these chaps, and they gave a graphic and amusing account of these ructions.

Mandelbaum met an early death by drowning, off a steamer of the Detroit and Cleveland line, on its passage between this port and Cleveland. He left a widow and daughter. The widow is a sister of John Senter, now of Houghton, Mich.

* * *

The residence of Thomas C. Sheldon stood on the corner of Wayne Street. After the death of Mr. Sheldon the corner passed into the hands of the First Congregational Society, on which they erected a church that was eventually transformed into the present *Detroit Journal* office. Thomas C. Sheldon was a brother of the John P. Sheldon who, in company with E. Reed, published the *Detroit Gazette*. They came here in the early days and were classed among the pioneers of the western country. Thomas C., unlike his brother of the *Gazette*, was a powerful man, not very tall, but thick set, with broad shoulders, and endowed with great strength. I have seen him handle a 200-pound barrel of pork as if it were a child's toy, ending it up and over and so on. Withal, he was a kind and genial man, a good citizen, husband and father; but he would not stand any nonsense—what he said he usually meant. He was a close friend and adviser of Governor Stevens T. Mason.

The Sheldons have been mentioned in a former article, then in connection with their residence on Jefferson Avenue in the thirties, and also in connection with their relationship to the Labadies, Piquettes, Navarres and others.

* * *

At the edge of the curb, south side of this street about the center of the block, between Shelby and Wayne Streets, was made the experiment of boring for water. Rufus Wells, Phineas Davis, Jr., Lucius Lyon, and A. E. Hathon in 1829 secured the contract to supply the city with water until 1850. They formed the Detroit Hydraulic Co. They went down about 200 feet, but found no water and did find much salt, but the latter was not what they were looking for, and much to their apparent disappointment the quest was abandoned. The workmen brought from beneath the surface large quantities of water-washed pebbles, indications, it was thought, of an underground stream of water. I have mentioned this slightly in a former article, but as I occasionally witnessed the boring, do not think it out of place to allude to it here, and boy that I was, I could not but think it a queer freak for four such brainy men as Wells, Lyons, Davis and Hathon to be hunting for water way down beneath the surface of Fort Street, when oceans of the purest, freshest water in the world was rushing right past the city's very doors, which could be had without asking.

* * *

Dr. Henry came next and he built the first brick house on this street. Dr. Henry was a nephew of the celebrated explorer and Indian trader, Alexander Henry. The latter was present at the massacre of Fort Mackinac by Pontiac in June, 1763, and was an eye witness of the atrocities committed. The same would have been meted out to the garrison at Detroit, but thanks to the Indian maiden "Oucanasta," Pontiac did not have "any show."

Alexander Henry visited the historic Lake Superior Copper Rock in 1766, when it lay in the bed of the Ontonagon River, and cut from it 100 pounds of fine copper, which is now in the British Museum, London, and is held to be one of its rarest mineral specimens. The only one before him visiting this rock, of whom we have any account, is said to have been the Jesuit missionary, Father Menard, in 1664.

This copper rock, as most people know, is now in the Smithsonian Institution, Washington.

Alexander Henry can share with a very few others the proud distinction of giving to the nation the knowledge of this then wonderful copper specimen, which led to the discovery of those vast deposits of that mineral which capital and enterprise have developed to such extent that the imagination can scarcely realize the limit. The total amount of wealth realized by the Calumet &

Hecla mine alone, to the present time, makes the brain whirl to contemplate.

In a narrative of his adventures, Mr. Henry says in regard to this copper rock: "On my way (April, 1776), I encamped a second time at the mouth of the Ontonagon, and now took the opportunity of going ten miles up the river with Indian guides. The object which I went most expressly to see, and to which I had the satisfaction of being led, was a mass of copper, of the weight, according to my estimate, of no less than five tons. Such was its pure and malleable state that with an ax I was able to cut off a portion weighing 100 pounds."

Mr. Geo. Wilson, a college graduate, in 1830 was teaching an English classical school in Detroit at the same time the Misses Farrand were conducting a young ladies' seminary. Miss Emily Mason, sister of Governor Stevens T. Mason, attended this school of the Misses Farrand, as did Isabella Cass, the Misses Campbell, Jane Dyson, Isabella Norvell, Emma Schwarz and many others.

Mr. Wilson was, I used to think, a remarkably homely man, but had the reputation of being a fine classical scholar and teacher. He married one of the Misses Farrand, as did Dr. Henry of Fort Street (being his second wife). D. Farrand Henry, civil and mining engineer, of this city, is a son of theirs.

Mr. Wilson resembled Dr. A. L. Porter, another homely man, but a good doctor, who was here in 1845 and before, and had his office and dwelling at 255 Jefferson Avenue, near Beaubien Street. I presume many will remember him.

Dr. Henry, when he lived below the Michigan Exchange, before he removed to Fort Street, had two children, a son and a daughter, by his first wife. The children were exceedingly well behaved, so much so that they attracted the attention of the dwellers in that vicinity. Hand in hand they wended their way to church or school, daily unattended. Aubry, the son, was a schoolmate and chum of mine, and the daughter a favorite of my aunt, and with her brother always welcome guests at the house, which they always made it convenient to pass on their way to church or school. The daughters name I have forgotten, or what became of her, but the boy after leaving school took to the printing business, was at it for many years, and after went into the bill-posting business. Aubry died some eight or ten years ago. He married, had two or three sons, one of whom is of the well-known firm of Jas. E. Henry & Son, bill posters.

After the doctor's death, Mr. Shadrach Gillett lived in the Henry house for a while until he moved further down the street to the southwest corner of Third, which corner Geo. S. Frost occupied after him. Mr. Nehemiah Ingersoll, after, occupied the Henry House. In it, one of his daughters (Delia), was married to the late Judge B. F. H. Witherell. The house is still standing. Dr. Abbott built the fine large residence on the southeast corner of Cass Street. He was succeeded as a tenant by Mr. Daniel Dunning, and he by H. Norton Strong, who became by purchase the owner of the property.

Dr. Marshal Chapin's residence and ample gardens were on the opposite corner. Dr. Chapin became the owner of this lot, quite a while before he vacated his home on Woodbridge Street. He cultivated during that time quite a garden here. Among other vegetables that he cultivated was the tomato, or "Love Apple" as it was then familiarly called, and grown for ornament only. It was shunned by most people as being poisonous, and classed among poison ivy, wild parsnips, etc. My aunt, Mrs. Hinchman, thought different, and had the temerity to use the vegetable freely in her household. She had the doctor's permission to visit his garden and use as many as she liked of the tabooed tomato, which she did in spite of the caution of the neighbors. I often visited the doctor's garden with her, just to procure the fruit of this plant. I then came to know, as all the world has since known, what a boon to the human race this excellent product of the soil was. What could we do without the tomato.

Dr. Chapin lived there until he died. This corner is, I think, owned by his heirs yet.

Theo. H. Hinchman built a brick residence on a portion of this lot. Wm. S. Driggs, just after the opening of the Cass farm, built two brick residences, very fine and palatial for that day, on the southeast corner of Second Street. Silas N. Kendrick built and occupied a fine residence of brick next this side and adjoining Fort Street Presbyterian Church.

My earliest recollections of Detroit center about Dr. Chapin and his family. I was familiar with the members of the latter when they occupied their cottage-like residence on Woodbridge Street, nearly opposite Uncle Ben Woodworth's Steamboat Hotel, and also when they moved to the corner of Fort and Cass Streets, and so continued. I also used to see much of the doctor when he was conducting his drug, medicine and grocery store on the south side of Jefferson Avenue, scarcely half a block distant from our residence on the southeast corner of Griswold, and he had at the time for his chief clerk the late John Owen, who a short time after became his partner. When he came into the partnership the firm name was Chapin & Owen, and they changed their location to the Cooper Block, a short distance down the street. After a while Dr. Chapin retired from the concern, Mr. Theo. H. Hinchman taking his place. In the meantime the latter had married the doctor's eldest daughter Louise, and the firm name was changed to John Owen & Co. The latter firm, after conducting a successful business for some years, dissolved partnership. Mr. Hinchman associating with himself his brother James, continued the business and the firm name became T. & J. Hinchman. All are familiar with the subsequent career of the Hinchmans.

Dr. Chapin had four children, two boys and two girls. The eldest boy, Charles, died young; the second, Marshal W., lived to see service in the Civil War, was first lieutenant Fourth Michigan Volunteers, then captain in the same regiment; then colonel of the Twenty-third Infantry, August 23, 1862. Resigned for disability, contracted in the service, April 15, 1864. A daughter, the eldest, married Theo. H. Hinchman (as said). The other daughter, Helen, married H. Norton Strong. Mrs. Hinchman survives, and is passing her declining years in quiet retirement with her children.

Dr. Chapin rendered most efficient service during the two cholera seasons that visited Detroit (1832 and 1834).

In 1832 the house of Engine Co. No. 2, was on Fort Street, at the northeast corner of the Campus and Griswold Street. A cut of this engine, from the late Geo. W. Osborn's collection, was in the Sunday *Free Press* May 21, 1905. This machine, it appears is now owned by an Ionia Fire Company, and is still in use.

I first saw this engine at a fire in the winter of 1831-2, on the corner of Jefferson Avenue and Griswold Street (Ives corner). It was then a spick and span new machine, glorious in paint and gilding.

The widow Griswold, relict of Griswold, the hatter, and sister of Mrs. John Palmer, occupied the house adjoining the Baptist Church, and resided there until she died. Mr. Charles Vail, manager for D. J. Campau when in the dry goods business in Detroit, married a daughter of Mrs. Griswold.

Jonathan Keeney, owned and lived in the adjoining house, still standing, and at present owned by the Kirby heirs. It may not be out of place to say that Mr. Keeney was a kind, modest, retiring gentleman; a foundryman and machinist, and master of his trade. He had a daughter and several sons. The daughter (Eloise) married Mr. Geo. Hunt, owner of the Hunt farm, and from whom the trustees of Elmwood Cemetery derive their title. Mr. Hunt had a son, Lewis, a schoolmate of mine, who entered West Point, served with distinction through the Civil War, and died a retired brigadier-general.

Another Hunt that also gained distinction during the Civil War was a native of Detroit and was, I think, the son of Henry I. Hunt. At all events, he was a graduate of West Point and later chief of artillery of the army of the Potomac. He died a brigadier-general, having won his laurels at Gettysburg repelling Pickett's persistent and desperate charges.

One of Mr. Keeney's sons, Willis G., was a cripple from childhood, one leg shorter than the other, but for all that he was as lively as the rest of the boys of his age. We were schoolmates and chums. That around Fort Shelby was a dangerous locality during the war of 1812 may be inferred from the fact that Willis and I used to go around the common, near by, with a wheelbarrow gathering up the fragments of exploded bomb-shells that came from the British batteries posted on the opposite side of the river. On one occasion we were out all day, and gathered up nearly the full of a French cart. All this for the benefit of the iron foundry. Willis died young. Another son, Charles, was older than Willis; and there are some, perhaps, who will remember Charles Keeney, and what a pleasant, genial good fellow he was. Rather fastidious as regards dress, it must be confessed, but he was an untiring medical student and ranked among the first in his profession. He and Dr. Louis Davenport studied under Doctors Terry and Russell. He was prominent on the boards of our "Detroit Lyceum" in the old University building on Bates Street, in the thirties.

The lot on the northeast corner of Fort and Shelby Streets (the residence of the late Hiram Walker) was vacant for many years after Hull's surrender, until Uncle Oliver Newberry built the present substantial building there, declaring that it was really the first good home for himself he ever had. Homes with others he had had, of course, but this was for "Oliver" alone. The "Old Bachelor Commodore" occupied it until his death.

On the northwest corner of Fort and Shelby Streets was the residence of Judge John McDonnell. It was formerly quarters for the officers stationed at Fort Shelby. I have already alluded to these quarters and the McDonnells at length in a former article. Next to Judge McDonnell's was a two-story wooden dwelling that had once formed a part of the officers' quarters adjoining. Sheldon McKnight occupied it at one time, as did Harry Guise, Frederick P. Markham and many others.

Dr. G. B. Russell built a fine brick residence adjoining this relic of Fort Shelby. He lived here for quite a while until he vacated the premises for upper Jefferson Avenue or Hamtramck. Wm. Chittenden, of the Russell House, succeeded him.

Mason Palmer owned the adjoining grounds to the corner of Wayne Street, and occupied the corner with a substantial brick residence. He lived there for many years.

John A. Welles, cashier of the then Farmers' and Mechanics' Bank, built the residence on the northwest corner of Fort and Wayne Streets, since the quarters of the Detroit Club, and later the Michigan Club. It was considered, by all odds, the finest residence building in the city and the state at that date, about 1837. It is a fine one to this day. He occupied it for a while. Theo. Romeyn occupied it after Mr. Welles and lived there until he removed to upper Jefferson Avenue.

Governor Mason occupied this house before Romeyn, for a short season. Henry Ledyard lived here for quite a while and after him General Pope, U. S. A., commanding this department. The general had his headquarters in this house.

* * *

N. P. Jacobs, who at one time was in drugs and groceries and after in the same business with John J. Garrison, and later was United State consul to Calcutta, occupied the next residence, and after him George C. Bates, the brilliant lawyer and silver tongued orator, who lived here many years. I think the house is still standing.

Governor Stevens T. Mason at one time occupied this house also for a short period. Miss Emily V. Mason, when here a short time ago, reminded me of the fact, and saying that Tom Sheldon, who lived nearly opposite on the corner of Wayne Street, and who was an ardent adherent of her brother, would often sing out "Come over here, Tom, I have something spicy to tell you." She added that it was fair to presume that her brother attended to the call, if he could.

Major Henry Whiting, U. S. A., built a fine brick residence adjoining just before he vacated his Jefferson Avenue house opposite the Michigan Exchange, and lived here until the Mexican war. Major Whiting had been stationed here for many years as United States quartermaster, and was an accomplished officer and gentleman. He had traveled extensively and often delivered lectures on his foreign travels before the Young Men's Society. One I remember particularly and that was on Genoa, Italy. It impressed me so much that many years after, when I had the good fortune to visit Genoa myself, I seemed to see it as the major had described it. He was something of a poet also, having composed a poem entitled "Sanilac" and one entitled "The Emegrant." I heard him recite the latter at a banquet at the Mansion House tendered to Governor Cass by the citizens of Detroit on the eve of his departure for Washington to assume the duties of secretary of war. I give below a few verses from "The Emigrant," as I have never forgotten the talented author nor the occasion:

> Upon the Clinton river, just through the country back,
> You'll find in shire of Oakland, the town of Pontiac,
> Which, springing up of a sudden, scared wolves and bears away,
> That used to roam about there, in Michigania.

> And if you follow downwards, why, Rochester is there,
> And further still Mt. Clemens looks out upon St. Clair,
> Besides some other places within Macombia
> That promise population to Michigania.

If you had rather go to a place called Washtenaw,
You'll find the Huron lands the best you ever saw,
The ships sail to Ann Arbor right thro' La Plaisance bay
And touch at Ypsilanti, in Michigania.

Or if you keep a going a great deal further on,
I guess you'll reach St. Joe, where everybody's gone;
There everything, like Jack's bean, grows monstrous fast, they say,
And beats the rest all hollow in Michigania.

Then come, ye Yankee farmers, who've mettle hearts like me
And elbow grease in plenty, to bow the forest tree,
Come, take a quarter section, and I'll be bound you'll say
This country takes the rag off, this Michigania."

Ex-Mayor K. C. Barker remodeled this house and almost made another one of it. He lived here until his untimely taking off by accidental drowning.

Geo. V. N. Lothrop became the next owner, and lived here while in the city, until he died, only a few years ago.

Lawyer Asher B. Bates, one time recorder of the city, built and occupied a wooden residence on the corner of Cass Street (NE.) He went to the Sandwich Islands to reside, and the property came into the hands of John P. Clark, of the Springwells Dry Dock, and how it got into the ownership of the Detroit club I do not know. John Chester, however, occupied it quite a while after Bates left.

General Cass, after he returned from the French mission, occupied the large wooden dwelling on the northwest corner of Cass Street, until the completion of Mrs. Canfield's brick residence, southeast corner of First Street, when he took up his abode with her, where he remained until he died. Major Lewis Cass, the son, did not go with the general, but remained with the art treasures the family had collected, keeping bachelor's hall, until the late Governor Baldwin succeeded him and became the fortunate possessor of all the rare and costly things the house contained. Governor Baldwin erected on the site of the house the fine brick residence that is there now.

Colonel Joshua Howard, U. S. A., after he had completed the Dearborn arsenal, occupied the adjoining wooden building for quite a while until he took up his residence again at Dearborn, where he died.

For many years Fort Street, below Colonel Howard's residence, to the lower line of the Cass farm, was with the exception of the Log Farm house, entirely destitute of buildings of any sort. The west or north side to Michigan Avenue was an unbroken common, where the cows wandered at will, and where the citizen soldiers held their encampments and went through their evolutions. Here the militia gathered once every year, to find out how much they did not know about marching, counter marching and the science of arms in general. Here on this ground was held the great Whig mass meeting and barbecue (campaign of 1840) at which meeting among the array of distinguished orators who addressed it was Wm. M. Evarts, who afterwards became secretary of state.

VISITING FIREMEN.

GENERAL CASS AND THE FIREMEN.

WHILE occupying the house on the northwest corner of Fort and Cass Streets, General Cass entertained at lunch a company of firemen from Syracuse, N. Y., just after he arrived home from France. I gave an account of the affair in the Sunday *Free Press* of October 4, 1903. I will reproduce it, in part, here:

The Syracuse company came without an invitation and unheralded. The first intimation the Detroit fire department had of their arrival was a notice from Uncle Oliver Newberry that a fire engine company from Syracuse, N. Y., with their apparatus had landed at his dock and wanted to know what he should do with them. The fire alarms were sounded at once and out came the whole department. In cases where the location of a fire was not known, the practice was to assemble at the corner of Woodward and Jefferson Avenues, and ascertain its whereabouts, then pitching for all they were worth. On coming together at the point I have named, the chief engineer gave the information that an eastern fire company was at our gates, knocking for admission. The entire department with its apparatus headed by the chief engineer and James A. Van Dyke, its president, at once repaired to Newberry's dock at the foot of Second Street, where they found the Syracuse company modestly waiting, as their foreman said, to see what their welcome would be, coming as they did, uninvited and unannounced, though down in their hearts they were sure it would be cordial, as indeed it was.

President Van Dyke, in his usual happy manner, welcomed them to the city and to its hospitalities, assuring them that they could have the best there was "in the shop." Then all hands repaired to the Firemen's hall, corner of Larned and Bates Streets, where more speech-making was had, a brief welcome by the mayor, etc. The foreman of the Syracuse company was elevated to the top of a convenient barrel in No. One's house, and told his story amid much laughter and applause—that his company had determined to visit the Detroit fire department, whose reputation was being continually buzzed in their ears, and see for themselves. He at the same time alluded to General Lewis Cass in happy terms, intimating that the citizens of Detroit ought to be proud to count among them as one of the citizens such an eminent statesman, and intimated that it would give himself and his brother firemen from the salt district great pleasure to pay their respects in person to the general, if the opportunity was afforded them. Word to that effect was gotten to the general directly, who responded, saying he would be much pleased to welcome the Syracuse firemen, as well as the Detroit fire department, at his residence on West Fort Street that afternoon at 3 o'clock.

ENTERTAINED BY GENERAL CASS.

At the appointed hour the fire laddies were on hand. The general and family welcomed them very cordially. Refreshments were served in the large dining room and after the boys had made a terrible slaughter of the sparkling champagne and rare wines that the general had brought from France, the foreman of the visiting company, a nervous little chap, made a eulogistic speech to the host that fairly staggered him.

The general, perhaps, had no idea until he was informed of it on that occasion, that he was so distinguished a personage. He, however, replied quite briefly, and in chosen words expressed the pleasure and gratification it afforded him to welcome at his home the Detroit firemen and their guests.

After a characteristic speech from President James A. Van Dyke, the firemen took leave of their host and his family, with warm expressions of pleasure the visit had afforded.

The Syracuse firemen left for their homes the following day, highly delighted with their visit, and, as they put it, "overwhelmed with hospitality."

ANOTHER VISITING COMPANY.

The following summer another fire company from the east visited our fire department. This time it was the Ithaca (N. Y.), Hook and Ladder Company No. 3. They also enjoyed the hospitalities of General Cass. An account of it appeared in *The Detroit Free Press* Tuesday, August 12, 1845, and is as follows:

"The Ithaca Fire Company arrived in this city on Monday morning on board the Illinois, accompanied by a fine band. They are a fine looking company and composed, we should judge, of the business men of Ithaca. Their uniform is neat and comfortable. They were handsomely received, considering the short notice, by our excellent fire companies, and hospitably entertained at the National Hotel."

Also, in *The Free Press,* August 13, 1845:

"The guests of our fire department left for the east last evening and were gratified at the manner in which they were treated while here. Our department never exerted themselves more than they did yesterday and the day before to make them at home. They succeeded well and everything passed off agreeably."

Extract from an old letter, dated Detroit, August 14, 1845, and written by myself to a friend in Monroe, Mich., in regard to this visit of the Ithaca firemen:

"Rest and quietness once more prevail in our city. We firemen have been kept in a complete ferment for the last two or three days, occasioned by a visit from a company of firemen from Ithaca, N. Y., and such times! We had a magnificent torchlight procession, which for length, brilliancy of light, and disposition of torches, could scarcely be equaled. We moved through the principal streets, and gave the towns folks a pretty good chance of seeing how the thing could be done up, and it was allowed by all to be pretty near beyond parallel. We escorted our Ithaca friends to the boat, Tuesday evening (12th), where they assured us that language was inadequate to express how much they had been gratified with their visit to the 'City of the Straits,' and the hearty reception accorded them by its citizens, coming as they did uninvited and unheralded. They meant it, too, every word of it, for all firemen and citizens in general seemed to vie with each other in rendering them hospitalities."

One of the Fort Street girls (Miss Mary Palmer, sister of Senator Palmer), writing to a girl friend in Monroe, Mich., August 12, 1845, among other things has this to say in regard to the visit of the Ithaca firemen:

"Our firemen are having a terrible time just now; a company of firemen from Ithaca, N. Y., have come to visit them; they leave for home this evening. Last night they had a splendid torchlight procession; today they are to have a dinner served on the ground where the Brady Guards camped, just below the residence of General Cass, on Fort Street. They are all fine looking men; their uniform is green jacket and white pants; a delightful band of music with them. General Cass has invited them all to his house to partake of a light lunch, and they have just passed our house (corner of Fort and Shelby Streets), on their way down accompanied by a number of members of our Engine Co. No. 2. The general is going to dine with them this evening. They have received a good deal of attention during their sojourn among us."

On Fort Street, north side, below the Howards, and where is now the residence of the late Allan Shelden, was the commodious log farm house of the Cass Farm; still further down and located on the DeGarmo Jones farm, was the palatial mansion of the widow Jones, erected by her after his death. My wife and I attended the house warming she gave on its completion, and it was a sumptuous affair. It is now used as a sanitarium. Generous hearted, whole-souled man that DeGarmo Jones was, it is a pity that his widow's last days were clouded by the fear that she would end them in the poor house, an unfortunate hallucination under which she labored.

THE CASS FARM.

When I came to Detroit the farmer that operated the Cass farm and lived in the log farm house down Fort Street, was an Englishman by the name of Nelson. When Mr. Rice succeeded him, he moved out on to Woodward Avenue, west side, about where Virginia Avenue crosses. The house (brick) is still standing. A daughter of his married Mr. Foster, a manufacturer of furniture. The latter bought three or four lots of my uncle Thomas Palmer, way out on Montcalm Street, or in that vicinity; anyway, it was before any streets were open out that way—a wide, common, quite destitute of houses. Foster agreed to pay for the lots in furniture; started in, put up his dwelling and shop, adjoining, and began business; but of all the slow workers I thought he was the slowest, and I reckon my aunt thought so too. Among the articles of furniture he was to make for my uncle in payment were two large rocking chairs, a set of parlor chairs, all rush bottomed, two or three settees and one or two other pieces. My aunt kept me dancing attendance on this Foster, and it was no light task for me to trudge from the corner of Fort and Shelby Streets over to his place on Montcalm Street, rain or shine, once a week at least, and hurry him up. We got the furniture at last, and the high-backed rocking chairs and the set of parlor chairs yet survive, and are now in the parlor of the Log Cabin at Palmer Park, large as life and twice as natural. Every time I see those chairs, I seem to see Foster and his comely wife, and in mind I again trudge over the hill to his shop on my hurryup errand. Perhaps Foster was not so much to blame, after all, as besides his furniture business, he had quite a little family to look after, and I think he had but one assistant in his employ. Foster and his wife may have some survivors in this community; in that case the sight of those articles of furniture I mention as being in Log Cabin at Palmer Park may be of interest to them, and that is why I bother the reader with a mention of Foster or Nelson at all.

In this connection I give something in relation to the "Old Cass (St. Martin) House" that stood on the river bank, from the pen of the late Judge James V. Campbell::

THE OLD CASS HOUSE ON THE RIVER BANK.

And threescore years were ended
    And the lily flag was down,
When Pontiac and his allies
    Encamped before the town,
But safely stood the mansion,
    Unspoiled of bolt or bar,
For the Indians loved St. Martin
    And the gray hairs of Navarre,
Sprung from an old and kingly race
    The glory of his dwelling place
Came from his honored children more
    Than from his ancestry of yore,
Bedecked with cross and star.

Behind the dormer windows
    That open on the strait,
First cradled were the Anthons,
    Renowned in church and state,
The good and wise physician
    Of all the red men known
Had love of the German forest,
    Of star and mine and stone;
And the slender, dark-eyed mother
    That held them on her knees,
Sang songs of the Spanish border,
    The land of the Pyrenees,
Who knows what golden threads of thought
Before the infant memory brought
In manly eloquence were wrought
    Beneath those waving trees?

FORT STREET.

There on the New Years gathered
    Within the largest room,
Around the roaring chimney
    The household of Macomb,
Straight sat the keen DePeyster,
    With learning quaint in store,
But, first at the sound of the fiddle,
    To dance on the well-rubbed floor.
And there were the great fur traders
    Whose will in the woods was law
With the heart of a Highland chieftain
    And grip of the lion's paw.

The hale old house had flourished
    A hundred years and ten—
Above the Fort was floating
    The flag of stars again.
A brave and honored soldier
    Came up to hold the town,
A wise and manly ruler,
    A scholar of renown.
And here he made his homestead
    And lived in quiet state
Before the wandering emigrants
    Began to crowd the strait,
Along the sloping bank-side,
    In front of his open door,
The tents of the forest's chieftains
    Are mustered as of yore.
And painted warriors as they pass
    Or smoke in groups upon the grass
Smile, grim applause when stately Cass
    Moves downward to the shore.

The spreading town has shouldered
    The useless fort away,
The grasping hands of Commerce
    Are closing on the bay,
The garden and the orchard
    No ripened fruit retain,
And idlers cross the wheat-fields
    And trample down the grain,
Alas, for the brave old mansion!
Alas, for its ancient fame!
Old things make room for the present
    As ashes follow the flame!

The last individual to operate the Cass farm before it was cut up into city lots was, if I mistake not, Harvey King, who was quite successful in its management.

CORRECTIONS.

EDITOR FREE PRESS:

It would appear from my article on Fort Street, in your issue of July 23, that Governor Mason occupied the John A. Welles house after Theo. Romeyn, whereas I meant to say that the governor occupied for a short time the house on the southwest corner of Woodbridge and Rivard Streets, before Mr. Romeyn, and that Henry Ledyard lived in the same house for quite awhile, and after him, General Pope, U. S. A., commanding this department. The general had his headquarters in this house. It is still standing.

And another correction. N. P. Jacobs occupied the Welles house after Mr. Romeyn vacated it, instead of the one next beyond it. FRIEND PALMER.

HARVEY KING.

In my last I mentioned that the late Harvey King was the last one to operate the Cass farm. He leased it in 1842 at a yearly rental of $150, and kept it until some time in 1880. He cleared off the dense growth of timber from Ledyard Street out. He was the first to deliver milk in the city. Driving his milk cart himself, with his large milk can beside him, going from customer to customer, ringing his bell before each residence to tell them that he was on hand, and to hurry up, as many had their ears open listening for the vigorous clang of the milk man's bell. King, with his son, John R., continued the milk business during the latter years of the farm lease quite extensively.

Harvey King was the first president of the board of public works, being appointed to that position by Mayor Moffatt. He was the builder and sole owner of the first street railroad, on Grand River Avenue—this about 1868. He also, in 1860, purchased a large tract of land from General Cass on the north side of Grand River Avenue, and established there (what was familiarly known for years) King's cattle yards. Also built and owned the Brighton house adjoining, a hostelry patronized almost exclusively by drovers and cattlemen. Previous to the establishment of this cattle yard, people having stock to sell had to expose them for that purpose on the Campus Martius in front of the Andrews Hotel. This action and foresight on the part of King was a great convenience to all concerned. Many will call to mind the crowded state of things in front of Andrews Hotel in the days I mention.

Harvey King purchased the wooden addition to the National Hotel (Russell House), which addition was on what is now Cadillac Square, and sold the same to his son John R., who removed it to the northeast corner of Montcalm and Cass Streets, and sold it to Mr. Ryan. It is still standing and doing duty as a five-apartment tenement house. The large front door of the old National is yet in commission as the backdoor of this tenement house, with its big brass knobs and the figures 1856 and 1858.

The house on the north side of Fort Street, beyond and adjoining the one built by Oliver Newberry (which latter was afterwards occupied by General Cass and the major), was built and owned by John Hulbert, who succeeded Henry R. Schoolcraft here as Indian agent. Mr. Hulbert was a brother-in-law of Mr. Schoolcraft, he marrying the latter's sister, and came here in a batteau from the Soo in 1836. He disposed of his property after awhile and built a brick residence at the northeast corner of Cass and Congress Streets (the same house later on was occupied by John Stephens, of Stephens & Field), which many years after was destroyed by fire, with Gray & Baffy's furniture warehouse.

THE CASS COMPANY.

In 1835 a company, styled the "Cass Company," was formed, its object being to build docks, warehouses, etc., for the improvement of the city, and to increase facilities for commerce, and as this undertaking was one of great importance to the city, it may not be out of place here to give a brief sketch of it, and a history of titles as they passed from hand to hand. The Cass farm was conveyed by the government by patent, dated April 20, 1811, to John W. Macomb, William Macomb and David B. Macomb, who were agents of the government, and were extensively engaged in trade here as early as 1777. David B. and William Macomb sold their thirds to General Cass by an act of congress. The old Macomb (St. Martin) mansion, subsequently occupied by General Cass, stood on a bluff on Jefferson Avenue, near the river, and upon the sale of the farm front, the building was removed to lot 142, West Larned Street, occupied by William Beal, ice dealer. The building was built of blocks of hewed timber and clap-boarded. It was in a good state of repair in 1863, and when it was demolished some years later it was found on examination to be in fit condition to last 100 years or more. There was some talk at the time of its purchase by the city and its removal to East Grand Circus Park, but that was all there was to it, and the historic landmark had to go.

The Cass Company consisted of DeGarmo Jones, Oliver Newberry, Eurotas P. Hastings, Major Henry Whiting, Shubael Conant, Charles C. Trowbridge, Elon Farnsworth, Henry S. Cole, Edmund A. Brush and Augustus S. Porter. The organization was a very powerful one financially, and the enterprise was looked upon by many of our citizens as one promising a very great reward, but there was some who had misgivings. The company raised the sum of $125,000, which they paid for the front, the deed bearing date June 18, 1835. On June 18, 1840, the property was mortgaged to General Cass, but the debt was discharged the following year.

The Cass Company deeded the property to Augustus S. Porter, as trustee, and on Mr. Porter leaving the state, Charles C. Trowbridge was appointed his successor. The property consisted of all that portion of the city embraced within the boundaries of the east and west lines of the Cass farm, and from the south line of Larned Street to the river. The company expended about $100,000 in docking and grading, and subdivided it into lots. A few of these they sold; but a financial crisis came on, and the entire property, with the valuable improvements the company had made, reverted to General Cass. But Mr. Newberry had obtained from the company lots Nos. 1 and 2, upon which he built a warehouse. The adjoining lot, No. 3, having reverted to General Cass, Mr. Newberry purchased it, which with the other two, constituted for many years what was known as Newberry's dock. This dock for a long period had been the scene of the greatest activity during the season of navigation, and it was Mr. Newberry's favorite haunt, even for years after he sold it. On the 13th of August, 1855, J. L. Hurd & Co. purchased this property, for which they paid the snug sum of $68,000. The lots Nos.

1, 2 and 3 extend from Second Street west 248 feet, comprising one-third of the Cass front, from Front Street to the river.

The unfortunate termination of the Cass Company's speeulations proved disastrous to several of the parties.

While recalling scenes and incidents in this portion of the town, I am reminded of General Cass and his parrot. He had a pet parrot brought from France, of which the family and himself made much, and he was taught to say many things. When the general was running against Taylor for the presidency, some one taught the bird to "Hurrah for Taylor." The bird enjoyed it so much that he kept at it, in season and out of season. It annoyed the general so he had to get rid of it, and he gave it away.

In my article on Fort Street (south side, Kinzie house), I omitted to say that one of the early dwellers in that house was Geo. W. Martin. He was of the firm of Martin & Townsend, hardware, corner of Woodward Avenue and Larned Street (southwest). He was a gay young man, but possessed of good business qualifications. He died of cholera in 1834 at the mansion house. Townsend associated himself with Harmon DeGraff in the same business on the same corner under firm name of DeGraff & Townsend. Many will call to mind Harmon DeGraff, what a staid, methodical, business individual he was, to be sure. Townsend was an equally good business man and quite genial. The firm after continuing in a successful business for a while was broken by the untimely and much regretted death of Mr. Townsend. After this Mr. Ben Vernor took Mr. Townsend's place in the firm, and it became DeGraff & Vernor. The former married the latter's sister. Vernor came here some years before with a stock of fancy dry goods and located in the Republican Hale Block where is now Edson, Moore & Co. The death of Mr. DeGraff caused the discontinuance of the firm and the business. Vernor went into the insurance business with Edward A. Lansing. The firm were successful, I believe for quite a while, then it became Lansing & Anderson, Vernor branching out for himself in the same business, which he continued until his untimely and much regretted death, especially so among the young business portion of the community. Vernor was not a Brady Guard, nor a Light Guard, but he was a most enthusiastic member of the Old Volunteer Fire Department, an all around good fellow and in all social functions he was ever at the front.

Mr. DeGraff during most of his life here, was associated with Mr. Silas N. Kendrick in the iron foundry business, corner Larned and First Streets, which they successfully conducted, Mr. K. being an expert in the business. The latter built for himself a fine brick residence adjoining the First Presbyterian Church on Fort Street, which property Mr. H. B. Joy has lately acquired. Mr. and Mrs. Kendrick were fine people, full of all good impulses and kindly deeds. Mr. Townsend was survived by Mrs. Townsend, and two daughters. One married Geo. B.. Sartwell, for some years cashier of the American Exchange Bank. Mr. Sartwell and the late Alex. H. Dey were closely associated in business for many years. He is still living and has retired on his laurels. Mrs. Townsend and Mrs. Sartwell died some years since. Miss Townsend is still living.

The Strongs have always occupied a prominent position on this street. The Strong family (John W. Strong, Sr.) when they first came here in 1838, occupied the Knaggs house down the river (Bela Hubbard's) for quite a while, then moved into the city. He was for some years forwarding merchant on Second Street. He was also at one time justice of the peace.

H. Norton Strong became the owner of the Doctor Abbott house after Mr. Dunning vacated it. Norton Strong, a neat, precise, fastidious individual, became quite prominent as a vessel owner and shipper in the forties and fifties. He quit this busy life in mid-career, leaving to his heirs a presumably comfortable fortune. Mr. Strong married the beautiful and accomplished Miss Helen Chapin, a daughter of Dr. Marshall Chapin. They had sons and daughters. Mr. Thomas Pitts married one of the daughters. Norton Strong, during the last years of his life, had the distinction of owning, with the exception of E. W. Hudson, the largest fleet of sailing vessels on the lakes, and the steam tug to help them along. John R. Gillett, who was his manager, right hand man, etc., published a lithograph print in colors, of large dimensions, showing five or six of his vessels heavily grain laden in tow of his steam tug Champion, passing Windmill Point light, headed down the river, a sight that will never be seen again. John W. Strong, Jr. (brother of Norton), married a daughter of Colonel Joshua Howard, U. S. A. John Strong was a very handsome man; indeed, they all were fine looking men, including the father. The daughters were all beautiful and accomplished. One married G. Mott Williams, son of General John R. Williams; another Henry T. Stringham, bank man; another Henry H. Brown, cashier Peninsular Bank, whose fine brick residence was on the site of the old hydraulic reservoir, corner of Wayne Street. Mr. Brown lived here for many years dispensing princely hospitality, an estimable man, and when he passed away he was much regretted. The house is still standing. The late John Moore, who at one time kept the Merchants' Exchange, that was on the southeast corner of Woodbridge and Griswold Streets, was in the employ of H. H. Brown for many years as coachman, etc. John died rich. He owned at the time of his death a fine residence and grounds, northwest corner of Washington Avenue and Grand River Street. Brown had two children, Warham and his sister Mary. The former was a very handsome, interesting boy, and when he grew to manhood was employed in the bank with his father as teller for many years. During this time he made the trip to Europe, in company with D. Bethune Duffield and Jas. C. Ladue. After the bank ceased operations his father and himself engaged in the insurance business until the death of the former. After the death of his father he was in the employ from time to time of the Detroit & Windsor Ferry Co., and then in the Detroit water office. He was in the latter employ at the time of his death, which occurred only a few years ago. In his prime Warham Brown was the handsomest young man in Detroit, and of the most polished and engaging manners. Those that attended the costume ball at the Russell Hause many years ago will, I am sure, call to mind the elegant appearance Warham made in his magnificant court suit of the time of Louis XIV., the observed of all observers. He was a guest at the various entertainments or banquets that Senator Palmer gave some years ago to the "Old Boys," the last one of which was at the "Log Cabin," Palmer Park, May 12, 1896. The daughter Mary, charming and bright, grew to a graceful womanhood. She married Wallace Osborn, of Rochester, N. Y., son of N. Osborn, the builder of the present city hall. Mrs. Brown, widow of H. H. Brown, passed her declining years with her daughter, Mrs. Osborn. She passed away but a few years ago. Mrs. Osborn died in Rochester nearly two years ago.

HOW JUDGE SOLOMON SIBLEY WAS NOMINATED FOR DELEGATE TO CONGRESS IN 1821.

Governor Cass having designated Pontiac as the county seat of Oakland County, Colonel Stephen Mack (Mack & Conant), of Detroit, who had become interested with many other citizens of Detroit in forming an association known as the "Pontiac Company," for purchasing, jointly, a tract of land for the purpose of laying out and establishing a town on the same, turned his attention to constructing a road from Detroit to the new city (Pontiac), and also to building mills on the Clinton River, near by. A company for the latter purpose was formed, consisting of Stephen Mack, Shubael Conant and Solomon Sibley, who completed the first saw and grist mill in Oakland County in 1821, and the event was duly celebrated. The occasion was one of great importance to the few scattered settlers in that region, not less to the enterprising company at Detroit who had originated and completed that important undertaking. There was as large a gathering on the occasion as the sparse settlement in Oakland County could furnish, then consisting of about a dozen families, the number present being increased by several gentlemen of Detroit who had been so rash as to embark in what was at that time considered a very doubtful enterprise, an undertaking that some were sure would result in failure and bankruptcy. A good dinner was provided, toasts were drunk and various sports ensued.

At that time the question of electing a delegate to congress was about to come before the people. But no nomination had been formally made. The company present resolved itself into a committee of the whole on the condition of the territory of Michigan. It was deemed to be a fit occasion to nominate in a formal manner a candidate for congress. There were three persons present, who, by education and position, were deemed to be qualified for the post, namely: Daniel LeRoy, A. B. Woodward, and Solomon Sibley. It was no easy task for the company to determine the merits of the respective gentlemen. The question had been unexpectedly sprung upon the candidates themselves, and they had no time to prepare elaborate speeches and answer all sorts of impertinent questions, whereby to prove their qualifications. The facetious Judge Woodward proposed that each candidate should be put through the mill, one at a time, and the one whose maniplations and skill in the hopper should produce the best meal should be declared the candidate. Colonel Mack and the miller being appointed umpires.

The suggestion was adopted by acclamation. It was agreed that Judge LeRoy should go through the ordeal first. He mounted the hopper, and it was agreed by all that he went through the performance admirably. Next Judge Woodward tried his chances, and won great applause.

The mill was beginning to work well, the meal could scarcely be excelled, but it remained for Judge Sibley to carry off the palm. He took his stand, and an appreciative constituency could not fail to see his superior merits. The miller took up the meal, handful after handful, and was enthusiastic in its praise. Colonel Mack did not at first quite agree with him, but finally was convinced, not only that the meal was finer, but the performance of the judge himself so unique and beautiful as to place his competitors in the shade. It was only a question of time to determine which of the three candidates was to be nominated. The judge was making good time in the hopper, when the umpires with watch in hand at the proper moment, declared him the successful candidate. His competitors acknowledged the corn. He was formally announced as the favorite candidate of Oakland County. His nomination was responded to in Wayne, Macomb and Monroe, and he was elected delegate to Congress for the Territory of Michigan, which position he filled with honor to himself and satisfaction to his constituents.

Judge Sibley's family when I knew them consisted of eight children, four boys and four girls. Henry, after attaining his majority, went to Wisconsin, when it was a territory, and was delegate to Congress from there. He also was appointed Governor of Minnesota.

Ebenezer Sproat entered West Point and after the usual time graduated into the artillery. He was afterwards transferred to the Quarter-Master's department, with the rank of captain, and served with great distinction in that capacity during the Mexican

War. He had charge of the immense military depot at Camargo, the center of supplies for General Taylor's army. The transactions of his department at that point were enormous, involving a large expenditure of money, and a necessary accumulation of much public property. On the breaking up of the depot at the close of the war and disposing of the public property under his charge, Captain Sibley found but little time to close his accounts with the department at Washington, so brought all his papers to Detroit, to which point he was ordered to take charge of the quartermaster's department in the military department of the lakes. I am able to testify that the transactions of his department at Camargo were very extensive from the fact that I, being his clerk while stationed here, made up his Camargo accounts and settlements with the United States; they were closed to the entire satisfaction of all concerned. To the initiated in such matters, the magnitude of the job will, I am sure, suggest itself. The knowledge I then and there acquired of the manner of settling accounts with the treasury department at Washington, stood me in good stead when in after years the task devolved on me of settling the accounts of the State of Michigan, against the general government, for expenses incurred on account of the Civil War.

Captain Sibley was stationed here about two years, and during that time Lieutenant U. S. Grant was stationed at the Detroit barracks with his regiment, the Fourth U. S. Infantry. From here Captain Sibley was ordered to Santa Fe, New Mexico, and remainded there, I think, until the breaking out of the Civil War, when he was elevated to the position of deputy quartermaster-general with rank of lieutenant-colonel, and stationed at Washington.

General M. C. Meigs was quartermaster-general at that time; and he, as first lieutenant of engineers, was stationed at Detroit, building Fort Wayne, at the same time that Captain Sibley was stationed here as quartermaster. The former used to draw from the latter his monthly commutation for fuel and quarters. Quite as odd, if not more so, were the different positions Captain Sibley and Lieutenant Grant occupied in after years. While Grant, the modest, retiring first lieutenant was stationed here with his regiment, he held the position of regimental quartermaster, or quartermaster of that portion stationed at the Detroit barracks, and as such drew all his supplies, cash, etc., from his superior officer, Quartermaster Sibley. After the Civil War broke out, the progress of events brought the obscure lieutenant very much to the front, far outstripping Captain Sibley, although he too attained distinction, rising to the rank of lieutenant-colonel. I think Sibley made a mistake when he sent in his resignation. I am told he realized it after a while, and when Grant got to be president he made a move to get re-instated, but the former found it impossible to do it, for military or army reasons. Colonel Sibley resigned April 15, 1864. He was a splendid man in every way. My two years' service with him made me appreciate his fine qualities of head and heart. A truly Christian gentleman and of the strictest integrity.

Alex H. Sibley I knew quite well as a young man, and while teller in the Bank of Michigan. Afterwards he and Samuel P. Brady were sutlers to Colonel Bennett Riley's regiment when it was ordered to California in 1849. They made the voyage by sea in sailing vessels around the Horn, taking quite an assortment of goods along, sufficient for the needs of the regiment, and for probable outside customers. They freighted an extra vessel with their supplies. When they arrived at Valparaiso, they first learned of the discovery of gold in California at Suter's mill. After a short stop they proceeded to Monterey, their objective point in California, but not being satisfied with this location, the Colonel after a brief period abandoned it for the Golden Gate and San Francisco, and there established his headquarters. The gold discovery created an immense excitement through the entire country, and thousands had already flocked to that point in quest of the precious metal. As a consequence provisions and supplies of every kind got to be very scarce, and when these supplies of Brady and Sibley were landed and get-at-able, the demand for them from outsiders, miners and others, amounted almost to a frenzy. They hastily stored their goods in tents, no other shelter being available, and did the best they could to answer the wants of the crowd, mostly miners, with their fat gold dust pouches. The cry was not "How much do you ask?" but "Can I have the goods?" and so it went on, until the other vessel of goods arrived from New York.

In the meantime supplies in a limited quantity had begun to arrive from points along the Pacific coast, which relieved the pressure some, but Brady and Sibley reaped a rich harvest and continued for some time. I had this account from Edward M. Pitcher, nephew of Dr. Z. Pitcher, and J. Mott Williams, son of General John R. Williams, both of this city, who went out in the employ of the firm as sutler's clerks.

After his return to the States, Sibley entered quite extensively in mining operations on Lake Superior, particularly the "Silver Islet" mine, and I understand gained quite a competency.

Frederick B., the youngest, I was always familiar with from our schoolboy days on. When the Sibleys acquired the lime business and stone quarry down the river near Trenton, Fred took charge of it, and established a stone yard and lime kiln on the river front between Rivard and Orleans Streets, which he carried on until a few years ago, when he disposed of it, as well as the stone quarry down the river.

When McClellan's army was before Richmond, Alex and Fred Sibley were engaged in furnishing Major Ingalls, quartermaster of the army of the Potomac at West Point, Va., with forage. They had an office in New York over which Fred presided. I was told they dispatched two or three vessels a day from that port loaded with forage for that army.

C. C. Trowbridge married one of the daughters, as did James A. Armstrong, of Armstrong, Sibley & Co., and Charles S. Adams, of the firm of Whitney & Adams. One of the daughters (Miss Sarah) survives.

Of all the sons of Judge Sibley, I think Alexander was the most strenuous, pushing and agressive. Mr. Trowbridge used to relate this of his father-in-law, which has been mentioned, I think, in an article some time ago: "I am reminded of a remark made to me not long ago by the venerable General Cass. The General said that, while a stout boy, he was one morning occupied at a hollow stump standing before his father's house on the Muskingum River, pounding corn for the family breakfast. He looked down the road and espied two persons approaching on horseback. They proved to be Mr. Sol. Sibley and his young wife, the daughter of Colonel Sproat of Marietta, Ohio, on their way to Detroit, where Mr. S. had decided to practice law. According to the custom of the country, they alighted without ceremony, partook of a welcome breakfast and resumed their long journey."

Solomon Sibley was one of the judges who presided at the trial of the wife murderer Simmons, July, 1830.

Colonel A. T. McReynolds, who lately died in Grand Rapids at an advanced age, was a prominent attorney here in the early days. He was a man of sterling worth and also quite military. At the outbreak of the Mexican War he organized a company of dragoons, of which he was commissioned captain. John T. Brown, of Tecumseh, was first lieutenant and J. C. D. Williams, of Detroit, and Frank Henry, of Wisconsin, were second lieutenants.

"Dev" Williams, as he was familiarly called, had the air and bearing of a soldier, but little else in that line, Captain McReynolds, however, left the drilling of the company entirely to "Dev." The company rendezvoused at the old Detroit barracks, corner Russell and Gratiot Streets. He used to go up daily, and with the aid of the sergeant of the company, who had once belonged to a British cavalry regiment, put his men through their paces.

* * *

Captain McReynolds and his command left here in due time, and saw service in Mexico under General Winfield Scott, and participated in the taking of Chapultepec and the City of Mexico. In the last affair Captain McReynold's company made a gallant charge across the causeway leading into the city, losing quite a number of men and horses. In this charge the captain received a severe wound in the arm, as did Lieutenant Dev. Williams. The wound of the former lasted him through life, the latter soon recovered. After the war both returned to Detroit, McReynolds to his profession and Williams to his father's hearth. During the Civil War McReynolds was given command of a Michigan regiment and served with distinction. Subsequently he took up his abode in Grand Rapids and died there recently. Lieutenant Williams died in Mt. Clemens a few years ago.

* * *

John McReynolds, brother of the colonel, was a man of sterling worth. He was associated with Henry Doty, also a man of the strictest integrity, in the auction and commission business for many years on Woodward Avenue. Associated with them was Wm. P. Doty, brother of Henry, who was a bright business young man and one of the society leaders of that day. David R. Peirce was also with this firm for many years.

Tom Edmonds, as he was familiarly called, was the auctioneer for McReynolds & Doty. He was an eccentric character. Unfortunately he was addicted to periodical sprees, that lasted sometimes a week or ten days. On these occasions he was a conspicuous object on the streets minus coat and hat, and in a dilapidated condition otherwise, he would declaim on the corners in an unintelligible jargon, always ending his sentences with "down goes the hammer." When he was himself, however, he was correct in every particular and faultlessly dressed.

As an auctioneer he had no superior. He was a great favorite with all the community.

* * *

In addition to Wm. P. Doty as one of the leaders of the young society of this city, I call to mind the names and personalities of Edward M. Pitcher, Dr. L. H. Cobb, Albion Turner, Geo. A. Cooper, Wm. A. Heartt, L. B. Watkins, J. C. D. Williams, John B. Palmer, Charles and George Dibble, Henry Schoolcraft, Eben N. and O. B. Willcox, Norman Emmons, Lafayette Knapp, Barney and Alex Campau, Henry A. Wight, Alex Lewis and W. G. Lee. The older set of society gentlemen—I think I have mentioned some of them before—who used to mix in on occasions with the younger, were John T. Hunt, Frank Hunt, Henry M. Roby, Chandler Seymour, Addison Mandell, Jed P. C. Emmons, Walter Ingersoll, John W. Strong, J. Norton Strong, A. H. Guise, Sam Lewis, Dr. Geo. B. Russell, Chas. S. Adams and H. C. Kibbee.

Of all the sons of General John R. Williams, Theodore was the most liked in this community, and the most active in the life of the city. Ferdinand, G. Mott, John C., T. Mott and J. C. Devereaux were good, respectable members of the community, and filled their roles as all good citizens are expected to do. Thomas Williams, as said in a former article, was a graduate of West Point, entered the infantry, served with distinction in the Mexican and the Civil War. During the latter war he attained the rank of brigadier-general. He was killed at the battle of Baton Rouge, where he commanded the union forces. He was a good soldier.

Among the bachelors who used to flourish here in the early days in addition to Curt Emerson, Josh Carew, Dr. Rufus Brown, Sax Kellogg, Sam Suydam, W. B. Alvord and Alf Hunter were Marsh Mead, Delos Davis and Charles Richmond. Mead and Davis, though not society men, were gentlemen of elegant leisure, favorites among their male friends. Charles Richmond, a most genial bachelor, was not exactly a gentleman of elegant leisure; but he made the tour of Europe and for a long period he was assistant postmaster here, and through fortunate ventures acquired quite a property. He became the owner of the Odd Fellows' Hall that order had erected on Woodward Avenue. The Odd Fellows were unable to hold it on account of lack of funds, and Richmond became the fortunate owner. Many with myself will remember him with feelings of admiration and pleasure. His early death was much regretted.

* * *

Few and perhaps no one now will remember Obed Waite. He was a man of much promise and was the architect of the state capitol building. He died in 1830. I remember his funeral (Masonic) was largely attended. He was a friend of Thomas Palmer, father of the senator, also of Colonel D. C. McKinstry, Shubael Conant, Oliver Newbury and indeed all of the prominent men here at that day. He was a remarkably fine looking man, and an accomplished architect.

*

OLIVER M. HYDE.

There was a row of wooden buildings on the west side of Woodward Avenue, between Woodbridge and Atwater Streets (Abbott Block), in which were the business places of Waller & Jaquith, Jenness, and others, but they did not extend to the corner of Woodbridge Street. Between was the leather store of Ingersoll & Kirby, and the store of Oliver M. Hyde; the latter extended to the corner of Woodbridge.

Mr. Hyde dealt in almost every conceivable thing, it was said that you could buy of Uncle Oliver Hyde, or he would furnish for a price anything from a mousetrap to a meeting house. He also carried on the platform and counter scale business with A. A. Wilder, under the firm name of Hyde & Wilder, at the same locality, the manufactory and scales room being in the upper part of the building. Wilder was an engineer, machinist and inventor, always inventing something of practical utility, but failed to derive much profit from his inventions, and as is often the case, others reaped where he had sowed and are even now enjoying the benefits of his genius. Mr. Hyde about the same time established an extensive foundry and machine shop on Atwater Street, near the foot of Dequindre Street. He was engaged here for some years in the manufacture of engines and steamboat machinery.

Oliver M. Hyde had an able assistant in the person of Captain Morgan L. Gage. The captain emigrated to Saginaw and died there. A son of his is at present and has been for some years bookkeeper for the extensive lumber and salt firm of Charles Merrill & Co., of that city. About 1852, O. M. Hyde built a steam saw mill on the west bank of the Saginaw River, opposite the town of East Saginaw, which he sold in 1854 to a company composed of Charles Merrill, R. N. Rice and U. Tracy Howe.

Mr. Hyde lived for many years, and until he died June 28, 1870, on the corner of Michigan Avenue and Griswold Street, in an attractive cottage, where is now the Whitney building. Uncle Oliver left a widow and three children, two sons and one daughter, in comfortable circumstances. One of the sons, Henry, was for a while in the dry goods business on Jefferson Avenue, he buying out Mr. Edward Graham. He married for his first wife Miss Wasson, whose father was an extensive car builder, of Springfield, Mass. He abandoned the dry goods business in this city, and took up his residence in Springfield, entering into partnership with his father-in-law. Louis, a younger brother, joined him in the business, Mr. Wasson having died in the meantime. They are both alive and carrying on the business vigorously. In addition to the car business, Henry is president of a bank in Springfield, a position that he has held for many years. Both enjoy in an eminent degree the confidence and respect of the citizens of that hustling New England city.

Mr. Asa D. Dickinson, brother of Hon. Don. M. Dickinson, married the daughter of O. M. Hyde, Harriet, an exceedingly bright and charming girl. After many years of happy married life Asa passed to the beyond. He died in 1904 and his remains rest in Elmwood. President Cleveland appointed him consul to Nottingham, England, a position that he retained until a short time before his death, relinquishing it at his own request.

Many will call to mind Asa's ("Little Dick," as he was familiarly called) career in the river steambot business in the early days. He was popular and successful, full of joke, repartee and a wonderful flow of spirits. He was afterward in company with John J. Gafrison (Garrison & Dickinson). The latter's extensive acquaintance with steamboat people and the inhabitants on both sides of the river up and down, from Malden to Port Huron, brought to the concern a vast volume of trade. But he sought a wider field, severing his connection with Mr. Garrison, and embarking in business in New York City, where he continued with varied fortunes until his appointment to the Nottingham consulship.

Uncle Oliver Hyde married in Poultney, Vermont, Julia Sprague, the sister of Judge B. F. H. Witherell's first wife, Mary Ann Sprague. He was uncle by marriage to Colonel Spencer Sprague, who with his son, Henry, composed the well-known patent right firm of Thos. S. Sprague & Son. The business is carried on under the same firm name today. Spencer Sprague was also for many years in the agricultural implement business on the east side of Woodward Avenue, between Jefferson Avenue and Atwater Street. Hon. James Mercer, of Ontonagon, was a clerk in his establishment for some time. Spencer saw service in the Civil War. He was a very genial, companionable man. A large number of our people will call to mind Colonel Spencer Sprague, and with pleasurable emotions.

After some years a brother of Mrs. Hyde's, Henry Sprague, came with his family and took up residence in Detroit. He died after a few years sojourn here, leaving a widow and several children. One of the daughters married Henry. Hopson, who was for many years a hardware merchant on upper Woodward Avenue, and is now a retired capitalist. Another daughter married Silas Bullock, who was for many years bookkeeper for Merrill & Palmer (Charles Merrill and T. W. Palmer). Bullock had seen service in the Civil War, was taken prisoner and confined for many months in the rebel prison at Andersonville. He never entirely recovered from the severe treatment he underwent in that southern prison pen, and no doubt it hastened his death. He left a widow, a son and a daughter. The daughter is married to Dr. J. Knox Gailey, of this city; the son, Earle Bullock, is also a physician, and is in the service of the government.

The late Benjamin F. Hyde, a prominent Democratic politician, was a nephew of O. M. Hyde. Very many will remember "Ben" Hyde. The old-time Democratic politicians, I am quite sure, will. He was by profession a lawyer, but it seemed to me that he always held office, either in the customs or somewhere else. He did though, about 1849, embark in the banking business, but not for long. He was very popular with all classes, and deservedly so.

My connection by marriage with a niece of Mrs. O. M. Hyde (Miss Witherell) made me quite familiar with the Hydes, and all akin to them. We were almost of the same family.

* * *

HENRY A. NAGLEE.

Henry A. Naglee, coming here in the early thirties, from Philadelphia, was the pioneer in the soda water, mead, ice cream, fancy cake and candy business, ice cream though had made its appearance here, a short period before, in a limited way, but Naglee advertised to furnish the above specialties in quantities as might be desired. He also served oysters in season and did a limited restaurant business, minus liquors. He also kept fine cigars and smokers' articles. He was brother of Mrs. H. D. Garrison, the principal milliner in the city at that time, somewhat eclipsing Miss Moon in the same line.

Naglee was a fine looking, pleasant mannered man, unmarried, and drew a large trade. His store was on Jefferson Avenue, opposite Rood's bookstore, midway between Griswold and Shelby Streets. He, however, was unfortunate in business through a mistaken venture, and had to retire. Emboldened with his success in his ice cream saloon business, he started a restaurant on an extended scale, corner of Wayne Street and Jefferson Avenue. His bill of fare was most elaborate, including almost everything in season. He also had a stock of fine wines and liquors and cigars. His venture was not a success, and both concerns were wrecked. Naglee entered the service of Sidney L. Rood, books and stationery, in which concern I was clerk and bookkeeper. Naglee's specialty with Rood was traveling through the state, disposing of books, stationery, blank books, etc. For this purpose Rood bought a fine span of horses and a strong peddler's wagon. It was a substantial outfit in every way, as indeed it had to be to stand the rough, primitive roads in the state at that early day. Naglee did not venture far outside of Wayne County, sometimes to Ypsilanti and Ann Arbor. This was the first time a rig of this description had ever visited the places he ventured into, and the people gave him an ovation. His graphic descriptions of the various incidents occurring on his trips were most interesting and amusing. The rough, muddy roads came in for a good deal of vigorous talk on Naglee's part, and well they might, judging from the condition of the goods returned unsold; shaken almost to pieces and requiring much repair. This venture was fairly successful, and what became of Naglee after he left Rood's employ, I never knew.

The incidents related were a part of my life at the time and mixed in with the daily happenings. Naglee was at that time and while in business here an important member of the community. He was not at the start a rival of Bull & Beard, the restauranters, under King's corner; he catered more particularly to the female portion of the community, which Bull & Beard did not.

A NOTED FIRM.

A NOTED FIRM AND ITS EXTENSIVE OPERATIONS HERE AND ELSEWHERE.

THE style of architecture in brick structures here in the early days was peculiar, in that they were all after the same pattern and severely plain. As a sample of the style then prevailing, the reader is referred to the Whiting & Wendell house, nearly opposite the old Michigan Exchange, and now used by commercial agents, the Kearsley House, northwest corner Jefferson Avenue and Randolph Street. This style of building continued without change until some time in 1855 or 1856. J. C. Devereaux Williams broke the spell when he erected the building where is now the Hotel Gies, Monroe Avenue, and his other building near the foot of Woodward Avenue, east side, between Atwater Street and the river. Five or six years after this the Merrill Block followed.

The Merrill Block was erected about 1860 by Mr. Charles Merrill, a wealthy lumberman from Maine, who had cast his lot in Michigan and made this city his permanent place of residence. Senator Thomas W. Palmer married his daughter, his only child, and was a most important and efficient assistant to Mr. Merrill. The Merrill Block was much more ornate and pretentious than the Williams buildings, and on its completion was the pride of the city, and continued so for many years. It became at once the center of its life and trade until about 1895, when Woodward Avenue, above the campus, seemed to become the center of attraction and gradually drew trade and public attention to that part of the city. The glory and fame of the Merrill Block departed, but not until it had proved to be a great financial success to its originators.

* * *

A short sketch is here given of the lumber operations of Mr. Merrill in Saginaw, when head of the firm of Charles Merrill & Co., of that city.

NOTED FIRMS.

About 1852, O. M. Hyde, of Detroit, built a mill on the west bank of the Saginaw River, opposite the town of East Saginaw, which he sold to a company composed of Charles Merrill, R. N. Rice and U. T. Howe, also of Detroit, in 1854. This mill had two Mulay saws and a siding machine for making six-inch strips. In 1856 they remodeled the mill, taking out the siding machine and putting in a small gang with an eight-inch crank, being the first flat gang ever placed on Saginaw River. This made the capacity of the mill six million feet per year. The mill was managed in 1857 by Mr. Cushing. It was a hard year for lumbermen, and money was lost. In 1858 the mill was placed under the management of Joseph A. Whittier, also from Maine, who in 1864 acquired a quarter interest in the firm, at the same time Thomas W. Palmer bought a quarter interest.

Mr. Merrill died in December, 1872. His daughter, Mrs. T. W. Palmer, inherited his interest (one-half), and the business was continued under the name of Charles Merrill & Co. In 1880 the mill was taken down, Joseph B. Whittier, son of Joseph A., became a member of the firm and a new mill was built, which contained all of the modern improvements and could saw about twenty-five million feet per year. In February, 1903, when J. B. Whittier died, the business of the company was closed, the timber (about 650,000,000 feet) on its lands had been cut and since then its affairs have been in the process of settlement. It was a remarkably successful company in that it never had any losses, of any amount, by fire, water or bad debts.

Aside from the Merrill Block, which as long as it stands will serve to perpetuate Mr. Merrill's memory, I call attention to the white marble fountain which conspicuously adorns the Campus Martius, erected to his memory by his daughter, Mrs. Thos. W. Palmer.

The first occupants of the Merrill Block after its completion were: Morrison & Conklin, jewelers; Staring & Wittemore, pianos; Higby & Stearns, druggists; Farrel Bros., dry goods; Forsyth Bros., dry goods; L. L. Farnsworth, boots and shoes; F. Wetmore, crockery; G. & W. Doeltz, dry goods and millinery; David Preston, banker; Isadore Kaufman, clothing; Yates ("Hold your horses") clothing; John Palmer, insurance; Detroit Gas Light Co.; Walkers & Russell, Barstow & Lockwood, law offices.

Nicholas had a Daguerrean gallery in fourth story, corner of Larned Street, and after removed to the northeast corner of Woodward and Jefferson Avenues (fourth story). Mr. Mellus succeeded him in the Larned Street corner. A large number of rooms in the fourth story of the block were occupied as sleeping rooms, tailors rooms, etc. St. Andrew's Society also had a large room in the block. Merrill Hall, occupying a large portion of the second, third and fourth stories, was the finest and largest hall in the city, except the Firemen's Hall, which it excelled in the facilities afforded the public for ingress and egress. It became immensely popular at once. There was scarcely a night that it was not in commission. The Detroit Musical Society, under the leadership of Professor Abel, held its weekly meetings there for many years. The hall continued to enjoy its popularity until "Pop" Wiggins captured it and turned it into "Wonderland." The Farmers & Mechanics bank at one time in the sixties occupied the northeast corner, first floor, upstairs. David Whitney, Jr., succeeded it and continued there for many years.

* * *

One great factor in the success of the firm of Charles Merrill & Co., in its early days, was John Mark, born in Alsace-Loraine. After completing his education in the common branches, and serving his term in the French Army, he, with his wife, emigrated to this country in 1846, coming directly to Detroit. He at once entered the service of Samuel Pitts (Pitts's saw mill) at 62½ cents per day. Mr. Pitts gradually advanced his wages until he received $5 per day as inspector of lumber. While with Mr. Pitts he acquired a complete knowledge of the lumber business, becoming master of all its details. In 1858 he went to Saginaw to measure some lumber that Mr. Merrill had sold. He soon found plenty of work and became an authority in Saginaw as inspector. He was also of great assistance to Mr. Whittier, the resident partner of Merrill & Co., who knew nothing about running a lumber mill. After a few years David Whittier, Jr., secured his services to handle his Saginaw interests, which he did very successfully, buying logs, having them sawed and shipping the lumber. He handled one year over seventy million feet for Mr. Whitney.

The good offices Mr. Mark rendered to Mr. Whittier, in showing him the way to make and handle lumber, enabled the latter to become, at the close of the first year, as expert as the best manufacturer in Saginaw. In rendering a deserved tribute to Mr. Mark, he says: "He was a thoroughly honest man, and gradually made his way to the front rank of the business men of Saginaw. He was one of God's noblemen."

Mr. Mark died not many years ago in his fine home on Jefferson Avenue, leaving his heirs quite wealthy. During his declining years he was a familiar figure around the Merrill Block and the offices of Hon. T. W. Palmer and David Whitney, Jr., and also in the haunts of his German friends. Many, no doubt, will call to mind his stalwart, erect form and genial manners.

The death of Joseph B. Whittier in February, 1903, no doubt hastened the close of the business of C. Merrill & Co. This gentleman from his long service with the company, as employe and partner, became an efficient lumberman, so much so that he took the entire management of the concern, the other partners deferring to his judgment in conducting the affairs of the firm. He was singularly successful, and his early death was deeply deplored by his surviving partners as well as by the entire Saginaw valley.

Mr. Jos. A. Whittier, father of Jos. B., still survives, and though the weight of years is upon him, is quite vigorous and sound of mind, and is at present busily engaged in closing up the affairs of the firm, no light task for even a man who is in his prime. In his lovely home in Saginaw, surrounded by his children and grandchildren, he enjoys his well-earned competency to the full, passing his declining years peacefully, calmly and quietly, even as the sun goes down.

* * *

Alexander H. Stowell came to Detroit in 1831, and went into the book business on the northeast corner of Jefferson Avenue and Griswold Street. After a while Sidney L. Rood became a partner of Mr. Stowell, and later bought him out, carrying on the business alone until he bought out Snow & Fisk and removed to the Cooper Block. Stowell was after this an auctioneer at the corner of Woodward Avenue and Woodbridge Street. He continued in the business (real estate, etc.) until he died about 1867. He was a full faced man of short stature and chubby; a glib talker, and rather inclined to "pull the long bow," could tell a good story, and all together was a good companion and shrewd individual. He was a Democrat, and a successful one, being elected alderman in 1839, also in 1851-2-3, when he represented the fifth ward. He was city marshal in the early forties, state senator in 1852 and assessor from 1854 to 1856. He lived on Grand River Avenue, where the Y. M. C. A. building is.

Stowell was a member of the Methodist Church. John Owen was also a member of the same church and it was supported mainly through the latter's liberality. It was deeply in debt nevertheless. On one Sunday after the conclusion of the sermon, the minister requested the members to remain and hold a business meeting. Among those who remained was Stowell, who was quite conspicuous in conducting it. "Now," he said, "we have all to contribute according to our means. We must not ride a willing horse to death, and I object to Mr. Owen's giving anything, as he has given too much already." Stowell took the subscription paper and headed it with $3,000 with a grand flourish. Then he passed it around, and the others, inspired by his liberality, gave large sums in proportions to their means. Mr. Owen desired to subscribe, but Stowell would not hear of it. The amounts subscribed were collected slowly, for cash was quite scarce in the early days of Detroit. Finally, some months afterward, the committee, headed by J. Wilkie Moore, waited on Mr. Stowell and said: "We have collected every subscription except yours, and we would like you to pay up." Stowell's face was a picture. He looked daggers at his fellow-churchmen. "What," he said, "do you think I am a darned fool? I won't give a cent. I did my part in raising the money from those stingy fellows, and that is sufficient. If it had not been for me the church would have been bankrupt and the property sold."

The committee was surprised, and even J. Wilkie Moore, who knew Stowell's peculiarities better almost than anyone else, was asked when they got out-of-doors: "What do you think of that?" "I can't think," was the answer. However, when Stowell was buried in 1872 two of his pallbearers were John Owen and J. Wilkie Moore.

I did not come much in contact with Stowell, though I knew him quite well. He was a familiar figure in the crowd of city solons who used to make Rood's book store their headquarters. I being the only clerk in the establishment, saw much of him of course. Later on when I was in business myself, I indorsed the paper of a Mr. Barrowman, a hatter, doing business in the Masonic hall building, to the extent of $100. He was a good fellow, a member of the Methodist Church in good standing, but he was not a success in business, and seeing he must go to the wall called a meeting of his creditors, and Stowell was one of the number. It appeared that all Barrowman's creditors were members of the Methodist Church, except myself. Stowell, on entering the room where we were assembled, seeing me, exclaimed to Barrowman, "Good gracious, man, what makes you go out of the church for help?" The idea seemed to tickle him immensely. It is needless to say I had to stand the $100.

Many will call to mind the firm of Pattison, Stowell & Jones. I think it was formed in the forties. Pattison was at one time in the printing business, later in real estate and later proprietor of a second-hand bookstore on Michigan Avenue, near Griswold Street. He was in this business at the time of his death a few years ago. He was quite an authority on old scarce and rare editions. He owned quite a nice farm out at Birmingham where he died.

Czar Jones at one time kept the Cass Hotel, now the Wayne. It was there I first knew him. He was an eccentric character. I did not know him very well until late in life. Along in the eighties I used often to encounter Jones, J. Wilkie Moore, Chas. Sanford and Pattison, and talk over the happenings in the early days. Jones owned and lived in a small brick building to the rear of Watson's drug store, corner of Jefferson Avenue and Riopelle Street. He was the inventor of a carpet tack that was a great improvement on the old one. He busied himself in disposing of these up to the time of his death, which happened only a few years ago. Pattison, Stowell & Jones transacted a real estate, auction and commission, brokerage and general information business.

In the year 1836 the governor appointed A. H. Stowell, William Driggs and Mr. Berry as a committee to locate the county sites of Midland and Gratiot counties. It took four days, with good horses, to get from Detroit to Saginaw. Saginaw had a trading house and about one hundred inhabitants, and there were three houses between Flint and the Cass River.

From Saginaw the party went about four miles up the Tittabawassee River, in canoes, and from there on foot to Midland. They then returned to Pontiac, and from there journeyed through the woods to Lyons, which then had about fifty inhabitants. From Lyons they took the trail on foot for about sixteen miles to the house of a trader by the name of Campau, it being the only house on the route, and from there to Midland, on foot, camping out at night, to Gratiot County. On their return a heavy rain had fallen and it was almost impossible to get along. Arriving at Pontiac, and taking an early start, it still took a whole day to get from Pontiac to Detroit.

In this connection, in relation to travel in the early days, General Cass went to Chicago to hold a treaty with the Indians, and this was, beyond doubt, the most wonderful canoe voyage in American history. Let the reader trace on the map the following route from Toledo to Chicago, which was given in the Geneva, N. Y., *Gazette* of October 3, 1821:

"General Cass, on his route to Chicago, ascended the Maumee to Fort Wayne; from thence his canoe was carried over a portage of about nine miles to the head of the Wabash. This river he descended to the Ohio and then descended the Ohio to the Mississippi. The latter he ascended to the mouth of the Illinois, one of whose tributaries approaches within ten miles of Chicago."

The reader will see, that in order to avoid a land journey of 300 miles, through a wilderness, a circuitous course of five times that distance was endured.

In this manner the government agent reached Chicago, where he held a council with the Indians. The direct journey can now be made in as many hours as it then took weeks, and during the extraordinary canoeing the party had to live on fish and game. Their route took them past St. Louis, and yet this was the easiest and safest way of reaching their destination.

A fine likeness of Stowell is preserved in a painting by the artist, Cohen, which is the property of D. J. Campau.

* * *

Warren Hill when he came here was a widower, and married for his second wife, Mrs. Hazard, nee Peirce, sister of Mrs. Ellis. Doty, Mrs. Randall S. S. Rice, Mrs. Wm. Moore, mother of Wm. P. Moore (the latter for so many years with Brady & Trowbridge and S. P. Brady & Co.), also the mother of Mrs. Henry L. Newberry, who is the mother of Mrs. Austin Ladue.

Mrs. Hazard, whom Mr. Warren Hill married, was also sister of the Mr. Peirce who was the father of our good friend and well known fellow townsman, the late Mr. David R. Peirce. The father of David was in business in this city many years, before 1820. He and Thomas Palmer, father of the senator, were engaged together in many mercantile ventures. He went to Ogdensburg, N. Y., where in 1827 our friend David was born. Mr. Peirce subsequently removed to Montreal, where he died.

David R. Peirce has given quite an exhaustive account of his own career since he came to this city, which appeared in *The Free Press* June 14, 1903. In addition to what appeared in that article, I desire to add that Mr. Peirce, when he first came to this city from Montreal, entered the auction and commission house of Doty & McReynolds and after Doty & Abbott, who carried on business on Woodward Avenue, where the Merrill Block now is, and remained with the latter firm until they retired from business. He next took service with Z. Chandler & Co., as bookkeeper, and after in the same capacity with the Detroit Locomotive works, where he remained until the company quit building locomotives and was merged into the Buhl Iron Works. He remained with the latter as manager until the death of C. H. Buhl and assisted in closing up his affairs. His service with the two concerns extended through a period of over forty years. He then entered the service of Hiram Walker as confidential secretary, and remained with Mr. Walker until his death, rendering valuable assistance in closing up his affairs. In the above varied interests in which he was engaged, Mr. P. had the reputation of being an expert bookkeeper as well as a first-class business man in every way, and also one whose integrity was never questioned.

After Mr. Hiram Walker gave to his sons his entire interest in Walkerville, Canada, he embarked in other enterprises that were successful, so much so that he was enabled solely and alone to bestow that splendid charity on this city, "The Children's Free Hospital" and also to liberally endow it—a monument to his memory for all time. In these enterprises of Mr. Walker, Mr. David Peirce was his right hand man, and to his integrity and business ability, Mr. Walker was in a great degree indebted for his success after he had given up his interest in Walkerville.

Since the foregoing was written David R. Peirce, our good friend for nearly sixty years, departed this life, January 21, 1905, deeply regretted by all who had the pleasure of his acquaintance. *The Free Press* at the date of his death paid a fitting tribute to his memory, but I desire to add, that I knew him intimately from the day of his advent here until his death, and during all of the fifty-six years of his residence in this city we were on the most intimate terms. Not a shadow ever came between us. We were members of the "Light Guard" together, as also of the old volunteer fire department. He was its last secretary and was a great factor in closing its affairs after the sale of the Old Fireman's hall to the water board.

After Senator Palmer had taken possession of his new residence adjoining Palmer Park, in the fall of 1897, Mr. Peirce was a frequent and welcome visitor. Every Sabbath saw him there at dinner, rain or shine, until his failing health, the result of the paralytic stroke that came to him, made his visits there few and far between. The Senator counted on his appearance so faithfully, on these occasions, that he might say, as did Julia in the play of "The Hunchback," when alluding to Master Walter's devotion to her, "I have seen the snow on a level with the hedge, and yet there was Master Walter." I desire to say further in regard to his obituary in *The Free Press* of the 25th of January, 1905, that it contains many interesting incidents of his early and late life in this city, aside from what I have related in this article.

Mr. Rodney D. Hill, a son of Warren Hill, was a college graduate, a pronounced book lover, a lawyer and member of the Detroit bar. He died many years ago, leaving a son and daughter in very comfortable circumstances. The son, George B., established the bolt and nut works in Hamtramck, with which all are familiar, and at the time of his death he was the manager and principal stockholder. Before Mr. R. D. Hill's death, he built for himself a fine brick dwelling on Jefferson Avenue, second east of Orleans Street, where his daughter, Miss Sarah Bacon Hill, now resides.

Mr. Bristol Hill, another son of Warren Hill, was a tall, fine looking man, pleasant and agreeable in his manners. I do not know what occupation he followed, if any. My impression always was that he assisted in managing the varied interests of his father, who was quite wealthy. He won for his wife, one of Mr. Lyman Baldwin's handsome daughters. After a brief married life, he passed away. His widow, who inherited all his fortune, which was said to be considerable (large for those days), married the late Wm. B. Wesson, and is still living in the family mansion, on Jefferson Avenue, with her daughter, Mrs. Colonel Seyburn.

Warren Hill built, in 1845, a four-story brick building on Woodward Avenue, west side, between Fort and Congress Streets. Geo. F. Macey, of the then well-known firm of Macey & Driggs, married Miss Tomlinson, a niece of Mr. Warren Hill.

* * *

Dr. Hosea P. Cobb, who built and lived so long in the house, still standing, next this side of the flat on southwest corner of Jefferson Avenue and Riopelle Street, was a well known physician here. He was born in Woodstock, Vt., in 1796, and married in that state a daughter of Warren Hill, and sister of Rodney D. and Bristol Hill. Mrs. Cobb died after a very brief married life, leaving an infant son, Lucretius H. Cobb. Dr. Cobb then removed to Detroit with his father-in-law and Rodney and Bristol and established himself in practice. He was quite successful in his profession, but unsuccessful in a venture in the drug business in connection with Mr. C. W. Wickware. Their store was next below the offices of the Cincinnatti, Hamilton & Dayton railroad, corner of Jefferson and Woodward Avenues. Mr. Wickware was quite a prominent citizen here in the early days. He held many offices of trust, besides the business association with Dr. Cobb. He married the sister of Mr. Townsend, of the firm of Martin & Townsend.

Cobb when he first came to this city had his office in the Connor building on the southwest corner of Jefferson Avenue and Bates Street, and after in the wooden addition to the American Hotel (Biddle House), where he and his son, Lucretius, boarded. They remained here until the great fire of 1848 swept the hotel and its surroundings away. After this disaster the doctor established his office in his new dwelling on Jefferson Avenue, which was luckily completed about that time. The doctor and his son, Lucretius, kept bachelors' hall in the new residence for a brief period, until the advent of the second Mrs. Cobb. The latter was a charming lady, and a great acquisition to the social side of Detroit. Along in 1845, Lucretius, who had studied medicine with his father, attended the Medical College in Cleveland, and after the usual time had elapsed he secured his "sheepskin" and returned home, a full-fledged doctor of medicine. He was successful, had a large practice, but was not in love with his profession to any great extent, and sighed for others paths to fame and fortune. He and Wm. B. Wesson were engaged quite extensively in real estate and building operations and must have made considerable money. After awhile the doctor associated himself with Freeman Norvell, H. N. Walker and others in the Spur Mountain Iron mine, Lake Superior. The venture at the outset was successful, and gave great promise in the near future. I know that at one time Norvell himself and the others could have sold their interests at a large advance on cost. They waited too long, the ore began to give out, disaster overtook them and the mine was abandoned, with what loss to the parties I do not know. Dr. Cobb spent about two years at the mine overseeing it, etc. While in charge there one winter he entertained the Michigan legislature on their Lake Superior trip with lavish hospitality and gave them a good time.

After quitting Lake Superior, returned to Detroit and took charge of the Hargraves Manufacturing Co. Mr. H. having resigned, the affairs of the concern were found to be in a terrible muddle, financially and otherwise. After a brief period, the doctor brought order out of chaos; put the concern on its feet and at the time of his death it was in a flourishing condition. The doctor died May 4, 1879, and on the day of the funeral the entire force of the establishment, a very large number, attended it in a body, besides the fire department and a host of personal friends, making an imposing spectacle. He made a gallant fight for life, as he had not arrived anywhere near the "sere and yellow leaf," but was in the full strength of his intellect and manhood. That "locomotar ataxia," the result of the rupture by accident of a nerve, clung to him with unrelenting tenacity until he was forced to succumb.

Dr. Cobb joined the fire deprtment August 13, 1842, and ran with Engine Co. No. 2. He was one among the younger members of the department who were all full of the fire of youth, daring and courage, as for instance, Eben N. Wilcox, Orlando B. Willcox, Stanley G. Wight, Barney Campau, Wm. B. Wesson, Henry L. Newberry, Kin S. Dygert, Jack Connor, Joseph Cook, Frank M. Farrer, Charles S. Cole, Wm. Duncan, John T. Walker, W. W. Duffield, Wm. P. Doty, David R. Peirce, L. L. Farnsworth, Henry P. Dequindre, David Esdell, John D. Fairbanks, Tom S. Gillett, Anson Burlingame, Henry J. Buckley, Lafayette Knapp, Leon Lafluer, Ike Warren, Clint Whitman, myself and some others of the younger element, whose names have escaped me. These were the members of the department, who talked engine, dreamt engine, haunted the houses containing their idolized "machines," and were always on hand at the first tap of the bell, eager to get as wet as drowned rats, and as eager to go wherever sent, and oft times without being sent. To illustrate the feeling of daring and adventure that pervaded the younger element of the department, the members of No. 4 (The Boys' Company) desired to decorate their meeting or business room with an appropriate motto, to be placed on the wall behind and over the foreman's chair, and this was what was adopted at a meeting one evening:

"When danger calls we're prompt to fly,
And bravely do, or bravely die."

The author of this brave declaration was Eben N. Wilcox, Dr. Cobb was a leading member of the old fire department. He was its president from 1864 to 1866, and chief engineer in 1850 and 1851. He was one of the first commissioners of the paid fire department appointed in 1867, just after its organization, and served in that capacity until his death in 1879. He was also city physician in 1848-1851, and again in 1863-65, county physician in 1865 and school inspector for the old seventh ward in 1858-59.

From his advent here as a youth until his demise he was a conspicuous figure in the social swim. In that gay Fort Street circle of feminity he was most welcome, and with the rest of the younger set of masculines disputed the supremacy of their elders, who sought to push them to one side. He was always in favor with the fair daughters of Detroit and could easily have had his pick from among them, yet he never married. It is useless to conjecture why, yet I am satisfied he passed away heart whole.

In the giddy whirl that dominated society here in the early days, from 1838 to about 1855 (and it seems to me has never been repeated), Dr. Cobb was ever a prominent figure and always on hand, never needing a second call. From almost the day he came here with his father, to make it their home until death, the closest relations existed between the writer and himself, and never a shadow clouded our friendship. He was my family physician always after he entered the profession, until his departure for the Lake Superior iron mines.

Dr. H. P. Cobb, just after he was admitted to practice, and

before his marriage, was invited by an invalid friend to accompany him to Europe in the capacity of companion and medical adviser. They traveled quite extensively in the British dominions and on the continent. They spent much time in Rome and the doctor brought back many souvenirs of that city, particularly engravings of some of its most prominent structures, the Colosseum, Pantheon, Castle of St. Angelo, etc. He would often get quite enthusiastic, dilating on the wonders of the "Ancient City," as well as of the wonders of other places that he had visited and the many interesting incidents connected therewith.

Prof. Williams, of Ann Arbor, at one time president of the University of Michigan, married a sister of Dr. H. P. Cobb. They had two daughters. One married Thos. S. Blackmar, a graduate of the university, and after a member of the Detroit bar and partner in the law firm of Moore & Blackmar (William A. Moore) and later circuit court commissioner for Wayne County. He was found dead in his office one morning, presumably from heart disease. Many will remember genial "Tom" Blackmar with emotions of sincere pleasure and regard, and also deep regret at his early taking off. The writer knew him intimately, and passed many delightful hours with him in his home and at other places, socially, in the society of congenial spirits. "Tom" Blackmar had one son, Paul, who, on the death of his father, engaged in mining in Colorado, which vocation he followed for a short period, returned to Detroit, and entered the service of W. E. Tunis, bookseller, where he continued for a brief period, and then entered the service of the Hon. Thos. W. Palmer, taking charge of the Detroit office, in the Merrill Block. He continued here for two or three years, and then became partner in the extensive lumber firm of McGraft & Montgomery, Muskegon, of which Senator Palmer was then a member. This firm was quite successful, but from some cause it was decided to discontinue the partnership, the affairs of the firm were closed with very gratifying results to all parties concerned. The Senator and Blackmar after this embarked in a lumbering venture in Big Rapids of considerable magnitude. It did not prove a very profitable enterprise, but they met with no losses, and I understand came out something more than even. After this he was appointed receiver of an extensive concern in Minneapolis, whose affairs were apparently hopelessly involved. He succeeded in bringing order out of chaos and confusion, and the result was exceedingly gratifying to all concerned. After this he was appointed to the position of cashier of the Chicago World's Fair. He also filled the same position at the San Francisco Exposition, in both of which he acquitted himself with singular ability. He afterwards became manager of the extensive business enterprises of Mr. F. A. Peck, of Chicago, and when the latter was appointed United States commissioner to the Paris Exposition took young Blackmar with him as assistant commissioner. While acting in this capacity he attracted the attention of the promoters of the extensive bottling works (Bass's ale) of London, England, who engaged his services, to take charge of their business, which he did. He visited this country two or three years ago, and placed on sale in every prominent city in the union, the output of this concern. At a meeting of the stockholders, held in London in 1904, they expressed themselves as being gratified with the year's business, and attributed the happy result, mainly, to the efforts of Mr. Paul Blackmar.

The other daughter of Prof. Williams married Prof. Dubois, of the University of Michigan. She still survives, and is at present living in Lansing.

* * *

When, in 1840, Sidney L. Rood quit the book and stationery business and vacated the store in the Cooper Block on Jefferson Avenue, he was succeeded by the firm of R. S. Babcock & Co. with a stock of dry goods (odds and ends) brought from the east. Mr. Babcock's partner was Silas M. Holmes. They gave it the name of "the Old Manhattan Store."

The firm continued to do business here for a few years and then dissolved, Mr. Babcock going to Kalamazoo and Mr. Holmes, taking in partnership with him his brother Jabez, opened up an extensive dry goods store on Woodward Avenue, opposite the present Merrill Block, under the name of Holmes & Co. They continued here for some years and prospered greatly, when they built and occupied a four-story brown stone front, importing the stone from the east, adjoining the Presbyterian Church on the same avenue. They filled it with an extensive stock of dry goods, carpets, etc.

The late R. E. Roberts, in his sketches of Detroit issued in 1855, says of this establishment:

"With the hope that it will not be considered invidious,

where there are so many extensive and well-managed dry goods, carpet and furnishing houses, the following description of one is ventured:

"The store has a free stone front, is four stories high, occupies a front of fifty feet and exceeding in depth one hundred feet. Comprising ten rooms, each twenty-five feet in width and one hundred feet in depth, giving an area of twenty-five thousand square feet, all of which are filled to their utmost capacity with foreign and domestic dry goods, carpets, cloths, millinery and clothing, in addition to which the firm occupy a storehouse in the rear. The retail rooms are four in number, furnished in the most gorgeous style. About three hundred gas lights are required to light the several apartments.

"From sixty to seventy-five salesmen and from 10 to 150 persons are employed in the several departments, and including those outside, seamsters and seamstresses the firm gives employment to about 600 persons. Their invoices of merchandise, imported during the year 1854, amounted to more than $700,000. This is believed to be the most extensive and best managed dry goods store in the United States, outside of New York."

While Holmes & Co. were occupying the premises on Woodward Avenue, opposite the Merrill Block, they had with them in their employ a number of bright, active young men who contributed much to the success of the concern; indeed, it may truthfully be said that they laid the foundation of the reputation the house gained and so long enjoyed. Their names were Gunn, Locke, Eaton, Irwin and Noble. They followed the firm into their new location, next to the Presbyterian Church. Many readers of these papers will, I am sure, call these young men to mind.

I give this extensive notice of the firm of Holmes & Co. for the purpose of showing the contrast between it and the mammoth establishments that Detroit can boast of at the present day, such as the Newcomb-Endicott Co., Hunter & Hunter, William H. Elliott, Pardridge & Blackwell, Taylor, Woolfenden Co., Goldberg Bros., Sparling, Kerns, Tuomey Bros., L. A. Smith & Co., and many others. I knew the firm of Holmes & Co. well and had many business transactions with them. They did a fine business for years, made much money, and if Silas had kept out of politics, the firm would never have met with disaster. When at the hight of their prosperity he (Silas) was induced to run for state treasurer on the Republican ticket, this about 1854-5. Kingsley S. Bingham was on the same ticket for governor (he was one of the organizers of the Republican party "under the oaks at Jackson"). The Republicans were successful and Holmes became at once "Big Injun" in the party and throughout the state. He became owner of the *Detroit Daily Advertiser* (Republican) and tried to run it for a while. He had already become the owner of the *Democrat* and *Enquirer,* and he merged it into the *Daily Advertiser.* If there is any one thing in this world that is hazardous to run, it is a newspaper or the printing business in any shape, unless you have served an apprenticeship at it from the "printer's devil" up. I know, for I was in the job printing business quite extensively once myself. After a while Holmes came to see what an elephant he had on his hands; he came to me and wanted me to run the paper in connection with my business and made a flattering offer, but having already "bitten off as much as I could chew," conveniently, I declined. After awhile R. F. Johnstone & Co. became the proprietors, on what terms I do not know, but it is safe to say Holmes must have parted with it at a loss of considerable magnitude.

As before remarked, Silas M. Holmes was a dominant spirit in his party. I readily saw that, for during his term of office I was a bidder for the contract to furnish the state with stationery, and could not help observing how all gave in to Mr. Holmes. He was one of the board of state auditors who had the giving out of the contract. There did not seem to be anyone else in evidence; he it was who named the successful bidder or bidders. These were the firm of Kerr, Morley & Co., of Detroit, represented by Colonel Fred Morley, one of the firm. There were at Lansing on business at that time and stopping with Morley and myself, at the old Hudson House, Thomas W. Palmer, then a young man just married, and the veteran editor, Rufus Hosmer, who had considerable fun at Tom's and my expense. Those who knew Rufus Hosmer will call to mind what a good natured joker he was. Morley had to remain at Lansing to get his contract formally accepted and approved, and was not with us on the home trip. He felt so elated at his success that he gave me sufficient cash with which to buy an oyster supper, etc., at Howell on the way home. We reached the latter place about midnight, and you had better believe we had a good old time. The landlord gave us the "best he had in the shop." The ride in the stage from Lansing to Howell was cold and chilly, and one can readily imagine how welcome a "hot Scotch" and a dish of steaming oysters would be under the same conditions. John Blessed, the grocer, I think was the driver of the stage on this occasion.

Well, Holmes & Co. went on from bad to worse, and being unable to stem the tide, went under. Jabez attended more to the purchase and sale of wool, he being the largest buyer of that staple in the state at that time. I saw Jabez in 1881, in Stonington, Conn., where he was living in comfortable retirement with his wife, who, I was told, had inherited money. Silas M. Holmes died in June, 1905, at Corning, Cal., at which place are living at present his married daughters, Mrs. A. Chittenden and Mrs. C. C. Chittenden.

Of the young men who were with Holmes & Co., Gunn and Locke went into the dry goods business on Woodward Avenue, between Congress Street and the Russell House, and were in it for many years. Charles Eaton was for some years, along in the later seventies, with Edward Lyon, Michigan Exchange, as manager. Mr. Irwin died early in life, much regretted. Mr. Noble continued in a subordinate position in the dry goods business until his death. Gunn and Locke and Noble are dead, and I presume Mr. Eaton is also.

* * *

LEWIS FAMILY.

The Lewis family (Villier Dit St. Louis) traces back to Louis Villier, born 1766, son of Jean and Marguerite Gatineau of Toule Loraine, France. This Louis Villier came to Quebec, Canada, and from thence to Detroit about 1745. He was married here April 26, 1746, Marguerite Moran, daughter of Pierre and Josette Drouet. Through her mother Marguerite was related to Drouet Sieur de Richardville, a French officer; to the Creviers and Le Neuf de Herrison, one of the oldest and most remarkable families of Canada. Louis was called St. Louis, on account of his great piety. He died in 1765, leaving the following children:

First. Louis, born 1747, married, 1770, Charlotte Requindeau, dit Joachin. She was related to Gaultier De Varennes, Governor of Three Rivers, Petit Lefebres, and many other prominent families.

Second. Christopher, married 1785, Josette Suzor.
Third. Marie Louise, married 1767, Jos. Thos. Dajot.
Fifth. Jennie, born 1754.

Louis and Charlotte Requindeau had several children. First. Louis Vitus, born 1776, who served in the War of 1812 and was promoted several times for his bravery. He settled at Sandwich, Canada, and died at an advanced age. Second, Josette, married Reaume. Third. Hubert, married Therese Barthe, daughter of Jean Baptiste and Genevieve Culleur de Beaubien. Fourth Francois X.

Jennie St. Louis, married April 3, 1804, Thomas Lewis, son of Thomas Lewis and Josette De Loraine of Three Rivers, Canada, whose children are Joseph, who married Fanny Sterling, two of whose children reside in Boston, Mass., one at Detroit. Sophie, married Narcissus Tourner dit Jeanette. Thomas, called "the good natured Governor of Grosse Ile," a man bubbling over with fun, witty sayings, anecdote and kindly, generous deeds, married Jeanette Francheville de Marentette, widow of William Macomb, whose only daughter married Dallas Norvell, son of Hon. John Norvell. This Macomb was brother of General Alex. Macomb, who was General Scott's immediate predecessor as general of the army. Thos. Lewis, married a second time Mary Brown, by whom he had a large and interesting family. Anne married Richard Godfroy. Charlotte married Dr. Fay, a distinguished physician and partner of Dr. Thos. B. Clark. She married a second time Henry P. Bridge, formerly of Boston, ex-Controller of Detroit, and one of its most prominent and respected citizens. He passed away many years ago. Mrs. Bridge is still alive, the weight of years sitting lightly upon her. She occupies the family home on East Congress Street. Samuel married Jennie Fenton, sister of Governor Fenton, of Michigan, and Colonel Fenton, Eighth Michigan Infantry. He died abroad in 1878. He was a successful business man, a genial companion, and a Christian gentleman beloved by all. Alexander married in 1850, Elizabeth, daughter of Justus Ingersoll and Ann Buckley. He has a large and exceptionally charming family. He has held many offices of public trust, mayor, fire commissioner, etc. He possesses in an eminent degree that courteous manner which was the peculiar inheritance of the French residents. We were boys together here, and through all our lives, have been on intimate terms, and am pleased to know that the ex-mayor is still in the land of the living, enjoying his well-earned wealth, the society of his children, and that his step is as sturdy and his faculties as clear and as bright as they ever were.

Referring to the marriage of Samuel Lewis to Miss Jennie Fenton, calls up the names and personalities of Mr. Jos. Clark and his wife. The latter was the sister of Miss Jennie Fenton, and at the time of the engagement of the latter to Mr. Lewis, they were all guests at the Michigan Exchange. At this particular time a series of weekly subscription parties were given at this house, which drew the elite of Detroit to its parlors. The city was also well stocked with officers of the U. S. A. The field and staff of the Fourth U. S. Infantry, and other officers of the army stationed here on detached duty, and their wives. So that coupled with the men of the city also the maids and matrons, composing the 400, enabled the management to present a delightful entertainment to their patrons. Detroit was cut off from water communication with the outside world, during the close of navigation and with no railroad, its citizens had to depend upon their own resources for amusement, and it is idle to say that we did not have plenty of fun, "fast and furious."

Joseph Clark and his wife were an exceedingly agreeable couple, and contributed much to the pleasure of those making their homes at this hostelry, among whom were Josh Carew, Judge Wagner Wing, Colonel J. B. Grayson, Wm. E. Whilden, Samuel Lewis, Curtis Emerson, even staid Uncle Shubael Conant was often forced to acknowledge their influence. Mrs. Clark died some years ago, leaving a son, who is now on a ranch in California. The widow married Prof. Edwin Sanborn of Dartmouth College, father of Miss Kate Sanborn, the authoress.

(All that relates to the Lewis family before "Governor Thomas Lewis of Grosse Ile," I am indebted to the late Mrs. Hamlin's "Legends of Detroit.")

An interesting article from the pen of Mr. C. M. Burton that appeared in the December (1904) number of *The Gateway*, in regard to the "Early Schools of Detroit," contains a sketch of Father Gabriel Richard, accompanied by a faithful likeness of the good old man. J. O. Lewis, a sketch artist, steel and copper plate engraver and printer, located here in the early days, engraved the plate from which the original of this was printed.

His studio was in a frame building, first floor, on the northwest corner of Griswold Street and the alley, in the rear of the present Michigan Mutual Life Insurance building. My uncle, Thomas Palmer, after the fire of 1830, occupied this first floor (as an office) with Mr. Lewis. I was around there almost daily and was much interested in Mr. Lewis's work, particularly this likeness of Father Richard. The latter I used to see there often clad in his priestly garb. With his straw hat, the broad brim of which was lined on the under side with green silk, to protect his eyes from the sun, carrying in his hand the almost ever present cotton umbrella. Lewis about this time engraved the likeness of Governor Lewis Cass, the same that appears in Mrs. Sheldon's "Early Michigan."

Mr. Lewis was with Governor Cass, Henry H. Schoolcraft and party, who made that canoe voyage to Lake Superior in 1820, to obtain a more correct knowledge of the Indian tribes inhabiting that region, and also to find out more about the presence of copper in the vicinity of the Ontonagon River, and other points, but more particularly did they look after the copper boulder lying in the bed of that river, some distance from its mouth. This copper rock had been known to the Indians and early explorers for a great number of years. By the former it was guarded from outside knowledge with jealous care.

A sketch of this rock as it appeared (at that time) lying on the shore of the Ontonagon River, partly in the water and partly out, is given in Schoolcraft's Journal of the expedition, page 177. I furnished the Sunday *Free Press* with an extended article in regard to this copper rock, which appeared in that paper one or two years ago.

* * *

LEVI B. TAFT.

Levi B. Taft, when he first came here in 1834, clerked in the store of Levi & Olney Cook, who were his uncles. He at the same time finished the study of the law. In 1839 he entered Dartmouth College, graduating in 1843. He returned to Detroit the same year and studied law with Hon. Jacob M. Howard. In 1848 he was admitted to the bar by the state supreme and federal courts. After practicing here awhile he went to Niles, where he was associated with Hon. George H. Jerome and Judge Hiram F. Mather. He afterwards went to Chicago, where he resided sixteen years. He was for twelve years a member of the board of education, and a portion of the time its president. In 1868 he came to Pontiac on account of poor health and bought a farm, where he resided eight years. Later he took up the practice of law in this city, and in 1873 was appointed judge of the sixth judicial circuit. He died at his home in Pontiac April 29, 1895. He was born in Bellingham, Norfolk County, Mass., August 6, 1821.

LEWIS GODDARD.

Referring again to Lewis Goddard, who erected the brick building on the site of the F. & T. Palmer store, on the corner of Jefferson Avenue and Griswold Street. He was quite an energetic man, and progressive, it would seem, as he, in 1831, sent a stock of goods, in charge of a Mr. Sanford Collins, to Toledo, Ohio, that town then quite in obscurity. The goods were placed in an old deserted blockhouse that was built in 1816. It had been so long deserted that it was perfectly surrounded with an undergrowth of timber of considerable size. It was said that this was the first fair sized stock of goods ever brought to Toledo. The present citizens of Toledo ought therefore to honor his memory. Those there at the time did him honor, for it appears that the event was celebrated by a ball given in an old log warehouse, then standing at the mouth of Swan Creek. He established his son, Alonzo (a schoolmate of mine), in the forwarding and commission business there, which he carried on successfully until his death.

A writer in a Detroit paper of January, 1858, relates what a Mr. Haile, of Newark, told him in relation to Toledo. He says: "They took passage on the steamboat Niagara, Captain Stannard, for Toledo. Left Buffalo Creek just before sunset and after steaming all night they found themselves back at Buffalo in the morning. After passing two nights on Lake Erie, the third day they reached Toledo. This was September 1, 1833. The town then consisted of a wharf, a small frame storehouse and two log houses. Mr. Haile was offered four acres on the hill, in what is now the heart of Toledo, for his team. Not considering it an offer worth looking at, he told them that if they would skim the scum from the Maumee River, perhaps he would stay with them."

Levi B. Taft was a member of the Detroit Lyceum and Debating Society, in which society he took an active part. He was its first librarian. He, Anson Burlingame and J. Hyatt Smith were always close friends.

JOHN PATTON.

The late John Patton was one of the best "dialect" readers in Detroit's celebrated amateur group, which included that versatile genius, Johnny Enright, and Frank Morton, and on occasions Peter White, of Marquette. Our friend Jim Scott might be included in this group, but he is more on the order of dialect story telling, in which role he is unapproachable.

On one festive occasion Patton told an Irish story with a delicious brogue that would have delighted all the senses of an evicted peasant of the "old sod," and followed it with a recitation of Burns' "Tam O'Shanter" in unimpeachable Scottish dialect. "Faith," exclaimed an Irish member of the company present, "pwhat is he anyhow? I think he's Irish and thin again I think he's a Scotchman." "He was born in Ireland," was the expianation. "Begorra! I might have knowed it, from the beginning ave his name—Pat!"

A fine sketch of his life that appeared in one of the city papers said, among other things:

"In 1840 he read the Declaration of Independence on the Fourth of July where the Presbyterian Church now stands, on Jefferson Avenue. This was at the time in the woods, and the city had its celebration there in the open."

Well, he did read the Declaration of Independence on the day and at the place mentioned, but the celebration was not in the woods nor in the open, but in an immense tent, and was participated in by the citizens generally, as well as by the Brady Guards and the Williams Light Infantry from Rochester, N. Y., the guests of the Bradys. The two companies went into camp and pitched their tents in close proximity to the big tent. They had a grand banquet in the latter, on the Fourth of July night, and had a good time, of course. I was at the banquet and at the reading of the Declaration of Independence, and can testify to John's masterly delivery of that piece of literature. It challenged the admiration of the large crowd assembled to listen to it, and from that hour Patton became a figure in the public eye.

Any one who heard John recite "Tam O'Shanter" will acknowledge his gifts in that direction.

John was fond of the drama and everything that tended in that direction. At one time when the stage of the Metropolitan Theater, opposite the Biddle House, was idle, he got up an amateur company and produced the play of "Damon and Pythias," John taking the part of Pythias. I do not remember another one of the actors. I knew John so well and was so much interested in seeing him get through his part all right, that I lost sight of the others cast in the play. His reading of the lines was fine throughout, but he lacked the physique that should accompany this part. He did not make much of a figure "mopping the stage" with that chap who slew his horse, or said he did. Forrest with his powerful frame was the man to do that "up to the handle." John next tried "Ion" in the play of that name, written by Thomas Noon Talfourd. He did fairly well, but it is a somber production.

The masterly rendering of the Declaration of Independence, on the occasion named, turned the gaze of the public upon Patton, and he rose step by step from the obscurity of his blacksmith shop to be mayor of the city, which office he held for two terms with honor and dignity. He was an enthusiastic member of the old volunteer fire department, and at one time its chief. For thirty years he carried on the blacksmithing and carriage making business successfully. He held every position in the fire department from "greaser" to chief, the latter from 1852 to 1854. While mayor he started the movement for building the present city hall, introduced the first steam fire engine and secured the first street railway. He was six years county auditor (1864-1869), and then sheriff of Wayne County for two years. He was elected justice of the peace in 1880 and served twelve years. He was appointed United States consul to Amherstburg by President Cleveland in 1893. He served in that capacity to the satisfaction of all, particularly the citizens of Amherstburg, until a change came in the administration and John had to go.

* * *

RESIDENTS OF CAPITOL SQUARE.

Referring again to the residents in the vicinity of the State house, where is now Capitol Square, along in the early thirties, I mention Mons. Girardin, who lived in one of my uncle's houses near Mr. Thomas Rowland. He was a tailor by trade, a native of France, and a professor of its language. He was highly educated and an old school gentleman. When he appeared in public, he was always faultlessly dressed, ruffle shirt, high hat, etc. In addition to his other accomplishments he gave lessons on the violin. He left two sons, bright young men, one of whom was a captain on the police force for some time, and died while such official many years ago. I do not know what pursuit the other followed, but he was quite an authority on "Old Detroit," and articles from his pen on that theme appeared often in the city papers. He also died many years ago.

* * *

Hiram B. Andrews, one time sheriff of Wayne county, was located not very far from the State capitol. He was the proprietor of the Railroad hotel that occupied the present site of the Detroit opera house. The Detroit & Pontiac railroad depot was in the rear of this hotel. Mr. Andrews was largely assisted by his wife, who was an energetic, hustling business woman. He at one time had for a partner Mr. Patrick, under the firm name of Patrick & Andrews. The business was successfully carried on until the death of Mr. Andrews, when the premises made way for the Detroit opera house.

Mrs. Andrews had a pretty daughter by her first husband, Mr. Eddy. She was bright, vivacious and had many admirers. One of them, "Joe" Webb, of the firm of Tinker & Webb, grocers on Woodward Avenue, and nephew of B. L. Wood, forwarding and commission merchants, finally captured her. They were married in St. Paul's Church on Woodward Avenue by Bishop McCoskrey.

* * *

"The Railroad-hotel, as many will remember, was three stories high. The two upper stories had balconies across their entire fronts and commanded fine views of the campus and Woodward Avenue. The former in those days was always crowded with farmers' teams from the surrounding country, far and near, filled with the produce of the season, dressed hogs, etc., all of which contributed to make it an animated scene. Mr. Andrews catered more particularly to the farmer element, as did Perkins, the proprietor of the tavern of that name on Grand River Avenue. I used to be a frequent visitor at Andrews' hotel, as my friend

Judge Caniff, having taken to himself a second wife, in the person of a maiden lady, Miss Roe, a native of New York City, made this house his home, and continued to do so until his wife's death, which occurred after a brief married life. I attended her funeral, and after it was over, the mourners, as well as myself, met in the apartments of the judge to hear the reading of the deceased lady's will. He requested me to read the will. I did so. After a few minor bequests, she left the remainder of her fortune, amounting to a little over $30,000, to her husband, the judge. When I came to the latter paragraph the judge burst into tears, which were quite uncontrollable for a few minutes, so much so that I was unable to proceed. After he had quieted down, I finished the document. This was a wrinkle in the make-up of the judge that I was unprepared for. It appeared that Miss Roe at the time of her marriage to the judge had a fortune of $30,000 in cash. This sum was never touched during her lifetime, but allowed to accumulate, and this was the fortune she willed to the judge, less the few bequests she made as stated.

This hotel was the headquarters at that time for ward caucuses, political meetings, etc., and many a stirring meeting was held in the large room in the rear of the office and bar on the ground floor. I remember one occasion when a laughable incident hapened, though at one time it looked as though it might end in disaster. It was on a summer night and the meeting was assembled at the call of some ward official. The audience was large and most enthusiastic. I happened to be there, but on the outside in the alley, looking in at the open window. At the conclusion of a telling harangue by one of the elect, the audience rose to their feet and cheered and stamped so vigorously that the floor gave way, and the whole "shootin' match" went into the cellar, without any serious damage, however, but much laughter was indulged in when the fright was over.

* * *

REV. J. HYATT SMITH.

The late Rev. J. Hyatt Smith came to Detroit with Webb, Chester & Co., from Albany. He was an odd genius, exceedingly bright and much given to literary pursuits. He was a prominent member of our Literary and Debating Society, a good debater, and, on every question up for discussion, he was assigned and accepted a position, either pro or con. He was also quite stage-struck, fond of the theaters, and was always trying to imitate Forrest and other actors of fame at that time. He was also a member of our Thespian Society, that held forth weekly, during the winter, in the upper part of the University building, where now are Williams, Brooks & Co.

In George Doty's jewelry store, was Seth P. Ranger, a young man, a clerk for Doty, who was also an odd genius at watch repairing, good at argument and debate. He, too, was a member of our Debating society. He and J. Hyatt Smith always took opposite sides, and, one time, during a heated debate, the "Lie" was given and a challenge followed the next day. A meeting was arranged for and the parties met with pistols, in old Fort "Nonsence," an earth fortification that stood on the Sibley farm, a short distance from Woodward Avenue and a little above High Street (which fort had been mentioned before). They exchanged shots, but the result was bloodless as well as harmless. Each one was convinced of the bravery of the other, they shook hands and were friends from thence on.

A young lad, "Jimmie" Jones, a nephew of Enoch Jones, was the only witness to the affair, and he never would tell, whether the balls in the pistols were lead or cork. Most every one believed they were the latter and no doubt they were.

This Seth P. Ranger died a few months later, much lamented by us all. The Literary and Debating society passed appropriate resolutions and appointed a committee composed of William B. Wesson, Anson Burlinghame and Eben N. Wilcox, to procure the means from the members to provide a tombstone to mark his grave. It was done. He was buried in the cemetery on the corner of Gratiot Avenue and Russell Street. His body was subsequently moved to Elmwood cemetery.

Smith and Anson Burlingame were great chums, and, in discussing their futures, they each resolved to go to Congress, and what's more, they did so. Smith went to Albany and got a position in the Albany City bank, studied for the ministry, was ordained and took charge of a Baptist church in Brooklyn and soon became a noted divine; had all Brooklyn at his feet, so to speak.

He made a trip to Europe, Egypt and the Holy Land, and upon his return lectured throughout the country on what he had seen. He gave one lecture here in Detroit at the Whitney opera house, where the new postoffice is now. His lectures were very humorous (after the Mark Twain order) and drew crowded houses. His congregation, with others, sent him to Congress, thus making good his compact with Burlinghame, where he served through one session and declared himself satisfied.

Smith was fond of relating his experience while here in Detroit. Telling of the wild life he had led with the rest of the "boys," always into something he ought not to have been. I happened to be in New York during his ministry in Brooklyn and saw by a morning paper that the various Protestant congregations of Brooklyn would get together in the Brooklyn Tabernacle on a certain evening. It gave the names of the pastors who would address the meeting and among the number I saw the name of Rev. J. Hyatt Smith. I made up my mind to be there too, and I was.

When it came to Smith's turn to speak, he gave a very eloquent and vivid account of his early struggles and the incidents thereto. When he came to relate his experiences while in Detroit, I was much surprised to learn what a bad, bad boy he had been. He pictured himself as having been, to use a slang phrase, "one of the worst bugs on the vine," and so thankful that he had been "plucked like a brand from the burning." Now I was with Smith as often as any one while he lived in Detroit, saw him almost every day and night, and never saw anything very bad in him. It is true, he liked fun and frolic as well as most boys, but we behaved ourselves as well as any community of boys are apt to do. I don't think he would have been so eager to tell the story the way he did if he had known that I was in the audience.

* * *

BUSINESS HOUSES PRIOR TO 1850.

The following persons in business here prior to 1850, I have omitted to metion: John G. Norton, furniture, on Woodward Avenue; S. P. Wilcox & Co., dry goods, on Jefferson Avenue, after this in boots and shoes; Winchell & Co., furniture, on Woodward Avenue; Brady & Trowbridge, grocers, on Jefferson Avenue, between Woodward and Griswold; E. Chope, carriage and wagonmaker, on the northeast corner of Larned and Randolph Streets; George D. Crossman, dry goods, on Jefferson Avenue; Fortier & Berthelet, dry goods, also on Jefferson

Avenue; A. E. Mather, crockery, on Woodward Avenue; George M. Rich, grocer, on the southwest corner of Jefferson Avenue and Randolph Street; William Sowersbey, grocer, on Woodward Avenue; Stevens & Zug, furniture on Jefferson Avenue; Marcus Stevens, afterwards on Campus Martius, near Andrews hotel; Charles W. Penny, clothing, on Jefferson Avenue; N. O. Sargent, boots and shoes, on Jefferson Avenue; John Bigley was with his father in the City Hall market.

Mr. Eardley Ives was a genial English gentleman, an expert bookkeeper, and as such was in constant demand. He was the father of the late Lewis Ives, to my mind the best portrait painter in the United States. His work will, I am sure, bear me witness. His son, Percy Ives, follows closely in the footsteps of his father and bids fair to equal if not eclipse him. Another son, Augustus, is a prominent physician.

William Gilbert, father of the late J. W. Gilbert, roofer, was a brick and stone mason, with his residence on Columbia Street; Daniel F. Webster, son of Daniel Webster, the god-like, practiced law here in 1837.

Dr. Hall was a prominent physician here in 1837; Calvin C. Jackson, private secretary to Governor Stevens T. Mason, afterwards a purser in the United States navy, married a daughter of his. His son, Amos T. Hall, was at one time deputy state treasurer, and afterwards was auditor of the Illinois Central Railroad, Chicago.

Major O'Callahan, in the feed business, had a mill on Atwater Street, about where is now the plant of the public lighting commission. He was a most genial Irish gentleman. The Emmons family were quite prominent here in the early days, and a great many of the present day will remember Jed. P. C. Emmons. Halmer Emmons was for many years a distinguished member of the law firm of VanDyke & Emmons. He later became judge of the United States court and died a few years ago. He was a most exemplary man in many ways and a high-toned gentleman.

Jed Emmons was an exceedingly bright young man, served a brief term with Z. Chandler in the dry goods business and then entered the law. He was one of the founders of the Detroit Lyceum and Debating society, and at the preliminary meetings in Eben N. Wilcox's barn, in the rear of his mother's dwelling on

Jefferson Avenue, his remarkable readiness in debate soon won the admiration of the rest of the boys and he at once became a leader. He was an ever-ready speaker on all occasions and became quite distinguished in his chosen profession. He severed his connection with Detroit on account of his health and emigrated to Florida, where he became attorney-general of the state. Norman Emmons was also a bright and gifted young man; he also served an apprenticeship for a time behind a dry goods counter, then entered the law office of VanDyke & Emmons, was admitted to the bar, and, with John VanDyke, opened a law office in Milwaukee, where, I think, they carried on a very successful business.

It was Mr. Throop's father who, in a letter published in the Geneva, N. Y., *Gazette,* many years ago, accorded to Mr. Elkanah Watson, of Albany, N. Y., the distinguished honor of being the originator of the movement that culminated in the building of the Erie canal.

Lawyer George B. Throop lived, about this time or a little later, in the house next beyond the VanDyke residence on Jefferson Avenue, occupied later on by George Doty. I do not know much about the legal ability of Mr. Throop or otherwise, but I was intimately acquainted with two of his sons. Aeneas and Montgomery. The former was clerk of Wayne county at one time, and afterwards moved to New York and became identified with the lithographic firm of Hatch & Co. The latter was a member of the bar here and afterward removed to New York state. Alex. M. Campau married Eliza, a daughter of Mr. George B. Throop.

Referring again to the Emmons family, I desire to say that Thad P. Sheldon, somewhat prominent in the law and a right good fellow, married Hester, a daughter of Mr. Emmons. They owned and lived in a small cottage on the corner of Adams Avenue and Park Street, where Mr. Linn now lives. I think Major Ford Rogers also married an Emmons.

Mr. James A. VanDyke, the partner of Halmer H. Emmons, was one of the most brilliant lawyers of his time, as all will remember. He was very popular in all walks of life, particularly in the law, and in the old fire department, of which he was the president.

Referring again to the firm of Jas. A. Hicks & Co. John B. Palmer was a member of this concern for some years, and a brother-in-law of Hicks. Many will remember him as a bright, handsome, young man, with a charming personality and one of Detroit's then 400. I fail to remember what became of the firm, but I think it went out of existence upon the death of Mr. Hicks. At any rate, John B. Palmer fell in love with and married a daughter of Major Kirby, paymaster United States army, who was stationed here at the time. Sometime before the outbreak of the civil war the Major was ordered south and with him went Palmer and his wife. After the fall of Fort Sumter, the Major joined the southern confederacy as also did his son-in-law (the wife of the latter being an ardent secessionist). John B. had some command in the C. S. A., but just what it was I fail to remember. At any rate he had charge of the prison for captured northern prisoners at Salisbury, N. C., at about the close of the war. After things got smoothed over a little he came north and visited Detroit, but the reception from his old friends was so cool that he left in disgust, returned to the south and went into business in Columbus, S. C. I met him some time afterwards in New York and he told me he was doing well and prospering.

John and Jerold Gray, brothers of Willie Gray, were somewhat prominent here in the early forties. The former was a lawyer, I think; at any rate he was a most entertaining debater at the Young Men's society. He was commissioned by the regents of the Michigan University to select and purchase the first invoice of books for their library.

Jerold was the broadest kind of an Irishman, genial and witty. He was for awhile a clerk for Hunt & Roby, on the dock, and often for J. Nicholson Elbert. Both John and Jerold returned eventually to Dublin from whence they came. Jerold was of the "Fighting Irish" and although a thoroughly good fellow would sometimes get into little scraps with the boys.

I refer again to the incident when Levi Bishop lost his arm by the premature discharge of a cannon on the Campus Martius. Tom Peck, as he was familiarly called, a boot and shoe dealer in the Republican block (where is now the Edson-Moore Co.'s store), when he heard of the mishap to Bishop, "procured a sledge hammer, went to the Campus Martius, and with it, knocked the cannon off its carriage, spiked it and otherwise unfitted it for anything but the melting pot, saying, as he did so:

"I'll be d—d if that gun will ever hurt anyone again." It had already injured one other person besides Bishop.

JUDGE EMMONS.

A large share of the community wondered why Hal Emmons located down at the Ecorse, and why he spent so much money on that swamp of a place. What a world of evergreens and other fine trees, and flowering shrubs, he planted there. When he was holding court, he was quite a picturesque character, mounted on his horse, with his saddle-bags behind him, going to and from his farm in Ecorse. It reminded one of the itinerant Methodist preacher, who in the earlier days rode his circuit on horseback with his saddle-bags behind him, and also the doctor of those days, visiting his patients by the same means, up and down the river, the River Rouge district. How often have I seen Dr. Hurd starting out on these excursions, rain or shine, and while roughing it on my uncle's farm in St. Clair, in my boyhood days, have I seen that Methodist circuit rider coming up the river road (the road that runs in front of the Oakland) of a Saturday, to fill the pulpit in the St. Clair county court room (no church building of any kind). This before the Rev. O. C. Thompson located himself there as permanent preacher.

"Judge Emmons, though not a professing Christian, was a very exemplary man. His wife was a devout Christian and a sincere believer in God's word. She also believed in the efficacy of family prayer and had family worship every day in her own chamber with her children. She also felt that grace should be said at the table, and that duty seemed to devolve on her. Laying aside her timidity, she determined to ask a blessing herself at each meal and set a time when she would begin. That evening Judge Emmons brought Chief Justice Field and Governor Alpheus Felch, to dinner. Mrs. Emmons, in speaking of the occasion, said: "I felt as if my heart would fly out of my mouth, but I asked the blessing, and I never again felt the least timid. God's grace was all sufficient."

Adonijah Emmons, the father, died in Detroit, April 15, 1843. Harriet L., his wife, died in Detroit January 20, 1874.

Judge McNeil, of Port Huron, married a sister of Judge Emmons. Their son, Hal E. McNeil, saw some service in the civil war. Entered service November 8, 1861, sergeant Company G, Fifteenth infantry, second lieutenant October 13, 1862, first lieutenant January 1, 1863. Resigned September 17, 1864, and honorably discharged. He married a daughter of Wm. Wallace, of this city.

PROFESSOR ASA GRAY.

Professor Asa Gray came to the state in 1838, to take the chair of natural history in the then new University of Michigan. The university had no building at that time erected at Ann Arbor, so Prof. Gray asked for a year abroad before taking up his work here. This was readily granted him by the regents, and they put $5,000 into his hands with which to lay the foundations of the university general library. Geo. P. Putnam, of the firm of Wiley & Putnam, booksellers, New York, was then resident in London, and through him the professor managed the expenditure of the money in a manner that proved satisfactory. On his return from Europe the university was still not ready for him and he was given another year's vacation. Finally it ended by his resigning and taking the Fisher Professorship of Natural History at Harvard, under President Quincy.

Houghton, Mifflin & Co., Boston, issued in 1894, two volumes, Letters of Asa Gray, edited by Jane Loring Gray.

LEVI BISHOP.

I have something further to say about the accident that happened to Levi Bishop. It is furnished by my friend, Richard R. Elliott, Esq., histographer of Detroit. He says: "It was not Dr. Hurd who amputated Levi Bishop's arm, but Dr. Zina Pitcher.

"The policing of Camp Payne, on the Cass farm, July 3-7, 1839, was placed in charge of the Washington Lancers, under command of Captain Henry B. Clitz. They were all young men, and I was a non-commissioned officer. The National Guard had a brass cannon of antiquated shape, which was being fired in rapid succession at the noonday salute, sixteen times in seventeen minutes; the piece became quite warm. It was primed from the vent, in charge of Sergeant Abraham McHose; Bishop and a swabber had charge of loading the gun. After it had been swabbed, Bishop inserted the charge, which was in a flannel bag, rammed it home once and while ramming the second time the premature discharge occurred, blowing out the ramrod, which fractured Bishop's hand and wrist and prostrated him. Captain Clitz ordered me to procure a cot, on which was placed the wounded man, and he was carried by his comrades to the house of Eralsey Ferguson, northeast corner of State and Griswold Streets, where he boarded. In the meantime Lieutenant H. A. Schoolcraft, of the Lancers, had been sent to Dr. Pitcher's residence, where he was .fortunately found. Captain Clitz ordered me to detail a guard of six men to escort the wounded man to his residence and to keep the near vicinity of the house clear during the operation; this I did. Chloroform was not in use at that time, and Bishop's screams were frightful.

"McHose stated that the piece had become quite hot at the vent, so much so that his thumb became blistered; while Bishop was ramming the charge McHose raised his thumb an instant, the air entered the vent, the swabbing not having been thorough; a spark had been left, which ignited the powder and the explosion followed."

This account of the affair differs a little in some particulars from the one I gave in an article published some months ago.

Mr. Francis Raymond, I am plesaed to know, is with us yet. As all know, he was one of the firm of Hallock & Raymond, in the clothing business, in the early days, and later on was of the firm of F. Raymond & Co., booksellers and stationers. He bears his eighty odd years exceedingly well, and is almost as able to put in as good a day's work at the desk as he did for so many years in the office of receiver of taxes.

WILLIAM HALL.

William Hall, another old-timer, is also with us (in 1901, when this was penned) yet, although well along in the eighties. As most know he carried on the watch and jewelry business for many years, in the forties and early fifties, where is now the old Masonic hall building, on Jefferson Avenue; later on he was for many years with the firm of M. S. Smith & Co. A peculiarity of Hall's was his rapid gait in the street when going to and from his place of business, not unlike John Owen, Theodore Hinchman and his brother, Lewis Hall. The boys all used to say that the four always went as if they had been sent for.

LEWIS HALL.

Lewis Hall had his jewelry store and watch making establishment on the south side of Jefferson Avenue, adjoining the Bank of Michigan (now Michigan Mutual Insurance Co.) In the rear, on the alley, lived John Hawley, saddler and harness maker, whose store was on the north side of Jefferson Avenue, between Woodward Avenue and Griswold Street. Mrs. Hawley was a sister of Uncle Shubael Conant. Between the Hawleys and Halls and the stores of William Wells and Mason Palmer, adjoining, was quite an area, a "patio," as it were, filled with trees and flowering shrubs, but no fountain; the latter could not be a possibility in those days. The front of the Hawley dwelling was really facing this area, a charming retreat in which to pass a summer afternoon. The occupants of the Jefferson Avenue front enjoyed it immensely. I passed many a pleasant hour there. Lewis Hall was an expert at chess and passionately fond of the game. And here, in the rear of his store, looking out into this garden (as it were), William Hammond, the Irish gentleman of leisure, whom I have before mentioned, and he would play by the hour at this fascinating game, with nothing to disturb them but the twitter of the birds and the humming of the bees. It is difficult to imagine that such a charming spot ever existed in that locality, an "oasis in the desert," so to speak.

Mr. Hammond, an enigma to Detroit society, passed his days here, his declining years smoothed and solaced by many kind friends, chief among whom were Judge B. F. H. Witherell and Lawyer "Billy" Gray. Mr. Hammond, when the "sere and yellow leaf" came upon him, and his step had lost the firmness of earlier days, could be seen nightly at Tom Gallagher's in the Fireman's hall building (now the water offices) enjoying his glass of steaming brandy toddy, one and only one, quitting the place at 9 o'clock, invariably, for his quarters nearby. He was somewhat addicted to snuff in his later years, which he took with the grace of a Chesterfield or a Talleyrand.

Quite a prominent citizen that I have omitted to mention heretofore was "Pat" McGinnis, and nearly all of the present day will, no doubt, recall him to mind. I first knew him about 1840, as a member of the Engine Company No. 4. After many struggles, incident to the life of a poor boy, he became an autioneer, also kept for years a small store on Bates street, in the rear of the Normandie hotel, filled with odds and ends, particularly remnants of dry goods, bargains in laces, ribbons, etc., which drew to his place of business the first ladies in the city. •His custom was large. He branched out as he prospered, bought real estate, notably McGinnisville at the Woodward

Avenue railroad crossing, became alderman of his ward and went to the legislature. He died in a fine residence of his own on Cass Avenue, a few years since.

Does anyone, I wonder, call to mind Pat's father? I remember him well. When I was clerk in Rood's book store he used to haunt Jefferson Avenue places of business, in the person of an itinerant peddler, who always had about him a ring or other piece of jewelry, sometimes rare and antique, rare coins and other articles of like character, which he would exhibit for inspection and, perhaps, purchase. Always quiet, gentlemanly, unobtrusive and invariably humming a tune. I presume his two boys, Peter and Pat, looked after his declining years, as they were fairly well to do at that time.

MATHEW GOODING.

Another prominent fireman and somewhat noted citizen in the forties, that has until now escaped my notice, was Matthew Gooding, ship carpenter and boat builder, on upper Atwater Street. He was a member of Engine Company No. 3. What particularly attracted attention to him was his magnificent physique, long flowing hair and beard, black as the raven's wing. In the Harrison campaign he went with the Detroit delegation of "Hard Cider Boys" to a celebration at Fort Meigs, Ohio, June 13th, 1840, garbed as a typical woodsman. In the capote of his hunting shirt Gooding carried a live raccoon securely fastened to his coat collar with a light metal chain. He marched some distance in advance of the delegation, and the oddness of his attire, coupled with the stalwart appearance of the man and the presence of the live "coon," attracted universal attention, and he was the observed of all observers at Fort Meigs, which was the most imposing and popular demonstration that at that time had occurred in the United States. The fort and grounds and the presence of some of the most distinguished actors who were associated with one of the most interesting events recorded in American history. General Harrison himself was present, as from this city, Governor Woodbridge, George C. Bates, George Dawson, Colonel Edward Brooks and many other citizens of note. Nine or ten military companies from adjoining states were also present. It was said at the time that the entire number of people present was something near forty thousand. Our friend Gooding died of cholera in 1854.

Leete & Ray, furniture dealers, were in business on Woodward Avenue; Peter Lee, baker, on the corner of Atwater and Brush Streets (foreman of Engine Co. No. 3); William Clay, hairdresser and perfumer, in the National Hotel building in 1845 (he was styled the "learned barber"); Hiram Joy and George Robb were ice dealers in 1845 and previous, and were pioneers in the business. Mr. Leete, of Leete & Ray, was the father of Attorney Leete of the Detroit bar.

* * *

William Clay was born in Bath, England, and first took up the vocation of a barber in Canandaigua, N. Y. He at one time used to shave Wm. H. Seward, legal agent at the time, of the Great Holland Land Company. He came to Detroit in 1833, and opened a shop in Ben Woodworth's hotel, where I first used to see him. He had the finest and best appointed barber shop in the city at that time. When Mr. Seward visited Detroit, he always inquired the whereabouts of his old friend, and when Jacob M. Howard, who always patronized Clay, and he came together in the little shop, then would come up problems in metaphysics, abstruse topics, and historical and political matters, that would be discussed at length. Clay was altogether a remarkable man. Geo. C. Bates, in his interesting "By-Gones of Detroit," published in *The Free Press* some years ago, gave an admirable pen picture of our learned and worthy friend. In 1852, the Northwestern University, at Chicago, bestowed on him the title of master of arts. Clay, in many respects, resembled Elihu Burritt, the "Learned Blacksmith."

* * *

"BIJAH" JOY.

Abijah Joy ("Bijah") assisted his brother Hiram, above metioned, in the ice business. He later drifted into the police force and was assigned to the central station, and to the call of "Hiz-oner," the police justice, where he remained many years, until his transfer to other stations.

Abijah was a faithful officer, of undoubted integrity, pluck and courage; besides he had been an old fireman, a member of hand engine No. 4. "M. Quad" (Mr. Lewis of *The Detroit Free Press* staff), through his admirable sketches of the proceedings of the police court, at that time, made Abijah's name a household word throughout the land.

Bijah was passionately fond of children, and many a little

truant waif was restored to its anxious parents, its little heart gladdened and its tears dried, through his fatherly ministrations. He was always provided with an ample supply of candy for the little ones.

Joy was appointed doorman at the central police station September 21, 1867. When the Trumbull Avenue station was built he was transferred to it in the same capacity, and with the opening of the Twentieth Street station, the scene of his services was again moved westward. He continued to act as doorkeeper at the last named station until he was retired by the commissioners in consideration of his long and faithful services. He died in 1885. I knew him well, always. Geo. P. Goodale has paid a fine tribute to "Bijah," which appeared in the Sunday *Free Press* some time last May.

* * *

E. B. and Dan Whipple succeeded Hiram Joy in the ice business; Abbott & Beecher had dry goods, corner of Jefferson Avenue and Bates Street; Toles & Allen were painters and paper hangers, on Woodward Avenue; D. W. Fiske (grandfather of Edward Locke), hardware on Woodward Avenue.

Doctor Lemcke (Dr. Klein married his widow), was practicing here in 1845. He became assistant surgeon of the First regiment of Michigan Infantry, that went to Mexico, under Colonel Stockton. Mrs. Klein is still living, her pretty daughter by Dr. Lemcke, married Mr. Dan Loring, an extensive dealer in boots and shoes here for many years. Both are dead.

* * *

JOHN HULL.

John Hull, that sturdy butcher, had a stall in the City Market. John lived on Washington Avenue, west side, near the corner of Grand River, in an unpretentious house. I think he died there. I knew him when he first became prominent in his trade. At that time (1848-9), I was in the employ of the United States Military Department here, and John used to supply it with cattle on the hoof, which of course led me into close contact with him. He was always honest and upright in his dealings with the government. He was an uncompromising Democrat. He left four sturdy boys and quite a large estate. The boys embarked in the grocery business, extensively; the largest retail grocery store in the state, which they managed successfully for some years. Disaster finally overtook them, and after a brief struggle they had to succumb. One of the brothers, Robert, is at present in the meat business in this city.

* * *

THE "SHADES."

In 1845, and later, Alfred Kennedy kept the "Shades," corner of Shelby and Larned. Afterwards he moved nearer to Jefferson Avenue, on the corner of the alley, opposite the building formerly occupied by the Calvert Lithographing Co. in the Evers homestead. Kennedy was celebrated for his fine wines, liquors, ales and cigars. He was also first to introduce here that appetizing morsel, the Welsh rarebit. I appeal to anyone living who ever partook of that delicacy at his establishment, if the memory of it does not linger with them yet. Here, at this place, used to meet nightly to enjoy the games of dominoes and "Rounce," Henry J. Buckley, Armory A. Rice, Uncle Oliver Newberry and many others. Mr. Newberry was very fond of the game of "Rounce" and enjoyed it hugely.

* * *

Ed. Franks had a small furniture store on Jefferson Avenue. He afterwards removed to Mackinac, and kept the Mission House there for many years. He married a daughter of Abraham Smolk. The latter had the contract for filling in and docking out the front of the Cass farm, and after its completion removed to Mackinac, and died there. One of Ed. Franks' daughters married Mr. Ed. E. Kane, of this city. Mr. Franks was a very genial, companionable man and a good citizen. The filling in and docking out the Cass farm front, was an enormous undertaking, as any engineer will see, on looking over the premises.

* * *

John W. Strong, Jr., grocer at about 99 Jefferson Avenue; A. & T. McFarlane, merchant tailors, on Jefferson Avenue; also T. & J. McGrath and P. McTerney; J. Wilkie Moore, had a fancy goods store on Jefferson Avenue, near Randolph Street; P. & W. Fischer dealt in watches, clocks and jewelry at the same place that they occupied until 1903; George W. Tucker (colored, as before mentioned) kept the swellest barber shop in the city on the north side of Jefferson Avenue, between Shelby and Griswold Streets. He also kept a fine stock of hair goods, perfumery, toilet articles, etc. W. K. Coyl, in 1837, had a grocery store on Woodbridge Street opposite the Eagle Tavern; he afterwards moved to the corner of the Campus Martius, on Woodward

Avennue, where are now Wright, Kay & Co., jewelers. Nathaniel Prouty had a grocery store on Woodbridge Street on the same side as Coyl's, but further down (before mentioned). William Phelps, late of the firm of Phelps & Brace, once taught school over Prouty's store. Mayor Patton had a blacksmith shop and carriage factory on Brush Street near Woodbridge Street; John Hanna had a tobacco factory at the foot of Bates Street; John was once warehouseman with J. L. Whiting, and after was on Woodward Avenue, between Congress Street and the Russell House, same side.

Morris M. Williams, who was once a member of the firm of Sidney L. Rood & Co., was for many years a distributing clerk in the Detroit postoffice. He had become so expert at it that people wondered who could be found to fill his place if he should die, and in harness, and strange to record, his successor was speedily found. Morris was a genial gentleman, also an old Brady Guard, and his death was generally regretted.

The old bank of Michigan had a number of bright employes. Besides E. P. Hastings, president, and C. C. Trowbridge, cashier, they were Norman Rawson and James A. Armstrong, bookkeepers; Alex H. Sibley and E. Steele, tellers; and W. W. Dean, discount clerk, and Mr. Sill. Sill was employed in the bank in some capacity; think he was appointed cashier. He was sent on by the Dwights, of Geneva, who subsequently wrecked the institution.

Major Robert A. Forsyth, formerly a paymaster in the U. S. army, after First Street was opened through the Cass farm, built and occupied a small cottage house, midway between Fort and Congress Streets, where the Union depot is now. The major was widely known here in his day and was universally popular. He and his family were intimately connected with the Cass, Kercheval, Jones and Mason families, and indeed all that went to make up the social side of Detroit. He was very fond of horses and with his fast nag Spider, was usually the first one out when the snow began to fly or when the ice on the Detroit and Rouge rivers was in any sort of bearable condition. I have seen him venture on the river in front of the DeGarmo Jones residence when the ice was so thin that it would rise and fall beneath the runners of his sleigh and the hoofs of his horse, but Spider, goaded on by the fierce yells of his driver, would always come out all right. He never used a whip. The Major and Lieutenant Grant were often pitted against each other when the ice and snow were in good condition. In the summer time Detroit could not boast of any good place to speed horses, but in the winter the Detroit and Rouge rivers and Jefferson Avenue gave the owners of fast nags ample opportunity to do so.

The Major passed away at the early age of 51 years. At the time of his death we youngsters used to look upon him as an old man, and he had somewhat that appearance, with his iron-gray hair and whiskers, a grizzled old veteran, as it were. Many years after his death Dr. Lucretius H. Cobb, Henry A. Wight and myself were one day in the cemetery on the corner of Gratiot Avenue and Russell Street and came across the Major's grave. On the tombstone above it we found, to our surprise, that he had died at the early age I have mentioned and we had always thought him an old, old man. A son of his, Lewis C. Forsyth, a retired colonel U. S. A., lately died at a summer resort near Washington, D. C. * * *

STATE CAPITOL AND SUPREME COURT.

Referring once more to the state capitol, the building possessed the full-length portraits of Washington, Lafayette, Governors Cass and Mason. I think the same are in the state building at Lansing at the present day.

The Supreme Court held its sessions here. I do not remember much about the personnel of the judges, but I do of "Day," the crier.

The former was an eccentric individual, tall and thin, and an old-timer, inasmuch as he clung to knee breeches, ample coat skirts and waistcoat. He wore his hair long, brushed straight back from his head and tied in a queue. He died in harness and was succeeded by John Gibson, quite Day's opposite. Gibson was "large and stout," had a stentorian voice, and at the least noise or disturbance in court he would shout "Silence in the court!" in a voice loud enough to paralyze a person. It was said of him that one day while dozing at his post there came up a thunder storm; a loud clap of thunder brought him to his feet with "Silence in the court!" shouted at the top of his voice, which much amused the judges, lawyers and spectators. On the occasion of Day's demise, two or three of the lawyers practicing before that court delivered themselves of poetic effusions to his memory, and I give them here. They appeared in public print (many years ago), but they are so witty and humorous, and as I know all the parties, I think they will bear repeating, since they will be new to many, as also the short notice of "Day" preceding them:

"For a number of years up to 1835 there flourished here a character whom many of the old residents will remember. His name was Isaac Day and his calling was that of "Crier of the Court" for the County of Wayne, Territory of Michigan. Among the well known members of the bar were Charles Cleland, John L. Talbot and Jacob M. Howard, neither of whom had then attained to such dignity of years as to despise a joke, even if it had a touch of ghastliness in it. One sad day the crier, Isaac Day, died, and Cleland, Howard and Talbot each contributed an obituary in verse. Those effusions are given here.

The record of Day's death is in the following form:

Territory of Michigan,   Circuit Court,
    County of Wayne.   May Term,
                                                                         1835.

"And now John Gibson, the present crier of the court, comes and presents the following Epitaph on his renowned and illustrious predecessor and prays the court that the same may be entered of record.

       First Contribution—Cleland.

           "Step light! The light of Day's expired.
           Silent is he who silence oft required.
           That stentor's voice and that majestic staff
           That raised the bearer and suppressed the laugh
           Are heard by Day no more—nor yet by night;
           ·Yet when the evening came, Day still was bright.
           But Day today no more shall utter speech,
           Since Day's in darkness far beyond our reach.
           Alas! our Day has gone! No ray of light
           Bespeak the Day—no morning radiance bright
           Shall ever restore to this dark court, its Day.
           Darkly they are left to feel this crooked way
           Since, as we are told, in Day's report,
           Day hath no more Day in court.
           None cry for Day, who oft have cried
           To please the court, when men were tried,
           Yet now that Day's eclipsed, we say,
           Peace to his manes! Poor Isaac Day."

Second Contribution by next mourner—Howard.

"His soul is fled from this, his daily scene
Downward, to search the gloomy caves of spleen.
He left few children in the legal way,
With mighty wail, to mourn the loss of Day;
He left no friend, no picture and no foes,
No face of bronze and no carbuncle nose,
Nor tooth, nor jaw, nor tongue, left he behind,
For heirs to quarrel for and none to find.
Yes, he's defunct, and no more the morning ray
Shall glad the rubicund nose of rising Day.
No more from whisky, ashes, rugs and straw,
Shall rising Day salute the halls of Law;
No more with silver-headed cane shall tread,
Proud as Apollo, from his orient bed,
The cost compelling hours of ten to two,
Big with defaults against the hapless few,
Whose dinner-loving souls and beefward views
Divert from law, the juries and the stews."

Third Contribution by next mourner—Talbot.

" 'Tis true the light of Day has fled
And night and silence reign, for Day is dead.
No more he cries but has the task assigned
To the sad spouse on earth now left behind.
But Day will dawn again in the courts much higher,
And take his place in them once more as Crier.
No need there'll be amid that glorious band
Of his once harsh reproof, or noise repressing wand.
Nor will there be as of that Court, the crier
To break his old back in making up the fire.
Nor growl on Sundays, as he casts his looks
In charge of records, papers, lamps and books.
In that abode his tasks will be far fewer,
Indeed his station there's a sinecure.
Instead of Whisky, nectar there will flow,
Instead of ashes, sausages will grow,
And ragged rugs exchanged for robes of Snow,
And brilliant stars and gaudy clouds will be
His daily couch and slumbering canopy.
From thence he'll rise and to the angels open
Heaven's Court whenever Day shines forth as broken.
Here from his wife, from culprits, lawyer's free
He'll eat and drink to all eternity."

THE LAST EXECUTION.

Referring again to the hanging of Simmons, I came across an article in an old newspaper, some time ago, that said:

"One Watson was a fifer and presented a claim to the Michigan Legislature at Lansing many years ago. It was for three days' service as fifer and playing the dead march for S. G. Simmons, from October 17 to 20, 1830, from the jail to the scaffold."

Also another newspaper article I came across regarding the same:

"An English gentleman who made a tour of the American lakes in 1830 and published a book of his travels, printed in London in 1833, was in Detroit at the time of the trial of Simmons, and on the 26th day of July, 1833, he was present in the courtroom when sentence of death was pronounced. Among other things, he says: 'As the murderer was conducted to the bar to receive the sentence of the law, I observed in him a noble human form, erect, manly and dignified; of large, but well-proportioned stature, bearing a face and head not less expressive than the beau ideal of the Romans, etc.'"

The judges who occupied the bench at the trial were Sol. Sibley, Henry Chipman and William Woodbridge. B. F. H. Witherell was the prosecuting attorney. Simmons was defended by Lawyers George A. O'Keefe and Cole and Porter. Simmons, on the scaffold, joined in the hymn sung on the occasion:

"Show pity, Lord; O, Lord, forgive,
Let a repenting sinner live—"

in a loud voice that I could distinctly hear from where I was on the roof of Lawyer Witherell's woodshed.

* * *

DETROIT BOAT CLUB.

Boat clubs flourished here sixty years ago, but of course not as much as now. The Detroit Boat Club was organized sixty years ago, February 18, 1839, by Edmund A. Brush and others.

I knew all the members of the Detroit Boat Club, not intimately, of course, but by sight, as at that time I was only a slip of a lad and trained with the younger set. Their boat house was located in a slip on the river front, between the large yellow warehouse of John Chester & Co. on the west, and the Campau warehouse at the foot of Randolph Street on the east. It was the pride of the city at that day, and all its members were quite enthusiastic. It was indeed a noticeable feature in the social life of the city.

In the great fire of 1848 the boat house was destroyed and the contents with it, except the boat called the Wolverine. The club was reorganized in 1856 and the old members were placed on the honorary roll. The club is booming at this day and is in splendid condition financially and otherwise. For further and fuller details of the club's doings, etc., I quote from the Detroit *Free Press* of February 19, 1899:

"First among the attractions of the City of the Straits is its unrivaled situation on the most beautiful river that flows. Nowhere else in the world can there be found so broad an expanse of flowing water with the same advantages of boating as are presented by the Detroit, and that this fact was appreciated by the earlier residents of the city is attested by the existence here of the oldest boat club in America.

The Detroit Boat Club had always included in its membership many of the foremost and most representative men of the city, and no other organization in the state has held the enthusiasm and spirit of the older participants in its benefits so well as has this one. They are interested today, although the gray may have crept into their hairs, in hearing of and assisting the welfare of the club. Their muscles twitch and the fire comes into their eyes as they talk of the good old days, when they were in their prime with the other 'boys.'

"It was just sixty years ago, on the evening of February 18, 1839, that a little company of gentlemen met in the office of Mr. E. A. Brush for the purpose of organizing a boat club. There were present James A. Armstrong, John Chester, J. H. Farnsworth, A. T. McReynolds, Alfred Brush, Alpheus S. Williams, A. H. Sibley and E. A. Brush. A constitution was drawn up and adopted and the list of members was filled out by adding the names of A. S. Kellogg, John Winder, J. S. Rowland, D. C. Holbrook, A. Ten Eyck, George C. Bates, Rufus Brown, John McReynolds, J. Nicolson Elbert, Samuel Lewis, William T. Pease, A. M. Campau and Wesley Truesdail. E. A. Brush was chosen president and James A. Armstrong was made the first secretary. For the sum of $225 a barge, thirty-eight feet long, was bought in New York. It was a six-oared Crolius racing barge. Previously a four-oared clinker boat, named the Georgiana, was bought and was manned by James A. Armstrong, E. A. Brush, James H. Farnsworth and Alpheus S. Williams. The larger of the two boats, which was successively called the 'E. A. Brush,' 'Frolic,' and 'Edmund,' was brought to this far western country through the Welland canal. It did service until 1877."

In those early days the club was largely a social organization and barge parties on the river were extremely popular. One of the features at this time was a stunning uniform adopted by the members. It consisted of a chip sailor hat covered with white linen and broad black band; sailor pantaloons of white duck with black belts around the waist; shoes with low sewed heels, and white socks; black silk handkerchief knot; blue shirts with white figure and broad square collar; coat of Kentucky jean. Garbed in this natty uniform the young sailors were wont to take the barges up the river on balmy, moonlight nights, the foremost young ladies of Detroit's society by their sides, sending the little craft steadily and swiftly along under the impulse of their strong, regular stroke. May 24, 1842, the first club contest took place, with the competing crews as follows:

"Race boat—Alfred Brush, stroke; E. A. Brush, No. 2; J. H. Farnsworth, No. 3; Lieutenant Brooks, No. 4; A. Ten Eyck, coxswain.

"Club boat—George Deas, stroke; J. N. Elbert, No. 2; A. S. Williams, then representative in Congress, No. 3; W. Truesdail, No. 4; Ed Brooks, coxswain.

"The race-boat crew won the event handsomely. The contest aroused considerable interest, as it was the first aquatic event of the kind anywhere in the western waters. The course was two miles straight away from the club house, a plain structure on the site of the present Detroit, Grand Haven & Milwaukee depot, to 'Hog' Island, the euphonius title in those days of our beautiful Belle Isle.

"It was the custom of the club members to spend every Fourth of July on the island, which then knew nothing of its present improved loveliness, but it was unexcelled in its wild and tangled beauty. Writing in the *Free Press*, December 2, 1877, George C. Bates described one of these holiday excursions:

"'On the third a detachment was sent to clear away the grounds, pitch marquees and tents borrowed from the army, and there they entertained among their guests Misses Isabella Cass,

Emma Schwarz, the Misses Griswold, sisters of Purser George R. Griswold, of the navy, and all the elite of Detroit society; Major Robert A. Forsyth and Henry Ledyard were always assigned to the duty of brewing a big bowl of sailor punch, half and half, a duty that was performed to the satisfaction of everybody; and toasts were drunk to the memory of George Washington, John Adams, Thomas Jefferson, and so on down to General Harrison in successive goblets filled to the very brim, and just tipped and touched on the edge with pineapple rum and arrack.

"'There, on the Fourth of July, 1841, the guests of the day were General George M. Brooke and his handsome adjutant, George Deas, who married Miss Garland; subsequently went with his brother-in-law, General Longstreet, into the confederate army and, after the rebellion, broke down and died of a broken heart. General Brooke, colonel of the Fourth Infantry, U. S. A., was the gallant old Virginia hero who, in 1813, at the sortie of Fort Erie, opposite Buffalo, when the American batteries were shooting wild because they could not find the British troops, volunteered and took a large glass lantern under his military cloak, crept inside the British lines, quietly clambered up a tree, tied the lantern to a limb and instantly dropped to the ground and ran, while a hundred cannon blazed away at him ineffectually, and he came back safe to camp. He was as brave as Ney, as gallant as Murat, and most elegant old Virginia gentleman.

"'Today,' continues the writer, 'Belle Isle is the abode where in summer the young men of society congregate, where good dinner, music and dancing, flirting and picnicking and sporting, all the elegancies of fashion, all the enjoyments of cultured life may be found; but of these club men only here and there remains an antiquated specimen. Its president and elegant secretary, the coxswain and bow-oarsman, and all the Philadelphia attaches have long since mingled with their mother earth.'"

* * *

Of all the persons mentioned above as members, only one is alive at this date, Alex. M. Campau.

Another boat club was organized about 1845, by the younger set of the young men of the city. It was not so pretentious as the older club, having but one boat, a twelve-oared barge called the Eliza, after Captain Inman's youngest daughter. Captain Inman was in command of the U. S. S. Michigan at that time.

Among the members present were Edward M. Pitcher, Lucretius H. Cobb, George Shepard, Leonard Watkins, George A. Cooper, Albion Turner, L. W. Tinker, William P. Doty, Charles L. Dibble, L. F. Knapp, H. A. Schoolcraft, J. C. D. Williams, Friend Palmer, and some others whose names I do not recall. We used to have a heap of fun, rowing on the river and at picnics at Belle Isle, then Hog Island. We often had dancing parties on the island in the old brick boat house that stood at the foot of it. Our boat would accommodate twenty-four people, all told, quite comfortably. The music and refreshments went up on another boat, of course. So it can be seen that we could always get up a dance during the summer because we had the facilities and the girls were always willing. We had many friends across the river, living at Windsor and along the shore to Sandwich, and also at the latter place. So we used to take them in, of course.

I don't think the older club had as enjoyable a time as we. True, they had the society of Miss Cass, Miss Schwarz, the Misses Griswold and others, but we had the society of the younger portion of Detroit's feminine contingent, and with the latter, the former were not "in it," so to speak. The club broke up after a few years from natural causes, and I do not remember what fate befell the dear old "Eliza." But the memory of these delightful excursions to Hog Island will remain with me always.

None of the "boys" mentioned above is at the present time living except myself.

OLD RESIDENCES.

When I came to Detroit in 1827, and until about 1840, business was transacted almost exclusively on Jefferson Avenue, and between the latter and the river (Woodbridge and Atwater Streets).

There was no places of business of any description on any of the streets north of Jefferson Avenue. Woodward Avenue could not boast of a single place of business. The nearest approach to such a thing was General Charles Larned's law office opposite the Merrill Block and adjoining his residence on the corner of Larned Street, and Dr. Hurd's office and residence on the corner of Congress Street. Larned, Congress, Fort, Wayne, Shelby, Griswold, Bates, Randolph and Brush Streets were all sparsely occupied by private residences.

Woodward Avenue was occupied by private residences, and as far as the Grand Circus only. The residences were not pretentions in any sense and were far behind buildings of like character at the present day.

The first residence building in the city to attract attention, was one erected by John A. Welles, cashier of the Farmers' and Merchants' Bank, on the northwest corner of Fort and Wayne Streets. It is still standing. At the time it was built it was considered a wonder and a show.

Soon, however, the example set by Mr. Welles in building was followed by others and residences of a better character than formerly began to prevail.

Business did not invade Woodward Avenue until about 1843, and then to a small extent, and only between Jefferson Avenue and Larned Street. Jefferson Avenue from the Cass farm line, and the streets between it and the river were quite busy streets, as far up and including Beaubien Street. Woodbridge Street, as now, was a busy street, but only up to Bates Street, beyond which point it was devoted to private residences. Atwater Street, from Woodward Avenue to Beaubien Street, was a business street solely. Randolph Street was the center of the grocery and provision trade, and indeed, from Jefferson Avenue to the river, was the busiest part of the city, as on this street were Woodworth's Hotel and the Berthelet market. Nearby were Eldred's store, tannery and ox mill; the Farrand & Davis pumping works, Harvey Williams's large blacksmith shop and the Detroit & Black River Lumber Co.'s steam sawmill.

Stead Brothers kept a large grocery and provision store on the southwest corner of Woodbridge and Randolph Streets, in the Berthelet Row, so-called. One of the brothers died many years ago, the other in January, 1903.

* * *

STAGE COACHES.

Ben Woodworth's Hôtel was the headquarters of all the stage lines running out of Detroit, which added much to the busy character of this locality, particularly in the winter. The stage drivers of those early days used to take great pride in their turnouts, coming into the city and going out with a great flourish. But it was coming into the city that they put on the most style.

They would allow their horses to go at an easy pace and take a rest, for a few miles before entering the town and until they crossed the Savoyard creek bridge on the river road between the Jones and the Cass farms, then they would come on with a rush and a run, until they reached the Mansion House, situated on Jefferson Avenue, about where Cass Street now is. After getting rid of the passengers desiring to put up at this hostelry, they would make their best show up Jefferson Avenue to Uncle Ben's, horns blowing, whips cracking and attended with all the clatter of hoofs, and rumble of stage coach incident thereto. It was inspiring to a degree, and brought every one on the route to the door or window to witness the passing show.

The foregoing was on the road between this city, Monroe and Toledo, more particularly; the other lines equaled this one in demonstration, but did not have so numerous an audience.

* * *

Jefferson Avenue at that day presented quite a different appearance from what it does now. Then all the retail dry goods stores (strictly wholesale dry goods houses there were none) were located on this street, and, with two or three exceptions, on the river side of the avenue (the "dollar" side, it used to be called).

It was then the custom of the merchants to make a display of their goods on the outside of their establishments; they used to call it "ragging out." In the spring, summer and fall, when the weather was fine, the avenue was exceedingly gay with fluttering dry goods, displayed by the merchants to catch the eye of their fair customers, who shopped then as eagerly as they do now. It was also the custom for the merchants to pile their empty dry goods boxes on the curb in front of their stores and allow them to remain for quite a time after the arrival of the spring and fall stocks, as an advertisement. The authorities never protested against this arrangement, nor did they against the custom of piling fire-wood by the merchants and sawing the same in front of their stores. I have seen fifteen or twenty cords of wood piled in front of Z. Chandler & Co.'s dry goods house, opposite the Merrill Block, and remain there until a convenient time came for sawing it up. Imagine such a state of things at the present day!

Merchants then made visits to the east in the spring and fall for the purchase of their goods. There were no railroads, no commercial travelers, and selections had to be made in person at eastern head centers.

* * *

Before leaving the eastern part of the city, I will mention that just above the foot of St. Aubin Avenue. Mr. McHoose had an extensive brewery; his "brew" was widely known. He was succeeded by Robert Fitzpatrick, and the last to occupy it was Mr. Carnes, formerly of the firm of Carnes, Carew & Co. (Josh Carew), who I think made some money here. His "Wine of Malt" was extensively patronized.

Many of the present generation will remember Mr. Carnes, as also Josh Carew. The former I think was from London, England, and had acquired his knowledge of the brewing business in the extensive establishments of that city. When he appeared on the streets, he was always faultlessly dressed, but in the brewery he was quite another character in attire. He was an acknowledged authority on whist.

Josh Carew will be remembered with pleasure by many of the present day. He was a "bon vivant" of the most pronounced type, and no function, ball or otherwise, was considered complete unless he was among the promoters. He was a thorough good fellow, ever ready to help the needy or assist in a charitable enterprise. The other partner in the concern of Carnes, Carew & Co. was Curt Emerson. All will acknowledge that Carew being so closely associated with Curt, as he was, could not have been otherwise than he was. Death long since claimed both Curt and Carew. Carnes is yet alive, I think, in New York.

The ale they brewed in the old brewery that stood on the southeast corner of Larned and Second Streets, had an extensive reputation. William Duncan succeeded to the brewery and the ale and kept up the excellence of both until "lager beer" gradually usurped both in popular favor.

* * *

Going back into the thirties I will relate an incident that occurs to me, before it escapes my memory.

Governor Stevens T. Mason appointed the late Peter Desnoyers state treasurer in 1835 or 1836. About a year before his death Mr. Desnoyers visited Lansing in company with his son-in-law, the late William B. Moran, and was struck with amazement at the splendid proportions of the new state capitol.

"Oh, my dear boy," he remarked, "there have been great changes in Michigan in my day. When I was state treasurer I used, every night, to carry the funds of the state home in my hat."

* * *

The only buildings of 1827 that now remain in the city are the wooden building on the southwest corner of Larned and Randolph Streets, occupied then as a Catholic sisters school, and the brick residence of the late Tunis S. Wendell, nearly opposite the old Michigan Exchange, and now used for commercial purposes. Also the small wooden warehouse of Shadrach Gillett next above the D. & C. line warehouse. I say "small" but it was considered large in its day.

ADDITIONAL RECOLLECTIONS OF MEXICAN WAR.

At the breaking out of the Mexican war, Colonel Bennet Riley's regiment, the Second United States Infantry, was stationed at the Detroit barracks, on the corner of Russell Street and Gratiot Avenue. Colonel Riley was a bluff old soldier and a fighter. Many will call him to mind, as also some of the officers of his regiment, among them, Captain Hoe and Lieutenants Canby and Granger. Only a portion of the regiment was stationed here, the remainder being assigned to garrison the forts up the lakes. The regiment was soon called on for duty in Mexico, where it rendered efficient service. Colonel Riley, on his departure, said he was going for "death or a yellow sash."

This gallant old soldier was born in St. Mary's County, Ind. He entered the army as ensign in a rifle regiment in the year 1813; served through the war with Great Britain, and through the Florida and Black Hawk Indian wars. Breveted colonel U. S. A. for galantry at the battle of Chokachatta, Florida; brigadier-general for galantry at Cerro Gordo, and major-general for gallantry at Contreras, Mexico. He was the first military governor of our newly acquired territory of California.

Lieutenant E. R. S. Canby, adjutant of the regiment, attained the rank of brigadier-general during the Civil War, and was killed in the "Modoc campaign." Lieutenant Gordon Granger also attained the rank of brigadier-general during the Civil War.

After the departure of the Second Regiment the barracks were left in charge of an ordnance sergeant, who looked after the government property as well as the welfare of some fifteen or twenty laundresses and their children belonging to the absent members of the regiment.

During the Mexican war the barracks were also the rendezvous for recruits raised in this state and in Wisconsin to fill the depleted regiments in the field. They were also the headquarters of the Fifteenth United States Infantry, of which Colonel Joshua Howard was lieutenant-colonel, Thornton F. Brodhead adjutant, and William D. Wilkins major, all of this city.

The First Regiment Michigan Volunteer Infantry, also rendezvoued here. Colonel B. F. Stockton was in command, and Alpheus S. Williams was his lieutenant-colonel, John V. Reuhle was major, Dr. Adrian R. Terry was surgeon, Lieutenant James E. E. Pittman was adjutant, and Dr. Lemke was assistant surgeon.

The regiment was not filled until the middle of the winter months and then was ordered to Mexico. Five companies under command of Lieutenant-Colonel Williams were ordered to march to Cincinnati, to take transports down the Mississippi, which they did. The other five companies with the colonel and staff engaged transportation by water to Cleveland. The river and lake were open and apparently there was no impediment to navigation in that direction.

Captain Sewel L. Fremont, the United States quartermaster ordered here to equip this regiment, contracted with Captain Gager, of the Steamer Albany, to take the five companies to the point above mentioned. Colonel Stockton's command, with baggage, etc., got on board the steamer all right at the foot of Woodward Avenue and started for their destination.

Before leaving the dock it was currently reported that Captain Gager had induced the quartermaster to pay him in advance for the transportation of the troops to Cleveland. But on arriving at Malden the steamer was met by a sudden change of temperature and threatening weather. The captain tied his boat up at the dock and informed Captain Fremont that he would not proceed a rod further under the circumstances, as he feared for the safety of his vessel and his passengers. He would not budge an inch, notwithstanding the threats of the officers, backed by loaded pistols (no revolvers in those days). They tried the engineer, but he, too, was obdurate. Finally the colonel and his command were forced to get to Gibralter, on the American side, as best they could, and that was on foot, across Grosse Isle and on scows across the river.

How Captain Fremont, if such was the fact (the prepaying of Captain Gager), ever squared himself with the war department at Washington I never knew. As for Captain Gager, he could take care of "No. 1," as all who knew him will testify.

* * *

On the breaking out of the war with Mexico Captain S. P. Heintzelman (afterward a major-general in the Civil War), was in charge of the quartermaster's department here. He was soon ordered to the front, and as there were no regular officers of the quartermaster's department available, General Brady was forced to place any United States army officer he could get on duty here, in charge of both the quartermaster and commissary departments. He accordingly selected Lieutenant Frank Woodbridge, his aid, to succeed Captain Heintzelman. Lieutenant Woodbridge was also soon ordered to the front to join his regiment and the department was filled by the following officers in succession, who happened to be here either on sick leave or detached duty: Captain J. B. S. Todd (brother of Mrs. Abraham Lincoln), Lieutenant Gordon Granger, Captain Carter L. Stevenson, Captain J. A. Whital and Lieutenant Andy Merchant.

Finally, the war being over, Major E. S. Sibley, of the United States quartermaster's department, and Major J. B. Grayson, of the United States commissary department, were ordered here in charge by the secretary of war. Both of the latter officers served with distinction in the Mexican war.

Directly after Major Sibley assumed charge the Fourth United States Infantry was ordered here. A portion of the regiment occupied the Detroit barracks, the remainder were distributed around at posts on the upper lakes.

Colonel William Whistler was in command of the Fourth Infantry. I have mentioned him and his family before, but I will add something that I think interesting, viz.: That is Captain Curtis, of the Second United States Infantry, brother-in-law of Colonel Whistler (having married his sister), was stationed at Green Bay and was in command there May 21, 1821. He died prior to 1830 at Prairie due Chien, leaving a daughter, Irene, who became an inmate of Colonel Whistler's family. She married Captain Daniel H. Rucker, United States army, who served with distinction throughout the Mexican and Civil War. The widow of the late Lieutenant-General P. H. Sheridan is a granddaughter of Captain Curtis's, whose daughter, Irene, now Mrs. Rucker, is Mrs. Sheridan's mother.

The other officers of the regiment I fail to call to mind, except Lieutenants Langebeil and Henry.

There was something peculiar in the assignment of the Fourth Regiment to this department. In the spring of 1812, this regiment was ordered to join General Hull at Detroit. A short time after they reported to Hull, he surrendered his entire command to the British.

The regiment, after the close of the Mexican war, was distributed at different points on the lakes between Fort Gratiot, Mackinac and Pittsburg. The headquarters with a portion of the regiment were established in this city at the Detroit barracks, where the Arbeiter Hall now is. The building used for headquarters is still standing next to the hall. It formerly stood facing Catherine Street, as before mentioned.

This was Grant's regiment. He was acting assistant quartermaster and was stationed with headquarters at Detroit barracks. I was a clerk in Major Sibley's office at the time and knew him well. His official duties often brought us into contact with each other. He was always the gentleman, quiet and retiring, never obtrusive. I do not think he was over fond of his office, as his quartermaster-sergeant told me that he detested papers and accounts, but on the other hand he was considered one of the best officers in the regiment for handling and maneuvering it, a soldier, every inch of him. Subsequent events verified the sergeant's opinion of him.

Colonel Wm. Whistler was a captain in the Fourth New York Infantry when it was engaged in the battle of Monguagon, fought the 8th of August, 1812. His younger brother, John Whistler, was an ensign in the same regiment and also present. He was fatally wounded. They were brothers of Mrs. James Abbott, whose father was then a captain in the army, and stationed at this post.

Lieutenant Geo. Johnson commanded the Michigan cavalry in this action. He behaved with the greatest gallantry, charged with the utmost impetuosity, and showing the courage of a lion. He had a horse killed under him. Johnson was called the Murat of the cavalry. Jesse Johnson, at one time a merchant here, and his brother, Thomas J., a young lawyer here, were sons of his. Lieutenant Johnson died in Green Bay, Wis., in 1850, at an advanced age.

Nathaniel Champ fought in this battle and was a sergeant in a company of Ohio volunteers, who fought with Colonel Antoine Dequindre at our left and gallantly entered the enemy's works at the point of the bayonet. Major Muir, of the British army, commanded the enemy's forces, which consisted of 200 regulars of the Forty-first Regiment; 100 militia and 450 Indians, in all about 750 men. Tecumseh, Walk-in-the-Water, Mainpot, Lame-hand, Split-log, with many chiefs of lesser note, led the Indians.

* * *

FALL OF FORT DEARBORN (CHICAGO) AND SIEGE OF FORT WAYNE.

The following letter was written by Captain D. Curtis, Fourth United States Infantry, from Fort Wayne, Ind., October 4, 1812, to his friend and former comrade, Cullen Colburn Witherell, uncle of Senator Thomas W. Palmer, and relates to the fall of Fort Dearborn, Chicago, and the siege of Fort Wayne:

FORT WAYNE, October 4, 1812.

Friend Cullen:

As our difficulties for the moment have in some measure subsided, and as I have been so fortunate as to survive the siege, it affords me the highest satisfaction to have it in my power to communicate to you some among many of the most important occurrences since my arrival at this place. I arrived here on the 5th of June after a successful passage, and killed two deer on my way. I was, on my arrival, and still continue to be, highly delighted with the place, and my situation, except, perhaps, I might have been a little better suited with a more active employment than I have had till about the 4th of last month.

Shortly after my arrival Lieutenant Whistler left for Detroit, and has not yet returned, we presume he has gone to take a peep at Montreal with the other unfortunate beings, included in the capitulation of General Hull, to the British.

Nothing here of an important nature transpired till about the 7th of August, when our captain received a note from General Hull, stating that Fort Dearborn was to be evacuated, and requesting the captain to communicate the same to Captain Wells and Wm. Stickney, and for them to point out the most safe and expeditious route for Captain Heald to take from Chicago to Detroit. The gentlemen were consulted on the subject, and concluded that by way of this place would be the best route, and in order to secure as much of the public property at that place as possible, Captain Wells thought proper to use his endeavors to that effect. Accordingly, on the 8th Captain Wells, with a party of thirty-five Miami Indians with their pack horses and one of our soldiers with five of the public horses, started to assisted Captain Heald in the evacuation of Chicago. On the morning of the 19th one of the Indians that accompanied Captain Wells returned, bringing intelligence that on the morning of the 15th (or as he calculated time, four nights ago), Captain Heald and his company, with Captain Wells, were all cut off; the particulars of which he thus related. They arrived at Chicago on the 13th, where were encamped then about 500 Indians of different tribes, some of whom were known to be at enmity with our government. Captain Wells being well acquainted with Indian customs, and seeing the difficulties likely to attend Captain Heald in getting away from his post, used every exertion in his power to effect an evacuation without the loss of men; he even gave up all the arsenal and magazine stores to satisfy their savage ferocity, but to no effect, and then agreed to deliver up all the cattle (about 100 head) and made them several other valuable presents in hopes of being permitted to depart in peace. The fatal morning arrived, and while the bloodthirsty savages were killing and dressing their beaves, the garrison was evacuated. Captains Heald and Wells marching in front, the baggage wagon next, the women and children next to it, followed by the soldiers and the thirty-five Indians with their pack horses bringing up the rear. They had not passed one mile from their little asylum when the alarm was given that the enemy, about 400 in number, was close upon them. A kind of hollow square was formed immediately, encompassing the women and children, and two rounds fired, but being overpowered by numbers, the brave, the innocent fair and the helpless, fell a prey to the savage cruelty of the tomahawk and scalping knife. We have since been told by another Indian that Captain Heald and lady (both wounded), W. Flanzay and wife, Lieutenant Helms and wife, and nineteen soldiers were made prisoners and sent to Detroit, from whence they are to be transported to Montreal or Quebec, with other prisoners taken at the capitulation, which perhaps you know more about than I do. Thus ends the fate of Chicago and its worthy commander, the success of this post and the fate of its great worthy and intrepid commander.

I now proceed to relate, and in some instances particularize. The Indians, since the news of Chicago, except some of the Miamies, have expressed and manifested a very different disposition from anything discovered in them previous to that event. Many attempts have been made to send expresses through to Detroit and other places, and many failed, either by being killed or driven back by Indians. A. W. Johnston on express to Piqua, Ohio, was killed on the evening of the 28th (August), before he had gone half a mile from the post. He was shot through the body, tomahawked, scalped, stabbed in twenty-three places and beaten and bruised in the most cruel and barbarous manner. The Indians came within hearing of our sentinels and hailed, requesting admittance into the garrison. This was the first instance since my acquaintance at this place of an Indian hesitating or expressing any fear in approaching the garrison. His business was to request of our captain a white flag, that some of the chiefs might come and speak with him and the Indian agent, A. W. Stickney. The flag was granted under a promise of its being returned that day, but the rascals kept it several days, during which time they were constantly plundering our gardens and cornfields, and even killing and carrying away our cattle and hogs immediately under our guns, and we, poor soldiers, either from cowardice or some other agency in our captain, were not suffered to fire a gun, but obliged to suffer their repeated insults with impunity. On the evening of the 4th of September the flag returned, accompanied by several chiefs, and after being asked whether they wished to remain at peace with us or be considered in an open state of warfare, the head chief among them observed: "You know that Mackinaw is taken, Detroit is in the hands of the British and Chicago is fallen, and you must expect to fall next, and that in a short time." Immediately upon this our great captain invited the savage rascal over to his quarters and after drinking three glasses of wine with him, rose from his seat, observed: "My good friend, I love you, I will fight for you, I will die by your side, you must save me," and then give him a half-dollar as a token of friendship, inviting at the same time to come and breakfast with him the next morning. The chief and his party retired to their camp, but instead of accepting his invitation to breakfast, sent five of their young warriors, who secreted themselves behind a root house near the garrison, where they shot and killed two of our men about sunrise as they were passing from a small hotel near that place.

The night of the 5th arrived and our captain had not drawn a sober breath since the chief left the garrison the night before. From the movement of the Indians in the course of the day, Lieutenant Ostrander and myself expected to have some sport before the next morning, and we were not disappointed in our conjectures, for at about 8 P. M. a general shout from the enemy was heard, succeeded by a firing of small arms on every side of us. The alarm post of every man, as well as the respective duties of Mr. Ostrander and myself, having been regulated during the day, the enemy had not time to fire a second round before we were ready, and opened three broadsides upon them and sent them a few shells from our howitzers, which we presume must have raked the shins of many. We exchanged the general shots, when I discovered from the flash of their guns that they were secreted behind the buildings, fences and shrubberies near the garrison, and ordered the men to cease firing till further orders, thinking the enemy would conclude that we were either frightened or scarce of ammunition, and perhaps would venture a little nearer. Although our ceasing to fire did not appear to bring them nearer, yet it tended to concentrate them more in a body, though they continued an irregulated fire about half an hour, without our returning a shot. As soon as a large body had collected at one point we threw a couple of shells from our howitzers which soon made them disperse, and but few shots were received from them the remainder of the night.

The next day they kept up a firing from behind fences, buildings and shrubberies near the garrison, till about 3 P. M. in order, we presume, to disturb our rest, knowing that we had been all night on the alert. Our captain still continued drunk as a fool, and perfectly incapable of exercising rationality on any subject whatever, but was constantly abusing and ill treating every one that came in his presence.

The night of the sixth approached, and as we are told that caution is the mother of safety, we had the roofs of our houses all watered as well as the pickets on the inside, our water casks all filled and buckets all ready in case of the enemy's attempting to throw fire, which they had endeavored several times to do, without success. This was all done and every man at his post before dark. Between 8 and 9 P. M. we heard a most tremendous noise, singing, dancing and whooping, and when they had arrived within a proper distance they hailed and aksed us in plain English what we intended to do, whether to surrender or fight? They said they had 500 men with them and that they expected 700 more the next day, and that in three days' time they would show us what they could do. We answered them that we were ready and bade them come on, that we were determined, to a man, to fight till we should lose our lives before we would yield an inch to them, and then gave a general shout round the works, in true Indian mood, which they instantly returned, commencing at the same time a general fire, which was kept up on both sides, with much warmth, till about 11 o'clock without the loss or injury of a man on our side, but from appearance they must have lost many, as they were very quiet till towards night.

The siege continued from the morning of the fifth till the morning of the tenth, both day and night, much in the manner above described, and the fears and troubles of our great and intrepid commander continually drowned in the excessive use of the ardent. Our fears and apprehensions, from the disorder and confusion he created among the men, were one of our greatest troubles, and we had everything prepared at one time to silence his noise and clamor by coercive measures. He would frequently talk of surrendering if the Indians were likely to be too much for us, and particulary if they or the British were to bring on one or more pieces of cannon which they took at Chicago and plant them near the garrison, when he knew that the largest piece at Chicago was only a three-pounder; and when told by one of his subalterns that the first person in the garrison who should offer to surrender to the Indians or the British at the approach of no heavier piece than a three-pounder should instantly be shot, he offered no resistance, but remained silent on the subject.

After the tenth we rested in tranquility, but could see large bodies of Indians, between that time and the 12th, running in great haste across the prairies, and many without arms. We were at a loss to determine the cause of this movement, but concluded that they must have met with some opposition as they discovered the approach of an army between this and Piqua, as they were running from that quarter.

About 3 o'clock P. M. of the 12th to our great joy we discovered the approach of a small troup of horse, and on their coming up to the garrison, we learned that it was the advance guard of an army of about 5,000 under the command of Brigadier-General Harrison. You may rest assured, friend C., that we lost no time, after the general had pitched upon and regulated his encampment, in making known to him the late conduct of our great, worthy and mortal captain, James Phea. The general, after hearing with great attention what we had to relate, expressed his great astonishment at the breach of confidence in the captain, and requested us to have everything reduced to writing and the charges produced in regular form; which was done that evening, and the next morning handed in. About 10 o'clock the captain was honored with a note from the general requesting him to deliver the bearer his long knife, and consider himself under arrest till his late conduct should be brought to a public investigation.

Shortly afterwards the general sent one of his aids to us requesting to know whether we would withdraw the arrest in case the captain would resign. We at first declined, but in a further request of the general we consented, on the consideration of his having been a long time in service, but more particularly on account of his having a young family. His resignation was sent in and accepted, to take effect on the 31st of December next, and in two days he left this for the State of Ohio.

Thus ends the success of this place so far, and thus you see the evils, the loss, the disappointments and mortifications attendant upon cowardice and intoxication, in mortal man.

D. CURTIS.

BUSINESS MEN OF SEVENTY YEARS AGO.

SOMETHING ABOUT BUSINESS MEN OF THE CITY SEVENTY YEARS OR MORE AGO.

WATKINS & JOY were saddlers and harnessmakers at 125 Jefferson Avenue. This firm continued in the business for quite a while, dissolved, and the firm became Watkins & Shaw.

Ferry Moores was the first to embark in the storing of ice for summer use, but only in a small way. He did not follow it up. The next was Abraham Smolk, and he, after one or two seasons, also discontinued the business.

Hiram Joy embarked in this business, succeeding Moores and Smolk. He made a success of it, filling a long-felt want. After Joy made the ice business a permanent thing, a chunk of ice was not quite so much of a luxury in the summer as it had been; for, in the absence of refrigerators and ice chests, it had to be kept in the cellar, or some cool place, wrapped tightly in a woolen blanket, to preserve it.

Joy continued the business four or five years. He was succeeded by James Robb (Robb the Ice Man), and he by E. B. and Dan Whipple. Joy was the brother of "Bijah" Joy, whom "M. Quad" made famous through the columns of the *Free Press* many years ago, as police attendant on central station court.

Hiram Joy married about 1838 or 1839 the widow of Newell French, city street inspector, and brother of David French, of French & Eldred, by whom he had one child, a daughter. After a brief married life, the wife died and the infant daughter was adopted by David French. This daughter of Hiram's grew to lovely womanhood, and was known as "Carrie" French. She became the wife of J. Sterling Morton, of Monroe, Mich. J. Sterling moved to Nebraska. After some years of a happy married life the wife passed away, leaving sons and daughters. Morton entered President Cleveland's cabinet as commissioner of agriculture. When Mr. Cleveland was replaced by Mr. Harrison, Morton retired to Nebraska, where he died. One of his sons, Paul, recently had the distinguished honor of being appointed to a seat in President Roosevelt's cabinet, as secretary of the navy. His subsequent career is known to all.

I knew Hiram Joy well, and seem to see him now when he came into Rood's book and stationery store (where I was' clerk) one morning to purchase some note paper, and told me, with great glee, of his approaching marriage, and what the purchase was for (invitations). And a day or two after the wedding, when he made his appearance at the store, how effusively all the crowd that usually assembled there congratulated him. Joy had another brother (Hartford), who was a master mariner and sailed the lakes.

Chas. W. Penny had an extensive stock of clothing at 92 Jefferson Avenue. Penny was of that set who boarded with Mrs. David Thompson on Fort Street, the Randolphs, and others. He was an ardent member of the Brady Guards, and with the exception of Geo. G. Bull was said to be the handsomest man in its ranks. In evidence of this fact (as stated in a former article on the Brady Guards) his full length figure, clad in the uniform of the guard, is represented on the flag presented to the company by General Hugh Brady. Mr. Penny removed to Jackson, where he carried on the same business until his death.

About 1838 Newbould & Strong were in the hardware business on Jefferson Avenue, south side, midway between Woodward Avenue and Griswold Street. The firm consisted of Alex. H. Newbould and John W. Strong, Jr. In the same block were G. & T. G. Hill, groceries and drugs; A. C. McGraw, boots, shoes and leather; Warren, candies, nuts, etc.; Hallock & Raymond (before mentioned); Howard's restaurant; the printing establishment of the *Detroit Advertiser* (George Dawson); Nelson, groceries; Mather & Hall, crockery (before mentioned); Edward Bingham, drugs; Salisbury, groceries. The Goddard building stood on the northeast corner of Jefferson Avenue and Griswold Street. In it was located the McKinstry museum (in the upper stories). On the ground floor, Griswold Street side, was located the offices of the United States customs. In this block also was the New York and Ohio house, a large wooden structure midway between Jefferson Avenue and Woodbridge Street, west side, and Mrs. Colonel Anderson's residence, northwest corner Woodward Avenue and Woodbridge Street, where is now the Mariner's Church.

This block was completely swept by fire on the night of January 1, 1842, the flames originating in the New York and Ohio house, burning out all the concerns I have named. This same block was visited by a destructive fire in 1830. Both fires have been described at length in former articles.

Charles M. Bull had a grocery store on Jefferson Avenue, south side, between Griswold and Shelby. He was at the same time in company with Geo. Beard in the restaurant business under King's corner, Jefferson and Woodward. He lived at the northwest corner of Michigan Avenue and Park Street. There was not a residence beyond him out Michigan Avenue for some years. He died in this home, leaving a wife and nine children. After a becoming period the widow married Judge E. Smith Lee, by whom she had one son, Charles Lee, who is now manager of some eastern railroad. After a while the judge and family removed to Washington, D. C., where he and his wife died. One of Bull's daughters married General Lucius Fairchild, at one time governor of Wisconsin, consul to Liverpool and minister to Spain. He is now a widower and living at Madison, Wis. Another of Bull's daughters (Miss E. C. Bull) is now living in Washington.

Judge Lee came here from Rochester, N. Y., with his wife, son and daughter in the late thirties, and engaged in the practice of law with David Stuart. His daughter, Mary Lee, married here, to whom I fail to recall; the son, Wm. G., was teller in the bank of St. Clair for three or four years, resigned and went to New York, after which I lost sight of him.

Mrs. Charles M. Bull was the sister of Captain Gager, of the steamer Albany, a steamboat that flourished in the forties, and a fine one for those days.

Gideon Paul had groceries, etc., at No. 71 Woodbridge Street. Gideon after this engaged in various ventures, but I do not think they proved very successful. He was an expert bookkeeper, and quite a jolly Englishman, being secretary of "the Old Countrymen's Benevolent Society." He finally drifted into the Peninsular Bank as bookkeeper, under H. H. Brown, cashier, where he continued until he died.

The Beaubien Bros. were in the dry goods business in the

Republican block, south side of Jefferson Avenue, between Bates and Randolph Streets. They were sons of Lambert Beaubien, one of the owners of the Beaubien farm. They were succeeded by the Watson Bros. (John and James), and they by Chas. Moran, son of Judge Moran.

The Detroit & St. Joseph Railroad was commenced in the spring of 1836. Forty miles was under contract, thirty of which was in operation, or stated would be during the summer of 1837 (to the mouth of St. Joe River—196 miles—was the objective point).

In a former article, I failed to mention the following very prominent citizens, who were here in 1827:

Francis D. Browning, James Sanderson VanAntwerp, father of Fr. VanAntwerp; Lemuel Goodell, Colonel Edward Brooks, Sheldon McKnight, Gildersleve Hurd, Israel Noble, Chas. Howard, Judge Jas. May, Lambert Beaubien, Antoine Beaubien, John Wright, Andries, Ord, Watsons, Clarks, Sheriff Champ, Sheriff Thompson, Sheriff Wilson, Louis Dequindre, Wm. Pettie, Archie McMillan, Conrad Ten Eyck, Dexter Merrill, Captain Pearson and Oliver Miller.

THE CITY IN 1834.

In March, 1834, a census was taken by A. E. Hathon. The four wards of the city contained 4,964 persons (2,904 males, 2,060 females), 477 dwellings, 64 stores and warehouses. In 1837 there were 9,763 inhabitants, and the number of stores and dwellings exceeded 1,300. The principal municipal officers were: Levi Cook, mayor; aldermen, Oliver Newberry, Thomas Palmer, Julius Eldred, Darius Lamson, John Farrer, David Cooper, John Owen; city clerk, Geo. Byrd; city attorney, Jas. A. VanDyke; collector, A. C. Canniff; city surveyor, A. E. Hathon; treasurer, David French; superintendent hydraulic works, Noah Sutton; justices of the peace, John W. Strong, David E. Harbaugh, Lemuel Goodell, Chas. Moran, B. F. H. Witherell, Henry V. Disbrow.

Supervisors of highways—District No. 1, Newell French; district No. 2, Lorenzo Pratt.

Clerks of the markets—Washington market, Israel Noble; Berthelet market, D. Hayward.

Wood measurers—James H .Cook, Israel Noble; weighmaster, Chas. M. Bull; superintendent of water works, David French; marshal, David Thompson; constables, Jacob McKinney, Robert R. Howell, Richard J. Conner; sexton, Israel Noble.

Fire department—Chief engineer, H. V. Disbrow; assistant engineers, John L. Whiting, R. S. Rice.

Fire wardens—Ward No. 1, Silas Titus, Alex. McArthur, James O. Graves, Geo. W. Gallagher. Ward No. 2, Shubael Conant, Enoch Jones, Chas. Bissell, James Hanmer, Marshal J. Bacon. Ward No. 3, David Dwight, G. Mott Williams, John Winder, Z. Kirby, R. Ingersoll. Ward No. 4, Mason Palmer, Jerry Dean, James Williams, Asher B. Bates, John Palmer. Ward No. 5, Henry Howard, Justin Rice, H. H. Brown, Benj. F. Larned, Edward Brooks.

* * *

The Ann Arbor mail arrived every other day; Chicago and western, every other day; eastern and southern, every day during the time of the close of navigation, and other times the mail arrived and departed by regular steamboats. Grand Rapids mail arrived Tuesdays; Mt. Clemens, every Tuesday, Thursday and Saturday; Pontiac, every Monday and Friday; Lapeer, every Saturday.

The officers of the Detroit & St. Joseph Railroad Co. were: President, John Biddle; directors, C. C. Trowbridge, Oliver Newberry, Shubael Conant, E. A. Brush, Henry Whiting, J. Burdick, H. H. Comstock, Mark Norris, C. N. Ormsby; chief engineer, John M. Berrien; assistant engineer, A. J. Center; secretary and treasurer, Alex. H. Adams.

* * *

The city hall was a two-story brick building with a hammered stone basement and was 100 feet long and 50 feet wide, the height of the first story 16 feet, and from the base to the top of the cornice 36 feet. On the front of the roof was a handsome cupola. The principal entrance was from the public square (Campus Martius). The first story was occupied by the city market and clerk's office, and on the second story was a spacious hall, used as a council chamber and court room. The building was erected in 1835, and cost about $20,000.

Young Men's society, chartered March, 1836. President, George E. Hand; vice-president, Silas Titus; corresponding secretary, Asher S. Kellogg; recording secretary, Francis Raymond; treasurer, David Harbaugh; auditor, Walter W. Dean; managers, John Chester, John L. Talbot, James A. Van Dyke, A. T. McReynolds, Jas. F. Joy, John S. Magruder, Alpheus S. Williams.

* * *

The Detroit *Daily Advertiser* was conducted by Geo. L. Whitney; its editor was Geo. Corselius.

* * *

The principal hotels were: American Hotel, by John Griswold; Michigan Exchange, by A. Wales; National Hotel, by H. K. Haring; Steam Boat Hotel, by B. Woodworth.

Captain Thomas Hunt was register of the United States land office. He was a brother of Henry I., William B. and Geo. Hunt. The business of the office was quite extensive in those days, emigration being at a fever heat in 1836-'37 and '38. The captain had two very pretty daughters, Eunice and Ellen. The former married Dr. Tripler, surgeon, U. S. A.; the other married Chas. Bissell, dry goods merchant (his second wife).

* * *

John McReynolds, northwest corner of Jefferson and Woodward Avenue, had drugs, medicines, etc. John was a brother of Colonel Andrew T. McReynolds. (Dr. Thos. B. Clark married a sister). He was afterwards in the auction and commission business with Henry Doty, also with Tom Edmonds, the principal auction and commission house in the city at the time. General O. B. Willcox, U. S. A., married for his second wife a daughter of his. A very companionable man in every way was John McReynolds.

* * *

Wm. P. Wing occupied Colonel McKinstry's circus building (that was near the present public library) after it was given up as such, as a planing mill, and gave out that in addition or connection therewith he had in opperation a circular saw, which would slit to great advantage door, sash, etc.

* * *

Dr. M. L. Cardell, an exceedingly quiet and retiring gentleman, was a skilful dentist, and had his office in the Desnoyers

Block. When the Lake Superior copper excitement was in full blast he removed to that part of the state, Hancock, I think. He was the father of Mrs. Joseph H. Chandler, of Chicago, and Mrs. Holland, of Detroit. A daughter of the latter married Mr. McClellan Brady, a son of Mr. Geo. N. Brady.

* * *

F. A. Hickox had an extensive stock of hardware at 127 Jefferson Avenue, west side, between Woodward Avenue and Griswold Street. After a while he removed to Ann Arbor. Mr. Fred Buhl married a sister of his. Another sister married James Platt, of Ann Arbor.

Henry Keeler, No. 22 Randolph Street, opposite the Berthelet market, kept jewelry, watches and clocks, repaired watches and clocks, and was an engraver on metal and wood.

C. Coggeshall & Co., 38 Woodward Avenue, had a fine assortment of hardware, also sperm oil and candles. This Coggeshall was the father of Mrs. David W. Fiske (Fiske was after in the same line of business). Chas. Locke, of the firm of Gunn & Locke, married a daughter of Mr. Fiske, and a son of Locke's married a daughter of the late Guy F. Hinchman. A son of Coggeshall had an extensive drug and grocery store in the Sheldon Block, on Jefferson Avenue, opposite Rood's book store, Cooper Block, in the early forties. Chas. Paddock, who was afterwards with T. H. Eaton, was his prescription clerk. Coggeshall was quite a society man and an all around good fellow.

Chas. M. D. Bull (he was a relative of the Widow Doty.) had an extensive stock of dry goods and groceries, at 94 Jefferson Avenue, in a brick building of Mr. Conant's, adjoining the residence and store of Joseph Campau. Mr. Bull was a fine looking, prompt, energetic business man. A society man withal. He married Miss Swathel, an interesting daughter of an influential family in Ann Arbor. After a brief married life, he passed away The widow after a few years married Mr. Sinclair, a prominent miller in Ann Arbor. The Sinclairs, Swathels, Hawkins, Brighams, Platts, Hickoxes were the society leaders in the University City, and drew around them all the gay and socially inclined students, among which were Thomas W. Palmer, Joseph Smith, Willis Ransom, Jas. B. Witherell, Geo. Kellogg, Cleveland Whiting, David, James and Thos. Blackmar.

Kingsbury & Burnham published the Detroit *Evening Spectator* in the Republican Hall Block (where is now the store of Edson, Moore & Co.). They had a reading room attached, to which all strangers were invited. Quite an attractive lounging place it was.

Dr. E. A. Theller, in addition to his drug and grocery store on Atwater Street, had an office at 119 Jefferson Avenue. Associated with him was Dr. Starkey, whose specialty was the eyes. Dr. Starkey was the father of Henry and Richard Starkey, both of whom were well known by many of the present day.

* * *

CAPTAIN SCOTT UPDIKE AND OTHERS.

Snow & Fisk were in the book and stationery business in the Cooper Block. They sold out to Sidney L. Rood in 1838, who continued the business.

Josiah Snow was a short, fat man, quite genial and endowed with a wonderful amount of energy. He was engaged in so many outside ventures that he had no time to devote to the book business. The last I knew of him was fifteen or twenty years ago; he was then engaged in laying telegraph wires in New York state. He never during his waking hours was without a cigar in his mouth, but it was rarely ever lit. I think Snow married Fisk's sister.

Scott W. Updike was a nephew of Josiah Snow. If there are any members of the old Brady Guard alive, they must remember Updike, the trim-built, prompt soldier; indeed, citizens of 1837 and later, who are alive now, cannot fail to remember Scott Updike, who was as well known as the "town pump."

At a military encampment, held in Cleveland, one Fourth of July, and many days thereafter, Scott Updike, then of Rochester, N. Y., was present with a company from that city, of which he was the captain, and a fine company it was. It was a very large encampment, comprising companies from various states, and in fine discipline and condition. Captain Updike invited myself and Dr. Lucretius H. Cobb to be his guests during the show. We went, and the captain gave us the time of our lives. I never can forget it. I have forgotten the year of the encampment, but it must have been in the late forties.

During this encampment the city of Cleveland entertained

the officers connected with it and a few prominent citizens at a banquet given at the principal hotel in the city at that time. The doctor and I, not being encampment officers, nor prominent citizens of Cleveland, did not have any show for an invitation, but Charles, Noble, a native of Monroe, Mich., and a friend of our boyhood days, happened, luckily, to be Cleveland's city attorney at the time and it was he who piloted us safely in. He also kindly included in the invitation a friend of ours from Saginaw, Colonel Little. It was a swell affair and no discount. Champagne flowed like water.

Charles Noble later on removed to this city and went into the real estate business. He had for a partner George L. Frost. Hosts of people will remember them.

Sidney L. Rood, before he bought out Snow & Fisk, was in the bookbinding and blank book manufacturing business in the old wooden building on the northeast corner of Jefferson Avenue and Griswold Street. Rood and A. H. Stowel had been, the year or so before, associated together in the book business. In a former article I mentioned Rood at considerable length.

* * *

Rufus Brown was a wholesale grocer, wine and spirit merchant at 83 Jefferson Avenue, opposite the residence of Joseph Campau. Brown came here from Albion, N. Y., in the early thirties, and with him Dr. J. B. Scovill, though I do not know if the latter came from Albion or not. He was the contemporary of Alfred Cox, Kintzing Pritchette, Governor Stevens T. Mason, Isaac Rowland, Franklin Sawyer, George C. Bates, E. A. Lansing, Humes Porter, Jacob M. Howard, Dr. Farnsworth, Alfred Brush, Major Lewis Cass, J. Nicholson Elbert and others. After a period he quit the grocery and liquor business, studied medicine and surgery under Dr. Scovill, and was admitted to practice. He never practiced the profession, but went into the drug, medicine, fine grocery and liquor business. After continuing in this awhile he sold out to Higby & Dickinson; they in turn sold out to Higby & Stearns. Dr. Brown after this took a trip to Europe, spending some time in England and on the continent. On his return to Detroit he became a gentleman of elegant leisure, and so remained until his death. He married late in life a lady who I think was related to Mrs. DeWitt C. Holbrook and Mrs. General F. W. Swift. She was an estimable woman and made him a devoted wife. They had three children, two girls and one boy. One of the daughters, Jessie, a charming girl, died just on the verge of womanhood, casting a gloom over the members of the circle in which she moved, one of whom was my eldest daughter. They were the closest friends, and had been from their childhood. The parents felt the blow most keenly. The doctor, after enjoying an almost uninterrupted period of good health, died after a brief illness. His widow and the two remaining children removed to Albion, N. Y.

Dr. Brown had two brothers, one, Joseph, a surgeon in the United States army, and the other, Robert H., a member of the Detroit bar. The doctor was possessed of elegant manners, always a gentleman, ever at his ease and a faultless dresser. What wonder is it that during his early bachelor life his society should be courted by all with whom he came in contact? He was of the set of beaux who fluttered around the belles of that day, including among their number the Misses Cass, Mason, Brooks, Cornelia Platt (daughter of Attorney-General Zepheniah Platt), Emma Schwarz, Isabella Norvell and others. Dr. Scovill and Dr. Brown were most assiduous in their attentions to the Misses Mason for quite a period. As an evidence of the gallantry shown by Dr. Brown, I will relate an incident that occurred one afternoon when the former was parading on Jefferson Avenue in company with Miss Emily Mason. The unpaved streets were a little muddy, particularly on the crossings. When they reached Griswold Street, at what was then called Sherlock's corner, the doctor observed that the gutter was in no fit condition to accommodate the daintily-booted feet of his fair companion, though beyond it was all O. K., so he drew from his pocket his ample white linen handkerchief and, emulating Sir Walter Raleigh when escorting Queen Elizabeth under similar conditions (though Sir Walter used his cloak), spread it on the ground over the muddy spot, and the lady passed on with boots unsoiled. I happened to be an eye-witness.

The doctor also had a desperate flirtation with Miss Belle Cass. So warm did it get that the general, fearing it might have a matrimonial termination, set his face against it decidedly, which put a stop to it. I do not know why the general opposed it; presumably, he hoped for a better mate for his daughter, though the doctor was desirable in every way except financially. I often heard the doctor allude to the affair in an amused sort of a way. The doctor and myself were always intimate, though he was some years older, especially during the latter years of his life, from 1868 until his death.

The foregoing was written many months ago, long before Miss Emily Mason had brought to fulfillment her dream of bringing the remains of her brother, the "Boy Governor of Michigan," to rest forever beneath the soil of the city and state he had loved so well. What a reunion it would have been, if, on that 4th of June, the parties I have mentioned above could have been present. All are now dead but Miss Mason.

Dr. Brown and Major Cass were always intimate friends.

* * *

E. Steel was teller in the Bank of Michigan. He was the father of Albert Steel and the brother of the late Mrs. A. H. Dey. His widow, a charming lady, married Mr. Oaks, who for many years operated a saw mill at St. Clair. It was said that she was the love of his early youth, and from some cause best known to themselves, Mr. Steel came out ahead. Old members of the Audubon Club will remember Mr. Oaks, I know.

John and Simeon Leake were tellers in the Farmers and Mechanics Bank. They came here from Albany, and had seen service in the Albany City Bank. They were bright young men, with pleasant manners, and were soon initiated into society, which was quite gay at that time. They were great favorites with all. They remained here in the bank for three or four years, and then returned to Albany and to the service of the bank from which they came, where I saw them in 1843.

Mrs. Johnson, a widow, had a small grocery at 22 Griswold Street at the corner of the alley. It was in an old wooden building belonging to Joseph Campau. It is a source of great pleasure to me to say a few kindly words in remembrance of this motherly woman. She was the especial favorite of all the young boys that lived anywhere near her. She catered to their tastes in the way of pies, turn-overs, and cakes; also candies, firecrackers, marbles, tops, etc. Besides she had an ear for all the little troubles that boys will have, which endeared her to them more than anything else. She got the most of our spare change, of course, but the loss of that did not worry us; the wish was that it could have been more. After a while she moved to the corner of the alley between Jefferson Avenue and Larned Street, on Shelby, before Ike Flowers occupied it. She continued in the same business there. What became of her I do not know. She had a son, engaged in some lucrative employment, who lived with her, and he, I believe, looked after her in her declining years. What fun we did used to have at good old Mrs. Johnson's. The memory of it and of the good old soul cannot be wiped out.

* * *

OLD BUSINESS HOUSES.

S. W. Higgins had an office in the Museum building, southeast corner Jefferson Avenue and Griswold Street. He was a surveyor, a most prompt and energetic man and thoroughly up in his profession. He built the first house on the Witherell farm, north of Gratiot Street. It was an attractive cottage, situated some distance back from the street in the then dense woods. He used to call it the "Higgins Retreat." Perhaps there are some living who will remember him.

Thomas J. Hulbert was in 1837 assistant cashier of the Bank of Michigan. How long he retained this position I do not know, but presume, until the bank went out of existence. The next that I remember of him he was in the ice business here, and after that he was in the paymaster-general's office, Washington. General B. F. Larned was paymaster-general. The latter was stationed here many years as major and paymaster, U. S. A. Mr. Hulbert married a daughter of Colonel Gad Humphrey, U. S. A. Colonel Humphrey's wife was the sister of General Larned. After General Larned's death, Mr. Hulbert entered the office of Mr. Spinner, treasurer of the United States, Washington, in which office he remained until his death. Mr. Henry P. Sanger, of this city, married a daughter of Mr. Hulbert.

In this connection, Major B. F. Larned, way long in the early days married the widow of a son of Elkanah Watson (Joseph B. Watson), the grandfather of Eugene W. and James B. Watson, late of this city.

Nathan Goodell, before 1827, was steward of the steamboat Henry Clay. He left the Clay and started a restaurant on Woodward Avenue, opposite the old market. Lemuel Goodell, his brother, came here in 1828 and hired out to Nathan. When the latter went into the mercantile business Lemuel purchased his interest in the restaurant and carried it on until about 1830, when he sold out and became steward of the steamer Henry Clay, and remained there through 1831. He was at one time justice of the peace, also deputy sheriff under John Wilson, and succeeded him in that office about 1832-3. He was also warden of the state prison under Governor John S. Berry, in 1842. He married Persus McMillan, daughter of the widow McMillan, and sister of Ananias. I think he went to live with a son in Oshkosh, Wis.

Thomas O. Hill was teller in the Michigan State Bank, of which F. H. Stevens was president and John Norton, Jr., cashier. He was the brother of G. & J. G. Hill, grocers and druggists. Mr. Hill and his wife were a handsome couple, the latter a lovely character. Presumably many will remember them. They had one daughter who, in after years, married Frank C. Markham, of the bookselling firm of Markham & Bros.

Horace Hallock and Francis Raymond had a clothing store on the southwest corner of Jefferson and Woodward Avenues. William A. Raymond, a brother of the latter, came on and joined them in the business. William A. was a very clever, bright young man. He was quite gifted as a sketch artist and made many spirited sketches of Detroit and vicinity as they appeared at that time. The late R. E. Roberts gave some of them publicity in his articles on Detroit in the early days. He died quite early.

It is not necessary to dilate on dear old Horace Hallock, the saintly man, as he so recently passed to his reward. Mr. Frances Raymond is with us yet, and "to the fore," I am happy to record.

There was a Mr. and Mrs. Harvey keeping a bake shop in 1815, Mr. McCabe's directory says on Jefferson Avenue, between Woodward Avenue and Bates Street, east side (where Lamson's store was). The house was moved to Woodbridge Street about 1827, and became the United States Hotel, where it remained as such for a long period of years. Perhaps the wife of this Mr. Harvey may have been the Mrs. Harvey who helped one Sam Kenton and his three companions to escape from the fort, before 1805.

De Mill & Goodell (Alex.) were dealers in groceries and provisions at No. 155 Jefferson Avenue and Bates Street. They were the successors of Campbell & Goodell. Henry M. Campbell was the father of Judge Jas. M. Campbell. Peter E. De Mill has been mentioned at length in a former article. Goodell had a brother (Elijah) who was clerk (later on) for H. P. Baldwin, who was quite a stirring, go ahead individual. He it was that was mainly instrumental in getting up the movement through which the name Hog Island was changed to that of Belle Isle, in honor of Miss Belle Cass.

The Watsons, Johnsons, Andres, Clarks, Ords and Whipples all at one time lived in the vicinity of the intersection of Larned and Randolph Streets. The Watsons, were John, James and Thomas, and a sister. They lived with the mother, a widow. John and James were dry goods merchants in the Republican Block, Jefferson Avenue. Thomas was a lawyer. The daughter married Judge O'Flynn. John married a daughter of Peter Godfroy. James married a daughter of Whittemore Knaggs, and removed to Saginaw. John continued the business here. Johnson, who was related to the Watsons, commanded the Michigan cavalry at the battle of Monguagon, 8th August, 1812, as mentioned in former article. The Andres and Clarks and Whipples I have mentioned in a former article.

Major Elias C. Andre, one of the Andre family, and born here, died in this city not very long ago. He passed most of his life among the Indians in northern Michigan. Was also engaged in lumbering. He, it was said, amassed quite a fortune, but unfortunately investments took it all or nearly all away from him. He was quite an inventor, and patented many inventions. I knew him here when he was quite a boy of 16 years.

* * *

JOHN COLLINS, CHAUNCEY HULBERT, ET AL.

A prominent resident here in 1827, and some years after, whom I have omitted to mention, and who influenced the advent here of two individuals who became distinguished citizens of Detroit, was John Collins. He came here in 1820, bringing with him his cousin, Daniel Goodwin, and later (1825) he induced another cousin, Chauncey Hulbert, to cast his lot in this city. Collins was quartermaster of the Kentucky Rifle Brigade in the war of 1812, and was present at the massacre of the Raisin. He settled in Detroit after the war and engaged in merchandizing and the manufacture of soap and candles and the packing of pork and beef. He supplied the government posts on this frontier for many years after the war of 1812. He had large transactions with John Hale (Hale & Bristol) and the Palmers (Friend and Thomas), who were also extensively in the soap and candle business.

Collins had a partner by the name of Woolsey (another cousin of his). They continued in business quite a while, until disaster overtook them, and failure was the result. This happened in 1836. What became of Woolsey I do not know. Collins retired to the Goodwin, now the Chestnut ridge, farm. He died in 1875. Woolsey left two sons; one, Melancthon, was a schoolmate of mine. I subsequently lost sight of him. The other son was adopted by Lawyer Daniel Goodwin, and was known in the family as "little Dan." "Little Dan" took the name of Daniel Goodwin, adopted the law as a profession and became a distinguished member of the Chicago bar. He died only two or three years ago.

John Collins lived while in Detroit on the northeast corner of Bates and Woodbridge Streets. A daughter of his, Lucretia Goodwin Collins, born in 1830, is the mother of Benj. F. Comfort, principal of the Cass School. Daniel Goodwin was for many years United States district attorney for Michigan, was subsequently appointed district judge, and served repeatedly in the Legislature. He was president of the constitutional convention of 1850. He appeared for the people in 1851 in the great trial known as the railroad conspiracy case. He was judge of the Circuit Court for the northern peninsula of Michigan, and I think he held this office at the time of his death.

The first knowledge I had of Chauncey Hulbert, he was in partnership with Jerry Dean in the saddlery and harness trade. A burn-out in 1832 dissolved the partnership. His subsequent career is too well known for me to expatiate on it; suffice it to say that his services in the interest of the city water works, and his munificent endowment of Water Works Park, will endear his memory to the citizens of Detroit forever.

I was up at the water works for half a day last summer, admiring the lovely park and its miniature lakes, and also lingered for an hour in the power house and watched the almost noiseless movements of the ponderous pumping engine. While contemplating it with wonder, I could not help contrasting it with the small affair, with its clatter, that used to do the pumping for the Detroit Hydraulic works, which was located on Woodbridge

Street in the rear of Edgar's sugar house, and forced the water up into its reservoir at the southeast corner of Fort and Wayne Streets. I could not help being reminded, also, of the water works of Farrand & Davis, the wooden pump at the foot of Randolph Street, and the miniature wooden reservoir at the corner of Jefferson Avenue and Randolph Street, where is now the water office.

* * *

The Baggs flourished here sixty years ago. John S. Bagg, of Bagg & Harmon, Dr. Joseph H. Bagg, A. Smith Bagg, Silas A. Bagg. Hosts of people will remember this family, though most of them have left us. John S. was the editor and one of the proprietors of the Detroit *Free Press*. A. Smith had a book and stationery store on Woodward Avenue, on the east side, between Jefferson Avenue and Woodbridge Street. He continued there for some years, then removed to Jefferson Avenue, just above King's corner. With him at this time was P. R. L. Pierce, who afterwards removed to Grand Rapids, became quite prominent there, was county clerk, member of the Legislature, etc.

I do not know how long A. Smith Bagg continued in the book business. The last I knew of him he was a farmer out Woodward Avenue, just beyond the railroad crossing. He was a very genial, companionable man, bubbling over with good spirits. He died not so many years ago. I do not know how many children he left. I knew only one—Charley Bagg, for many years until his death, the efficient and popular clerk of the Recorder's Court, and like his father, one of the most genial and companionable of men, as many will call to mind.

John S. Bagg, I did not know much about. He always appeared to me cold and austere, as a newspaper editor ought to be, I suppose; though I have been told that he was easy of approach and most kind. His daughter is the wife of Mr. Geo. H. Russell, the banker.

Silas A. was county register for two terms, I think.

Dr. Joseph H. Bagg was quite prominent in his profession. Mrs. Bagg, his wife, was first cousin to the late Thos. C. Sheldon, Dr. Randall S. Rice, the first Mrs. Dr. Pitcher, Mrs. Sheldon McKnight, and Mr. John P. Sheldon, who in conjunction with Mr. E. Reed conducted the Detroit *Gazette*. Mrs. Bagg when a girl attended the female seminary at Clinton, Oneida County,

N. Y. There was then at Clinton a preparatory school for boys in connection with Hamilton College, which was also in that village. The girls and boys of the two institutions often took their meals together at the same boarding house, and Mrs. Bagg well remembered taking her meals there at the same table with three sprightly young gentlemen who hailed from Detroit. These were Sproat Sibley, Edmund A. Brush and Peter Desnoyers, all well known Detroit names in the early days.

Dr. Bagg and his wife came here in 1838, and it took a full week to come by steamer from Buffalo to Detroit. He was appointed surgeon of the expedition (1839), to remove the Chippewa Indians beyond the Mississippi. The doctor also made several voyages of exploration into the Lake Superior country. His companions in one of those expeditions, were the following, then familiar names: Lucius Lyon, Dr. Douglas Houghton, Jonas H. Titus, Omar D. Conger, and Anthony Ten Eyck. They made the entire circuit of the lake in birch-bark canoes. The doctor was the father of Hon. B. Rush Bagg, member of the Detroit bar, and who was for years known as the efficient police justice of Detroit. It will perhaps be remembered by some, that when he ran for that office the last time, as a party candidate, it was ascertained about noon on election day that the "roughs" were making a strong effort to defeat him, so the respectable portion of the electors, without distinction to party, rallied to his support and elected him by a strong majority. He died young.

Dr. Bagg lived on the northeast corner of Brush and Macomb Streets for eighteen years after his removal from Woodward Avenue. He was for one term what was then known as "side judge" of the Circuit Court. He was a member of the common council of Detroit for two or more terms, and member of the State Constitutional Convention of 1850. He was also judge of probate of Wayne County for four years, from 1853 to 1857.

Rush Bagg married one of the daughters of Lyman Baldwin (sister of Mrs. William B. Wesson), one of the most beautiful women that ever lived in Detroit. She, too, died young. It is said the doctor originated and carried through the common council the celebrated resolution of order to tear down the house of the notorious "Peggy Welch" as a public nuisance. It was torn down by order of the council by Alex. H. Stowell, then marshal of Detroit. I have alluded to this incident at greater length in a former article. Of all the members of the Bagg family it was generally conceded that John S. was the head and front and received the most consideration. The events of his long and honorable life are of public record.

BUSINESS BUILDINGS SIXTY YEARS AGO.

Business buildings that stood in Detroit sixty years ago have gone out of existence, except the Abbott Block, corner of Griswold and Atwater; Desnoyers building, northwest corner of Jefferson Avenue and Bates Street; Shelden Block (now Willis Block), Jefferson Avenue (west side), between Griswold and Shelby Streets; White buildings (now Waverly Block), opposite Michigan Exchange. The others were commercial buildings, west side Woodward Avenue, between Jefferson Avenue and Larned Street; Connor's building, northeast corner Jefferson Avenue and Bates Street; King's building, corner of Jefferson and Woodward Avenues; Law buildings, corner Woodward Avenue and Woodbridge Street; Republican Hall, where Edson, Moore & Co. now are; Smart buildings (Merrill Block); Wardell Block, southeast corner Woodward Avenue and Woodbridge Street, a portion still standing.

Harsha and Chas. Willcox had a book and job printing office at No. 80 Sheldon Block (up stairs). Harsha was the father of Walter Harsha, so well and favorably known. He was an exceedingly well read man, quiet and unobtrusive, great in argument. He was one of the learned crowd that used to gather at Rood's book store and discuss the affairs of the nation. Joseph Campau and he were great friends. I have often seen the two together in the printing office, discussing the Catholic Church, priesthood, etc. Chas. Willcox was the brother of E. N. and General O. B. Willcox.

Atkinson & Godfrey were house, ship and sign painters, Woodward Avenue, east' side, one door above Atwater. Both partners were jolly, genial men and quite conspicuous in the busy life of the city, and enthusiastic members of the volunteer fire department. Many no doubt will remember Jerry Godfrey well, as I do. The firm after this was, I think, Godfrey & Dean.

William Cole was sailmaker and rigger, corner Woodward Avenue and Atwater Street. Perhaps some will call to mind this bluff, hearty sailmaker.

Smith, Glover & Dwight (R. G. Smith, Henry Glover, A. A. Dwight) had foreign and domestic dry goods at No. 118 Jefferson Avenue.

J. W. Tillman had a fine stock of furniture at 69 and 71 Jefferson Avenue, opposite the Michigan Exchange. J. W. Tillman was quite a factor in the life of Detroit, both in business and socially. At the breaking out of the Civil War he was very much interested in military affairs. He was quite active in the organization of the Lancer Regiment, was temporary colonel until Colonel Arthur Rankin, an English-Canadian, and capable officer from Windsor, Canada, was commissioned as its colonel, this in 1862. It was recruited mainly from Canada. It was mustered into service with the maximum number, fully equipped, with the exception of horses. It would have left the state for the field in fine condition, but was disbanded by order of the war department, contrary to the repeated protests of the governor, and without giving any reason for such procedure, losing to the service of the Union a remarkably fine regiment of officers and men. The late W. G. Thompson was an officer in this regiment. Lieutenant H. M. Whittlesey, quartermaster of the camp of instruction at Fort Wayne in 1861, and after quartermaster of the freedman's bureau, under General O. O. Howard, U. S. A., was a brother-in-law of Tillman's, the latter marrying the sister of the former. Will Tillman, a son, was major and paymaster of volunteers during the Civil War. He now resides at Louisville, Ky.

Colonel Tillman married for his second wife, Miss Martha Conant, of Monroe, Mich. After Colonel Tillman's demise, his widow married General A. G. Williams, then member of Congress from Michigan.

Frederick Wetmore had a crockery store at 125 Eldred Block, north side of Jefferson Avenue. Scores of the present day will remember Fred Wetmore, also his nephew, Charles H., men of character and strict integrity.

They afterwards moved to Woodward Avenue, north side, between Larned and Congress.

George E. Egner had a confectionery store and ice cream parlors at 172 Jefferson Avenue. They were generously patronized by our first citizens, and everything furnished was of the highest order.

James Stewart had copper, tin and sheet iron ware, stoves,

etc., at No. 83 Woodward Avenue. Stewart was at one time a partner in the same business with M. F. Dickinson, brother-in-law of William B. Wesson. Mr. Stewart was an enthusiastic member of the old fire department, a most estimable man and a good citizen.

William T. Pease was forwarding and commission merchant, foot of First Street. He was also agent for the Troy & Erie line. Earlier than this Pease had been captain of several steamers plying between here and Buffalo. He and his clerk, Charles Harrington, were immensely popular with the traveling public, and deservedly so.

Charles Howard & Co. were forwarding and commission merchants at the foot of First Street, also they were agents for many eastern transportation lines. Charles Howard was at one time mayor of the city, and was one of the first projectors of the Detroit & Pontiac Railroad. He built two enormous warehouses, where is now the Grand Trunk depot. One of them was occupied by Brewster & Dudgeon. During the Civil War he invented a musket, not a breech loader exactly, but the cartridge was inserted through an aperture in the side of the barrel. He called it the "Thunderbolt." The war department looked upon it with some favor, but with not sufficient to adopt it. What became of it I never knew. Many will remember Mr. Howard, one of the very best of men.

N. T. Ludden had domestic and fancy goods, also dry groceries, at No. 96 Jefferson Avenue and corner of Woodward and State Street. Ludden was at one time sheriff of Wayne County. His son is, I think, city or county surveyor.

John I. Herrick had books, stationery and paper hangings at 98 Jefferson Avenue, where the Conant Block now is. Herrick also had a circulating library, the first of the kind here of any account. It filled a long felt want and was well patronized.

Theodore H. Eaton had groceries, drugs, medicines, dye stuffs, etc., at 188 and 190 Jefferson Avenue. It is needless to say, I presume, that his son (Theodore H. Eaton) is now in the same business, but not in the same locality.

THE OLD TEN EYCK TAVERN.

FAMOUS WAYSIDE INN AT DEARBORN, WHERE PIONEER TRAVELERS FOUND WELCOME SHELTER IN MICHIGAN'S EARLY DAYS.

THE recent destruction by fire of the ancient stables, formerly a part of the "Old Ten Eyck Tavern" at Dearborn, obliterates one of the very few remaining local landmarks of the early pioneer days of Michigan.

The Old Ten Eyck Tavern stood for over fifty years on the Chicago road, about nine miles west of Detroit, at a point on the banks of the River Rouge where the ancient highway forks—the southerly branch running westerly to Saline, Adrian and so on, and the northerly branch, known as the Howell road, running to Ionia and Grand Rapids.

It was a typical wayside pioneer tavern, spacious, substantial and comfortable, and in some respects the most memorable and illustrious one in Michigan.

The old barn or stable, which stood just across the street and which burned to the ground a few nights ago, was perhaps equally famous, for it afforded shelter to the pioneer teams and also to many of the men, for the house itself was generally filled to overflowing with the women members of that great stream of pioneers that surged westward from the city about 1820 and 1840.

If the reader will glance through the volumes of the Michigan Pioneer and Historical Collection, he will find more references to the Old Ten Eyck Tavern than to any other hostelry. Indeed, almost every settler in the southern and southeastern portion of the state who has there left a record of the memorable wagon journey westward from Detroit refers in almost affectionate terms to the Old Ten Eyck Tavern at Dearborn.

There is good reason for this, for it was at this house that those hardy and hopeful pioneers passed their first night after plunging into the wilderness on their long-contemplated journey by wagon and ox team to their new homes in the wild and glorious west.

To appreciate the attitude of mind in which those hardy travelers approached the Old Ten Eyck Tavern, one should remember that they had come to Detroit by boat from Buffalo, where they had gathered from various parts of New York and other eastern states, full of expectancy and hope and intense interest, and some perhaps not without an occasional misgiving and even a shade of fear and dread.

THE JOURNEY THROUGH THE WOODS.

Arriving at Detroit, they at once set about fitting out for the long-expected journey through the woods. Getting an early morning start, they would proceed out Michigan Avenue, then called the Chicago road, but would not get farther than to where the Clippert brick yards now are located before they struck the "swamp" and its attendant calamities.

The "thirty-mile swamp," as it was called, extended from just west of Detroit nearly to Ypsilanti. It was not really a swamp, for it yielded perfectly to subsequent drainage, being a low, level, heavily-timbered and very wet plateau, broken only by the sandy and gently-rising banks of the River Rouge. On one of these sandy knolls, the Old Ten Eyck Tavern stood, a welcoming beacon to the anxious traveler journeying over the corduroy or floundering hub-deep in the thick and sticky mud. Not a house nor habitation had they seen during that first long, hard day of struggle through the somber, elm-shaded, swampy trail. It is a forty-minute ride by trolley now, but in those days the stage or emigrant wagons that made it in a day did well.

Emerging at nightfall as the sun cast its setting rays upon the broad facade of the substantial old tavern, and greeted by the genial beams of its famous proprietor, "Old Coon" Ten Eyck, as he was affectionately called, the weary pilgrims began to feel something of the glow of that fellow feeling which makes us wondrous kind.

"Sally, have some more wolf steak put on," Old Coon would call out in a cheery voice, as each new load of hungry pilgrims would drive up.

Sally was the proprietor's wife, and, like him, one of the famous characters of those early days. Many years later I knew her well, a dear, kindly old lady in white cap and prim kerchief. She had been long blind, but her mental faculties were keen, and she was full of interesting reminiscences of the olden time.

GENIAL OLD "COON" TEN EYCK.

Conrad Ten Eyck was accounted one of the prominent men of Detroit as long ago as 1815. He was United States marshal for Michigan, and, I think, the first sheriff of Wayne County when that county embraced the greater part of the lower peninsula. He came here from Albany, N. Y., being a member of the old Ten Eyck family of that city. He was a very genial and shrewd man. When the stream of settlers surged into lower Michigan, he went out to where the Chicago road crossed the Rouge River, afterward called Dearbornville, and built the "Old Ten Eyck Tavern" about 1820. The location selected was a happy one. The tavern and its business prospered. All the pioneers had money. Land speculation was rife. Conrad got his share. All his descendants were left well off. His oldest son, the late William Ten Eyck, died about twelve years ago, one of the very wealthy men of the county. The Ten Eyck farm at Dearborn originally contained several thousand acres. Mr. George Hendrie bought five hundred acres of it twenty or twenty-five years ago for $100,000, and still owns it. A part of a farm at Grosse Pointe owned by the Ten Eyck family is now the site of the Country Club.

The pleasantry about the "wolf steak" was one of "Old Coon's" stock jokes. He was wont to perpetrate it upon the newcomers, perhaps for the purpose of awing the juvenile pioneers. Once a particularly pretty and jolly girl emigrant, coming out of the tavern dining-room, with the taste of the juicy Ten Eyck lamb chops still in her mouth, asked, "And have I really eaten wolf steak?"

"Surely, my pretty miss," replied Old Coon.

"Then I suppose I am a wolverine," exclaimed the fair traveler.

"That you are," said Mr. Ten Eyck, "and will be from this on!"

The remark caught the ears of some gallant young swains

who forthwith claimed that they, too, were wolverines, doubtless wishing to be as much like their fair fellow traveler as possible. So the nickname "caught on" and was passed along, and in time the settlers, after they had passed the Old Ten Eyck Tavern, came to call themselves "wolverines."

Whether this was the origin of the term "Wolverine State," the official nickname of the state of Michigan, I do not know for a certainty, but Clarence Burton does.

REMEMBERS THE OLD DAYS.

The writer spent an evening recently with Mrs. Sarah Ten Eyck Tompkins, widow of the late Daniel D. Tompkins, of Dearborn, who is the only surviving member of Conrad Ten Eyck's large family. She was born at the Ten Eyck homestead adjoining the Old Ten Eyck Tavern in 1828. She remembers distinctly the exciting times of her childhood when the old tavern was filled to overflowing with the wayfaring settlers bound for their new homes.

"Many a night," she remarked, "have I seen every floor in the house covered with the sleeping women and children of the pioneer travelers, while the men and boys took refuge in the lofts of the tavern barn or camped in or under the wagons clustered about the yard or along the roadside.

"No, I do not think we ever cooked wolf meat. Father was very fond of a joke. I often heard him telling with solemn awe about the wildcats and wolves that were wont to prowl around at night.

"Father gave up the tavern while I was still quite young, and rented it to Dr. King, who ran it for many years, but as our house was so near by, we always knew what was going on.

"There were eight children of us, six girls and two boys, and all grew up and lived to good age, but I am the only one left. The generation that witnessed the trials and triumphs of those thrilling pioneer days is rapidly passing. They were interesting days. Their like will never come again."

MARRIAGE AND DEATH NOTICES.

The marriage and death notices mentioned below were furnished to the *Detroit News* by Mr. C. M. Burton some months ago. I have reproduced them, and have added to each some personal recollections of the parties which may give them more interest than a plain notice would possess.   FRIEND PALMER.

MARRIAGES and deaths of prominent people. Notices taken from the *Detroit Gazette*, 1820-1821:

March 24—Married at St. Clair, Jas. Fulton, Esqr., sheriff of the County of Macomb, to Miss Hannah Thorn.

NOTE—James Fulton, who married Miss Thorn, sister of John Thorn, of Port Huron (Black River), was the original owner of the ground on which the city of St. Clair is platted, and from whom the Palmers (Friend and Thomas) acquired it. Abraham Cook, of Detroit (Cook farm) also married a Miss Thorn. John Thorn was the original owner of the site of Port Huron, and was a "high roller" in the early days.

Captain Gleason, U. S. A., married Miss Hunt January, 1820. Sister of Henry I. and Wm. B. Hunt.

NOTE—The captain died at Fort Mackinac March 27, 1820. The widow married Tunis G. Wendell, merchant, this city. Mrs. Gleason gave the name of "Lover's Lane" to that lovely driveway which once existed on the outskirts of the city, in the vicinity of Fort Wayne. Mrs. George E. Curtis, 45 Madison Avenue, is a daughter of the Wendells. Her sister, another daughter, Mrs. V. Wendell Doolittle, of Chicago, is spending the present winter (1906) with her.

November 22, 1820—Died near Sandwich, U. C., Mrs. Archange Askin, aged 71 years. She was a native of Detroit, lived much respected and died without an enemy.

NOTE—Mrs. Askin was the mother of Mrs. Colonel Brush, who was the mother of Mr. Edward A. Brush, this city. Colonel Brush had a command under General William Hull.

November 30, 1820.—Married in Williamson, Ontario County, N. Y., Jeremiah Moores, of this city, to Miss Sophronia Kelly.

NOTE—Jerry Moores was a master stone and brick mason. He was one of the city magnates in the early days, with Levi Cook, Judge Caniff, Oliver Newberry and others.

December 24, 1820.—Married, in this city, by Rev. Mr. Monteith, Mr. David Cooper to Miss Lovicy Mack.

NOTE—Miss Mack was the daughter of Stephen Mack, of the firm of Mack & Conant (Shubael), extensive merchants here before the destruction of the city by fire in 1805. Mr. David Cooper was later a prominent merchant and capitalist. He was the father of Rev. David M. Cooper, the widely-known and respected divine.

December 25, 1820.—Married, by Rev. J. M. Monteith, Captain Henry Whiting, Fifth United States infantry, to Miss Eliza Macomb.

NOTE—Captain Henry Whiting was United States quartermaster, stationed at Detroit. He continued on duty here until the breaking out of the Mexican war, when he was ordered into the field. His wife was the sister of General Alexander Macomb, United States army.

On the same day and by the same minister, Lieutenant Aeneas Mackay, corps of United States artillery, to Miss Ann Macomb.

NOTE—Miss Macomb was a sister of Mrs. Whiting.

January 18, 1821.—Married, in this city, by Rev. John Monteith, Mr. Benjamin B. Kerchival to Miss Maria Forsyth.

NOTE—Miss Forsyth was the sister of Major Robert A. Forsyth, paymaster U. S. A. Mr. Kerchival was a prominent citizen and merchant here for many years.

February 2, 1821.—Died, at Chicago, 27th December last, Miss Maria Dodemead, of this city.

NOTE—Miss Dodemead, who died at Chicago, was the sister of Mrs. Charles Jackson, of Detroit. The Dodemeads owned for years the southeast corner of Jefferson Avenue and Shelby Street.

February 16, 1821.—Married at Hudson, N. Y., Dr. John L. Whiting, of this place, to Miss Harriet C. Tallman, daughter of Dr. M. John Tallman, mayor of that city.

NOTE—Dr. Whiting came directly to this city with his bride.

He was a prominent citizen here for many years. Was eminent in his profession and rendered most efficient service during the cholera seasons that visited Detroit. He is well and favorably remembered.

June 1, 1821.—Married, in this city, Sunday evening, by Rev. John Monteith, Mr. Eben Beach to Miss Elizabeth M. Owen, both of this city.

NOTE—Mr. Beach was of the firm of Willcox & Beach, hatters. Willcox was the father of Eben N. and General O. B. Willcox. Miss Owen was the sister of Mr. John Owen. Mr. Beach was the father of Eben Beach, the capitalist, who was a resident of Lafayette Avenue for many years and died on that street not many years ago. I think he has a daughter yet living in Pontiac.

"OLD OAKEN BUCKET."

March 30, 1821.—Married, Sunday evening last, by Rev. John Monteith, Mr. William Russell to Miss Abbey Woodworth.

NOTE—Miss Woodworth was the sister of Benj. Woodworth, who kept the Steamboat hotel that was on the northwest corner of Woodbridge and Randolph Streets. She was also sister of Sam Woodworth, author of the "Old Oaken Bucket." Uncle William Russell lived for many years until 1837, on the southeast corner of Hastings and Woodbridge Streets.

April 3, 1821.—Married at Hudson, N. Y., in the evening, A. G. Whitney, Esq., of this city, to Miss Anne Eliza, daughter of John Tallman, Esq., formerly mayor of the former city.

NOTE—Miss Tallman was the sister of Mrs. Dr. M. J. L. Whiting. Mr. Whitney's name is often seen in the early public records of Wayne County.

May 3, 1821.—Married, by Rev. John Montieth, Lieutenant John Mellen, of the U. S. corps of artillery, to Miss Elizabeth Scott, all of this city.

NOTE—Charles Mellen, a son of theirs, was well known here in the forties and fifties. The Smarts, the Williams's and the McKinstrys were always great friends of the Mellens.

May 3d, 1821.—Died at Sandwich, Canada, Lieutenant Otis Fisher, of the Eighth Regiment, U. S. Infantry, who fell a victim to those false notions of honor which have recently deprived our country of so many valuable officers and citizens.

Mr. Fisher was an officer of much merit and served his country in the second war with Great Britain with distinguished reputation. In the glorious battle of Bridgewater, on the Niagara frontier, he lost an arm, and was just about retiring from the army to enjoy the consideration to which his services entitled him.

Lieutenant Otis Fisher's antagonist in the fatal duel was Lieutenant Farley, of the same regiment. The affair occurred near Sandwich, and Liuetenant Fisher fell mortally wounded, and died the next day. Lieutenant Farley was the brother of the late Mrs. William Brewster, of this city.

November 22, 1822.—"The last mail brought us the melancholy intelligence of the death of our friend, James B. Witherell, on board the U. S. schooner Peacock, while on her return from Havana, Cuba, to Norfolk, Va. He was the son of Judge James Witherell, of the Supreme Court of this territory, and a young man universally esteemed among his acquaintances. There are few officers in the navy better qualified than he was to shed a luster on that arduous service. Our readers will recollect that last week we published a letter (dated October 10, 1822) from him dated a few days before his death, full of hope, patriotism and of enterprise. He was then engaged in chastising the pirates of the West Indies, and it is due to the peculiar hardships of that service that his death may probably be attributed. He was appointed midshipman March 10, 1820, and died October 20, 1822.

NOTE—He was uncle of the Hon. Thomas W. Palmer.

May, 1831.—Lieutenant E. G. Sibley (Sproat Sibley), U. S. A., was married to Harriet L. Hunt, daughter of Judge Hunt, of Washington, D. C., by Rev. Richard Berry.

NOTE—They were married at the cottage residence of General Charles Larned, southwest corner of Woodward Avenue and Larned Street, in the afternoon, in the presence of a distinguishd gathering composed of the elite of Detroit society. The groom and the other military officers were in full uniform. It was a brilliant affair. Mrs. Larned was an aunt of the bride. Lieutenant Sibley was a son of Judge Solomon Sibley and was born in this city. He served with distinction in the Black Hawk war, the Mexican War and the Civil War. In the last named war he rose to the position of colonel and assistant quartermaster-general.

Colonel Sibley was stationed in this city for two years directly after the close of the Mexican war, as quartermaster of the department of the lakes.

I had, though quite a lad, the pleasure of being present at the above ceremony.

September, 1831.—Mr. John Owen was married at Mt. Morris, N. Y., to Miss Lucy B. Beach.

NOTE—Miss Beach was the sister of Mr. Beach, of the firm of Willcox & Beach, hatters, this city. This was Mr. Owen's first venture in matrimony.

October, 1831—Colonel John Winder was married to Elizabeth C. Williams, daughter of General John R. Williams, by Rev. Richard R. Bury.

NOTE—The colonel's first wife. The marriage ceremony took place in General Williams's residence on Woodbridge Street, north side, between Randolph and Bates Streets.

The above last three notices were taken from *The Detroit Free Press*.

Two other marriage notices that may be of some interest, but not taken from the *Detroit Gazette:*

June 25, 1807.—Captain Samuel Dyson, U. S. A., commanding the garrison at Detroit, to Ann Dodemead, daughter of Mr. John Dodemead. Stanley Griswold, Esq., justice of the peace for Michigan territory, performed the ceremony.

NOTE—They were married in the Dodemead residence, southeast corner of Jefferson Avenue and Shelby Street. Griswold Street got its name from this Squire Griswold.

Mrs. Dyson afterward married Chas. Jackson of Detroit. Captain Dyson was quite prominent in the battle of Monguagon in 1812.

May 7, 1834—Dr. F. A. Breckinridge, of Brockville, N. C., to Catherine Ann, daughter of Hon. John McDonnell.

NOTE—Judge McDonnell was occupying at the time the abandoned officers' quarters, Fort Shelby, which stood where the new postoffice building now is. I was at the wedding. Miss McDonnell was the aunt of the present superintendent of the Detroit house of correction.

SOME RESIDENTS THAT I HAVE OVERLOOKED.

MRS. JOHN R. WILLIAMS was buried on the corner of Woodward Avenue and Adams, where is now the First Methodist Church. The land was owned by the general. The grave, with conspicuous headstone, was a short distance from Woodward Avenue and in plain sight of the passer-by. Where her body rests now I do not know.

* * *

Judge B. F. H. Witherell's circuit, when he was first elected judge, embraced the counties of Wayne, Washtenaw, Jackson and Oakland. In after years it was narrowed down to Wayne.

* * *

J. W. Brooks, who was the first superintendent of the Michigan Central Railroad, after it had been sold by the state, wrote a shocking bad hand, as many will remember. He once answered a letter written to him by James W. Sutton, who carried on a pail factory near the road on Fort Street, in relation to some trespass by the company. Well, Jim rode on that letter for ever so long, the conductors taking it for a pass, the writing was so bad. All who knew Jim Sutton can readily realize how much he enjoyed the joke.

Speaking of newspapers, there was one that very few persons ever saw or heard of. It was published about 1840, during the Harrison campaign, by the late Henry Campau, of the register's office. It was a small sheet, 7x9, and was called the *"Castigator."* Henry was at that time a clerk in his cousin's (D. J. Campau's) store, and he got out the paper in a room over the premises. It was anti-Harrison in politics, and, as its name implied, full of vinegar, and castigated much, so much, indeed, that his employer, D. J., ordered it suppressed. I think Mr. Richard R. Elliott has preserved a copy. It was unique, and those that knew Henry Campau can well believe it. Campau graced the top of the first page of his paper with the figure of an "owl," with the legend:

"The owl is out,
In vain the raging blade
Shall court the midnight shade."

In addition to those proprietors of the National Hotel (Russell House) from time to time (heretofore mentioned), I have failed to name H. D. Garrison, former dry goods merchant on Jefferson Avenue, about 1840. If any call him to mind they will remember him as a model landlord, possessed of a fine presence, winning, prompt and energetic. I was forcibly reminded of him a short time ago by a visit from one of the old clerks in his dry goods store, Orson Wooden. Orson has been for the past thirty years employed in the postoffice in this city, but has now retired from public life to the St. Luke's Home, with a comfortable competence, and says he intends to pass his remaining days in peace and quiet. The last time I heard of Garrison he was keeping a hotel in Chicago.

One of the proprietors of the old National Hotel, and one whom I have mentioned before, John R. Kellogg, had a beautiful daughter, Amanda, with whom our family were quite intimate. She was an interesting girl, admired by all and had many suitors. But she fell a victim to the smallpox and died in the hotel, much regretted by all the community. Strange to say (at this day) her sickness in the hotel with that dreaded and malignant disease did not cause any alarm among the guests of the house for their own safety. How much different from now. Mr. Kellogg was a man of distinguished appearance, polished manners, etc., but I do not think he was a success as a hotel keeper. He died in Allegan a few years since.

* * *

Many will remember Signor Martenez, that supreme master of the guitar. He was the finest player on that instrument that Detroit has ever known. He was the especial pet of Colonel Grayson and other United States officers here at the time. Although so skillful on the guitar, he was an out-and-out vagabond, so to speak, and tolerated only on account of his musical gift. He married a pretty French girl here, and the two lived with his wife's mother. He gave lessons on his instrument to Colonel Grayson and many other army officers, as well as some citizens. Colonel Grayson once made him a present of a gold watch and chain, with which he seemed highly pleased. A short time after, when he came to give the colonel a lesson, the latter noticed the absence of the chain and asked the signor what had become of it and the watch.

"Well, colonel," said he, "I got awful hard up and put 'em up spout."

Imagine the colonel's ire. On another occasion the signor received from some one an order on Brady & Trowbridge, grocers here at the time, for $10 in goods from their store. He was asked how he would have it, and he replied:

"Guess I will take nine dollars' worth of brandy and cigars for myself and one pound of tea for the old woman (meaning his mother-in-law) so she will not make a fuss."

He, poor fellow, got caught in a cattle guard on the Michigan Central Railroad near the city and was run over by a locomotive. He was under the influence of liquor at the time, it was supposed.

Colonel McIntosh was the most peppery United States army officer I ever came in contact with. He was, in appearance, about like the late General Wheeler, of the United States Volunteers. He commanded at Fort Winnipeg in 1834.

I mentioned Colonel McIntosh briefly in a former article, in relation to the boarders at "Dunning's" on Fort Street in 1845. I said he was killed in Mexico, and on "General Taylor's line." This was error. He died from wounds received at the battle of "Molino del Rey" (King's Mill) and not on Taylor's line. The men under his command used to call him "Old Smash Pipe," because he would not allow smoking. He was born in Georgia and commanded a brigade in General Worth's division in the above battle. Colonel Isaac D. Toll, now of Petoskey, this state, was in the "Molino del Rey" battle and gave me the above facts.

THE PLAT OF THE TOWN, KNOWN AS "WOODWARD'S PLAN."

THE GOVERNOR AND JUDGES' PLAN.

THE wide avenues and public squares and parks of Detroit are evidences and enduring monuments of the wisdom and good taste and judgment of the governor and judges who adopted the plan, they having been authorized by an act of Congress after the destruction of the city by fire in 1805.

The plan was designed and proposed by Judge Woodward, and was known in the early days as "Woodward's plan." The governor and judges who adopted the plan were William Hull, governor; Augustus J. Woodward, James Witherell and James Griffin, judges.

The original plan, which has been described as "resembling one of those octagonal spider webs, with a center and lines leading out to the points around the circumference and fastened to spires of grass," was designed for military defense, and to communicate information by signal telegraph from all points to a common center (the Grand Circus), but only in part carried out. At the time of the adoption of the plan a large portion of the site was covered by the fort, cantonment grounds, military gardens and fields, which were reserved to the general government, and when granted to the city twenty years later, was laid out in regular square blocks.

The original plan was in twelve sections. In the center of most of them there were large triangular spaces of ground, dedicated for specific public purposes, to-wit: educational, scientific, fire protection and religious. Of these one is occupied by the public library, one formerly by the high school (now Capitol Square), and one formerly by St. Anne's Church (now the Auditorium). The others are known as the east, west and north parks. Besides which, two large spaces were dedicated as public grounds, which have now become most conspicuous on the plat. These are the Campus Martius, which is crossed by Woodward Avenue, and which is 600 feet long and 250 feet wide. On the west line of the square there was a lot with a front of 280 feet on Griswold Street, which at one time, about seventy-five years ago, was donated by the city to the trustees of a female seminary, on which they erected a large brick building which for many years was operated as such, but it did not prove a success, and by the terms of the donation the property reverted to the city, and is now occupied by the present City Hall. An extended account of this seminary has been given in a former article.

The governor and judges' plan embraced all between the Brush farm on the east and the Cass farm on the west (except the military reservation, covering all west of Griswold Street between Congress Street and Michigan Avenue) and from the river to Adams Avenue; and all north of which to a point about three miles from the river, was platted into lots, designated as park lots, containing ten acres more or less, and were sold by the acre. Those park lots are now platted into city lots and are for the most part compactly built upon."

The foregoing is from the late R. E. Roberts's book, "Sketches of Detroit," issued in 1854.

Here is a contemporary description of Judge Woodward's surveying process written by John Gentle, and published in a Pittsburg paper:

"Judge Woodward, appointed to lay out the town, deposited his instruments, astronomical and astrological, on the summit of a huge stone, and for the space of thirty days and thirty nights viewed the diurnal revolutions of the planets, visible and invisible, and calculated the course of the blazing comets. To his profound observations of the heavenly regions the world is indebted for the discovery of the streets, alleys, circles, angles and squares of this magnificent city—a theory equal in magnitude and splendor to any on earth."

Colonel McKenney in his book, "Tour of the Lakes, 1826," has this to say in regard to Judge Woodward's plat of the city:

"I have seen a plat of this city (Detroit). I wish, for the sake of the designer, towards whom, personally, I entertain the kindliest feelings, that it had never been conceived by him. It looks pretty on paper, but is fanciful—resembles one of those octagonal spider webs which you have seen on a dewy morning, with a center, you know, and lines leading out to the points round the circumference, and fastened to spires of grass. The citizens of Detroit would do well, in my opinion, and their posterity would thank them for it, were they to reduce the network of that plan to something more practical and regular."

Mr. Smith, father of Mrs. Judge McDonnell, died at Sandwich, Canada, March 3, 1833. He laid out this city after Michigan's first organization as a territorial government, under the direction of Governor Hull and Judge Woodward; the plan was designed by the latter, to which Mr. Smith, as a scientific man, was much opposed; he considered it visionary, and ill adapted for the purposes for which it was intended. He was when he died 79 years of age, and by birth a native of Wales.

Mr. C. M. Burton's library is rich with information in regard to this plan of Judge Woodward's.

BUFFALO TO DETROIT BY STEAMBOAT IN 1821.

GENERAL HERBERT E. ELLIS, in Wisconsin Historical Collections, Vol. 7, gives an account of a trip from Buffalo to Detroit on the steamboat Walk-in-the-Water, June, 1821, in which he says:

"There was not a good harbor on Lake Erie (south shore) except Sandusky. At Erie, Ashtabula and Cleveland bars, had formed across the mouths of the streams, and goods had to be lightered off. We reached Detroit at the end of the third day."

The general had something to relate in regard to our city which I quote:

"The town (Detroit) was not as large as it is now. It was built on a single street, parallel with the river and something over half a mile in length. There was one brick house, that of General Macomb, built by Governor Hull, a rather respectable structure, but the general had left it under orders from the war department to go to another part of the country. There was beside this house of General Macomb's, a small brick market house, a new structure, the pride of the city; a tavern of wood, of moderate pretentions; a council house of poles, set on end and the joints filled with lime mortar. There were besides, some hundred or less small houses and shops; and last but not least, Governor Cass's dwelling, a square structure of logs, lathed and plastered inside and out, and quite out of town, down the river bank at least three-quarters of a mile.

"The population of Detroit was mixed, the French-Canadian prevailing. There were many halfbreeds, and it being the season of the year when the Indians usually came in from their wintering grounds, the wild Chippewas seemed to be in undisputed possession. They did not appear over select in their language or manners; still they were quite inoffensive to the whites, especially the French traders, to whose every order and command they rendered instant obedience. No police existed or was necessary.

"Woodworth kept the principal hotel, which was well patronized. It was at Woodworth's that I observed the wall ornamented with a large map of Michigan, laying down nearly the whole interior of Michigan (on authority said to have been derived from the war department), as a swamp.

"The court was in session, held at the afore-mentioned council house, made of poles set on end. The whole court consisted of his honor the judge, three lawyers and as many suitors. One of the counsel, a Mr. Biddle, was discussing some obscure questions involving title to land; the court seemed in much perplexity; the opening counsel only made darkness more visible.

"The lawyers at length paused for the decision from the bench. It was in the afternoon of one of the hottest days in June; the court room seemed to broil—the judge being the chief victim. He wiped the perspiration from his naked poll with no seeming relief; at length, rising with much dignity, he proceeded, not to a decision of the case, but deliberately through the council room, and without explanation of any kind, marched into the street and thence to the wharf at the river, and sitting down with his feet hanging over the river, having on neither coat nor vest nor hat, amused himself for an hour or more, throwing sticks and pebbles at the fishes. Having, at length, apparently cooled his head and quieted his nerves, he rose, and with the same deliberation observed in his egress, returned to the court room and resumed his seat. The suitors and counsel being, probably, accustomed to his moods, had all quietly maintained their places during the recess, and were ready for a resumption of the case. The judge, as if nothing unusual had happened, proceeded to give his decision, which, if it did not please both parties, evidently satisfied them, as immediate acquiescence followed.

"I learned that with all his eccentricities, he failed not of securing the confidence of the people, both of the bar and of the suitors.

"Though a majority of the inhabitants of Detroit were of plebian order, Canadian and mixed blood prevailing, yet there was not wanting a good proportion of well-educated, intelligent, cultivated people, who would have graced almost any society; for open, free-hearted manners to strangers, and genuine hospitality, they were an honor to our common humanity.

"Detroit river presented most creditable improvements along its banks; the farms being occupied on the old French plan of one of three arpents (an arpent is one-seventh less than an English acre) in width and extending eighty arpents deep—the houses were generally a few rods apart on the river bank, and there was a halo of antiquity in their appearance. Orchards of apple and pear trees invariably occupied their front—the trees indicating a growth of a hundred years. Every point on the river bank was garnished with a windmill—water mills being unknown at that time in this part of the globe."

* * *

Referring again to Mr. Busby, the keeper of the yellow tavern (Cliff's) out Woodward Avenue near Grand Circus:

His son, Thomas Busby, now residing at Ypsilanti, furnishes a few particulars in regard to his father that may, perhaps, be of interest.

His father came here from London, England, in 1830, and opened the tavern in 1831, and continued it until 1838. He then sold the lease to a Mr. Cliff, who gave it its name, "Cliff's Tavern," which it afterwards retained until it was purchased and removed by the late H. H. LeRoy.

While Mr. Busby had the premises it was called the "Eagle Tavern," and the following is a copy of the printed card setting forth to the community what he proposed to furnish at his hostelry, prices, etc.:

EAGLE TAVERN.

GOOD ACCOMMODATIONS FOR TRAVELERS.

Rates as follows:

Boarding by the week	18s 0d
Ditto, by the day, with lodging	4s 6d
Ditto, by the meal	1s 6d
Cold meals	1s 6d
Span of horses to hay one night	3s 6d
One horse to ditto	1s 6d
Each carload of goods drawn for customers	1s 0d
Lodging	1s 0d

Good pasture for cattle.

One yoke of cattle per night.................................... 2s 0d

JAS. BUSBY.

Mr. Busby removed to Saginaw in 1836, it taking him three days to get there by land, with family and household effects. They camped out over night where Flint now is, there being but one dwelling there. They found but a few dwellings in Saginaw, one of them of considerable dimensions, owned by Mr. Campau, which they occupied. (Since this was penned this building has been torn down.)

Strange to relate, when they essayed to build themselves a home in Saginaw, they were compelled to import lumber for the purpose from Detroit.

* * *

Mr. LeRoy, some time after he bought the Cliff tavern site and adjoining lot, said he never expected to get his money back—things looked so blue out Woodward Avenue. The ground was so swampy that no one seemed to care to take it off his hands, so he was forced to occupy it himself, improving the grounds by draining, etc. He lived there for many years until Mr. David Whitney, Jr., persuaded him to take very much more than the property cost him—indeed so much more that Mr. LeRoy never regretted his Woodward avenue innvestment.

ELKANAH WATSON AND THE ERIE CANAL.

THAT Hon. Elkanah Watson, of Albany, N. Y., the projector and originator of the Erie canal, was closely identified with our people may be inferred from the fact that one of his sons, Joseph B., married a daughter of the Hon. James Witherell, and sister to Mrs. Thomas Palmer, mother of the senator. She dying, Mr. Watson married again. After a brief period Watson died and his widow married Maj. B. F. Larned, paymaster U. S. A., of this city. A daughter of Elkanah Watson (Emily) married George B. Larned, brother of General Charles Larned, of this city, and uncle of Sylvester Larned. He served in the war of 1812, with the rank of captain, and after the war was stationed in Detroit. He died at the home of his brother, General Charles Larned, southwest corner of Woodward Avenue and Larned Street, January 27, 1825.

Joseph B. Watson had by his first wife two sons, Eugene W. and James B., and by his second wife one son, George. Eugene W. was nearly all his life in the U. S. navy, served during the Civil War, and was during the latter part of his life in charge of one of the life-saving stations on the upper lakes. He married one of the St. Aubin girls (Matilda). He was the father of the late Lewis C. Watson, circuit court commissioner. James married a daughter of Judge Charles Moran.

B. Watson was a member of the Detroit bar. George Watson was a sutler at Fort Gratiot for some years. He married a daughter of James Williams (Eliza) of this city. He died in St. Louis many years ago.

This Elkanah Watson was a well-to-do merchant whose portrait was painted by Copley, the eminent British portrait painter, which was in itself a guarantee of respectability. He saw little of volunteer service, but during much of the revolution was in Europe, engaged in mercantile transactions. On his return he interested himself in many matters of public concern, particularly in the building of the Erie canal. While in Europe he investigated thoroughly the canal system in Flanders and Holland, and saw how easily the same system could be made to prevail in the United States, if capital or state aid could be induced to venture in the construction. By persistent effort he induced the canal commissioners of the State of New York to take hold of his project, and hence the Erie canal. That he was the projector of this canal, which proved such a vast boon to the country and particularly to the great west, is evidenced in a communication from the Hon. Robert Throop that appeared in the Geneva (N. Y.) *Gazette* February 19, 1819, in which he says:

"The successful progress of the Erie canal, and the immense benefits likely to arise from its completion, have lately excited a laudable curiosity to know who was the projector of the canal policy in this state. A just regard to the reputation of the state seems to require that the projector, if alive, should be favored with some decisive proof of public gratitude; and in case of his death, that his name should be handed down with becoming honor to posterity. It is fortunate for the reputation of the state that the projector is both known and alive; and I now, without fear of contradiction, declare him to be Elkanah Watson, of the city of Albany.

"The sagacious and comprehensive mind of that truly patriotic gentleman, in the year 1791, conceived the sublime idea of uniting, by means of navigable canals, the waters of the great lakes with those of the Hudson and Susquehanna."

The author of this letter, Hon. Robert Throop, of Geneva, N. Y., was the grandfather of the late Mrs. Alex. M. Campau, of this city.

In 1779, Mr. Watson sailed in a United States packet to France, in charge of dispatches from Congress for Dr. Benj. Franklin, then our minister at the Court of St. Cloud, and Monsieur De Vergennes, the prime minister of France, which he delivered in person as directed. He was in Paris at the time of the surrender of Cornwallis. Later on he was in London and was on the floor of the house of lords, December 5, 1783, and heard King George III. read his speech formally recognizing the United States of America as in the rank of nations.

In writing (September, 1791) in relation to the project of a canal to unite the waters of the Hudson and the great lakes, Watson said:

"In giving a stretch to the mind, into the womb of futurity, I saw those fertile regions, bounded west by the Mississippi, north by the great lakes, east by the Allegheny mountains, and south by the placid Ohio, overspread with millions of freemen, blessed with various climates, enjoying every variety of soil, and commanding the boldest inland navigation on the globe; clouded with sails, directing their course towards canals, alive with boats passing and repassing, giving and receiving reciprocal benefits from this wonderful country, prolific in such great resources, or, perhaps, passage boats, bearing distant travelers on their surface, with horses trotting on their embankments. In taking this bold flight in imagination, it was impossible to repress a settled conviction that a grand effort will be made to realize all my dreams —perhaps delusive."

Mr. Watson made a brief visit to his daughter, Mrs. Larned, in this city, arriving Sunday, July 2, 1818, on the schooner Franklin from Buffalo, which port they left on the 23d of June. He does not appear to have much to say about Detroit only in a general and pleasing way. He participated in a celebration of the Fourth of July, which was held in a field or orchard in the rear of the residence of Governor Cass, where he dined with a large collection of gentlemen and officers of the army.

PRINCE PHILIP AND QUEEN MARY.

THERE WERE GREAT DOINGS WHEN THEY WERE WEDDED AT WINCHESTER.

A SPANISH-ENGLISH ROYAL MATRIMONIAL ALLIANCE THAT DIDN'T HOLD VERY LONG.

THE approaching marriage of King Alfonso of Spain to the Princess Ena of Battenberg bring to mind a similar affair that occurred in 1554, when Prince Philip of Spain came to anchor in Southampton water, and, landing, proceeded to Winchester to Mary Tudor of England, an event heralded as being fraught with tremendous probabilities to Christianity.

After the contract was ratified and before Philip left Madrid for England the Spanish Marquis de las Navas was ordered to take Philip's first presents to his bride. We are told that the Marquis fitted himself out for his mission regardless of cost, and his splendor appears to have been equalled by the princely gifts of which he was the bearer and the noble hospitality extended to him in England.

Philip's offering to Mary consisted of "a great table diamond, mounted as a rose in a superb gold setting, valued at 50,000 ducats, a collar or necklace of 18 brilliants, exquisitely worked and set with dainty grace, valued at 32,000 ducats; a great diamond with a fine, large pearl pendant from it (this, it was said, was Mary's favorite jewel, and may be seen on her breast in most portraits). They were, we are told, the most lovely pair of gems ever seen in the world, and were worth 25,000 ducats. Then comes a list of pearls, diamonds, emeralds and rubies of inestimable value, and other presents without number for the queen and her ladies.

The account goes on to say that "each great noble—and there were 20 of them—took his train of servants in new liveries and the Prince (Philip) had a Spanish guard of 100 gentlemen in red and yellow, 100 Germans in the same uniform, but with silk facings, 100 archers on horseback, and 300 servants in the same gaudy colors of Arragon.

THE PRINCE'S VESSEL.

The ship selected to convey Philip and his suite to England was a fine merchant vessel, named the Espiritu Santo, and commanded by the bold Biscay mariner, Martin de Bertondona. A splendid sight it must have been with its towering, carved and gilded poop and forecastle. It was hung, we are told, from stem to stern with fine scarlet cloth, and aloft on every available spot were colored silk pennons. A royal standard, thirty yards long, of crimson damask, with the prince's arms painted on it, hung from the mizzen-mast. The fore-mast had ten pointed silk flags painted with the royal arms, and there were thirty other similar flags in the stays and shrouds. Three hundred sailors in red uniforms formed the crew, and we are assured that the effect of the ship was that of a lovely flower garden—as well it might be—and the cost of the decorations was 10,000 ducats.

It is further related how the queen (Mary) was anxious for her consort's arrival, and how she had ordered 1,000 gentlemen to await him with as many horses.

On the 12th of July Philip and his suite embarked in a sumptuous galley of twenty-four oars manned by sailors in scarlet and gold, with plumed hats of scarlet silk, and amidst music, singing and daring gymnastic feats of the marines, went on board the Espiritu Santo. The next day, Friday, at 3 in the afternoon, they set sail. They arrived without mishap in Southampton water Thursday, the 19th of July, where they were welcomed with a national salute by the combined English and Flemish fleets of thirty sail assembled to receive them.

On landing at Southampton Philip found awaiting him a beautiful white charger caparisoned in crimson velvet and gold, that was champing its bit hardly. The prince, it is said, must have looked an impressive figure with his dapper, erect bearing, his yellow beard, and close cropped yellow head, dressed as he was in black velvet and silver, his massive gold chains and priceless gems glittering in his velvet bonnet and at his neck and wrists:

EXCHANGE MESSAGES.

The queen was at Winchester and had learned post-haste of the landing of her future husband, and messengers were actively scurrying backwards and forwards through the pitiless rain of the next three days.

Early on Saturday morning the earl of Pembroke arrived from the queen with an escort for the prince of 200 gentlemen dressed in black velvet with gold chains and medals, and 300 others in scarlet cloth with velvet facings, all splendidly mounted.

The next morning, in a pouring rain, the royal cavalcade set out for Winchester, 3,000 strong. On the road 600 more gentlemen dressed in black velvet with gold chains met the prince, and when nearing Winchester six of the queen's pages, beautifully dressed in crimson brocade with gold sashes, with as many superb steeds, were encountered, who told Philip that the queen had sent the horses to him as a present. On their arrival at Winchester the party proceeded at once to the grand cathedral, which, it is said, impressed the Spaniards with wonder, and above all, to find that mass was as solemnly sung there as at Toledo.

A group of mitred bishops stood at the great west door, crosses raised and censers swinging and in solemn procession to the high altar, under a velvet canopy, they led the man whom they looked upon as God's chosen instrument to permanently restore their faith in England.

When the prince started for Winchester he was immediately surrounded by seventeen of the principal nobles of England and fifteen Spanish grandees. He was dressed in a black velvet surcoat adorned with diamonds, leather boots, and trunks and doublet of white satin embroidered with gold, but this delicate finery had to be covered by a red felt cloak to protect it from the rain. Notwithstanding this it was too wet for him to enter Winchester without a change, so he stayed at a hospital that had been a monastery one mile from the city, and there donned a black velvet surcoat covered with gold bugles and a suit of white velvet trimmed in the same way, and thus he entered, passing the red-clothed aldermen with gold keys on cushions and then to the grand cathedral.

After admiring the cathedral Philip and his court went to the dean's house, which had been prepared for his reception in order to allay the maiden scruples of the queen with regard to his sleeping under the same roof with her at the bishop's palace before the solemnization of the marriage.

A LITTLE DIVERSION.

The narrator goes on to say that after Philip had supped and presumably was thinking more of going to bed than anything else, the Lord Chamberlain and the Lord Steward went to him, it being 10 o'clock at night, and told him that the queen was waiting for him in her closet and wished him to visit her secretly with very few followers. He at once put on another gorgeous suit, consisting of a French surcoat embroidered in sliver and gold, and a doublet and trunks of white kid embroidered in gold. The party traversed a narrow lane between two gardens, and on reaching a door in the wall the Lord Steward told the prince that he could take with him such courtiers as he chose.

Philip did not seem disposed to run any risks, and construed the invitation in a liberal spirit, taking into the garden twelve or fifteen of his most distinguished followers. They found themselves in a beautiful garden with rippling fountains and arbors, which reminded them of the books of chivalry. The prince and his party entered by a little back door, and ascended a narrow winding staircase to the queen's closet. She was in a "long narrow room or corridor where they divert themselves," surrounded by four or five aged nobles and as many old ladies, the bishop of Winchester being also with her, and the whole party, we are told, were marvelously and richly dressed, the queen herself wearing a black velvet gown cut high in the English style, without any trimming; a petticoat of frosted silver, a wimple of black velvet, trimmed with gold, and a girdle and collar of wonderful gems. She was walking up and down when the prince entered, and as soon as she saw him went quickly towards him and kissed her hand to him before taking his. In return he kissed her on the mouth, in the English fashion, and she led him by the hand to a chair placed by the side of her own under a canopy. The queen spoke in French and her future husband in Spanish, and thus they made themselves well understood. The two lovers sat under their brocade canopy chatting for a long time, but this probably seemed somewhat slow to the bridegroom, who, after asking the queen to give her hand for all his Spaniards to kiss, as they loved her well, begged to be allowed to see her ladies, who were in another room. The queen went with him, and as the ladies approached, two by two, he kissed them all "in his way," with his plumed hat in his hand, "so as not to break the custom of the country, which is a very good one," the narrator says. Whether the queen thought it good on this occasion is not clear, but when her lover wanted to leave directly the extensive osculation was over she would not let him go, but carried him off for another long talk with her. When he had to leave her she playfully taught him to say "Good night," and he made this excuse for going to the ladies again to say it to them, but when he reached them he had forgotten the outlandish words and had to return to the queen to ask her, "whereat she was much pleased," but probably less so when he found it necessary to go back once more to the ladies to salute them with "God ni hit."

Philip slept late the next morning, and as soon as he was up the queen's tailor brought him two superb dresses, one made of very rich brocade profusely embroidered with gold bugles and pearls, with splendid diamonds for buttons, and the other of crimson brocade. His highness went to mass in a purple velvet surcoat with silver fringe and white satin doublet, and then after his private dinner went in great state to see the queen. She received him in the great hall of the palace with the courtiers ranged on a raised platform on each side. The great officers of state preceded her, and she was followed by fifty ladies splendidly dressed in purple velvet, and, having met her consort in the middle of the hall, she led him to the dais, where he stood in sweet converse with her for some time. Then Philip went to vespers and the queen to her chapel, and after supper they met again.

THE WEDDING.

The next day the wedding ceremony was performed by the bishop of Winchester. There were four services of meat and fish, each service consisting of thirty dishes, and minstrels played during the feast, while the solid splendor and pompous ceremony appear to have impressed the Spaniards with wonder not unmixed with envy.

Then after the queen had pledged all her guests in a cup of wine, and a herald had proclaimed the titles of Philip as king of England, France, Naples and Jerusalem, prince of Spain and count of Flanders, the royal party retired to another chamber, with the English and Spanish nobles, where the time passed in pleasant converse until the ball began.

After dancing until nightfall supper was served with the same ceremony as the dinner, and then more talk and gallant compliment, after which all retired for the night.

HAPPINESS SHORT-LIVED.

It appears that the couple got on very nicely for a while, at least, as a letter written from Richmond of date 19th August, says:

"Their majesties are the happiest couple in the world, and are more in love with each other than I can say here. He never leaves her, and on the road is always by her side, lifting her into the saddle and helping her to dismount. He dines with her publicly and they go to mass together on feast days."

Great preparations were made for the entrance of the queen and her consort into London, which they did amidst the greatest rejoicings. The signs of vengeance visited upon the Wyatt rebels had been cleared away and the city was as bright and gay as paint and gilding could make it. The "galluses" from which the fifty dead bodies of the London trainbandsmen who had deserted to Wyatt at Rochester bridge were cleared away from the doors of the houses in which their families lived and the grinning skulls of the high offenders were taken from the gates and from London bridge.

Despite all this Philip and the Spanish nobles found, instead of a submissive people ready to bow the neck at once to the new king and his followers, a country where even the native sovereign's power was strictly circumscribed, and where the foreigner's only hope of domination was by force of arms, and this they saw in the present case was impossible.

Philip, recognizing that his sacrifices had been in vain, and that he could never rule in England, made the best of an unfortunate speculation, and in September of the following year, with all gravity, courtesy and dignity, left Mary to die of broken heart, alone, disappointed and forsaken.

THE "FORT STREET GIRLS."

FORT Street West in the early days was the aristocratic street of the city, where ebbed and flowed almost the entire social swim of Detroit. I recall the faces, forms and names of many of the fair daughters of that street and immediate locality who ruled the hour. Misses Cornelia and Julia Howard, daughters of Colonel Joshua Howard; Misses Eliza and Mary Inman, daughters of Captain Inman, United States navy (who had command of the U. S. S. Michigan); Misses Rosa and Alexandrine Sheldon, daughters of Thomas C. Sheldon; Miss Frank Gillett, daughter of Mr. Shadrac Gillett; Miss Lizzie Whiting, daughter of Dr. J. L. Whiting; Miss Sarah Gillman, niece of Mr. Mason Palmer; Misses Mary and Julia Palmer, daughters of Mr. Thomas Palmer; Miss Mary Palmer, daughter of Mr. John Palmer; Misses Helen and Louisa Chapin, daughters of Dr. Chapin Miss Marion Forsythe, daughter of Major Robert Forsythe; Miss Eliza (Puss) Knapp, daughter of Mrs. John Owen (nee Knapp), Miss Jane Cook, sister of Mrs. Owen; Misses Mary and Harriet Larned, daughters of General Charles Larned; Misses Eliza, Mary and Harriet Williams, daughters of James Williams; Miss Louisa Heath; Miss Kate Hinchman, daughter of widow Hinchman; Misses Eunice and Ellen Hunt, daughters of Major Hunt, paymaster U. S. A.; Misses Brooks, daughters of Colonel Edward Brooks; Misses Kercheval, daughters of B. B. Kercheval, and Misses Stewart, daughters of Charles Stewart.

These young ladies, joined with those that upper Jefferson Avenue could furnish, such as Miss Adeline Rice, daughter of Dr. R. S. Rice; Misses Sarah, Martha and Harriet Brewster, daughters of William Brewster; Misses Kate and Matilda Connor, sisters of Mrs. Darius Lamson; Miss Emily Trowbridge, niece of Mrs. Lamson; Misses Martha and Harriet Witherell, daughters of Judge B. F. H. Witherell, and Miss Sue Dibble, the daughter of Colonel Dibble; the two daughters of Chancellor Farnsworth; Miss Cornelia Platt, daughter of Attorney-General

Platt; Miss Louisa Whistler, daughter of Colonel Whistler, U. S. A., and Misses Louise and Francis Ladue, daughter and niece of Andrew Ladue, presented as brilliant a galaxy of feminine youth and beauty as could be found west of Albany. In this category must be included Miss Eliza Throop, daughter of Lawyer Throop; Misses Eliza, Elizabeth, Mary and Harriet Ingersoll, daughters of Justus Ingersoll; Miss Martha Mullett, daughter of John Mullett; the Misses Godfroy, daughters of Peter Godfroy; Miss Cornelia Wales, daughter of Austin Wales; Misses Garland (Virginia and Louise), daughters of Colonel Garland, U. S. A.; Misses Chipman, daughters of Judge Henry Chipman; Miss Martha Kearsley, daughter of Major Kearsley; Miss Fannie Truax, daughter of John Truax; Miss Sophia Griswold, niece of Mrs. John Palmer; Miss Anna Jackson, daughter of Mr. Charles Jackson; Miss Charlotte Chase, daughter of Mr. Thomas Chase; Miss Mary Williams, daughter of General John R. Williams; Misses Moran, Matilda, Julia and Mary, daughters of Judge Charles Moran; Miss Mary Clark, daughter of Dr. Thomas B. Clark; Misses Davenport, Anne, Sarah and Matilda, daughters of Mr. Louis Davenport; Miss Elizabeth Gardner, sister of Mrs. John Y. Pettie; Miss Maggie Moore, niece of Dr. R. S. Rice; Miss Julia Willcox, sister of E. N. and O. B. Willcox.

Perhaps I might add Miss Emily V. Mason, but she really belonged to an older set, which included Miss Isabella Norvell, daughter of Hon. John Norvell; Miss Jane Dyson, daughter of Captain Dyson, U. S. A.; Miss Emma Schwarz, daughter of General John E. Schwarz; Miss Isabella Cass, daughter of General Cass; Miss Maggie Biddle, daughter of Hon. John Biddle; Miss Samantha Brush, sister of Edmund A. Brush; Miss Sarah Roby, sister of Henry M. and Reuel Roby; Miss Josephine Desnoyers, daughter of Peter Desnoyers; Miss Annie Dequindre, cousin of Miss Desnoyers; Miss Annie McDonnell, daughter of Hon. John McDonnell; Misses Sibley, daughters of Judge Sibley; Miss Sarah Abbott, daughter of Judge James Abbott; Miss Cassandra Brady, daughter of General Hugh Brady; Miss Caroline Whistler, niece of Mrs. Judge James Abbott; Miss Brevoort, daughter of Commodore Brevoort; Misses Adelaide and Catherine Campau, daughters of Mr. Joseph Campau; two daughters of Mr. Barnabus Campau; two daughters of Colonel Knaggs; Miss Watson, sister of John and James Watson; Misses Larned, daughters of General Charles Larned (Jane, Kate and Julia.)

On the other hand the list of beaux contained such names as John W. Strong, Jr., John T. Hunt, Frank Hunt, Barney Campau, A. M. Campau, Henry M. Roby, Samuel Lewis, Charles S. Adams, Dr. Rufus Brown, Dr. Scovell, Dr. Farnsworth, Edwin M. Pitcher, William P. Doty, Albion Turner, Dr. L. H. Cobb, George A. Cooper, Charles Dibble, George Dibble, Henry A. Wight, J. C. D. Williams, Joshua Carew, H. Norton Strong, La Fayette Knapp, James C. Parsons, Dr. George B. Russel, Benjamin Vernor, Leonard Watkins, Decatur Norris, William A. Heartt, John Rucker, Charles J. Paddock, nephew of Mr. Charles Jackson, Charles A. Trowbridge, E. A. Lansing, John B. Palmer, Friend Palmer, Alex. Lewis, William Gray, James A. Armstrong, A. S. Kellogg, Alfred Cox, Walter Ingersoll, Chand. W. Seymour, H. T. Stringham, James W. Bradford, William P. Doty, W. L. Whipple, Addison Mandell, H. A. Schoolcraft, Eben N. Willcox, O. B. Willcox, J. P. C. Emmons, Norman Emmons, Frank P. Markham, William G. Lee, Simeon Leake, Frank B. Phelps, A. H. Guise, Jerrold Gray, Dr. Egge, Alex K. Howard, John Rumney, Will Rumney, Albert Crane, W. B. Wesson, George W. Bissell, Griffith Jones, Samuel Suydam, Alfred Hunter, and H. J. Buckley. No greater gallants than they in their day could be found. To these might be added officers of the United States army stationed here from time to time as well as the officers of the United States navy attached to the U. S. S. Michigan and their ladies.

I do not know what became of Alfred Cox and A. S. Kellogg.

James Bradford went to Milwaukee and engaged in the piano business.

Henry A. Schoolcraft drifted to New York, after he had finished his law studies and enlisted in General Stevens's regiment, then organizing for duty in California. The regiment reached its destination in due season and, after serving his time, he entered the employ of Captain Sutter, and was in his employ when gold was discovered in his sawmill race. He died out there many years ago.

Ted P. C. Emmons became a distinguished member of the Detroit bar and, after some years practice here, went to Arkansas and became its attorney-general. I think he died there.

Norman Emmons, like his two brothers, the judge and Ted, took up the law, and he and John Van Dyke (brother of James A.) started practice in Milwaukee. They were quite successful for years, when the partnership was dissolved, and Norman returned to this city, where he died only a few years ago.

William G. Lee died a few years ago in New York city. ·He was agent there for a large insurance company.

Ferrold Grey returned to Ireland, where he died many years ago.

Griffith Jones drifted to El Paso, Texas, engaged in business, and died there many years ago.

Samuel Suydam, while here, was the representative of the extensive New York house of Suydam, Sage & Co. His manners were pleasing, he was lavish in the expenditure of money, and a faultless dresser. He soon became quite a favorite and flourished until disaster overtook the firm of Suydam, Sage & Co., when he returned to New York.

Alfred Hunter and Suydam were warm friends and associates. The former was not quite the lady's man that Suydam was, if anything, a more faultless dresser. He never appeared on the street except in the most correct attire. The lining of his coat, which was usually a sack of black cloth, was invariably of white silk. Hunter was the proprietor of an extensive flouring mill at Ypsilanti. What the end of these two gentlemen was I never knew.

John T. Hunt, of the firm of Hunt & Roby, was a remarkably handsome man, a general favorite and deservedly so. He died many years ago, unmarried.

Dr. Rufus Brown led an easy bachelor life for years and finally married the sister of Mrs. General Swift. He died about 20 years ago.

Edward M. Pitcher served in the Mexican War, as a lieutenant in the First Regiment Michigan Volunteers. On his return here, he engaged in the boot and shoe business with Alfred Knight. After a while he severed his connection with Mr. Knight, and on the departure of Colonel Bennet Riley's regiment for California he and James Mott Williams joined the sutler's department and went out with it around the horn. Pitcher remained there, and died there. Williams after some years returned to this city.

William P. Doty was for many years with his brother, Henry Doty, in the auction and commission business. Finally he and his two brothers, George and Henry, built a sawmill at Saginaw and engaged in the lumber business. After a few years of success William died there, unmarried.

Albion Turner, after many years' service with his brother-in-law, Benj. G. Stimson, caught the California fever, then quite prevalent, and journeyed there across the plains. He was at first fairly successful, but went into an unfortunate venture, the freighting of a vessel with a stock of miscellaneous goods for trading along the Pacific coast towards Alaska. He and his vessel got away from San Francisco all right, but they were never heard of after.

Geo. A. Cooper, after quitting school, took service with his father, David Cooper, assisting him in the care of his various interests. He died unmarried, about 1864.

Charles Dibble, son of Orville B. Dibble, joined his father in the proprietorship of the Biddle House. When his father died, Charles retired from the hotel business and went into other pursuits. He and Mr. Higham engaged in the manufacture of a burning fluid. Their establishment was located on Dequindre Street, northeast corner of Guoin. They were progressing quite successfully when one morning an explosion completely wrecked the whole concern, instantly killing Dibble and Higham, besides one or two of the employes. Dibble married Miss Davis, a sister of Clayton Davis, a Lake Superior mining operator. She survived him and married Henry Warner Newberry.

Geo. Dibble entered the United States navy, and died many years ago in California. Both of the Dibble boys will be remembered as two bright, genial attractive young men.

Devereaux Williams (son of General John R.) was a favorite in the young society of that day. During the Mexican War he saw service as a lieutenant in Captain A. T. McReynolds's company of dragoons. He was wounded in the arm at the capture of the City of Mexico. He went to California in 1849 and spent some years there. He returned shortly before the death of his father and remained here, employing his time in the care of the inheritance left him. He married the widow of Captain Stanton, U. S. A. Mrs. Stanton was a niece of General Alex. Macomb. Both died many years ago.

Joshua Carew, after severing his connection with Carne, Duncan & Emerson in the brewing business, went to New York city for a while. He returned, however, and took hold of the old brewery that was where Dwight's lumber yard now is, and operated it for a short time, but failing health compelled him to give it up. He died many years ago. He was the last one to do business in the "Old Brewery."

William A. Heartt left our circle early and branched out in the northern part of the state. He, I understand, is at present a citizen of Caro, and in comfortable circumstances.

John A. Rucker is yet alive and is a prosperous farmer and land owner at Grosse Isle.

Henry L. Newberry was with his Uncle Oliver in the vessel, steamboat and warehouse business for many years. He married Miss Maggie Moore, sister of William P. Moore, and niece of Mrs. Dr. R. G. Rice. Henry died some years ago in New Orleans, where he had gone on a business venture. His widow still survives him.

Charles J. Paddock, nephew of Charles Jackson, drifted away to Cincinnati many years ago. He was for some years chief clerk for Theodore H. Eaton, druggist.

Marion Forsythe and Eliza (Puss) Knapp were the most vivacious of all that bright galaxy that went by the name of the "Fort Street Girls," and were among the leaders in the social swim. Marion had at that time quite a flirtation with a Scottish nobleman, the "Laird of Inches," visiting here, and it was thought he might carry her off, but nothing came of it. She married Prof. Antisell, attached to some department in Washington, a widower with two daughters.

Eliza Knapp married Frank Hunt, son of Judge Hunt, and after married Mr. Albert Prince, barrister of Sandwich, also a member of parliament from Essex County.

I will try and give, as far as memory serves, the after life of the remainder of the feminine, as well as that of the masculine members of Detroit's gay society of that day.

Cornelia Howard married John W. Strong, capitalist.

Julia Howard married Walter Ingersoll, cashier Michigan Insurance Co. Bank.

Eliza Inman married a son of Bishop Odenheimer, of Philadelphia.

Rosa Sheldon married Henry A. Guise, commission merchant, of this city.

Alexandrine Sheldon married Barney Campau, and after his decease, became the wife of R. Storrs Willis.

Miss Frank Gillett married Oren Howard, son of Charles Howard.

Sara Gilman, niece of Mrs. Mason Palmer, married Charles Young, a lawyer in this city. After his demise she spent twelve years in Paris, France, engaged in studying the system of street cleaning and sewerage of that city, also the construction of flats or apartment houses. She returned to this country to reside in Hartford, Ct., after having made herself proficient in these specialties.

Martha Palmer, niece of Mason Palmer, married John Rumney, grocer of this city.

Miss Mary Palmer, daughter of Thomas Palmer, married Henry M. Roby, of the forwarding and commission firm of Hunt & Roby. The firm dissolving, Mr. and Mrs. Roby removed to Monroeville, Ohio.

Julia Palmer married Henry W. Hubbard, of Kenosha, Wis. After a few years' residence in the latter city, they removed to New York. After a residence there of some years, Mr. Hubbard contracted some permanent stomach trouble, and with his wife visited the home of her father here, in hope that a change of scene might afford him relief. But he died soon after their arrival in this city. After a while she married Hon. Hugh Moffat, at one time mayor of this city.

Mary Palmer, daughter of John Palmer, died early, unmarried.

Helen Chapin, daughter of Dr. Chapin, married H. Norton Strong, vessel owner of this city, brother of John W. Strong.

Jane Cook, sister of Mrs. John Owen, Mrs. Owen dying, she, after the death of her sister, married Mr. Owen.

Mary Larned married Alexander K. Howard, son of Col. Joshua Howard.

Harriet Larned married Will P. Rumney, son of Robert Rumney, of this city.

Eliza Williams married George Watson, son of Mrs. Major B. F. Larned, by a former husband. Mr. Watson was at the time sutler at Fort Gratiot.

THE "FORT STREET GIRLS." 941

Mary Williams married Henry J. Buckley, of the firm of G. O. Williams & Co., commission merchants.

Louisa Heath married Mr. Stone, of New York City, of the firm of Bowen, McNamee & Co.

The daughters of Col. Edward Brooks: The eldest, Margaret Ann, married Judge Charles Whipple, of the Michigan Supreme Court. The second, Adeline, died of consumption, unmarried. The third, Octavia, married Chandler W. Seymour, connected with the Farmers' and Mechanics' Bank, of this city. After many years they removed to San Francisco. The fourth, Emma, died just on the verge of womanhood, a most charming girl and the admiration of all who had the pleasure of knowing her. Rebecca, the fifth, married Dr. J. B. Scovell, of this city. The sixth, Mary, married Mr. Whitney, a rich gentleman of New York. Emily married Francis P. Markham, of the dry goods house of Thompson & Markham. Elizabeth married Henry Scovell, son of Dr. Scovell. Carrie married Philip Guliger.

Elizabeth Hale, daughter of John Hale, married William F. Driggs, of the firm of Macey & Driggs, land agents, this city.

Eliza Kercheval married Lieutenant Frank Woodbridge, U. S. A., aid at the time to General Hugh Brady. Harriet, the second daughter, married Mr. Hudson, from Lake Superior. Alice, the third daughter, died unmarried many years ago. Mary, the fourth daughter, married Moses W. Field, of the firm of Stephens & Field. Later Mr. Field became member of Congress from this district.

The Misses Stewart, daughters of Lawyer Charles Stewart: One became the wife of Lieutenant, afterwards Commodore, William D. Whiting, United States navy, and son of Major Henry Whiting, at one time stationed in this city as quartermaster, United States army. The other became the wife of William Gray, lawyer, this city.

Adeline Rice married Henry Kibbee, of Mt. Clemens.

Sara Brewster married Joseph G. Hill, of the firm of G. & J. G. Hill, grocers of this city. Martha died many years ago unmarried. Hattie married Jonathan Thompson.

Matilda Connor, sister of Mrs. Darius Lamson, married Dr. Egge, of this city.

Emily Trowbridge, niece of Mrs. Lamson, married a gentleman from Rochester, N. Y.

Martha Witherell died of consumption just on the verge of womanhood, widely lamented.

Harriet Witherell married the writer of these recollections, and after twenty-eight years of happy married life passed to the beyond.

Sue Dibble died in early life, about 1846, unmarried, leaving a wide void in the young social circle of that day.

The two daughters of Chancellor Farnsworth—one married Lieutenant O. B. Willcox, U. S. A., afterwards a retired brigadier-general, U. S. A. The other married a gentleman, a non-resident of Michigan, whose name I do not recall.

General Willcox married for his second wife, Julia, daughter of John McReynolds, Detroit.

Louise Ladue married Colonel William W. Duffield.

Miss Frank Ladue married Mr. Anson Eldred, of Milwaukee.

Jennie Fenton, of Flint, sister of Colonel W. M. Fenton, of the Eighth Michigan Infantry, resided here with her sister, Mrs. Joseph Clark. She married Samuel Lewis, of the firm of Lewis & Graves, forwarding and commission merchants, this city.

Alex. K. Howard, after the loss of his wife, married Lizzie Whiting, daughter of Dr. J. L. Whiting.

Eunice and Ellen Hunt, daughters of Major Hunt, paymaster, U. S. A. The former married Dr. Tripler, surgeon, U. S. A., stationed here; the other married Charles Bissell, forwarding and commission merchant, this city.

Cornelia Platt married a gentleman in Brooklyn, N. Y.

Louisa Whistler married Wm. Helm, a gentleman from Kentucky, who joined the southern confederacy.

Julia Willcox married David A. McNair, druggist, here.

Charlotte Chase married Dr. Casgrain, of Windsor.

Mary Williams (daughter of General John R.), married, first, David Smart, of this city; second, Commodore James P. McKinstry, U. S. N.

Matilda Moran married Jas. B. Watson, this city; Julia Moran married General Isaac D. Toll.

Mary Moran married William Robert Mix, Cleveland, Ohio.

Benjamin Vernor married the sister of Mrs. William L. Whipple.

John Rucker married Miss Fannie Traux.

Mary Ingersoll married Mr. Carmen, a merchant residing at Lockport, N. Y.

Eliza Throop married Alex. M. Campau, this city.

Elizabeth Gardner married Mr. Miller, an extensive lumber dealer, Chicago.

Anna Jackson married, first, Leonard Watkins, and second, Jonathan Thompson.

Laura Chipman married General Henry L. Chipman, U. S. A.; Eliza, William Baby, Windsor. Katherine died unmarried.

Martha Kearsley married J. Howard Webster.

Louisa Chapin married Theodore H. Hinchman.

Sophia Griswold married Charles Vail.

Martha Mullett married Mr. Forster, a Lake Superior mining engineer.

Elizabeth Godfroy married John Watson, dry goods merchant, this city.

Carrie Godfroy, the other daughter, is still living.

Kate Hinchman married Joseph Law, this city.

Cornelia Wales married, first, Mr. LaFayette Knapp; second, Alex. H. Newbould.

Virginia Garland married Lieutenant George Deas, adjutant Fifth United States Infantry.

Louise Garland married Lieutenant Longstreet, U. S. A.; during Civil War, Lieutenant General, C. S. A.

Eliza Ingersoll married Frank B. Phelps, this city.

Elizabeth Ingersoll married Alex. Lewis, this city.

Harriet Ingersoll married Anthony Dudgeon, this city.

Mary Clark, daughter of Dr. Thos. B. Clark, married James C. Parsons, Detroit.

Maggie Moore, niece of Mrs. Dr. R. L. Rice, married Henry L. Newberry.

Dr. Farnsworth married Kate Connor, this city.

Henry A. Wight married Sara Davenport.

William B. Wesson married Mrs. Hill, widow of Brittan Hill.

Albert Crane married a lady from the east and moved to Chicago.

James A. Armstrong married, first, Miss Sibley, daughter of Judge Sibley; second, Miss Bates, of Canandaigua, N. Y.

H. T. Stringham married a daughter of John W. Strong, this city.

William L. Whipple married Miss Fairchild, of Cornell, N. Y.

Eben N. Willcox married Louise Cole, daughter of Henry S. Cole, this city.

Addison Mandell married Miss Chittenden, daughter of William Chittenden, this city.

Frank P. Markham married a daughter of James O. Hill, this city.

Dr. George B. Russel married Miss Anne Davenport.

General John H. King, U. S. A., married Matilda Davenport.

Charles S. Adams married Miss Sibley, daughter of Judge Sibley.

General Henry R. Mizner married a daughter of Colonel Joshua Howard.

BELLES AND BEAUX OF BYGONE DAYS.

In a previous paper I omitted to mention Martha and Clara Griswold, daughters of John Griswold, who kept the American Hotel (Biddle House) in 1844-5. Martha, the elder, married Captain Carter L. Stevenson, Fifth U. S. Infantry. Clara married Lieutenant Paul Guise, of the same regiment. Guise was the brother of the late Harry Guise, of this city.

Also Frances Roberts, daughter of Colonel E. J. Roberts, father of Colonel Horace L. Roberts, First Michigan Volunteer Infantry. Miss Roberts married George R. Griswold, son of John Griswold.

Martha Kearsley was married to J. Howard Webster, a young hardware merchant, in 1840. Mrs. Webster died in the house (Kearsley house) she was married in, which is now standing at the northwest corner of Jefferson Avenue and Randolph Street, in 1862. Mrs. Webster was secretary of the Mt. Vernon Association when it was started in Michigan by Mrs. Elon Farnsworth as state agent. She was a life member of the Protestant Orphan Asylum and for many years on its board. She was the first president of the Home of the Friendless. Being the granddaughter and daughter of soldiers, she was earnestly interested in army work at the beginning of the Civil War. Dying at the early age of 42, the second year of the war, Detroit lost a notable woman.

John W. Strong, Jr., was first in the hardware business, as partner of Alex. H. Newbould, and then in the grocery business for himself, and next in real estate. He acquired a competency.

Barney Campau had all he could do to take care of the large estate left him by his father. His tragic and early taking off will be well remembered.

John B. Palmer married a daughter of the confederacy, which took him south. He entered the rebel service and remained in it until the close of the war. He returned to Detroit, but the feeling was so strong against him that he concluded to take up his residence at Columbus, S. C. He died there many years ago.

A. L. Kellogg was at one time in partnership with Marsh Mead, in the forwarding and commission business. He was an expert bookkeeper, and his services in that capacity were much sought after.

Samuel Lewis was associated with many prominent men in the forwarding and commission business on the dock, from time to time, and acquired wealth and a first-class business reputation. He died in Europe many years ago while on a trip there.

Charles S. Adams, a brother of Mrs. Sheldon McKnight, was of the firm of Adams & Ashley, painters and decorators; afterwards of the firm of Whiting & Adams, tax, insurance and real estate agents. A very popular gentleman. He was gifted with a fine voice, and was the leader in St. Paul's Episcopal choir. Many will remember this choir, composed of Dr. and Mrs. Terry, Charles S. Adams, Charles A. Trowbridge and one or two others whose names have escaped me.

E. A. Lansing married Miss Annie Dequindre, granddaughter of Peter J. Desnoyers. Lansing was a well known insurance agent here for a long time. He died here many years ago.

Dr. Geo. B. Russel, though classed among the older set, thought himself young enough to claim the hand of Miss Annie Davenport in marriage. All will remember Dr. Russel, he died so recently.

H. Norton Strong was an extensive vessel and steam tug owner. He died many years ago. Thomas Pitts married a daughter of his.

Lafayette Knapp was in the drug business for quite a while on Woodward Avenue, west side, between Fort and Congress Streets. After his marriage to Miss Wales, he quit business, retired to a farm in Erin, Macomb County, and after two or three years died there.

Simeon Leake came from the Albany City Bank, was teller in the F. & M. Bank here for three or four years and then returned to Albany.

Dr. Egge will be remembered favorably by many. He was a skillful physician and enjoyed a large practice.

John Rumney was a successful grocery merchant for years, until the day of his death. William Rumney was for a short time with his brother, John. He was for some years secretary of the Board of Trade.

Frank B. Phelps was an extensive fur dealer for years, also dealt heavily in beans. He was acting mayor of Detroit when a negro riot occurred in front of the jail on Beaubien Street.

A. H. Guise was a native of Philadelphia. After his advent here, he became one of the firm of Armstrong, Sibley & Co., forwarding and commission merchants. He continued in the business for quite a period, and then engaged in other pursuits. He will be remembered most favorably by many of the present as a man of strict integrity and as a finished, courteous gentleman.

James C. Parsons was of the firm of Parsons and Croul, until he removed to Chicago. He passed through the fire there and met with great loss. He died quite recently at Whitestone, Long Island, N. Y.

William Gray, the witty, genial Irish barrister—the large number of persons of the present day who knew him regret that he died so young.

Dr. Scovell came to this city with Dr. Rufus Brown. He was a gay society man, a fine gentleman and a skillful practitioner.

Mr. Henry T. Stringham was a bank man during his residence here. A fine, courteous gentleman.

Frank Hunt, brother of John T. Hunt, went to Winnipeg, Canada. It was almost a wilderness then. He took up government lands, near the latter city, and resided on them until his death, which happened the fore part of 1905. He became quite familiar with the language and habits of the Indian tribes in that locality and wrote an elaborate and extended account of their manners, customs, etc.

Dr. J. H. Farnsworth was the dentist of the city almost up to the day of his death. He was exceedingly clever in his profession.

Dr. L. H. Cobb will be well and favorably remembered as the skillful practitioner, the, at one time, efficient head of the old Volunteer fire department, one of the first commissioners of the paid fire department and manager of the Hargreaves Manufacturing Co. He died in the service of the latter company.

Leonard Watkins was the nephew of Mr. Geo. W. Bissell. After his marriage to Miss Jackson he removed to Milwaukee, and died there a short time after.

Walter Ingersoll will be well remembered as the cashier of the Michigan Insurance Company Bank. A very companionable gentleman who had hosts of friends.

Addison Mandell came here with Theodore Romeyn, with whom he was associated for some years. He later became clerk of the United States Court and remained in that capacity until his decease. Mrs. Mandell survives him.

Henry A. Wight, son of Buckminster Wight, and brother of Stanley G. Wight, with both of whom he was associated in the lumber business, died early in life and in the midst of a successful career.

William B. Wesson, from a small beginning in the real estate business, amassed a large fortune. He died comparatively early in life, leaving to his widow and heirs his large possessions which they are now enjoying.

Alex. M. Campau is yet very much alive, and I am pleased to say enjoys his comfortable fortune and the society of his surviving family and friends.

Benjamin Vernor—"Ben" has not been gone from among us sufficient years to blot out his memory, but with the many who knew him in life, it is as fresh as ever. And all his good qualities are remembered; bad ones he never had.

Henry J. Buckley was a very bright business man. He was the right hand of Uncle Gurdon Williams, and the first manager of the Detroit & Pontiac Railroad, built in 1842, or about that date. After this he was associated with Mr. Williams in business on the dock. On the death of the former he succeeded to the business, which he carried on successfully, and at his death left a fine fortune to his widow. He was at one time a member of the legislature from this county.

James A. Armstrong, of the firm of Armstrong, Sibley & Co., on the dock, foot of Cass Street. He afterwards filled many responsible business positions, among which was the head of the freight department of the Detroit & Milwaukee Railroad.

Alexander Lewis, I am happy to say, is with us yet, hale and hearty, enjoying life, the companionship of his children and the society of his numerous and attached friends.

Charles A. Trowbridge, of the firm of Brady & Trowbridge, grocers, and later of the firm of Trowbridge, Chipman & Rood, forwarding and commission on the dock, was a very genial, companionable man, fond of music and socially inclined. He was largely interested in Lake Superior ventures, and at the time of his death, which occurred in New York not many years ago, he was agent for the Silver Islet Mining Co.

Mr. R. B. Ross recently published an article on the old Catholic seminary, still standing on the corner of Randolph and Larred Streets. He covers almost the entire ground. I will supply some deficiencies. I was, as he states, a pupil of Edwin Jerome when he taught school in this building, and my sister was a pupil of the Sisters conducting the seminary. I will give as near as maybe the names of the boys attending Mr. Jerome's school, about 1830: Thos. Williams, J. Mott Williams, George Doty, Lewis Rowland, Barney and Alex. M. Campau, Henry Chipman, Wm. Miller, Sam Woodworth, Alex. Sibley, Henry Brevoort, Tom Biddle, Edmund A. Kearsley, Jim Clark, Friend Palmer, Geo. Jerome, Ordo Watson, Andries, Henry and Wm. L. Whipple.

Mr. Sears had a boys' school, about this time, in the upper part of the old council house. It was a rival partially to the one kept by Edwin Jerome, and intended more particularly for boys of more advanced years. Most of the scholars I call to mind. Their names were: Theo. Williams, Dan Campau, Tom Biddle, Joe Norvell, Isaac Rowland, Alex. H. Sibley, Henry W. Roby, Henry J. Canniff, Lewis Cass, Jr., Humes and Andrew Porter, Ben May and others.

Names of the young girls who attended the Sisters' seminary in same building, but later: Misses Biddle, Sibley, Chipman, Kearsley, Schwarz, Norvell, Hurd, Brooks, Palmer, Brush, Desnoyers, Dequindre, Campau, Rowland, Doty, Watson, St. Aubin, Larned, Dyson, Abbott, Bronson, Campbell, Willson, Chapin, Brevoort, Berthelet and Whipple.

The Andries were influential citizens, and lived opposite this building, as did the Clarks. Adjoining the convent, towards Jefferson Avenue, lived the Watsons, John, James and Thomas, also their sister, who married Judge O'Flynn. The Jerome family occupied this convent building during the time the son Edwin had his school in it.

The Whipples lived on the northeast corner of Larned and Randolph Streets. From this family came Chief Justice Charles Whipple; Henry L. Whipple, at one time deputy auditor-general; Wm. L. Whipple, conspicuous in the Mexican and also in the Civil War, and a daughter who was the second wife of Peter Desnoyers.

In the rear of the Whipple house was Noyes's livery stable, and between it and Miss Lyons's school house, was a vacant space, where the circus people pitched their tents. It was here that I first saw Dan Rice, the renowned clown of those days. Father Richard also lived close by, on Randolph Street, south side, between the latter street and Larned. I do not remember the elder Clarks, but I recall the son, "Jim" Clark, who was a tall and powerful athlete, whom no one cared to tackle. He was a Democrat and invariably their champion. He was quiet and peaceable enough when not molested; otherwise a terror. Placidius Ord married a sister of his. Ord was at one time a member of the territorial legislature from Chippewa County, and later was its librarian. General E. O. C. Ord, U. S. A., a West Point graduate, and a distinguished officer in the Civil War, was a brother.

The Johnsons also lived in this vicinity. Johnson was at the battle of Monguagon, commanding the cavalry, and on account of his impetuous riding was called the Murat of the American cavalry. He had two sons—Jesse, who was in the dry goods business with John Watson; the other (I think) entered the priesthood. It is my impression that the Johnsons were relatives of the Watsons.

Judge Sibley lived on the northeast corner of Jefferson Avenue and Randolph Street.

It has been lately asserted that Miss Lyons was teaching school in the convent, southwest corner of Randolph and Larned, when the St. Clair sisters came in 1833, and after their departure in 1837, remained in the same convent Charity. This is a mistake, as Charles Trombley, of this city, whose wife, Miss

950   EARLY DAYS IN DETROIT.

Elizabeth Knaggs, an adopted daughter of Miss Lyons, asserts to the contrary. I also from my own personal knowledge make the same statement that he does.

Miss Lyons's schoolhouse and residence was directly opposite Father Richard's. I have some reason for remembering it, as my two cousins (Senator Palmer's sisters), attended her school, and when the streets were in a muddy condition, which was generally the case in the spring and fall, it was always up to me to harness the horse onto the French cart, and take them to and fro. Miss Lyons and her two adopted daughters were familiar figures to me in my young days. I knew Miss Lyons well, or as a boy might know a person old enough to be his mother. The school room was in the residence, which she owned. Many of the first families in the city sent their daughters to her school.

In the immediate vicinity on Jefferson Avenue and Randolph Street, was the Hull House (later on Biddle House), the Council House, residences of Colonel John Biddle, E. A. Brush, Detroit City Bank, Counselor O'Keefe, Major Jonathan Kearsley, Dr. Wm. Brown, Swan's tavern (Swan was at one time sheriff of Wayne County. He was brother-in-law of J. C. Sheldon), John Truax, Thos. F. Knapp, Barnabas Campau, Dr. McCrosky, Judge Henry Chipman, Oliver Miller, Captain Fearson, Ellis Doty, Peter T. Desnoyers, John Y. Petty, Simon Poupard, Wm. Krinze, Wm. Brewster, D. R. L. Rice, Sheriff Wilson, Henry M. Campbell, Mrs. (widow) Wilcox.

Pat Palmer's tavern was near by on Jefferson Avenue, east side, midway between Randolph and Bates Streets. Palmer was the father of Captain Perry Palmer, of Wesley Truesdall's ill-fated propeller Goliath, Geo. Egner, confectionery and ice cream parlors, and Geo. Doty, watches, clocks and jewelry, some time later occupied the Palmer tavern site with new and substantial brick structures.

General John R. Williams lived on Woodbridge Street, close by Woodworth's Hotel. His first residence was on the southeast corner of Jefferson Avenue and Bates Street, where is now the dry goods house of Edson, Moore & Co. The house was a wooden cottage painted yellow, with white trimmings. An immense willow tree completely shaded its front. Felix Hinchman occupied this house for a while, after the general vacated it. All the latter's children were born in this house. There also lived on this street, Dr. Marshal Chapin, Thomas Rowland, Knowles Hall, Mr. Sanderson, father of Mrs. Geo. W. Bissell, Henry Berthelet (of the market), while nearby on Bates Street were located McDurell and his furniture store, John Collins, soap and candle manufacturer, David Isdell, Mrs. Hanks, widow of Lieutenant Hanks, who was killed by a stray shot from a British battery, located on the opposite side of the river, just before Hull's surrender, Theo. Williams's grocery store, Hon. Austin E. Wing, H. H. Le Roy, who afterwards owned and lived on the block where is now the Whitney building (Woodward Avenue), the Detroit garden, northeast corner of Bates and Atwater.

Names of prominent citizens of Detroit who, in the thirties, lived between Antoine, Congress and Cass Streets and the river:

Wilcox, John Truax, Wm. Brewster, E. A. Brush, John Biddle, Judge Sibley, Andre, Watsons, Ords, Johnsons, J. Kearsley, Dr. McCrosky, B. Woodworth, Oliver Miller, Thos. Rowland, Dr. Chapin, General John R. Williams, Sanderson, Knowles Hall, H. H. Le Roy, Judge Austin E. Wing, Judge Henry Chipman, Dr. Wm. Brown, Henry M. Campbell, Barnabas Campau, Ellis Doty, Felix Hinchman, Peter Desnoyers, Lewis Davenport, Colonel Edward Brooks, Arthur Bronson, Colonel Dick Smith, Mrs. Colonel Anderson, Judge James Abbott, John J. Deming, J. P. Browning, Julius Eldred, David French, Dr. R. L. Rice, Dr. Justin Rice, Chauncey Hulburt, John Roberts, R. E. Roberts, Edward Bingham, Rev. Noah M. Wells, Thos. F. Knapp, Wm. Pettie, Presque Cote, Tunis L. Wendell, Major Henry Whiting, the Cicotts and Beaubiens, Simon Poupard, John Y. Petty, William Durell, Isdell, Dr. T. B. Clark, A. C. McGraw, T. B. Vallee, T. L. King, Lebot, Horace Hallock, T. Bour, Dr. Henry, Judge Canniff, Jerry Dean, Dr. J. L. Whiting, John Hale, Levi Cook, Lewis Goddard, Shubael Conant, John Garrison, Robert Smart, Henry S. Cole, Dr. Z. Pitcher, M. Paulding, Dr. H. P. Cobb, Colonel Dibble, B. F. Farnsworth, Phineas Davis, N. Rossiter, Nathaniel Prouty, William Nesbitt, John Hanmer, Dr. E. A. Theller, P. Berthelet, Henry Howard, E. O. Graves, Thomas Gallagher, Elliott Gray, H. D. Garrison, Alvah Ewers, Jas. A. Van Dyke, Levi Brown, Colonel L. B. Mizner, Eugene St. Armour, A. D. Frasier, Judge James May, William Duncan, Thiebault, Melvin Dorr, William B. Alvord, J. R. Dorr, Dr. Rufus Brown, Dr. J. B. Scovell, Marsh Mead, Joseph Campau, Charles Piquette, Chauncey L. Payne, Thomas L. Chase, William Harsha, Eustache Chapoton, Gideon Paul, General Charles Larned, Dr. Ebenezer Hurd, Henry V. Disbrow, Alex. McFarrand, Shadrach Gillett, Reynolds Gillett, Stephen Wells, A. H. Stowell, Garry Spencer, A. B. Calhoun, Judge Elliott, John and Charles Wells, Pierre Tiller.

Some of the above citizens, those living in close proximity to the Hull House (Biddle House) and the old Council House, southwest corner Jefferson Avenue and Randolph Street, I mentioned in a former article, January 1, 1905. The others mentioned, though living at a greater distance from this business center, recognized it as such and were seen almost daily somewhere around Uncle Ben Woodworth's Steam Boat Hotel, Wales's American Hotel, and Berthelet market.

This Randolph Street and Jefferson Avenue corner, and near vicinity were in the twenties, and in fact earlier, and almost up to 1848, the year of the great fire, the social center of Detroit, and if we include Randolph Street to the river, it was the business center as well, I might say, of the entire state. In the immediate vicinity, on the southeast corner of Jefferson Avenue and Randolph Street, was the Governor Hull House, later on the American Hotel, and later the Biddle House. The old Council House, where is now the water office. On Randolph Street, as many old settlers know, was located Uncle Ben Woodworth's Steam Boat Hotel, southwest corner of Woodbridge Street. On lower Randolph Street, southwest corner of Atwater, was the Berthelet market, the only cattle market in the city. It had adjoining it on Randolph Street, quite a space fenced in and paved with cobble stones, for the convenience of horses and cattle exposed for sale.

The extensive industries of French & Eldred close by on Atwater Street, the pumping works of Farrand & Davis, at the foot of Randolph. Also on Randolph Street were located the principal retail grocery stores in the city. Augustus Kunze had his soap and candle factory, southeast corner of Woodbridge and Randolph; a grandson of his is, or was, an employe in the water office. At that time Mr. Kunze, General Schwarz and Mr. Uhlman, keeper of the Mansion House, were about the only Germans of prominence in the city.

At foot of Randolph was the extensive forwarding and commission house of Howard & Wadhams, and later on Brooks & Hartshorn, and later on J. Nicholson Elbert. It was indeed a busy center then, teeming with life and activity.

RANDOLPH STREET.

When the Sibleys vacated the premises on the northeast corner of Jefferson Avenue and Randolph Street, the wooden house was moved away and the brick one torn down, leaving an open space of nearly half the block. On this open space the circus people pitched their tents in preference to their former location on Randolph Street, and continued to do so until 1848. Here, also, the Whigs erected their log cabin in which to hold their meetings during the stirring campaign of 1840, "Tippecanoe and Tyler too," which many now living will call to mind, with all its hard cider and coon skins.

When the platform scales came into use the old city hay scales and building at the corner of Larned and Wayne Streets were abandoned and the platform scales took their place, but not in the same locality. These were established in front of the American Hotel, on the opposite side of the street. They were for a long time the only hay scles in the city with the exception of the ones at the northwest corner of Jefferson Avenue and Wayne Street.

In the large room on the first floor of the Council House the territorial court held its sessions, and continued to until the territorial capitol was completed (1824 or 5). The common council also held its sessions here until about 1830 or 31, when the Presbyterian Church people, at the sale of the Old Cantonment buildings, Fort Shelby, purchased the long Hall building that had been used by the troops for balls and other purposes, and moved it to the rear of their new church, northeast corner Woodward Avenue and Larned Street, and on their own lot, for use as a session and a Sunday school room. It suited their purpose admirably, and it came in very opportune for use by the common council of the city. The latter, for some unexplained reason, had leased the Council House to Mr. Lillibridge for his "Tontine Coffee House," and therefore they were gratified enough to secure a room in which to hold their sessions. The city continued to use this church session room until the Firemen's hall (brick) was erected on the adjoining lot, northwest corner Bates and Larned Streets, clearing away the old wooden shed-like structure that had accommodated Fire Engine Co. No. 1 so many years. The upper part of this new building was devoted to the uses of the common council, the fire department and city offices.

Services of the Church of England, were held in the Council House from 1824 to 1828. It was here that the first St. Paul's parish was organized in 1824. It is said it was the cradle of the first Episcopal Church in Michigan. Rev. Richard F. Cadle was the pastor. Wardens and vestrymen were: Samuel Perkins, Levi Brown, John Biddle, A. J. Whitney, Jonathan Kearsley, James Abbott, Henry Chipman, John Garland, John L. Whiting and Jerry Moores.

I mention the minister, wardens and vestrymen, as I knew them all by sight. The Rev. Mr. Cadle I heard in the pulpit. Samuel Perkins was a United States ordnance officer and keeper of the arsenal here. Levi Brown was a jeweler, and inventor of the gold pen. John Biddle was Major Biddle, after whom the Biddle House was named. A. J. Whitney held some county office. Jonathan Kearsley was United States receiver. James Abbott was postmaster. Henry Chipman was a judge and father of Hon. J. Logan Chipman. John Garland was a colonel in the United States army. John L. Whiting was a prominent doctor. Jerry Moores was a master stone and brick mason.

In the large room of the Council House, first floor, Dr. Douglass Houghton was first introduced to the public through his chemical lectures, which were largely attended. They were very interesting, illustrated as they were by brilliant experiments. They were the first lectures of their kind ever given here to the general public. D. Z. Crane, our old schoolmaster in the University building on Bates Street, was a regular crank on chemistry. Crane had a fine laboratory, apparatus, etc., and gave frequent illustrated lectures to his scholars only. So we youngsters who were attendants at Crane's school, were somewhat familiar with chemistry and "caught on" when we came to hear it expounded by Dr. Houghton.

After this Lillibridge (a queer character), established here "the Tontine Coffee House," the first of its kind in the city. It was a little ahead of the times and did not prove a success.

Upstairs in the southwest corner of the Council House was the Masonic lodge room, with the curtains to the windows always tightly drawn, and outwardly all looked dark and ominous, owing, no doubt, to the cloud cast on the order by the Morgan affair that happened in New York State in the early twenties, and with which all Free Masons are familiar. It was said the feeling entertained against them here, at that time, by the anti-Masons, was so strong that they did not dare to appear in public, in their regalia with music, etc., as they formerly had been in the habit of doing. Perhaps this may have been so, generally speaking, but I know of two occasions when they did appear in full regalia; these were at the funeral of my father and later that of Mr. Obed Waite, architect of the territorial capitol building. Not being a Free Mason I do not remember when the lodge resumed its former sway. I (boy that I was) was full of the mystery of this alleged Morgan abduction business. Before my mother and the rest of our family left Canandaigua for Detroit, I accompanied her to the jail there to see Mr. Cheesbro and Mr. Sawyer, prominent Free Masons, who were confined on suspicion of being concerned in the kidnaping. Mr. Cheesbro was one of my father's most intimate friends, as also was Mr. Sawyer. The latter was a tenant of his, and a very near neighbor.

There was no evidence against them, or of sufficient character to convict them, and they were released. Mr. Cheesbro died at a good old age in Canandaigua, and Mr. Sawyer emigrated to Grand Blanc, in this state. He too lived to see many years and died at Grand Blanc.

The last to use the Council House building were James A. Hicks, dry goods, and after him Sandford Brittan as furniture store. Then came the fire of 1848.

* * *

Between the Council House and Randolph Street, was a vacant lot where had been the reservoir of Farrand and Davis. On this lot Eldred & Co. erected a two-story wooden building, and used it a while for a hardware store. They vacated it for larger premises further down Jefferson Avenue. Geo. M. Rich succeeded them in the building with a stock of groceries. He too was dirven away by the fire.

When the Governor Hull House became the American Hotel, it was extended to cover the vacant space between it and Randolph Street. The first story was finished for business purposes, and the two upper stories for the hotel. The corner store was occupied by Riley & Ackerley, drugs and medicines, then by David A. McNair, same business, and later by Theo. H. Eaton. The latter occupied the premises at the time of the fire. The adjoining store was occupied first by the Cicotts, with dry goods, and after by Fortier & Berthlet, in the same trade.

Near the American Hotel, on Randolph Street, and fronting Michigan Avenue (now Cadillac Square), Mrs. O. Hartwell kept a boarding house. Mrs. Hartwell, a widow with two children, son and daughter, came here from Canandaigua, N. Y., about 1845. One of her boarders was Attorney Jeremiah Van Rensselaer, a member of the Detroit bar and a lawyer of rare ability. He took quite a liking for the widow's son, Thomas H. Hartwell, who was a bright, studious lad, and induced him to enter his office as a student. After the usual time had passed, Thomas was admitted to practice and became a full-fledged limb of the law.

In 1852-53 Van Rensselaer was county clerk, and Hartwell was his deputy. They were both practicing their profession here in 1855 and later.

Hartwell became quite interested in the public school system of Detroit and was at one time president of the board of education. He unfortunately sustained a serious paralytic stroke, which incapacitated him from attending to business of any sort for some years. These years he spent in travel west and other parts of the Union, mostly on horseback. Being young, he gradually won back his health, and is now practicing his profession in New York City, or was a few years ago.

Lawyer Van Rensselaer married Hartwell's sister. After a few years of married life she passed away, and he married Miss Sarah Morse, daughter of Mr. Chauncey Morse, the bookseller. Mr. Van Rensselaer died some years ago. His widow survives him.

✧   ✧   ✧

Garry Spencer also lived on Randolph Street, fronting Michigan Avenue. It was at Spencer's house that our schoolmaster, Edwin Jerome, met his fate in the person of Mrs. Spencer's sister. The boys of the school knew all about it, at the time—for during this period he was particularly gracious.

Alpheus White, a rugged and noted character at that time, lived near by the Spencers, and Mrs. Hartwell, in the log cabin farm house of the Brush estate. I remember his personality well, but I do not call to mind his occupation.

Cullen Brown, with his extensive harness and saddlery establishment, was located on Jefferson Avenue, near Randolph Street. The boys all knew Cullen Brown, and it was at his shop all went to get their skates strapped. We went there more particularly on account of William Duncan, who was his head man. Duncan will be remembered as that energetic member of the old Volunteer Fire Department of Detroit, of which he was at one time chief.

About the time Chancellor Farnsworth built on upper Jefferson Avenue Cullen Brown built on the southeast corner of Rivard, where is now the residence of ex-Mayor Alex. Lewis. After some years' residence in this locality, and on the opening of Jefferson Avenue across the Dequindre, Witherell and St. Aubin farms, Mr. Brown sold this corner to Mr. Lewis, and built a brick residence further up on the St. Aubin farm, where is now the city residence of Mrs. Addison Mandell. Mr. Carnes, the brewer, succeeded him. The Mandells succeeded the latter, supplanting the old-fashioned brick structure with a more modern one.

Mr. Brown married for his second wife the sister of Mrs. Geo. Jerome and Mrs. Homer Warren. They had one son, the present Cullen, whom every one knows, and favorably. The Brown house that was on the southeast corner of Jefferson Avenue and Rivard is now doing duty as the residence of Mr. W. Q. Hunt, northwest corner of Jefferson Avenue and Leib Street.

* * *

ALEX. CAMPAU AND BELLE ISLE.

Mr. Alex. M. Campau has deposited in the Detroit Museum of Art, historical department, about sixty papers, mostly original, in regard to Hog Island (Belle Isle), derived from his father, Barnabee (Labie) Campau, all of which are valuable, either historically or because of the signatures. They are at present in a somewhat dilapidated condition. In due time they will be mended and catalogued so as to make them easy for reference for any one interested.

Mr. Campau related to the writer the version of the charge that the $5,000 his father paid Wm. Macomb for the island was in wildcat money, and that he (Macomb) never realized anything from it. He said: "The $5,000 my father paid Macomb was in 'red dog' (or wildcat) money, issued by some chartered bank in Ohio, and about the only currency in circulation here at that time, and considered good. Macomb was owing this bank in Ohio $5,000 on a promissory note, and he went down post haste to pay it, as it was past due. On arriving at the bank he noticed an unusual crowd in and around it. On demanding that the teller produce his note, the latter hesitated, and finally referred him to the cashier in an adjoining room. After some palaver with the latter official he paid over the $5,000 and got his note. It appears that the bank had failed, and the officials, knowing Macomb was good for the $5,000, had expected or hoped to retain this good piece of paper, and let their 'red dog' promises-to-pay go to the dogs."

So it will be seen that Macomb did not lose in the transaction.

* * *

B. F. FARNSWORTH AND PHINEAS DAVIS.

"I did not know Mr. Farnsworth intimately during the latter's years of his life, but saw much of him during the first two years after his arrival here, as he was an inmate of my uncle, Thos. Palmer's home, when he occupied the upper part of the store, southeast corner of Jefferson Avenue and Griswold Street, and it is of that period of his life that I write.

"He first came to the city in 1829 as the accredited agent of Phineas Davis, Jr., of Boston. Mr. Davis had just purchased a stock of general merchandise for the western market, which he committed to the charge of young Farnsworth, and a start was made from Boston by water during the month of September. The goods were loaded on a small schooner and conveyed to Albany via Long Island Sound and the Hudson River. The voyage was an extremely tedious one, occupying six days in its first stage as far as New York City. After a day's delay in that city, he took the steamer for Albany and reached there five days in advance of the schooner, which occupied five days in its voyage up the river. At Albany the cargo was transferred to a canal boat, and the weary westward journey was taken up. Mr. Farnsworth left the freight boat to Utica, and journey in advance by packet to Buffalo. The delays had been so many that when the cargo reached that city the last steamer of the season had started for Detroit, and the only recourse was a belated schooner. Upon this he shipped his stock and took passage, fortified by instructions from his principal that if his journey were arrested he should land and dispose of his goods wherever possible. This did not prove necessary, however, as he reached Detroit safely and without incident on the 13th day of October, 1828. He at once purhased the stock of F. & T. Palmer, remaining in the brick store, southeast corner of Jefferson Avenue and Griswold Street, and rented the premises from Thomas Palmer, father of Senator Palmer. His authority was absolute, as if he had been in business for himself, for he held an unconditional power of attorney from his principal, witnessed by James Witherell and Thomas Palmer and acknowledged before Judge Solomon Sibley.

Though I was quite a small boy at the time of Mr. Farnsworth's advent here, his personality is very vividly impressed on my memory. He was an exceedingly clean cut, handsome man, and precise in all his movements—Boston from the crown of his head to the sole of his foot.

Henry L. Ball, assistant editor and publisher of the *Detroit Gazette* at that time, was, with his sister, also an intimate of my uncle's family. Mr. Ball and Mr. Farnsworth became intimate friends. The latter, so recently accustomed to the busy life of Boston, would have found existence extremely monotonous here, through the long winter, but, as he said, for the amusement he found in reading the exchanges of the *Detroit Gazette* furnished him by his friend Ball. The calm, quiet, cool and deliberate demeanor he brought with him from Boston, he always maintained. His integrity was unquestionable. After severing his connection with Phineas Davis, he associated himself with Amos T. Hall and A. E. Mather.

Phineas came here with his family in August, 1828.

Farnsworth managed "Phin's" business here for some time, but was taken ill and went back to Boston. In 1836 Phineas was placed in charge of an important enterprise, and wishing to relinquish his store, went to Boston and held a conference with Farnsworth. As a result the latter returned to Detroit in December, 1836, and formed the partnership mentioned above. They bought out the entire business interest of Davis. Besides this venture of Mr. Farnsworth's with Mather & Hall, he engaged in some other enterprises, notably the hotel business (Eagle Tavern on Woodbridge Street, near Griswold, which he built and owned); the shoe business which he conducted for many years, and he was also at one time connected with the assessor's office. He was, in addition, quite an extensive owner of real estate.

Mrs. Davis was the sister of Colonel Sylvanus Fair, of the United States Engineer Corps, who was a distinguished soldier in the war of 1812. At that time Colonel Fair was the superintendent of the military academy at West Point, and his statue stands there now to perpetuate his fame.

Davis in 1829 was connected with Detroit's water supply. He was in company with Rufus Wells, Lucius Lyon and A. E. Hathon, the common council giving to them the exclusive right of furnishing water in Detroit until 1860. The reservoir was located on the south side of Fort Street, between Shelby and Wayne. The company did not give good service and its charter was revoked in 1836.

Phineas was a stout man of medium hight and blond complexion, magnetic and pushing, and somewhat eccentric in his ways. He was engaged in many enterprises, notably the Gibraltar and Flat Rock canal. He induced Daniel Webster to invest, he buying stock to the amount of $2,500, giving his note for it. The note was discounted by the Bank of Michigan, but it never realized a cent from it.

A bank was established at Gibraltar under the wildcat banking law of 1837, with a capital of $100,000. Its directors were Joshua Howard, Enoch Jones, Benjamin Porter, Alanson Sheeley, Theo. Romeyn, H. B. Lothrop, N. T. Ludden, Eldridge Morse and Griffith H. Jones. Joshua Howard was president and J. C. Ringwalter cashier. The bank went down like the rest of the brood of wildcat banks; as did the Flat Rock Canal Co., and Phin Davis was a ruined man.

In 1837 Webster visited Detroit to see his son, Fletcher Webster, who was at that time practicing law here. While here Daniel Webster spoke in the Cass orchard, rear of the old mansion. Cass was not here at the time; was United States minister to France. The use of the grounds was kindly tendered to the Whigs by Edmund A. Brush, Democrat. All the Whig notables of Detroit were present, as well as the officers of the new state. After dinner, served to 500 persons, the speech was delivered on the questions of the day. I was present.

Davis was finally forced to make an assignment for the benefit of his creditors, to Alanson Sheeley and N. T. Ludden, and directly after removed to Pontiac, where he kept a general store for many years. He died in Pontiac in 1850, in his fiftieth year. I do not know the date of Mr. Farnsworth's death. Mrs. Farnsworth died in this city February 7, 1904, at the advanced age of 91 years. I remember when her husband brought her here as a bride. She was prominent in society for many years. I think three daughters survive her.

The immediate associates of Mr. Farnsworth, directly after he came here, were Henry L. Ball, assistant editor *Detroit Gazette*; Obed Waite, architect of capitol building; Sheldon McKnight, Sidney D. Hawkins, J. V. R. Scott, Mr. Pettie and Walter L. Newberry.

FIRST PROTESTANT SOCIETY.

IT was due to the labors of Rev. William Case, a Methodist Episcopal clergyman, that the first Protestant society was formed in Detroit in 1810, with seven members; Robert Abbott, Betsey, his wife; William McCarty, Mamia C., his wife; William Stacey, Betsey, his wife, and Sarah Macomb. These people were organized into a church, the membership of which was increased to thirty before the war of 1812, when it suffered in the general demoralization attending the conflict, though Mr. Abbott and Mr. McCarty kept up the religious services as far as possible. The little company held together, and when Rev. Joseph Hickox, of Hartford, Ct., came to this region as a missionary, the original seven members were again established as a Methodist Episcopal Church, occupying the Council House, southwest corner Jefferson Avenue and Randolph Street, as a place of worship, with preaching once in three weeks.

Robert Abbott was the first English-American born in Detroit. His mother was the first English-speaking woman who settled in Detroit.

Wm. McCarty was born on Grosse Ile. His wife was the sister of the wife of Robert Abbott, and they were born in Philadelphia.

William Stacey and his wife lived on the River Rouge. Mr. Hickox preached regularly on the River Rouge, and at Monroe, as well as in Detroit.

In June, 1816, Rev. John Montieth, a graduate of Princeton Theological Seminary, a missionary commissioned by the board of missions of the Presbyterian Church, began his labors in Michigan. At that time the population of Detroit was about 1,000. In May, 1819, a lot on Woodward Avenue, running from Larned to Congress Street, was granted to the First Protestant Society, which was the title taken by the church and congregation. The deed was signed by Lewis Cass, governor of Michigan territory, and Solomon Sibley and John Hunt, two of the judges of the territory. The witnesses were Henry Chipman and Edmund A.

Brush. In 1818 a church was organized, having some of the doctrines of the Presbyterian Church, but not so rigid as to repel those of other religious beliefs from uniting with them. The first elders were John J. Deming, Levi Brown and Lemuel Shattuck. In the year 1820 the church edifice was completed. The signers of the first constitution were Charles Larned, Austin E. Wing, Thomas Palmer, Jas. Duane Doty, Thomas Rowland, Stephen C. Henry, Frances Audrian, Wm. Woodbridge, John Hunt, Justin Rice, James Abbott, Henry I. Hunt, Henry Sanderson, D. G. Jones, John P. Sheldon, John J. Deming, Lewis Cass, Benjamin Woodworth, A. Edwards, B. F. H. Witherell.

In 1825 the church was reorganized and regularly adopted the Presbyterian form of government.. At that time there were forty-nine members, thirty-eight of which were women. Their names were: Margaret Audrian, Seth Beach, Maria Brewster, Cullen Brown, Lucy Brown, Catherine Bronson, Elijah Converse, Phoebe Crosby, Rebecca Converse, William B. Hunt, Sarah Hubbard, Matilda Hurd, Melicent Hunt, Catherine Jones, Jane Kelly, Mary Chapin, Louisa Cooper, Elizabeth Cass, Nancy Caniff, John J. Deming, Ruth Edwards, Lucretia Goodwin, Mary Gillett, Stephen C. Henry, Ann Henry, Lydia Sanderson, Sophia Seymour, Martha Ten Eyck, Almira Willcox, Ashbel W. Wells, Asenath Lee, Temperance Mack, Fanny Mack, Mary McMillan, Mary Owen, Jane M. Palmer, Justin Rice, Hannah Roby, Mary Rice, Mary J. Scott, Ann Hunt, Mary Hunt, Eurotas P. Hastings, J. W. Woolsey.

In 1825 Stephen C. Henry, Eurotas P. Hastings, John J. Deming and A. S. Wells were elected elders of the church. E. P. Hastings, Henry I. Hunt, Shubeal Conant, Levi Cook and Austin E. Wing were trustees.

ILLUMINATIONS.

The custom of illuminating public buildings and private residences to celebrate any important event was much in vogue here in the long ago.

In 1837, when Michigan was admitted into the Union as a state, there was a grand illumination to celebrate the event. Sperm candles, inserted in three-cornered tin candlesticks, were used. A projecting corner of the latter was stuck into the wooden sash inclosing each pane of glass in the windows. It was quite general throughout the city.

The lighting was simultaneous, at the sounding of the bell from the Presbyterian Church steeple, on Woodward Avenue and Larned Street. The effect was striking and quite spectacular. The night was without a moon, and as dark as a "stack of black cats." Seen from the middle of the river, or from the Canada shore, the aspect the city presented was brilliant.

The Michigan Exchange Hotel, then just completed, presented a splendid sight. Every pane of glass in the entire structure had its gleaming light. Other prominent buildings did their share, but I think the Michigan Exchange excelled them all. Jefferson Avenue was a blaze of light from end to end, and bonfires lent their aid to turn night into day.

There was another illumination of a like character, in every way, more brilliant, perhaps, some ten years later, on the ending of the Mexican war. The city had grown larger in the meantime, and the display was more imposing.

I do not call to mind another illumination, and think this was the last. Housekeepers were no doubt glad of it, as the spluttering candles must have caused them no end of bother.

THE FAREWELL TO JUDGE A. B. WOODWARD.

ENTHUSIASTIC SPEECHES IN OLD-TIME STYLE OF OVER-PRAISE—SINGULAR CONTRAST BETWEEN THE WOODWARD ADDRESSES AND THE JUDGE'S REAL SELF.

FRIEND PALMER offers an interesting selection. He had gone into *The Detroit Gazette,* Feb. 20, 1824, and found important details of the farewell to Hon. A. B. Woodward, for 18 years territorial judge. The gathering of citizens included all the well-known men of the day. It was held at Woodworth's hotel. Hon. John McDonnell was called to the chair and Philo E. Judd was chosen secretary. The report continues in the quaint phraseology of the day:

After the organization, the chairman was requested to explain more fully, the purpose for which it was called. He did so in a concise, but feeling manner, stating that it was to take into consideration the public services of the Hon. Augustus B. Woodward, during his residence in Michigan territory. The chairman dwelt on the intrepid conduct pursued, and the inestimable services rendered by Judge Woodward to this country, and to our fellow-citizens in the most trying scenes—scenes, too, in which the chairman himself was an actor. Whereupon the following preamble and resolutions were considered and unanimously adopted:

JUDGE WOODWARD PRAISED.

"Whereas, by the recent organization of the judicial department of this territory, we lose the services of the Hon. Augustus B. Woodward, late chief justice of the Supreme Court, who has faithfully and honorably, discharged that important trust, during a period of more than eighteen years. And, believing it to be our duty to express the sentiments of this meeting, which are in unison with those of our fellow-citizens generally, in relation to his merits and public conduct; therefore,

"*Resolved,* That the extreme legal information, incorruptible integrity, splendid talents, correct and gentlemanly deportment, tried patriotism, and the great literary acquirements of the Hon. Augustus B. Woodward, eminently entitled him to the respect of every American.

"*Resolved,* That during the long period he has served as chief justice, his research, impartiality, independence and urbanity have been such as to merit the entire approbation of this meeting; and his unceasing exertions for the good of the country, command our warmest gratitude.

"*Resolved,* That the intrepid course pursued by him during the prevalence of the power of the enemy in the territory, and his zeal in the protection of our unfortunate citizens and prisoners, have lastingly endeared him to us; and that we shall ever cherish the most grateful recollections of his fortitude and active philanthropy.

"*Resolved,* That Mr. John Burnham, Mr. Calvin Baker, Mr. J. O. Lewis, Mr. Obed Wait, Mr. James Byrne, and Mr. John Roberts, Jr., be a committee to prepare a suitable address, expressive of the sentiments of this meeting and those of the public."

The said committee then retired and after some time returned and reported an address which, having been considered, it was further unanimously

"*Resolved,* That the address be adopted, and that the committee present the same together with a copy of these resolutions, to the Hon. Augustus B. Woodward.

"*Resolved,* That the proceedings of this meeting be signed by the chairman and secretary, and together with the address, be published in the *Detroit Gazette* and *National Intelligence.*

JOHN MCDONNELL, Chairman."
"PHILO E. JUDD, Secretary."

HIGH RESPECT SHOWN.

Judge Woodward was deeply affected by the sincerity of the resolutions but managed to make a felicitous reply, couched in the polished style of the day.

In addition to the resolutions, the committee offered the judge a memorial signed by John Roberts, Jr., brother of Robert E. Roberts, city clerk and secretary of the Detroit water board; John McDonnell, progenitor of the present superintendent of the Detroit

House of Correction; James O. Lewis, sculptor, whose work is seen in the statues of Father Richard and Lewis Cass; Obed Wait, the designer and architect of the territorial capitol building; James Burnham, Calvin Baker, James Byrne. This somewhat flowery address, prepared by these gentlemen, reads as follows:

A portion of your fellow-citizens, who have learned with unfeigned regret that, in the recent arrangement of judges for this territory, they lose the benefit of your services in a situation which you have filled for so many years with such honor to yourself cannot, in justice to their own feelings, suffer this occasion to pass without assuring you of the high respect they entertain for you personally, and the estimation in which they have invariably held your virtues and your patriotism. In the expression of our sentiments we refrain from adulation and panegyric, because we conceive they could add little to the meed of praise which is already justly your due. Our subject is fully accomplished if we have conveyed to you, in the unaffected language of simplicity and truth, the testimony of our confidence—our regard, and our gratitude—and we hope that our feelings will not be measured by the brevity which we shall observe in their expression.

Coeval with the existence of our territory we find you commence the discharge of an office, than which none within the range of civil government is more arduous and important an office, the faithful discharge of which sustains the good order and happiness of society. The duties which devolved on the judges of this territory were, indeed, of no ordinary magnitude. Not only were they judicial, but they were also of a legislative character; and sure we are, that whatever success may have attended their labors, your individual exertions were never wanting to their accomplishment. If these duties were performed in any manner to merit praise, and that they were, we believe few will feel disposed to dispute, certainly no small share should belong to you.

LAUD HIS WAR RECORD.

Since the year 1805 we have beheld you presiding on the bench of the Supreme Court if we except the period during which a foreign foe waved over our city a "flaming brand," and with what dignity, strict integrity, assiduous research and true independence of character you have discharged the functions of that station, because it must be acknowledged, not only by the citizens of this territory, but also by those beyond it who have perused your learned and elaborate opinions that none could possibly possess these qualities in a more eminent degree than yourself. It is unquestionable that you possess no common share of legal as well as scientific knowledge qualities which enabled you to discharge the duties of your station in the most unexceptionable manner, it is equally true that your strict attention and unwearied exertions in whatever conduced to the public prosperity, could not be surpassed in any country or in any age. With such qualifications, your sensibility of heart, your sound judgment, and your perspicuous and penetrating understanding rendered you peculiarly calculated in every respect for that office.

When our country was plunged in the deepest horrors of war, and the ruthless savage exercised his uncontrolled domination over our devoted city, from a review of your conduct in that mournful period, we profess to be at a loss which to admire most, the former enlightened judge upon the bench, or the now intrepid patriot in the hour of danger. During the lapse of eighteen years you have presided in our Supreme Court you have continued to accumulate that debt of gratitude which your country now owes you and which, we will venture to assert, she can never repay. And so indefatigable have been your exertions, that even when the hand of sickness laid you low, you hesitated not to attend to the duties of your station at the imminent hazard of your life.

FIRMNESS.

Who that has heard of our late war with Great Britain and pretends to know anything of the history of that sanguinary period in which it raged, but must be aware of your patriotic exertions in vindication of the rights of our citizens? Who that remembers the bloody massacre of the River Raisin, that does not remember also the more than Spartan firmness you manifested on that occasion? When the articles of capitulation were violated—when the lives, the liberty and the property of our citizens were in jeopardy, you alone were their "guardian and their shield"—and you alone had the firmness to step forth to save them. And this bold stand you maintained to your eternal honor until the sword of the enemy repelled the advancing forces of your country. Neither captivity nor death had any terror to deter you from pursuing the laudable course which you deemed necessary, to insure the safety of your countrymen; and you have now the consolation to reflect that you were not only instrumental in guarding their liberty and property, but had even saved the lives of others. But why need we detail the signal actions you performed? We only repeat what is already on record. We only glance at deeds, the details and proofs of which are now in the archives of the government.

REPROACHED CALUMINATORS.

Think not, sir, that your country will be ungrateful. If foul play has been used—if impure feelings have prevailed, the actors in unholy transactions will learn that in a land of freedom, merit cannot be depressed.

It were to be wished that we could stop here; but we cannot do so in justice to you. The example which you set to others they could not imitate, even in the distance; and jealously envied you the fame and the honor you so meritoriously acquired. After time will do you justice, and the page of history will be devoted to your actions and your name. It is melancholy reflection that the character of the virtuous citizen often finds no shelter from the storm of calumny. Imputations, odious, absurd and unjust, deserve no reply. You have discharged your public duties in a manner to elicit the approbation of the virtuous part of the community. You drifted not with the current. You sailed not in the wind of opinion and prejudice.

In conclusion, be assured that the memory of your virtues, your talents and your actions will be forever green in the remembrance of your countrymen. Accept, sir, the assurance of our high consideration and respect.

M'DONNELL'S SPEECH.

With great formality the resolutions were presented to the judge by Chairman McDonnell, as follows:

A meeting of your fellow-citizens was held agreeably to public notice in this city, on the evening of Saturday last, the avowed object of which was to take into consideration the services of an officer, who has with singular felicity, in the discharge of his public duties, continued, for a series of years, to command the admiration of which he is a member. Need I scarcely add that I allude to you, sir? If on the one hand, we lament the occasion that called us together, we hope that on the other, we see nothing that can justify us in drawing a conclusion of any intended ingratitude by your country towards you. No, sir, whatever the present appearances of the horizon may indicate, we trust, that without pretending to a spirit of prophecy, we can venture to assert, that the sun of your fortunes far from being set, is merely eclipsed by a passing cloud that will soon vanish from the sight, and will at no distant period become more resplendent than ever.

In presenting you, sir, with the resolutions and the address which the unanimity of the meeting deemed to be due to you, permit me to assure you for myself and the rest of the gentlemen of the committee appointed to wait on you, that we derive peculiar pleasure from the performance of the duties which the meeting enjoined on us; that we fully concur in the sentiment of approbation in relation to yourself and I beg to add the assurances of our high consideration for you personally.

FOND REMEMBRANCES.

Be assured, sir, that when the little bickerings and prejudices of the transient hour are buried in the vale of oblivion, when the pulse of the caluminator shall have ceased to beat, when his organ of detraction will no longer furnish a banquet to the worm; and when himself and his character are sunk in forgetfulness, a generation, yet unborn, will do justice to the man in whom were united the philosopher, the patriot, the judge and the philanthropist. In that day, the cultivation of the sciences will add an additional ray to the light which will shine around your name, and a grateful posterity will venerate the memory of him whose labors have enlarged the boundaries of their knowledge.

JUDGE WOODWARD'S RESPONSE.

This is Judge Woodward's response: The affectionate address I have had the honor to receive from you, while it is an evidence of your attention and kindness, cannot be otherwise than gratifying to a mind of sensibility.

To find my humble qualifications thus appreciated, and my

inadequate services, in the cause of my country, so applauded, is a reward sufficient to satisfy a higher ambition than mine.

In the various labors which have diversified a situation and scenery so peculiar as those in which I was placed, my only merit is that I have been uniformily governed by a severe sense of duty, and while I can have no claim to exemption from error, it is not in the lot of human nature that exertions, however well intended should be viewed in the same aspect by all. A steady and uniform approbation is not anticipated, even in the most exalted stations of our republic; nor is it to be regarded as a matter of surprise than those in less elevated capacities should not always escape censure or obloquy.

In that melancholy and sanguinary hour, when a hostile banner overshadowed our land, and during which I could perform no official act, my feelings imperiously compelled me to stand by my fellow-citizens, to combat for their rights, to share their dangers, and participate in their sufferings; and, according as they should stand or fall, to stand or fall myself. Nor, at this day, would my heart or head dictate an alteration in my course, were a destiny so deplorable again to attend the fortunes of my country.

Be pleased to accept, gentlemen, for yourselves, and for your fellow-citizens, my sincere thanks for the respect and politeness with which the communication of your sentiments has been accompanied; and believe me, your welfare and prosperity are objects which will be ever dear to my heart.

COMMENTS.

It may not seem inconsistent to add that the judge, while praised for his urbanity and high social qualities, had according to Henry A. Cherey, "a temper of his own." Mr. Cherey's comment is as follows: "He was a marvel of personal untidiness, even among pioneers, and his imperious will was such that no mortal man could get along with him unless he submitted to it. During the British occupation, in 1812, he was General Proctor's secretary in civil matters, but he bullied Proctor as he had previously bullied Hull."

C. M. Burton says of him, "His life in Detroit was among a frontier people who were not at that time overcleanly themselves; and if he was so untidy as to call the attention of his neighbors to the fact, he must have been filthy indeed. We are assured that he drank liquor more than was usual even in his day; that he was not very punctual in the payment of his debts; and continually quarreled with Governor Hull. He was never married. This may have been because he found no lady who was willing to risk her life and happiness by a union with him."

Mr. Burton comments on the fact that in New York City, about the time Judge Woodward was born, there was baptized there one Elias Brevoort Woodward, who may have been identical with the judge; but no explanation is at hand to indicate why Woodward changed his name, if indeed such is the fact.

EARLY SOCIAL CONDITIONS.

THE VENERABLE MICHIGAN HISTORIAN EXAMINES NEWSPAPER FILES FOR 1823, AND THROWS A FLOOD OF LIGHT ON EARLY SOCIAL CONDITIONS—UPS AND DOWNS OF LIFE IN THE VILLAGE OF DETROIT.

FRIEND PALMER again looks over the *Detroit Gazette* for the mid-winter of 1823, and finds quaint historic suggestions of life in the old town. That there is historic value in advertisements may no longer be doubted. Friend Palmer's method of looking over the people's wants, to find what was going on in the village community smacks of the scientific method of original discovery. For example, with proper classification of the advertising columns of today, much that would prove difficult to understand, of the passing period, would be revealed, say in 100 years, if the public notices of merchants were read. Friend Palmer's advertisements from the *Gazette* throw a flood of light on the old village days—what was paid for butter and eggs; how the housewives saved the ashes; how lands went begging for owners; how men fell in debt, and other interesting transactions of a long-forgotten day. Among the notices which came under Friend Palmer's critical eyes are the following, which he offers without additional comment, each paragraph being self-explanatory:

GREAT LAND TRANSACTIONS.

To enterprising capitalists and mechanics: The subscribers, having contracted with the governor and judges of the territory of Michigan to erect a courthouse or capitol in the city of Detroit, and having received from them a transfer of all the city lots and land remaining of the 10,000 acres, which was granted to the said city by an act of Congress, of the 21st April, 1806, have thought proper to offer for sale 6,640 acres of land and 144 city lots. It will be only necessary to state briefly, in order that an estimate may be made of the value of the land, that it lies in the immediate vicinity and adjoining the city of Detroit, a place which for advantageous location is not equaled by any on the borders of Lake Erie, which is rapidly increasing in its population and business, and will always be the commercial, if not the political, capital of Michigan. The most important highway in the territory, that leading from Detroit to Saginaw, passes directly through the tract offered for sale. The quality of the soil is various, but by far the greatest proportion is of the first description, and very heavily timbered. The value of the timber may be estimated by a knowledge of the fact that the average price of wood in the city of Detroit during the two winters last past was $2.50 per cord. It may also be truly said that the proximity of the above land to an excellent market for all kinds of vegetables, grain, fowls, etc., aside from the certainty of a rapidly increasing population and consequent rise in the price of real estate, greatly enhances its value and importance over all lands now offered for sale on the western waters. The city lots are pleasantly situated, and are mostly in the immediate vicinity of the capitol (the cornerstone of which was laid the 22nd inst.). Some of the lots offered by the subscribers extend from the shore of the river to the ship channel, and afford excellent locations for wharves and storehouses.

The terms of sale will be liberal, a credit of from one to three years being given if required. Masons, carpenters and joiners will have an opportunity next summer to purchase for their labor such lots or pieces of land as they may select. Thomas Palmer, one of the late firm of F. T. & J. Palmer; David C. McKinstry. Detroit, September 25th, 1823.

N. B.—Thirty-three quarter sections of bounty land in Indiana, Illinois and Missouri, fifteen village lots in Pontiac, and twelve out-lots adjoining, containing from three to twenty acres each, will be exchanged for personal property.

Four or five good carding machines will be received for any of the above property. David C. McKinstry.

OLD TIME SALES.

Cash Establishment.—F. Hinchman has just opened a new store, in the building formerly occupied by Colonel D. G. Jones, on the corner of Jefferson and Woodward Avenues, where he offers to the public as handsome an assortment of dry goods, groceries, crockery and hardware as can be found in this city, and he pledges himself to all to whom these presents shall come to sell as cheap if not cheaper than any of his neighboring tape-cutters.

He will receive in exchange for goods purchased of him, the following commodities, to wit: Cash, grain of all kinds, furs, ginseng, beeswax, and hides. Also, uncurrent money at a discount. Detroit, January 5, 1823.

Messrs. Sheldon & Reed: We observe in your paper of the 26th inst. prices of several articles of produce, calculated to mislead and disappoint the expectations of people who trade to this market. We have on hand 100 kegs butter, 250 bbls. flour, 50 do pork, a few barrels beer and 3,700 lbs. cheese, which we will sell at the following prices: Butter, first quality, 12½ cents per pound; inferior, do 10 cents; flour, $6.75 and $7 per bbl.; pork, $10 do; beef, $7 do; and cheese, 7 to 3 cents per pound. Dorr & Jones, Detroit, December 29, 1823.

Postoffice, Detroit, January 1, 1824.—The mail for the eastern, southern and western parts of the United States will in future be closed on Wednesday evening, precisely at 9 o'clock. James Abbott, postmaster.

DEBTS AND ASHES.

CITY OF DETROIT, Feb. 18, 1824.

I offer for sale all my property, personal and real, on Saturday, the 18th day of September next.

I wish soon to go to Washington, in order to dispose of some property to pay my debts here. I would like to see those to whom I am indebted before I go; and as I suppose, I shall have to resume the practice of law, I shall accept of any professional business in which it is conceived I may be of service, for a moderate compensation. A. B. Woodward.

NOTICE.—The office of the Clerk of the Supreme Court and Register of Probate, is kept in the brick building on the n. e. corner of Jefferson and Woodward Avenues, over the store of Mr. Darius Lamson.

All writs, transcripts, or other writings required from his office, must hereafter be paid for before they are taken away. Those who are indebted for such writings are requested to settle accounts without further delay, and those who have left deeds, etc., with the Register to be recorded will please to call and receive the originals and pay the fee. J. V. R. Ten Eyck, Register of Probate, etc., Detroit, January 22, 1824.

VILLAGE PRICES.

"Idleness is the mother of vice." What would some of our neighboring competitors do if they could? "Ashes, Ashes, Ashes," or "Grain, Grain, Grain!", The subscriber will pay in goods, at cash prices, the following prices for grain, delivered at his store: Oats, forty-four cents; wheat, $1.12; corn, sixty-nine cents; rye, eighty-two cents.

Not having but one store in Detroit he is not as well prepared to sell goods at various prices as some of his neighbors; and he hopes the public will not suffer themselves to be deceived by the enhanced price offered for ashes, when they can call at the old and well known store of John Hale's at the sign of the Pot Ash kettles and grind stones, and purchase their goods without extortion. John Hale.

THE public will please to take notice, that Messrs. F. & T. Palmer, my competitors in the purchase of ashes, have had the offer of 400 bushels at thirteen cents per bushel (that being the price which they have advertised to give, as per a late notice in the Detroit *Gazette*), and they refused to take them at that or any other price and transport them.

This is very like "the dog in the manger;" vide old fables of Esop. John Hale, Detroit, January 14, 1824.

EARLY LUXURIES.

One hundred and fifty mococks maple sugar of a very superior quality and suitable for the use of families has just been received, and is offered for sale by C. S. Payne & Co., July 10.

To sell or let.—That most valuable farm, situated at Grosse Pointe, in the territory of Michigan, belonging to the estate of the late Hon. A. Grant (Commodore Grant). It is only ten miles from the city of Detroit, and would form an eligible residence for a respectable family.

There is an excellent orchard on the premises. For terms apply to Thomas Drekson, Esq., Queenstown, or to James Woods, Esq., Sandwich, Upper Canada, April 18, 1820. (This Grant farm is now (1906) owned and occupied by T. P. Hall).

The subscriber, in connection with Mr. James Lockwood, has commenced the manufacture of tin ware, and will hereafter keep on hand a full assortment of articles in that line (at the building recently occupied by him as a Silversmith's shop), which he will sell at prices from thirty to fifty per cent lower than articles of the same description have usually been sold in this market.

This ware will be made by Mr. Lockwood, of the best materials; and those who may wish to purchase either by wholesale or retail, are respectfully invited to examine it—as by purchasing at this establishment, it is believed, a considerable saving may be effected, besides the expense and risk of transportation. C. S. Payne & Co., Detroit, November 29, 1823.

Watches, clocks and timepieces of every description, carefully repaired and warranted, by Levi Brown, of the firm of C. S. Payne & Co. His time in future will be entirely devoted to that branch of their business.

A general assortment of watches, jewelry, silver work, and other articles in their line, kept constantly for sale at low prices by C. S. Payne & Co. Detroit, November 20, 1823.

Willcox & Beach's hat factory, Detroit. The subscribers continue their business one door south of the *Gazette* office, Griswold Street, where hats of every description are made, of the best materials, and warranted equal in workmanship to any manufactured in the United States. They flatter themselves that by the most unremitted attention to business, and a determination not to be excelled as to the durability, beauty or cheapness of their hats, they will merit a liberal portion of the public patronage. Willcox & Beach. Detroit, May 17th, 1823.

BUSINESS CHANGES.

Dissolution.—The co-partnership heretofore existing under the firm of F. T. Palmer and J. Palmer, is by mutual consent, dissolved. All those having demands against said firm are requested to present them for payment, and all those any wise indebted to said firm, either by note or book account, are notified that in consequence of the late dissolution, they are obliged to call for immediate payment to F. & T. Palmer, who are authorized to settle all the demands, either for or against the late firm. Friend Palmer, Thomas Palmer, John Palmer. Detroit, August 2, 1823.

NOTICE.

The business will be, as usual, continued at the old stand, corner of Jefferson Avenue and Griswold Street, by F. & T. Palmer. Detroit, August 25, 1823.

Bar and pig lead.—Two thousand five hundred pounds of bar and pig lead is just received from the mines of the Mississippi, and for sale by C. S. Payne & Co.

Washtenaw County.—Messrs. R. Smyth, J. L. Leib, A. E. Wing, J. McCloskey, and T. C. Sheldon, have been appointed by Governor, Commissioners for fixing the seal of justice in the new County of Washtenaw, and will next week proceed to execute that duty. The county seat will probably be established on the River Huron of Lake Erie, about 40 miles from its mouth. Emigration is taking a direction that way, and we have no doubt but it will be in a short time a flourishing and well settled country. It is the ninth in the territory, and the seventh that has been organized within four years.

At this time, when our national legislators and government begin to be informed of the rising importance of this territory, and of its value to the Union, there are some objects which should be sought for, and which, with a little exertion, we believe, can be obtained from Congress.

Within the compass of this city the United States possess a reservation which would be of much value to the corporation or to the country. In its present situation it is of little use, and as there is a great probability that Detroit will not soon become a military post of any consequence two-thirds of this reservation could at this time be disposed of without injury to the public service. It would be well if government should direct the immediate sale of such of the reservation as can be dispensed with, but it would be far better if it should be made a gift to the city of Detroit, or to the County of Wayne; and we contend that for one good reason it would be no more than an act of justice on the part of government to make a free gift of this reservation. It is well known to almost every inhabitant of Wayne County that for several years past they have been at an enormous expense for the support of paupers; and it is as well known that a large proportion of these paupers were discharged soldiers from the different posts in this territory. Indeed, there has been every year a number of helpless mortals discharged from the posts in the upper country, many of whom, learning that our laws are very liberal in respect to poor and helpless people, have made Detroit their residence, and have been supported at the expense of the community for years. This fact alone should go far to induce our national legislature to give to this community the military reservation in this city, or at least a considerable portion of it.

There is little doubt but improvements in laying out and making roads in this territory would yield a greater profit to the national treasury than a like quantity and kind of improvement made in any of the other United States territories. Why, then, should not Michigan receive more aid in this respect than any other section of the national domains? Why should there be any hesitation in making appropriations for roads through the public lands when it is known that a trifling expenditure for this purpose will insure a rapid sale of the lands and greatly increase the receipts of the national treasury? (The Hon. Austin E. Wing secured, when in Congress, a grant of this reservation to the city of Detroit).

THE FIRST THEATERS IN DETROIT.

THE first theater I attended in Detroit was about 1828. It was up stairs over a grocery store, in a wooden building on the southwest corner of Woodward Avenue and Atwater Street, with the entrance in the rear. The only play that I can recall was "The Honeymoon." I have seen the same play many times since but, looking back through all the years that have passed, I do not, to my mind, think I have ever witnessed a better rendering of it or one that pleased me more. The "Mock Duke" was simply wonderful, and so very funny. The names of the actors I do not recall.

The next theater, Parson & Dean's, was in Ben Woodworth's Hotel, in the rear on the corner of the alley, over the stables, entrance on the alley and in rear of the present water works building. The accommodations were rough and primitive, the scenery improvised for the occasion, but the acting was all that could be desired, at least as far as I was concerned. Of the plays given there, the one I distinctly remember before all others was "The Stranger," with Mr. Parsons in the title roll, and Miss Clark took the part of Mistress Haller. Parsons was celebrated in the theatrical world at that time, about 1832. He afterwards became a distinguished Methodist divine. This theater had a good financial career, though Detroit could not boast of but four or five thousand population.

The next theater was in a brick building near the public library. It was originally a Methodist church. I attended divine services there often; indeed, it was our church, so to speak. Dean & McKinney, of the Eagle Street Theater, Buffalo, were the lessees. Dean was the father of Julia Dean, who in after years became that charming actress and beautiful woman, whom many will remember. I have often seen many a celebrated actor and actress tread the boards of this theater, notably Mr. Ingersoll, a pupil of Edwin Forrest, Charlotte Cushman, Mr. Burton, Mrs. McClure, William Warren, Mr. and Mrs. Trowbridge, the Isherwoods, the Clark sisters, Mr. Ince and daughter, Parker and daughter Julia, Little Billy Forest, J. E. Murdock, Dan Marble, Mr. Hackett, and others.

Mr. Ingersoll was a fine actor and bid fair to rival his tutor, but he died early, shortly after his engagement here. He appeared as Virginius, with Mrs. Dean as Virginia. Miss Cushman appeared as Romeo, with Mrs. Dean as Juliet; Portia in "The Merchant of Venice," with Mrs. Dean as Nerissa, and Mr. McKinney as Shylock. Miss Cushman's engagement with Dean and McKinney was in 1837. She was the guest of Governor Stevens T. Mason. Captain Marryatt, R. N., author of "Midshipman Easy," etc., was entertained by the governor at the same time.

* * *

Mr. Dean was famous as "Balie Nicol Jarvie" in "Rob Roy." Mr. McKinney, besides enacting the part of Shylock, used to take the part of "Arbaces" in "The Last Days of Pompeii," with Mrs. McClure as "Nydia," the blind girl, and also "Wacousta" in the play of that name, with Mrs. McClure as "Oucanasta." The scene of "Wacousta" is laid in and around Detroit, the siege of Pontiac. Major Richardson, author of "Wacousta," was a retired British officer, residing in Windsor. Mr. McKinney was also fine in "Shylock," at least I thought so, though a youth of 18 or thereabouts. Those who would care to see a representation of Nydia, the blind girl of Pompeii, and Mrs. McClure almost very self in that character, can easily do so, by visiting the Detroit Art Museum, where is the statue of the "blind girl" in marble, by the celebrated Michigan sculptor, Randolph Rogers, and kindly loaned that institution by Senator T. W. Palmer.

* * *

One of the specialties of one of the Isherwoods (Harry) was such characters as "Sir Giles Overreach." Mrs. Trowbridge usually playing with him. The latter used to get quite carried away with her part and once, during her excitement, she stabbed Isherwood with a dagger, almost fatally; so serious was it that a doctor had to be called immediately, and he was laid up for a week in consequence. I was present at the play. Isherwood was also a first-class scene painter, and was later on employed in that capacity at Wallack's Theater in New York for many years. He was a fine actor, of the robust class.

* * *

Mr. Ince and daughter were in light opera, such as "LaBayedaire," the first opera that I remember to have seen and the first of its kind to be presented to the citizens of Detroit, I think.

Mrs. Parker, of Parker & Ellis, looked after her charming daughter, Julia, who was a danseuse and a fine one, too.

* * *

The patrons of the theaters in those days used to get their money's worth, and more, too, as the price of admission was low, it being from 25 to 75 cents, according to the location of seats. Two plays were always given, the first usually a heavy one, and the second, a light, amusing farce. Between the first and second play, a comic song or dance was given to fill up the time. Here Miss Parker, whose stage name was "Miss Honey," used to get in her work, so to speak, and she used to dance the hearts of the "boys" right out of them as well as the hearts of some of the older heads.

* *

Little Billy Forest, whom many old-timers will remember, was an excellent low comedian. Later on he was with Parker and Ellis, then with McFarland and Ed Sherlock, at the Metropolitan Theater, opposite the Biddle House. Dan Marble was an admirable personater of the "Yankee," and won fame and fortune. He was also fine as William in "Black-eyed Susan," Diggory in "All the World's a Stage."

* * *

William Warren appeared here in "O'Callahan, or On His Last Legs," and other characters. He afterwards became a celebrated comedian, and died in Boston a few years ago. Here Winchell, the impersonator of odd characters used to appear. His sketches were of the same character as those that Lingard gave in recent years.

This theater was quite a distance from the heart of the city at that time. One reached it from the corner of Monroe Avenue and Farmer Street, by a wide plank sidewalk that ran across-lots to the entrance, but it was well patronized, nevertheless. Colonel McKinstry, the owner, finally sold the property and built a large wooden circus, opposite the northeast corner of State Street. It did not prove a success as a circus so he turned it into a theater, and continued it for awhile, but neither as a theater did it turn out to be a successful venture, so he finally abandoned it altogether. After this, the old city hall was used occasionally for entertainments. It was, in fact, about the only place for the purpose in the city from 1841 to 1848.

Mr. J. S. Potter and wife were the first to give theatrical entertainments in the city hall. Garry Hough used to appear here, as also did a Mr. Ryer, who had considerable talent. He used to take the leading male characters in "Evadne," "Blanca, the Italian Wife," etc. Isaac S. Merritt was at that time a strolling actor and he, too, appeared here. Some years later he wrote his name "Isaac Merritt Singer," because he was the inventor of the Singer sewing machine. He had no use for the stage after that. The Detroit *Free Press* of July 5, 1848, has this to say in regard to the city hall and J. S. Potter: "Mr. J. S. Potter from the eastern states is now fitting up the old city hall in a neat and commodious style, as a theater, and when completed will open it with a fine company. The building is being thoroughly cleaned and painted and will be arranged with a pit and a tier of boxes capable of seating 300 persons."

Christie's Minstrels occasionally appeared here. They were the pioneers in this class of entertainment, and they took at once, being such a novelty. Christie was a host within himself. He was aided by his brother, George, and a youth named Pearce, as end men. The remainder of the troupe were all first-class musicians. Presume many will remember Christie, the leader. He was quite distinguished in appearance when off the stage, and then always faultlessly dressed, and usually accompanied by two dogs of a fine breed, but not of the bulldog variety. What became of him I do not know. The minstrels gave the newest and most catchy songs of the day, and were immensely popular. Many years after this George Christie, with Burch, Backus and Wambold (also former members of Christie's Minstrels), opened a music hall on Broadway, New York, opposite the Metropolitan

Hotel (Niblo's Garden), and continued there for a long period with great success.

Charley Backus was of an influential Rochester (New York) family. He was a fine singer of the minstrel order. Burch was a better story teller than singer I used to think. Wambold was a fine singer. His "Sally in Our Alley" was one of the many popular songs of the day that he used to render bewitchingly. I often heard this trio at the above music hall.

The National Theater (Metropolitan) was built and first opened by Parker & Ellis in 1848. After Parker & Ellis came James Sherlock, who gave place to his son, Ed T. Sherlock, for two years. In 1855 came Asa McFarland, and during his reign, which lasted up to the year 1861, the theater was known as "McFarland's Metropolitan Theater."

PARKER AND ELLIS.

Mr. Parker was an old-time comedian, reveling in large check trousers, and boasting a red nose. He was a good comic singer, an indispensable accomplishment for a comedian in those days. His song, "The Seven Ages of Man," with the chorus of "Hey Down, Ho Down, Derry, Derry, Down," I am sure will be remembered by some of the old theater-goers of the present. In their repertory they had an excellent farce called "The One Hundred Pound Note," in which Parker had the comedy role of "Billy Black." The fun of the part consisted in asking conundrums, which, of course, no one must answer; and whenever the farce was put up Parker always collected a batch of new (?) conundrums. I remember one of the awful ones that he prided himself on. In making an exit he would say something like this: "What becomes of all the pins? Eh, you can't tell? Well, I will. They all go into the earth and become terrapins, see?" And another: "Why am I like the old year? Can't tell, eh? Because I am going out." Exit Billy. As a "gagger" and "mug-ger" he did not have his equal.

Parker also was very good in "Sir Harcourt Courtly," in "London Assurance," and in the song of "The Seven Ages of Man," spoken. "My grandfather was a most wonderful man. He sailed up to the north pole, and all around it, cut it down, and brought it home with him, and my grandmother uses it now to prop up her clothes line. Then why not come here every night, listen to a good play, hear a good song, and go home singing 'Hey Down, Ho Down, Derry, Derry, Down, all to fill up this farcical scene O.' "

Ellis sometimes ventured on the stage in different roles, but I call to mind only that of Claude Melnotte in "The Lady of Lyons," which he rendered fairly well.

Mrs. Farren also appeared at this theater as Lucretia Borgia. Miss Weymess, as Blanca in "The Italian Wife," and like characters, supported by Mr. Perry, who at one time played the leading male roles with Julia Dean.

Joe Whiting, a fine all-around actor, and genial gentleman, played here. His rendering of the "Seven Ages of Man," in Shakespeare's "As You Like It," Act 2, Scene VII, was fine. He was very chummy with the members of the Detroit Boat Club. Mr. Whiting, I understand, makes this city his permanent home.

There appeared here from time to time, The Denin Sisters; Charlote Cushman; the Payne & Harrison troupe in opera; Edwin Booth and his brother, J. Wilkes; Maggie Mitchell; Lawrence Barrett; Ada Isaacs Menkin; E. L. Davenport; Dan Marble; Little Billy Forest; Fuller; Barney Williams; Billy Florence; J. W. Wallack, Jr.; the Webb Sisters (Ada and Emma); Frank Chanfrau; the Cooper opera troupe, also Campbell and Castles; William Crisp; Matilda Heron; E. L. Tilton. Couldock appeared here often and was a decided favorite. His acting in "The Willow Copse," "Louis XI," "Richelieu," etc., was fine. Fuller was almost a fixture at this theater. He was most efficient in old men's characters, such as Sir Peter Teazle in "The School of Scandal."

Lola Montes did not happen to appear on the Metropolitan "boards," but she did appear at the old "Firemen's Hall," in a lecture. She was a small but most attractive woman, and had wonderful eyes. No wonder she made a fool of King Louis of Bavaria.

Two old play bills of the National, June 7, 1855, and January 15, 1856. In the first, the play was the drama in four acts, entitled "Capt. Kyd." The cast was as follows:

CAST.

Robert Lester...	⎫
Herbert Morel...	⎬ Charles Barry
Robert Kyd..	⎪
Housebeam Hemlock...................................	⎭
(A Yankee with comic songs)..........................	J. H. McVicker
Mark Meredith	Mr. Barrett
Old Man	Mr. Deering
Laurence	Mr. Pratt
Kenard	Mr. Healey
Hans Schenck	Mr. Hackett
Countess	Mrs. Durivage
Grace	Mrs. McFarland
Jost Stoil	Mrs. Deering
Tunell	Boswell
Karl	Terrill
Jacob	Vanderin
Custa	Cheney
Kate	Mrs. Armstrong
Elpsey	Miss Deering

The performance concluded with Morton's comedy, "Sketches in India," in which Lawrence Barrett was the Count Garloux, a character dialect comedy part.

The second bill, January 15, 1856, announces "a complimentary benefit to Mr. A. Macfarland, on which occasion the popular actresses, Celia and Olive Logan, will appear." There is a letter to Mr. Macfarland, from the members of the company, begging him to accept the benefit. The following were the signers: Miss Celia Logan, Miss Olive Logan, Miss Rosa Kingsley, Mrs. George Burt, Mrs. T. T. Fannin, Mrs. Nelson Kneass, Miss Anna Kneass, Mr. W. D. Lacy, Mr. J. T. Fannin, Hy E. Mehen, L. P. Barrett, George Burt, Frank Willis, P. C. Cheney, A. S. Black, Nelson Kneass, W. S. Lennox, John W. Roberts, James Jamison, E. Macfarland. Then follows Mr. Macfarland's reply excepting the compliment. The performance began at 7:30 o'clock, precisely, with the tragedy of "Pizarro," cast as below:

CAST.

Rolla	Mr. Macfarland
Pizarro...	Lacy
Ataliba	Fannin
Orezembo	Mehen
Almagro	Cheney
Sentinel	Lennox

Alonzo	Barrett
High Priest	Kneass
Orano	Willis
Davilla	Black
Elvira	Miss Celia Logan
Cora	Miss Olive Logan
Highland King	Miss Macfarland

The farce was "Bombastes Furioso" in which little Charley Kneass, Mr. Kneass, Miss Kneass and little Agnes Kneass appeared. The prices of admission were: Private boxes, $5; dress circle and parquet, 50c; orchestra arm chairs, 75c; gallery, 25c; single seats in private box, $1.00.

* * *

Edwin Booth appeared here in his usual round of characters, with which most of the theater-goers of today are familiar. I liked him best in "Hamlet." I have seen Macready, Forrest, Charles Kean, Murdock, Davenport and Fechter in this character and think he excelled them all.

* * * *

Adah Isaacs Menken appeared in the play of "Mazeppa." She rode the "Wild Horse of Tartary."

> "To me the desert-born was led,
> Wild as the wild deer and untaught.
> It was but a day that he had been caught,
> They bound me on, that menial throng,
> Upon his back, with many a thong."

She was at that time a most beautiful woman, and possessed a captivating form. The mad rush of the steed, up the artificial stage hills, with the "Menken" lashed to its back, was most thrilling.

Dan Rice, the circus man, broke the untamed steed upon which she used to ascend and descend to and from the flies of the theater. This horse accompanied her on her travels, through this country, to London and Paris. In the latter cities her success was phenomenal, much more so than in the United States. In London she was the rage of the male population. She had young lordlings dangling at her heels, and in Paris her debut was even more of a success than it was in England. Among her admirers in the gay capital, it is said, was the Emperor Napoleon III, at the time in the heyday of his power.

It was not so much the excellence of her acting and riding as her fascinating personality. Her features were perfect. Her glossy dark hair fringed her forehead in short crisp curls, while her form was a study for a painter.

She died in Paris in the height of her career, and was buried in Pere-la-chaise. A simple slab with the name "Adah Isaacs Menken" marks the spot.

* * *

Mrs. Matilda Herron appeared in "Camille" through two engagements, and drew crowded houses. It was the first time this play was presented in this city.

* * *

Barrett's first appearance was as Murad, in "The French Spy," June 28, 1853. He was then a little over 15 years of age.

Barrett's manner in acting was severe and abrupt, and otherwise cold and reserved. It is told that his first appearance was a failure. He rushed out of the theater at the conclusion of the play, and did not appear again that evening, he was so chagrined. But his indomitable will and perseverance ultimately secured him success, and in two years after this failure he was the Romeo to Julia Dean's Juliet. I saw him often during his early career, and later.

* * *

Hackett, the elder, also appeared here in his celebrated characters, Falstaff, Rip Van Winkle and Monsieur Mallet. It was said he was the best Falstaff that ever appeared on the American stage. Two other actors followed him here later on in that character, Ben Debar, of St. Louis, and Charles Bass, and though good, could not hold a candle to Hackett.

His representation of Rip Van Winkle was considered a wonderful and realistic production, at that time, but later on Joseph Jefferson eclipsed him.

* * *

During Charlotte Cushman's engagement here, she made a specialty of her great character Meg Merrilles. Presume many will remember what a thrilling and effective piece of acting it was. "When Meg Merrilles sprang forth in the moonlight and stood, with towering figure and extended arms, tense, rigid, terrible, yet beautiful, glaring on the form of Henry Bertram, the spectator saw a creature of the ideal world and not of earth."

* * *

I heard Couldock many times at this theater, in "Richelieu," "Willow Copse," and "Louis XI." 'I have seen Irving in the latter character, and do not think he surpassed Couldock. The latter's Louis XI was as devilish, and diabolical, as it could well be. All will acknowledge, who ever heard him, his superiority in "The Willow Copse."

* * *

I saw Madame Celeste, the famous French dancer, at the Metropolitan in the "Green Bushes," and as Mathilde in the "French Spy." She and Fanny Ellsler divided the honors of the world at that time in that line. They have not since been eclipsed.

Bonfanti, a French dancer of some fame, appeared here also. Perhaps many will remember how she used to walk across the stage on her toes, and then throw one leg straight out and whirl around on the other like a top. Mrs. McFarland, wife of the once proprietor, used to essay the same thing, but it was a miserable failure.

* * *

J. W. Wallack, Jr., played here as Fagan in "Oliver Twist," and as Mercutio in "Romeo and Juliet." His rendition of Queen Mab, Act 1, Scene 4, was a delicious treat.

Miss Caroline Richings and her father appeared at this theater often. Mr. Richings did not come before an audience here, that I remember, except posing in the character of George Washington; he merely chaperoned, as it were, his talented daughter. Miss Caroline, though an adopted daughter, was the apple of the old gentleman's eye, and she had a brilliant career until she married that little insignificant opera singer, whose name I have forgotten. She died early, much regretted.

It was said of the late Peter Richings that on his benefit night he would stand on a pedestial surrounded by set clouds and red fire, made up as George Washington, the father of his country, while his adopted daughter Caroline, dressed in white, and an American flag draped around her, would warble "The Star-Spangled Banner," and that during that time Peter really imagined he was the original G. W. It is said that while waiting one night for the curtain to go up an unfortunate super strayed in the clouds, where Peter was. He exclaimed: "Here, you fellow —you—what are you doing up here? This is heaven, and only Caroline and myself are allowed here."

Miss Richings also appeared at the Fireman's Hall, and gave recitations from Longfellow's "Hiawatha," in character, which were fine. She made a charming looking "squaw."

* * *

Susan Denin was a fine actress. She and her sister, Kate, appeared at the Metropolitan and were very popular. I call to mind only one of the many characters personated by the former; that one was Parthenia to Mr. Kent's Ingomar. She rendered the part charmingly. Mr. Kent was a very strenuous and wild barbarian. I think that Miss Susan appeared at this theater during the following season, in the same character, with Mr. Albaugh as Ingomar.

* * *

Maggie Mitchell was often seen at this theater in her charming characters, "Fanchon," "Pearl of Savoy," etc.

* * *

Julia Dean and her father appeared many times on the boards of this theater. Miss Dean was a charming actress, as well as woman, and of the many characters she essayed, the one which overshadows all the others in my memory, is that of Julia, in "The Hunchback," with her father as Master Walter. I have seen Eliza Logan and Mary Anderson in the same character, and to my mind Miss Dean excelled them both.

* * *

Dan Marble was always a favorite and drew crowded houses. He was inimitable in Yankee characters, as well as William, in "Black-Eyed Susan," and Diggory, in "All the World's a Stage."

* * *

William Warren was almost a fixture at the Eagle Street Theater, Buffalo, in 1842-3-4, where he played his usual round of characters, Sir Harcourt Courtley, O'Callaghan on his Last Legs, etc. This was before he associated himself with the Boston Museum, where he was for nearly fifty years. Dan Marble married his sister, Anna Warren. The widow of Joseph Jefferson is a niece of the late Mrs. Marble. Dan Marble and wife resided in Buffalo at the same time I did, 1842-3-4 and 5, and years after. They lived in a neat brick cottage of their own quite a distance up Main Street. The personalities of Marble and his wife I was quite familiar with on the stage and off. By the papers, September 24, 1903, I see that a daughter of theirs, Mrs. Mary Myers, appeared at the Detroit Opera House in the play of "The Eternal City." Mrs. Marble was by marriage an aunt of Mary McVicker, who was the second wife of Edwin Booth. Dan Marble died of cholera in Louisville, Ky., fifty-four years ago.

* * *

Little Billy Forest was the oddest and funniest man on the job. It did not make any difference whether he was in tragedy or comedy, he always created a laugh. His impersonation of "Sam," in the "American Cousin," was fine, also as Sir Peter Teazel, in the "School for Scandal."

The Cooper Opera Co. were very fine, I thought.

De Lussan also appeared here, early in her career. I heard her in "The Bohemian Girl," as Arline; she was superb.

The Pyne & Harrison Opera Co. also appeared at the Metropolitan. They were fine.

Mr. William H. Crisp appeared here in "Don Caesar de Bazan." I think he was the father of Mr. Crisp, at one time speaker of the lower House of Congress.

* * *

E. T. Tilton was leading man at the Metropolitan in 1855, and afterwards assisted in opening the Detroit Opera House. In the same year Lawrence Barrett had a benefit here, and gave "The Rake's Progress," "The Soldier's Daughter," and a scene from "The Iron Chest."

Wilkes Booth was a very handsome man, of slighter build than his brother Edwin. He played but one engagement at the Metropolitan, I think. I remember to have seen him as Iago to Mr. O'Neill's Othello, also as Richard Third; Fazio in the "Italian Wife," "Macbeth" and "Hamlet," "The Widow's Victim," "The Two Gregories," and "Family Jars." He played about two weeks and his share of the receipts, it was said, was $116. This was under Ed. Sherlock's management.

The Campbell and Castle Opera Company appeared often at this theater and were great favorites. It was almost a revelation to hear Campbell render "Then You'll Remember Me." in "The

Bohemian Girl," "A Heart Bowed Down," Seguin and wife were with them also, the former as Devilshoof and the latter as the Gypsy Queen.

* * *

Sothern played here in "Rich Poor Man and Poor Rich Man," his first appearance.

Brougham appeared here in "Pocahontas," as the Indian Chief Powhattan; a rythmetical burlesque of his own creation. A remarkably fine actor and gentleman he was. During his life on the stage he gave an immense amount of pleasure and he did no harm.

Mrs. John Drew, lately deceased, on her first appearance here as Mrs. Hunt, was young, vivacious and most attractive. She essayed sprightly parts, such as Maria in "The Spoiled Child." I first saw her in this character and have never forgotten it. Mr. Hunt I do not recall, but I do her second husband, Mr. Mossop, as also her third, Mr. Drew. The latter was an exceedingly good comedian, and justly popular. Mr. Mossop was fine in Irish characters and a good comic singer. Mr. Drew I saw in "Handy Andy," and in a play I think was called the "Hypocondriac." It was very funny and he kept the audience in a continual roar of laughter. His Handy Andy was a revelation. Mrs. Mossop-Hunt-Drew also acted in after years Julia in "The Hunchback," Constance in "The Love Chase," and Francine in "Grist to the Mill." But her crowning success was in the character of Mrs. Malaprop, in "The Rivals." Her rendering of it will be remembered as long as the traditions of the stage endure. She engaged with Mr. Joseph Jefferson in 1887 to travel with him and act Mrs. Malaprop, and from that time till 1892 continued to do so. Mrs. Drew passed away recently and is buried in Glenwood Cemetery, Philadelphia, and before her death she bade her son, John Drew, inscribe on her tomb the stanza given below, from Mrs. Barbauld's poem:

> "Life, we've been long together,
> Through pleasant and through cloudy weather
> 'Tis hard to part when friends are dear,
> Perhaps 'twill cause a sigh, a tear;
> Then steal away, give little warning.
> Choose thine own time;
> Say not Good-Night, but in some brighter clime,
> Bid me Good-Morning."

Lawrence Barrett, as said before, made his first appearance at the Metropolitan. He had been bellboy at the Michigan Exchange and after, parcel boy in Holmes & Co.'s dry goods house. While serving in the above capacities he found time to work as supe at this theater. I often witnessed his early efforts on the stage, and must say he did not give much promise of attaining the high position in his profession that he did. It was said of him that during his after brilliant career he had no memory of those who assisted him in his early struggles, nor the chums of his early days.

Mr. Murdock appeared here in various characters and it was said of him in his day, from about 1840 to 1850, that he was one of the most delightful actors on the American stage. His Charles Surface in "The School for Scandal," it was said, was never excelled, and his Hamlet was pronounced fine. I saw him in both characters.

The Logan sisters (Eliza, Olive and Celia) appeared here from time to time. Eliza was most effective in the character of Julia in "The Hunchback" and plays of that character. She was not as attractive in person as Julia Dean, but she was a fine reader, an appreciative actress and a great favorite. Olive was perhaps the finest looking of the three, but did not impress me with the idea that she was much of an actress. She, after a little, gave dramatic readings through the country and met with much success.

I refer again to Miss Julia Dean to say that on the occasion of her first engagement here at the Metropolitan Theater it was determined that she must have a benefit tendered her, whereupon a number of her admirers met in the rooms of Mr. J. D. Jones, the sculptor, at the Michigan Exchange (Mr. Jones, from Cincinnati, was modeling in clay a bust of General Cass for the Young Men's Society). The Hon. John Norvell presided and drew up the tender of a benefit to the fair Julia, which was agreed to by those present.

I give herewith Mr. Norvell's effort, as well as the names of those signing it.

"Miss Julia Dean:

"The undersigned citizens of Detroit, having frequently witnessed your finished and excellent representations; having with pride and pleasure seen the genius which you exhibit in each part you play, and knowing the purity and excellence of your private life, beg leave to tender you a complimentary benefit.

"They do this to evince not only to yourself, but to other ladies in your arduous profession, that true genius, a ready and earnest disposition to become a finished artiste, and an exercise of the graces and virtues of their sex, will receive as they merit, universal approbation.

"We would suggest Friday evening next for the benefit, and such a bill as may best suit your own taste."

Henry Ledyard,	E. A. Brush,
William Gray,	Marsh J. Bacon,
Wm. D. Wilkins,	George C. Bull,
J. N. Elbert,	Samuel Suydam,
A. R. Terry,	Chas. S. Adams,
J. W. Strong, Jr.,	C. Harvard,
S. P. Purdy,	Dallas Norvell,
W. T. Rice,	Wm. T. Smith,
J. C. Gordon,	E. S. Throop,
John Hosmer,	W. C. Cole,
Friend Palmer,	W. P. Moore,
Chas. A. Trowbridge,	T. D. Jones,
Geo. C. Bates,	A. G. Gray,
Alex Davidson,	J. E. Martin,
J. B. Scovell,	A. Mandell,
Barry Norvell,	J. Lake Henry,
J. Logan Chipman,	W. S. Stevens,
Frank C. Markham,	H. H. Dunckley,
Sheldon McKnight,	John Norvell,
Col. John B. Grayson,	Henry R. Mizner.

Detroit, October 4, 1849.

Miss Dean responded in graceful terms and chose for her bill the play of "The Hunchback," with herself as Julia and her father as Master Walter. The theater was crowded on the night of the representation, and it is needless to say the artist acquitted herself with credit.

Barney Williams and Billy Florence almost began their career on the boards of this theater. They married sisters (Pray). Barney's wife used to act with him.

Barney Williams was fine in Irish characters, and a great favorite. In addition to his Irish characters he played "Mose" here. Chanfrau had just introduced it in New York at the

Bowery in "A Glance at New York," and it was all the rage. Williams was fairly good in the character, but he did not come up to Chanfrau in my estimation. I saw the latter in the role of "Mose" shortly after it was put on the boards at the Bowery. I say Bowery, but it was either that or the Olympic, on Broadway. Anyway, a man by the name of Mitchell was the manager. It is related of him that he used to talk to the boys in the pit, who paid their shilling for admission, and if they were particularly noisy, or misbehaved themselves in any way, he would go on and make a speech, saying, "Perhaps, boys, if you don't behave, I'll raise the price to a quarter, as sure as you live." A very effectual threat.

The characters that I most admired Florence in were Captain Cuttle and Sir Lucius O'Trigger. The late Mrs. John Drew once said that Florence was the best Sir Lucius O'Trigger she ever saw. What a treat it was to see and hear him and Jefferson in "The Rivals," the former as Sir Lucius and the latter as Bob Acres, not forgetting Mrs. Drew as Mrs. Malaprop. It was a delicious bit of acting and memory recalls it with pleasure. Florence died November 19, 1891, in Philadelphia.

Mr. and Mrs. Florence came out first, just about Chanfrau's time, and played as the "Irish Boy and Yankee Girl," also "Born to Good Luck" and "Mischievous Annie," in which Mrs. Florence appeared in six different parts, introducing songs and dances. Mrs. Florence's "Bobbing Around" and "Away Down in Maine" were whistled and played from north to south.

EDWIN FORREST.

Edwin Forrest was in his day the grandest figure on the American stage. The first time I saw him was in the winter of 1843 at the Eagle Street Theater, Buffalo, in the character of Claude Melnotte. He was then in his prime, and had not acquired the athletic proportions he gained in after years. He had just returned from Europe after his marriage with Miss Sinclair. I saw him many times in later years, both in Detroit and New York, in the characters of Othello, Hamlet, Richelieu, Jack Cade, Damon, in "Damon and Pythias," Spartacus, Richard III, Metamora, Virginius. I think Edwin Booth excelled him as Hamlet only. Edwin Booth and his brother, J. Wilkes, both essayed the character of Richard III, at the Metropolitan here. It was thought by some that Edwin was superior to his father in that character, ahead of Forrest even. I have seen somewhere a criticism on his acting in the fifth act, where Richard falls asleep in his tent and is tormented by the ghosts of his victims, who file before him, denouncing and threatening him. When the ghosts vanish Richard wakes from his uneasy, horrid slumbers, and springing from his couch, grasps his sword and cries out, "Bring me another horse, bind up my wounds," etc., and whirling round and round, brandishing his weapon at his imaginary foes, drops on one knee at the footlights, his countenance the perfect picture of horror and dismay, and his whole frame shaken with fright. After assuring himself it was but an idle dream, he exultingly says so. The critic in question declared Edwin Booth's representation of this scene, as terrible beyond description, and unapproachable. In my opinion Forrest excelled him in this character.

"Forrest had a grand body and a glorious voice and in moments of simple passion he affected the senses like the blare of trumpets and clash of cymbals, or like the ponderous, slow-moving, crashing and thundering surges of the sea." At one time in his early youth, it was said, he acted a female part, and on being hissed by a young person in the audience whom he recognized, he came to the footlights and addressed the offender in these words: "Damn you, damn you, you wait till I get through with this part and I'll lick you like hell."

Sir Wm. Don, baronet, and Lady Don appeared here, he as Sir Charles Coldstream in "Used Up." I do not remember what character Lady Don took. Sir William was at one time a cornet in the Fifth dragoon guards, British army. Baronets were not so common in that time as they are now, and as people were curious to see one, he drew very well. He went to Australia, where he died still a young man.

Forrest was one of the most athletic men of his time, and possessed great physical force. In view of this the characters of Spartacus, Metamora and Damon were created for him and I think Jack Cade was also. "He was a great egotist and thought himself the greatest of actors and of men. Caricatures of himself, no matter how delicate or how comic, he could not endure."

Regarding Forrest's marriage with Miss Sinclair, his divorce and his trouble with Macready, most all theater going people are familiar. He acquired great wealth, having reached a professional position where he could command his own terms. He gained the admiration and applause of the theater-going world, and there was no reason, outside of himself, why he should not have lived a triumphant and happy life. Yet his existence was a tempest and his career a splendid failure. "There was always a fly in his ointment, a Mordecai at his gate, sullen resentment in his heart and scorn on his lip."

The present generation have seen McCullough, Salvini, and many of them Forrest in the character of Othello, and I will venture the assertion that all will agree with me that Forrest was the grandest Othello that ever trod the American stage. I mention this character particularly, because his rendering of it pleased me the most of all. And further quoting from William Winter: "Forrest's hyena snarl when as Jack Cade he met Lord Say in the thicket, or his volumed cry of tempestuous fury when, as Lucius Brutus, he turned upon Tarquin under the black midnight sky—those are things never to be forgotten."

I saw Forrest impersonate both of the above characters, and can truly say, with Winter, they can never be forgotten.

After the verdict in the Forrest divorce case in 1852 crowds at Christy's Minstrels, in New York, nightly, for months, encored the song of "Jordan am a Hard Road to Travel," for one verse—

> "For sixty-nine nights the immortal Forrest played,
> And sixty-nine crowds he had accordin';
> In Macbeth, Damon and Jack Cade,
> He's the greatest actor on this side of Jordan."

After his trouble with Macready, Forrest clubs and Forrest associations filled with youthful enthusiasts, deified him and defied his traducers. His last performances and readings in 1871 and 1872 were comparative failures, the great, generous, magnetic but lonely and unhappy man died December 12, 1872.

Lady Don, after the death of her husband, appeared in Vincent's theater, where is now the new county building, in the character of the Earl of Leicester in "Kenilworth." It was a rythmetical play, after the burlesque order, and quite amusing. She may have appeared in other plays, but this is the only one that I remember. It had quite a run and to crowded houses. Mrs. Don was a very handsome woman of fine presence, and she acquitted herself admirably at least in this play.

McKee Rankin made his first appearance on the boards of the Metropolitan. The character he represented I do not call to mind. Later on he tried his hand at "Rip Van Winkle." He was farily successful in this character, but he had to yield the palm to Jefferson.

"Uncle Tom's Cabin," when it first came out, had a very successful run of many weeks at the Metropolitan. I think Mrs. Macfarland took the character of Topsy. It was admirably rendered, whoever essayed it.

After Macfarland, in 1861, came John Ellsler and his wife from Cleveland for a short period. They presented "The Old Curiosity Shop." I have forgotten who played the character of Little Nell, but I call to mind quite vividly how admirable Ellsler was in the character of Quilp, and Mrs. Ellsler in that of the Marchioness. They also gave "Aladdin, or the Wonderful Lamp," with Mrs. Ellsler as Aladdin. The scenery and spectacular appointments were gorgeous for that day. The play had quite a run for two weeks, and was a drawing card.

After Ellsler came Yankee Robinson for a short season in his various characters, then came Mrs. H. A. Perry, who had for her leading man John W. Albaugh, who at this engagement played Ingomar to Miss Susan Denin's Parthenia.

In 1862 Mr. Bayless opened the Metropolitan as a variety theater, and he was followed by Welch & Jacobs. The latter retired and Chas. M. Welch became manager, and so continued until fire swept the theater away in 1877. Welch made much money here, clearing, it was currently reported, $1,000 per month. The young men's hall in the Biddle House had from time to time been used for theatrical purposes; notably Ristori with her troupe appeared here for two nights in January, 1876, in the characters of Queen Elizabeth and Marie Stuart, under the management of Garry Hough. The latter paid her $5,000 for the two performances, and said he lost money in the venture.

J. W. Lanergan and wife opened here, shortly after the Metropolitan was destroyed or about that time. Lanergan was a fine versatile actor. He was particularly good in "Still Water Runs Deep," "The Love Chase," "She Stoops to Conquer," etc. His wife was very good, but inclined somewhat to the emotional. Under their management here, Castle, of Campbell & Castle's opera troupe, appeared as Don Caesar in the opera of "Maritana."

Edwin Booth also appeared here as Claude Melnotte in "The Lady of Lyons," and Charles Kean as Cardinal Wolsey in a portion of the play of "Henry VIII." and as Hamlet in the play of that name. Both were remarkable productions, particularly that of Cardinal Wolsey.

Brignoli and Clara Louise Kellogg gave some selections from operas here. The former's rendering of "Good-bye, Sweetheart, Good-bye," was particularly fine. They were then in their prime and it can readily be imagined what a rich treat their engagement here was.

Lanergan was quite successful in his venture here. He quit to engage in the grocery business, however, with sample room attached, on the northeast corner of Larned and Griswold Streets. That popular young man, Charles A. Mack, was associated with him. They always appeared to be doing a good business, and I presume they were successful.

ON THE CANADIAN SIDE.

OUR GOOD FRIENDS AND NEIGHBORS ACROSS THE BORDER.

THERE were many prosperous farmers on the Canadian side of the river in the early days, and their wives frequented the old market on Woodward Avenue, near Jefferson, in the season, with their stocks of apples, pears, poultry, eggs, early vegetables, etc. They usually squatted down on the space between the market and Jefferson Avenue, surrounded by their possessions. They came across the river in their own dug-outs or canoes in the early morning, did these thrifty French matrons.

The farmers up and down the river on this side did not seem to have any surplus to dispose of, at least, I do not remember seeing any of them vending their produce at this market, except one, and he was not French, and that was Judge Jedediah Hunt, who had leased the Abraham Cook farm in Hamtramck, and was on hand daily, during the season, with an abundant supply of vegetables, eggs, chickens, etc. He also supplied the Berthelet market, as did the French housewives from Canada. At these markets in the fall of the year, were found in perfection the delicious white fish, also muscalonge and sturgeon, and all so fine and cheap. One could always get white fish in the season and at these markets from the up and down river French fishermen, for five and ten cents each, and this until twenty-five or thirty years ago.

Discharged British soldiers married into French families on both sides of the river, and from these unions have sprung many of our most influential citizens.

In those early days our Canadian friends and neighbors were more closely interwoven into our social life than at the present time. The Watsons, Askins, McKees, Rankins, Beaubiens, Princes, Mercers, Richardsons, Dougalls, Elliotts, Lewises, Woods, Cowans, McIntoshes, Halls, etc., were large land holders, most if not all of them, and wealthy for those days, Colonel Prince quite so. It was said that he brought with him, when he came from England, $300,000 in gold. Colonel Gardner, who lived on the River Aux Canard, just below Sandwich, was also a wealthy English gentleman. Besides these, the officers of the British army stationed from time to time at Malden and Sandwich were always welcome guests at our firesides, and on all festive occasions they contributed much to embellish the social life of this then gay city. I say gay city; it was eminently so, it seems to me, more so than at present, particularly during the winter months, shut out as we were from contact with the eastern world. There was not much else to do then only to have a good time, and we had it. All seemed like one family, as it were. The interchange of civilities was constant. Many of the families intermarried. Bob Woods married Miss Emma Schwarz, daughter of General Schwarz. Mr. H. S. McDonald, Windsor, married Miss Brodhead, sister of Colonel Thornton Brodhead. Alex. Lewis married Miss Libbie Ingersoll, of this city. Samuel Lewis married Miss Jennie Fenton, of this city, sister of Colonel Fenton, of Flint. William R. Wood married Miss Caroline Whistler, niece of Mrs. Judge James Abbott and Colonel William Whistler, U. S. A. Hon. Albert Prince, M. P., married Mrs. Eliza Hunt, nee Knapp. William Baby married Miss Eliza Chipman, daughter of Judge Henry Chipman. Theodore Williams married Miss Hall, and Tom McKee married Miss Mary Gager, daughter of Captain Gager, of the steamer Albany. So it will be seen that the tie that bound residents of both communities together was no fickle one.

Colonel Gardner, who lived with his niece, Mrs. Sutton, on the banks of the Canard, had seen service in Spain under Wellington, was at Salamanca, also Vittoria, where the duke drove Napoleon out of that kingdom. I dined with him often on the banks of the Canard, and on one occasion my brother-in-law, James B. Witherell, was with me. The latter had been in Spain, and was familiar with many of the localities where Colonel Gardner had been, so the meeting was very agreeable and interesting on both sides, and doubly so to me. The colonel had been associated, for a while after he came to Canada, with Tom D. Babcock (late of St. Clair) in the dry goods business in Windsor in 1837-8. The Colonel and Sidney L. Rood, bookseller of this city, were always warm friends, the former invariably making the book store his headquarters when in the city. He was a bluff, hearty, typical Englishman, and somewhat resembled Colonel Prince in appearance. The Mrs. Sutton with whom Colonel Gardner made his home was the wife of Mr. Sutton, druggist in Windsor.

The Mercers lived about an eighth of a mile above the ferry landing. There were three daughters. One married a gentleman near Chatham by the name of John Duck; another married Johnson Richardson, brother of the Major Richardson who wrote "Wacousta;" the other married a gentleman named Blackwood. There were three boys, I think. John Mercer was appointed sheriff for the County of Kent, and held the office until his death in 1897. Jos. Mercer was clerk of the court of Sandwich, and was killed on the Great Western Railway at Chatham in 1862. Mrs. Duck died in 1852, Mrs. Richardson in 1881. James Mercer, the youngest son, cast his lot early in the United States. He came to Detroit when quite young, was clerk for John J. Traux and later for Colonel Spencer Sprague in his agriculture store on lower Woodward Avenue, and after that, he got married and emigrated to Ontonagon, where he engaged in the forwarding and commission business, was quite successful and acquired a comfortable competency. He was quite a factor in electing to the Unites States Senate Hon. Thos. W. Palmer. He is at present in Ontonagon, enjoying his well earned fortune. Mr. Mercer, a Republican in politics, represented his country in the legislature (House, session of 1881; and in the Senate, session of 1883). When Captain Marryatt, R. N., author of "Midshipman Easy," "Peter Simple," etc., was in Windsor he was the guest of the Mercers during his stay.

When I came to Detroit the brick store and warehouse of John and James Dougall was a conspicuous object, located down as it was almost under the bank of the Detroit River, on the Canadian side and directly opposite the foot of Griswold Street. The firm carried a large stock of general merchandise, imported exclusively, and they pledged themselves to sell carpets, hearth rugs, etc., as cheap, duty included, as they could be bought in New York. I was a frequent visitor to their establishment, when it was in the heyday of their fortunes, and, boy that I was, was amazed at the display of foreign goods they made. One of the firm, James, was mixed up a little in the rebellion of 1837, but not on the Patriot side. He was a participator in the battle of Windsor on December 4, 1838, and on seeing the two-starred flag of the Patriot forces borne by Colonel Harvell, cried out, "A hundred dollars to the man who shoots the standard bearer." Harvell was shot and fell on the flag, which was captured by Lieutenant, afterwards Colonel Rankin. Harvell was then bayoneted. Mr. Dougall married the daughter of Mr. Baby, a very beautiful and accomplished young lady. The homestead of the latter was situated just across the street from Dougall's store, and I think they made their home with old Mr. Baby. Mr. Dougall was mayor of Windsor four years, serving in 1859-60 and 1869-70. One of his sons was at one time of the clothing firm of Mabley & Co. on Woodward Avenue. The Dougalls had an immense American trade for years. They were heavy importers of hardware, iron and steel, and were hustling competitors of Erastus Corning & Co., Albany, N. Y.

The Richardsons were quite a distinguished family in Windsor, Robert Richardson being a surgeon in the British army. One of the sons, John, was a major in the same service and spent some time in Windsor. He was quite literary, and wrote among other books, the Indian novel of "Wacousta," as before said; it was very popular and widely read. Some one dramatized it, and it was brought out here by Dean & McKinney at the theater on the southeast corner of Gratiot and Farrar Streets (house still standing). This about 1837. Charlotte Cushman was here at the same time, playing at this theater. The major and herself were guests of Governor Stevens T. Mason. A son of the major married a daughter of my jolly good friend, Dr. Donnelly, who was so well and favorably known on both sides of the border. I had an experience with the doctor and it was a jolly one, too. The late Governor Dave Jerome shared it also. The latter, in his early days, chartered the steamboat Chataugue one season for the purpose of tugging on Lake and River St. Clair, making his objective point at Algonac. He invited the doctor and myself to make a ten days' visit, which we did. It is needless to say we had a thoroughly good time.

I think some of the members of the Richardson family are residents of Windsor at the present time. One of them was engaged for two or three years on the Detroit *Journal* in the circulating department, when it was under the management of Hon. William Livingstone.

The first time I remember to have seen Colonel Rankin and notice him particularly was at an entertainment given by Mr. Robert Watson at his hospitable home, on the river bank, just below Windsor, and where is now the Canada Southern depot.

Gathered there at the same time were Bob Woods, now Judge Woods, of Chatham; Mr. and Mrs. Mercer with their sons and daughters; Colonel and Mrs. Prince, with their sons and daughter, Miss Belle Prince; the Babys, the Dougalls and other prominent people who went to make up the social and business life of that side of the border. The gay company was, of course, plentifully sprinkled with the representatives of both sexes of Detroit's social side. Colonel Rankin was then in his prime, and just married to Miss McKee, daughter of Colonel McKee and sister of Tom McKee, of Sandwich, lately deceased, and who was for so many years connected with the Canadian customs. I never could get on terms of intimacy with the colonel, he was so imperious, but I was quite intimate with the McKees.

Colonel Rankin in 1862 obtained permission from the war department to raise for the United States service a regiment of lancers, which he did, recruiting the members almost entirely from Canada. It was mustered into service with the maximum number, fully equipped with the exception of horses. It would have left the state in fine condition, but was disbanded by order of the war department, contrary to the repeated protests of the governor (Blair) and without giving any reason for such a procedure, losing to the service of the United States a remarkably fine body of officers and men.

Colonel Rankin in a very happy manner presented, on behalf of the Windsor town council, to the Detroit fire department a silver trumpet in recognition of its opportune services in staying what promised to be a disastrous fire on the night of the 6th of April, 1849. The loss, anyway, was about $30,000.

The colonel died March 13, 1893, at the Hotel Dieu in Windsor. He was a familiar figure on the streets of Detroit and Windsor for many years. He was a powerfully built man and vigorous to the last. His individualism was strongly asserted in his facial contour, which indicated firmness, determination, shrewdness, and iron will. His bronzed, resolute face and gleaming eyes were surrounded by a mass of white hair and long whiskers and mustache, which gave him a resemblance to a French marshal. Nor did his appearance belie his record. He was a gallant soldier, fire-eating duelist, belligerent politician and successful speculator and man of business, and wrote his name on more than one page of Canadian history. He and Judge Woods of Chatham were lifelong friends.

Shortly after his marriage Rankin proceeded with a band of Indians from Walpole Island to England, where he attracted marked attention in London from the extravagant and gorgeous display of his troop, driven by himself, as an Indian chief, in a van made for the purpose, with his team of six gorgeously caparisoned cream-colored horses drilled to the quick step of a brass band in attendance. He sold out to Catlin (Indian showman) for a large amount and returned to Canada.

Rankin was born at sea (Atlantic). His marriage with Miss McKee was clandestine, though why was not known.

On the river front and near the Fellers, Benjamin mansion, is his old, time-worn home. It is a strong, old-fashioned wooden structure with dormer windows. It was built by Wm. R. Wood, lawyer and town treasurer of Sandwich, somewhere about 1840. Wood was allied to one of the prominent Detroit families, having married Miss Caroline Whistler, niece of Mrs. Judge James Abbott, as before said. Wood, in addition to the above, owned Bois Blanc Island, both of which he sold to Colonel Rankin some time in the late forties.

Colonel Rankin had two remarkably fine boys. Both grew to manhood; one took to the stage and has been before the public for many years. I always thought him a very fine actor. The other, George C., I hardly know what vocation he did follow. The first I had my attention called to him particularly, he was the proprietor of an opera company down at Manhattan Beach, just below Sandwich. Their entertainments were given under a large tent, and were very good. I thought they drew remarkably well, anyway. He was also the author of a work on Canada, a dialect novel, which was fine. He was quite an authority on French dialect. Not long before his death he had a controversy with Dr. Wm. H. Drummond, the Montreal professor and author of "L'Habitant," because the latter claimed to be the author of the poem, "The Wreck of the Julie Plante." Though it had been popularly credited to him, he maintained that Frank Morton, of Detroit, Michigan Central ticket agent and cousin of Hon. J. Sterling Morton, was responsible for the verses. The latter was widely known on both sides of the river, but more particularly on this side, where he had hosts of friends, and they all upheld

Rankin's contention as correct. I presume that by this time the matter has been settled in Dr. Drummond's favor. Morton's rendition of the poem was certainly admirable, as was that of Hon. Peter White, of Marquette, and Hon. E. W. Cottrell, of Detroit.

COLONEL JOHN PRINCE.

The late Colonel Prince was without doubt the most noted person that ever settled in Sandwich. He came from England somewhere about 1832 with his wife and four children, born in that country. It was said that he brought with him 75,000 gold guineas, besides a fine breed of English setters and several brace of pheasants, being a keen sportsman. He was a man of splendid physique, about five feet ten inches in hight, powerfully developed chest and shoulders and a voice of thunder, but it was said "so controlled and modified that at times it filled the audience with wonder at his powerful denunciations and his electric flights of oratory. A striking type of Daniel O'Connell, the renowned Irish patriot. He purchased in Sandwich what is called the Park farm, and from the quaint homestead he and his charming wife dispensed princely hospitality. In a short time he won his way into the hearts of the people; was elected to parliament, and was a very active member of that body. He was quite conspicuous during the Patriot War, on the Dominion side. It was thought at the time on both sides of the border that his treatment of those patriots who fell into his hands after the battle of Windsor was extremely harsh. It may have been, but the provocation was great. Put yourself in his place. An armed body of irresponsible men from a foreign soil, led by irresponsible officers, invaded Canada with murderous intent, threatening not only his peaceful home and the lives of those near and dear to him, but the homes and lives of his neighbors as well. Aside from this, an act of barbarity perpetrated by the Patriots on the person of one of his dearest friends, almost an inmate of his household, drove him to frenzy. But a few hours before this visitation of his vengeance on his patriot prisoners, his eyes had been filled with the horror of the mutilated body of this friend, who had been in his house in the full possession of youth, health, strength and intelligence, on the evening preceding this eventful day.

On the evening before the third of December, 1838, Dr. Hume, assistant staff surgeon—only child of Dr. John Hume, of

Almada Hill, Lanark, Scotland, in whose family the medical profession was hereditary; the father being in Egypt under Abercrombie, and a cousin—German surgeon to the duke of Wellington—dined at the house of a friend in Sandwich. He wore his undress uniform and during the evening went to the Park farm, partly to see the colonel, as times were exciting, partly to give professional advice for Mrs. Prince, who was ill to distraction from nervous fever, partly to prescribe for the colonel himself, who was ill and worn out, and chiefly to see the third ill person in this afflicted family, Miss Rudyard. Hume was a fair-complexioned fellow, of easy and gentlemanly manner, with a look and countenance peculiarly mild; altogether a pleasing personality, handsome and distinguished looking. On the morning of the attack, he and Commissary Morse directed their steps from the Park tavern to where the sounds of firing came, the former to tender his professional services. They rode, the staff-surgeon still in uniform, and the horse in its usual military trappings. Some one suggested that to be in plain clothes might be safer, but he laughingly replied that no one would touch a doctor. As the incendiaries returned from burning the steamer Thames they met the two. Hume mistook them for Loyalists. A woman came out from her house and warned him that they were a detachment of patriots, but she was too late. The patriot account is that their captain demanded Hume's surrender. To his question "To whom shall I surrender?" came the answer, "To the Patriots." He then quickly dismounted, with the uncomplimentary rejoinder, "Never, to a —— —— set of rebels." Then a dozen bullets pierced him. "Only a part of our force fired—the rest, among whom I was one, thinking it quite unnecessary to go to extremes with so brave a man." The surgeon's body told a different story. Colonel Prince's official dispatch says that, not content with firing several balls into him, they stabbed him in many places with their bowie knives and mangled his body with an axe. One Loyalist appears to have been near enough to call out, "Don't shoot that man; he is the doctor." This interruption and their absurd query, "Then why does he not surrender?" enabled him to slip past the corner of a house under the cover of which he tried to reach a friend's. The first man who fired must have been satisfied with his aim, for he turned to a companion and said, "You may go and take his sword; he won't run farther." At any rate, he retreated, pistol in hand, facing his enemies.

Some of these details of the atrocities have been contradicted. Hume's companion fared better; he was shot at, but the balls passed through his hair.

All the details of the Patriot War and the incidents connected with the battle of Windsor, including a minute account of the part Colonel Prince took in it, as also the cruel fate of Dr. Hume, have often been written and commented upon, and must be quite familiar to the present generation, but I have never seen quite so detailed an account of the tragic death of Dr. Hume as is given here, which is taken in part from "Rebellion Times in Canada" by the Miss Lizars—I myself was an eye witness of this affair in Windsor in 1838, from Jones's dock at the foot of Shelby Street, and also from the room of the David Cooper building on Jefferson Avenue.

It was in the fifties that Colonel Prince went to the Canadian Soo, as first judge of the Algoma district. It was then partially a wilderness. He served with credit until his death, which occurred there November 30, 1870. He was buried on an island opposite Bellevue, where he lived. Mrs. Prince did not desire to accompany him to the Soo, and was not with him when he passed away. The island is owned by some eastern parties, and is called Deadman's Island. His son, Albert Prince, Q. C., erected a tablet to his father's memory. Deadman's Island, lying where the Little Rapids first begin to break over the gravel set with large boulders, on the Canada side, between Topsail Island and the main land. Quiet and secluded as if in the heart of the wilderness, then, and known to but few, but now in the very whirl of traffic and commerce.

Mr. F. J. Hughes, of the Canadian Soo (who is living there yet), nursed the colonel, almost in his arms, during his six months' sickness of heart disease, and after his death, saw him buried on Deadman's Island, as he promised he would. This Mr. Hughes was a relative in a way. He married the colonel's step-granddaughter, Miss Hunt, daughter of Mr. Frank Hunt, of Detroit.

Despite the ill feeling that existed among some of the Canadians against Colonel Prince on account of his course in this affair, he was more of a hero than ever. His journeys were ovations. It was said that Hamilton, Chatham and London testified to a general appreciation. In Chatham the incorporated companies saluted him not only with their arms, but with hearty cheers. At London the Union Jack was run up on his hotel and fire balls were thrown about to make the night brilliant. He was dined in Toronto, and made a triumphal progress home. The portion of the Eighty-fifth regiment stationed at Sandwich were ready to draw him to the Park farm on his arrival, substituting themselves for his horses, and immediate preparation was made to dine and wine him, which was done, and the dinner was set in an arbor of oak boughs adjoining the barracks.

In an account of the battle of Windsor, given by a Canadian writer, this passage occurs:

"Perhaps the unkindest mention of the battle was the report given, as the events progressed, by the Detroit *Morning Post,* fresh from the wonderful spy-glass of the reporter. The infantry are evidently citizens, and as near as we can judge by means of a spy-glass, are like men employed in an unwilling service. They move at the rate of two miles an hour, and have several times stopped, as though irresolute about proceeding."

The author of the article in the *Detroit Morning Post* was correct, for I was an eye-witness of the march of the British infantry from Sandwich. They came up along the river road almost like a flock of sheep, without any hustle or double-quick, although they could plainly see the smoke from the burning barracks in Windsor and hear the reports of the patriots' guns. I saw them from the top of the Cooper building, and I did not have any spy-glass, either. They were quite conspicuous in their red coats. The five sons of Colonel Prince were conspicuous in Canadian life. Albert became a distinguished barrister and member of the dominion parliament from Essex. The one daughter, Arabella (Belle) was a charming girl, of the English type, attractive in every way. She always graced our social functions, given at the National hotel (Russell House) and elsewhere. She is the sole survivor of the immediate Prince family and is passing her declining years at the Park farm.

Albert Prince married Mrs. Lizzie Hunt, of Detroit, daughter of Mrs. John Owen by her first husband, Thos. Knapp. They lived at the "Firs," just below Sandwich on the bank of the river; an ideal home, where they dispensed princely hospitality, and drew around them all who were distinguished in the dominion, politically or otherwise.

FELLERS & BENJAMIN.

In after years, when worried with the cares of business, Mr. Fellers (of the firm of Fellers & Benjamin, hotel proprietors) occupied the old Johnson Richardson homestead for a while, and in 1859, bought the Scott residence, which he occupied until his death; then it passed into the hands of his former partner Benjamin. It will be remembered that Fellers & Benjamin at one time kept the National Hotel (Russell House); also the Michigan Exchange. Benjamin married the only daughter of his partner Fellers, somewhere in the late fifties.

The National hotel and the Michigan Exchange under the management of Fellers & Benjamin, were in their prime, and not excelled by any west of Albany. Benjamin, during the civil war, kept the Adams House in Chicago, which was situated near the Michigan Central railroad depot. The house had a fine reputation. After his retirement from the above, he and his wife joined Mr. Fellers in Canada where he passed his remaining days in rest and retirement. He died in 1900. A fine man was "Ben." Fellers I was not so well acquainted with.

NOTED ENGLISH OFFICERS.

Between the years from 1829 to 1839 several noted men from the British army and navy settled along the bank of the St. Clair River in the townships of Sarnia and Moore. There were Captain Hyde, Commodore Crooks, Captain Vidal, Admiral Vidal, Captain Wright, Captain Graham, Captain Sturgeon, and Surgeon Donnelly's family, also Sergeant Minton, and several other minor subordinates. Sergeant Minton was one of the bodyguards of Napoleon on the island of St. Helena. Admiral Vidal built a spacious house. It had knees under the beams and in the corners, like those in a ship, to stand a gale without twisting. Dr. Donnelly was sent by the government to Upper Canada during the cholera epidemic of 1834 and died of that disease in London, and his family moved to their lands in Moore.

Captain Wright had been captain of the guardship, man-of-war Griffin, and had charge of Napoleon on the island of St. Helena. He married Miss Jane Leach, one of the belles of the island, about whom an interesting story is told. While attending a ball on the island, given in honor of Napoleon, he honored her with considerable attention. She remarked that she had a great favor to ask of him, and he replied he would grant it if it were in his power, that he had never refused a lady anything he could do. She then asked him for a lock of his hair. This, he said, he would give with pleasure, but she must honor him by cutting it off with his sword, which she did, and this lock of hair is set in a beautiful brooch, now in the possession of Mrs. Wright, widow of the late Dr. Henry Wright, of Ottawa. Captain Wright was colonel of the frontier regiment during the Mackenzie rebellion, 1837 and 1838, and also captain of one of the earliest steamers that floated the Rivers Detroit and St. Clair, called the Minacetunk (an Indian word meaning the spirit of the wave). Her average time between Malden and Sarnia, by steam and sail, was four days, and it is said she sometimes tied up over night to a tree. For the first four years she was a failure; her paddle wheels did not dip enough in the water and her boiler capacity was insufficient. During those four years the steamer Gratiot came out and ran between Detroit and Port Huron, as did the steamers Huron and Macomb.

Dr. Donnelly was the head surgeon in the British navy, under Admiral Nelson, and was on the man-of-war St. Joseph when the British and French fleets were approaching each other. Nelson sent an order for him to come on board his ship, the Victory, which was to have the principal weight of the fight. This he did, taking with him six surgeons from other ships. He attended Nelson when he was wounded, and held his hand when he died. But few of the children of these old settlers are living. Senator Vidal, of Sarnia; P. M. Wright, of Detroit, and J. P. Donnelly, of Port Arthur, are all the writer knows about; but there are a great many grandchildren.

The above is taken from an article which appeared in some one of our daily journals and purports to be from the pen of Mr. E. P. Wright, of Detroit, date missing, as also name of journal publishing same.

Dr. Donnelly, of Windsor, was a son of Surgeon Donnelly. He occasionally practiced on this side of the river. A large number of people on both sides of the river will, I am sure, remember the doctor well, as his geniality and ready Irish wit made him a great favorite among those who had the pleasure of his acquaintance. He died in Windsor not many years ago.

INDEX.

EARLY DAYS IN DETROIT.

Abbott, James W., 533, 714, 782.
Abbott, John S., 378.
Abbott, John T., 783.
Abbott, Judge James, 99, 103, 124, 243, 271, 275, 308, 312, 323, 376, 386, 435, 459, 533, 536, 577, 735, 733, 737, 879, 975.
Abbott, Madison, 736.
Abbott, Mary, 369.
Abbott, Robert J., 367, 369, 376, 418, 482, 591, 963.
Abbott, Wm. G., 335, 577, 736.
Adair, Wm., 114, 357, 451.
Adams Alexander H., 362, 647, 890.
Adams, Alvin, 204, 211.
Adams, Charles S., 183, 234, 241, 244, 357, 401, 521, 532, 671.
Adams Express, 204.
Agnew, Mrs. Sam'l, nee Platt, 781.
Agnew, Professor, 781.
Albaugh, J. W., 998.
Alery, E. F., 238.
Alger, General Russell A., 409.
Alvord, Wm. B., 223, 386, 401, 727.
Allen, Capt. Levi, 31, 47, 176.
Allen, Mrs. Lewis D., 732, 739.
Allen, Mrs. Orville, nee Nellie Guise, 624.
Allen, Orville, 624.
Allerie, Prof. F., 479.
Alley, Col. John, 227.
Allor, Max, 648.
American Express Co., 194, 198, 211, 474.
American Fur Co., 100.
Amsden, C. F., 408.
Anderson, Mrs. Colonel, 455, 682.
Andre, Joseph, 20, 690.
Andre, Major Elias, 899.
Andre, Major John, 464.
Andries, George, 889, 908.
Andrews, Hiram B., 678, 849.
Anthon, George Christian, 606, 614.
Anthon, Prof. Charles, 615, 616.
Anthon, Rev. Henry, 616.
Apel, Professor, 828.
Archambault, Josephine, see Mrs. George C. Kelly, 624.
Archambault, Mary J., see Mrs. Chas. M. June, publisher of this book, 624.
Archambault, Mrs. L. J., 624.
Armstrong, Capt. Benj., 34.
Armstrong, Capt. James A., 115, 170, 180, 371, 729.
Armstrong, J. A., 391.
Arnold, Benedict, 464.
Asher, John, 367.
Ashley, John J., 169.
Ashley, Wm., 749.
Askin, John, 106, 107, 405.
Aspinwall, J. & P., 61, 391, 732.
Astor, John Jacob, 493, 537.
Atkinson, John, 714.
Atterbery, Rev. John, 175.
Atterbury, Mrs. Samuel G., 732.
Atwood, Capt. F. S., 35, 40.
Audrain, Peter, 367, 369.
Aumale, Duke d', 261, 262.
Avery, Chas. H., 490.

Babcock, Thomas D., 1001.
Babillon, Peter, 507.
Baby, Chris., 557.
Baby, James Duperon, 103.
Baby, Mrs. Raymond, nee Josephine Ch 631.
Baby, Wm., 74.
Backus, Charley, 983.
Backus, Col. Electus, 227, 535, 737.
Backus, Fred W., 228, 238, 419.
Bacon, Judge M. J., 243, 375, 890.
Bacon, Marshall J., 166, 168, 223, 723.
Bacon, Rev. Dr., 367.
Bacon, Urilla, see Mrs. James Burns,
Bacon, Washington A., 524, 556.
Bagg, A. Smith, 493, 498, 901.
Bagg, B. Rush, 901.
Bagg, Charles R., 633, 901.
Bagg, Dr. Joseph H., 591, 691, 715, 901
Bagg, John D., 460.
Bagg, John S., 243, 901.
Bagg, Miss, see Mrs. G. H. Russell, 9c
Bagg, Mrs. C. R., nee Cicotte, 683.
Bagg, Silas A., 901.
Bagley, A. S., 498.
Bagley, Governor John J., 181, 348, 45 552.
Baker, Colonel, 86, 318, 378, 645.
Baker, George A., 238, 696, 789.
Baker, J. B., 76.
Barker, Mayor K. C., 553, 800.
Baldwin, Lyman, 902.
Baldwin, Governor H. P., 175, 358, 45 724, 750, 781, 800, 899.
Ball, Henry L., 961.
Ball, Miss Sophia, see Mrs. Hancock, 2
Ball & Petit, 273.
Barclay, William, 356, 774.
Barker, Chauncey, 90.
Barnerd, Henry, 478.
Barnes, Henry, 182, 183.
Barnum, C. W., 401.
Barnum, Henry V., 117.
Barrett, Lawrence, 985, 988, 991.
Barry, John S., 182.
Barston, Samuel, 723.
Barstow, Homer, 224.
Barton, "Ben.", 36, 176.
Basden, Col., 170, 173, 177, 179.
Bates, Asher B., 243, 725, 800, 890.
Bates, Capt. Kinzie, 789.
Bates, George C., 735.
Bates, Geo. C., 166, 168, 170, 172, 17 178, 181, 184, 215, 217, 220, 222 242, 282, 294, 414, 695, 720, 723 861, 870, 894.
Bates, Morgan L., 243.
Baubie, Maria Logan, 486.
Baubie, Mrs. Wm., nee Chipman, 486.
Baubie, Mrs. Wm. E., nee Julia Beatt
Baubie, Raymond P., 486.
Bauhie, Wm., 486.
Baubie, Wm. E., 486.
Beach, Col. Samuel E., 594, 602, 661.
Beal, Wm., 810.
Beatty, James, 486.

Beaubien, Antoine, 526, 528, 889.
Beaubien, Chas., 598.
Beaubien, J. B., 20, 510, 515.
Beaubien, Lambert, 20, 523, 528, 889.
Beaubien, Peter, 680.
Beaubien, T., 510.
Beeson, Jacob, 477.
Belanger, Joseph, 622.
Bellair, Oliver, 135, 551.
Belles and Beaux, 1840, see also Fort Street Girls, 944, 948.
Bemis, Geo., 210.
Bemis, J. D., 210.
Benjamin, Capt. J. C., 39.
Beniteau, Capt., 634.
Beniteau, Israel J., 634.
Berczy, Wm., 90.
Berge, Elisha N., 90, 512.
Berger, J. M., 514.
Berger, Wm., 120, 122, 501.
Berkey, Chas., 183.
Bernard, Frank, 467.
Berrien, Col. John M., 221, 227, 416, 417, 737, 784, 785, 890.
Berrien, Judge John, 417.
Berry, Governor John S., 898.
Berry, Taylor, 145.
Berry, Thos., 728.
Berthelet, Henry, 369, 674, 675.
Berthelet, Peter, 255, 674.
Bertrand, Marshall, 261, 262, 263.
Biddle, Edward, 156.
Biddle, E. M., 236.
Biddle, Maj. John, 44, 144, 324, 372, 487, 512, 675, 698, 890.
Biddle, Miss Sophie, 156.
Biddle, Wm., 236, 237.
Bidwell, Barnabas, 67.
Big Beaver, 140, 142.
Bingham, Edward, 344, 453.
Bishop, Levi, 167, 723, 729, 855.
Bissell, A. E., 391, 738.
Bissell, Bishop, 738.
Bissell, Chas., 373, 391, 450, 777, 890.
Bissell, E. W., 391.
Bissell, Geo. W., 61, 236, 316, 391, 677, 751.
Black Hawk, 155, 156, 219, 280, 515.
Black Hawk (Young), 156.
Blackmar, David, 892.
Blackmar, James, 892.
Blackmar, Paul, 838, 839.
Blackmar, Thomas S., 838.
Blackmar, Thomas W., 524.
Blackmar, Wm., 892.
Blades, Rev. F. A., 598, 673, 706.
Blake, Capt. Chelsea, 46, 51, 59, 70, 216, 270, 390, 447.
Blair, Gov. Austin, 227, 348, 409, 424, 598.
Bloody Run, 559, 561, 566, 630, 772.
Bloom, John, 268, 767.
Bloom, Nelson, 767.
Blossom, "Bill," 210.
Boncher, Pierre, 251.
Bond, Wm., 402.
Bonfanti, Signora, 989.
Bonnell, John C., 235.
Book, Dr. J. B., 440.
Book, Mrs. Dr. J. B., 440.
Booth, Edwin, 985, 999.
Booth, J. Wilkes, 985, 991.
Bouchard, Lieutenant, 522.
Bour, J., 522.
Brackett, Col. A. G., 546.
Bradford, James F., 236, 727.
Bradford, John, 234.
Bradley, 39, 291, 292.
Bradish, Alvah, 581.

Brady Guards, 114, 163, 168, 172, 179, 183, 187, 190, 192, 233, 345, 418, 474 534, 597, 695, 847, 878, 893.
Brady, Genl. Hugh, 114, 121, 164, 168, 173, 175, 177, 179, 180, 181, 187, 191 487, 512, 594, 737.
Brady, G. N., 77, 182, 892.
Brady, Preston, 238.
Brady, L. P., 391.
Brady, McClellan, 892.
Brady, Cassandra, 542.
Brakeman, Louis J., 101.
Brakeman, Mrs. Anna, 99.
Brakeman, Peter F., 100, 101.
Brevoort, Anne, see Mrs. Charles L. B 609.
Brevoort, Commodore Henry, 61 372, 577 609, 645, 727.
Brevoort, Elias, 609, 610, 611.
Brevoort, John, 609.
Brewster, Chas., 183.
Brewster, W., 531.
Brewster, Wm., 421, 533, 675.
Briscoe, Benj., 59.
Bristol, Capt. R. C., 38, 62.
Bristol, Chas. S., 342, 494, 680.
Britton, Calvin, 740.
Britton, Sanford, 345, 502.
Broadhead, Col. Thornton F., 460, 486 577, 586, 594, 877.
Broadhead, Lieut. John, 577.
Broadhead, see Mrs. Webster, 486.
Brock, Gen'l., 61, 136, 147.
Brodie, Dr., 714, 774.
Brooke, General, 227, 228.
Brooks, Adeline, 626.
Brooks, Col. Edward, 163, 165, 213, 240
Brooks, J. W., 200, 915.
332, 450, 527, 619, 625, 627, 661, 730
Brooks, Mary, see Mrs. Whitney, 625,
Bronson, Alvah, 87, 219, 271, 387.
Bronson, Arthur, 34, 455, 681.
Brown, Capt. Wm., 99, 101, 446.
Brown, Col. Simon, 215.
Brown, Cullen, 554, 559.
Brown, Dr. Rufus, 223, 353, 383, 473 747. 894, 895.
Brown, Dr. Wm., 233, 369, 675, 725.
Brown, Ephraim, 733.
Brown, General Joseph E., 109, 110, 11
Brown, H. H., 401, 457, 791, 813, 890.
Brown, John, 732.
Brown, Joseph, 895.
Brown, Levi, 121, 125, 316, 407, 409, 629.
Brown, Mr. and Mrs. H. H., 117, 727.
Brown, Noah, 45, 82.
Brown, Robert H., 507, 510, 898.
Brown, Wareham S., 235.
Brown, W. M., 466, 813.
Browning, F. P., 265, 267, 283, 470, 728 889.
Browning, Sam'l, 267, 728.
Brownson, D. Orestes, 477.
Brownson, Henry F., 477.
Brow, Andrew J., 357.
Brougham, John, 992.
Brush, Alfred, 383, 512, 894.
Brush, Edmond A., 234, 260, 335, 344 383, 512, 526, 529, 533, 611, 668, 675 737, 788, 868, 890, 902.
Brush Elijah, 367, 703.
Buckley, Henry T., 227, 357, 507, 740.
Buel, Alex. H., 556.
Buffalo City Guard, 174, 175, 176, 191.
Buffalo Light Guard, 174, 175, 176.
Buhl, C. H., 357, 494, 496, 526, 728.

INDEX.

Buhl, F., 494, 495, 684, 760.
Buhl, Frederick, 892.
Buhl, Walter, 496.
Bull, Chas. M., 166, 412, 436, 489, 682, 741, 889, 892.
Bull, Miss, see Mrs. Gov. Fairchild, 741.
Bull, Mr. and Mrs. G. G., 58, 166, 174, 191, 475, 741.
Bullock, Dr. Earle, 823.
Bullock, Miss, see Mrs. Dr. J. Knox Gailey, 823.
Bullock, Robt., 684.
Bullock, Silas, 823.
Bullock, V. W., 183, 507.
Bunce, Judge Z. W., 124.
Burbank, David, 19.
Burch, "Billy," 983.
Burchard, L. Y. B., 725.
Burdick, Justin, 221, 890.
Burgess Corps of Albany, 174.
Burke, Capt. Edward, 37.
Burke, Oliver, 357.
Burke, P. B., 211.
Burlingame, Anson G., 166, 244, 357, 488, 490.
Burns, James, 68, 316, 323, 403.
Burns, Jimmie, 100.
492, 698, 851.
Burt, Charlotte, see Mrs. Ralph W. Kirkham, 624.
Burt, Miss Nina, 624.
Burt, Mrs. O. P., nee Labadie, 624.
Burtis, Capt. John, 25, 40, 74, 76, 78, 80, 256, 390, 668, 740.
Burnett, Mrs. Charles, 656.
Burnham, Thomas, 343, 452, 720.
Burton, Clarence M., 391, 392, 396, 406, 844, 909, 910, 920, 971, 972.
Burton, Wm., 981.
Busby, James, 713, 923.
Busby, Miss, see Mrs. James Fraser, 713.
Busby, Thos., 923.
Bush, Mrs. Edward, 631.
Bushnell, City Treasurer, 507.
Butler, W. A., 494.
Byrd, Geo., 889.

BUSINESS HOUSES AND FIRMS.

Bank of Michigan, 497.
Bank of St. Clair, 497.
Baughman, Hubbard & King, 493.
Beaubien, T. & J., 510.
Beecher, Rice & Ketchum, 497.
Bissell & Lauderdale, 481.
Buhl & Ducharme, 496.
Buhl, F. & C. H., 494, 495.
Buhl, Newland & Co., 496.
Buhl Sons & Co., 496.
Bull & Beard, 488, 490, 695.
Business Firms, 1835, 866.
Business Firms, 1845, 863.
Calvert Litho. Co., 863.
Campbell & Goodell, 102, 481.
Campbell & Linn, 466.
Carpenter & Rice, 497.
Chandler & Bradford, 493.
Chandler, Zachariah & Co., 243.
Chapin & Owen, 270, 418.
Chittenden & Whitbeck, 239.
Cicotte Bros., 511.
Crane, J. G. & Co., 513.
Dean & McKinney, 285.
Doty & Palmer, 501.
Eaton, Theo. H., 481, 482.
Edson, Moore & Co., 184, 892.
Eldred & Son, 513.

Elliott, W. H. Co., 840.
Farnsworth, Mather & Hall, 513.
Farrand & Davis, 674.
Farrand & Wells, 502.
Freedman Bros., 205, 481.
Freedman Bros., 205, 481, 732.
French & Eldred, 297, 341.
French & Eldred, 502.
Gardner, M. T. & Co., D. M. Ferry successors, 504.
George, P. & J., 524.
Godfroy & Beaugrand, 590.
Godfrey & Dean, 903.
Godfroy, P. & J., 591.
Goldberg Bro., 840.
Graham & Lacey, 542.
Hale & Bissell, 494.
Hicks & Palmer, 493, 502.
Hunter & Hunter, 840.
Hutchinson & Titus, 514.
Ingersoll & Kirby, 514, 523.
Kern, Ernest, 840.
King, R. W. & Co., 514.
Loomis & Jaquith, 683.
Mack & Conant, 57, 288, 430.
Martin & Townsend, 514.
McArthur & Hurlbert, 493.
Michigan State Bank, 497.
Moore & Carpenter, 497.
Nall, Jas. & Co., 510.
Newcomb, Endicott & Co., 840.
Pardridge & Blackwell, 840.
Poupard & Petty, 391, 523.
Saunders & Kittredge, 501.
Sheldon & Reed, 274, 317, 325, 333.
Smith, L. A. & Co., 840.
Sparling, J. & Co., 840.
Stephens & Zug, 514.
Taylor, Wolfenden & Co., 840.
Truax & Booth, 510.
Tuomey Bros., 840.
Walton & Lacey, 542.
Wilcox & Beach, 481, 484.
Wright, Kay & Co., 864.

Cabell, Mrs. Nancy, 265.
Cadillac de La Motthe, 25, 27, 93, 95, 38 619.
Cadman, C. C., 238.
Calhoun, 89, 463.
Callender, F. D., 670.
Campau, Albert, son of Barnabas C 624.
Campau, Alex M., 94, 345, 501, 564, 60 871, 957.
Campau, Angelique, see Mrs. John P 629.
Campau, Angelique, see Mrs. Louis L 623.
Campau, Barnabas (L'Abie), 295, 46 503, 564, 567, 577, 606, 629, 67! 732, 733, 957.
Campau, Charlotte, daughter of Barnaba pau, 624.
Campau, Daniel J., 439.
Campau, Daniel J., 426, 436, 438.
Campau, Daniel J. W., 426, 432, 55 832, 915.
Campau, Denis, 436, 439.
Campau, Henry, 426, 915.
Campau, Jacques, 606.
Campau, James J., 436, 438, 440, 50 582.
Campau, J. Barnabas, 71, 94, 234, 34
Campau, Joseph, 426, 438, 566, 598.
Campau, Louis P., 439.

EARLY DAYS IN DETROIT.

Campau, Major Joseph, 103, 104, 105, 136, 150, 284, 291, 325, 334, 367, 369, 374, 420, 433, 438, 439, 440, 562, 567, 570, 606, 662, 673, 727, 746, 892, 894, 896, 903, 500, 564, 624, 633, 695, 715, 820, 945.
Campau, Matilda, see Mrs. Eustache Chapoton, 631.
Campau, Miss Adelaide, see Mrs. W. G. Thompson, 439.
Campau, Monique, see Mrs. Gabriel Godfroy, 590.
Campau, Mrs. Alex., nee Eliza Throop, 854, 926.
Campau, Mrs. Barnabas, nee McDougall, 295.
Campau, Theo., 439.
Campau, Thomas, son of Barnabas Campau, 624.
Campau, Timothy, 440, 510.
Campbell, Alex., 323.
Campbell, Colin, 466.
Campbell, Henry M., 102, 898.
Campbell, H. M., 481.
Campbell, John, 323, 357, 687.
Campbell, Judge James M., 481, 724, 898.
Campbell, Sher., 985, 991.
Campbell, Walter E., 77.
Campbell, W. P., 76, 77.
Canann, John, 285, 386.
Canby, General E. R. S., 666, 876.
Canniff, Henry J., 337, 357, 425.
Canniff, James, 425.
Canniff, Judge A. C., 121, 398, 412, 419, 425, 497, 701, 727, 759, 850, 889.
Canning, E. B., 283.
Cardell, Dr. M. L., 891.
Carne, 227, 559.
Carpenter, N. B., 497.
Carpenter, Wm. N., 337.
Carpenter, W. N., 234, 243, 357, 454, 497, 534.
Carson, Kit., 609.
Carson, James, 228.
Carson, Miss, see Mrs. A. S. Williams, 720.
Carson, Mrs. James, nee Hanmer, 749.
Carson, Mrs. Samuel, 720.
Carew, Josh, 28, 226, 228, 394, 695, 749.
Casgrain, Mrs. Senator C. E., 464.
Casgrain, William, 233, 477.
Caskey, S. I., 358, 449, 453.
Cass, Governor Lewis, 18, 20, 48, 97, 127, 138, 140, 142, 146, 160, 166, 219, 250, 252, 261, 266, 278, 289, 291, 311 339, 356, 364, 371, 382, 412, 444, 471, 499, 527, 533, 571, 595, 614, 616, 634, 645, 663, 666, 673, 708, 756, 778, 800, 808, 845, 921, 927, 967.
Cass, Major Lewis, Jr., 86, 234, 383, 778, 780, 800, 894, 896.
Cass, Miss Elizabeth, 384.
Cass, Miss Isabel, see Baroness Von Limbourg, 384, 648, 778, 870, 845.
Cass, Miss, see Mrs. Canfield, 384, 778, 800.
Cass, Miss, see Mrs. H. Ledyard, 384.
Cass, Mrs. Governor Lewis, 384.
Cass, Mrs. Major Lewis, Jr., nee Ludlow, 780.
Castle, Wm., 985.
Cauchois, Capt. Chas., 100.
Cecil, Mrs. Capt., nee Duncan, 750.
Celeste, Madam, 989.
Center, Lieut, Alex J., 221, 227, 417, 737, 890.
Chaffee, Amos, 353.
Chamberlain, Dr. Harmon, 323.
Chamberlain, Olmstead, 105, 325.
Chandler, Zacharia, 358, 493, 528, 777, 853, 874.
Champ, Sargt. Nathaniel, 782, 880.
Champ, Sheriff Wm., 782, 889.
Chandler, Mrs. J. H., 892.
Chanfrau, Frank, 985.

Chapin, Col. H. L., 188, 243, 337, 358 675.
Chapin, Dr. Marshall, 335, 342, 358, 418
Chaplin, Rev. J. E. and Mrs., 753. 675, 795.
Chapoton, 561.
Chapoton, Alexander, 631, 728.
Chapoton, Alexander, Jr., 631.
Chapoton, Cecile Martha, see Mrs. Chas tier, 622.
Chapoton, Dr. Edmond, 631.
Chapoton, Dr. Jean, 630.
Chapoton, Dr. Jean Baptiste, 630.
Chapoton, Emile, see Mrs. Edward Bush
Chapoton, Eustache, 440, 524, 630, 728.
Chapoton, Josephine, see Mrs. Raymond 631.
Chapoton, Miss, see Mrs. Antoine Dequ 622.
Chapoton, Mrs. Eustache, nee Coquillard
Chapoton, Mrs. Dr. E., nee Martha She 631.
Chapoton, Mrs. Alex., nee Montreuil, 6
Chapoton, Mrs. Alex., Jr., nee Mariam tier, 631.
Chapoton, "Tash," 440, 631, 675.
Chapoton, Therese, see Mrs. Louis St. 631.
Charton, Peter, 369.
Chase, Alex. R., 290.
Chase, Capt., 47.
Chene, 562, 563.
Chene, Isadore, 641.
Chene, Gabriel, 642, 643.
Chene, Mrs. Chas., nee Catherine Baby
Chester, John, 168, 170, 180, 222, 344 453, 891.
Chicago, 123, 515, 880.
Chilvers, Capt. Thomas, 76.
Chipman, Hon. J. Logan, 243, 358, 546.
Chipman, Judge John, 486.
Chittenden, Lieut. W. F., 505, 746.
Chittenden, Mrs. A., nee Holmes, 842.
Chittenden, Mrs. C. C., nee Holmes, 842
Chittenden, Wm. F., 190.
Chittenden, W. J., 238, 239, 413, 798.
Chope, E., 852.
Christiancy, Hon. Isaac P., 590.
Christie, Geo., 983.
Cicotte, Capt. Francois, 20, 374, 634.
Cicotte, Edward, 20, 633.
Cicotte, E. V., 377, 524, 595.
Cicotte, F. X., 633.
Cicotte, Geo., 20.
Cicotte, Jean B., 634.
Cicotte, James, 20, 633.
Cicotte, Miss E. V., see Chas. Peltier, Jr
City Guards, 163.
Clapp, Paul, 271.
Clark, Benj., 357, 566.
Clark, Darius, 347, 349, 350.
Clark, Dr. T. B., 332, 450, 463, 505, 89
Clark, Emmons, 349.
Clark James, 90, 565, 690.
Clark, J. P., 29, 40, 844.
Clark, Joseph, 228.
Clark, Rev. Rufus W., 641.
Clark, Winnie, see Mrs. T. P. Sheldon
Clay, Wm., 217.
Clay, Wm., 686.
Cleland, Chas., 218, 294, 395, 866.
Clemens, Miss Elizabeth, 274.
Clements, Samuel, 357.
Clemmens, Col. Christian, 153, 304, 30
Cleveland. Rev. J. P. 626, 726.
Clinton, Capt. W. C., 76.
Clinton, Capt. W. R., 76, 77.

Clitz, Admiral John, 775, 777.
Clitz, Edward M., 776.
Clitz, Frances, see Mrs. General De Russey, 776.
Clitz, General Henry B., 775, 776.
Clitz, Harriet L., see Mrs. Lieut. Sears, 776.
Clitz, Lieut. John, 775.
Clitz, Mary, see Mrs. Major Pratt, 776.
Clitz, Sara, see Mrs. General Anderson, C. S. A., 776.
Clitz, Wm., 776, 783.
Cobb, Dr. H. P., 534, 835.
Cobb, L. H., 245, 357, 418, 506, 556, 698, 835, 893.
Codd, Geo. C., 358.
Coggeshall, C., 892.
Colclazer, Rev., 37, 706.
Cole, Chas. S., 316.
Cole, D. B., 686.
Cole, Harry S., 218, 316, 335, 380, 383, 747, 476, 479.
Cole, Miss, see Mrs. Eben N. Wilcox, 316.
Cole, Wm., 243, 685, 903.
Collender, Capt. F. D., 600.
Collins, John, 749, 899.
Combs, General Leslie, 159.
Comfort, Benj. F., 900.
Coming, Erastus, 211, 227.
Comstock, Elkanah, 265.
Comstock, H. H., 890.
Conant, Shubael, 20, 28, 222, 224, 227, 260, 291, 323, 335, 414, 436, 444, 471, 495, 598, 700, 762, 890.
Conger, Col. J. L., 448.
Conger, Omer T., 902.
Conhehan, Mrs. Chas., 621.
Conklin, M. J. S., 501.
Connor, Andrew J., 525.
Connor, Henry, 153, 614.
Connor, John, 369, 654.
Connor, Matilda, see Mrs. Dr. Egge, 524.
Connor, Miss, see Mrs. Darius Lamson, 524, 533.
Connor, Miss, see Mrs. J. H. Farnsworth, 524, 533.
Connor, Mrs. Henry, nee Trombley, 153.
Connor, Richard, Jr., 654.
Connor, Richard J., 151, 525, 533, 654, 664, 890.
Cood, Edward, 73.
Cook, Abraham, 19, 369, 562, 581, 582, 585, 593, 653, 910.
Cook, Eliza, see Mrs. John Owen, 584, 587, 588.
Cook, Eliza, see Mrs. Thos. Knapp, 562, 584, 587, 588.
Cook, Hon. Eli, 347.
Cook, James H., 584, 890.
Cook, Jane, see Mrs. John Owen, 584.
Cook, John, 183, 584.
Cook, Joseph, 59, 245, 584, 701.
Cook, Levi, 676.
Cook, Mayor Levi, 286, 291, 316, 362, 402, 419, 598, 700, 733, 751, 889.
Cook, Mrs. Abraham, nee Thorn, 582.
Cook, O. & L., 316, 323, 402.
Cook, Otis, 584.
Cooley, Horace, 117.
Cooper, David, 114, 120, 272, 319, 335, 412, 427, 429, 439, 498, 692, 889, 911.
Cooper, Geo. A., 414, 507.
Cooper, Rev. David M., 272, 376, 415, 427, 480, 560, 911.
Copeland, A. P., 355.
Coquillard, Thomas, 435.
Cornell, Mr. and Mrs. Richard, 623.
Cornwell, B. B., 202.
Corselius, Geo., 891.

Cote, Presque, 369, 730.
Cotton, Capt. L. H., 31, 47.
Cotrell, Col., 101, 582.
Cotrell, David, 100.
Cotrell, Hon. E. W., 101, 583.
Couse, Adam, 408.
Couldock, 985, 989.
Cowles, Dr. E. W., 274.
Cox, Alfred, 894.
Coyle, W. K., 562, 716, 863.
Cranage, Thos., 416.
Crane, Albert, 785.
Crane, Ambrose, 698.
Crane, D. B., 454.
Crane, D. B., 549.
Crane, Walter, 785.
Crane, Walter, 26.
Crapo, Governor, 516.
Crisp, W. H., 985, 991.
Crocker, Chas., 268.
Crocker, Chas., Jr., 743.
Crocker, Mrs. Chas., 742.
Croghan, Col. Geo., 130, 139, 533, 704.
Crongeyer, 186.
Crooks, Commodore, 1010.
Crosby, C. P., 236.
Crossman, G. D., 510, 852.
Croul, Col. Jerome, 187, 439, 504, 506,
Croul, Col. Frank, 530.
Croul, Alvah, 357.
Cummings, T. J., 704.
Curtiss, Asa H., 82.
Curtiss, Capt. D., 44, 579, 880.
Curtiss, Mrs. Geo. E., 411.
Curtiss, Mrs. George F., nee Wendell, 9
Cushman, Charlotte, 981, 988, 1003.
Custer, General, 228.

CHURCHES.

Baptist, First, 264, 385, 540, 701, 736.
Catholic, 284, 285, 286, 522.
Cemetery, 688.
Congregational, 521.
Convent of Sacred Heart, 526.
Episcopal, First.
First Protestant Society, 962.
Fort Street Presbyterian, 795.
German Lutheran, 703.
Huron Indian Church, 618.
Mariners or Bethel, 458, 460, 682, see Taylor, 458.
Methodist, 300, 670, 673, 706, 713, 715, 962.
Presbyterian, 395, 540, 626, 644, 670, 70, 722, 726.
Presbyterian, Jefferson Avenue, 525.
Seminary for Girls, 690, 948.
St. Phillipe's, 643, 654, 670.
Ste. Anne's, 281, 296, 573, 613, 642, 66, 689, 691, 772, 718.
St. Joseph's, 665.
St. Peter & St. Paul, 528.
St. Paul's, 540, 644, 670, 722, 945, 953.

Dalzell, Capt., 370, 559, 566.
Dana, Miss, see Mrs. H. W. Whipple,
Dana, R. H., 621, 710.
Davenport, Dr. Louis, 76, 164, 238, 550, 730, 197.
Davenport, E. L., 985.
Davidson, "Gill," 227.
Davie, Geo., 183, 727.
Davis, Caleb F., 169, 512.
Davis, Capt. Ira, 57.
Davis, George, 515.
Davis, J. B., 111.
Davis, Jonathan D., 164.

Davis, Mrs. Phineas, nee Fair, 960.
Davis, Phineas, 243, 258, 332, 959.
Davis, Rev. Henry, 264, 265, 268.
Davis, Solomon, 268, 701.
Dawson, Geo., 242, 344.
Dean, Jerry, 121, 276, 333, 409, 752, 759, 900.
Dean, Julia, 980, 988, 990 993.
Dean, Walter W., 891.
Deas, Lieut. George, 234, 408, 871.
De Bar, Ben., 988.
De Graff, Harmon, 357.
De Graff, Judge Jesse D., 605.
De Graff, Major Isaac, 603.
DeGraff, Major John J., 603.
Demas, John, 657.
Demill, Peter E., 168, 398, 898.
Demill, P. E., 357.
Deming, Geo., 255.
Deming, John J., 267, 335, 742.
Deming, Mary, see Mrs. Chas. Crocker, 742.
Densmore, Wm. B., 211.
Dequindre, Annie, see Mrs. E. A. Lansing, 284, 478, 479.
Dequindre, H. P., 245, 357, 478.
Dequindre, Louis, 20, 140, 558, 666, 889, 476, 478.
Dequindre, Major Antoine, 150, 275, 332, 450, 453, 529, 582, 673.
Dequindre, Miss, see Mrs. W. H. Wells, 667.
Dequindre, Miss, see Mrs. Rev. Rufus Nutting, 667.
Dequindre, Timothy, 666.
Dermont, Robt., 732.
Desnoyers, Chas. R., 163, 357, 476, 477, 688, 787.
Desnoyers, Dr. Edwin, 474, 532, 556.
Desnoyers, Edward, 479.
Desnoyers, Emilie, see Mrs. Prof. F. Allerie, 479.
Desnoyers, Frank, 476, 478.
Desnoyers, J. P., 246.
Desnoyers, Miss Josephine, see Mrs. Henry Barnard, 284, 479.
Desnoyers, Peter J., 121, 150, 166, 314, 317, 367, 438, 467, 468, 469, 472, 476, 480, 570, 598, 673, 675, 727, 737, 787, 875, 902.
Desnoyers, Philip James, 477.
Desnoyers, P. T., 471.
Desnoyers, Victorie, see Mrs. Henry S. Cole, 479.
Detroit Boat Club, 345, 868, 869, 871, 872.
Detroit City Guard, 190.
Detroit Gas Light Co., 828.
Detroit Historical Society, 550.
Detroit Light Guard, 181, 183, 188, 598, 634.
Detroit Light Infantry, 189.
Dey, Mrs. A. H., 812, 896.
Dibble, Chas L., 183, 229.
Dibble, Miss Susan, 229.
Dibble, Orville B., 223, 234, 529.
Dickinson, Capt. A. D., 236, 822.
Dickinson, Capt. Wm., 37.
Dickinson, Hon. Don. M., 547.
Dickinson, M. F., 362, 493, 783, 905.
Disbrow, H. B., 121, 466, 733, 734, 889.
Dodemead, Alice, see Mrs. Joseph Wilkinson, 405.
Dodemead, Ann, see Mrs. Capt. Dyson and Dodemead, Betsey, see Mrs. Chas. Jouet, 405.
Dodemead, Catherine, see Mrs. Jacob B. Varnum, 405.
Dodge, General H., 156.
Dodemead, John, 270, 367, 369, 399, 405, 527.
Dodemead, Mrs. Jane, 405.
Mrs. Chas. Jackson, 405.
Dodge, Surveyor, 109, 111.
Dolson. Peter, 680.

Donnelly, Dr., 1003, 1010.
Donnelly, J. P., 1011.
Doolittle, Mrs. Reuben, 408.
Dorr, J. R., 243, 314, 335, 386.
Dorr, Melvin, 218, 314, 335, 385.
Dorsheimer, Philip, 202.
Doty, Ellis, 500, 514, 555, 562, 675.
Doty, Geo., 166, 170, 185, 191, 193, 337 463, 477, 501, 507, 555.
Doty, Henry, 514, 555, 819, 891.
Doty, Jas. D., 277, 290.
Doty, Mrs. Geo., 501.
Doty, Wm. P., 176, 357, 704.
Douglass, C. C., 228.
Douglass, Sam'l T., 724.
Douglas, Stephen A., 221.
Dougall, James, 354, 1002.
Dougall, John, 1002.
Dougall, Mrs. James, nee Baby, 1003.
Dousman, Michael, 469.
Doyle, Lieut. M., 594.
Drake, Mr. and Mrs. Rush, 625.
Dresser, Aaron, 115, 117.
Drew, Hon. John, 584.
Drew, John, 992.
Drew, Mrs. John, 992.
Drew, Mrs. John, see Mrs. "Sol" Whit
Driggs, Capt. U. S. N., 623.
Driggs, Frederick E., 405.
Driggs, Mrs. Wm. S., 623, 795.
Druillard, Joseph, 106.
Dryer, Capt. Hiram, 597.
Duck, Mrs. John, nee Mercer, 1002.
Ducharme, Chas., 228, 695, 704.
Dudgeon Anthony, 553, 686.
Dudgeon, Mrs. Anthony, 523.
Dudley, Col., 157, 161.
Duffield, D. Bethune, 509, 517, 598, 72
Duffield, Rev. George, 28, 712.
Duffield, W. W., 188.
Duncan, Wm. C., 245, 353, 357, 747, 74 875.
Dunks, Chas. H., 404.
Dunning, Daniel, 196, 202, 474, 786.
Durrell, Wm., 500, 680.
Dustin, Capt. Selah, 57.
Dwight, A. A., 463, 904.
Dwight, David, 268, 463, 714, 890.
Dygert, Kin S., 245, 343, 357, 501.
Dyson, Jane M., 405.
Dyson, Samuel T., 399, 405.

Eastman, Lieut. Ahira G., 594.
Eaton, Mrs. Theo. H., 417, 497.
Eaton, Theo. H., 268, 341, 415, 417, 51 784, 892, 905.
Eddy, Orson, 678.
Edmonds, Capt. J. L., 35.
Edmonds, Thos. 473, 476, 891.
Egge, Dr. W., 473, 524, 695.
Edwards, A., 288, 296, 533.
Edwards, Capt. Arthur, 40, 47, 400, 442
Edwards, John, 77, 685.
Elbert, J. Nicholson, 344, 391, 674, 684,
Eldred, Anson, 245, 357, 465, 539.
Eldred, Elisha, 357, 465, 704.
Eldred, Francis E., 337, 357, 715.
Eldred, Julius E., 236, 247, 249, 25 297, 415, 674, 718, 889.
Elert, Jacob, 291.
Elliot, Col. R. T., 158, 160, 238, 35 611, 724.
Elliott, James R., 357.
Elliott, Mayor Robert T., 188, 357.
Elliott, Richard R., 185, 265, 458, 52 857, 915.
Elliott, Wm. H., 714, 840.

Ellis, General Herbert E., 921.
Ellis, John, 243, 725.
Ellis, Surveyor General, 86.
Ellsler, Fannie, 989.
Ellsler, John, 998.
Elwood, S. Dow, 503, 506, 703, 724.
Emerson, Curtis, 224, 227, 451, 695, 749.
Emerson, Thomas, 224, 227, 431.
Emmons, H. H., 724.
Emmons, Jed, 695, 937.
Emmons, J. P. C., 244, 510, 723, 853.
Emmons, Norman, 937.
Esdell, David, 357.
Ewers, Alvah, 357, 746.

Fales, Timothy, 335, 739.
Fair, Col. Sylvanus, 960.
Fairbanks, Col. John D., 188, 357.
Fargo, Chas., 203, 208.
Fargo, Francis F., 197.
Fargo, James G., 208.
Fargo, Wm. G., 196, 198, 202, 208, 404.
Farmer, John, 244, 362, 419, 497, 701, 704, 706, 733.
Farmer, Silas, 739.
Farnsworth, B. F., 958.
Farnsworth, Chancellor, 243, 401, 554, 666, 687, 737.
Farnsworth, Col. Fred E., 189.
Farnsworth, Dr. J. H., 94, 120, 394, 473, 513, 524, 534, 894.
Farnsworth, L. L., 727.
Farnsworth, Elon, 398, 740, 787.
Farrand, Bethuel, 256.
Farrand, Jacob S., 257, 341, 357, 450, 453, 502.
Farrar, Frank, 35, 59, 245, 701.
Farrar, John, 163, 165, 244, 317, 335, 342, 362, 680, 683, 701, 889.
Farquher, Col. Francis U., 731.
Fellows & Benjamin, 224, 233, 235.
Fenton, Col., 228.
Fenton, Governor, 623.
Fenton, Miss Jennie, 228.
Ferro, James Dewitt, 117.
Ferry, Dexter M., 454, 504, 512.
Fenwick's Restaurant, 730.
Ferguson, Eralsey, 739.
Field, Moses W., 236, 454, 765.
"Fielding May," 625.
Firemen's Ball, 233, 361.
Fish, Capt. Job, 84.
Fisher, Mrs. M. M., nee Ten. Eyck, 699.
Fisher, P., 556.
Fisher, W., 556.
Fiske, David W., 732, 892.
Fitch, Prof. C. M., 525.
Fitch, Andrew, 698.
Fitzpatrick, Robt., 875.
Flaharty, Capt., 46, 71.
Flannigan, Col. Mark, 357.
Florence, W. J., 995.
Flowers, Isaac, 744, 897.
Floyd, Capt. G. W., 37.
Foley, Bishop John S., 688.
Folger, Capt. Thos. P., 57.
Folsom, J. L., 234.
Foote, Geo. W., 342, 356, 684.
Forbes, Capt. Jas., 76.
Forrest, Edwin, 400, 981, 995.
Forrest, Little Billy, 981, 985, 991.
Forsythe, Col. Lewis C., 865.
Forsythe, Major Robt. A., 97, 221, 290, 335, 633, 670, 737.
Forsythe, Marion, 596.
Fort Dearborn, 123, 880.
Fort Wayne, Ind., 880, 881.
Fox, Col. C. Crofton, 581, 722.

Fox, Col. Dorus M., 708.
Fox, Mrs., nee Miss Rucker, 722.
Fox, Rev., 580, 722.
Franklin, Sir John, 116.
Franks, Edward, 863.
Franks, Miss, see Mrs. Ed. E. Kane, 86
Fraser, A. D., 102, 501, 527.
Fraser, Alex., 236, 627, 628.
Fraser, A. J., 236, 627, 661.
Fraser, James, 369, 713.
Fraser, Mrs. C., 656.
Freelen, Thomas, 594.
Fremont, Capt. Sewell L., 58, 877.
French, David, 465, 676, 889.
French, Newell, 889.
Frink, John B., 507.
Frost, G. L., 894.

Gage, Morgan L., 190, 357, 595, 597, 68
Gager, Capt. C. L., 31, 50, 57, 59, 877.
Gager, Miss Mary, 58.
Gager, Mrs. Capt. C. L., 58, 741.
Gailey, Dr. J. Knox, 823.
Galup, E. C., 308.
Galup, Mrs. E. C., see Mrs. Sidney D. kins, 307.
Gardner, Col., 1000.
Garland, Col., 86, 44, 125, 408, 534.
Garland, Louise, see Mrs. Gen'l Jas. street, 408.
Garland, H., 226.
Garrison, H. D., 223.
Garrison, John J., 357, 598, 684, 693, 79
Garrison, Willis, 693.
Gallagher, G. W., 450, 890.
Gallagher, Thos. 686.
Gay, Thos., 90.
Geer, Kye, 203.
George, Edwin S., 496.
George, P. & J., 732.
Gibbs, Miss, see Mrs. W. N. Carpenter,
Gibson, G., 774.
Gibson, J., 774.
Gilbert, Wm., 853.
Gilkerson, Jasper, 661.
Gillett, Frances, 596.
Gillett, John P., 81.
Gillett, Shadrach, 40, 335, 390, 477, 56
Gillett, Thos. S., 40, 183, 357.
Girardin, James A., 103, 105.
Gladwin, Capt., 560, 770.
Gleson, Capt., 398, 648.
Glover, Henry, 268, 393, 457, 904.
Goodale, George P., 862.
Goddard, Alonzo, 208.
Goddard, Lewis, 268, 450, 846.
Godfroy, Alexandine, L., 592, see Mrs. P. Hale, 591.
Godfroy, Caroline Anne, 501, 502.
Godfroy, Caroline, see Mrs. Colwell, 5
Godfroy, Col. Jaques Gabriel, son of J 589, 590.
Godfroy, Elizabeth, 591.
Godfroy, Elizabeth, see Mrs. Isaac P. tiancy, 590.
Godfroy, Gabriel, Jr., 367, 369, 590, 764.
Godfroy, Jaques, 588, 589.
Godfroy, Jaques B., 591.
Godfroy, John Bapti, 590.
Godfroy, John Bapt, 588.
Godfroy, Jeremiah, 357, 903.
Godfroy, Melinda, see Mrs. John Askin,
Godfroy, Miss, see Mrs. W. B. Hunt, 59
Godfroy, Mrs. Gabriel, nee Elizabeth 590.
Godfroy, Mrs. Gabriel, see Monique C 590.

Godfroy, Mrs. Gabriel, nee Therese de Bondy, 590.
Godfroy, Mrs. Jaques, nee Chapoton, 589.
Godfroy, Nancy, see Mrs. Joseph Visger, 591.
Godfroy, Pierre, 588.
Godfroy, Pierre, 372, 373, 493, 591, 592, 899.
Godfroy, P. & J., 591.
Godfroy, Richard, 598.
Godfroy, Sophie, see Mrs. James B. Whipple, 502, 619.
Godfroy, Susan, see Mrs. Morton, 591.
Godfroy, Susanne, see Mrs. Jas. McCloskey, 590.
Godfroy, William, 591.
Godfroy, William, 591.
Godfroy, Zoe, see Mrs. Benj. Abbott, 591.
Goodell, Elijah, 899.
Goodell, Lemuel, 218, 682, 714, 889, 897.
Goodell, Mr. and Mrs. Alex., 102, 898.
Goodell, Nathan, 682, 897.
Gooding, Mathew, 241, 357.
Gooding, Wm., 243.
Goodnow, Daniel, 223, 226.
Goodnow, Wm., 223, 226, 457.
Goodrich, Simon B., 117.
Goodsell, Capt. J. B., 76.
Goodsell, N., 110.
Goodwin, Judge Daniel, 123, 166, 243, 737, 900.
Goodwin, F. G., 238.
Goodwin, Lieut. John B., 594.
Gordon, Hannah W., 265.
Gore, Capt., 552, 556.
Gouin, Chas., 560.
Graham, Capt., 1010.
Granger, General Gordon, 408, 666, 876.
Grant, Commodore Alexander, 659, 976.
Grant, General U. S., 181, 225, 408, 488, 528, 552, 556, 633, 666, 670, 816, 879.
Grant, John, 117, 659.
Grant, Mrs. Alexander, nee Therese Barthe, 660.
Grant, Mrs. U. S., 225.
Gratiot, Col., 608.
Graves, Col. Frank, 549.
Graves, J. O., 450, 890.
Gray, Prof. Asa, 857.
Gray, Wm., 506, 508, 556, 684, 695, 723, 767, 855.
Grayson, Col. J. B., 182, 185, 187, 227, 358, 413, 506, 554, 695.
Grayson Light Guards, 180, 182, 185, 187, 684.
Green, C. K., 596.
Green, Wm., 331, 343, 358.
Greenslade, John, 74.
Greusel, Col. Nick, 184, 186, 357, 549, 621, 717.
Greusel, Hon. Joseph, 184, 621.
Griesbach, 428.
Griswold, Chas., 231.
Griswold, Clara, see Mrs. Paul Guise, 231.
Griswold, Dr. Alex., 511.
Griswold, Dr. J. A., 231.
Griswold, Geo. R., 231, 243, 511.
Griswold, H., 332, 450.
Griswold, John, 230, 511, 797, 891.
Griswold, Martha, see Mrs. C. L. Stevenson, 231.
Griswold, Rufus W., 337.
Grosvenor, Col. E. O., 227, 424.
Guise, A. Henry, 231, 464, 624, 745, 798, 820.
Guise, Lieut. Paul, 231, 511.
Guise, Mrs. A. H., 464, 631.
Guise, Philip, 624.
Guise, Richard, 624.
Guise, Thos. 624.

Gulliger, Mrs. Philip, nee Carrie Brooks
Gunn, C. K., 238.
Gunn, Dr. and Mrs., 235.

Hackett, Capt. James, 37.
Hackett, James, 981, 988.
Hale, John, 90, 311, 402, 412, 494, 623 752, 900.
Hale, Mrs. John, see Labadie, 402, 623.
Hale, Wm., 243, 412.
Hall, Amos T., 853.
Hall, Frank, 244, 379.
Hall, General Wm., 121, 144, 232, 311 371, 654, 680, 682.
Hall, Knowles, 342, 675, 680, 881.
Hall, Lewis, 442.
Hall, Lewis, 768, 774, 858.
Hall, Miss. see Mrs. Bronson Rumsey,
Hall, R. H., 682, 732.
Hall, Theodore Parsons, 591, 660, 663.
Hall, Wm., 768, 858.
Hallock, Horace, 267, 455, 556, 742, 89
Hamilton, Mrs. Major Frank, see Miss 422, 548.
Hamlin, Mrs. Caroline Watson, 480, 60
Hammond, Chas G., 682.
Hammond, Wm., 859.
Hamtramck, Col. John F., 469, 582, 60 662, 664.
Hand, Judge G. E., 218, 223, 891.
Haning, S. K., 223.
Hanmer, Jas. H., 163, 165, 747, 890.
Harbaugh, D. E., 759, 889, 891.
Hardee, General W. J., 546.
Harper Hospital, see Nancy Martin, 2
Harper, Walter, 26, 28.
Harmon, John, 114.
Harnden, Wm. F., 211.
Harring, H. K., 891.
Harring, S. K., 238, 717.
Harrington, Chas., 905.
Harrison, General W. H., 146, 160, 16 456, 590, 610, 612, 626.
Harsha, Walter, 401, 903.
Harsha, Wm., 243, 903.
Hart, Mrs. Capt., nee Watson, 554.
Hart, Rev. Edson, 90, 92.
Hartwell, Thos. H., 236.
Harvey, Andrew, 698.
Harvey, John, 368.
Harvey, Mr. and Mrs., 898.
Haskell, Rev. Samuel, 265.
Hastings, Eurotus P., 274, 328, 335, 53 645, 724, 727.
Hastings, Henry, 211, 724.
Hathon, A. E., 114, 258, 376, 418, 46 889.
Hawkins, Capt. Rufus, 48.
Hawkins, Sidney D., 307.
Hawley, Cleveland, 226.
Hawley, Emmor, 323, 444.
Hawley, John, 463, 858.
Hazzard, Capt. Morris, 38.
Hayward, Capt. Samuel, 100.
Hayward, D., 889.
Healy, 237, 717.
Heintzelman, General S. P. 221, 248, 39 580, 878.
Helm, Capt., 134.
Hendrie, Mr. and Mrs. Strathern, 477.
Hendry, Mrs. Dr., see Mrs. Chas. C 395.
Henderson, Don C., 467.
Henry, Alex, 252.
Henry, D. Farrand, 120, 794.
Henry, Dr. Jas., 120, 367, 369, 431, 79

INDEX.

Herrick, John I., 905, 442.
Herriot, Geo., 126.
Herter, Mrs., nee Mary Miles, 627.
Heyerman, Mr. and Mrs. Oscar, 486.
Hicks, Jas. A., 502.
Hickox, F. A., 464, 892.
Higby, L. E., 235.
Higham, 200, 230.
Higgins, 897.
Hill, Bristol, 834.
Hill, Col. Edward, 188.
Hill, G., 344, 453, 898.
Hill, J. G., 344, 453, 898.
Hill, Rodney D., 834.
Hill, Thomas S., 898.
Hill, Warren, 832, 834.
Hinchman, Felix, father of Guy, 23, 335, 498, 586, 622, 675, 678, 974.
Hinchman, Guy F., 23, 381, 498, 555, 747, 749, 892.
Hinchman, Jas. A., 270, 674.
Hinchman, Jas. W., 335, 796.
Hinchman, Joseph B., 747, 749.
Hinchman, Kate, 727.
Hinchman, Mrs. C., 90, 91, 381, 555, 795.
Hinchman, Theo. H., 236, 270, 357, 419, 423, 426, 555, 768 795, 796, 858.
Hinchman, Theo. H. & Son, 270.
Hinchman, T. & J., 270.
Hittel, Robt., 684.
Hoban, Mrs. James, nee Elsie Piquette, 629.
Holbrook, Benj., 164.
Holbrook, Mrs. De Witt C., 894.
Holmes, Jabez, 732, 839.
Holmes, J. H., 206.
Holmes, Silas M., 732, 839, 841.
Homan, Capt. Phin, 182.
Hopkins, Mark, 742.
Hopkins, Robert, 335, 358.
Hopkins, Samuel, 742.
Hopkins, Wm., 355.
Hopson, Henry, 823.
Hopson, Richard, 551.
Horn, Capt. W. L., 77.
Horn, John, 746.
Horner, A., 369.
Hosmer, John, 696.
Hosmer, Rufus, 182, 841.
Hough, Garry, 983.
Houghton, Douglass, 234, 248, 252, 502, 723, 902.
Houghton, Jacob, 255, 260, 357.
Howarth, J. B., 440.
Howard, Alex. K., 183, 190, 595, 597.
Howard, Charles, 256, 390, 391, 686, 707, 747, 889, 905.
Howard, Col. Joshua, 109, 530, 594, 595, 778, 877.
Howard, Cornelia, see Mrs. John W. Strong, 596.
Howard, Daniel, 595.
Howard, Henry Dearborn, 595, 596, 597, 517.
Howard, Jacob M., 166, 169, 243, 286, 410, 540, 723, 724, 731, 845, 866, 894.
Howard, Julia, see Mrs. Walter Ingersoll, 596.
Howard, Lawson, 591.
Howard, Lizzie, see Mrs. Henry R. Mizner, 596.
Howard, Mayor Henry, 517, 674, 890.
Howard, Miss, see Mrs. C. K. Green, 596.
Howard, Mrs. Alex K., nee Larned, 596, 732.
Howard, R. R., 187.
Howe, Geo. W., 746.
Howe, W. B., 503.
Howe, U. Tracy, 822.
Hoyt, D., 211, 412.
Hoyt, Starr, 211.

HOTELS.

American Hotel, 511, 952, 953, 955.
Biddle House, 487, 944, 950, 954.
Cass Hotel, 831.
Eagle Tavern, 687, 923, 959.
Finney's, 716.
Mansion House, 571, 685, 799, 952.
Michigan Exchange, 716, 964.
National Hotel, 463, 627.
Railroad, 849.
Russell House, 463, 627, 717, 747, 759 1009.
Seamen's Home, 685.
St. Clair, 703.
U. S. Hotel, 687.
Woodworth's Hotel, 686, 873, 952.
Yankee Boarding House, 693.

Hubbard, Bela, 95, 129, 571.
Hubbard, Henry G., 169, 248, 252.
Hubbard, Mrs. Nancy, 232.
Hudson, Bay Co., 96.
Hudson, Henry, 657.
Hudson, J. S., 90, 92.
Hughes, F. J., 1008.
Hughes, Mrs. F. J., nee Hunt, 1008.
Hull, John, 862.
Hull, Robert, 863.
Hume, Dr. 118, 1006.
Humphrey, Col. Gad., 897.
Hunt, Cleveland, 317, 592, 652, 666, 740
Hunt, Col. Henry J., 20, 272, 276, 29 371, 389, 398, 405, 460, 553, 607, 61 688, 891.
Hunt, Frank, 587.
Hunt, General Lewis C., 553, 797.
Hunt, G. W., 236, 891.
Hunt, G. Wellington, 552, 592, 650, 66
Hunt, Harry P., 587.
Hunt, Jedediah, 90, 585, 1000.
Hunt, John T., 228, 234, 421, 587.
Hunt, Judge, 587, 732.
Hunt, Mrs. H. J., 379, 751.
Hunt, Mrs. W. B., 591, 666.
Hunt, Thomas, 587, 648, 650, 891.
Hunt, W. B., 398, 591, 650, 740, 891.
Hunt, W. Z., 317, 957.
Hurd, Alanson M., 335.
Hurd, Gildersleeve, 111, 729, 889.
Hurd, Dr. Ebenezer, 120, 167, 728, 27 556, 559.
Hurlburt, Chauncey, 788.
Hurlbut, Chauncey, 357, 684, 899.
Hurlbut, John, 391.
Hurlbut, Thomas J., 897.
Hurst, Thos., 358.
Hyde, Captain, 1010.
Hyde, Benj. F., 822.
Hyde, Henry, 822.
Hyde, Louis, 822.
Hyde, Mrs. Henry, nee Wasson, 822.
Hyde, O. M., 358, 457, 682, 821, 823,

Imson, 39, 203.
Imson, Captain, 39.
Ingersoll, Jerome, 553.
Ingersoll, Jesse, 237, 553.
Ingersoll, Justus, 523, 553.
Ingersoll, R., 890.
Ingersoll, Miss, see Mrs. Alex. Lewis,
Ingersoll, Miss, see Mrs. Carman, 553.
Ingersoll, Miss, see Mrs. Frank Phelps,
Ingersoll, Walter, 234, 236, 401, 457, 47 695.
Inman, Captain Wm., 784, 785.
Inman, Eliza, 596.

Inman, Mary, 596.
Inman, Miss, see Mrs. Bishop Odenheimer, 784.
Irving, George, 720.
Irving, Major, 181.
Isdell, David, 500, 680.
Isherwood, Harry, 981.
Ives, Albert, 460, 732.
Ives & Black, 391.
Ives Bros., 24, 370.
Ives, C., 460, 853.
Ives, Eardley, 460.

Jacklin, Mary, 28.
Jackson, Andrew, 166, 325.
Jackson, Anna, see Mrs. Jonathan Thompson, 405.
Jackson, Calvin C., 183.
Jackson, Chas., 120, 163, 165, 244, 398, 405, 416, 419, 692, 701.
Jackson, Col. Carus W., 598.
Jacobs, N. P., 732, 798.
Jadot, Col. Louis, 614.
Jadot, Genevieve St. Martin, see Mrs. G. C. Anthon, 615.
Janvier, Rev., 315, 317.
Jaquith, C. H., 401.
Jarvis, G. W., 236.
Jasperson, Geo., 100, 102.
Jasperson, Henry, 102.
Jasperson, Miss, see Mrs. Alex. Goodell, 102.
Jenkins, Capt. Geo., 76.
Jenkins, Shadrach, 78.
Jones, De Garmo, 23, 243, 288, 380, 387, 390, 449, 568, 645, 670, 681, 762.
Jerome, Edwin, 123, 372, 690, 697.
Jerome, Geo., 245, 446, 506, 691, 728, 741.
Jerome, Governor David, 81, 691, 1003.
Jerome, Horace, 691, 728.
Jerome, Judge, 124, 676.
Jerome, "Tiff," 81, 733.
Jenness, J. S., 357.
Jennison, Judge Wm., 625.
Johnson, Annie, see Mrs. Ephraim Brown, 759.
Johnson, Col. Richard M., 148, 245.
Johnson, Jesse, 880.
Johnson, Josiah, 625.
Johnson, L., 69.
Johnson, Lieutenant George, 880.
Johnson, Miss, see Mrs. Louis F. Tiffany, 759.
Johnson, Sheriff A. S., 759.
Johnson, Thomas J., 880.
Joinville, Prince De, 261, 263, 309.
Joncaire, Chabert de, 642.
Jones, David A., 188.
Jones, Enoch, 450, 890.
Jones, General De Lancey Floyd, 227.
Jones, G. H., 450.
Jones, J. L., 234.
Jones, Mrs. Col. De Garmo, nee Sanger, 759.
Jones, Senator, 156.
Jouet, Chas., 405.
Jouet, Jane, see Mrs. Samuel Northington, 405.
June, Chas. M., publisher of this book, 624.
June, Mrs. Chas. M., nee Mary J. Archambault, 624, 666.
Joy, Abijah ("Bijah"), 245, 357, 861.
Joy, Hiram, 861.
Joy, James F., 539, 723, 739, 891.

Kane, Mrs. Ed. E., 863.
Kanter, Edward, 722, 765.
Kaufman, Isadore, 827.
Kearsley, Edmond, 245, 357, 482, 485, 487, 679.
Kearsley, Major E. R., 170, 182, 358, 485, 522, 675, 677, 698.

Kearsley, Major J., 87, 256, 271, 484, 67 718.
Keeler, Henry, 892.
Keeney, Benj. R., 357, 797.
Keeney, Geo. W., 337, 797.
Keeney, Jonathan, 21, 559, 774.
Kellogg, Asher S., 890.
Kellogg, James, 642.
Kellogg, John R., 213, 233, 238, 916.
Kellogg, Geo., 305, 670, 892.
Kellogg, Mrs. Serena, 642.
Kellogg, Sax, 532.
Kelly, George A., 624.
Kelly, Josephine M., 624.
Kelly, Mrs. G. C., nee Archambault, 62
Kendrick, Silas V., 795.
Kennedy, Alfred, 683, 355.
Kercheval, B. B., 380, 443, 645, 683.
Ke-Tan-Kah, 315.
Ke-Wa-Bis-Kim, 315.
King Bros., 208, 301.
King, Daniel, 477, 502.
King, Edward, 243, 245, 502.
King, General John, 550.
King, Geo., 301, 502.
King, Harvey, 808.
King, . E., 468, 492.
King, J. L., 343, 489, 492, 502, 667, 673
King, John R., 808.
King, Marion, 477.
King, R. W., 357, 514.
King, Wm., 468, 492, 714.
Kinniff, A. C., 243, 272.
Kinzie, John H., 788, 790.
Kinzie, Lieutenant, 90.
Kinzie, Mrs. John H., 645, 788.
Kirby, Z., 853, 890.
Kish-Kan-Ko, 20, 140, 142, 144, 146, 151 528, 664, 667, 729, 772.
Knaggs, Captain James, 22, 24, 36, 48, 6 370.
Knaggs, Geo., 261, 284.
Knaggs, Whitmore, 370, 614, 899.
Knapp, Bela, 101.
Knapp, Captain, 247.
Knapp, Eliza, see Mrs. Albert Prince,
Knapp, H. T., 112.
Knapp, Lafayette, 231, 245, 357, 587, 7
Knapp, Sheriff Thos., 231, 283, 562, 584 795, 733.
Kundig, Bishop, 283, 285, 691.

Labadie, Alexandrine, see Mrs. O. P. 624.
Labadie, Antoinette, Mrs. Joseph Langley
Labadie (Badichon), Antoine Louis, 623 631, 661.
Labadie, Chas. F., 628.
Labadie, Delphine, see Mrs. V. E. Mare 628.
Labadie Eleanore, see Mrs. Thomas C. don, 623.
Labadie, Eleonore Descompts, see Mrs. Baptiste Piquette, 629.
Labadie, Elizabeth, see Mrs. J. G. N tette, 628.
Labadie Francoise, see Mrs. Isadore Na 608.
Labadie, Laura J., see Mrs. Jos. Archam 624.
Labadie Lizzie, see Mrs. Wm. S. Driggs,
Labadie, Marguerite, see Mrs. Judge 625.
Labadie, Miss, see Mrs. John Hale, 402,
Labadie, Medard, 148, 149.
Labadie, Mrs. Louis, nee Charlotte B 623, 661.

INDEX.

Labadie, Peter Descompts, 370, 372, 402.
Labadie, Pierre Barthe, 661.
Lacey, Col. Herman A., 542, 543.
Lacey, Miss, 543.
Lacey, Mrs. Julia A., 542, 729.
Ladue, Andrew, 529, 538.
Ladue, James C., 539, 813.
Ladue, Mayor John, 182, 373.
Ladue, Miss, see Mrs. General W. P. Duffield, 539.
Ladue, Mrs. Austin, 832.
Ladue, W. N., 538.
Lafferty, 372, 636.
Lafountaine, Francois, 372, 641.
Lafountaine, Lucy, see Mrs. James McBride, 642.
Lafoy, Augustin, 369.
Lafoy, Lambert, 20.
Lamson, Darius, 335, 362, 493, 533, 765, 889.
Lamson, Mrs. Geo., nee Stephens, 766.
Lamson, Mrs. Geo., nee Stephens, 766.
Lanergan, J. W., 998.
Langdon, Mayor, 668, 749.
Langham, Col. John, 125.
Langley, Captain T., 73.
Langley, Jos. L., 182, 238, 623.
Lansing, "Gat," 478.
Lansing, E. A., 238, 478, 731, 811, 894.
Lansing, Miss, see Mrs. Sylvester Larned, 731.
Larned, Catherine, see Mrs. Samuel G. Atterbury, 732, 890, 897.
Larned, Col. Sylvester, 245, 282, 371, 661, 731, 732, 925.
Larned, General Benj. F., 535, 925.
Larned, General Charles, 20, 81, 218, 271, 283, 596, 678, 727, 730, 731, 925.
Larned, General Frank, 737.
Larned, Geo. B., 925.
Larned, Harriet, see Mrs. Wm. Rumney, 732.
Larned, Jane, see Mrs. General A. S. Williams, 732.
Larned, Julia, see Mrs. Lewis D. Allen, 732.
Larned, Mary, see Mrs. Alex. K. Howard, 732.
Lathrop, G. V. N., 575, 588, 723, 800.
Lathrop, Mrs. Chas., 556, 580.
LaSalle, Jacob, 613.
LaSalle Sieur de, 42. 98.
Lau, Joseph, 186, 238.
Lauzon, Francis, 100.
Lebot, Alderman, 501, 674.
Leake, John, 896.
Ledyard, Henry, 260, 412, 798, 808, 871, 994.
Ledyard, Mrs. Henry, 384.
Lee, General R. E., 227, 546, 599.
Lee, Sam, 196.
Lee Wm. G., 339, 357, 695.
Lefevre, Bishop, 691.
Leib, Judge, 317, 476, 645, 661.
Leib, Lieutenant G. C., 44, 169.
Leib, Louis, 476.
Lemcke, Dr., 862.
Leroy, Daniel, 105, 325.
Leroy, H. H., 342, 713, 923.
Leroy, Joseph, 358.
Leroy, M. A. H., 357.
Lester, C. Edwards, 731.
Lewis, Alexander, 71, 358, 391, 450, 507, 523, 620, 678, 820, 843.
Lewis, Anne, see Mrs. Henry P. Bridge, 843.
Lewis, Anne, see Mrs. Richard Godfroy, 843.
Lewis, Edgar, 620.
Lewis Family, 842.
Lewis, Gleason F., 457.
Lewis, Joseph, 843.
Lewis, J. O., 444, 844, 967.
Lewis, Lieutenant, 44.

Lewis, Miss, see Mrs. Dallas Norvell, 8
Lewis, Mrs. Alex., nee Ingersoll, 843.
Lewis, Mrs. Edgar, nee Whipple, 620.
Lewis, Mrs. Joseph, nee Fanny Sterling
Lewis, "M. Quad," 861.
Lewis, Mrs. Samuel, nee Jennie Fenton
Lewis, Mrs. Thomas, nee Jennie St. 843.
Lewis, Thomas, 234, 237, 357, 450, 843.
Lewis, T. O., 252, 533, 565.
Lincoln, Abraham, 188, 424, 492, 878.
Linn, Thomas, 466.
Lilibridge, 214, 400.
Little, Chas., 508.
Livingston, Crawford, 195, 202.
Livingston, Wm., 195, 548, 1003.
Logan, Celia, 986.
Logan, Olive, 986.
Log Cabin, Palmer Park, 806, 813.
Longstreet, General Jas., 408, 666, 754.
Loomis, Leonard, 265.
Loring, Mrs. Daniel, nee Lemcke, 862.
Louis, Samuel, 843.
Love, Tobias, 413.
Lowe, P. J., 733.
Luce, Theo., 39, 506, 723.
Lucas, Benj., 20.
Lucas, Governor, 109.
Ludden, N. T., 243, 915, 714, 721.
Lum, Col. Chas. M., 188, 357, 766, 854.
Lum, David O., 245, 357.
Lum, Steward, 245.
Lum, W. H., 357.
Lyon, Edward, 224, 226, 233, 534.
Lyon, Farnham, 224.
Lyon, Lucius, 258, 903.

McArthur, General, 295.
McBride, Capt. D. H., 38.
McBride, James, 642.
McBride, Miss, see Mrs. Fitzimmons, 6
McBride, Miss Nellie, 642.
McCabe's Directory, 1815—898.
McCrae, J., 355.
McCarthy, John, 337.
McCarthy, Jonsy, 276.
McClain, D., 369.
McClellan, Robert, 223, 537, 740.
McClintock, Wm., 107.
McCloskey, James, 292, 317, 590.
McCoon, Samuel, 82.
McCoskrey, Bishop, 53, 415, 516, 67 722, 783.
McCoskrey, Dr., 686.
McDonald, Mrs. H. S., nee Broadhead
McDonnell, Judge John, 329, 332, 450,
McDonnell, Mrs. Judge John, 107.
McDougall, George, 103, 218, 254, 26 292, 294, 563, 577, 605, 614.
McDougall, Robert J., 582, 606.
McDonough, Commodore T., 603.
McDowell, General Irwin, 227.
McEwan, John, 355.
McFarren, Alex., 467, 724.
McGraw, A. C., 243, 344, 449, 453, 46 709, 783.
McGraw, E. M., 244, 783.
McGraw, Virgil, 163, 243.
McGinnis, Patrick, 859.
McGinnis, Peter, 357, 860.
McIntosh, Angus, 607, 614.
McIntosh, Miss Catherine, 607.
McKay, Col., 175.
McKay, Lieut. Aeneas, 290.
McKay, Wm., 74, 111.
McKenzie, Capt. James, 43.
McKenney, Thomas L., 250, 252, 533.

McKinney, Col., 97, 561, 571, 616, 890.
McKinstry, Capt. "Gus," 34, 47, 56, 452, 551.
McKinstry, Charles, 452, 698.
McKinstry, Col. D. C., 56, 75, 276, 285, 291, 330, 335, 449, 451, 553, 702, 707, 711, 721, 891, 974, 982.
McKinstry, Commodore J. S., 532.
McKinstry, James P., 452, 485.
McKinstry, Judge Elisha, 452.
McKinstry, Justus, 452.
McKnight, Sheldon, 105, 325, 329, 333, 401, 459, 489, 798, 889, 901.
McLean, Dr. Donald, 750.
McLoughlin, Prof. Andrew, 127.
McMillen, 18, 22, 138, 694.
McMillan, Ananias, 357, 694, 898.
McMillen, Archibald, 19, 22, 889.
McMillen, Arthur, 680.
McMillen, George, 714.
McMillan, Robert, 357.
McMillan, Senator, 550, 555.
McMuir, Alexander, 82.
McNair, David A., 415, 515.
McNeil, Hal. E., 856.
McNeil, Judge, 856.
McNiff, Judge, 367.
McNicol, Archie, 590.
McQueen, Robert, 82.
McReynolds, Andrew T., 168, 538, 599, 676, 779, 819, 891.
McReynolds, John, 169, 473, 514, 890.
McVey, William, 19.

Macaunse, 150, 152, 434, 447, 664.
Macey, G. F., 437.
Mack, Charles W., 219, 337, 999.
Mack, Col. Andrew, 155, 219, 325, 330, 387, 428, 668.
Mack, Col. Stephen, 431, 815.
Mack & Conant, 51, 288, 430, 656.
Mack, Major S., 287.
Mack, Mrs. Andrew, 220.
Mack, Mrs. Hannah, see Mrs. John Farrer, 317.
Mackintosh, Angus, 369, 379.
Macomb, Alexander, 581, 606.
Macomb, A. & J., 578.
Macomb, Capt. J. M., 760.
Macomb, David, 577.
Macomb, Elias T., 609.
Macomb, Eliza, see Mrs. Capt. Henry Whitney, 272.
Macomb, Gen'l Alex., 221, 291, 292, 293, 294, 576, 580, 606, 613, 615, 708, 755, 771, 921.
Macomb, Henry Navarre, 609.
Macomb, John, 577.
Macomb, John (father of above), 577.
Macomb, Mrs. Wm., nee Navarre, 578.
Macomb, Miss, see Mrs. Henry Brevoort, 577, 609.
Macomb, Miss, see Mrs. Col. Broadhead, 577.
Macomb, Miss, see Mrs. John Anthony Rucker, 578.
Macomb, Miss, see Mrs. John Wendell, 577.
Macomb, Miss, see Mrs. Col. Whiting, 578.
Macomb, Navarre, 611.
Macomb, Wm., 577, 578, 609, 611.
Macomb, Wm., 577.
Madison, Asa, 335, 687.
Madison, Dr. W. F., 315.
Maffit, Rev. John N., 299, 300.
Magruder, J. S., 891.
Mallaby, Capt. Frances, 43.
Mallory, Norman, 117.
Mandelbaum, Simon, 228, 791.
Mandell, Addison, 58, 554, 704, 820, 957.
Mann, Capt. Parne, 37.
Manning, Robert, 243.

Marble, Dan., 285.
Marble, Dan., 985, 990.
Marentette, Jas. G., 628.
Marentette, Mrs. J. G., nee Labadie.
Marentette, Mrs. V. E., nee Labadie.
Marentette, Victor E., 628.
Mark, John, 828.
Markham, Frank C., 898.
Markham, Francis, 503, 505, 626.
Markham, F. P., 503, 506, 514.
Markham, Mrs. Frances, nee Emily 626.
Marriage and Death Notices in 1820—91 914.
Marris, Lieut., 86.
Marsh, Capt., 738.
Marston, Major, 67.
Martin, George B., 169, 223.
Martin, Hon. Luther, 646.
Martin, Jas. E., 183.
Martin, Morgan L., 223.
Martin, Nancy, 26, 28, 466.
Martinez, Signor, 234.
Masons, F. & A. M., 502, 951, 955.
Mason, Governor John T., 756.
Mason, Governor Stevens T., 108, 11 169, 183, 221, 282, 452, 719, 73 779, 792, 799, 875, 894, 1003.
Mason, Kate, see Mrs. Isaac Rowland, 7
Mason, L. M., 484.
Mason, Miss Emily, 778, 799, 895, 896.
Mason, Thomas, 244.
Mather, S. J., 183.
Maxwell, Major T., 87, 271.
May, Benj., 526.
May, Caroline, see Mrs. Alex. D. Fraze
May, Judge James, 104, 106, 369, 370 526, 590, 619, 625, 889.
May, Marguerite, see Mrs. Col. F Brooks, 625.
May, Mrs. Judge James, nee Labadie,
May, Nancy, see Mrs. Jas. Whipple, 62
Mead, Marsh, 695.
Meads, John, 82.
Meigs, General M. C., 228, 429, 816.
Meldrum, James, 20, 369.
Meldrum, George, 367.
Meldrum, William, 20, 140.
Meloche, 560.
Menard, Pere, 251.
Menkin, Ada Isaacs, 985.
Mercer, Hon. James, 823, 1002.
Mercer, John, 1002, 1004.
Mercer, Joseph, 1002.
Meredith, G. R., 419, 513.
Merriam, Silas, 90.
Merrifield, Lieut. E. R., 594, 602.
Merrill Block, 449, 453, 485, 532, 727,
Merrill, Charles, 531, 822, 823, 826, 82
Merrill, Charles & Co., 822 (Rice R U. T. Howe).
Merrill, Dexter, 335, 783, 889.
Merrill, Fountain, 827.
Merritt, Adna, 442.
Merritt, Perez, 335.
Mettez, Joseph, 691.
Metcher, 468.
Methodist Church, 396.
Miles, Capt., 46.
Miles, F. D., 530.
Miles, Marcus H., 323.
Miles, Mary, see Mrs. Herter, 237, 627.
Miles, Milly, see Mrs. Alex. Frazer, Jr.,
Miller, Capt. Fred S., 38.
Miller, Chas. H., Express Co., 39, 200.
Miller, George, 686.
Miller, Hon. Daniel B., 642.

Miller, Lynus W., 117.
Miller, Mrs. W. Van, see Josette McBride, 642.
Miller, Oliver, 501, 675.
Miller, Sidney T., 642, 556.
Miller, T. C., 89, 235, 237, 498, 551.
Miller, T. C., Jr., 551.
Miller, W. Van., 506, 642.
Mills, Capt. A. H., 76.
Mills, Major Frederick, 594.
Mills, M. I., 516.
Mills, Wm., 337.
Mitchell, Maggie, 985.
Mitchell, General, 629.
Mitchell, Lieut. Ormsby, 629.
Mitchell, Gen'l Henry R., 187, 237, 245, 357, 377, 532, 535, 596, 627.
Mizner, Mrs. General J. K., nee Stephens, 766,
Mizner, Thos. W., 237.
Moffatt, Henry, 404.
Moffatt, Hugh, 357, 358, 782.
Monteith, Rev. John M., 272, 431, 911.
Montes, Lola, 985.
Montesquieu, Viscount, 262.
Montgomery, "Bob," 39.
Montholon, Count, 262.
Moon, G. C., 267, 493, 531.
Moon, Matthew, 674.
Moon, Sallie, 265, 267, 493.
Moore, B. V., 163, 166.
Moore, Geo. W., 399.
Moore, Franklin, 243, 341, 342, 497, 684.
Moore, J. Wilkie, 830.
Moore, Thos., 161.
Moore, Wm., 187, 357.
Moors, Jeremiah, 244, 335.
Moran, Alfred, 531.
Moran, Catherine, see Mrs. Strathearn Hendrie, 477.
Moran, Charles, 510, 529, 666, 889.
Moran family, 529, 530.
Moran, George, 163, 375, 658, 660, 661.
Moran, James, 530.
Moore, John, 813.
Moran, John Vallee, 531.
Moran, Louis, 19, 20, 139, 668, 889.
Moran, Judge Charles, 529, 645, 668, 740, 925.
Moran, Julia, see Mrs. Isaac D. Toll, 529, 695; Barnard, Moran, Kitty, see Mrs. Henry D. 478, 531.
Moran, Louis, 666.
Moran, Maurice, 598.
Moran, Miss, see Mrs. James Watson, 925.
Moran, Mrs. Charles, 529.
Moran, W. B., 476, 477, 531.
Moran, Wm. B., 876.
Morass, C., 448, 556.
Morgan, Col. Geo. W., 530, 594.
Morgan, General, 517.
Morley, Col. Frederick, 696, 841.
Morley, Col. Frederick, 596.
Mormon, A. P., 286, 358.
Morrell, Judge, 218, 221.
Morrison, Capt. John C., 161.
Morius, Julius, 237.
Morrow, Col. Henry A., 548.
Morrow, Henry A., 541.
Morton, Frank, 847, 1005.
Morton, Hon. J. Sterling, 1005.
Morse, Chas. R., 474, 521.
Morse, Chauncey, 474.
Morse, Commodore, 1007.
Morse, Rev. Ashael, 265.
Morse, O. B., 674.
Mott, Richard, 206.
Mullett, Henry, 337, 370, 409.
Mullett, James H., 123, 169, 337, 701.

Mullett, John, 244, 379, 420.
Munger, Daniel, 243.
Munson, H. N., 473.
Murray, Michael, 117.
Myer, Mr. and Mrs. Harvey, 619.

Nagle, Henry A., 402.
Nall, James, 510.
Napoleon, 1010, 1011.
Napoleon Prince, 73.
Navarre, Alexis, 612.
Navarre, Isadore, 608.
Navarre, James, 612.
Navarre, Pierre, 611, 612.
Navarre, Marie Francoise, see Mrs. Ge McDougall, 606.
Navarre, Marie, see Mrs. Henry Bre 609.
Navarre, Marrianne, see Mrs. Dr. Geo. thon, 607, 614, 662.
Navarre, Miss, see Mrs. General Alex comb, 581.
Navarre, Monique, see Mrs. Wm. M 611.
Navarre, Mrs. Isadore, nee Francoise compts Labadie, 608.
Navarre, Robert, 234, 372, 606, 611.
Navarre, Robert, Jr, (Robishe), 607, 66
Neglee, Henry A., 353, 874.
Nesbitt, Wm., 751.
Newberry, Henry L., 267, 357, 420, 55 832.
Newberry, John G., 553.
Newberry, Oliver, 34, 51, 53, 56, 59, 213, 221, 243, 330, 333, 368, 388, 39 420, 446, 452, 471, 550, 719, 75 802, 810, 889, 890.
Newberry, Walter L., 223, 333, 335, 9
Newberry, Thankful, 265, 267.
Newberry, Miss, see Mrs. Austin Lad
Newberry, Mrs. Henry L., 832.
Newbould, A. H., 28, 227, 231, 394, 4 695, 704.
Newhall, Clark, 100.
Newhall, Roswell, 100.
Newland, Henry A., 495, 768.
Newell, Steve, 35, 59.

NEWSPAPERS.

Detroit Daily Advertiser, 783, 841.
Detroit Evening News, 491, 612, 751.
Detroit Gazette, 575, 687, 748, 770, 7 961, 965, 973, 976.
Detroit Journal, 1003.
Free Press, 687, 729, 746, 983.
Morning Post, 1009.
National Intelligencer, 966.
The Castigator, 915.

Nicholas, 35.
Nichols, 202.
Noble, Charles, 894.
Noble, Israel, 216, 285, 890, 706.
Norris, Mark, 890.
Norton, John, 497.
Norton, John, Jr., 808.
Norton, Capt. Walter, 23, 30, 47.
Norton, Capt. Wm., 69.
Norvell, Col. Freeman, 182, 183, 836
Norvell, Hon. John, 220, 222, 243, 459, 460, 559, 895.
Norvell, James, 389.
Norvell, Joseph, 389.
Noyes, Wm. R., 260, 357, 730.
Nutting, Mrs. Rufus, nee Dequindre
Nutting, Rev. Rufus, 667.

Ockford, C., 357.
Odd Fellows Lodge, 532.
O'Flynn, Judge Cornelius, 460, 889.
O'Keefe, George A., 102, 254, 482.
Oliver, Jerry, 37.
O'Malley, Charles, 490.
Osborn, Mrs. Wallace, nee Brown, 813.
Osborne, George, 358.
Osmer, Eunice, 90, 92.
Ormsby, C. N., 890.
Overton, Mrs., 405.
Owen, Capt. Griffith, 588.
Owen, Catherine, see Mrs. Horace Turner, 588.
Owen, Edward, 588.
Owen, Fannie, see Mrs. Chas. Lothrop, 588.
Owen, John, 270, 353, 354, 357, 403, 413, 419, 422, 423, 424, 425, 426, 442, 562, 701, 728, 768, 783, 790, 796, 830, 858, 889.
Owen, John, 588.
Owen, J. V. D., 515.
Owen, Lafayette, 588.
Owen, Lieut. Edward T., 588.
Owen, Mrs. John, 562, 584, 585, 1000.
Owen, Thomas, 227, 332, 381, 450.

Paddock, Chas. T., 416, 780.
Paddock, Mrs. Bishop, nee Sanger, 759.
Faldi, Signor Angelo, 598.
Palmer, Friend, 30, 55, 57, 59, 60, 76, 78, 79, 80, 81, 91, 101, 102, 112, 113, 118, 124, 146, 150, 155, 184, 185, 187, 190, 194, 195, 196, 107, 199, 200, 201, 203, 204, 205, 206, 210, 219, 220, 221, 222, 225, 230, 234, 238, 240, 242, 244, 245, 252, 256, 261, 266, 268, 274, 281, 284, 286, 294, 296, 300, 301, 303, 304, 305, 306, 307, 324, 329, 331, 333, 335, 336, 337, 338, 342, 344, 346, 347, 356, 372, 373, 375, 379, 383, 384, 388, 391, 392, 396, 410, 415, 416, 419, 420, 421, 423, 424, 425, 435, 442, 448, 454, 457, 463, 473, 474, 478, 479, 480, 484, 488, 491, 495, 498, 501, 506, 507, 508, 523, 524, 525, 528, 529, 539, 540, 545, 562, 563, 571, 573, 583, 584, 592, 595, 598, 609, 616, 620, 626, 631, 642, 649, 655, 656, 669, 678, 682, 683, 684, 696, 699, 703, 705, 717, 723, 725, 732, 745, 753, 768, 779, 824, 831, 836, 837, 841, 844, 865, 872, 909, 950, 955, 994, 1003, 1008.
Palmer, Friend, Senior, 23, 25, 266, 274, 286, 291, 402, 444, 689, 703, 791, 977.
Palmer, F. & T., 23, 267, 272, 314, 329, 332, 447, 449, 452, 474, 523, 570, 571, 592, 629, 676, 733, 900, 910, 978.
Palmer, F., T. & J., 288, 311, 974, 977.
Palmer, George, 105, 305, 447.
Palmer, Jane M., 743.
Palmer, John B., 183, 244, 238, 288, 362, 436, 441, 442, 457, 502, 507, 733, 736, 737, 787, 820, 855, 890.
Palmer, Julia, 596.
Palmer, Miss Catherine, see Mrs. Felix Hinchman, 88, 90, 499, 586.
Palmer, Mary, 596, 804, 805.
Palmer, Martha, 596.
Palmer, Mason, 362, 441, 458, 479, 736, 798, 859, 890.
Palmer, Miss Sarah, 236.
Palmer, Mrs. Friend, nee Witherill, 542.
Palmer, Mrs. Thomas, Senior, nee Miss M. A. Witherill, 25, 26, 88, 90, 92, 93, 307, 384, 540, 586, 741.
Palmer, Mrs. Thankful, see Mrs. George Kellogg, 266, 267, 305.

Palmer, Mrs. Senator T. W., 548, 553, 827.
Palmer Park, 616, 834.
Palmer, Pat, 500.
Palmer, Perry, 500.
Palmer, Senator T. W., 90, 120, 121, 156 187, 245, 268, 307, 316, 334, 422, 479, 507, 543, ("Old Glory") 545, 553, 749, 752, 769, 788, 790, 821, 823 834, 838, 841, 880, 892, 1002.
Palmer, Thomas, Senior, 23, 24, 25, 41, 7 88, 90, 92, 93, 101, 120, 121, 150, 256, 259, 269, 286, 323, 324, 329, 373, 376, 386, 396, 402, 418, 419, 444, 445, 447, 449, 471, 540, 559, 645, 676, 678, 683, 701, 714, 717, 764, 778, 782, 805, 844, 974, 977, 925.
Palmer & Whipple, 620.
Palms, Francis, 439, 440.
Palms, Miss Catherine, see Mrs. Dr. 440.
Pangborn, Zadok, 77.
Parent, Jaques, 560, 561.
Parker, Julia, 981, 984.
Parker, "Ferd.," 554.
Parker, Rev. Theodore, 426.
Parker, T. A., 554.
Parks, H. C., 203, 709.
Parsons, General Samuel Holden, 66?.
Parsons, James C., 504, 505, 506.
Parsons, Philo M., 454, 738.
Partridge, Asa, 322.
Partridge, General Benjamin, 323.
Partridge, Timothy, 323.
Partridge, T. L., 316.
Patterson, Richard, 427.
Payne, Major H. C., 174, 175, 187.
Patton, Hon. James, 177.
Patterson, John, 187, 357, 358, 847.
Patterson, G. N., 357.
Paul, Gideon, 686.
Patrick, Capt. W. P., 591, 746.
Patterson, Mayor John, 598.
Paterson, Wm., 418.
Paulding, M., 463, 464.
Paulding, John., 464.
Paxton, Mrs. Thos., nee Hunt, 651.
Payne, Chauncey S., 125, 272, 407, 408.
Pearson, Capt., 889.
Pease, Capt. W. T., 30, 47, 69, 391, 905.
Peck, Thomas, 167.
Peck, W. B., 194, 198, 200, 202.
Peirce, D. R., 507, 833.
Peltier, Charles, 622.
Peltier family, 560, 619, 620, 621, 622.
Peltier, Marianne, see Mrs. Alex. Cha Jr., 631.
Pence, D. R., 358.
Penfield, W. S., 728.
Penfield, Miss, see Mrs. C. H. Buhl, 728
Penny, Charles C., 475.
Penny, Charles W., 169, 101, 513.
Penny, James, 788.
Perkins, Capt., 318, 387, 388.
Perry, Mrs., 301.
Perry, Commodore O. H., 31, 61.
Petit, Dudley, 274.
Pettie, Wm., 889.
Petier, Lucy, see Mrs. Lacey of Niles, 6
Petier, Madeline, see Mrs. Joseph Bela 622.
Petty, J. T., 357, 523, 675.
Phelps, Brace & Co., 387.
Pheatt, Capt. J. T., 37.
Phelps, Mayor Frank B., 516, 523, 553,
Phelps, Mrs. F. B., 523.

Phelps, Wm., 682.
Pierce, Capt. Loring, 31, 62.
Pierce, David R., 187, 714.
Pierce, Lieut. John J., 290.
Pierce, P. R. L., 498, 901.
Pike, Capt., 141.
Pinckney, Col., 86.
Piquette, Charles, 402, 405, 463, 469, 477 623, 629.
Piquette, Elsie, see Mrs. James Hoban, 629.
Piquette, Elsie, see Mrs. Lieut. Ormsby Mitchell, 629.
Piquette, Emelie, see Mrs. F. P. B. Sands, 629.
Piquet, Father Francois, 629.
Pittman, General James E., 182, 187, 391, 493, 506, 532, 620, 695, 877.
Piquette, John B., 369, 402, 463, 469, 500, 623, 629.
Pitcher, Dr., 244, 346, 901.
Pitcher, Dr. Zena, 765.
Pitcher, Edward M., 176, 245, 695, 698, 818.
Pitcher, Nat., 235.
Pitts & Cranage, 416.
Pitts, Mr. and Mrs. Thomas, 812.
Pitts, Samuel, 731, 828.
Pixley, Frank, 413.
Platt, Attorney General Zepheniah, 491, 529, 780, 895.
Platt, Cornelia, 780, 895.
Poe, Lieut. C. M., 237.
Pomeroy's Express, 42, 194, 198, 200, 204, 206, 210.
Pomeroy, George E., 195, 196.
Pomeroy, Lieut., 86.
Pomeroy, "Thad," 196.
Ponchatrain Fort (Old Detroit), 769.
Pond, Charles, 586.
Pontiac, 370, 383, 560, 589, 611, 614, 630, 769, 772.
Porter, Augustus S., 218, 380, 645, 737.
Porter, General Andrew, 371, 527.
Porter, George F., 250, 335, 533.
Porter, Governor George B., 281, 371, 525, 527, 645.
Poupard, Simon, 335, 523, 675.
Powers, Mrs. J. Newton, 476.
Pratt, Capt. Amos, 36.
Pratt, Ralph, 82.
Preston, David, 457, 827.
Pretty, John W., 168.
Pridgeon, Capt. John, 553.
Pridgeon, Mayor, 525.
Prince, Albert, 587, 1008.
Prince, Col. John, 118, 587 1001, 1004, 1006, 1008.
Prince, John, 587.
Prince, Miss A., 587.
Prince, Miss Arabella, 588, 1009.
Prince, Miss Constance, 587.
Prince, Mrs. Albert, nee Knapp, 1001, 1009.
Pritchette, Kintzing, 756, 894.
Proctor, General, 121, 136, 153, 157, 160, 232, 345, 612.
Prouty, N., 243, 686.
Provencal, Catherine B., see Mrs. Judge James Weir, 639.
Provencal, Mrs. Pierre, nee St. Aubin, 638.
Provencal, Pierre, 369, 639, 661.

Rankin, Col. Arthur, 355, 356, 904, 1003, 1005.
Rankin, George C., 1005.
Ransom, Governor E. P., 601.
Rankin, McKee, 998, 1005.
Rankin, Mrs. Col., nee McKee, 1005.
Randolph, Edgar, 473.

Ransom, Willis, 892.
Rathbun, Benj., 23.
Raymond, Francis, 243, 357, 888, 890,
Raymond, W. A., 898.
Ray, Eleazor, 680.
Reed, C. M., 70.
Reed, E., 325, 327, 402.
Reeve, T. V., 238.
Reeve, Nathan, 238.
Reeves, Selah, 394, 732.
Reuhle, Major J. V., 186, 187, 877.
Rhodes, Joseph P., 355.
Rhodes, Martha, 265.
Rice, A. A., 357, 497.
Rice, Amoray S., 581.
1010.
Rice, Dan., 690, 987.
Rice, Dr. Randall S., 244, 283, 286, 52 901.
Rice, George S., 505, 532.
Rice, Justin, 668, 980.
Rice, R. M., 716, 822.
Rich, George M., 401, 503.
Richards, Capt. Thomas, 37.
Richardson, Col. J. B., 620, 1003.
Richard, Father Gabriel, 212, 281, 296 444, 479, 642, 670, 675, 690, 692 967.
Richardson, Mrs. Johnson, nee Mercer,
Richardson, Robert, 1003.
Richings, Caroline, 989.
Richings, Peter, 989.
Richmond & Backus Co., 120, 314, 728.
Richmond, Charles, 532.
Riese, Bishop, 643, 691.
Rivard, Antoine, 158, 582.
Richter, Charles, 696.
Riley, Col. Bennet, 599, 876.
Riley, James, 20, 21, 290.
Riley, John, 21, 22.
Riley, Judge and Mrs., 478.
Riley, Peter, 20, 21.
Rionelle, Joseph, 20.
Rivard, Francois, 582.
Roberts Col. E. J., 114, 243.
Roberts, Col. Horace S., 115, 188, 237 411, 467, 507.
Roberts, John, 25, 342 675.
Roberts, R. E., 25, 52, 163, 166, 244, 35 675, 700, 705, 782, 839, 898, 919.
Roberts, Mrs. R. E., nee Champ, 782.
Robertson, General John, 183, 188, 712.
Robertson, Wm., 369.
Robinson, 134, 143.
Robinson, Eugene, 188.
Robinson, General, 227.
Roby, Henry M., 234, 237, 241, 243, 33 421, 521, 532, 704.
Roby, John S., 270, 421, 422.
Roby, Henry S., 471, 532.
Roby, Mrs., 395.
Roby, Reuel T., 421, 426, 698.
Rochester, General W. B., 39.
Roe, Wm., 100, 103.
Rogers, Capt. Jedediah, 44, 46, 69, 85, 270, 276, 317, 320.
Rogers, Ebenezer, 526.
Rogers, Mayor Ford, 854.
Root, Capt. Aaron, 35.
Roland, Capt., 114, 120.
Roland, Isaac S., 163, 168, 170, 175, 19 894.
Roland, Louis C., 337.
Roland, Thomas, 292, 309, 335, 460, 675
Rolshoven, F., 463, 714.
Romeyn, Theodore, 28, 243, 767.
Rood, A. N., 237.

Rood, Ezra, 393, 400, 420, 555.
Rood, Gil F., 242, 398, 412, 419, 403.
Rood, Sidney L., 28, 242, 261, 286, 331, 397, 419, 454, 501, 514, 704, 824, 893, 894.
Roosevelt, President Theodore, 575, 611, 625.
Roosevelt, Judge, 625.
Roosevelt, Marcia, see Mrs. Edward B. Scovell, 625.
Rosenberg, J. P., 355.
Ross, J. B., 559.
Ross, R. B., 274.
Rossiter, Seymour, 336, 337.
Round Head, 147.
Roy, Robert B., 261.
Rucker, General Daniel H., 182, 227, 579, 610.
Rucker, John A., 191, 524, 578, 580, 722.
Rucker, Miss, see Mrs. General P. H. Sheridan, 579, 879.
Ruland, John, 20.
Rumney, John, 237.
Rumney, Robert, 501, 524.
Rumney, W. Y., 237, 732.
Russell (of Russell House), 233.
Russell, Alfred, 187.
Russell, Capt., J. B., 76, 550, 759, 798.
Russell, Capt. J. B. F., 221.
Russell, Dr. G. B., 76, 550, 759, 798.
Rust, P., 207.
Ryan, W. C., 357.

Sabine, J. C., 156, 513.
Sager, Dr. Abraham E., 169.
Sands, Rear Admiral, 629.
Sands, Mrs. F. P. B., 629.
Sanderson, Henry, 315, 342, 670, 675.
Sanderson, Miss, see Mrs. G. W. Bissell, 677.
Sanger, H. K., 759, 768.
Sanger, Henry P., 236, 499, 759, 897.
Sanger, General Joseph P., 759.
Sargent, N. O., 29, 436.
Sawyer, 210.
Sawyer, Franklin, 166, 243, 720, 723, 894.
Schoolcraft, Hon. H. R., 85, 94, 247, 249, 253, 290, 418, 740, 845.
Schuyler, 196.
Schwarz, Emma, see Mrs. Robt. Woods, 29, 895.
Schwarz, General J. E., 28, 73, 163, 182, 192, 219, 295, 387, 392, 678, 695, 737.
Schwarz, John, 73, 295.
Schwarz, Mrs. J. E., 29.
Scott, General Winfield, 52, 170, 177, 180, 219, 221, 280, 389, 446, 599.
Scott Guard, 184, 186, 598.
Scott, "Jim," 420, 440, 728, 753, 791, 847.
Scott, John, 420, 728, 753.
Scott, J. V. R., 308.
Scott, Mrs. Hester, see Luther Martin, 646.
Scott, Mrs. Hester;. pupils at her school (1840), 646.
Scott, Mrs. James, 438, 440.
Scotten, Daniel, 498, 552.
Scovell, Dr. J. B., 227, 400, 473, 625, 695, 894, 895.
Scovell, Edward Brooks, 626.
Scovell, Harry, 626.
Scovell, Mrs. E. B., nee Roosevelt, 626.
Scovell, Mrs. Harry, 626.
Seaman, Ezra C., 715.
Seek, Conrad, 369, 412, 715.
Seek, Wm., 715.
Seereiter, John, 694.
Selkirk, Earl of, 85.
Senter, John, 228, 792.
Sevenack, Charles, 700.
Seward, Wm. H., 347.
Seyburn, Col. S. Y., 834.

Seymour, J. C. W., 625.
Shanaway, Megesh, 52.
Shaw, Father (of Ste. Anne's), 691.
Shaw, Wm., 686.
Sheeley, Alanson, 243, 275, 666, 714.
Sheeley, George M., 517.
Shelden, Allen, 549, 743, 760.
Shelden, Alexandrine, see Mrs. R. Storrlis, 590, 623.
Shelden, Chauncey, 117, 118.
Shelden, John P., 273, 288, 330, 792, 9
Shelden, Mrs. Thomas P., 469, 661.
Shelden, Ransom, 228.
Shelden, Rose, see Mrs. A. Henry Guise 623.
Shelden, Thomas C., 221, 234, 311, 335 792, 799, 901.
Shelden, Thomas P., 187, 237, 623, 97
Sheridan, Mrs. General P. H., nee R 579, 879.
Sheridan, General P. H., 409, 579, 879.
Sherman, Capt. Roger, 30, 91.
Shepard, Edward, 210, 358, 714.
Sherlock, Edward, 991.
Sherwood, Wm., 220.
Shields Guards, 598.
Shields, Thomas, 695.
Shoepack Recollections, see General O. B cox, 520, 567, 573.
Shook, Capt. John, 36, 261.
Shook, "Jim," 36.
Shurley, Dr. E. L., 624.
Sibley, Alex. H., 234, 240, 244, 521, 642 791, 817.
Sibley, Frederick B., 428, 818.
Sibley, Judge Solomon, 139, 218, 292 428, 484, 499, 511, 533, 645, 662 675, 814.
Sibley, Major E. S., 225, 413, 414, 415 816.
Sibley, Major Sproat, 732, 791, 902, 913 818.
Sibley, Miss, see. Mrs. C. C. Trowbridge
Sibley, Miss, see Mrs. Jas. A. Armstron
Sibley, Mrs. Alex. H., nee McBride, 642
Simmons, John H., 117, 231.
Singer, Isaac Merritt, 893.
Skinner, Henry W., 710.
Skinner, Mrs. Edward, 621.
Slaves in Detroit, 104, 105.
Slaymaker, Judge James A., 684.
Sloss, Capt. John, 76.
Sloss, Dr., 326.
Sloss, Wm., 394.
Smart, Robert, 121, 531, 727, 466.
Smith, Colonel, 44.
Smith, Col. Jas. R., 227.
Smith, Col. Richard, 134.
Smart, David, 243, 356, 473, 524, 531, Smith, Edward J., 187.
Smith, Glover, 904.
Smith, Jack, 20.
Smith, Jacob, 125, 408.
Smith, J. Hargrave, 505.
Smith, J. Hyatt, 244, 373, 698, 850, 832
Smith, Joseph, 892.
Smith, Major Henry, 594.
Smith, M. S., 456, 760.
Smith, R. G., 904.
Smith, Sergeant, U. S. A., 226.
Smith, U. J., 333.
Smolk, Abraham, 221.
Smyth, Richard, 307.
Snelling, Capt. Josiah, 650.
Snelling, Harry N., 337.
Snelling, Lieut. J. G. T., 754.
Snow, Electa, 456.

Snow, Josiah, 388, 418, 893.
Snow, Mrs., 456.
Snow, Samuel, 117.
Snow's Sanitarium, 714.
Society Men, 1840 to 1850—820, 821.
Southern, 992.
Sparling, Benj., 357.
Speed, Wm. J., 188.
Spencer, Garry, 163, 165, 463, 676, 691, 715.
Sprague, Ara. W., 190, 595.
Sprague, Col. Spencer, 823.
Sprague, John, 117.
Sprague, Julia, see Mrs. Oliver Hyde, 823.
Sprague, Henry, 823.
Sprague, Miss, see Mrs. Henry Hopson, 823.
Sprague, Miss, see Mrs. Silas Bullock, 823.
Sprague, Mrs. Dr., 415.
Sproat, Col. Ebenezer, 500, 663, 815.
Squeirs, Heber, 36.
Squires, Captain, 63.
Squires, Captain, 63.
St. Amour, Eugene, 677.
St. Aubin, Francois, 638.
St. Aubin, Francois, 638.
St. Aubin, Gabriel, 560, 562, 582.
St. Aubin, Louis, 638.
St. Aubin, Matilda, see Mrs. Eugene Watson, 638, 639.
St. Aubin, Matilda, see Mrs. Eugene Watson, 925.
St. Aubin, see Mrs. Antoine Moross, 638.
St. Aubin, see Mrs. Henry Beaubien, 638.
St. Aubin, see Mrs. John F. Godfroy, 638.
St. Aubin, Mrs. Louis, nee Therese Chapoton, 631.
St. Aubin, see Mrs. Pierre Provencal, 638.
St. Aubin, see Mrs. Richard Connor, 638.
St. Martin, Antoine, 614.
St. Martin, Jacques (La Butte), 606.
St. Martin, John Bapte, 614.
St. Martin, Mrs. Jacques, see Navarre, 614.
Stannard, Capt. Chas. C., 34, 47.
Starkey, Dr., 893.
Starkey, Henry, 893.
Starkey, Richard, 893.
Starkweather, Captain, 62.
Starr, Reuben, 265.
Starring, Ford, 317, 701.
Stead, Benjamin F., 120, 311, 337, 393.
Stead, Wm., 714.
Steel, Albert, 896.
Steel, E., 896.
Stephens, Col. Albert S., 496, 621.
Stephens, John, Jr., 554.
Stephens, John, 444, 765.
Stephens Mrs. John, Jr., nee Watson, 554.
Stephens, Wm., 444, 766.
Sterling, Col. J. T., 486, 561.
Stetson, Turner, 243, 387.
Stevens, Captain, 100.
Stevens, Elijah, 117.
Stevens, F. H., 514, 525.
Stevens, Henry, 496.
Stevens, Robert, 106.
Stevens, Sears, 237, 526.
Stevens, W. H., 496.
Stevenson, Capt. C. L., 230, 511.
Stewart, Capt. John, 37.
Stewart, Charles H., 767.
Stewart, Dr. Morse, 27, 497, 537, 898.
Stewart, Duncan, 390, 391.
Stewart, James, 904.
Stewart, Joseph B., 82, 117.
Stewart. Riley M., 117.
Stiles, Captain, 70.
Stilson, James, 719.
Stimson, B. G., 236, 357, 543, 684, 710, 712.

Stockton, Col. T. W. B., 58, 306, 408, 620.
Stone, Capt. W. B., 37.
Story, Alfred M., 715.
Story, Martin, 715.
Stowell A. H., 286, 692, 830, 894, 902.
Strelinger, 695.
Strelinger (Samuel of Posen), 696.
Stringham, H. T., 235.
Strong, H. Norton, 81, 236, 391, 812.
Strong, John W., 235, 391, 419, 453, 596
Strong, John W. Jr., 626, 813.
Strong, Judge, 481.
Stuart, 100, 537, 554.
Sturgis, General, 609.
Sumner, Chas., 492.
Sutton, James W., 163, 183, 241, 243, 507, 521, 915.
Sutton, Noah, 259, 358, 889.
Suydam, Samuel, 227.
Swan, Sheriff, 311.
Swathel, see Mrs. C. M. D. Bull and Mrs clair, 802.
Swift, F. W., 188, 894.

SOCIETIES, ETC.

Detroit Musical Society, 828.
Detroit Thespian Society, 698.
Firemen's Hall, 596, 694, 700.
Hamtramck Driving Park, 586.
St. Andrew's Society, 828.
Vingt Club, 506.
Young Men's Society, 723.

Taft, Levi, 698, 845, 847.
Talbot, John L., 223, 243, 866, 891.
Tallman, Dr. John, 272.
Tallman, Harriet, see Mrs. Dr. L. J. W 272.
Tallman, Mrs. Fitz, nee Mack, 220.
Tanke (the Crane), 146.
Taylor, Charles A., 515.
Taylor, Col. J. P., 227.
Taylor, Elisha, 505, 514.
Taylor, General Zachariah, 180, 597.
Taylor, Joseph, 24.
Taylor, Mayor of Buffalo, 174.
Taylor, Miss, 455, 458.
Tecumseh, 146, 149, 157, 159, 161, 245 493, 660, 664, 880.
Teller, Pierre, 357, 467, 473, 524.
Ten Eyck, Anthony, 223, 243, 567.
Ten Eyck, Conrad, 125, 166, 325, 658 889, 906, 908.
Ten Eyck, Jerry, 125.
Ten Eyck, J. V. R., 291, 301.
Ten Eyck, Miss, see Mrs. Fisher, 658.
Terry, Dr. A. R., 241, 671, 723, 877.
Thayer, George N., 224.
Theller, Dr. E. A., 114, 173, 633, 685, Thiebault, Joseph, 369, 399.
Thomas, General George H., 546.
Thompson, "Brad," 707.
Thompson, David, 375, 419, 497, 670, 78 890.
Thompson, E. H., 227.
Thompson, John, 493.
Thompson, Jonathan, 405, 410, 514.
Thompson, Mrs. David, 375.
Thompson, Mrs. W. G., nee Campau, 43
Thompson, Rev. O. C., 856.
Thompson, W. G., 268, 439, 455, 538,
Throop, Aeneas, 854.
Throop, George B., 90, 854.
Throop, Hon. Robert, 926.
Throop, Montgomery, 854.
Throop, Wm. A., 188.

Thorn, Capt. Wm., 99, 101.
Thorn, John, 101, 583.
Thorn, Reuben, 732.

THEATRES.

Circus, 511, 690, 953, 983.
City Hall Theatre, 983.
Dean & McKinney's, 980, 1003.
Detroit Garden, 342, 675, 679, 951.
Detroit Opera House, 705, 991.
First Theatre in Detroit, cor. Woodward Ave. and Atwater St., 980.
Lyceum, 702.
McFarland's Metropolitan (National), 847, 982, 984, 993.
Parsons & Dean's, 980.
Vincent's Theatre, 997.
Welch & Jacobs, 998.
Young Men's Hall (Biddle House), 998.

Tillman, J. W., 401, 904.
Tillman, Major W., 904.
Tinker, L. W., 245, 391, 476, 678, 733.
Titus, Jonas, 39, 362, 493, 902.
Titus Platt, 594.
Titus Silas, 493, 890.
Todd, Capt. J. B. S., 878.
Toll, Capt. Daniel, 603.
Toll, Gen. Isaac De Graff, 530, 594, 599, 601, 602, 603, 917.
Toll, Capt. Philip R., 603.
Toll, Mrs. Nancy De Graff, 603.
Tompkins, Mrs. D. D., 909.
Tompkins, see Mrs. Sarah Ten Eyck, 909.
Torrey, Joseph W., 335.
Townsend, Ambrose, 223.
Travers, Capt. Jacob, 39.
Tripler, Chas. S., 183, 891.
Tromblev, Gazette, 151, 153, 154, 664.
Trowbridge, C. C., 97, 244, 282, 335, 372, 399, 401, 439, 452, 490, 499, 512, 521, 555, 562, 582, 585, 645, 653, 688, 719, 737, 890.
Trowbridge, Captain, 372.
Trowbridge, General C. A., 241, 357, 670, 711.
Trowbridge, S. V. R., 711.
Truax, Fannie, see Mrs. J. A. Rucker, 580.
Truax, John, 524, 580.
Truesdail, E. S., 234.
Truesdail, Wesley, 73, 500, 587, 476, 497.
Truesdail, Zeke, 476.
Trumbull, Jonathan, 378.
Tryon, Charles, 490.
Tucker, Rev. Elisha, 265.
Tuffts, Lieutenant, 86.
Turnbull, Lieut. C. N., 237.
Turnbull, Reverend, 268.
Turner, Albion, 176, 245.
Tunnicliffe, Doctor, 348.
Tyler, Captain, 47.

Uhl, 388.
Uhlman, M., 29, 219, 387.
Ulrick, Charles, 315.
Updike, Scott W., 418, 893.
Underwood, Joseph R., 161.
United States Express Co., 194.

Van Allen, Captain, 35, 57.
Van Antwerp, James Sanderson, 680, 889.
Van Antwerp, Rev. F. J., 889.
Van Armen, Col. John, 347, 350.
Van Derventer, Captain Eugene, 594.
Van Dorn, General Earl, 546.
Van Dyke, Elsie, see Mrs. W. B. Moran, 477.
Van Dyke, J. A., 242, 260, 356, 363, 397, 473, 477, 479, 651, 723, 802, 854, 889, 891, 937.
Van Dyke, Josephine D., see Mrs. I Brownson, 477.
Van Dyke, Philip, 477.
Van Dyke, Rev. Ernest, 477.
Van Dyke, Victoria, 477.
Van Every, Peter, 585, 653.
Van Rensaeler, Mrs. Sarah, 475.
Van Vleit, Mrs. Captain, nee Stephens,
Vail, Charles, 357, 426.
Vallee, Mrs. J. B., 630, 668.
Vallee, T. R., 668.
Vananden, J. C., 237.
Vananden, J. W., 231.
Vanderpool, Father, 670.
Vanhusen, 227.
Varnum, Doctor, 406.
Varnum, Gen. Joseph M., 663.
Varnum, Jacob B., 405.
Varnum, John, 117.
Vary, Capt. Samuel, 37.
Verhoff, Peter E., 100, 355.
Vidal, Admiral, 1010.
Viger, Alexander, 631.
Viger, Mrs. Alexander, nee Elizabeth ton, 631.
Vingt Club, 506.
Visger, Joseph, 20, 591.
Von Limbourg, Baroness, see Miss I Cass, 384.
Von Thoultz, Colonel, 116.
Voyez, Joseph, 369.

Wagner, James, 117.
Wagstaff, Capt. "Bob," 34, 56, 243, 452 726.
Wagstaff, Henry C., 337, 726.
Waite, Obed, 313, 335.
Wales, Austin A., 214, 223, 230, 231, 587, 891.
Wales, Cornelia, see Mrs. Lafayette F 231.
Wales, George, 467.
Wales, E. A., 222, 231, 245, 511, 695, 6
Wales, E. B., 222.
Walcott, Alexander M. D., 290.
Walker, Capt. Augustus, 32, 39, 47, 34
Walker, C. I., 724.
Walker E. C., 454, 698.
Walker, Hiram, 457, 833.
Walker, Henry N., 243, 460.
Walker, Hon. C. L., 598.
Walker, H. D., 682.
Walker, J. T., 245, 550.
Walk-in-the-Water, 144, 146, 435, 493.
Wallack, James W., Jr., 985.
Walsh, Captain Michael, 400.
Ward, Capt. E. B., 37, 40, 60, 82, 391,
Ward, Capt. Samuel, 40, 60, 446, 584.
Ward, Mrs. E. B., see Miss McQueen,
Ware, Dr. M., 473.
Warren, Anna, see Mrs. Dan Marble, 9
Warren, Homer, 957, 990.
Warren, Wm., 981, 982.
Washington, General George, 417, 485.
Washington Lancers, 175, 176.
Waterbury, Captain and Mrs., 625.
Watkins, Kittie, 405.
Watkins, Leonard, 410.
Watson, B., 925.
Watson, Charles, 529.
Watson, Col. Joseph B., 86, 650, 925.
Watson, Elkanah, 529, 925, 927.
Watson, Eugene W., 650, 897, 925.
Watson, George, 59, 74, 727, 927.
Watson, James, 690, 889, 899.
Watson, James B., 529, 559, 897, 925.

Watson, John, 234, 337, 369, 510, 592, 690, 889, 899.
Watson, Lewis C., 650, 925.
Watson, Mrs. Eliza, 480.
Watson, Mrs. Eugene W., see Matilda St. Aubin, 638.
Watson, Robert, 1003.
Watson, Samuel G., 553, 766.
Watson, Thomas, 510. 899.
Wayne, General Anthony, 144, 278, 608, 616, 651.
Weaver, Miss, see Mrs. David Thompson, 375.
Weaver, Mrs., 375.
Webb, I. Watson, 755.
Webb, B. L., 202, 390, 523.
Webster, Capt. John W., 37, 244, 476.
Webster, Daniel, 179, 221, 853.
Webster, Daniel F., 223, 853.
Webster, J. Howard, 236, 244, 481, 484, 486, 728, 943.
Webster, Fletcher, 960.
Webster, Sallie, 237.
Weir, Miss Isabel, 639.
Weir, Mrs. Judge James, nee Provencal, 639.
Welch, James M., 234.
Welch Thomas, 369.
Welles, John A., 184, 223, 415, 417, 737, 767. 784, 788, 798, 873. .
Welles, Henry H., 236.
Welles, Wm., 784.
Wells, Augustus L., 466.
Wells, Col. W. H., 441, 667.
Wells, C., 81, 184, 474, 697.
Wells, Fargo & Co., 39, 55, 194, 209, 211.
Wells, Henry S., 195, 201, 209.
Welton, Mrs. Alanson W., 92.
Wells, Rev. Noah M., 726.
Welton, Rev. Alanson W., 90, 92, 317.
Wells, Rufus, 256, 258.'
Wells, Stephen, 328, 333, 410, 444.
Wells, Wm., 726.
Wendell, Capt. Charles E., 188, 393, 398, 411.
Wendell, Henry, 393, 398.
Wendell, John, 577.
Wendell, Tunis G., 120, 270, 393, 397, 398. 410, 412, 576, 648, 651, 910. .
Wesson, Mrs. W. B., nee Baldwin, 834, 902.
Wesson, W. B., 244, 331, 537, 698, 835, 905.
Westbrook, Captain, 18, 56.
Westbrook, Colonel, 101, 399, 446.
Western Express. 198, 202, 204.
Weston, Allyn, 237.
Wetmore, F., 514, 827.
Wetmore, Fred, 904.
Wetmore, C. H., 237. 904.
Wetmore, Mrs. C. H., nee Buel, 550, 556.
Wheaton, W. W., 404.
Wheeler, ——, 668.
Wheeler, ——, 196.
Wheeler, Capt. Fred S., 38, 51, 71, 695.
Whilden, Maj. C. E., 182, 185, 238, 506, 684.
Whipple, Catherine S., see Mrs. Edwin Skinner, 621.
Whipple Col. W. L., 457, 620, 625, 690, 695, 698.
Whipple, Commodore Abraham, 621.
Whipple "Dan," 36, 71, 72, 409, 694, 862.
Whipple, Eliza S., see Mrs. Chas. Conaghan, 621.
Whipple, Henry W., 621.
Whipple, James Burdick, 592, 619.
Whipple, James, of Monroe, 627.
Whipple, Judge Charles W., 165, 182, 183, 228, 330, 476, 560, 619, 625, 690.
Whipple Major John, 17, 21, 476, 533, 592, 627, 688.

Whipple, Margeretta T., see Mrs. Chas. 621.
Whipple Major W. S., 188.
Whipple, Mary Walcott, 621, 690.
Whistler, Col. Wm. D., 181, 183, 187, 357 508, 536, 556, 579, 594, 596, 684, 8
Whistler, James Mc. Neil, 536.
Whistler, Miss Caroline, 307, 736.
Whistler, Miss Louise, 237.
Whistler, Miss, see Mrs. Capt. Curtiss, :
Whitaker, Capt. Harry, 32, 39, 49, 54 204, 581.
Whitale, Capt., J. A., 227.
Whitall, Major J. A., 59, 190, 344, 609.
Whitbeck Mrs., 120, 239.
Whitcomb, W. N., 391.
White, Captain ———, 46.
White, Peter, 228, 501, 598, 676, 791, 8
Whiting, Admiral Wm. D., 393, 768.
Whiting, Cleveland, 892.
Whiting, Col. Henry, 24, 120, 227, 393,
Whiting, De Garmo J., 237.
Whiting, Dr. J. L., 156, 164, 244, 272, 335, 341, 357, 596, 890.
Whiting, Henry D., 219, 272, 393, 579, 698, 799.
Whiting, Joseph, 985.
Whiting, J. T., 235, 698, 760.
Whitman, Peleg O., 680.
Whitney, A. G., 291.
Whitney, Col. Henry, 399.
Whitney, David, 829, 924.
Whitney, George L., 50, 480.
Whitney, Mrs., nee Brooks, 626.
Whittier, Joseph A., 827, 828.
Whittier, Joseph B., 827.
Whittlesey, Hon. Elisha, 109, 358.
Whittlesey, H. M., 188, 358, 424, 739,
Wickware, C., 463.
Wight, Buckminster, 549.
Wight, Edwin B., 550.
Wight, Henry A., 50, 549.
Wight, Stanley G., 191, 242, 245, 356, :
Wilcox, Charles, 484, 515, 903.
Wilcox, Eben N., 243, 245, 277, 357, 479, 484, 514, 516, 519, 698, 717, 837, 903.
Wilcox, General O. B., 245, 277, 357, 484, 514, 516, 519, 555, 566, 698, 903.
Wilcox, G. G., 739.
Wilcox, Mrs., 514.
Wilcox, W. W., 739.
Wilkins, Major W. D., 530, 877.
Wilkins, Ross, 221, 218, 300, 529.
Wilkins, T. D., 236.
Wilkinson, Capt. David, 31.
Wilkinson, Joseph, 405.
Willard, Lather B., 349.
Williams, A. L., 234.
Williams, Capt. G. R., 35.
Williams, Davis, Brooks & Hinchman's 270.
Williams, Ezra, 493.
Williams, Gardiner, 712.
Williams, Gen. Alpheus S., 170. 181, 187 357, 452, 460, 487, 491, 493, 520, 6 695, 712, 731, 877, 891, 904.
Williams, Gen. John R., 105, 121, 163, 165, 325, 330, 346, 359, 367, 498, 500 619, 675, 678, 713, 714, 722, 739.
Williams, George, 90.
Williams, Gurdon, Jr., 323.
Williams, Gurdon M., 223, 391, 767, 890.
Williams, Gurshom· M., 740, 813.
Williams, Harriet, Mary and Eliza, 532,
Williams, Harvey, 275, 335, 387, 676.

Williams, James, 362, 688, 695, 712, 733, 890.
Williams, John C., 117, 369.
Williams, J. C. Devereaux, 510, 826.
Williams, Light Infantry, 174, 175, 177, 847.
Williams, Morris F., 419.
Williams, Morris M., 521.
Williams, Morris M., 241, 243, 419, 532, 581, 647.
Williams, Mrs. A. S., 720.
Williams, Mrs. and Mrs. Julian, 637.
Williams, N. G., 237.
Williams, Oliver, 676.
Williams, O. B., 676.
Williams, Rev. Eleazar (alleged Dauphin of France), 261, 262, 309.
Williams, Salt, 223.
Williams, Theo. G., 243, 335, 473, 500, 525, 528, 678, 605.
Williams, Thomas, 164, 165, 512, 619.
Willis, Mrs. R. Storrs, nee Sheldon, 464, 500, 537, 596, 623, 631.
Willis, N. P., 501, 624.
Wilson, Major James C. 549.
Wilson, Major M., 165, 657.
Wilson, Sheriff John M., 708, 889, 898.
Winans, Capt. Frazer N., 594.
Winder, Col. John, 58, 168, 507, 532, 703, 890.
Wing, Col. Warner S., 165, 227.
Wing, Hon. Austin E., 28, 292, 309, 322, 330, 675, 678, 727, 758, 979.
Wing, J. T., 679.
Wing, Talcott E., 678, 698.
Wing, W. P., 891.
Winget, Wm., 501, 686.
Winter, George, 494.
Witherill, Charles I., 547.
Witherill, Cullen C., 880.
Witherill, Harriet, see Mrs. Friend Palmer, 542.
Witherell, James B., 182, 486, 507, 543, 545, 547, 684, 892.
Witherell, Judge James, 26, 67, 87, 93, 145, 167, 271, 316, 334, 384, 539, 557, 562, 566, 570, 592, 638, 645, 662, 729, 925.
Witherill, Judge B. F. H., 102, 134, 142, 146, 148, 151, 157, 283, 304, 329, 336, 435, 455, 493, 531, 535, 540, 542, 549, 559, 561, 598, 638, 645, 705, 729, 737, 795, 823, 868, 889.
Witherill, Julia, see Mrs. Col. H. A. 542.
Witherill, Martha E., 542.
Witherell, Miss (Mother of Senator Pal 93.
Witherill, Mrs. B. F. H., first nee Ma Sprague, 542.
Witherill, Mrs. B. F. H., second nee A. Ingersoll, 542.
Witherill, Mrs. B. F. H., third nee Cass S. Brady. 542.
Witing, Dr. J. L., 761.
Wittemore, Gideon O., 105, 325.
Wood, Joseph, 111.
Wood, Mrs. Robert, nee Schwarz, 1001,
Wood, Mrs. W. R., nee Caroline Wh 1001.
Woodward, Judge A. B., 218, 254, 292, 527, 972.
Woodbridge, Judge Wm. L., 218, 242, 292, 371, 378, 386, 392, 508, 645, 737
Woodbridge, Lieut. Frank, 594, 878.
Wooden, Orson, 916.
Woods, Mrs. Robert, 29.
Woodworth, Benjamin, 41, 74, 75, 87, 166, 213, 215, 217, 219, 229, 271, 273 307, 345, 705, 727, 890, 921.
Woodworth Capt. Samuel, 45, 215, 321,
Woodworth, Samuel, 912.
Wool, General, 177, 221.
Woolsey, 367, 900.
Woolsey, Daniel, 900.
Woolsey, Melanchton, 900.
Wormley, 35.
Worth, General, 170, 174, 177, 180, 22
Wright, Captain, 1010.
Wright, Capt. John F., 31.
Wright, Kay & Co., 716.
Wright, Mrs. Henry, 1011.
Wright, P. M., 1011.
Wright, Stephen T., 117.
Wright, T. T., 115.

Young, Andrew, 355.
Younglove, C., 202.
Young, W. T., 295, 388.